INTEGRATED MARKETING COMMUNICATIONS

INTEGRATED MARKETING COMMUNICATIONS

Dr. NIRAJ KUMAR

M.Com. (Bus. Admin.), Ph.D., Ll.B., A.M.S.P.I., F.M.S.P.I., F.A.I.M.C.
Gold Medalist, National Awardee & Paul Harris Fellow
Advisor: Columbia Holistic University, California, U.S.A.

Former Head & Director
Deptt. of Business Administration
Lucknow University

ISO 9001:2015 CERTIFIED

First Edition : 2009
Edition : 2011
Edition : 2015
Edition : 2022

Published by : Mrs. Meena Pandey for **Himalaya Publishing House Pvt. Ltd.,**
"Ramdoot", Dr. Bhalerao Marg, Girgaon, Mumbai - 400 004.
Phone: 022-23860170, 23863863, **Fax:** 022-23877178
E-mail: himpub@bharatmail.co.in; **Website:** www.himpub.com

Branch Offices :

New Delhi : "Pooja Apartments", 4-B, Murari Lal Street, Ansari Road, Darya Ganj, New Delhi - 110 002. Phone: 011-23270392, 23278631; Fax: 011-23256286

Nagpur : Kundanlal Chandak Industrial Estate, Ghat Road, Nagpur - 440 018. Phone: 0712-2721215, 2721216

Bengaluru : Plot No. 91-33, 2nd Main Road, Seshadripuram, Behind Nataraja Theatre, Bengaluru - 560 020. Phone: 080-41138821; Mobile: 09379847017, 09379847005

Hyderabad : No. 3-4-184, Lingampally, Besides Raghavendra Swamy Matham, Kachiguda, Hyderabad - 500 027. Phone: 040-27560041, 27550139

Chennai : No. 34/44, Motilal Street, T. Nagar, Chennai - 600 017. Mobile: 09380460419

Pune : "Laksha" Apartment, First Floor, No. 527, Mehunpura, Shaniwarpeth (Near Prabhat Theatre), Pune - 411 030. Phone: 020-24496323, 24496333; Mobile: 09370579333

Lucknow : House No. 731, Shekhupura Colony, Near B.D. Convent School, Aliganj, Lucknow - 226 022. Phone: 0522-4012353; Mobile: 09307501549

Ahmedabad : 114, "SHAIL", 1st Floor, Opp. Madhu Sudan House, C.G. Road, Navrang Pura, Ahmedabad - 380 009. Phone: 079-26560126; Mobile: 09377088847

Cuttack : Plot No 5F-755/4, Sector-9, CDA Market Nagar, Cuttack - 753 014, Odisha. Mobile: 09338746007

Kolkata : 108/4, Beliaghata Main Road, Near ID Hospital, Opp. SBI Bank, Kolkata - 700 010. Phone: 033-32449649; Mobile: 07439040301

Printed at : Geetanjali Press Pvt. Ltd., Nagpur, On behalf of HPH.

OM ASATOMA SATGAMAYA
TAMASOMA JYOTIRGAMAYA
MRITYORMA AMRITAM GAMAYA

(1-3-28, BRIHADARANYAKA UPANISHAD)

LET US LEAD FROM UNTRUTH TO TRUTH
FROM DARKNESS TO LIGHT
FROM MORTALITY TO IMMORTALITY.

GAYATRI MANTRA

OM BHUR, BHUVAH, SUVAH
TAT SAVITUR VERENAYAM
BHARGO DEVASYA DHIMAHI
DHIYO YO NAA PRACHODAYAT
(YAJURVEDA 36-3)

OM, WHO IS DEARER THAN OUR BREATH
IS SELF SUBSISTENT.
ALL KNOWLEDGE AND ALL BLESS.
WE MEDITATE UPON THAT ADORABLE EFFULGENCE OF THE
RESPLEDENT VIVIFIER OF THE MARCROCOSM, SAVITA,
MAY HE ILLUMINE OUR INTELLECTS UNTO THE RIGHT PATH.

IN MEMORIUM

Of

My Father, Prof. Gyan Chandra Gupta

And

My Mother, Smt. Kamla Gupta

TO WHOM I RESPECTFULLY

DEDICATE

THIS HUMBLE PRESENTATION

Preface

Now there remains no doubt that 'communication' is an in-word in the twenty-first century. Today, it has become a cult. Now marketing is not just confined to develop a good product and put it on the shelves in the market. There exists a good possibility that the potential customers may not recognize the product. It is also possible that they could not be persuaded of the product's good qualities.

For the most non-marketers, integrated marketing communications is the whole of marketing. Like an iceberg, only the tip is visible; the common consumer do not see product development, pricing policies or distribution in the same way as they see communications.

There is a popular belief often expressed in marketing circles that the consumer is regularly 'bombarded' with marketing messages, implying that there exist a kind of warfare. Quite true, in a single day an individual is exposed to thousands of messages; yet this is in the nature of human being. As human beings, we distinguish ourselves from the other animals by our unique ability to communicate on a subtle level. We talk to each other in many ways, showing pictures, using body language and gestures to communicate over distances. We invent novel ways to make contacts with each other and exchange ideas, feelings, emotions, sentiments etc. If some of these ideas are about new products, or special offers, or better ways of meeting needs, this is really no different in concept from any day-to-day communication between two people. Far from being a kind of war, integrated marketing communications, in an ideal world, should be waging a kind of peace, in which the communications are welcomed as being helpful and positive.

Today, the interest that is shown by people in number of T.V. campaigns, the animated conversations they have with salespersons, in articles in magazines and news papers about various products, very clearly demonstrates that now consumers do not see integrated marketing communications as 'bombardment' at all. Only in cases if a communication is so poorly phrased or poorly targeted, that it is either irritating or offensive – most of the time consumers simply screen out the uninteresting one and concentrate themselves on what is of importance to them. This is in the same way as one concentrates on an individual conversation during a noisy party.

Today, every company is cast, by the very nature of customers and competition, into the role of communicator and marketing communications. Now, all companies, whether professionally managed or not, hire specialized people, the sales forces to carry messages in order not only to persuade but to impress upon the customers, advertising agencies to develop attention-getting ads; sales promotion consultants to develop exclusive sales campaigns, and trained public relations' firms, just to enhance the company's image. No doubt, not all the companies feel good about all of such activities, and some positively act if promotional expenditures were among the less productive made by the firm. Yet they all continue to spend a hefty sum on integrated marketing communications' activities. Why? The answer is obvious; it pays in the long run.

We have started with the concept of communication and later on with that of marketing. We have tried to fuse them together in the preceding chapters. Therefore, we advocate consumer awareness and demand stimulation rather than pure manufacturing of demand. Because of this approach, it emphasizes the duality of our view; on the one hand we need expertise in the process of communication and on the other hand these interactions should be soundly based on the philosophy of marketing management. Therefore, there are numerous sub-themes to our approach while dealing with integrated marketing communications.

We hope that the present text will not only be useful to the students of management especially those who intend to specialize in marketing, but also to marketing managers, advertising managers, public relations' practitioners and many more in practice. It is expected that this humble presentation will serve them not as a text but as a practical guide to integrated marketing communications. The generic skills discussed will provide them a practical framework in the present era of competitive world of marketing, which is now much different than few decades ago.

As a communication, no book is the product of one communicator. There are numerous people whose ideas and practical assistance have contributed to this presentation. The list being too exhaustive, it is rather impossible to pen down all of them here. Therefore, keeping them a bit anonymous the author expresses his heart felt gratitude to all of them.

The author is deeply grateful to the authors and publishers of the various works from which consciously or unconsciously material has been drawn to prepare the present volume. However, every attempt has been made to acknowledge the debt as and where required to the extent as far as possible. The author is also grateful to Anuj Pandey and Niraj Pandey of Himalaya Publishing House who took all pains to present it before you in this form. Any remaining errors or omissions are of course of the author and he willingly accepts them.

Dr. NIRAJ KUMAR
C -4/8, River Bank Colony
LUCKNOW – 226 018
Email: kumarniraj1000@rediffmail.com
nirajklko@yahoo.com

Contents

CHAPTER

1 BUSINESS IS COMMUNICATION

The business world you are planning to enter moves around the consumer, and is based on the exchange of information, co-operation, utility and finance. No business can survive in isolation. To start and run your business successfully, you have to gear yourself to communicate effectively with everyone associated directly or indirectly with your enterprise so as to gain co-operation, finance and information as well as to publicize your product/service among your consumers.

Communication, though bereft of physical attribute, affects the existence of the enterprise. You may find evidences where sincere efforts and qualitative work have failed to bring about desired results because these remained invisible to the person concerned, or differed from the actual requirement due to a lack of proper understanding and effective communication. Major business activities indicate the importance of communication skill.

Why is communication important to business? Couldn't we just produce graduates skilled at crunching numbers? Communication matters because business organizations are made up of people. An enterprise is begun with the registration of the unit, obtaining licenses and approvals, finances, machinery, raw material, manpower etc. All this needs communication skills.

As Robert Kent, former Dean of Harvard Business School has said, "In business, communication is everything." Research spanning several decades has consistently ranked communication skills as crucial for managers. Typically, managers spend 75 to 80 per cent of their time engaged in some form of written or oral communication. Although often termed a "soft" skill, communication in a business organization provides the critical link between core functions.

The first place of business communication is the market. Before the selection of the product/service, you require information regarding the size, requirements, purchasing, power, nature of the market and the specifications of different product and their demand. For this, interaction with different people, such as general merchants and professionals, in the field is a must. The interaction may be in the form of individual discussions, interview, surveys etc. Each of these needs a different style of communication. In an interview and discussion with a person at a time you can use the language and analyse the information revealed, keeping in mind that particular person. On the other hand, if you are using a questionnaire, the format should be according to the language being used, educational social and economic status of the particular target group.

In the market, you will come across all kinds of people, directly or indirectly. This process may feed you with a lot of irrelevant information. To check it, focus on the subject leading to useful and conclusive direction. This will save time and energy, which is of utmost importance. An appropriate response is possible only if the message has been understood in the right perspective, so make sure your message is comprehensible to your target group. It should also be easy to respond to.

Second comes the power to convince the authorities concerned. After selecting your product/ service, you require registration, license and approval according to the nature of the selected item. These are issued if the authorities concerned are convinced of the viability of the project and its implications. Hence, you should clearly provide whatever the answers the information agencies are seeking. Raising funds for implementing the project leads you to deal with financial institutions, resource persons, including your parents, relatives, and friends etc., from where you can get financial help. In a financial institution or bank, you will be dealing with a person whose job is to ascertain that the money he is distributing will be properly utilized for the promotion of the enterprise and returned within the stipulated time with interest. The way one explains it and presents the various facts and figures, alongwith all the pros and cons of the institution, showing clearly the feasibility of the project, will be the most effective factor in ultimately attaining the finances.

To increase this skill you should understand financial analysis, market analysis, the technicalities involved in the project etc. Remember, that the best way to impress and convince others of your intentions and abilities is a thorough used, pitch and tone of the voice, body language and facial expressions play a very important role. This does not mean that you speak only to impress others. You should also listen attentively to whatever is said and understand what type of response is required of you. Sometimes, the other person may try to provoke you, de-motivate you or even try to confuse you, in such a situation, you should keep your cool and, at no cost, lose your temper or patience. These are but a few of the tricks to judge your determination, clarity of goal and understanding of the proposal you are submitting/ presenting. Learning from the experiences of others also unfolds various dimensions of the business world hitherto unknown to freshers. Communication with the suppliers should clearly define the terms and conditions of a project and give full assurance of prompt payment etc., as this may help you when you require material on credit. Although this does not require much expertise, your skill in dealing with the supplier and your bargaining power may save some money, time and effort.

At the production stage, your work place is the most important area of communication, which takes place in different directions, which, directly or indirectly, influences the growth and development of an enterprise.

Communication within the enterprise can be classified into formal and informal mode. The formal communication comprises official communication, such as instruction reports, inquiries, explanations etc. These can be understood in three ways Superior to subordinate to superior and between colleagues working at the same level. In formal communication, the status of the receiver should be kept in mind. On the other hand, informal communication takes place irrespective of the requirement and the designation. For a smooth working culture in your enterprise, you not only need to communicate effectively but you also require, keeping the communication within the enterprise formal or informal. Lack of proper communication leads to anarchy, frustration, slow work, and misunderstandings etc., which are detrimental to the growth of your organization.

With your product/service, you shall be going to the market or to the consumer where, again, your communication skill will play a vital role in the sales strategy. Here, your approach is to provide certain utility to the consumer in exchange for money. You will be selling your services/ products, directly or indirectly, to the target group. Hence, you should be able to convince the consumer of the veracity and usefulness of your service and should be able to motivate him/her to buy it. With this one-point programme in mind, you should highlight the benefits derived from the usage of your product/services.

To achieve this, you can use different publicity channels, like the newspaper, television, radio, door-to-door publicity, hoarding, posters, handbills, kiosks etc. As each of theses has a different degree of impact on different segments of the society, it has its own limitations. It is imperative that the selection of the message, language, size and colour of the display must be very carefully selected and produced so as to have the optimum impact. A feedback of the publicity and sales thereof should be minutely noted and analyzed so as to make necessary amendments to the publicity campaign adopted.

People receive information from different sources therefore, they become selective in actually receiving and responding in their final decision. For instance, if a society believes in simple living, it would not try to understand a message emphasizing fashion and show business.

When people communicate with each other, they exchange various forms of meaning, such as ideas and information, through a common system of symbols. Typical communications can include writing in a diary, watching television, talking with friends, and speaking on the telephone. It has been estimated that people spend more time communicating than they spend on any other complex activity in life. Human communication takes place on many levels, from the simplest interpersonal and small-group exchanges among friends to mass communication, as experienced in public speeches, magazines, or news broadcasts.

Communication is not limited to exchanges between people. It also refers to activities that do not involve people—for example, the word communication may be used to describe the ways that animals relate to each other. Similarly, it is often said that electronic devices communicate with each other. All such communication happens because participants in the process share an understanding of certain symbols and exchange them in a systematic or orderly way.

Technological developments have changed the way people receive daily news. Just as radio broadcasts replaced newspapers as the main carrier of breaking news, so television news eclipsed radio. Television has become one of the most important sources of news information in the United States. In the early 21st century, however, people were just as likely to turn to multiple sources for their news. Newspapers, magazines, Internet news sites, radio, and television in combination provide more information than they have ever before encountered.

Information is rapidly becoming even more available because of these advances in technology. Personal computers, cable television, DVDs, and video recording devices are finding their way into more and more homes, classrooms, and businesses. Computers have already dramatically changed the storage, analysis, and retrieval of information by students, teachers, businesses, and governmental agencies. Individuals can receive such items as sports scores, weather reports, and stock prices through their cell phones.

Instantaneous communication of text, audio, and video information became a reality when digital technology made it possible to compress, store, and transmit large volumes of data efficiently. This development increased the speed and reduced the cost of distance communication for offices and homes. Business teleconferences with people in far away cities became affordable and routine. Friends increasingly keep in touch with instant messaging or send each other pictures through their telephones. Computers link offices, families, and friends through e-mail, Web sites, and intranets. Electronic fund transfers give banks and businesses great flexibility in managing money.

New technologies have created opportunities in the entertainment industry as well. Increasing number of households receive their television programming through coaxial cable or satellite signals. The many methods of recording television programs for later playback increase both the quantity and variety of materials people may view in their homes. The actual content of entertainment also changed as computer animation created entirely new styles and visual effects in cartoons and films.

Computers are an increasingly important part of the communication process. Large computers in central locations store enormous amounts of information and permit other computers to use it if desired. Internet connections permit people to see information from a library or other program sources.

No matter what technical advances in communication may occur in the future, the actual meaning of any communication will still exist only in the minds of people. Technology is a means of helping people to share ideas and feelings, but it will never replace the fundamental human need to exchange and interpret information.

Any industry is part of the world economy and make an attempt to buy and sell in world markets. Businesses need efficient communications to keep in touch with their suppliers and customers. Parts of an American industrial enterprise may be spread over the globe. One of the leading computer manufacturers in the world, for example, is International Business Machines (IBM). It is based in the United States and has about 80 foreign subsidiaries. To remain competitive, IBM's managers need to gather information from all parts of the world. Even the smallest local business depends on accurate and up-to-date information to be delivered to them by mail, telephone, fax, computer, television, newspapers, and magazines.

The communication industry uses the most advanced technology. Messages are sent via satellite, along tiny glass cables, or on laser beams. The increasing use of semiconductors has led to a revolution in modern communication's equipment. Computers store and deliver messages and converse with other computers. Word processors and minicomputers are linked in networks that can move messages and ideas rapidly around an office, making office communications far less dependent on books, papers, telephones, and the postal service.

Management is concerned with combining all the other inputs of production. Managers decide what to make and how to make it. They choose from the available inputs and work out the right mix. Management must organize production to meet the goals of the company, which normally include keeping manufacturing costs low and producing a profit.

The first industrial managers were men like Richard Arkwright and Thomas Edison, both inventors and businessmen. They owned their companies and made all the management decisions. As the scale of production increased in the 19th century, ownership of companies was divided among shareholders. Management gradually became separated from ownership, and a class of professional managers emerged.

The division of labour has been successfully applied to management. In the modern factory, managers specialize in one function: production, finance, marketing, personnel, or public affairs. Management is a skilled occupation, and the amount of education needed to become a professional manager is increasing. Managers are schooled in all aspects of production and business before specializing in one field. Many of today's managers are college graduates who also have advanced degrees in business.

The emphasis on well-trained managers reflects the belief that good management is essential to industrial success. Companies can go bankrupt very quickly if they are poorly managed. Each nation and company develops a style, and the management techniques of leading industrial nations and of individual companies are admired and copied. Japanese forms are currently imitated in many industrial nations. Yet as economic fortunes rise and fall, the popularity of management styles changes.

Many small groups are also part of a larger group called an organization. An organization is, simply, a body of people organized for some specific purpose. Among the major organizations in society are churches, temples, schools, colleges and universities, businesses, corporations, libraries, military services, service organizations, city, county, state, and national governments.

Because organizations are complex, it is important for each to establish a formal communication network. The communication network in a business or public agency is often drawn up in an organization chart that identifies the titles of people who hold positions in the organization and indicates who reports to whom. While the organization chart identifies the path formal communications will travel, it is understood that informal communication networks will develop without conforming to any chart. These two types of communication networks thereby provide for both formal and informal exchanges of ideas.

It is important in organizations that communication networks provide for a two-way flow of information. It must flow from a company president's office to all of the individuals and groups who need that information. But it should also flow in the other direction. Workers are more satisfied when they feel that their ideas are being heard by persons higher in the organization chart.

Organizational communication is also important because conflicts inevitably arise between individuals and groups. Engineers in a company, for example, may produce product designs that shop foremen consider too difficult to make. When such differences arise, the communication network must provide for conflict resolution—a system through which workers can settle their differences.

CORPORATE COMMINCATIONS

"Some people change their ways when they see the light; others when they feel the heat."

Extend this Caroline Schoedar's aphorism to cover the widespread misconception about 'Corporate Communications' in the Advertising, Public Relations (PR), Marketing Communications and financial advertising industries and chances are that you will find yourself confounded, if not dumbstruck.

The maze of paradoxes involving public relations and corporate communications is so entrenched in the world of 'Image Makers' (positioned as PR firms, financial ad agencies offering the incentives of 'press coverage' and the one-stop -communications-shops') that it is often difficult to decipher them on this count.

Nevertheless, one cannot completely disregard their potential to see the 'light' but possibly after the 'heat' is felt to have been turned on them by the clients who have, thanks to the changing business environment, begun to feel the 'heat' themselves to have a more comprehensive and yet a distinct corporate image.

Before reaching the stage of hoping to see the light of change in a 'world' where everyone appears to be gorging 'Corporate Communications' and 'PR' mantras with great felicity. Consider the case of a few a leading financial ad agencies claiming that they offer apart from every thing, 'PR and Corporate Communications'. Self-styled 'largest PR firm in India' claims that it offers 'Public Affairs' (read as lobbying with the establishment). Media Management (that's management' for securing press coverage) and 'Corporate Communications'. Yet another boasts of providing everything under the banner of 'Public Relations' including 'Corporate Communications'.

The list of those who have managed to conveniently appropriate 'Corporate Communications' -predictably due to the high sounding effect that this phrase creates - is a never ending one. A close scrutiny will reveal that the phrase finds its place more to embellish the menu of services for impressive spiel than anything implied to provide veritable substance to the clients.

COLLUDING TO CAST A SHADOW

So you wonder why is it so? What could be the possible difference between corporate communications and PR? Is one the part of the other? Is the role complementary? What qualifies a PR firm or financial ad agency to provide the Corporate Communication's solutions? And whether they will do justice. The questions that elude answers abound, but then who bothers as long as the client can be influenced and stays amenable to hogwash and as long as favourble press stories can be generated occasionably through 'contacts, friends and former colleagues' in the media to keep the clients 'satisfied'.

The situation on the other side of the fence or the clients' side is no better either. The label of 'Corporate Communications' has found its popular adoption as a mere brag-tag for those entrusted with PR (call it rather press liaison) or even advertising coupled with assorted jobs. However, one must acknowledge some path-breaking work that the internal corporate communications wing of many organisations keeps churning out periodically. They single mindedly pursue their objectives through integrated corporate communications' programmes to create and promote corporate equity. Many of them today enjoy an enviable corporate reputation and image.

From the dominating hodge-podge that one comes across in the industry emerges a picture where PR is mistaken for corporate communications and *vice versa*, even by professionals who claim to be 'Practitioners'. So much so that it has been reduced to being an exalted qualifier for many to describe the 'efforts' at securing press coverage which is still considered the planned and sustained work towards image- building aimed at promoting understanding between an organisation and its public.

There is a need to clear the clouds that surround corporate communications and create awareness about it as a stand-alone discipline that it is and its role in creating, nurturing and protecting corporate equity.

THOSE WHO CREATE THE SMOKE-SCREEN

And today many of them exist in the most elementary form experiencing only occasional bumps of activity which are handled with an equal measure of incompetence and non commitment.

On the flip side, the new found interest in image building and reduction in media spending triggered a spurt in demand for 'PR activities' which made it a lucrative business proposition. This saw a large number of people cashing in on the opportunity and launching PR outfits as their second or third career option. There was nothing wrong with that *per se* as long as the focus on capability and competence development was not lost. Instead, the industry pushed investment in training and infrastructure to the background and considered it a taboo in its scheme for rapid survival. Unfortunately, this mindset by and large still continues.

Consequently, the discipline was strapped of innovative ideas, freshness of approach and extraordinariness of work content which are the mainstays of any discipline. And without these basic elements, the dilution is bound to take place which precisely is corporate communications and PR's case today impelling it to gasp for fresh air.

If this discipline has to grow along the lines of other functional areas then it is imperative that 'PR / Corporate Communications' Professionals' initiate work on developing and expanding the functional scope with the same zeal that they display for the bottomline.

Moreover, as the clients look for more value for the fee and come to terms with the reality of creating, nurturing and protecting corporate image. Merely listing down the services may no longer sustain the aura that is sought to be created every time a presentation or pitch is made which only leaves more and more clients to discover later that what was packaged originally cannot be stretched beyond a few coverage clippings.

THE SIEGE AROUND: LET THERE BE LIGHT

The first step to correct the misnomer would be to recognise that corporate communications is not a poor cousin of either corporate advertising or PR but by itself an independent discipline having PR and corporate advertising as two of its important elements: and when adopted, applied and practiced by following what it entails for comprehensive image building helps an organisation build corporate equity.

Corporate Communications is a discipline that integrates and encompasses all elements of mass media whether corporate advertising, identity management, events, public affairs or media coverage. The selection of components is a function of situation and programme objectives. It is the holistic approach to building and sustaining a distinct and relevant corporate image through reinforcing the understanding and relationships of an organisation with all publics primarily through various means of information dissemination and sharing.

Corporate Communications programs cannot be conceived and implemented without having premises of substance. It involves projecting and building reputation of an organisation covering its activities, quality of products, management, manpower, philosophy, culture, vision, fulfillment of responsibilities as a corporate citizen and contribution to the society and environment. The nature and quality of these aspects of an organisation contribute to the creation of reputation which in turn transforms into image. While the reputation is largely action driven, corporate communications can only highlight various contributory aspects and help an organisation strategize, evolve and implement programmes that could strengthen and emphasize those aspects and in turn create and reinforce its reputation.

It is through reputation that an organisation builds its corporate equity which not only breeds familiarity and thereby favourable disposition of the target groups but yields an opportunity to be heard when a danger lurks from hostile quarters having potential to hamper the operation and impact the image.

In the changing scenario where one can witness a debate on corporate governance, a call for transparency and greater accountability-on the one hand, and a marketplace where the product/brand differentiation is getting diminished across all categories coupled with proactive consumer fora, fastidious consumers and a plethora of competing players, on the other - corporate communications can help organisations build a meaningful rapport with the marketplace, internal stake holders or any other group by opening channels of communication through a sustained image-building exercise and ensure a balanced share of voice and recognition which in turn would lend a competitive advantage to the organisation.

However, one must be clear that providing undue smoke-screen in troubled times invities more trouble and that constructive criticism from media and pressure groups, which corporate communications can help tone down and build the information bridge that could enable an organisation present its case and help the interest groups take note of the organisation's perspective also.

There is a school of thought (specially in the ad industry) which believes that a corporate should be treated like a product brand for promoting the corporate as a brand and that the traditional product-brand building principles should be applied. While the merit of this argument, to a certain extent, cannot be discarded, the point to be borne in mind is that branding the corporate is an entirely different ballgame, distinguished from building product brand equity. It involves multiple target audience which cannot be influenced through a brilliant corporate ad campaign alone or its short term hoopla which proves insufficient to create and sustain, in all circumstances, a long term 'top-of - the-mind' awareness.

Corporate Advertising, as one of the important components of corporate communications, can be used only as a supplementary and short term measure. The task of integration of the ad campaign with other programmes will have to be carried out for a universal impact which is why corporate communications must be considered as an umbrella discipline that can perform an integrated orchestra for the brand building of the corporate. It looks at and beyond conventional advertising towards areas such as events, literature, A/V, identity management, avenues for financial and internal communications, communications with the pressure groups and institutions, and integrates multi-directional efforts for strengthening the corporate reputation. In marketing, it lends the advantage of corporate image and opens scope for greater marketing successes while tilting the balance in favour of the organisation. It is therefore necessary that a strong corporate identity is developed and managed, but in contrast to a planned approach to developing and sustaining an identity, what happens often is that it is treated as an exercise in visual gimmickry.

In the process, the significance and relevance of this potent vehicle which could otherwise effectively reflect the heart and soul of an organisation and differentiate it in the marketplace is pushed to irrelevance and drudgery. Corporate Communications can be employed to address the issue of evolving and integrating the corporate identity with the overall communications programme in a way that it becomes a true representation of an organisation and reflects various traits of its personality.

The fact remains that the misconception about the discipline of corporate communications, and the confusion that follows it, is unfortunately all pervading. But we, whether clients or ad and PR industries, must take a beginning to put things in the right perspective and derive maximum advantage from what this discipline is capable of delivering. While the clients should demand, more than a few coverage clippings, the work that could lend a competitive advantage to them through proper exercise in image-building and be willing to pay a price for it. As for PR firms, if they want to reap the real benefits of using corporate communications, should focus on capability development and training.

Initially, the change in approach may cause a little heart burning and possibly effect a shake out among the 'Image Makers'. But mustn't it be done if it can lead to the good of the clients in terms of building corporate equity and the PR/financial as industries in terms of their own growth and stable future. As for the audience, whether press or pressure groups, availability of relevant information, which at times seems so difficult to come by, and proper response to queries would certainly turn out to be reasons to celebrate.

Communication Need Felt by Government Companies too – A Case of LIC

The life insurance industry in India dates back to 1818, when a British firm Oriental Life Insurance Company opened its office in Kolkata, followed by Bombay Life Assurance Company in 1823. During the British rule in India, 'The Indian Life Assurance Companies Act' was enacted in 1912, which was followed by the Indian Insurance Companies Act, 1928 enabling government to collect the data regarding life and non-life business conducted by both Indian and foreign insurance companies. The 1928 Act was amended and a new Act; 'Insurance Act' was formed in 1938.

By the mid-1950s, 154 Indian insurers, 16 foreign insurers and 75 provident societies were operating in the country. The life insurance business was concentrated in urban areas and was confined to the higher strata of the society. In 1956, management of these companies was taken over by the Government of India. LIC was formed in September 1956 through the 'LIC Act 1956' with a capital of Rs 50 million. One of the main objectives of forming LIC was to spread the insurance cover and make it available to the lower segments of the society. In 1972, government formed General Insurance Corporation (GIC) when it took over management control of 106 private general insurance companies. Over the years, LIC expanded its network all over the country emerging as one of the largest corporations in India.

Insurance industry's growth in the India was minimal in 1960s and 1970s due to factors like low savings, low investment, inadequate infrastructure, and illiteracy. However, changes in the economy in 1980s, such as growth in the rate of industrialization, infrastructure, the capital markets, savings rate and capital formation resulted in a tremendous growth in the life insurance industry, which in other words meant growth of LIC. Over the years, LIC launched several schemes aimed at expanding its reach in the rural areas. Many group insurance and social security schemes were started by the company to enhance its reach over the rural. LIC had seven zonal offices, 100 divisional offices, 2,048 branch offices and army of agents totalling 6,28,031.

Need for reforming the industry was felt in the early-1990s for providing better coverage to the Indians and to increase flow of long-term financial resources to finance the growth of infrastructure. In 1993, the Indian government constituted the 'Malhotra Committee' to suggest reforms in the industry. The Committee submitted its report in 1994, with recommendations for opening the insurance sector to private players, improving service standards and extending insurance coverage to larger sections of the population.

The Committee's suggestions faced stiff opposition from various labor unions and political parties in the country. They opined that entry of private players would lead to job cuts by the nationalized players in order to compete with them. There were a host of other arguments against these reforms. The government sought to address them by restricting foreign stake in insurance companies to only 26%, which was well below 51% needed for managing the company in the Insurance Bill.

Though one of LIC's basic objectives was to 'provide insurance cover to all Indians,' insurance penetration in India was considered to be very low. According to reports, only 65 million people were covered by insurance. R. N. Jha, LIC's former Executive Director commented in his book, 'Insurance in India,' "Insurance coverage has been extended only to about 25% of the insurable population in 40 years," indicating the huge uncovered market potential in the country.

It was reported that per capita insurance premium in developed countries was much higher as compared to India. In 1999, per capita insurance premium in India was only $8 while it was $4,800 in Japan, $1000 in Republic of Korea, $887 in Singapore, $823 in Hong Kong and $144 in Malaysia. In the world market, in terms of gross insurance premium also, India's share was only 0.3%, though population wise it ranked second in the world. The corresponding figures in 1999 for Japan was 31%, European Union 25%, South Africa 2.3% and Canada – 1.7%. Further, in 2001, while the ratio of insurance premium to the Gross Domestic Product (GDP) was 9% for UK and Japan, and 5% for US, it was only 1.9% in India.

Attracted by the huge untapped potential, many private players entered the market after the Insurance Bill was passed in late 2000. A majority of these were collaborations between an Indian company and a leading MNC insurance/financial services company (See Table 1.1).

According to industry observers, one of the main reasons for the low insurance penetration in India was the ineffective distribution and marketing strategies adopted by LIC. The company reportedly never had any strategic marketing game plan, and due to its monopolistic nature the need for serious marketing efforts was never felt. The communication through advertising initiatives were limited to some print and electronic media advertisements that typically talked about LIC's products being great tax saving tool for salaried individuals who came under the income-tax bracket. Despite all this, LIC was synonymous with insurance in India and it had established an enviable brand image for itself, especially in the rural areas and small towns. However, with the entry of new players, the insurance market changed almost overnight. Analysts commented that the private insurers seemed all set to make the industry marketing-driven, wherein technical and service excellence would be the key factors of success. The private companies, in a bid to make their presence felt and their brand noticed, initiated a series of aggressive marketing and promotion initiatives, something that buyers of insurance were not accustomed to. Such frenzy prompted IRDA to frame an advertisement code for companies.

TABLE 1.1.

Private Players in the Indian Insurance Market

Compay	*Indian Partner*	*Foreign Insurer*	*Area*
Birla Sun Life	Aditya Birla Group	Sun Life, Canada	Life
Om Kotak	Kotak Mahindra Finance	Old Mutual, South Africa	Life
HDFC-Standard Life	HDFC	Standard Life, UK	Life
Royal Sundaram	Sundaram Finance	Royal Sun, UK	Life and Non-Life
ICICI-Prudential	ICICI	Prudential, UK	Life
Max New York Life	Max India	New York Life, USA	Life
Tata-AIG	Tata Group	AIG, USA	Life and Non-Life
ING Vysya	Vysya Bank	ING Insurance, Netherlands	Life
Aviva	Dabur	CGU Life, UK	Life
MetLife India	Jammu & Kashmir Bank	MetLife, USA	Life
Bajaj Allianz	Bajaj Auto	Allianz	Life & Non-Life
AMP Sanmar	Sanmar Group	AMP, Australia	Life
SBI Life Insurance	SBI	Cardiff, France	Life

Source: www.knowledgedigest.com

In July 2002, India's state owned insurer, Life Insurance Corporation of India (LIC) announced aggressive marketing plans with a budget of around Rs. 1 billion. The aim of this unusual decision was to woo customers across the country through a multimedia campaign including advertisements on the radio and the press media, the outdoor media and the television. However, this did not come as a major surprise to industry observers who said that LIC did not have too many options.

With the insurance bill being passed in 2000, the Indian insurance sector saw a host of private players enter the market with multinationals as their partners. These new players resorted to aggressive marketing communications strategies – something the market had never seen earlier.

This sudden spurt of marketing communications' strategies – advertisements and awareness programs was visible on all the media channels. Print, electronic and outdoor advertisements of the new private insurers flooded could be seen everywhere. This prompted many comparisons of such behavior of insurance companies with the advertising frenzy of the dotcoms in India not too long ago – with similar full-page advertisements, huge hoardings and costly electronic media advertisements.

According to a survey conducted by a leading marketing research firm, ORG Marg, brand awareness of private insurers in India was increasing in the early 21st century. The difference in the level of awareness of these new players as compared to the hitherto monopoly of LIC was decreasing fast because of the aggressive advertising measures adopted by private insurers.

The new insurance companies used all channels of advertising from newspapers and the television to insurance agents and direct mailers. A fierce battle seemed to have begun among Indian insurance companies to make one's own brand win over the other.

A majority of Indian customers being very conservative and averse to risk, trust was an extremely important factor in the insurance business. Since LIC was a government owned body, there was an element of security embedded in its services and products. This proved to be the biggest hurdle for the new insurance companies as Indian customers were reportedly rather skeptical about them. Hence, the new companies focused their campaigns primarily on building an image of trustworthiness and reliability for themselves. Secondly, their advertisements focused on insurance as an investment option and not a mere tax saving tool – another first for the Indian market. Most of these advertisements carried messages like the family's happiness, human bonding, etc., with underlying emphasis on the security that insurance could provide. Also, instead of projecting the idea, that an insurance policy actually starts working only after the death of the insured, the new campaigns projected that insurance protects people throughout their lives.

In one of its TV commercials, ICICI Prudential showed a series of scenes depicting the childhood, marriage and old age of an individual. The purpose of using these visuals was to translate the company's message 'I will protect' into real-life incidents. In order to project its commitment towards consumers to 'protect at every stage of life,' the company brought in the concept of sindoor, which symbolizes protection. Sindoor was shown throughout the commercial as a mark of auspiciousness and protection, and at the end, it became the red line below the ICICI Prudential logo.

Max New York also resorted to depicting positive emotions such as trust and protection in its print advertisements. The company released two print advertisements. While one of them carried an image of the revered deity Goddess Durga, the other projected three teenagers standing together, with their faces painted green, white and saffron – like the Indian national flag. Reportedly, Max New York wanted to convey the message that 'insurance is your partner for your life.' Suhel Seth of Equus Advertising the ad agency, which created the advertisements for Max New York – said, "We had to break the clutter, as insurance as a category has largely communicated doom and fear. Therefore, the campaign lent itself better to an emotional route." Max New York Life also carried out an extensive outdoor media campaign across the country, focusing on 'India-specific' images such as traditional wrestlers and village people.

In addition to such TV commercials, the private insurance companies were trying to make their presence felt by organizing blood donation camps, contests and sponsoring various events. ING Vysya tied up with leading US-based Columbia Picture's Indian arm to carry out promotional activities using the blockbuster English movie 'Spiderman.' In the metros, ING Vysya distributed free movie tickets to its customers. A similar exercise was carried out for another English movie 'Mitr' (Friend). Reportedly, Columbia Pictures and ING Vysya had planned to join hands on a long-term basis. The latter also organized the Green Mumbai Drive and several blood donation camps in association with the Red Cross, besides sponsoring the action replay of the India-West Indies cricket match series in May 2002 and also in November 2002.

Om Kotak and Birla Sun Life took to sponsoring events in a major way, to attract prospective customers. In 2001, Birla Sun Life sponsored a play to which a few Citibank credit card customers were invited. A company official said, "Sponsoring plays and events like these give us good mileage. They may not directly give us leads to sales, but certainly give us better visibility." According to company sources, Birla Sun life was considering the sponsorship of premier shows and offering tickets to corporate agents like Citibank and employees of Deutsche Bank, who helped in the sale of policies. A senior company official said, "It is all about building relationships with our corporate agents."

Om Kotak initially highlighted in its advertisements the credibility and trustworthiness of individual partners (Old Mutual & Kotak Mahindra) through its generic campaigns. The TV commercials featured men and women 'meeting' themselves in the future - happy, healthy and secure, thanks to insurance. In early 2002, company also launched product - specific campaigns. Om Kotak was also considering sub-branding of products.

Allianz Bajaj went a step ahead. Apart from bringing out TV commercials and putting up hoarding and billboards, it entered into a two-month long contract with Shoppers Stop. According to the contract, every Shoppers Stop outlet had an Allianz Bajaj kiosk that provided information about policies in order to attract customers. According to company sources, its plans were to try any kind of activity that would generate awareness about company and its policies and 'leads' (interest by a prospective customer) and converting the same into its customers. Allianz Bajaj's entire communication package included print advertisements, outdoor media campaigns and direct marketing methods. All its print advertisements carried a visual of human hands, which symbolized partnership and care to stress on the concept of care.

Similarly, Tata AIG entered into an agreement with Westside to set up information kiosks in all its outlets in order to attract people's attention. Also, Tata AIG was one of the first insurance companies to adopt the celebrity endorsement strategy. Tata AIG chose the Hindi movie star, Naseeruddin Shah (Shah), as its brand ambassador for endorsing its personal accidental death insurance policy. According to company sources, Shah was selected because he had the image of being an intelligent and reliable individual. Another private insurer AMP Sanmar, roped in former Australian cricket captain, Steve Waugh for endorsing its life insurance policies.

MetLife came up with simple, lucid advertisements that could be easily understood by all. One of its advertisements read, 'Why does anyone need insurance? Well, why does a car need a spare tyre?' According to analysts, this marketing communications strategies successfully projected the importance of insurance for an individual. MetLife's advertisements carried cartoons from the popular 'Peanuts' series and carried emotional messages.

In addition to all the above, private players in the insurance sector charted out various innovative marketing plans to establish their products. For instance, ICICI Prudential launched the 'TruLife Club' for its high-value policyholders as part of its marketing strategy. Through TruLife Club, the company offered a wide range of health-related products, health and fitness equipment and membership in gyms, health resorts and clinics in India. Policyholders with a sum assured of Rs 0.5 million or more were included into this club. According to company sources, the purpose of this whole exercise was to encourage a healthy life of its customers.

During the late-2001, when SBI Life was concentrating on building its brand it was offering packaged products to its customers. S Muralidharan, Chief of Marketing & Sales, SBI Life, said, "We are slowly and steadily building our brand. Very soon we will be launching print advertisements in regional languages too. As for launching a club for the premium segment, it's certainly a possibility which we are now evaluating." According to Muralidharan, SBI Life was also exploring the possibility of advertising on the Internet in its bid to reach out to its target audience.

Another interesting development was regarding the punch lines used by private insurance players that invariably tried to associate positive emotions with insurance products. While ING Vysya said 'Adding life to insurance,' ICICI Prudential said, 'We Cover you. At every step in life.' Similarly, HDFC Standard advertisements projected a happy man asserting, 'Now I can continue enjoying a comfortable lifestyle even after I retire.' AMP Sanmar commercials carried the line 'The joy of living life to the fullest, with a 153-year old expert taking care of your insurance needs.' Om Kotak highlighted its campaigns with 'Jeene ui czaadi' (Freedom to live)' and Allianz Bajaj stated 'Allianz Bajaj, Life insured by care.'

With private players paying much attention to advertising and promotional activities, LIC, too, was forced to make efforts to increase its visibility and enhance its brand image. The company commenced intense, systematic and well-focused public relations and publicity activities both at the corporate and operational levels. LIC came out with a corporate advertisement on TV with the punch line, 'Zindagi

Tumhari Roshan Rahe' (May your life be glorious). In addition, LIC established a broad-based frame for external communication aimed at building a stronger brand image. Several sports events were co-sponsored by the company and special publicity activities with a social purpose were undertaken.

Traditionally, LIC used to target either middle-aged people or elderly ones. But private insurers targeted individuals in all age groups, in their advertisement campaigns. Analysts pointed out that LIC was also biased against women; most of its policies were designed with men in mind, whereas private insurers' products covered women's needs, too. Thus, LIC was forced to modify its advertisement campaigns and communication in order to appeal to all groups. It made its marketing communications strategies - advertisements carry universally applicable messages, focusing particularly on the young executive or the working woman, in order to tap the market comprised of people in the age group of 18-35 years. Ultimately the Government owned company too recognized the importance of communication in order not only to survive but also to face the upcomming competition of private players in the insurance sector in the twenty-first century.

Why Good Communication Is Good Business?

Let's examine three reasons why good communication is important to individuals and their organizations.

Reason 1. Ineffective communication is very expensive.

Communication in a business organization provides the critical link between core functions.

The National Commission on Writing estimates that American businesses spend $3.1 billion annually just training people to write. The Commission surveyed 120 human resource directors in companies affiliated with the Business Roundtable, an association of chief executive officers from U.S. corporations.

According to the report of the National Commission on Writing:

- People who cannot write and communicate clearly will not be hired, and if already working, are unlikely to last long enough to be considered for promotion.
- Eighty percent or more of the companies in the services and the finance, insurance and real estate sectors—the corporations with greatest employment growth potential—assess writing during hiring.
- Two-thirds of salaried employees in large American companies have some writing responsibility.
- More than 40 percent of responding firms offer or require training for salaried employees with writing deficiencies.

Tips for Communication

- Whether writing or speaking, consider your objectives. What do you want your listeners or readers to remember or do? To achieve an objective, you need to be able to articulate it.
- Consider your audience. How receptive will it be? If you anticipate positive reception of your message, you can be more direct.
- Consider your credibility in relation to your audience. Also, consider the organizational environment. Is it thick or flat, centralized or decentralized? Each will have communication implications.
- How can you motivate others? Benefits are always your best bet. And if you can establish common ground, especially at the opening of a message, you can often make your audience more receptive.
- Think carefully about channel choice, about the advantages and disadvantages of your choice, and the preferred channels of your audience.
- If you want to have a permanent record or need to convey complex information, use a channel that involves writing. If your message is sensitive, email may not be the best choice; the immediacy of face-to-face communication can be preferable, especially when you would prefer not to have a written record. (Adapted from Research on Communication Strategy by Mary Munter of the Tuck School at Dartmouth and Jane Thomas of the University of Michigan).

In a New York Times article about the Commission's findings, Bob Kerrey, president of New School

University in New York and chair of the National Commission on Writing, put it this way: "Writing is both a 'marker' of high-skill, high-wage, professional work and a 'gatekeeper' with clear equity implications. People unable to express themselves clearly in writing limit their opportunities for professional, salaried employment." The ability to communicate was rated as the most important factor in making a manager "promotable" by subscribers to Harvard Business Review.

Reason 2. The changing environment and increasing complexity of the 21st century workplace make communication even more important.

Flatter organizations, a more diverse employee base and greater use of teams have all made communication essential to organizational success. Flatter organizations mean managers must communicate with many people over whom they may have no formal control. Even with their own employees, the days when a manager can just order people around are finished. The autocratic management model of past generations is increasingly being replaced by participatory management in which communication is the key to build trust, promote understanding and empower and motivate others.

Because the domestic workforce is growing more diverse, an organization can no longer assume its employee constituencies are homogeneous. Employees reflect differences in age, ethnic heritage, race, physical abilities, gender and sexual orientation. Diversity is not just a matter of social responsibility; it is also an economic issue. Companies are realizing the advantage of making full use of the creativity, talents, experiences and perspectives of a diverse employee base.

Teams are the modus operandi in the 21st century workplace. In a recent survey of Fortune 1000 companies, 83 percent reported that their firms use teams; teams are all about communication. The collaboration that allows organizations to capitalize on the creative potential of a diverse workforce depends on communication.

Reason 3. The world's economy is becoming increasingly global.

By the end of the 20th century, 80 percent of U.S. products were competing in international markets. The direct investment of foreign-based companies grew from $9 trillion in 1966 to more than $300 trillion in 2002. Many products we assume are American, such as Purina Dog Chow and KitKat candy bars, are made overseas. Brands we may think are international, Grey Poupon mustard, Michelin tyres and Evian water, are made in the United States.

Complicated and uncommon words should be avoided in all types of publicity mode and material. What is more, ideas couched in faulty phrases may change the meaning of the message and goal. Furthermore, in business dealings, correct facial expressions, body movements and right tone are necessary.

Effective communication considerable reduces the chances of failure. Following certain golden rules of communication can improve your skill use of simple language well-planned and structured outline clear concept flow in writing and speaking expression suitable to the message and understanding the recipient's background.

WORDS ARE IMPORTANT, BUT...

As we converse or communicate, little do we realize that while we are communicating, messages are being flashed to the receiver through the strategies, which we adopt? In other words, together with the import of the message, a sub text of the content is also transmitted to the recipient.

The most common and prominent of these strategies is the domination stand taken by the people. They try to bulldoze their way into close-knit circles where, probably, high-level confidential exchanges are taking place. Why go to that level? Even the mere exchanges of information, if interrupted repeatedly by an interact ants who refuses to ease the surfaces tension results in the cessation of communication. The individual, by his domination or bulldozing, technique, transmits the message. "I am too superior to be bogged down by your communication. I and I alone will do the talking."

While, on the one hand, we have the domination kind of people, on the other, we have the type who would prefer to remain uninvolved in the whole exchange. If there is an exchange of messages at the formal of informal level, unless they are, not asked, they would prefer to steer clear of the entire pretence of trying to communicate. Two underlying themes can be interpreted through this strategy of talk. Either the not-so-active co-communication is an introvert or he/she considers himself/herself for to superior to the rest of his communicators, that is, he/she does not feel the necessity to interact.

Making too many queries, related or unrelated to the topic, reveals a skeptical kind of person. Excessive queries pertaining to the message sent transmit that all is not clear and that further explantions are needed. If the queries are unrelated, the sub text reads as follows: "Okay, enough of what you are saying, I am sick of it already let us branch out into more interesting topics".

The next defective yet self-revelatory strategy is of giving advice whether you are asked to or not. No one likes to be told that this is how things ought to be done. Couple it with criticism and praise, interpretation and judgment and finally, sympathy. You have done your best where severing of bonds in concerned excessive criticism or praise is basically destructive communication. A negative element is ticked off in the mind of the communicator, resulting in a placid attitude. Too much praise makes the other person wonder instead of concentrating on the communication: Now, what I have done to deserve this kind of excessively favorable attitude? He/she smells a rat! Trying to indulge in lateral thinking, that is, trying to read between the lines is more than his been actually said, and trying to pass judgment along similar lines, together with a sympathetic clucking of the tongue: "God! Stay away!" The co-interactant shouts, albeit mentally. All these devices, when adopted, reveal a superiority complex where a person wants to impose himself on the other person by sounding as if he were really his well-wisher!

All persons like to be thought of highly if they are not actually so. Supportive communicative strategies like "name – dropping" or relating anecdotes bolstering the self-image to impress the other person who would be least interested in the inter act as big connections or even bigger stories. Sub text: Person suffers from an inferiority complex and is trying to play big or resort to big name spelling games.

The ability to read through the main text of the message sent, and reach a conclusion which is only apparent to the effective communicator's eye helps you to decide which strategy to choose which can countermand the effect of the interactant's detective strategies. It should be kept in mind that it is only a game. If all the rules of the game are observed and followed truthfully, your effectiveness can be improved tremendously. At the end of it all, the co-communicator would leave the scene of interaction, feeling that he/she been successful in delivering his/her message to an interactants whose communicative skills were great!

SIMPLICITY IS THE RULE OF COMMUNICATION GAME

Communicating through juggling with alphabets seems to have suddenly caught on. What it can possibly have to do with the basic concept of communication is a question, which has puzzled may a student just before interviews as well as during interviews.

These alphabets are being used by communication gurus as basic building blocks for understanding the concepts of communication and a starting point to test the communicative competence of the candidate. Amongst the many alphabets used to convey the import of the discipline, the most important are the seven C's, four S's, three R's and six O's.

The first two are relevant in almost all spheres of communications, be it mass, managerial or marketing. The last two are the by-product of marketing communication.

Let's begin with C's the first alphabet of the word communication. Effective communication depends on understanding the essence of the seven C's. The first of the lot is credibility – the sender's credibility. Unless and until the speaker is viewed as a credible source for delivering the goods, communication cannot become reliable, or for that matter, sustainable.

Issues then are floated and discussed without really influencing the listener or eliciting any response from him.

This is followed by the context of the message. In which context has a message been delivered? This would certainly encompass the time-span, the

Fig. 1.1

situation, as well as the preceding interaction. The third C- the content — becomes relevant when viewed in the light of the context. Whilst the content has to be more thoroughly researched and rehearsed before presenting to the superior, it can be more relaxed when being presented to a subordinate. For the message to be correctly and accurately conveyed, it is imperative that the message should be as clear as possible to the listener.

The fifth C is for channels - the channels adopted to communicate the message. Part of the clarity of the message depends upon the channel chosen to send across a message.

Suppose the sender is credible, clear in content in the appropriate context and correct in selection of channels, would he be an effective communicator? Not unless he has the mastery over the last 6 C's.

One of them is consistency. A consistent thought-process, as opposed to an inconsistent one, carries more weight. The receiver dose not has to necessarily shift from a logical sequence to an illogical one. Ideas and thoughts get attuned to the speaker and start crystaillsing even while the speaker is speaking.

The last C concerns the capability of the audience. Gauging the capability prior the speaking enables the sender to modify his message according to the capacity of the receiver.

Now come the four S's. Remember the initial lessons at school? Adhere to simple short sentences. Avoid verbosity. Well, the same has been transferred to communication skills, whether verbal or non-verbal. Brevity in writing and speaking is to be strictly observed. Sentences that are too long can make hearing or reading extremely painful, resulting in frequent wandering of attention.

The simpler the message, the easier it is to comprehend it. Convoluted ideas lead to convoluted expressions or the mere impression of the presence of knowledge. Avoid them and move on a simple path for an effective response from the audience.

The third S stands for strength — the strength behind the message. Is it one of those inane pieces of conversation leading to desultory remarks, on after another, or is it something substantial?

In other words, it is all about testing the real value of the import of the message? The last of the four S's connotes sincerity on the part of the sender. Just look at the options which can probably harass the listener - Is he credible but insincere? Is he incredible but sincere? While trying to sort out these issues, he probably misses the most important thing—the message.

The three R's of marketing communication are based on the theories and principles which govern marketing. The first R, which is of primary importance, stands for undertaking responsibilities in an adult and mature manner.

The corporate image is built upon responsibilities undertaken and executed in a manner appropriate for the industrial sector.

This brings us to the second R—relationship. This can only be built and maintained when there is an efficient flow of communication. You cannot expect a good relationship with anyone if you are in disagreement with him all the time. Proper and conductive relationship leads to the development of result-oriented strategies, which is absolutely imperative in marketing of any kind.

The last of the alphabets reveal a solitary O with six sub-divisions explaining the basics of marketing communication. The first denotes occupants, the potential customers. Knowledge of this can lead to devising strategies for maximum return. The next O specifies objects currently being used by customers. In other words, what do the consumers currently buy, and why do they buy, what they buy?

This brings us to the next O — the objectives of the customer.

Remember, there is no close link between what is acceptable and not-so-acceptable to the consumer. Unless it is communicated in a manner which is appreciated by them, they will not accept the new product or may even give it up for an alternative product.

To come to the fourth O — the organization. The brand name of the organization communicates quality, respectability, and familiarity to the consumers. If a new product is introduced in the market, it will sell more because of the name of the company and the organization rather than for its intrinsic quality. The intrinsic worth of the product will be realized subsequent to its initial sale.

The last two O's clarify when and the where of marketing, i.e., the occasion and the operations—when do the clients buy, what they do and where do they buy them?

The first of these two would give a clue as to what has to be communicated so that consumers feel that this is the appropriate product for all occasions. The second of these would be contingent upon the retailer or distributor. A retailer or distributor's relationship will decide the fate of a new product. Good rapport would elicit more cooperation from them and a greater flow of positive consumers. Much is clarified about the subject through pnemonics. Understanding of the same, whilst playing or juggling with alphabets can reveal some known, but not well thought of principle and concepts.

COMMUNICATION ENHANCES MOTIVATION

Communication is not merely the transmission of ideas and messages but also a process by which we secure the participation of the members of a group by motivating them. Merely exchanging information with the desired feedback can make communication short-lived if participation is not sought. It can be primarily achieved through a search for ideas and reactions by an empathetic attitude. Unless all concerned are made to feel that they are important, none would be willing to participle or communicate in a group where they have no standing.

After the completion of the first step, the rest naturally falls into place. Not only should communication be an elicitation of feedback on the comments made but also the creation of opportunities, which would excite comment. This would greatly help in decision-making where brainstorming is a necessity. Sharing ideas, problems, plans, information and balancing of viewpoints all help in securing the participation of the individuals.

Participation itself is not sufficient. A lot needs to go into motivation if participation is to be of more than a superficial nature. There thus remains the level of the 'motivator' and the 'motivated'. The job of both is equally tough. Despite the likes and dislikes, the 'motivator' if he/she wants full cooperation and participation at work of otherwise, has to improve work relationships by showing keen interest in the worker plus respect for him which will make him reciprocate and work in a similar vein. He/she has to put in more labour by identifying the job requirements and specifying personal preferences regarding it. If he/she has managed to earn the respect of the workers by respecting them, he/she should have no difficulty in securing their co-operation on specifying his/her own job preferences.

Subsequent to this, recognition of one's performance, coupled with praise, goes a long way in building up confidence plus inculcating a willingness to outshine the performer.

It is not necessary for everything to be rosy for members on the other side of the table. Errors, practical mistakes and other loopholes in performance are bound to crop up in any organization. The tactful handing of those responsible is necessary. If on the contrary, the mistakes are pointed out crudely a withdrawal of the self-raises barriers that go on widening till relationships and all ideas of participation are ripped apart. For this, it is imperative to work in unison to develop a participatory programme for improvement and future progress of the group. But for this, the motivator has to realize his/her potential where understanding others, organizing matters, integrating and developing ideas is concerned. Until he/she is not sure about it, his/her communication would fall short of expectations – his/her own and group's.

At the end of the scale lie those members of the group who have to be motivated to put in their usually with proper and effective motivation which they feel and can voice openly and freely, be it opinions, aspirations and problems. These could be personal as well as related to the job. Once they secure the necessary encouragement, they are motivated to made worthy and useful suggestions with the use of special talents in their possession. If that, however, does not happen, they have the confidence that they can spell out reasons for their inability to accomplish that task. This, however, does not prove to be the ultimate cause of failure. If encouraged properly, they can be encouraged to overcome their own limitations and improve their performance, which would be beneficial to the organization as well as to themselves. Finally, they would be able to perceive their own shortcomings and scale the barriers, if any.

All this would not be possible if participation was not sought and achieved through appropriate motivation. If participation was not sought and achieved through appropriate motivated through appropriate motivation. If participation is to be complete, both parties, that is, the ones who motivate and the ones who are motivated, should work together to achieve the goal of totality in performance and excellence.

A COMMUNICATION MANAGER

Are you a manager or on the way to becoming one? Are you aware of the magnitude of the tasks assigned to you? If the answer to all these queries is yes, then it necessitates rethinking, resorting the reassembling ideas and concepts so that one emerges as a prosperous manager. As all problems start and end at the level of communications, a reallocation of roles is what is needed and desired.

Five differing roles have to be considered where a communicating manager is involved. An executor of tasks; a leader a subordinate an information source and a contributor to the development of the organization. At the elementary level, it is a combination of all these qualities, which would strengthen the functioning of an organization. As a major link between the top management and the people under him, the manager has to take a firm stand while passing information both upward as well as downwards. Messages have to be carefully shitted at his/her level, and the pros and cons weighed so that the final outcome or result is a perfect co-ordination between the people at the top rung and bottom rung.

As an executor of tasks, the communicating manager has both problems solving as well as decision-making to do. What conflicts would he encounter, how would he sort them out with the help of his peers and colleagues, and how much of his personal decisions thrust upon them need careful screening and pruning at the personal level. After all, it is how and what he communicates that will motivate people to work or shelve it. Having accepted authority and initiative, he has to anticipate problems, if any, before taking any stand, as he would be accountable to his superiors. Finally, after cognizance of the problems, which might arise, he has to learn to be effective in the transmission so that there is one-to-one correspondence between his mental set-up and the people with whom he has to work or who will work for him.

The next role of the communicating manager is that of a leader. How effectively he unites the group members, conjoins them to put in their best efforts and make contributions to the hilt. A proper delegation of the job to those concerned is what is of paramount importance. He has to motivate them into putting in their best by various communicative strategies. This could only come about as a result of proper and correct involvement of the people and development of potential. To be able to recognize the same by repeated counselling and listening to problems, reconciling himself to facts pertaining to almost any problem necessitate leadership qualities. If has to be a happy mix of conviction and contention so that the contention meter stays upright and there is neither 'flight nor fight' leading to dissatisfaction and discontentment. Whilst the communicating manager happily takes on the leader's role, he has to remember too that he is subordinate to certain members within an organization. His integrity, loyalty to those high up in the hierarchy is absolutely imperative. In other words, establishing "sender credibility" on the part of the communicating manager is a must. The amount of discretion, tact and self-discipline, which he exercises, will help him in establishing his integrity with his superiors and his subordinates. An old adage, "Practice what you preach" will go a long way in enabling him/her to communicate the messages with conviction and strength.

As the manager receives his/her input from the top management, the job of information and transmitting messages mounts as more and more members fall within the group. Taking on a prejudiced or biased opinion in no way helps. It is primarily listening with both ears and then interpreting according to the facts presented which will help in selection and transmission of important contributions.

The final role which the communicating manager has to undertake is that of a contributor to the organization's development. Keeping the progress of the organization in mind, a proper, thinking, planning and then proposing of ideas and concepts should be done. But while the final step being taken, he/she should remember that it should come in the form of suggestion with appropriate question answer techniques, which would enlist as well as ascertain a correct and desired feedback from the interactants. This does not mean that he/she should accept and agree with all that has been proposed, as he would be accountable for wrong decisions, if any. He should have the capacity to disagree on issues, which are not in favour of the organization in a tactful and diplomatic manner.

All these roles, when observed and adhered to be managers, lead to the overall growth and development of the organization. None of these are absolutely independent. All of them overlap each other, with the manager adopting differing roles on differing occasions. However, understanding and appraisal of these roles is absolutely imperative for any manager if he/she wants to be an effective communicator and effective manager.

For managers, having international experience is rapidly moving from "desirable" to "essential." A study by the Columbia University School of Business reported that successful executives must have multi-environment and multinational experience to become CEOs in the 21st century. The ability to compete in the global economy is the single greatest challenge facing business today. Organizations will want to negotiate, buy and sell overseas, consider joint ventures, market and adapt products for an international market and improve their expatriates' success rate. All of this involves communication.

Products have failed overseas sometimes simply because a name may take on unanticipated meanings in translation: the Olympic copier Roto in Chile (roto in Spanish means 'broken'); the Chevy Nova in Puerto Rico (no va means 'doesn't go'); the Randan in Japan (randan means 'idiot'); Parker Pen's Jotter pen ('jockstrap' in some Latin American markets). This type of mishap is not an American monopoly: A successful European chocolate and fruit product was introduced into the U.S. with the unfortunate name "Zit."

Naming a product is communication at its simplest level. The overall implications of intercultural communication for global business are enormous. Take the case of EuroDisney, later renamed Disneyland Paris. For the year 1993, the theme park lost approximately US $1 billion. Losses were still at US $1 million a day in 1994-95. There were many reasons for this, including a recession in Europe, but intercultural insensitivity was also a very important factor. No attention was paid to the European context or to cultural differences in management practice, labour relations, or even such simple matters as preferred dining hours or availability of alcohol and tobacco. EuroDisney signals the danger for business practitioners immersed in financial forecasting, market studies and management models when they overlook how culture affects behaviour. Few things are more important to conducting business on a global scale than skill in intercultural communication.

For all these reasons, communication is crucial to business. Specialized business knowledge is important, but not enough to guarantee success. Communication skills are vital.

Gary Lessuisse, the new assistant dean for master's programs at the School of Business, who recruited UW students for many years for Ford Motor Company, found effective communication in the workplace to be essential. His advice? Think before you communicate. Be an active listener. Be focused on your audience in your response. Be brief and be gone.

MEANINGFUL COMMUNICATION ENHANCES LEARNING

Learning to respond in accordance with the intent of the communicator is contingent upon a number of factors. The amount, the speed and the participation in learning are factors pertaining to the individual who perceives the same.

The strength of importance of the need greatly affects the speed of learning. For instance, during examination time the process of learning is highly charged with the desire to secure high grades. Couple this with total reinforcement. Nothing would be easier to grasp or retain than the subject being learnt. If on the other hand, there is only partial reinforcement problems arise, as learning is more resistant to change in such circumstances. Contradictions in presentation or contradictory statements can hamper the initial learning with the participant trying to figure out the correct way.

Another way of improving is procedure of learning is establishing the stimulus respond – reward cycle. Like Pavlov's dog, which was conditioned to respond in a manner if a reward is offered on a platter, the process of learning could be faster and quicker.

Not only the reward but the amount of it also pays a significant role in learning or "unlearning" of a particular message. In other words, the rewards, the amount of it and the immediacy of the same, condition the responses of the individual.

As more and more learning takes place along the same line, that is with the original stimulus-response association, anything which is in accordance with the original stimulus is grasped easily and retained for a longer period. As and when the stimulus is changed for a novel one, which is at loggerheads with the original stimulus, it results in a mental block leading to queries for easing truant learning situation and content. Learning is always maximum at the beginning and in the end in the order of symbols or words used by the facilitator. This is why ideas and concepts are repeated again and again in different words on in differing terminology with emphasis on different parts of the same idea.

Trying to elicit feedback or entail participation from the receiver speeds up the process of learning as the participant, while taking part, negates partial reinforcements, clarities doubts and builds towards a more concrete and wholesome picture or a meaningful (from the perspective of the receiver) one. But if the message is consolidated or contradictory to learning, the process is slowed down. There would be initial self-despondence and futile attempts to sort out the implication of the message.

Subsequent to this, clarifications would be sought so that the learning process moves with ease and without any barriers.

A message which is presented in isolation rather than with competing messages is normally learnt faster and retained for a greater span of time. For example, eradication on theories presented by various scientists if done one at a time with sufficient time gap would lead to greater comprehension, better learning and excellent retention. Simplifying the message, making it easier to remember by use of simple words and uncomplicated ideas result in a simple long-lasting and well-learnt response. The more complex or consolidated the message, or for that matter response, the higher the probability of getting the original stimulus.

To be aware of the basic factors, which help or hinder the learning process is absolutely imperative for any good communicator. A communication is never a one-time process but an on-going one; it is effective communication is aimed at.

Realizing the need of the interactant, the communicator should provide the stimulus in a manner that it becomes meaningful and concrete for the receiver. Once the initial stage is over, reinforcement along similar lines is what is needed. Learning would be complete, responses would be conditioned and communications would be effective and excellent.

THE ART OF PRESENTATION

Communicating with an audience can be frightening, even scary, with each sitting there, ready to pounce on and kill the presentation or the presenter. To empathies with the presenter, who has to face probably 40-50 strange faces, is not the task assigned to the audience. It is the presenter who has to empathiese with his audience, trying to understand their viewpoint and how he/she can best fit in his/her message in the cognitive scheme of the audience.

To excel in the art of presentation, one has to learn how to exercise control – control over the material to be presented, the self and the audience. The first stage is the preparation of the material. There is absolutely no harm in preparing more material than necessary. Once this is ready, use your brain and give it structure – what should come first, what should follow it and so on. Learn to differentiate between the objective and the assignment that has fallen to your lot. Your attempt should merely be the satisfaction of the purpose not the elucidation of the assignment. Once you have done the brainstorming, delete the extra material. Emphasize on the opening. If you do not capture your audience right at the start, you have lost them forever. Any amount of persuasion or the use of stylistic devices will not help you to regain the confidence where your abilities for presentation are concerned.

Thereafter, have your key areas marked out in order of importance and, finally, have the summary ready. A pertinent question, which often plagues many minds, is whether the material to be presented should be memorized. Memorization can bring the mind under pressure, with thoughts cluttering up the brain. Try to learn the thoughts behind the words. Let the audience know right at the start what you are talking about so that they understand and when you give them the bottom line they are not left floundering in the dark while presenting your material, remember to grip the audience's attention and to keep them interested.

COMMUNICATION AND PARTICIPATION

Communicating in a group many a times cannot only be tedious but also problematic. Clash of egos, attitudes and interests with vacillating behavioural syndromes may result in loss of money, time and energy. Participatory communication within groups, thus, entails a high-level of communicative competence together with recognition of each individual as a separate entity, with a free will and volition to express his views effectively.

Within a group, all cannot and will not speak. The more vocal ones will definitely have and edge over the rest. It is comparatively simple to study them. The other lot necessarily have to be studied with the aid of techniques devised specifically for the study of non-verbal behaviour.

NON-VERBAL COMMUNICATION

The mute/silent sorts are to be first analyzed in a group by studying the two aspects of their personalities. The first of these is kinesic, i.e., the use of gestures, posture and hands etc., to communicate.

The second of these is a variety of Para-language/ voice and articulation used for expressing various motions.

Object, language, clothes and things, which you carry, also cannot various messages. Are you formally attired for a formal meeting or you are still in your pajamas and chappals? How frequently do you forget to carry the important papers and how do you carry them?

Then comes the space and distance which you maintain or proxemics. Do you prefer to maintain a safe distance or lean over the other interactants in a group or insist on proximity when lest desired?

The last of the lot is time or chronemics. Time managements, within and outside a group is of paramount significance. Adherence to or negligence of the same tell about the individual.

Remember, for participatory communication, studying these aspects of non-verbal communication is absolutely imperative. They help you to gain an insight into the other interactants, silent or otherwise; assist you in analyzing their traits, and co-ordinating them towards higher goals. These behavioral patterns are mostly involuntary. Therefore, they should be studied as they have a major impact on our relationships with other members of the group.

ESSENTIALS FOR GROUP PARTICIPATION

If group participation is needed and desired, it is of primary importance to first acquaint oneself and the organization with the goals to be achieved. The may be positive or negative. Awareness of the same and strategic action along the same lines is to be attempted. This can be brought about by providing accurate, necessary and adequate information to all group members.

Merely providing date is not sufficient. If the group members are not adequately motivated, try as you might, you will not succeed. Urge them, motivate them, to overcome hurdles and obstacles while maintaining their morale. Needless to say, higher the morale, higher will be the level of efficiency or work input.

For building up the morale of the group members, develop and atmosphere of mutual confidence and understanding. If I let you weep on my shoulder, you must also be willing to do the same. In other words, all should be on the same level, either some will have to sleep or some will have to rise. The balance should be maintained. In this mutually, reinvigorating environment, you can get the best individual performance as well as the team input.

It is not easy to stimulate everyone within the group so as to elicit maximum cooperation from all. Understanding communicants as individuals and as members of a group through their verbal and non-verbal communication strategies, the network within which they operate, and finally, the essentials of participation, requires keen perception and an analytical eye. But once accomplished, the bonds are strengthened, ties are reinforced and results are magnified.

COMMUNICATION A KEY TO LEARNING

Communication is a process by which the sender transmits his/her message and the recipient gets and responds to it accordingly. Moving a little-beyond the learning at school and college levels, where the focus is primarily on books and rote memorization learning in the arena of life with dimensions of rewards, acknowledgement and other unrewarded areas have a greater impression on the communicative input and output of the individual.

Business Communication is communication used to promote a product, service, or organization; relay information within the business; or deal with legal and similar issues.

Business Communication encompasses a variety of topics, including Marketing, Branding, Customer relations, Consumer behaviour, Advertising, Public relations, Corporate communication, Community engagement, Research & Measurement, Reputation management, Interpersonal communication, Employee engagement, Online communication, and Event management.

Primarily, the response is conditioned on the temporal dimensions of effects of learning. These could be short-term or long-term, immediate of delayed. Subsequent to this is the nature of affect of a stimulus, which helps us to perceive an object as it is and communicate about it in a verbal or non-verbal manner. In other words, this would be contingent on the receiver, his mental state and how the sender transmits the message, together with medium and channel used by him/her. If the communicator is insensitive to the needs of the receiver, the communication would probably not reach the targeted audience. But this is one of those rare occasions when the communication is processed without taking cognizance of the receiver. How effectively or efficiently the recipient grasps the communicative intent would be a result of his/her cognition, comprehension, emotional arousal, identification, attitude, overt behaviour and interest. All these would act as determining factors, which would induce or lessen the learning process and result in his/her grasp of the transmitted message.

Awareness of a particular issue is subsequent to direct experience or through second-hand reality which, in other words, would be a symbolic representation of the known world. Whilst in the former instance, extensive knowledge is required to grasp the message, in the latter, it could also lead to an unwitting bias, a bias resulting in a prejudiced perception of the message. The cognition on the part of the receiver based on the aforementioned points, would also help him/her to develop personal or socially relevant interest or disinterest in the subject. The next stage is how well he/she (receiver) comprehends the message subsequent to his/her perception. What relationship does the receiver perceive between the content and his own attitudes and values? Do all of them fit in neatly? If yes, communication is effectively countered with a desired feedback if not, problems arise, with more and more elucidation and example.

Not only the content but also the context is equally important. Together with the cognitive scheme of the recipient, the patterning of the response is based on our learning, regarding motivation, plus the correct mood for effective arousal of and production of the feedback. Many a times, difficult, moody behaviour can lead to a communicative impasse when the best solution is "Let's discuss it some other time."

Identification would lead to an empathetic understanding and learning of various normal and abnormal situations with stress arousal or change, leading to instigating conditions, which would modulate the resultant behavior. Recognizing the need to transmit with a similarity in approach and behaviour can lead to psychological gratification with responses formulated accordingly.

The attitude of the recipient of a message, which, while receiving it, is primarily focused on either a conservation, or reinforcement of existing views determines the response. Anything in accordance with it is accepted and the rest either shelved or really not taken cognizance of. Overt behaviour or response would then be naturally contingent upon the attitude of the recipient.

The interest of the receiver is dependent on the aforementioned points. Social, personal and educational determinants, which mould a person's perception develop interest and enable him/her to respond in a particular manner, are all by-products of learning which has taken place and which will continue to take place. There might be instance when he will change his mode of thinking and suitably responsive operations will be undertaken. So long as the sender recognizes the perceptual needs which if moulded according of the learning to the receiver, or the other way round, chances of miscommunication are minimized to great extent.

Does business language have to be dull? And full of jargon? And generally mind-numbing? Brian Fugere, Chelsea Hardaway and Joan Warshawsky don't think so. In 2003, the three former consultants at Deloitte Consulting released a software program called Bullfighter. It includes a "jargon database" and "Bull Composite Index calculator" that allow you to measure just how bad your communication is.

Better yet, it has a feature that allows you to copy and paste any awful office memo that crosses your electronic inbox, rate it for readability—or lack thereof—and email the rating anonymously to the transgressor.

Now the light-hearted trio has a new book on the same "Why Business People Speak Like Idiots: A Bullfighter's Guide" (176 pages, Free Press, New York) The book attributes failures in business communication to four common missteps: the obscurity trap, the anonymity trap, the hard-sell trap and the tedium trap. In fact, they maintain "jargon, wordiness and evasiveness are the active ingredients of modern business speak." But fear not: The book uses humour to help you devise ways to communicate your message —in a sales pitch, a web page, even an annual report—and avoid "corporate-speak."

HOW TO ORGANISE MEETINGS

The most interesting thing about a meeting which, if not chalked out properly, is the accompanying goodies. The number of breaks and their duration, coupled with light delicacies, which would appeal to the palate of all and sundry, make a meeting successful. If on the contrary, meetings are properly prepared, things can be more exciting and challenging.

Motivation is what is basically lacking at official get-togethers. The group leader first has to decide the agenda of the meeting, as he/she must be clear about what he/she wants to achieve. Finally, he/she has to devise ways through which he/she can solicit the complete co-operation of all the participants.

The first step is good and sound planning of the agenda, with sufficient time given to the participants to sort out the matters relating to the main issues. This is done so that subsidiary or ancillary topics pertaining to the main issue can be through out in advance. This is done with the basic objective of keeping the participants fully aware of the plans so that they do not come as a surprise. In case of queries about the agenda or suggestion, if any, they should always be handed over a day in advance so that the flow of communication at the time of the meeting is effective and efficient without there being any discussion on the validity of the question and their subsequent answers. While this comprises taking care of the basic issues to be discussed, it is also imperative for the group leader to ascertain that the physical environment is suitable and conducive to a proper exchange of information. This should naturally be of secondary importance and should not take on a major role.

Once proper arrangements have been made, scheduling has been done and participants informed, the rest of the communication is postponed for the final session. The group leader has to take on the role of a facilitator, merely guiding and directing and not issuing orders. This does not mean that things should get out of hand, with each member voicing his/her opinions on a particular issue. The facilitator has to keep the group in order, having stress on the objectives and activities that would strengthen the group.

A brainstorming session would just be ideal, as it would involve a majority of the participants. The facilitator should again be able to exercise control, be open to suggestions, and control emotions, if any, when issues pertaining to the personal element are tackled. He/she should also be an active listener and should inculcate this quality in the rest of the group, as it would lead to greater harmony and accord between all. Listening should, in such cases, be hundred percent without interruption so that there is no break in the flow of thought. Active listening, however, does not entail acceptance. In cases of dissent, differences should be sorted out by resorting to the question-answer technique.

The participants at a meeting should be bold enough to be creative instead of adhering to the hackneyed traditional thoughts and concepts. Whether they are accented or not by the group is another matter, but the incentive should be there. Who knows the members or some of them might come up with an ingenious idea.

At meetings such as these records should be maintained systematically, preferably in a manner that is visible to all the participants. This obviates the chances of miscommunication on the recorder's part. At the end, a summary of the accepted details and facts should be read out to enlist the approval of all the members.

It is necessary for the participants to realize that, the meeting is important and that their time has been well spent. If the group leader can accomplish these two tasks, he/she can be sure that further meetings are going to conclude on a successful note with equally positive and useful inputs from all participants.

Dealing with Difficult People While Making a Sales Call

As a working sales executive one often come across with different type of people. You must have experienced some tough moments during the calls.

Your clients include almost all variety of people from all segments of the society. No policy of strategies can be generated in tackling these clients. Almost every person becomes restive in nature when it comes to spending money.

Hereby I include some of the interesting moments you may encounter in your sales carrer.

You can classify your clients into the following categories:

(a) Angry or short tempered persons
(b) Rude people
(c) 'Know – it – all' clients
(d) Who refuse to deal with man
(e) Who user abusive language
(f) Who cannot take decisions.

ANGRY OR SHORT TEMPERED CLIENT

Hostile aggressive behaviour is probably the most difficult to deal with whatever form it comes inputs underlying antagonism can make even the strongest person sun for cover. Some of the characteristics described by seminar delegates are aggression calling people unmentionable names, playing points – stabbing comments, causing conflict in any way possible.

Hostile aggressive can appear out of control at times, but don't be fooled; they usually know just what they are doing. If you show any signs of weakness you will open yourself up and possibly become their prey.

Their behaviour says. I want it now, regard of your needs.

There are six strategies for dealing with hostile – aggressive :

(1) Wait for the time to turn out of steam
(2) Don't take their behaviour, leave if need be
(3) Get help when you need it
(4) Show your disapproval
(5) Change what they say into something more acceptable, and repeat it back to them.

EXPLOSIVES

How to recognize the symptoms and avoid being the target.

Explosives become out of control, often without any warning. They are loud, slamming a look on the table or shaking a finger while yelling at you they are accusatory, name calling techniques such as "you don't" or 'How could you be so stupid? They interrupt you to tell you how wrong your point of view is: 'only an idiot would think that way'.

When dealing with as explosive, you feel as if you can't say anything without causing more abuse. You feel you want to hide. Explosives reduce many people to tears. They can and do make others appear out of control by taking charge of the situation by force. Explosives have learned this behaviour and perfected it because it works to accomplish what they want, at least at that particular moment. Often you will find these people in a position of authority which adds to your fear of communicating with them.

If you seen to be a victim of this type of behaviour, examine what makes you an easy target.

We can ask ourselves these questions:-

1. Are you timid, using a faint, soft voice?
2. Do you feel unsure of yourself?
3. Do you lack confidence that the information you are discussing is correct and up to date?
4. Are you an experienced, or new to the job?
5. Do you have low self-esteem?
6. Do you put up with this behaviour hoping that it will stop or go away?

If the answer to any of their question is 'yes', the first step is to change these traits that makes you an easy target.

If your voice is weak, record it and listen to it then start working on it until you can hear a definite improvement.

End sentences with a downward tone when making a strong statement, an upward one for a question.

If you are feeling unsure of yourself, the best thing to do is to remain silent until you are confident about what you have to say.

An adage I like is: - If you have nothing to say, don't let any one persuade you to say it.

Are you new to the job? Inexperienced?

Once you know that there is an explosive to deal with, move every attempt to stay out of his way until you have more experience. Don't act like an expert before you are one.

How self-esteem is something many people suffer from. I often hear the statement he makes me feel bad / lowers my self-esteem.

Remember 'NO ONE MAKES US HAVE LOW SELF ESTEEM'. It is an inside job, something we do to ourselves through years of self-abuse and poor self-talk. Being by being more positive about yourself. Don't put yourself down using phrases like 'I was so stupid' 'This is a dumb question' or 'I am sorry'.

Begin by telling yourself that you are smart, useful, and correct. Now add two adjectives of your own. Remember 'You are what you say you are all day long'.

If your self-esteem is high and none of the personal issues above apply to you, may be you have put up with the explosive behaviour because you didn't know how to deal with it.

There will being more reasons to be a victim if you follow their basic strategies for dealing with the explosive.

1. Don't use fighting words like, you are wrong. You can never win a fight with an explosive. Do say things like 'In my opinion 'or I don't agree with you but I want to hear more of what you are saying.
2. Use the explosive's name at the beginning of the conversation or whenever you want to take control.
3. Keep eye contact at all times. You will appear more in control of yourself. When you look away it appears that you are weak or afraid, and the explosive will know he has his next victim.
4. Don't tell him about you weaknesses, whatever it is? He will not have sympathy and will only point it out to you at every chance he gets.
5. Let him explode until he has seen out of powder. Once that happens and you begin to speak he may interrupt you.

6. Stop the explosive from interrupting you by telling him 'You interrupted me', then continue with what you were saying. Each time he interrupts, you must stop him with the same sentence, 'You interrupted me'. If you allow him to continue interrupting, he wills see you as weak again and your point of view will never be heard.
7. Don't take his attacks personally; an explosive would say the same thing to anyone who was is available.
8. Make sure that your communication is at eye level, either sitting or standing. Don't stay seated when he is standing over you.

RUDE OR INSULTING ATTACKERS

The verbal attack is a particularly difficult kind of 'hook'. The attackers object is to get the victim emotionally involved in a no-win situation, when the attack is successful; the attacker feels superior to his victim.

There are many varieties of verbal attack, but the most common uses a negative presumption to hook the victim. There are some examples together with responses to keep you from becoming a victim.

REMEMBER: THE BASIC STATEGY FOR THE VERBAL ATTACK IS TO RESPOND TO THE PRESUMPTION, NOT THE ACCUSATION OR INSULT.

Not this fault.

There are some basic strategies for dealing with the first type of Know All:

1. Be prepared
2. Listen carefully
3. Don't make mistakes
4. Double-check all your work and facts, this type of knows - alls is influenced by facts.
5. Don't challenge, but offer alternative ideas if you know he is wrong.
6. Make friends not enemies.

Some strategies for second type of Know - All too.

1. Ask question let him to elaborate — Remember that he is all headlines and no news and that therefore he will soon run out of back up information.
2. Cope with him alone.
3. Point out that his opinions may not be accurate, while his giant size ego is intact.

KNOW – ALLS

KNOW - ALLS are people who always have the perfect answers, at least in their own minds. They are insensitive to any one's opinion except their own.

This type of know - all actually does know most or all the answers. He is smart and has a way of pushing his projects or ideas through to completion.

1. The second type of know - all's is all headlines and now news. He will act as if he has the answers to everything. But most of the time his facts are incorrect or unrehearsed. You may learn the hard way that he is a phony, because he sounds so convincing. He does not take any responsibility for his mistakes and will have a mile long list of plausible reasons as to why the mistake was.
2. Decide if it is worth your time to be with this person.

LISTENING

There are many skills that will help us in dealing with difficult people "Successful listening" is one of them. As it is the most often used, yet least understood and researched of the communicating processes. We do it all day long. Usually without thinking about it, yet we often do it badly.

Good listening requires a number of skills. They include concentration, a desire to understand the other person's point of view, an awareness of what is meant. The listeners can away the directing of the conversation and he is free to observe minutely. Here are some tips to improve your listening skills.

(a) Don't interrupt to demand clarification of insignificant or irrelevant details.

(b) Try not to anticipate what the other person will say.

(c) When someone mentions a particular reaction or emotional response, repeat it so he knows you understand it.

(d) Let your body give reassuring messages. Maintain eye contact and avoid fiddling with your fingers or thumbs. Make sure your body indicates an understanding & interest.

Thus, we can say active listening is a skill which consists of reflecting back to the speaker a statement of what you think you heard which will surely solve the problem of the subordinates about their manager "he / she never listens".

Refuse to Deal with 'Men'

We have talked about many different types of difficult behaviour in variety of situations, the innate difference between men and women can make for challenging situations regardless of any other circumstances.

The male body & mind are significantly different from the female body & mind.

While men focus on one_thing at a time. Women focus on many things at one time. Men understand that women's talent are different from yours. Acknowledge their ability to do many things well and stop considering them scattered or unfocussed.

Men smile less, causing them be seen as strong and powerful, women smile more, inciting interruption and causing them to be seen as less of a leader but more approachable and helpful.

CLARIFY YOUR THINKING
OBTAIN FAVOURABLE ATTENTION
MAKE EFFECTIVE USE OF FEED-BACK
USE "YOU" APPEAL
NOTE SOCIAL CLIMATE AND SPECIFIC SITUATION
INCLUDE BENEFITS TO THE RECEIVER
CONSIDER TONE AS WELL AS CONTENT
ALWAYS PLANT MENTAL PICTURES AS GOAL IMAGES
TALK ONLY IN POSITIVE TERMS
IMPRESS, REPEAT, ASSOCIATE TO GET RETENTION
OFFER AND EARN LIKING AND RESPECT
NULLIFY BARRIERS TO TRANSMISSION AND RECEPTION

One must always keep in mind that business is conducted through various channels of communication, including the Internet, Print (Publications), Radio, Television, Ambient, Outdoor, and Word of mouth.

There are several methods of business communication, including:

- Web based communication - for better and improved communication, anytime anywhere ...
- E-mails, which provide an instantaneous medium of written communication worldwide;
- Reports - important in documenting the activities of any department;
- Presentations - very popular method of communication in all types of organizations, usually involving audiovisual material, like copies of reports, or material prepared in Microsoft PowerPoint or Adobe Flash;
- Telephoned meetings, which allow for long distance speech;
- Forum boards, which allow people to instantly post information at a centralized location; and
- Face to face meetings, which are personal and should be succeeded by a written follow-up.

Internal and External Business Communication

There are two main aspects of business communication: the one in which communication takes place within one organization, among it's members (internal), and the other one where the organization communicates with another organization, or another external subject (external).

Internal communication includes communication of corporate vision, strategies, plans, corporate culture, shared values and guiding principles, employee motivation, cross-pollination of ideas, etc.

External communication includes branding, marketing, advertising, customer relations, public relations, media relations, business negotiations, etc.

"It is vital for the success of our companies that businessmen and women emerge as real leaders and demonstrate their ability to communicate effectively, internally and externally." says Sir Colin Marshall, chairman, British Airways.

"Communication in stressful change situations requires sustained and extensive interpretation and reinforcement. Competent, high-trust firms are in a position to communicate the same basic messages to all levels, from middle management to shop floor, with nothing left out on the grounds that those below would not understand it." Tony Eccles, London Business School

According to Sir John Harvey-Jones,former chairman ICI and renowned European 'troubleshooter' "No manager can be effective in his job unless he is able to communicate. It is the most essential single skill. I hope that managers everywhere will seek to improve their ability, for it is one that can be learned."

"Effective communication needs to be built around this simple foundation and realization: communication is a dialogue, not a monologue. In fact, communication is more concerned with a dual listening process." So said Dr. Heinz Goldmann, Chair, Heinz Goldmann International Foundation for Executive Communications, Geneva.

MARKETING IS COMMUNICATION

The five W's and one H of communication. That is Who, What, Where, When, Why and How are applicable not only to interpersonal communication but also in in the area of marketing. Spell out around advertisement at a wrong time and the money goes down the drain, for example the product like cold drinks or thirst quenchers, that are needed more in summers, if advertised extensively during peak winter season. But time it well, after selecting the TGA (Target Group Audience), word it accurately and with the bang you hit the market. All it needs is the little bit of perceptive thinking.

According to experts in the area of marketing communications, there are some immutable laws which if well understood can lead to success, improved finances and overall increases in clientele. For instance, it is always better to be first in advocating the idea than to be better. What is said, heard or ready initially finds an imprint in the mind of customers, the rest if it falls along the same line, is a mere addition or an appendage to the initial statement. For example take the very recent ad of 'Coke' on television whereby they use the punch line "Too Aaj to Jashn Mana Ley" and that of 'Thumps-up'. It even reinforces the initial learning with the customers trying to figure out where he had read or seen it first. Many a times, it so happened that you try to be first in the advocacy of an idea but some one beats you at it, for example the ad of 'Pepsi'. In instances such as these, trap your level best to set up a new category where your idea could perhaps be the first in the long chain of similar or closely resembling ideas to follow.

At the time of launching of a new product if you can possibly strive for communications rather than bringing out the product itself it is bound to have a lasting impact as the "Ponds" did for their "Seven day anti ageing and anti wrinkle' cream. Marketing communications could be in almost any form: T.V./ Radio/ Print Media/Exhibitions etc. The prospective customers should get to know about it long before the product itself takes its final shape and makes it first appearance in the market place. Basically, the quarrel between rival companies is not over the product itself, rather it is the battle over trying to gain supremacy over the perceptions of the customers. For instance take the case of "Ponds" and "Garnier" for their anti wrinkle face creams along with "Shanaz Hussain's" and many more similar products. This can only be down attempts that are made to reach out to the for flung customers, to measure their likes and dislikes regarding particular product and then to play upon their perceptions in such a manner they are convinced that this and this alone is the only product for me. It can be accomplished through written or oral communication, specially designed for this purpose.

While transmitting ideas or messages, it is extremely important to keep in mind the fact that two companies cannot use the same key word. If one company or organization is banking on one word which happens to convey the brand image, no matter how hard the other company might try, it just cannot impress upon the mind of the consumers its product by using similar well-associated key words. A negative re-play is needed. For example, 'the official drink' and 'nothing official about it' used by different Cola based soft drink companies during the World Cup Cricket matches ads telecasted on television.

Communications in the market place necessitates that you establish and maintain sender credibility. If you claim to be No. 1 when actually you are No. 2, the customer is unable to figure out the accurate positioning of the product, that is, there is a dichotomy between the claimed and mentally decided position. To be on the safer side, claim your actual position plus the strife for the higher rung in the ladder of success so that things come your way easily.

The strongest of all the laws is the law of the opposites.

Take the "Law of Leadership," for example. The Rieses have a one-liner to explain it: "It's better to be first than it is to be better." And they cite known brands- Coca Cola, McDonald's, and IBM. That looked unarguable, at first glance and there is another law that seemed to contradict the first, according to one participant- the "Law of Opposite"- which is also a one-liner: "If you're not the leader, then you need to be the opposite." They cited Pepsi Cola, which became the cola of the "younger crowd"- and thus was born the "Pepsi Generation." Coke is 120 years old. So, on the midst of such seeming contradictions, why are the Rieses so credible? The reason could be that one law works for one, and another law works for another. They are not actually contradictory; they may be stand-alone laws that work.

Many a times, when you find yourself placed on the second position, remember to play the game of building up on your opponent's strengths. Use them as a weapon to fight away their customers. In the market battle between 'Coke' and 'Pepsi', the latter hit out on an effective marketing strategy. An age old tradition – bound "Choice of new generation". In this illustration, while you have the tradition-bound consumers on one hand, and on the other hand you have the newer sect or those who are bold, brazen ready to rebel against anything that is or claims to be age-old or traditional.

Part of the success or failure of a product depends on its ability to catch the attention of the consumer or to keep it well-focused. The minute the attention wanders, it perceives a similar product of a different company by more eye-catching marketing strategies. So what becomes essential if an organization is to survive in the market place is its communication has to be impeccable, effective and self revelatory.

Communication for Social Cause

If social communication can benefit from branding exercises, can consumer product branding be based on social messages? How can brand promise and volunteerism create loyalty within the organisation?

These and other current branding issues were discussed on 'Brandwidth 2005,' a conference to discuss how successful brands are built and nurtured. Pranesh Misra, President and CEO, LOWE India, illustrated how consumer products can benefit from branding through social communication and not just the other way round. For instance, Lifebuoy's Little Gandhi and Surf's `Save two buckets' have benefited tremendously from public service communication. "With increasing competition and little differentiation in product features, organisations need to explore areas of a higher order and give better value to consumers," he said, adding, "but not all brands have the stature to move into this kind of communication."

Subroto Bagchi, CEO, MindTree Consulting, talked of the need for corporate branding driven by top leadership. "Not only should it be able to deliver value, but give it to employees ahead of expectations," he pointed out. He felt that organisations should create value for employees and fulfil the brand promise, which will result in volunteerism and employee loyalty. Other must-haves for corporate branding are customer inclusion, interactivity and consistency. I. S. Sivakumar, CEO, Agri-business, ITC Ltd., also threw light on the benefits of co-creation of brands with customers. ITC's e-choupal for instance, started as a supply-chain initiative, but has transformed itself into a platform that offers dignity of choice and informed transaction opportunities to farmers who are its customers, he said.

Let us examines this new and exciting genre that's grabbing eyeballs and attention and challenging the old order that defined advertising solely as a one dimensional, sell-sell-sell game!

Advertising communication is the public face of marketing with an uncomplicated, one-point-agenda to make products disappear from the shelves to the right hands and homes, with consistency and speed. Over time, areas like patriotism and social service have deployed advertising, but, at best, they were cute to watch tickling the feel-good glands... at worst, boring and preachy. Predictably these efforts came from the government quarters. Typically the issues tackled were 'safe' ones, never remotely touching sensitive themes like caste, religion or politics. As far as they were considered, these subjects were taboo and totally off-limits.

Much water has flown under the bridge since those politically correct and sanctimonious times with 'Social

Messaging' coming centre-stage as a powerful, persuasive and significant agent of social change. Ravi Naware (Chief Executive, Food Division, ITC) lays it on the line when he says that way beyond the much touted CSR, 'consumers today seem to be interested in more than just a great ad or quality product. They are interested in products that echo their own values.' Adds Ajit Varghese (MD, Max India, an agency that works closely with Britannia), 'We are witnessing a strong trend where brands are utilising issues that surrounds the consumer's immediate environment and addressing them through mainstream ads.'

Advertising communication, from time immemorial, has been consistently bad-mouthed by a section of society labelling them as shameless promoters of excess and useless mass consumerism. This has been fiercely defended by the ad fraternity citing examples where advertising communication has indeed attempted to be an effective and a powerful agent of social change. At least three ads of this 'genre' are presently occupying center-stage and inviting both attention and admiration.

The first - an Airtel ad - shows kids on either side of a barbed wire fence, (fig. 2) jump the barrier to indulge in a game of football in no-man's land. In an extraordinarily simple but powerful way, it works as a magnificent metaphor for communication as a solution to end all conflicts, wars and battles. Says Arvind Mohan (Chief Strategist Officer, Rediff DY&R), ' We wanted to create branding that went way beyond the purchase intent and made people proud to be associated with the brand.' Adds Amatesh Rao (National business head, Rediff DY&R), 'Admittedly commercials with social messages don't immediately bring about change, but they reflect strongly the change that is happening in society... a change that may not be perceptible or articulated but definitely taking shape in collective fashion, in the sensibilities of new age youth in a resurgent India.'

The Airtel Ad is creative, it breaks the clutter and it has been voted the best. Bharti Airtel Ltd., latest television advertisement-featuring two children on opposite sides of an international border getting together to play football in the no man's land has scored the highest (93 in ad reach index) in brand recall and awareness in Mint's survey of top ads in December. The ad from the cellular services firm scored a high of 99% in likeability, but slipped slightly on the believability and claim criteria. Its evocative tag line, "Barriers break when people talk", was believed by 81% of the people.

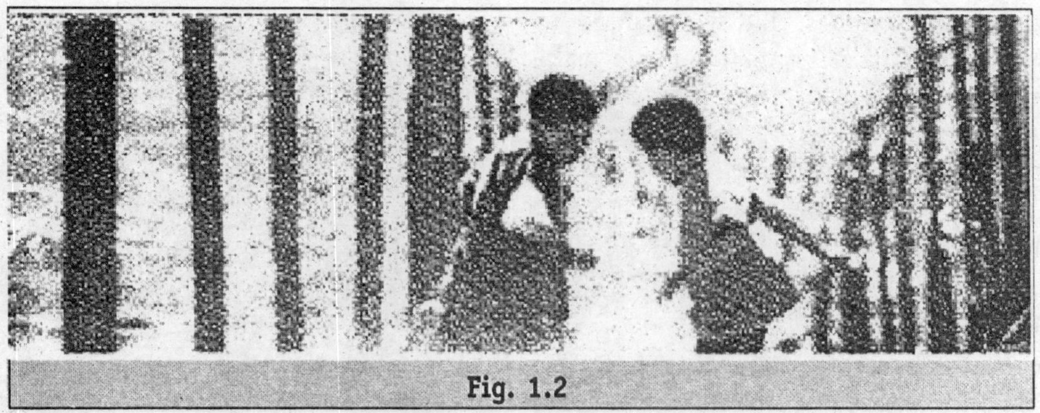

Fig. 1.2

Keeping it simple

How the idea that 'barriers are what you make of them' helped make the Airtel ad a winner. Telecom firm Bharti Airtel Ltd., new television ad (TVC), which topped Mint's monthly ad survey in 2008, was created by Rediffusion DY&R Pvt. Ltd. Amitesh Rao, its national business head, explains how the campaign took shape. "We wanted a campaign that would go way beyond the kind of communication we have been seeing in this sector. In the past, Airtel featuring world leaders — there was a need to produce an iconic campaign like that. A campaign that has stature and scale, and establishes the brand's credentials beyond product and service. So, the brief essentially was to convey the thought: Communication dissolves boundaries". They further elaborated.

Fig. 1.3

This campaign is not about a particular situation or context, it is about people. So we picked a neutral context, which would not lend itself to any association, and focused on the core idea. The original script went through a lot of editing. It started out as a fairly complicated script around these two little boys from countries which were at war with each other and with fathers who felt strongly about the situation. We explored several routes but at the end, the only thing that mattered was the simplicity of the message. In the end, we took everything but the two kids out of the script.

Some say featuring teenagers who knew the significance of those boundaries could have strengthened the message. If we had used teenagers, then it would come across as a conscious decision to communicate, to build bridges. But we wanted to focus on the idea that "barriers are what you make of them". And to a little kid, the space between those two boundaries looked like a good place for a game of football. It is a pure thought there is no construction behind it. They are clueless, and their actions are spontaneous, none of them are thinking like Miss World and consciously communicating to bring world peace.

The Tata Tea ad comes next. Fig. 1.4. The communication thought is truly clutterbusting, attempting to migrate tea from being a physical and emotional vitaliser to becoming a catalyst for social awakening. Percy Siganporia (MD, Tata Tea Ltd) quite categorically emphasises that the focus is to emotively connect the product with issues that drives the heart, mind and soul of India's emerging social consciousness. Executive Creative Director Amer Jaleel of Lowe (the agency behind this ad) sensed the restlessness among today's youth and extended the concept of 'waking

Fig. 1.4

up with tea' in a stunning communication package that embraced social awakening, giving a whole new dimension to the term 'Jago re'.

Lowe struck target again (group creative director Nikhil Rao, take a bow) with yet another brilliant, breakthrough concept that redefined the very meaning of Idea. Executive Chairman Balki was clear about the focus - how to position the brand as a better Idea' than anyone else and elevate it from transactional issues like price and value. Tar-geting politics as a platform and humorously-yet pointedly-dramatizing the so-cial inadequacies that plague the nation, with a mobile number (not a name) as an identity tag, the Idea Cellular communication truly deserves the fulsome 'What an Idea, Sirjee' salute! Fig. 1.5.

Fig. 1.5

Amidst the accolade and approval that has greeted these ads, there have been dissenting voices too. Is this brand of advertising relevant to the basic job it's meant to do? The popular consensus seems to be a resounding, yes. In today's environment, marketing and branding are increasingly becoming real, rooted, and relatable. Hence, they have a legitimate and deserved space. Besides, these ads reflect that magical, seamless embrace with reality. Do today's 'I-Me-Myself' generation really connect with the Jago Re or the Idea Cellular communication-without-barrier stuff, absorbed as they seem to be in living life, king-size? Fig. 1.6.

Fig. 1.6

Of course, they are! It's a total myth that today's youth only believes in celebrating life and are totally blind, uncaring and insensitive to the social inadequacies, causes and concerns. Never before has there been such passionate and dramatic demonstrations of rooting for justice (Jessica Lal case) or such immense acceptance for movies like Rang De Basanti. Sure, today's youth enjoy life, but their hearts continue to be in the right place, solidly re-affirming the validity and relevance of social messaging in advertising! Truly a great idea, sirjee!

Soulful social circuit: Corporates mix consumerism with conscience

Feeling philanthropic? Buy a pack of the Whisper brand of sanitary napkins. Or brush your teeth with Colgate toothpaste, bathe your kid with Doy soap, wear a Benetton T-shirt and Acuvue contact lens, have Kelloggs packaged cereal for breakfast, wash it down with tea made with Nestle milk powder, then make sure you drive down to the marketplace in a Maruti car which runs on Shell engine oil, pay your bills with your American Express credit card.

Make this your ritual if you care about blind adolescent girls, air pollution, AIDS, racism, destitute children, iron deficiency among pregnant women, world hunger... In short, if you care about the world, buy! Buy anything that comes with a social cause. And that would not be a tough job considering that the retail shelves today are choc-a-bloc with products that claim to have a heart and a penny for the poor and needy.

Call it a marketing gimmick or cause-related marketing, 'social service' is the new mantra in corporate boardrooms, even if it means throwing Philip Kotler out of the window. Says Suhel Seth, Chief Executive, Equus Advertising, "Cause-related marketing is a strategy that links the company or its brand with a social cause. Here, the corporate is giving two reasons to buy the product: one, the product benefit itself, and two, the intrinsic satisfaction of participating in a social cause. In a way, it is transaction-based philanthropy, which says, 'I am a responsible corporate citizen, so you can buy from me'. This kind of promotion creates a differentiating platform for the corporate in a marketplace where everyone is trying to push his own product, especially in a scenario where the consumer is increasingly growing cynical of self-laudatory advertising."

Which is why Procter & Gamble speaks very little about the product specifics of Whisper sanitary napkins. Instead, its ads talk about the superstitions associated with the subject. But the real 'cause' is that the company donates one rupee from every pack of Whisper sold towards educating blind adolescent girls. Called 'Project Drishti', P&G launched this programme in the wake of Whisper market-share falling from 51.1 per cent to 44.9 per cent in the first half of 1999. Says a P&G spokesperson, "Our product and the brand identify the women of today — it's modern, not forgetting the traditional values and has a heart too."

And how far has the 'cause' helped boost sales? "Well, considerably. We have gained in volume significantly," he says. "A study showed that quite a few of the women interviewed responded that they bought Whisper for three dominant reasons — charity value, community feeling and functionality." The hygiene factor came last for a sanitary product.

But Whisper will definitely not feel lonesome in this 'social' circuit. Sample this: Maruti Udyog has associated itself with environment with its air pollution campaigns and pollution checking counters, Kelloggs contributes towards creating awareness on ills of iron deficiency, Doy Soap (kids soap) makes a contribution towards giving a home to destitute children, MRF Tyres have espoused the cause of promoting stress-free driving on roads by highlighting the value of the smile through half-page colour advertisements, Benetton has internationally been associated with creating awareness about AIDS, safe sex, and fight against racial inequality and capital punishment even as American Express works for eradication of world hunger.

Then there are the health-freaks such as Johnson & Johnson which promotes eyecare clinics across the country, Nestle sells milk powder and the fact that mother's milk is the best babyfood, while Tata Steel contributes towards creating more healthcare centres in small towns and villages, and cosmetics MNC Avon makes a gesture towards creating awareness about breast cancer. Not to mention the computer literacy drive kicked off by computer companies NIIT and Zenith Computers.

Says Joe Plummer, executive vice-president, McCann-Erickson Worldwide, says, "The consumers that these companies want to reach out to are the socially and politically active trend-setters. They are receptive to such causes. In fact, a survey shows that the receptivity of cause-related marketing is highest among those between the age-groups of 19 and 49. Cause-related marketing is gaining ground world-wide.

In the United States, about 7 per cent of the marketing spend goes toward cause-related marketing. Statistics reveal that social causes as part of business culture has increased 8 per cent since 1993. The reason is that it creates a strategic positioning in the consumer's mind and increases brand loyalty and brand switches from competition. A survey reveals that eight in ten customers have a more positive image of a firm which supports a cause close to their heart. About two-thirds of them say they would like to switch to brands or organisations with a cause." Which probably explains women citing charity value — and not hygiene — as a reason for buying Whisper!

What prompts a company to pick a social cause? Says marketing guru Shunu Sen, "Theoretically it is in the latter part of a company's growth chart — when a brand has attained certain maturity — that it transcends to the emotional or psychological level. As in the sanitary market, when the market got highly competitive, P&G decided to give Whisper a different push by making it more humane."

However, Doy Soaps, targeted at children, used this strategy — by contributing towards giving destitute children a better life — as its launching pad. At times, an organisation planning to diversify or multiply its portfolio also takes the 'social' route. For instance, when J&J launched its new Vision Product division, which sells Acuvue and Vistavue brands of disposable contact lenses, the company decided to donate a percentage of its sales proceeds to eye-care societies. Says S. Nadkarni, representative of J&J in Delhi, "Consumers respond to brands in a holistic way, irrespective of what lifestage the brand is in. Cause-related emotions play a key role in creating involvement and bonding. In fact, the earlier a brand dons the role of a cause-related emotion, the quicker will be the bonding process with the consumer. Hence, when we launched our eye-care programme we were not just aiming at creating sales. It was meant to be an awareness programme because eye-care is a problem in India. and what better way to do than linking it up with our own brand."

"In a way, a company which sells contact lens creating awareness about eye-care or a company which sells milk powder promoting mother's milk or car manufacturers working towards green air adds to the credibility of the company itself. But it depends a lot on the cause that one associates with. It has to be in tandem with the product and the target audience, otherwise it could backfire," says Plummer.

In fact, in what marketing gurus' term as Lazarfelt/Merton analysis, there are three conditions that need to be fulfilled for an effective cause-related campaign. First, there must be a mass feeling for that particular social communication such as concern for blind girl children. Second, there must be a real or psychological monopolisation of the media, which implies the absence of any counter propaganda for the given social cause. Third, supplementation, that is the effort to follow up the promo with other contacts as and when desired, such as eye-care clinics.

Warns Sen, "The potential problem with cause-related marketing is that it does not directly promote the brand's benefit. Hence, if the cause is not a good one or relevant to the target consumer, or if the execution is shoddy, not convincing enough, the money would have been badly spent. In worst cases, it might even adversely impact the brand's image."

Brands Communication that Prick the Conscience

This may be the start of a trend. You can't have helped but notice how some brands have been piggybacking on social causes. If HLL brands like Surf Excel and Ponds are doing it, so are ITC's Sunfeast and Aashirwad. Is it a one-off tactical thing or does it make strategic sense? Also is it about the product or the corporate brand?

Some kids in Mumbai's Bainganwadi slums are grateful to Surf Excel. The Rs. 485 crore brand in turn has them to thank, for a feel-good marketing campaign - the Surf Excel 10/10 drive. This saw Excel buyers in the four cities of Mumbai, Delhi, Bangalore and Kolkata SMSing an amount to HLL. The company in turn donated that amount to an NGO that was imvolved in educating underpriviledged children.

Keeping Surf company is HLL's Rs. 355 crore Ponds, that's tied up with the United Nations Development Fund for Women. For every flap of Ponds cold cream mailed by the consumer, the company would contribute Rs. 2 to the fund to fight domestic violence. Even though, the proportion of adspends from its Rs. 1,000 crore advertising and promotion budget have been minimal, HLL says most of its brands will look for long-term strategic linkages with social causes.

Vice President, Skincare, HLL, Ashok Venkatramani told CNBC-TV18, "If the activity is not housed in brand promise, then it looks like a charitable activity and in my view, those activities are difficult to sustain in the long run. In our case, specific to Fair and Lovely, or even Ponds, these are strongly housed in what the brand stands for and what brand promise is all about, hence they are easy to sustain and will reap huge benfits."

Industry watchers say that HLL has moved gingerly towards backing this creative tack. Four years ago, it did an on-ground activation on Lifebuoy under the 'Swasth Chetana' campaign, and saw sales go up by 20% in 17,000 villages. With such proof of better sales, the company is set to extend that initiative to urban areas. Further, the soap has extended the idea of social focus to their mainline TV advertising, featuring little Gandhi. Creative gurus think brands walking the social talk are welcome.

Executive Creative Director, Lowe, R. Balakrishnan explains, "There are so many causes which are so fresh and which have not been tapped, so, they are all potentially great ideas lying there. Only look at it that way, I won't look at this as a tack that'll be the focus of corporates in the future."

Here's another difference to note. Corporate social responsibility, CSR, is being used to build individual brands rather than the corporate brand. A case in point is the Rs. 16,000 crore ITC, that ran their CSR campaign, about putting India first for its e-choupal initiative two years back. Cut to the present. The company has linked the Sunfeast brand to its social forestry campaign, where the company chips in with 25 paise for every pack of Sunfeast biscuit and pasta sold, and consumers who buy the atta brand, Aashirvaad, contribute towards ITC's rain harvesting campaign.

Divisional Chief Executive, ITC, Ravi Naware says, "Consumers like to connect with the brand, if the brand is seen as a responsible brand, then consumers get an emotional connect thats far beyond just usage of the brand and consuming it. It's this higher level of connect that we are attempting to create through this campaign. So, in an attempt to connect with consumers at several levels, we will run this campaign, parallel to other campaigns that talk about differentiated innovative products under the Sunfeast brand."

Back home too, experts say that brand loyalty is passe. For the shopper, both Rin and Tide offer stain removing benefits at a similar price and soon the retailer's in-store brands will add to that list of me-too brands. Marketing consultant & Founder of Nobby, Nabankur Gupta adds, "Product differentiation is completely drying up, service aspects are narrowed out, so the brand value question will come up in the durables sector as well. It will come up in the auto sector in my view. This will be a very live issue as we move forward in time."

But if from detergent to TV sets, all brands chase consumers for a cause, there will be clutter. At the same time, experts say it's important to find the right fit between brand and cause that lasts longer than a passing fad, using effective communication techniques, media and channels.

CHAPTER 2

MARKETING COMMUNICATIONS — A PREVIEW

LOOK OUT SONY-THE KOREANS ARE COMING!

Have you ever heard of Samsung? Probably not, unless you own a microwave oven (the company's preeminent U.S. brand presence). But then again, not too many people had heard of Sony back in the early 1960s. Like Sony, which was initially known for its clock radios and small black-and-white TVs and was a secondary player relative to Motorola, Philips, and Zenith, Samsung has been known in the United States for low-end products, such as VCRs, TVs, and micro-wave ovens. Now the company wants to be like Sony in another way—by becoming a well-known, market-leading electronics brand. In fact, Korea-based Samsung has Sony in its crosshairs-its goal is to be a stronger brand name than Sony by the year 2005.

Not likely, you say? Well, don't tell that to Samsung. Consider this: While the Japanese com-panies Fujitsu, Hitachi, Matsushita, NEC, and Toshiba have all been losing money and Sony has been struggling. Samsung has been on a roll, turning a $2.2 billion profit on sales of $24.7 billion in 2001. Not only that, but Samsung now manufactures laptops, DVDs, cell phones, and flat-screen TVs (among many other products) and is ranked fifth in the world in patents, behind IBM, NEC, Canon, and Micron Technology. The firm's growth has caught the attention of the competition, who now no longer doubts that Samsung can do it.

Samsung's strategy is to reposition its current brands upward. The company's most well-known brand, Sanyo, produced copycat products-cheaper versions of Sony or Mitsubishi products. But since 1997, the company has changed its image by producing more upscale, top-of-the line offerings. It is pulling out of big discount chains like Kmart and Wal-Mart, which focus on price over quality, and moving in to Best Buy, Circuit City, and other specialty stores. And while its brands are still slightly lower priced than the very top names, the Samsung label is right there with them in quality.

The change in image has been supported by changes in advertising and promotion. A new campaign, "DigitAll Everyone's Invited," attempts to position Samsung products as exciting, cutting edge, and reasonably priced. The company's 55 different advertising agencies were consolidated into one. Over $900 million was to be spent on global IMC marketing campaigns in 2002. $70 million of it in the United States, including the cost of a redesigned 65-foot-high electronic billboard in New York's Times Square and a high-profile presence at the Olympic Games in Salt Lake City. The current advertising campaign is designed to raise awareness, as well as to enhance the brand image. The focus of the ads is surreal, many featuring the "snow woman"—a hauntingly beautiful woman who imparts an expensive and classy feeling to the viewer and, hopefully, to the brand. The ads appear on television, in print, and on retail and out-door billboards.

Samsung's Olympic sponsorship typifies the repositioning strategy the company has undertaken. Samsung's objectives in Salt Lake were "to provide Olympic fans, athletes and their families with entertaining and memorable Olympic experiences" and "to showcase [its] leadership in digital convergence by letting spectators touch and feel products that will soon be unveiled to the U.S. market" (II-Hyung Chang, head of Samsung's Olympic projects). The Olympic Rendezvous was the centerpiece of the sponsorship. Located in Salt Lake Olympic Square, the sponsorship provided daily entertainment shows, athlete appearances, future product displays, free phone calls, and other forms of enter-tainment. More than 240,000 people visited the Rendezvous during the 16-day period, and it was rated the top attraction in Olympic Square by visiting fans. Perhaps more important 74 percent of the visitors stated they now had a more positive image of Samsung, and 76 percent indicated a willingness to purchase a Samsung product in the future.

The Internet is also a major part of the new IMC program. Samsung have front-page sponsorships on 50 major websites, including Fortune.com, Forbes.com, BusinessWeek.com, and other business publication sites. CNN.com and EW.com was also included in an attempt to reach 300 million "hits" per month. By being on these sites, Samsung associated its brand with other well-known, and well-expected, brands. Joint product development ventures with strong-brand-image companies such as Sprint, Texas Instruments, and Dell are also working to reposition the brand.

So far, the efforts appear to have gone well. According to Interbrand—a brand consulting firm in New York—Samsung's brand-value rank is 43 (Sony's is 18). While still behind Sony, the brand's value rose 22 percent in 2001, with only Starbucks doing better. The Samsung brand ranks number 1 in flat-panel monitors and DRAM semiconductor memory chips. It is number 2, behind Sony, in DVD players and number 3 in mobile handsets. Samsung is, by far, the largest corporate presence in South Korea. Overall. Samsung is the second most recognizable consumer electronics brand in the world, according to interbrand. A very strong player in China, Russia, and Korea, Samsung has now become a global brand as well, with 70 percent of its sales outside these three countries.

Can Samsung overtake Sony? As of now, the company has less than half the revenue of Sony, but it is no longer just making cheaper versions of Sony products. Robert Batt, of Nebraska Furniture Mart, thinks Samsung can outstrip Sony. To quote the $300 million retailer, "Someone shook that company up. It's moving up with the big boys." Look out big boys!

Sources: Christopher Saunders, "Samsung Ramps Up Web Efforts in New Campaign," InternetNews.com, May 24, 2002, pp. 1-2; William J. Holstein, "Samsung's Golden Touch," Fortune, Apr. 1, 2002, pp. 89-94; Frank Gibney, Jr., "Samsung Moves Upmarket," Time, Mar. 25, 2002, pp. 49-52; Heidi Brown, "Look Out, Sony," Forbes, June 11, 2001, pp. 96-98.

Buyers and sellers come into trading contact under marketing communications. Social and technological changes are introduced and resources come within the reach of buyers whose demands are intense through marketing communications.

Moreover, trading partners are able to negotiate transactions because of logistic information received in the process. Potential buyers and sellers are able to collect information being circulated by trading partners when they search the market. Persuasion is an effective tool both for buyers and sellers. Persuasion can help sellers to create demand for their marketed product, while buyers can manipulate or negotiate price concessions from sellers. Executives, on their part, while solving problems can help mobilise and allocate market resources on the basis of feedback received on performance data.

The feedback received enables marketing organisations to direct and co-ordinate their marketing activity and strategy. Feedback also helps decision makers because this information helps them to solve problems. The information received may prove to be elusive or incorrect because it is difficult to correctly forecast or prospect marketing future. Because of this, marketing executives have a pressing or sound reason to postpone decisions till the future proceeds and come close to the present. Executives, therefore, "trade off" or keep "options open" because of uncertainty between errors of delay due to postponement of decisions and errors arising from fluctuating or oscillating data due to imperfect information about the future.

Placement of orders indicate successful negotiations. Communication channels get automatically established when pairs of buyers and sellers motivated by their demand and need respectively, that is, the intent to purchase or demand and keeness to sell or need, mutually search for each other. Once, this step is over, negotiations for terms and conditions for exchange take place and finally culminates in the placement of orders. Post-negotiatory service agreements are also vital when negotiations for buying and selling have been finalised and the nature of the transaction requires reciprocal obligations on trading partners.

CLASSIFICATION OF COMMUNICATION CHANNELS

Communication channels can be broadly classified into three categories:

(i) Logistic: This communication channel is of the natural kind, where buyers and sellers enter into a trading contract leading to the direct delivery of goods.

(ii) Persuasive: This communication channel entails a continuing contact between buyers and sellers to finalise transactions.

(iii) Problem Solving: This communication channel helps organisational chains in transaction channels in allocating resources for mutual benefit and shape their marketing pattern to changing marketing conditions.

Trading partners, once a trading contact is established, have reason for continuing the transaction relationship because of the cost intensive nature of communication involved in the process of searching each other. Every organisation would like to economise on time, money and effort for attaining its avoided objective, which can be called the principle of least efforts for maximum results. Thus, the survival of a communication channel is linked to the trading-benefit involved and the cost of searching it as determined by money, time and effort needed. It can be initially presumed that the possibilities of a link between successive trading partners will be the same in the future and in the past, once a communication channel structure has been identified and adopted. The possibilities of the link through the accepted communication channel can be minimised or reduced in present phase once the uncertain future overtakes it.

A transaction channel could get dissolved or destroyed due to various reasons. It can happen when trading partners fail to reach an agreement. It may also be due to the exit from the market of a buyer or buyers whose demands have been met. It can also be caused by the seller's inability to meet or fulfil the buyer's demand. Communication channels and networks are also liable to change because producers may achieve additional economies or bag increased profits by discarding ineffective or unproductive middlemen. The change may also be due to employment of communication specialists who can achieve the same or better results at lower cost.

Economy in operations and improved skill helping conserve efforts and curtailing cost of negotiating transactions may also bring about changes in communication channel pattern and structure.

BASIC CONCEPTS

COMMUNICATION PURPOSES

Three purposes are served by communication in marketing:

(1) Acts as the means for striking and continuing a trading contact needed for completing a transaction.
(2) Acts as a conduit for conveying and exchange of persuasive messages to both the trading partners for arriving at an agreement.
(3) Acts as a source of receiving "feedback" of results regarding productivity, efficiency and effectiveness of marketing activity.

A particular type of communication is needed for serving each of the three purposes. Availability of goods, prices and demands are conveyed by Logistics Communication. Messages motivated and designed to clinch or. effect transactions is the role played by Persuasive Communication. Regulated information on marketing information received by an organisation enabling it to change or modify subsequent performance is the objective of Feedback Communication. Marketing communications also help to organise the economic system.

(1) Logistic Communication and Persuasive Communication help to bring the buyer and seller into trading contact:

Buyer-seller communication regarding terms of exchange or terms and conditions for selling and buying helps in finalisation of transactions. This leads to sellers identifying buyers whose demands are pressing and urgent within the structure of money prices.

For example, if a producer comes to know that he is likely to fetch higher prices prevailing in market A as compared to those offered in market B, the producer is bound to shop or transport his products to market A, unmindful of additional cost of transportation or shipment because he is confident of recouping the extra expense because of the price differential between the two markets. A farmer too studies market prices and the additional gain which he can secure with the help of price differential. The farmer listens to market news on the radio or by studying newspaper reports of commodity prices in the main markets within his shipping or commercial area. Market news agencies giving information may also lead to distribution of goods in extractive and intermediate goods markets.

Buyers and mass production suppliers in the final-goods markets can easily be brought into trading contact through advertising which constitutes the cheapest means for achieving this end. Advertising comprises the most effective method for communicating with millions of prospective buyers. Moreover, communication is almost simultaneous with millions of buyers. It is largely true that cost incurred per individual contact through the advertising process works out lesser than the cost incurred on personal selling to scattered consumers. Despite this truth, there are some categories of final goods that sell best through the traditional bazaar and the farmers 'haat' or market methods of sales achieved by higgling and haggling. These goods are such that they sell best through this method where the buyer and seller negotiate best when they are face-to-face and settle the price for the transaction. This method of higgling and higgling may not apply to organised markets. This is the pattern of saletransactions mostly in congested slum markets or in far away markets locked within unapproachable rural markets which retain their social and also business function. These markets are unapproachable to normal customers of regular markets with the result that slum and rural markets continue to adhere to the traditional procedure of buyer-seller negotiations of arguing and settling the price for affecting a transaction.

(2) Cultural change through Advertising and Selling together acting as agent :

A fast developing technology is easily introduced to consumers when advertising and selling go together hand in hand. The benefits of such technology are best appreciated when advertising and selling are used as a combined package. This process can easily introduce a new product to consumers who take on to it because of a strong advertising campaign offering sales of the product simultaneously. A survey revealed that persuading users to try new drugs, pharmaceutical firms and drug manufacturing companies effectively users to try new drugs, pharmaceutical firms and drug manufacturing companies effectively promoted adoption for the new drug by influential and successful physicians, ultimately inspiring other lesser physicians and medical practitioners to begin prescribing the new drug. This method yields fruitful results for a wide range of products. Herbert Menzel and Elihu Katz[1], in their article on "Social Relations and Innovation in the Medical Profession" published in the public Opinion Quarterly, "Winter" have elaborated how new drugs are adopted by physicians and how users accept the use of such drugs. In the case of other products, for example, detergents, face creams, shampoos, razors, kitchenware and soaps, users accept new brands because of the advertising appeal and simultaneous sales offered by the companies, either because of the consumer's urge to discover better products, or due to the apparently low and bargain prices at which these products are being offered for sale by advertising vans or agents. Distribution of free samples of such products are being offered for sale by advertising campaigns adds another incentive to boost sales and ensure acceptance by consumers accustomed to other popular brands. Technological superiority of a new product suitably advertised also accelerated sales. Yet another example may be quoted how advertising and selling can go hand in hand in another sector. Local agricultural agents or influential politicians can persuade farmers in underdeveloped countries to adopt new advances in agricultural technology. They can convince such farmers in giving up their hand operated threshers, winnowers and harvesters for diesel or power-operated units. These farmers can also be persuaded to give up traditional Persian wheels and other conventional gadgets for drawing water for irrigation from wells in favour of power or diesel operated pumps. This process can be called the "Demonstration effect" which may invariably "break the cake of custom" in the words of Veolen. This helps to convert a backward class of people and liberate them from the conventional methods of agriculture raising their lives from starvation and disease to affluence and health.

The beneficial effects of a planned cultural change are seldom accepted or realised by social critics of marketing. The social critics think that it is morally wrong to effect a cultural change or a transformation of the attitude of consumers using advertising and selling as an agent to achieve the end. These social critics often disapprove of the introduction of new drugs through advertising and selling without testing them properly. They often consider it to be dangerous or undesirable to introduce untested drugs to consumers. They seem to forget or fail to appreciate the truth that persuasive advertising and selling is morally neutral. It is, in fact, perfectly harmless, rather innocent, that advertising and selling used as an instrument of cultural change. This process can both enrich or impoverish the lives of the user. It can either raise the standard of life or reduce its level. The user's morality contributes materially to the success or failure of the process. The changes in the buying attitude of the purchaser brought about by this process cannot be denied. Marketing organisations realising the efficacy of this process use it to bring about cultural change amongst consumers. These marketing organisations know full well that advertising and selling can induce a craving for new goods and products and services offered, although may be real or unreal. They know that this process can ensure cultural change amongst consumers. The social effects persuasion produced by the subtle or gentle process of advertising is quite different to that produced by persuasion employed by dictators and tyrants.

(3) Use of Information by Business Organisations for reducing risk in decisions related to resource allocation:

The business executive is often faced with the problems of matching resources to ensure the highest marginal productivity. These problems arise when resources have to be allocated to their utmost productive uses. The business executive or an organisation must correctly estimate future marginal productivity of management, labour and capital. On correctly estimating marginal productivity of these three parameters, the executive or the organisation can confidently choose the product amongst the many others before him, which merits development. After having done this, the executive or the organisation can select the appropriate level of inventory to be maintained for the goods to be produced, distributed and sold. The organisation of the executive can safely frame the sale price and invest in building and necessary equipment. In fact, the executive or the business organisation through this process, has discovered how best can available resources be directed to their most profitable use not merely with the marketing area, but also in other activities of the organisation.

Estimation of future costs and revenue poses the greatest problem. The problem lies more in the correct assessment of future costs and revenue rather than in a general appraisal. Some errors are bound to creep into the information and facts gathered about the future. Frequent appraisals, alteration or modification of plans have to be made as the future for which the plans were formulated draws closer to the present. Market risk is bound to arise and is rather unavoidable because of the impossibility of precisely knowing the time shape of market demand. Moreover, the supply flow of the product from the manufacturing firm or company is also regulated by quite a few uncertain and unanticipated factors. These factors may include a strike in the firm or company holding up production and supply. The resignation by a key functionary of the firm or company or a key executive's death or failure of the mode of transport used, or disruption in packaging material, poor supply of raw materials, failures in power supply or the manufacturing plant, labour problems causing a go slow action by the work force or change in management, comprise some other factors that may disrupt market supplies.

Natural causes also tend to increase business pressures. A snow storm hitting out at the peak Christmas season is bound to unsettle or decrease sales. A dust storm can similarly undo a market place, a riot may also make buyers run for safety deserting the market, even a quarrel or a minor brawl or exchange of violence in a section of the market would ruin it. Although a riot, quarrel, brawl or violence do not fall in the category of natural causes, but their evil effect on undoing market activities cannot be denied. But, a fire which breaks out in a market either through a power short circuit or a burning cigarette or 'bidi' bit carelessly thrown by a smoker or the toppling of a coal oven or even a fire caused by other sources, can be classed as a natural cause which disrupts marketing activities.

Marion Harper Jr., President of McCann Erickson Advertising Agency has correctly stated that "to manage a business is to manage information[2]." It is worthwhile appreciating that some risks can be eliminated, shifted, shared or diversified, yet the risk arising out of inadequate, incomplete or casual information used for decision making have to be shouldered and faced by the manufacturer or producer of the product. Even the marketing channels used by the manufacturer or producer are adversely affected by the risk of marketing information. The best that can be done in the situation is that the adequately strong information network can anticipate and identify the most probable risks. These probable anticipated, unanticipated and even identified risks ruin marketing activities on the one hand and on the other, have to be unavoidably borne by channel members of the marketing system.

MARKETING COMMUNICATIONS

Communication is the base of all human activity. Talking, singing, acting in a play, teaching in class, question answer sessions inside classrooms, making speeches, giving orders, getting tasks executed by individuals and virtually all kinds of human activity has communication content.

Communication, in general, is the act of conveying a message. The process involves not just conveying the message, but involves a complete cycle from the sender of the message to the receiver and feedback from the receiver to the sender. The sender, of the message has, first, to identify the message and choose the media for communication, because the message must match the media employed. The sender, after identification of the message, has to frame the message in the words that match the media used for communication. This process is known as codification of the message. After the message has been codified, it is put in the communication channel for being received by the receiver of the message for whom it is meant. The receiver, on his part, on receipt of the total message, interprets it. This process is called de-codification of the message. The receiver after identifying the message and interpreting its objective, reacts and has something to say in reply. The receiver, therefore, frames his reactions or response to the message received frames his response in words which, means, that he codifies his response. This is called the 'feedback' of the receiver of the message. The receiver, like the sender of the message once again uses the same media for communicating his feedback message. The sender of the message on receiving the feedback message once again de-codifies it to interpret the feedback message.

Marketing communications has to be limited to three kinds of messages which are relevant to effort of directing, soliciting or persuading consumers or users of the product offered for sale. These three kinds of message are as follows:

(*i*) Logistic information
(*ii*) Persuasive or promotional information
(*iii*) Problems solving information.

The mechanics involved in any kind of human communication is similar or identical to the act of communication in marketing activity. An individual in the process of communicating with another through some channel or media does so with the objective of producing the desired effect. In marketing activities too, the producer or manufacturer in their attempt to sell their product must necessarily produce an awareness or induce an urge amongst existing consumers of the product or help create a new sector of consumers, if the product is new and needs proper introduction.

Harold D. Lasswell to explain the process of marketing communications has outlined five questions in his book "The Structure and Function of Communication in Society" as follows:

(1) Who is the communicator? (Control Analysis)
(2) What is the content of the message? (Content Analysis)
(3) Who is the audience for which the message is intended? (Audience Analysis)

(4) What information media or means of transmitting the message are employed? (Media Analysis)
(5) What behaviour follows receipt of the message? (Effect Analysis)[3]

It would be worthwhile to consider each of these effects and how and in what manner these effects influence business transactions. Let us take up each of these effects in detail.

CONTROL ANALYSIS

Trading contract between buyers and sellers is established leading to negotiation of transactions after logistic messages are exchanged between buyers and sellers. The seller has to make several logistic communications for achieving trading contract with the buyer, and all those intermediaries which help in the final execution of the sale. The seller or his agent, for example, will have to convey messages to rail and road transport centres for ensuring prompt delivery of goods in the marketing sector. Similarly, the seller will have to communicate with financial institutions for making monetary arrangements backing non-cash sales. The seller has to employ yet another communication to materialise sale of his product. The seller has to use all means of persuasion to motivate, inspire or even entice the buyers into negotiations so that the sale of his product could take off. These persuasions continue during all phases of sales, namely, before, during and after the negotiations so that trading remains uninterrupted and continues without break for the sellers benefit and advantage. The seller has also to solve problems that might confound, confuse or discourage the buyer into snapping of trading relations. Solving of such problems is an activity which the seller or his decision-makers have to undertake by collecting all relevant information from the market which might disrupt his trading relations. Such problems might also be tackled by internal groups within the organisation firm or company selling the product. Problems are sometimes difficult and elude solutions. Thus, in solving problems the seller will have to use all logistic or persuasive information that is relevant to tackling the problems before him.

Control analysis is not a superficial or causal exercise. The main task in control analysis is to convey the message of the sender or seller with clarity so that it is correctly understood and properly grasped ruling out any kind of mis-interpretating. If the identity of the sender of the message is known the probability of the message being correctly understood, believed and acted upon is higher than when the sender's identity is not clear or uncertain. There may be exceptions, however, to this process of communicating such messages. For example, message conveyed by the sender or the seller or his advertiser may be dismissed, disbelieved or even be ineffective if it loaded with self interest. Such messages will be received with disbelief or misinterpreted or may be taken at a heavy discount, if they fail to assure and promise the receiver or buyer the expected benefits or considered important by the receiver. Advertisers employ various methods to allay fears or apprehensions of the buyers. They may substantiate their message or solicitations with testimonials from prominent users of the product if the product has already been introduced in the market. If the product is new and is in the introduction stage, the advertiser may secure and publicise their product with testimonials from reputed laboratories which have tested the product or from giant organisations which vouch safe for the efficacy of the product. All these methods, including the testimonials, are used to impart the hallmark of credibility to the product proposed to be sold. A case in point is the giant fabric manufacturer Vimals which has allowed its trade market to be prominently displayed on the package of Surf International, a new product, backed by the advertisement in which film actress Shabana Azmi first appears on the TV screen saying that she will not believe the efficacy of Surf International without proper verification. Shabana is first shown going to a testing laboratory and the scientist there testifies to the fact that a fabric is weakened and loses its gloss and shine in texture when the fabric threads snap into fine fibres which he calls "wobbling." Shabana next steps into the laundry section of Vimals where the lady superintendent shows her the difference between a fabric washed by an ordinary detergent causing wobbling or damage in the fabric texture and compares it with the same fabric washed with Surf International which retains its original shine and texture even after 40 washings. The lady superintendent of Vimal's laundry section also answers another query by Shabana saying that

Surf International is an ideal and harmless detergent for all kinds of fabrics like silk, cotton, terrycot and terrylene. Shabana next appears on the TV screen and conveys the real message that after having satisfied her normal/questioning nature and sticking to her habit of not making any claim without verification, announces that had it not been for the super quality of the new detergent, surf international, Vimals, the top fabric manufacturer of the country would not have permitted, surf international to use and display Vimals trade mark on its package. This advertisement by the manufacturers of surf international along with testification by Vimals conveys a message for the new product about its superfine quality which is bound to be believed by the prospective buyers.

In a competitive market where the atmosphere is tense even a causal rumour or an innocent comment or an artless innuendo tending to discredit a product is likely to upset the sender's message and adversely affect the prospects of the sale of the product. Sometimes, the sender of the message may himself float a rumour which drives the market in the direction desired by him. A large producet market has been plagued by frequent rumours under a conspiracy amongst producet buyers to float the rumour that prices of the particular producet are falling. In such a situation, commission agents are left with a few options. The commission agents that is, commission merchants, finding that buyers are bidding prices lower that those prevailing in other parallel markets, may invariably exercise the option of reshipping the producet to a market where the prevailing prices are higher. The other option before the commission agent is to hold back the producet, including even perishable goods in the hope or expectation that the prevailing low prices would soon pick up and take to an upward trend. It requires intelligence in a seller that before exercising his options, he is able to discover whether the rumour set afloat making prices to fall is artless or unintentional or intentional or conspiratorial.

The audience of the message, that is, the buyer is often endowed with an intuition and armed with the capability or possesses the ability to discover the real intention of the sender in conveying a particular message. Quite often the sender of the gullible, loaded or diabolical message is easily identified and his intentions and objection of the message is disciphered or discovered. In such a case. there is no problem whatsoever. The content of the message is often indicative of the sender's purpose behind it. Even the motive behind a message which tends to affect marketing activity may not remain hidden for long from the buyer. Motive, as we all know, may be laudable or mischievous, constructive or destructive and innocent or loaded. There are many other subtle ways in which the sender may convey his message to achieve his desired objective. Sometimes, the message may be framed in such a way so as to dissuade the buyers from entering into sale transactions. In fact, control analysis is a matter of opinion. In the absence of positive evidence it can be dismissed as a mere surmise compared with other substantial matters contained in the literature on marketing. Thus, it does not require more than passing notice.

CONTENT ANALYSIS

As stated earlier control analysis or assessment of the content of the message in marketing communications is next important factor.

Economics literature from Alfred Marshall to E.H. Chamberlin and Kenneth Boulding has clearly distinguished between combative and constructive (or informative) advertising. Alfred Marshall has expressed his views in a industry and trade, E.H. Chamberlin in 'The Theory of Monopolistic Competition' and Kennth Boulding has done so in 'The Image; Knowledge in Life and Society.'[4]

David Ogilvy has said 'I will let these dons in on a curious secret. The combative persuasive kind of advertising which they approve.'[5] Moreover, the distinction drawn between combative and constructive advertising is an imaginary concept. A message that is informative possesses an immense persuasive appeal. For example, a warning sign at the edge of a desert that there is no petrol pump within 200 kilometers would make motorists check their automobiles and get their petrol tanks full before entering the desert. Thus, this informative message would boost the sales of the petrol pump at the edge of the desert. Similarly, the announcement in the advertisement that some new gadget to eliminate household drudgery was available in the market, would make housewives form a beeline or make a queue for getting a chance to purchase the gadget.

Communication made in both an explicit or implicit manner or that which is either factual or symbolic is deeply rooted in reality which is the way in which people think and talk. In the world of symbols the language is not a spoken one. Symbols constitute an entire gamut of feelings, including that of friendship, status, pain and pleasure, achievement or failure, elation and despondence, desire and vacuum, enthusiasm and rejection. A product has a want satisfying power if imagery is employed to produce a convincing or forceful psychological intensity. The seller in order to produce this effect presents the product that gratifies both desire and need of the prospective customer and which he can afford to purchase. Symbolic language produces images which is, however, conditioned by the ever changing value system of the recipients or the audience. Consumers respond to the images produced by symbolic language in a rather irrational manner because these images are related to the real world fantasies expected to maximise utility.[6] Mostly people prefer a combination of satisfactory results in which the criteria of contentment are changeable factors of human behaviour.

American businessmen chiefly depend upon image building while operating and soliciting customers in other countries. An American sales manager himself visited a Minister of a Latin American country because he wanted to purchase the American equipment and did not rely upon his Latin American agent. Unmindful of the psychology of the Latin American client in which friendly personal relations would have been fruitful, the American sales manager tried to persuade the customer in the same manner as he would handle a customer in America, his own country. The American sales manager insensitive to cultural difference between the two countries requiring a longer time for striking a personal friendly relationship with the Latin American client, had pressed for an unsuccessful speedy close to the transaction. The American sales manager failed to identify the association between friendship and after sales service ingrained in the mind of the Latin American customer. The Latin American minister gave his order to a Swedish firm because the American sales manager was neither imaginative nor practical.[7]

It cannot be presumed that all business communication and its content is subtle. Businessmen should adopt objective and a long range viewpoint about the constituents of a transaction while establishing contacts and maintaining relationships with trading partners whom they have dealt with earlier. The terms of exchange quite often take standard accepted forms or get institutionalised because of continued and routine usage. The key to success lies in modifying the terms of contract for each transaction suiting the ever changing psychology of the purchaser. In fact, the terms of exchange have to be properly understood by the buyer and seller for each transaction for successful completion of trade transactions. Edward T. Hall's views expressed in Harvard Business Review under the title of 'The Silent Language of Overseas Business' are as relevant for transacting overseas business as Edmund D. McGarry's observations in the journal of Business under the caption 'The Contactual Function in Marketing' in the instant case. The American sales manager failed in winning the Latin American client because he did not realise that a time factor was needed for striking a friendship and for giving an assurance of after sales service and ultimately the Swedish firm got the contract, although the client preferred the American equipment.

McGarry's views on 'The Contractual function in marketing' may be quoted to illustrate the relevance of communication content in trading contacts: 'The techniques of contact which tend to break down the barriers of distrust and suspicion between the parties are fairly well-known to businessmen... they must talk the same language. This means not only that the words and phrases used must mean the same thing to each of them but also that they must have a clear understanding of all the qualities and characteristics of the goods traded in as well as of the business techniques which they employ. Precision in communication is the major factor in agreement.'[8]

Stable trading relations are established through frequent contactual communication because it helps in the firm linking of combination and sequence of agencies in the minds of the contacting parties. These are known as 'consensus demand systems' which comprise channel relationships. Once these channel relationships get established, the channel system or channel organisation grows and develops. The channel members gradually develop precise language well understood by the trading partners and whose vocabulary is distinctive and well accepted by both the parties to the trading relationship.

Logistic and problem solving information evolves from trading transactions. More information is generated from the processes of trading relations. These processes like buying and selling, physical distribution of the products, financing techniques and methods adopted educate the decision makers of participating firms and companies for assessing and appraising how their actual performance is close to or far away from the performance they had planned.

Marketing research is yet another important factor in content analysis. Product planners through marketing survey and research are able to assess how consumers or customers have responded to the offers made by their firm or companies compared with parallel offers of rivals or competitors. It also helps the sales manager to discover the hitherto untapped segment of customers and also enables them to identify the potential segments of customers where with concerted marketing efforts trade returns could be improved.

Marketing research and surveys also enlighten the advertising strategist and expert. It helps the advertising expert to find out how the firm or company's advertising compaign in different media has cast an impact on customer audience, as to whether it has understood, believed or fully grasped the message given by the advertisement campaign.

There is yet another aspect of marketing research and survey. Marketing research helps the firm or company in making a proper distribution cost analysis. This serves two distinctive purposes. It enables the firm or company to examine both the demand serving and demand stimulating efforts and measure it in terms of income or returns secured under achieved marketing performance against the planned marketing performance. Any advertising campaign for product has two distinct objectives. One is to serve the existing demand for the product. The other is designed to stimulate a demand for the product by creating new clientele or customers. Both the demand serving and demand stimulating efforts have to clearly understood and executed for real benefits for the firm or company.

Feedback information-of a trading campaign is important and relevant for successful trading activities. Problem solving information in feedback helps the executives of a firm or company to chalk out, plan and moderate their trading campaign. The executives can in the backdrop of this information choose a course of action fairly sure of the outcome or result of adopting one of the several alternatives for the trading campaign. Decision makers with the help of logistic information received, using persuasion in appropriate measure, and analysis of feedback information, can properly give direction, effect co-ordination and control marketing activities. Decision maker would be well advised to use all this information for planning, executing and supervising marketing or trading activities. Those who fail to rely on this information or do not take notice of indications given by this kind of information may miserably fail in their trading activities. Like the hunter going out in the forest for a choice kill, must aim properly at his target once sighted for success, so should the decision maker aim his campaign in trading activities. He must first identify and spot out the customers whom he wants to bag, but he can only succeed if he has all the information needed for success.

AUDIENCE CUSTOMER ANALYSIS

The audience for trading information is constituted of buyers and sellers. The buyers and sellers are divided into homogeneous groups like markets. For example, brokers and commission agents in commodity exchanges receive information about transactions with the same speed and pace as transaction are executed. Within a few hours the information becomes common knowledge of a larger audience comprising farmers and suppliers.

Advertising and selling messages through mass media is meant an audience comprising household and industrial consumers. We have seen while discussing demand and market segmentation how audiences which are homogeneous with regard to age, residence and other distinguish characteristics are likely to fulfil their need by purchasing identical products or services or opting for same stores marketing the product.

Markets are segmented and comprise totally different categories of customers who react in peculiar ways to advertising appeal. Housewives, for example consulting and keeping in touch with women's magazines comprise an audience which is self-selective.

Women gleaning through these women's magazines imbibe their own ideas for running a home. Advertising therefore, matching these ideas will help purchase of these products advertised in a manner that caters to the preferences of women buyers.

Similarly, industrial markets are differently segmented into self-selecting vertical and horizontal markets. Customers in the industrial markets would be guided by the information they gather from horizontal media magazines and will make their purchases accordingly. Customers in the industrial markets conditioned by the horizontal media magazines horizontally out across industry, trade and professional sections. On the other hand, customers or audiences influenced by vertical media magazines make their choice in purchases in a particular manner.[9] Self selection of products by such audiences also applies to professional media, religious magazines and farm publications and also institutional journals. Advertising in this special category of the media for having the desired impact has to be framed in technical or symbolic language so that it can be comprehended more by the special interest groups than the people or customers in general.

The audience for problem solving communication comprise staff advertisers and decision makers. Executives on their part, are keen to know how well their directives or commands have been executed and how the result match or fall short of the planned outcome. Executive needs proper information and even additional know-how for rectifying their errors at the earliest of their commands or directives have failed to produce the anticipated results. Inability of technically oriented staff researchers to understand the problems faced by executives often precipitate the problem of delay in feedback of marketing research results. Research audience too has its complaints. Either researchers fail to understand the problem or remain pre-occupied with techniques instead of grappling with executive problems or remain engrossed or imprisoned in their technical jargon and communicate in it instead of making simply worded statements or findings or recommendations.

Research findings and sales reports or reviews can always be framed in a language to suit the comprehension ability and desires of the audience. Research investigators often produce three separate reports about a single problem. One report stresses upon the major findings and the associated policy implications for operating executives. The second report would deal and advise staff advisers the details of the method for implementing the major findings and also indicates the researcher's confidence in his results. The third report is intended for use by sales managers and their sales staff indicating how the major findings of the research can be used in their day-to-day method of soliciting customers or converting them or making them opt for the product being pushed up for sale.

MEDIA ANALYSIS

Communication channels for specific messages are the subject matter for media analysis. This is in the narrow sense. In a broader sense, media analysis covers study of all matters like risk-organisation, physical distribution and financial flow of marketing. Invariably in media analysis done in the narrow sense, the marketing network has to undertake communication for getting goods from the producers to the users or customers. The setup for communicating messages has undergone a change due to development and modernisation of communication technology and simultaneously the technological organisation has changed the pattern and structure of marketing channels.

Transmission channels have undergone a vast change with the advancement of technology. There has, virtually been an explosion in sophistication of communication media. Advertisement and market news messages can be transmitted by a host of modern media or communication channels via., the radio, telephone, television, satellite and inter net networks, besides advanced electronic devices. Data processing is a modern marvel. Data processing technology makes it possible to report sales outcome instantaneously and co-ordinate it simultaneously with inventory-ordering activities along with details of production, advertising and marketing support services. Buyers of supermarkets can, with the help of this technology inform a food dealer or broker the details of the purchase made from him the previous week are on the shelves, how much of the product was sold out during the period and the price at which it was sold. For example, a chain-stores could brief supplier's representative with this data and also place their demand order on the suppliers to make further suppliers both as regards the quantity needed and the price at which it should be dispatched. A supplier who makes mistakes in recommendation of supplies needed is likely to be replaced by another. This situation arises in an extreme case of use of market information. Salesmen can however, utilise cost data of current distribution for fixing prices and terms of sale on the basis of details of company cost. Use of internal problem-solving information can help fixation of external prices offered to customers. With this background, salesmen can effectively co-ordinate their marketing activities in tune with the capacity of the firm marketing the product. Speedy transmission of messages have materially accelerated transactions in a number of industries.

Computer to computer data exchange or telephone communication of messages help to coordinate production with inventory information from warehouses spread all over the country and also within departmental wholesale and retail stores. Information about future sales and inventory requirements can be created both for existing and future conditions.

Computer simulation process adapted in industries with short production inventory final sales cycles can generate highly dependable information which can soundly give guidance when to reorder, how much to indent and to choose and regulate transportation which can help to minimise distribution costs. Logistic information systems may become more realistic and sharp in ascertaining long-term trends that will appreciably affect demand serving activities. This result will flow when more experience is gained from simulation models.

Media analysis is helpful in several ways. In a restricted sense media analysis helps to locate areas in which advertisement prone audience can be found. It could also indicate the money quantum needed for sending messages that would cover fully or partially cover a specific market segment and the degree to which audiences would get duplicated by messages through a particular mass media. It is a difficult task to secure the latest about audiences of any particular mass media. Buying of media space by advertising agencies for anticipated results is a highly developed skill. This is called a top or sophisticated skill because it is dependent upon knowledge of shifts in market segments and the changes in audience character.

EFFECT ANALYSIS

EFFECTS OF LOGISTIC COMMUNICATION

There are some mute signs and symbols or scenes which convey a message or make a logistic communication. A famous or well-known example is of a broker entering the Chicago Board of Trade with a wet umbrella during a bad drought. The result was that price of wheat futures contract feel steeply. The mere sight of the wet umbrella scared traders in the chambers who were banking on wheat futures but on sighting the wet umbrella assumed that the contracts they had purchased would fall steeply in value if the drought had ended. In the example just cited there was no link whatsoever in the climate at Chicago and in distant Kanas-Nebraska wheat belt. The symbolic interpretation from the wet umbrella immediately precipitated selling panic. This instance indicates how ineffective logistic communication can be highly effective in conveying a message. Effect analysis comprises the relationship between content of the message and the subsequent behaviour of the audience. In the example cited while the message conveyed through the wet umbrella was effective and deep yet the message itself through the symbol wet umbrella was both superficial and unintentional.

EFFECTS OF PERSUASION

Mass media acquires immense power over the minds of the audience through "hidden persuaders" like signs and symbols, howsoever controversial may be the effects produced by these factors hidden persuaders. Brilliant or clever "brain washing" efforts do not produce spectacular effects whether it is logistic information or mass communication process. It is wrong to infer that such information or process, despite such brain washing efforts could produce instantaneous results. Joseph Klapper in his work on "The Effect of Mass Communication" has stated: "(1) Mass communication ordinarily does not serve as a necessary and sufficient cause of audience effects, but rather functions through a nexus of mediating factors and influences; (2) these mediating factors .... typically render mass communication a contributory agent, but not the sole cause in a process of reinforcing the existing conditions."[10] According to Raymond Bauer "the hidden persuaders are made of straw." Bauer has said this in an article titled "Limits of Persuasion," published in the Harvard Business Review.[11] Persuasion results rarely touch the degree of efficiency anticipated by the sender.

EFFECTS OF PROBLEM-SOLVING

Robert F. Bales in his article, "Task Roles and Social Roles in Problem-solving Groups" and several other experts have deeply studied the effect of problem-solving communication in organisations taking it up.[12] Inability to produce problem-solving communication by task oriented groups is often due to people connected with marketing, finance and production who think and act in a limited area because they lack a proper perspective or do not have adequate or sufficient information. The intelligence of the decision taken is closely linked to the command on organisation performance. The command also regulates and conditions the quality of the feedback information.

Marketing organisations for the desired success have to closely co-ordinate all the three kinds of information, namely, logistic, persuasive and problem-solving. Efficient and effective marketing results can be secured if wholesale, retail, physical distribution units and financial specialists are cooperating constituents of a closely knit network, although it may be complex in character. Sometimes, it is surprising to find that well planned and designed communication fails to reduce the desired results. Analysis of failure involves not merely examining the major sources or causes of failure itself, it also includes the need for a sharp perception and understanding of each aspect of marketing communications discussed in the foregoing paragraphs. It also requires a proper knowledge and grasp of the complex control mechanism of organisations.

Study of Feedback Adaptation and Search Needed for Problem-Solving :

Feedback may be described as the difference or discrepancy between the desired and a achieved result of performance. Electrical engineer using the term label it as the correction process needed to rectify or cure the discrepancy between the desired and achieved performance. Norbert Weiner in his book "The Human Use of Human Beings" has labelled it as the concept of "cybernetics" or steermanship to a wide public.[13] Weiner has indicated how the control centre can be effective in applying or taking corrective measures on the basis of feedback information through appropriate channels to it. Weiner has compared the marketing control centre to the steering mechanism of a ship designed for keeping it in the right direction. He has also compared it with the human nervous system which on receiving feedback signals, instantaneously flashes corrective commands for body action. For example, when the human hand during sleep suddenly comes in contact with a hot object, despite the person being asleep, the nervous system through the sub-conscious centre immediately flashes the corrective command and the man asleep without waking up removes his hand. This concept in a large measure has to be applied to social organisations or marketing networks as well.

FEEDBACK

Experience acquired through sustained cause and effect process guides human affairs in a large measure. Past experience is not just a rule of the thumb amongst human beings because they possess the brain which, in turn, is armed with analysing power based on logical deduction. Decision makers are able to solve problems chiefly from the errors that make an appearance in the existing system. Moreover, these errors also teach lessons and help decision makers to anticipate changes that might affect performance. Records comprising sales and distribution costs reports in the control mechanism uncover discrepancies when actual results of an organisation do not meet the desired output. The discrepancies or 'errors' constitute such information which the decision makers use for taking corrective action for the organisation. The 'Feedback; along with information received on competitive conditions in the market helps the decision makers to plan and execute the adjustments needed for taking corrective action. The sales department of an organisation may face innumerable problems that may ruin results. It may cause sagging of sales due to market conditions, evoke a keen competition between rival groups pushing their products or a poor adjustment of the 'marketing mix.' The 'marketing mix' includes several things, like arrangements made for product line, pricing strategy, promotion and physical distribution. With correct information, the sales manager could easily take decisions so that performance may achieve the desired objectives.

ADAPTATION

A sales manager has to grow wise and learn from experience. He is not one who is born with infinite wisdom. Like all humans he has to learn, either by trial and error, or through failures or from the experience of rivals. When the sales manager learns how to adjust his organisation to prevailing conditions in the market, he is supposed to practice 'adaptation.' Adaptation involves changing the organisation's marketing campaign in accordance with the alternative searched out and formulated and finally executed with the result that the organisation achieves its goal effectively or satisfactorily. Adaptative behaviour may be of different kinds or forms. Risk averting behaviour undertaken by competitors in the market like price resale maintenance, is one kind of adaptation. Yet another kind may be the risk minimising behaviour of firms or companies engaged in co-operative performance of marketing. Similarly, information flows from interlocking complementary activity networks, which is necessary for undertaking ownership transfers, physical distribution of goods and for materialising financial arrangements.

Learning from illustrations or examples or from the performance, both success and failures, of others is a rather complex process. Neither exposure to new methods or successful procedures adopted by others, nor receipt of feedback information from one's own experiments in marketing or of others, can help a sales manager to learn, educate himself or improve his performance. Sometimes, learning can be acquired without additional information, namely, of performance or feedback results. Quite often, a sales manager blessed with a proper insight and imagination can learn more than by trial and error, or through one's performance or from the performance results of others or from logical deduction simpliciter. We can, however, safely conclude that a sales manager who is a decision maker can learn a lot if he has the capacity to properly analyse and understand feedback and other logistic information flowing into his organisation through his marketing network.

SEARCH

'Search' is an important step whereby information would be got. Information flows into an organisation only if it is available. The process adopted for collecting information constitutes a search, which results in collection of information which has to be sorted out for study. Information is available, if a sales manager has an eye for it. It has to be located and identified, information just does not arrive by itself or suo motto. Such information emerges automatically from the activities of rivals or prospective trading units. Information may also flow from trading partners. For example, a grocer or a general merchant makes a 'search' for the product which could be a "hot seller" and on discovering such an item makes an "impulsive purchase" which secures him the desired result. Similarly, when a consumer prior to going in for the purchase of a product scan various advertisements for deciding upon the right product that could fulfil his needs, he is supposed be engaged in a "vicarious search." The consumer does so to avoid a cumbersome shopping procedure of visiting a chain of shops for a choice of the desired product.

Sellers, on their part, undertake an even more intensive 'search' for choosing a product because they want to put up on sale a product that would prove to be 'hot seller.' For the sellers as well advertisements and all other varieties of persuasive appeals and messages through various kinds of advertising media provide the sellers the areas to which they would direct their search. On the same pattern, a problem-solving search or a solution finding search comprises the capital seeking search when done in corporate long range planning like soliciting at subscriptions to share capital. Equilibrium positions are sought by planners in all sectors of the economy at higher levels of the organisation. The equilibrium position is sought in the context of the full use of national resources that will promote full employment, ensure balanced growth of economy or honour other national objectives.

Decision makers and complex organisations ensure coordination in their multi faceted efforts by the proper and judicious utilisation of feedback information, adaptation processes and search exercises. The general model of the process is shown in Fig.2.1, where all the elements of the act of communication in marketing are clearly present.

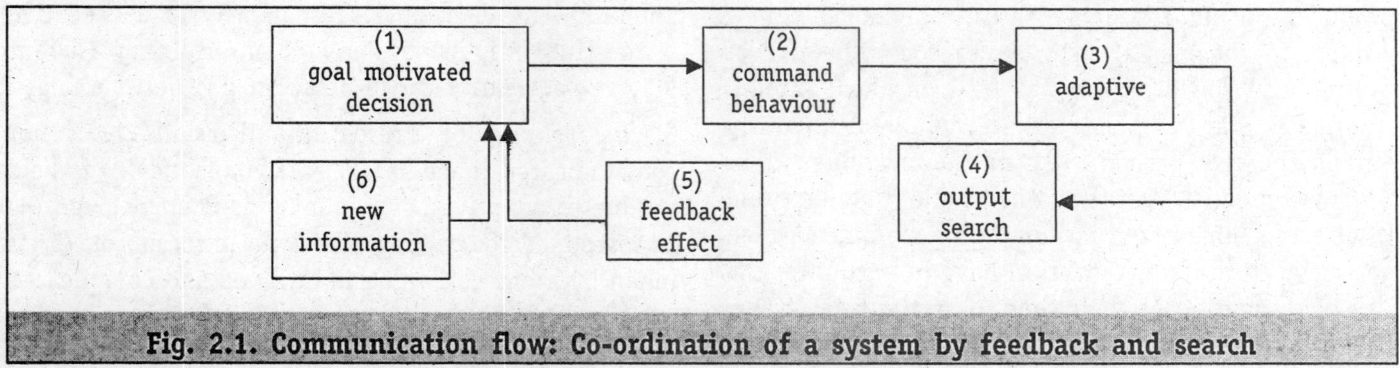

Fig. 2.1. Communication flow: Co-ordination of a system by feedback and search

Search enables a decision maker to send appropriate commands based on the feedback and new aspects of information received from the ground situation or environment of the market. The command message given by the decision maker is not arbitrary, but formulated from adaptive behaviour based on past outcome and also external information. Interplay of different kinds of information which in turn depends upon errors reported for correction of adaptive behaviour comprising various inputs like the work, acts, flows and inter-industry transaction flows of marketing helps to achieve coordination in all activities. This theoretical concept or model of a system can be thrown out of gear if the model is taken in its simplified form. If the information in feedback or collected through a search is incorrect or misleading, the results based on execution of the corrective measures are too obvious, that is, bound to be infructuous.

POSTPONEMENT OF CORRECTIVE ACTION BASED ON FEEDBACK ERROR

"Feedback error" is incorrect information received. Performance error is a different category of information. "Feedback error" and "Performance error" are different and can be distinguished from each other. Performance error arises from complex causes and which produces feedback information which can be used to correct future performance. Performance cannot be corrected if the feedback information is incorrect, and, if however, inspite of an inaccurate feedback performance gets improved or corrected, it can be called an accident or sheer luck. Decision-makers as well as administrative set up often get incorrect information. Even marketing network is not spared from the problem of receiving incorrect information. The problem confronts a sales manager and equally the national marketing policy makers planning for sale of agricultural produce or for drawing up policy programmes for international trade.

The situation arising from receipt of incorrect information creates a gigantic problem. The problem obviously cannot be solved immediately and the best way or option available is to delay the decision till such time as correct information is available. Wroe Alderson in a monthly journal in his newsletter has stated "changes in form and identity to the latest possible point of time" automatically comes within the reach of the marketing network, once its decision-makers in the context postpone their corrective action.[14] Although action-oriented decision-makers may neither approve nor accept postponement of their corrective decisions, yet postponement of corrective decisions is the only way to avoid the risk arising from incorrect information.

Albert G. Hart in his book, "Anticipations, Uncertainty and Dynamic Planning" has observed "Fuller information about the future will come as it draws towards the present and many decisions can be postponed until the information is available."[15] On the contrary, decision-makers, quite often, decide to take corrective action with or without correct information. They do so because they are averse to postponement and do not prefer delays in decision making. But, the truth is that these decision-makers rarely have as much knowledge about the future as actually needed to act confidently for positive results.

MAGNIFICATION OF DELAY

When an executive or decision-maker decides to reduce risks by waiting till such point of time when enough information is available, a delay in communication of corrective action takes place. A producer opting for delay in introducing his new product in the market in order to cover the risk of failure and deciding to wait till he has enough information about the market, he simultaneously entails the risk permanently in the introduction of the new product. On the other hand, retailers and wholesalers already opting for the new product which gets delayed in its introduction have to encounter the risk of stagnation of their capital. In the final event, if the new product because of delayed introduction, fails to catch the market, the wholesalers and retailers might find their capital permanently blocked or which may be eventually lost for good. The wholesalers and retailers also run the risk of losing loss of reputation in the market. They may also lose their "customer franchise" so termed in trade terms. In other words, the well set groups and sections of customers may lose interest in their wholesalers and retailers and seek new markets and traders in them as a substitute. The delay if any, has to be measured and weighed against the much awaited additional information and the degree to which its use could help reduce risk and uncertainty. This delay becomes irrelevant and redundant if the decision-maker is blessed with the necessary foresight and imagination which could help him make dependable and reliable forecasts and for him the additional information or market feedback is hardly necessary.

An executive or decision-maker may have to encounter delays in decision-making and in giving directives or commands, due to various causes. Amongst these, one may be that he is unable to solve a problem which he has chosen to tackle. Yet another situation would arise when the executive or decision-maker does not agree with the advice or suggestions given by advisers. A third kind of situation entailing delay comes up when the executive or decision-maker postpones a decision himself in the hope of getting correct information about the demand of the product and the effort that would be needed for meeting it. Sometimes, a delay may be caused by technical failure to communicate the directive or command in a corrective action despite the correct decision having been taken at the right time. Moreover, delays may be caused by some unanticipated factors as well. A secretary of a company or organisation, or an executive or a sales manager having taken ill suddenly like catching a severe cold may helplessly delay a decision. Similarly, the decision-maker, namely, and executive on getting fatigued because of entertaining a client may unnecessarily cause delay in decision-making.

Delays may be caused if a decision (1) is not communicated immediately as a command (2) is held up due to adaptive behaviour (3) is itself delayed (4) is postponed for getting additional information (5) is taken by a process which is involved and complicated (6) is subjected to a long procedure for the purposes of studying output and effect (7) is subjected and stayed in favour of conducting a search for more information which consumes a long time. Similarly, feedback delay may be due to a failure in completing a distribution cost analysis or in formulating a market search or survey on time.

Delay causes an oscillation in the interaction between the market and the organisation which helps to keep the system balanced and in control. Postponement of a decision beyond a certain critical reaction time often results in competitive losses due to delays often gripping large-scale systems like centrally administered super markets or variety chain organisations. The too well-known oscillation is the trade cycle in which information on market conditions arrive too late so that the company or organisation may have to cancel its orders for capital equipment or other items on trade unit's inventory for producing the product, because of declining demands for the new product proposed to be launched.

MARKET OSCILLATIONS

Oscillations in market conditions is a phenomenon which confounds the best of managers of a commercial organisation. Oscillations have to be properly interpreted and understood for planning out preventive or corrective action. Even if that be done, and well intentioned and well thought out action is taken, the result may not be as anticipated. Refer to Figure 2.1.

Market oscillations with the passage of time get magnified. At times, if it is discovered that the adaptive behaviour, that is, preventive or corrective action, is either more or less forceful compared with the available information, the outcome of action taken may be entirely different than the output desired. This happens because the feedback information about adaptive action (preventive or corrective action) automatically involves a time lag due to which the decision-maker's adaptive action fails to incorporate the intelligence from feedback information. The decision-maker may at times succeed in bringing performance within tolerable expectations or limits, if his reaction time to the feedback information is fast enough.

At some occasions, the decision-maker may press the panic botton, giving orders to stop adaptive action or giving orders rapidly in succession, which may plunge the organisation or the company in utter disorder and confusion. Quite often, the feedback information in unclear or ambiguous that the decision-maker is unable to get cue for adaptive action, both preventive and corrective.

FATE OF PANIC DECISIONS

Well thought out or well planned decisions taken fast on feedback information do hold out promise for results close to output desired. But, there is also the case of panic decisions taken arbitrarily or without reason or may be to satisfy the ego of the decision maker heading the organisation or company. In such a case, the sales of the product are bound to nose dive. If the decline in sales is the outcome of certain market factors beyond the knowledge of the management, the safest bet for the manner or decision-maker is to do nothing, that is not to take any adaptive action till a proper survey of market conditions reveal how the market factors have eroded the sales of the product. In fact, the correct approach for taking adaptive action or to pursue a strategy for reversing the decline in sales is to act on information that promises the best results.

EGO DECISIONS

The worst case is of the manager or decision-maker who takes adaptive action to serve his ego. Being at the top of the organisation of company gives him the feeling or imparts to him the inflated notion that he is the last word on decision-making; his subordinates or co-workers down the ladder or even those associated with the sales drive possess neither the status nor the capability to advise the manager or decision- maker at the top of the management.

Peter F. Drucker in his exposition in "Managing for Results" has ascribed some failures to "Managerial Ego." He has also cited a case which illustrates his point of view. He has stated that it is not at all surprising to find skilled managers having an inflated ego investing millions of dollars in product whose market feedback reports are "failures."

The case cited by Drucker is that of an American car whose market survey reported that it was the best engineered car and the American public raved over it and virtually loved it. The market survey revealed the same information for nearly a quarter of a century.

Surprisingly, the American people did not buy it. Each successive year the car failed in the market; there were hardly any buyers. But, each year market forecasts for the next year repeatedly stated that the car would finally take off and become the successful leader in cars which its engineering excellence deserved. The company believed and also relied on the market feedback information and pumped in more money every year in its project. The worst part of the affair was that the company's top management invested all its key resources — managerial, technical, marketing and its working personnel — in the almost failed project. Moreover, any person in the company who claimed some kind of talent, especially if he was engaged in pushing up sales of the company's other good selling models of cars, was removed from the assignment and pushed into the campaign of the "sick model" and, if that employee or worker failed to make the failed model a success, he was thrown out of employment.

After 24 long years when the unsuccessful car model was finally abandoned, it had drained out the company of its power, success and growth.[16]

FORMATION, SURVIVAL & DISSOLUTION OF COMMUNICATION CHANNEL

Communication channels are created when the seller and the buyer search each other. This is what may be called a "Double Search." A communication channel is not a one-way search, that is, the seller alone or the buyer singly cannot establish a communication channel.

FORMATION OF CHANNELS

Communication channel is the demand of trading obligations and a necessity for carrying on business of selling and buying. Here we are talking of the marketing channel, which is essentially a communication channel between the seller and the buyer, and how they are formed.

Marketing channels are needed by business firms or companies to attain economies of scale and skill. The marketing channels enables the business firm or company to bridge existing gaps between goods supplied by producers or manufacturers and the demand and need of the consumer.

The existence of marketing agencies or communication channels between the producers and consumers helps the latter in a big way. The consumers through these marketing agencies can assess their requirement or demand for goods and guide them to time their purchases. The consumers, because of these agencies, can either go in for immediate purchase of goods or can postpone their purchases with a view to appraising their future demand for the goods. These agencies also enable the consumer or purchaser to decide the quantum of goods needed and the time when the requirement would arise.

On the other hand, even wholesalers derive reasonable advantage from these marketing agencies. The wholesalers with the assistance of these channels can relive pressure upon retailers to indent goods for sale. The wholesalers can assist retailer by advising them to postpone indenting or seeking supplies of goods for specific areas and locales till the consumer-demand for goods both as regards their variety and quantum is clearly evident.

Intervening marketing agencies automatically get included in communications channels due to necessity especially when the distance between the producer and consumer increases. For example, a manufacturer located in the eastern region can successfully sell its products in the eastern region or nearby areas. But, the difficulty arises if the manufacturer has to catch distant markets say in the western region. For this purpose, the involvement of an intervening marketing agency as a link between the eastern manufacturer and the western consumers is bound to work out cheaper. The intervening marketing agency already in trading contact with western buyers, if hired is bound to be less costly than the eastern manufacturer trying to spread its sales organisation in the west. Measurable economies develop with the passage of time which enables buyers and sellers to find each other while searching the market for trading partners. It is thus clear, that the preliminary step in the formation of a channel segment begins with a double search.

RESEARCH FOR CHANNEL

A producer for making sure of winning over unexplored market, often prefers to hire a research organisation or firm to make a survey and advise him in planning the sales campaign for the product suited to meet the demand which exists but which has been met. Capable and competent market managers use feedback information derived from consumer research or consumer survey for planning the marketing of their product to suit consumer demand. The market research or market survey serves as a useful guide for a producer before introducing his product in the market. If product-planning so made managed to receive consumer acceptance, the consumers themselves "pull" or purchase the product from wholesale or retail outlets. On the contrary, the product producer in the absence of market survey or research has to search for these consumer outlets in order to "push" or organise sales in consumer markets. In the process of searching customers or searching activity in general, which may include advertising and personal selling, the product manufacturer, at times, is successful in locating and selling his product to customer pools of latent demand which gets converted into real market demand.

THE SEARCH CYCLE

Trade contacts are established through a search cycle. Retailers are needed by wholesalers to help them in locating customers for their products, which they buy from manufacturers. On the other hand, retailers need a trading contact with producers because they are the purchasing agents on behalf of the consumers. Retailers, on their part, may either make their purchases from wholesalers or directly from producers or manufacturers depending upon the quantity they want to purchase for the consumers. The purchases by retailers depend upon the consumer demand and the source of their purchases is chosen accordingly; bigger quantities directly from producers or manufacturers and lesser quantities from wholesalers.

The search cycle is a two way affair. It is not merely the wholesalers seeking the retailers for selling their products, *vice versa* the retailers also seek the wholesalers to meet consumer demand. Lower down, the consumers search for the retailers who can meet their demands, while the retailers search and locate consumers for selling products procured by retailers from wholesalers. The entire chain from the producer or manufacturer to the wholesalers and therefrom to the retailers and further downwards to the consumers is necessary for an effective trading channel.

It is obvious, therefore in the process of double searching from segment to segment, that is from the producer or manufacturer to the wholesaler, from the wholesaler to the retailer, and from the retailer to the consumer, a communication channel gets established for a particular trading contact. When a pair of trading partners complete negotiations for a single product and begin operating on it, they can be said to have formed a successful communication-channel unit.

The single communication channel for a single product ensuring smooth flow of the product from the selling to the purchases with the passage of time gets secure and may easily be expanded for the sale of an entire class or type of goods. In fact, the act of communication and not the variety of products that helps to establish independent entities in trading contact and convert them into channel segments.

Finally, it can be said the communication link in establishing a trading contact is formed in three phases:

(*i*) Pre-negotiatory Double-Search
(*ii*) Negotiation for Settlement of an Order
(*iii*) Pre-Negotiatory Agreement on Services.

Pre-Negotiatory Double Search

"Double-Search" is a term which refers to the search by a selling for customers and the search by customers for suppliers. This mutual search and efforts for establishing trading contact are termed as a "pre-negotiatory double search."

Sometimes, a buyer's minor purchase search may commence and end with an impulsive selection of an item that suits his fancy. When the search is just in a routine transaction, the time taken for the search and the efforts involved are invariable minimal. In the process of "double-search" the terms of exchange for the trading contact are well-known to the trade seeking partners and well settled. The seller in his search-effort makes goods and products freely and widely available and also well known to the buyers, so that a simple impulsive selection by the buyer satisfies his demand. Purchases made by housewives through super-market transactions or purchases made in industry for maintenance supplies, fall in this category of transactions. They are causal transactions during the pre-negotiatory search.

The carefully considered and thought out purchase which often ends in a fully negotiated transaction, is the purchases at the other extreme compared with the causal purchase. In the fully pre-meditated purchase, the purchaser is influenced and persuaded by advertising and he also consults other buyers who has purchased similar products. Brokers or buying services may also be sought to give advice for negotiating terms of exchange. Communication with transportation agencies, banks, and installation engineers is also necessary for assuring delivery and for securing payment in accordance with the terms of exchange negotiated and finally settled.

Negotiation for a Settlement

During the negotiatory phase for finalising a transaction additional communication is often required for settling terms of exchange. After settlement of terms of exchange the buyer and seller arrive at an agreement after finalising a transaction. The buyer and seller under the agreement have to examine several factors and also concur on these terms of exchange. The buyer and the seller have to agree on the amount of money to be exchanged for a product. The exchange factor of purchase of a product includes time and place of delivery, time and place of payment and the services that the buyer and seller agree to exchange after negotiations are over.

Some more conditions, may form part of the agreement when the negotiated settlement is a transaction for exchange of durable item needing after-sale repair and maintenance. It is common for the buyer to agree to deliver the durable item to the seller and the seller is bound by an undertaking to complete repairs or carry out maintenance at a pre-settled cost schedule. Used cars, fall in the category of a durable item or product, which under the negotiated settlement includes, repair and maintenance. For example, used cars are often sold enjoining the seller for bearing the burden for the total cost replacement of worn-out parts and 50 per cent labour cost. Sellers do not expect much of the cost burden that might otherwise be expected because spares and parts of the car are not needed frequently. The buyer, on his part, feels that he is insured against an impossible hazard he fears to encounter.

Negotiations take to a routine from when the transaction includes agreement on certain major factors like standard repairs, standard prices market clearly on merchandise, pre-packaging, advertising and branding. These factors enable the buyers to get cues permanently for making an approximate estimate of the goods offered. Customers usually accept the product offered on conclusion of routine transactions. Unless the goods found defective and returned. Goods delivered to the checkout counter of which receive acceptance of customers and those which are consumed automatically terminate the negotiation.

Pre-negotiatory Agreement

Trading partners are bound by reciprocal obligations in fully negotiated or semi-negotiated transactions. These fall in the category of "Service Agreements" because these obligations constitute a host of logistic and persuasive communication included in the trading agreement to finalise a sale in which the commitment is for performance of services after negotiations are completed. Buyer services normally have limitations. For example, unpaid balances may be made at specified repair stations or presentation of goods according to a scheduled agreement included in the negotiations. On the other hand, seller services include commitments like warranty, maintenance and repair agreements. Basic goods sold on an annual delivery contract have to abide by and fulfil an agreed delivery schedule falling which the seller may have to pay specified penalties on each default in delivery. A parallel example is of construction contractors or contract construction sellers who stand to earn a bonus or extra profit for an early completion of the construction project but are required to pay a fine under the penalty clause in the agreement for a belated delivery of the project like a finished power station, dam or some other construction unit. Similarly, "free advice" or engineering assistance assured on the use of a product after completion of sale comprises a part of service-agreement communication.

CHANNEL SEGMENTS

Channel segments are formed in three stages of a transaction when communication is related to specific goods or products.

(1) The pre-negotiatory stage in which buyers and sellers exchange communication in their double search for each other.
(2) The negotiatory stage in which trading partners, namely, buyers and sellers, arrive at an agreement on the terms and conditions of the sale by placing an order for supply of goods or products, while in routine transactions give physical delivery of goods in exchange for an agreed upon or negotiated price.
(3) The pre-negotiatory stage in which the trading partner execute their commitments in accordance with their mutual service agreement.

ONE TO ONE LINKAGE

There is one-to-one linkage if only a single buyer and seller are reckoned at each stage as depicted in Figure 2.2.

If the initial transaction has proved satisfactory, trading partners, that is the buyer and seller, are invariably keen on renewing trading contacts because of strong reasons and incentives as the cost of double-search is fairly high. The seller considers a transaction satisfactory if the product or products he is selling meets his requirements of the expected stock turnover and anticipated profit margin. A consumer, on the other hand, re-enters the market on the basis of arousal of his needs and satisfactory fulfilment.

Both in household and industrial buying decisions, the buyer is most likely to renew his trading contact with the same trading partner if he has experienced the anticipated degree of satisfaction in the previous trading contact purchase. Trading partners, that is, the buyer and the seller, are said to form an institutional channel segment when they maintain trading contacts after specific goods are no longer being exchanged, namely, after the obligations under the previous trading contact have been finally met by them.

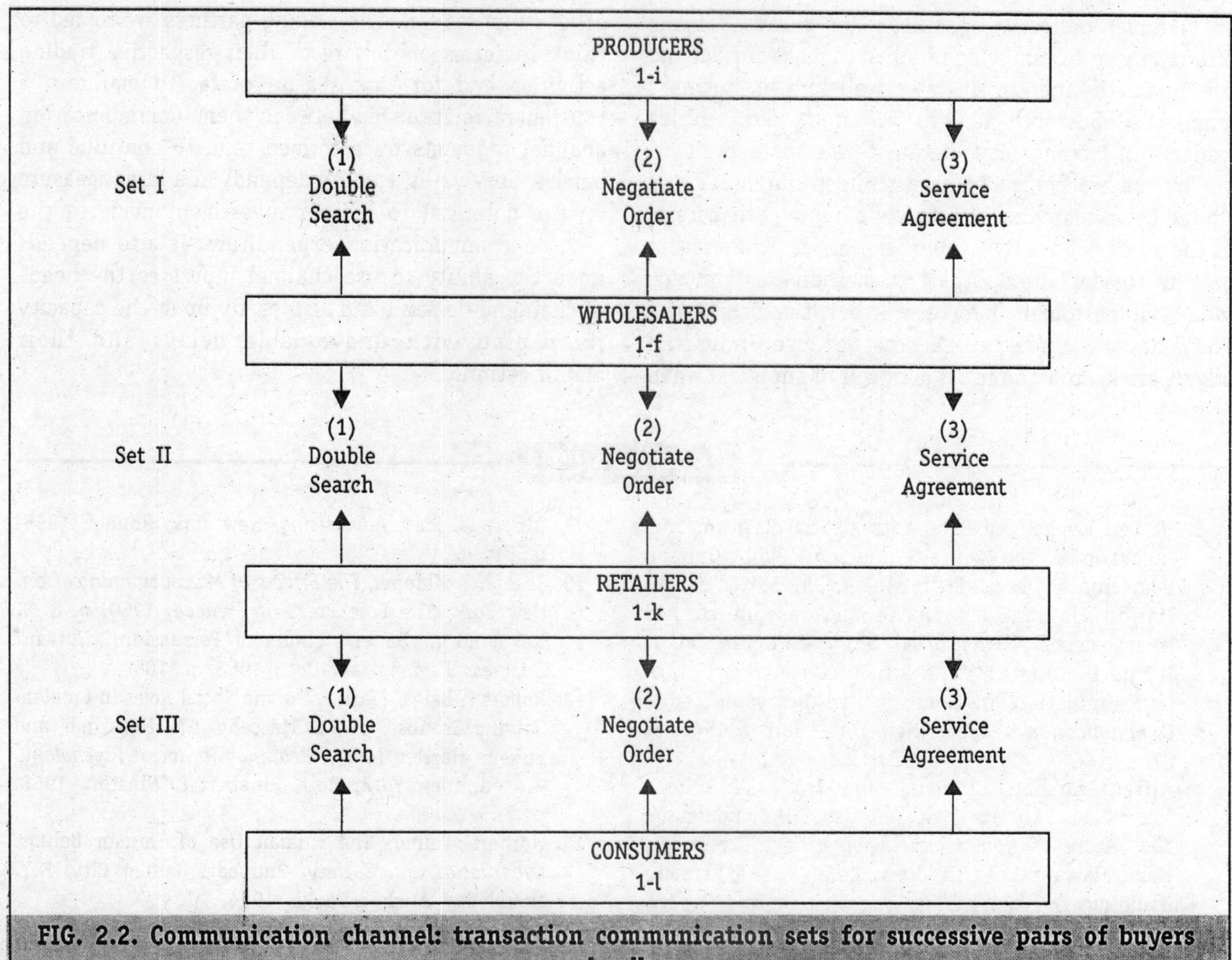

FIG. 2.2. Communication channel: transaction communication sets for successive pairs of buyers and sellers

Edmund D. McGarry in his article on "The Contractual Function in Marketing" published in the Journal of Business has stated:[17]

"As the chain of contacts between the producer and the consumer develops, it tends to become institutionalised, that is to say, each agency tends to look upon itself less as an isolated and independent unit in the business world and more as a part of a greater entity which has an *esprit de corps* of its own. Thus, it becomes the interest of each agency to preserve, protect and defend every other element in the chain, in order to maintain the structure as a whole and thus provide continuously profitable business for all. The chain of contacts, once established, provides the mechanism for a continuous two-way line of communication between the producer and the consumer and a linkage of their interests."

The development of time-stable sets of trading relations between pairs of buyers and sellers is not accidental because producers and marketing agencies continually alter merchandise offers. In the hope of winning additional customers, sellers keep on expanding merchandise variety. Sellers also keep on experimenting with variety and stock quantum due to competitive pressures. In the event of goods getting exhausted in the seller's supplies in the initial trading contact, the buyer associated with the earlier trading contact may still prefer to remain associated with the know services of the seller in view of the time, effort and money cost that would be required to search for another seller.[18]

A buyer prefers a specific seller because of the efforts known to him which he has to make for getting the goods he needs. It is a well-known business maxim. "Goods well bought are half sold." "Price leaders" in trading may dictate terms for a product, but buyers are known to have stopped purchases and slowed down searching efforts while buying other items in the stocks of another seller who offers a concession on one "leader" item. Apart from individual buyers, industrial customers may also react the same way. They have a different reason because industrial buyers are keen on building goodwill of suppliers when other suppliers fail. The trading partners are forced to think in terms of welfare of their respective trading activities and for that reason prefer to maintain a continuous relationship between them. Communication channel segments once formed tend to continue and persist. Survival in trading depends in a large measure on the potential to recover investment made in the past on communication expenditure. It also depends upon the ability to use channel inputs to the needs of changing demand and also partly upon the capacity for coping with unavoidable delays and their amplification.

REFERENCES

1. Herbert Menzel and Elihu Katz, "Social Relations and Innovation in the Medical Profession," Public Opinion Quarterly, *Winter*, 1955-1956, pp. 337-352.
2. Marion Harper, Jr., "A New Profession to Aid Management," *Journal of Marketing*, Jan. 1961, p. 1.
3. Harold D. Lasswell, "The Structure and Function of Communication in Society," in L.Bryson (ed.), *Communication of Ideas*, New York, Harper, 1948, p. 27.
4. Alfred Marshall, *Industry and Trade*, New York Macmillan, 1919, p. 304. See also E.H.Chamberlain, *The Theory of Monopolistic Competition*, Cambridge, Mass., Harvard University Press, 1950, p. 157; Kenneth Boulding, *The Image: Knowledge in Life and Society*, Ann Arbor, University of Michigan Press 1956.
5. David Ogilvy, *Confessions of an Advertising Man*, New York, Atheneum, 1964, p. 152.
6. I.J. Good, "How Rational Should a Manager Be?" *Management Science*, July, 1962, p. 391.
7. Edward T. Hall, "The Silent Language of Overseas Business," *Harvard Business Review*, May-June, 1960, pp. 93-95.
8. Edmund D. McGarry, "The Contactual Function in Marketing," *Journal of Business*, Apr. 1951, pp. 96-113. Reprinted by permission of The University of Chicago Press.
9. Albert W. Frey, *Advertising*, New York, Ronald, 1955, p. 314.
10. Joseph T. Klapper, *The Effects of Mass Communication*, New York, The Free Press of Glencoe, 1960, p. 8.
11. Raymond A. Bauer, "Limits of Persuasion," *Harvard Business Review*, Sept-Oct., 1958, p. 105.
12. Robert F. Bales, "Task Roles and Social Roles in Problem Solving Groups," in C.E. Macceby, T.M. Newcomb, and Eugene Hartley (eds.), *Readings in Social Psychology*, 3rd ed., New York, Holt, Rinebert & Winston, 1958, pp. 437-447.
13. Norbert Weiner, The Human Use of Human Beings: *Cybernetics and Society*, 2nd ed., Garden City, N.Y. Doubleday Anchor Books, 1954.
14. Wroe Alderson, *Cost and Profit Outlook*, Philadelphia, Alderson and Sessions, Sept., 1950 (a monthly four-page newsletter).
15. Albert G. Hart, *Anticipations, Uncertainty and Dynamic Planning*, Reprint, New York, Augustus M. Kelly, 1961, p. 55.
16. Peter F. Drucker, *Managing for Results*, New York, Harper, 1964, p. 61.
17. McGarry, *op. cit.*
18. *Marketing Systems: An Introductory Analysis*, George Fisk, Harper & Row, New York, 1967. pp. 281-313.

CHAPTER

3 COMMUNICATION — CONCEPT & PROCESS

EDS REBUILDS ITS IMAGE

Until 2000, if you asked the average person what, if anything/he or she knew about a company called Electronic Data Systems (EDS), you would probably get a blank stare. Some might associate the company with Ross Perot, the company's founder and former presidential candidate, and know that he later sold EDS to General Motors, but it is unlikely they would know any-thing more. Perot founded EDS in Dallas, Texas, in 1962 with the somewhat radical notion that organizations would hire an outside company to handle all of their computer operations. At the time, the word "outsourcing" had not even entered the business lexicon. However, the idea caught on quickly and EDS came to rule the industry it created, which was evolving beyond just computers into information technology services (ITS). EDS grew exponentially after being acquired by General Motors in 1984 and became a $14 billion giant before splitting off from the automaker in 1996 and becoming an independent company. In many ways the success EDS had under General Motors' wing turned out to be a competitive handicap. A hefty annuity from GM provided a steady revenue stream that lulled the company into complacency and fostered an unwillingness to change even though the world was changing all around it, particularly with the rapid growth of the Internet.

In early 1999, EDS hired a new CEO, Dick Brown, who realized that he and his management team had to do more than reinvent the company—they had to remake its identity and brand image. EDS was perceived as a stodgy, old-economy firm in a new-economy industry and was being eclipsed by flashier firms such as Razorfish, Scient, and Viant, which focused purely on eservices, as well as a reinvented IBM, which had rebuilt its identity around the themes of e-business. Brown hired Don Uzzi, whose record included leading a marketing turnaround for Gatorade in the 90s, as EDS's senior vice president of global marketing and advertising and put him in charge of rebuilding the company's image. Brown wanted Uzzi to build awareness of EDS and make the company a household name. However, there was also a second, equally critical goal: to market EDS to its own employees and make them feel good about working at the company.

The first area Brown turned to in establishing EDS as a power brand was advertising. EDS began working with the Fallon McElligott agency, which came up with a new tagline, "EDS Solved," that was chosen to position the com-pany as a problem solver in the complicated, ever-changing world of e-business. While print work broke in the fall of 1999 with full-page ads in The Wall Street Journal, New York Times, and other major publications, the company did not limit its newfound boldness to advertising. Uzzi decided the Y2K fervor provided an opportunity for EDS, which had a thriving year-2000 conversion practice in place, as a publicity opportunity. He arranged for EDS's strategic command center in Piano, Texas, to be opened to the media on New Year's Eve night.

More than a dozen journalists showed up, and CNBC and CNN did live feeds from the command center, as did local TV crews. Uzzi noted: "We showed the world what EDS does and how we do it. That's something the company never would have done before." Once the New Year passed with few glitches, EDS celebrated with a full-page "Y2KO" ad in The Wall Street Journal, calling attention to the role the company played in helping the world get ready for the date change.

The risk taking continued when EDS ran its now-famous "Cat Herders" ad during the 2000 Super Bowl. The Super Bowl is advertising's biggest showcase and is usually reserved for major advertisers rather than companies such as EDS, which was nearly invisible in the ad world. The commercial was shot in the style of a John Ford old-style western—big sky, big country, stirring musical score— and featured cowboys herding 10,000 house cats. Uzzi noted that herding cats is an information management metaphor for organizing an overwhelming amount of varied data and captures perfectly what EDS does: "We ride herd on complexity. We make technology go where clients want it to go." The commercial was one of the most popular of the Super Bowl ads, and the EDS website received 2 million hits in the first 24 hours after the ad ran and 10 million hits in the first week. Clients called from all over the world, asking for tapes of the commercial to play at meetings, and EDS parlayed the ad's suc-cess into a high-profile presence at trade shows.

EDS followed the "Cat Herders" spot with two more high-profile commercials including an ad that debuted on the 2001 Super Bowl called "Running with the Squirrels," which was a spoof of the traditional running of the bulls in Pamplona, Spain, and sent a message about the importance of staying nimble in business. The second commercial was called "Airplane," and it compared what EDS does to building an airplane while it is in the air. Follow-up research shows that the trilogy of commercials resulted in a doubling of the percentage of people associating EDS with e-business solutions and a 50 percent increase in overall brand awareness.

In 2002, EDS moved its advertising in a new direction with a series of commercials and print ads designed to move beyond creating awareness and provide businesses with a better understanding of each of the EDS lines of business—information technology outsourcing, hosting, and security/privacy. In just two years, a lot more people in the corpo-rate world have become aware of EDS and now view it as a hip, hardworking company that can provide solutions to information technology problems. In addition to helping generate business, EDS's advertising has created excitement among its employees and helped attract new talent to the company. EDS wants its advertising to continue to lead, surprise, and impress its customers as well as its own employees. It is likely that it will.

Sources: Suzanne Vranica, "Cats Corralled: EDS Ads Go Back to Basics," The Wall Street Journal, Feb. 8, 2002, p. B9; Tom Wasserman, "Brand Builders," Brandweek, Feb. 11, 2002, pp. 17,18; "Reinventing the Brand," Fortune, October 2001, p.

A concept means what its definition says it means. If it does not say this clearly so that we know when we do or when we do not have an instance of it, then the concept may be criticised legitimately as being inadequately defined.[1]

A concept is the effect of generalisation of a mental operation. It is a generic mental image abstracted from percepts, and generally relies on an originally inductive process rooted in objective reality. It is basic and fundamental to theory and theory formulation, since it is the point of research origination, and radically effects the determination and reaching of the desired destination or goal. It serves as a real, if unstated, rule for making observations and organising experience. In theory formulation the primary function of a concept is to define the behavioural field observed, which at length affects the principles derived which, in turn, gives a colour to the hypotheses constructed. This, in turn, again affects the laws and the system of laws stated which all put together composes the theory generated. The understanding and perception of individual acts or realities lead to the grouping of percepts as well as the nomenclature of such groupings. Ernest Bormann states it in this way, "The setting up of classes in such a way that knowledge can be ordered related and explained is dependent upon concept formation."[2] Abraham Kaplan observes that "what makes a concept significant is that the classification it institutes is one into which things fall, as it were of themselves."[3] Although psychologists and Psycho-linguists have studied concept formation, it is the philosophers who have concentrated on the subject and made an in-depth study of it.

Briefly, concepts can broadly be divided into two categories:

(*i*) Ordinary, common concepts

(*ii*) Extraordinary, scientific concepts.

(*i*) Ordinary, common concepts include everyday concepts such as 'dog', 'food', 'cloud', 'thunder', 'table', 'hunger', 'colour', etc. which seem manifest to all and impinge willingly or unwillingly on all of us. The terms of common sense name these vanguard daily experiences.

(*ii*) Extraordinary, scientific concepts include those features of the world which are recognised only by a more subtle, pervasive and critical examination of nature, man and society then it is made in everyday life, things and objects. 'The function of scientific concepts is to mark the categories which will tell us more about our subject-matter than any other categorical sets.'[4] Scientific terms like 'mass', 'IQ', 'Primary group' and 'repression' etc., name attributes which do not stand out explicitly as do ordinary, common concepts such as 'love, 'hunger', 'green', 'round', and 'huge' etc.[5]

Interpretation of Concept in terms of 'Communication'

The concept of communication is vital to the study and understanding of communication in its proper perspective. It substantially effects any addition to existing theories of communication or any efforts directed toward the development of a new theory. Kaplan raises[6] two issues about communication concepts. The first issue is concerned with the objectivity of the concepts. *i.e.*, are the communication concepts objective? The second issue poses a question, 'Do communication concepts clearly delineate the paths for moving freely in both logical as well as experiential space?' One way of assessing the usefulness of any given concept of communication stand out explicit in the same way as do the scientific concepts. But our experience in this direction is otherwise.

The vagueness of communication concepts is clearly discerned in the vagueness of the field or fields identified with the study of communication. The concept of communication, as defined by scholars and theoreticians, is not only loose but also includes contradictory components, and does not allow the synthesization of a single internally consistent definition.

The definitions of communication examined here were drawn from divergent fields and diverse publications. These were subjected to expert evaluation as well as content and critical analysis. The substantive terminology in each term was listed and collated into a master list which revealed evidence of repetitive terms as redundancy of themes. Out of approximately 4,560 words or tokens comprising approximately 2,612 types, thirty different terms were classified. Out of these thirty terms were derived fifteen which were regarded to be distinct conceptual components.[7]

These fifteen distinct conceptual components each followed by a definition representative of those definitions including the component, include both intentional and extensional components. It is to be seen that every definition contains more than one conceptual component, and the sample definitions are not meant to reproduce only the component for which they serve as examples. These are briefly examined here:

(1) Process: 'Communication: the transmission of information, ideas, emotions, skills, etc., by the use of symbols — words, pictures, figures, graphs, etc. It is the act or process of transmission that is usually called communication.[8]

(2) Commonality: "It (communication) is a process that makes common to two or several what was the monopoly of one or some.'[9]

(3) Transfer/transmission/interchange: '... the connecting thread appears to be the idea of something's being transferred from one thing, or person, to another. We use the word 'communication' sometimes to refer to what is so transferred, sometimes to the means by which it is transferred, sometimes to the whole process. In many cases, what is transferred in this way continues to be shared; if I convey information to another person, it does not leave my own possession, through coming into his. Accordingly, the word 'communication' acquires also the sense of participation. It is in the sense, for example, that religious worshippers are said to communicate.[10]

(4) Understanding: 'Communication is the process by which we understand others and in turn endeavour to be understood by them. It is dynamic, constantly changing and shifting in response to the total situation.'[11]

(5) Symbols/Verbal/Speech: 'Communication is the verbal interchange of thought or idea.'[12]

(6) Stimuli: "Every communication act is viewed as a transmission of information, consisting of a discriminative stimuli, from a source to a recipient."[13]

(7) Discriminative response/behaviour modifying/response/change: 'Communication is the discriminatory response of an organism to a stimulus.[14] "So, communication between two animals is said to occur when one animal produces a chemical or physical change in the environment (signal) that influences the behaviour of another...."[15]

(8) Replicating memories: 'Communication is the Process of conducting the attention of another person for the purpose of replicating memories.'[16]

(9) Linking/binding: 'Communication in the process that links discontinuous parts of the living world to one another.'[17]

(10) Reduction of uncertainty: 'Communication arises out of the need to reduce uncertainty, to act effectively, to defend or strengthen the ego.'[18]

(11) Intentional: 'In the main, communication has as its central interest those behavioural situations in which a source transmits a message to a receiver(s) with conscious intent to effect the latter's behaviour."[19]

(12) Interaction/relationship/social process: 'Interaction, even on the biological level, is a kind of communication; otherwise common acts could not occur.'[20]

(13) Channel/carrier/means/route: '(pl.).... The means of sending military messages, orders, etc., as by telephone, telegraph, radio, couriers.'[21]

(14) Power: '... communication is the mechanism by which power is exerted.'[22]

(15) Time/Situation: 'The communication process is one of transition from one structured situation-as-a-whole to another, in preferred design.'[23]

Analysing the above fifteen conceptual components, one can conclude that there are basically three aspects upon which the definitions critically divide. These three aspects of critical conceptual differentiations are:

(*i*) the level/extent of observations made,

(*ii*) presence or absence of 'intentionality' on the part of the sender, and

(*iii*) the normative judgment (qualitative), such as goodness-badness/successful-unsuccessful, of the act.

(*i*) The above definitions of communication reflect the diverse fields of observation ranging from all behaviour to significant, purposive behaviour of human beings in conscious interaction. Of course, the theories needed and the theories predicated will vary to considerable degree upon the level /extent of observations made. It also indicates wide divergencies in behavioural fields as well as in the number and interpretations of observations and the consequent theory formulation.

(*ii*) The conceptual component of 'intentionality' denotes those aspects of human behaviour which stand opposed to considerations of reality and experience. It greatly delimits the behavioural field observed. For example, if one chooses only those acts which can be labelled 'intentional' for the purpose of communication, then our behavioural field and the consequent observations become ridiculously restricted. Acts revealing objectivity or accident, resulting in acquirement of information or altering of one's behaviour as a result of interaction of another person will be out of the picture.

(*iii*) The conceptual component of normative judgment is also greatly restrictive of the observational field. If we interpret only successful interaction (in which the purpose of sender is achieved) as illustrative of communication. Then our range of observation becomes all the more selective and restrictive.

An essential concept in understanding communication is that it is a system, the interplay of messages sent and received, rather than a one-way process. Social science research provides many helpful insights into the techniques of effective communication, but communication today is far from being a science. For such a varied and complex a concept, a variety of approaches and methodologies are necessary for understanding the intricacies of the subject in its proper perspective. It seems well-nigh impossible to arrive at a single, rigid, exclusive definition. But the supreme importance of concept and its far-reaching consequences on our scholarly research and professional behaviour cannot be over-emphasised.

Kaplan has suggested the creation of a family of concepts. According to him, "the meaning of a term is a family affair among its various senses."[24] The members of the family may consist of 'attitudes', 'belief', 'opinions', 'communication', 'human communication', 'animals communication', 'effective communication' etc. The phenomenon of a family of concepts helps to enlarge the scope study of communication and treat it in a systems fashion. Moreover, the identification of the familial members requires serious attention of the researchers. It would greatly facilitate systematisation of scholarly research, elimination of conceptual inconsistencies and professional contradictions, and formulation of a precise, methodical and uniform theory of communication.[25]

THE COMMUNICATION PROCESS

In a general sense, one can very easily say that communication means exchange of, or act of imparting thoughts, ideas, messages, experiences, wishes, emotions, moods, opinions, etc. Some social scientists have defined communication as an exchange of information. The American Management Association has defined Communication as, "any behaviour that results in an exchange of meaning."[26] The Special Committee on Communication in Business and Industry (National Society for the Study of Communication, U.S.A.) has tentatively defined it as follows, "Communication is a mutual exchange of facts, thoughts, opinions or emotions. This requires presentation and reception, resulting in common understanding among all parties, this does not necessarily imply agreement."[27] In a series of lectures delivered on the uses of communication by managers for the benefit of students in the Graduate School of Business at Columbia University, New York, Willard V. Merrihue has further defined communication as "any initiated behaviour on the part of the sender which convey the desired meaning to the receiver and causes desired response behaviour from the receiver."[28] We can give a general working definition of communication as thus, "Communication is an interactional process in which meaning is stimulated through the sending and receiving of verbal and non-verbal messages." The key to the definition is process. More than 2,000 years ago, Heyraclitus provided a basic insight into the concept of process when he stated that a man can never step in the same river twice (the very act changes the man and the river, i.e., they both have been affected by the passage of time). Communication is not static for it cannot be properly understood as fixed elements in time and space. Perhaps all communications begin and end with the work "and." Communication is an irreversible and unrepeatable process. Mortensen states, "Communication does not necessarily stop simply because people stop talking and listening."[29] By communication, we mean here the broad field of human interchange of facts and opinions rather than the working of the telephone, radio, television, telegraph, and the like.

Communication is, in the first instance, the process of transferring a particular information or message from an information source to a definite and particular destination. It sets employees in individual jobs, regulates their flow of work, coordinates their efforts and secures better and higher work accomplishment. Management in action comes into existence as a direct human efforts and activities towards the successful execution of action plans. It is the essence of organised activity and is the basic process out of which all other functions are derived.[30] Peter Drucker identifies four fundamentals of communication which show the nature of the process. These are briefly stated below:

(a) Communication is perception. This implies that it is only the recipient who communicates, because if he does not perceive what is transmitted, no communication takes place. The effectiveness of communication is limited to the recipient's range of perception.

(b) Communication is expectation. People perceive only what they expect to. The unexpected is ignored or misunderstood.

(c) Communication makes demands. Experiments have shown that words with unpleasant emotional charges or threats tend to be suppressed while those with pleasant associations are retained longer. In other words, communication makes a demand on the recipient, in terms of his emotional preference of rejection. It also demands him to become somebody or do something.

(d) Communication and information are different. Information is logical, formal and impersonal, while communication is perception. The less tied up information is with human factors, the more valid and reliable it becomes. However, both these are interdependent.[31]

THEORY OF COMMUNICATION

As early as 1938, Chester Barnard observed that, "in an exhaustive theory of organisation, communication would occupy a central phase, because the structure, extensiveness and scope of the organisation are almost entirely determined by communication techniques."[32] If this is the case, it is apparent that central to the study of organisation is communication. It is the one aspect that allows an organisation to be an organisation. Think about it. If we removed all forms of communication from the organisation, would there be an organisation? Recent research studies indicate that depending upon your position within the organisation, it can range from 50 percent to 95 percent of your working day. Can there be any doubt that "organisation man" depends upon communication?[33]

The message may be transmitted as spoken or written words, pictures, or in some other form. In oral communication, the transmitter is the voice box. In telegraphy it is the telegraphy key (Morse Key) which codes the messages into dashes and dots. The receiver decodes the transmitted message in an understandable form to the information destination. The receiver may be, for example, the mechanism of the human ear, which converts sound waves into a form which can be recognised by the brain; a television receiver decodes the electromagnetic waves into recognisable visual representation.[34]

Communication process involves an apparently simple procedure consisting of only a few steps. Berlo has provided one technical model for understanding the process.[35] See Fig. 3.1.

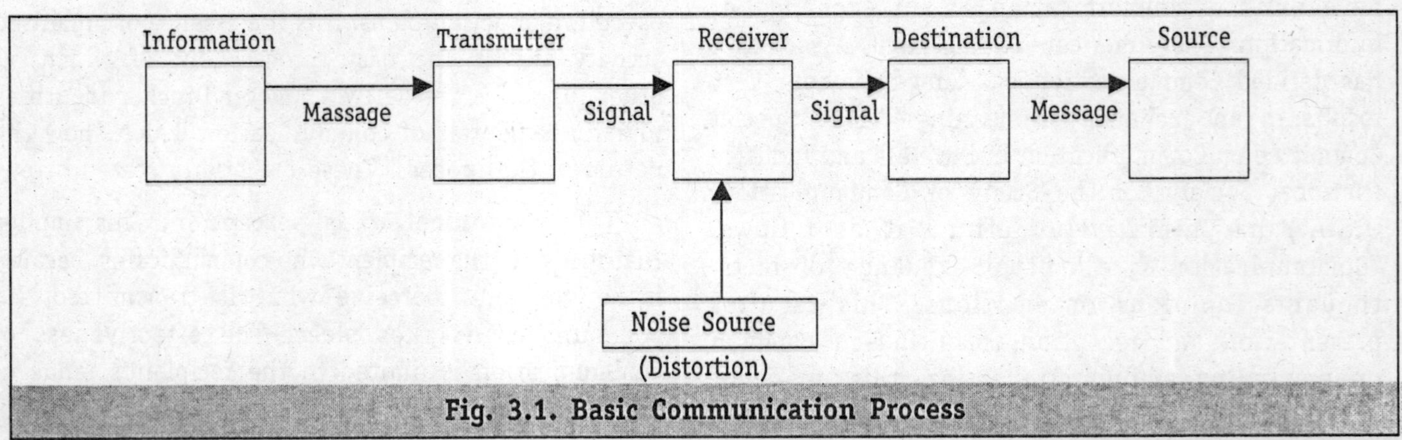

Fig. 3.1. Basic Communication Process

1. A communication source
2. The encoder
3. The message
4. The channel
5. The decoder
6. The communication receiver.

These elements are not necessarily always separated and exclusive, since a person can send a message to himself, and, therefore, he would be both the source and the receiver and do both encoding and decoding. They are mutually inter-dependent, and the whole process is a unity in conveying a meaningful information. Furthermore, the elements are not restricted to people only, since machines may be used in the communication process.

ELEMENTS OF COMMUNICATION

We can say that the communication activity, whether human, mechanical, electrical or electronic, consists of mainly six elements, i.e., a code, a channel, a process of encoding, an encoder, a process of decoding, and finally a decoder. These are briefly described below:

(1) Code

We know that no communication is possible unless there is a code of some kind through which information can be conveyed, and which is comprehended both by the transmitter and receiver. The necessity of human code system arises, as in other systems of communication, to successfully convey the messages to other people. Computer language provide the link between the 'sender', (i.e., the magnetic tape conveying the information needing to be processed), and the 'receiver' which is the electronic complex designed to store the information, think about it and produce the required answer. The computer is able to do this, because it understands the code, but if any code alien to it is fed into it, it would not be able to do its work, and thus, the process of information conveying communication cannot even start. A telecommunication engineer, speaks of binits or bits which are self-contained units of meaning attached to particular signals, each of which is used with greater or lesser frequency according to the type of information transmitted. A similarity between the mechanical code system and the human code system can be seen, because a language consists of the totality of all the words theoretically available to all its speakers but in actual practice, any one speaker will use only a proportion of these words in his life-time and that too, according to his educational or cultural range.

A code, unless it is activated is useless. It can very easily be compared to an electric charge stored up in battery which can work only if a circuit is completed by the touch of a switch, and the current has a channel to flow. The same thing applies also to human code impulse. The technical means by which this code is structured and made audible or visible are highly complex and belong to the domain of physiologist.

(2) Channel

Channels of communication codes often create environmental disturbances which prove beyond the ability of communication to control. Speech sounds between people quite close to each other are transmitted in the most natural way through vibrations set up in the air spaces between them. But if the range of distance is more wider, the message will become less audible and there may also arise the possibility of distortion and interference. Visual images and codes of various kinds which are transmitted similarly through electrical and atmospheric channels are subject to distortion in the same way. But in written communication the channel is comparatively free from distortion, and the impact on the mind of the receiver is visual only and offers no obstacles to clear reception especially in the case when bad hand writing or faulty printing produces illegibility.

(3) Encoding

Encoding is an important element in communication activity. Mechanically, this is a simple process which involves a human operator writing instructions for a computer to operate in series of codes (or a programming language) which the computer can understand. In human terms, encoding is the means whereby a person puts and arranges his ideas in a socially recognisable form for conveying them to other people. Although, thinking or reflection may exist without a process of encoding but when an attempt is made to communicate, the thinking to other people, the code has to be used for this purpose.

(4) Encoder

Encoder is a human agent since the arrangement and delivery of code signs and signals must always be the acts of volition or initiative. A machine is not a free agent because it has to have its code fed into it, and programme originated by a person. A person is also not so free an agent, because the code he uses is enforced upon him by his social environment. Moreover, the mass of experience which he absorbs throughout his life constitutes part of his 'programming' and it is not under his relations with society and social movements, that freedom is circumscribed by external pressures and, constraints. Thus, the encoder himself contains as many factors of distortion as any other element in a communication activity.

(5) Decoding

Decoding is the most important element in a communication activity because on it depends the whole of the comprehension process. We know that the code is certainly psychologically very remote from the reality itself. With the use of codes representing the ordinary and everyday objects of experience, difficulty in understanding the concepts will not arise. But in the codes of more abstract concepts of experience, not having the same clear cut connotations behind them. The message will be received and interpreted differently by different people according to their knowledge and experience of life. If the idea conveyed to two parties is shared in all particulars. Communication between them will be complete and perfect. Hence, the importance of mutually agreed definitions of codes, particularly those codes referring to abstract conceptions where the scope for interpretative variations is wide, cannot be over-emphasised.

(6) Decoder

The sixth element in a communication process is the decoder. In fact, he is a passive element. He has to wait for the words to be uttered or written and to make what he can of them according to his knowledge, experience, assumption and attitudes. When two people communicate who are equally matched in intelligence, social background, and grasp and range of vocabulary, the advantage and disadvantage pass from one to the other without embarrassment.

The encoder; the initiator of communication activity chooses his subject and the channel of communication and makes the first impact upon the mind of the decoder. He has thus the primary responsibility for saying precisely what he intends to say. The decoder will give only a secondary reaction which is bound to be coloured by the quality of the first utterance.

It is true that the management must frequently become the decoder as well as the encoder, *i.e.*, it must listen carefully to the information received from the factory and office floor through all levels of junior management, and in this process, it should decode and interpret the information correctly as it ought to be at encoding its original information. All communication from below comes as a secondary reaction to the primary communication emerging from the management, and thus, the quality of the second activity will quite certainly depend upon the quality of the first.

Shannon and Weaver[36] while working in the context of communications engineering, computers and telegraphy, represent the communication process in the diagram given on the next page, Fig. 3.2 originally developed for physicists and mathematicians, in their book, entitled, the mathematical theory of communication.

AN ENGINEERING THEORY OF COMMUNICATION

The classical information theory studies the effect of noise on the probability that the received message and the transmitted message are identical. It explores the means for reducing interference between adjacent channels and other sources of internal noise while increasing the rate of transmission through a given system. Its purpose lies in constantly improving the design of the communication channels and input output facilities, and in deciphering received signals at the decoding stage to minimise the probability of error.

Telephone and Radio engineers have to tackle continuously difficult problems in communication. Their task is not only to clarify the meaning of message, but also to take the message as given whether a music programme, or a reservation request in airlines and deliver it to destination with high fidelity and accuracy. For performing this job, they need to design the transmitting equipments. Dr. Claude Shannon, as expert in telephonic switching, and his coauthor, Warren Weaver have put forward several questions, of which two, particularly concern us.

(1) How accurately can the symbols of communication be transmitted. This is an engineering problem ?

(2) How precisely do the transmitted symbols convey the desired meaning. This is a problem concerned with semantics ?

Dr. Shannon has propounded a very useful theory which deals with problem no 1. Weaver brings in problem no 2. Shannon's twenty two theorems include the use of Boolean algebra, the Stochasio process, the Markoff chain, theory of probability, etc., and finally they end in a special form of the concept of entropy. With the help of these theories, emerges a design for a system which can handle a maximum of messages with a minimum of 'noise.' This theory in now being applied to the practical operation of radio and television, computing machines and guided missiles and many other modern electronic devices.

What about problem No. 2, the meaning of the message? As a social scientist, Weaver tackles the second problem, following the well-known demonstration of the twenty-two theorems. For question No. 2 he says, another box might be inserted just after the receiver box in the diagram (Fig. 3.1) to be called the 'Semantic decoder.' This will serve to give the 'message' a second decoding in terms of its meaning to the receiver. Also 'noise' which is always mechanical on level I, should be expanded to cover 'semantic noise' or distortions of meanings not intended by the sender. It is an axiomatic truth that we shall never be able to communicate perfectly; 'noise' will always get in. But we can improve the present performance. The diagram, after allowing for level 2, would look like this Fig. 3.2.

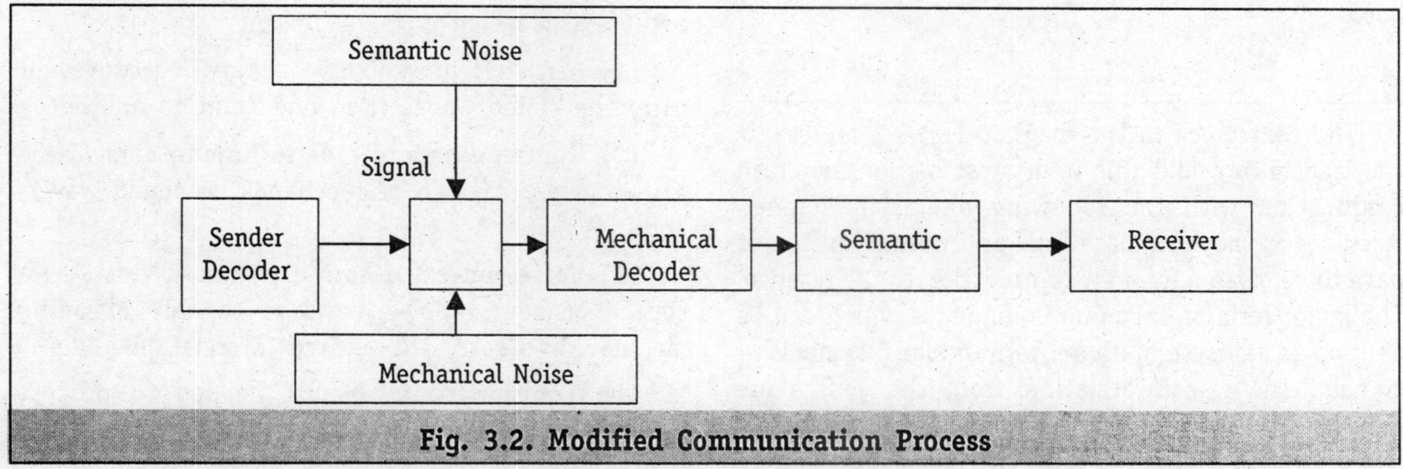

Fig. 3.2. Modified Communication Process

Some loss in communication is bound to take place, particularly, in human organisations — a phenomena described as 'Entropy', the second law of Thermodynamics. It reveals 'the degree of ignorance, chaos, and randomness in a system.' This suggests a prevailing tendency towards equilibrium which accounts for a certain amount of 'slippage' in performance, resulting from shortcomings in communications. It can be counter-acted by the organisation, because according to Wiener's theory, an organisation primarily depends on information. The question of Entropy on level No. 1 does not arise, and it probably operates on level No. 2 as well as in the transfer to meaning. Semantic entropy can take us into question of the total situation, the mental alertness and condition of the receiver, and so forth.

INFORMATION SOURCE

The information source originates or generates a message. It is the logical beginning of the communication process. The source consists of raw information and includes some form of intent and purpose on the part of the sender. Accounting, statistics, and computer data are the examples of raw information which must be given meaning and purpose in the information source. For this purpose, a selection is made of one particular message from any set of messages. Any ensemble of possible messages consists of several individual messages which may be distinguished from one another. When one indicates that a word or a group of words is a particular message, it is understood that the person acting as a source of information has made a choice of a particular set of words from his own vocabulary. However, information is conveyed by a message only to the extent that the destination a second person is unable to predict which particular message word will be selected. If in a conversation one is able to predict with certainty the next word or the next sentence or paragraph, no information is conveyed by that word or paragraph which had already been anticipated with certainty.

The essence of information is unpredictability. Once a choice has been made, resulting in a signal, the element of unpredictability is no longer there unless the performance of some of the portions of the system itself is unpredictable because of failure or introduction of noise indistinguishable from the signal.

In any conversation under adverse conditions, a word or several words may be heard indistinctly, incoherently or missed completely. If, from the context, the listener is able to replace the missing words without ambiguity, nothing is lost. The ability to replace missing portions of a message is facilitated by redundancy in the language because it enables one to replace the missing or doubtful portions without asking to have the entire message repeated. In some messages, there is no redundancy, as for example, "B" will follow "A" or when a bank clerk informs a depositor as to his current bank balance by writing a figure on his pass book.

THE TRANSMITTER

The next block in the diagram Fig. 3.1 represents the transmitter, and this item must be considered in conjunction with the following one, the channel. Messages as they originate from an information source have to be given a form for transmission to the receiver. The major form of encoding is language which can be defined as any systematic pattern of signs, symbols or signals. The raw information from the source are encoded into a meaningful language, e.g., accounting, statistics and computer data are translated into a message. This message is then transmitted by means of sound waves, electrical impulses, light waves or pieces of paper. Here it may be worthwhile to distinguish between a chosen word, a message and a spoken word, a signal.[37] The chosen word involves information, while the spoken word converts it into acoustic energy; it can be described as a pressure or sound wave carrying, a certain power and a specified set of sound frequencies. Its time duration can be measured and it can be picked up by a microphone. Two persons who wish to communicate must be in contact with each other through a channel which serves to convey signals. In a spoken conversation, the channel is the air, which serves to transmit sound waves. The sustained tone in speech carries information only when it is modulated by syllables, when its pitch, loudness and timber are varied, and when voiced sounds — vowels — are attended by appropriate unvoiced sounds — the consonants. The information, thus, is conveyed approximately at the syllabic rate, i.e., several syllables per second, rather than at the frequency of the sound used as a carrier, several hundred to several thousand cycles per second.

Successive transmissions of the same message are decreasingly accurate. A portion of the information transmitted is lost in the process of transmission. Additions to the original communication and distortions are quite often and a general feature as sharp specifics become more blurred with each handling. But this obstacle to effective communication operate more in oral communication. Recent research indicates that in oral communication something about 30% of the information is lost in each transmission.[38]

Acoustic waves can be used for communication because three elements are present:

(1) Air. It is present as a channel to convey or carry the sound waves from one point to another.

(2) Human ears and aids to human ears. These exit, and are capable of receiving the sound waves: and

(3) Voice-source of sound power. It exists as a source of sound power, and is capable of being modulated to carry the desired information.

The transmitter is a unit needed to process information from an information source for rendering it usable for transmission as a signal over a channel. The method of impressing the information on the carrier varies from system to system. For this, we have amplitude modulated radio transmitters, frequency modulated radio transmitters, pulse modulation etc.[39] In wire telephone, there is one-to-one correspondence, the pressure variations arising due to human voice and the changes in the magnitude of the electric current in the telephone wire. In this case, the conversion device is a microphone.[40] In other systems, and encoding process may be used, such as converting a written message into morse code, to render the message suitable for transmission over a telegraph channel, while at the receiver's end, the inverse decoding process is to be employed.[41] In this method, an arrangement exists between source and destination regarding the coding process. Further, there is also an agreement as to the language to be employed in transmission of the information or message.[42]

The ultimate purpose of any transmitter is to process a message generated by an information source to render it suitable for use in a communication channel. The input to the transmitter thus is a message, and its output is a signal, capable of being conveyed to the next unit in the communication link. During its passage through the transmitter, the signal may change in character, perhaps its frequency spectrum is altered, or its power level is increased. as it passes from one portion of the system to another. For example, one may consider the signal as it comes from a speaker through the various parts of a transmitter for eventual radiation.

After a word has been chosen and spoken, it constitutes a signal which travels from the vocal organs of the speaker to a microphone by a relatively short acoustic transmission channel. The microphone is an electro-acoustic transducer, i.e., it is a device which accepts as its output signal varying electric currents to carry the information. The choices of a communication channel as well as the various kinds of messages to be conveyed are the chief determination of requirements to be placed on the transmitter.

All the symbols in a communication process are transported through a channel. Air waves deliver words from one person to another, while gestures, and facial expressions are delivered by light waves. Sound and light are the channels used most often in human communication. Although a tender feeling can be conveyed by a delicate touch or a mood created by a whiff of seductive perfume. Touch and smell commonly function as secondary channels. By increasing the number of channel used to convey a message, one can substantially increase the likelihood of successful communication.

COMMUNICATION CHANNELS

Channel of communication is the mode that is used for conveying the message from the source to the receiver. In other words we can say that communication channels are the paths along which messages travel either from one person to another, or from one group to another, or both. A message could be verbal, written, face-to-face, telephonic, mass-media etc. The appropriateness of channel selection contributes to effectiveness of communication. Communication channels have been compared to the nervous systems of organisms because they perform the same function. Both carry messages, or impulses, from one place to another to keep the organism, or organisation informed about any changes taking place in the environment. The impulses carry signals from one portion of the complex system to another and to a central coordinating agency through which the entire system is kept in balance and functioning. However, to transfer message along organisation communication network is not so easy a task to be accomplished as the transfer to impulses through the nervous system. In organisation communication, comprehension does not form the only test of the effectiveness of a message. In an organisation, a message must pass the following tests:

(*i*) it must be comprehended;
(*ii*) it must be trusted;
(*iii*) it must be accepted; and
(*iv*) action must take place.

It has been observed that in large and complex organisations, mostly messages do not pass these tests. One reason for this state affair is that the formal communication channels used to convey messages are one-way channels only, and opportunities for feedback do not exist. Again, a large volume of communication is transmitted in black and white. Even where some facilities for feedback exist; they are not immediately applicable. Like face-to-face communication, in organisational communication also immediate feedback is a *sine-qua-non* for achieving understanding credibility and acceptance of the messages conveyed to others.

We have already given brief description of the uses of acoustic channels, visual channels are used in signalling with the help of searchlights, semaphores, and hand signals from automobiles etc. Generally, some type of code is employed in a visual communication system. The colour used for traffic or for lights used to inform the operator of the train, has significance only because in the signalling system, an agreement exists as to the meaning to be attached to the display of light of a given colour. Wide use is made of wire and radio communication channels in broadcasting, telephone, intercom, television (both closed circuit and open circuit), radio receivers, etc.

SIGNALS AND SIGN

An account of the process of communication would be incomplete without discussing the component parts of the mechanism of communication itself. The component parts, the outward and visible (or audible) elements, used in the practical manipulation of the means of expression by the projector, and conversely, in the identification and interpretation of that expression by the receptor. These visible and outward forms manifest themselves into signs and signals. Both these words, signs and signals, derive from the Latin,

"Signum" meaning a mark or a token, and more particularly, have a legionnaire standard. As both sign and signals are used to convey information of some kind, a message or a warning which can, if necessary, be translated into language if the sign or language is not in a linguistic form. Although there exists a relationship between them but there is clearly a difference in meaning which would prevent us using them as absolute synonyms. A sign is always static while a signal is dynamic. When we speak of a sign, we mean a mark or an object of some kind which has no element of movement in it. It bears its message in its design or colour and that message remains the same in all circumstance until regulation, custom, or time changes it. As opposed to this, the signal has element of movement in it. We can say that a sign is like a still photography remaining the same and carrying only a single unchanging meaning and is always visual; whereas a signal is like a moving film conveying a number of meanings from a single source and can be both audial and visual. The traffic signal, with its changing lights of green, amber and red, will be called a signal because its elements of communication are always on the move. The very essence of the signals of spoken language is movement, i.e., the movement of the nerve centres, movement of the organs of speech and movement of air through disturbance by the impact of the voice. In written or printed language, the code is expressed by visual marks, and these are, of course, the letters of the alphabet and the various punctuation marks. Once these have been written in a certain order, the marks are fixed and unchanging, rather like a series of still photographs, and therefore, these marks are not signals but signs. Language, therefore, is series of sign or signal arranged in patterns of a simple or complex nature, according to the simple or complex nature of the information to be conveyed. When a person speaks he emits audible signals; when he writes he sets down signs which are conventional visual equivalents — or rather, approximations — to those signals. The various stages in which these signs and signals are used and the cumulative process by which they build up as a language system.

In any type of communication system, a choice is made in the information source of a particular message from the set of possible messages. This set of selected messages is processed by the transmitter to convert it into a signal. The signal itself may assume a variety of forms, depending upon the system of communication. It may be a sequence of sound waves radiated from the vocal organs of a human being, or a set of electric impulses propagated along a transmission line, as used in telephone or telegraph, or a sequence of modulated electromagnetic waves radiated from the antenna of broadcasting station used for voice or television transmission.

The most omnipresent sign without words, nowadays is the red, amber and green traffic light, whose one way message is to "stop", "get ready" and "go." Highways are also using symbols rather than words: for "cross roads" — for "by road on the right," "Z for zig-zag turning" etc.

Before the machine age, non-verbal signals include fire beacons, smoke columns, mirror flashes, drums, tree blazes, horns, whistles, uniforms, insignia, etc. But science has now added such useful items as whistling buoys, block signals for railroads, emergency alarms, fire alarms, Geiger counters and ethyl mercaptan — which, if transmitted into the ventilating system of a mine, can warn miner of any possible danger by its penetrating smell.

The question now arises: Is sign language verbal or non-verbal? The answer is that it can be both, i.e., verbal and non-verbal. Deaf and dumb people spell outward signs for expressing their thoughts, and feelings, but when two normal persons, with no knowledge of each other's language meet, they express their acts, feelings and ideas by means of gestures. For example, if one of them is thirsty, he pretends to drink by making outward signs for drinking, i.e., making a glass or cup by a curved palm, and then taking it to his mouth he thus makes the other person understand the meaning of this gesture. Frowning indicates anger, fidgety hands anxiety; averted eyes, a dislike of other person.

KINESICS OR NON-VERBAL COMMUNICATION

It is true that there is a language of the body, the scientific study of which is known as Kinesics. These Kinesics are also known as "Body language."

Non-verbal communication plays a vital role in getting through to other people. It can be as effective or ineffective as words themselves. It can also occur on a level at which no words can possibly convey meaning. What words, e.g., can adequately describe the experience of holding a new-born child in one's hands or the love of mother for a child? There are a number of bodily channels through which unspoken communication is carried out. Touch (tactile communication), proximity, the loudness as well as softness of the voice, gestures, facial expression, and the chemistry of human emotions and channels used in non-verbal communication. Non-verbal communication studies head shaking for no or bad news, laughing, nodding, raised eyebrows, squints, deadpan expression, wins, whistles, sneers, eye-contact, glares, kisses, pouts, arm-waving, pointing, hand-shaking, shoulder shrugs, beckoning, drumming with fingers, shuffling feet, crossing legs, teetering of toes, clapping, weeping, and so on. There are about 300 symbols which represents bodily movements alone.

An awareness of Kinesics is of supreme importance, not only in business and marketing, but in every aspect or our inter-personal relationship. Those persons who are able to interpret and use Kinesics signals successfully have an edge over others in dealing and achieving success on their own, the list of masters of Kinesics would certainly include politicians who have been able to inspire considerable influence and loyalty in people.

The face acts as an extremely significant organ of communication for revealing, concealing and dissembling stages of emotions, desires, feelings, and intentions. The face we present to the outer world is rarely our face. A smile on the face is a sign not only of humour, or pleasure, but also of an apology, defence of even an excuse.[49] We can conceal our social feelings with some effort by maintaining a "poker face." Similarly, we can communicate feelings which we do not virtually possess by "acting." Thus, each facial contortion is unique in meaning and significance.

It goes without saying that gestures and facial expressions convey meaning, and therefore, a distinct form of communication. Ignoring them often leads to undesirable consequences. It would definitely add to the defectiveness of an organisation, if businessmen should become thoroughly conversant with the 'modus operandi' of Kinesics type of communication theory. With a proper understanding of Kinesics signals, they can avoid many personal anxieties, pitfalls etc., and understand, analyse and rejuvenate many human relations, mix-ups, when mistaken meaning is the crux of the problem. A very effective formal, sales message can be neglected by the body language of the person who delivers it; while a master — perhaps an unconscious master — of positive body language can spellbound an audience while delivering only a mediocre message.[50] An awareness of how our actions as well as our words, communicate things about ourselves also helps us to a considerable extent in our dealings with other people.

Postures also provide a number of communication signals. They send signals to another person during the course of conversation. When a person starts to speak, he looks on at first. When he finishes speaking, he looks back at the listener. The lowering of the head may indicate the end of a statement while of the head punctuates the end of question.[51]

It should be borne in mind that cultures differ from each other in the use of non-verbal communication signals. There is no universal code of body language. Differences are found in the kinds of signals used and in the meanings given to body movement, eye-contact and even distance apart between people. Comparisons can be made between cultures in the non-verbal expression of emotions and in greeting behaviour.

THE RECEIVER

The last block in the diagram (Fig. 3.1) of Shannon and Weaver is that of the receiver. Under this step of the model, the communication has passed from the sender's side of the process to the receiver's side. Decoding of the message now taken place. An interpretation may be and understanding must be gained of the accounting, statistical, or computer information. Besides knowledge requirements, perceptions and listening enter the reception phase of the process model. Receivers in communication systems are as varied as the systems themselves, are. A radar receiver and its display system furnishes an example of a communicated receiver, while a crystal set and a head-phone is an example of a relatively simple receiver. The key processes in the receiver are demodulation and sometimes decoding as in the case of telegraphy, and are inverse to these used in the transmitter. However, in a telephone transmitter or intercom set, for example, there is a conversion from acoustic to electric power, while in the receiver there is conversion from electric into acoustic power.[52]

NOISE

Noise — our communication villain — is any interference that takes place between transmission and reception of a message, and includes anything moving in the channel other than the signal desired by the sender.[53] It is perhaps, most easily understood as anything that causes distraction from the communication process. It can be static, electrical, semantic problem with the language or deliberate distortion of the message. Any communication problem that cannot be fully explained can be categorised as noise. Noise is a "black box" concept. It pervades like an umbrella over the entire communication system, reducing the accuracy of communication, and is responsible for miscommunication. It also covers errors in shorthand and typing, misprint by a teleprinter or misprint in a book. The office grapevine may also be called as a noise.

BASIC CATEGORIES

Noise can be separated into two basic categories, internal and external. Internal noise refers to the uniqueness of human beings that causes them to bring different perceptions to a message. These internal noises have become an entire field of study called, 'semantics' — the study of meaning, of language, and its effects on man. In addition, internal noise is also caused by an abnormal psychological or physiological state. For example, while reading, your stomach signalled strongly that food was needed, naturally, you would be experiencing at the moment that your hunger distracted your attention from the reading, i.e., internal physiological noise.

External noise refers to those environmental qualities that interfere with communication effectiveness, for example, temperature, light, room size, acoustics, etc.

In all communication systems, noise is associated with the chosen signals. During the process of transmission, a signal may degenerate because of distortion inherent in the system, because noise is introduced during the operation of the process or during transmission so as to mask the signal or message. In general, the effect of noise is to produce distortion, ambiguity, and uncertainty in the communication system limiting its performance, and obscure or mask a signal which usually is a relatively weak one.[54] Only one noise source has been shown in Fig. 3.1 but noise may be introduced at any point between the source of information and the receiver, which is its destination.

Thus in radio reception, under adverse circumstances. The mixture of static or atmosphere and of music actually heard from a receiver may or may not meet the standards or excellence set by a discriminating musical taste. In telephony, electrical interference from power lines, cross talks and ringing signal from other telephone circuits, or noise from repeaters used in long distance calls, may give rise to unsatisfactory communication. Communication does not take place in a vacuum; the receiver is constantly being bombarded with more than one signal at a time. For instance, during a business, noise will be produced by the secretary typing in the next room, the sound on the street, and the shuffling of papers by those present at the meeting. Consequently it acts as a stumbling block to the smooth flow of communication in an organisation, necessitating a message to be repeated until ambiguity is totally removed.[55]

Two people may talk with one another, using an ordinary speaking voice, and then increase the distance between them until ambient noise interferes with transmission. One solution, of limited utility, is increase the power in the voice by shouting to improve signal-to-noise ratio, but a better one is to make changes in the design of communication system, perhaps by using a different type of communication channel. Many communication systems are operated with a high signal-to-noise ratio so that the operator may not be aware of noise as the factor which limits performance in a given system. Effectiveness of a communication system be enhanced by reducing noise when it is amenable to such reduction just as communication, efficiency may be enhanced by increasing signal power. However, when satisfactory performance under limiting conditions is required — extreme range or reliability in the transmission itself with equipment that is cheap, light, rugged, and simple, and finally that requires low power from inexpensive sources for its operation, close attention must be paid to those attributes in design which considerably help in maximising the signal-to-noise ratio.

VARIETIES OF NOISE

It is worth-while distinguishing between three varieties of noise at this stage:

(*i*) Non-Mechanical noise
(*ii*) Mechanical noise
(*iii*) Non-Verbal noise

The first kind, i.e., non-mechanical noise may eliminate completely if one is willing to make the required effort or pay the price for it. For example, in television reception, interference from the ignition system of automobiles may be reduced to any desired level, if one is at liberty to locate his antenna and set at a considerable distance from automobiles. In television, the electric impulses from the ignition system of an automobile may interfere with the synchronising pulses from the transmitter, which serve to hold a picture stationary, creating annoyance, and that is amenable to improvement.

However, there is no remedy for the second variety of noise, i.e., mechanical noise. For example, any electrical noise is generated in the resistor used in the input circuit of a high gain amplifier. Similarly in vacuum tubes, transistors and photocells, an inherent noise level is found which makes itself felt when low-level signal are amplified and picked up.

Non-verbal 'noise' can also occur because of contradictory messages sent by the sender. For example, if a politician while addressing an audience says that he has plenty of time to speak, but very often sees his watch, he is thus sending two distinct and conflicting messages. Significantly enough, the non-verbal message (seeing the watch, very often implying thereby that his time is precious) will have a much more powerful impact than his verbal statement. Similarly, while advising our employees to remain punctual in their daily attendance and work, if we do not keep time in our appointments with others, this will mean two distinctive and contradictory messages, creating confusion and acting as non-verbal noise to the employees.

CHARACTERISTICS OF NOISE

One may occasionally obtain information on noise by observing the time function associated with it. The wave forms in ignition systems may be viewed on an oscilloscope and photographed, as is the case with wave forms associated with lighting discharges. Similarly, noise arising in a resistor as modified by an amplifier may be displayed on an oscilloscope screen. One may also obtain information on noise wave forms by observing the frequency range over which appreciable noise energy is observed.[56] We shall deal only with electrical noise sources for illustration purpose, but with no intention of minimising the importance of noise in acoustical or other problems. For example, one may find that speaking tubes are practical on tug boats but not on aeroplanes.

If noise consisted of a sequence of unit impulses, interference would be observed over an infinite frequency range. Electrical interferences in any particular instance arising from a given source of impulsive disturbance are observed from a low frequency. For example, 100 kc, up to perhaps 30 mega cycles with abroad maximum at 2 mega cycles, may be taken to indicate that a large fraction of noise impulses has duration in the neighbourhood of 1/2 m Sec., but some of it is as short as 1/30 m Sec.[57]

The term 'noise' mentioned by Shannon and Weaver means distortion which affect the messages while en route from transmitter to the receiver. One of the basic characteristics of noise is that portion of the message which people do not want to hear. The following instance from the life of the great Greek philosopher Socrates illustrates this point:

"The wife of Socrates, Xanthippe, was a woman of a most fantastical and furious spirits."

At one time when she had vented all the reproaches upon Socrates her fury could suggest, he went out and sat before the door.

His calm and unconcerned behaviour irritated her so much the more; and, in the excess of her rage, she ran upstairs and emptied a vessel upon his head, at which he only laughed and said that "so much thunder must need to produce a shower."

Alcibiades, his friend, talking with him about his wife, told him that he wondered how he could bear such an everlasting scold in the same house with her.

He replied, "I have so accustomed myself to expect it, that it now offends me no more than the noise of carriages in the street."

A COMMUNICATION MODEL

We may now with the help of a model see as to how communication process takes place. The flow of a stimulus reaches the brain in a continuous stream. The density, speed etc. of the stimuli varies and this flow reaches the brain. The stimuli passes through the perception screen, and are given meaning. Each perception screen is unique in itself because attitudes, opinions, beliefs, personality, emotions, knowledge, thought, experiences, values etc. of individuals are not identical. Now since we see that each perception screen is unique, and since meaning is assigned to the stimuli as it filters through this screen, it becomes obvious that the meaning assigned to a given stimulus will also be unique in the case of each individual to a large extent. The reaction to this stimuli may be predominantly or entirely physical or verbal. Generally, in most of the cases, an individual's reaction to a given stimulus is to communicate conversationally. Hence, in order to perform this conversation process, he selects some type of symbols. These selected symbols can be in words, facial expressions, gestures or a combination of all the three activities.

The competence of any communicator at this stage largely depends upon the size and knowledge of his vocabulary and the ability to choose the correct words which must accurately express his meaning. The greater number of word symbols one knows, the more precise one would be able to express his meaning.

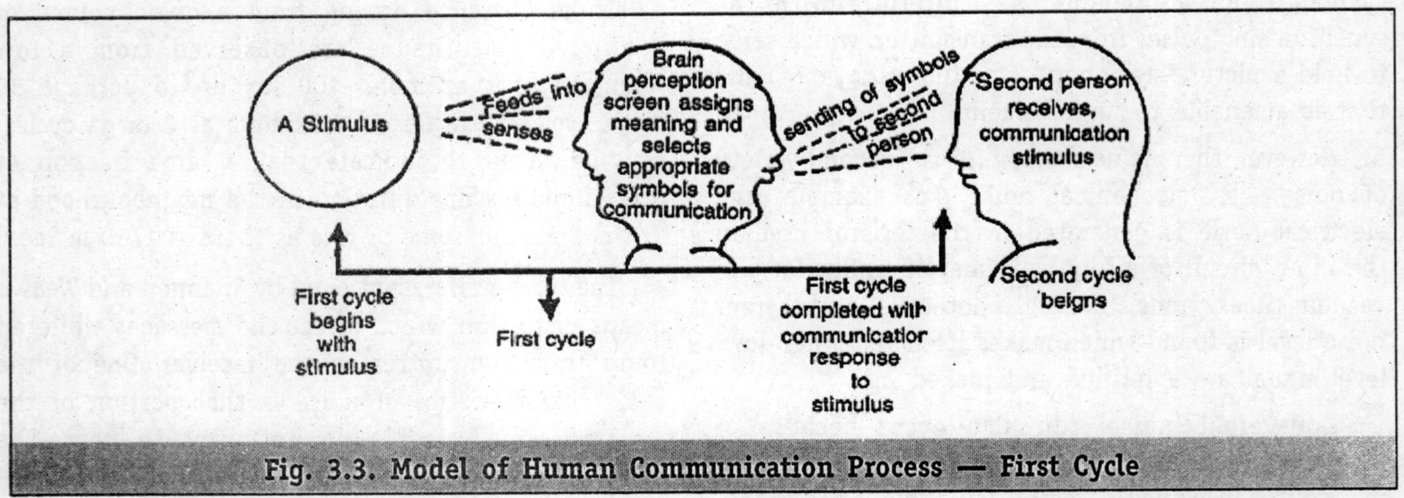

Fig. 3.3. Model of Human Communication Process — First Cycle

A person can well understand the difficult limitations and shortcomings of a small vocabulary on the part of a child struggling to express himself. Moreover, words have multiple meanings, many are vague and general. Of course, a person has ample liberty to select words while writing from a large vocabulary, but in verbal face-to-face conversation, he tends to require an almost instantaneous response.[58]

Now at this stage symbols are selected and the individual sends his response to another individual (See Fig. 3.3). This completes the first cycle of the communication process. The same process is repeated when the second person responds to the stimulus of the communicated message of the first individual. It must always be borne in mind that the second person also has his own personal perception screen, and hence there is always a chance for him to misinterpret the meaning of the first individual, in which case, instead of communication miscommunication results.[59]

THE MEANING OF MEANINGS

Since communication is defined as the interchange of meaning between and among individuals, "meanings", plays a vital and significant role in the philosophy and psychology of communication. Brown defines meaning as "the total disposition to make use of or react to a linguistic form."[60] There exist innumerable components in the meaning evoked by a word or a sentence. As Brown further adds: "A man might give all his productive years to spelling out the meaning of a single utterance and find the task unfinished in the end."[61]

DETERMINANTS OF MEANING

We frequently feel difficulties in transferring information and understanding to each other. These difficulties arise due to certain determinants of meanings which include the following categories:

(1) Words
(2) Semantics
(3) Emotions
(4) Frame of reference
(5) Situational context.

These are briefly described below:

(1) Words

(a) Cultural context

"Words"[62] are symbols and do not have meaning in and of themselves. They refer to ideas or objects outside themselves and derive their meaning from their continual use in a given culture. Thus, the meaning of a word is formulated by the society and culture in which it is used. Over the years the vocabulary grows, and the meanings of some words change. The fact becomes evident if one looks in a dictionary for 1930 and one for 1997. It would then become obvious that not only has the number of words increased, but the number of definitions for each word has also grown. With a view to communicating with another person successfully, we must be aware of the words and the different meanings associated with those words.

The meaning of words exists within ourselves

People when in doubt often pose the question, "What do you mean by that?" Most people confronted with that question assemble their thoughts into new combinations of words and phrases, and try to get the meaning across in different words. Empirical evidence reveals that the meaning does not change, but the words do change. Meaning exists within ourselves, and not in the words we use to express that meaning.

Learning and meaning are highly inter-related

One can grasp certain more subtle meaning for words only after learning the ideas and concepts for those subtle meanings. Further, meaning differs among separate culture or sub-cultures. For instance, the word "sing" normally refers to the act of producing musical tones by means of the voice. A bird is said to sing when it emits sound. In certain sub-cultures, however, the word "sing" refers to the act of confessing to the authorities, particularly, the police. Criminals have been said to "sing" to the police about gang operations. Again, the word 'tree' has no meaning in itself. English-speaking people use the word to denote to a wooded plant. It is, thus, obvious that different cultures and societies have given different interpretations as well as meanings to the same words.

Basic categories

Writers have categorised two types of words i.e., (*i*) denotative, and (*ii*) connotative. The denotative meaning of a word is that to which the word points. It is the explicit identification of the referent as well as the social consensus or accepted definition. For example, the commonly accepted definition of the word 'rich' is of someone or something well-supplied with lend, goods, or money — the denotative meaning is wealth. The language of mathematics and of science is considered to be exclusively a denotative and objective language — 'a thing language.' Objective meaning in mathematics and science can be communicated because in those "language systems" one term is never allowed to have more than one meaning. There can be no ambiguity in a term, e.g., 'plus' can never mean 'minus', and it can also never imply 'equal to.' The rules of mathematical language leave, absolutely no room for disagreement. On the other hand, the word 'happy' can signify 50 different interpretations to 50 different people. Moreover, it can also denote twenty different things to the same person in twenty different sets of circumstances. It is self-evident that what makes on person happy can cause another to become sad, but 'ten and ten equals twenty' always denotes the same thing to everyone of us. So far as dictionary meanings are concerned, they are as close to being objective as it is possible for non-mathematical meanings to be.

The connotative meaning of a word is the emotional or evaluative meaning which is different for each individual. It refers to a wider penumbra of ideas and feelings and action tendencies which cluster about a word to the implicit and the attitudinal components of the meanings. For example, the word 'rich' has different connotative significance for each person as discussed earlier. A person receiving more money than an individual who gets his income from charity might be considered rich. A middle income person who is not worried about paying his bills may be considered rich. A millionaire having no children or close friends may consider a person with many children or close friends a rich person. Thus, each of us has a different connotative meaning for most words which include: attractive, expensive, bad, frugal, frank, liberal, socialist, conservative and radical etc. Thus, a word's connotative or subjective meaning is the personal that word has for an individual. For many persons, the term 'singing' means stimulating, exciting, rhythms, singable melodies and amusing or provocative lyrics. On the other hand, the same term may denote to other persons disagreeable sounds to the human ear, with no perceptible melodies and inaudible lyrics. Empirical evidence reveals that almost every word we use has different emotional and intellectual meanings for each of us. Even the most ordinary, everyday term will have a multitudinous variety of meanings attached to it because the meaning attached to any object or experience is always personally experienced. Julius Laffal in his investigations on subjective and connotative aspects of communications has found that:

"Relationships between words and things exist only by virtue of and within the minds of the people who use the words."[63]

Again two words may have exactly the same denotative meanings, but altogether divergent connotative significance. For example, the words, call-girl and whore, both point to the same object but the emotional overtones evoked by the two words are explicitly different.

Meaning and its measurement have attracted the attention of researchers for a long time chiefly because of the supreme importance of the subject in human affairs and the consequent frustrations encountered in its measurement. The difficulties arising out of communication problems can to a large extent be overcome when difference in meaning are considerably lessened.

Meanings are in us, not in messages

Messages can be conveyed to other persons, but the meanings reside in the message-users. Empirical evidence suggests that when we convey a message, we hope that the other person's 'meaning' will overlap or be similar to our own, and that we will be understood. It has been found that the more our messages relate to and overlap the other person's mental and emotional experiences, the more effectively we communicate with each other.

Experiences are always changing, so are meanings. Consequently, the meaning can never be fixed. Hence effective communication demands a high tolerance for ambiguity, especially since the most abstract the term, the more meanings it has. For example, some words as 'justice', 'freedom', and 'faith' have different meanings for different people. Researchers in communication are having positive belief that effective communicators are person-oriented, not word-oriented. Although one word may have many meanings, people always give their own meanings to all words.

(2) Semantics

"Semantics is the systematic study of the meaning of words."[64] It is directly related to the study of perception. People may interpret the same stimulus in different ways, depending on their background and past experience. We are not familiar with the different cultures of the world as to how they interpret words. It so happens that on many occasions when we are talking with another person, we develop a problem in semantics in the sense that the receiver does not decode the message in the same way as we have encoded it. This problem is not confined to communication between distinct cultures, but takes place within an organisation. One's family background, religious teachings, cultural level, knowledge, etc., influence to a considerable extent one's interpretation of the words being used. The same stimulus evokes different attitudes due to the way each person perceives the stimulus. Words are, in fact, 'events' — environmental stimuli perceived by an individual. All events pass through the overall process of perception. Obviously the problem is that decoding is not identical among all recipients of the stimuli.

(3) Emotions

The emotions of the sender greatly affect the meaning of a message. The same is the case with the receivers also. A person will interpret an identical message in different ways depending on his emotions at the time of its receipt. Emotions form a part of the thinking process, and, therefore, their influence on meaning cannot be overemphasised. In a recent study conducted by the Opinion Research Corporation,[65] it was revealed that the employees reacted differently to words or phrases that essentially meant the same thing. Since many times people think with their emotions also, it becomes rather a hard and tough job to do away with the disfunctional consequences of emotions on meaning and content of the message.

(4) Frame of Reference

The Term 'frame of reference' refers to one's prior knowledge, attitude, perception, family background, early experience etc. We cannot ignore the consequences of events in our lives since they remain in our minds, and considerably affect the interpretation of future course of events. Consequently, one's frame of reference plays a vital role in affecting the meaning and content of the message. For example, an American who has suffered the bad effect of depression will have a different frame of reference than the one who has seen the affluent period of 1950s and 1960s. Both will interpret the same phenomena but with their different frames of reference.

(5) Situational Context

The term 'situational context' is a concept that refers to the preceding and following contents of the message in question. Many times, politicians complain that their statements have been interpreted out of context. If someone has picked up one or two sentences out of a longer message without knowing what preceded or followed that message, he will encounter difficulty in arriving at the correct meaning since he has not understood the full situational context of the message. For example, if we say, "we greatly need more cases like that." Without understanding the full situational context in which this statement has been made, it is well nigh impossible to ascertain the exact meaning and significance of this statement. However, if we precede this statement with a report about court cases, then the statement would imply the need for more clients. On the other hand, if we had been discussing about a management course of an Institute, then one might think about the case-study approach to class-room presentation.[66] Again, the word "call" may mean many different things, depending upon the situational context in which it is used. One can call someone else in a loud voice; one can use the telephone to call a friend; a poker player may call the bluff of a fellow-player; a creditor may call for payment of a loan, or one may use an expletive to describe a person — call him a name. Specificity or situational context is required to ensure that the meaning intended is being communicated. Moreover, the environment in which the message has been sent also constitutes a part of the situational context since the message does form a part of the stream of events being perceived at that moment. Each observed stimulus may greatly influence the meaning and significance attached to the other stimuli. Hence, the importance of the environment as a part of the situational context in influencing the meaning and content of the message in question cannot be over-emphasised.

THE MEANING OF INFORMATION

In English language, the word 'information' is used for identifying different concepts. However, it is well-nigh impossible to define it precisely. Differentiation between terms like fact, data, knowledge, information, understanding, etc., are not easily amenable to definitive interpretation. For overcoming such difficulties, a great deal of pure research of a fairly abstract and philosophical nature needs to be developed. Despite this barrier, an understanding of how different individuals have tried to define and quantify information is useful. Recent research indicates that there are very many views as well as interpretations on the nature of information itself.

The following is probably a useful way in which information may be defined, "Information is a statement that describes an event or an object or a concept in a way that help us distinguish it from others." A garbled sequence of unintelligible signals is, therefore, not information since it cannot enhance our ability to distinguish between events, objects or concepts.

Information flow in a communication network is the lifeline of business enterprises; it is like blood flowing through the veins and arteries of the body. It was Drucker[67] who said, "the manager has a specific tool; Information. He does not 'handle' people; he motivates, guides, organises people to do their own work. His tool — his only tool — to do all this, is the spoken or written word or the language or numbers." And because this tool is so essential to the working of an enterprise, large resources of personnel and finance are devoted to the development and upkeep of communication systems.

Many systems analysts differentiate between information and data. 'Information' consists of data which have been measured or appraised as good or bad, and emphasises how much meaning is conveyed, relative to standard believed to be compatible with the objectives and goals of business enterprise. 'Data' are regarded as the raw materials from which information is produced and in this sense the definition of information is again different from the one employed in information theory.

MEANING AND INFORMATION

Every kind of communication is directed towards the achievement of one basic and fundamental objective, *viz.*, the give and or receive some information in one form or another. Actually speaking, information cannot be called 'Information' unless it is given expression in some way, either in language — spoken or written — or in some other system of signs, signals or symbols. There must also be some agency capable of receiving and interpreting that expression briefly and unambiguously, so that it might become an impression. Information is something that passes between two parties at least. The embryo of information generally lies latent in the mind of the potential communicator. Here the information remains only as an idea, or sometime, as a sequel to ideas. The difference between an Idea and Information, is that whereas an 'Idea' is purely a mental activity; 'Information is the mental activity only when it emerges into the light of the day by means of a physical activity, i.e., it is translated into a physical activity, becoming intelligible to another party. Undoubtedly, an 'Idea' can be translated into its appropriate symbols with a view to passing on information. Moreover, an idea, in its most elementary form, is a mental image of some aspect of our experience of life. This image may be tactile, audial, visual, gustatory, or olfactory. Hence we can also conclude that an idea is a psychical reflection of a physical sensation.[68] The human mechanism is subtle complex of sense organs. It enables an individual to receive information and gain experience through sight, sound, taste, and smell, operating either individually or in combination. Consequently, the information is received by the individual in a very specialised and particular way according to the senses being used. There are two kinds of such images, i.e., (*i*) the images of things and (*ii*) the images of events. Thus we can very easily distinguish the idea of, say, a motor car as a static object lying on the road, and that of movement of the motor car as it moves into position and starts off; an event as distinct from an object. In general, the term 'referent' has been coined by Ogden and Richards[69] to cover both types of things and events which are subject to human thought and the begetters of mental images. Consequently, the 'referent' is the object or event itself as a part of external reality, whereas the idea or thought ('reference' according to Ogden and Richards[70]) is the mental image of that created reality, by the activating mechanism of one or more of the five sense.

It goes without saying that although there is a close connection between the referent (object or event) and the reference (idea, image, or thought), the reference could not occur without the referent. There is also a close connection between the symbol (code, sign, or signal) and the reference, since the reference, with a view to conveying precise information, must embody itself in the symbol. Of course, there is no such connection between the symbol and the referent.

We have discussed at length the word 'idea' in its original Greek sense, *i.e.*, the image or appearance of referent in connection to its reality. A real and tangible object is supposed to be the most elemental type of idea experienced by all living beings including animals as well as human beings. One of the most basic and fundamental things were the material objects and events for which the ancients had to find language codes to express them properly. Consequently, the most primitive parts of any language are what the grammarians called the concrete nouns and verbs representing physical objects and events in the world. As civilisation advanced, and more realism became apparent, he interpreted these developments in abstract terms, since it was very convenient for him to do so in making useful generalisations. A major communication problem arises when we make use of the terms referring to highly abstract reference believing that we know precisely what we mean in the sense of being able to define the terms exactly. We also arrive at a conclusion that our listener always understands us, and he agrees with the definitions and arguments advanced by us, while the obvious fact is that he might or might not agree with us.

All codes, whether of language or of any other type of sign, or signal, exhibit the symbols of some kind of realism either in a concrete or abstract form. Obviously, the symbols refer to the tangible and concrete objects. Words dealing with complex abstract ideas represent the most potent cause of ambiguity, uncertainty and confusion. These should be dispensed with at all costs, besides calling for the clear cut definition by critically evaluating and examining the reality with reference to the referents behind them. Certainly, it is a herculean task for a manager to perform.

It is, therefore, obvious that an idea should be translated into its appropriate symbol for conveying its significance in its proper perspective. If the communicator's grasp of the system of codes is perfect, there arises no difficulty in conveying the proper sense, and consequently, it crystallises into meaningful action. Everything depends ultimately on the problem of definition, and clear thinking is a *sine-qua-non* before any communication can be made effective.

REFERENCES

1. M. Brodbeck, "General Introduction", in M. Brodbeck (ed.), Readings in "The Philosophy of the Social Services", Macmillan, 1968, p. 5.
2. E.G. Bormann, 'Theory and Research in the Communicative Arts', Holt, Rinehart & Winston, (1965), p. 34.
3. A. Kaplan, 'The Conduct of Enquiry', Chandler,1964, p. 50.
4. A. Kaplan, *op. cit.*, p. 25.
5. M. Brodbeck, *op. cit.*, pp. 3-4.
6. A. Kaplan, *op. cit.*, p. 35.
7. F.E.X. Dance, 'The "Concept" of Communication', in *Journal of Communication*, Vol. 20 (1970), pp. 201-10.
8. Berelson, B., and Steiner, G.A., "Human Behaviour", Harcourt, Brace & World (1964), p. 254.
9. A. Gode, 'What is Communication?' *Journal of Communication*, Vol. 9 (1959), p. 5.
10. A.J. Ayer, 'What is Communication?' in *Studies in Communication*, Communication Research Centre, University College, London, Secker & Warburg (1955), p. 12.
11. M.P. Andersen, 'What is Communication', *Journal of Communication* (1959), Vol. 9, p. 5.
12. Hoben, J.B., 'English Communication at Colgate Reexamined', *Journal of Communication* (1954), Vol. 4, pp. 76-86.
13. T.M. Newcomb, 'An Approach to the Study of Communication Acts' in A.G. Smith (ed.), *Communication and Culture*, Holt, Rinehart & Winston, p. 66 (1966).
14. S.S. Stevens, 'A Definition of Communication', *Journal of the Acoustical Society of America* (1950), Vol. 22, pp. 689-90.
15. H. Frings, 'Animal Communication', in L. Thayer (ed.), *Communication: Concepts and Perspectives*, Spartan Books, p. 297 (1967).
16. F.A. Cartier,& K.A.Hardwood, 'On Definition of Communication', *Journal of Communication'* (1953), Vol. 3, pp. 71-5.
17. J. Ruesch, 'Technology and Social Communication', in L. Thayer (ed.), *Communication Theory and Research* (1957), Charles C. Thomas, p. 462.
18. D.C. Barnlund, 'Toward a Meaning-Centred Philosophy of Communication', *Journal of Communication* (1964), Vol. 12.
19. G.H. Miller, 'On Defining Communication: Another Stab', *Journal of Communication*, (1966), Vol. 16, pp. 88-98.
20. G.H. Mead, 'Mind, Self, and Society', in Broom, L., and Selznik, P. (eds.), *Sociology*, 3rd ed., (1963), Harper & Row, p. 107.
21. *American College Dictionary* (1964), Random House, p. 244.
22. S. Schacter, 'Deviation, Rejection, and Communication', *Journal of Abnormal and Social Psychology* (1951), Vol. 16, pp. 190-207.
23. B. Sondel, 'Toward a Feld Theory of Communication', *Journal of Communication* (1956), Vol. 6, pp. 147-53.
24. A. Kaplan, *op. cit.*, p. 48.
25. F.E.X. Dance, 'The 'Concept' Communication', in *Journal of Communication*, Vol. 20(1970), pp. 201-10.

26. Quoted in the book, 'Managing by Communication' by Willard V. Merrihue (1960), p. 15.
27. *American Journal of Communication,* Vol. 4, No.1, *Spring*, 1954.
28. Willard V. Merrihue, *op. cit.*, p. 16.
29. C. David Mortense, 'Communication: the Study of Human Interaction', McGraw-Hill, New York, 1972, p. 11.
30. Allex Bavelas and Dermot Barrett, 'An Experimental Approach to Organisational Communication', *Personnel*, Vol. 27, March 1951, p. 368.
31. Peter F. Drucker, *The Practice of Management*, N.J., Prentice Hall, 1970.
32. Chester Barnard, 'The Functions of the Executive', Harvard, Cambridge, Mass, 1939, p. 4.
33. Gerald M. Goldhaber, 'Organisational Communication', Brown, Dubuque, Iowa, 1974, p. 7.
34. Claude E. Shannon and Warren Weaver, 'The Mathematical Theory of Communication', 1949, pp. 98-99.
35. David K. Berlo, 'The Process of Communication', New York: Holt, Rinehart and Winston, Inc. (1960), p. 32.
36. Claude E. Shannon and Warren Weaver, *op. cit.*
37. Norbert Wiener, 'The Human Use of Human Beings', 1954, pp. 28-29.
38. Koontz & O'Donnell, 'Essentials of Management', Tata McGraw-Hill Publishing Ltd., New Delhi, p. 401.
39. J. Atkinson, *Telephony*: Vol. I, 1968.
40. *Ibid.*
41. J.W. Freebody, *Textbook on Telegraphy — 1970*, Sir Isaac Pitman & Sons, Ltd., London.
42. Royal Sysol, *Transmission Handbook* — pt. I, 1971.
43. Jack Halloran, *'Applied Human Relations* — An Organisational Approach', Prentice Hall of India Private Limited, New Delhi - 110001, 1978, p. 58.
44. *Ibid.*, p. 59.
45. Robert Dubin, 'The World of Work' (Englewood Cliffs, N.N., Prentice Hall, 1958), p. 336.
46. R.L. Birdwhistell, 'Introduction to Kinesics', 1974, Preface.
47. Julius Fast, 'Body Language', May 1972, Pocket Books, New York, M. Evans & Co., Inc., New York, p. 1.
48. Stuart Chase, 'Power of Words', 1955, pp. 23-24.
49. Julius Fast, *op. cit.*, pp. 53-54.
50. Benthall, 'Body as a Medium of Expression', 1972 (Pocket Book Ed.)
51. Julius Fast, *op. cit.*
52. Leifer and Schreiber, 'Advances in Electronics', Vol. 2 & 3, L. Marton, Ed., 1951.
53. Colin Cherry, 'On Human Communication' (New York: Science Edition, 1961), p. 42.
54. J. Atkinson, 'Telephony', Vol. II, 1968, Pitman Publishing, London, 1972, pp. 823-25.
55. J. Atkinson, *Ibid.*, p. 823.
56. J. Blitz, 'Elements of Acoustics', 1964, p. 84, and Charles A. Marshall, 'Communication', 1960, pp. 36-42.
57. Leifer and Schreiber, 'Advances in Electronics', Vol. 3, L. Martorn, 1951.
58. George A. Miller, 'The Psychology of Communication', Penguin Books Ltd., 1974, pp. 52-54. J.E. Hochberg, 'Perception', Prentice Hall Inc., N.J., 1969, 3rd Ed., pp. 100-112 and D.E. Broadbent, 'Perception and Communication', Pergaman, N.Y., 1966, pp. 14-20.
59. Julian E. Hochberg, 'Perception', 3rd Ed., N.J. Prentice Hall, Inc., 1964, pp. 10-13.
Wendell Johnson, 'The Fateful Process of Mr. A Talking to Mr. B', Harvard Business Review, January-February, 1953, Vol. 31. No.1, pp. 49-56.
William Scholz. 'Communication in the Business Organisation': N.J. Prentice Hall, Inc., Oct. 1963, pp. 31.
George A. Field, John, Douglas, and Lawrence X. Tarpey, 'Marketing Management: A Behavioural Systems Approach', Columbus, Ohio, Charles E. Merrill Publishing Co., 1966, first Ed., pp. 62-84 and D.E. Broadbent, 'Perception and Communication', N.Y. Pergaman, 1966.
60. A.C. Spence, 'Management Communication: Its Process and Practice', Macmillan and Co. Ltd., 1969, pp. 84-85.
61. Brown, *op. cit.*
62. David K. Steward, 'The Psychology of Communication' (New York: Funk and Wangnalls Company, 1968), pp. 3-4.
63. Julius Laffal: Pathological and Normal Language Atherton Press, Inc., New York:1965, p. 272.
64. Dalton E. McFarland, 'Management: Principles and Practices', 3rd ed., New York: The Macmillan Company, 1970, p. 572.
65. Verne Burnett, 'Management's Tower of Babel', Management it, p. 412-413.
68. A.C. Spence, *op. cit.*, pp, 84-85.
69. C.K. Ogden and J.R. Richards, 'The Meaning of Meanings', 2nd ed. pp. 7-9.
70. *Ibid.*, pp. 9-10.

CHAPTER 4

MARKETING COMMUNICATIONS IN THE MARKETING PROCESS

Branding has become more important than ever to companies competing in today's marketplace. At a time when battered investors, customers, and even employees are questioning whom they can trust, the ability of a familiar brand to deliver proven value has become extremely important. A belief in the power of brands has spread beyond the traditional consumer-goods marketers, and branding has become a very important part of the marketing strategy for companies in almost every industry. Purveyors of products ranging from Gillette razors to BMW automobiles to Starbucks coffee have been able to use their strong brands to keep growing without succumbing to the pricing pressure of an intense promotional environment. However, many of the traditional big-brand companies are striving to reinvent themselves and to restore value to their venerable brands. And as they do so, many are looking to their advertising agencies to help them determine the best way to build strong brands and connect with their customers.

Advertising agencies often conduct research studies for their clients, using techniques such as surveys, focus groups, and ethnographic studies to help them better understand their customers and determine the best way to communicate with them. However, in recent years a number of agencies have been conducting branding research and developing proprietary models to help better identify clients' customers and determine how they connect to their brands.

DDB Worldwide provides clients with branding insights through its Brand Capital Study, which amasses information on more than 500 brands ranging from Wal-Mart to Yahoo and from Budweiser to Michelin. The proprietary branding research is based on a global marketing study consisting of quantitative surveys conducted among 14,000 consumers in 14 countries. The surveys consist of a battery of questions focusing on consumer attitudes, interests, desired self-image, values, and product use as well as various subjects and issues including family, religion, politics, advertising, and brands. The agency uses the information from the Brand Capital Study to compare the desired self-images and lifestyles of consumers who love a brand with those who have a less strong connection. The study also measures brand magnetism, which is the brand's ability to strengthen its connection with consumers and is based on four factors: high quality, leadership in the category, growth in popularity, and uniqueness in the category. According to the agency's worldwide brand planning director, the success of a product or brand is tied to how it is perceived in popular culture: "In category after category, around the world, the evidence is clear. As a brand's breadth of connection with consumers increases, its depth of connection increases exponentially." DDB describes this phenomenon of each consumer's feelings about a brand being directly affected by other consumer's feelings as "brand contagion."

Young & Rubicam is another agency that has developed a proprietary tool for building and managing brands, a tool it refers to as the Brand Asset Valuator The agency has invested over $70 million and conducted over 120 studies in building a comprehensive global database of consumer perceptions of brands. This tool views brands as developing through a very specific progression of four consumer perceptions, including differentiation, relevance, esteem, and knowledge. Differentiation measures the strength of the brand's meaning, while relevance measures the personal appropriateness of the brand to consumers. These two measures together form brand strength, which is viewed as an important indicator of future performance and potential. Esteem is the extent to which consumers like a brand and hold it in high regard, while knowledge represents awareness of the brand and what it stands for and is the culmination of brand-building efforts. Esteem and knowledge form brand stature, which is a more traditional measure of the status of a brand and its current performance, which is a strong strategic indicator of the health of a brand. The Brand Asset Valuator uses measures of these four factors to identify core issues for the brand and to evaluate current brand performance and potential.

Advertising Agencies Find Ways to Build Stronger Brands

The Leo Burnett agency relies on its Brand Belief System to guide its global brand-building philosophy and practice. This system focuses on the development of the brand-believer bond, which is at the core of the relationship between a brand and its believers, and considers four fundamental questions. The first question involves the category and asks, Where does the brand truly belong? The second involves the content and asks, How will the brand inspire belief? The third question considers the culture and asks, What shapes belief in the brand? The final question involves the customer and asks, With whom and how will the brand belong? Leo Burnett uses a set of proprietary esearch tools to provide information that can be used as part of the Brand Belief System and provide the agency with a basis for brand analysis and planning.

Nearly all the major agencies are conducting branding research and/or developing models or systems that they can use to gain better insight into con-sumers and develop more effective campaigns for their clients. The importance of building and maintaining strong brands is likely to become even greater in the future. This will put even more pressure on agencies to develop new and better tools and techniques that can be used to guide their clients' advertising campaigns.

Sources: Kathryn Kranhold, "Agencies Beefing Up on Brand Research," The Wall Street Journal, Mar.9,2000,p.B) 4; Brand Asset Valuator White Paper, www.yr.com; "DDB Worldwide Explores What Makes Big Brands Big," www.ddb.com, March 2000.

The child, from the time he comes out of his mother's womb, shouts or screams whenever he wants something. This act of the child is in order to sell his idea of his own hunger, thirst or something else. As he grows older he is more sophisticated in his manner in which he communicates his needs and wants. His reactions are more complicated. The same idea of selling holds true in business. Selling is the foremost of all the activities, implying the selling of ideas, services and goods. As selling becomes more competitive and as the ideas generated become more sophisticated, year after year, decade after decade, marketing becomes more imperative.

The author of evergreen, world famous novel, Alice in Wonder Land, Lewis Carrol very aptly remarked "One of the hardest things in the world is to convey meaning accurately from one mind to another." This is true equally to both individuals and organisations small, medium or even large. If we focus our attention in light of the marketing communications, it would clarify why even some of the well reputed and established organisations miserably fail to promote a good product idea or service, after spending a huge amount which was at their command. Let us consider the example of Second World War. During the war period, the allied forces dropped a huge quantity, probably millions of leaflets in Japan, suggesting the Japanese to surrender. To utter surprise this had just the opposite effect. But later on, when the contents of the leaflets were drastically modified to the idea of cessation of fighting honourably, the dropping of the leaflet had a great positive effect. Let us consider another example when one of the leading manufacturer of cigarettes released unique campaign, in order to grab the market share, emphasising the idea of companionship and refreshing cool by adding the word 'Menthol Puf', it changed the product personality from cigarette not meant for men, rather than to cigarette especially meant for women. To illustrate our point, let us again consider the example of 'Maggie Noodles' in relation to 'Top Raman Noodles.' Both the products are distributed through well established channels and backed by tremendous promotional effort. 'Top Raman' has failed to persuade the prospective customers more precisely the younger generation and the children. Similarly, the promotional campaigns of 'Rasna' and 'Hajmola', effectively able to strive to persuade their prospective customers or not? The answer to the above queries would lie in the understanding of the marketing communications process.

ROLE OF MARKETING COMMUNICATIONS

Communication is a unique tool in the hand of marketers, which they can use very effectively and intelligently to persuade their present and prospective consumers to act in a desired way to make a purchase to a certain product or to patronise a certain store. Even the political parties and voluntary organisations with the tool of marketing communications are able to turn the table in favour of their candidate and compel the voter to cast their vote or make a donation to their organisation marketing.

Marketing communications can evoke emotions and are able to put consumers in a more receptive frame of mind. It encourages purchases to solve problems on one hand and avoid negative outcomes on the other hand. Marketing Communication plays a pivotal role in bridging the gap between marketers and consumers. It also bridges the gap between consumers and their socio-cultural environments.

Manufacturing a product and making it available in the market is only a part of the company job. It is equally important, or perhaps rather more important, to make it known to the consumers that the product is available in the market. Today's market is a competitive market where several firms are striving hard to win over consumers. Now, only it is not enough if the availability of a product is made known to the consumers. It is also equally important to let the consumers know the distinctive features of the product. The process does not end here. The company should also get the feedback as to how the consumer accepts its product and interprets its messages. This multifaced function is carried out only through an effective, continuous and two-way flow of information between the producer and their customers.

There are a number of ways — written messages, symbols, pictures, quality products, window displays, salesmen, attractive and colourful packages, centrally located show rooms etc. by which a company tries to communicate with their consumers. When these different stimuli are perceived and interpreted by consumers, marketing communications takes place.

Now companies practising modern management concepts realise the role which marketing communications play to corporate success. For example, Du Pont, the giant U.S.Chemical Company describes collecting information from the market and distributing information to the market is the essence of marketing. Du Pont's, marketing communications department suggests that marketing communications be treated as a strategic resource by being planned and integrated with other critical corporate decisions and not just as something that is done to accomplish current needs. In other words. Du Pont's decisions are guided under a philosophy that marketing communications when treated as a strategic force and not just as a tactical tool, represents a critical corporate resource for building and creating market share and profits.

If a company and the consumer are viewed as two separate systems, we would notice that both share certain common characteristics. First in the company system the company finds itself in some position where it wishes to improve or at least maintain its current position. The company may wish to enhance its reputation further among its close competitors and its customers to increase profit and its market share or be perceived as an innovator and market leader in its area of operation. The list is just an illustrative one. These desires of a company has some gaps to close of needs to fulfil. In a similar way, the consumer also perceives his present position and the personal goals he wishes to attain. He also has some gaps to close. These gaps are his needs. For example, a consumer may wish to perceive himself as masculine wealthy as well as spotty. The purchase of a new WWF mobike may help this person to move much closer to the way he would like to himself being projected see Fig. 4.1.

The Common element which permits both the systems — company and the customer to move closer to its goals is the total product offering — a bundle of satisfactions which a company offers to its prospective buyers or probable customers. There is a

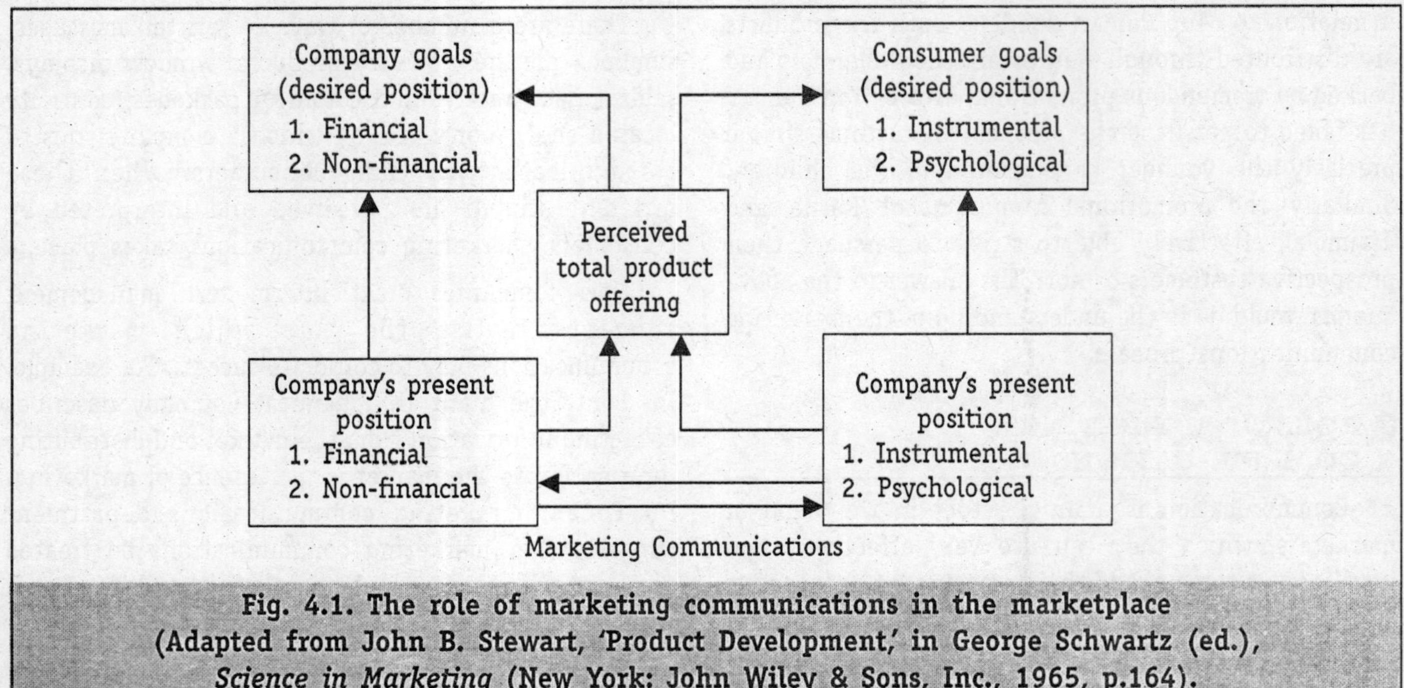

Fig. 4.1. The role of marketing communications in the marketplace (Adapted from John B. Stewart, 'Product Development,' in George Schwartz (ed.), *Science in Marketing* (New York: John Wiley & Sons, Inc., 1965, p.164).

natural tendency among buyers that they do not make a purchase of a product for the product's sake. They make a purchase for the meanings the product has for them and for what it will do for them instrumentally as well as psychologically.

Therefore, the basic role of marketing communications is to share the meaning of the company's total product offering with its consumers is such a fashion as to help the company to move closer to its goals and at the same time help the consumers to attain their goals.

WHY MARKETING COMMUNICATIONS

In recent years, the importance of marketing communications has increased many fold.[1] A major factor contributing to the increased importance of marketing communications is the basic fact that it is practised against a backdrop of ever changing social, economic and competitive developments. The following major developments and their implications are basically responsible for the importance of marketing communications.

Increased International Competition

The process of liberalisation and globalisation in India, which was knowingly or unknowingly, started by the then Prime Minister, Late Rajiv Gandhi has overtaken by the events of communication revolution. This has forced the companies to alter their marketing programmes as marketers and competitors have begun to span the globe. Even the advance counties like U.S.A. has not remained affected by this.[2] While formulating the advertising goals and allocating budgets the world market is kept in mind. Media are selected from around the world rather than confining to local markets. Advertising messages are created in such a fashion so that they can appeal to different cultures at the same time. Sales force which once were confined to domestic levels, are now spread across various world markets.

Government Policies

Widespread deregulation of many industries and change of government policies have led to numerous mergers and acquisitions. For example, opening of the airline sector to private companies has been able to break the monopoly of Indian Airlines in domestic sector, with competitors may be fewer, entering in this area. These developments have influenced the marketing practices through changes such as increased advertising expenditures and a variety of special promotion programmes such as frequent-flyer programmes and one fare return travel on certain routes. Effective image-marketing has steered Indian Airlines clear out of the doldrums. From being the least preferred airlines in 1994, it has become to the most preferred in 1996. The number of passengers carried by IA declined from 88,85,600 in 1991-92 to 76,35,268 in 1994-95. Net losses amounted from Rs. 15.24 crore in 1989-90 to Rs. 258.46 crore in 1993-94. the people had preferred to travel by other competitive private airlines.

It was March 1994 onwards that a major image-control exercise was embarked upon and far reaching decision taken to put Indian Airlines back on the runway. In February 1995 a committee under the chairmanship of Union Petroleum Secretary Vijay Kelkar, was set up to pull Indian Airlines out of the red. So a variety of sound marketing measures were introduced. For example, new pricing for senior citizens, new pricing for return ticket buyers, better lounging facilities, ticketing at last minutes, removal of cancellation fee, wider reservation network, simplified reservation procedures, and easy accessibility to the customer. But the most clinching proof of image enhancement has been the surveys of passenger opinion done by IMRB and other agencies. The IMRB Image track reports saw a progressive improvement in the ratings awarded to IA by frequent fliers. In the last two tracks IA emerged as the Most Preferred Domestic Airline. MARG, MODE, MUDRA, and Apeejay School of Marketing surveys too indicated IA as the most preferred airline. The Apeejay survey also confirmed discernible improvement in IA services in the last two years. A survey commission for Tata Singapore Airlines found IA the best domestic airline and also concluded that IA would continue to be so for a few years even if Tata-Singapore Airlines starts its operations.

Indian Airlines' ebbing confidence got another boost when it won the Hotel & Food Services Award for the Domestic Airline in 1995. While on the one hand the award took IA completely by surprise, on the other it strengthened its hope of taking private airlines head on. The icing on the cake was the Delhi Advertising Club Gold Award for the Best English Campaign to the IA corporate campaign and A & M Award for the Best Campaign of the year to IA's international flight campaign. Indian Airlines had embarked upon a major damage control and image enhancing exercise by way of a series of beautifully conceived and excellently executed campaigns which compelled the drifter to return home to Indian Airlines.

The Indian Airlines embarked upon focused advertising communication in May 1995. The three part campaign, created by Nexus Equity, has already caught the imagination of the people. The first campaign (May-July 1995) consisted of a series of five ads and projected the intrinsic strengths of Indian Airlines in a credible manner. Research has shown that a sizable number of fliers considered attributes other than in flight service in decision-making and it was here that Indian Airlines scored well. The five ads, therefore, focused on the following areas of Indian Airlines' superiority Fleet strength/choice of aircraft, in flight comfort due to greater leg space extensive maintenance infrastructure wide, spread network and greater baggage allowance. Apparently negative sounding headlines (We admit Indian Airlines does not give you the same choice the others do. We concede Indian Airlines planes are constantly grounded etc.) were used to attract attention and focus on the benefit being highlighted. This approach also gave credibility to the communication since it subliminally conveyed that IA was not trying to gloss over the negatives of its past image.

The second phase of the campaign (August-November 1995) endeavoured to further underline the strengths of Indian Airlines in terms of experience and consequent peace of mind for the flier by using a testimonial approach. It turned the emotional link the flier had with Indian Airlines into a positive force by lending meaning to the theme 'Come Home to India Airlines.' Tracking studies done by IMRB during the campaign period showed that image ratings improved from 3.2 to 4.0 on a 5 point scale. Moreover, from being one of the least preferred of the domestic airlines, Indian Airlines became the most preferred.

The six ad campaign (September-November 1996) goes a step further by clearly conveying that the customer benefits from the various strengths of Indian Airlines, in terms of its size, infrastructure and network. And it helps in further reinforcing the already growing realisation that there is more to choosing an airline than just in flight service. Visually aerial pictures of various parts of India have been used to enhance the Indian skies and of being the only true national airline.

Similarly, deregulation in the banking institutions and financial industry has encouraged banking institutions and many financial institutions to employ aggressive marketing communication techniques and to use many forms of special events, services and giveaways to attract new customers and also to retain their old clients.

Acute Time Pressure

With majority of Indian women now preferring to be part of the work force and with the changing concept of two income households, both men and women have less time at their disposal for spending on traditional shopping and thus changing the consumption behaviour. This has ultimately resulted in towards a growing trend for seeking greater time control and management. The consumers of the present day society now are more determined than ever to tailor daily schedules to their needs rather than having schedules imposed on them.[3] This hold equally true to the present Indian society. The overwhelming usage of videocassette recorders and increasing usages of ATN's (automatic teller machines) by bands for their various banking activities reflect this trend. In both the cases the consumer engages in behaviour whenever he or she wants to rather than having a television network or bank imposing the servicing hours. There are numerous of other manifestations of time management and control, all of which have created new challenges and opportunities for marketing communications.

Increased Health Consciousness

Today, there is an increased concern for personal physical fitness and health. This has resulted in a boom in the growth of a fitness industry, including health clubs, aerobic and yoga centres. The people have changed their eating habits. They are now preferring to eat more nutritious food like eating more fresh leafy vegetables, poultry and cheese but less red meat. This has resulted in marketing of such products which offer consumers better health and physical appearance (e.g., weight loss products, less calorie sugar — Sugar Free of Equal brand of sugar substitute and cosmetic products of Shahnaz). Today, consumers have changed — how they eat, how they play, when they recreate, how they dress-up, how they groom and what they expect from life and from products that they consume. Dramatic societal changes have been responsible to create many challenges; and opportunities for responsive and creative marketing and finally marketing communications practices.

Once, Nursing homes which used to sit back and wait for patients to show up now actively promote their various services through news paper advertisements, hoarding and T.V. commercials. They are coming up with novel schemes of health care and providing services at the clients' door step in certain cases. For example, the Ochsner Hospital in New Orleans developed a promotional programme aimed directly at men. It was so that they decided to direct their programme at men because men are more likely to neglect their health care in comparison to women. Ochsner's marketing communications programme comprised of aggressive television advertising which evoked interest in men to seek medical checkups and carefully trained telephone receptionists that received inquiries generated because of the aggressive television advertising and fixing an appointment with the appropriate physicians.[4]

Marketing Communications Mix

Now the vital question arises, as to what tools does a company have to its disposal so that a comprehensive communications programme for its product can be chalked out. Basically, these are all the elements which make up the company's promotional effort. In its widest sense, promotion means to move forward. The word promotion is derived from a Latin word promovere: pro meaning forward and movere meaning 'to move.' However, in business promotion has a somewhat similar meaning, namely, to motivate (or move in a sense) customers to action (to make a purchase). In marketing communications its general meaning may be confined to those communication activities which include advertising, personal selling, sales promotion, publicity and POP (point of purchase) communication. A brief description will amply clarify the fine distinctions among these promotional elements.

Advertising is a form of mass communication through news papers, magazines, periodicals, radio, television and other media like bill boards, handouts etc., or directly to consumer communication involving direct mailing of information. These advertisings are paid for by an identified sponsor the advertiser, and are purely non-personal, as the sponsoring company is communicating at one and the same time simultaneously, to a very large number of receivers rather than communicating with an individual, a specific person or a small group.

Personal selling is person-to-person communication. Here the seller tries to persuade his prospective customers to purchase the company's product or service. Basically, personal selling involves face-to-face communication but now-a-days, telephone sales and many other forms of electronic communications are being increasingly employed.

Sales promotion encompasses all such marketing activities that attempt to promote immediate sales of a product by acting as an incerting and stimulating quick buyer action, thereby giving the name 'sales promotion.' Advertising personal selling and publicity are excluded from the activities of sales promotion. Advertising and publicity are basically designed to accomplish other objectives, such as, creating brand awareness and influencing customer attitudes. Sales promotions are directed both at the trade level, wholesalers and retailers and at consumers. Trade-oriented sales promotion employs the use of various kinds of display concessions quantity discounts and merchandise assistance. Consumer-oriented sales promotion techniques include discount coupons premiums, free samples, contests, rebates and the like. The above three promotional activities advertising, personal selling and sales promotion are such variables over which the company has its control.

Publicity, the fourth promotional activity of a company, the company generally has no control over its presentation. Publicity like advertising is also a non-personal form of marketing communications to a large segment of people in a particular society unlike advertising, publicity is not paid for by the company usually in the form of news items or editorial comments about a company's products or services. These items of information or comments receive free print space in newspapers and magazines or even broadcast or telecast time because of the mere fact that media consider the information relevant and news worthy for their readers or listeners. Therefore, it is in this light, publicity is 'not a paid for' by the company who is receiving all the benefits of the publicity.

Point of purchase (POP) communications include displays at the counter as well as at the show windows, trial packs, posters, hangings, glow signs and a variety of other promotional materials that are especially created and designed to influence buying decisions at the point of purchase. This is traditionally done at the supermarkets and reputed retail outlets. Table 4.1 represents the number of specific tools that fall within the categories of marketing communications and promotion activities of a company.

A blend of above referred activities is known as a promotional mix which is actually a part of the marketing communication mix. Therefore, the promotional mix which has been till recently viewed as the company's sole communications link with the consumers may lead to sub-optimization of the company's total communication effort. This is so, because if viewed in isolation, promotion can work contrary to other elements in the marketing communication mix, for a successful marketing requires careful integration of all promotional and non-promotional elements. Advertising, sales promotion, personal selling and publicity ought to be coordinated with all other actions of the company that communicate to customers something about a company activities such as product design, price choice of dealers and the like.[5]

Therefore, the other communication elements with which promotion is linked and coordinated are price, product, retail outlets and other company actions which consumers perceive as communicating some information about the company's total product offering (T.P.O.).

The likelihood that a prospective customer will attend to a message can be expressed as:

Likelihood of attention =

$$\frac{\text{Perceived reward strength} - \text{Perceived punishment strength}}{\text{Perceived expenditure of effort}}$$

TABLE 4.1
Common Communication/Promotion Tools

Advertising	*Sales Promotion*	*Public Relations*	*Personal Selling*	*Direct Marketing*
Print and broadcast ads	Contests, games,	Press kits sweepstakes, lotteries	Sales	Catalogs Presentations
Packaging — outer Packaging inserts	Premiums and Sampling	Speeches gifts Seminars	Sales meetings Incentive Programs	Mailings Telemarketing
Motion pictures	Fairs and Trade	Annual reports shows	Samples	Electronic Shopping
Brochures and booklets	Exhibits	Charitable donations	Fairs and trade shows	
Posters and leaflets	Demonstrations	Sponsorships	TV shopping	
Directories		Couponing	Publications	
Reprints of ads		Rebates	Community relations	
Billboards		Low-interest financing	Lobbying	
Display signs		Entertainment	Identity media	
Point of Purchase displays	Trade-in allowances	Company magazine		
Audiovisual material	Trading stamps	Events		
Symbols and logos	Tie-ins			

Therefore, beside promotional elements the marketing communications mix of a company also considers the fact that:

Product Communicates

Price Communicates

Place Communicates

Promotion Communicates.

When we say that product communicates we mean that any product or service whatsoever, communicates to its consumers much about itself through its size, shape, brand name, package design and colour. These product eves or product messages communicate something about the product carrying certain impressions and its total product offering. For example, recall the reaction of people to the 'Tata Tea' packaged in green, giving the impression of garden fresh tea. Let us focus our attention how these different constituent elements of a product function as marketing communicators:

Physical Features of a Product Communicates

Any product whichever it may be communicates through its physical features. The colour, shape, design, packaging material, finish and the like all such features convey a message to its buyer. Lavender perfume, round shape, smooth and silky feel, handy, pocket size are some of the product features which possess high communicative and persuasive value.

Package Communicates

Packaging provides the first appeal to the buyer. The actual product is the secondary element. For example, consider the festival gift packs of sweets and dry fruits. People are willing to purchase the box at exorbitant prices even knowing that the contexts of the box are not worth the price that they are paying for. Why? The package is there to be seen and felt. Its colour, its shape and size, the brand name, the material used and the innovative idea, they all carry some specific marketing communication cues.

The colours of the package also possess great communicative impact. Some colours are bright and exciting while some of them are dull. It is not mere a co-incidence that a large number of products displayed on the shelve have different shades of yellow and red combinations. There are ample research evidence that yellow and red colours are in a better position to get attention in comparison to other colours. This combination of colours also helps to look the package a little bigger than what it really is. Blue colour is associated with peace contentment and security. A toilet soap in light blue package, for example, 'Ganga soap' has greatest possibility to capture the attention of a cultured young lady, a book with a subdued yellow and brown cover may attract an intellectual, a toy in a bright red package is more attracted by young boys, whereas frozen food in light orange packing attracts a middle aged housewife and if in a green packing attracts more to health conscious people. Red being associated with vitality, power and an urge to win, manufacturers of cigarettes and soft drinks like Wills, Pepsi, Coke, I.T.C. are extensive users of red and blue colour for packaging their products. By the right choice of colours the company is able to make the initial selling through these communication cues because the colours on the package communicate instantly.

Brand name as a component of the total product has great communication value. In fact this is the age of brands. No woman asks for just facial make up, she asks for Pond's or Lakme. She does not ask for shampoo, She asks for Halo, Sunsilk, Tiara or Gleem. It is not toothpaste that she wants but Cibaca fluoride or Cibaca Top, Colgate or Signal, Forhans or Promise. Any toilet soap is not welcome, she wants Lux or Rexona, Hamam or Jai, Mysore Sandal or Margo. From the utility angle any of these products may serve the purpose. But the buyer identifies the products and distinguishes one from the other through the brand name. And this is the main function intended of a brand name to communicaters with the prospective buyers by evoking positive meanings and associations in their minds. Halo or Pond's Dream flower, Sunsilk of Signal Angel face or Gleem, Godrej or Swan they convey a message to the buyer. A good brand name should be able to suggest to the buyer, what type of product it is and what distinctiveness it claims. Even if there are no real differences between the two products through a successful brand strategy, psychological product differentiation can be created. Quite often the brand names are supported by slogans which can be easily remembered or which have great reminder value in the market.

In the Indian market, Lifebuoy, Lux, Vimal, Nirma and Rasna are examples of brand names that have succeeded remarkably in their communicative role. Besides the brand name, if the company has earned a name and reputation in the market, they also use the company name for marketing communications. For example, generally Tatas carry the suffix — 'A Tata Product,' Products from Godrej ranging from toilet soap to steel almirah or white goods carry the company name Godrej in addition to the brand name.

In another example of how the physical attributes of a product and brand name communicate with the buyer, consider the detergent 'Aerial' which now has multicoloured granules which purport to perform various functions on dirty clothes. The white granules takes out the dirt, the green granules bleach clothes to make them white, while the blue granules make clothes whiter than white.

Price Communicates

Price communicates something more than the price. Price is generally used by the sellers to connote in the product offering. In certain cases, price, becomes a symbol of prestige and status for the buyer. The experience of a jewellery store owner in Arizona clearly explains price's communication role. During the peak tourist season, a jewellery store owner was not able to sell the turquoise jewellery to her expectations. She tried a number of merchandising and sell technique with no success. While she was departing for an out of station buying trip, she wrote a note for her salesman, 'Everything in this display case, price X1/2'. When she returned several days later she was astonished to find that every turquoise jewellery in the shop was sold out. She was more surprised when she learnt that the salesman had misread the note and actually doubled the price of each item rather than cutting the price of each item to half according to the note. It appears that when the turquoise jewellery was sold at double its original price, tourists perceived it as a more valuable item and therefore more worthy as a gift item for their dear ones or for their personal use.[6]

On the contrary in the case of certain products, consumers develop an idea of reasonable price based on prices of similar products available in the market. When the actual price is higher than the reasonable price what the buyer has assumed they are reluctant to make a purchase. However, if the actual price is much lower than the expected or reasonable price, the consumer is reluctant to buy the product, suspecting the quality. Therefore, the price has a major communicative role in order to make the total product offering to consumers more attractive.

Place Communicates

Place where the product is sold, i.e., retail store, also have significant communication value to customers. Two stores selling a similar product can project entirely different product images to their prospective buyers. For example, Raymond's suitings sold exclusively through the high class company, exclusive retail show room at a good location and well displayed counter, project a premium quality product image rather than if the same clothing is sold at a store where discounted items are sold.

It is not as though the consumers go through the process before each store visit. If past experiences with a store have been satisfactory, the store is usually utilised without reevaluation. Again, it is not as though the consumer elaborately thinks out all the four steps, making a store choice, but the process does take place. In certain cases, the very name of the store, as its category, guidely higges off in his mind the required responses and the decision, e.g., he may have in his mind certain ready associations with names like 'Supper Market', 'Cooperative Store', 'Discount Shop' & 'Exclusive Shop.' So the store is a good communication tool. The chain of exclusive VIMAL show- rooms established throughout the country by the company is a telling example of channel becoming a powerful tool of marketing communication and promotion.

Now, it should be amply clear that promotion is only one of the several activities in which a company engages itself to communicate their total product offerings. All the Four 'P's of marketing have a positive role in marketing communications. The blend of all these variables as perceived by existing and prospective customers of a company is being referred here as the marketing communication mix instead of marketing mix, a notion which was popularised by Neil M. Borden and Martin V. Marshall in their book *Advertising Management* (Home wood, I ll Richard. D. Irwin, Inc., 1959, p. 23).

WHAT IS MARKETING COMMUNICATIONS?

Marketing communications can be best understood by evaluating the nature of its two constituent elements — communication and marketing. As said earlier, communication is the process whereby commonness of thought is established and some meaning is shared between individuals or between organisations and individuals. Marketing has been viewed by American Marketing Association as 'Marketing is the performance of business activities that directs the flow of goods and services from the producer to the consumer or user.' Marketing can be said to be the set of activities in the process of asserting consumer needs, whereby businesses and other organisations create transfers of value by converting them into products or services, between themselves and their customers or users in order to satisfy such needs and wants of specific consumer with emphasis on profitability and getting the optimum use of resources available with the organisation. Hence, one may argue marketing is more general than marketing communications, but one should not forget that market does involve communication activities. Considering together marketing communications represent the collection of all elements of marketing mix that facilitate exchanges by establishing shared meaning with the company's customers and clients.

MARKETING TO MARKETING COMMUNICATIONS

A doubt ponders here, how does marketing differ from marketing communications. After all both involve the four basic Ps — price, product, place and promotion — the major decision variables of marketing. One school of marketing argues that 'the market mix is in reality a marketing communications mix in which all activities integrate sometimes in a mutually reinforcing way, sometimes in conflict with one another to form an image that can be favourable or unfavourable.'*

Another school of thought differentiates between marketing communications and marketing. They consider marketing communications take place at a later stage of the marketing in the total marketing process. According to this view:

Marketing effectiveness depends significantly on communications effectiveness. The market in reality

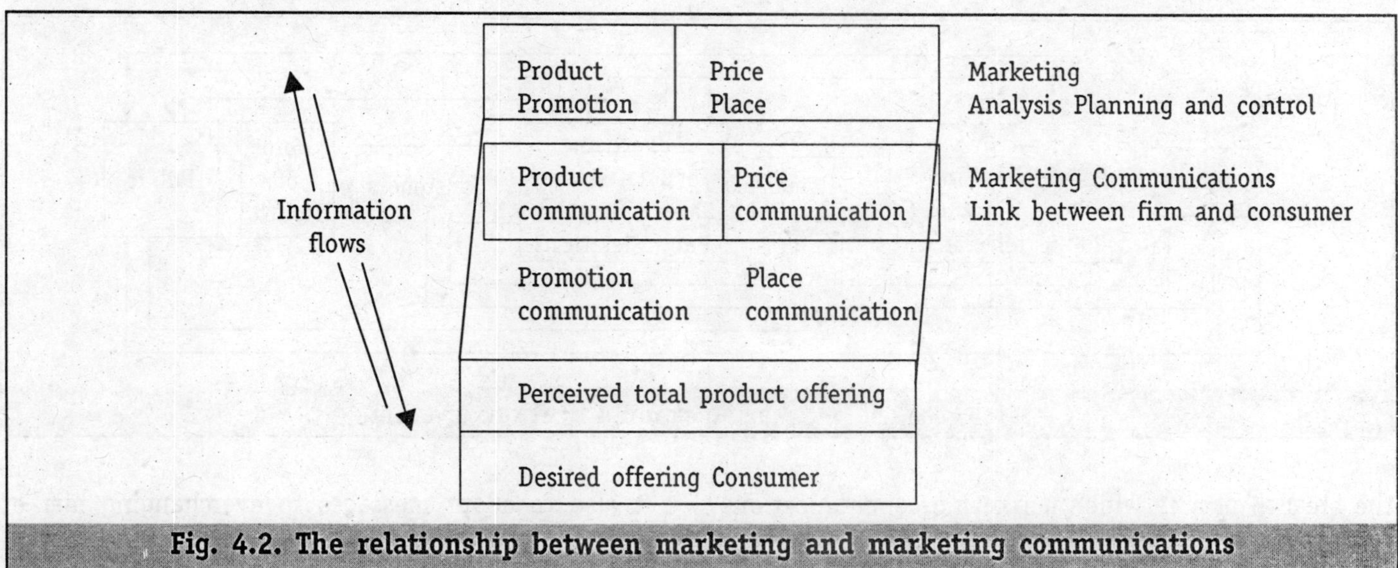

Fig. 4.2. The relationship between marketing and marketing communications

is energised (or activated) through information flows. The way a buyer perceives the market offering of the sales is influenced by the amount and kind of information he has about the offering and his reaction to that information.[8]

The Fig. 4.2 suggests that marketing is heavily based on decision-making activities, whereas marketing communications is the implementation of marketing decisions.

This results in two-way information flows between the company and its buyers. Implementation of marketing decisions requires the help of communications process. Unless these marketing decisions are manifested in the market through marketing communications the system is at a standstill.

It should be quickly pointed out that a good marketing communications system provides for information flows from the consumer to the firm. Marketing communications is a dialogue between buyer and seller, not simply a monologue from seller to buyer. Stidsen and Schutte support this point when they say:

Effective communications also involves the availability of suitable media for a consumer-producer dialogue. The emergence of organised consumer groups has been helpful in this respect. The establishment of direct telephone lines to some corporate customer service departments and the 'we-listen-better' campaign launched by Ford Motor Company, have at least the appearance of exemplifying a communications model of the marketing process. But these are very limited examples of what could have been accomplished to implement the spirit of the marketing concept through the development of effective communications channels from consumers to corporate decision centres.[9]

In today's competitive environment a company has to manage a complex marketing communications system (see Fig. 4.3). It is compelled to switch over to marketing communications instead of only marketing. The company constantly communicates with its middle men, consumers and publics. The company's middle men communicate with their consumers and publics. Consumers have word of mouth (WOM) communication with each other and with other public, who may be prospective consumers of the product. Not only this, each group provides feedback to every other group.

This discussion brings us to the central theme of this book. Significantly, the market is a place where buyers and sellers share common platform to give and share meanings about total product offerings. Marketing communications is the process which permits such sharing to continuously go on uninterrupted.

MARKETING COMMUNICATIONS DEFINED

So far we have made an attempt to make a distinction between marketing communications and marketing. Therefore, till now we have not given any definition of marketing communications. We are sure by now the reader must have got a positive feel for

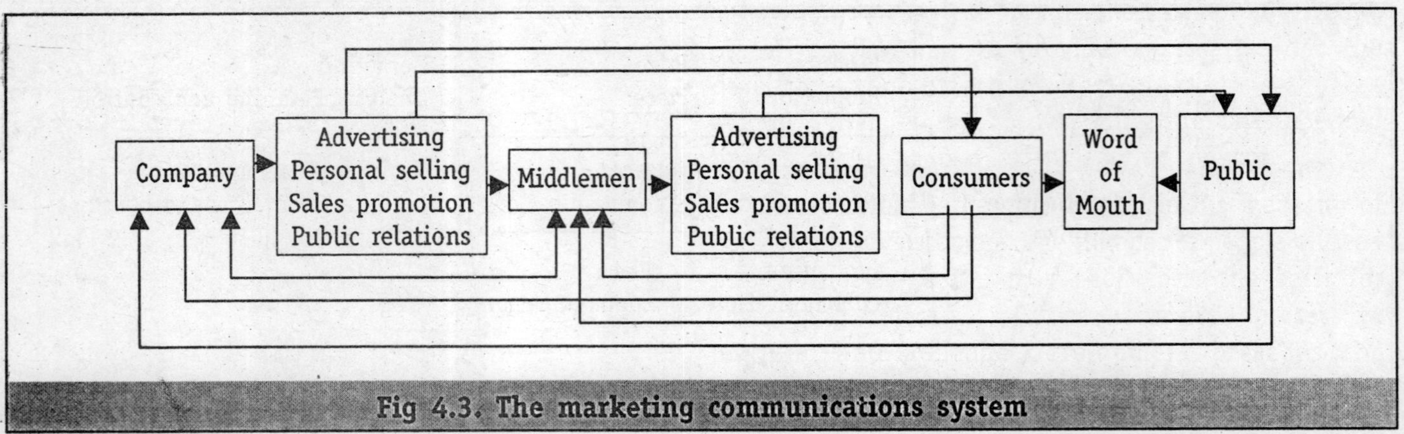

Fig 4.3. The marketing communications system

the breadth of area which marketing communications deals with.

To give a very broad definition of this process, one can say that marketing communications is a continuing dialogue between sellers and buyers in a market place. However, this definition of marketing communications might be viewed as a 'macro' definition and might serve as a mere philosophical definition rather than a practical one from the management point of view.

From the managerial angle, we may define the process of marketing communication as (1) It is a complex process of presenting an integrated set of stimuli to the target market (buyers with the intention of evoking positive set of responses within that target market and (2) setting up appropriate channels to receive, interpret and thereby act upon the messages received from the market for meeting the objectives of modifying present messages sent by the company and also identifying new communication opportunities.

This definition of marketing communications emphasises the fact that the company is a sender of market messages as well as a receiver of market responder. As a sender of messages, the company in the competitive environment attempts to inform and persuade consumers to purchase the company's brand in order to achieve a certain level of profits. The company communicates with the market only through promotional stimuli but also through, price, product, point of purchase or place. As a receiver of market responses, the company gathers all the relevant information through market research and marketing information systems, in order to realign its messages not only to its present consumers or market targets but also to adopt messages to everchanging market conditions.

The above definition of marketing communications is in tune with the notion that all marketing mix variables not only the promotional variable, communicate with customers. This definition further expands the scope that marketing communications can be either intentional, as in the case of personal selling or advertising, or unintentional or a combination of both as when any of the product feature price cue or package cue symbolises something to customers that the marketing communicator may not have intended when he had sent a message.

MARKETING COMMUNICATIONS PROCESS

As discussed earlier, the three essential elements of a communication process is source, message and the receiver. Effective Communication takes place only when any meaning assigned to a message means the same thing to both the parties — the sender of message and its receiver.

Marketing communication involves sharing of meaning, information and concepts by the source and the receiver about products and services and the information about the company selling them. The effective communication takes place when a sender, i.e., source sends an information in terms of message in a favourable manner that satisfies the sender because both sender and the receiver response to the message in a favourable manner that satisfies the sender because both — sender and receiver, have assigned identical meaning to the message.

TABLE 4.2
Elements of Communication

1. **The Source:** A marketing company, a sender of message.
2. **The Message:** The commercial idea, sales story, the copy theme.
3. **The Channel:** The vehicle carrying the message, a salesman, an advertising medium, sales literature sent through the mail. Telephone, radio, or television, newspaper, etc., can also act as the channel of promotion.
4. **The Receiver:** A person or a group of persons; the receiver is a potential customer, purchase influencer or a reseller.
5. **The feedback:** A response, a reaction or message sent back by a customer to the marketer. The feedback improves the effectiveness of communication.
6. **The Noise:** Noise creates many obstacles reducing effectiveness of the communication process.

For marketing communications, marketer is the source who tries to deliver a message to the customer, the receiver, in order to promote his product or service.

The message is transmitted in a variety of ways. All available forms of promotion are media or channels of communication for transmitting the message. The receiver is the target market segment — a group of existing and potential consumers for whom the message has been sent. When this transmitted message is received and interpreted by consumers and if they find something common in the message with that of the sender, they come into action, i.e., they make a purchase. Feedback is the reverse of communication flow, from the consumer to the marketer. Therefore, the marketing communications process can be diagrammatically represented as in Fig. 4.4.

When the message is transmitted through personal salesmanship, the seller may have prompt feedback from the receiver. The sender can find out how the message is being received as we have face-to-face direct communication through sales talk and conversation. The salesman can balance the message on the basis of feedback from the buyer. This is the real advantage of personal selling. Personal interaction is the most efficient form of communication. Under mass communication or advertising, mass sellers must rely for information feedback (returned message from buyer) on dealers, consumerism, complaints from consumers, marketing research or total sales results given through sales analysis. Mass communication is essentially one-way communication. Feedback is

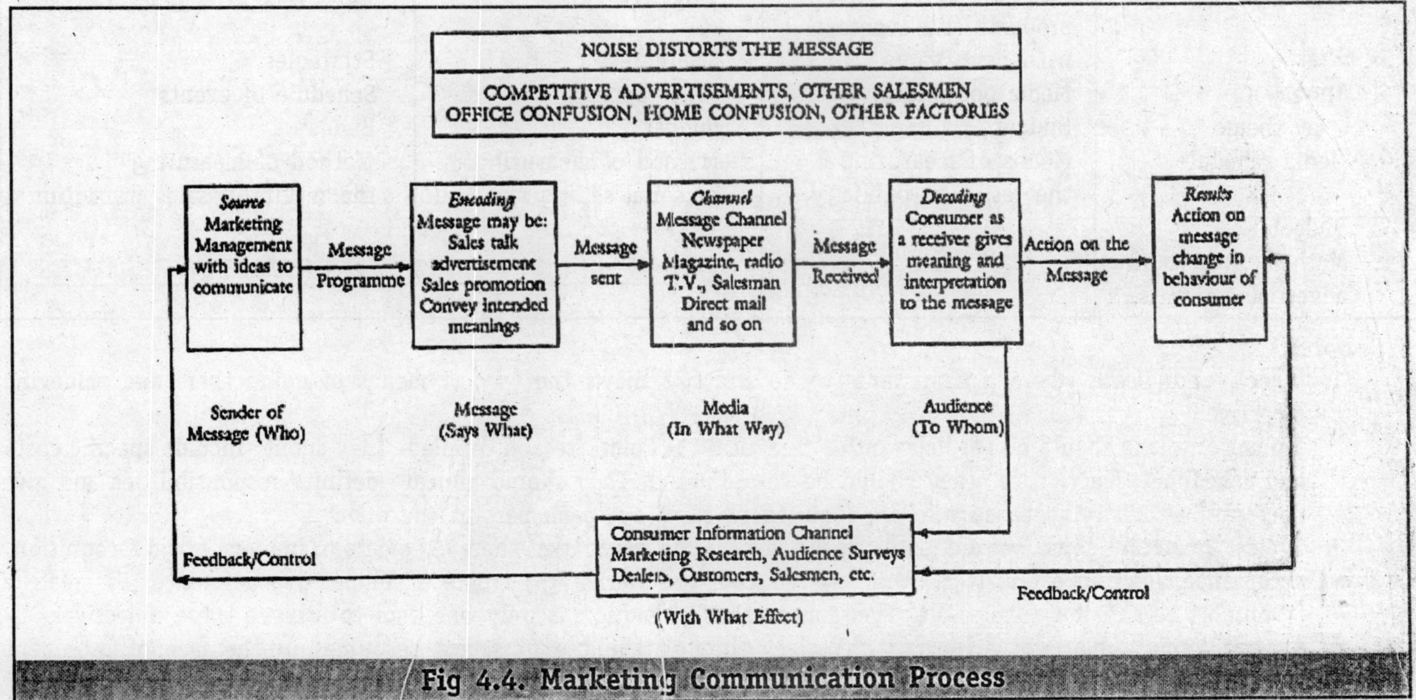

Fig 4.4. Marketing Communication Process

difficult and usually delayed. Consumer surveys, electronic devices and other types of marketing research are used to get the feedback. However, this feedback is delayed and it is of no use in altering a message already sent. Of course, it is useful in altering the future advertising message.

All kinds of promotion play the role of communication channels between the marketer (the source and the sender of message) and the consumer (receiver of the message). Promotion as an element cuff marketing mix has broad objectives (*a*) information (*b*) persuasion, (*c*) reminding. The oven objective of promotion is of course, influencing the buyer behaviour and predispositions (needs, attitudes, goals, beliefs, values and preferences).

Table 4.3 and 4.4 summarises the various marketing communication plans and types of communication influencing the buyer behaviour at different stages respectively.

MARKETING COMMUNICATIONS MODEL

By now we have seen that marketing depends heavily upon communication process. It would be appropriate to develop a marketing communications model that corresponds to the general communication model developed earlier. Naturally, When we talk about a model, a question ponders in our mind, what is a model? A model is a representation of important elements and its relationship to real world phenomenon.

Building a model begins with a series of simplifying assumptions which result in a reduced set of descriptions of the real world entity. These assumptions form the basis for the formulation of relationships among elements believed to be extant in the real world system. These relationships may be based upon previously conducted research along with the model builder's own observations of the phenomenon under investigation.

TABLE 4.3
Promotion Plans

Advertising Plan	*Publicity Plan*	*Personal Selling Plan*	*Sales Promoting Plan*
An advertising plan covers advertising	A pubicity plan above	A personal selling plan covers	A sales promotion plan covers
1. Targets	Targets and objectives	Sales targets	Sales promoton targets
2. Objectives	Schedule of company products and events	Objectives	Objectives
3. Strategy	with news value	Strategies	Strategies
4. Appeal	Media possibilities	Major appeals	Schedule of events
5. Copy theme	Budget	Budget	Budget
6. Media schedule	Means of measuring the resuls of publicity	Method of measuring personal selling results	Method of measuring the results of sales promotion
7. Budget			
8. Method of measuring advertising results			

Notes:

1. Objectives indicate where a firm wants to go strategy shows the way or means of going there and achieving objective
2. Promotion plans should be (1) Relevant (2) Practical (3) Complete and detailed. They should include specific costs and schedules of activities. They should be co-ordinated. They should allocate definite responsibilities and give necessary authority to those who are required to carry out each part of the plan.
3. Typical promotion objectives are (1) increase sales (2) improve market share (3) create or improve brand recognition, acceptance, insistence etc. (4) inform and educate the market (5) create a competitive deference (6) create a favourable climate for future sale. Please note that promotion is only one tool to achieve these objectives.
4. A strategy is a plan for achieving objectives through the use of scarce resources in the face of inteligent competition.

TABLE 4.4

Types of Communication Influencing Various Stages in Buyer Behaviour

Components or Dimensions of Attitude	*Movement toward Purchase (Six stage Sequence)*	*Types of Communication Relevant at each stage*
1. The Conative (Behavioural) Dimension It is the region of drives or motives, i.e., activated un-satisfied wants. Advetisements and sales promotion must stimulae and direct desires so as to motivate the consumer to buy a product. The buyer should be made ready to respond and he should have conviction that the purchase would be wise. Purchase is the last step converting this attitude into actual purchase.	6 Purchase 5 Conviction	Point of purchase material, retail store advertising, special advertising, special deals, last chance offer, price appeals, testimonials, source credibility, i.e., Expertness and trust-worthiness of the source, personal selling, inter-personal communication, word of mouth communication, are essential in evaluation and adoption stages. Believability of company as a communicator is called source credibility.
2. The Affective (Feelings and Emotion) Dimension It is the region of feelings and emotions, consumer moves from knowledge to liking and preference. He develops a favourable attitude toward the product liking and then develops the point of preference. Promotion tools must stress the affective aspect of behaviour, i.e., the area of feelings and emotions must be tapped. Advertisements and sales promotion will change emotions and feelings.	4 Preference of buyers 3 Liking	Competitive advertising argumentative advertising copy, image advertising, status, glamour appeals stress on changing emotions and feelings opinion leaders are used as a good source of information and opinion to change attitude of buyers through inter-personal communication.
3. The Cognitive Dimension It is the region of awareness and knowledge. Promotion tools must emphasise the cognitive aspects of buyer behaviour in order to create awareness and knowledge. Advertising provides adequate information and facts.	2 Knowledge 1 Awareness	Announcements advertising, descriptive advertising copy, classified advertisements, slogans, jingles, sky writing, television, radio advertisements. Mass media must be adopted to create awareness and provide knowledge and information.

Notes:

1. Buying process involves six stage sequences related to three basic psychological states: (1) The cognitive dimension (Awareness and Knowledge), (2) The affective dimension (Liking and Preference), and (3) The conative dimension (Conviction and Purchase).
2. A firm does not have separate strategies of advertising selling and sales promotion. It has one promotional mix and this mix is an integral part of the overall marketing plan. The elements of promotion mix are not independent strategies. Each one supports the other. They are complementary tools of promotion. Taken together advertising, personal selling and sales promotion are the 'Three Musketeers' of marketing programme. Their motto is: 'All for one and one for all.' An integrated marketing mix means this, and nothing short of this can be thought by the marketer.
3. Promotional plan should be in harmony with overall corporate objectives, policies, organisation and its competence. Promotional plan should be evaluated against specific promotional objectives as well as against the rest of the marketing mix.
4. The proper coordination and integration of selling, advertising and sales promotion produces a far more efficient programme than an attempt to carry out these activities without regard to their effects upon each other.
5. Movement towards purchase is upwards. It starts from awareness and ends at purchase action or decision.
6. The company reputation, created through advertising and other forms of mass communication, can enhance the effectiveness of the salesman. Company image is the personality of reputation of the company as perceived by customers, prospects, suppliers, shareholders and the general public company image is created by communication, particularly through public relations.

The efficiency of the model may be determined by testing the empirical system. If the model proves reliable, it may be found useful in predicting events in the real world or in discovering relationships which were not before observed.

THE MODEL[10]

Fig. 4.5, represents a descriptive model of marketing communications. The communications process can be initiated by either internal or external stimuli. In this model examples of external stimuli are awareness of market opportunities and information, about how well existing products are performing. These external stimuli are the result of some form of feedback from the market. Internally, company executives or employees can make suggestions which may eventually affect the company's total product message. In either case the firm is continually besieged with information which defines its present position in the marketplace or which may alter its conception of its desired position in the marketplace. Where this position discrepancy is perceived by company decision-makers as either too far out of line or closing at an unsatisfactory rate, the firm must make decisions to correct the situation.

These decisions may be in the form of a policy change or policy formulation mapping of new strategy or alteration of the set of tactics to implement the strategy. The decisions also include formulation of a desired set of consumer responses. Because of their importance, these consumer responses are broken out of the decision parameters box of comparison against actual consumer responses. This comparison process sets up controls which the company can use to measure its progress and if necessary to change its total product message. These decision parameters are comparable to the communicator parameters of the general model.

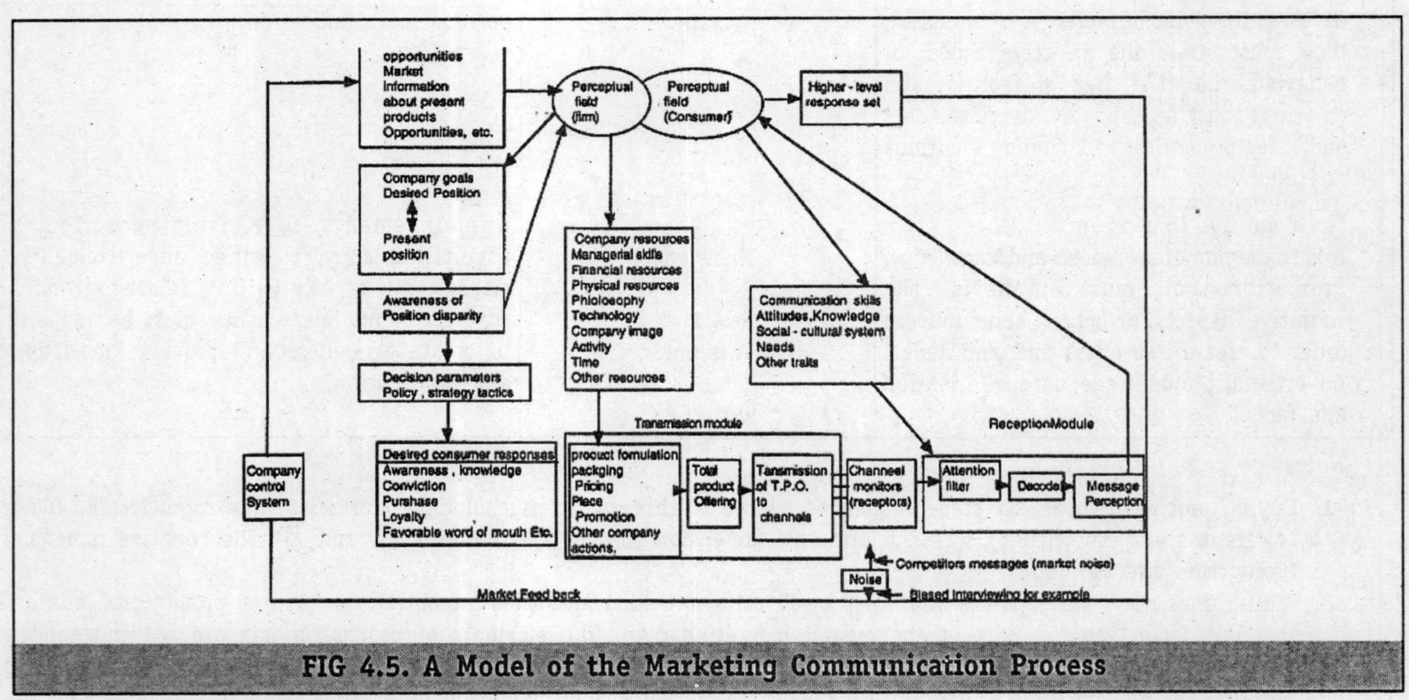

FIG 4.5. A Model of the Marketing Communication Process

The decisions made by the company necessarily involve assessment of and eventual change in the use of company resources. The company's resources are analogous to an individual's communication skills, knowledge etc. Both company resources and decisions related to their use affect the construction of the total product message. Product characteristics, Packaging, price, retail image, promotional themes etc., are all components which are encoded into a unified total product message and transmitted to the channel's members.

The channels through which the firm's message travels are varied and complex. For example, an advertising agency acts as a relay earlier referred to as transceiver which receives a message often modifying it and transmits it further through the channel to radio, TV, newspaper, magazine, and other transceivers. These transceivers in turn transmit the message in different forms, namely, through visual aural and olfactory channels to consumers. Some target consumers receive the message directly. Others receive the message indirectly from other members of the target market (opinion leaders for example). Many consumers receive the message through both personal and non-personal transceivers.

Transceivers are critical links in the communications channels because they represent sources of potential distortion in the final message. Newspapers make print errors, radio announcers mispronounce words or leave parts of the message out and opinion leaders add their personal biases to the message. Each link is of vital concern to the marketing communicator.

In the supermarket the package is a silent communicator. If store personnel do not know the brand free from dust distortion in this message cue may occur. The consumer may perceive the brand differently from a brand free from dust. He may think, for example this brand has been sitting here a long time. If no one else is buying it, may be something is wrong with it so I better not buy it either.

The sales representative who has unpolished shoes noticeable personality defects or bad breath affects the way in which the total product is perceived by the consumer.

All these things communicate undesirable messages to the consumer. Each is due to message distortion in the channels of communication.

From this point the marketing communications model is similar to the general communications model described earlier. The message must penetrate the consumer's attention filter. It must be decoded and perceived with varying degrees of perceptual distortion as influenced by the individual's personal set of needs, attitudes, values etc. And finally different levels of consumer responses feedback through the system to the firm all subject to various forms of noise (e.g., interview bias in the case of surveys). The feedback of actual response is compared with the desired set of responses. The discrepancies between the two are further inputs to the perceptual field of the firm which may result in alteration of the total product message.

Admittedly, the explanation of the process presented here is an oversimplification. For example, all components are not received simultaneously by the receiver; lags exist in the system. However the model should be useful in understanding the process at a general level.

It must be pointed out that the firm should begin by attempting to learn what the characteristics of its consumers are. Questions which should be answered are: What consumer needs, attitudes, communication skills, knowledge levels etc., are likely to influence; how the message is received? What set of stimuli is best at gaining attention and reducing perceptual distortion so that the message is perceived as intended? How can the firm use this understanding of its consumer to combine its resources in such a way as to evoke the intended product meaning within its target consumer? Thus, the process should begin with careful analysis of the intended receiver and a total product message formulated on that basis.

The Best Media Plans – A Truth

Each year, Adweek selects the best media plans of the year. The selection is made by a number of top execu-tives of advertising and media agencies, with category winners including "Best media plan spending more than $25 million," "... between $10 and $25-million," "... between $1 and 10 million," and "..less than $1 million." In addition, there are winners in specific cate-gories such as "best use of cable TV," "best use of outdoor," "best use of new media," and so on. While we would like to report on all of them, space permits only a few. However, this sampling will demonstrate what successful plans include.

- **Spending more than $25 million:-** Dunkin Donuts (Hill Holliday Agency): Dunkin Donuts has over 3,500 franchises in over 120 markets, with multiple products and varying advertising budgets. Trying to find a positioning statement that serves everyone is no easy task. Hill Holliday's creative "Loosen Up"-designed to help consumers overcome guilt associated with eating donuts-required a very unique media strategy to communicate. To be effective for all franchisees, a "modular" strategy was developed from which individual locations could pick and choose what would work best given their needs and budgets. For example, sponsorships were created for early morning shows such as the Today show. Drive-time and in-office radio spots were purchased, as was space on the Captivate Network, which places advertisements on screens in high-rise elevators. Local TV spots at prime time and late fringe were included on shows like Friends, Every-body Loves Raymond, and the Letterman and Jay Leno shows. A 20-foot-high inflatable coffee cup was hung over the Massachusetts Pike in downtown Boston, and mobile billboards were common around Dunkin' Donuts sites. While no endorsement deals were made, the brand was able to receive the co-operation of radio and TV personalities while effectively communicating the "have fun" message through a "have fun" media strategy.

- **Spending between $10 and $25 million:-** Baskin-Robbins (Initiative Media): Changing lifestyles, super-market sales of ice cream, and a limited media investment restricted for years to spot TV and radio led to flat sales for the ice-cream purveyor and its franchisees. Armed with what the agency considered to be "a ton of proprietary research," the agency realized that the target audience included both children and adults and that the strategy had to change in respect to communications with consumers, field organizations, and promotional partners. Baskin-Robbins first teamed up with DreamWorks to promote the animated film Shrek. Movie signage appeared in stores,a "Free Scoop Night" promotion was initiated,and new products that tied in with the movie were developed. Initiative Media's plan was to leverage this success through media buys.TV spots were placed on Nick, Nick at Nite, Fox Family, Hallmark, and the Discovery channel, among others. Oprah, Jack Hanna, and Home Improvement also received shorter (10-second) spots. Cable included the Hallmark channel, VHl, and the TV Guide channel. Most of the ads were accompanied with sales promotions like "Flava of the Week," "Birthday Scoops," and others.
- **Spending less than $1 million:-**Archipelago (Fallon Minneapolis): Archipelago's goal was to attract stock traders away from traditional brokers to online trading. A $245,000 budget employing street protests, pennies, and other nontraditional media was allocated to reach the traders-most of whom were unhappy with their current means of trading. Fallon developed a creative strategy that capitalized on this dissatisfaction with the campaign slogan "Don't Get Pennied," which referred to the New York Stock Exchange's switch to expressing stock transactions to the penny rather than in increments of 6.25 cents-a practice that many traders perceived to be to their disadvantage. The agency actually organized demonstrations along Wall Street and in Boston's Post Office Square-where many traders had offices. An armored truck drove past the traders' offices playing the Beatle's "Penny Lane," and out-of-work actors took to the streets chanting "A penny saved is a penny earned. Choose Archipelago and don't get burned." Direct-mail pieces including advertising specialties and a roll of pennies followed, as did handouts in Boston subway stations and wallscapes in specified Manhattan communities. A full-page ad was placed in regional editions of The Wall Street Journal, The website was also altered to reflect the "Don't Get Pennied" campaign.

As these plans clearly demonstrate, a variety of media are now employed to get one's message across. They also demonstrate that effective plans don't have to cost millions and millions of dollars-but don't tell that to the media people!

Sources: Kate Macarthur, "Dunkin' Donuts Tries New Tag," Advertising Age, Aug. 12,2002, p. 8; Eric Schmuckler and Todd Shields, "Media Plan of the Year" Adweek, June 17,2002, pp. SR 1-16; "Green Giant Produces Big Sales for Baskin-Robbins," Potentials, July 2002, p. 13.

REFERENCES

1. The following articles are just a few of the many publications that have highlighted the importance of marketing communications: 'Marketing — The Mew Priority,' *Business Week*, January 9, 1984, pp. 70-72, 'A New Survival Course for C.EO's Marketing Communications,' September 1985, pp. 21-26, 94, 'Marketing's New Look', *Business Week*, January 26, 1987, pp. 64-69.
2. For an interesting discussion of competition in United States from Asian competitors refer to 'The Four Tigers — Start Clawing At US Markets', *Business Week*, July 22, 1985, pp.136-142. (The 'Four Tigers' refers to the competitors from Korea, Taiwan, Hong Kong and Singapore).
3. '31 Major Trends Shaping the Future of American Business', *The Public Pulse* (A publication of the Roper Organisation), Vol. 2 No.1, 1986, p. 1.

4. 'Marketing Medicine to Men', Cable News Net Works, *'Health Watch'*, January 16, 1988.
5. John Fitzgerald, 'Integrated Communications' *Advertising Age,* Feb. 15, 1988, p.18.
6. Robert B. Cialdini, 'Influence: How and Why People Agree to Things', New York, William Morrow and Company, 1984, pp. 15-16.
7. Harper W. Boyd. Jr. and Sidney J. Levy, *Promotion: A Behavioural View,* Englewood Cliffs, N.J., Prentice Hall Inc., 1967, p. 20.
8. Thomas A. Staudit and Donald A. Taylor, *A Managerial Introduction to Marketing,* Englewood Cliffs, N.J. Prentice Hall Inc., 1965, p. 353.
9. Bent Stidsen and Thomas F. Schutte, 'Marketing as a Communication System: The Marketing Concept Revisited,' *Journal of Marketing,* Vol. 36, p.25, October 1972.
10. Adapted from M. Wayne DeLozier, *The Marketing Communications Process,* McGraw-Hill Kogakusha Ltd., Tokyo, 1976, pp. 170-172.

CHAPTER 5

COMMUNICATIONS MODEL IN MARKETING

COMMUNICATING WITH THE HISPANIC TEEN MARKET

A few years ago, Jeff Manning, the executive director of the California Milk Processor Board (CMPB), was considering ways to reverse a decline in milk sales in the heavily Hispanic southern California market. As he reviewed a report on the Latino market, a potential solution to the problem came to him: target one of the fastest-growing market segments in the United States, which is Hispanic teenagers. The results from the 2000 census show that over the past decade the Hispanic market grew by 58 percent, compared with only 3 percent for the non-Hispanic white segment, and another 35 percent jump for Hispanics is forecast over the next 10 years. Moreover, the ranks of Hispanic teenagers are projected to swell to 18 percent of the U.S. teen population over the next decade, up from 12 percent in 2000. Nearly one in five children born in the United States today is of Latin American descent, and more than half of all children in Los Angeles alone are born to Latino mothers.

While marketers are recognizing the importance of appealing to the Hispanic market, they are also finding that communicating with this fast-growing segment can be very challenging and requires more than creating an ad in the Spanish with tried-and-true Hispanic themes. They have to decide whether to use ads with a Hispanic-focused creative, dub or remake general market campaigns into Spanish, or run English-language ads and trust that they will be picked up by bilingual Hispanics. Contributing to the challenge is the fact that Hispanic teens often live in two worlds: one rich in traditional Latino values, such as strong commitment to family and religion, and the other in which they eagerly participate in mainstream teen America. They bounce between hip-hop and rock en Espanol; watch Buffy the Vampire Slayer with their friends and Spanish tetenovelas (night-time soap operas) with their parents; and blend Mexican rice with spaghetti sauce and spread peanut butter and jelly on tortillas.

Advertising and marketing executives have different perspectives on how to best reach these "young biculturals." For example, research manning conducted for the California Milk Processor Board on targeting English versions of its popular "Cot Milk?" ads to Hispanic teens found that they reacted enthusiastically to the ads. The CMPB had considered doing the ads in Spanglish (a combination of English and Spanish) but found that the language used was not a major issue for teens, as they reacted to ideas, not language. However, a 2000 study of Hispanic teens by the Roslow Research Group found that advertising to bilingual Hispanics in Spanish is significantly more effective than advertising to them in English. English ads were 28 percent less effective than Spanish ads in terms of ad recall, 54 percent less effective in terms of persuasion, and 14 percent less effective in terms of communication.

The California Milk Processor Board has decided that it is important to develop ads that appeal to bicultural teens. Recently, its ad agency worked with Latino students from the Art Center College of Design in Pasadena to develop a commercial based on a Hispanic cultural myth that has long been used to scare kids straight. When Hispanic kids misbehave, their parents threaten that La Llorona ("the weeping woman") will come to claim them. Basically, she's a boogiewoman for bambinos. In the spot the ghostly figure, clad in flowing gown and veil, wails as she wanders through a house. Walking through a wall, the specter enters the kitchen and opens the refrigerator. Rather abruptly, her tears terminate. "Leche!" she exclaims, lunging at the half gallon of milk needed to wash down the Mexican pastry she clutches. But sadly for La Llorona, the carton is empty, so the tears resume and the "Got milk?" tagline appears.

While the La Llorona ad targets bicultural teens through mainstream media, it relies on only one word of dialogue and thus may appeal to non-Hispanics as well. In fact, marketers are finding that by targeting Hispanic youth they may also attract the more general teen market. Many have noted the tremendous popularity of Hispanic entertainers such as Ricky Martin, Jennifer Lopez, Marc Anthony, and Shakira, and their crossover appeal to non-Hispanic teens. As one agency executive notes: "It's very cool to be Hispanic at this age. It almost makes them more attractive, exotic."

Sources: Becky Ebenkamp, "A House Lacking in Lactose? Intolerable," Brandweek, Jan. 21, 2002, p. 23; Jeffery D. Zbar, "Hispanic Teens Set Urban Beat," Advertising Age, June 25,2001, p. S6; Rick Wartz-man, "When You Translate Got Milk' for Latinos, What Do You Get?" The Wall Street Journal, June 3,1999, pp. Al,10.

In Chapter 2 simple models of the communication process and some essential features to the process were discussed. These models provide us with a foundation for a more elaborate and integrated model in order to attempt to answer the following questions:

How is communication initiated?

What are the critical factors that effect the communications process?

What changes are likely to occur in a receiver as a result of receiving a message?

GRAPHIC MODELS

Fig. 5.1 represents a more comprehensive communication model. It represents that the sender selects the information (message), encodes this message, and selects an appropriate channel (medium) through which he transmits the encoded message to the receiver. After receiving this encoded message, the receiver decodes (interprets) the message according to his own frame of reference and then responds or does not respond, depending on the accuracy of

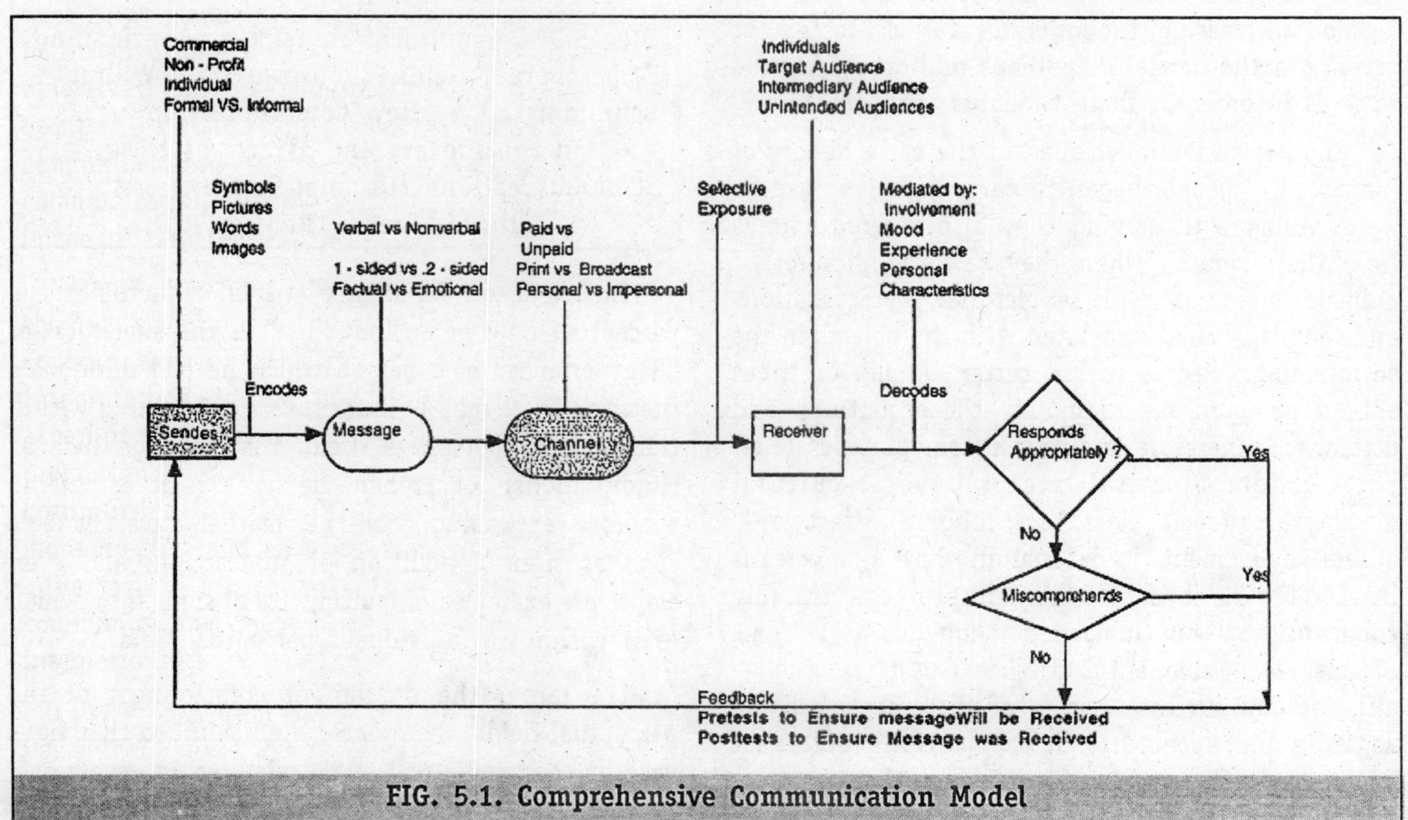

FIG. 5.1. Comprehensive Communication Model

interpretation and the persuasiveness of the transmitted message.

In all the communications model discussed so far, comprehension — the amount of meaning accurately derived from the message, i.e., encoding and decoding the message has a significant importance. Comprehension is a function of the message characteristics, the receiver's opportunity and ability to process the message and the receiver's motivation.[1] Human beings share their thoughts with other members of the society. Contact with the environment, which includes other people also, is through the sensory system — eyes, ears etc. A person's thought, as a mental unit, cannot be detected by another person's sensory system. Thought itself cannot simply be picked up and placed in another person's head. Therefore, there must be some vehicle that both sender and receiver can use which is detectable by their sensory systems.

One way of sharing a thought with another is simply by way of showing a thing. He would be able to see it, touch it or even smell it. And further, if the person wants to share a thought about another thing with you, he would show you the next thing. Once again you see it, touch it, smell it and taste it. This method of sharing thoughts creates a problem of carrying a thousands of, perhaps millions of objects with us in order to share thoughts with others.

Another system developed in the early history of human race, people began to carve pictures on cave walls. Along with carving they also uttered sounds from their mouths when they saw the pictures of animals and people. These pictorial representations and sounds became associated with the objects in the surroundings. People within certain family or tribes shared common meanings for these pictures and utterances. Therefore, a person's demographics (e.g., age, gender, marital status), socio-cultural memberships (social class, race, religion), lifestyle — all are key elements in determining how a message is interpreted. A bachelor may interpret a friendly comment from his unmarried neighbour as a 'come on' message. Personality, attitudes, past learning — all affect how a message is decoded. Perception based as it is on expectations, motivations and past experience, influence message interpretation to a great extent.

Therefore, the sender stores within his mind, a set of signs which are used to represent his thoughts. He transmits his encoded thoughts into the receivers environment, through the transmitting system, in this case through the voice box. The receiver detects the sound waves which after passing through the air, by using his sensory system, his ears in the present example. The receiver decodes the received encoded stimuli (messages in the form of sign), using his mental sign system, in order to share thoughts with the sender.

This process of communication can be effective only when the sender uses signs which the receiver can decode. The sender has to encode his thoughts using signs which are common to both his and his receivers field of experience. Schramm[2] has illustrated this point by using overlapping circles, as shown in Fig. 5.2.

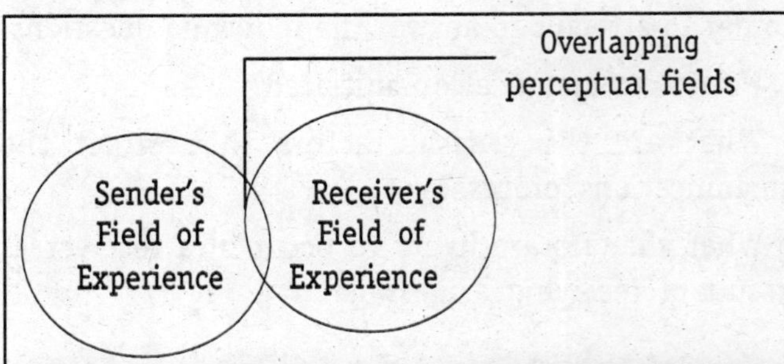

FIG. 5.2. Communication requires overlapping perceptual fields. (Redrawn from Wilbur Schramm (ed.), "How Communication works," in the Process and Effects of Mass Communications (Urbana: The University of Illinois Press, 1965), p. 6)

The field of experience, which is actually the perceptual field of an individual, is the sum total of all experiences of a person which he had during his lifetime. There may be numerous signs coming within the scope of perceptual field. His language such as Hindi, English or French, gestures such as raising eyebrows or waving good-bye, mathematical symbols such as sign of addition or subtraction, and even smiles are examples of multiplicity of signs form which exist within an individual's perceptual field.

The larger the overlap of commonness of the perceptual fields, the greater the likelihood that signs used by the sender will be decoded by the receiver. If the sender uses signs not common to both fields, the receiver will be unable to decode the message. To illustrate, consider a sender who sends you a message in Morse code. If you have never learned the code (i.e., if it is not in your perceptual field), you will not be able to share thought with the sender. So, while transmitting the message in marketing communications, the marketer has to keep in mind the overlapping perceptual fields to whom the message is intended to, in order to force the buyer to become in action. This overlapping perceptual field is one of the essentials of good communication process in marketing. Good communication is stimulating as a mug of black coffee and just as hard to sleep after.

Therefore, keeping in view the marketing communications aspect, the model of the communications process can be depicted as in Fig. 5.3. The reader will notice that in this model for meeting the objective of clarification and emphasis, the important elements in the communications process, discussed so far, have been intentionally diagrammed outside the perceptual fields of the sender and the receiver.

VERBAL MODELS

Till now we have discussed the graphic models of the communications process. Harold Lasswell has given us a useful verbal model of communications process by posing certain basic questions[3]:

Who?

Says what?

In which channels?

To whom?

With what effect?

Laswell model of communications process describes the elements in communication but fails to describe their inter-relationships. Even then, its real value lies in the area of research. This model identifies five basic areas of analysis which have been shown in the Table 5.1 given below:

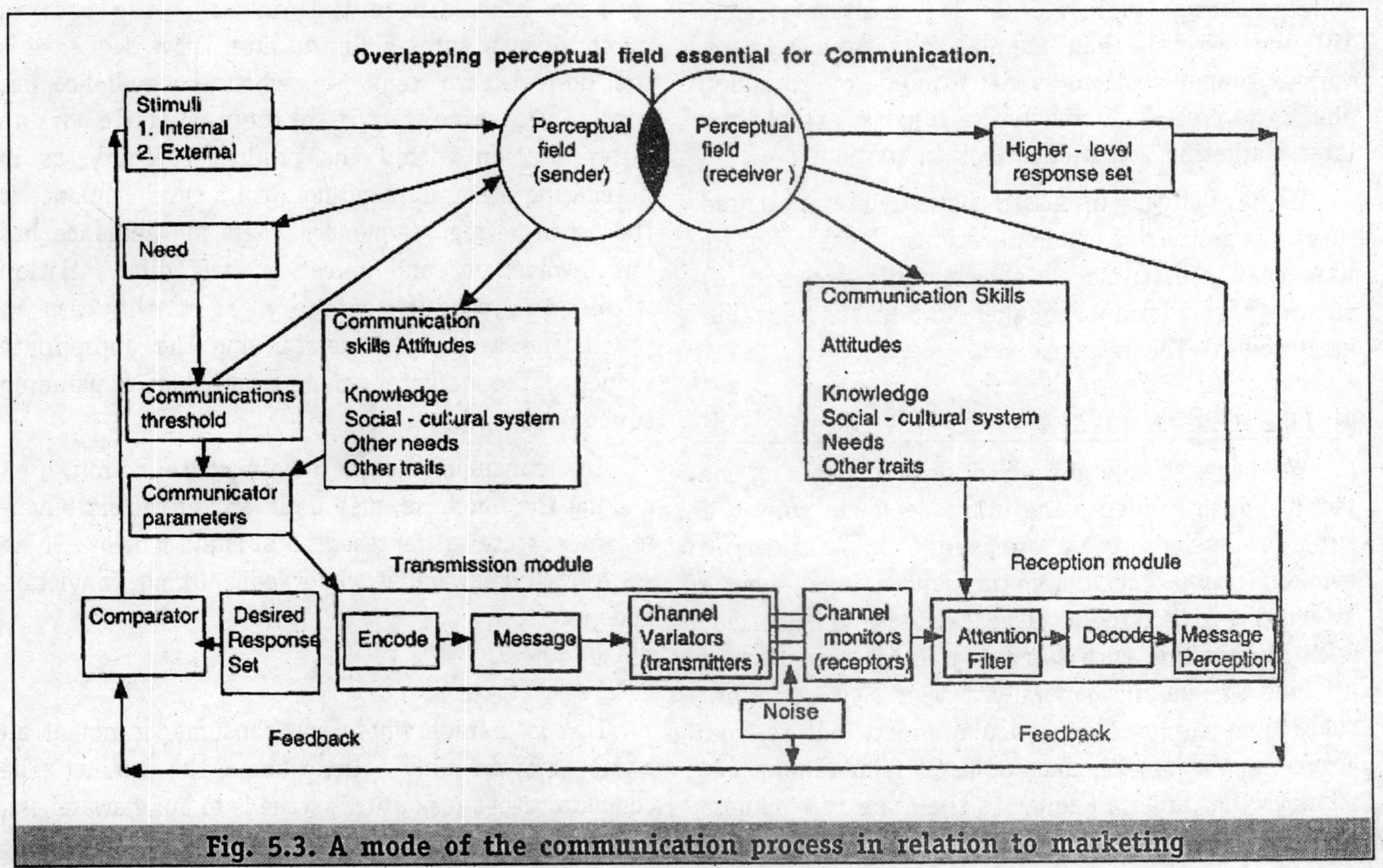

Fig. 5.3. A mode of the communication process in relation to marketing

TABLE 5.1
Basic Areas in Laswell Model

Model	*Areas of Analysis*
Who?	Source analysis
Says what?	Content analysis
In which channel?	Media analysis
To whom?	Audience analysis
With what effect?	Effects analysis

Source analysis is concerned with who is talking, content analysis with what is being said, media analysis with channels, audience analysis with who is listening, and effects analysis with audience impact.[4]

Though the Lasswell model is useful from the standpoint of posing critical questions for research, most verbal models are of limited usefulness. Generally, they will fail to show the dynamism of the communications process. This failure is in part due to the static nature of words.[5]

As we have seen, a number of models come in different forms, according to the intended use by the model builder. Some models are useful for conceptualising a process, others for guiding a research. Till now, we have had an elaborate discussion on various communications model to guide our thinking about the process of communications as a whole and later marketing communications in particular.

We have already discussed the two ideas presented in our definition of communications. Specifically, we have examined (*i*) models of communication and (*ii*) the ways of sharing thought. Now let us turn our attention to 'The response set.'

THE RESPONSE SET

We have already discussed briefly some of the factors which influence the initial set of responses, a receiver makes to a message. In marketing communications, generally, the sender (marketer) is attempting to gain the receiver's (customers) agreement with his position with some degree of conviction or attitude change and generally a desired overt action, such as purchase of a particular product or service. Therefore, a marketing communicator should know how to move the target audience to the state of readiness to make a purchase.

The marketer can be seeking a cognitive, affective, or behavioural response from the target audience. That is, the marketer might want to put something into the consumer's mind, change the consumer's attitude, or get the consumer to act. Even here, there are different models of consumer-response stages. Figure 5.4 shows the four best-known response hierarchy models.

All of these models assume that the buyer passes through a cognitive, affective, and behavioural stage, in that order. This sequence is the 'learn-feel-do' sequence and is appropriate when the audience has high involvement with a product category perceived to have high differentiation, as is the case in purchasing an automobile. An alternative sequence is the 'do-feel-learn' sequence, when the audience has high involvement but perceives little or no differentiation within the product category, as in purchasing aluminium siding. Still a third sequence is the 'learn-do-feel' sequence, when the audience has low involvement and perceives little differentiation within the product category, as is the case in purchasing salt. By understanding the appropriate sequence, the marketer can do a better job of planning communications.[6]

The consumer before coming into action, *i.e.*, making the purchase, may be in any of the six buyer-readiness states as represented in Fig. 5.5 below. These states include awareness, knowledge, liking, conviction and purchase.

Awareness

This is a stage where the consumer is not at all aware or aware only a little about the product. The communicator's task at this stage is to build awareness, may be letting the consumer let know the name, the

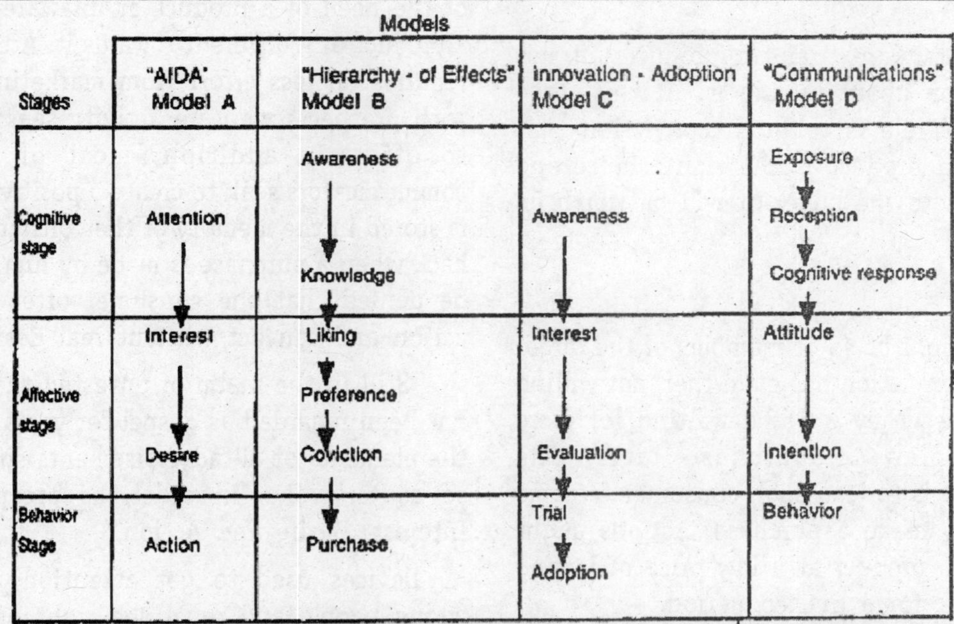

FIG. 5.4. Response Hierarchy Models Sources:
(a) E. K. Strong, The Psychology of Selliing (New York: McGraw. Hill, 1925), p.9;
(b) Robert J. Lavidge and Gary A. Steiner, "A Model for Predictive Measurements of Advertising Effectiveness," 'Journal of Marketing, October 1961, p. 61;
(c) Everett M. Rogers, Diffusion of Innovations (New York; Free Press 1962), pp. 79-86;
(d) various sources.

process can start with simple messages repeating the name of the company, product or service.

Knowledge

The next stage of consumer readiness is knowledge state. There exists a possibility that the target audience might have some information-knowledge about the company, product or service. But there is all possibility that the target audience might like to have much more knowledge about it.

Liking

Let us assume that the target market has the knowledge about the product, the vital question arise, as to how do they feel about it. If the response looks unfavourable, the communicator has to find out why the response is unfavourable. After finding this fact, the communicator has to develop his communication campaign.

Preference

There is a possibility that the target market might like the product but even then not to prefer it to make a purchase. In such a case, the communicator has to promote the various qualities, utilities, value, performance, and other features of the product.

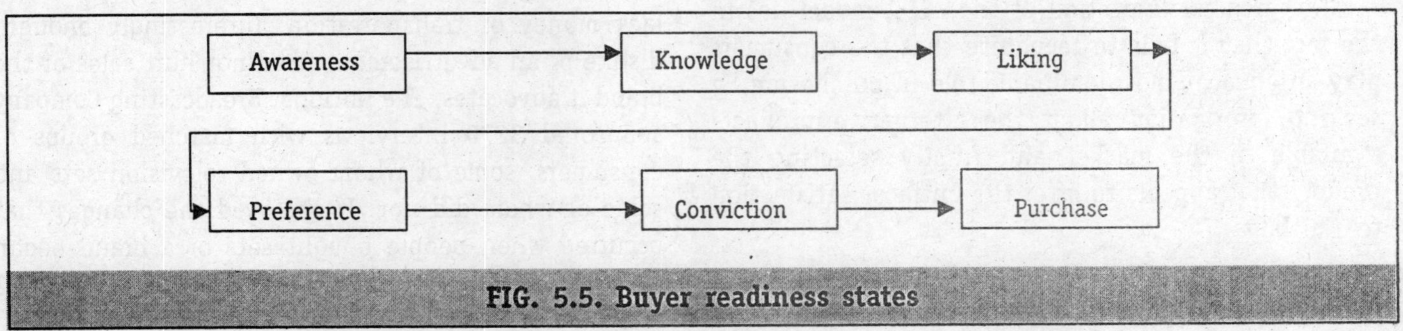

FIG. 5.5. Buyer readiness states

Conviction

A target market might prefer a product but not develop a conviction about buying it. At this stage the communicator's role is to build conviction that purchasing the said product is the right choice and would be beneficial to the buyer, it will be worth its money.

Purchase

Finally, there might be some members of the target market who have conviction but even then not willing to make a purchase. They may be waiting for more information or plan to purchase later. The communicator's role is to lead such consumer to come into action, i.e., to make a purchase. Actions might include offering the product at a low price or letting the consumer try it for a limited period.

Let us have some more insights into this aspect as several models and theories have been developed from time to time by various researchers to help the marketing communications to interpret the buyer's purchase process.

AIDA Model

The letters in the acronym denotes — Attention, Interest, Desire and Action. This is perhaps one of the early models developed as far back as twentieth century. According to this model of marketing communications, even any effective impersonal sales presentation attracts Attention, gains Interest, arouse a Desire and ultimately results in Action. No doubt, this is a passive model depicting the consumer as basically submissive to the self serving interest and promotional efforts of marketing communications. In this model, the consumers are perceived as impulsive and irrational purchasers. They are considered ready to yield to the arms and aims of marketers much easily.

The greatest limitation of the AIDA model lies in the fact that it fails to recognise that the consumers play an equal, if not dominant, role in purchasing by seeking information about the alternative products available in the market and finally selecting the product that appears to offer the outmost satisfaction to the buyer.

No doubt a message or information generates interest and desire if the target audience is not aware of the need of a product or unaware of any need for a product or indifferent towards it. Attracting attention requires far less effort from marketing communicator with prospects who are activity seeking what he has to offer. In addition, most of the marketing communicators seek to create a positive attitude, which is stored in the memory of the consumer to be recalled back when a purchase is made by him. The fact cannot be denied that the consumer often desires without action and can act without real desire.

Still in the realm of untested theory, although it has been regarded as gospel for years, is the idea that the elements of all advertisements should be ordered, so as to evoke, in order, as prospects Attention, Interest, Desire and Action.[7]

Devices used to get attention may attract the wrong people and repel the right ones: 65% in one test audience recalled the girl in a white bathing suit who appeared in a TV commercial, but only 10% could remember what she was advertising.

Understanding does not necessarily create change in attitude. When groups of 500 to 1000 soldiers in World War II were shown a film, Battle of Britain, designed to increase their motivation to serve in the armed services, a familiar 'funnel effect' was shown.[8] Some 78% of those who saw the film (compared with 21% who did not see it) could tell how the British safeguarded planes on the ground from enemy attack. The film caused an increase of 27 percentage points in agreement that British resistance gave the United States time to build up its own military strength. But the film did not cause GI's to look more favourably on their involvement in the war. Films on prejudice or socio-economic attitudes have shown similar results: learning of facts but failure to accept the conclusions that the facts imply.

Not everyone who believes a message will act on it: the drugstore may be closed, or the prospect may lack money or transportation. Interestingly enough, dislike of an advertisement need not hurt sales of the brand it advocates. The National Broadcasting Company sponsored 3270 interviews with matched groups of consumers, some of whom owned television sets and some of whom did not. It observed the changes that occurred when people bought sets or a brand began to advertise on television, studying purchases of 12 different products including gasoline, cigarettes, toothpaste, and coffee.[9] Viewers, even those who disliked a commercial, bought more of brands advertised on TV than did non-viewers. On the other hand, a study was done in which matched groups of soldiers were exposed to several messages which had been rated on a 100 point like-dislike scale urging them to take care of their shoes.[10] A subsequent check of actual shoe care showed it improved most among men exposed to the best-liked messages and least among those who got messages ranked in the middle. An advertising man says that when consumer juries pick advertisements they like, positive appeals win out; coupon tests of the same advertisements show that actual buying behaviour favours negative appeals.

Mere repetition of a brand name, however irritating, may fix it so firmly in our minds that when someone says toothpaste we reply 'Pepsodent' as automatically as we say 'cat,' when someone says 'dog.' Neither awareness nor understanding nor belief seems to be involved. Behaviour need not result from attitudes. It may be unrelated to them or it may be cause rather than effect. Living in integrated housing has changed the attitudes toward integration. Making speeches saying that college students face three years of military service has changed attitudes toward the draft. Pupils induced to argue in favour of a type of comic book they did not like, have changed their comic-book preference.[11]

Even if research were to provide guidelines for designers of both marketing mix and message, we seem to be a long way from programming such guidelines for a computer. Creative individuals are needed to design mix and message, and the environment needed for such a job.

LAVIDGE-STEINER MODEL

These two behavioural scientists suggested a conceptualised model of covert responses through which an individual moves to the overt behaviour of action, i.e., finally purchasing a product or service. He suggests that there is a definite sequence of events which occurs from initial awareness to a final action such as a purchase. This model was developed as far back in 1961 and is depicted in Fig. 5.6.

According to this model, the sequence of events — unawareness, awareness, knowledge, liking, preference, conviction and purchase always occurs for familiar events. The only difference between new and familiar message is the amount of time spent at each stage of process.[12]

Each of the steps is tied to three basic psychological states — cognitive, affective, and conative. The cognitive dimension refers to the realm of thought, the affective dimension to the realm of emotions, and the conative dimension to the realm of motives. The distance between each step varies. Lavidge and Steiner point out, for example, that "The distance from awareness to preference may be very slight, while the distance from preference to purchase is very extreme." Furthermore, the length of time to move through the sequence of stages can vary with the commitment required on the part of the receiver.

The model is not without its critics. One of the staunchest critics is Kristian Palda, who contends that, with few exceptions, there is no empirical evidence to support the sequential assumption or the theory that the outcome of previous stages has a mediating effect on succeeding stages.[13] In effect, he suggests that there are no surrogate measures of communications effectiveness. Further- more, he believes the only measure of success is the actual achievement of behaviour modification. In business this would mean a change in the level of sales.

Though the Lavidge-Steiner model has not been supported by empirical evidence, it does provide a conceptual framework for thinking about the sequence of events which occurs from initial awareness to a final action such as purchasing.

McGUIRE MODEL

Another model of information processing to help the marketing communicators was presented by William J. McGuire. This model was similar to that of Lavidge and Steiner that it also hypothesises a hierarchy of effects.[14] According to the proposer of the model — McGuire — there exists five sequential events. Each of these events having a probability of occurring which determine the likelihood that a person will be persuaded to perform a given behaviour a sixth event, such as making a purchase. The probability of an actual purchase taking place is the joint probability or product of all the six events occurring.

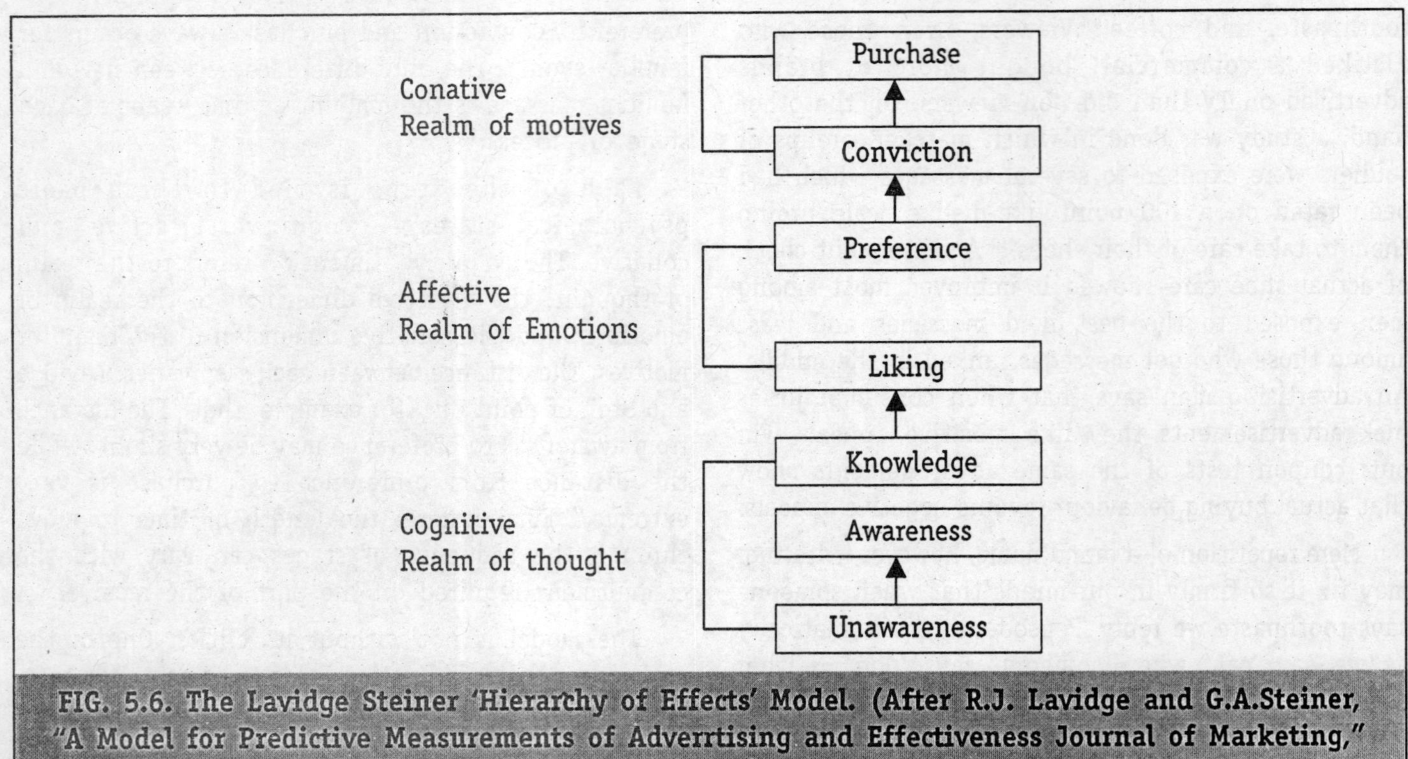

FIG. 5.6. The Lavidge Steiner 'Hierarchy of Effects' Model. (After R.J. Lavidge and G.A.Steiner, "A Model for Predictive Measurements of Advertising and Effectiveness Journal of Marketing," Vol. 25, pp. 59-62, October 1961.)

As represented in Fig. 5.7, above, the message has associated with it a certain degree of probability with it of being presented to a person. Similarly, there is a degree of probability attached to the event that the consumer will attend to the message given to him and so on. The possibility that the person will reach to a given stage in the hierarchy, such as attitude change, is contingent upon the probabilities attributed to each of the stage upto and including 'yielding' stage. Thus, **Probability of Attitude Change = P(p). P(a). P(c). P(y).**

For the purpose of marketing communications, it is not necessary to be more concerned with the

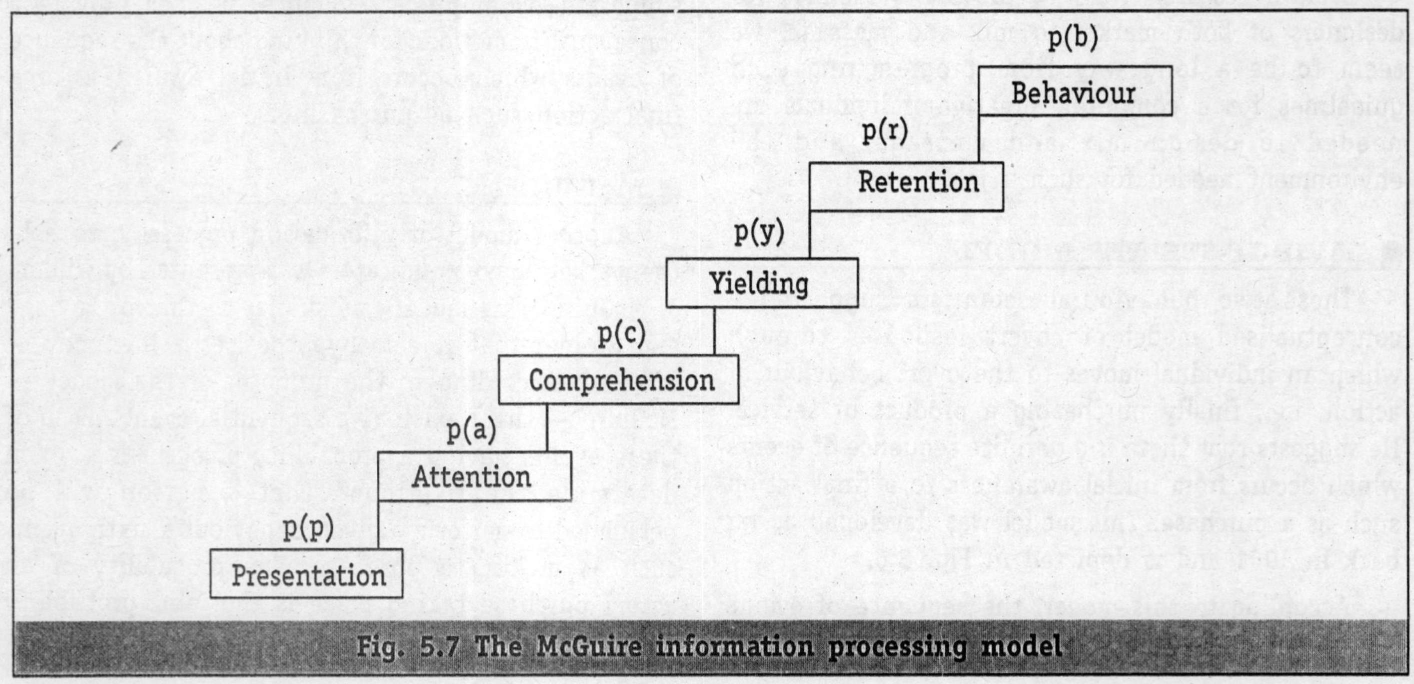

Fig. 5.7 The McGuire information processing model

mathematical aspect of this model, but rather to recognise the conceptual thinking involved in the information processing stages. More significantly, one should recognise the mediating processes occurring between the presentation of the message and the final outcome or behaviour that the marketing communicator is attempting to achieve.

DAGMAR MODEL

In the past, companies defined advertising objectives in terms of sales, for example a likely objective for advertising would be to increase sales by 10 percent. With this kind of objective, advertising bore the entire responsibility for sales. When the Association of National Advertisers sponsored a study entitled, 'Defining Advertising Goals' in 1961, it turned the thinking of a lot of people around about 180 degrees on this whole matter of copy testing.

What Russell H. Colley, had to say was this:

Advertising's job, purely and simply, is to communicate to a a defined audience information and a frame of mind that stimulates action. Advertisings' success or failure, depends upon how well it communicates the desired information and attitudes to the right people at the right time and at the right cost.[15]

Colley emphasises that relating advertising to sales is totally unrealistic. He stressed that sales are influenced by the total mix of the marketing variables, where advertising is only one ingredient blended with personal selling, price, package and various other marketing forces.

According to Colley, before an attempt at defining the goals is made, one must look into the various marketing forces which move the people towards buying action. The second set of forces is the countervailing forces which move the people away from the product such as competition, memory lapse, sales resistance and marketing attrition. Having studied both the positive and negative forces, one must study the target audience to be reached, who like the colours of a rainbow are at successive levels of 'communications spectrum' ranging from Unawareness, Awareness, Comprehension, Conviction and Action. Though one may have reservations regarding the movement of people through successive stages, yet it does provide a useful frame for definition of advertising goals. For instance, in case of a new product, one may define the advertising goals as creation of say 50 percent of awareness in the first year amongst the target audience. As regards established products, the goals may be defined by changing the various levels of communications spectrum.

He further stresses that marketers should focus their attention upon the achievement and measurement of communication goals, for which measuring tools exists. What should be measured of course is the anatomy of a sale; by answering the following questions:

1. How well did I get your attention?
2. How great did I make your desire?
3. To what on extent did I convince you?
4. What amount of action did I get?
5. How well did I succeed in communicating the knowledge of the product to my customers?

If I succeed measurably well, I got their money's worth. If I failed they did not get their money's worth.[16]

Thus, Colley's model more popularly known as Dagmar model where,

D stands for Defining
A for Advertising
G for Goals
M for Measured
A for Advertising
R for Results

suggests a series of stages through which a prospect moves from total unawareness of the firm's offering to purchase, like the Lavidge-Steiner and McGuire models. These stages can be represented as in Fig. 5.8.

Although the model is quite simple, its effect on the advertising community has been substantial. The model has made business executives conscious of the desirability of measuring the results of the firm's total marketing communications efforts at several points in the process rather than looking only to sales.

Colley distinguished fifty two possible advertising goals for measured advertising results in his outlined method — DAGMAR — for turning advertising objectives into specific measurable goals. An advertising

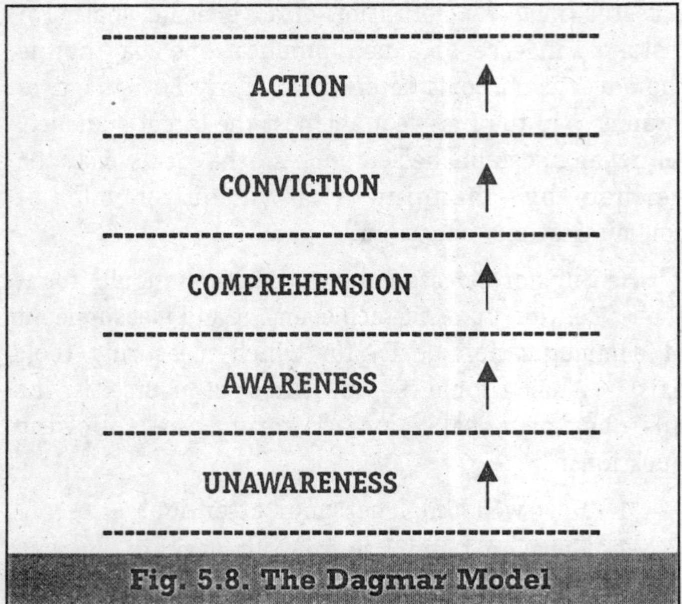

Fig. 5.8. The Dagmar Model

goal is a specific communication task to be accomplished among a defined audience in a given period of time.

The development of operational objectives usually starts with a consideration of the ultimate behaviour that advertising is to influence. Is it to maintain the loyalty of existing customers, to attract new ones or to generate insights to a retailer operational objectives provide criteria for decision-making and standards against which to evaluate performance, and serve as a communication tool. Short run sales usually do not provide a basis for operational objectives for two reasons:

(*i*) Advertising is usually only one of the many factors influencing sales and

(*ii*) The impact of advertising often occurs primarily over the long run.

Whatever the ultimate behaviour, it should be possible to conceptualise and perhaps estimate its value to the firm hopefully in terms of the profit stream over time. There may be behavioural measures, For example, the number of new customers attracted that may provide the basis for advertising objectives. However, it is usually helpful to consider the communication and decision process that will lead to the desired behaviour and to identify key intervening variables in that process. These intervening variables, such as brand awareness, image or attitude will then, either by themselves or it can function with behavioural measures, provide the basis of advertising objectives. Further, to provide information for the development of objectives it is useful to study the market dynamics and to determine the various brand images and consumer attitudes that prevail.

One possible target for advertising is made up of potential new customers. The number of people enticed into trying the brand may then form the basis for advertising objectives. Often, however a process of learning and attitude development precedes the decision to try the brand, and advertising concentrates more profitably on this process. It may also attempt to increase or maintain the loyalty of existing customers. Advertising may also increase the product usage of existing customer. This approach to setting objectives is a refinement and extension of DAGMAR's approach. DAGMAR defines advertising goal as a specific communication task, to be accomplished among a defined audience in a given time period. Thus a communication task is based on a hierarchy model of the communication process involving awareness, comprehension, conviction and action. The goal is specific, with a definite measure, a starting point, a defined audience and a fixed time period. In defining the audience, a particularly useful segmentation scheme is based on the steps in the hierarchy model. Thus, it may be useful to direct a campaign to an audience that is not aware of the brand to aid those implementing the approach. DAGMAR suggests that the decision maker analyse the situation in terms of merchandise, markets, motives, messages, media and measurement.

Although it is often difficult to trace the effect of advertising on sales, it is fairly easy to trace the effect of advertising on ideas. One can tell whether the advertising has impressed you, or gotten across to you, or convinced you or interested you, or fixed something in your mind. And what is more interesting, one can tell you to what extent the advertising has done the above things in comparison to the competitor's advertising.

By introducing the behavioural science theory into advertising management, DAGMAR provides the framework for the development of more operational objective. However, this has been challenged through the years on several fronts. Some critics are of the opinion that the only appropriate measure of advertising is to sell. Another objection is that it is difficult to select a hierarchy level on which to base objectives, and to know how to move people up the hierarchy.

Others believe that the approach is limited by measurement problems and noise in the system. By providing guidance to operating people, DAGMAR is said to inhibit the development of the great idea. The most fundamental attack is that the hierarchy model of the communication process is not appropriate. There is for example, empirical evidence that changes in behaviour may precede and cause changes in attitudes in some situations.

Refinements of DAGMAR made an attempt to draw research to improve the communication model on which DAGMAR was based. In refinement, the emphasis has to determine which of the many models of the communication process will be appropriate in a given application. Of late, more analytical models have been developed that make the link between intervening variables and behaviour.

An important question in many advertising campaigns is to determine which intervening variable should be the focus of the campaign. Our approach is to determine to those hierarchy levels that have not yet been reached by a large number of potential customers. An extension would not only consider the size of the segment but the difficulty and therefore the cost of moving them up the hierarchy, as well as the likelihood of their eventually making the desired decision once they have moved up.

To implement the DAGMAR approach people often need to be influenced about the particular intervening variable. For a durable product one method is to compare it with the brand image of other brands. Another method was given by CLAY CAMP and LIDDY in their model, which made an attempt to specify the primary variables which determine the achievement of adequate levels of awareness and trial purchasing. A model test showed that advertising expenditures were important contribution to awareness if the advertising quality was high and that the awareness level in turn, contributed to trial purchasing.

COMPARISON OF RESPONSE MODELS

We have discussed the models of communications responses in the field of marketing. The intention was to bring out the fact that a receiver's response to a message involves more than a simple observable form of behaviour in marketing communications. Instead, we observed that normally several mediating covert responses occur between the presentation of a message and an action sought by the communicator. In many instances, none, or only a selected few of the intervening responses occur.

We can compare the similarities in the three models of communications responses and the resulting synthesis can serve as a foundation for discussing these responses in detail in our next chapters. Glancing Table 5.2, below, one can notice that like McGuire model, all the models begin with an initial stage of unawareness. The initial response is an awareness of or attention to a message. The next stage in the process, above awareness stage, is known as 'comprehension' or 'knowledge' stage. Both of this imply that some level of understanding should take place

TABLE 5.2

A Comparison and Synthesis of the Lavidge-Steiner, McGuire, and DAGMAR Models

Lavidgesteiner	*DAGMAR*	*McGuire*	*Synthesis*
Purchase	Action	Behaviour Retention	Action Learning
Conviction Preference Liking	Conviction	Yielding	Attitude development and change (persuasion)
Knowledge	Comprehersion	Comprehersion	Understanding (a function of the perceptual process)
Awareness	Awareness	Attention	Attention/awareness
Unawareness	Unawareness	Presentation	Unawareness

next in the response hierarchy. This response is the outcome of the perceptual process and the receiver applies his learning experiences to the messages so that he may assign some meaning to it.

The next stage in the response process is 'yielding' or 'conviction.' The Lavidge -Steiner model of communications responses precedes conviction with 'liking' and 'preference.' These are basically the refinements of the same notion of attitude development and change. This response is responsible for directing our attention to the field of persuasion.

The McGuire model of communications responses, is the only model, which emphasises that the previous response to a message should be necessarily retained. This aspect has been referred as 'retention.' Basically this is a function of learning process. The positioning of 'retention' between yielding and behaviour is arguable. There exists all possibly that can and more often does occur at earlier response stages, also. Let us consider an example, there is all likelihood that a person might retain a large amount of information regarding a brand, also during the comprehension stage. It is not necessary that during the comprehension stage the person has 'yielding' to the persuasive components of a message.

However, the final response, common to all these models is referred to 'action.' Lavidge and Steiner refer this action stage as 'purchase', whereas McGuire uses the term 'behaviour' instead of 'action,' No doubt, 'action' is a more general term since marketers are often interested in influencing other forms of behaviour also beside purchase. But even all these three terms can be termed as synonyms, for discussion in marketing communications.

ANOTHER PERSPECTIVE

Does Advertising Ignore Older Consumers?

In early 2002, a battle was waged between two of the major television networks, CBS and ABC, over The Late Show with David Letterman. ABC was trying to lure Letterman's show away from CBS to replace Nightline, the news show hosted by Ted Koppel, which it had been airing in the late-night time slot for 22 years. The battle was being fought mainly because Letterman is more popular among younger viewers between the key ages of 18 to 32 and brings in $100 million more in advertising revenue each year than Nightline. Observers argued that the tug-of-war over Letterman is just another example of advertisers' obsession with younger consumers. While aging baby boomers may argue they are more active, more fit, more adventurous, and more experimental than their predecessors, they are still of less interest to advertisers than younger consumers.

It has often been argued that people who work in advertising are different from the typical consumers who represent the target markets for their clients' products and services. Some say advertising may better reflect those who work in the industry than the consuming public, as it is really about the people who create it, not about the consumers who actually buy the products being advertised. A study conducted a few years ago on ageism in advertising considered potential problems that might arise because of age differences between agency personnel and older consumers. The study found that professionals who work in advertising agencies are much younger than the U.S. adult population. Nearly 40 percent of ad agency professional staff are between the ages of 30 and 39, while only 20 percent of all adults are in their 30s.

The youth bias is particularly evident in the creative departments. Agency employment drops like a rock after age 40, particularly among those involved in creating the ads. As a result, agencies rarely have creative professionals with a true understanding of life after age 40, not to mention life after 50 or 60. Richard Lee, a principal of High-Yield Marketing, the company that conducted the study, notes: "Most young agency staff, reflective of their life phase, are fixated on creating advertising that is hip, cool, impressive to their peers, and award-winning. This is more fulfilling than creating advertising for people with out-dated tastes, who wouldn't know Smashing Pumpkins if they stepped on them."

Advertisers who are unable to connect with older consumers may be squandering opportunities to reach a valuable market. While nearly 40 percent of American adults are 50 or older and they control more than 50 percent of the U.S.'s discretionary income, they receive only 10 percent of the advertising messages. Many observers wonder why advertisers remain focused on consumers in their teens, 20s, and early 30s when spending power is becoming progressively more concentrated among those age 50 and older. Some point to the conventional wisdom in marketing and advertising that brand loyalties and consumer preferences form early and once formed, stay pretty much the same. Older people are stereotyped and are unlikely to change brands and try something new.

Another reason for the youth bias stems from the problem of advertisers' not wanting to have their brands perceived as being for older consumers for fear of damaging their image among younger people. As the senior vice president of Zenith Media notes: "For a lot of brands we work with, it's sexier to advertise to the younger consumers who are trendier, much more fashion forward, very social and very much in the public eye. With marketing dollars so limited and precious, you want to bet on the future."

Of course, not everyone in the advertising industry agrees with the findings of the ageism study. One agency executive calls the conclusions ridiculous, noting that "we have people of every age segment here." There are, of course, examples of excellent advertising targeted at mature consumers, and new media are being introduced to reach the over-50 crowd.

Many believe, however, that the youth bias in advertising is still a major problem. They note that the best hope for the demise of the primary focus on youth in advertising is the marketing people who are growing and maturing themselves. Some feel that it has finally dawned on advertisers that they ought to follow the green, which is quickly going gray, and that older consumers are more hip. As one ad executive noted: "Sixty-year-olds don't think like they did in the last generation. Sixty-year-olds in the last generation wore plaid pants."

Sources: Hillary Chura, "Boomers Hope to Break Age-Old Ad Myth," Advertising Age, May 13,2002, p. 16; Richard Lee, "The Youth Bias in Advertising," American Demographics, January 1997, pp. 47 50.

REFERENCES

1. David Glen Mick, 'Levels of Subjective Comprehension in Advertising Processing and Their Relations to Advertising Perceptions, Attitudes and Memory', *Journal of Consumer Research,* 18, March 1992, pp. 411-24.
2. Wilbur Schramm, 'The Process, and Effects of Mass Communications', Urbana, The University of Illions Press, 1965, p. 6.
3. Harold D. Lassewell, 'The Structure and Function of Communication in Society', in Wilbur Schramm (ed.) *Mass Communications,* Urbana, The University of Illions Press, 1960, p. 117.
4. *Ibid.*, pp. 117-118.
5. John Ball and Francis C. Byrnes (eds.), 'Principles and Practice in Visual Communications,' National Education Association, Washington, 1960.
6. Michael L. Ray, 'Advertising and Communications Management', Englewood, Cliffs, N.J. Prentice Hall, 1982.
7. Kristan S. Palda, 'The Hypothesis of a Hierarchy of Effects: A Partial Evaluation', *Journal of Marketing Research,* Vol. 3, pp. 13-24, February 1966.
8. C.I. Hovland *et al.*, 'Experiments on Mass Communication, (Princeton, N.J.: Princeton University Press,1949).
9. Thomas E. Coffin and Jack B. Landis, How Television Changes Strangers Into Customers (New York: NBC television,1955).
10. *Ibid.*
11. Herbert C. Kelman, 'Attitude Change, as a Function of Response Restriction,' Human Relations, Vol. 6, pp. 185-214.
12. Robert J., Lavidge and Gary A. Steiner, 'A Model for Predictive Measurements of Advertising Effectiveness', *Journal of Marketing,* Vol. 25, pp. 58-62, October 1961.
13. Kristan S. Palda, 'The Hypothesis of a Hierarchy of Effects: A Partial Evaluation', *Journal of Marketing Research,* Vol. 3, pp. 13-24. February 1966.
14. Thomas S. Robertson, Consumer Behaviour (Glenview, III: Scott, Foresman and Com. 1970), pp. 46-77 in reference to Wiliam J. McGuire, 'An Information Processing Model of Advertising Effectiveness,' paper presented at the Symposium on Behaviour and Management Science in Marketing Centre for Continuing Education, the University of Chicago, July 1969.
15. Russell H. Colley, 'Defining Advertising Goals,' in Tayor W. Meloan, Samuel V. Smith, and John, J. Whealty (eds.), 'Managerial Marketing Policies and Decisions' (Boston: Houghton Miffin Com. 1970), pp. 326-335, Reprinted from 'Defining Advertising Goals for Measured Advertising Results' (New York: Association for National Advertisers, Inc., 1961). pp. 49-69.
16. *Ibid.*

CHAPTER 6

INTEGRATED MARKETING COMMUNICATIONS

EVERYTHING OLD IS NEW AGAIN

Advertising generally prides itself on being ahead of the curve and helping to create and define popular culture rather than trying to revisit it. However, recently many advertisers have been bringing back some of their classic advertising characters and commercials rather than looking for new creative ideas. The D'Arcy Masius Benton & Bowles agency brought back the original "Mr. Whipple" the stern grocer known for his famous request, "Please don't squeeze the Charmin," in commercials for the brand. The ads, which ran over a period of 18 months, resulted in an onslaught of e-mails and letters from consumers indicating their fondness for the iconic character. The Quaker company brought back the classic "Mikey" commercial for Life cereal, which first aired in 1972 and ran for 12 years. The spot features a cute three-year-old boy who hates everything but likes the taste of Life cereal when he tries it. The director of account planning at the FCB agency noted that the commercial was successful because people had a warm and fuzzy feeling about Mikey, and it is still relevant today.

Other popular advertising characters from the past have resurfaced recently. Isuzu brought back Joe Isuzu, the sleazy pitchman with a creepy smile who satirizes the cliches of car ads, to hawk its Rodeo SUV after he had been off the air for 2 years. Several animated characters have also returned to the airways, including the Jolly Green Giant for Green Giant vegetables and Charlie the Tuna for Starkist. Music and fashion from the 1980s are also back in vogue, so advertisers are bringing back some of the decade's iconic TV stars to appear in their commercials. Alien puppet ALF, whose show was popular in the late 80s, appears in ads for discount phone service 10-10-220, while Mr. T, from the hit show The A-Team, endorses 1-800-COLLECT. Robin Leach, who hosted the celebrity-watching show Lifestyles of the Rich and Famous, appears in ads for Courtyard by Marriott hotels. Robert Thompson, director of Syracuse University's Center for the Study of Popular Television, says that there's usually a two-decade break between a TV show and the resurrection of its stars.

Astute marketers recognize they cannot rely solely on the recognition and nostalgia generated by past ads and simply bring back the same thing. Thus, advertisers are seeking to avoid the inherent risks associated with retrospective marketing, primarily by contemporizing the classic elements of their ads to make them relevant to current consumers, especially young people. For example, Pepsi created an extravagant commercial featuring pop star Brittany Spears taking a trip through generations of Pepsi advertising and revisiting jingles while dressed in period garb. Although the commercial has a nostalgic tone, it also has a modern, forward-looking ending as it transitions to the current image for the brand. Fruit of the Loom recently brought back the "fruit guys," four obnoxious little men who dress up as pieces of fruit and appear in humorous commercials for the brand of underwear. However, the new ads indirectly poke fun at the four middle-aged fruit guys from the old days.

Reviving time-tested advertising characters, spokespeople, and commercials has long been a popular advertising tactic among marketers, particularly during uncertain times, such as the post-September II era. Experts note that new creative ideas are often put aside for the reassuringly familiar. One brand identity consultant notes: "When we feel less secure, with less control over our daily lives, we reach out in brands to connect with a time when things felt better and and more comfortable. It's about finding security, what we can trust." However, marketers recognize that they must recalibrate the familiar if they want to make their ads relevant to the modern-day consumer.

Sources: Vanessa O'Connell "Ad Campaign Again Bears Fruit Guys." The Wall Street Journal, July 19, 2002, p. B2; Stuart Elliott, "Ads from the Past with Modern Touches," The New York Times, Sept. 9, 3002, p. C8; Julia Cosgrove, "Listen Up Sucka, the '80s Are Back," Business Week, Aug. 5,2002, p. 16.

Since many decades now, the promotion function has been predominated by mass media advertising. Most companies have generally relied on their preferred advertising agency's guidance in almost all areas of marketing communications. On the advice of their agencies, some of them have used additional promotional tools such as sales promotion, direct marketing, etc. The general view has been that sales promotions, or direct marketing, publicity, and package design were helping only services. Agencies dealing in these services were often contracted on a project basis. These activities were not viewed as being in the main stream and an integral part in the marketing communications process.

Different marketing and communication functions were being managed as totally separate entities. They had their different views about the market, different objectives and goals, and different budgets. Such companies did not realise that marketing communications tools should be co-ordinated for communication effectiveness and present a consistent image to target markets.

Many companies, in developed countries, during the 1980's recognised the need for increased strategic coordination of different promotional elements. Integrated Marketing Communications (IMC) is an attempt to coordinate various marketing and promotional activities in such manner that marketing communication to target customers becomes more effective and efficient. New terms such as "new advertising, orchestration and seamless communications" have been used with the concept of integration.[1]

In the beginning of the 90's, when mass advertising had slowly being replaced by target market advertising, the ways of being more effective in order to reach and persuade the target audience had also being rethought. Parente (2000) in his statement support this idea by saying that "as firms apply the lessons of market segmentation and product differentiation, they target smaller parts of the overall market. As firms speak to consumers with an increasing number of voices, locating the sources of all of a company's communication within the same organization can be more efficient." So, by that time it was felt that simply placing a message in a specific media was not enough to give the desired result by the companies. Some form of strategic synergy should be thought that could put together the message spread out in different media and used by the different communications tools. Belch (2001) mentioned "during the 1980s, many companies came to see the need for more of a strategic integration of their promotional tools." He says that "many agencies responded to that call for synergy among the various promotional tools by acquiring PR, sales promotion, and direct marketing companies and touting themselves as IMC agencies that offer one-stop shopping for all their clients." The main idea was to develop marketing and communication program that the activities defined strategically in the plan would work direct and synergic to achieve the company's marketing objective using the same message. As the result of this, new think appeared the Integrated Marketing and Communication plan (IMC) that has been discussed and used by various authors, researchers and marketing and advertising people.

The first definition of IMC, formulated by American Association of Advertising Agencies (the 4As) says:

".... a concept of marketing communications planning that recognizes the added value of a comprehensive plan that evaluates the strategic roles of a variety of communication disciplines – for example, general advertising, direct response, sales promotion, and public relations – and combines these disciplines to provide clarity, consistency and maximum communications impact."[2]

The focus of the above definition, formulated by the task force of AAAA, is on using all the promotion elements to create maximum promotion impact. However, Don E. Schultz, of Northwestern University, advocates for an even broader perspective that considers "all sources of brand and company contact that a customer or prospect has with a product or service." Schultz and others are of the opinion that "integrated marketing communications calls for a 'big picture' approach to planning marketing and promotion programmes and co-ordinating the various communication functions. It requires firms to develop a total marketing communications strategy that recognises how all of a firm's marketing activities, not just promotion, communicate with its customers."[3] According to Schultz professor at Northwestern University (1993), "Integrated Marketing Communication-IMC, is the process of developing and implementing various forms of persuasive communication programs with customers and prospects over time". He also states that, "the goal of IMC is to influence or directly affect the behaviour of the selected communication audience. IMC considers all sources of brand or company contacts which a company or prospect has with the product or service as potential delivery channels for the future messages. IMC, makes use of all forms of communication which are relevant to the customer and prospects, and to which they might be receptive."

According to Belch, the Schultz's definition involves all sources of brand or company contact given a broader picture of the relationship between the company and its diverse publics. His definition does not deal only with the delivered message. It deals also with the different contacts that a firm has such as personal selling, PR, suppliers, non-profit organizations, direct marketing, general advertising, and today we must ad, the Internet advertising, the company's home page, electronic mail, etc. Belch mentions that in order to develop an IMC program, a firm must develop a total marketing communications strategy that take into account how all the marketing activities developed by a firm, not just promotion, communicate with its public etc.

The American Association of Advertising Agencies, on the other hand, says Belch, concentrates on the process of using all forms of promotion to achieve maximum communication impact. The 4A's definition in others words gives importance to the communications activities as strategy to reach the consumer based on data bases.

The two definitions mentioned above deals with the IMC in the way that the marketing communication plan must work synergically in order to reach efficiently the target public. However, the Schultz definition, once deals with the entire company's audience (retailers, suppliers, personal selling, etc.), requires more knowledge by the company about all audience, while the 4A's concentrates more in the impact that the message in the final consumer.

Throughout the 90's mention Wells and others (2000) that the IMC continued to grow and has been used more widely by different companies. However, we have to mention that during the 90's not only the IMC had grown but also a new fact in marketing and communication plans had grown— the use of the new media Internet.

Amstrong (2001) says that "it is impossible to measure cyberspace accurately and many experts disagree on which metrics should be used for sizing the web, but everyone agrees that the Internet growth is a phenomenon. Web sites appear faster and faster every day." He continues saying that " NEC Research estimates that there are approximately 1.5 billion Web pages at the current time, an 88 percent increase from the previous year. This suggests that 1.9 million Web pages are created every day."

As the IMC suggests, the marketing and communication plan must work in a synergic way. So, the new media Internet which has been growing tremendously and has been used largely by the companies to do business, to sell and advertising its products, to maintain relationship with its target public, etc., must be thought as an important part of the IMC.

If we analyze the IMC Schultz approach (broad picture), the Internet is extremely useful for all marketing and communication activities because throughout the Internet, as mentioned above, a company can do business, advertise its products, maintain contacts with the customer, do PR and so on. So, if a company wants to do efficient IMC program, the Internet is an essential media for the success of it today. So, we cannot use the Internet as main point of our strategy, but, we have to use advertising on the Internet as part of the IMC.

Some authors have defined the integrated marketing communications as a management concept that is designed to make all aspects of marketing communication such as advertising, sales promotion, public relations, and direct marketing work together as a unified force, rather than permitting each to work in isolation. While others state that it is a management concept that is designed to make all aspects of marketing communication such as advertising, sales promotion, public relations, and direct marketing work together as a unified force, rather than permitting each to work in isolation. While to some it means a planning process designed to assure that all brand contacts received by a customer or prospect for a product, service, or organization are relevant to that person and consistent over time. Some define integrated marketing communications as a concept of marketing communications planning that recognizes the added value of a comprehensive plan that evaluates the strategic roles of a variety of communication disciplines—for example, general advertising, direct response, sales promotion, and public relations—and combines these disciplines to provide clarity, consistency, and maximum communications impact.

According to businessdictionary.com IMC is Synergistic approach to achieving the objectives of a marketing campaign, through a well co-ordinated use of different promotional methods. As defined by the American Association of Advertising Agencies, IMC " ... recognizes the value of a comprehensive plan that evaluates the strategic roles of a variety of communication disciplines—advertising, public relations, personal selling, and sales promotion—and combines them to provide clarity, consistency, and maximum communication impact."

WHAT IS IMC?

Let's see if you can guess how many Ph.D.s it took to create this definition of IMC provided by Northwestern University?

"IMC is the integrated management of all communications to build positive and lasting relationships with customers and other stakeholders. It is a customer-centric, data-driven approach to marketing and branding that stresses communicating to consumers through multiple forms of media and technology".

The answer is, too many. If this definition did not help much, permit to translate. IMC stands for "integrated marketing communications," a process that aligns university communication efforts in order to speak with one compelling voice. In other words, it's how you prevent your school from having multiple, conflicting messages sent out by individuals who shouldn't be sending them out.

According to advertising marketing guru Bob Sevier, "IMC plans balance an institution's responsibility to create awareness with its need to generate results." Sevier breaks the IMC process down into three distinct functions: brand marketing, direct marketing and customer relationship management.

BRAND MARKETING

According to Sevier, brand marketing is "Pre-funnel" communications that differentiates you from competitors and increases awareness of your school's brand promise." Think establishing the brand through advertising and PR. For Sevier, a brand promise should:

(1) matter to customers,
(2) be unique to your school and
(3) be believable.

The brand promise helps you position yourself in the minds of your prospective customers. Brand marketing deals primarily with perception and is typically handled by the organisation's marketing communications department.

DIRECT MARKETING

Direct marketing, Sevier says, is "An interactive, integrative prospect communication and contact program that spans the traditional funnel of search though measurable action or behavior." This IMC function specializes in getting people to take action on your brand promise. Think supporting the brand through efforts like direct mail and events. Whereas brand marketing positions you in the customers' mind, direct marketing asks the customer to do something like log onto your Web site, fill out an inquiry card or visit the campus. Direct marketing efforts are typically handled by admissions, alumni and development departments. In all cases, your direct marketing efforts should be consistent with and flow from your school's brand marketing plan.

CUSTOMER RELATIONSHIP MANAGEMENT

Finally, customer relationship management, according to Sevier, is "What is done from application forward that impacts yields, retention, and eventually the support and participation of alumni." In other words, this is where you and everyone else working for the college delivers the promise. The goal here is repeat business.

Brand marketing, direct marketing and customer relationship management that's IMC in a nutshell.

Therefore, IMC can be defined as a process in which messages communicated by each of the promotional elements are harmonized, so that consumers will receive a consistent message regarding the brand or the company. It can be defined comprehensively as a process for managing the customer relationships that drive brand value.

More specifically, it is a cross-functional process for creating and nourishing profitable relationships with customers and other stakeholders by strategically controlling or influencing all messages sent to these groups and encouraging data-driven, purposeful dialogue with them. The growing importance of IMC can be attributed to various factors.

This include increasing competition, decline in effectiveness of mass advertising, more information sources for consumers and technological advances. Implementing the IMC process in an organization is not an easy task and it cannot be done at one go. The implementation of IMC in a company requires proper planning.

The American Productivity & Quality Center has devised a four stage process to integrate the marketing communication function. The four stages are tactical co-ordination of marketing communication, redefining the scope of marketing communication, application of information technology and financial and strategic integration. Though the awareness about IMC is on the rise, implementation has been slow.

This is because of three key barriers, namely lack of top management support, organizational barriers and cultural barriers. To implement the IMC process effectively company needs to follow certain guidelines. It should adopt a flexible organizational structure and change the mindset of the employees. It should adopt a customer centric strategy to design communication campaigns from the consumer perspective.

A collaborative strategy is needed, that enables coordination and co-operation between various departments in the organization. Entrusting all its creative activities to a single agency will help the company in reducing costs and increasing consistency in communication campaigns.

To fully appreciate the IMC perspective, one has to look through the consumer's eyes. Many consumers' views of advertising include not only the advertising in TV, print and other media but they also consider door-to-door selling, shopping bags and even community sponsored events as advertising. The perceptions of consumers about a company's image, its products, or services depend on a number of elements other than promotion alone. Besides advertising, personal selling, sales promotion, publicity, direct marketing, and messages on the Internet, etc., other elements such as, package design, price of the product or service, selected distribution outlets, displays, news reports, word-of-mouth, gossip, experts opinions and financial reports also communicate powerfully.

All such communications, whether sponsored or not, create an integrated product in the consumers' mind. This means that consumers, on their own, integrate all brand-related messages originating from the company or any other source and this determines their perception of the company.

Modifying the definition used by the American Association of Advertising Agencies for more practical purpose, one can say, "Integrated Marketing Communications is a concept of marketing communications planning that recognizes the added value of a comprehensive plan that evaluates the strategic roles of a variety of communications disciplines—for example, general advertising, direct response, sales promotion, and public relations—and combines these disciplines to provide clarity, consistency, and maximum communications' impact through the seamless integration of discrete messages."

When Southwest Airlines started flights out of its new Baltimore hub in September 1993, they knew they had to familiarize East Coast travellers, unaware of what Southwest stood for, with the no-frills, low-fare, high-frequency service that it offered. Five weeks before the first flight, they staged a public relations event: Southwest Airlines Chairman Herb Kelleher and the Maryland Governor jointly announced Southwest's entry into Baltimore, and Kelleher handed the Governor a floatation device, calling it a "lifesaver" from high fares for the people of Baltimore, Another public relations event followed to launch the $49 fare to Cleveland, Southwest flew 49 elementary schoolchildren free to the Cleveland Zoo. Next, the Company sent a direct mail piece to frequent short-haul travellers in the Baltimore area, offering a special promotion to join Southwest's frequent-flier program. Another consumer promotion followed that featured employees handing out fliers and peanuts at Baltimore street corners, promoting the airline's low "Just Peanuts" fares. And, only then did TV and print ads kick in. This combination of public relations, direct mail, sales promotions, and advertising led to a company record for advance bookings-90,000 passengers bought advance tickets even before service began.[4]

This case is an excellent example of an increasingly popular approach called integrated marketing communications, or IMC for short-to combining and integrating different elements of the communication mix. The key idea behind IMC, however, is simply that advertising has various strengths and weaknesses and that it thus has to be combined with the other elements of the communications mix— for example, direct marketing, consumer and trade promotions, publicity and public relations, and event and sports marketing, and others—in an integrated and consistent way.

In addition, these different elements of the communications mix have to be used in a way that the strengths of one are used to offset the weakness of another. For instance, one of advertising's weaknesses is its frequent failure to induce immediate action. Very often advertising can create high awareness and favorable attitudes, but it cannot create the final "push" needed to get the inquiry, trial, or sale. When such a situation appears, a marketer must use direct marketing, or sales promotions, to get the necessary action, possibly after an advertising campaign.

What marketers must understand is that everything they do, or do not do, sends a message. That is, every corporate activity has a message component. There are four company/brand related messages that consumers and other stakeholders receive. They are :

1. **Planned messages:** Planned messages are say messages, representing what companies say about self. These messages represent typical marketing communications such as advertising, personal selling, sales promotion, direct marketing, publicity, etc. Such messages often have the least impact because they are viewed as marketer controlled and self-serving. Planned messages should aim to accomplish the determined set of communications objectives. This is the most basic aspect of Integrated Marketing Communications.

2. **Product messages:** Product or service messages are do messages, as they communicate what the company does. Messages from product, its price and distribution elements are referred to as product messages. Customers and others receive totally different messages from the Rs. 75 lakh BMW and Rs 2.36 lakh Maruti 800. Product messages cause great impact because when a product performs as promised, the consumer gets a positive and reinforcing message. On the other end, if there is a gap between the product's performance and the communicated promises, the customer is more likely to get a negative message.

3. **Service messages:** Company's employee interactions with consumers also become a source of messages. In many service-providing companies, customer service personnel are supervised by operations, and not marketing. The service rendered sends messages, which have greater impact than the planned messages.

4. **Unplanned messages:** Such messages are confirm messages as they represent what others say and confirm/not confirm about what the company says and does. Companies have little.[5] or on control over the unplanned messages that result from employee gossip, news stories not under the control of the company, comments that traders or competitors pass on, word- of–mouth rumours, or major disasters. These unplanned messages, favourable or unfavourable, may influence consumer attitudes quite significantly.

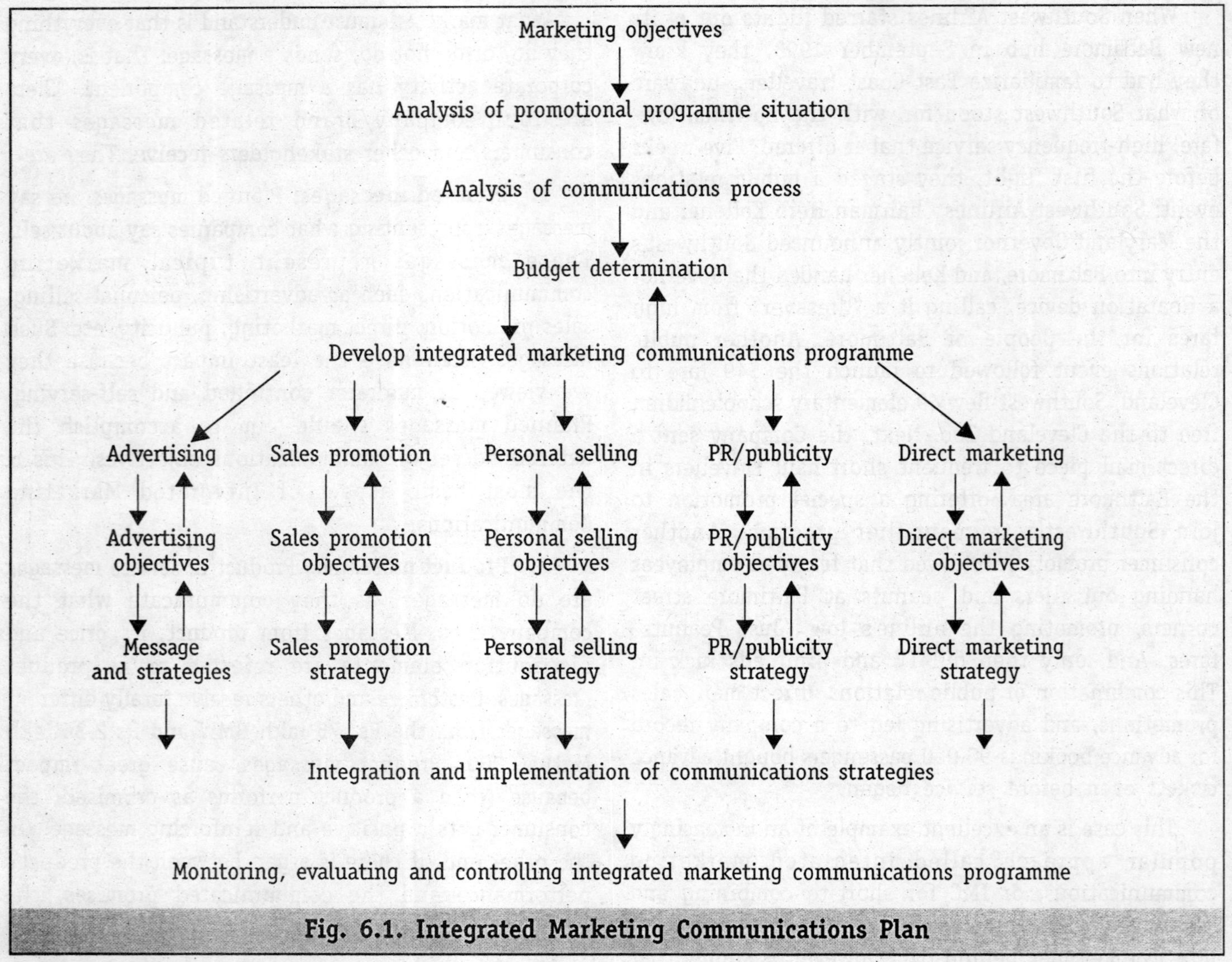

Fig. 6.1. Integrated Marketing Communications Plan

The objectives of integrated marketing communications are to co-ordinate all of the company's marketing and promotional efforts to project and reinforce a consistent, unified image of the company or its brands to the market-place. The IMC approach is an attempt to improve over the traditional method of treating promotion elements as totally separate activities. IMC is increasingly helping companies to develop most suitable and effective methods to contact customers and other interested groups.

John Deighton, Thomas, R. Duncan and Stephen E. Everett have called IMC as one of the most significant marketing developments of the 1990s. A very important and fundamental reason, besides others, is the value of strategically integrating various communications functions and taking advantage of the resulting synergy among various communication tools in developing more effective and efficient marketing communication programmes. Experts say that IMC is one of the easiest ways to maximise return on investment in marketing and promotion.

Despite the increasing use of the term "integrated marketing communications" by both practitioners and academicians in recent years, there is little agreement on what the term actually means. According to one recent review.[6] at least two related ideas are involved:

ONE-VOICE MARKETING COMMUNICATIONS

As consumers increasingly begin to be addressed by the same marketer in a variety of different ways-through image-building advertising, public relations, direct marketing, sales promotions, point-of-sale material, collateral material e.g., brochures and catalogues, and sales force calls-there is the obvious need to ensure a consistency of positioning, message, and tone across these different media. Such consistency is a vital as well as essential element of brand-building. Ideally, these different communications would all begin from the same vision of what the consumer was supposed to be hearing from the marketer so that they all operate seamlessly, reaching the consumer with one voice. At the very least, this implies that the different marketing communications elements-mass media advertising, direct marketing, sales promotions, package graphics, point-of-sale material, events, trade shows, employee communications, and public relations-need to be created in a tightly co-ordinated manner by the many different agencies and organisations like the PR firm, direct response agency, sales promotion firm, ad agency, client company etc., that work on the different elements.

INTEGRATED COMMUNICATIONS

A marketer's consumer communications need to not only confine itself and raise brand awareness, or create or change brand preference and image, or to get sales trial or repurchase, but it is supposed to do all of the above at the same time. Increasing image without getting a sales result is not good enough and getting short-term sales e.g., via sales promotion at the expense of a brand's long-term image is also courting disaster. Thus, it is argued that all marketing communication materials, particularly ads, should attempt to simultaneously achieve targeted communication goals e.g., raising attitudes or building image and lead to some behavioural action e.g., trial or repurchase.

WHY IMC HAS GROWN?

A major reason for the growing importance of IMC is the ongoing revolution in global business practices that is changing the rules and concepts of marketing and the role of the traditional advertising agency. Some major features are:

- More budget allocation for sales promotion due to intensifying competition.
- In general, advertising has become more expensive and less cost effective.
- Escalating price competition is resulting in more price promotions than advertising.
- Power of trade compels companies to offer fees and allowances for promotion.
- This takes away money from advertising to produce short-term sales results.
- Companies are using computers to build databases containing customer names; geographic, demographic, and psychographics profiles; purchase patterns; media preferences, and other relevant characteristics.
- Companies are increasingly relying on direct marketing methods, rather than relying on mass media.
- Top management wants more accountability from brand managers.
- Advertising agencies are being made more accountable.

As should be apparent from the two conceptualizations of IMC above, the need for IMC has grown in parallel with the trend to allocate marketing communications budgets away from their mainstay of mass media advertising. Both consumer goods and industrial goods marketers have moved increasingly large proportions of marketing resources into direct marketing and sales promotions. The amounts of money being spent in direct marketing and in sales promotions have thus grown dramatically.[7] These trends in spending patterns have occurred for various reasons, including the increased splintering and fragmentation of consumer media, the increasing segmentation of consumer tastes and preferences, the easier access to consumer databases and computational resources, the increased pressure on marketers to maintain the momentum of short-term sales, the increased power of the retail trade, the recognition of the importance of reinforcing consumer loyalty and repurchase via relationship marketing, and so on. At the same time, marketers have also been forced to recognize the vital importance of building and increasing a brand's image-based equity.[8]

Thus, marketers in the twenty-first century now must accommodate more complex and multiple commu-nication objectives simultaneously, must spread their marketing communications resources over a much wider array of techniques and media, and usually must im-plement these multiple communications programs through a larger number of vendors or agencies. The multiplicity of markets and media and objectives and organizations can very easily lead to a fragmentation and dilution of message consistency and impact, unless steps are taken to integrate these various communications efforts.

IMC STRATEGIES AND TACTICS

According to Thomas Duncan, a company that thinks it is doing IMC should begin by conducting an audit: check to see the real degree to which it is co-ordinating its various communications activities and the real degree to which it is sending out messages that are integrated and consistent. Most companies that do this find they are actually doing less IMC than they first thought.[9] There are many barriers to doing real IMC, among them a lack of appreciation for its value especially among top management, a lack of skills and training, and organizational structures and systems that create territorialism. We will discuss organizational issues further below, and providing skills and training and an appreciation of its value are obvious prerequisites to implementing IMC: But is there anything more to IMC than the commonsensical idea that all communications to the consumer about a particular brand should be "synergized," which is hardly a novel or earthshaking idea.

There is no clear answer to this last question, and only a few interesting implementation-oriented ideas have emerged. Most of these borrow heavily from the concepts of database or direct marketing. Don Schultz and colleagues, for instance, have suggested that marketers should build a comprehensive database of customers and prospects and then think through what different time and place opportunities exist for the company to contact each segment of customers such as loyals, switchers, new prospects, etc., what medium or communications mode, with what message and tonality, and for what overall marketing objectives. An overall communications strategy must then be developed that guides the integration of the different communications tactics. Each communications contact with the target must then not only deliver the intended message, but also solicit a response, which is then added to the database for further analysis.[10]

For example, the following sequence of questions should help develop an integrated marketing communications program:

1. What is target customer's information gathering, decision, and shopping process?
2. Who or what are all the media, institutions e.g., retailers, and people or influencers e.g., pharmacists with which the target customer comes in contact? In what sequence do these contacts occur? What communications opportunities do these contacts create for us?
3. For all these people, what attitudes and/or behaviours do we want to affect?
4. Therefore, for each communication opportunity, what are our communications needs? What are our quantitative goals?
5. For each communications opportunity, given what we need to accomplish, what is the best programme(s) to accomplish it—advertising, direct mail, public relations, sales promotion, or other?
6. Given this choice and sequence of programmes, how should the budget be allocated?
7. Who is to be responsible for implementing which part?
8. How will we measure the degree of success of each part?

The key to ensuring the desired integration and consistency in these various contacts is having organizational arrangements that facilitate rather than impede such integration, and we now turn to discussing these.

ORGANIZING FOR IMC

Obviously, the easiest way to organize for IMC is to have just one outside communications supplier, such as an ad agency, and to have centralized responsibility for all brand communications within the client company, at either a brand/product manager or marketing vice president level. In terms of outside suppliers, ad agencies are more likely to have the expertise to perform multiple communication tasks such as advertising, direct marketing, sales promotions, public relations than stand-alone single-function suppliers such as public relations, direct marketing, or sales promotion firms. Indeed, large ad agencies have for long claimed an ability to or chestrate all of a client's communications efforts if they were all done by that agency and its affiliates and have used this claim to solicit all of a client's communications budget, not just the ad budget. Such orchestration should obviously be better for the consistency of message and tone necessary for brand building. Agencies also claim that if they handled all of a client's communication needs the client would have greater control, because overall responsibility for all those efforts would lie with one account supervisor at the agency rather than being dispersed. The agency would also supposedly be more responsive to the client's needs if it handled all these communications because the client's total billings with that agency would now be a larger percentage of the agency's revenue.

However, many clients have balked from giving their lead ad agency these multiple responsibilities because of a perception that a single ad agency might not have the best sets of skills in all these different areas, so that the client might get better expertise by mixing and matching skills from several specialized communications suppliers, instead of relying on "one-stop" shopping, while relying on the client organization staff itself to perform the necessary integration especially among larger client firms.[11] Some even argue that an ad agency will never get the best talent in the non advertising communications areas simply because such people will always be "second-class citizens" in ad agencies. Consolidating all of a client's business at one agency also potentially reduces the motivating effect of having several suppliers compete with each other to come up with the best com-munications ideas for that client. In addition, most ad agencies themselves have had trouble integrating the different functions, especially if the functions are organized as affiliate companies or departments instead of being organized as people with different resources and skills working as part of one integrated account team. Many clients are thus skeptical that the different functions will be better integrated if they are combined under a single agency umbrella, instead of being at multiple unaffiliated suppliers, although they do believe the potential for miscommunication would be reduced.[12]

It is not entirely clear, however, that, the many people involved in communications programs at the client organization themselves perform the integration of which they believe they are capable. The sales force, trade account management, public relations, sales promotion, direct marketing and other staffs within client companies sometimes run programs that are not adequately co-ordinated with the mass media programs typically managed by brand or advertising managers and with each other.[13] Many organizations such as IBM are. experimenting with cross-functional teams as a solution.[14] At McDonald's, the various departments involved in a marketing project are all represented on a strategy review board led by a project manager, so they have input into the decisions and know what actions are to be taken by whom.[15] It is obviously important to train everyone involved in the concept of integrated marketing, in the skills necessary to make it work, and to create a shared vision in them about what is to be communicated, with what tonality and with what effect.

Ad agencies too often have problems in properly incentivising the use of a truly integrated approach by their account staff. If PR direct mail, sales promotions, and mass media advertising are structured as separate profit centers, the managers of these divisions battle for budgets instead of doing what is best for the client. Again, cross-functional account teams led by one "communications director"-who could be a direct marketing specialist, not necessarily the ad agency account manager-appear to be a superior organizational arrangement when combined with a financial structure that measures total account billings, not billings by function. It thus appears that the key needs in organizing for better IMC are:

(1) better communication and common goal-sharing among the various client personnel themselves and
(2) better integration of the various functions within the major ad agencies that offer all or most of these different communications functions.

ROLE OF ADVERTISING *VIS-A-VIS* MARKETING PROGRAMME

Advertising planning and decision making take place in the context of an overall marketing programmes. Obviously, there are several marketing tools that can be used to help an organization achieve its marketing objectives. Its product or service can be developed or refined. A distribution network can help match an organization's output with its clientele. Pricing strategy is another marketing decision variable.

The most appropriate way to improve the sales of a brand may not involve promotion or advertising at all, but may involve more extensive distribution, better relationships with the trade, a lower price, or simply better product quality.

A brand manager needs to spend considerable time pinpointing the exact source of a brand's poor sales before deciding that the core problem is inadequate or poor advertising or promotion. For instance, if research data indicate that consumers are trying the brand but are not repurchasing it, it may well be that the firm's advertising is successful, since consumers are trying the brand, but that the brand's product quality needs attention, since people who try the brand do not repurchase it. The marketing plan thus should be based on the specific problems or opportunities uncovered for the brand by the kind of situation analysis.

In addition to placing the advertising plan in this total context, the brand manager must also take care to develop a marketing program in which the component parts work in a coordinated, synergistic manner instead of at cross-purposes. For instance, when a company develops a prestige product with a premium price, it is important that the advertising reinforce that idea of high quality and prestige. This can be done by associating the product with prestigious people, situations, or events. If the advertising objectives are written to encourage the use of advertising copy and advertising media incompatible with a prestige image, the whole marketing program may be jeopardized. Alternatively, when a company offers a low-priced product, the job of advertising might be to stress the price differential by using hard-hitting copy.

As another example, the role of advertising will also depend on the distribution channel selected. If door-to-door selling is employed, advertising may be used only to introduce the salesperson, or it may not be used at all. If wholesalers, retailers, or other middlemen are employed, different advertising strategies are available. The advertising and selling effort may be primarily directed to either the consumer or the trade. In the former case, the intent would then be to have con-sumer interest "pull" the merchandise through the distribution channel; in the later case, distributor margins would get the emphasis, consumer advertising would be less, and the intent would be to "push" it through the channel. Generally, the nature and significance of advertising will differ according to whether the company is stressing a push or pull strategy and whether its distribution strategy is intensive, the use of many outlets to maximize customer convenience, exclusive, the use of a few outlets to maximize retailer interest, or selective or intermediate arrangements.

THE ROLE OF ADVERTISING *VIS-A-VIS* "COMMUNICATIONS MIX"

Once it has been determined that a key problem or opportunity for the brand involves its communication with consumers, it should not be immediately concluded that more money needs to be spent on advertising. Advertising is only one part of the communications mix: a firm can also communicate with its consumers through the sales force, through publicity or public relations, and through various consumer and trade promotions techniques.

Within this mix, advertising has various strengths and weaknesses. Unlike the high cost of a sales call which by some estimates now exceeds $225 per call once all relevant costs are considered,[16] advertising is a much cheaper way to reach target consumers often pennies per exposure, since it uses mass media. And again, unlike sales calls, advertising can use complex visual and emotional devices to increase the persuasiveness of the message. However, salespeople can often communicate more complex information, often necessary in industrial or big-ticket purchases, better than advertising can, can tailor the nature of the message much more closely to the message recipient, and are much more likely to "close" the sale by getting an order. Thus, direct marketing may be needed to target certain prospects with a more customized message, provide them with detailed information, and induce them to act.

Advertising is notorious for this inability to actually get the sale: while the effects of advertising in increasing brand awareness and favorable attitudes for the brand are easily documented, effects on sales are harder to find. It is thus often useful, after advertising creates awareness of a brand, to supplement advertising with sales promotions, both consumer promotions and trade promotions, which are often more effective in actually getting consumers to try the brand. Such sales promotions may be especially required if research shows, during the situation analysis, that target consumers are aware of the brand and think it has the features they are looking for but have not gotten around to trying it.

Finally, advertising is also weak in another respect: it is widely perceived as biased. Many consumers often do not trust advertising and are skeptical about its claims. In such situations, it is often useful for a marketer to try to communicate his message to consumers through media that are perceived as more credible and unbiased, such as editorial endorsements obtained through publicity and public relations (PR) campaigns.

Thus, an integral part of the advertising planning and decision-making process is an assessment of the role that advertising is meant to play as one part of a firm's communications mix and as one part of the total marketing mix. Once this perspective has been gained, the brand manager must design a marketing and communications plan in which the different elements complement each other in increasing the sales for the brand. An advertising plan can only be developed in the context of a total marketing and communications plan for the brand.

DIRECT OR DATABASE MARKETING

Direct marketing includes not just direct mail, but also telemarketing and direct response advertising on TV and radio and other media, in which the ad aims to generate an action response such as calling a toll-free number. Direct marketing has two key advantages that differentiate it from regular, mass advertising:

(1) the ability to target specific, individual consumers not just demographically described segments with an offer that is tailored to that consumer and
(2) the ability to directly measure response. For example, the script used by a telemarketer can be tailored to what is known about the person being called. The response or lack of it can then be entered into a computerized database so that the next marketing effort aimed at this individual can be customized to whatever the direct marketer knows about this specific individual.

Unlike traditional mass media advertising, the goal of most direct marketing efforts is not simply to build awareness or change preference, but to generate an action: either an order or request for more information, a visit to a dealer or a store, and so on. This need to generate action is another distinguishing element of direct marketing and has implications for its creative requirements, which we will discuss further below.

These features of action orientation, targetability, customization ability, and measurability have led to the tremendous growth in direct marketing over the past decade and have led to the current popularity of so-called database marketing[17] While the first cataloge in the United States was offered as far back as 1744 by Benjamin Franklin, today about 4,000 catalogs go through the mails each year in the U.S. and almost 100 million Americans shop every year by mail or telephone, spending over $50 billion.[18] By one estimate, Americans today receive 62 billion pieces of direct mail and 18 million telemarketing calls per year. Taking a clue from their western counterparts, now Indian companies too have employed extensive use of telemarketing techniques.

To share in this growth, all the major ad agency groups now own direct marketing units. The leading direct marketing agencies in the United States include Ogilvy and Mather Direct (New York), Wunderman Cato Johnson (a division of Young and Rubicam, in New York). Rapp Collins Marcoa (a part of the Omnicom group, and based in New York), Kobs and Draft Worldwide (Chicago), and Bronner Slosberg Humphrey (Boston).[19]

This explosion in direct marketing has occurred because more and more traditional "mass market" advertisers have taken to combining direct marketing efforts with their regular advertising efforts, in an effort to not only sharpen their ability to win new customers by mailing more targeted offers to prospects but also to retain the loyalty of existing customers, to cross-sell new products and services to these existing customers, and to increase the amount or frequency of usage.[20] As some examples of such databases, consider these: Pizza Hut now has a database of 10 million pizza eaters in the country; Kraft General Foods has one on 25 million of its customers; Seagram knows the names and addresses of over 10 million liquor buyers, and Marriott Hotels and Resorts has one on 4 million of its regular guests.

Uses and Examples

As an example of the first goal mentioned above that an advertiser may have-customer acquisition-a magazine advertisement for a new General Motors car may feature a coupon inviting the reader to write in for a free copy of a book that will help him make a better automobile-buying decision. The coupon collects not just the reader's name, address, and telephone number, but also information on his present car and how soon he expects to buy his next car. The coupon-sending customer is then sent further collateral materials such as brochures and catalogs on the car, with an invitation to test-drive the car at a local dealership. The dealership will also be sent that coupon information on the reader so that the dealer can follow up with a telephone sales call, called outbound-telemarketing. Other ways of building up databases might involve inducing customers who use a grocery coupon to also write in their name and address, as part of a sweepstakes entry. The easiest way, of course, is simply to rent a mailing list.

Obviously, this marketing effort may or may not result in a sale. Whatever the response or lack of it, all the information now known about the consumer and his response is entered into a computer database and this database is subsequently utilized to target certain individuals for further mailings or telemarketing efforts. For example, if the car in the example above is a luxury Cadillac model, a mailing for it may be sent to those known to own a competing model of luxury car such as BMW or Lexus using a mailing list obtained from automobile registration data. Every subsequent response or no-response that can be directly tracked and attributed to a specific mailing piece or phone call is entered into this database, and the cycle of targeting and measuring response continues.

As an example of the second goal-customer retention, or loyalty building—a company such as DuPont Automotive might send all its present customers a regular newsletter on its new research and new products to build up its relationship with these customers. In many businesses, a key 20 percent or so of customers account for 80 percent or so of volume, so building relationships with these key customers is obviously vital. To enhance customer satisfaction, a company might offer a toll-free telephone number for service questions, customer enquiries, or product complaints. Such a telephone service is an example of inbound telemarketing. An airline might send all its frequent-flyer programme members a newsletter with special loyalty-building offers. Axis Bank, formerly known as UTI Bank mail their quaterly newsletters regularly to their "Priority" customers. A credit card might use an envelope stuffer mailing to induce its present customers to charge even more, like ICICI Bank Credit Card Division. Many of these loyalty programs offer free gifts or incentives to a company's best customers: American Express offers the top 5 percent of its card members special restaurant and travel offers that vary by the zip code in which the card member lives.[21]

Such mailings can be used not only to strengthen relationships and build loyalty, but also to accomplish the third and fourth goals-cross-selling products or increasing the usage rate. Thus, a large financial services company such as American Express might attempt to sell new insurance or financial planning services to its charge card membership base, or a large foods company like Kraft General Foods might try to get a customer of one low-fat product to try its other low-fat products by mailing them coupons or samples. As an example of direct marketing to increase the usage rate, or amount of repeat consumption, an automobile dealership or repair facility such as General Motors and Maruti Ltd., track the mileage of the cars brought in for service and send mailed reminders to these customers to bring their cars in for service at regularly scheduled intervals.

Because of the high cost of personal sales calls, companies also often use direct marketing in after-market sales for e.g., selling copier supplies to people who bought copiers and whose names and addresses and phone numbers are now in a database, and in generating sales inquiries that can then be followed up by telephone and personal sales calls. The use of databases also allows companies to use direct marketing to target mailings of coupons and samples to only high-opportunity individuals and households. The traditional users of direct marketing have always been magazines and newspapers who use it to sell subscriptions, the marketers of insurance-by-mail, the record and book clubs, in what are called the negative option continuity programs, through which customers are sent something every few weeks till they say no, and, of course, the catalog retailers such as Spiegel's, Lands' End, etc.

TARGETING

The targeting ability of direct marketing can be greatly enhanced by a systematic development of the direct marketer's database. Someone who knows your address and, thus, your postal zip code or census block group, can obtain information from database companies about various characteristics such as the median income, average age, etc., of the area code in which you live, based on the average for the geodemographic cluster in which you live. This information is then used to assess whether you are a likely prospect for a particular product, on the assumption that your individual profile is similar to the average data available for your area code and every household can be classified into one of these clusters based on its area code.

CLUSTER CODE	
1	Highest SESI, highest income, prime real estate areas, highest education level, professionally employed, low mobility, homeowners, children in private schools
2	Very high household income, new homes and condominiums, prime real estate areas, highly mobile, high education level, professionally employed, homeowners, families with children
3	High income, high home values, new homes, highly mobile, younger, high education level, professionally employed, homeowners, married couples, high incidence of children, larger families
4	High income, high home values, high education level, professionally employed, married couples, larger families, highest incidence of teenagers, homeowners, homes built in 60's
5	High income, high home values, high education level, professionally employed, low mobility, homeowners, homes built in 50's and 60's
6	Highest incidence of children, large families, new homes, highly mobile, younger, married couples, above average income and education, homeowners
7	Apartments and condominiums, high rent, above average income, high education level, professionally employed, mobile, singles, few children, urban areas
8	Above average income, above average education, older, fewer children, white collar workers
9	Above average income, average education, households with two or more workers, homes built in 60's and 70's
10	High education level, average income, professionally employed, younger, mobile, apartment 'dwellers, above average rents
11	Above average income, average education, families with children, high incidence of teenagers, homeowners, homes built in 60's, small towns
12	Highly mobile, young, working couples, young children, new homes, above average income and education, white collar workers
13	Older, fewer children, above average income, average education, white collar workers, homeowners, homes built in 50's, very low mobility, small towns
14	Retirees, condominiums and apartments, few children, above average income and education, professionally employed, high home values and rents, urban areas
15	Older, very low mobility, fewer children, above average income and education, white collar workers, old housing, urban areas
16	Working couples, very low mobility, above average income, average education, homeowners, homes built in 50's, urban areas
17	Very young, below average income, high education level, professionally employed, highly mobile, singles, few children, apartment dwellers, high rent areas
18	High incidence of children, larger families, above average income, average education, working couples, homeowners.

Source: Donnelley Marketing Information Services

CHART-1 Demographic characteristics of selected Cluster PLUS^{SM} neighbourhood clusters.

In addition, data are also available that apply to consumers as individuals: lifestyle, hobby and activity information supplied on product warranty registration cards can be purchased, as car driving license and automobile registration data in most states. Any other source to whom consumers reveal their incomes or age or anything else may also sell this information to the large database companies such as Donnelley, Metromail, Polk, etc. that maintain household data-bases on almost every household in the United States. Databases on business establishments are maintained by companies like Dun & Bradstreet, containing information on the businesses' sales, number of employees, and nature of business using the Standard Industrial Classification, or SIC, code.

Companies can also acquire names from their databases in other creative ways: a company making diapers, like Kimberly-Clark, may acquire the names of all those expectant mothers who take a childbirth class before delivery-or from newspaper birth announcements after the delivery. Many packaged goods companies attempt to "capture" the names and addresses of users by obtaining them from sweepstakes entries, from those sending in mail-in offers for promotional premiums and gifts, from those who cash in rebates or writing in response to free sample offers, or from those who include a sweepstakes entry form as part of a regular grocery coupon that is redeemed in a store. The consumer who writes in a name and address on the redeemed coupon thus not only receives the coupon's promised cents-off but also enters a sweepstakes. Retailers build up lists of customers by obtaining names and addresses as part of the regular sales process. Obviously, the availability of such information on consumers raises all kinds of concerns about privacy.[22]

MEASURING AND IMPROVING RESPONSE

Typically, the direct marketing companies compute response on a response-rate-per-thousand-mailings basis, abbreviated as OPM (orders per thousand). They can tell which mailing to which a customer responded by using code numbers called key codes on the response coupons that uniquely identify a mailing package. Companies continually test different mailing packages to see which ones "pull" best. Thus, different mailing pieces may be sent to random samples of 10,000 to 25,000 individuals, with the mailing pieces varying systematically in the size and colour scheme of the envelope, the copy in the sales letter, the size and illustrations in the brochure, and the price and payment terms. The objective in such tests is to see which of these many new test packages yields a response rate or order rate greater than the mailing piece being used currently, called the control package.

Response rates-which can be very low, often just 1 to 2 percent of the packages mailed are a function of many factors. First, of course, there is the product being offered, at a certain price and payment term, and with or without a premium or free gift. These are collectively called the offer. Response rates are higher if the product is unique and not available in regular retail channels, if the price is credibly low, and if the payment terms are easy, and so on. Second, there are the quality and responsiveness of the names in the mailing lists that the direct marketer is renting, through a list broker or list compiler perhaps paying $100 for every thousand names mailed. Are the people on the list really interested in this product or service? Third, of course, is the quality of the creative message: the letter, the brochure, the envelope, and so on. Even with such low response rates, and even with production and mailing costs of 50 to 60 cents per mailing piece, a mailing can still be profitable if the gross profit per response is high. Conversely, if the gross profit per sale is low, and/or if the target market is reached more efficiently by mass media than through targeted direct marketing, mass marketing and advertising may make more economic sense than a direct marketing programme.

Direct marketers also spend large sums of money building analytical models of the responses to their mailings. For example, a logit or logistic regression model might be estimated on a previous mailing, which can be used to forecast which of the prospects for an upcoming mailing are most likely to respond to it, and the mailing can be limited to only the most likely responders. Such models to a company's existing customers often model the likelihood of response as a function of how long it has been since that customer's last order ,called recency, how many times that customer has purchased in the past, called frequency, and how much money that customer has spent with the company in the past called monetary value. Such RFM models for the first letters of these three concepts are very often used by traditional catalog direct marketers, but newer and more sophisticated modelling methods—some even using artificial intelligence techniques called neural nets are often superior to such RFM models.

In building a direct marketing business, a direct marketer is concerned not just with maximizing the response rates to a mailing called the front-end of the business, but also the back-end profitability of the customers acquired. For example, a book club can very easily boost response rates to a mailing by giving away more books free of charge, and requiring no commitment from the new member to buy any more books ever. Such a soft offer would obviously boost response rates. However, the members acquired through such a mailing may well not end up buying many books over the lifetime of their memberships with the book club and may thus be relatively unprofitable to acquire. In contrast, a hard offer that offers fewer free books and requires bigger and longer commitments to buy a certain number of books may well result in a lower overall response, but more profitable members in the long-term. A direct marketer is concerned not just with immediate pay-off but with the lifetime value of its customers.

MAILING LIST RENTAL AND PROCESSING

Mailings or telemarketing campaigns can obviously be made to a company's list of existing or past customers, called its house list. For mailings to prospects, however, outside lists usually have to be rented. Mailing lists are usually rented on a per-use basis, rather than bought and sold. Compliance with rental conditions is monitored by inserting dummy or decoy names into the list to which the renting mailer will unknowingly send mailings, which can be tracked for frequency of use.

Such outside lists are of two primary kinds. A response list is a list of the customers of another business. Such a list will obviously contain a name and complete address, but may also contain information on the recency, frequency, and monetary value of the name on the list, the terms were defined above. If these are customers who ordered from that business very recently, the list may be called a hotline list and command a higher price. In contrast, a compiled list is a list put together from directories and other sources, and is usually cheaper to rent, since it is unknown how likely the people on the list will be to respond to the mailing.

Such outside lists are usually rented through a list broker, who represents the people who own or compile the lists, for a commission, of course. List brokers offer access to a huge number of lists-over 40.000 by one count including every conceivable occupation and profession. Lists are rented on a per-thousand-names basis, with the charge varying on the desirability of the list. Since a renter may end up renting several hundred small lists, the multiple lists used are first merged and purged of duplicate names, and payment is usually made on a net basis, after deleting duplicate names. This merge/purge is done by computer bureaus. The actual mailing of the mailing pieces, using the mailing labels or names supplied by the list broker, is done through lettershops.

CREATIVE GUIDELINES

Good direct mail pieces are built on an intuitive understanding of the psychology of inducing action. Think about the state of mind of a consumer opening a direct-mail solicitation. He or she has doubts about the quality of the product, since it cannot be physically inspected. There is no salesperson to answer questions and overcome objections. And, there is the very human tendency to postpone things: even if the consumer feels vaguely interested, there will typically be a reaction of "I'll get around to this later, not now."

What good direct marketing copywriters have discovered—and this is wisdom that even non-direct marketers can benefit from—is that direct-mail copy that gets action tries hard:

(1) to use testimonials and guarantees to develop confidence;
(2) to use as much information as is necessary in the letter to clarify doubts, overcome objections, and increase the reader's level of desire for the product;
(3) to make it easy for the consumer to take action, by having easy-to-use response cards or toll-free telephone numbers:
(4) to "involve" the reader, through devices such as peel-off stamps and scratch-off numbers; and

(5) to express urgency about the need for immediate response, by saying that the offer or free premium is good "for a limited time." expires by a certain date, and so on.

In direct marketing, as in all marketing, the key barrier to getting consumers to act is sheer inertia, and ads that target such inertia directly are most likely to obtain action.

Although the advertisement is not a one-time effort but part of a continuing campaign, its primary goal is intended to precipitate immediate response and its effectiveness can be properly measured by this response. Direct marketing advertising has long been recognized as being perhaps the only area in advertising in which immediate sales are a reliable indication of advertising performance. As a result, advertising professionals look to the experience of mail-order advertisers to learn what works and what doesn't.

SALES PROMOTIONS

Sales promotions are of two broad types: consumer promotions, such as coupons, sampling, premiums, sweepstakes, low-cost financing deals, and rebates; and trade promotions, such as slotting allowances, allowances for featuring the product in retail advertising, display and merchandising allowances, and the like. They are used to get consumers to try or to repurchase the brand and to get the retail trade to carry and to "push" the brand.

Additionally, promotions are also used by manufacturers to '"discriminate" between different segments of consumers—for example, only those consumers who have the time to clip coupons will clip and use them and obtain a lower price for themselves, while those consumers who are time-pressed won't use coupons and ultimately will end up paying a higher price. Finally, retailers use promotions to clear their inventory of slow-moving, out-of-season, or shelf-unstable products for example those products, such as fresh produce, that will spoil if they are not sold quickly. Retailers thus run their own promotions aimed at consumers, such as price cuts, displays, frequent shopper programmes, and so on.

Sales promotions are a key element in inducing trial or repurchase in many communications programs in which advertising creates awareness and favorable attitudes but fails to spur action. One of the reasons they spur action- compared to simple price cuts—is that they are typically run for a limited duration,' which means that the consumer must act quickly, before the promotion ends. Other reasons they spur action is simply that many consumers feel they get value for their money if they buy "a good deal" and consider themselves as "smart shoppers", in fact, many consumers automatically assume that if a brand is being promoted it must be a good deal but this is not always true. By one estimate, 80 percent of U.S. house-holds use coupons, 75 percent of the appliances bought in the U.S. are bought on deal, and 70 percent of the packaged goods sold to retailers are sold with a trade promotion.[23] Simillar tendencies are now also visible in Indian purchasing behaviour and with the opening of Super Stores like, Big Bazar, Vishal Mega Mart, Spencers and many more. Thus, it is important to understand the complementary roles of advertising and sales promotion in order to conduct situation analyses properly and to set communications, advertising, and sales promotion goals.

According to a 1993 survey held in U.S. of promotional practices in seventy leading companies, sales promotions constitute about 73 percent of marketing expenditures of which about 27 percent is spent on consumer promotions, 46 percent on trade promotions, whereas advertising constitutes about 27 percent.[24] The share of the marketing dollar spent on trade promotions has risen rapidly in recent years, in large part due to the growing power of ever-larger retail chains. For instance, America's largest retail chain, WalMart, now accounts for 10 to 15 percent of the sales of many of America's largest packaged goods companies. Some of the power of retail chains also comes from their access to accurate checkout scanner data, which reveals which brands are moving fast off the retail shelves (and which are not) and to their ownership of the precious retail shelf-space "real estate" that the manufacturing companies covet and are willing to pay for. Other reasons for the growth in promotional spending are the trend to more local and regional marketing programs and the greater price competition posed to national brands by store-label (private label) brands.

Clearly, since advertising expenditures take place in this total promotional context and not in isolation, it is essential that the advertising manager have a good understanding of sales promotions as well. While the implementation details of sales promotions and advertising are handled by different individuals in most marketing organizations, brand managers usually are responsible for both areas. In order to be able to offer "integrated" sales promotion services, many of the major advertising agency groups own one or more sales promotion companies such as Alcone Sims O'Brien, owned by Omnicom, or Lintas: Marketing Communications, owned by Interpublic, although many of the leading firms in this area are still independent.[25]

Advertising and sales promotions operate together in their impact on the consumer. When designed and run in tandem, they yield powerful synergies that magnify their individual effects. For example, a coupon offer in a Sunday news paper free-standing insert (FSI) can have a higher redemption rate if theme ads for that brand are run concurrently. On the other hand, if advertising and sales promotion efforts are designed and run in isolation, they can lead to effects that hurt each other-poorly designed promotions, in particular, can quickly erode the long-term image of the brand that advertising has worked hard to build up over several years. This longer-term brand equity dilution effect of promotions is probably greater for brands in highly involving image and "feeling" product areas, because promotions might "cheapen" a brand's image. Brands in product categories in which choices are based on "economic," price-minimizing criteria are not as vulnerable to brand equity dilution.[26] Even if the brand's image is not hurt, most promotions end up only drawing volume from existing users who would have bought anyway, so that the promotion may end up costing the company more money than it brings in.

COUPONS

Coupons are perhaps the most frequently used consumer promotion-over 300 bil-lion coupons were distributed in the United States through print media in the early 1990s, but only about 3 percent were redeemed.[27] Although over 75 percent of all coupons are currently distributed through newspaper FSIs,[28] coupons distributed through direct mail are more targeted than are those distributed through print me-dia like newspapers and magazines and thus have much higher redemption rates (about 9 to 10 percent in direct mail versus about 2 to 3 percent in newspapers). Whereas coupons that are in or on the pack are specifically designed to build repeat purchase and loyalty, those that are carried in other products consumed by a similar target market (such as coupons for a baby shampoo carried in a diaper product) are designed to attract new customers. These latter coupons are called cross-nuff coupons. Coupons (or cash checks) are often offered as straight price rebates for durable products, such as cars or appliances, and are sometimes offered as refunds, mailed to consumers who send in proof of purchase. Manufacturers often hope that many consumers who buy products because of a mail-in rebate never in fact mail-in the rebate, and this is often the case.

From an advertising perspective, it is important in couponing to design the coupon ad in such a way that it builds on, and reinforces the positioning and key benefits developed in theme advertising, rather than having a different theme or no theme at all, other than the price incentive. Similarly, a rebate offer might be creatively designed to highlight a brand strength—for instance, an offer to pay for a car's gas consumption or maintenance expenses in its' first year might better highlight the car's gas economy or repair record than a simple rebate check. In addition, of course, the coupon must be designed so it is easy to clip, shows the package prominently, has the appropriate legal copy, and so on.

From a media standpoint, another key objective in couponing is to make sure it really gets new users instead of merely going to existing users who would have bought it anyway. The easiest way to deliver coupons, to gain mass reach, is to use newspapers. However, it has been estimated that only one-third of coupon usage, from such mass-distributed coupons such as those in Sunday newspaper FSI's, comes from new users. As a result, many more companies are either mailing coupons via direct mail to those known to be nonusers, or using new in-store services which prints a coupon for a brand at the point-of-sale to someone who has just bought a competing brand. The coupon is "triggered" by the scanned purchase of the competing product.

This synergy can work the other way as well: coupons or other promotional offers can be used to increase the effectiveness of an ad by increasing readership. Apple Computer supported the introduction of its Macintosh with a "Test Drive a Macintosh" promotion, which allowed customers to leave computer showrooms with $2,400 worth of equipment.[29] The budget was $10 million, of which $8 million went to advertising and the rest supported such activities as in-store displays and carrying the inventory costs. Around 200,000 Macintoshes were test driven, at a cost of only $5 each.

CONSUMER PROMOTIONS

Consumer promotions are designed to offer consumers an incentive such as a lower price or a free or low-cost premium or gift to try a brand for the first time, to switch back to it, or to repurchase it. The different types of consumer promotions vary in their trial versus repurchase orientation, as will be pointed out below. A few consumer promotions, such as sweepstakes and premiums, can be designed with a view to enhancing the key imagery equities of the brand.

PRICE PACKS

Price packs are those packs that offer a lower than usual price, or greater than usual quantity are another kind of consumer promotion that can both attract switching and reinforce loyalty. Here again, it may be more supportive of the brand's advertised image to offer "extra" product volume than to simply lower price. For some products such as tea, coffee, detergents, etc., it may be possible to offer the "extra" volume in a special container such as a glass carafe or plastic dispensing unit that reinforces some aspect of the brand's image.

SAMPLING

Giving people free samples or trial packs by door to door, at street corners, in stores or shopping malls, or through the mail is another promotional technique and is an excellent but expensive way to get consumers to try a product. Chesebrough-Pond's; for instance, distributed 80,000 full-size samples of its new products, plus coupons and literature, in five shopping malls. A new product launch could include a small sample mass-mailed to possibly half of the nations households. Alternatively, for an existing product, small trial packs could be mailed to households known—as part of a databased marketing effort—to be current users of a competitive product. New and creative avenues for in-store sampling include sampling children's products in toys stores such as Toys R Us, sampling products aimed at teenagers in college bookstores, and so on. In such sampling programmes, care must be taken to provide enough product quantity to convince the 'trier' that this is indeed a better product, while simultaneously minimizing product, packaging, and mailing expenses.

SWEEPSTAKES

Sweepstakes are another kind of consumer promotion, and these offer the greatest potential to reinforce a brand's advertising platform. McDonald's, for instance, ran a sweepstakes promotion at the same time that its ads were featuring a "McDonald's menu song" in which consumers had to play a plastic record to find out if they had won-with the record featuring the same menu song. Benson & Hedges cigarettes, around the time it launched a 100-mm-length version, ran a sweepstakes in which consumers had to pick which one of a hundred mini contests they wanted to enter, in which each of these mini contests had as their prize 100 units of something such as 100 pints of ice cream.

SUBSIDIZED FINANCING

This incentive is frequently used in the promotional programs for many durable products, including automobiles. Since these products are often purchased by consumers on monthly installment plans, the consumer is more concerned with the monthly payment amount, including the monthly interest payment, than the total amount paid. Companies therefore attempt to lower this monthly amount by offering a subsidized interest rate, often through a captive financing subsidiary such as General Motors Acceptance Corporation, in the case of General Motors. The key thought in the foregoing discussion on consumer promotions is that promotions are needed to move the consumer along to making the needed "action" step, or needed to build loyalty and promote repurchase, after advertising has done its job in creating awareness and preference. However, promotions can sometimes hurt a brand's image by cheapening it, but this is not necessary if the promotion is designed with a view to working with and strengthening the brand's advertised image.

PREMIUMS AND GIFTS

The same kind of thinking can be used to select premiums that are offered to consumers are "free" products that are provided in the pack or mailed if multiple proofs of purchase are sent in, either at no cost or at below-retail prices. If the latter, they are called self-liquidating premiums because the company recovers its out-of-pocket costs. An intelligently selected premium can be used to reinforce a brand image: Mueslix cereal from Kellogg, from instance, which built its initial advertising campaign around a European heritage, offered consumers a packet of Eu-ropean currency notes if they sent in the required number of proofs of purchase. In-pack premiums such as toy characters in children's cereals can also be designed to build a brand's image. The cigarette brand Marlboro offers loyal con-sumers-those who collect enough boxtops-merchandise with an outdoorsy. Western, cowboy theme that reinforces the brand's classic imagery. Since such premiums typically require multiple proofs of purchase, they are designed most often to build repeat purchase and customer loyalty.

TRADE PROMOTIONS

Trade promotions are financial incentives given to the trade to stock the product, to buy in larger quantities, to move merchandise from the warehouse onto the re-tail shelf, to display the brand in end-aisle displays, or to feature the brand in local retailer advertising such as on "best food days"-Wednesdays or Thursdays, for example the cheapest "Sale Day" is Wednesday in Big Bazar, including offering retailer coupons, and so on. Another purpose served by trade promotions is that they give the manufacturer some degree of control over the final price charged to the end-consumer: if the price to the retailer is cut, it should lead to at least slightly lower prices for the consumer.

These trade promotions often have the objective of "buying" retail shelf space and getting additional retailer "push" by loading the retailer with extra inventory or of giving the retailer a temporarily lower price in the hope that some of the price cut is passed on to the consumer. Unfortunately, retailers have begun to keep back for themselves much of the price incentive they are expected to pass on to the consumer, the pass-through percentage is often only about 50 percent. In addition, many retailers often forward buy more deal-promoted product volume than they can sell at that time, either using the extra volume for non-promoted future time periods, or "diverting" that volume to other dealers at a slight mark-up. As a consequence of these practices, trade promotions have begun to account for a very large percentage (20 to 30 percent) of retailers' total profits.

Because of these problems, manufacturers have recently begun to cut back on these promotions, often by substituting a lower everyday low price (EDLP) for a sometimes-high, sometimes-low (high-low) price and promotion policy. Since cutting back on trade promotions will obviously hurt retailers' profits, manufacturers have begun to compensate for these cuts by also trying to hold down the costs that retailers incur in warehousing, transporting, and stocking that manufacturer's products through processes called efficient consumer response. The hope is that the retailers' direct product profitability (DPP) on these manufacturers' brands does not suffer.

In addition, many companies have begun to offer advice to retailers on how to maximize their income return from each section of the store, by showing them how to allocate their retail shelf space optimally among the different brands, using planograms. This approach is called category management, and has led to many manufacturers developing closer relationships with each retail chain so that they can understand the retailer's needs better, often on a store-by-store or market-by-market basis.

Some of the types of trade promotions frequently used by manufacturers are described briefly below.

Off-Invoice or Buying Allowances

These incentives are the simplest form of trade promotion and are nothing more than a price cut of a certain percentage applied to the volume bought by a retailer during the promotional period e.g., 5 percent may be taken off the invoice, hence the name. No retailer performance such as displays, feature ads in retail store circulars, etc., is required. As mentioned, retailers often purchase more than they can sell during such promotional periods to have enough stock to last them to the next promotional period, a practice called bridge buying or forward buying. A variant of such promotions is the offer of free goods, such as one unit free per dozen purchased. This has the advantage of requiring the retailer to actually sell the free good before the gains from the promotion are financially realized, putting greater "push" pressure on the retailer.

Count-Recount Allowances

Under this type of trade promotion, the discount is applied not to the quantity the retailer buys from the manufacturer during the promotional period, but only to that quantity that is moved from the retailer's warehouses into the retailer's stores. As a consequence, the retailer is given a greater incentive to pass the price cut on to the consumer so that the product "moves" from the store into consumers' hands.

Billback Allowances

These allowances are paid by the manufacturer to the retailer on a per-case basis only if certain performance criteria are met. While they have the advantage of "pay-for-performance," they have the disadvantage of requiring sales force and administrative time to monitor compliance.[30] The kinds of "performance" expected from the retailer could include in-store displays, feature ads in the retailer's circulars, and so on.

Display Allowances

These allowances are incentives to the trade to display the product prominently, in an end-of-aisle or store-window display. These have been found to be very effective, because many time-pressed consumers simply pick up those brands that are made salient by such displays, assuming they are on sale which is not always the case. Stores like such allowances because they are a good source of revenue a grocery chain might charge $200 per week per store for a display. For durable goods, such displays are often a very valuable tool to educate both the consumer and the retail salespeople about the special features of the product.

Slotting or Facing Allowances

These allowances are one-time fees paid by the manufacturer to the retailer to get a new brand on the retailer's shelf, paid to compensate the retailer for the brand removed to make space for this new brand and for associated inventory and administrative costs-and the risk-involved with the new brand. These fees may cost manufacturers anywhere from $10,000 to $100,000 per item per chain.[31]

Trade Inventory Financing or Delayed Billing

These financial incentives are used most often in durable goods industries, such as appliances or automobiles. The manufacturer lowers the cost to the retailer to pur-chase products to stock on the retail floor or in inventory, either by offering a reduced-rate financing facility, by delaying billing, or both.

In-Ad Grocer Coupon

This type of payment by the manufacturer is made to the retailer in return for which the trailer features a coupon for that brand in the retailer's weekly advertising circulars, the coupon is redeemable only in that retailer's store. The manufacturer pays the coupon face value, plus handling costs.

SWEEPSTAKES, CONTESTS, AND SPIFFS

These are incentives used to reward retail salespeople who meet their sales quotas for the manufacturer's good, usually for durable goods, paid for by the manufacturers of those products. Ideally, these are timed to run concurrently with consumer promotions.

There is emerging consensus that, in addition to the several negative consequences discussed earlier, these trade promotions also have the potential to erode a brand's franchise and image. They do this by reducing the amount spent on advertising and in increasing the extent to which the consumers buy the brand in the supermarket because it is "on deal" that week, rather than because of its ad-vertised image. This leads to an increase in the perception that the brand is a commodity, or parity product, rather than something with unique added values. Here, again, the smart advertiser must strive to focus these trade deals on advertising-enhancing activities such as thematically linked displays or thematically consistent retailer advertising.

In the longer run, of course, only an advertiser with a strong brand consumer franchise-built up through consistent advertising-will have the market clout to withstand retailer pressure to provide higher and higher trade allowances. Strong brands with demonstrated "sell-through", advertising-induced consumer demand, will not have to give as much to the retailer although the trade will often "push" stronger brands of their own accord and will thus end up as more profitable brands.

Another form of interaction pertains to their timing: consumers are more likely to notice the advertising for a brand and the promotions for it if both are run concurrently rather than in separate time periods. Such a co-ordinated campaign is more likely to break through the clutter. This is likely to enhance the effectiveness of both the advertising campaign through higher readership or viewership and of the promotional programmes through greater coupon redemption or in-store sales from special displays.

OTHER ACTION-ORIENTED COMMUNICATIONS

Retail Advertising

Another example of advertising that has direct, action objectives is the advertising of retailers, or retail advertising. What are the advertising practices of successful retailers? The best retail advertisements are those that provide the consumer with a lot of specific information, so that the consumer can see immediately that he or she must indeed visit the store. It is not enough, therefore, for example, that the shirts on sale are available in various colours and sizes: it is much more action-inducing to list the exact colours, sizes, and prices, any piece of missing information could hinder action. It is also important to create a sense of immediate availability and urgency, by stressing that this availability and these prices are 'for a limited time only." Such tactics are frequently used by Big Bazar and Vishal Mega Mart in India too.

While there is probably little carryover effect of advertising of a specific storewide sale, retail advertisers are very particular that every retail ad fit and enhance the specific long-term image of the store. Every ad from Bloomingdaie's, Lord & Taylor, and so on is carefully tuned to the particular character-the "look and feel"-that the store has carefully developed over the years. For durable products, such as large appliances and automobiles, an appropriate behavioural objective for advertising might be to entice customers to visit a dealer's showroom. For large-ticket consumer items, the final phases of the selling process are usually best handled by a person-to-person sales effort, with advertis-ing used appropriately to draw people to the showroom. In such situations, "traffic-building" advertising becomes key, and once again the advertising must try to create a strong sense of desire, curiosity, and urgency to get the reader or viewer to make that store visit.

Co-operative Advertising

A situation closely related to retail advertising is that of co-operative advertising, in which a manufacturer offers retailers an advertising program for the latter to run.[32] The program may include suggested advertising formats, materials to be used to create actual advertisements, and money to pay a portion quite often, half of the cost. It also often includes requests or requirements that the retailer stock certain merchandise quantities and perhaps use certain displays. By some estimates, almost one-half of retail advertising is some form of co-op advertising.

There are three types of co-op advertising:

(1) vertical, when an upstream manufacturer or service provider, such as Royal Cruise Liners, pays for a down-stream retailer's ads, such as a travel agent's ads;

(2) horizontal, when local dealers in a geographical area pool money, as in automobiles or fast-food chains; and

(3) ingredient producer co-operatives, when the producer of an ingredient, such as Nutrasweet, pays part of an ad run by the user product, such as Diet Coke.

Recent estimates have put the amount of co-op advertising in the U.S. at about $1(1 billion per year, of which about two-thirds are spent through newspapers.[33] Co-op ads thus constitute a large portion of newspaper advertising revenue, and newspapers have set up set up organizations such as the Newspaper Co-op network, and the Newspaper Advertising Co-operative Network to alert local retailers to manufacturer co-op programs they may not be fully utilizing.

The intent of cooperative advertising, in part, is often to stimulate short-term sales. The advertising is well suited to this task because it is usually specific as to the product, the place at which it can be purchased, and the price. However, co-op advertising also has other longer-term objectives: namely, to reinforce the brand image of the original manufacturer or service provider and to maintain the manufacturing company's leverage with the retail trade. The former is especially important because retail store buyers and salespeople often favor products that come with large allowances, to the extent that a product not having the expected co-op amount can find itself losing distribution.

The latter implies that the manufacturer needs to monitor and control co-op advertising content carefully, to ensure that it is consistent with the national ad campaign. Weak control over the creative content and media placement of co-op ads run by small retailers can contribute to a lack of consistency in the image of the brand and even the creation of negative associations with the brand, potentially hurting the brand's equity. Such creative control can be obtained by providing the local retailer with advertising slicks created by the manufacturer's agency, which can then be customized by the local retailer while still being consistent with the national campaign for the brand.

Given the pressures from the retail trade and from one's own sales force to maintain and even increase co-op advertising allowances; a marketer is often tempted to allocate more money into co-op advertising at the expense of national advertising, in deciding how much money to allocate to co-op advertising, the marketer needs to determine if the product will really benefit from being associated with a store's image. Such benefits are typically higher for the case of fashion goods, hi-fi stereo equipment, and so on, which are expensive and image-driven products about which consumers seek retail information and endorsements: these benefits are lower for inexpensive, frequently purchased products such as toothpaste or shampoo about which the consumer does not seek retail advice. The key question is: What are the relative roles of national advertising and store advertising in influencing consumer brand choice processes?

In addition to looking at consumer decision processes, the advertising planner must also be concerned with the need to acquire or expand distribution; a high need typically compels higher co-op allowances. Further, legal and administrative requirements must be met. For example, co-op allowances have to be offered on an "equally available to all" basis unless it can be demonstrated that certain stores to whom proportionately higher allowances are being offered will lead to a greater gain in new customers to the manufacturer.[34]

A co-op programme is likely to yield greater benefits to the manufacturing company if the program is tightly monitored (e.g., limited to certain slow-moving sizes of products rather than all sizes). The administrative burdens of a co-op programme, also need to be remembered: claims need to be documented and compliance checked before payments are made, and this can be a tremendous headache if hundreds of retail accounts are involved. Software packages exist to streamline this process.[35]

Reminder, Point-of-Purchase, and Specialty Advertising

Sometimes, the primary role of advertising is to act as a reminder to buy and use the brand. The brand may be established and have a relatively solid, stable image. Reminder advertising then serves to stimulate immediate purchase and/or use to counter the inroads of competition. A good example is the Budweiser advertisement. Other examples of reminder advertising are the "shelf talkers" or other point-of-purchase (P-O-P) materials placed in stores at or near the place where the brand is on display. Such P-O-P materials often feature the package, price, and a key selling idea.

Reminder advertising can work in several ways. First, it can enhance the top-of-mind awareness of the brand, thus increasing the probability that the brand gets included on the shopping list or gets purchased as an impulse item. A media plan that aims to enhance or maintain top-of-mind awareness through reminder ads might utilize shorter ads such as fifteen second commercials with a high level of frequency or use media such as outdoor billboards or transit that are suited to such reminder advertising. Second, it can reinforce the key elements of the national campaign at the point-of-purchase. It has been shown in research by Kevin Keller that if there is a match between the type of information used in the P-O-P material and in an ad for the brand seen previously, the consumer is more likely to re-call the information in the ad successfully, and this leads to more favorable judgments about the brand involved.[36]

In addition, it is often useful in such situations to use items of specialty advertising, useful products given free to consumers that have the manufacturer's name and related information on them. Specialty advertising items go beyond the usual calendars, ball-point pens, coasters, and Rolodex cards to all kinds of creative, high-quality products such as a refrigerator magnet for Domino's Pizza that reminds a hungry but time-starved consumer which phone number to call for quick, home-delivered pizza. Manufactured by supplier companies, such specialty advertising items are not usually handled by traditional advertising agencies but by organizations called specialty distributors or specialty advertising agencies.[37]

In addition to maintaining top-of-mind awareness for a particular brand, reminder advertising can also increase the motivation for the use of the product class as a whole. In this context, the advertising may tend to simply increase the purchase and use of the product class and thus work to the advantage of the leading brand. Thus, reminder advertising for Royal Crown Cola may tend to increase purchases of other colas, to the advantage of Coke and Pepsi. Similarly, Maggi's Noodle, Soups and Sauces is the brand that is in the best position to conduct reminder advertising.

In-store Advertising and Merchandising

In-store advertising is a rapidly growing area of advertising, in large part because of the increasing realization among marketers that most consumer decisions about which brand to buy are made after the consumer enters the store and scans the brands on the aisles.[38] As a result, a variety of new in-store media have become available to the advertiser, such as electronically scrolling ads in the aisles, ads on TVs near the checkout lanes, ads in radio programs played in-store while the consumer shops, on-aisle coupon dispensers, even ads on shopping carts equipped with special video screens. While some of these new services have shown rapid sales growth, others have had to shut down after an experimental run, in part because of the difficulty in measuring results. Actmedia, Catalina, Advanced Promotion Technologies, and Video cart are some of the companies that are very visible in this rapidly growing area.[39]

Another frequently neglected type of in-store communication is the merchandising environment, by which we mean the displays, signs, and positioning of the brand in that particular store. Creative and attention-getting displays in the store serve to do much more than stock the product: they can greatly add to a sense of excitement about the product and lead to much greater involvement by the consumer in that product. An example would be the in-store "'computers" used by cosmetics companies such as Noxell that lets consumers make their own colour matches. Service establishments, such as banks like Citibank or fast-food restaurants like McDonald's, are constantly experimenting with better branch displays and signage to increase cross-selling opportunities as well as to create the particular kind of image and ambience that are so vital to creating a service company's brand image and equity.

Industrial Marketing: Sales Leads

Industrial (business-to-business) marketing is similar to the marketing of durables in that advertising can rarely be expected to make the sales. Rather, a salesperson is usually required to supply information and to handle the details of the transaction. Advertising, in this case, can provide the engineer or buyers with the opportunity to express interest in the product by returning a card which is a request for additional information. These inquiries or leads are then typically qualified by a tele-marketing callback to determine if an in-person sales call is necessary and cost effective. Often this telemarketing call can itself lead to a sale. Once qualified, the salesperson then follows up these leads by calling on the prospect, discussing his or her requirements, and trying to "close" the sale. Thus, for industrial advertising, a useful objective is to generate such inquiries or leads. The reader can get specific information by calling the toll free number in the ad.

Public Relations

Because consumers are exposed to so much advertising these days, they often try hard to avoid it-and are very skeptical of it when they do get exposed it. To reach these hard-to-reach consumers and to convey messages to them in a manner that is more credible partly because it is more subtly delivered, more and more companies today are devoting a portion of their communication budgets to the use of public relations (PR) for marketing purposes. Some of the different ways in which this is done are reviewed below, but what most of them have in common is the delivery of a message about the brand not through paid, explicit advertising, but rather through an implied or explicit endorsement of a credible third-party media source, such as the editorial content of a newspaper or magazine, or by associating themselves with a sports or cultural event, or a charitable organization.

Public relations is usually regarded of as a way to build a corporation's public image before stakeholders such as government, shareholders, employees, and so on, and as a way to counteract negative publicity such as the scare about Tylenol after it was involved in cyanide murders in 1982. While these corporate reputation and crisis communications uses of public relations are still very important, it is being used more and more in the form of marketing public relations.[40] Budgets for such uses of public relations are rising-one estimate puts the total annual amount of PR spending in the U.S. at about $8 billion. Most leading PR agency groups today own one or more PR firms, including two of the biggest: the WPP Group owns Hill & Knowlton, and Young & Rubican owns Burson-Marsteller.

The following are some examples of public relations used as an essential element in integrated marketing communications.

Event and Sports Marketing

Ed Bernays, considered the father of modern public relations, pulled off a huge publicity coup for General Electric by orchestrating the celebrations for the fiftieth anniversary of Edison's invention of the light bulb, in which then-President Herbert Hoover-and millions of others-switched on their electric lights after an NBC announcer gave the signal. Budweiser sponsored the concert tour of the Rolling Stones, Pepsi that of Michael Jackson, both gaining tremendous visibility. Fast food and other companies often run tie-in promotions with movies. Cigarette companies sponsor sports events, like Virginia Slims Tennis and Winston Cup NASCAR racing. Most athletes' at most major sports events today are paid to wear the logos of sponsoring companies.

The sponsorship of big events and sports competitions-such as the Statue of Liberty Centennial, or the L'eggs 10K Mini Marathon for women is a multi-billion-dollar business involving its own specialist firms. Obviously, the key issue here is the "fit" between the event being sponsored and the desired positioning and image of the sponsoring brand or company.

News Stories and Media Editorial Coverage

Cabbage Patch Dolls became a toy craze in 1985 after being featured in a Newsweek cover story, appearing in network and local TV and radio broadcasts, and after first lady Nancy Reagan was shown worldwide giving them to two Korean children hospitalized for heart treatment. New products of various kinds-from Ford cars like the Taurus, to fat substitutes like Simplesse-achieved very high levels of brand awareness even before advertising for them broke because of favourable news coverage. To convey an image of industry leadership, many industrial marketers try hard to have trade magazines carry articles by-lined by their top executives.

Product Placement

Sales of Reese's Pieces candy soared after they were shown in the hit movie E.T. When Ray-Ban provided actor Tom Cruise sunglasses to wear in the movie Top Gun, sales reportedly rose 30 to 40 percent. Auto makers provide cars for free for use in Hollywood TV shows. Almost 75 percent of local TV stations are reported to make use of video news releases, including those on the making of commercials.[41] A study by Advertising Age found 1,035 instances of "product plugs" in a single day of programming on the four major networks.[42] Again, specialist companies exist that, for the necessary fee, will "place" your product in movies and TV shows.

Contests

Salisbury's bake-off recipe contests lead to big sales increases after they are held annually and have made Pillsbury synonymous with baking. Pepto-Bismol sponsors a chili-cooking contest. Combat roach killer sponsors a contest for the World's Largest Roach.

In all of these cases of marketing public relations, the benefit to the brand is not only that the message is delivered through or in the context of a perceivedly neutral, objective, and trustworthy organization or institution, but also that it is relatively cheap. Unlike ad budgets, which can run into the hundreds of millions of dollars, most public relations programs cost well under $1 million. The downside of this cheapness and credibility of course, is the lack of control: you can hope the media will present your story the way you want, but you have no way of ensuring that is what will happen. Public relations payoffs are also hard to quantify. Most companies simply attempt to add up the seconds or minutes of free media exposure for their brand names or logos and then value that exposure at advertising rate equivalents. A few companies actually test for increases in brand awareness, attitudes, or sales in markets with versus without the PR campaign.[43]

Obviously, the standard way to try to get PR coverage is to send out news releases to the media or to hold a news conference. These are more likely to be used by the media if they contain something that is genuinely newsworthy in the context of the publications that are targeted. Ask yourself: If 1 were the journalist receiving this news release, would I consider it news that my readers should see? Following this logic Quaker Oats sponsored and publicised research about the health benefits of eating oats, which was picked up by most media because they thought most readers would in fact benefit from that information. Other ways include the creation of events such as McDonald's sale of its 50 billionth hamburger or the opening of its restaurants in Moscow and Beijing, or the contests described above.

Cause-Related Marketing

Pampers diapers are distributed free at mobile baby care centers at state and county fairs across the country, gaining not only trial but much goodwill for the brand. American Express asks card members to "charge against hunger." donating a few cents from every card use to hunger-fighting organizations. Hall's cough suppressant tablets are distributed free in many concert halls. Phillip Morris, IBM, and AT&T have sponsored major art exhibitions at the Metropolitan Museum of Art in New York and at other museums. Local McDonald's restaurants take the lead in raising funds for Ronald McDonald children's charities and Houses. Campbell Soup gives elementary schools free equipment in return for collected labels for its products.

INTEGRATING THE DIFFERENT ELEMENTS

Thus far in this chapter, we have discussed some of the other communication elements that a communications manager can and should use in addition to advertising. It should be clear that a huge variety of these communication elements exist, and the purpose of this chapter was merely to introduce you to what they were and to refer you to sources for further information. Obviously, the best communication programmes manage to use many of these elements in ways that reinforce each other. The Southwest Airlines case cited in this chapter illustrates such mutual reinforcement of these elements and is an example what is today being called integrated marketing communications (IMC).

Impact of IMC on Advertising Practice

Two major studies of the attitudes toward, and use of. IMC were conducted in 1991 in the United States, by researchers from Northwestern University and the University of Colorado.[44] In both, almost 80 percent of the respondents surveyed marketing and advertising managers from client firms said the concept of IMC was valuable to them by potentially providing greater consistency to their communi-cations, reducing media waste. Their expectation was that the use of IMC would increase, provided that the key barrier to its use-turf battles and egos within their companies and in outside agencies-could be overcome. There was disagreement, however, on who should do the integrating. While marketing managers from larger, higher-expertise companies surveyed in the Northwestern study felt that the companies themselves should do the integrating, managers from smaller companies in the Colorado survey felt that such integration was the responsibility of the outside agencies. Clearly, how best to organize for IMC is a key issue in implementing it, and we will return to it below. Meanwhile, both clients and agencies have clearly become conscious of the need for IMC, and many companies and agencies have begun programs to train their managers to take a more integrated approach to marketing communications.[45]

Therefore, whereas Advertising has many strengths (reaching mass audiences, creating awareness, building preference, etc.), but it also has major weaknesses (targeting individual consumers, making them believe a message, and pushing them to action). Thus, its use has to be combined with that of other communications elements (such as direct marketing, sales promotions, and public relations). And, this usage of all these elements has to be integrated in terms of its message, tone, and effect.

Direct marketing is one communications approach that aims to evoke action. Its distinctive features are the ability to target small segments of consumers, to measure response to different offers, and to build customer databases. Direct marketing ads try to get consumers to respond immediately by building confidence, providing information, making it easy to order, involving consumers in the order process, and creating a sense of urgency that can overcome the natural tendency to inertia.

Sales promotions can be designed to create trial purchases, to stimulate short-term sales, to enhance purchase volume or brand loyalty, or to affect the brand image. Consumer promotional devices include coupons, samples, price packs, premiums, and sweepstakes. Trade promotions attempt to obtain or maintain shelf space, build retail inventory, get retail "push," and lower retail prices. More money is spent on sales promotions than on advertising, and it is essential that sales promotion efforts be co-ordinated with advertising efforts, to maximize the effectiveness of each and to ensure that the sales promotions do not dilute the long-term image of the brand.

Retail ads aim both to build the store's image and to create immediate sales, through building store traffic. Co-op ads, paid for by both the retailer and the manufacturer, are another important form of retail advertising. Reminder advertising seeks to maintain high top-of-mind awareness, through high frequency and other visibility-enhancing means. In-store ads try to increase brand salience at the point-of-purchase. Industrial ads seek to generate leads and inquiries that can then be followed up through sales calls.

Public relations as a part of marketing tries to increase the credibility of a marketer's communications by appearing subtly in a third-party editorial vehicle.

Techniques include news and editorial mentions, event and sponsorships, product placement, contests, and cause-related marketing. Genuine newsworthiness makes for easier placement. Such PR events are relatively cheap to create but harder to control.

The emerging discipline and philosophy of integrated marketing communications tries to make all these elements work with one voice and in mutually reinforcing ways. A detailed IMC plan for every brand and situation need to be thought through. The key problems issues in implementing it are those of training and organization, both internal and external.

REFERENCES

1. Scott Hume, Advertising Age, September 23,1991.
2. Don E. Schultz, "Integrated Marketing Communications : May be Definition in the Point of View", Marketing News, January 18, 1993, p.17.
3. *Ibid.*,
4. Jennifer Lawrence. "Integrated Mix Makes Expansion Fly," Advertising Age. November 8. 1993, p. S-l0-S-12.
5. Duncan and Monarty, Driving Brand Value: Using Integrated Marketing to Manage Stakeholder Relationships.
6. Glen J. Novak and Joseph Phelps, "Conceptualizing the integrated Marketing Communications' Phenomenon: An Examination of Its Impact on Advertising Practices and Its implications for Advertising Research," Journal of Current Issues and Research in Advertising, 16, no. 1 (Spring 1994), pp. 49-66.
7. See Novak and Phelps for some recent statistics on growth rates and spending estimates.
8. Many of these trends are discussed in detail in Tom Duncan. Clarke Caywood, and Doug Newsom, "Preparing

Advertising and Public Relations Students for the Communications Industry in the 21st Century," Report on the Task Force on Integrated Communications, December 1993.

9. Tom Duncan, "Is your Marketing Program Co-ordinated?" Advertising Age, January 24, 1994, p. 26.
10. Don E. Schultz, Stanley I. Tannenbaum, and Robert F. Lauterborn, Integrated Marketing Communications (Chicago: NTC Business Books, 1993).
11. Adrienne Ward Fawcett, "Marketers Convinced: Its Time Has Arrived," Advertising Age, November 8, 1993. p. S-l.
12. See the Caywood. Schultz, and Wang report, *op. cit.*, for more details on these client perceptions.
13. Tom Duncan, "Is Your Marketing Program Co-ordinated?" Advertising Age, January 24. 1994, p. 26.
14. Wayne McCullough, "Organizational issues in Integrating Marketing Communications: The Relationship Between Structure and Functioning." Marketing Science Institute Report pp. 94-109, July 1994. Conference Summary on "Marketing Communications Today and Tomorrow."
15. Roy T. Bergold. "Integrated Marketing and the McLean Deluxe," in "Integrated Marketing Communications," Northwestern University, Medill School of Journalism, June 1991.
16. The median cost per call was $225, according to Sales and Marketing Management, February 26. 1989, p.75.
17. For a discussion of database marketing issues, see Lisa Petrison, Robert C. Blattberg, and Pail Wang, "Database Marketing: Past, Present, and Future." Journal of Direct Marketing, 7 Summer 1993, no. 3, pp. 27-44.
18. For these and other statistics, see the "Catalog Review'" supplement to The New York Times, March 27, 1994.
19. See Advertising Age, July 12, 1993, Special Report on Direct Response.
20. For information on databased direct marketing, consult David Shepard Associates. Inc. The New Direct Marketing: How to Implement a Profit-Driven Database Marketing Strategy (Homewood. IU., Dow Jones-Irwin, 1990). For more general information on direct mar-keting, see Robert Stone, Successful Direct Marketing Methods, 4th ed. (Lincolnwood, IU.,: National Textbook Company, NTC Business Books, 1988).
21. Advertising Age, May 24, 1993, p. 13.
22. For a discussion, see Glen J. Nowa[1]- and Joseph Phelps. "Understanding Privacy Concerns," Journal of Direct Marketing. 6. no. 4 (Autumn 1992). pp. 28-39.
23. See, for example, Robert C. Blattberg and Scott A. Neslin Siles Promotions: Concepts, Methods, and Strategies (Englewood Cliffs, N J: Prentice Hall. 1990); John A. Quelch, Sales Promotion Management (Englewood Cliffs, N J: Prentice Hall, 1989); Don E. Schultz and William A. Robinson, Sales Promotion Management (Chicago: Crain Books. 1982); John C. Totten and Martin P. Block. Analyzing Sales Promotions: Text and Cases (Chicago: Commerce Communications. 1987): and Stanley M. Ulanoff, (ed). Handbook of Sales Promotion ("New York: McGraw-Hill, 1985).
24. Progressive Grocer, 72, no. 10 (October 1993), p. 69.
25. Advertising Age has special reports on sales promotion agency revenues; for example, May 17, 1993.
26. Blattberg and Neslin, Sales Promotions, p. 474.
27. Advertising Age, various issues.
28. Advertising Age. April 3, 1989. p. 38.
29. William A. Robinson and Kevin Brown, "Best Promotions of 1984: Back to Basics," Advertising Age, March 11. 1985, p. 42.
30. Food and Beverage Marketing, Nov. 1, 1992, p. 30.
31. Food and Beverage Marketing. May 1991, p. 30.
32. Robert F. Young, "Cooperative Advertising, Its Uses and Effectiveness: Some Preliminary Hypotheses." Marketing Science Institute Working Paper, 1979.
33. Sales and Marketing Management, May 1992, p. 40.
34. Isadore Barmash, "FTC Plans Rule Change on Co-op Ads," The New York Times, February 21, 1989.
35. Sales and Marketing Management, May 1986, p. 90.
36. Kevin L. Keller, "Cue Compatibility and Framing in Advertising," Journal of Marketing Research, 2 (Februuary 1991), pp. 42-57.
37. For details, see George L. Herpel and Steve Slack, Specialty Advertising: New Dimensions in Creative Marketing (Irving, TX: Specialty Advertising Association International,) and Charles S. Madden and Marjorie J. Cabailero-Cooper. "Expectations of Users of Specialty Advertising," Journal of Advertising Research, July/August 1992. p. 45.
38. Marketing News, May 14. 1990.
39. See, for example. Business Week, March 29, 1993. p. 60, and Advertising Age, July 19, 1993, p. 31.
40. This phrase, and many of the examples that follow, are taken from Thomas L. Harris, The Marketers Guide to Public Relations (New York: John Wiley, 1993). The interested reader is strongly encouraged to read this book.

41. See, for example, the The Wall Street Journal, September 24, 1993, p. Bl.

42. Advertising Age, July 12, 1993, p. 21.

43. Advertising Age, Special Report on Event Marketing, June 21, 1993.

44. Clarke Caywood, Don Schultz, and Paul Wang, "Integrated Marketing Communications: A Survey of National Consumer Goods Advertisers," Department of Integrated Advertising/Marketing Communications, Northwestern University, June 1991, and Thomas R. Duncan and Stephen E. Everett, "Client Perceptions of Integrated Marketing Communications," Journal of Advertising Research, 33 no. 3 (May/June 1993) pp. 30-39.

45. Rajeev Batra, John G. Myers and David A. Aaker, Adverstising Management, Prentice Hall of India, 2000 pp. 71-107.

CHAPTER 7

FACETS OF INTEGRATED MARKETING COMMUNICATION

THE PERPETUAL DEBATE: CREATIVE VERSUS HARD-SELL ADVERTISING

For decades there has been a perpetual battle over the role of advertising in the marketing process. The war for the soul of advertising has been endlessly fought between those who believe ads should move people and those who just want to move the product. On one side are the "suits" or "rationalists" who argue that advertising must sell the product or service and that the more selling points or information in the ad, the better its chance of moving the consumer to purchase. On the other side are the "poets" or proponents of creativity, who argue that advertising has to build an emotional bond between consumers and brands or companies that goes beyond product advertising. The debate over the effectiveness of creative or artsy advertising is not new. The rationalists have taken great delight in pointing to long lists of creative and award-winning campaigns over the years that have failed in the marketplace, such as the humorous commercials for Alka-Seltzer from the 1960s and 70s and the Joe Isuzu spokes-liar ads from the late 80s. They also point to the recent dot-com explosion that brought with it a lot of creative and award-winning ads but proved that great advertising alone cannot make consumers buy a product or service they really do not want or need.

There are many examples of creative campaigns that moved consumers' emotions but were terminated because they failed to move the sales needle and they put accounts and reputations on the line. In 1998 Levi Strauss & Co. terminated Foote, Cone & Belding, of San Francisco, from its Levi's jean account after 67 years because of declining sales, even though the agency had consistently earned rave reviews and awards for its creative work. The company moved its account to TBWA/Chiat/Day, which won accolades for its creative work on campaigns such as "Opt for the Original" and "Make Them Your Own." However, the popularity of Levi's among young people plummeted 74 percent from 1996 to 2001, with only 8 percent citing the brand as their favourite jean, down from 31 percent in 1996. In early 2002 Levi Strauss parted company with TBWA/Chiat/Day and moved its business to Bartle Bogle Hegarty, the agency that has handled advertising for Levi's in Europe for a number of years.

Another company that had differences of opinion with its agency over artsy versus more hard-sell advertising is Norwegian Cruise Liners. The company's marketing director, Nina Cohen, felt that the sensual "It's different out here" campaign produced by Goodby, Silverstein & Partners in the mid-90s was gorgeous but irrelevant. She said, "Every frame of those ads was frameable, but we're not in the framing business." Cohen added that "while there are some creative icons out there who feel they have some higher voice to answer to, as clients, we're the ones you have to answer to." However, the agency's co-creative director, Jeff Goodby, considered his agency's creative work for Norwegian both beautiful and effective and argues that the impact of creative and entertaining advertising on sales isn't always quantifiable for good reason. He notes: "It's where the magic happens in advertising, and you can never predict that.

It's dangerous to be suspicious of that." Many of the "poets" on the creative side agree with Goodby and like to cite the teaching of legendary adman Bill Bernbach, who preached that persuasion is an art, not a science, and that its success is dependent on a complex mix of intangible human qualities that can be neither measured nor predicted.

Most of the "poets" who support advertising that connects on an emotional level insist that selling product is as much a priority for them as it is for those on the rational side of the debate. One top agency executive notes, "We've proven that this kind of advertising works; otherwise we wouldn't be in business, us or the agencies that practice the craft at this level." However, Brent Bouchez, founder of Bouchez Kent and Company and a creative director for 20 years, argues that the poets are losing sight of the fact that advertising is about selling things and that being really creative in advertising means solving problems and building interesting brands that people want to buy. He notes; "It's time we stopped teaching young creative people to consider it a victory if the logo in an ad is hard to find, or if the product doesn't appear in the commercial at all. It's time we stopped using "break through the clutter" as an excuse to say nothing about what it is we're selling or why you should buy it."

It is unlikely there will ever be peace between the warring factions as long as there are "rationalists" and "poets" who make a point of arguing over which approach works best. Steve Hayden, vice-chairman of Ogilvy Worldwide, says, "It's the ad industry's reflection of the essential Platonic/Aristotelian split in the world, pitting two groups of people against each other who usually can't agree which end is up." However, Nina Cohén, who has worked on both the agency and the client side of the business, is bewildered by the intense opinions held by people on each side and asks, "Aren't we all here to do the same thing?" meaning to build brands and business. While the answer is, of course, yes, the debate over how to do it is likely to continue.

Sources: Alice Z. Cuneo, "Bartle Bogle Tapped to Cure Levi's Blues," Advertising Age, Jan. 14, 2002, p. 6; Brent Bouchez, "Trophies Are Meaningless" Advertising Age, July 30,2001; Anthony Vagnoni, "Creative Differences," Advertising Age, Nov. 17,1997, pp. 1, 28,30

Marketing communications are vital for the success in selling a product. It is not a simple process of selling and buying. The seller must use all the potential at his command to convince the buyer to induce him for a purchase. It can, therefore, be imagined that the process of selling requires several inputs, including, management of advertising, advertising as applicable to Indian customers market and sales promotion.

Effective communication between a company offering a product and the consumer or customer is the key to good and successful marketing. Good marketing means that the product offered for sale must find a large number of buyers. The test of good marketing is determined by the end result. The end result may not be a 100 percent sale; it may be less, say 90, 80, 70, 60, 50 per cent or even less. The end result is not tested in isolation. It has to be compared with the end results of other rival companies offering a similar product under a different brand name. We may leave this discussion at this stage for the time being.

Resuming the discussion of what good marketing or effective marketing communications could be, may be evaluated against the following steps that constitute it.

(1) The company making a particular brand of product, must make it known to the customer market that it is producing such a product.

(2) The next step of effective communication is to make it known that the product is available in the market.

(3) The company should also inform as to where is the product available or identify the point of sale.

(4) The company should project the distinctive features of its product so that it is able to stand out as a class product amidst the brands of similar products being marketed by rival companies.

(5) The company should also be able to convince customers that its product is the best in the market, not merely by a simple claim or statement, but through sound logic.

(6) The company offering the product should be able to secure a proper 'feedback' from the customer-market about how well or ill received is the product.

(7) The company in order to get a proper 'feedback' should develop and build a trustworthy

Marketing Information System and Marketing Research.

(8) The company should also develop and build a strong wing or department, which can analyze the 'feedback' and arrive at specific findings.

(9) The company's advertisement department should also be manned by experts who can modulate the advertising campaign and plan and launch and alternative marketing communication programme.

The traditional view or concept of marketing communications has undergone a sea change. The conventional method of marketing personnel of offering a 'promotion-mix' which includes personal selling, advertising, sales promotion and publicity, is not enough in toady's marketing communication. Market-literature, like folders, leaflets, or handouts issued by marketing wings of companies also depend upon the 'promotion-mix' elements of conventional marketing communication, as mentioned above.

Today, in addition to the traditional 'promotion-mix' other elements that matter for the customers have also become relevant. These new elements like product information, price factor, place of availability and promotion constituent, have become important for vital marketing communications.

Moreover, the company today also concentrates and gives importance to publicizing the product-quality, pays attention to product-packaging making it more colourful and attractive, delivers tell-tale messages or important cues to product-suitability, uses pictures, symbols, insignias, brand-markings or credible logos, that help to make its showrooms more attractive and employs efficient, persuasive, polite and soft-spoken sales personnel. A proper impact of these new elements or stimuli on customers, inducing a favourable response in them, helps to make marketing communication effective.

CONTENTS OF MARKETING COMMUNICATION

The above discussion can help us now to define marketing communications and help us discover its vital elements, as follows:

(1) Constructing or framing a realistic message for the customer.

(2) The message should be drafted by efficient copy-writers which can direct it effectively to the customers target group to who the product is being offered for sale.

(3) The message should be composed of multiple cues or stimuli aimed at activating the target group.

(4) The message of the company offering the product should be conveyed through a suitable media.

(5) The company, if need be, should opt for a media-mix in order to cover the largest chunk of the target group.

(6) The message should be aimed with the objective or intention of promoting a favourable response in the target group, conveying the company's total product offering.

(7) The conveying of the message should be coupled with the company's efforts at securing a proper 'feedback'.

(8) The 'feedback' on collection by the company should be oriented for improving or modifying, if necessary, the company's total product offering.

The company, therefore, while making marketing communications plays a dual role, namely, that of a sender of the message and also as a receiver or market response or 'feedback'. Thus, the company communications with its target market, both through the traditional or conventional constituents of the 'promotion-mix' augmented by the modern promotional stimuli through product, price and place or point of sales communication. The company, in its role as a receiver of market response or feedback, collects information through market surveys and research and its marketing information machinery or infrastructure. This work, as stated earlier, is done by the company's wings or departments of Marketing Research and Marketing Information System.

As stated earlier, the new stimuli of modern marketing communications, which can also be called the 'communication', are as follows:

(1) Product communicates
(2) Price communicates
(3) Place (point of sale) communicates
(4) Promotion Communicates

Marketing Communication Through Product Communicates or Cues

A product no longer is considered an inanimate or lifeless object. A product speaks for itself; it is not dumb. When a marketing communication is made about a product, it actually delivers two messages:

(1) The product possessing a 'live identity', delivers a 'product message' to the customer comprising the meaning and significances of the product to the consumer. The 'product message' makes consumers derive and interpret or attribute a meaning and significance or the 'product message' is conveyed by its physical attributes like its colure, its shape and size, its package, labels, logos, appearance, its brand name and the name of the company or manufacturer.

We know well and recognize the wrappers of toilet soaps, toothpaste packages, a shampoo displaying pictures of women exhibiting hair and styles, an aftershave lotion showing a clean shaven male face in the midst of macho-waves or a package of a ground condiment like 'garam-masala' exhibiting a steaming hot 'chola' dish.

The companies or manufacturers marketing the product load it with innumerable cues both attractive and persuasive, which enables the consumers to attribute meaning and significance to a particular brand of the product in preference to others.

(2) The second message is also from the product identifiable as its image, identity or personality.

Both the above message together create a 'personality of the product' or materialize an 'image in totality', which communicates with the consumer.

We have mentioned that the product gives certain cues or 'product messages' to the consumer, which motivate him for decision-making. It would be worthwhile to examine the messages or cues, which emerge from the total personality or image of a product and how they influence the consumer. In other words, we will now examine how these cues or 'product messages' from various constituents of the product act as 'effective communicators'.

The various elements or constituents of the product, which function as communication can be broadly classified into three categories:

(1) Physical features of the product: six size, shape, form design, colour, layout, finish, odour etc.

(2) Product: Brand name and company manufacturers name.

(3) Product Package: Colour, size, design, label, logo etc.

PHYSICAL FEATURES AS PRODUCT COMMUNICATE

A physical feature of the product is an effective 'product communicates'. These features of the product include the material of the product, its size, shape, from, design, colour, layout finish, odour etc. All these physical features of the product convey messages to the consumer or purchaser and motivate him in his purchase-decision.

For example, an extra large size of a product package conveys the message that the package contains additional quantity of the product. A pocketsize package of the product, gives the impression that it is a convenient carry-size of the product.

The colour of the product package emits different messages. For example, pink colour ensures health assurance; blue colour emits an effect of peace and favourable outcome.

Likewise, shape of the product in an egg container promises strength, oval shape a feeling of elegance, rectangular shape creates an impression of ruggedness and durability, a square-six size assures that the product solves every problem with equal effectiveness.

Product design evokes confidence, convinces or assures the consumer with dependability, trustworthiness and faith.

Product odour like rose, jasmine, etc., arouses a feeling of delicacy, refinement, pleasure, etc.

Similarly, the finish of the product indicates the care and concern with which the company or manufacturer has prepared the product.

On the other hand, a silky touch of the product package infuses in the consumer a feeling of elegance.

These communications from the product can be:

(1) Visual communication, which the consumer acquires through his sight

(2) Tactile communication which the consumer gets through touching and feeling the product, and

(3) Performance communication, which the consumer experiences through seeing the performance or use of the product.

Visual, tactile and performance communication make an early impact or take precedence in influencing the customer or consumer.

When a customer wants to buy a pair of jeans, the colour, finish or appearance makes a first impact, which is the visual communication of the product. When the customer feels the fabric of the pair of jeans, as to whether the denim makes or the material of which it is made, he comes under the influence of tactile communication and finally when the customer goes inside the dressing-room, wears it and tests or examines its fitting on his person, he is getting the performance communication of the pair of jeans.

Similarly, a woman customer who enters a readymade garments shop, opts to buy a 'salwar-kameez' suit, first comes under the impact of visual communication by having a look at the suit, its design, colour, stitching. Next when she feels the fabric used for making the suit, holds it in her hand and feels the various parts of embroidery, frills, lacing, etc. She is acting on the tactile communication emerging from the suit. Finally, going inside the dressing room, she wears it and examines its impact on her person by looking at her image in the mirror; she is examining the performance communication from the suit.

Tactile communication is very important, especially when the customer is purchasing a non-aesthetic product or a utility product. For example, he pushes his hand inside a bag of seeds or a bag of chemical fertilizer, to feel the texture of the seeds or the quality of fertilizer. Customers while buying a scooter, motorcycle or a car are deeply interested in the performance communication of the product. They invariably demand rigorous trial test runs of the vehicles for satisfying themselves about their performance, petrol average, noiseless running, operational smoothness, seat comfort, driving-ease and other aspects which vouch safe for the suitability of the scooter or car brand.

The performance 'communicate' of the product becomes vital when the item of luxury or comfort is being purchased by the buyer. In such instances the performance of the item is more important then the visual and tactile communication of the item, the ability of to perform has to be proved by the product, especially when the product, is a highly-priced durable like scooter, cars, washing machines, a vacuum cleaners; music-systems, television set, tape recorders, computers, printers, etc.

PACKAGE 'COMMUNICATES' FROM THE PACKAGE

The package of the product, whether it be on the shop shelf, show-window or in the sales-counter showcase, functions as a 'silent salesman'. Companies and manufacturers have, fully realized the power and potential of the product-package. They, by making the package colourful, attractive and appealing, have converted in into an effective 'communication tool'. The package make the first impact on the customer, the actual product comes later. The colour, shape, size, labels, logo, manufacturer's name, product-utility, brand name, lettering, product message and the material used for the package, together make a visual impact, comprising the 'visual communicate' and as well as the 'physical communicate' felt by the customer on touching and feeling the package, comprise two vital communication cues.

COLOURS ON THE PACKAGE 'COMMUNICATE'

Colours emit a communicative message. Colours have a wide range - dull, soothing, provocative, appealing, convincing, motivating, bright, sparkling, emotive and so on.

Dull colours may fail to attract, soothing colour which pacify, colours that arouse appetite, colours that appeal or motivate, bright colours that infuse energy in the viewer, colours that soothe and induce sleep. Colours are also associated with prosperity; colours also symbolize love and romance. Colours also invoke belligerence, war and aggression; colours that are linked to festivals, colours connected with mourning, sorrow and grief. Climate, age, level of literacy or education religion and psychology determines or influences colour preferences. Association of events with colour, or tragedies linked to colour cannot be ruled out. Some colours are considered auspicious; others inauspicious. Colours are also associated with feelings and emotions, like pink in the dining hall is reported to excite appetite, green symbolizes prosperity and progress, blue for bedrooms is reported to be soothing and helps induce sleep. Yellow in the kitchen indicates or is associated with cleanliness. Thus, colours seem to be endowed with powerful communicative potential.

A judicious combination of colours on the packaging of a product, therefore, has a great appeal for the customer. An intelligent colour scheme both in packaging of a product and in the layout and design of an advertisement ensures good results and response.

Business houses engage psychologists and researchers and spend a lot of money for deciding the colour scheme of the packing of their product. Similarly, advertising agencies too invest large amounts of money for deciding the colour scheme of the advertisement layout and design. It is a universally accepted fact shades of red and yellow on packages and displayed on shelves of shops and stores, appear bigger than their actual size.

Researchers have reached findings that the red colour is associated with "vitality, power and an urge to win" Cigarette and soft drink manufacturers make extensive use of the red colour on their packaging because the vital selling point of their product is their product have the potential of imparting vitality, infusing power and makes their users winners in life.

On the other hand, blue colour symbolizes "peace, contentment and security". This colour is used extensively by car manufacturers and banks in their logos and symbols. Similarly, yellow colour represents progress, well-being, prosperity and intellectual power.

The colour impact has been aptly described by V.S. Ramaswamy and S. Namakumari in their book on Marketing Management in the following words.

"The colours on the package communicate instantly. A cake of soap in the light blue package may capture the attention of a cultured young lady, a toy in a bright red package may attract a young boy, frozen food in light orange packing may attract a middle-aged housewife, chocolates in a light blue and pink package may attract a girl in love, a book covered in subdued yellow and brown may attract an intellectual. So, the colour plan of the package can have telling communicative effect. The right colour scheme will communicate the nature of the contents; it will capture the attention of consumers; it will reflect the neatness and elegance of the product inside; it will facilitate easy reading of the instructions; and is effect, it does the initial selling through these communicative cues."

DESIGN OF THE PACKAGE

Package design is a powerful 'communicative' cue. The package design should be eye-catching. It should not strain the eye of the consumer and printed matter on it should be easily readable because the customer not merely looks at it, but also examines it holding it in his hands. There is a great possibility that the good and high quality product may not evoke response from customers if its package is badly designed, its colour scheme is poor and the printed matter on the package cannot be read by the customer. In fact, the package design and its colour scheme must together be able to make package communication effective. The illustrations, pictures or photographs, labels, logo and other elements in the package get-up should be blended in such a manner so as to enhance the communicative value of the package.

BRAND NAME 'COMMUNICATES'

The brand name of any product contributes to the overall product personality. The brand name also possesses several theoretical dimensions. We are, however, considering that the brand name communicates or communicative cues which it transmits.

The brand name of a product, in fact, distinguishes it from the products of its rivals in business. Brand names are judiciously chosen because it communicates to prospective/customers a positive meaning, associations and images, which make them take the 'buying decision'.

A good brand name communicates to the prospective customer the product's type, quality, distinctiveness, and also its status amidst rival products. A successful brand strategy often creates and establishes a psychological product differentiation although the product being propogated through, may not be very different to rival products.

V.S. Ramaswamy and Namakumari in their book on Marketing Management have summed up the impact and the role of the brand of a product in the following words:

"Brand name as a component of the total product has a great communication value. No woman asks for just facial make-up; she asks for Ponds, or Lakme. She does not ask for shampoo; she asks for Halo, Sunsilk, Tiara or Glean. From the utility angle, any of these products may serve the purpose. But a buyer identifies products and distinguishes one from the other through the brand name. And this is the main function intended of a brand name—to distinguish the company's product from its competitor's products".

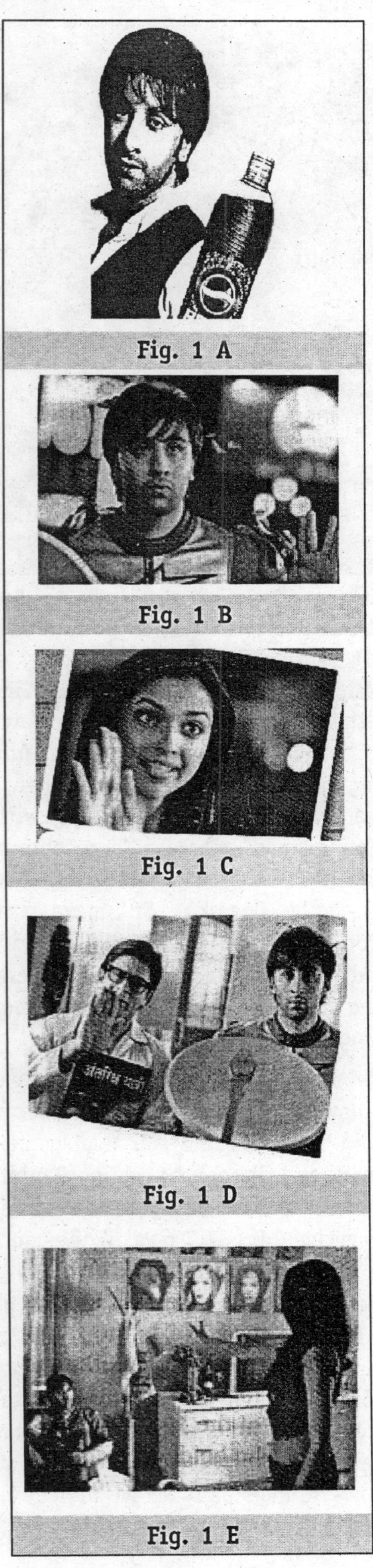

Fig. 1 A

Fig. 1 B

Fig. 1 C

Fig. 1 D

Fig. 1 E

The authors for illustrating the role of the brand name for conveying to prospective buyers a positive meaning and associations in their minds thus: "Halo or Ponds Dream flower, Signal, Angelface, Godrej or Swan, all convey a positive meaning and associations in the minds of the buyers.

Often, slogan supporting brands names, can be easily retained in the purchasers' mind. Virtually, they have a significant 'reminder value' in the market. The authors state: "in the Indian market, Lifebuoy, Lux, Vimal, Nirma, Close-up, Savlon, Ujala etc., use the slogan mode or punch line to fix these products in an unique way in the customers' mind. Like Lux uses 'Mera Sabun – Lux aur Kiya'. Savlon- 'Sau Pratishat Shampoona Snan:' Ujala- Ujala Safedi.

Let us consider the example of "Pepsi' and their latest ad launched in March 2008. This is the latest Pepsi" effort to hit the younger generation, who happens to be the heavy consumer of soft drinks. The story started from 'Oye Babli' to gain from visiting 'Youngistan', developed by JWT with a baseline "Yeh hai Youngistan meri jaan'. See Fig. 7.1 A to F.

Ranbir drops Deepika home and asks whether he can find a Pepsi in her room. Deepika says that he wouldn't just find Pepsi but her bodyguard brother as well. Pepsi-crazy Ranbir climbs up Deepika's balcony but slips and falls down, when SRK comes out and asks him where he is from, Ranbir looks at an electronic board that reads, 'Young Hindustan Supermarket' and he says in a robotic tone from 'Youngistaan' - another planet, adding that he plans to become his sister's bodyguard. SRK allows Kapoor into Padukone's room, where they enjoy their privacy-and Pepsi!

Fig. 1 F

The three hottest names in Bollywood team up in this latest Pepsi campaign, which comes with a new slogan: Yeh Hai Youngistaan Meri jaan'. Single-minded focus of the ad (after 'Hoo haa India, Aaya India') is to re-position Pepsi as a cool & happening drink of the young generation (at a time when summer is showing all the signs of coming back with a bang!), USP is Youngistaan,' where a large chunk of India's population lives in (youth - the. target audience in this case). Ranbir, Deepika & SRK make excellent brand ambassadors - and are utterly convincing. The storyboard, though a tad unreal and over the top, is interesting and will definitely strike a strong connect with Young India. Ek dum right choice, baby!

A few months ago, when the creative brains at JWT sat down to conceptualise a new campaign for Pepsi India little did the top management at Pepsi know that they will soon be adding Ranbir & Deepika to their brand ambassadorial team. Soumitra Karnik, V.P. & Executive C.D., JWT says, 'While conceptualising the new campaign, we didn't write the script with stars in mind. Once the campaign was planned, we suggested to Pepsi who will be the best fit as there needs to be a commonality between the brand and the endorser.' So last year's two most talked about debutantes in Bollywood, Ranbir Kapoor and Deepika Padukone joined hands with Pepsi to start a new revolution - Youngistaan. No we aren't talking about a newly formed state (or country for that matter). We are talking about Pepsi's latest expression for the youth. The cola company has come out with a star studded campaign to reaffirm its youthful imagery.

According to Hari Krishnan, VI! JWT, 'Yeh Hai Youngistaan Meri Jaan is the new expression of India's confident, upbeat youth. They're excelling in everything they do. They are changing the rules of every game and playing it their way. Youngistaan is their new attitude, it is their new world, where they are busy creating the lives they want to live. Adds Karnik, 'Youngistaan' is inspired from the spirit of today's generation. They are opinionated, look for solutions and change things, be it in the field of sports, experimental cinema, politics *et al.* Even 'Lead India' as a concept is all about influencing change.'

With a star studded cast of Shahrukh, Ranbir & Deepika, the Youngistaan campaign has immediately caught the eyeballs of all and sundry. The ad that has been directed by Abhinay Deo of Ramesh Deo Productions interestingly has SRK playing a stoic, over-protective elder brother to the youthful nerve of Ranbir & Deepika. But being the seasoned actor that he is, SRK can do any garb & essay any role with great finesse. Adds Karnik, 'SRK was exposed to the idea of Youngistaan much before Ranbir & Deepika came on to the scene.' Incidentally the creative brains at JWT had trashed some 20-30 scripts for Youngistaan before zeroing in on this one.

For Pepsi, which swears by its A-list of Bollywood brand ambassadors, there was always a doubt that the stars might just overshadow the concept. Counters Karnik, 'The idea behind Youngistaan is much bigger than the celebrities involved. They, in fact, enhanced Youngistaan with their presence.'

The ad is a first in a series and is part of a large campaign that JWT is planning for Youngistaan, to be supported by radio, on-ground, web and wireless media. Guess it won't be long before 'Yeh Hat Youngistaan Menjaan' will begin resonating with the Indian youth. After ail, Pepsi does have a knack for producing memorable taglines. Remember Yehi hai right choice baby, Oye Bubbly and Yeh dil maange more!

COMPANY NAME AS A 'COMMUNICATE'

Big business houses, companies and manufacturers often use their company name with the product in order to highlight its acceptability and excellence. In such cases use of the company's name is done along with the name of the product. Like, almost all products manufactured by the Tata's, carries the company's name as a suffix to the product name like 'A Tata Product' Gores Product like a refrigerator or almirah or locks- 'Gogrej – A House of Quality'.

MULTI-PRONGED "COMMUNICATES' OF A PRODUCT

A product emits various messages or communication for the customer. These messages, as we have seen, emanate from the product/and its colour, shape, touch, design, smell, aroma, appearance etc.; the product package also conveys messages from its size, shape, lettering of printed matter, labels, their colour scheme, pictures and illustrations on the package, brand name of the company or the manufacturer, slogans logos, etc. The entire spectrum of the above mentioned product and its packages communicates, as discussed earlier, convey a convincing meaning to the customer and all of these are positive 'communicates' which enable the customer in decision-making. When all these 'communicates are positive and successful and all the product and package cues are complementary to each other, they tend to produce and, in fact, do materialize a total product image that appeals, convinces and influences the purchaser.

PRICE CUES VITAL TO MAKE MARKETING COMMUNICATION

THE PRODUCT PRICE IS MORE THAN THE PRICE CUE

We are not discussing here the strategies, rationale or basic concepts and other parameters that are taken into account while fixing the price of a product. Under this heading we are analyzing and evaluating the communicative role of price. In other words, the point under examination is how does the price of a product convey something more than the indicated price.

Here we will consider the following aspects:-

1. Price-quality equation
2. Price-status equation
3. Price-technological superiority
4. Price-reasonableness squation.

1. Price-Quality Equation

Quite often, the price of a product, especially when it is higher than, those of similar products, acts like a cue to quality. The product in the higher price range, somehow, tends to give a higher quality assurance to the purchaser. The same consideration comes into play when a person wants to make gift to someone; he or she chooses a higher priced gift rather then the cheaper one. In both the cases, the higher price is associated to brand name, company name etc., because reputed brand name or company name conveys the higher quality assurance.

2. Price-Status Equation

Price is also linked to status; the higher price is somehow synonymous of higher status. The purchaser uses the price, rather the higher price as a cue to higher status; It is a normal buyer behaviour. This applies even to lower-income or middle-income group of buyers. By purchasing the higher priced brand, buyers from these financially less well off income groups, tend to project themselves among their relatives and friends a higher status. Almost all buyers are status conscious when they take the purchase decision. Companies and manufacturers of products, especially, consumer items, use the price-tag to boost their business. This buyer instinct is fully exploited by established brand or company names. The buyer while informing his circle of friends, relatives and admirers about having purchased the higher priced brand, he is actually using the price-tag as his status-symbol, or is parading it as a symbol of prestige.

3. Price-Technological Superiority Symbol

Technological improvement that introduce product superiority or innovations often lures customers and in such cases the price tag, even if it is on the high side, is used by them as the most dependable information cue for making a purchase decision. The customers may come across a wide range of a single product marketed under different brands, say a television or a washing machine, each brand claiming technological superiority, special engineering features, technical excellence, which may confuse even a knowledgeable person, who knows how to take a purchase decision. In such cases customers who are laymen, not aware of technological niceties, may rely on the high price tag as a cue for product excellence for making a purchase decision.

'Reasonable Price'- Consumers' Fad

Customers, somehow, develop an image or concept of what should be the reasonable price of a particular product. The company or manufacturer while marketing its products must, for ensuring good sales or their product, remembers that price, necessarily, may not work as an effective economic tool to attract customers. The price offered for a product must be near the customers' concept of a "reasonable price." The "reasonable price" factor is a psychological factor and has a communicative role, which must be fully exploited for enabling customers in taking a purchase decision.

It may well be appreciated that customers are not aware of the company's cost of production or the margin of profit, which they intend to make in a certain product or about the high quality material, which the product of a particular brand is offering. This concept of "reasonable price" which customers nurture may be based on the prices of similar products available in the market. But, the "reasonable price" factor operates in a peculiar manner. The customers are reluctant to buy a product if its price is more than the "reasonable price" concept, *vice versa* they also decline to buy a product whose price is/lower than the "reasonable price" concept because they are prone to suspect the quality of the product.

MARKETING COMMUNICATION – PLACE, A VITAL COMPONENT

In general, the 'Place' from where the product is bought also determiner the customers' preference in making a purchase decision. We often come across customers who relate the quality of a product to the place from where they have purchased it. They are invariably heard saying that a particular stores stocks all brands of a product which helps in making a choice, that is, so and so shop offers a wide choice, it is a lovely shop, the service is good in a particular shop; so and so shop sells quality products, it is in a good and easily accessible location, it offers competitive prices of a product and so on.

The Image of the stores

The stores where different products are sold also project an image just like the product and its various manifestations as discussed above. The place or the stores which customers visit possesses a number of parameters or factors that attract customers to the exclusion of other similar stores or places in the markets. The stores, its location, its exterior ambience or looks, its display projections, the range of merchandise it has on its racks, its price policy, its reputation in the market, the status segment of customers that visit it, its sales promotion practice, courtesy of its salesmen or sales girls, politeness, hospitality like cold water and soft drinks, the patience taken in offering selections of product, etc., are vital marketing communication cues that attract customers.

Customers normally do not patronize a poorly stocked shop or stores. They also do not prefer any stores or shop in an isolated place; preference normally is for such places centrally located in the center of a posh marketing complex or market place. Price display boards both outside and inside the stores is an additional attraction for customers because it gives them a feeling or impression that the shop is well stocked with a wide variety of merchandise.

The youth would normally prefer a store which has flashy display of goods or which welcomes them to the softly played music of popular numbers of songs. Modern external and interior decoration of the shop is an additional factor to attract young customers. Young ladies may find it inconvenient to buy their stock of cosmetics from a cheap looking shop. On the other hand, they would like buying their inner garments from a store, which allows privacy. The elderly, however may patronize old-fashioned stores which the young would avoid. The physical features of the stores, the department and behaviour of the sales personnel, politeness, mannerisms and patience also work as additional factor to attract customers in general.

Merchandising at Stores Level

Merchandising at Stores Level is vital to customer satisfaction. It is determined by the speed with which the items selected by the customer proceeds from the display racks to his shopping bag. This is possible only when the items selected are quickly billed and paid for by the customers. The customers do not relish an endless wait after selecting their purchase items.

Shoppers crowd may be welcome to the shop owner, but an individual customer's agony is if he finds himself or herself lost in the crowd of other customers necessitating an endless wait. A customer may switch over to a competing brand of a product, if the product of his choice is not displayed on the racks. Sale of a competing brand of product may be instantly beneficial for the stores, but it does no augur well in the long run with it or the company whose brand-addiction with customers is the crucial selling point because such customers are bound to search out the shop or stores where the favourite brand is available. In order to remedy such situation, several companies in the face of stiff competition from producers of similar products, ensure that the shops and stores, which market their product, are an attractive display unit of their products. To ensure this, they often supply the shops and stores with specially crafted and portable display racks or improvisations so that customers do not miss their brand of the product in the stores.

Communication Potential of Stores

An ingenious and judicious organization of stores display, both the exterior and its interior, add or highlight the communication potential of stores or a shop.

Stores-Image is vital to Stores-Preference

The communicative potential of a shop or stores is vital for attracting customers. Customers, on their part, sub-consciously decide stores preferences on several psychological factors. These factors are not considered by customers in deciding their stores choice according to any mechanical order or a pre-set sequence, but operate in the customer's mind sub-consciously. No set rules or preference order can be delineated which function in the customer's mind. Some of the factors that operate in the minds of customers for deciding stores preferences include the formulation of the customer's own criteria of a 'good stores', namely, its character, status and reputation comparison with similar stores, customer-dealing etc.

Quite often customers exercise their preference for a shop or stores on the basis of 'category' or 'specialty' or 'name' of the stores. For example, a "Super-Market" or "Chain-Stores", a "Co-operative Stores", "Exchange-Stores" "Discount-Stores" or an "Exclusive-Stores", act as a powerful communication cue for stores-choice.

"Specialty-Stores" is a pretty old concept in marketing practice for drawing customer. Such old examples are "Lal Imli" or "Dhariwal" retail stores marketing woollens of their quality hallmark for which they have been reputed for decades both for quality and variety. The "Raymond" and "Digjam" retail stores for woolen suiting are later versions of the same marketing concept. "Reliance" retail shops for the modern and updated suiting matching the western or foreign producers of woollen and other suiting is also another example. These and the nationwide range of showrooms of 'Titan' or 'HMT' watches vouch safe both for the entire range of these watches and also for after-sale service for genuine repairs of these watches. The Maruti showrooms, besides the Maruti service stations guarantee both, namely, a genuine purchase and a reliable after-sale service. The 'Bajaj' two-wheelers also have nation-wide showrooms. Moreover, the country-wide stores chains of Cooptex for Tamil Nadu handlooms, 'Tantuja' showrooms for the Bengal handlooms, attract customers who are addicted to their textile products. Even the "Gandhi Ashram" showrooms are a big attraction for the wide range of 'Khadi' products, namely, Khadi cotton, silks, woollens both cloth and readymade garments, honey, powered 'masala', footwear, woodwork, metal ware etc.

"PROMOTION-COMPONENT" IN MARKETING COMMUNICATION

"Promotion-Component" is the most vital factor in marketing communication, besides the three other factors, namely, 'Product', 'Price' and 'Place' as already discussed earlier.

"Promotion" has, for long, been considered synonymous with marketing communication; hence it is important and the most vital factor.

"Promotion" can be studied under the following four heads: -

1. Personal Selling
2. Advertising
3. Sales Promotion
4. Publicity.

Under this head, we shall examine in detail 'Personal Selling' and 'Publicity'. In fact, 'Advertising' itself, 'Advertising' itself is a vast subject, which merits exhaustive and as well as 'Sales Promotion' which has wide manifestation and, therefore, requires separate discussion.

Taking up the first factor of Personal Selling, which again falls within the ambit of Sales Management, we will take up mainly the communicative role of personal selling.

Face-to-Face Transactions

Face-to-face transactions are the first aspect or personal selling. This comprises the inter-action between the sales personnel and customers. Well-trained sales personnel can be very effective as communicators. With the passage of time the well-trained sales personnel can be result-oriented communicators. The sales personnel need to have several qualities to be effective communicators. They should know everything about the product, namely, its quality, technical efficacy, performance, its superiority by elements over rival brands and its after-use satisfaction and harmlessness.

The sales personnel should be able to understand the customer; namely, his nature, strong and weak points, his likely preferences, all of which the sales personnel can size up in the first few minutes. The sales personnel should also be able to understand whether the customer is new to his stores or a casual customer or a regular customer, or is one who can be won over by effective salesmanship.

The sales personnel should also have firm faith and convictions in the company's products, which he is trying to sell, possess a high degree of motivation for recommending the product backed by technical know-how, and exuding confidence in the efficacy of the product.

Product-knowledge

As we have stressed upon product-knowledge in the sales personnel as a vital factor in communicating effectively with the customer, it would be worthwhile to examine it in detail.

Product-knowledge is essential for sales personnel for effective communication with customers, whether the product is a consumer item or a unit of machinery or electrical gadget.

Products of a technical or semi-technical nature are such items about which the sales personnel should have complete knowledge. The customer who arrives to purchase such an item is a lay person, not knowing anything about it and, hence solely depends upon the sales personnel to convince him about the technological aspects and good performance of the item. If the sales personnel fails in educating the customer, they fail in effecting a sale. The knowledgeable salesman or sales girl is a winner with customers. Product-knowledge of sales personnel about such items enables them to fully convince customers about the technical excellence, performance and efficiency of the mechanical or electrical gadget. The sales personnel should also be product-knowledgeable of rival brands of the product.

For example, a customer intending to purchase a 'mixie' can buy a particular brand if the sales personal are able to tell him about how the brand being offered to him is not merely the best mechanical and electrical unit, but is superior to rival brands in the market performance and durability-wise. The same applies to the purchase of a washing machine by a customer who wants to be assured of its performance technical superiority and efficiency.

Customer-Salesman Equation

The customer-salesman equation is also relevant in marketing communication. Identity of the salesman with the customer in the matter of age, culture, language, dress pattern or style, manners etc., at once strikes an identity equation between the two an develops and automatic rapport which helps in effecting a sale.

Apart from technical knowledge, product know-how and customer-sales similarities, the salesman should, as mentioned earlier, be polite, well mannered and a patient listener. The salesman to be successful in his work, should develop this quality because listening patiently to the customer is interpreted or casts an impression on the co-operation on the customer. Communicative efficiency and communicative image is mightily enhanced by the salesman's ability to listen to the customer with patience.

Correct Sales Message

A correct sales message is vital in communication

through personal selling. The salesman may be well equipped with product-knowledge, technical know-how and be well versed with other details, the sales message comprising its content, language, its presentation and its style, is a vital communicative cue in personal selling.

In the sale of technical products it has been found that sales messages prepared judiciously well in advance and presented extempore in an effective and natural manner have worked effectively and favourably with knowledgeable customers. Slip-shod messages in content and construction do not work and lack communicative effectiveness. The companies and manufacturers have, of late, thought it worthwhile to prepare good and effective sales messages, possesses the right or correct communicative contents and train salesmen handling sales of their product. This has been found to pay off in increased sales of the products.

It has been well established that personal selling as a marketing communication instrument or tool proves more effective in the trial stage of the purchase cycle, while advertising proves more result-oriented in the awareness campaign and evaluation stages. The marketing personnel must remember that personal selling while being an effective communication tool has to be supplemented by other marketing components, if it were to become more effective in its communicative role. The role of the correct marketing message must be well appreciated and its function in the entire process properly identified for making the marketing efforts more productive and for achieving better result.

PUBLICITY

Publicity, as stated earlier, is the fourth major cue in marketing promotion and communication. Publicity is not easy to control by the firm, while advertising, personal selling and promotion are within its control.

The firm must plan its publicity campaign carefully. A well-planned and carefully crafted publicity campaign helps in building a good and effective publicity story which describes the improvement, innovations and quality enhancement in the products and services offered by the firm. A publicity story may also centre around some issue of importance to the public at large, so that it can attract the full attention of the people. The most important content or a publicity story must by newsworthy, credible and convincing and arouse the interest of the largest segment of the public at large.

Publicity – A Potential Marketing Tool

Big companies and manufacturers and giant industrial corporates engage themselves in a continuing publicity exercise. They do so by organizing frequent press conferences. Issuing press releases at regular intervals, publicizing their activities through newsletters, leaflets, pamphlets, surveys, opinion polls, and letters to the editor.

It has also been noted that they also issue publicity advertisements for the sake of keeping intact their brand name in public mind. But, it is not easy for companies and firms to control publicity in its favour. Media, especially the print media may publish adverse reports about a specific product or brand that may cause permanent damage to the company's name and reputation. In order to prevent publication of such adverse reports, it is in the interest of product manufacturers or companies to maintain good relations with the media. It is also a well known fact, that howsoever attractive or persuasive may be an advertisement message, a news item in the media has a higher degree of credibility. An advertisement message may be ignored by a customer because they are aware that advertisements of products are designed to promote or enhance sales of the product. Thus, publicity campaigns in the media serve as potent tools in marketing activities. Advertisements do not constitute the entire publicity campaign; congenial or favourable reports about the product or company appearing as news items in the media ensure better response and improve the image of the firm or company.

MARKETING COMMUNICATIONS – A VITAL FUNCTION

We have already seen that the entire four 'Ps' are vital to marketing communications. Just for purposes of recalling the four 'Ps' we may put them in the same order in which they were discussed in detail earlier: Product Communicates; Price Communicates; Place (Point of Sale) Communicates and Promotion Communicates. The obvious conclusion is that marketing communications are a dynamic process, not static one. It is a proactive process in which efforts are made in anticipation of well planned and conceived results. The communication initiated is according to plan. Consumer preferences, price options, suitability of place that is, the point of sale, where the product is available.

Releasing an advertisement is not enough for sales promotion, nor is it sufficient for creating an exceptional demand for the product. It also does not make any product superior to rival products. It is has been over-advertised. Repeated advertisements also do not certify product-quality. Advertisements and their repeated appearance helps to make the customers permanently aware of the product and keeps it embedded in the customers' mind which enables him in decision-making at the time of making a purchase.

Similarly, offering reduction in price of a product is a motivating factor for the customer in making a decision to purchase. It may, sometimes, generate a bias in the customers' mind that the rebate offered might be a cover-up for poorer quality of the product offered for sale. It may also make customers wary of purchasing the product with a reduction tag.

An attractive packaging focuses the attention of customers and makes them inclined to examine the product inside. The colour used in the package sends different messages to the customers. Quite often the colourful packaging of a product tends to make customers doubt the product quality. The packaging and product-quality is an equation, which must not get disbalanced.

Marketing communications has a much deeper meaning. It is a major process and should be continued uninterrupted. It is virtually a continuous dialogue between the firm, company or manufacturer of a product and its customers patronizing the product. As in a dialogue, the communication has to be modified, modulated for effective outcome, similarly the marketing dialogue between the firm, company or manufacturer of product and their customers has to be continually altered, changed, modulated or modified for effective results.

Moreover, the firm, company or manufacturer has to continually adjust and modify their product-message in the context of the changing social and business culture and environment. All the tools of communication have to be employed judiciously and

Fig. 7.2

with imagination for securing the optimum results. All such tools possess a potential of their own. The potential has to be fully used, but in a manner that such potential of each tool supplement each other, rather than counter each other. Thus, marketing communications have to be formulated and executed within the format of a unified and effective strategy.

The present chapter, which deals with marketing communications, provides an overview. The other components in marketing activities include: Advertising Management, Advertising in India and Sales Promotion. These areas of activities are complementary to the overall marketing communications.

Advertising is vital to marketing activities. Advertising has been aptly summed up thus: "Advertising is telling and selling." It has, over the years, matured into a separate discipline. It has become a specialized art and technique. Innumerable innovations have been incorporated in the art of advertising. It has added many subtle components to advertising making it somewhat complex exercise before a modern advertisement is formulated.

Advertising Management is a vital component of Marketing Communications. Advertising Management itself has several elements all of which have to be kept in mind and put to practice for making the management of advertising effective.

Advertising Management must necessarily be examined from different angles. Of late, in the fifties, advertising began to be treated as a commercial or management tool. The first step is to understand the meaning of advertising. Advertising has been defined as "any paid from of non-personal presentation and promotion of ideas, goods or services by an identified sponsor." Advertisements help to spread the advertiser's ideas about his products, offerings or service facilities to their customers.

Before framing an advertisement, the advertiser has to fully make an appraisal of buyer-behaviour. An advertisement drawn up subsequently alone can influence the buyers. It is well established that buyers and their purchase-behaviour can be influenced only if the advertisement matches the psychology and metal perceptions. Some of the other components of advertisement should be that it is of interest to the buyers or the target group. Further, the advertisement message should be interpreted by members as intended by the advertiser. Additionally, the advertisement message should influence the target group.

Just go through Fig. 7.2, a copy of the TV advertisement of Asian Paints created by O&M, using the baseline 'The ultimate weather paint'.

The above ads tells a story somewhat like this. Through the years, a rich man's barber cuts his hair. They discuss the rich man's bungalow, how come wind, come hail, come dust storm - nothing seems to take away the glow of the paint. Years pass and finally, the ever-faithful barber tells his 'huzoor' that may be it's time for a fresh coat of paint. The old man is surprised and asks, 'Rang lagane ka? Par bangle to abhi bhi chamak raha hai' The barber agrees. In the end, the VO says, 'Huzoor bahari deewaron pe dhool tikne na dey. Asian Paints ka Apex Ultima.'

After Asian Paints has flaunted its collection of paints for home interiors saying, 'Har ghar kuch kehta hai,' guess it's time to move out-side! Single-minded focus is to promote Asian Paints' Apex Ultima range of colours that withstand anything - even the unpredictable weather. The USP is the weatherproof factor - highlighted clearly at different seasons, through the years. The story-board is interesting, and grabs the attention by using the dialogue format between the house-owner and his faithful barber (the colloquial language that is used also helps!). Reward to the prospect is, of course, the name that is trusted by Indians over years: Asian Paints. So what do we say about the brand now? Guess, it's safe to say, it's a paint for all seasons!

Before we embark upon discussing the appeals in marketing communications which influence buyer behaviour and induce him for a purchase, we must study buyer behaviour itself. This will be of immense help in conceiving and shaping buyer appeals in marketing communications.

BUYER BEHAVIOR

In earlier times, marketers were able to understand buyer's behaviour because there used to be lesser number of buyers, too few competitors and the product manufacturers or services providers could easily come in contact with their prospective buyers through direct contact or direct selling.

Over the years, the buyers increased in numbers and instead of being concentrated in accessible areas

Fig. 7.3

they spread out in far-flung regions making direct selling a difficult task. Secondly, product manufacturers too increased in numbers with the result that utility products of innumerable brands flooded the market. The product manufacturers became competitive, offering better deals, discounts, and lesser price for similar utility products.

In the changing scenario, product manufacturers were compelled to undertake research into consumer behaviour. As in journalistic communication process in the dispensation of news or in its dissemination in the print or electronic media, the basic rule of 5 W's and one H also became relevant to research in buyer behaviour in order to shape effective marketing communications.

The earlier marketing concept was somewhat colourful. One such approach was "Find wants and fill them". Yet another was "Make what you can sell instead of trying to sell what can make". Also another method: "Love the customer and not the product" and "Have it your way" (Burger King), quoted by Philip Kotler. Further, "You're the boss" (United Airlines) J.C. Penny's motto summarizes this attitude: "To do all in your power to pack the customer's dollar full of value, quality and satisfaction."

Levitt in "Marketing Myopia" has made the following observation: -

"Selling focuses on the needs of the seller; marketing on the needs of the buyer. Selling is preoccupied with the seller's need to convert his product into cash; marketing with the idea of satisfying the needs of the customer by means of the product and the whole cluster of things associated with creating, delivering and finally consuming it."

Reverting to the theme of marketing communications, buyer behaviour and the appeals in the communication message to influence the buyer to the point of purchase, the answer to the basic tenets of 5 W's and one H, would be of great help.

The six questions, namely five related to the 5 W's and one to H, would enable the marketing communicator to frame marketing communication effectively and help him to include in them the appropriate appeals.

These questions are as follows:

1. Who buys or who are the buyers?
2. What do they buy or would like to buy?
3. When do they buy?
4. Where do they buy or want to buy?
5. Why do they buy?
6. How do they buy?

Further, a seventh question would be "Which kind of product would they like to buy?

Every manufacturer of goods or provider of services wants to ascertain and understand why, how when people or consumer buy goods and avail services and how do they derive satisfaction. This understanding helps to mould and shape effective marketing communication for exploiting consumer patterns of buyer behaviour. Producer of goods, provider of services and advertisers must be able to understand the basic forces that shape human behaviour in the marketing environment.

Consumer of buyer behaviour has been defined thus: "The behaviour that consumers display in search for, purchasing, using and evaluating products, services and ideas which they expect will satisfy their needs."

Marketers for success should understand consumer behaviour. The song often quitted is "If I knew what mood you are in, then I know I could win". Analysis of human behaviour indicates a predictable buying habit. On this basic producers of goods and advertisers could model and shape their marketing and advertising programme. Many studies have been conducted to find common factors that could approximately indicate the buying pattern of consumers. Several models representing consumer behaviour have been developed, consumer behaviour basically can be studded through two approaches: namely (i) Rational or Substantive approach and secondly (ii) Emotional or the non-substantive approach.

It is difficult to define as what is rational. What is rational for one may not be the same for some other person. Every person, however, presumes that he is rational, whereas he may be quite irrational or purely emotional or impulsive.

Even when a person is not considered rational by social standards, he can continue to claim that he is rational. For example, a terrorists is a murderer in the eyes of society, he may be considered hero for those for whom he indulges in terrorist acts.

Generally, a consumer would be considered rational if he takes into account economic considerations in decision making for a purchase, on the other hand, he would be considered irrational if he takes a purchase decisions on emotional values of his needs and desires.

Consumer behaviour has been studied by experts and marketing analysts from different angles and perspectives. But, in general, the consumer behaviour theory is that person is a rational consumer if his purchase decisions are based on economic consideration and taken after examining the pros and cons of the purchase in order to minimize the risks involved in taking wrong decisions. The other kind of purchaser or the non-rational buyer is that person whose purchase is impulsive and whose choices are random and unplanned or without any forethought.

This is an animation feature developed by O&M for Asian Paints, claiming themselves to be the ultimate weather proof paint, with an ape being a slave to a donkey, pulling his sledge while the donkey takes it easy. They stop to rest under a tree where the ape finds a packet of Mentos and offers it to the donkey but the donkey refuses; the ape pops one into his mouth. Next we see the ape super-energised as he starts running, hunting, wearing clothes, inventing fire, lighting torches and finally walking erect - as a man. Finally, the man enslaves the donkey for his own leisure ride. In the end, the VO says, "Mentos, dimag ki batti jala deyl"

We had seen Cadbury, another candy brand, taking the animated route last year - and it was successful! What's more, this Mentos ad uses what looks like the Shrek donkey (that will have instant connect with kids). The single-minded focus is to promote sale of Mentos candy targeting the kids as well as the youth. The USP: the taste opens up your mind and sharpens your grey cells. The story board is interesting (and will, again, have great connect with kids) and articulately depicts an animated evolution of mankind. A good, fun ad (which is also educative) that factors in the impulse purchase mindset! Who knows, probably the makers of the ad popped in a Mentos before thinking up this one!

BUYER: CHARACTERISTICS

Advertisers who make marketing communications for influencing and motivating persons for making purchases have always been keen in isolating and studying the factors that influence buyer behaviour. They are equally interested to know the factors that tend to bring changes in buyer behaviour.

Buyer characteristic or traits can be studied properly for making effective marketing communication by finding answers to questions to the 5 Ws and one H. For example, a lady buys a semi-professional digital camera. The advertiser for making effective marketing communication would like to find answer to these questions:

1. Who would like to buy such a camera?
   Only ladies; would men also like to buy such cameras; whether children would also buy it or professionals and as well semi-professionals and also amateurs.
2. When would people would like to buy such cameras?
   Are these cameras bought for special occasions like birthdays, festivals as gifts or for amateur or professional purposes.
3. Where would they like buying such cameras?
   From retailers, wholesalers, agencies or directly from manufacturers.
4. What do customers want to buy?
   Just any camera, a digital camera of any brand or of a particular brand, with special or desirable features.
5. Why do they buy a camera?
   For pursuing a hobby or for using it to ultimately become a professional or for recording memories of the family or social activities.
6. How do they (customers) buy cameras or how would they like to do so?

Cash down; installment-basis or through financial assistance or loans.

Besides the characteristics of the buyer already discussed above there are other external elements which also influence the buyer's decision making process for making a purchase.

The following are the external elements :

1. The Product. Characteristics of the product include its quality, price, utility, competitive advantage as compared with similar products of other brands, etc. if the product gives or promises to extend a higher degree of satisfaction to both physical needs and as well as psychological and emotional desires, it would prove to be a better and favourite products for the consumer.

2. The Seller. The image and reputation of the company selling the product are important for the consumer. These factors generate a sense of confidence about the product in the mind of the consumer. The image and reputation of the company is exhibited by the concern which the company practices in its dealing with customers like refund or replacement of defective products, back-up services for the product like warranties, after sale services etc., which boosts the image of the company in the minds of consumers or buyers.

3. Situational Characteristics. A situation sometimes creates an unusual demand for a product for availing some kinds of special service. This means that a particular situation creates related demands. For example, unexpected rains may make customers rush to the market for buying umbrellas; sudden sickness may create a need for taking an insurance policy or the offer of a sudden trip to a tourist spot might induce the need for buying a camera or knowledge about a discount sale is likely to rush people to the point of sale for a purchase of items thereby saving money.

FACTORS INFLUENCING CONSUMER BEHAVIOUR

The consumer, that is, the buyer is the most important factor in making a purchase decision. The other factors discussed above do influence his decision to make a purchase, but the characteristics of buyers or purchasers must be analyzed and studied in detail for successful marketing that is for making effective marketing communication.

FMCG giant HUL looks really inspired by its earlier online initiative Sunsilk Gang of Girls, as it can now boast of another social networking website for Lux called wivzv.magicof-black.com. This online ad just adds oodles of glamour to the website. The visual is rocking with the three hot chicks (though animated) successfully become what they want to, by letting

Fig. 7.4

loose the provocater within. The communication is bang on with the three stunning girls doing justice to the web-site, with their looks inspiring both the wannabe women of today and those who are looking for a major makeover. The three captions with the different types of girls is an interesting read - be a daring damsel like the bombshell, frolick in the heavens like an angel and follow your darkest desires as the wild cat. The USP is an offer to live your own fancy fairytale with you and your crush on the website - wwzv.magicof-black.com. Rewards to the prospect, of course, HUL's globally trusted name as well as the globally trusted brand, Lux. After Sunsilk's success with the Gang of Girls, guess HUL is again betting big with Lux's tvtvw.magicojblack.com. Here's wishing them all the best to get lucky again!

Studies have been conducted to analyze the major factors that influence consumer behaviour and purchasing decisions. Some of these factors are classified as follows:

(A) PSYCHOLOGICAL FACTORS

1. Motivation
2. Perception
3. Learning
4. Beliefs and attitudes

(B) PERSONAL FACTORS

1. Age and life-cycle position
2. Occupation
3. Economics
4. Life style and personality

(C) SOCIAL FACTORS

1. Role & status
2. Family
3. Reference group

(D) CULTURAL FACTORS

1. Culture
2. Sub-culture
3. Social Class

(A) PSYCHOLOGICAL FACTORS

1. Motivation

The motivation process commences with some basic needs. Basic needs are those which a consumer wants to satisfy on as his first priority. Thus, the difference between needs is what you must have or that which you already possess, while subsequent needs are or those items which want to possess or satisfy to meet some deficiency.

There are two kinds of needs (a) Biogenic (b) Psychogenic. Biogenic needs are those which arise from physical tension, worry or requirements like income, food, drink, physical comfort-houses, electricity, sex, protection against heat, cold, rains, etc. Psychogenic needs, on the other hand, are those which a person requires for status in society, attainment of prestige and acquisition of recognition, etc. They are related to social urges or tension or craving. If these needs are pressing, an "inner drive" for acquiring of fulfilling these needs. Once these needs are fulfilled the motivation process ends.

This motivation process is represented by a model framed by Sam Dennis; as follows: -

Need—Drive—Response—Goal—Goal achievement.

Maslow has classified the process of motivation, according to the hierarchy of needs as follows:

(a) "A human being may have many needs that are different in nature ranging from biological needs at the lower level to psychological needs at the upper extreme".

(b) "These needs vary in importance and, therefore, can be ranked in an hierarchy."

(c) "People seek to satisfy the most important needs first and they will focus their total attention to this."

(d) "Only when this need is satisfied, will it cease to be a motivator, until it arises again."

(e) "When the first need is satisfied, the person will turn his attention to the next important need. These needs in order of impoftance can be summarized at five levels of hierarchy as illustrated below: -

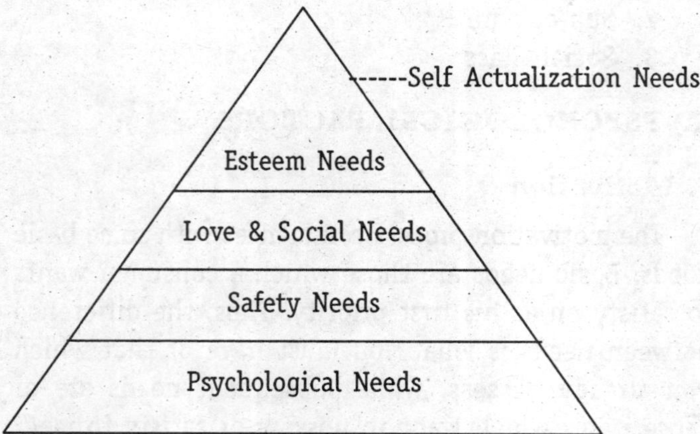

(i) Psychological Needs. These needs arise primarily from physiological or biological reasons, which sustain life itself and include the needs for food, water, sex and shelter. Sexual need and desire are not to be confused with love, which is a third-level priority. On the fulfillment of these basic needs, the needs of other levels arise, become important and begin to act as a motivator.

(ii) Safety Needs. Gratification of psychological needs, the needs at the next level become predominant. These needs include the need for self-preservation, while the psychological needs are for survival. Safely and security needs amount to provision against deprivation in the future. They induce a sense of protection against danger and threats.

(iii) Love and Social Needs. After the bodily and security needs are satisfied, the sense of belonging and acceptance become prominent and operative for motivating and acceptance become prominent and operative for motivating consumer behaviour. These needs are love, friendship and social interaction. Everyone seeks an environment were where we are understood, respected and wanted. These demands are common, hence it leads to "polarization" what is, people of similar background and thought tend to group together.

(iv) Esteem Needs. Esteem needs include the urge for achievement, prestige, status and power. It also includes the desire to ensure self-respect and also to command from others. Self-respect is a state in which a person cherishes internal recognition. Commanding respect from others is external recognition and also appreciation of one's individuality, image and contribution. Fulfillment of these needs result in self-confidence, independence, state, reputation and prestige.

(v) Self-Actualization Needs. This need arouses in the person the urge or the need to develop oneself fully and to achieve one's capacities and potentialities to the fullest. This is the highest level of need in Maslow's hierarchy of needs. This need is activated as a motivator when all other needs have been reasonably fulfilled.

Maslow's model is of a general nature. In which all the needs are interactive to some degree. These needs are not bound in a rigid sequence. Their relative priority is continually changing, shifting and variable.

The advertisers knowing these needs, their relative importance, varying nature, changing preferences and importance are able to shape their marketing communications to motivate consumers for a purchase.

See Fig. 7.5 in which Max New York Life have successfully attacked this need through their Ad released in 2008 with the baseline 'Ab Koi Samjhota Nahin' created by RSCG Ad agency.

Euro RSCG created this Ad for their client Max New York Life using the baseline Ab koi samjhauta nahi! A school kid sees a bunch of guys jump into the water from the bridge; he wants to jump too but his parents stop him. In the next shot, he's a young man; his boss yells at him, and he wants to yell back, he remembers his pregnant wife at home. In the end, he's grown old and is driving with his wife towards the bridge from where his parents had stopped him from jumping. This time, he jumps in the water, and VO says, "Zindagi bhar kitne samjhaute kiye, apno ke liye, apni zimedaariyon ke khatir, ab to apne liye jiyo. Max New York Life leke aaye hain pension plan. Ab koyi samjhauta nahi."

A cracker of an ad, full of emotions - but to sell something as mundane as insurance. Power idea is to beautifully depict the sacrifices a man makes throughout his life - from his childhood till he grows old. But in the end, he's able to take chances, thanks to sensible investments. Communication is effective, slice-of-life & poignant. USP is the pension plan from Max New York life that makes you say: Ab koyi samjhauta nahi (showing the reward one reaps after retirement through the pension plans as the man drives the car he wanted to once purchase and jumps into

Fig. 7.5

the water, from the point where he couldn't jump as a kid). Reward to the prospect is the globally trusted name of Max New York. Good stuff on a tension-free, pension-full life.

2. Perception. Perception is a mental process through which information enters our minds after which it is interpreted. Perception is the outcome of /interaction of the senses of hearing, seeing and general feelings.

A human being has five senses, seeing, hearing, taste, smell and taste. The sixth sense is discretion. Perception is the first stage of INTRA-PERSONAL COMMUNICATION, through which decision-making is completed through three stages: (i) Perception (ii) Judgment and (iii) Adoption.

The general rule or the accepted truth/about perception is that a person sees what he wants to seek; a person was to hear what he wants to hear and wants to do what he wants to do. Adoption of an idea itself passes through five stages:

(i) Awareness: The first stage is that person learns about a new idea or proposal; **(ii) Interest:** In the second stage the person seeks more information and considers its merits; **(iii) Evaluation:** In the third stage the person applies his mind, weighs its merit, examines the pros and cons of the new idea or proposal; **(iv) Trial:** The persons in the fourth stage applies the idea, proposal, service offered etc., on a small scale, that is, tests it and **(v) Adoption:** The person in the fifth and final stage approves the idea, proposals or service offered and adopts or accepts it. In other words while analyzing the process, it is apparent that perception plays an important part in human and also in organizational behaviour. The well-known maxim is what may be one man's meat may be another person's poison.

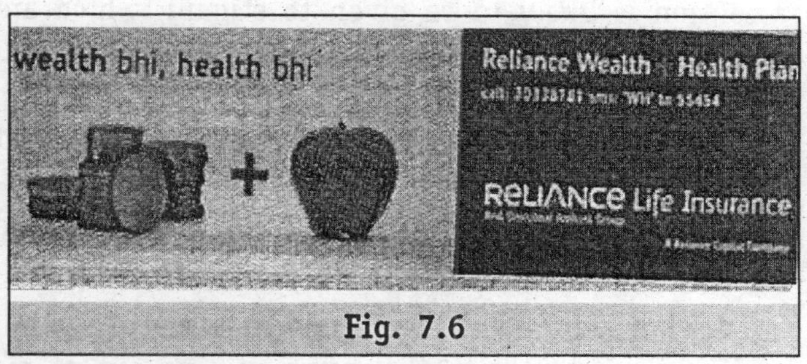

Fig. 7.6

Guess what Reliance Life Insurance stands for? It is a combination of two essential elements in life that keep us going health and wealth. And simply stated without buying a life insurance scheme, how can health and wealth complement each other? An apple a day keeps the doctor away, but in this billboard, Reliance Life Insurance is all set to become a permanent doctor for you by offering a great treatment to all your today's problems. The visual is very appealing with a fresh blood red apple symbolising good health on one side and the other side comprising of gold coins that indicates wealth. The communication with the baseline - 'Wealth bhi, health bhi', delivers the insurance giant's objective clearly and furthermore, the USP of Reliance Life Insurance is a remarkable blend of both wealth and health plan. What's more, a simple call or an SMS, and the agent will be right there on your doorstep. Reward to the prospect - Anil Dhirubhai Ambani's desi name. The billboard ad does outstanding work for the brand and why not, when health is the real wealth for all!

Fig. 7.7

Perception may be studied from three different perspectives, as follows: -

(i) Selective Exposure: Consumers may accept certain stimuli and avoid or reject them. Advertisements, which are colourful or larger in size, are likely to attention of consumers, which they can also conveniently or deliberately avoid. Similarly, more attention is likely to be given to stimuli, which are surprising, novel and catching. According to James R. Battman, "new products, special sales, colour brochures, new packaging, discounts, gift schemes, value-based special discounts, free additional items on quantum-value purchases, may prompt the consumer to respond to such stimuli immediately.

A man sits on a bench alone at a metro station and listens intently to the music coming out of his Vodafone Magic Box (next to his ear). In no time, everyone around get attracted to the old Hindi Bollywood track, 'kabhikhushi, kabhigham, tara rum pum pum...' and start grooving and dancing to the music. Next, the man then gets a call from his office (his cell phone starts to ring from inside the box) and everyone looks else-where as the man talks on his phone. In the end, the caption reads, 'Magic Box with FM Radio for Rs.1,999. 2-year, replacement warranty. Make the most of now.'

Around Diwali in the year 2007, Vodafone announced its Magic Box offer to Indians and the power idea was to lure consumers with the same. This ad takes the power idea further with the added USPs: FM Radio for Rs.1,999 only and a 2-year replacement warrant}' to customers. The communication is effective through the depiction of metro passengers (who have time to hill when they are waiting for a train - or travelling on it!) remaining glued to the FM Radio on the phone. Reward to the prospect: the global brand name of Vodafone, i.e., the song grabs all ears, then the attractive Magic Box draws all eyes too! Quite an out the box delivery, isn't it?

(ii) Selective Distortion: This implies the ability of people and also the tendency to twist or distort information into personal concepts. The information received that strengthens their already held beliefs is easily accepted by people and reject/or ignore such information which is against such beliefs. The most important example is the warning; Smoking is injurious to health" which is ignored by smoking addicts.

(iii) Selective Retention: Contrary to selective distortion, is selective retention, which implies that information which matches people's attitudes and prejudices and ignore those portions of information which is counter to it. A consumer makes a purchase remembering only the good points or plus points of a product or gadget enumerated by a salesman, while overlooking or ignoring the negative points.

Note: (iv) Selective Perception: As already discussed, this trait of human nature is 'to see what one wants to see and to hear what one wants to hear.' This explains why a group of persons remember certain aspects of the political leader's speech and hails that leader as the best choice of being voted to power, while another group politically opposed will consider that leader is useless in the context of the same public speech and refuse to vote for him.

3. Learning: Learning indicates the changes in an individual's behaviour through experience. The major part of human behaviour is based upon learning. This excludes instinctive preferences or responses like food, hunger, fatigue, etc. Learning induces experience, which in the long run shapes into a habit. Brand loyalty is built upon continuous buying of a quality product.

4. Beliefs and Attitudes: Belief is based upon knowledge, opinion or faith. Attitudes, on the other hand, are relatively more endorsing and take root in feelings, concern sympathies and behaviour tendencies towards other persons, groups, ideas or objects. Attitudes are basically acquired, learnt or imbibed but not inherited and are fairly long lasting. Sometimes, external phenomena influence attitudes and bring about a change in them.

(B) PERSONAL FACTORS

(1) Age and Life Cycle position: Buying habits vary with age and are also different at various ages. The young are fond of flashy things in dress, motorbikes, cars etc., while the middle aged and older people prefer sober and sophisticated versions of everything which are also lower in price range. Two aspects determine buyer behaviour, namely the psychographics profile and the demographic profile of buyers.

Fig. 7.8

Demographic profile of a person or prospective buyer includes details about status, single, married, with or without children, married and young children, married with older children and all settled in life, etc., exert a decisive influence on the purchase behaviour of buyers.

The psychographic's profile of a person or prospective buyer indicate other parameters like social groups, income, beliefs, ideals, life-style, etc., which in their own way influence the purchase decisions of buyers.

Well, the Aditya Birla Group is now going the designer way! The single-minded focus of this ad is to promote its linen club fabric venture - a line that hotshot fashion designer Rohit Bal himself (no less!) is endorsing! So it's Rohit Bal who himself communicates to the consumers about the USP of the product: timeless charm and all-season fabric. (What more do you want but a dashing designer speaking aloud for your designs?) The visual is attractive with the classy designer holding ccntre-stage (and stvay!). The ad scores full points on building the trust factor for the brand and the product is positioned clearly. The trust factor is further highlighted as the ad warns you to look out for Linen Club stamp of authenticity to make sure you own the purest of linen. The reward to the prospect? Aditya Birla Group's desi name that has established itself as a big success story in the international markets too! With that comes the power idea: the fact that the line is 'European'. Guess you need a global vision to come up with something that's European (read: fashionable), right?

Advertisers which soliciting consumers for their products or services, make use of the factors of both the profiles and for framing effective marketing communication.

(2) Occupation. The occupation of a person determines that kind of purchase he/could turn out. The occupation and the income of the person also reveal the quantum of money or the disposable income, which he can employ for making purchase. A white-collar worker is liable to purchase luxury items coppered with a person who has an average income because he would give priority to essential items of sustenance. A photographer would prefer to purchase more of photographic equipment, while a doctor would give preference to life insurance policy. An executive of a corporation would go in for/and expensive car, which a schoolteacher would never think of purchasing. A person's occupation indicates the kind of marketing group to which he belongs to and advertisers design their marketing campaigns and marketing communication aimed at winning over consumers from the group.

(3) Economic Circumstances: The economic condition and environment of an individual indicates his purchasing behaviour. For example, a doctor in financial difficulty might not buy a car, but a business executive in better economic circumstances would purchase a car on credit or on hire purchase. Thus,

FIG. 7.9

the purchase behaviour depends upon a person's income, savings, assets, borrowing power etc.

Holding on to a long rope, a man goes to Paris for a vacation with his wife and kid. A jingle plays in the background: 'Latka dejo! The man carries the rope with him everywhere he goes. Next, the family is roaming around in a bus with the man holding the rope; the other end is tied around one of the MakeMyTrip.com's executive who boldly asserts, "Latka dejo!" "Harnare saath trip mein koi kamimile, toh aadhapaisa mat dejo!" The caption reads, 'Pay 50% after you return.' And the VO says, 'MakeMyTrip I loliday Plus... Humne toda vaada, toh pay only aadha.'

This MakeMyTrip.com ad does not talk about any new added destinations to their list - or, for that matter, the fact that they are offering the cheapest rates. Instead, the USP this time is that the company will pay half the amount of the holiday package if they don't fulfil any of their promises while their customers are on holiday. In the wake of competition between travel agencies - who are offering 'cheap' deals - the single-minded focus is to win over consumers by reinforcing the trust factor. The reward to the prospect is conveyed through the MakeMyTrip. coms executive - who is clearly shown as walking the talk! Promises, it seems, are never meant to be broken, eh?!

Personality & Life Style: The personality of a person determines his life style. Life style indicates a distinctive mode of living, which may be adopted by

Fig. 7.10

an individual or his entire family. Life style determines how people spend their time and money; adopt hobbies and practices and chart out their preferences and activities. The rich would plan their holidays in spare time, students would opt for adventurous excisions, the family man would plan his trips to fulfill his social responsibilities or commitments like attending a marriage or birthday get together. These distinctions help the producers of goods and product plan out their advertising strategies so that people of various life style segments are persuaded to make a purchase.

Someone rightly said, 'Majority wins' and Bajaj XCD 125cc has collected all the votes of the jury to its credit. Launched to upgrade 100cc customers to the 125cc XCD DTS-Si drive, power idea is to introduce 125cc bikes on Indian roads. In fact, the brand proposition goes one step ahead - and boldly announces phasing out of 100CC bikes in the near future, now' that the 125cc one is here! Now, isn't that quite a power statement?! The communication is bang on - making you wonder why the headline states that 100cc bikes will soon be history - and grabs the eyeballs instantly. Great hook! Visual is appealing with a sexy bike in royal blue hogging the lime-light. And in case you're wondering if Bajaj will be able to walk the talk, then do please check out the body copy that reinstates the consumer's faith in the product by stating how the Bajaj XCD 125cc has already bagged three different 'Bike of the 'Year 2008' awards! The body copy also lists the USPs; at 109 kmp, the bike is India's most fuel-efficient one, boasts of a digital console et ah. The positioning is clear — targeting bikers and speedsters who believe in experiencing an adrenaline rush each time when they hit the roads. Reward to the prospect? Bajaj's desi name in the Indian market. So what do we say? That not only is Bajaj's new product innovative, powerful and high-speed, the company's strategy is fast and furious too! A real punch of power!

C. SOCIAL FACTORS

(1) Role and Status: Role comprises the pattern of activities that a person is expected to exhibit according to the expectations of persons around him. For example, a student who is not bound to wear the school uniform may dress casually like donning a shirt and, while an executive is expected to present himself amidst his employees.

Status, on the other hand, is embodied by the general esteem in accordance to the role of a person. For example, the status of a Supreme Court Judge differs from that of an ordinary employee, worker or citizen.

(2) Family Influence: "Family atmosphere" and "parental value system" play a significant role in shaping general attitudes towards life, including purchasing patterns. The family influence induces amongst its members, which makes them develop a particular frame of mind, which in turn induces "brand loyalty". For example, a toothpaste brand loyalty may pass down from generation to generation. Advertisers while targeting their prospective purchases have to keep family influence in mind while framing their purchasing appeals.

(3) Reference Groups: Reference groups are such collection of people which consumers respect and tend to identify themselves with/which become dominant influencing factors in purchase decisions. These reference groups are primarily of three types as follows:-

(1) **Primary Groups:** Close friends, neighbours, fellow-workers and colleagues along with family members/constitute such groups whose opinions are sought by a prospective purchaser before making a purchase decision which shopping for specialty goods like a refrigerator, television set, an expensive camera or a car.

(2) **Secondary Groups:** There are some organizations and professional associations, which case and influence. For example, senior groups in high school or big her classes tend to influence all girls, even if they are not their members. Similarly, a member of a professional photographic society is likely to be influenced by his associates in purchasing a specific brand of a camera.

(3) **Asp rational groups or Opinion Leaders:** Aspirational groups comprise such people who have acquired an unusual distinction. The also tend to influence purchase behaviour in customers. Such persons are also known as "Opinion leaders" because their opinion influences people who want to be associated with such opinion leaders. Such opinion exist in all fields of activities, like film celebrities, sports stars etc. A product endorsed by a film celebrity or done by a sports star has a deep impact upon a prospective purchase. Similarly, an endorsement by a doctor would help establish brand goodwill like a toothpaste brand or a painkiller.

D. CULTURAL FACTORS:

Cultural factors or characteristics can be classified in three categories as follows: -

(1) Culture: Culture casts a subtle influence on the members of a family. A child learns or, rather, imbibes a certain set of values as it grows up. These values have a wide range like ideas, values, perceptions, preferences, like strong likes and dislikes, habits, mannerisms, etc. Some of these values are also imbibed through social interaction. These values remain ingrained in the child as he grows up into an adult, which in turn influences his purchase behaviour. Even professions adopted by children are because of such family or social values. A young man is likely to use the expensive camera of his father and family for taking pictures, which may shape him into a professional photographer. The same expensive camera in the hands of a tribal group may not influence its members in the art of taking pictures because there is no family tradition of doing so. A sophisticated

Fig. 7.11

camera in the hands of anyone in a family of photographers has immense appeal, but not so in the tribal group.

(2) Sub-Culture: Every cultural group comprises of smaller groups, namely smaller group distinguishable by their belief, faith and worship or ethnic entities which determine their purchasing preferences and buying behaviour. These sub-cultural groups with respect to their purchasing behaviour are distinctive target marketing groups. Even geographic areas impart their own influence on purchasing preferences quite different to those residing in another geographic area. Similarly, a rural sub-culture is different to that of an urban area. For example, iced tea may be popular in an urban area but totally unacceptable in rural areas.

(3) Social Class: A social class may be described as a group of people whose members hold similar attitudes and beliefs and subscribe to the same value system. Social groups may be classified in the following three categories according to their characteristics: -

(i) Persons within a social class tend to have similar preferences and would behave in a similar manner.

(ii) A social class is governed by several variables like income, education, occupation, beliefs and values, all of which are inter-related and these factors may act or influence behaviour singly or as a result of the combination more than one factor. The similar life style of such groups provide the advertiser an unique marketing segment, for which an effective marketing communication can be designed or framed.

(iii) A social class in not static; its members move up and down and so do their purchasing preferences and priorities. This upward or downward movement of a member of social class depends upon environmental changes, which change like style of that person. For example, a member of a social class may be having one kind of preference, is bound to have entirely different preferences when he moves upwards and qualifies as an engineer or doctor.

With the baseline India. On schedule. Climbing gear delivered to Kabmpong. 10:30 am. Adventure. On sched-ule. It takes First Flight to give you adventurous spirit, wings to fly high with! Great communication that, together with a bang on visual! The single-minded focus is crystal clear: in the wake of stiff competition between courier service providers who deliver goods in no time, First Flight takes a step up further by harping on its USP: the fact that it has 800 branches, that can reach 1,800 destinations covering over 5,200 PIN codes. Whew! Quite a network, what say? And if those figures weren't enough, body copy adds that the company does 100 million shipments a year and that it delivers a whole range of stuff - from parcels/gifts to cargo assignments to perishables (rewards to the prospect). USP is 'On schedule' - in the Indian market: with that the company strikes an instant chord with Indian consumers. So what do we say about the ad? It's at the right place, at the right time!

Future Group release this Ad with the baseline India Tomorrow. We saw the earlier two print ads of the Kishore Biyani-promoted Futurê Group using kids to make their point strongly - talking about the services and products that the group offers, without getting into specifics. This one uses the same means once again - kids - to talk about its insurance division specifically, other than brand-building for everything else. Leaving aside insurance, the ad also talks about the other key businesses of the Future Group - en-tertainment, fashion, retail, capital, restaurants, shopping malls, consumer finance *et al.* The communication is via the strong body copy, and the headline - Sone ki chidiya aayegi. Har fikar dur uddjayegi! - talks about a tension-free life, thanks to the insurance offered by the Future Group (the USP).

Fig. 7.12

The 'Sone ki chidiya is, again, borrowed from 'The Bird of Gold: the Rise of India's Consumer Market', a report prepared by McKinsey on the booming Indian market. So why do you think that the company is using kids to endorse a product like insurance? Well, because India is a young country, just beginning to grow. And if you plan sensibly, we can all reap the benefits of a Golden Age! Now, isn't that a great promise?!

ROLE OF OPINION LEADERS

Every social group has few members who are opinion leaders or tend setters towards whom members of the group look forward to for guidance in their activities including purchase decision.

These opinion leaders are likely the first people who purchase new products and adopt new gadgets. They serve as reliable sources for information on the new products and gadgets. The members of the group seek decision-making for purchase.

These opinion leaders being educated like information from all kinds of information sources like newspapers, radio, television and other modern mass media which helps them to draw conclusions on all matters which identify such opinion leaders who give information and advice to members of their groups and often focus their communication appeals on such leaders. Theses opinion leaders are often used as information outlets for introduction of new products. These opinion leaders are important for members of their reference of these leaders.

Fig. 13

The marketers who design a marketing mix and leaders, effective communication appeals which arouses the interest and attracts the attention of theses opinion leaders, the chances are that such communication messages and marketing appeals will also influence members of the opinion leader's group.

The activities and characteristics of these opinion leaders have a great value for members of their groups. A social, professional or other kinds of groups may have more than one opinion leader, namely one for seeking advice on social issues, another for professional preferences and so on.

A man is sipping tea on a rainy night standing at a dhaba, when his cell rings (the Airtel tune) and he touches his chest pocket emotionally. A college boy keeps his hand on his heart when his phone rings. A peon, a monk, a man on a wheel-chair, a farmer, all do the same thing. Enter Shahrukh Khan, and he does the same thing too! As the Airtel tune plays in the background, SRK takes out the phone from his chest pocket and says, 'Jab Airtel our Nokia ek saath milen to garv se bolo, hello.' In the end, the caption reads, 'Airtel + Nokia, Lifetime prepaid.' This Ad was developed for Airtel by JWT.

This ad achieves a lot of things - at the same time. It strikes an emotional connect, rises above the clutter and is a great effort in co-branding. And, of course, it uses Shah Rukh Khan for the telling effect. While the single-minded focus of the ad is to promote the latest tie-up between the telecom service provider (Airtel) and the Finnish handset maker (Nokia) for a lifetime of prepaid service (the USP of the ad), the power idea is simple: brand building. SRK, as most of us know, is brand ambassador for both Airtel and Nokia, and 'talking to' Airtel users and Nokia's loyal consumers (as well as other potential consumers), he doesn't let us down - yet again! Guess, emotions and Airtel have always been directly proportional to each other (and Nokia was, of course, connecting people) - and yet again with this 'touching' Airtel and Nokia win hearts all around.

We have studied buyer's behaviour, which provides a sense of direction and insight for making effective marketing communications. If we have carefully studied customer behaviour the next legitimate question is should we also undertake marketing research, preferably advertising research. Advertising research would help us to appreciate or evaluate the effectiveness of advertising; the appeals in advertising communication that have worked or have aroused or motivated purchase decisions. It will also make us understand how to make advertising communications properly oriented for motivating purchase decision. Advertising communications which fail to evoke purchase decisions would be waste be time and labour and also the huge costs which would be incurred in such advertisements. This takes us to the next question as to what is the role of research?

ROLE OF RESEARCH

Top managers and experts use research findings in taking the most complex decisions whether they are in the field of marketing research or advertising research or management research. Scientific methods are being used for this research. All kinds of business operate amidst uncertainty about results, but research would help to eliminate such uncertainties.

MEANING OF RESEARCH

Research is neither a set of techniques; nor an elaborate collection of facts or an aimless fishing expedition. In fact, research is purposeful investigation. If helps to impart a sensible shape and structure to decision making.

Investigation done in research comprises three components:

1. The problem, which is implicit;
2. The solution or answer; which is explicit.
3. The collection, interpretation of information derived from the process from the problem to the answer.

In business, research is needed in all areas of activity. It plays a key role in each of these areas, namely advertising, marketing, production, management, purchasing, materials-use; selling, baking, management of human resources, banking, resource mobilization, image building, customer care interaction with government and so on.

MARKETING RESEARCH

Marketing begins much before actual selling of the product. This is based on the analysis of the needs and wants, priorities and preferences of the buyers. Marketing today continues even after selling of the products by examining whether the product satisfies the buyer or not.

Marketing today has matured into a specialized exercise, which keeps the buyer or consumer in the centre while designing a product mix.

These days' products are made to satisfy the needs and wants of the buyers like his requirements of health, entertainment, speed, comfort etc.

Customers today comprise a wide range dependant upon their preferences, like some may love freedom, be bound by conservatism, or like an aristocratic life-style or believe in economy. Further, there are some customers who possess a negative attitude while others may have a positive attitude. For example, vegetarians would shun or exhibit an aversion towards eggs, meat sandwiches or burgers and prefer to buy other items like shirts and jeans.

Market research is an effective tool, which helps the producer of the product in several ways, the information and data generated through it enables the decision-makers to design a proper product, chart out its development, fixation of price, promote it effectively, finalize the distribution process and in shaping and formatting an effective marketing communication. Marketing research, therefore, helps to evaluate all areas of the marketing programme. In others words, marketing research is research pertaining to any problem in the field of marketing.

Let use examine some of the definitions on marketing research:

"Marketing Research (MR) is the systematic, objective and exhaustive search for the study of the facts relevant to any problem in the field of marketing". Crisp, R.D.

MR is "the application of scientific method to the solution of marketing problems."—Luck, Wales, Taylor

MR is "the systematic and objective search for the analysis of information relevant to the identification and solution of any problem in the field of marketing". – Green and Tull

MR is "the systematic recording and analyzing of data about problems relating to marketing." American Marketing Association.

The various vital elements outlined in the definitions above may be explained as follows:

1) MR is database findings: The data collected is related to all areas of marketing functions. Facts are collected related to product reach, price, distribution and promotion. Decision maker analyzes and interprets the collected data for chalking out success strategy in all the aspects associated with the marketing process.

2) Methodology of data collection: Data collection must by methodical and systematic. The first step before collecting data is to identify the problem. Once the problem is identified the collection of data becomes meaningful because it remains associated with the problem. For example, the problem is that lack of response to the sale of a product; the problem is obviously the ineffectiveness of the advertising communication. The problem having been identified, the next step is to collect data from a representative sample, which are analyzed and interpreted in the form of a report. On its basis, advertising communication is objectively reframed in order to make advertising communication effective.

(3) MR should be objective: The research should be problem-oriented, that is, objective in order to discover reasons for the ineffectiveness of the advertising communication. The research should not be subjective, that is, to collect data in a manner in order to justify or support a pre-determined result or solution of the problem. MR research should be aimed at finding a well-reasoned and data-supported solution to the problem.

(4) MR data becomes useful information for corrective action. The MR data systematically collected on analysis and interpretation enables the decision-maker to frame corrective action.

(5) MR should be a continuous process: Marketing activity is a continuous process hence marketing research should also be in continuous manner; neither be slip shod nor choosy, but data collection should be a continuous process and also carried out even after corrective action has been taken. This is necessary because the product-mix, promotion-mix and pricing pattern are ever changing.

(6) MR is a multi-dimensional process: MR is a multi-dimensional and also cross-disciplinary process. MR Marketing research collects data influenced by various disciplines like, Economics, Psychology, Sociology, Statistics, Political Science, Operation Research, and Computer Science.

(7) MR is a decision-making tool: MR is merely a decisions-making tool and to not a substitute the decision-making process. MR provides valuable inputs in aid of decision making. There may be several other variables that may make the decision-maker reject the findings of a MR exercise and may undertake yet another MR exercise based on the variables vital to decision making.

Marketing research has a wide scope and may cover a wide area. It also helps in writing of effective marketing communication and in framing of advertising communication.

IMPORTANCE OF MR

Marketing research is important in many ways:

(1) Marketing activity becomes realistic with the back up of the marketing research function. It ensures consumer satisfaction.

(2) Marketing effort becomes effective with the input of the critical element of marketing research.

(3) Marketing research helps in transforming a sellers' market into the desirable and profitable buyers' market.

(4) Marketing research fortifies an organization in meeting challenges of business environment and successfully faces the ups and downs in marketing.

(5) Marketing research helps to reduce business risks. These risks arise because of the vast geographical expansion of markets.

(6) Marketing research has become vital to undertaking of product innovation, in tackling distribution problems and in studying price sensitivity of Indian markets.

MARKETING RESEARCH IS SCIENTIFIC RESEARCH

Marketing research is no longer random research. It has acquired a scientific basic. Marketing research has achieved a scientific basic. Marketing research is now considered a science for the following reasons:

(i) A step-by-step method is adopted for a systematic study of the problem. The marketing problem or hypothesis is tested or verified against the data collected.

(ii) Marketing research today is an objective study; not a subjective one, that is, it does not rely upon any kind of presumption or subjective basis. The first step is to identify the objectives, fixed and settled, which are subjected to an objective methodology. The data collected according to the objectives outlined are subjected to an objected analysis.

(iii) The results are derived in a scientific manner using sophisticated tools like Latin Squares, Markov Chains, Multi-dimensional scales, etc.

Marketing research is completed in five phases. The following are the steps or phases of this research. Moreover, the marketing problem may have to be changed into an operational marketing research task, if a problem audit and background analysis reveal that further marketing research is required. Analysis reveal that further marketing research is required. For this, research objectives, research questions and research hypothesis are identified and settled.

The operational marketing research task is tackled as the first step or phase in marketing research, which is a follows: -

(i) Marketing objective or Task: The marketing research task comprises a specific set of marketing research objectives. These objectives determine the scope of marketing research effort which indicate as to what information is needed which can be generated by research data. The information generated in this manner may be heeded for decision-making. The decision-making information may be useful for external environment, namely competitors and competing markets. The information could be useful for the organization itself like sales levels, distribution networks, pricing pattern, and packaging.

"Research questions are refined statements of research objectives." A marketing research may be initiated at the instance of the Marketing Manager to assess the awareness of potential buyers of a new brand of house décor *vis-a-vis* other décor packages being offered by the same company.

The above research objective can be converted into specific research questions as follows: -

(i) "What is the unaided recall of the company's brand?"

(ii) "What is the aided recall of the company's branch?"

(iii) "What is the awareness of the specific brand features?"

"Research questions are further refined into one or a series of research hypotheses. Hypotheses are tentative statements about relationship between two or more variables." For example, the primary reason why customers buy a product of a particular brand is the low price of that product. "When operational hypotheses are stated using symbolic notation, they are commonly termed as 'statistical hypotheses'.

The first step in the field of marketing research is identifying or crystallization of the marketing problem. It can also be called or labelled as a search of a marketing opportunity.

The identification of the marketing problem or the search of a marketing opportunity is a process, which helps to pinpoint the task for the researcher.

(ii) Research Design: The second step in marketing research is to formulate a Research Design. After the marketing research task has been identified and finalized, the next step is to develop a marketing research plan. The plan is also known as a marketing research design. The plan provides a direction to the research process by indicating as to what kind of data should be collected, how the data are to be collected and the manner in which it would be analyzed. Thus, the marketing research plan specifies research data that is to be collected and also specifies that research procedure, namely the procedure for analyzing the data.

(iii) Collection of Data: Data collection comprises three stages, namely measurement decisions, the manner of data collection and indicates the format that should be deployed for data collection. The first two stages outlines the steps needed for implementing the marketing research design. The third stage of data collection sets out the steps or the manner in which the data is to be physically collected, like drawing out samples, questionnaire process or other methods, including surveys.

(iv) Interpretation of Data and Analysis: This step in marketing research comprises three stages: Preparation of raw data, Preliminary data analysis and, thirdly, cetailed data analysis and interpretation. This is the fourth stage in marketing research. It comprises data analysis and interpretation. The raw data from the previous stage is systematically arranged, and analyzed with the help of statistical methods. The next step is to interpret analysis results of the data and conclusions related to the research objective or problem are drawn and finalized.

(v) Research Report: The final stage in marketing research is the preparation of the research report. This report forms the basis of decision-making by the managerial section of the company or industrial house. The report mentions in brief the research process, which had been adopted and provides the solutions to the marketing problem on which marketing research had been undertaken. The report also enlists the feedback loops of all the five stages of the research process which arise from the anticipated and unanticipated events and development which occur along the research process.

Marketing research is a systematic and scientific process and is also a continuous one. Feedback on developments in the marketing sector may, sometimes, necessitate repetition of the entire marketing research process, which might be modified according to the requirements of the current marketing objectives.

The marketing research report is the end result of the research process, while its recommendations and conclusions are actionable. The current demand is to design a Marketing Information System of which the marketing research report is a part.

There are various market survey techniques. It is beyond the purview of the present discussion as we are talking about the critical analysis of marketing communications. The analysis is of the marketing research report and not the methodology methodologies of the research process.

It would suffice here to dwell here on the various methods adopted for marketing research. One of the methods may be a survey conducted by personal, telephonic and mail interviews.

ADDITIONAL RESEARCH METHODS

The following are in brief the alternative marketing research processes:

(1) Panel Research: In this research method, a researcher interviews the same sample group two or more times and collects data from them on two or more occasions. Respondents may be individual customers, retailers, wholesalers, dealers, distributors, agents, etc. Panel research has an advantage. It can measure small changes in purchases, purchase habits, purchasing behaviour, purchase priorities, etc., over a period of time. In non-panel type research, different groups are assessed each time a study is conducted. Panels are constituted from respondents who report their buying behaviour in a regular manner.

(2) Consumer Purchase Panel: The consumer purchase panel is much in vogue these days. Family units, which keep a regular record or maintain a diary of weekly or monthly purchases of items of daily or immediate use, are chosen. The data so recorded includes the type of items purchased, the number of units bought, price, brands and the sources of buying. These family units receive cash or gifts from research sponsors to motivate them to maintain such records or diaries. The consumer purchase panels are used to evaluate or test a new product, new package or to find solutions to research objectives.

Utility of Consumer Purchase Panel:

(i) It helps to assess consumer preferences, attitudes and changing trends in demands for specific products.

(ii) Used for testing product samples.

(iii) Helps to study market trends.

(iv) For identifying brand loyalty and brand changes.

(v) To probe consumer attitude to packaging.

(vi) For finding out the relevance and importance of retail outlets.

(vii) For measuring consumer response to price pattern and advertising.

(viii) For carrying out a marketing test while launching a new product.

Benefits of a Consumer Purchase Panel: Consumer panels have mainly three benefits. These panels provide such information, which is useful for organizing or modifying marketing activities.

(i) Panels provide an inside view of buyer behaviour, which can help in studying buyer characteristics.

(ii) Reveal changes in buyer behaviour, which can help in reorganizing the market mix.

(iii) Help in studying changing trends in buyer behaviour on examining information from consumer panels if studied over a period of time.

(3) Pre-testing of new products: Before launching new products, they need to be pre-tested as to the response they would evoke from consumers. Thus, new products are tested by a panel or by surveying the response of identified buyer-sectors like housewives, girls, and young men etc., who are given samples of a new product for trial and comments. When the product samples distributed for trial are unidentified, it is called a blind-fold test. The objective of such an exercise is to compare products and the response to them.

We have discussed in the previous pages how buyer-behaviour is crucial to successful marketing. Along with this we have dealt with the relevance of six major questions and their answers, namely who are the buyers; what do they like to buy; when or at which time the buyers would like to make their purchases; where would the buyers like to make their purchases; why, after all, do they want to buy and finally how, or in what manner the buyers make their purchases. In other words, the manufacturer of a product must be well acquainted with buyer characteristics. This helps, inspires or makes the manufacturer rationalise his approach and make it effective so as to reach the prospective purchaser through an advertisement with an appeal that convinces him.

Understanding the characteristics of the buyer proves to be a vital aid in framing advertisements with the right appeal that motivates the prospective buyer to make a purchase.

We have also discussed how motivational factors move the prospective bye to buyer to the point of purchases and helps in decision-making for buying a product of a particular brand. Advertising appeals capable of striking the right chord of motivation succeed in inspiring a buyer to make a purchase decision for the product positioned in the advertisement.

Advertising appeals cannot be framed in the air rather they have to be related to ground realities. We have all pointed out earlier that the needs of the buyer are important. Advertising appeals based on these ground realities click and convince and win over prospective purchasers.

These ground realities include the various needs of the prospective purchaser. It is obvious that advertising appeals that cater to these needs would be more effective and result oriented. Customer needs comprise a broad psychological needs, safety needs, love and social needs, esteem needs, and self-actualisation needs.

We have dealt with all these needs of the customer earlier. The psychological need of the customer is important because only that product would be purchased by a buyer which tallies with his or her mental attitude and preferences.

Products which match the safety needs of the prospective purchaser also sell well. Each and every product may not be welcomed by a purchaser; the safety factor or the absence of harmful effects motivates the purchaser in a big way. The ready, shavers of different brands have flooded the market and customers have patronised the various brands according to their individual safety preferences. It is because of these ready shavers that 'safety razor blades' which had to be fixed manually in the safety razor instrument faced lower demand.

It may be recalled that the safety-razor replaced the cut-throat razor of old time which had to be sharpened on a hone (sharpening stone) then given the fine cutting edge on a leather strap or on a smooth wooden slab. The use of cut-throat razor either by the barber or by the individual for a self-shave used to be a risky affair. The advent of the safety-razor blade quite easily replaced and ousted the cut-throat razor because of the safety needs of the user customer.

Yet other customer needs discussed earlier are the esteem needs and actualisation needs. Quite a many customer in order or satisfy rather gratify their esteem needs prefer a particular brand compared with other brands. Here status-consciousness of the customer comes into play. The purchases are made of high equality-brand products compared with rival brands. The esteem need of customer, in fact, is linked to social status of the customer, because in the midst of his social groups he wants to be classed in its top or creamy later.

We have mentioned earlier as to what is the actualisation need of the customer. It comprises the urge of the person who makes a purchase of particular brand of the product to develop oneself fully. It also includes the inclination of the customer to achieve one's capacities and potentialities to the fullest. We may recall here the words of Maslow who has stated that in the hierarchy of needs, the self-sctualisation need is at the highest level amongst various other needs of the customer. Maslow, however, said that all the needs of the customer are inter-active, namely their relative priority is continually changing, shifting and variable.

We have clearly mentioned earlier that advertisers knowing these needs, their relative importance, varying natures, changing preferences and importance are able to shape their marketing communications to motivate consumers for a purchase. This leads us to the conclusion that only such marketing communications would click which are able to motivate customers for a purchase. The intelligent advertiser in the backdrop of the relative needs of customers, their preferences and priorities, strive to make their advertisements effective by including such marketing appeals which would win over customers.

Before discussing the various advertising appeals that make advertisements effective and result-oriented, we should also recall how four kinds of factors influence customers. We have discussed these factors in the earlier pages. These parameters which influence customers of going through advertisements are psychological factors, personal factors, social factors and cultural factors.

The psychological factors include motivation, perception, learning and beliefs and attitudes.

The personal factors comprises age and life-cycle position, occupation, economics and life-style and personality.

The next is the social factor which includes role and status, family and reference groups.

The cultural factor is also important which comprises culture, sub-culture and social class.

We have already discussed marketing research and have seen how it helps in securing marketing results. The study of advertisements and their impact on consumers is another area from which the advertiser can learn a lot. With the inputs of advertising research, the advertiser can reshape, remodel and re-format his advertising communications to make it more effective and result-oriented.

It would be worthwhile to recall how four Ps help achieve success in marketing communications, that is, through advertising communications.

In the world of marketing four Ps, namely,

- Product
- Place (Distribution)
- Price and
- Promotion

are vitally relevant in successful selling.

The product manufacturer in order to achieve successful selling must be able to make "TOTAL OFFER" to the consumer. The 'Total offer' concept must be fully understood by the advertiser in order to make an effective marketing or advertising communications.

The 'Total offer' concept to the consumer comprises three ingredients (1) the offer should be able to fully meet the needs of the consumer; (2) all aspects of the offer are acceptable and beneficial to the consumer, and (3) all the organisational goals, including profits, are achieved in the process. Incidentally, the four Ps mentioned above constitute the Marketing Mix of the firm, company or manufacturer.

It was the American marketing experts James Culliton, who evolved the concept of 'Marketing Mix'. He defined the Marketing Manager as a 'mixer of ingredients'. To quote him, "The marketing man is a decider and an artist - a mixer of ingredients, who sometimes follows a recipe prepared by others; sometimes prepares his own recipe as he goes along; sometimes adapts a recipe of the ingredients immediately available; sometimes invents some new ingredients; and sometimes experiments with ingredients as no one else has tried before".

Neil H. Borden popularlised the concept of marketing later on. It was the well-known American professor of marketing Jerome McCarthy who defined 'marketing mix' in terms of four Ps, listing its variables under four heads, each commencing with the alphabet 'P'.

We will not deal with the four 'Ps' of marketing here, these may be taken up later in a separate chapter. Such a chapter can discuss at length the various elements of not merely the four 'Ps' of marketing mix and its different variables, but also the 'environmental variables of marketing' and 'behavioural variables of marketing'. For the present, we are concerned only with advertising communications and the appeals in them that can arouse interest of consumers and prompt them for a purchase.

The Significance of Advertising

The essence of advertising has been aptly summed up in a pithy statement: "Advertising is telling and selling". Although, advertising is one of the several functions of marketing, it has acquired the stature of an independent discipline, fit only to be handled by advertising experts.

There exists a voluminous literature on the subject of advertising. During the last two decades with the influx of literature on the subject, advertising grew and developed in a full-fledged field of study. More that 1,500 books on advertising appeared during the period 1990 to 2000 covering various aspects of advertising, such as social, economic and psychological elements of advertising communications.

These books have examined at length the task involved in advertising. They also deal with the ethics of advertising, began treating experts and authors of book began treating advertising as an exclusively commercial or management subject from the fifties onwards. Authors like Nell Borden, Marting Marshall, Boyd & Newman and Aaker & Myers treated advertising as a management and marketing tool.

In the marketing context, advertising has been defined "as any paid form of non-personal presentation and promotion of ideas, goods or services by an identified sponsor," The term advertising has originated from the Latin word, 'adverto', which means to turn around, Thus advertising comprises the means employed to draw attention to any object or purpose. The, advertiser through his advertisement intends to spread his ideas about his products or offerings among the customers and prospective purchasers in order to turn him around for a purchase.

UNDERSTANDING THE BUYING PROCESS KEY TO EFFECTIVE ADVERTISING

Mere transmission of an advertising message does not mean that the advertiser has established proper communication with the consumer-audience. The customer must see the advertisement, catch his attention, understand it and grasp what it conveys and finally the customer's purchase behaviour, that is, of the target, audience should get influenced and converted into a purchase decision. This amounts to a successful communication from the advertiser to his target audience Thus, the advertiser should not merely know but understand the intricacies of buyer behaviour. In effect, the advertiser is attempting to capture the attention of his target-audience and influence it, behaviour towards making a purchase. In brief, the advertisement should be of interest to the target-audience, the target-audience should interpret the message (advertising message) in the manner intended and the advertisement should influence the buying-attitude of the target-audience (customers).

ATTITUDE VITAL TO MARKETING

Attitude and 'Attitude Construct' constitutes the core of advertising management. The traditional view is that 'Attitude' comprises three inter-related components - congnitive, affective and conative.

To quote, "the cognitive component deals with cognition, or knowledge; it is the faculty of knowing or perceiving or conceiving ideas; it is the sphere dealing with knowledge. The affective component deals with affection and emotions, namely, feelings of likes and dislikes towards objects are treated on the affective plane, and, the cognative component deals with behaviour or action, (V.S. Ramaswamy & S. Namakumari).

We need not go into discussions of Theories on Attitude Change because it would be out of context here.

The main concern of marketing communications is to see and analyse how attitude change takes place through such messages (advertising), in other words, we should examine how marketing communications can be made more effective and result oriented.

At this stage, it would be worthwhile to examine the factors in the advertising message which can effectively persuade the target audience. The two most influential factors of an advertising communications are the source of the message and content of the message itself, or rather, the appeal in the message.

The Source of the Message

The source of the message, that is, the advertiser, is an important element in the success of the advertising message. Three elements are necessary, namely, credibility of the sources, likeability or attractiveness of the sources and the approach of the sources towards the view and disposition of the target audience.

THE MESSAGE

Message in the advertisement is equally important as the source in Audience Persuasion.

There are two main features in the advertising message that bring about 'attitude change' in the target audience. They are (1) The Message Structure and (2) The Message Appeal.

Message Structure

Message structure means how the various elements of the message should be organised and arranged in the advertising communications. The question that often bogs down the advertiser is whether the message should be a one-sided argument for the product or a two-sided argument. Extensive research has concluded that if the audience is already in agreement with the communicator's viewpoint, a one-sided argument in the message will surely win it over. If however, the audience is initially in disagreement with the communicator's viewpoint, a two sided argument would be helpful in winning over the target-audience.

A two sided argument would be greatly helpful in winning over and sustaining an audience which comes across counter-arguments later on and because the audience has been made aware of both the kinds of arguments for and against the advertised product.

A two-sided argument in fact, desensitizes the audience against counterarguments that may crop up later, because it has been made aware of both sides of the proposition. It has been noticed that a two-sided argument is effective in winning over an audience with a high educational level. Such audience possesses the potential and capability to appreciate and assess both sides of the argument. When the message is one-sided such an audience is likely highly to reject it as being partial and subjective. The one-sided argument goes well with an audience of a low educational status, because it is likely to accept it as explained to them in the message. It may not be swayed by counter arguments that come up before it subsequently.

The order of presentation of ideas in the message is equally important in the message structure. Like a nail that cannot be fixed into a wall by a single stroke of the hammer, it has to be nailed in by repeated stroke of the hammer on the nail-head. Similarly, the advertising message has to be put into the mind of the customer through an organised, well designed and orderly message format. Incidentally, the same message from two different sources can have different impact on the target-audience, depending upon how and in what logical manner the message has been delivered.

The persuasive influence of the source of the message depends mainly on three factors: (1) Credibility of the source (2) Likeability or attractiveness of the source, and (3) The approach of the source to the views and disposition of the targets audience. We may leave the analysis of the source and its vital factors to a later stage, when we choose to discuss it in detail.

THE COMMUNICATION MESSAGE APPEAL

The most important element of the advertising communications is the advertising message. It is as important as the source in the persuasion of the target-audience.

The message appeal in marketing communications is vital because it catalyses and helps to achieve an attitude change of the customer. The message appeal caters to important needs and desires of the target audience. Message appeals are addressed to both the emotional and logical requirements of the target audience.

Message appeals can be broadly grouped into two main categories:

(1) Product-oriented appeals

(2) Consumer-oriented appeals

Product-oriented appeals highlight the main features of the product offered for sale. These appeals emphasis the physical features of the product or functions of the product or may also compare the product with rival brands available in the market. This has to be done in a subtle manner without running down rival brands or defaming them; if done in an offensive manner it may amount to unfair trade practice. Moreover, lowering the reliability and usefulness of rival brands of the product may not be accepted as credible by the consumer. Legitimate puffery of a product brand, that is highlighting the qualities of the particular product brand persuades the target-audience, while denigration of a arrival brand of the product may not evoke the trust of the consumer. He would see through it as a game plan to boost a product-brand through unhealthy or unintenable criticism.

The consumer-oriented appeals, on the other hand are directed at the attitudes, faith and beliefs of the target-audience. The consumer-oriented appeals may endorse attitudinal and behavioural patterns of the target-audience. These appeals say also sustain the lifestyles of the targets audience or the sought after social change of the consular. As a practical measure, advertising messages choose to combine both the product-oriented and consumer-oriented appeals for better and effective results.

Sticking to our broad classification of message appeals into product-oriented and consumer-oriented appeals, we may examine them briefly as to what they mean in actual practice.

Product-Oriented Appeals

The following are the main product-oriented appeals:-

(1) **Physical Features Oriented:** The advertising message in this kind of appeal highlights the physical features and characteristics of the advertised product.

(2) **Function Oriented Appeal:** These advertising message appeals stress upon the functional utility of the product or upon the operational mechanism the advertised product.

(3) **Brand-to-Brand Comparison Oriented Appeals:** Such advertising message appeals draw a comparison of the superiority of the product-brand with other rival brands of the same product available in the market.

Consumer-Oriented Appeals

The consumer-oriented appeals may be broadly classified as follows:-

(1) Attitude Oriented Appeal: The advertising message is designed to appeal to the beliefs, faith and values of the target audience.

(2) Class Oriented Appeal: The advertising message is framed in such manner so as to appeal to a social class as a whole which normally uses the advertised product. The social class in this case is usually held in high esteem by members of the target audience to which the appeal is directed.

(3) Lifestyle Oriented Appeal: In such an advertisement the message an appeal which is directed or matches the lifestyle of the target audience, including its social activates, recreations, its pastimes, etc.

It has been noticed that advertisers often evoke some human emotions in consumer oriented appeals. Sometimes, pleasant sensations and moods are aroused in the minds of consumers. Quite a few advertisements of consumer oriented appeals tickle the sense of luxury and distinctiveness. Some use fantasy to catch attention. The sense of fear is rarely used in such appeals. Humour is also employed in some of these appeals, the impact of which is doubtful.

Appeals Evoking on Pleasant Sensation and Moods

Advertisements on textiles, cigarettes, soft drinks, chocolates, cosmetics, peromes, etc., are often seen to use such appeals. Arousing a vast variety of emotions and feelings such as love, affection, sense of belonging, leisure, etc., are included in such appeals.

Appeals Evoking Sense of Luxury and Distinctiveness

Some consumer-oriented appeals attempt to arouse the feeling of luxury and distinctiveness. Such appeals are used in advertisements of consumer goods of established brands.

Humour Appeals

Advertisers are not unanimous on whether humour appeals attract the attention of the consumer? The persuasive have concluded that humour appeals do attract attention, but the question is whether they bring about change in consumer attitude? Yet another view is that humour appeals are likely to be taken lightly by the consumer.

TYPES OF APPEALS

Successful advertising develop such message content which would attract the attention of the consumer. The ad content is designed around a convincing appeal both related to the product utility and consumer psychology. Ads often contain in the appeal a catchy idea or an 'Unique Selling Proposition' or, in short, known as the USP of the product.

Appeals may also be broadly classified into there major categories:-

(1) Rational appeals

(2) Emotional appeals

(3) Moral appeals

Rational Appeals

Rational appeals are designed to arouse the thinking faculty of the target audience. These appeals stress upon or highlight the functional benefits of the product.

(a) High quality: These appeals containing this UPS are mostly used in ads for consumer durables. Consumer goods without high quality would generally not be welcomed by the consumers.

(b) Low price: Purchasers would consider it a rational decision in purchasing a product at lower price which functions equally well or slightly less than a product of some established brand.

(c) Long life: An electric bulb claimed to last a specific period of time, say 1,000 hours, before getting fused, would motivate the customer to purchase it compared with a bulb of a reputed brand which is silent on its life-span. Such an appeal in an ad that is, of assured long life, is a rational appeal.

(d) Performance: The performance-oriented appeal for rugged roads of a two -wheeler motor vehicle and an assured better mileage per litre of fuel is a rational appeal, which would motivate purchasers for a purchase to the exclusion of other established brands with gives lesser mileage.

(e) Ease of use: Ease of use of a gadget or home appliance say a washing machine of a new brand, which cleans, rinses dries clothes like a machine of a reputed brand, the former incarnating easy operation switches, would be a rational appeal.

(f) Resale value: Better resale value of a Bajaj scoter is a very attractive rational appeal, compared with two-wheelers of other brands, even if available at lower price, which have little or no resale value.

(g) After sale-service: After sale-service ensured by the manufacturer for a motor vehicle at conveniently accessible network of garages is a powerful rational appeal.

(h) Economy in operating expenses: A geyser which has effective switch on and switch off gadgetry which can be set at different temperature levels or a regulator which switches on and switches off power promptly, the ruby saving power consumption is also an effective and powerful rational appeal.

It may be noted that industrial products are mostly sold on the strength of rational appeals. Purchases are invariably made on the basis of declared specifications like technical, physical, chemical, etc. Even products purchased on the basis of emotional appeals are based on rational justification.

Emotional appeals

Emotional appeals as their name suggests arouse emotions, excite the human mind and arouse the heart for taking purchase decisions. Such appeals do not operate on a well designed pattern, because the heart is moved for making the purchase. Emotions may arise from a sub-conscious process. Emotions could be both positive and negative. We may examine both the negative and positive emotional appeals.

Negative emotional appeals: Such appeals highlight the likely harm if care is not taken. This would also fall in the category of the fear appeal like warning against possible tooth decay if a particular brand of toothpaste is not used which contains anti-decay ingredients.

Positive emotional appeals: These appeals incorporate the emotions of love, price, humour, prestige, joy, mother's love, etc. Parental love is also invoked.

The advertiser has over the decades been experimenting with the means necessary to evoke human emotions, move the heart of the consumer, and is employing all kinds of methods for ensuring successful selling of his product. Thus, it can be said as time passes, human psychology, emotions and values, preferences and almost all the human traits would generate a host of advertising appeals, fit for detailed study and research later.

CHAPTER

8 COMMUNICATION DIFFUSION PROCESS

Whatever message we communicate through advertisement, the first thing is that it must enter the mind of the receiver so that he may be persuaded to buy the product. Until and unless the message is entered in the mind of the receiver, he cannot be in a position to gain the knowledge about product or create or change an attitude or image about product or producer. This part of communication process is referred to as perception. There are two prerequisites for a successful advertising message first, an individual must be exposed to it and pay some attention to it. Second he must interpret it in the way in which advertiser intends it to be interpreted. Perception, therefore is the process by which an individual maintains contact with his environment. An individual receives stimuli through various senses and interprets them, is known as perception. Thus, it has two stage: attention and interpretation. There are two important factors that influence the perception—stimulus and individual factors. Perception is always referred to selectiveness. Only selective stimuli are perceived.

Perceptual skills are learned through experience and therefore, advertiser must pay mome attention to learning process. As soon as stimulus is perceived, the perceiver wants to learn about the product characteristics. If he is satisfied, and gains some advantages of using the product over the competitors product which he was using earlier, be may purchase the product. Thus, a relationship between stimulus and response is learning. The success of learning process may be imagined from (i) receptivity of learner's mind, and (ii) the environment of learning. As learning is quite slow in the beginning, repetition of message be necessary. It helps in changing attitude in favour of the product.

If, after learning, the attitude of the public is changed, it is good for the profitability and stability of company. The acceptance or rejection of a new product as in other words, the image of the product further diffuse the information about the characteristics, among other people. This is called diffusion of information. There are too many theories of diffusion.

PERCEPTION PROCESS OF COMMUNICATION

A perception starts as soon as the message is released for onward transmission to the destination. Before a message can transfer knowledge, create or change an image, or an attitude or a precipitate behaviour, it must enter the mind of the receiver. This part of communication process is referred to as perception and is itself a process made up of elements, flows and forces that enhance or inhibit messages to which an individual is exposed.

Perception has been defined as "the process by which an individual maintains contact with his environment." In other words, it is "the process whereby an individual receives stimuli through the various senses and interprets them" Stimuli here can refer to sets of advertisements, to a single advertisement, or to a portion of an advertisement.

There are two important prerequisites for a successful advertising message. First an individual must be exposed to it and pay some attention to it. Second, he or she must interpret it in the way the advertiser intended it to be interpreted. Each represents, in some sense a perceptual barrier through which many advertisements fail to pass. Some advertisements fail to stimulate sense organs in the recipient to a minimum threshold level of interest and awareness. There are some other advertisements, the meaning of which are distorted by the recipient in such a way that the effect of the advertisement is quite different what the advertiser intended. Both these elements—attention by the receivers and the desired effect—are necessary to make the message or advertisement successful. Thus, the perception process as conceptualized in Fig. 8.1 includes two stages—attention and interpretation. The perception process is influenced by such stimulus characteristics as its size intensity message, etc., and by the variables reflecting the differences across people, such as their needs, attitudes, values and interests.

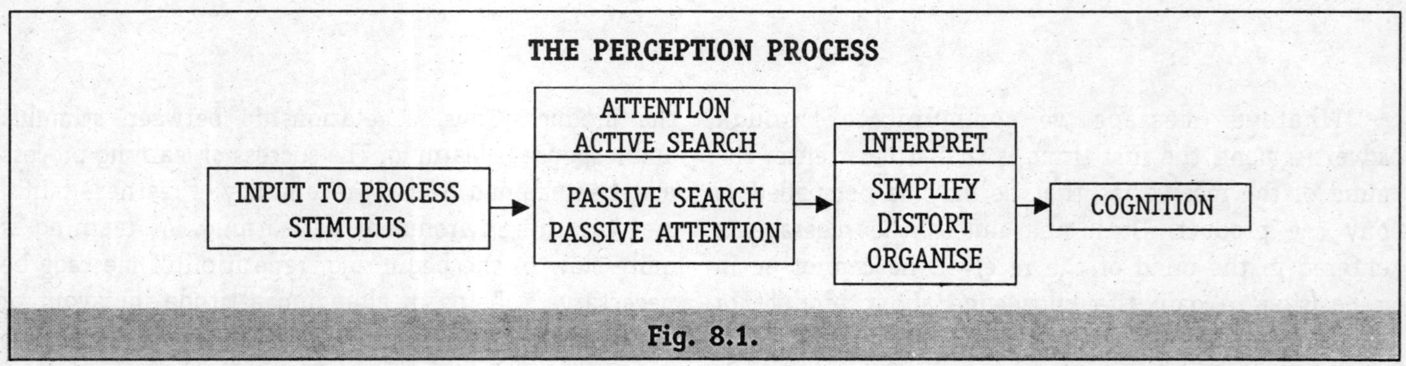

Fig. 8.1.

The first stage in the perception process is the attention filter, individual overtly or accidentally avoids exposure to stimuli, receiver reads only certain publications, see only selected television programmes and listens to radio programmers which he or she thinks to be interesting or which affect his or her needs, attitudes, uses and interests. Furthermore, most stimuli (advertisements) to which a person is exposed, are screened out or remain unseen, unlistened or unread because he or she considers them uninteresting and irrelevant. Thus, only a small fraction of all advertisements are exposed to a given person. Also, only a portion of those advertisements to which an individual is exposed will get through the attention filter.

The second stage in the perception process is the interpretation process. An individual organised the stimulus contents into his or own models of reality, models that may be very different from those of other individuals or of the sender. In doing so, the person often simplifies, distorts, organises and even creates stimuli. The output of this process is a cognitive awareness and interpretation of stimulus—a cognition.

Individual behaviour resulting from motivation is affected by how we perceive the stimuli. Perception has the meaning that each person attributes in incoming stimuli received through the five senses—

To Perceive is	To see To hear To touch To taste To smell	Some	Thing Event Idea

Psychologists previously assumed that perception was an objective phenomenon, that is, an individual can perceive only what was there to be perceived. Only recently have researchers recognised that what we perceive is as much a result of what we want to perceive of what is actually there. This does not mean that people view ants as elements. We may distinguish temples from petrol pump stations; but a petrol pumping station with good service and repair facilities, is perceived quite differently from an ordinary petrol pumping station having no such facilities. Thus, the perception is not what the advertiser intends to be perceived but the receiver perceives what they want to perceive out of what is actually there and thus their self concept, group pressures, role, and reference groups influence the perception to a great extent.

Factors that Influence the Perception Process

There are two types of factors that influence our perception process.

(1) Stimulus Factors—These are inputs to the process. Stimulus factors are characteristics of the physical object that affect both stages—attention and interpretation—of the process. Such factors are size, intensity, colour, shape, message, novelty, position and context; and

(2) **Audience or Individual Factors** – There factors reflect individual characteristics or differences. These factors include not only sensory processes but also past experiences with similar items, and basic motivations and expectations. Factors to be considered are information's needs, attitudes, values, interests, confidence, social context and cognitive style.

These factors can be depicted in the following ways :

Stimulus Conditions	Audience Conditions
Intensity	Attitudes
Size	Values
Message	Interests
Position	Confidence
Context	Social Context
	Cognitive Style.

The process of perception is not identical across people, even for the same stimulus. On the contrary, there are extreme differences among people in terms of their exposure, to what they are attracted and how they interpret information. A most important aspect the study of the perceptual process is to determine what variables explain these differences. Thus, different people will perceive differently the same stimulus at different times according to their needs, is interests, values, attitudes and confidence.

Principles of Perception

Perception is the process by which an individual receive interprets and responds to Stimuli in his environment. From advertising point of view, it is the process by which a mental impression is formed from the stimuli within the consumer's field of awareness. The consumer attaches significant meaning to what is observed because this meaning depends upon personal experience, memories beliefs, and fantasies and so on. No two people have the same meaning of any given observation. Let us approach the problem of understanding perception by four principles—

(1) **Perception is selective** - An individual will perceive selectively. In other words, he will not perceive all the stimuli. He will perceive only those stimuli which concern him.

(2) **Perception is organised** - Perception is well organised in the individual because it has meaning for the individual. Perceptions do not represent confusion.

(3) **Perception depends upon stimulus factors** - The nature the physical scuttles itself helps determine perception. Various stimulus factors such as size, colour, intensity, position and context. Effect the perception of the message. It is, therefore, relevant whether mediam advertisement in a magazine is in colour or black and white, a till page or a half from the perception point of view.

(4) **Perception depends upon personal factors**—Personal factors such as needs, moods, memory, experiences and values, affect the message reception. What the individual brings to the situation governs perception the ability to see or hear the message. A person who is interested in cricket is more likely to perceive an advertisement for stereo equipment than one for power hack-saw. A person's need at the moment will also determine perceptual selectivity. The thirsty man is more likely to perceive an advertisement for cold drink during a match. Past experience also shows that people have developed a taste for product preferences, and therefore, like to see some ads than others.

Perhaps, the most significant aspect of perception from marketer's point of view is its selectivity. The individual consumer perceives a product in terms of its brand image resulting from experience with the product and any promotion or advertising. The product name, package, design, and consumer's behaviour—all contribute to the consumer's perceptual performance.

Product price also has special significance. Every customer has two price limits in his mind a lower limit and an upper limit. Anything above the upper limit is expensive and will fail in. perceiving the customers. Any price below lower limit will create doubt, about quality of the product. The price perception is only part of the total brand image to be maintained.

Selective Perception

The manufacturer most often bombard the target consumers with commercials on T.V. and advertisements through different media but all are not perceived by them. Most of them are ignored, many are seen or viewed uninterestingly and probably a few are retained in the mind. The main problem of every marketer is how to stimulate the target consumers or in other words, what are those stimuli which consumers may respond to. How can they gain the attention of the individual, so that be may read and perceive the message in the advertisement? There are two basic factors (stimulus and individual) that affect the selectivity of the message i.e., size, colour, intensity, position and the needs, motives, attitudes etc., decide the perception process. As every individual is different in motives, interest, attitudes etc., so he selects only those ads that meet his requirements. Thus, there is a great deal of selectivity going on, in the process of perception. A popular word in the lexicon of the consumer behaviourist is 'Selective Perception'. Three kinds of selectively occur:—

(i) **Selective exposure** - The costumer attempts to encounter only those media and messages that interests him and are important to him and consistent with his deeply held values and beliefs. He will not attend to the. exposures which are not in agreement with his beliefs and values.

(ii) **Selective perception** - The customer will 'see' or 'hear ideas, messages and appeals which are relevant to him and can screen out others. It generally happens that persons do not see or view the advertisements that do not interest him or concern him at the time. Either they take them lightly or read hurriedly or do not see them at all. It means they have not perceived the message or appeal.

(iii) **Selective retention** - The people will remember what they like to remember and the rest they forget. It is neither desirable nor feasible to remember what is irrelevant for them.

These selective processes help to explain why some people are not at all affected by advertising, even by offensive advertising because they do not care to see and remember the advertisement messages.

A person's attitudes and pre-disposition to wards the market in question affect these selective processes. Furthermore, decisions that the consumer in currently making and typically concerned about will affect the pre-dispositions which are relevant. For example, if a consumer is thinking about buying a scooter, he will perceive the message in advertisements relating to scooters and the people attitude towards the existing brands of scooters available in the market. He will not even see advertisements concerning land dealings.

In case of introduction of new product in the market, the manufacturer will bombard the target consumers with commercials or advertisements on T.V. and in magazines with a view to inform and perceive the target consumers. In the beginning, it brings a little change in sales because for some time, most of the consumers would have no knowledge of the new product, though heavily advertised—Why? Because this information simply never penetrated their perceptual filters. Consumers perceive incoming stimuli on a selective basis. They perceive only those incoming stimuli which they wish to perceive or in other words which serve their interests with such selectivity at work, it is easy to see the importance of the marketer's efforts to obtain a consumer franchise for his product in the form of brand loyalty. Satisfied customers will not like to seek much information about competing products. If this information is forced upon them, they will not pass it to others through their perceptual filters. They will tune out such information which is not in accord with their beliefs and expectations.

Subliminal Perception

Subliminal perception is a stage of subconscious level of awareness. It is possible to communicate with persons without their being aware of the communication. The words 'Drink Campa Cola' flashed at the cinema screen frequently during the interval only for one second the message may be too short to be recognised at the conscious level. Still it may increase the sale of Campa Cola. This is why the advertising agencies become intensely interested in subliminal perception. It avoids perceptual screens of viewers. The goal of original research in this area was to induce the buyers of consumer goods without their awareness of the source of motivation. But later findings have not been successful. The subliminal advertising has been widely condemned throughout the world over, it is unlikely to conclude that such advertising will induce the buyers and will increase sales except in such cases where buyer himself is interested in purchasing the item. There are several reasons for this—

(a) Stimulus factors are absent in such type of advertising which are very necessary to gain attendance.

(b) Only a very short message can be transmitted.

(c) Individuals vary greatly in their thresholds of awareness. Message transmitted in such cases for one person may not be perceived at all by other people who have not seen it on the screen. Moreover, when exposed subliminally. The message may carry a confused version. For example, the message 'Drink Campa Cola', may go unseen by some viewers. Some others may take it as 'Drink Coca- Cola' or Drink Cocoa etc., and in this way competitors may gain. Contrary to earlier research, it has been established that consumers cannot be forced to purchase what they do not want to purchase.

Thus, subliminal advertising is not used in the present day advertising world.

Role of Attention in Perception Process

The term attention can be viewed as the state of focusing one's mind upon something. When consumers attend to advertising, they focus their perception upon it. They distinguish advertising from other elements of environments. Attention can also refer to as an information filter—a screening mechanism that controls the quantity and nature of information. Often, advertisers experience difficulty in gaining attention of target consumers who are encircled with an infinite number of stimuli to which an individual could be exposed and an infinite variety of parts or components of a stimulus to which he or she might attend. Clearly, it is possible for an individual to absorb only a small fraction of the available stimuli. The advertiser, generally, are faced with the need for taking steps to make their advertisements stand out and say or do something to attract consumer's attention in the midst of all this clutter of competing stimuli.

One of the ways of gaining attention is to design the advertisement copy in such a way that consumers may take it different from other elements in the environment. The marketers will try to induce consumers to attend to the advertisement by designing the message and utilising the media that is quite different from others. Usually, target consumers are likely to attend to those ads which are in colour, that feature a well-known personality, that are larger than others (in print media) or louder than others (in broadcast media). If the target consumer's perceives a particular type of advertisement in preference, to others, it means, it Is effective in capturing the attention of consumers and they themselves differentiate it from the others to which they are exposed. Exposure is a must without exposure, there can be no communication.

Only a small percentage of the exposed advertisements get through the attention filter i.e., are actually 'seen' or 'attended to' The attention filter operates at three levels of effort and consciousness they are as follows :

(a) Active Search - At one extreme level is the process of active search wherein, the receiver actually seeks information. He or she might collect information through opinions of friends and relatives or search through old newspapers and magazine, not generally read.

(b) Passive Search - This is another extreme where the receiver seeks fox information only from sources to which, he or she is exposed during the normal course of events.

(c) Passive Attention - The final level might be called passive attention. In such cases, the receiver does not make any serious attempt to obtain the information because he or she does not need it. But some information may nevertheless enter the system.

Motives which Stimulate Consumers to Obtain Information

At all the three levels, it would be appropriate to search why a person obtains information. There may be, as many reasons as there are situations and individuals. However, it is instructive to examine four general motives for attending to informative stimuli. In a sense, these are audience conditions influencing attention. Four motives are: —

(1) To obtain information that has practical value for the person;

(2) To obtain information that supports their opinions-supportive exposure;

(3) To obtain information that stimulates; and

(4) To obtain information that interests.

(1) Information that has Practical Value

Advertising, undoubtedly, is a source of information. Psychologists are of the view that people do expose themselves to information that has practical value of them. The information seeker or target audiences are in a practical need for product information and effective advertisements tend to fulfill this need. Such information is used in making decisions. If an advertisement contains certain information of practical value, people will actually search it out in certain circumstances and will be willing to read the copy to others.

Advertisements that provide useful information enhance the company image. For example, Indian Oil Corporation disseminates information to its customers that may help the consumers against any risk from the gas leakage. Burnkrant applies a general theory of motivation that the behavioural tendency to process information is based upon three factors;—

(i) Information need for some product which are costly, complex or some what unknown because they are new or for some other reason.

(ii) The second factor is expectancy that processing a particular stimulus will lead to relevant information exposure.

(iii) The third would a measure of the value of the message as a source of relevant information. It is measured in terms of goodness or badness of the message as an information source.

(2) Information that Supports — The Consistency Theories

It is a psychological truth that people have a preference for supportive information and avoid non-supportive or discrepant information For example, here is a statement of a comedian Dick -Gregory "I have been reading so much about cigarettes and cancer that I quit reading." It means drives or motives that do not support the customer's view, he disregard them. We can term this type of derive as 'selective exposure'.

Selective exposure can be explain here by the consistency theories such as dissonance theory, which suggest that people have a cognitive drive to develop consistent cognitions and behaviors about the existence of conflicting cognitive elements, is discomforting and that people will try to reduce it. One mechanism to reduce dissonance is selective exposure that is perceive such exposures which are supportive to their views and avoid which are not.

Sometimes, involuntary exposures threaten the selective exposure that tend to increase due to non-supportive information. If a person receives any negative information about the brand or product he is loyal to, he will become sensitive to information that supports his view—that the brand is quite reliable. In such cases, the advertiser might therefore stand ready to respond immediately to any negative information, his customers are likely to receive or received. Such a campaign would capitalise on selectivity and could be very effective.

In combating such selective exposure, the advertiser can offer rewards, contests or premium to get people to read the message. An alternative is to approach a certain segments of markets indirectly through opinion leaders and rely on words of month to reach others. Another approach may be to broaden the media used i.e., to use certain non-conventional media inspite of high cost of advertisement per thousand.

(3) Information that Stimulates—The Complexity Theories

A third motivation is to obtain variety to combat boredom. The argument is that when an individual's stimulation level is sufficiently low, he will cease screening out discrepant information, and actually seek out information that is complex, novel, and even inconsistent with his existing attitudes. Theories supporting this view are termed 'complexity theories' Mr. Maddi, who holds prime position as a complexity theorist, has put forth the theory as follows :

"Its essence is that novelty, unexpectedness, change and complexity are pursued because they are inherently satisfying. The definition of novelty and unexpectedness must stress the difference between existing cognitive content and current or future perceptions, and hence, the experience of variety is very likely to also be the experience of inconsistency".

This theory is based on the very reasonable assumption that people get bored and are motivated to reduce that boredom by seeking stimuli that are novel, unusual, and different. People are always curious what is around them and this curiosity will influence exposure patterns. In other words, they may be motivated to seek out information that does not support their positions.

The complexity theories have empirical support of their own. Studies have revealed that when a new element is introduced in the environment. People are very much anxious to know about it. Studies have also indicated that variety in the form of novelty and unexpectedness is pleasurable whereas completely predictable events become boring. It is thus obvious that advertising should avoid being predictable, especially in situations wherein selectivity can easily operate to screen out advertisements. Another empirical conclusion is that variety is not only pursued and enjoyed, but is actually necessary to normal living.

(4) Information that Interests

People are attracted to the information that interests them or in turn, they are interested in subjects with which they are involved or people or situations with which they are identified. In an attempt to attract attention, an advertiser can adjust the stimulus, the advertisement and its environment. Studies show that people are more apt to look and remember things in which they are interested than things in which they are not. Normally, people are interested in information concerning benefits that they feel are important in a product. He, thus, applies benefit segmentation to the task of penetrating the attention barrier.

A most effective approach for gaining interest is to run an advertisement about the person or persons to whom it is directed, mentioning the name and discussing his activities. Advertisements can be developed with which people can readily identify. For example, an insurance company runs a series of advertisements in which agents may be presented in a most personal way. Their hobbies and life styles may be discussed in a manner that made it easy for readers to identify with them. Such advertisements of course, are sure to have an enormous impact on the company's agents.

Another approach is to present a communication involving topical issues—those in which the audience is likely to be heavily involved.

An advertiser should not forget that to attract attention is not his only concern. It will be worthless if attention diverts interest from the important aspect of the message. In particular, it is not useful to attract an individual with a highly interesting subject if the brand and its message get lost in the process.

The adoption level theory suggests that it is not the focal stimuli that determine perception, but also the contextual stimuli (background) and residual stimuli (past experience). Attention is enhanced when the stimulus deviates markedly from that level. Thus, a colour advertisement will attract more attention than it is seen in black and white environment. In an advertising context, a humorous advertisement may attract attention, if it is surrounded by more conventional copy approaches. However, if many humorous advertisements are involved, the attraction will be less.

Thus, there are four motives that stimulate the audience to read the advertisements or that attract the attention of the people. These motives are—(i) information of practical value, (ii) information that supports the audience view, (iii) information that stimulates or (iv) information that gain interest.

INTERPRETATION PROCESS

Interpretation is the second prerequisite of the perception process. By interpretation, we mean that the target audience must carry the same meaning of the message that the advertiser wants to communicate. In other words, the audience must interpret the message in the way, the advertiser wants it to be interpreted. If it is not interpreted in that way, the whole efforts and cost go waste.

Two concepts from the Gestalt psychology help up to understand the interpretation process. The first is that stimuli are perceived as a whole. What is important in an advertisement interpretation is the total impression that it leaves on the minds of the audience. The second is that an individual has a cognitive drive towards an orderly cognitive configuration. We shall now discuss these two concepts (i) organised whole and (ii) cognitive drive, in detail.

(1) The Organised Whole

The stimuli should be viewed as a whole and not in parts. Various experiments draw conclusions that even when the stimuli are incomplete, people seem to strive to form a complete impression of a person or object. Advertising copy does not necessarily have to tell the whole story, an individual will naturally fill in the gap to form an impression. The studies indicated that stimuli are seen in interaction. The intelligence of different persons will differ. Because of such interaction effects, the total impact of an advertising campaign needs to be considered. An appeal or an advertisement may prove effective by itself, but it may not be effective in terms of the whole campaign. Studies show that there are some attributes that are more central to the conceptual process than others. Experiments also indicated that first few traits formed a context within which others are interpreted. Thus, an advertiser should be concerned with the first impression that advertisement generates.

The stimuli are viewed as a total configuration suggests that brand must be considered as an organised whole. Thus, alteration or addition of a single component may indeed affect the total configuration. We might see that there are interactions among various dimensions, If one dimension is changed or a new dimension added, the perception of the brand along the others may change radically to consumers. If perception is indeed an organised whole, then the system of interrelationship among components stimuli has meaning of its own. All the stimuli could change, but if the relationship among entities remain, the perception may not be affected.

The concept of orgnised whole also dictates that perception of a stimulus cannot be considered in isolation from its context. The selling of the stimulus is part of the total field and will influence the perception. A salty expression would be perceived quite differently at a football game that it would be in the middle of wedding ceremony.

The context of an advertisement will effect how it is perceived. Advertisement appeared on advertising vehicles will have different perception. The feature material in a specific edition may create a mood chat will effect interpretation. Furthermore, the company involved and all its interactions with an audience member will also affect interpretation.

(2) The Cognitive Drive

The next important tenet of the Gestalt Psychology is that there is a cognitive drive to obtain a good configuration, one that is simple, familiar regular, meaningful, consistent and complete. The following principles are related to the cognitive drive—

(a) Closure—If a subject realises that something is missing from a picture or from a copy, the audience will fid in the gap. This process is called 'closure'. Strong perception may be seen in closure copy. An advertiser can use the closure process to make a campaign more effective. A 69 second commercial may be run several times on TV. To combat forgetting, a shorter spot of 5 or 10 seconds long may be spotted. A viewer may visualise the omitted materials. Thus, the material contained in the 60 second commercial will have been transmitted in a much shorter time, reducing the risk of boring the viewer.

Another use of closure concept is leaving a well known jungle uncompleted. Those exposed will have a strong cognitive drive to effect closure by mentally completing the jungle.

Closely related to closure is the process of interpreting an ambiguous stimuli. The interesting part of the process is the involvement of participants. The advertiser will leave the advertisement ambiguous in any of ways. An advertisement has three main components—a picture, a written message and the brand name. The ambiguity can be introduced into any of these elements. This ambiguity with stimulate sufficient interest to sustain cognitive activity necessary to figure it out. But advertisement should not be too ambiguous.

(b) Assimilation-Contrast—Another principle of perceptual psychology is called assimilation-contrast. This principle is used by the audience member to remove ambiguity from a stimulus. A host of audience conditions may influence interpretation among themselves. Here values, brand preference, social situations, cognitive styles and cognitive needs are of importance. For example, some people have a need for cognitive clarity, a need to impose meaning and organisation, on their experiences with the world. Such people tend to exert a greater effort to understand an ambiguous communication than those with low need for cognitive clarity. It is useful to attempt to measure advertising, specially while it is being developed, to determine its impact on the attention and interpretation stage of the perception filter. Among the approaches to the measurement of interpretation in a pretest is the direct questioning of those exposed in a laboratory setting, for example, projected techniques such as word association arid unstructured interviews.

LEARNING PROCESS

Psychologists believe that learning is possible in all human behaviour. Gary Stener defines learning as "all those changes in behaviour that results from previous behaviour in similar situations'. There is confusion in its meaning when we try to discover how learning works. The most important theory from advertising point of view is the 'stimulus—response approach'. According to this approach, 'learning is what takes place when a link is established between a particular stimulus and a particular response'. Drivers stopping their vehicles at red light, and audiences applauding a performance are examples of stimulus-response learning.

Learning Process and its Important Variables

Perceptual skills are learnt and this fact has led some adver-tisers to pay special attention to learning process. Learning theorists have isolated a number of steps in the learning process. Learning process begins with a drive a strong stimulus—that motivates the individuals to learn. Depending on the cues, ads signs and other stimuli relevant to the situation existing in the environment, the individual chooses certain specific response in an effort to satisfy the drive. The specific response thus chosen depends very much on the cues and previous experience. Man behaves in the way in which he satisfied the drive earlier.

The reinforcement of the learning process occurs when the response is followed satisfaction i.e., a reduction in drive tension. Reinforcement strengthens the relationship between the environmen-tal cue and the response, and may lead to similar response next time the drive occurs. Repeated reinforcement leads to the development of a habit. It becomes a routine for the satisfaction of the drive.

John Dollard and Neal Miller have formulated the stimulus-response relationship in more sophisticated term by breaking it down into four important variables of learning process. They are drive, cue, response and reinforcement. The term drive refers to inner need of an individual that invites action. For example, hunger, fatigue, fear, insecurity and so on. These inner drives call for action. A cue is a stimulus in the environment that stimulates an individual to work. A commercial on T.V. providing a solution to the inner drive may be the cue. If hunger is a drive, a commercial for 'pulao' or biscuits may be a cue. Cue links the drive and the response. The response is the action of an individual what he does in response to the cue. For a hungry man, getting something to eat as suggested in the cue is a response.

Reinforcement is the strengthening of the cue-response relationship and is directly related to the degree of satisfaction the response brings to the original drive. The individual reinforces the response, if degree of satisfaction is high otherwise he seeks alternatives, if a response is reinforced regularly, the result is habit formation.

We can depict these four variables as follows.

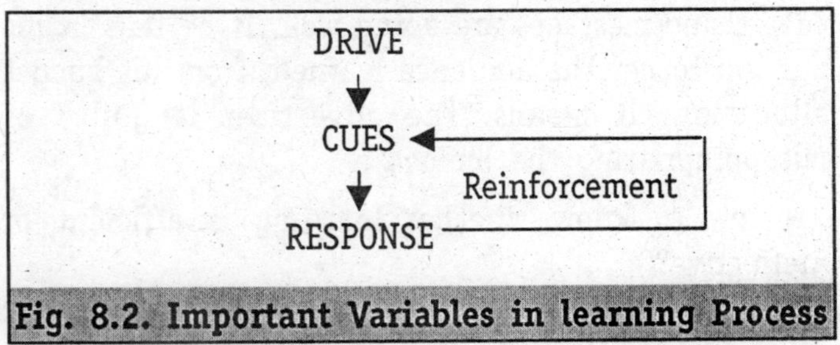

Fig. 8.2. Important Variables in learning Process

The above description seems to be very simple and straight forward. But, it is not so, if we consider the possible alternative response. The response may be immediately or deferred. If our response is immediate, our hungry consumer, watching a pulao commercial may immediately go to the kitchen or out to some restaurant and may have some pulao to satisfy his hunger. Or, if the commercial simply focusses attention on hunger drive, it may lead the consumer to any response necessary to satisfy the need i.e., he may go to chicken or nons or any other ordinary food. On the other hand, if our hungry consumer is observing fast on that day, he may negate the need for food.

Regardless of the immediate response, the consumer may respond several days later when he goes for shipping. Remembering how appealing it was in the commercial, he may look for it in a restaurant. At this, point another intriguing element intervenes, if the consumer notices that the ordinary cooked rice is cheaper than the advertised pulao. This may act as a cue to his drive of economy. The response would be to buy ordinary cooked rice unless the advertisement convinced him that his need would be better satisfied by paying extra for pulao. Anticipating and dealing with such chains of stimuli-response relationship is one of the most absorbing elements of the advertising.

The learning theory is that body of interrelated principles which deals with human money. The notion that the learning theory may be relevant to, and helpful in, in advertising, suggests, the role of the advertiser as:

(a) disseminator of information;
(b) an audience;
(c) a disseminator who may have a measurable impact on the audience.

The learning laws which govern education may be conveniently applied to advertising.

Every advertiser is interested in knowing that his advertising messages are doing well. If he fails in his mission to get the audience learned, from his budget allocation, it means, the advertiser is guilty of misappropriating the budget.

How to know whether learning is efficient or ineffective?

How an advertiser comes to know whether or not learning is efficient or totally ineffective depends upon two factors:

(a) The 'receptivity' of the learner's mind; and
(b) The environment of learnings.

(a) The Receptivity of Learner's Mind— The receptivity means grasping power of the learner's mind and that depends upon two important elements—(i) interest level and (ii) the intellectual capacity to grasp things. The disseminator has no control or little control over the receptivity of the learner's mind. There are no doubt, certain techniques to develop interest and draw attention of the learner, but these techniques will not be of much help unless the learner has some prime interest in the first place.

(b) The Environment of learning—The second element for the effectiveness of learning is the environment of learning—the conditions under which the exposure is made, can, to a large extent, be controlled by the disseminator. The body of laws or principles that we call the learning often specifies the best environment for effective learning.

The average person is exposed to several messages each day. Indeed such messages are so ubiquitous that we may seem to have come a long way towards developing a filter within ourselves that reduces our annoyance to tolerable levels. Thus, there are certain advertisements that attract our attention most while there are others that draw our attention not to that degree. The most memorable commercial exposure, the commercial message that produces the most lasting learning experience, is in some way differentiated from the run of the mill commercials. The laws of the learning theory suggest the manner in which differentiation may be developed and exposed. Instead of tall claims of quality, the learning theory suggests that we can associate the product with some other product which is well established in the minds of people. For an advertisement of Cadbury chocolate, we may advertise like. 'Rolls Royce is a car—Cadbury is a chocolate'. This manner of conveying the notion of quality utilises the psychological law of belonging. The learning percept that specifies that ideas or objects that are naturally related and organised into meaningful relationship can be remembered better than those that have no logical connection.

An important group of attitude change theories rests on an assumption that attitudes change through a process of cognitive conflict arousal and reduction. The change takes place in an effort to resolve the conflict situation and the resolution results in a new attitude. The motivation for resolving conflict is considered a general human tendency to seek consistency, harmony and balance in cognitive structures. As a group, they are thus called consistency theories.

There are three basic theories comprising in consistency theories of attitude change i.e., the balance theory. The congruity theory, and the dissonance theory.

The Balance Theory

The balance theory deals with three elements (a) an individual or "perceiver", (b) another person, and (c) sonic object, and relations among the elements. Relations may be positive or negative. The main preposition of this theory is that a cognitive structure can be balanced or unbalanced depending upon the configuration of rela-tionship among the elements. Furthermore, balanced structures are essentially stable and create no force or tension for cognitive, affective or behavioural change. Unbalanced structures, on the other hand, are unstable and set up a force requiring some sort of change to regain balance.

The major attitude change implication is that balanced states are stable and should resist change whereas on the other hand unbalanced states are unstable and should change as to generate a balance. Thus, an unbalanced state is one in which psychological tension is aroused, and it is this tension that leads to attitude change towards the balanced state.

This theory, from marketer's point of view is of wide importance. An advertiser can view a market or a market opportunity from this relatively primitive theoretical prospective. The basic idea is to design a message that would create an unbalanced state in the minds of a receiver. This state of mind could motivate the receiver to restore the balance by changing his attitude for the product. If the message were such as to imply the restoration of balance by developing a favourable product attitude, the advertisement would succeed in changing attitude.

The balance framework is applicable to a wide variety of other market situations as well.

The Congruity Theory

Unlike the balance theory, in which only the direction of relation is considered, congruity theory considers both direction and magnitude of the relation. Focussing on the strength of the relation also draws attention to the degree of change to be expected in a particular cognition. A cognition that is strongly held will tend to change less. The theory introduces the idea that changes in degrees of positiveness or negativeness occur and that predicting the attitude change potential of a persuasive communication is altered accordingly. These theories after insights why an advertising communication be a motivating communication.

The Dissonance Theory

This theory is also flowing out of the same kind of cognitive, balance reasoning. The contribution of dissonance theory is that it emphasises the significance of the actual purchase involved in forming or changing attitudes. The theory focus attention on the actual product choice and use behaviour as a source of attitude formation and change. A basic assumption of this theory is that choice of one product over another involves psychological tension or conflict. Following choice of one of the products, the consumers go through a cognitive reappraisal process best known as rationalising the decision to choose the one over the other. In the reappraisal process, cognitions that are consonant and supportive, of the choice are reinforced in the positive direction. Those that are dissonant with the choice (and perhaps consonant with alternative not chosen) tend to be suppressed or rejected. In effect, positive attitudes develop for the alternative chosen and the negative attitudes for the one not chosen. The process of tension arousal and tension reduction is basic to this theory of attitude change. Dissonance theory also points out the significance of what actual purchase and use of the product can do to develop values, like styles and a wide variety of related attitudes.

Consistency theories — the balance theory, the congruity theory and the dissonance theory—provide an insight into the probable persuasive impact of individual advertising messages and an explanation for that persuasive impact. An advertiser's capacity to change brand attitudes on one exposure is limited. One advertisement might initiate trial but the flow from the trial itself may develop or change a brand attitude. Individual advertisements can never be judged on their persuasive potential by viewing them as being made up of components or parts, each of which is capable of encouraging some measure of receiver's

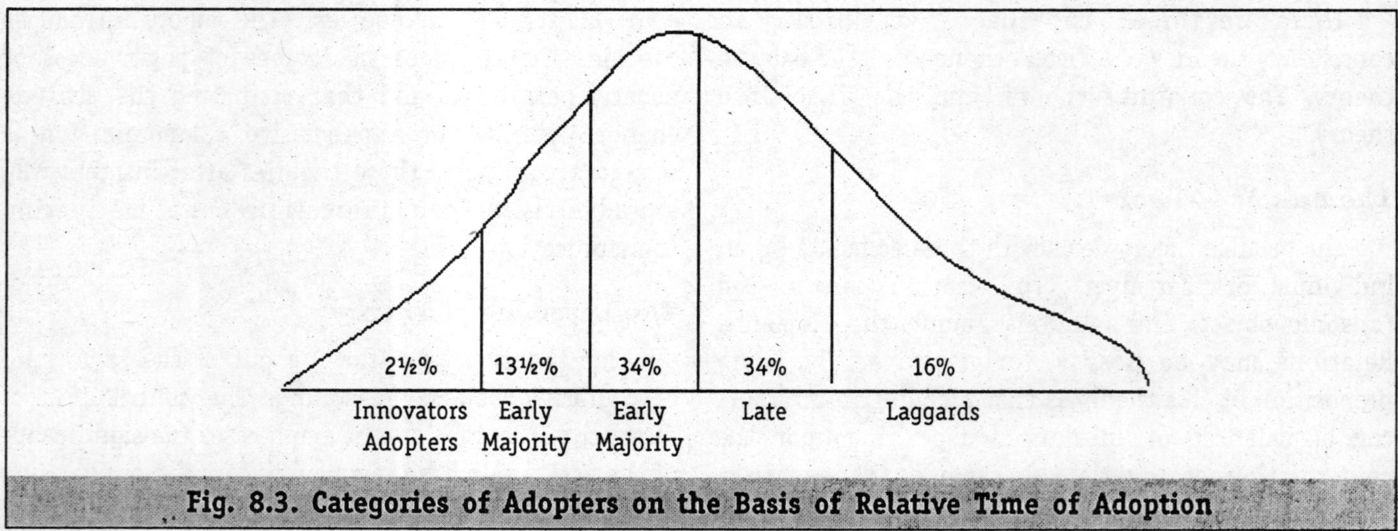

Fig. 8.3. Categories of Adopters on the Basis of Relative Time of Adoption

'involvement. Moreover, the relation among the components, as seen by a receiver, may be used to judge the degree of psychological tension that the message is likely to arouse in a particular receiver or market segment.

Significance of Repetition in Increasing Retention

Advertising plays a very important role in providing cues to the product and the product's performance. The prospects learn through the cues barring is quite slow at the beginning and it increases rapidly with repetition until plateau is reached. The central concern is how long the cues are retained and what values repetition has in increasing retention. Repetition adds to memory and one cannot retain a cue for long unless new exposure is received. The researches show that massive repetition of an advertisement may be sufficient to induce the consumer to buy the product advertised. This introduces the opposite side of learning forgetting, and the intriguing question of the decay of advising effects. If the earlier learning involved reinforcement or rewards, the fact would have an effect on decay rate. There are evidences that after several repetitions (or a fewer, if ad is memorable), forgetting is not complete for many years or in some cases for many decades. The effects of advertising message may be difficult to eradicate completely ever after many years after the campaign came to an end.

The conclusions of some psychological experiments dealing with retention and forgetting are :

(i) In the very beginning, immediately following learning, forgetting is the greatest. Learning in the beginning is slow and forgetting is fast.

(ii) Retention increases with repetition. Repetition can result in increased liking for the repeated stimulus.

(iii) A more meaningful and vivid material is better retained than a less meaningful and less vivid material.

(iv) The more completely the material is initially learned, the greater is the retention.

(v) The material presented first (primacy) or last (recency) is better retained than the material presented in the middle.

(vi) The effects of repetition in advertising depend upon the given advertising situation. These effects are likely to be influenced by factors such as the type of product or brand, the appeal, and format of the ad, and the media frequency schedule.

(vii) The effects of repetition seem to be less on measures of behaviour, such as purchasing action, than on measures of affect such as brand evaluation or intention to purchase.

Repeated advertising messages have better chances of being retain if they are spread over a period of time rather than concentrated over a limited period. The scheduling decision, may, however, depend upon the product advertised long term continuous advertisement may be preferred for well established products. However, new products may require the impact of concentrated messages to reach consumer awareness.

DIFFUSION PROCESS OF COMMUNICATION

The diffusion process refers to the acceptance of new products and services by the members of a community or a social system. When a manufacturer introduces a new product to the market, it is pertinent to let the people know about that product. So, a marketer or manufacturer must know the process by which people learn about new products, try them, and eventually accept or reject them In an age of changing technology and rapid obsolescence, the growth, profitability and stability of many companies depend upon consumer acceptance or rejection of their new products. In order to get the acceptance of the people for the new product, the information about the product must reach the people in time so that they might learn all about the product. This is called diffusion of information. The diffusion process refers to this acceptance of new products and services by the members of a community or a social system. Central to the diffusion theory is the concept that there is a process of diffusion by which an innovation spreads from its source of invention or creation to its ultimate users or adopters. This process involves four elements:

(i) **An innovation**—It is an idea, or a product that is perceived as new. The innovation need only be new in the eyes of its beholder and may actually be quite well known to others.

(ii) Its communication from one individual who has come into contact with the innovation to another.

(iii) Its permeation into social system.

(iv) Its use over a period of time.

Ultimately, the extent to which an innovation permeates a social system depends upon the number of people who adopt it. The term adoption refers to the buying decision of the individual as a token of acceptance of the innovation. If the products are accepted by a few, the adoption rate is slow.

Categories of Adopters—Adopters are person' who use the product or accept it by taking buying decision. All people do not accept the product in the very beginning. Only few take decision to buy the new product, others only follow them. The following curve shows the various categories of adopters on the basis of relative time of adoption in a normal distribution—

Fig. 8.3 shows that a few people (make up only 33% of total population) only adopt the innovation at first. Yet they are the key elements in the success of the new products. They are the first to try out the product. If the innovation is successful they pass it on to a large group (13½ per cent), the early adopters. These early adopters pass it again on to the early majority, the late majority and the laggards respectively. The rate finally diminishes, only a few potential consumers remain in the non-adopter category. Since the above categories are based on a normal distribution, standard deviations are used to partition each category. The first 2½% of the individuals who adopt the product are innovators and the final 16% are the laggards.

Locating the first buyers is the main challenging task for the marketing manager because these first buyers serve as a test market. They would evaluate the product at the introduction stage and possibly make suggestions for necessary modifications. Since the early purchasers are the opinion leaders, they communicate their advice or attitude to others or others seek their advice while making a decision about the purchase of the product. The acceptance or rejection of the product by these innovators serves as a warning signal for the marketing manager, indicating the expected success of the new product. Unfortunately, the first adopters of one new product may not necessarily be the innovators for the other new products of the company.

The characteristics of innovators differ from product to product and from area to area or from culture to culture. A large number of studies have established some general characteristics of most of the first adopters:—

(a) The first adopters are younger, have higher social studies, are better educated and enjoy a higher income. They feel proud of being the first adopters.

(b) They are more mobile than later adopters and change both their job and home address frequently.

(c) They are more likely to rely upon impersonal information sources than later adopters. More often, they rely upon print media and other impersonal sources for product information. The rarely rely upon personal sources such as friends, relatives, associates and salesmen.

(d) Innovators are not to be confused with opinion leaders. The later are not necessarily to be the first to adopt a new product.

Next category of adopters is early adopters and they are responsible for the diffusion of innovations. If, suppose, they do not accept the product or the new idea and pass it on to the early majority, the product has no chance to live long. It may be assumed to die without further chance of acceptance. This being the case, the marketers of new products attempt to identify the innovators and early adopters and to direct their efforts at them rather than at the target consumers at large. They are really the opinion leaders.

Once the early adopters accept the new idea or product, the pass it on to the early majority, a group of persons who wait for others to try the innovation before becoming involved in it. The late majority—another group is very slow to accept the new concept, preferring to wait until it has achieved substantial popularity. Finally, the laggards adopt an innovation only when it has become firmly entrenched in the ranks of the other four groups.

CHARACTERISTICS OF INNOVATION

The above process—passing the innovation from innovators to laggards—is known as innovation process. This process may take a very short time (over several weeks) or a very long time (many years). The adoption rate is influenced by the following five characteristics of the innovation:

(1) Relative Advantage—The superiority of the innovation over the existing product decides the adoption rate. Superiority might be in its performance, price, better appearance or convenience in use as compared to other products or services. For example, the adoption rate of black and white T.V. was greater than the colour T.V. The reason, being its convenience and price.

(2) Compatibility—Innovation has compatibility if it fits with the values and life style of the group in question. T-shirts, when introduced in India were quite successful because of their design suitable for the tropical climate of the country.

(3) Complexity—It means the degree of difficulty, the consumer experiences in understanding its working or in using it. Very complex ideas take time m innovation where as ideas or products which are very simple to operate spread very rapidly.

(4) Divisibility —Divisibility of the ideas or product also establishes the adoption rate. It is the extent on which innovation may be used on a limited basis. Consumers tend to accept divisible innovations faster than those that one quite indivisible. Customers may try out a new detergent in small packs and may use it to clean the clothes. If found suitable, they may purchase a big package of the product. But, on the other hand, a consumer cannot purchase a small unit of portion or a car.

(5) Communicability—The adoption rate of innovation is high if its quality or characteristics are communicable or described to other persons effectively. A T.V. salesman can describe a new T.V. model in terms of its quality and can demonstrate the quality of its reception if needed. On the other hand, a life insurance policy cannot be featured easily, so, it is communicable.

All these factors will affect the degree to which information about the new product is passed along and the extent of word of mouth advertising that takes place The above factors except complexity are essentially the supportive factor in the diffusion and personal influence process, whereas complexity will tend to retard the process.

DIFFUSION MODELS

Diffusion is the process by which something spreads through a population. Although much research is devoted to the study of the adoption of an innovation as the something being diffused, it should be recognised that the diffusion of information of any kind can be considered from the same perspective. Information, whether about an innovation or otherwise can be diffused through some form of communication channel. Channels may be vertical or horizontal, formal or informal.

A vertical channel exists if there is meaningful difference in the interests, social status, demographic or economic characteristics of the communicating units. In marketing, the relations among manu-facturer, wholesaler, retailer and consumer are often considered of as a vertical channel. A horizontal channel, on the other hand, exist when these similarity of interests, social status, demographic or economic conditions among the members of a group. This type of communication takes place among the members of the same group.

A formal channel is that is established by some one intentionally and is under the direct control of communicator. Thus, an advertise has a formal channel to a target audience that is established by choosing various media or direct exposure channel. An informal channel is one not intentionally established and not under the central of communicator. It is word of mouth aspect of advertising.

Trickle-Down Thesis of Diffusion

Another important aspect of the time of adoption research relates to the manner in which opinions are diffused in general public. Generally, the opinions are diffused in an informal vertical channel. The word 'diffusion' as we employ it here, means the process of transmission of ideas, points of view, or preferences of the population, if we whispered an idea in the ear of a person in an auditorium full of people and asked him to convey that idea in the ear of another and further asking everybody to communicate the idea likewise. We would thus create a miniature diffusion sequence. Here members worked under instruction to spread an idea. We are more immediately concerned with a natural diffusion proceeds, one in which pass along procedure is voluntary.

A natural diffusion process is amplified by the transmission of the awareness of new products, political issues, information about books and movies. How does this diffusion process work? Perhaps, he most frequently encountered theory of diffusion assumes that notion may be referred to as "Trickle Down Thesis" of diffusion which presumes a satisfied or layered, social system. A good illustration of trick-down flow is given by Elmo Roper. He suggested that ideas flow from 'great thinkers' to 'inert citizens' in the following sequence :

Great thinkers → great disciples → great disseminators → lessor disseminators → participating citizens → inert citizens.

The same theory applies to the innovations of new products, it assumes that the innovation in a social system is first adapted by people in the higher social classes and then later picked up by those in lower classes. The basic notion behind the theory is that subordinate social strata look to the levels above them for guidance in matters of taste and fashion. There are several reasons why this trickle down phenomenon is observed in the society. Hundreds of years ago, Royalty was considered to be an act of style innovators. The nobility copied royalty and some of the middle classes copied nobility. Moreover, we can see some trickle down influence in matters of fashion. We observe that new style appears first in the upper strata of the society or at the level of exclusive high fashion shops, then high quality ready-to-wear outlet, and finally at mass appealing stores. To the extent, each of these types of retail outlets caters to a clientele of a descending social class, a kind of trickle down phenomenon is observed.

The study of social class is in itself a very large subject about which much theory, empirical research and controversy exist. We can classify a society in the following classes: upper, lower-upper, upper middle, middle, upper lower and lower and show the trickle down process in the following diagram:

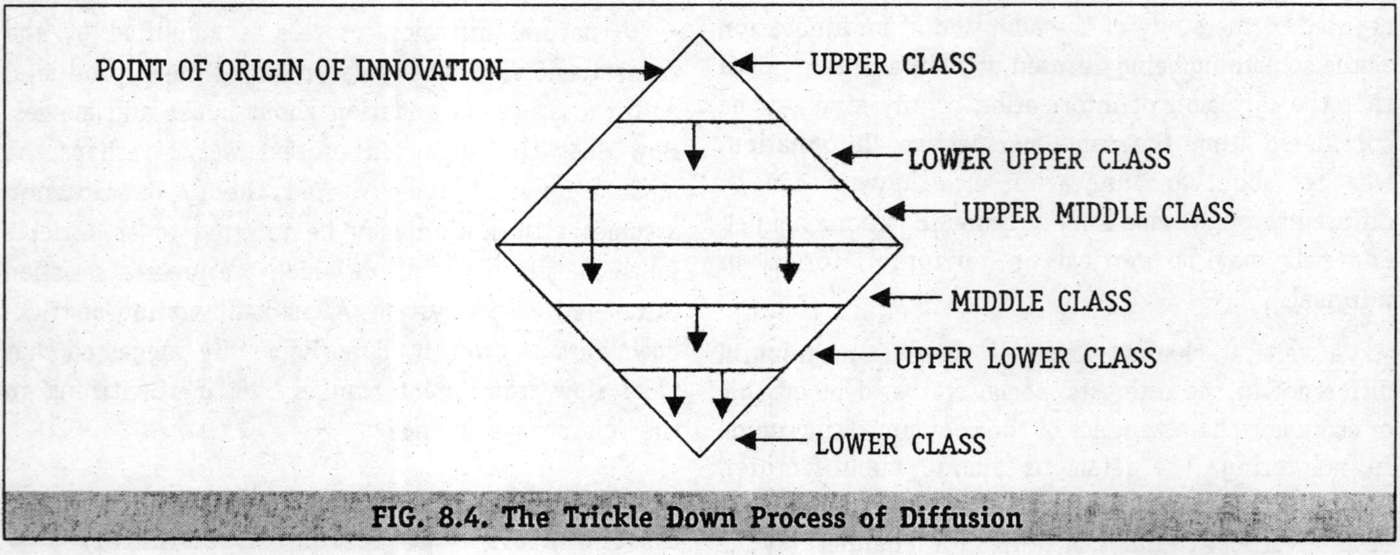

FIG. 8.4. The Trickle Down Process of Diffusion

Although the trickle down thesis of diffusion seems logical and operative in some context, yet there are many critics of the theory. These critics argue that the applicability of the theory is limited now-a-days and that it errs. This theory assumes that opinion leadership necessarily originates at the top of the social hierarchy. The fact is that such leadership may, and in fact, does, originate at ail levels of the social system. There is an opposing theory which supports this view. Those has been named as 'horizontal influence thesis'. This theory assumes that opinion leaders or influential, are present in every social and economic stratum and that such opinion leaders tend to specialise in terms of their realms of expertise i.e., there is very little overlap of leadership. A leader in one sphere may be influential in other unrelated spheres as well. Generally, educated people at all socio-economic level hold the position of opinion leaders.

The trickle down process is very significant from advertiser's point of view because they should consider that the innovation first took place in elite class and then it trickled down to another class. If trickle is less than desired, the mass media may be used to hasten the adoption process. But under horizontal influence thesis, it has been assumed that opinion leader resides throughout the social structure is a very complicated fact. The notion that opinion leaders are also specialists (rather than generally influential) tends to complicate the matter further.

There are other kinds of flows that are also significant from advertiser's point of view. Some styles, products and customs are introduced into a society by a reverse process. They begin at the bottom or middle and spread to other social classes upward.

The Booster Station Theory or The Two Step Flow Model

The two step flow model developed by Katz Lazarsfeld presents an explanation how mass communication works. The theme of the model is that mass communication information flows from the commercial sponsor (sender) of the message to the ultimate consumer in two steps. First the disseminated information is received by some relatively small proportion of the total potential audience called opinion leaders through the media. These individuals, (influentials or opinion leaders), in the second step then disperse or discriminate the information to others in their primary social group. This second step of communication is an extremely persuasive or influential personage. This can be clarified by means of the following figure.

There may distinct economic advantages in concentrating sales efforts on persons who act as influentials. Thus, influential, if properly persuaded may sell, in turn, what the manufacturer sells them. To be of the greatest value, the message that is transmitted to the prospects through influentials has a greater impact on them because the heart of the two step flow of influence lies in the relatively greater persuasiveness of the influentials. Thus, this theory emphasises that certain individuals, called opinion

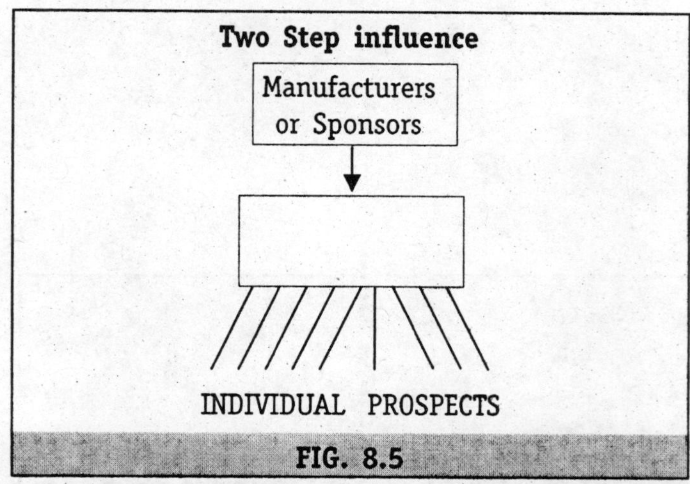

FIG. 8.5

leaders, tend to receive the information first and then they disseminate that in the population by using their influence.

The notion is theoretically interesting because it suggests that certain individuals tend to receive the message before others and serve as an important link between manufacturer and the audiences-by disseminating the information. It is also interesting from marketing point of view that such opinion leaders should be identified in certain market conditions and all advertising efforts should be concentrated around these people alone. It is yet another way to think about market segmentation.

The key idea is that certain individuals tend to receive the mass communication messages before others, decode and interpret them and then pass them along. These individuals—opinion leaders— should under the circumstances be considered the principal target of an advertising campaign because of the important role they play in getting a product or an advertising idea accepted by the market as a whole.

But, in practice, there are certain difficulties— in identifying these opinion leaders in any market situation opinion leadership may be general or specific. A general leader exerts influence across product categories or interest areas. A specific leader is specific to particular product. Which one is to be pursued by the manufacturer? Another issue is whether opinion leaders sense as gatekeepers of information—are they likely to be exposed more often to mass media information? This appears to occur at the time of exposure to relevant media but not to mass media as a whole. The two step flow model is extended by elaborating the other steps involved in it, and the robs of mass communication and personal influence at various stages in the adoption process. In the adoption process, mass communication exerts a stronger influence: during the early stages of the process, and personal influences during the later stages. The marketing mix variables may also effect the adoption rates. Price, distribution, advertising and the product itself all exert some influence.

An advertiser should determine the degree to which personal influence and opinion leadership are important forces insofar as his product is concerned. In some cases, opinion leaders may be singled out and treated as market targets, at which the initial phases of the advertising programme may be directed. Copy tactics may be developed and evaluated to enhance the diffusion and personal influential process.

CHAPTER 9

CONSUMER COMMUNICATIONS

SAVIN ADVERTISING CONNECTS WITH CUSTOMERS

In the late 1970s and early 80s Savin Corp. used a very effective comparative advertising campaign to overtake Xerox and become the top brand of office copiers in America. With the help of small, inexpensive copiers made by Ricoh-Corporation of Japan but sold in the United States under the Savin brand, the company caught Xerox off guard by running advertising comparing its products directly against the market leader. However, a decision to manufacture the copiers in-house at a new factory in Binghamton, New York, caused a severe financial crisis that ultimately led to Savin's filing for bankruptcy protection in 1992. A year after emerging from bankruptcy proceedings in 1994, Savin agreed to be acquired by Ricoh. Since being acquired, Savin is getting back to what it did best: marketing copiers made by Ricoh under its own name primarily through its own network of dealers that sell directly to companies. And creative advertising has been an important part of its strategy for gaining market share by positioning Savin as a feisty and committed company with the best prod-ucts, service, and support, as well as willingness to take on the competition.

Savin's first campaign after being purchased by Ricoh was launched in 1996 and used the tagline "We're going to win you over." The goal of the campaign was to build awareness of and add value to the brand name and to place Savin on the "considered list" of the middle managers who influence or make the copier purchase decisions for their company. A year later, Savin launched the second phase of the campaign, which focused on document management and product line attributes, and the tagline evolved into "We've got what it takes to win you over." The first two phases of the campaign leveraged Savin's renewed focus on people, products, and programs and positioned the company as faster and easier to do business with. However, the market was changing rapidly with the emergence of digital technology that offered improved output quality in black and white and colour as well as network connectivity.

The merging of printing and copying functionality changed the marketing focus, as more companies were offering products with similar benefits to the same customers. However, the target audience within companies was shifting. The traditional copier buyer, such as an office manager, was no longer the only person involved in the purchase decision or was losing power to information technology (IT) departments. Moreover, Savin's competitors such as Xerox, Canon, and Hewlet-Packard were seen as the safe choice, and there was still a need to position the company as a viable player in the digital office equipment market.

In 1998, Savin launched the "Alternative to Xerox" campaign. The comparative ads piggybacked off Xerox's efforts to promote new digital copiers and mocked Xerox for wanting to be the "biggest" document company. Savin's ads positioned the company as the "fastest, most responsive and easy to work with name in the business." Savin's CEO, Jim Ivy, noted: "Going toe to toe with Xerox is part of our history. People remember Savin going after Xerox." And since there was a need to reach both existing copier buyers and new customers in the IT space, Savin felt the ad campaign would ring a bell with them. When the comparative campaign began in mid-1998, Savin had a small 2.9 percent share of the U.S. office-copier market, placing it a lowly eleventh out of 14 brands, while Xerox led the industry with a 16.4 percent market share. However, in 1998 and 1999 Savin's growth in sales outpaced that of all major providers of document output systems, and the company nearly doubled its digital sales.

While Savin's comparative campaign was very successful, by 2000 market conditions had changed, causing the company to reconsider its creative strategy. Negative press reports about financial, sales, and marketing issues at Xerox raised concern about using the company as a reference point in Savin advertising and positioning itself as an alternative to the troubled competitor. Also, with the growth of the Internet, intranets, e-mail, and fax machines, the office environment was changing from a "print and distribute" approach to more of a "distribute and print" process. Thus in 2001, Savin decided to take its advertising in a different direction to position the company as an attractive player in the digital office equipment market with its "Think Inside the Box" campaign.

The objective of the new creative strategy is to convince decision makers that Savin provides both the advanced digital imaging solutions they need and the customer-focused attitude they want to support all of their network printing and copying requirements. A softening of media costs due to the advertising recession opened the opportunity for Savin to use television advertising for the first time in recent years as part of the campaign, and three 15-second spots were created. The shift to TV makes it possible to broaden awareness of Savin, maximize impact, and generate excitement among its dealer partners. However, creativity was important to enable the spots to break through the clutter, which they have done successfully. Savin is enjoying almost double-digit growth in a category that has experienced a 2 percent annual decline in recent years.

Companies have been responding very favourably to Savin's easy-to-do-business-with philosophy and its ability to provide solutions to all of their printing and copying needs. They also have been responding well to Savin's advertising, which has helped build awareness of the company and position it as a major player in the digital office equipment market.

Sources: Personal correspondence with Louise Stix, Manager of Corporate Communications and Creative Services, Savin Corporation; Raju Narisetti, "Savin Hopes Campaign Will Boost Image," The Wall Street Journal, May 19, 1998, p. BlO; "Savin Corp. Having Award-Winning Year," Business Wire, June 8, 1999.

Communication is an important tool through which the marketers persuade consumers to act in a desired way e.g., to vote, to make a purchase, to make a donation, to patronize a retail store. Communication takes many forms. It can be verbal either written or spoken. It can be visual an illustration, a picture, a product demonstration, a frown, or a combination of the two. Communication can also be symbolic represented by a high price, or premium packaging, or a memorable logo and convey special meaning the marketer wishes to impart. Communication can evoke emotions that put consumers in a more receptive frame of mind, and it encourage purchases to solve problems or to avoid negative outcomes. In short, communication is the bridge between marketers and consumers, and between consumers and their socio-cultural environments. While there are many ways to define communication, communication has been defined as the transmission of a message from a sender to a receiver via a medium of some sort. There are many people who believe that the fifth essential component of communication is feedback, which alerts the sender as to whether the intended message was in fact received.

The term communication has been defined in different ways. According to Peter Little, "Communication is the process by which information is transmitted between individuals and/or organisations so that an undertaking response results". W.H. Newman and C.F. Summer Jr., define communication as an exchange of facts, ideas, opinions, or emotions by two or more persons. In short, most writers would argue that communication is the transmission of a message from a sender to a receiver via a medium of some sort.

COMPONENTS OF COMMUNICATION

Marketers need to understand how communication works. Lasswell said that a communication model will answer (1) who (2) says what (3) in what channel (4) to whom (5) with what effect. Over the years, a communication model with nine elements has evolved. Two elements represent the major parties in a communication - sender and receiver. Another two represent the major communication tools - message and media. Next represent major communication functions—encoding, decoding, response, and feedback. The last component represents noise in the system. These components are defined as follows:

The sender, as the initiator of the communication, can be a formal or an informal source. A formal source is likely to represent either for profit (commercial) or a not-for-profit organization, an informal source can be a parent or a friend who gives product information or advice. Consumers often rely on informal communication sources, the sender apparently has nothing to gain from the receiver's subsequent actions. For that reason, informal word of mouth communication tends to be highly persuasive. Research shows that consumers prefer personal information sources when they buy services because they have greater confidence in such sources.

The receiver of formal communications is likely to be a targeted prospect or a customer e.g., a member of the marketer's target audience. There are also many intermediary and even unintended audiences for marketing communications. Examples of intermediary audiences are whole-sellers; distributors, and retailers, who are sent trade advertising designed to persuade them to order and stock merchandize, and relevant professionals such are architects or physicians or surgeons who are sent professional advertising in the hope that they specify or prescribe the marketer's products. Unintended audiences include everyone who is exposed to the message, whether or not they are specifically targeted by the source. The unintended audiences offer include publics that are important to the marketer, such as shareholders, creditors, suppliers, employees, bankers, and the local community, in addition to the general public. It is important to remember that no matter how large the audience, it is composed of individual receivers, each of who interprets the message in his or her own special way.

The medium/or communications channel can be interpersonal — an informal conversation e.g., face-to-face, by telephone, or even by mail, between two friends, or a formal conversation between a salesperson and a customer. The medium can be impersonal — a mass medium such as newspaper or television programme. Mass media are generally classified as print like newspapers, magazines, billboards and broadcast e.g., radio, television, though electronic media are becoming more important daily (e.g., fax, computers). New modes of interactive communication that permit the audiences of mass media to provide direct feedback are beginning to blur the distinction between interpersonal and impersonal communication. For example, in some communities consumers can do their grocery shopping electronically as the TV camera scans the grocery shelves. Home shopping networks are expanding dramatically, as consumers demonstrate their enthusiasm for TV shopping. Direct marketers also called data-base marketers, they seek individual responsibilities from advertisements placed in all the mass media; broadcast, print, electronic, as well as from direct mail.

The term "mass media" has been used to describe impersonal media. However, there is a growing trend toward demassification as publishers shift their focuses from large, general interest audiences to smaller, more specialized audiences. Some media try to create "captive" audiences. For example, one communications company is providing free television equipment and programming to school districts that agree to run their special "school" channel, which includes two minutes of paid commercials during class time.

As already mentioned the message can be verbal or non-verbal, or a combination of the two. A verbal message, whether it is spoken or written, can usually contain more specific product (or service) information than a non-verbal message. Sometimes, a verbal message is combined with an illustration or a demonstration and together they may provide more information to the receiver than either would alone.

Sometimes, non-verbal information takes the form of symbolic communication. The study of semiotics is the study of the meanings implied by sign and symbols. Marketers often try to develop logos or symbols that are associated exclusively with their products. The Coca-Cola Company, for example, has trade marked both the words "Coke" in specific typographic style and the shape of the traditional coke bottle and both are instantly recognizable to consumers as symbols of the company's best-selling soft drink.

Non-verbal communications take place in interpersonal channels as well as in impersonal channel. For example, a good sales person usually is alert to non-verbal feedback provided by consumer prospects. These may take the term of facial expressions, (a smile; a look of total boredom, an expression of disbelief) or bodily movements (finger tapping, head nodding, head shaking). Because senders often can "read" meaning into such bodily reactions, these non-verbal actions sometimes are referred to as "body language".

Feedback is essential component of both interpersonal communications. Prompt feedback permits the sender to reinforce, to change or to modify the message to ensure that it is understood in the intended way. Clearly, it is easier to obtain feedback in interpersonal situations, but it is even more important for sponsors of impersonal communications to obtain feedback as promptly as possible.

Fig. 9.1 presents a more detailed model of the communications process. It notes that the sender selects the message, encodes the message, and selects an appropriate channel through which to send it. The receiver decodes (interprets) the message, and then responds or does not respond depending on the accuracy of interpretation and the passiveness of the message. The receiver's response constitutes feedback to the sender.

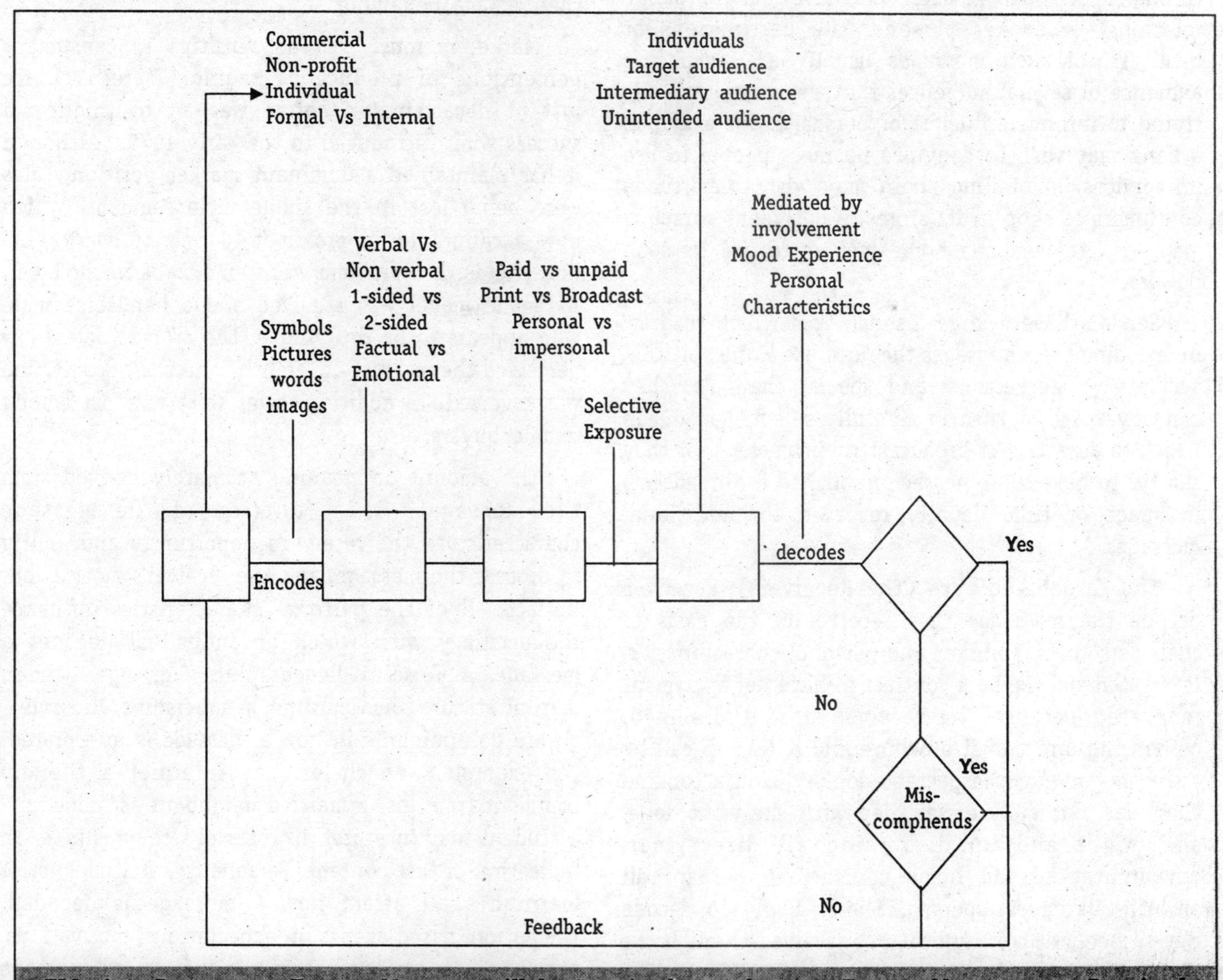

FIG. 9.1. Pretests to Ensure Message will be Received, Postfasts to Ensure Message was Received

Designing Marketing Communications

Company's marketing communications are design to induce, to create a positive attitude toward the product, to give the product, to give the product a symbolic meaning, or to show that it can shine the consumer's problem better than a competitive product (service) can.

The Message Initiator (The Source) : The sponsor, or initiator, of the message first must decide what the message should convey and to whom it should be sent, and then must encode the message in such a way that its meaning is interpreted by the targeted audience in precisely the intended way. The sources of impersonal communications usually are organizations that develop and transmit appropriate messages through special departments (i.e., advertising or public relations) or spokes persons. The destinations or receivers, of such messages usually are a specific audience or several audiences that the organisation is trying to inform, influence or persuade. For example, a bank may wish to convince business people to use its services, a retailing chain may wish to persuade consumers to shop in its stores, a detergent company may wish to persuade home makers to use its soap powder.

Senders have a large arsenal from which to draw in encoding their messages they can use words, picture, symbols, spokespersons, and special channels. They can buy space or time in carefully selected media in which to advertise or broadcast their message, or they can try to have their message published for broadcast) in space or time usually reserved for additional messages.

The Target Audience (The Receivers): Receivers decode the messages they receive on the basis of their personal experience and personal characteristics. If Mrs. Singhal signed a contract to have her apartment renovated because she received a well designed, convincing direct mail brochure and follow up call by a sincere-sounding, respectable-looking contractor, and then was extremely dissatisfied with the work done, she might end up disbursing all direct mail communications, all home contractors, perhaps all smooth-talking salesperson. She is likely to decode any subsequent communications received through the mail with great skepticism. Yet her neighbour Mrs. Verma, ordered some salwar and shirts from the Home Shopping Catalogue and was so pleased with the quality, the service and the fit that she studies all subsequent direct mail catalogues with great care and decides to do all her shopping by direct mail. The level of trust each neighbour displays towards direct mail communications is based on her prior experience.

Comprehension: Comprehension or perception represents one of the important stages of information processing, what is concerned with the interpretation of the stimulus. It is the point where meaning is attached to the stimulus.

Successful marketing is often based on thorough understanding of consumer's perception across a broad range of topics. Consumer's attribute-based perceptions of products and stores are critical determinants of their choice behaviour.

Marketers must also be sensitive to consumer's perceptions of product packaging. Taster's choice instant decaffeinated coffee was an overnight ma success what introduced in the early 1970s. Although it has maintained a dominant market position, sales were being lost in the single male segment, which now accounts for approximately one of every nine households. The problem was found to be in the label. A female model was removed and a handsome male who appears to be drinking in the aroma. Males now perceived the product differently, and the sales decline was reversed. In addition, sales were not lost among female buyers.

The amount of meaning accurately derived from the message - is a function of the message characteristics, the receiver's opportunity and ability to process the message, and the receiver's motivation. In fact, all of the personal characteristics influence the accuracy with which an individual decodes a message. A person's demographics e.g., age, gender, marital status, socio-cultural memberships, lifestyle - all are determinants in how a message is interpreted. For example, a bachelor may interpret a friendly comment from his unmarried neighbour as "come-on" a student may interpret a professor's comments as an indication of test content. Personality, attitudes, prior learning - all affect how a message is decoded. Perception, based as it is on expectations, motivations, and past experience, certainly influences message interpretation.

Further, how much attention is paid to the message depends upon a person involvement. This means that persons having low involvement with sound systems will pay less attention to an ad for specially designed speakers, but may note how compactly, they fit into a living room setting. On the other hand, people who are highly involved in sound reproduction may read every word of a highly technical advertisement describing the new speakers. Thus, a target audience's level of involvement is an important consideration in the design and content of persuasive communications.

In advertising, it is important to examine consumer's perceptions. Recent research, for example, has found that higher degrees of facial prominence produce more favourable perceptions about the person's intelligence; ambition and physical appearance. Consequently, visual ads might employ this principle for enhancing the spokes person's persuasiveness. Furthermore, accurate comprehension of a message, even a relatively simple one, cannot be assumed. However, a substantial number of people show at least some misunderstanding of what they view on TV, whether it is news, a programme, or advertising.

OBJECTS OF COMMUNICATION

A company's marketing communications are designed to induce purchase, to create a positive attitude toward the product, to give the product a symbolic meaning, or to show that it can solve the consumer's problem better than a competitive product or service can.

STEPS IN DEVELOPING EFFECTIVE COMMUNICATION

In the major steps in developing a total communication and promotion program, the marketing communicator must (1) identify the target audience; (2) determine the communication objectives; (3) design the message; (4) select the communication channels; (5) develop the total promotion budget; (6) decide on the promotion mix; (7) measure the promotion's results; and (8) manage and co-ordinate the total marketing communication process.

Communicators have been looking for audience traits that correlate with their degree of perishability. People of high education and or intelligence are thought to be less perusable, but the evidence is inconclusive. Women have been found to be more perusable than men, but men who feel socially inadequate also show this trait. Persons who accept external standards to guide their behaviour and who have a weak self-concept appear to be more perusable. Persons who are low in self-confidence are also thought to be more perusable. However, research by Box and Bauer and later by Bell showed a curvilinear relation between self-confidence and perishability, with those moderate in self-confidence being the most perusable. The communicator should look for audience traits that correlate with perishability and use them to guide message and media development.

Cartwright has outlined what must happen for a message to influence the behaviour of another person.

- The "message" (that is, information, facts, and so on) must reach the sense organs of the persons who are to be influenced.
- Having reached the sense organs, the "message" must be accepted as a part of the person's cognitive structure.
- To induce a given action by mass persuasion, this action must be seen by the person as a path to some goal that he has.
- To induce a given action, an appropriate cognitive and motivational system must gain control of the person's behaviour at a particular point in time.

1. The Message Initiator (The Source) - The sponsor, or initiator, of the message first must decide what the message should convey and to whom it should be sent. Then he must encode the message in such a way that its meaning is interpreted by the targeted audience in precisely the intended way. Usually, the sources of impersonal communications are organizations that develop and transmit appropriate messages through special departments such as advertising or public relations or spokespersons. The destinations or receivers, of such messages usually are a specific audience or server audiences that the organization is trying to inform, influence, or persuade. For example, a bank may wish to convince business people to use its services, a retailing chain may wish to persuade consumers to shop in its stores, a detergent company may wish to persuade homemakers to use its soap powder.

Senders have a large source to draw in encoding their messages" can use words, pictures, symbols, spokespersons and special channels, one can buy space or time in carefully selected media in which to advertise or broadcast their message. They can try to have their message published broadcast in space or time usually reserved for editorial messages. This is the result of public relations or publicity efforts. It tends to be more believable because its commercial organs or intent are not readily apparent.

2. The Target Audience (The Receivers) - On the basis of their personal experience and personal characteristics, receivers decode the message they receive. Suppose Ms. Agrawal signed a contract to have her apartment renovated. She received a well-designed, convincing direct mail brochure and a follow-up call by a sincere-sounding, respectable-looking contractor. But she was extremely dissatisfied with the work done. She ended up distrusting all direct mail communications, all home contractors, all smooth-talking salesmen. Now, she is likely to decode with great skepticism any subsequent communications received through the mail. On the other hand, her neighbour, Mrs. Gupta ordered some slacks and shirts from the Demon catalog. She was so pleased with the quality, the service and the fit that she studies all subsequent direct mail catalogs with great care, and decides to do all her shopping by direct mail. These examples show that the level of trust each neighbour displays towards direct mail communications is based on her prior experience.

IMPORTANT CHARACTERISTICS OF TARGET AUDIENCE

1. Comprehension - It is the amount of meaning accurately derived from the message. It is a function of the message characteristics, the receiver's opportunity and ability to process the message, and the receiver's motivation. The key determinants in how a message is interpreted are the personal characteristics which influence the accuracy with which an individual decodes a message. A person's demographics are such as age, gender, marital status, socio-cultural memberships such as social class, race, religion and lifestyle. A bachelor may interpret a friendly comment from his unmarried neighbour as a "come-on." A student may interpret a professor's comments as an indication of test content. Thus, personality, attitudes, prior learning all affect how a message in decoded. Based on expectations, motivation and past experience, perception certainly influences message interpretation.

2. Level of involvement - A target audience's level of involvement is an important consideration in the design and content of persuasive communications. A person's level of involvements plays a key role in how much attention is paid to the message, and how carefully it is decoded. For example, people who have a low level of involvement with sound systems may not pay much attention to an ad for specially designed speakers. They may note how compactly they fit into a living-room setting. Those who are highly involved in sound reproduction may read every word of a highly technical advertisement describing the new speakers.

3. Mood - Mood, or affect, plays a significant role in how a message is decoded. The term mood describes an individual's subjectively perceived "feeling state." For example, a consumer might be in a cheerful mood or in an unhappy or hostile mood. His mood affects the way in which an advertisement is perceived, recalled, and acted upon.

(i) Positive moods - Consumer's mood states are often influenced by the context in which the advertising message appears such as adjacent TV program or newspaper story and the content of the ad itself, which may affect the consumer's evaluation and recall of the message. Positive feelings are induced by a commercial which shows positive outcomes. It may enhance the likelihood that consumers will buy the advertised product such as a large screen TV.

(ii) Negative moods - On the other hand, depressing commercials may induce negative moods that may be congruent with the marketer's objectives. Consumers may be persuaded that a negative outcome will occur if they don't buy the advertised product such as accident insurance.

(iii) Non-cognitive moods - Besides inducing positive or negative cognitive moods, marketers can also induce no cognitive moods through the use of advertising stimuli such as background music. Telco creates a mood of timeless elegance and tradition in multi-page advertisements that serve to enhance consumer attitudes towards the company's merchandise. Denim Jeans uses the same multi-page advertising technique to induce a mood of total sensuality. The retail store image, the climate, even the weather are other extraneous factors that influence consumer moods and the subsequent decoding of marketing communications.

4. Selective exposure and selective attention - These also influence the reception of marketing communications. Consumers selectively expose themselves to various media. They selectively expose themselves to advertising messages. They exercise their right to ignore print advertisements. They exercise this same right with television commercials with the help of the remote control. TV remote controls offer viewers the ability to "wander" among program offerings with ease. They are used to "zap" commercials by muting the audio or by "channel surfing". These are used for switching channels to check out other program offerings during the commercial break. Some marketers try to overcome the last consumer practice by "road blocking" which means playing the same commercial simultaneously on competing channels.

By enabling viewers to fast-forward, or "zip" through commercials on prerecorded programs or rented videotapes, the VCR created problems for television advertisers. Patricia A. Stout and Benedicta L. Burda have found that the majority of subjects zip indiscriminately to avoid all commercials, while few attempt to evaluate commercials prior to zipping through them. By making the mistake of playing theme music at the beginning and end of a commercial break some marketers signal viewers that they can attend to other needs without missing program content.

Information processing begins when patterns of energy in the form of stimulus inputs react one or more of the five senses. This requires the communicator to select media, either interpersonal or mass, that reacts the individual at the time and place where he or she happens to be. Exposure occurs from physical proximity to a stimulus input such that the individual has direct opportunity for one or more senses to be activated.

This commonsense principle of media selection is more difficult to implement them it might appear, however, because the first step is a precise definition of audience target. It will not do, for example, to say that the target market for Friskie's dry cat food is all families who have a cat as a pet.

Thus, consumers selectively expose themselves to various media. Similarly, they selectively expose themselves to advertising messages.

A psychological constraint on whether or not exposure will take place is known a thresholds, the intensity of stimulus energy required to activate various sensation levels. There are three thresholds for each of the five senses.

(1) Lower or absolute threshold: The minimum amount of stimulus energy or intensity necessary for sensation to occur.

(2) Terminal threshold: The point at which additional increases in stimulus intensity have no effect on sensation.

(3) Difference threshold: The smallest change in stimulus intensity will be noticed by an individual.

(4) Selective attention: An incredible number of stimuli for attention any given moment. Mckeen Chic and Doyle give the following estimates:

(1) Information comes into the central nervous system from over million visual cells alone, (2) 48,000 cells are available for auditory perception (3) the other senses have at least 78,000 receptor cells; and (4) it would take the brain, the size of a cubic light year to process just the information received by the eyes alone. As we know that an individual's processing capacity have distinct limits. Consequently, consumers must be selective in what they attend to. For advertising, this means that an ad must dislodge the consumer's current thoughts so that the message can be processed.

The importance of capturing a person's "full" attention is clearly demonstrated by studies known as shadowing experiments. In a typical experiment, a different message is transmitted though headphones to each ear of the subject. The subject is then asked to "shadow" one of the messages; that is repeat aloud the content. Despite hearing two different simultaneously, subjects can easily shadow one of them. The interesting question, however, is what can be recalled about the message that is not shadowed? Some aspects of this unattended message are absorbed, such as whether it contained human speech versus a non-speech sound and changes in the sex of the speaker.

However, recall of any message content is non-existent. Indeed, even changes from normal speech to a nonsense speech sound (e.g., normal speech played backward) escape detection. Clearly, then a major imperative for marketers is to break through the tremendous clutter in the market place and grab the consumer's undivided attention.

Because consumers are selective in what they attend to, it is important to understand what factors influence attention. Such factors can be grouped major categories: personal or individual determinants and stimulus determinants.

5. Psychological Noise - It is a barrier to message reception like a telephone static, such factors as competing advertising message or distracting thoughts can impair reception of a message faced with the clutter of nine successive commercial messages during a program break a viewer may actually receive and retain almost nothing of what he has seen. Similarly, while driving to work a woman planning a management meeting may be too engrossed in her thoughts to "hear" a radio commercial. Similarly, a student daydreaming about a Saturday night date may simply not "hear" a question directed to him by his professor. He is as much a victim of psychological noise as the student who literally cannot hear a question because of hammering in the next room. To overcome noise, the best way for a sender is simply to repeat the message several times, just as a sailor does when sending an SOS over and over again to make sure it is received. The principal of redundancy is seen in advertising that use both illustrations and copy to emphasize the same points. Repeated exposure to an advertising message helps surmount psychological barriers to message reception and thus facilitates message reception.

SOURCE CREDIBILITY

The credibility of source affects the decoding of the message. The source of the communication — his or her perceived honesty and inactivity has enormous influence on how the communication is accepted by the receiver. If the source is well respected and highly thought by the intended audience, the message from a source considered unreliable or untrustworthy will be reserved with skepticism and may be rejected.

Credibility is built on a number of factors, the most important being the perceived intentions of the source. Receivers ask themselves, "just what does he (or she) stand to gain if I do what is suggested?" If the receiver perceives any type of personal gain for the message sponsor as a result of the proposed action or advice, the message itself becomes suspect. "He wants me to buy that product just to earn a commission".

Credibility of Informal Sources: One of the major reasons that informal sources such as friends, neighbours, and relatives have such a strong influence on a receiver's behaviour is simply that they are perceived as having nothing to gain from a product transaction they recommend.

Interestingly enough, informed communications sources, called opinion leaders, often do profit-psychologically if not tangibly - by providing solicited as well as unsolicited information and advice to friends. This ego gratification may actually improve the quality of the information provided, since the opinion leader will deliberately seek out impartial information in order to enhance his or her position "expert" in a particular product category. The fact that the opinion leader does not receive material gain from the action recommended increases the likelihood that this advice will be seriously considered.

Even with informal sources, however, intentions are not always appear to be. Individuals who experience post purchase dissonance often try to alleviate their uncertainty by convincing others to make a similar purchase. Each time they persuade a friend or an acquaintance to make the same brand selection, they are somewhat reassured that their own product choice was a wise one. The receiver, on the other hand regards product advice from "the person who owns one" as totally objective, since the source is able to speak from actual experience. Thus, the increased credibility accorded the informal source may not really be warranted, despite the aura perceived objectivity.

Credibility of Formal Sources: Such formal sources as neutral rating services or editorial sources have greater credibility than commercial sources because of the likelihood that they are more objective in their product assessment. That is why publicity is so valuable to a manufacturer: citations of a product in an editorial context, rather than in a paid advertisement, give the reader much more confidence in the message.

When he intention of a source are clearly profit making, then reputation expertise, and knowledge become important factors in message credibility. The credibility of commercial messages is often based on the composite evaluations of the sender, the retail outlet that carries the product, the medium that carries the message and the company spokesperson (the actor or sales representative who delivers the message).

Since consumers recognise that the intentions of commerce sources (manufacturers, service companies, commercial institutions, retailers) are clearly to make a profit, they judge commercial source credibility on such factors as past performance, the kind and quality of service they are known to render, the quality and image of other products they manufacture, the type of retail outlets through which they sell, and their position in the community (e.g., evidence of then-commitment to such issues as social responsibility or equal employment).

Firms with well-established reputations generally have an easier time selling their products than the firms with lesser reputations. The ability of quality image to involve credibility is one of the reasons for the growth of family brands. Manufacturers with favourable brand images prefer to give their new products the existing brand name in order to obtain ready acceptance from consumers.

The reputation of the retailer who sells the product has a major influence on message credibility products sold by well-known quality stores seem to carry the added endorsement of the store itself of product carried in a traditional department store usually is perceived as being of better quality than one carried by a mass merchandiser. Therefore, a message concerning the product's attributes is more readily believed. That is why so many national ads carry the line "Sold at better stores everywhere".

The reputation of the medium that carries the advertisement affects the credibility of the message. The image of a prestige magazine adds status on the products advertised therein.

People sometimes regard the spokesperson who gives the product message as the source of the message. In interpersonal communications, a salesperson who engenders confidence, and who gives the impression of honesty and integrity generally is more successful in persuading a prospect than one who does not have these characteristics. A salesperson who looks in the eye "may appear most honest than one who evades direct eye contact. For many products, a sales representative who dresses himself well and drives an expensive late model car may have more credibility" than one without such outward signs of success.

Further, interaction between the spokesperson and the medium affects the overall credibility of the presentation. Thus, in the experiments a "likeable" communicator's message was more persuasive in videotaped and audio taped form, while the "unlikable" communicator was more persuasive in written format.

In impersonal communication, the reputation or expertise of the advertising spokesperson may strongly influence the credibility of the message. This accounts for the popularity and effectiveness of testimonials as a promotional technique. If an audience perceives a message to be incompatible with its source, a high-credibility source will be no more believable than a low credibility source. Marketers who use testimonials must be sure that the specific wording of the endorsement lies within the recognised competence of the spokesperson.

Audience attitudes also affect credibility. The initial opinion that an audience holds prior to receiving the message can affect the persuasiveness of both high and low credibility sources. When the audience is favourable to the message prior to its presentation, moderately credible sources attitude change than highly credible sources. However, what the is opposed to the communicator's position, the high credibility source is likely to be more effective than the less credible source. The consumer's own experience with the product or the retail channel also serves to affirm the credibility of the message. A product or store that lives up to its advertised claim increases the credibility with which future claims are received. Fulfilled product expectations tend to increase the credibility accorded future messages by the same advertiser, whereas unfulfilled product claims or disappointing products tend to reduce the credibility of future messages. The significant increase in mail order sales in the last decade has been attributed to the fact that reputable catalog houses have lived up to their advertised claims of providing full and prompt refunds for merchandise returns.

Many companies sponsor special entertainment and sports events in order to entrance their image and credibility with their target audiences. The nature and quality of these sponsorships constitute a subtle message to the consumer "we are a great (kind, good-natured society-responsible) company; we deserve your business".

The Effects of Time on Source Credibility: The persuasive effects of high credibility source do not endure over time. Though a high-credibility source is initially more influential than a low-credibility source, research suggests that both positive and negative credibility effects tend to disappear after six weeks or so. This phenomenon has been termed the sleeper effect.

Studies attribute the sleeper effect to disassociation (in which the consumer disassociates, the message from the source) overtime, leaving just the message content. The differential decay interpretation of the sleeper effect suggests that memory of a negative cue simply decays faster than the message itself, leaving behind the primary message content. A study that examined the impact of the encoding of product information on consumer attitudes over time found that advertising messages that encouraged consumers to process the information elaborately were more likely to show increased effectiveness over time, despite an initial clue.

IMPACT OF ATTITUDES UPON CREDIBILITY

1. Initial Opinion - Prior to receiving the message the initial opinion that an audience holds can affect the persuasiveness of both high-and low-credibility sources. Moderately credible sources produce more attitude change than highly credible courses, when the audience is favourably disposed to the message prior to its presentation. However, according to Robert R. Harman and Kenneth A. Coney, when the audience is opposed to the communicator's position, the high-credibility source is likely to be more effective than the less credible source.

2. The Consumer's Own Experience with the Product or the Retail Channel - It also serves to affirm or deny the credibility of the message. A product or store that lives up to its advertised claims increase the credibility with which future claims are received. Fulfilled product expectations tend to increase the credibility accorded to future message. Reputable catalogue houses have lived up to their advertised claims of providing full and prompt refunds on all merchandise returns. Therefore, a significant increase in mail–order sales has been noticed in the last decade.

3. Special Events Many companies sponsor special entertainment and sports events in order to enhance their image and credibility with their target audience. The nature and quality of these sponsorships constitute a subtle message to the consumer that "we 're a great (kind, good-natured, socially-responsible) company; we deserve your business." For example, such firms as the Indian Tobacco Company, Sahara India and Amitabh Bachchan Limited (ABCL) have sponsored cricket matches (and now even film personalities like Shahrukh Khan and Priti Zinta) and beauty contests.

Other kinds of corporate sponsored special events include bands, fireworks displays, computerized sky writing, laser shows, and of course athletic events.

THE EFFECTS OF TIME ON SOURCE CREDIBILITY

The persuasive effects of high-credibility sources do not endure over time. Though a high-credibility source is initially more influential than a low credibility source, research suggests that both positive and negative credibility effects tend to dissipate after six weeks or so. Carl I. Hoveland and Arthur A. Lomodaine have called this phenomenon the sleeper effect. Though consumers forget the source of the message faster than they forget the message itself, reintroduction of the message by the sources serves to jog the audience's memory and the original effect remanifests itself. Thus, as Darlane B. Han and Brian Sterntha maintain the high-credibility source remains persuasive than the low-credibility source. Its implication for marketers who use high-credibility spokespersons is that they must rerun the ad or commercial regularly in order to maintain its persuasiveness.

CAUSES OF SLEEPER EFFECT

1. Studies attribute the sleeper effect to

disassociation in which the consumer disassociates the message from the source over time, leaving just the message content.

2. The differential decay interpretation of the sleeper effect suggests that memory of a negative cue such as low-credibility source simply decays faster than the message itself, leaving behind the primary message content.

3. A study that examined the impact of the encoding of product information on consumer attitudes over time found that advertising messages that encouraged consumers to process the information elaboratively or to "internalize" the information were more likely to show increased effectiveness over time, despite an initial negative cue.

FEEDBACK - THE RECEIVER'S RESPONSE

Marketing communications are usually designed to persuade a target audience to act in a desired way i.e., to purchase a product, to vote for a specific candidate, to pay income taxes early. The ultimate test of marketing communications is the receiver's response. Therefore, it is assent sender to obtain feedback as promptly and as accurately as possible. It is through feedback that the sender can determine if and how well the message has been received.

1. Interpersonal Communication - Interpersonal communication has the ability to obtain immediate feedback through verbal as well as non-verbal cue. Experienced communicators are very attentive to feedback. They constant modify their messages based on what they see or hear from the audience. Immediate feedback makes personal selling effective. It enables the salesperson tailor the sales pitch to the expressed needs and observed reactions of each prospect. It also enables a political candidate to selectively stress specific aspects of his or her platform in response to questions posed by prospective voters in face-to-face meetings. In the form of inattention, immediate feedback serves to alert the college professor to the need to awaken the interest of a dozing class. The professor may make a deliberately provocative statement such as "This material will probably appear on your final exam,"

2. Impersonal Communication - Feedback is just also important m impersonal (mass) communications. Due to the large sums of money expended on mass media, many people consider such feedback even more essential than interpersonal feedback. The organization that initiates the communication must develop some method for determining whether its mass communications are, in fact, received by the intended audience, understood in the intended way, and successful in achieving the intended objectives.

CHARACTERISTICS OF MASS COMMUNICATIONS FEEDBACK

1. Inferred - Contrary to interpersonal communication, mass communications feedback is rarely direct. It is usually inferred. Receivers buy or do not buy the advertised product. They renew or do not renew their magazine subscriptions. They vote or do not vote for the political candidate. From the resulting action or inaction of the targeted audience, senders infer how persuasive their messages are.

2. Test of Messages - By conducting audience research, advertisers often try to gauge the effectiveness of their messages. It is to find out which media are read, which television programs are viewed, and which advertisements are remembered by their target audience. If the feedback indicates that the audience does not note or miscomprehends the ad, the sponsor has the opportunity to modify or revise the message so that the intended communication does take place.

3. No Timeliness - Though retailers usually can assess the effectiveness of their newspaper ads by midday on the basis of sales activity for the advertised product, mass communications feedback does not have the timeliness of interpersonal feedback. Other commercial sources such as manufacturers are constantly seeking innovative methods to find out how effective is their consumer advertising. For example, an important feedback mechanism of food and other packaged goods is based on the Universal Product Code (UPSC) and tied to computerized cash registers. Supermarket scanner data can be combined with data from other sources such as media and promotion information to measure the correlation between advertisements, special promotions, and sales.

4. Degree of Consumer Satisfaction Dissatisfaction - Companies seek from mass audiences the degree of customer satisfaction or dissatisfaction with a product purchase. In order to retain the brand's image of reliability they try to discover and correct any problems that occur. Many companies have established 24-hour hotlines to encourage comments and questions from their consumers. By telephoning 2,100 customers chosen at random, Federal Express, U.S.A. conducts a quarterly customer satisfaction survey. MBNA America, a Delaware-based bank, used a Customer-First Index based on customer perspectives as a measure of its service quality.

5. Copy Testing - Advertising effectiveness research is called copy testing. It is done before the advertising, it is actually run in media (pretest sting) or after it appears (post testing):

(i) Pretests - These are used to determine which, if any, elements of advertising message should be revised before major media expenses incurred.

(ii) Posttests - There are used to evaluate the effectiveness of an ad: has already run, and to see which elements, if any, should be changed to improve the impact of future ads.

In U.S.A. a popular method for evaluating the effectiveness of magazine advertisements is through a syndicated service called the Starch React Service. Readers are given an issue of a magazine and are asked to point out which ads they noted, which they associated with the sponsor and which they read most. When compared to similar-sized ads, the resulting readership score is meaningful to competitive ads, and to the marketer's own prior ads. High noted Starch scores are correlated with a favourable attitude toward the advertised brand and a positive brand purchase intention. Thus, Starch scores may have validity bound immediate processing of the ad. They may indicate more lasting communication effects for the brand.

In U.S.A. syndicated services such as the A. C. Nielsen Company collect data on the size and characteristics of television audiences through electronic means, supplemented by diaries kept by a national sample of viewers. Recall and recognition post-tests are conducted to determine whether consumers remember seeing a commercial, whether they can recall its content, and to assess the commercial's influence on consumer attitudes toward the product and their buying intentions.

Communications Strategy: To develop its communication strategy the sponsor must establish the primary communications objectives these might consist of creating awareness of a service, promoting sales encouraging or discouraging certain practices, attracting retail patronage, reducing post-purchase dissonance creating goodwill, a favourable image, or any combination of these and other communications objectives.

Selecting the appropriate audience is an essential element of a communications strategy. Since individual has his own traits, characteristics, interests, needs, experience, and knowledge, it is essential that the sponsor segment the audience into groups that are homogeneous in terms of some relevant characteristics. This enables the marketer to create specific messages for each target group, and run them in specific media that are seen or heard by each target group. It is unlikely that a marketer could develop a single message that would appeal simultaneously to total audience. Efforts to use "universal" appeals phrased in simple language that all can understand invariably in unsuccessful advertisements to which few people relate. Since it enables the marketers to tailor marketing communications to the specific needs of like groups of people, market segmentation overcomes some of the problems inherent in trying to communicate with mass audiences. Let us take for example the problem of hostile audience. Even though people tend to avoid viewpoints opposite to their own, there are times when it makes sense to advertise to hostile audiences. Though it may not change the beliefs of those fully persuaded, an ad can prevent others from being infected with some degree of hostility. A study of a 1986 Chenon campaign directed to hostile audiences indicated that the company's promotional efforts resulted more positive attitudes as well as increased sales of the firm's gasoline campaign's greater impact in terms of attitude change and increased purchase behaviour was observed among a market segment described as inner directed to those consumers who "think for themselves".

Companies that have many adverse audiences sometimes find it useful to develop a communications strategy that consists of an overall communications message to all their audiences, from which they spin off a series of related messages targeted directly at the specific interests of each individual segment.

To maintain private communications with all their publics, organizations employ public relations counselors, or establish their own public relations departments, to provide favourable information about the company and to suppress unfavourable information. A good public relations person will develop close working relationship with editors and programme directors of all the relevant media in order to facilitate editorial placement of desired publicity campaign designed to promote the image of the company are becoming increasingly popular, and marketers have developed methods to monitor and increase their effectiveness.

Media Strategy: Media strategy is an essential communications plan. It calls for the placement of ads in specific media read, viewed, or heard by selected target markets. To accomplish this advertisers develop through research, a consumer profile.

Further, before selecting specific media vehicles. advertisers must select a general media category that will enhance the message they wish to convey, which category the marketers selects depends on the product or service to be advertised. the market segments to be reached, and the advertising objectives. Rather than select one media category to the exclusion of others, many advertisers use multimedia campaign strategy, with one primary category earning the major burden of the campaign, and other categories providing supplemental support.

Many research studies have pointed out the comparative effectiveness of one medium over others for various products, audiences, and objectives. In general, the findings have been inconclusive. Each media category has certain advantages and disadvantages that the marketer must consider in developing a media strategy for a specific campaign. Some media categories are more appropriate vehicles for certain products or messages than others, example, a retailer who wants to advertise a clearance sale should advertise in local newspapers, since that is where consumers are accustomed to looking sales announcements.

Once marketers have identified the appropriate media category, they can then choose the specific medium in that category that reaches their intended audiences. The major issues marketers must consider when selecting specific media are overlapping audiences, the characteristics of the audiences and the effectiveness of their advertisements.

Since many media especially those with similar editorial features and formats have overlapping audiences, advertisers usually place their advert messages simultaneously or sequentially in a number of media with similar audience profits. This enables them to achieve both reach and frequency. The term reach refers to the number of different people or households that are exposed to the advertisement, frequency refers to how often they are exposed to an individual number of a target group over an agreed upon time period. The effective reach thresholds suggests that 45% of the target group should be reached over the agreed upon time period. Figure given below illustrates how an ad in two similar media vehicles is likely to reach a unique audience in each medium, as well as an overlapping segment which reads both magazines, and thus receives two exposures.

Marketers use various syndicated marketing research services to obtain data on media audiences - their demographics, product purchases, brand preferences etc. Many marketers have adopted a media strategy called precision targeting. This strategy has been facilitated by media that seek a specific niche for themselves in the marketplace by catering to the needs and interests of a highly specific target segment.

Direct mail and direct marketing are excellent examples of precision targeting. Direct mail is advertising that is sent directly to the mailing address of a target customer. Direct marketing is not a medium, but a marketing technique that uses various media

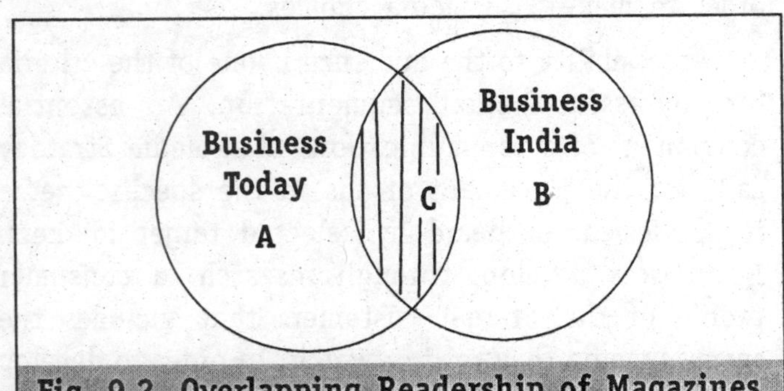

Fig. 9.2. Overlapping Readership of Magazines with similar Audience Profiles

for the purpose of soliciting a direct response from the consumer. A major advantage of direct marketing is measurable responses. This capacity enables direct marketers to profitability of their efforts directly through such variables as cost per inquiry, cost-per-sale, and income per advertisement, and to evaluate the frequency of campaigns.

A prime objective in direct marketing is to build and constantly refine electronic database of qualified buyers. This is done by soliciting both inquiries and direct others.

Many people are concerned that the direct marketing practice and building the shopping histories of customers in their database in an invasion of privacy. Mail-order catalogues are a prime example of direct marketing sent through the mails to carefully-homed databases. Given the huge competition in the field, some category retailers are trying to relationship marketing by including in their catalogues editorial content they think will make them more 'human" to their customers.

Electronic shopping is also considered direct marketing because it generates an electronic database of buyers. The popularity of electronic shopping stems from a shortage of free time among working women and the dislike of crowded shopping malls. In some cases, consumers simply find home shopping an entertaining way, while to relax in the comfort of their homes.

Some advertisers using fax machines to reach an upscale, educated market through numbers listed in fax phone books.

Clearly, marketers must be familiar with the characteristics of their audiences, the characteristics of their products, and the characteristics of media in order to make wise media choices.

Accessibility to the audience is one of the criteria for successful market segmentation. An essential component of a communications plan Media Strategy calls for the placement of ads in the specific media read, viewed, or heard by selected target markets. Advertisers develop, through research, a consumer profile of their target customers that includes the specific media they read or watch. In order to develop descriptive audience profiles. media also research their own audiences. A cost-effective media choice closely matches the advertiser's consumers profile to a medium's audience profile.

STEPS IN MEDIA STRATEGY

(i) Selection of a General Media - Before selecting specific media vehicles, advertisers must select a general media category that will enhance the message they wish to convey. This selection depends on the product or service to be advertised, the market segments too depends on the product or service to be advertised, the market segments to be reached, and the advertising objectives. Instead of selecting one media category to the exclusion of others, many advertisers use a multimedia campaign strategy. In it one primary category carries the major burden of the campaign, and other categories provide supplemental support.

(ii) Comparison - Numerous research studies have compared the effectiveness of one medium over others for various products, audiences and advertising objectives. Each media category has several advantages and disadvantages. The marketer must consider it in developing a media strategy for a specific campaign. Some media categories are more appropriate vehicles than others for certain products or messages. For example, a retailer who wants to advertise a clearance sale should advertise in local newspapers where consumers are accustomed to looking for sales announcements. A manufacturer who seeks to present a detailed argument in favour of its sewing machines should advertise in household magazines, where readers are accustomed to reading detailed articles and stories. A marketer who seeks to promote a power mower with unique cutting features should use a medium like television, on which the mower can be demonstrated in action.

(iii) Chance of Specific Media - After marketers have identified the appropriate media category, they should choose the specific medium in that category that reaches their intended audiences. The major issues that they must consider while selecting specific media are overlapping audiences, the characteristics of the audience, and the effectiveness of their advertisements or commercials.

(iv) Effective Reach - As many media especially those with similar editorial features and formats have overlapping audiences; advertisers usually place their advertising messages simultaneously or sequentially in a number of media with similar audience profiles. This enables them to achieve both reach and frequency. The term reach refers to the number of different people or households that are exposed to the advertisement either because they hear or watch the program or read the newspaper or magazine. Frequency refers to how often they are exposed to it during a specified period of time "term effective reach combines both reach and frequency. George B. Murry and John R. G. Jenkins define it as a minimum of three confirmed vehicle exposures to an individual member of a target group over an agreed upon time period. The effective reach threshold suggests that 45% of the target group should be reached over the agreed upon time period. An ad in two similar media vehicles is likely to reach a unique audience in each medium, as well as an overlapping segment which reads both magazines. It thus receives two exposures.

(v) Precision Targeting - To obtain data on media audiences-their demographics, product purchases, brand preferences marketers use various syndicated marketing research services. Many marketers have adopted a media strategy called precision targeting. It has been facilitated by media that seek a specific niche for themselves in the marketplace by catering to the needs and interests of a highly specific target segment.

(vi) Selective Binding - Magazine publishers are constantly locking for ways to refine their audiences. Selective binding is a new technique that enables publishers to narrowly segment their subscription bases. When readers subscribe, they are asked to provide demographic information which the publisher enters into a database. Through a sophisticated computerised system, the publisher selects specific subscribers to receive specific sections that are bound into a limited number of magazines. This is based on reader demographic policies. Selective binding enables magazines to target subscriber more precisely. It also enables them to offer advertisers a more specialized audience. American Baby magazine sends its parental edition to subscribers who have indicated pregnancy on their subscription applications, and substitutes its postnatal edition after the subscriber's expected due date. Gerber Products inserts coupons; into editions mailed to mothers with babies three months old.

ONE SIDED VERSUS TWO SIDED

The message is the thought, idea, attitude, image or other information that the sender wishes to convey to the intended audience. In trying to encode the message in a form that will enable the audience meaning, the sender must recognise exactly what he or she is trying to say and why. Senders must also know their audiences' characteristics in terms of education, interests, needs, and realms of experience. They must also try to phrase or encode their messages in ways that fall within then of understanding and familiarity.

Persuasive messages should begin with an appeal to the needs and interests of the audience, and end with an appeal relevant to the marketer's own needs. Marketer's have formed that the most effective ads conclude by telling the audience exactly what it is they want them to do. Advertisements that do not conclude with an action closing, tend to provoke much less response from those that do.

Nonverbal stimuli such as photographs or illustrations are commonly used in advertising to add meaning or to reinforce message arguments, showed that when verbal information was low in imagery, the inclusion of the pictures that provided examples increased recall of the verbal information immediate post test and a delayed post test.

A number of studies have tried to manipulate the proportions of and body copy used in print ads to determine the impact on recall and persuasion, but the findings have been fragmented and inconclusive. For example, one study showed that in some instances, body copy alone induced more favourable consumer evaluation than body copy used in conjunction with a picture; in other instances, the reverse was true. Other researchers found that the attractiveness of the picture in the print and influenced brand attitudes.

Should marketers tell that only the good points about their products, or should they also tell then Should they pretend that their product is the only one of its kind, or acknowledge competing products? There are vital strategy questions that face everyday, and the answers depend on the nature of the audience nature of the competition.

If the audience is friendly, e.g., if it uses the advertiser's prod initially favours the communicators position, or if it is not likely opposing argument, then one sided communication that stresses only if information is most effective. However, if the audience is critical or unfriendly (e.g., if it uses competitors products), if it is well-educated, or if it is likely to hear opposing claims, then a two sided message is likely to be more effective.

Two sided advertising messages are more credible then one sided advertising messages because they acknowledge that the advertised brand has short comings. A study that examined one sided and two sided celebrity endorsements found that two-sided endorsements were more credible, received higher effectiveness ratings, higher evaluation of the sponsor in terms of perceived overall quality of service, and provoked a significantly greater intention to use the advertised service.

Some marketers stress only positive factors about their products, and pretend that competition does not exist. Communication researchers have investigated ways to insulate existing customers from outside persuasion. Their findings suggest that two-sided messages containing both positive and negative arguments about the brand serve to insulate consumers against arguments that may be raised by competitors.

A comparative analysis of one sided and two sided messages for two totally dissimilar products found that two-sided messages produced higher evaluations and purchase intentions for deodorants.

Method of Presentation: The manner in which a message is presented strongly influences its persuasiveness. For example, people are much more influenced by word of mouth communications that they are by a printed format. However, research indicates that this effect is reduced or eliminated when a prior impression of the target brand is available from memory.

Researchers study not only the semantics of ad messages i.e., the meanings of the words used and resulting inferences but also the syntax (the sentence structure). One study found that ads using simple syntax produced greater levels of recall, regardless of the strength of the argument, than ads of greater complexity. A study designed to explore the differences between persuasive and non-persuasive TV commercials found that highly persuasive commercials tended to have stronger linkages between the visuals in the advertising. The findings concluded that this "wholeness" provided a mere complete or unified experience for the consumer.

Involvement Theory and Message Presentation: The central and peripheral routes-to-persuasion theory suggests that individuals are more likely to devote active cognitive effort to evaluating the pros and cons of a product in a high involvement purchase situation, and more likely to focus on peripheral message cue in a low involvement situation. Thus, for high involvement marketers should follow the central route to persuasion: that is. they should present advertisements with strong, well documented, issue relevant arguments that encourage cognitive processing. When involvement is low, marketers should follow the peripheral route to persuasion by emphasizing such non-content message elements as background scenery, music, or celebrity spokesperson. Such highly visual or symbolic cues provide the consumer with pleasant, indirect associations with the product, and provoke favourable inferences about its merits.

Despite the fact that many marketers have found that action closings tend to be more effective in encouraging consumer response, researchers have also found that, for high-involvement audiences, open-ended advertisements i.e., ads that do not draw explicit conclusions are more effective in terms of creating positive brand attitudes and purchase intentions.

Studies which examined message framing effects on persuasion have had mixed results. Researchers also have found that the presentation are consistent with consumer's self image triggers the cognitive processing information.

Some researchers tend to over simplify the two-route recommending the exclusive use of either emotional (i.e., right brain peripheral route) or rational (left brain, control route) message appeals. The destination between these two approaches is readily seen in advertisements that make heavy use of emotional, symbolic cues in their formats, as opposed to straight forward factual presentations.

Comparating Advertising: Comparative advertising has been used as marketing strategy by increasing numbers of marketers. It can be defined as advertising that claims product superiority only one or more explicitly named or implicitly identified competitors, either on an overall basis or on selected product attributes.

Comparative advertising is useful for product positioning, for target market selection and for brand positioning strategies that stress the differential advantage of the "underdog' product over leading brands. So reinforce credibility, some marketers cite an independent research organization as the supplier of data used for the comparison.

Although comparative advertising is used widely, some critics maintain that comparative ads may assist recall of the competitors brand at the expense of the advertised brand.

A study of comparative advertising using an information-processing perspective found that comparative ads elicited higher levels of processing activity, had better recall than non-comparative ads, and were perceived as more relevant.

Order Effects: Communication researchers have found that the order in which a message is presented affects audience receptivity. On TV. the position of a commercial in a commercial pod can be critical. The commercial shown: are recalled best, those in the middle the least, and the ones at the end slightly better than those in the middle.

When just two competing messages are presented one after the other evidences as to which position is more effective is somewhat conflicting. Researchers have found that the material presented first produces a greater effect while others have found that the material presented last is more effective.

Magazine publishers recognize the impact of order effects by as "preferred position" placement to front back, and inside covers of magazine which means they charge more for these position than for inside magazine because of their greater visibility and recall.

Order is also important in listing product benefits within an ad. If interest is low, the most important point should be made first to attract. However, if interest is high, it is not necessary to figure curiosity, and benefits can be arranged in a ascending order, with the most important point mentioned last.

DIRECT MARKETING

Direct mail and direct marketing are excellent examples of precise targeting. Direct mail is advertising that is sent directly to the mailing address of a target customer. Direct marketing is not a medium It is a marketing technique that uses various media such as mail, print, broadcast, telephone for the purpose of soliciting a direct response from a consumer. A major advantage of direct marketing is its ability to generate measurable responses. This capability enables direct marketers to measure the profitability of their effort, directly through such variables as cost-per-inquiry. cost-per-sale and income-per-advertisement and to evaluate the timing and frequency of campaigns.

OBJECTIVE OF DIRECT MARKETING

A prime objective in direct marketing is to build and constantly refine an electronic database of qualified buyers by soliciting both inquiries and direct orders. Computer analysis of the database can yield highly selective customer segments. For example, through an analysis of charge slips, American Express can target all cardholders who made purchases from golf shops, or who charged symphony subscriptions, or who travelled abroad more than once during the past year.

(i) Shop Histories - Many people are concerned that the direct marketing practice of preserving and building the shopping histories of customers in their databases is an invasion of privacy. In an effort to counter this concern, Equifax, one of the largest credit but bureaus of U.S.A. has set up a consensual database which contains the names of people who agree to be listed and who specify the types of information they would like to receive by mail. In order to induce participation, consumers are given up to $250 a year in discounts on products they want.

(ii) Mail-order Catalogs - There are prime examples of direct marketing sent through the mails to carefully-honed databases. Many companies in U.S.A. have experienced dramatic success in catalog selling, including L.L. Bean. The Sharper Image, and Lands' End. Given the huge amount of competition in the field, some catalogue retailers are trying to engage in relationship marketing by including in their catalogue editorial content that they think will make them more "human" to their customers. For example, Hawkins and Prestige cookware catalogs in India include recipes and menus. Some clothing catalogs include information about how silk fabric is produced. Woollen's catalogs tell how Cashmere sweaters are made.

(iii) Electronic Shopping - It is done through home-shopping TV channels, interactive cables, home computers, and stand-alone shopping kiosks. It is considered direct marketing because it generates an electronic database of buyers. Its popularity stems from a shortage of free time among working women and the dislike of crowded shopping malls. Sometimes, consumers simply find home shopping as an entertaining way to relax in the comfort of their homes.

(iv) Use of Fax - Some advertisers are using fax machines to reach an upscale, educated market segment through numbers listed in fax phone books.

To sum up, the marketers must be familiar with the characteristics of their audiences, the characteristics of their products, and the characteristics of media in order to make wise media choices.

[Donald R. Self, Jerry J. Ingram, Robin S. McChullin, and Roger Mckinney, have given the following comparable data in their article "Direct Response Advertising as an Element in the Promotional Mix." Published in Journal of Direct Marketing I (Winter 1987) :]

COMPARATIVE ANALYSIS OF DIRECT MARKETING MEDIA

1. Telephone - (i) Personal but not face-to-face; (ii) Relatively flexible; (iii) Individual approach; (iv) Slow market penetration; (v) Relatively costly presentation, usually to target customers; (vi) Two-way communication; (vii) Possibility, though more difficult of rebuilding interest; (viii) Ideas tailored to customer; (ix) Customer led through reasoning process; (x) Limited to audio stimuli; (xi) More control over purchasing decision; (xii) Direct, immediate feedback.

2. Interactive TV - (i) Less personal, may be face-to-face; (ii) Somewhat flexible; (iii) Selective approach; (iv) Relatively quick market penetrations; (v) Relatively costly presentation, not necessarily to target market; (vi) May be one or two-way communication; (vii) One shot at developing interest; (viii)Limited number of general ideas: (ix) Customer may or may not be led through reasoning process; (x) Visual and audio stimuli; (xi) May or may not have control over purchasing decision; (xii) May or may not be direct immediate feedback;

3. Broadcast - (i) Impersonal; (ii) Somewhat inflexible: (iii) General approach; (iv) Quick market penetrations; (v) Relatively costly presentation, not necessarily to target customers; (vi) One-way communication; (vii) One shot at developing interest; (viii) Limited number of general ideas; (ix) Suggestions offered; (x) Visual and audio stimuli; (xi) Little control over purchasing decision; (xii) Indirect, delayed feedback.

4. Direct Mail - (i) Somewhat impersonal; (ii) Relatively inflexible; (iii) Selective approach; (iv) Somewhat slow penetration; (v) Relatively economical presentation, usually to target customers; (vi) One-way communication; (vii) One shot at building interest; (viii) Ideas tailored to market segments; (ix) Customer may or may not be led through reasoning process; (x) Somewhat limited number of stimuli; (xi) Little control over purchasing decision; (xii) Indirect, delayed feedback.

5. Print - (i) Impersonal; (ii) Inflexible; (iii) General approach; (iv) Relatively quick market penetrations; (v) Economical presentation, can be geared to target market; (vi) One-way communication; (vii) One shot at developing ideas; (viii) Limited number of general ideas; (ix) Suggestions offered; (x) Limited number of stimuli; (xi) Little control over purchasing decision; (xii) Indirect, delayed feedback.

CRISIS CONSUMER COMMUNICATIONS

In June 1993, several incidents in which syringes were purportedly found in Pepsi cans around the country were widely reported. Although it was found that most of these incidents were hoaxes, the Pepsi company had to deal with the highly extensive media coverage that resulted.

In the past few years, many major companies have discovered unexpectedly that disasters like fires, deaths, oil spills, poisonings occur and if not handled properly these can have catastrophic effects on the company's business. To emerge unscathed from such disasters, companies had a crisis communications plan in place. They decided to meet with the press, had press releases ready to go, provided outlines for the public, gave the press telephone access and camera opportunities, provided constant updates on the situation and in general reassured the public and eliminated antagonism from the press. Some companies do not have a crisis communications plan ready to go in times of disaster. They are totally unprepared for the press and the public. These companies generally lose public confidence and a great deal of business. In U.S.A., in 1982, when seven people died in Chicago after ingesting cyanide-laced Tylenol capsules, Johnson & Johnson spent $ 100 Million on an immediate recall of their best-selling product. They spent another $ 30 million in replacing the product in tamper-resistant packaging and promoting the "new" Tylenol. As soon as the disaster occurred, the company chairman went on television to answer all questions and to alleviate consumer concern. While most marketing professionals thought the company would have to drop the Tylenol brand, even though the cause was traced to limited product tampering, but the product achieved even greater sales volume when it returned to the shelves due to the openness and frankness and rapidity of the company response.

On the other hand, there are companies with no crisis plans. In 1989, in U.S.A. when Exxon suffered a disastrous tanker accident that fouled the waters of Prince William Sound, Alaska, the company sent a mid-level manager to Alaska and the chairman of the company did not make a public response until weeks later. Therefore, the company's image had taken a severe beating that took years to overcome.

Today, sophisticated companies particularly MNC'S identify every possible kind of disaster that could befall their company. As Joseph Wisenbelt (1989) points out these companies develop detailed communications plans for each type of crisis so that, should disaster occur, they know exactly who should do what, who should speak to the press and what to say to calm public fears and to retain public confidence.

CHAPTER

10 COMMUNICATION MIX

SUBLIMINAL RATS OR PURELY COINCIDENCE?

One of the most controversial topics in all of advertising is subliminal advertising. Rooted in psychoanalytic theory, subliminal advertising supposedly influences consumer behaviours by subconsciously altering perceptions or attitudes toward products without the knowledge-or consent-of the consumer. Marketers have promoted subliminal self-help audiotapes, weight-loss videos, and golf game improvement tapes. Studies have shown that the majority of American consumers believe that advertisers sometimes use subliminal advertising and that it works.

The controversy hit national proportions in the last presidential election. In the Bush-Gore campaign, Democratic officials and some advertising experts accused the Republican National Committee of running a subliminal advertisement on television by having the phrase "bureaucrats decide" flashing around the screen and then, in larger print, flashing the word "rats" for a fraction of a second while an announcer criticized candidate Gore's Medicare plan. Republicans argued that the word appeared for one-thirtieth of a second on only one frame out of 900 and was purely an accident. Advertising analysts, including two experts on political advertising, disagreed, contending that there is no way such a thing could happen by accident. At least one noted that the word was "carefully superimposed." A Federal Communications Commission (FCC) investigation concluded that no further action would be taken.

The concept of subliminal advertising was introduced in 1957 when James Vicary, a motivational researcher, reported that he increased the sales of popcorn and Coke by subliminally flashing "Eat pop-corn" and "Drink Coca-Cola" across the screen during a movie in New Jersey. Since then, numerous books and research studies have been published regarding the effectiveness of this advertising form. Some of these have reported on the use of this technique by advertisers to manipulate consumers.

Numerous articles have reviewed the research in this area. Timothy Moore, after reviewing the literature three times (1982,1988,1992), has concluded that there is no evidence to support the fact that sublimi-nal messages can affect consumers' motivations, perceptions, or attitudes. Joel Saegart and Jack Haberstroh have supported Moore's conclusions in their studies. On the other hand, in 1994 Kathryn Theus concluded after an extensive review of the literature that "certain themes might be effectively applied by advertising or marketing specialists."

In more recent writings, opposite positions are again taken. In a study conducted in Australia by an ad agency and Mindtec (a consulting firm), 12 groups of television viewers were hypnotized and asked questions about specific commercials and programs. According to the study, 75 percent of the hypnotized subjects stated that sexy images were the main attraction for viewing, as opposed to only 22 percent of the non-hypnotised subjects. The researchers were surprised by the subliminal details that hypnotised participants were able to recall. In the ads, names and slogans that were visible only when the commercial was paused had high levels of recall, even when the brands recalled were not those being advertised. On the other hand, in his book, Ice Cube Sex: The Truth about Subliminal Advertising, Haberstroh reviews research and discussions with practitioners and concludes that subliminal advertising does not influence consumer behaviours, advertising recall, attitudes, or any other marketplace behaviour.

When Haberstroh asked ad agency executives if they had ever deliberately used subliminal advertising, 96 percent said no, 94 percent said they had never supervised the use of implants, and 91 percent denied knowing anyone who had ever used this technique. A study by Rogers and Seiler supported these results, with over 90 percent denying any use of subliminal implants.

Going even further, Haberstroh contends that subliminal advertising does not even exist except for a few pranksters playing around with artwork for fun. But not so fast! Fashion retailer French Connection is not only employing subliminal advertising but incorporating it into a tagline. Using print and posters, the tagline "subliminal advertising experiment" is arranged in such a way as to spell out the word sex if one reads vertically. Likewise, Master Lock has become the first company to run a one-second national print commercial. The goal of the ad is to reinforce the brand name. And, in upstate New York, a personal injury lawyer paid $35 each for one-second spots in an attempt to gain new clients. At this time, no one knows if any of these efforts have been successful.

Thus, while most consumers believe subliminal techniques are used and are effective, researchers are divided as to their effects. It seems few people in the advertising world think subliminal advertising works and even fewer claim to use it, but there are still those who feel they are wrong. Will there ever be an end to this controversy?

Sources: "Hypnosis Reveals Ad Effects" Adweek Asia, Jan.29,1999, p. 4; "Breaking French Connection," Ad Age, Mar. 22,1999, p. 52; "Blink of an Ad," Time, Aug. 3,1998, p.51; Jack Haberstroh, Ice Cube Sex: The Truth about Subliminal Advertising, New York Times Publishing, 1996; Kathryn Theus, "Subliminal Advertising and the Psychology of Processing Unconscious Stimuli: A Review of Research," Psychology & Marketing 11, no. 3,1994, pp. 271-90; Timothy Moore, "Subliminal Advertising: What You See Is What You Get" Journal of Marketing 46, no. 2 (Spring 1982), pp. 38-47; Timothy Moore, "The Case against Subliminal Manipulation," Psychology and Marketing 5, no. 4 (Winter 1988), pp. 297-316; Kalpana Srinivasan, "FCC Ends Probe on Republican Ad," www.individual.com, Mar. 12, 2001,pp. 1-2; George E. Condon Jr. and Toby Eckert, Flap over 'RATS' Latest to Plague Bush's Drive" San Diego Tribune, Sept. 13,2000,p. Ai; Bob Garfield," Subliminable Seduction and Other Urban Myths," Advertising Age, Sept. 18, 2000, p. 4.

"Communication" is defined as the sharing of an orientation toward a set of information signs. It is a process which requires the same perspectives of the sender and the receiver. It is a two-way channel which must have the same objective. It is a social process. It varies as society changes. The process, the message, the objectives, etc., change as the social values change. Culture tradition, social institutions etc., have a wide impact on the communication process.

The word "communication" is derived from the Latin communist, meaning common. The basic ingredient in communication is commonness. If the message is common or single for the sender and receiver, it will be communication. It means the same thing to the sender and the receiver. The audience must understand what the sender wants to communicate. The message of communication may be in a silent or subtle language or verbal language; it may be a written or pictured presentation. Thus, the word, the picture, the silence and the indication may be termed communication if the sender and the receiver perceive the same meaning of these messages.

INDIVIDUAL AND MASS COMMUNICATION

Communication is the social process by which two or more persons exchange views. The communication between two persons, i.e., the sender and the receiver, will be termed individual communication and where there are more than two persons, i.e., more than one sender or more than one receiver are involved, it is known as mass communication. Communication can be psychological and political, besides being social. The encoding; i.e., sending the message, and decoding, i.e., receiving the message, should be done in accordance with the objectives of communication. The objectives of communication may be social, economic, political or psychological. The receiver should accept or decode the communication in the form in which it has been sent.

In September of 1996, Sony Australia launched two television commercials as the first stage In a three-year campaign to help change Sony's image. Although the ads showed Sony's products, they did not mention features or benefits of the products, and had weird plot lines and strange images.

In the eyes of young Australians, Sony was no longer regarded as an innovative company, and arch-rival Panasonic was increasing its lead in the Australian consumer electronics market Sony's ad agency had been running product-specific commercial which did not integrate the company's image into a clear message about the brand. Mike Beckerleg, Sony Australia's advertising and promotions manager, said, 'When I joined in 1995, it looked as if we had seven different companies. All the product groups were running their own ad campaigns'.

According to Beckerieg, having a good-quality, technologically-advanced product is the point of entry to the market Sony had to come up with something more than that, if it was to increase market share beyond the 20 per cent barrier. For years Sony had relied on its technological lead, but with rivals cloning the products almost as soon as they hit the shops, the lead had been eroded to the point where the 16-24 age group (who represent 30 per cent of the population of Australia) saw the brand as irrelevant and old-fashioned. At the same time, the consumer electronics market has been hit by declining brand loyalty. Sony's premium price position, sustained by technical superiority, was now proving to be a positive disadvantage.

Sony Australia's new ad agency, Foster Nunn Loveder, decided that the company would need some innovative advertising to rebuild their image. One ad shows an angler catching fish by playing a videotape of a trout fly on a TV set in his boat; another ad shows giant tomatoes wired up to Sony headphones.

The campaign proved hugely successful: despite the total cost of $4.6 million; the results have been well worthwhile. Sony's market share jumped from 173% in October 1995 to 21.2% in October 1996, and to a remarkable 24.4% in December 1996.

Australia has now overtaken Panasonic as the country's number one consumer electronics supplier. Unaided consumer recall of Sony's ads had claimed to 56% from only 35%in 1995 (Panasonic's was only 32% in December 1996). At the same time, the company had made significant improvements in terms of unaided brand recall, with the crucial 16-24 age group, increasingly referring to Sony as innovative, reliable and technically superior.

In this case the company's innovative advertising had given the consumers an overall perception of the company as being innovative in its product design consumer responses to the company's campaign were exactly what the agency had aimed for.

Advertising is targeted communication by which advertisers try to convince the audience about the utility of the advertised products. It is a process of informing, persuading and motivating the targeted audience through effective communication. In order to develop the type of communication that will lead to favourable action on the part of consumers or potential consumers, the communication should be persuasive so that the product advertised may by bought. It should be effective in achieving the success of advertising. Advertisers should be made aware of the elements of effective communication so that they may communicate to individuals-or to mass audiences concomitantly. In persuasive and effective communication process the words-presentation, the indication and the silence should be carefully directed towards the objectives of communications. The model process of communication includes the communication mix and the hierarchy of communication effects.

In Fig.10.1 the source delivers the message to the receiver through a channel-magazine, television, radio or a newspaper. Some disturbances, known as noise, are observed at every step. The source, intending, channel, decoding, receiver and feedback are influenced by the environment which may be cultural, social,

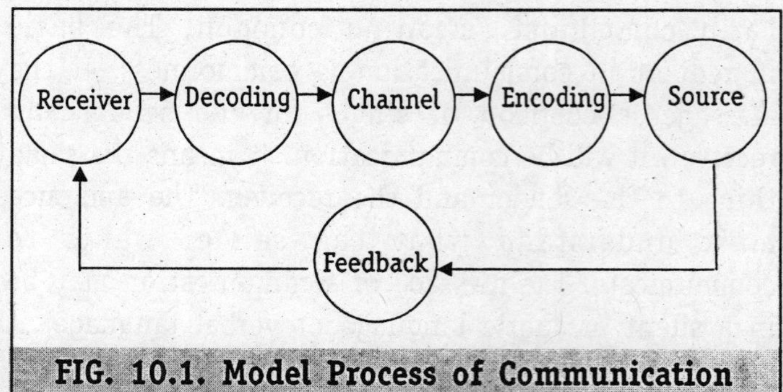

FIG. 10.1. Model Process of Communication

political, legal, economic and so on. The effectiveness of communication is disturbed by noise, The encoding is the translation of the message in words, pictures, indications, play, etc. These are transmitted through channels to the receiver who decodes, the message.

MODEL PROCESS OF COMMUNICATION

The model process of communication has been described under each component of the communication process, viz, source, message, perception, channel, receiver and effect are depicted in Fig. 10.2 below.

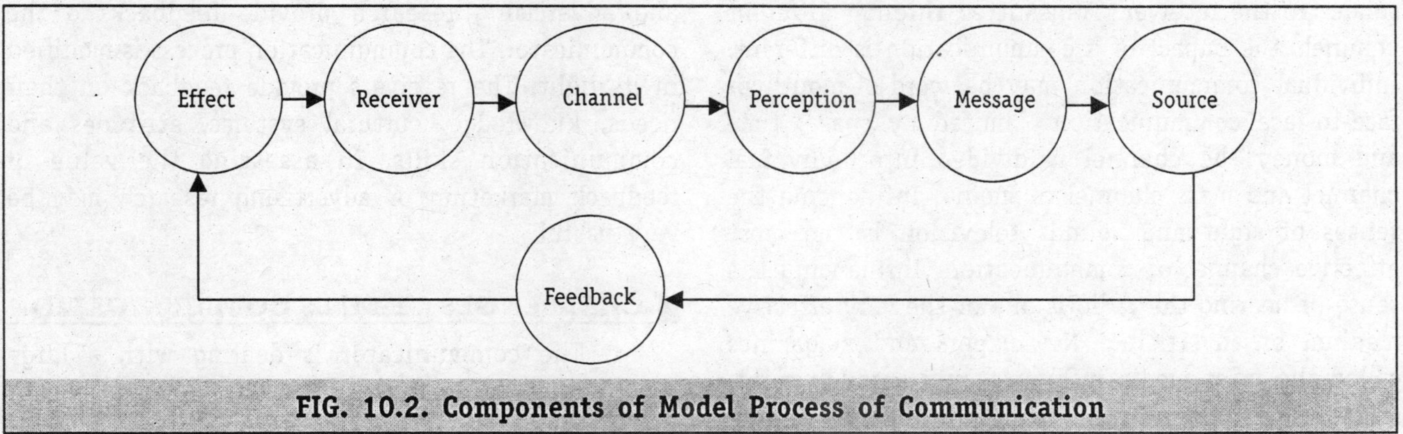

FIG. 10.2. Components of Model Process of Communication

1. Source - The source of a communication or message is called the encoder, sponsor, advertiser or sales representative. The source is the sender of the message. It is the place where the message originates. It is the spokesperson of the message of the advertising: The message is carried to the receiver through a channel, such as the newspaper, magazine, radio or television. It may relate to the brand, product, quality, price etc., which are to be brought to the knowledge of the receiver. It is encoded at the source and carried through a channel to the receiver who decodes the message. It may be perceived by the receiver who may be influenced on the basis of his culture, status, preference, knowledge and convictions. This process known as perception influences the message and the manner of decoding it by the receiver. Communication is complete when feedback is given by the receiver. Several disturbances, such as culture, perception, knowledge, etc., may weaken the message during the process of communication.

2. Message - The competence of the source depends on the credibility and attractiveness of the message, Message is the content of the communication. It is the creative idea of communication. It may include words, pictures, symbols, order of presentation, appeal, refuting or ignoring certain statements. Emotional, logical or rational approaches may be used in its preparation. The emotional appeal in advertising is very effective in message transmission. In insurance, the fear appeal motivates people to purchase life and non-life policies. In transmitting a message comparison or ignorance may also be taken advantage of as the message varies according to the objectives of the communication and the receiver's nature. The important principles in message preparation and presentation are the one-sided message climax, order, relevance, desirability, expertise and objectivity. Impersonal topics, non-conclusive statements, persuasive appeals, emotional appeals and non-verbal communication are included in the advertising communication and message.

3. Perception - The effectiveness of perception depends not only on the message and the channel used but also on the sender and receiver. The message can be perceived by the receiver according to his nature and culture,; its attention, interest, desire and action. The attitude and desire of the sender also influence the perception level. Their nature and features influence communication. Perception is influenced by cultural, psychological, educational, economical and political factors. The attention and interest of the audience depend on their perception of the message. Perception can be increased if the attention and interest of the receiver are aroused at a higher speed. Words, pictures and sounds are important factors influencing perception. If the audience does not perceive the message, it will not pay attention and will not take interest in the message.

4. Channel - In advertisement the message is carried through channels known as the media: newspaper, magazine, radio, or television-from the sender to the receiver. Transmitted through different channels the impact of a communication is different. Individual communication may be word-of-mouth or face-to-face communication. Limited by space, time and money (he channel is divided into individual channel and mass channel or media. Influencing the senses of sight and sounds television is the most effective channel of communication. Influencing the sense of hearing the radio is one of the very effective medium of advertising. Newspapers and magazines called the print media influence only through sight. Individual communication or face-to-face communication is the most effective channel because the receivers are analysed and evaluated in the course of the communication of the message. To influence and attract and audience, the sender or the communicator can change his mode of presentation. Advertisers cannot communicate effectively, efficiently and economically with the entire audience, through the individual channel.

5. Receiver - The target audience of the receiver's characteristics are evaluated to design the communication and message. To frame the content and medium of communication the number, location, type, awareness influence, knowledge, etc., of the receiver or audience are evaluated. The objectives of communication are information, persuasion and reminding the audience of the products. Individual communication may be effective for a particular objective. Advertisers try to create awareness, communicate information, develop the image of the product and company, create the attitude to purchase and precipitate consumer behaviour through the mass media. The audience is segmented on the basis of demographic, psychographic, geographic and other need factors.

To design the process of communication the advertisers should consider the receiver first. Advertising researches have been useful in determining the mode of communication. Advertisers should consider the value attitudes of the product, experience and responses of the audience while designing the communication process.

6. Feedback - An essential factor in making communication more effective feedback indicates how the communication process is working. It is received from the receivers or audiences. Marketing research and advertising research provide feedback to the communicator. The communication process is modified in its light. The receivers provide feedback on their needs, knowledge, cultural systems, attitudes and communication skills. In assessing the value of feedback marketing or advertising research may be very useful.

CHALLENGES OF MASS COMMUNICATION

1. The communicator is dealing with a large number of individuals unknown to her or him.
2. The communicator has no control on the circumstances under which the message will be received.
3. There is no opportunity for immediate feedback — that is, the communicator has no immediate opportunity to determine if the message is "getting through," and to change it if it is not.

ADVANTAGES OF THE MASS COMMUNICATION

1. The communicator can reach large numbers of people at far less cost per impression than would be the case with person-to-person communication.
2. The mass communicator can employ any number of artistic and graphic blandishments to make the message attractive. Celebrities can extol; cartoons can entertain; dazzling photography can enthrall; music can linger in the mind. And on and on.

THE FRAME OF REFERENCE

According to Muzafer and Carolyn W. Sherif the idea of the frame of reference is: "Psychological processing is patterned as jointly determined by operating internal and external factors, whether consciously experienced or not."

The behavior, as interpreted by the Sherifs, proceeds from psychological processing (PP) taking place within the individual at that given moment in time. This processing is patterned. It represents an order for that individual processing a particular set of stimuli at that particular moment as depicted in Fig. 10.3 below.

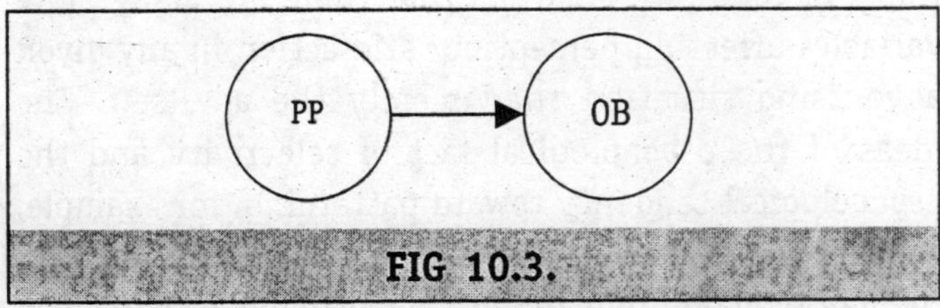

FIG 10.3.

VARIABLES DETERMINING PSYCHOLOGICAL PROCESSING

There are two type of variables that determine the psychological processing at any moment.

1. External Factors - These are all those things going on outside of you, at any given moment: For example, whether of not there are other people present and who those other people are; where you are; the weather; the kind of physical objects around you; the general state-of the environment-whether it is noisy or quiet; what kinds of things are there for you to pay attention to (e.g., ads); and so on.

2. Internal Factors - These are all those things going on inside you at the same moment. Your past experiences, your attitudes about different things; the state of your health at the moment-all of that "psychological baggage" that is called "beliefs" and "opinions" and so on.

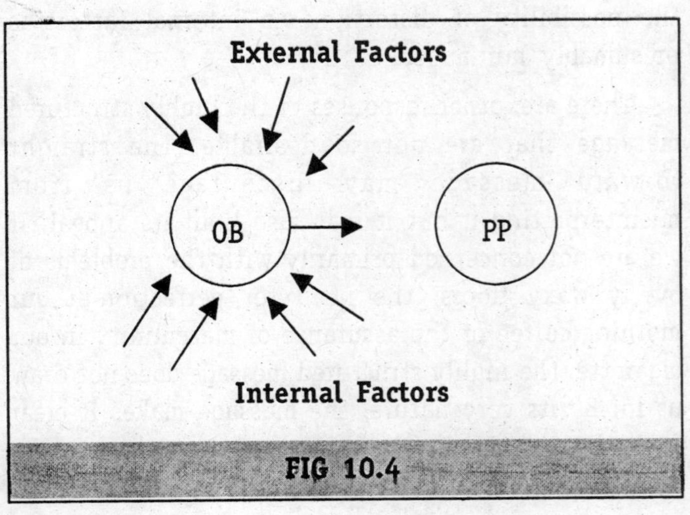

FIG 10.4

These internal and external factors are processed from moment to moment. They result in different behaviours depending on the psychological pattern — the order that has been given is those elements.

CHARACTERISTICS OF ONGOING PSYCHOLOGICAL ACTIVITY

(1) Selective

Both consciously and unconsciously, each of us is constantly selecting some things out of these internal arid external factors to attend to and act upon, arid ignoring the others. As the frame of reference concept suggests, our screening may vary from moment to moment because of operating internal and external factors.

1. Patterns of Selectivity - Over a period of time, our selectivity does begin to develop patterns. We are mort likely to be selective to some things rather than to others, although it is always possible that at any given moment our normal selectivity may be aborted. Some of the selectivity we develop is determined by that psychological baggage of attitudes, belief, opinions and past experiences that we carry with us. Thus, the selectivity of our ongoing psychological activity is crucial to the understanding of individual's responses to advertising.

(i) Voluntary - The exposure to communications media tends to be voluntary and selective. It is voluntary in the sense that people intentionally expose themselves to the medium. They turn the television set on and tune in particular programmes or purposely read certain magazines and newspapers.

(ii) Selective - It is selective in that people choose only a fraction of all media available and different people choose different things. The choices they make — the programmes, the magazines, the articles, the features-are generally likely to be those that gratify their expectations and compatible with their existing attitudes and opinions.

(iii) Involuntary - Whereas exposure to media tends to be voluntary, exposure to much advertising is involuntary that is the person does not always seek the advertisements. Generally, the ads come along with the programme or editorial content, and one becomes involuntarily exposed to the ads as a result of voluntary exposure to the medium. Exceptions, of course, are intentional exposures to classified ads, to the yellow pages, to mail order catalogue and to regular sources of shopping information such as grocery store and department store ads.

Thus the frame of reference at any given moment is determined in part by the selective nature of ongoing psychological activity. Each of us perceives (and acts) somewhat differently than everyone else, and this screening clearly affects the potential for advertising response (or the lack of it) or, as advertising practitioner Howard Gossage observed, "People don't read advertising *per se.* They read what interests them and sometimes, it's an ad".

2. Patterning of Experience - There are perceptions and actions that we seem to hold in common. Most of us complain that we never have enough free time. Yet, when we eventually do find ourselves with time on our hands, we often busy ourselves filling it up rather than pursuing more or less random activities, as free time might suggest. It is apparently not in the psychological makeup of humans to wish to experience prolonged instability — a loosening of "patterns" — at least in the long run.

The potential of advertising for creating and sustaining patterns of thought and action is at the heart of many critic's contentions that advertising restricts competition. By developing brand images through heavy advertising large companies are able to restrict competition by making it difficult for new entrants to dislodge these influential patterns. However, the potentials and resistances are by no means certain. There is a variety seeking within the general patterns of consumer behaviour. Hirschman and Wallendorf, note that variety seeking seems to have two components : Stimulus variation seeking involves varying the type of stimulation received by rotating one; usage among stimulus objects. Novelty seeking involves varying the type of stimulation received by seeking stimulus objects which are new and different. The advertisers to determine how firm are the patterns in the short and long run, and how much variety seeking, by brand or by product class, is present. Eventually, the tendency toward patterning asserts itself. It may or may not work to the benefit of the advertiser. So when our actions lead us to prefer the sure to the uncertain, the "old reliable" rather than the new, the predictable restaurant franchise to the untested roadside eatery, our frame of reference may be influenced by the tendency toward patterning of experience. It may be a blessing or a bane for advertising response.

3. Structured Stimulus, Limits to Alternatives in Psychological Patterning - The concept of the frame of reference suggests that there are many more variables affecting perception[1] arid action in any given advertising situation than merely the ad itself. The ideas of the psychological fact of selectivity and the psychological tendency toward patterning, for example, suggest that variables within the individual are likely to play a major role in how advertising is perceived and acted upon.

This proposition examines the potential influence of a major external variable — the degree of structure in the stimuli (including ads) around us. A structured stimulus situation may be defined as one that is clear cut, has a definite pattern and is unambiguous.

The proposition suggests that whenever the external stimulus situation is-relatively structured, the influence of internal factors such as our ability to see what we want to see will be lessened. It would seem to follow from the 'proposition that whenever an ad is highly structured, the opportunity for us to interpret it via our internal factors is limited. Now an advertising message that is relatively structured would have a clear, unambiguous message. A structured ad would possibly feature explicitly stated product/service characteristics and expectations. It would make clear what the message is and what action we are supposed to take as a result. Given this type of message, then, the possibility of distortion via internal factors is presumably minimized.

There are, other responses to the highly structured message that are not so desirable. The straight forward message may discourage us from misinterpreting it but it may also limit its appeal. If we are not concerned primarily with the problems of overly waxy floors, the need for perfection in our morning coffee or the assurance of masculinity in our cigarette, the highly structured message does not draw us in. By its very nature, the message makes it clear from the outset what it is about and we may not be interested.

With a highly structured ad message, alternatives in psychological patterning other than those intended by the advertiser are limited, simply because the message imposes its clear-cut pattern on the stimulus situation. Whether or not we respond to that pattern is determined by whether the, advertiser's patterning of reality matches our own.

4. In Unstructured Stimulus Situations, Alternatives in Psychological Patterning are Increased-Given the psychological tendency toward patterning of experience and given an external stimulus situation that is not clearly structured, it follows that the patterning will tend to be added by internal factors. Thus, many reports on unidentified flying objects have described them as "saucer" or "cigar" shaped apparently as a result of imposing a known pattern (structure) on a subject (the flying object), that is unstructured ambiguous, fluid and lacking clear definition. The individual must bring the pattern to the ink blot, since it has no structure to make a pattern clear. Here, then, the interpretations tend to be subjective, varying from individual to individual. It follows that relatively unstructured advertisements may be interpreted in different ways by different people. Many of the so-called soft-sell approaches used by perfumes, cosmetics, beers, liquors and even some politicians-are deliberately designed to be ambiguous enough so that individuals can impose their own structures on the situation.

By allowing room for many interpretations, the advertiser increases the possibility of attracting a wide range of customers, each of whom would potentially find something in the message that they could pattern from their own experiences. To the extent that the effort of patterning is that of the individual, there is potentially a greater sense of achievement, "involvement" in having "closed" the message structure to some meaningful whole.

HARD SELL AND SOFT SELL APPROACH

Thus, the response to advertising messages may be influenced by the degree of structure of the advertising message. When the message is relatively structured, the pattern is already imposed and the chances for individual interpretation and patterning are diminished. This is the advertising approach frequently associated with the so-called hard-sell school. In contrast, as the structure of the advertising message loosens, the patterning is more likely to be supplied by the individual in line with previous experiences and attitudes. Often interpreted as the soft-sell, this message approach implies a frame of reference with internal factors intended to fill in the gaps intentionally or unintentionally left in the message structure.

5. Human Psychological Functioning is Typically on the Conceptual Level - The most fundamental example of the interaction between internal and external factors in the frames of reference of individuals is the use of conceptual communication. Human conceptual communication is of a different order, than animal or mechanical.

It is, what makes humans different from animals. As anthropologist Loren easily observes with a touch of awe, "Man.....escaped out of the eternal present of the animal world into a knowledge of past and future." Carey observes, "Communication is a symbolic process whereby reality is produced, maintained, repaired, and transformed."

MEANS OF COMMUNICATION MIX

1. Verbal

In his wise and witty book on communication, Ton Fabun says, "When we act as if we believed that a word symbol is the event that was originally experienced, we ignore all the steps that have made, if something else....

Common words cannot possibly have meanings in themselves-only people can have meanings." Now some words are more structured than others, thus limiting our capacity for misinterpretation. But in trying to communicate on our level, advertisers are usually trying to persuade. And in the process they usually use words that cajole, suggest, flavour and hope that their meaning is also our meaning. As agency executive Jeremy Bullmore put it to his fellow practitioners. "We tend to believe that words are very explicit, but I'm not sure they are. I think they are stimuli with the audience filling in the gaps."

2. Non-Verbal

(i) Body Movement - While words are the most common symbols used in communication, they are scarcely the only ones. We communicate by gesture, by body movement of one sort, or another. You may have had the experience of misinterpreting the body movement of another. A nod of the head could mean "come here"; it could also mean, "I have a sore neck."

(ii) Colour - We communicate by colour; Generally within a given culture, colours will tend to be common meanings. In our culture, for example, blues and greens are considered restful colours; red and orange, hot or active colours; and black for mourning (in India white is the colour for mourning). The selection of colours "saying" the right things is increasingly important in package design, as well as advertising messages.

(iii) Time - Of course we communicate through time (keeping someone waiting says something to them) as well as space (the boss's office is bigger than mine). Even silence communicates, as each of us is probably painfully aware.

Edward T. Hall has called many of these non-verbal communication forms the "silent languages". They are part of the Advertiser's communication tools. Like words, they are powerful but imprecise predictors of advertising response.

Thus, the phenomenon of conceptual communication makes advertising (and every other form of mass communication) possible. Yet, at the same time, It makes the response to advertising messages uncertain, due to the many possible interactions of the external symbols (both verbal and non-verbal) with the internal factors at work within each individual at any particular moment.

6. Different Relative Weights of Various Factors in the Frame of Reference - This is because of the different reference points that are being used. In some primitive societies, the passing of the seasons is noted by the anchor (enduring reference point) of the scents of different blooming flowers. In our culture, our reference point is more frequently a calendar, or the activities of schools, or retail merchants. In other words, our frames of reference are influenced by factors that have the greatest relative weight.

One result of this anchoring phenomenon is the so-called assimilation/contrast effects. Simply, if an individual's reference point (or anchor) is deeply held on a controversial issue, all subsequent communications about that issue are evaluated from that reference point. Those that seem relatively close are assimilated — perceived as being closer to the individual's own position than they may objectively be. But those that are perceived negatively are contrasted — perceived as being farther away from the individual's position than they may be. Thus, an individual who feels strongly about the forced busing of school children might well think of someone who was neutral on the issue as being against them.

This assimilation/contrast effect can, be quite important with advertising by producers, government, and groups increasingly directed toward presenting views on such controversial issues as the environment and energy policy. This type of advertising is often directed toward sympathetic audiences but must also frequently attempt to persuade those whose points of view are at least neutral and possibly opposed to the position advocated.

Anchors can work either for or against advertisers. They may in some cases be a formidable influence in assessing relevant communications yet may be of little influence in matters of small concern to the individual. A strong anchor in support of free enterprise could be significant in evaluating a message calling for more government control of energy resources. On the other hand, a feeling that "It really doesn't matter what toothpaste brand I buy" suggests the absence of a strong anchor and the likelihood that the individual may be more influenced by transient external influences such as sales.

Many marketing communications are misunderstood or misinterpreted because of necessity, they tend to be brief. One way of overcoming this is to send the message by different routes, creating redundancy in the system, so that a failure in one route does not prevent the message from getting through.

The communication process effectively uses all the limits of the communication mix.

Communication mix includes the interdependent objectives of communication, communication components and variables. The objectives of communication are achieved by using the components of communication and modifying the controllable variables within the given non-controllable variables.

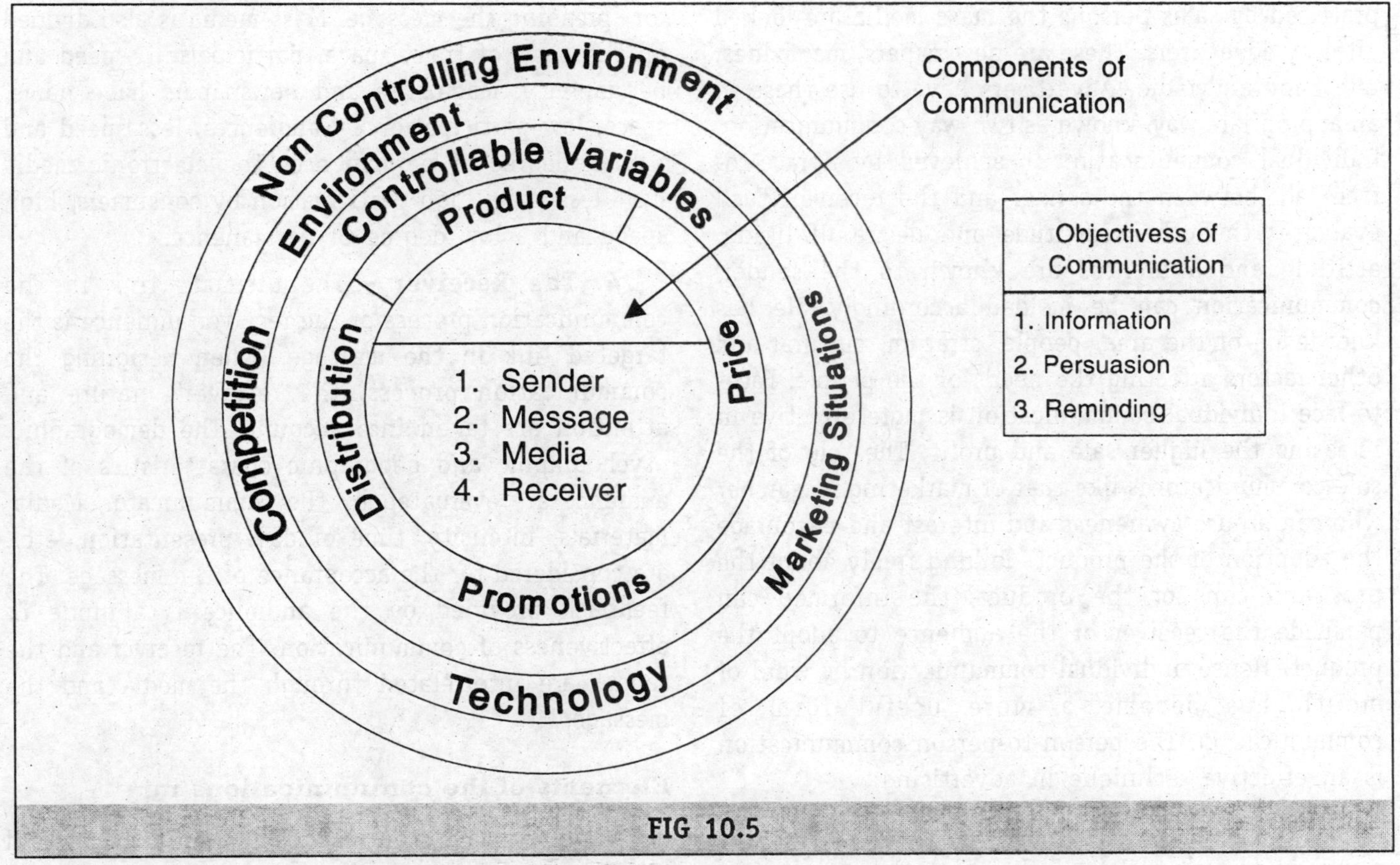

FIG 10.5

OBJECTIVES OF COMMUNICATION MIX

The objectives of communication mix are formulated after a thorough analysis of the environment, marketing situation, technology and competition. The strength and weakness of the controllable variables, i.e., product, price, promotion and physical distribution, are evaluated to find out the practical objectives of advertising. The main objective of communication is to communicate to the target audience. It is informative and mix persuasive. It reminds of the products of the company and its image. Russel Colley refers to four objectives of commercial communication, *viz.*, awareness, comprehension, conviction and action.

1. Awareness - Consumers must be informed about the attributes of the product.

2. Comprehension - If they are informed, they will comprehend what the product is and how it satisfies a particular want.

3. Conviction - The advertiser should convince the audience that the products are worth purchasing and will satisfy wants.

4. Action - The communication should be motivated in such a manner that the consumer takes the action and purchases the products. The communication should describe the product; remind the audience and relate it with other products so that the superiority of a particular product may be accepted by consumers. Many advertisers and producers concentrate on the corporate image through the communication process. The built-in image increases sales volume, sales share and profit.

COMPONENTS OF COMMUNICATION MIX

The components of communication mix are four-

1. Sender;
2. Message;
3. Media; and
4. Receiver.

1. The Sender - The sender is the person or advertiser who communicates or sends the message which may be prepared for mass media or for individual communication. While individual communication is practiced by sales persons the mass media are looked after by advertisers. These are newspapers, magazines, television and radio. Advertisers have to use these in an appropriate way, known as two-way communication, individual communication is achieved by a face-to-face talk between the sender and the receiver. Each evaluates the other's attitude and desire. If liking, attitude and awareness are known to the sender, communication can be molded accordingly. He has knowledge of the area, people, stratum, cultural and other factors affecting the needs of the people. Face-to-face individual communication is more effective in releasing the higher sale and profit. The role of the sole communicator is like that of marketing researcher who can arouse awareness and interest and encourage the adoption of the product. Talking freely about the pros and cons of the product, the informed can persuade the receiver or the audience to adopt the product. Hence, individual communication by word of mouth has become a more useful form of communication. The person-to-person communication is an effective technique in advertising.

2. The Message - The message, visual or verbal is a very important tool for influencing the audience or receiver. The success of advertising depends on how well the elements of the message are created and arranged. Bases of the message are the word, the picture, the symbol and other communicative elements. Formerly, the word was considered to be the vehicle of an effective message; but research has shown that the other elements are equally important. Advertisers have discovered that colour, illustrations, designs, the injection of sex etc., are effective factors in the advertising message. With the invention of the electronic media, i.e., television and radio, the message effectively achieves the advertising objectives. The factors of silence and indication are effective pans of the message through television, Advertisers have to mix the various elements of the message judiciously and logically to achieve success in use.

3. The Media - The media has been divided into mass media and individual media. Sub-classsified on the basis of frequency, coverage and ownership the mass media are newspapers, magazines, television, radio etc. Their message is accelerated by family, relatives, friends, neighbours, etc. who spread the message to other acquaintances. Advertisers use them effectively for spreading the message. Mass media is also divided on the basis of time, space, participation, speed and permanency. Magazines and newspapers have name, space, low participation by audiences, less speed and a high degree of permanence. The electronic media have less time, high participation by consumers, high speed and a low degree of permanence.

4. The Receiver - The ultimate link in the communication process or the receiver audience is the targeted link in the message. When designing the communication process, the receiver's nature and attention are taken into account. The demographic, psychographic and geographic characteristics of the audience are evaluated by the communicator. Media, materials, intensity, time of day, presentation, etc., are considered for the acceptance of the message. The feedback provided by the audience is a guide to effectiveness of communication. The receiver and the sender are interrelated through the media and the message.

Elements of the communications mix

Marketers have many tactics at their disposal, and the best marketers use them in appropriate ways to maximise the impact of their communications activities. A very basic taxonomy of promotional tools is the four-way division into advertising, public relations, sales promotion, and personal selling. This taxonomy is really too simplistic, as each of the elements sub-divides further, and there are several elements which don't readily fit into these categories. For example, T-shirt slogans are clearly communications, but they are not advertising, nor are they really public relations. Yet, T-shirts with brand logos on, or even adaptations of brand logos, are a common sight and can be considered as marketing communications. Table 10.1 lists some of the elements of the communications mix. This list is unlikely to be exhaustive, and there is also the problem of boundary-spanning - some elements of the mix go beyond communication and into the realms of distribution (telemarketing, home shopping channels), or even into new product development (as with the web site which allows students to sell successful essays to other students).

The range of possible tools at the marketer's disposal is obviously large, as creating a good mix of communications methods is akin to following a recipe. The ingredients have to be added in the right amounts at the right time, and treated in the right way, if the recipe is to work. Also, one ingredient cannot substitute for another: personal selling cannot, on its own, replace advertising, nor can public relations exercises replace sales promotions. Fig. 10.6 shows how the above elements of the mix relate to each other.

The interconnections between the various elements shown in Fig. 10.6 are only the main ones; in fact, every marketing communication impinges on every other in some way or another. The methods used will depend on the firm, the product and the audience.

VARIABLES OF COMMUNICATION

1. Controllable Variables - Producers have to communicate facts and reality to the receiver. Deceptive and false advertisements may damage the image of the product and the company. A communication should convey the truth about controllable variables such as product, price, promotion and distribution. Some criticism is very useful for product design, reasonable pricing, effective communications and distribution. While framing the components of communication these variables are considered. Information on quality, product line, price level and distribution is communicated to the receiver or audience. Promotion strategies other than advertising are evaluated. Unless the controllable variables i.e., marketing elements are

TABLE 10.1

Elements of the Communications Mix

Element	*Explanation*
Advertising	A paid insertion of a message in a medium.
Ambient advertising	Messages placed on items such as bus tickets, stamp franking, bill receipts: petrol pump nozzles and so forth. Any message that forms part of the environment - for example, 'art installations' in city centres.
Press advertising	Any paid message that appears in a newspaper or magazine.
TV advertising	Commercial messages shown in the breaks during and between TV programmes.
Radio advertising	Sound-only advertisements broadcast on radio.
Outdoor advertising	Billboards, bus shelters, fly posters etc.
Transport advertising	Posters in stations and inside buses and trains.
Outside transport advertising	Posters on buses and taxis, and (in some countries) the sides of trains. British Airways have recently carried other companies' logos on the tail planes of aircraft.
Press releases	News stories about a firm or its products.
Public relations	The planned and sustained effort to establish and maintain goodwill and mutual understanding between an organisation and its publics (Institute of Public Relations, 1984).
Sponsorship	Funding of arts events, sporting events etc., in exchange for publicity and prestige.
Sales promotions	Activities designed to give a temporary boost to sales, such as money-off coupons, free samples, two for the price of one promotions etc.
Personal selling	Face-to-face communications between buyers and sellers designed to ascertain and meet customers' needs on a one-to-one basis.
Database marketing	Profiling customers onto a database and sending out personalised mailings or other communications to them.
Telemarketing	Inbound (helpline, telephone ordering) or outbound (telecanvassing, teleselling) telephone calls.
Internet marketing	Use of websites to promote and/or sell products.
Off-the-screen selling	Using TV adverts linked to inbound telephone operations to sell goods. Also home shopping channels such as QVC.
Exhibitions and trade fairs	Companies take stands at trade fairs to display new products, meet consumers and customers, and raise the company profile with interested parties.
Corporate identity	The overall image that the company projects: the company's 'personality'.
Branding	The mechanism by which marketing communications are co-ordinated.

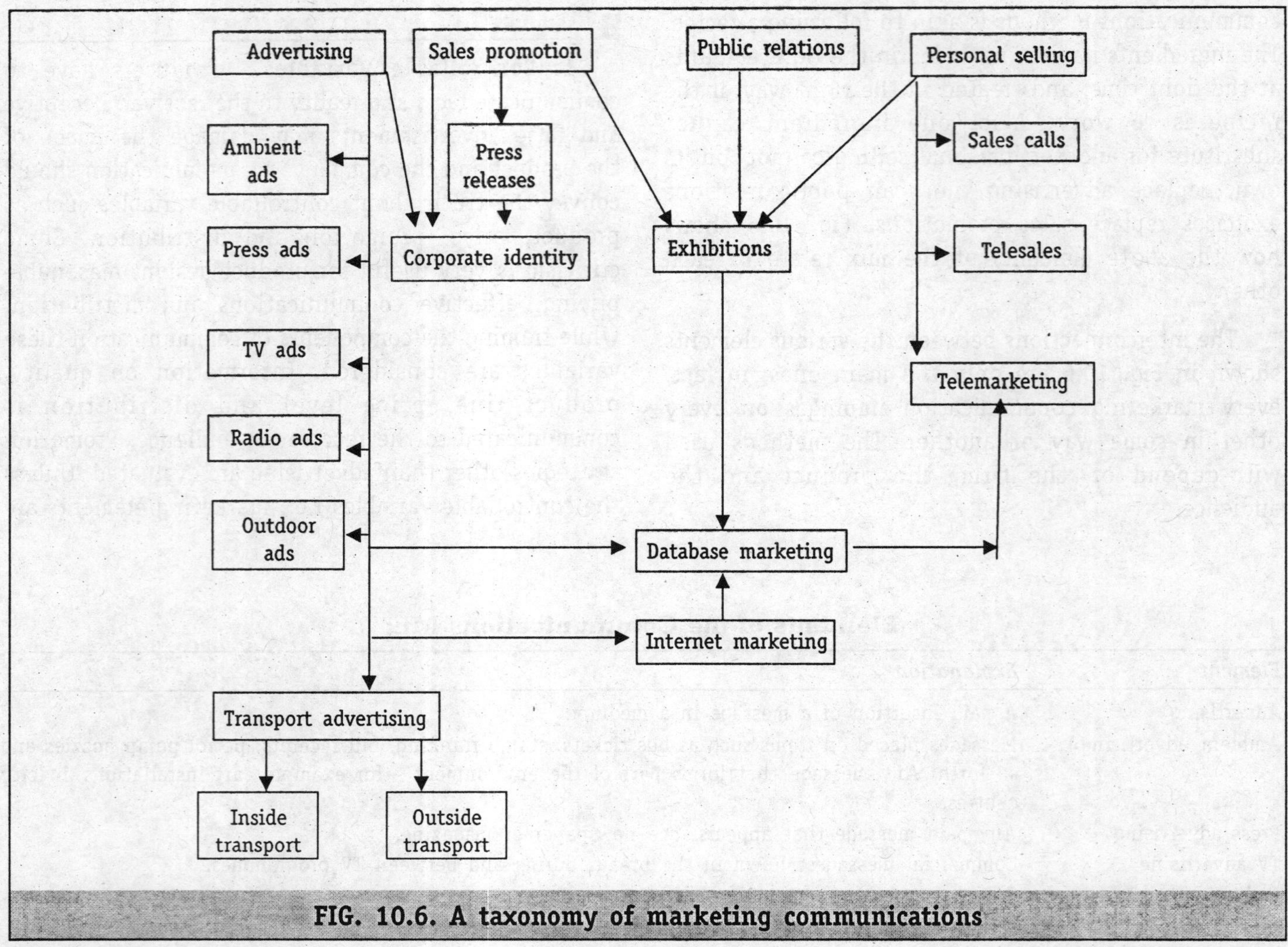

FIG. 10.6. A taxonomy of marketing communications

demonstrated truly and correctly no communication can be effective.

2. Uncontrollable Variables - The uncontrollable variables are environment, market situation, technology and competition. These have a long-lasting impact on the components of communication. As these cannot be changed or abandoned, the components of communication are modified by uncontrollable variables.

(i) Environment has a long-lasting impact on advertising and communication. It includes social, legal, economic and political factors.

(ii) The marketing systems in the economy also influence communication.

(iii) Personal selling, buyer's behaviour, seller's approach etc., are considered under the marketing system.

(iv) Competition also influences the components of communication. The buyer's competition, the seller's competition, product competition etc., have a direct influence on advertising. Competition for space and time in the print and electronic media also influences message creation and presentation.

Structuring the Communications Mix

Structuring the communications mix will differ from one firm to another indeed from one promotion to another within the same firm. Developing effective marketing communications follows a six-stage process:

1. Identify the target audience. In other words, decide who the message should get to.
2. Determine the response sought. What would the marketer like the audience to do after they get the message?
3. Choose the message. Write the copy, or produce an appropriate image.

4. Choose the channel Decide which newspaper, TV station, radio station or other medium is most appealing to the audience.
5. Select the source's attributes. Decide what it is about the product or company that needs to be communicated.
6. Collect feedback. Carry out market research (for example), to find out how successful the message was.

Communication is often expensive: full-page advertisements in Sunday colour supplements can cost upwards of £11 000 per insertion; a thirty-second TV ad at peak time can cost £30 000. It is therefore worthwhile spending time and effort to ensure that the message can be comprehended by the target audience, and is reaching the right people. Fig. 10.7. shows how the communication mix operates.

In the above diagram, messages from the company about its products and itself are transmitted via the elements of the promotional mix to the consumers, employees, pressure groups, and other publics. Because each of these group is receiving the messages from more than one transmitter, the elements of the mix also feed into each other so that the messages don't conflict. The choice of method will depend upon the message, the receiver, and the desired effect.

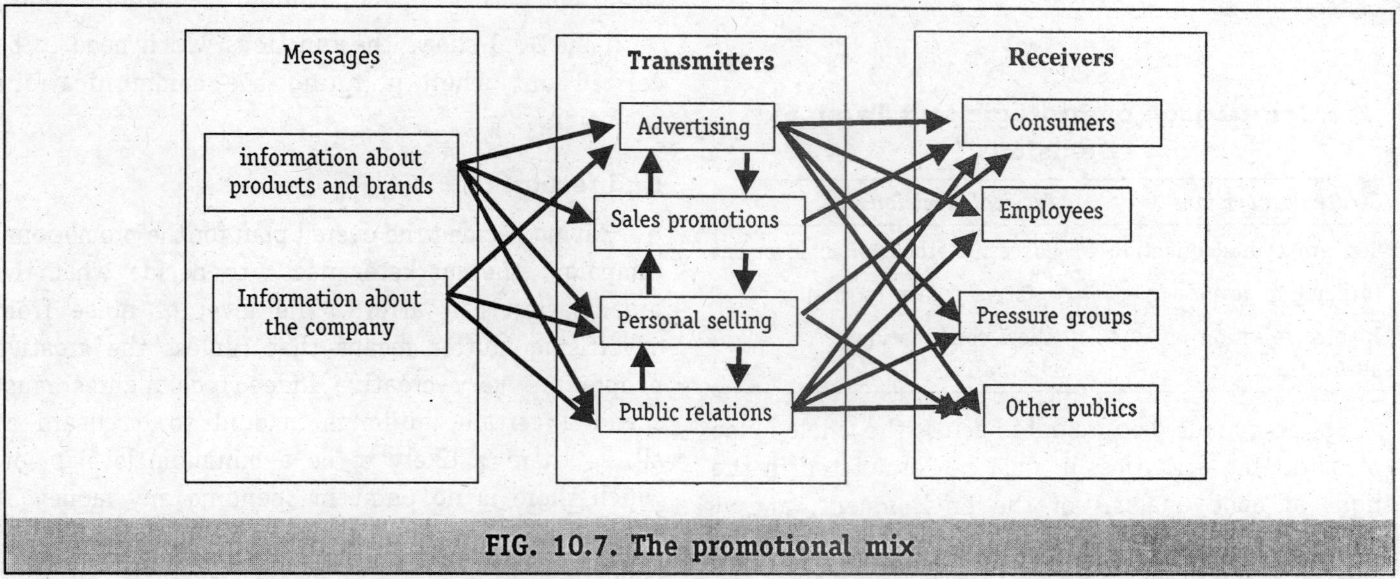

FIG. 10.7. The promotional mix

HIERARCHY OF COMMUNICATION MIX EFFECTS

The communication process effects on the receivers may be classified as low level, middle-level and high-level effects.

1. The Low-level Effects - These are observed when the difference between the competing brands is the least. The receiver does not assign any significance to such difference.

2. The Middle-level Effects - These are observed when product choice or alternative choice is not known to the receiver or audience. Sales persons can influence the effect on such audiences.

3. High-level Effects - These are observed when the audience is interested in learning, in knowing the product and brands.

Formulating a Strategy

The first step, as in any other issue in marketing, is to find out what the customers are looking for. In communications terms this means finding out which magazines the target audience reads, which TV stations they watch, what their leisure activities are, whether they are interested in football, opera or horse racing, and so forth. This is a substantial part of the market research that is carried out daily; consumers not only consume products, they also consume communications media. Knowing which media they consume enables the astute marketer to target accurately and avoid wasting the budget on trying to communicate with people who are not paying attention and have no interest in the product.

Strategic decisions concern the overall direction of the organisation. Strategy is about 'where we want to be. Tactical decisions are about 'how we're going to get there'.

Strategic decisions tend to be difficult to reverse. They usually involve a rejection of other strategic options, and they generally therefore involve a major personal commitment on the part of the decision maker. Tactical decisions are relatively easy to change, involve less commitment, and can often run alongside other options.

TABLE 10.2

Comparison of Strategic and Tactical Decisions

Strategic decisions	*Tactical decisions*
Concern overall direction	Concern methods of achievement
Difficult to reverse	Relatively easy to change
Involve rejection of alternatives	Allow combination of alternatives

Strategy must be integrated across the whole range of marketing activities, it must be formulated in the light of good analysis of the environment, and it must include a feedback system so that the strategy can be adapted according to environmental changes. Strategy is influenced by organisational objectives and resources, competitor activities, the structure of the market itself, and the firm's willingness to make changes and take risks.

Push versus pull strategies

Two basic strategic alternatives exist for marketing communications, at least as far as promotional activities are concerned. Push strategy involves promoting heavily to the members of the distribution channel, i.e., to wholesalers, retailers and agents on the assumption that they will, in turn, promote heavily to the end consumers.

In this way the products are pushed through the distribution channel. Pull strategy involves promoting heavily to end users and consumers to create a demand that will pull the products through the distribution channels. The ultimate pull strategy was adopted by Levi Strauss when they launched L501s into the UK market. The firm ran a series of TV adverts before the product was actually available in the shops. This generated consumer demand, which led to the shops demanding that Levi supply the jeans as quickly as possible.

Push strategies tend to place the emphasis on personal selling and sales promotion, whereas pull strategies tend to place the emphasis on mass advertising. The two strategies are not mutually exclusive, but rather represent opposite ends of a spectrum: most campaigns contain elements of both.

Table 10.3 shows the functions which need to be carried out when planning the communications campaign.

Budgeting

Having decided the overall plan for the promotional campaign, the marketer needs to decide what the organisation can afford. The level of noise from advertising clutter means that (unless the creative people are very creative indeed) companies must spend a certain minimum amount to be heard at all, so there is likely to be a minimum level below which there is no point in spending any money at all. Table 10.4 illustrates some methods for setting budgets.

In the real world, marketers usually adopt a combination strategy, using several of the above methods. Even an objective and task approach might begin by looking at what the competition are spending (comparative parity approach), if only to determine what the likely spend would have to be to overcome clutter. Likewise, a marketer may be part way through a campaign, and be told by the finance department that no more money is available (or perhaps be told that more than anticipated is available) and will switch to an 'all you can afford' policy.

MODELS OF COMMUNICATION EFFECT

The hierarchy to communication effects has been studied under the AIDA model, the effect model and the innovation adoption model.

TABLE 10.3
Communications Planning Functions

Planning	*Explanation*
Situation analysis	1. Demand factors. These include consumer needs and decision-making processes, cultural and social influences on demand, product category and brand attitudes, individual differences between consumers. 2. Identify the target, it is better to approach a small segment of the market than to try to use a 'scattergun' approach on everybody. 3. Assess the competition, other products, possible competitor responses etc. 4. Legal and regulatory restrictions that might affect what the strategy is able to do.
Defining the objectives	Deciding what the communications are supposed to achieve, it is essential here to give the advertising agency, PR agency, salesforce and indeed everybody associated with the campaign a clear brief. 'We want to raise awareness of the product to 50 per cent of the adult population' is a measurable objective. 'We want to increase sales as much as possible' is not measurable, so there is no way of knowing whether it has been achieved.
Setting the budget	This can be done in four basic ways (though this is expanded on later in the chapter): 1. The objective and task approach, whereby objectives are set and an appropriate amount of money is put aside. This method is difficult to apply because it is difficult to assess how much will be needed to achieve the objective. 2. The percentage of sales approach whereby the budget is set as a percentage of sales. This is based on the false idea that sales create advertising, and usually results in less being spent on marketing communications when sales fall, thus reducing sales further. 3. The competition matching approach whereby the company spends the same as the competition means that the firm is allowing its budgets to be set by its enemies. 4. The arbitrary approach whereby a senior executive (usually a finance director) simply says how much can be allowed within the firm's overall budgets. This does not take account of how the firm is to achieve the objectives.
Managing the elements of the mix	Media planning. This is about deciding which media will communications. There are two main decision areas: the reach (number of potential consumers the communication reaches) and the frequency of coverage (number of times each consumer is exposed to the communication). In advertising, the decision is frequently made on the basis of cost per thousand readers/viewers, but this doesn't take into account the impact of the ad or the degree to which people are able to skip past it. Briefing the salesforce, deciding whether it is to be a push or pull strategy, choosing the PR and support communications.
Creating the platform	Deciding the basic issues and selling points that the communicate convey. This clarifies the agency briefings, or at least clarifies on producing the communications.

1. The AIDA Model - Designed by Strong, AIDA model involves Attention, Interest, Desire and Action. The recipient of a message moves from awareness to interest and again to desire to reach the level of action-the purchase of the product. The advertiser should draw the attention of the consumers to create desire to buy the product. In the beginning of the advertisement the attention of the potential customer should be drawn. Now, interest should be aroused and held through the advertising process. Interest leads to desire. Customers can satisfy their wants or desires by purchasing goods.

The AIDA model is adopted by advertisers indirectly or directly adopting different messages and media.

TABLE 10.4

Promotional Budgeting Methods

Method	*Explanation*	*Advantages*	*Disadvantages*
Objective and task method	Identify the objective to be achieved, then determine the costs and effort required to achieve those objectives.	Has a logical basis, and if carried out correctly will achieve the firm's strategic goals.	Difficult to calculate the necessary spend to achieve the objective. Time-consuming and expensive in terms of market research.
Percent of sales method		Simple to calculate, also ensures that, if sales drop off, costs also drop.	Is based on the false premise that sales cause promotion, rather than promotion causing sales. Logically, if sales fall, promotion expenditure should be increased to bring the customers back in.
Comparative parity method	The planner simply allows a fixed percentage of the company's sales to be used for promotion. This promotional budget increases as sales go up, and decreases as sales go down. A very common method of budgeting.	Ensures that the firm remains on par with the competitors, and does not waste expenditure.	Takes no account of changes in the market, or opportunities that might arise (in other words, is not customer-orientated).
Marginal approach	The marketer matches expenditure to that of the competitors. Thus, the firm does not lose ground if a competing firm increases its budget.	This method would maximise profits since no excess spending would result.	Extremely difficult to calculate, given the changing nature of markets.
'All you can afford' method	Marketer only spends up to the point where any further spending would not generate enough extra business to justify the outlay. The marketer spends whatever money can be spared from other activities. Often used by small businesses when starting out.	Company cannot become over - committed or run into trouble by relying on sales which do not, in the end, materialise.	Again, bears no relationship to the state of the marketplace. Also relies on the marketer being able to persuade other departments within the firm to give up expenditure on their own pet projects.

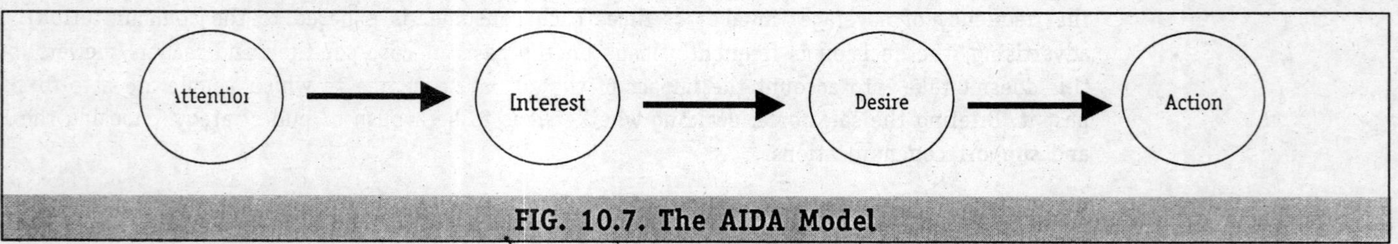

FIG. 10.7. The AIDA Model

2. The Hierarchy Effects Model – Conceived by Lavidge and Steiner hierarchy effects model shows that the awareness created by advertising imparts knowledge of the product's attributes and develops a liking for it, while the product's attributes and qualities are known.

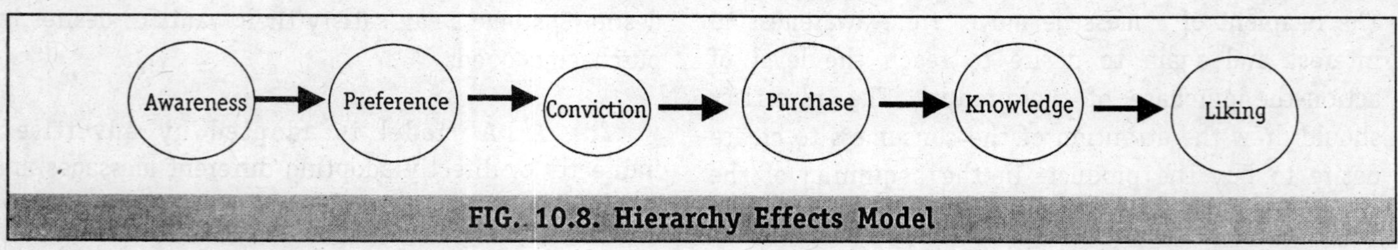

FIG. 10.8. Hierarchy Effects Model

Receivers of the message determine the priorities for the purchase of products. Believing that the preferred products would satisfy their wants and desire, they are led to the action of purchasing the products. Advertisers therefore, make the audience aware of their products.

3. Innovation Adoption Model - Devised by Rigors the term "innovation adoption model" refers to adoption by trial. In it, awareness and interest of the audience are created by advertisers, so that the audience may evaluate the message of advertisements.

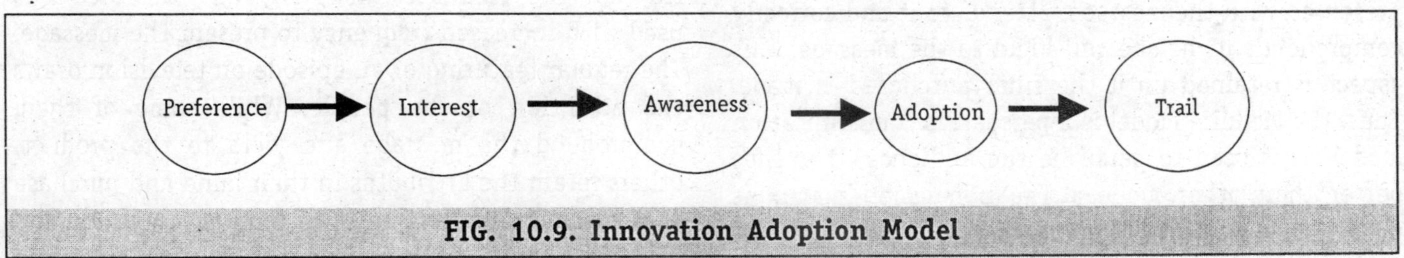

FIG. 10.9. Innovation Adoption Model

If satisfied with the attributes advertised the potential purchaser purchases a product on a trial basis, advertisers have to inform consumers and make them realise the worth of a product after the trial purchase. If customers are satisfied after a trial, they adopt the product. Mass and individual communication are used to make people aware of the product or product attributes. Then advertising is used to encourage a liking for the product. As consumers evaluate the qualities and attributes of the different product brands, product comparison is made to adopt a particular product, to prefer the innovation adoption model to the previous model.

THE PERSUASION OBJECTIVE

An important objective of advertising is persuasion. The prime function of advertising is communication of information. The advertiser influences attitudes and persuades the audience, the consumer and the prospect to purchase the article. He should know how and why attitudes develop and the manner in which they may be changed. He uses economic and psychological appeals to influence attitude. He persuades, audiences by stimulating attitudinal changes.

METHODS OF BRINGING ATTITUDINAL CHANGE

Persuasion matrix, source factors, message factors, perception factors, cognitive consistency and low-involvement learning are the important methods of bringing attitudinal changes in prospects :

1. Persuasion Matrix - It is a combination of hierarchy effects and communication components. The hierarchy effect is also known as the response hierarchy which according to Rogers may be awareness-interest-evaluation-trial and adoption. Though the hierarchical steps of Rogers' model are similar to the others; but his purpose is to illustrate the process of new product adoption. The McGuire information processing model known as PACYRE is better than those of his predecessors. PACYRE means presentation of message, attention to message, comprehension of message, yielding to the conclusion, retention of the new belief and behaving on the basis of the belief.

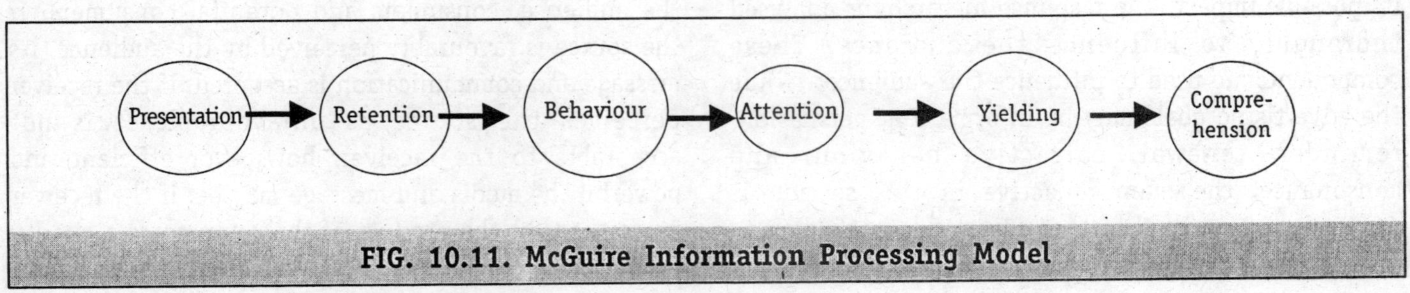

FIG. 10.11. McGuire Information Processing Model

According to McGuire, the appropriate view of a receiver is like an information processing machine or a problem solver, a silent acceptor of the message presented to him. The response model has many parallel characteristics in common with the hierarchy-effects models. This model emphasizes the elements of comprehension and behaviour. If the prospect is presented with the message, attends to it and correctly comprehends it, he she will yield to the message. This aspect is retained until the final purchased is made. Thus, the McGuire model is a persuasive communication model. It is used to persuade the audience. It is thus better than other models. The persuasion matrix is prepared on its basis. The communication components such as source message, media and receiver, are independent variables which influence the persuasion matrix. The response hierarchy, presentation of the message, attention to the message, comprehension of the message, yielding, retention and behaviour are the dependent variables. Each communication component influences every step of the hierarchy effects and any model may be used for the purpose. Being more effective and persuasive, McGuire model is used for persuasion purposes. From the presentation to the behaviour level communication, behaviour is the ultimate goal of persuasion. Not only the message, but the source, receiver and sender have to follow in sequence to the behaviour level.

Maximum utilization of a component of communication leads to persuasion as they pass serially through the responses hierarchy and the media is used with increased frequency to present the message. The regular featuring of an episode on television draws the attention of the people. While some of them comprehend the message and yield to the product, others retain the attributes in their mind and purchase it at the appropriate time. The receiver's attitude and interest are taken into account to influence the audience. The message may be presented in many ways using effective factors such as attractive colours movements, sex, sweet voices, joke etc., to draw the attention of the audience. When the probability of attention increases by communication components the probability of the subsequent hierarchy also increase. No subsequent step should be taken in the response hierarchy till the first step shows satisfactory results.

Communication Components	*Source*	*Message*	*Media*	*Receiver*
Response Hierarchy Presentation Attention Comprehension Yielding Retention Behaviour				

One can easily understand the probability of response of each component at each level by the persuasive matrix. The probability estimation is made on the basis of the magnitude of demonstration and its possible impact. The response hierarchy is analysed thoroughly to influence the audience. These components are used to influence the audiences. While the advertising goals may be information, persuasion, reminder, renewal, corrective behaviour and consonance, the main objective in this section is persuasion. Because the other advertising goals depend on persuasion, they are secondary.

2. Source Factors - These are the basic components of persuasive functions. The advertiser, the producer and the sender of the message are the source factors. These send the message to the receiver, the recipient, the audience, consumers and potential consumers. If the source is favourably perceived by the audience, its message and communication is accepted. If the receiver perceives the source as unfavourable it is not acceptable to the receiver, howsoever efficient and powerful the media and message may be. If the receiver perceives that the product of the company is a quality product, the communication or advertising is effective.

However, if the company's credibility is suspect, the communication is not persuasive. On the other hand, if the company's products give satisfaction to consumers and prospects, its advertising is accepted as true. Many organizations in India have doubtful credibility. Therefore, their sales do not materialize even after excessive advertising. Besides the company the product, the brand, the organization of markets alienation or alignment of advertising companies are the source factors influencing communication.

The individual, the spokesperson, the endorser and other source factors have a greater influence on the receiver or audience. Apart from the message and media their credibility and attractiveness are instrumental in influencing the audience. The impact of persuasive communication will be very great if these three factors acquire high credibility with the receivers. If the audience has a low opinion of the source about these factors, the acceptability of the product or the persuasive result will be very low.

KINDS OF SOURCE FACTORS

(i) Credibility - Credibility means the acceptability of or belief in the source. It is associated with the reputation of goodwill or the source. It determines the degree or chances of communication success. The greater the credibility of the source, the greater the change of success. It arises if the product is backed by the expertise of the producer and his unbiased altitude in marketing it. The term expertise "indicates" that the source is knowledgeable and a specialized producer. Unbiasness reflects the fairness of the source's opinion and its worth. The source should be credible to the audience, because the audience internalizes the arguments and believes in the message given by the source.

Pertaining to new products credibility has been more influential. If his credibility to the existing products has already been established the producer may launch another new product very effectively. The audience believes that the new product is likely to be of an equally acceptable quality. A new company may not be benefited by the credibility factor unless it is a subsidiary to the existing reputed company. To reap the benefits of credibility some well-known advertisers introduce the new products of such companies. If the source is fair and trustworthy the message and communication are accepted.

(ii) Attractiveness - This arises out of the receiver's perceptions of the source. The important components of attractiveness are the prestige, similarity and physical attractiveness.

(a) Prestige - It depends on past achievement, reputation and visibility. The prestige of the producer and the marketer are also taken into account by the receiver or the audience. The term "prestige" connotes the quality and satisfying attributes of a process.

(b) Similarity - It relates to the relationship of the product to the satisfying attributes. A film star or a distinguished player is used to demonstrate the product to create an impression that the product is of high quality because he prefers only quality products. As the opinion of the audience may change at a later stage it is essential to advertise constantly at regular intervals to remind the audience of the attributes of the product. There may be an attitudinal similarity of the audience with the source. The receiver and the sender may have similar attitudes to the' product and advertising. Group attitudes are also used as a similarity factor.

(c) Physical Attractiveness - Similarity and physical attractiveness have a profound influence on the audience. The use of sex in advertising has a persuasive effect. Education has also some impact on attractiveness. The advertisers use emotional figures to attract the audience. A cosmetic can be advertised successfully when beautiful ladies are shown to use it. Acceptance can be achieved through an advertisement showing that strong men prefer it. Thus, the similarity of the product and the source should be established to persuade the audience successfully to buy a product.

SOURCE INCONGRUITY

The receiver may like an advertisement but may dislike the product or *vice versa*. This conflict is known as source incongruity. The relative strength of product and advertising, determines the ultimate effect. The advertiser and the producer should try to increase the credibility and attractiveness of their products to bring them at the persuasion level. By regular and effective advertising the credibility and attractiveness of the source should be maintained throughout the life of the product.

3. Message Factors - The message transmitted through a channel has important effects on persuasion. However, the actual message may be interrupted during the period of transmission. A message familiar to an audience should be selected in such a way as to make the communication successful. As the source encodes and the receiver decodes the message the message should have commonness. The experience and attitude of the receiver and source should be brought to the same platform. Common experience of the sender and receiver may create a positive effect of the message on persuasion and action. The encoding and decoding of the message taking place outside the area of the experience of the sender and the receiver will have less or no impact on persuasion. Unless both the sender and the receiver conform to the existing attitudes, they are unlikely to be successful. Advertisers should use the message in the most favourably conditions. The sponsor should strive to create a favourable attitude to make the message successful. He should take note of positive resistant and changing negative attitudes.

KINDS OF MESSAGE FACTORS

1. Creating Positive Attitudes - The message should create a positive attitude to the purchase of the advertised product in favour of new and existing products through advertising by the adoption of focus message stating conclusions, two-sided arguments and emotional appeals.

(a) Message Focus - The advertiser should design the message to focus the attention of customers on new products by word, action, voice and role playing. Ethos, pathos and logos are important techniques for focusing the attention of the receiver.

(i) Ethos-When the attention of the receiver is focused by the action and voice of the advertisers, it is called the ethos method.

(ii) Pathos-The term "pathos" refers to the emotional nature of pie appeal to the receiver, which puts him in a pleasant mood and bolsters his ego. This creates a sense of closeness to the advertiser who focuses on the important points of the message.

(iii) Logos Method - It refers to the logical approach to the receiver's capacity on generally accepted principle that on reasonable grounds of capacity the receiver can be motivated to pay for the satisfaction of his wants.

(b) Stating Conclusions - As one may want to draw his own conclusions, the message should not burden the receiver with conclusions. If the intelligence of the receiver is attacked by stressing the conclusions of the advertiser in respect of a product it would be very unproductive. The right of drawing conclusions should be that of the receiver. The message should be appropriately and logically worded to help the receiver draw favourable conclusions and purchase the product. The receiver may be encouraged to enquire further about the brand and the product. If the target audience is less educated and less informed as it is in India, conclusions may be suggested by the advertiser through the message.

(c) Two-sided Arguments - While one-side of messages are more effective with people who are less educated and have a positive predisposition toward the product the two-sided argument presents both sides of the argument and leave the receiver to draw his own conclusions from the message. The advertiser puts the arguments in such a way that the receiver or audience like a favourable decision. Comparative advertising often adopts two-sided arguments. These offer more information to the audience and improve is decision making capacities and more effectively persuade the consumer in favour of purchasing the product. To avoid suspicion the leader does not compare products or brands. The follower and challenger may use the technique of comparative advertising to impress upon consumers that their products are superior to the leader's product.

(i) Emotional Appeal - By the adoption of several kinds of emotional appeal persuasiveness can be increased. Emotional appeal makes an explicit appeal to a particular mood : humour, fear, drive or sex. A humorous message attracts attention, facilitates comprehension and increases persuasion. As fear increases people's anxiety the persuasive message may increase fear to create (he attitude to purchase. Drive produces dynamic, energizing motivational effects on behaviour. Sex is entertaining and lures people to purchase the goods advertised. By using models of the fair sex, an emotional appeal is made to buyers to purchase the product.

(ii) Building Resistant Attitudes - Consumer attitudes developed by advertisers should be maintained. If advertising is not regular or periodical, the sleeper effect will "tarnish" the attitude. The altitude may change on account of product life cycle brand switching or competitive appeals. The attitude of consumers may be favourable in the beginning of the product life cycle, but, in the latter pan of this cycle, consumers may switch off from one brand to another. As competitive appeals may destroy the attitude and consumers may shift to any other product advertisers should assume that the attitude does not change. Either by the offer of attractive brands and products or by persuasive efforts consumers should be educated to resist competitive appeals. Advertising should be designed to maintain consumers self-esteem and enhance their ego. The brand should be used as a means of building the ego defense. The producer should lay emphasis on the product as an indicator of status-symbol. Word-of-mouth message becomes very important and effective. In this context diffusion theory may be pressed into service to promote the resistance altitude. Inoculation theory promoted by comprehensive and intensive advertising at certain intervals may persuade consumers to resist brand fall-out.

Explicitly or implicitly the refutation approach is applied to ensure that consumers continue to have a positive attitude to the brand and the product. Competitive appeals are used to persuade them to discard competitive products. To refute the claims of competitor the longer impact of advertising and competitive environment is taken into account.

Refutation advertisements are often found superior to others. They yield more fruitful results than other forms of advertising, particularly at the stage of maturity and competition. The competitive claims made by competitors are refuted logically. The claims of competitors are shown to be immature and unreliable. For example, the claims of some producers that hair oil nourishes the growth of long and black hair is refuted by showing that particular hair oil gives rise to allergic condition. The self-medicator refutes the theory that other medicines are of no use, only his medicine is appropriate and quick.

The refutational message should not be ambiguous or threatening. Some supporting arguments should be used along with it. As people do not pay much attention to such messages, supportive messages have not been useful in sustaining attitudes.

(iii) Changing Negative Attitudes - To face problems arising out of a negative attitude to his product the producer has to change it into a positive one. He has to demolish the arguments against his product through counter-arguments. He should convey the message of critical ability to immunize a person against the competitor's attack. By attacking resistance and negative viewpoints he should change the consumers' negative attitude into a positive one.

The distraction theory has been used to counter negative attitudes. As the commonly-used methods are not useful for the purpose, some new and drastic methods are used to counteract the feelings of the people. To emphasise the attributes of one's own products a film show may be screened at influential centres where the impact of the advertisement is long-lasting. The distracting messages are prepared after a thorough analysis and evaluation. The high commitment group is first approached. Distraction is effective only when the attitude change is more apt to be induced be interference with a counter argument. The interference with the counter-arguing process is called distraction which may take the form of product, audiences, channels and other factors. Before attacking or interfering with counter-arguments the counter arguing process is to be understood and analysed. The supportive and counter arguments are tested by the experimental groups. The test result may show whether the argument would be effective or not in countering the negative attitudes of consumers. The experimental groups put forward arguments for and against the message showing how the interfering message should be framed and presentation made effective. To find the most useful arguments to counter negative attitudes, the study should use mediators counter-arguments, source derogation and support arguments.

4. Perception Factors - Perception is the process between the message and the receiver which enhances or inhibits the message to be communicated. The perceptual barriers are the defeating factors of persuasion. If the perception factors are properly understood and utilised, the efforts of persuasion will be successful. Because of the perception factors involved in them the advertising effects may be different from the intended ones. The message or stimulus may or may not motivate the receiver to purchase the advertised product. Its immediate impact is to draw attention to the product. The audience attracted by it interprets the message or stimulus and accepts or rejects the message. This is called "cognitive awareness".

KINDS OF PERCEPTION FACTORS

(i) Stimulus - It is the message used for advertising. The stimuli used to persuade the audience to accept the product are effective, depending on their size, intensity, message, position and context. The message should be useful lo influence the different types of people. There may be a large number of stimuli to which the receiver's attention is drawn; though he may absorb only a few of them. The focal stimuli, contextual stimuli and residual stimuli are used to motivate people. The size and intensity of a stimulus influence attention and persuasion.

(ii) Attention - Effective stimuli gain the attention of consumers or audiences. Advertisers should know how to draw the attention of consumers to the product. A knowledge of the interests, reading habits, information needs, life styles of consumers enables advertisers to draw their attention. As many people do not bother to read advertisements, the advertisers must choose the right time and frequency to attract a large number of persons to their advertisements. Audience would talk about or interpret the stimuli only when they view the advertisements. Audience may be divided into active searcher, passive searcher and passive attention payer.

(a) The Active Searcher - He is the person who actually seeks information. He may read a newspaper, a magazine etc., or he may view a television programme or listen to the radio to find out which would be an appropriate product that would satisfy his wants. Simple advertisements may be sufficient to draw his attention.

(b) Passive Searchers - These are those who rely on ready-made information to determine their approach to the advertised product. They do not attempt to inquire much about the messages or sources of advertisements.

(c) Passive Attention Payers - Passive attention drawn is the involuntary attention. Though the receiver has no immediate need of the message but his attention is drawn to some specific purposes, such as practical utility, supportive exposure, stimulation and interest.

(iii) Practical Utility - When the receiver's attention is drawn to the practical utility of the stimuli, he may require product information that would assist in better purchase decisions. Recent studies have shown that advertisements have been read or viewed for the practical utility of the product. Consumers are interested in costs, utilities, comparative situations and information exposure of some products. Advertising should contain only that information and message which may be assimilated by the audience. Short but attractive advertisements may have a long-lasting impact on consumers. The long-copy advertisement may be used only for industrial products. While framing the copy message, the needs of the audience are taken into account. The impact of active search, passive search and passive attention is considered before designing the stimuli for consumers. While framing the copy of the stimuli, the appropriateness of the season and time are considered.

(iv) Supportive Exposure - Customer's attention is drawn to the information that supports their opinions and avoids discrepancies as they have a preference for supportive information. The principle of selective exposure has been applied to motivate audiences. The dissonance theory, also known as the consistency theory chosen for this purpose suggests that dissonance or contradictory factors should be reduced as far as possible to ensure a permanent impact on the audience. People develop a cognitive drive to certain behaviour. As the existence of conflicting cognitive elements is discomforting people try to avoid them. Selective exposure is choosen to motivate people, who develop interest and read advertisements which constantly appear in a newspaper or on the TV screen, although the product and the advertisement may not be very useful to them. They try to select advertisements of the products useful to them. They are motivated to purchase them.

When involuntary exposure to non-supportive information is made selective exposure develops. The advertiser should be ready to counter response to any negative information given lo his customers. The loyalists should be given adequate information so that despite criticism, they may remain with the brand.

(v) Stimulation - Advertisers persuade customers by novelty, unexpectedness, change and other motives. The audience is motivated by unusual and different messages as it gets bored with routine and repetitive advertising. People are curious about surroundings. The exposures to a snowy hill, dense forest etc., make people attentive to advertisements which have their backgrounds, new techniques, environments and methods are preferred by them and they listen to such advertisements. The content should have variety in the form of novelty and unexpectedness, which have pleasant and stimulating effects. Variety and novelty stimulate people toward the products. The quality and extent of stimulation depend upon the volume of the sales and the price of a product. A heavy purchaser needs more information about the product.

(vi) Interest - When the message is interesting the audience pays attention to it. Uninteresting information and message may not be read by them hence, interest and self-reflection are used for selection purposes. To arouse interest among the people, age-group, sex similarity, economic and homogeneous factors are taken into account. The most effective approach for gaining attention is to run an advertisement for the group of persons for whom the produce is made. Too much interesting content may destroy the very purpose of advertising because people get lost in the interest without information *per se* being influenced by it.

(vii) Interpretation - The target group interprets the message according to its intelligence, skill, determination and practical or cautious perception. Although the stimuli are partially presented the group can understand the message whose formation is differently perceived by a cold person and a warm person. The brand of a particular product should be considered as a whole. Alteration of a single component may affect the total quality of the product. The perception of a particular brand *vis-a-vis* other brands may change radically if one dimension is affected. The stimuli properly added to the existing advertisement may increase the perception of quality, but it should not be considered in isolation from the product. Stimuli should be a part of the product's attributes. If they are different from the attributes of products they will not make long-lasting impact on the target group.

Interpretation depends on stimuli product, and the perception of the buyer. If any one is missing, the receiver may supply that according to his perception. Stimulating efforts enhance the learning level of customers. Ambiguity used to stimulate sufficient interest to sustain cognitive activity can be exercised to complete the sentence, brand name and picture. The assimilation-contrast principle is used to stimulate the buyer. Assimilation-refers to the perception of a thing rather than its worth. Contrast is the apparent rather than the real difference between two products. Needs, values, preferences, group pressure, cognitive needs, cognitive style, etc., are the important factors influencing the interpretation of the stimuli.

5. Cognitive Consistency - The attitude can be changed through the process of cognitive consistency, *i.e.*, by resolving conflict. Consumers resolve conflicts through consistency, harmony and balance.

(i) Consistency Theory - These have been developed about physical objects, physiological response, social and psychological response.

(ii) Balance Theory - It describes positive and negative elements. Balanced structures create no force or tension for cognitive, affective or behavioural change. Unbalanced structures are unstable and set up a force leading to a balanced state. Balance theory believes in tension-reduction find direction of the relationship between consumers and the product.

(iii) Congruity Theory - Also used to ensure cognitive consistency, congruity theory assists in the development of a relationship between consumers and products and the enhancement of sales. Cognition of a product or a brand is presumed by a particular advertisement. Strongly held cognition tends to change less. If there is no positive or negative attitude to the product, that product attitudes shift more than attitude changes towards the endorser.

(iv) The Dissonance Theory - It focuses attention on actual product choice, It uses behaviour as a source of attitude change. It postulates that consumers go through a cognitive reappraisal process known as rationalising the decision. The reappraisal-process cognition supports choice in the positive direction. Positive attitudes develop for the chosen alternative product. Negative attitudes are developed to the non-chosen alternative. The dissonance theory may promote particular values, life-styles and a wide variety of related attitudes. It develops a relationship between the consumer and the source (endorser), the consumer and the message, the source and the message, the source and the product and the product and the message.

(v) Low Involvement Theory - It is based on the belief that advertisements have not been accepted by the audience in the way they were as perceived by the advertiser. Television viewers do not bother much about the commercials that flash on the TV screen as they observe them routinely. Some experts believe that the attention, interest and emotion cannot be creased by advertisers. The print media have been more effective in so far as the involvement of the target group is concerned because people generally read advertised matter. The low-involvement impact can be changed by extensive advertising causing a How of information from short-term to long-term memory system. The brand's conception should be changed to make the product interesting and attractive. Attitude change may be possible by behaviour when consumers have first-hand experience of the brand and product advertised.

For many years, effectiveness was measured in terms of sales results - the premise being that the purpose of advertising is to generate sales. The problem with this view is that sales can result from many other activities (personal selling, increased efforts by distributors, increased prosperity and so forth, so that it is difficult to assess the importance of advertising in the outcomes. A more recent view has been that the role of advertising is to communicate - to change awareness and attitudes (Colley, 1961). This view crystallised as the DAGMAR model (Defining Advertising Goals, Measuring Advertising Results) (Colley, 1961). DAGMAR implies that concrete and measurable communication objectives should be set for advertising, rather than sales turnover goals. Thus, the outcomes that are measured are usually things like awareness, brand recognition, recall of content, and so forth.

DAGMAR has been criticised on the grounds that it tends to lead planners to find out what can be measured easily, then set that as a goal (Broadbent, 1989). The simple objectives which can be measured do not tell the whole story of major-brand success. Advertising does other things which are hard to measure, such as encouraging brand loyalty or increasing word-of-mouth communication between consumers themselves.

Advertising effectiveness can be assessed by market research, by returned coupons, and (sometimes) by increased sales. The last method is somewhat risky, however, since there may be many other factors which could have increased the sales of the product. Table 10.5 shows some common techniques for evaluating advertising effectiveness.

TABLE 10.5

Advertising effectiveness

Technique	*Description and explanation*
Pre-tests	These are evaluations of the advertising before it is released. Pre-tests are commonly carried out using focus groups - research shows that this is the commonest method used by advertisers (Eagle, Hyde and Kitchen, 1998).
Coupon returns, or enquiries	The advertiser courts up the number of enquiries received during each phase of an advertising campaign. This allows the marketing management to judge which media are working best, provided the coupons have an identifying code on them
Post-campaign tests (post-tests)	The particular testing method used will depend largely on the objectives of the campaign. Communications objectives (product awareness, attitude change brand awareness) might be determined through surveys; sales objectives might be measured according to changes in sales which can be attributed to the campaign. This is difficult to do because of other factors (changes in economic conditions, for example) which might distort the findings.
Recognition tests and recall tests	In recognition tests, consumers are shown the advertisement and asked if they recognise it. They are then asked how much of it they actually recall. In an unaided recall test, the consumer is asked which adverts he or she remembers seeing recently; in an aided recall test, the consumer is shown a group of ads (without being told which one the researcher is interested in) and is asked which ones he or she has seen recently.

Any testing must be valid (must measure what it says it measures) and reliable (free of random error). A reliable test would provide consistent results every time it is used, and a valid test would enable the marketer to predict outcomes reasonably accurately. In order to ensure that this is the case, a set of principles called PACT (Positioning Advertising Copy Testing) have been established (Marketing News, 1982). A good advertising testing system should:

1. provide measurements that are relevant to the objectives of the advertising;
2. require agreement about how the results will be used in advance of each specific test;
3. provide multiple measurements because single measurements are generally inadequate to assess the advert's performance;
4. be based on a model of human response to communication - the reception of a stimulus, the comprehension of the stimulus, and the response to the stimulus;
5. allow for consideration of whether the advertising stimulus should be exposed more than once;
6. recognise that the more finished a piece of copy is the more soundly it can be evaluated. It should also require as a minimum that alternative executions be tested to the same degree of finish;
7. provide controls to avoid the biasing effects of the exposure content;
8. take into account basic considerations of sample definition; empirically demonstrate reliability and validity.

Planning the Campaign

Whether this stage comes before or after budget-setting will depend on whether the marketer is adopting an objective and task policy or not. In most cases, though, planning the campaign in detail will come after the budget is known and agreed upon; few companies give the marketing department a blank cheque for promotional spending. Campaigns can be carried out to achieve many objectives: a new product launch is often an objective, but in most cases the products will be in the maturity phase of the product lifecycle.

Image building campaigns are designed to convey a particular status for the product., and to emphasise ways in which it will complement the user's lifestyle. For example, Volvo promote the reliability and engineering of the car rather than its appearance, thus appealing to motorists who prefer a solid, reliable vehicle. Marlboro cigarettes promote a masculine, outdoor image.

Product differentiation campaigns aim to show how the product is better than the competitors' products by emphasising its differences. In most cases, this will take the form of the unique selling proposition or USP for short. The USP is the one feature of the product that most stands out as different from the competition, and is usually a feature which conveys unique benefits to the consumer. Mature products often only differ very slightly from each other in terms of performance, so a USP can sometimes be identified in terms of the packaging or distribution, and is very commonly generated by a prestigious brand. Of course, the USP will only be effective if it means something to the consumer - otherwise it will not affect the buying decision.

Positioning strategies are concerned with the way consumers perceive the product, compared with their perceptions of the competition. For example, a retailer may claim 'lower prices than other shops', or a restaurant may want to appear more upmarket than its rivals. Avis car hire said 'We're number two, so we try harder', thus positioning their product as number two in size (behind Hertz), but emphasising the positive aspects of this.

Direct response campaigns seek an immediate response from the consumer in terms of a purchase, a request for a brochure, or a visit to the shop. For example, a retailer might run a newspaper campaign which includes a money-off coupon. The aim of the campaign is to encourage consumers to visit the shop to redeem the coupon, and the retailer can easily judge the effectiveness of the campaign by the number of coupons redeemed.

Putting it all together

To make the best use of the promotional effort it is worth spending time planning how it will all fit together. The recipe will need to be adapted according to what the product is and how the company wants to promote it. The elements marketers need to consider are:

- size of budget;
- size of individual order value;
- number of potential buyers;
- geodemographical spread of potential buyers;
- category of product (convenience, unsought,, shopping, etc.);
- what it is the firm is trying to achieve.

It is impossible to achieve everything all at once, so marketers often plan the campaign as an integrated package. For example, Table 10.6 shows a product launch strategy designed to maximise penetration of a new food product.

TABLE 10.6

Example of a Promotional Calendar

Month	*Activity*
May	Press release to the trade press and retailers.
June	Sales campaign to persuade retailers to stock the product. The aim is to get 50 per cent of retailers stocking the product, so the salesforce tell them a big advertising spend is forthcoming. Begin a teaser campaign.
July/August	Denouncement of teaser campaign. Promotion staff appear in major retail outlets offering free samples. Press releases to cookery writers, possibly reports on daytime TV if product is newsworthy enough.
September/October	Once 50 per cent retailer penetration has occurred, start the TV campaign. Brief the advertising agency to obtain maximum brand awareness.
January/February	Begin a new campaign to inform consumers about the brand. Possibly use money-off sales promotion, linked promotions, etc. Review progress so far using market research. Possibly issue some press releases, if the product is innovative enough, to the business/cookery press.

Carrying out this kind of planning needs the co-operation of all the members marketing team. It is no use having the PR people doing one thing, and the salesforce doing something else that negates the PR efforts. If the campaign is to be effective it is important that all the team members are involved in the discussions so that unrealistic demands are not made of them.

PERSONAL INFLUENCE IN COMMUNICATION

Advertising succeeds by the diffusion and personal influence. Personal influence through the word-of-mouth communication achieves the objectives of advertising. While segmentation strategies stimulate the behaviour and altitudes of buyers, personal influence plays an important role in the decision-making process of consumers adopted. Under personal influence come the strategy, tactics and other aspects of advertising. Advertisers should know how far personal influence promotes the purchase and exchange situation. They should know the extent to which advertisements influence consumers. While some consumers can be persuaded more easily by advertisements, there are others who are susceptible to personal influence by social interactions, the opinions of friends, neighbours and relatives. The social influences operating in consonance with the product, service and other factors are also known as external or internal personal influences.

KINDS OF PERSONAL INFLUENCES

1. External or Explicit Personal Influence - It involves social interaction of two or more persons such as friends, relatives and neighbours, whose recommendations and suggestions influence purchase of some items. Buyers of industrial products seek the advice of industrial associates. This personal influence known as word-of-mouth advertising is different from mass communication. If has been very effective in motivating people to purchase goods and services.

2. Internal Personal Influence - It refers to the consumer's own mental process taking the form of a social process, when one consumer influences others by his choice of a product. One may purchase the product as a gift for other people. He may purchase an item as a status symbol i.e., to be the first with the latest product. No explicit social interaction takes place in internal or implicit personal influence. There is no specific conversation between a consumer and his acquaintances.

CONSTITUENTS OF PERSONAL INFLUENCE

Personal influence includes the decision-making unit, information acquisition and processing innovation motivational characteristics, reference groups and social classes.

I. Decision-Making Unit (DMU) - It may be an individual or group which takes a purchase decision. Many households take purchase decisions individually and do not seek the advice of any other person. They may consult their family-members-wife, children or parents known as an individual decision-making unit. On the other hand, a purchase decision may be taken by involving two or more external persons, including the family-members. When two or more families, two or more industrial associates, are involved, the decision-making unit is known as a group decision-making unit.

KINDS OF DMU

The decision-making unit may be of two types: individual decision-making unit and group decision-making unit, respectively known as "internal decision-making units" and "external decision making units." The target in the first case is an individual, in the second case it is a group. The advertiser should evaluate their role in advertising.

1. Individual DMU - In it the individual or family may be involved in the purchase-decision. Many individuals purchase an item for self-consumption while others may purchase the item for a family member or as a gift for others. Their attitudes will not be the same. The self-purchasers are generally known as consumers.

The non-self purchasers are known as customers. Consumers believe that the products to be purchased should be economical and durable, while customers purchase attractive and fashionable items.

(i) Group DMU - There are external decision making units influenced by external person or group. Advertisements should be addressed lo the real purchaser. The difference between consumers and customers must be taken into account while designing an advertisement. The success of advertising depends on how the decision-making units are approached, informed and persuaded.

2. Information Acquisition and Processing - Knowing how consumers acquire the information and process it the advertisers should assess the nature of information acquisition and its processing by the consumer or the decision-making units. The relationship between the information process and the product is also evaluated in order to make advertisements more effective. The face-to-face communication or word-of-mouth advertising plays a significant role in promoting the sale of the product. In involves a large number of consumers, heavy investment and risky decisions. Cosmetics, baby foods and other daily consumption products have the maximum number of consumers and personal advertisements would enhance their sales. Consumers seek the advice of family members, friends, neighbours, relations etc., in cases where financial investment is substantial. Individual advertisements by sales persons can positively influence the market share. Expert advertisers and producers employ salesmen to influence the decision-making units particularly the individual target groups.

Large investment and long-term commitments involving dissonance and conflict place consumers in a great deal of emotional tension and strain before and sometimes after the purchase of articles. A method of reducing this tension is to interact with friends and associates. In this context, external personal influence is more effective than internal personal influence. By providing a memory structure the advertiser can also influence personal decisions. To interact with other information and help increase the sale of the product, the brand and market share the stored information is transferred from long-to short-term memory. Personal influence is the distinguishing characteristic in a situation. The situation the purchase of a birthday cake which motivates people to have a particular brand of cake, should be used judiciously as it may also reduce the sale of the products. Therefore, the product should not be locked up in a particular situations' use. As the family decision has been a very useful component of the internal personal influence the family and the behaviour of its members should be taken into account while framing personal advertisements.

3. Innovation - New or innovated products are advertised by demonstrating their characteristics, relative, advantage, compatibility, complexity, communicability and divisibility to influence customers through advertisements.

The risk and habit factors inhibit the success of new products, because the products may not be accepted by consumers, who are habituated to the existing products. New products may fail because of entrenched social values and personal acceptance. Innovation succeeds when the advantages of new products are persuasively communicated to consumers and extensive advertising is used to make the product popular.

4. Motivational Characteristics - Before launching upon its extensive advertising advertisers have to assess the usefulness of motivations and attributes of a product. The advertisement campaign should provide some satisfaction to the audience. Its language and picture should concentrate on the needs and goals of the products. It must ensure product involvement, self-involvement, message-involvement and other persons involvement.

(i) **Product involvement -** It refers to the product to the pleasure and satisfaction to be derived from it and the excitement of having it.

(ii) **Self involvement -** It confirms the behaviour of producers suggests mission, status and goals of the company and asserts the superiority of the product.

(iii) **Message involvement -** It includes the message, motivational approach, word-of mouth communication and the focus of conversation.

(iv) **Other person's involvement -** It reflects the need and intent to help other people share their joy, care for friends and neighbours.

BASIC FACTORS

The basic factors in motivational characteristics are the sponsor's experience and interest of the audience. The sponsor should convince the audience about the value of the product, the credibility of sound, the connoisseur's. The goodwill of sponsor make a profound impact on consumers interest, the interest of the audience is aroused by the use of the needs-hierarchy. The product mainly satisfies a particular need; that fact should be emphasised in an interesting manner. As the car and the refrigerator satisfy the ego in India, the message of self-esteem arising out of owning a car will draw the attention of potential buyers.

1. Reference Groups - The reference group includes those individuals who have developed comparison points and who are aspired-person and perspective person. They may belong to a social class, an ethnic group, a subculture and outstanding achievements. If other people recognise it as a symbol of status and recognition, the product would be very desirable. If it is commonly used, it would not be a striking product. The person using a conspicuous product is known as a reference group person. His action is used as the frame of reference.

If the individual reference group uses the product, says something and accepts its merits, the people or consumers would be attracted to it. They would be influenced by its message, action and consumption. New products are popularised by the adoption of the techniques of the reference group. Consumption groups are mobilised to deliver their message on social and functional needs.

2. Social Class - If the advertiser uses the social class for personal influence, he can succeed in his advertising campaign. In India, many products are designated as belonging to a particular social and economic level. The car or a telephone are for the upper class. These products are used generally by professionals. Dresses have been symbols of teachers and artists. Refrigerators and coolers are used by office-assistants and officers. A good bag and water bottle are symbols for school-going children. Although the products are not exclusively earmarked for them, they are generally used by some social class.

Advertisements can be tested on two dimensions: those related to the advertisement itself, and those related to its contents. Since these two issues are sometimes difficult for the consumer to separate, there is no real certainty as to which is actually being tested.

Pre-testing and Post-testing

Pre-testing the advertisement to assess whether it is likely to be effective has a mixed history. There has been considerable debate as to whether it is really possible to predict whether an advert will work or not, and there is of course no certainty about this, even when sophisticated copy-testing methods are used. Testing almost certainly reduces the risk of producing an ineffective advert, and it is better to find this out before expensive space is booked in the media, and possibly before an inappropriate message is sent out.

Post-testing is concerned with researching the effectiveness of the advert after it has appeared. Finding out whether the advertising has been effective in achieving the objectives laid down is much easier if clear objectives were set in the first place and if the advertising agency was given a clear brief.

Laboratory Techniques

Testing can be carried out in the field or in the laboratory, and most pre-tests are carried out in laboratory conditions. Table 10.7 shows some of the available techniques.

TABLE 10.7
Laboratory Techniques for Testing Advertising Effectiveness

Technique	*Explanation*
Consumer juries	Groups of consumers are asked to judge whether they think the advertisement will work. This has the advantage that consumers (presumably) know what affects them most. The drawback is that they will sometimes 'play expert' and this will distort their responses.
Focus groups	A moderator conducts a loosely-structured interview with six to twelve respondents simultaneously. The respondents tend to discuss issues amongst themselves, so that a range of ideas is elicited. This data is qualitative (it is not usually possible or desirable to express it numerically), but it does raise issues effectively.
Portfolio tests	Respondents are shown test adverts (those the researcher wants to test) and control adverts (adverts whose effectiveness is already known) and asked to score them. The researcher can then compare the scores of the test adverts with the control adverts and see whether the test adverts will be as effective.
Readability tests	The copy is analysed for readability without consumer interviewing. The foremost method is the Flesch formula (Flesch, 1974). Readability is assessed by determining the average number of syllables per hundred words, the length of sentences, the human interest content, and the familiarity of words. Results can be compared with predetermined norms for the target audience.
Physiological measures	Eye cameras can be used to record the route an individual's eye takes when seeing an advert. This can be unreliable: lingering on one part of the advert might denote interest, but it might denote incomprehension. Galvanic skin "response and pupil dilation response measure different aspects of interest; pupils dilate and the electrical resistance of the skin decreases when an object of interest appears.

Laboratory measures at first appear scientific and therefore objective; unfortunately this is often not the case. While the researcher might be able to maintain objectivity, it is unlikely that the subject (respondent) will and the knowledge of the artificiality of the situation is likely to cloud the respondent's judgement. Furthermore, the results of (for example) a galvanic skin response or pupil dilation response still need to be interpreted. Interest or excitement at seeing an advertisement does not necessarily stem from the communication itself, and almost certainly does not translate into the achievement of the communications objectives.

Field techniques

Typical field techniques include street surveys and

self-completion questionnaires. Each has the advantage of being quick, relatively cheap, and relatively easy to interpret.

The main problems with these techniques are as follows:

- Interviewer bias. The interviewer (unwittingly or otherwise) leads the respondent to answer in a particular way.
- Design bias. The way the questions are worded elicits a particular response from the respondent.
- Sample bias. The wrong people are asked for their opinion, or an otherwise unrepresentative sample is taken.

These sources of bias are remarkably easy to generate. For example, a supposedly 'random' sample of people might be sought by standing in a shopping mall on a Saturday morning and stopping everybody who comes past. This will not actually be a random sample; some people will walk past without stopping, some people never shop in that particular mall, some people never shop on a Saturday morning. In each case, those people might have given very different responses to a questionnaire on advertising.

Equally, a question such as 'Have you seen this advertisement?' will provoke a 'yes' response from many people who have not actually seen the advert. This is because they do not want to appear stupid, or possibly because they genuinely believe that they have seen it.

Field surveys can certainly be very helpful, and they are still widely used. However, it is important to take care over the design and administration of the techniques.

Tactical considerations

The tactical possibilities in a marketing campaign are huge in number. Most of the tactics of marketing involve creativity on the part of practitioners, so it is virtually impossible to lay down any hard and fast rules about approaching different marketing problems. However, the list below might provide useful guidelines.

- Marketers should always try to do something that the competition hasn't thought of yet.
- It is important to consult everybody who is involved in the day-to-day application of the plans. Salespeople in particular do not like to be told what to do by somebody back at Head Office.
- Most marketing activities do not produce instant results, but results should be monitored anyway.
- The messages given to the consumers, the middlemen, the suppliers, and all the other publics should be consistent.
- Competitors are likely to make some kind of response, so marketers should try to anticipate what the response might be when formulating plans.

The SOSTT + 4Ms structure for planning gives a useful checklist for ensuring that the elements of strategy and tactics are brought together effectively. Table 10.8 shows how the structure works.

TABLE10. 8
SOSTT + 4 Ms

Element	*Description*
Situation	Current position of the firm in terms of its resources, product range, and markets.
Objectives	What the company hopes to achieve in both the long term and the short term.
Strategy	Decisions about the correctness of the objectives and their overall fit.
Tactics	How the strategic objectives will be achieved.
Targets	Formalised objectives, target markets and segments of markets. Decisions about the appropriateness of these markets in the light of the firm's strategic objectives.
Men	Both genders, of course! Decisions about human resources and having the right people to do the job.
Money	Correct budgeting and allocation of financial resources where they will do the most to achieve the overall objectives.
Minutes	Time-scales, deadlines, and overall planning to ensure that everything happens at the right time.
Measurement	Monitoring and evaluation of activities to ensure that they remain on course and work as they should.

Cost effectiveness will always be an issue in promotional campaigns, and it is for this reason that there has been a growth in direct marketing worldwide. The accurate targeting of market segments made possible by computer technology has enabled marketers to refine the approach, and hence increase the response rate. Marketers now talk in terms of response rates from promotions, not in terms of contact numbers.

RESEARCHING THE EFFECTIVENESS OF COMMUNICATIONS

Having developed and implemented the strategic and tactical plans, the next stage is to gather feedback as to the effectiveness of the communication. Much of the emphasis on effectiveness tests centres around advertising, since it is a high-profile activity and often a very expensive one. Four elements appear to be important in the effectiveness of advertising: awareness, liking, interest and enjoyment. There is a high correlation between brand loyalty and brand awareness (Stapel, 1990); likeability appears to be the single best predictor of sales effectiveness, since likeability scales predict 97 per cent of sales successes (Biel, 1989); interest clearly relates to likeability (Stapel, 1991); and enjoyment appears to be a good indicator in advertising pre-tests (Brown, 1991).

DIFFUSION IN ADVERTISEMENT

Diffusion is the process of spreading. Advertising is diffusive if the information is spread through the population. All advertising adopts diffusion through some form of communication such as through a channel; a two-step flow, the flow through an opinion leader, the adoption process and strategy.

MEANS OF DIFFUSION

1. Channel - The channel is an important medium of spreading information. It may be a vertical channel, a horizontal channel, a formal channel, an informal channel, a personal channel or an interpersonal channel.

Kinds of Channel

(i) Vertical Channel - It exists if there is a meaningful difference in interests, in demographic factors, social class and economic class. The emulation of an identification with the consumption behaviour among social classes is a kind of vertical channel. The relationships among producers, wholesalers retailers and consumers are other examples of the vertical channel,

(ii) The Horizontal Channel- It exists among the members of a group, who exchange ideas and information about a product. Members of a social class exchange their ideas about the product. Members of an economic class may spread innovative ideas. While the exchange of information between members of two and more groups is through a vertical channel the exchange of information among the members within the group is through a horizontal channel. Advertisers adopt these channels for diffusion purposes. Producers ask wholesalers who give information to retailers, the retailers inform consumers about the attributes of a product. If a higher social class wears a particular dress, the information of the dress is immediately diffused to a lower social class.

(iii) The Formal Channel- It is within the control of the sponsor or the sender of information. Advertisers can select the target group for purposes of diffusing information on television. Commercials for baby foods are addressed to mothers as they are the potential purchasers of baby foods. This kind of information addressed to customers is through a formal channel also known as mass-media or direct exposure channel. The informal channel is not within the control if advertisers, if it is not intentionally established.

(iv) Informal Channel- Unlike the formal channel, where the advertiser can prepare the message, picture, etc., for the audience according to his needs by placing ii in (he print media and/or electronic media, the advertiser has no control over the message disseminated through advertisements or by sales persons who choose their own words and designs.

(v) Personal Channel- It is within the control of the advertiser. He can directly ask the channel to adopt a particular set of information that may be disseminated through it.

(vi) Interpersonal Channel- In interpersonal communication the channel is not within the direct control of the advertiser. This is word-of-mouth information communicated by representatives. Channel information is designed to suit the needs of a particular category. A.H. Maslow's need hierarchy is used to frame and facilitate the flow of information. Diffusion theories refer to emulation and imitation, trickle-down information, life styles, etc. Information can flow upward or downward in a vertical channel. When preparing the diffusion of information the product, the nature of the members of a class, culture, religion, etc., are considered. Compliance or acceptance, identification, internalisation and other psycho-social processes are used to diffuse information.

2. Two-Step Flow- This process involves one person between the sender and receiver who is very important and well-acquainted with the diffusion process. He receives the advertising information from the sender or sponsor and inseminates it to the ultimate consumer. He accelerates the spread of information among the different segments of consumers. Receiving the advertising information before any other person does, he explains it to the prospects who are influenced by his meaningful communication with them.

3. Opinion Leader- Opinion leaders are representatives of society. Their actions and purchasing habits are followed by the other members of society. They may be leaders in the areas of marketing fashion, films or any other area of public life. They may be positive or negative opinion leaders. Advertisers try to influence customers through them by asking leaders to be a party to advertisements and diffuse information through helpers, business associates or middlemen. These opinion leaders demonstrate before the public the attributes of products. Being influential, they help diffuse information. They are used in mass media and personal media for this purpose.

4. Adoption Process

(i) Meaning- It is the product life cycle used to diffuse advertising information through innovators, opinion leaders, early majority, late majority and laggards. The diffusion process for each adoption is adopted differently.

(ii) Stages- Awareness, interest, trial and adoption are the five stages in the adoption process. While mass media have been very useful for creating awareness and interest personal media or word-of-mouth advertisements have been useful for evaluation, trial and adoption. Innovators and opinion leaders have been used for diffusion purposes.

(iii) Innovators- Having a more favourable attitude towards trying out new things innovators are known as experimenters. They are heavy purchasers of new products. They give serious attention to advertisements and take prompt decisions. They are frequently asked about their opinion of new products. The word-of-mouth advertising has been very effective in influencing innovators. In some areas, and for the purchase of products, personal influence has been very effective. For example, wine and liquor are strongly recommended by friends. Mass communication is very effective in other areas and in respect of other products.

(iv) The Late Adopters- These have different views from those of early adopters.

(v) High- risk Perceivers- They purchase a product very late.

(vi) Laggards- They have a lower income and brand loyalty. Therefore, the product, the adoption-process and the perception attitude should be considered while diffusing advertising information.

5. Strategy- The advertisers strategy to single out the crucial innovator and opinion leader has achieved success in the field of new products, new brands and new organisations. Age, income, education, social class, etc., are effective strategic categories diffusing information. The advertiser should simulate, stimulate and monitor personal influence and the diffusion process.

(i) Simulation- Simulation demonstrates to the people how and why to use these products. A person can use the simulation theory to function as a personal influence.

(ii) Stimulation- The information used for motivation to purchase a product is stimulation.

(iii) Monitoring- The monitoring strategy identifies the attributes of a product and the overall attitude of consumers to the producer. Direct mail has been used to give a personal touch to contacts with prospective consumers.

(iv) Promotion- Promotional techniques should by properly moulded to diffuse information. The components of communication within the uncontrollable premises should be mobilised for a proportional use of the marketing mix to achieve the objectives of advertising.

THE NEW COMMUNICATIONS ENVIRONMENT

Communications are being revolutionised by computer-based and cell-based electronic systems. Computer-based communications include database systems and web sites.

Databases can be merged to generate an increasingly accurate profile of the consumers on them. This in turn leads to much more accurate targeting of mailings, so that an individual consumer is able to receive a mailing which is unique. At its simplest level, the mailing can be personalised, putting the individual's name in the appropriate places, but at the more complex and subtle level marketers are able to identify which individuals are likely to be in the market for a given product at a given time, and target them exclusively (Evans, 1994).

Internet marketing uses web sites and e-mail to communicate with existing and prospective customers. The number of Internet users has doubled every year since its inception. With 57 million users worldwide, predicted to reach 1000 million by the year 2002, the potential for reaching high-income, educated consumers is enormous. By that time, on-line shopping, banking and entertainment will be available to 20 per cent of the world's population, generating 5I billion (US) of advertising revenues, according to analysts Morgan Stanley (Johnson, 1997).

Some commentators, however, are taking the view that the growth in Internet advertising will be smaller in some markets than in others. For example, US and Australian web users routinely leave the graphics switched on when surfing the Net because local calls are free in the US and are charged at a flat rate in Australia, unlike most of Europe where calls are charged according to the time spent. For this reason, the value of a web site is lower for European advertisers than it would be for their

US or Australian counterparts, and consequently the price may not represent value for money. Further complications arise because web sites charge for an 'impression' even if the surfer just passes through; and web ads are not passed on to friends, in the way that magazines are (Wright, 1997).

On the other hand, providers such as Double Click have networks of advertising sites using 'cookies' (files stored on a user's machine) which build a profile of consumers for segmentation purposes. This is something that few other advertising media can match, and provides a real benefit for some Internet advertisers.

INTEGRATION OF MARKETING COMMUNICATIONS

There is increasing interest in integration of marketing communications, and this is being extended to include all corporate communications (Nowak and Phelps 1994). The need for integration is because of the following factors (Borremans, 1998):

Changes in the consumer market:

- the information overload caused by the ever-increasing number of commercial messages;
- advertising in the mass media becoming increasingly irritating;
- media fragmentation;
- increasing numbers of 'me too' products, where differences between brands are minor;
- complexity and change in FMCG markets, with increased distances between suppliers and consumers making it harder for public to have an image of suppliers;
- increasing media attention on the social behaviour of companies, putting goodwill at a premium.

Changes in the supplier market:

- multiple acquisitions and changes in structure in and around corporations;
- interest of management in short-term results;
- increased recognition of the strategic importance of communication;
- increased interest in good internal communications with employees.

Integration offers the possibility of reducing the ambiguity of messages emanating from the firm, and also of reducing costs by reducing duplication of effort. These are barriers to integration (Petrison and Wang, 1996), and the factors below tend to mean that integration would actually detract from the effectiveness of communications.

- Database marketing allows customers to be targeted with individually tailored communications.
- Niche marketing and micromarketing mean that suppliers can communicate with very small and specific audiences, using different messages for each group.
- Specific methods and working practices used for different communication tools affect the message each transmits.
- Corporate diversification.
- Different international (and even national) cultures mean that a single message comprehensible to all is difficult to achieve.
- Existing structures within organisations mean that different departments may not be able (or willing) to 'sing the same song'. For example, salespeople may not agree with the public relations department's ideas on what customers should be told.
- Personal resistance to change, managers' fear of losing responsibilities and budgets. This is particularly true of firms with the brand manager system of management.

In practice, promotional mix elements often operate independently (Duncan and Caywood, 1996), with specialist agencies for PR, advertising, exhibitions, corporate identity, branding etc., all working in isolation. There are nine types or levels of integration, as shown in Table 10.9. Note that these do not necessarily constitute a process or represent stages of development - indeed, there may be considerable overlap between the types.

Part of the reason for separating the functions is historical. Traditionally, marketing communications were divided into above the line and below the line. Above the line means advertising; below the line means everything else. This came about because of the way advertising agencies are paid. Essentially, agencies are paid commission by the media they place adverts in (usually the rate is 15 per cent of the billing), and/ or by fees paid by the client. Traditionally, any paid for advertising attracted commission (hence above the line) and any other activities such as PR or sales promotion was paid for by fees (hence below the line). As time has gone by, these distinctions have become more blurred, especially with the advent of advertorials (advertisements which look like editorial) which are usually written by journalists, and with ambient

TABLE 10.9
Levels of Integration

Level of integration	*Explanation*
Awareness stage	Those responsible for communications realise that a fragmented approach is not the optimum one.
Planning integration	The co-ordination of activities. There are two broad approaches : functional integration, which co-ordinates separate tools to create a single message where appropriate, and instrumental integration, which combines tools in such a way that they reinforce one another (Bruhn, 1995).
Integration of content	Ensuring that there are no contradictions in the basic brand or corporate messages. At a higher level, integrating the themes of communication to make the basic messages the same.
Formal integration	Using the same logo, corporate colours, graphic approach and house style for all communications.
Integration between planning periods	Basic content remains the same from one campaign to the next. Either basic content remains the same, or the same executional approach is used in different projects.
Intra-organisation Integration	Integration of the activities of everyone involved in communication functions (which could mean everybody who works in the organisation).
Intra-organisation Integration	Integration of all the outside agencies involved in the firm's communications activities.
Geographical integration	Integration of campaigns in different countries. This is strongest in large multinationals operating globally, e.g., the Coca-Cola Corporation a (Hartley and Pickton, 1997).
Integration of publics	All communications targeted to one segment of the market are integrated (horizontal integration) or all communications targeted as different segments are attuned (vertical integration).

advertising and other new media which do not attract commission.

Overall, the advantages of integrating communications almost certainly overcome the drawbacks, since the cost savings and the reduction of ambiguity are clearly important objectives for most marketers. There is, however the danger of losing the capacity to tailor messages for individuals (as happens in personal selling) or for niches in the market, and there are certainly some major creative problems attached to integrating communications on a global scale.

International Marketing Communications

Single communications strategies rarely work for firms in the global arena. In fact, the few exceptions are so notable that they are used as examples time and again -Marlboro cigarettes, Coca-Cola, Levi jeans - and nearly all are American. It is possible that the overwhelming influence of Hollywood in exporting American culture worldwide means that people in most countries are able to understand American cultural references (the Marlboro cowboy, for example) in a way that would not work for, say, the Brazilian gaucho or the Japanese samurai.

There is some common ground between countries, and there are identifiable international markets. The market for women's magazines has expanded in Europe as a result of deregulation, and magazines such as Hello! (originally Hola! in its native Spain) have managed to cross over successfully. This means that some print advertising within those magazines should also be able to make the transition.

The main reason for standardising communications is cost. It is clearly much cheaper to produce one advert and repeat it across borders than it is to produce separate adverts for each country. However, the savings are most apparent in producing TV adverts, where the costs of production can easily approach the costs of airtime. This is not the case with press advertising, so the thrust to internationalise is less apparent.

There are five basic strategies for international communications, as shown in Table 10.10 (Keegan, 1984).

TABLE 10.10

Basic international strategies

Strategy	*Explanation*
Same product, same communication	Can be used where the need for the product and its use are the same as in its home market.
Same product, different communication	Can be used where the need for the product differs in some way, but the basic method of use is the same, or when the cultural references differ. For example, soy sauce is considered an exotic product in Western Europe, but is a regular purchase item in oriental countries.
Different products, same communication	Sometimes the product formula has to change to meet local conditions, but the communication can remain the same. For example, the formulation of chocolate is different for hot countries due to the low melting-point of cocoa butter, but this need not affect the advertising.
Different product, different communication	Applies to markets with different needs and different product use, for example greetings cards, or electrical appliances.

Most successful international campaigns are run on TV, which enables the advertiser to minimise or even omit words altogether. Standardising press communications is difficult due to language differences. Some difficulties in this connection are more subtle - Arabic reading from right to left, for example.

The following tips for translating advertising copy have been identified (Majaro, 1982):

1. Avoid idioms, jargon or buzz-words.
2. Leave space to expand foreign language text (Latin languages take 20 per cent more space than English, and Arabic may need up to 50 per cent more space).
3. Check local legal requirements and codes of conduct.
4. Ensure that the translators speak the everyday

language of the country in question. The Spanish spoken in Spain and Latin America differ, as does UK English and American English, or French French and Belgian French. For obvious reasons, people who are not native speakers of the language should never be used.

5. Brief the translators thoroughly so that they get a feel for the product, its benefits, the customer and competition. Do not just hand over the copy and expect it to be translated.
6. Check the translation with customers and distributors in the local market. This also gives local users the opportunity of being involved and raising any criticisms of the promotional materials before they are published for use.
7. Re-translate the materials back into English as a 'safety check'. They may not come back exactly as the original version, but there should be a reasonable commonality.

There are many (probably apocryphal) stories about translations of brand names and slogans that have gone horribly wrong: Pepsi's 'Come Alive with Pepsi' translating as 'Come back from the grave with Pepsi or the Vauxhall Nova translating as 'Doesn't go' in Spanish. Any regular traveller will be aware of humourous (or obscene) brand names on foreign products. Provided that a universally-recognisable icon is available, and that it is possible to produce meaningful hooks in each language, it should be possible to produce good internationalised press advertising. Certainly factual information (e.g., 'Open Sundays') should translate fairly easily, so sought communications are presumably more likely to transfer easily.

REFERENCES

1. Smith, P. R., (1998) Marketing - An Integrated Approach. London: Kogan Page. This has a good practically-orientated approach to the integration of communications.
2. Hart, N., (1998) Business to Business Marketing. London: Kogan Page. This has a very comprehensive opening section on strategy and planning.
3. Chee, H., and Harris, R. (1998) Global Marketing Strategy. London: Financial Times Pitman Publishing. This gives a clear analysis of international strategic planning, including some up-to-date and useful case studies and examples.
4. Mole, J., (1990) Mind your Manners. London: The Industrial Society. This gives some excellent insights into dealing with other cultures, and in particular gives some very readable and amusing examples of cultural conflicts which have led to disaster.
5. (1982) '21 Ad agencies endorse copy testing principles', Marketing News, February 19th.
6. Biel, A., (1989) 'Love the ad, buy the product?', ADMAP, (October).
7. Borremans T., (1998) 'Integrated (marketing) communications in practice: Survey among communication, public relations and advertising agencies in Belgium', Proceedings Annual Conference of the Global Institute for Corporate and Marketing Communications.
8. Broadbent, S., (1989) The Advertising Budget. Henley: Institute of Practitioners in Advertising and NTC Publications Ltd.
9. Brown, G., (1991) 'Modelling Advertising Awareness', ADMAP, (April).
10. Bruhn M., (1995) Intergrierte Untemehmensk-ommunikation: Ansatzpunkte fur eine Strategische and Operative Umseitzung Integreirter Kommuni-kationsarbeit. Stuttgart: Schaffer-Poeschel.
11. Colley, R.H.,(1961) Defining Advertising Goals. New York: Association of National Advertising.
12. Duncan, T. and Caywood, C., (1996) The Concept, Process and Evolution of Integrated Marketing Communication', in Thorson, E. and Moore, J. Integrated Communication. Synergy of Persuasive Voices. Mahwah: Lawrence Erlbaum.
13. Eagle, L., Hyde, K, and Kitchen, P., (1996) 'Advertising Effectiveness Measurement : A review of industry research practices', Proceedings of the Third Annual Conference of the Global Institute for Corporate and Marketing Communications.
14. Evans, M.J., (1994) : 'Domesday Marketing?', Journal of Marketing Management, 10(5) pp. 409-31.
15. Flesch, R., (1974) The Art of Readable Writing. New York: Harper and Row.
16. Nowak, G., and Pickton, D., (1997) 'Integrated Marketing Communications - a new language for a

new era', Proceedings of the Second International Conference on Marketing and Corporate Communications, Antwerp.

17. Johnson, T., (1997) 'An end to I-way robbery', Financial Times, 21st April.
18. Keegan, W., (1984) Multinational Marketing Management, Englewood Cliffs, NJ: Prentice Hall International.
19. Majaro, S. (1982) International Marketing. London: Allen and Unwin.
20. Nowak, G. and Phelps, J., (1994) 'Conceptualising the Integrated Marketing Communications Phenomenon', Journal of Current Issues and Research in Advertising, 16, (1), Spring, 49 -66.
21. Petrison, L. A. and Wang, P., (1996) 'Integrated Marketing Communication: An organisational perspective' in Thorson, E. and Moore, j. Integrated Communication. Synergy of Persuasive Voices. Mahwah: Lawrence Erlbaum.
22. (1984) Public Relations Practice - Its Roles and Parameters. London: The Institute of Public Relations.
23. Stapel, J., (1990) 'Monitoring advertising performance', ADMAP, (July/August).
24. Stapel, J., (1991) 'Like the advertisement but does it interest me?', ADMAP, (April).
25. Wright, C., (1997) 'Internet could be flat chat keeping up with the explosion', Australian Financial Review, 1 April.

CHAPTER 11

COMMUNICATION MIX VIS-A-VIS PROMOTION MIX

MCDONALD'S AND OTHERS LEARN THE PERILS OF PROMOTIONS

Contests, sweepstakes, and premium offers are often used by marketers to give consumers an extra incentive to purchase their products. However, when these promotions don't go as planned, they can embarrass a company or even create legal problems. A number of high-profile companies known for their marketing excellence have experienced problems with promotions over the years. Kraft Food and PepsiCo encoun-tered problems resulting from printing errors and computer glitches, while more recently McDonald's was the victim of a conspiracy to steal high-value game pieces from its long-running Monopoly game promotion. These botched promotions were embarrassing for the companies and resulted in the loss of goodwill as well as money.

Kraft was one of the first to learn how expensive it can be when a promotion goes awry. In 1989, a printing error resulted in the printing of too many winning game pieces for a match-and-win game promotion. Kraft cancelled the promotion but still had to spend nearly $4 million to compensate the winners-versus the $36,000 budgeted for prizes. The snafu gave birth to the "Kraft clause," a disclaimer stating that a marketer reserves the right to cancel a promotion if there are problems and hold a random drawing if there are more winners than prizes.

A few years later, PepsiCo had a major problem when a bottle-cap promotion offering a grand prize of I million pesos (about $36,000) went wrong in the Philipines. Due to a computer glitch, the winning number appeared on more than 500,000 bottle caps, which would have made the company liable for more than $18 billion in prize money. When the error was discovered, Pepsi announced that there was a problem and quickly offered to pay $19 for each winning cap, which ended up costing the company nearly $10 million. The furor caused by the botched promotion prompted anti-Pepsi rallies, death threats against Pepsi executives, and attacks on Pepsi trucks and bottling plants.

McDonald's also ran into a major problem with a promotion when winning game pieces were embezzled from its popular Monopoly game promotion. McDonald's ran its first Monopoly game promotion in 1987 and began running it annually in 1991. The company was able to run the game so long because it worked on many different levels. Consumers knew how to play the game, its big prizes generated excitement and interest, and its format — which required participants to collect all the Monopoly board game pieces to win-drove repeat traffic into the restaurants. McDonald's also spent large amounts of money on ads promoting the game and kept refining it with new iterations such as a Pick Your Prize twist. However, in August 2001 the Federal Bureau of Investigation arrested eight people for embezzling winning game pieces from the Monopoly game as well as the company's "Who Wants to Be a Mil-lionaire" sweepstakes in order to divert nearly $24 million worth of prizes to co-conspirators.

The conspiracy is believed to have begun as early as 1995, and the FBI investigation, which was conducted with McDonald's co-operation, lasted two years before the arrests were made. Fifty-one people were indicted in the case, nearly all of whom either pleaded guilty or were convicted following trial. Among those pleading guilty was the director of security for McDonald's promotional agency, Simon Marketing, who stole the winning tickets and conspired with the others to distribute them to a network of recruiters who solicited individuals to falsely claim they were legitimate game winners.

Following the arrests, McDonald's immediately fired Simon Marketing, as did several other of the agency's clients, including Kraft Foods and Philip Morris Co. To win back consumer confidence, McDonald's ran a five-day instant giveaway promotion over the Labour Day weekend in which consumers could win 55 cash prizes ranging from $1,000 to $1 million. The company also created an independent task force comprised of anti-fraud and game security experts to review procedures for future promotions.

The promotion scandal that rocked McDonald's sent shock waves through the industry and threatened to undermine consumer trust in contests and sweepstakes in general. Marketers are now more carefully reviewing their contests and sweepstakes as well as the companies that manage them. However, most industry experts maintain that McDonald's was a rare victim in an industry conducted honestly and legitimately and policed by many private and public watch-dogs. While marketers will continue to use contests, sweepstakes, and games, they will be taking extra precautions to safeguard them to avoid the problems Kraft, PepsiCo, and McDonald's encountered.

Sources: Kate McArthur, "Guilty Verdict for Four in McDonald's Sweepstakes Scandal," AdAge.com, Sept. 3,2002; Kate McArthur, "McSwindle," Advertising Age, Aug. 27,2002, pp. 1,22; Cara Beardi, "Scandal May Impact Other Sweepstakes," Advertising Age, Aug. 27,2002, p. 22; Betsy Spethmann, "The Perils of Promotion" Promo, November 1996, pp. 22,134.

Communication between the manufacturer and the consumers is indirect either through the middlemen, sales force or impersonal methods like; advertising, publicity and public relations. These all methods of communication-advertising, personal selling, publicity and sales promotion techniques are invariably used by almost all the manufacturers. A promotion strategy involves the coordination of all communicated efforts aimed at specific audience - consumer, whole-salers, retailers, government shareholders and so on. The main problem before the marketing or advertising manager is to co-ordinate and use all these communication methods in a compact manner and mix them in such a way as to product the best results taking market and product conditions, competitive situations, behavioural characteristics of target audience and the size of budget. Different communication mix will be required in different stages of product life cycle — introduction, growth, maturity, saturation and decline. In introduction stage, all promotional methods including adver-tising and personal stages, are necessary whereas in decline or obsolescence stage, many efforts will remain fruitless.

It is, therefore the responsibility of marketing or advertising manager to arrange an ideal promotion mix to achieve the objectives.

RULE OF FIVE OF COMMUNICATION

In the process of communication, out of six steps three are to be taken by the sender and last three by the receiver. There are two more steps which are generally desired by the sender from the receiver though these steps are not essential to the completion of communication. These steps are 'Acceptance' and 'Feedback' sender wants that his message must be accepted by the receiver in the same sense so that co-operation and motivation may be improved and the sender may came to know that the receiver has understood the message correctly. Similarly, sender wants feedback. It means that the receiver generates the message of the sender in response the sender's original message. This may help the sender, evaluating the effectiveness of the message and may improve it, if necessary, the next communication. Although these two steps of the receiver are not essential for completing the communication, yet these are essential in generating an effective long run working relationship.

If all these expectations from the receiver are considered, they are sometimes called the Rule of Five in communication i.e., (i) receiving, (ii) decoding or understanding, (iii) acceptance, (iv) action and (v) feedback. If these five steps are taken by the receiver, the communication is effective and successful.

HOW COMMUNICATIONS INFLUENCE THE ROLE OF PROMOTION

Mutually satisfying exchange being the ultimate goal of marketing, therefore the role of promotion is to encourage such as exchange through linking communications with the 'product adopted process' of the buyer. Then, motivating the adoption of promoted product as well as effecting the desire change in the consumer behaviour is the goal of the promotion function. The attainment of these goals presupposes that product purchase process be understood by the marketers before marketing communications are designed. While there are many models that help to conceptualise the buying process, the two very specific models that aid in understanding the buying process as well as in framing communication, are: (1) AIDA framework, and (2) Hierarchy-of-effects.

PROMOTIONAL STRATEGY AND COMMUNICATION PROCESS

Promotion is described as a process of communication between the seller and the buyer. By promotion here means sales promotion. Sales promotion may be described as the adhesive which bonds the two — the seller and the buyer-together. Its main application is in marketing situations where there are intermediaries between the seller or producer and the consumer-agents, distributors, wholesalers, retailers. Thus, the promotion bonds the two ends. The communication process of some type is necessary between the seller and the buyer. This process may also be called marketing communication process.

The marketing communication process is not much different from the general process of communication and may be applied to promotional strategy. The marketing manager or the person concerned with the promotion work is the source or sender. The idea originates there. The message is encoded in the form of sales representations, advertisements, displays or publicity releases. The transfer mechanism or the channel for the delivery of the message may be, according to the strategy used, a sales person, a public relations channel or the advertising media. The decoding step begins with the consumer's interpretation of the sender's message. This is probably the most troublesome aspect of marketing communication because the consumer does not always interpret the message in the same way as the sender does it. As stated, the fundamental difficulty in the communication process is decoding and encoding. The source (sender) must take the precaution in sending the message so as it may be translated by the receiver in the same sense. For this purpose, the message should be so worded that it may be easily translated or understood or decoded. This may be very tricky because the meanings attached to various words and symbols may differ, depending on the frames of reference and the field of experience of the two groups. If the message is received correctly, the receiver will take the necessary action to go for the purchase of items advertised. If the message is not understood or misunderstood or not received correctly, the efforts of the source go waste. A view of the marketing communication process may be shown with the help of the following Fig. 11.1

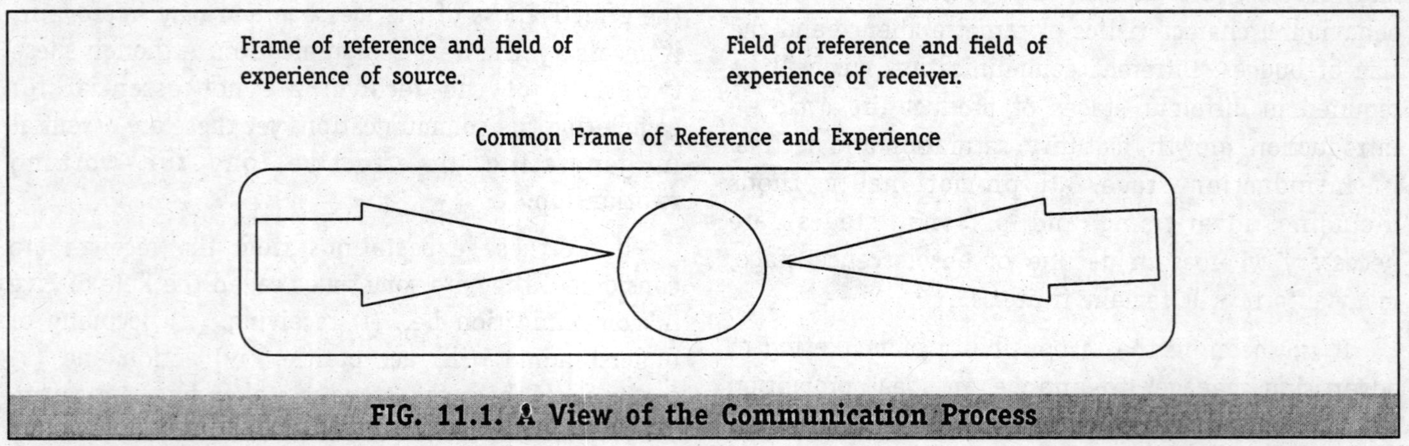

FIG. 11.1. A View of the Communication Process

As it is evident from the above figure, there is a common field of reference and experience of both sender and receiver. It means, there is an overlapping, of one's field of reference and experience into other's field. This overlapping is a must, if there is no overlapping, communication may be bad or impossible.

Information about consumer decision (whether to purchase or not) is feedback to the marketing manager. The marketing manager gets this feedback information through market research or the report of salesmen. The noise element is usually represented by competitive promotional messages transmitted through the same communication channels or by the random noise factor, such, as people taking snacks during T.V. commercial announcements.

Errors in communication may be minimised by knowing the relevant market dimension in terms of the needs and attitudes of the potential customers. These data should be available for strategy planning anyway, and here they should be especially useful.

Whether the message should emphasise only the positive features (one sided arguments) or the positive and negative features (two-sided arguments) depends on the attitude of target market. Sometimes, it is desirable to argue only the positive features, for it is less confusing, But if potential customers are awakened or know something of the pros and cons, it may be desirable to use a two-sided approach. The marketing manager should take care of such matters, as they affect the effectiveness of the message during implementation process. It is also a point worth noting that message should be transmitted via message channel. Consciously or unconsciously, the receiver may attach more value to a product, if its in a well respected newspaper or journal.

The whole process of marketing communication may be shown in the following Fig. 11.2

Thus, it is quite evident that the marketing communication process bonds the buyer and seller together provided, there is a good understanding between the two.

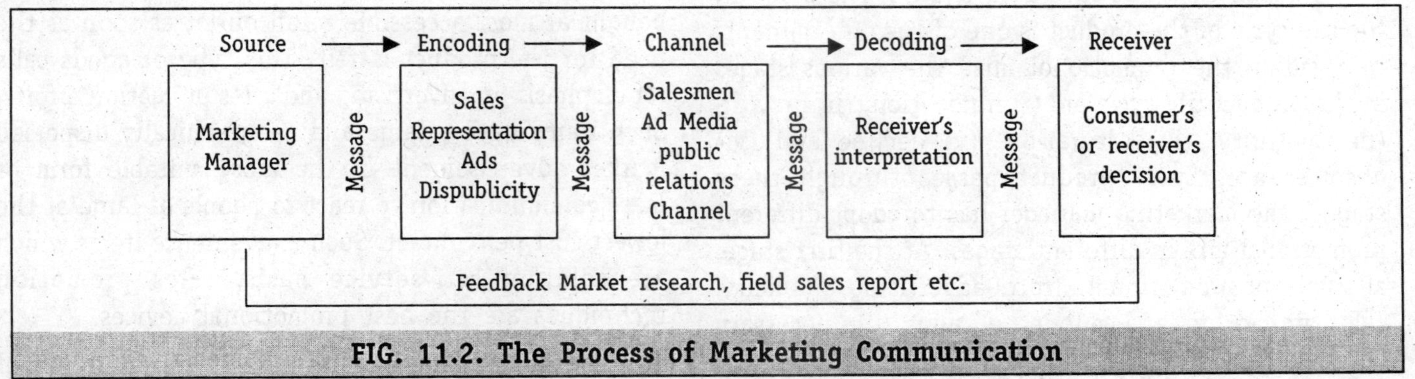

FIG. 11.2. The Process of Marketing Communication

What is Promotional Mix ?

Communication is a must in marketing process. The manufacturer (communicator or source) transmits the message to the target consumer through mass communication methods — advertising, personal selling, sales promotion and publicity — in order to create the demand for the product. This is invariably called promotion.

Promotion influences demand by communicating pro-product and pro-company messages to the market. A promotion strategy involves the co-ordination of ail communication efforts aimed at specific audiences-consumers, dealers, the government shareholders and so on. The most critical promotional question facing the marketing manager concerns the proper mix of communication methods advertising, personal selling, sales promotion and publicity. The promotion mix is usually co-ordinated on a campaign basis, making the campaign, the relevant unit of the promotion strategy campaign may last for a short fixed period i.e., a few week, months or a year or if successful, it may run over a pretty long period, i.e., several years. The most desirable marketing effort includes a total campaign with one unified theme. It is a co-ordinated effort of unifying various promotional strategies.

The four communication mix currents — advertising, personal setting, publicity and sales promotion are more or less used at every stage in the selling process, but their intensity differs at different stages and at different periods. Publicity is generally effective at the awareness stage. Advertising becomes less and less effective over a period of time. Personal selling is more effective as consumer needs dictate a more personal relationship. Sales promotion may be effective in providing added incentives for buyer's action.

To a marketing manager, it is difficult to arrive at the best kind of communication mix because results of communication efforts are hard to measure and it is very difficult to understand what a particular medium will do at a particular time for one product as opposed to another. Most marketing managers select more than one channel to promote a product. Their choices are affected by a number of factors.

Factors Deciding the Promotional Mix

There are various factors which are usually considered by the marketing manager in arriving at the promotional mix:

1. Stage of a Product Life Cycle - The stage in the life cycle of the product is one of the determinants in deciding the promotional mix. The various stages in the product life cycle are (i) innovation, (ii) growth, (iii) maturity, (iv) saturation, (v) decline and (vi) obsolescence. Every product passes through these stages. The marketing manager has to adopt different promotional mix in different stages. At the first stage, all types of promotional efforts-advertising, publicity, sales promotion and public relations are necessary because these efforts are aimed at informing the target consumers of the presence of the product in the market. Substantial expenditures on advertising are vital to inform the public on the other hand, personal selling programme is also undertaken that aids in generating product acceptance among retailers, wholesalers and industrial and institutional buyers.

Sales promotion efforts are made during growth period in order to check the entry of competitors. During the maturity stage heavy expenditure on advertising and personal selling are required to fight competitive situation and to maintain their share of market. During saturation and declining stages, the promotion expenditures are reduced to a great extent. Only a minority of organisations attempt to prop up lagging product with high promotional advertising. Some use aggressive personal selling programme to further penetrate the specific market segments where demands or the product exist. In obsolescence stage, all promotional efforts are stopped and it is thought better to withdraw the product from the market or substitute the product with the new product.

2. Type of Product - The characteristics of a product may also dictate its natural audience. A non-differentiated product (detergents or soaps) may be promoted with psychological advertising. A product with hidden emotional qualities of suitings, clothing etc., may be given a careful and subtle mass media promotion. The product is generally classified as consumer product or industrial product. The classification of product or service is an indicator of the most appropriate type of promotion mix that may be required.

(a) Consumer goods - Ordinarily, there are three types of consumer goods – convenience, shoppings and specialty. Each one requires a separate type promotion. Convenience goods are those goods that are frequently purchased, are low in cost and are bought at most accessible retail outlet as soon as the need for the product is felt. This type of goods calls for emphasis on advertising and sales promotion efforts. Such items have a large and geographically dispersed market advertisement in the most suitable form of mass communication to react to people at large at the lowest cost per contact. Such convenience items which are sold on self-service basis, sales promotion techniques are the best promotional devices.

Products purchased after careful consideration of quality, price style and durability are classified as shopping goods. The product, in this case, is a high unit value and are not infrequently purchased such as clothing and furniture. The marketer of shopping goods place more emphasis on personal selling because customer in purchasing such items require an advice from the salesmen and a comparison of goods with the other brands of the same product in the same store or in different stores. A good salesmanship will do the needful. However, advertising is also necessary just to inform the public of the existence of the product.

High unit value and infrequent purchase are also the characteristics of specialty goods, it is a branded item, which the consumer has become convinced is superior to all competitive brands. Here, the marketer employs a combination of the three primary methods of promotion — advertising, personal selling and sales promotion.

Personal selling technique helps the marketer in maintaining the image of the product, Advertising also serves the same purpose and reminds the people to keep the product in mind. Sales promotion techniques maintain the image of the product and remind consumers of the product.

(b) Industrial goods - Industrial goods are generally classified into five categories —raw n aterials, fabricating materials and parts, operating supplies, installations, and accessory equipments. In general, all types of industrial goods require more emphasis than consumer goods. On personal selling, because these goods are purchased and sold in bulk and moreover, salesman offer advice and assistance at the time of supplying such goods and in the post sales period. A computer supplier, unhesitatingly, allow his salesmen to spend many hours with an account after the sale has been completed just to ensure that the equipment is operating properly and the account is using it in proper a manner.

Advertising and-sales promotion are important elements of the promotion mix, for some advertising is helpful for salesmen in convincing the prospect about the product and the organisation and its product line. Once the prospect has achieved familiarity about the product and product line of the organisation through advertisement the sales person finds it easy to get an appointment. Some industrial seller use advertising to generate prestige. As far as sales promotion devices are concerned, the sellers of industrial goods use these devices not as extensively as the marketers of consumer goods do. Some marketers of industrial goods rely heavily on displays in trade fairs, exhibitions and conventions. Some use price deals such as 'Rupees off' or 'two for one' or "buy two get five free" or 'gifts' offers to generate sales. Still others allow premiums and trading stamps to the buyers.

3. Target of Promotion - The use of promotion mix is also affected by the type of person, to which it is directed. Promotion may be directed at four different groups — wholesalers, retailers, industrial consumers and final consumers. The right choice of promotion blend for each group is different.

(a) Promotion to Wholesalers - As wholesalers are less in number and more conscious to demand and cost, they respond to economic arguments. Any type of promotion which the producer intends to direct at retailers and final consumers will be sufficient promotion for wholesalers but they are more conscious about the personal selling representatives who cements the relationship between producer and wholesalers.

(b} Promotion to Retailers - If number of retailers are less, the personal selling may be feasible to manufacturers and wholesalers.

In case the number of retailers are numerous, the advertisings in trade magazine and newspapers are valuable. Sales promotion activities such as discount on sales or gifts on bulk purchases etc., also play valuable roles in marketing the goods. If the product is consumer item of high value, the bulk of promotion efforts is to serve the retailers through sales personnel. Personal selling will also be valuable where the product requires after-sales service or possesses some technical characteristics, because the sales person may answer the retailer's questions about the technical characteristics, the promotion will be directed towards the final consumer, the retailer's own part in selling the product, and important details concerning price, the marketers and promotional assistance. In other words, promotion to retailer is mainly informative in nature which he passes on to consumers. The promotion to retailers must also be persuasive so that his interest in selling the product may not be lost. In most cases, personal selling is the main promotion efforts to retailers because marketing mixes may have to be adjusted drastically from one geographic territory to another to meet competitive situations and moreover it creates and maintains good channel relationship.

(c) Promotion to Industrial Consumers - Industrial customers, being less numerous than final consumers have a justification for a promotion blend emphasing personal selling because the personal sales representatives may be more flexible in adjusting their company's appeal to suit each customer. They supply the necessary information as desired by the customer. Although personal selling dominate the scene in industrial marketing, advertising is also used widely, mainly for economic reasons,

(d) Promotion to Final Consumers - The large number of ultimate consumers practically force retailers, wholesalers and manufacturers to use the mass selling techniques in their promotion blends. So, advertising is preferred in most cases because it establishes brand preference to such an extent that little personal selling may be required. Sales promotion techniques are also used extensively. Self-service, discount, gift and novelties attest to this. Advertising may even be the way to supply the necessary information to those who are interested in seeking them.

4. Size of Budget - The amount allocated for the promotional efforts is an obvious limitation on the choice of promotional channels. If the budget is small, a firm cannot spend more on promo-tional activities because it cannot buy enough mass media advertising worth count. If accounts are limited, the organisation can safely rely on personal selling and publicity, and can manage within its resources. But, on the other hand, if accounts are numerous, the organisation will prefer advertising in local or regional newspapers, why be not of repute or it may use local radio or T.V.

On the other hand, if size of budget is big enough, the organisation may use national newspapers, or T.V. and radio. It will be economical per contact but it will require jumpsum amount which a small firm cannot afford. Some smaller manufacturers, out of necessity rather than choice, use personal selling as their major promotion method. A sales person may be employed for Rs. 5,000 p.m. or so plus expenses while the sponsoring of a single T.V, broad-cast may cost a sizable amount of money. A small firm having small promotion budget may also use sales promotion, public relation and direct mail over and about personal selling.

The size of promotion budget may have an impact on the composition of the promotion mix. Organisations with small budget may be forced to use promotion methods which are less effective because they are not in a position to afford heavy expenditure on other methods which are more effective such as advertising in national newspaper and national network on T.V. and radio which can be used only by the organisations that allocate a big amount for their promotional efforts. Smaller organisations prefer personal selling and publicity. They pay commission to salesmen which is payable only when sales are affected. Sometimes family members invest their time in personal selling. Though personal selling is costly per contract than the advertising, yet it is used because the payment is not made in one lump sum.

Thus, size of budget leads the management to use the methods which would not be employed otherwise even though they are less effective.

5. Push and Pull Strategy - In deciding on ideal promotional mix, the key variable is the direction of influence in the distribution marketing channel. In some cases, direction of influence is towards the middlemen whereas in some other cases, it is an end-user. This characteristic of the variable is called push-pull strategies.

Push Strategy- A push strategy is generally used in industrial product marketing — products have a high unit value and need adjustment for consumer needs. It is aimed at the middlemen with the goal of getting them to aggressively promote the manufacturer's brand to consumers. This strategy can favourably be used when consumers rely heavily on the advice of dealers for the product use. Thus, specially stores often emphasise the push strategy with a lesser emphasis on advertising. In this strategy, personal selling is the favoured promotional channel. Dealers promote the product line aggressively for which they are granted high margins and an exclusive distribution territory.

Pull Strategy- A pull strategy, in its extreme form, emphasises the importance of mass communication. It is aimed at stimulating the end-consumer demand to a sufficient degree so that the consumer may ask retailers for the product and retailers are forced to stock the brand in order to please their customers. The retailer will ask: the wholesaler to supply the brand demanded by the consumer and the wholesaler, naturally, will ask the manufacturer to supply. Thus, this strategy stresses on advertising in order to create a heavy demand of goods.

The promotional campaigns of most manufacturers are a blend of the two approaches. Deciding where to place the emphasis is not always easy, the choice of approach depends on the nature of the product and the buying habits of consumers. Push strategy is most effective where units value is high, whereas pull strategy is suitable for products having low unit value and are meant for broad public distribution. In most cases, marketers use both strategies; but one is always emphasised.

(6) Organisational Philosophy - The philosophy of the organisation too, affects the promotion mix.

Thus, it is evident from the above discussion, that no promotion blend is suitable for ail situations. Each mix should be developed as a part of marketing mix. A blend of personal selling and advertising may be expected when a firm sells consumer and industrial goods. More emphasis on advertising should be on advertising promoting consumer goods and or personal selling for industrial goods.

Stages in Product Life Cycle

Product life cycle is one of the very important aspect in evolv-ing an effecting advertising strategy. The stage in the life cycle of the product is the one of the determinants of the promotion mix. The product life cycle theory suggests that all products have certain length of life daring which they pass through certain identifiable stages. The theory recognises five phase process of development success and decline. These five phases are:

(i) introduction or innovation,
(ii) growth,
(iii) maturity,
(iv) saturation, and
(v) decline.

Since the conception of the product, during its development and to the market introduction, product remains in the prenatal stage. Its life begins with its introduction in the market. It follows a period during which its market grows rapidly, eventually, it reaches at maturity and then stands saturated. Afterwards, its market declines and finally its life comes to an end.

During the introduction stage, the sales will take some time before they pick up because the target consumer is not aware of the new product. The organisation must discover that the substantial promotional expenditures are necessary. Various promotional programmes are carried out to inform the target consumers of the existence of the new product stating the advantages of the product over the rival products that exist in the market. The product is made popular among its users through promotional activities. At this stage, high levels of advertising, sales promotion and publicity are vital to gain the consumer acceptance.

As soon as the product gains consumer acceptance, it enters in growth stage. During the period of market growth, the sales of organisation keep increasing as the product gains popularity among its target consumers. Consequently profits of the firm start go up and up because of the two primary reasons: (i) the firms gets large scale production economics due to increase in demand, and (ii) advertising and distribution costs per unit expenditure is reduced considerably due to increase in production. High profits are likely to attract the competitors in the field.

At the third stage, immaturity stage, the competition is severe, through the sales of the product go up but with a lower speed. The innovator has to struggle hard to survive. The total industrys, sales are high and a number of organisation, including the innovator must have a share in them. The competitive situation leads some organisations to spend, a substantial sum on promotional activities in order to retain at least this existing market share. At this stage, profit rate begins to decline. The producer makes search for the new markets. Market and marketing research expenditures go up.

Next comes the saturation point. The sales volume comes to standstill inspite of the best efforts but it is at all time high. Competition is also at its peak in this period. It brings the costs of promotional efforts and distribution at a new peak. Prices begin to fall and therefore profit comes down. Fresh efforts are made at this stage to survive the position and new markets are tried.

The last stage in the cycle is the decline stage. This stage is brought out by product gradual displacement by some new innovation or change in consumer behaviour. Technological changes and market conditions lead the competitors to enter the market with improved substitutes of the product which naturally reduces the demand of the existing old product. The sales and profits start going down and finally, the demand of the product dies hard. At this stage, it is advisable to stop the production of the product and shift to some other products.

Advertising Strategies and Product Life Cycle

Advertising is a life for the business. It is needed at each stage of the product life cycle, although, the strategy of advertising differs at each stage. The promotion mix, appeal, creativity and medium all carry different impact on target consumers at each stage. Now in the following discussion, we shall try to explain different strategies which are usually adopted by the manufacturing in advertising in the different stages of product life cycle.

1. Introduction - It is the first stage of the product life cycle. As the product is newly introduced in the market, the buyer or target consumer is not well informed. So, the prime objective of advertising at this stage is to inform the consumers about the characteristics and qualities of/the product taking into account the similarities and differences of the rival products. Heavy expenditures on advertising, sales promotion and publicity are made to inform the public of the existence of the new product. In case of industrial goods, personal selling may be useful but it should be effective, In case of consumer items, the promotional efforts should centre on generating a primary rather than a selective demand for the individual brand. Since there are few competitors at this stage, mass selling efforts may be concentrated on the basic information job. Initial advertisements should be designed to draw inquiries.

2. Growth - As soon as the product gains popularity among and recognition from the target consumers, it enters the second stage i.e., growth stage. Due to heavy dose of promotional efforts at introductory stage, the demand and sales volumes increase tremendously. Profits go high competitors are lively to enter the market. So the main aim of the marketer, at this stage is to capture the sizable share of the market and for this purpose, he concentrates on generating the selective demand of the brand. Due to increasing trend of sales and the likely competition, the marketer is induced to incur substantial promotion expenditure to obtain a differential advantage. The management now has a capacity to appropriate higher budget due to heavy profits, to capture a sizable market of the brand. At this stage, the main thrust of the marketer still is to persuade customers to buy and stay with the company's product, although informing and convincing them is still important. As now more potential buyers are trying and adopting the product mass selling may become more economical. The management may utilise sales promotion efforts like 'reduced price' of 'free samples' or 'off coupons' etc., in order to maintain or increase the sales. Likewise, 'advertising' and 'personal selling' expenditures are sizeable to overcome the efforts of the competitors to capture increasingly larger shares of the market.

3. Maturity Stage - The competition at this stage is severse. The total sales and profits of the concern go up but a lower speed. The producer at this point, is to struggle hard to survive and to spend a large sum on advertising and personal selling in order to retain its share of the market. The promotion approach is persuasive rather than informative. Mass selling efforts dominate the promotion blends of consumer products. The firms that have achieved a strong consumer support, use reminder type advertising rather than persuasive advertising, just to remind the customer of the product or producers name and this may be more economical.

4. Saturation Stage - The competition at this stage is at the peak. Sales are not getting tempo inspite of best efforts. At this stage, a balanced promotion mix is used to maintain the sales level. Moreover, the marketer must try to improve the product at this stage by expending more on the product or market research and to bring with the new usages of the product, or new markets should be tried.

5. Decline Stage - At this stage, the sales go down. The marketer is of the belief that any attempt to compete is unprofitable and therefore, he does not allocate more funds to advertising and promotion activities. Some organisations however use aggressive personal selling programmes to further penetrate specific market segments. In general, marketers slow down on all forms of promotion efforts at this stage. It may also invest in new market research to locate areas of weakness or possible improvement. Since the product, remains acceptable to some people, more targeted promotion is required to reach such customers, and such arms ma; reminder-type advertising.

Product life cycle theory assumes that every product has five phases in its life. It means every product is to die out inspite of best promotional efforts by the marketer. The period of life cycle may differ from product to product and from market to market. Experience shows that this theory does not apply to every product and there has been some criticism of it on these grounds.

There are three sophistications of the product life cycle that are also of interest in advertising and public interest -

(i) There is recycled product life cycle which applies to long lived product which suffers no decline, but has periodic market challenges. These threats are met by injections of product modification.

(ii) When one product is replaced by another this has leap frog effect.

(iii) There is the very interesting stair case effect where the life cycle continues to take off from the point of maturity as new uses and markets are discovered. Passengers shipping is the fine example of it, when shipping line met the competition of the aeroplane by developing car ferries ships and container ships.

Thus, the conclusion may be drawn that every product with few exceptions has this cycle and the advertising efforts differ with each successive stage till the product moves unprofitable.

ADVERTISING AND THE COMMUNICATION PROCESS

Our system of mass communication media acts principally as a purveyor of commercial and non-commercial information. Both the media of advertising, print media (newspaper, magazine; direct mail etc.) and broadcast media (radio and television) normally carry commercial and non-commercial (editorial and entertainment) content. Here we are concerned only with the commercial aspect of the mass communication.

Advertising is the impersonal communication of ideas, goods or services to a mass audience by an identified and paying sponsor. Advertising thus, is : (i) impersonal, (ii) a communication of ideas, facts, goods and services, (iii) aimed at a mass audience, (iv) by an identified sponsor, and (v) by a paying sponsor.

The two forms of mass communication — publicity and propaganda are invariably confused with advertising. To distinguish these two terms from advertising, if we eliminate the element of paying sponsor, it would have the element of publicity left. Technically speaking publicity is advertisement without payment. Similarly, if we eliminate the element of 'identified sponsor', the resulting communication is propaganda.

Advertising involves the communication of ideal goods and services in an attempt to sell goods and services offered by the sponsor. But the more important fact in advertising which we overlook, is to sell the ideas, it persuades the receiver with information and with emotion. Advertising is impersonal but it does not mean that it is cold or without compassion. It does only mean that the communication does not involve a face-to-face communication, The relationship between the buyer and seller is maintained through the media called channel newspaper, magazine, direct mail, radio, T.V., store signs, short length movies and cinema slides, poster, signboards, novelties etc. The impact of communication shall be different for different media.

The source of message in the advertising communication system is where the message originates. In case of advertising, two types of sources are involved. The first is the company or brand that is interested in communicating certain information to the audience, The second is the spokesperson, the model or personality featured in the advertisement. Each of these types of sources will have characteristics that will affect the communication system, such as the following:

Credibility (expertness, unbiasedness)

Attractiveness (prestigeousness, similarity, physical attractiveness).

The message refers to both the content and execution of the advertisement. It is the totality of what enters the perception of the receiver. The message execution can be described in terms of the approach, such as — soft sell versus hard sell, use of humour, use of fear appeals, use of two sided communication.

The receiver in an advertising communication system is the target communication. Thus, the receiver can be described in terms of audience segmentation, variable, life style, benefits sought, demographic and so on. A particular interest can be the involvement in the product and the extent to which the receiver is willing to search for and/or process information. The communication can have a variety of effects upon the receiver as it creates awareness, communicate information and precipitate behaviour.

PERSONAL SELLING AND THE COMMUNICATION PROCESS

Personal selling is another marketing tool that is primarily concerned with communication. Personal selling is for more effective communication method than advertising- It consists of-face-to face and person-to-person (communication between the sales person and their prospects. Unlike advertising, it involves personal interaction between the source and the destination (receiver). It aims at individuals. The message and its presentation can be tailored according to the unique characteristics of each individual prospect. Furthermore, inter personal interaction provides immediate feedback that permits the presentation to be adjusted. If feedback indicates that the message is not getting across, the sales person may immediately adjust it and present it in the way, it is intended.

Personal selling may be a very intense means of promotion because a destination or receiver cannot ignore the sales person, whereas it is possible in advertising. This is the most effective means of communication if the source could provide sales person to have a face-to-face contact with each largest consumer. But this system has been proved quite inefficient except in certain circumstances where the impact of personal call will be large i.e., when the product and a sale to one customer represent a significant amount of money or when contact is being made with a retailer or wholesaler who may buy large amounts of products. This method of face-to-face communication is not appropriate when a new product h being introduced to hundreds of thousands of consumers. In such circumstances only advertising (paid mass communication) is the most appropriate form of communication. Even when personal selling is appropriate, its effectiveness can be enhanced if it is supported by advertising. A sales person will be received more often and more sympathetically, if the prospect has already learned something about the mm and the product from advertising.

Thus, two methods of mass communication — advertising and personal selling differ in their approach. The communication process of the two differs to a great extent. The channels, the message or appeal, the receivers and the methods of feedback are all different in these two cases. Personal selling is much important in industrial marketing, whereas advertising is significant in consumer marketing. However, these two have complimentary effects.

WHAT IS CHANNEL IN THE COMMUNICATION PROCESS?

The message in the communication process is transmitted from the source to the destination or receiver through some channel. Channel is the path through which message is carried or delivered to the audience or destination. It might include any form of promotion.

The channel in the advertising communication system consists of the media such as radio, television, newspapers, magazines, bill board, and point of purchase displays and so on. The impact of the communication will be different for different media. There will be different communication channels in different forms of mass communications, i.e., personal selling, sales promotion and public relation. So, channel is the most important consideration in taking the decision for the form of communication to be adopted in communicating the message to the receiver.

1. **Vertical channel –** A vertical channel exists, if there is meaningful difference in the interests, social status, demographic or economical characteristics of the communicating units or groups. Thus, the communication among social classes that may occur largely as an emulation of or an identification with the consumption behaviour of another social class is a type of vertical channel. In marketing, the relations among manufacturer, wholesalers, retailer and consumer are often thought of as a vertical channel because these communicating groups differ from each other in various perspectives but still they provide a link (channel) between the manufacturer and the consumer.

2. **Horizontal channel -** If the communication flows among members of a group having similar interests, social status, demographic or economic characteristics, it is horizontal channel. A. group may be defined in many ways i.e., a social group, a workgroup, a professional group, a neighbourhood group and so on. The important point for consideration is that this type of communication takes place among the members of the same group and not between the members of two different groups, in marketing,

communication from one consumer to another consumer may be identified as horizontal channel.

3. Formal channel - A formal channel is one that is established intentionally and is under the control of communicator. The communicator has a choice of and control over the channel. Thus, an advertiser has a formal channel to a target audience that is established by choosing various media alternatives. The use of this channel is paid for by the advertiser and is sometimes exiled the mass media or direct exposure channel.

4. Informal channel - Opposite to formal channel, an informal channel is one, not intentionally, established and not under the control of communicator. The communicator is, is no way, in a position to control the nature of the information exchanged through such a channel. It is the word of mouth aspect of advertising and is sometimes referred to as interpersonal or indirect exposure channel. Although, an advertiser has no direct control over what is communicated through the channel, he can attempt to influence it in one way or the other.

A vertical channel can either be formal or informal. The manufacturer, wholesaler, retailer and consumer chain would be an illustration of vertical formal channel. A good illustration of vertical informal channel can be expanded through a society like this. A basic idea suppose, on economics is developed by a great thinker which is followed and extended by several academic disciples and disseminated by political leaders through policy decisions that have great impact on the people of the country, la marketing, one popular view of the way new product innovation, particularly in the fashion and clothing area are diffused through a population is called the trickle down theory. It assumes that the innovation is first adopted by people in the higher social classes and then later picked up by those in lower classes who emulate the behaviour of upper class.

SPECIAL PROBLEMS OF ADVERTISER IN COMMUNICATION

The elementary communication model message-receiver analysis is quite inadequate because the advertiser has to face certain basic problems, in this model that are of particular significance to him. These basic problems are: -

(1) Reception of Message - The characteristics of an effective communication are (i) the message must be so designed and delivered as to gain attraction of the receiver and (ii) it must use signals and words that are understood by the receiver in the same sense in which they are transmitted by the source. Obviously, there will be little or no communication if the receiver does not follow the message in the same sense in which they are transmitted by the source. Obviously, there will be little or no communication if the receiver does not follow the message by the receiver but it must be received by him psychologically as well as physically. The receiver must perceive and be able to understand what is seen or heard.

To follow the message, a field of experience and understanding common to both sender and receiver is a must, otherwise the message may be misunderstood or misinterpreted and may create confusion. Thus, common field of experience assures understanding of the message because, a close relationship between the advertiser and the consumer, does not exist, one of the primary problems in the creation of advertising is the translation of news and information (message) about the product from the language of the consumer.

(2) Interference or Noise - Interference is another problem, the advertiser must cope with. To a degree the noise or disturbance is present in almost all forms of communication i.e., radio, T.V. or newspapers. This consists of factors that affect or distort the message received from the source. In other words, noise or interference refers to conditions that distort the communication process or interfere with the transmission of the message.

Noise or interference may inhabit at any point in the process. It includes poor message planning, inappropriate media selection, the competition message, busy audience members and careless measurement of results. The phone rings while we are reading the newspaper or viewing the television or the baby cries for milk and mother leaves the TV set are some to the illustrations where the interference affects the right delivery of message. These all are external interference but the greatest danger to the advertiser is not due to external interference. Internal interference i.e., the other message competing the attention of the reader, the listener or the viewer – not only the news and entertainment, but advertising messages being transmitted by other competitors. Such transmissions, obviously, draw the attention of the receiver and more perhaps change the attitude of the consumer.

(3) Lack of Feedback - Another problem faced by the advertiser is lack of feedback. Feedback is, getting the results by the communicator or source about what the audience has learned or gained from the communication message or how he behaves in response to the appeal. It provides answer as to when and how the message should be altered or modified to be most effective. It is the last step in the communication process and helps the communicator in planning the further message. This feedback is not inherent in all types of communication. When we talk face-to-face with a person or even when we address a group, there is no problem of feedback because it can be known immediately how effectively our message is being delivered, indicated by the behaviour of the audience. The receivers or the audience may ask questions about points which are not clear to them and even though they do not talk back, their actions and expressions can indicate whether message is being received correctly or not. A yawn, for example from the audience may be a sufficient indication that the message is not getting through. Thus, interpersonal communication is a two-way communication and feedback is no problem.

But advertising is an impersonal and one way communication. The prospect or the receiver of the message has no chance to ask the questions or even to indicate to the advertiser whether he has got the message. Instead of feeding back the reactions, the receiver changes the channel. The advertiser subsequently finds through research or sales reports that only a few received the message. This fact cannot be known by the advertiser when he transmits the message and therefore, he cannot alter the message timely. It, thus, provides a hurdle in two-way communication. To overcome the obstacle, the advertiser must attempt to anticipate the audience's reactions when exposed to the message.

Thus, these are the special problems or noise factors or interferences that an advertiser has to face. These factors are present almost in every form of mass communication and the advertiser must be aware of them.

Broadly speaking, marketing communication is "the continuing dialogue between buyers and sellers in a market-place. However, looking from' marketers perspective, the marketing communication is the process of presenting an integrated set of stimuli to a target market with the intent of evoking a desired set of responses within that target market and setting up channels to receive, interpret, and act upon messages and indemnifying new communication opportunities." This definition is quite relevant to an individual firm. It recognizes that the firm is both a sender and a receiver of market-related messages. As a sender it first approaches customers to buy its products/brands in a competitive environment. As a receiver, it seeks to attune itself to its target market in order to realign its messages, to adopt messages to its changing marketing conditions and to spot new communication opportunities. The firm must be a sensitive receiver of market's needs if it is to survive and grow.

MARKET COMMUNICATIONS TRAVEL BEYOND PROMOTION

It may be clearly noted that traditionally, marketing communications was thought to be a function which could be charged with the task a informing the target customer about the nature and type of the firm's products, their unique benefits, uses, and features as well as the price and place at which those would be available in the market. In this way, since marketing communications was supposed to aim at influencing only the consumer behaviour in favour of the firm's offerings, these were thought to be persuasive, were commonly called 'promotion' and a study of marketing communications was assumed to be a study of the promotion function of marketing. For very long time, it has been seen as if promotion formed the only communication bridge between a company and its buyer. However, there has been a significant change in viewing marketing communications.

According to the changed modern view, all marketing communications are not directed towards ultimate buyers alone. Many are addressed to other manufacturers and some to opinion-leaders who are in a position to recommend the product. Each of them requires a different message. Thus, while a consumer may be impressed by the look of a particular brand of non-breakable synthetic cooking wares, dealers may need to know the margins available, its quality and attraction over the competing brands. The examples will include the regular publication newsletters to teachers from publishing houses for book purchase and recommendation. The advertisements inviting dealers/distributors for various product like, Washing Machines, Microwave Ovens, TV, Refrigerator etc., is another example of business-to-business communication.

Thus, it is important to note that the limited view of marketing communications that it forms the communication bridge between a company and its buyers and is known to be promotion, is now being replaced with a more correct and wider proposition that marketing communications travels beyond promotion. In its linkages with buyers, it encompasses everything including product, packaging, and distribution channels and forms as a vital part of overall marketing efforts towards buyers and also the other sections of the society.

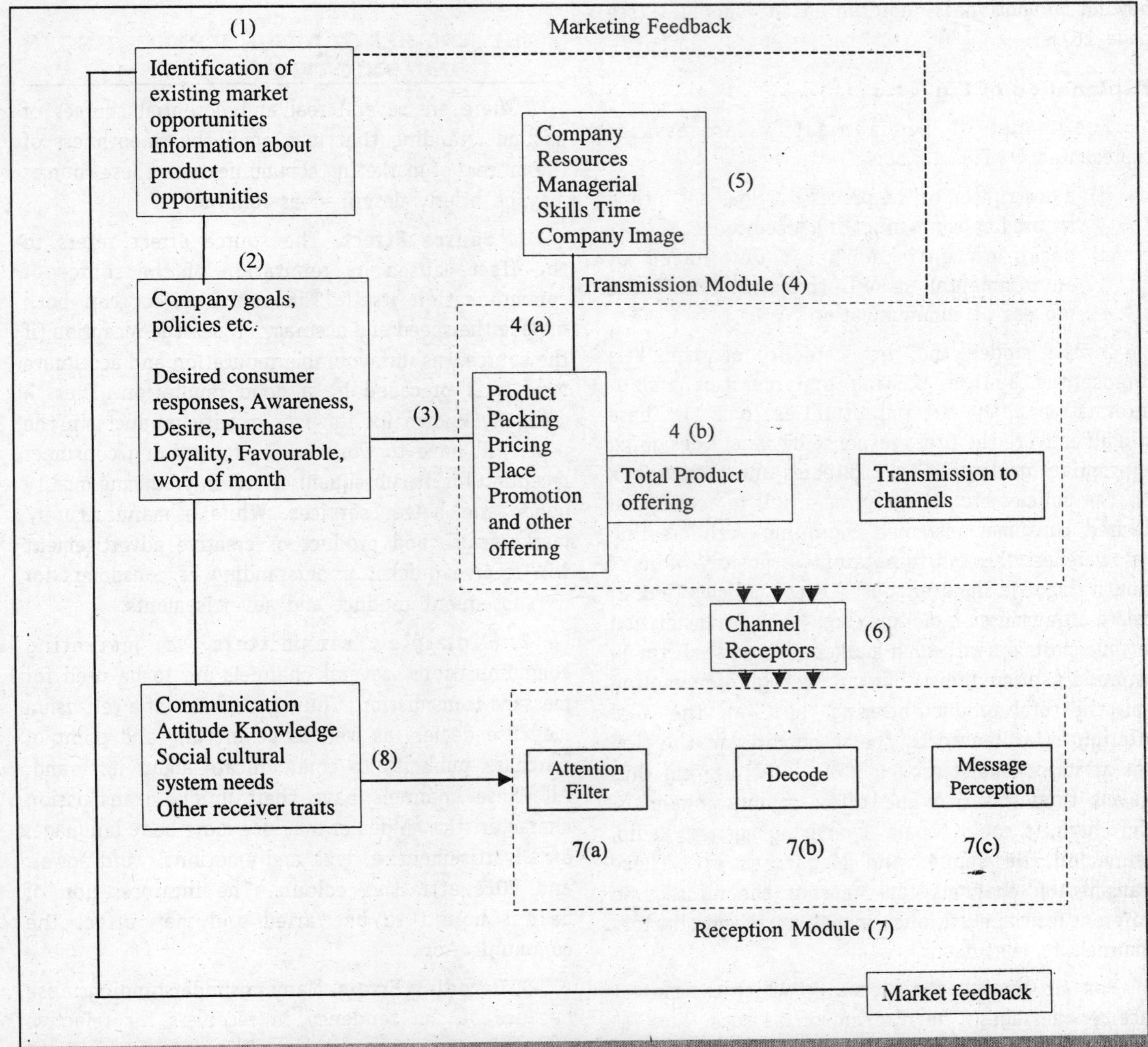

FIG. 11.3. Marketing Communication Process Travels Beyond Promotion

Communication is vital to non-profit organisations and social institutions too. Thus, the Help Age India of Delhi, and the Times of India foundation for Eye Bank would look forward to marketing communications with the same expectation as would probably the Proctor & Gamble and The Hindustan Lever. The anti-drugs campaign and the Family Planning & Welfare message at the TV Prime time are handy illustrations of the value of marketing communications in non-profit and social organisations.

The marketing communications process that travels beyond promotion is represented in Fig. 11.3 (see page 267).

Explanation of Fig. 11.3

The model of communication process, as represented by Fig. 11. 3 is :

(i) a description of the process. It does not intend to predict communication occurrence.
(ii) based on both marketer dominated or environmental stimuli that trigger off the process of communication.

In the model, the first category of stimuli is represented by the existing opportunities and/or information about the opportunities (box 1). These stimuli activate the firm's response by way of designing appropriate goals policies, strategies and tactics (box 2). The policies etc., then act as a null to accomplish desired consumer response beginning with creating an awareness through to obtaining a positive word of mouth (box 3). Simultaneously, these policies (box 2) create a transmission module (box 4). The transmission module starts off with such marketer-dominated stimuli as product, pricing, distribution, packaging, promotion i.e., the total product offering (box 4a). The total offering is influenced by the resources that the firm has at its command (box 5). The total offering thus travels though varied and often complex channels. The channels could be an advertising agency, Radio, Television, Newspaper and Magazines etc. These transmission channels can transmit the message in different forms i.e., through visual, aural and olfactory channels to consumers.

Box 7 represents the process in which the market receives messages. The filtering of message (box 7a) is a dependent upon communication skills of message receivers (box 8). The box (7c) indicates how messages have been perceived by target-receivers. This indication is given in the form of feedback, which travels back right through to the company's perception of existing and potential market opportunities and through to the transmission module (box 4) to turn the circle full.

It should be cautioned that the model may suffer from an over-simplification of the process. Further, there may be many hidden snags in proceeding from a stage to another. However, the model should be useful in understanding the process at a general level.

THE SOURCES OF MISUNDERSTANDING IN COMMUNICATION

There are several real and potential sources of misunderstanding that may spoil the smoothness of the process of marketing communication. These sources may be briefly described as follows:

1. Source Effect. The source effect refers to the effect caused by reputation of the source of communication itself. The source effect can both impede the speed and accuracy of message reception (if the source was unfavourable reputation and accelerate it if it is preceded by a good reputation. Thus, a company known for its poor quality products in the past, will have to work harder for gaining consumer reception for its subsequent efforts in producing quality goods and better services. While a manufacturer/ marketer-of good product or creative advertisement will receive quicker understanding of consumers for its subsequent product and advertisements.

2. Multiple Transmitters. In marketing communications, several channels are to be used for message transmission. Thus, a marketer of a television may use dealers as well as advertising and point of purchase publicity to communicate about its brand. All these channels have their unique transmission characteristics. A dealer may use more body language; an advertisement; a sleek and emotional word power; and POPs attractive colours. The interpretation of each is bound to be varied and may affect the communication.

3. Decoding Errors. Many misunderstandings arise because of the tendency in receivers for selective perception and interpretation. The classic example of this phenomenon is again the ONIDA television. The snag occurs more often when the message is unusual, shocking and substantially different from the current ones.

4. Communication Noise. 'Noise' represents an interference in marketing communication that is either deliberately or accidentally introduced and which blocks or distorts transmission . The noise could originate from the message itself (internal noise) either in the form of unknown words or any other stimuli. The communication could suffer from 'external noise' (TV commercials in a busy restaurant). The competitors could also introduce 'noise' by having similar messages or providing counter-arguments, Liril of HLL and Godrej's Lime are the recent examples of communication noise.

5. Inadequate Feedback. The final misunderstanding in communication may arise due to poor feedback given to the sender. This may affect the quality of subsequent marketing communication. No wonder, therefore, many marketing communicators spend lakhs of rupees to establish and monitor their feedback system.

MANAGING AND CO-ORDINATING THE MARKETING COMMUNICATIONS PROCESS

There are several promotion tools, such as advertisement, personal selling, sales promotion, and public relation and publicity. Members of the marketing department often have different views on how to split the promotion budget. The sales manager would rather plead to hire a few more salespersons than spent a lot of money on a single television commercial ad. The public relations manager may feel that he can do wonders with some money shifted from advertising to public relations. Similarly, the advertising manager may plead the efficacy of a commercial ad on television to attract more potential-buyers. In the past, firms left these decisions to different people. No one person was responsible for thinking through the roles of the various promotion tools and co-ordinating the promotion mix. However, today, more firms are adopting the concept of "integrated marketing communications" firm and its products can help customers solve their problems.

No matter who is in charge of marketing communications, people at all levels of the organisation must be aware of the growing body of laws and regulations that governs marketing communications activities. The firms should not only understand and abide by these laws and regulations but they should also ensure that they communicate honestly and fairly with consumers and resellers as well as without creating any kind of misunderstanding.

PROMOTIONAL STRATEGY AND TACTICS

A wide range of communication tools and procedures are available to a firm to communicate with its target markets. It is therefore imperative that they are well co-ordinated, other wise the communication process may not work to fullest advantage of the firm. In fact, the financial and non-financial resources sunk in any marketing communication programme are just too heavy to afford any misjudgment in promotional planning. Of course, there is need of giving a strategic orientation to the promotional efforts.

The strategic orientation to promotional activities is a necessary condition to a firm with a desire to survive and earn profit in a highly competitive marketing environment. Such orientation provides it with an orderly plan for putting marketing resources and for exploiting market opportunities. It is a design that guides promotional activities for a long period.

Strategy is the art of distributing and applying means to fulfill the end policy. It may be defined as the art and service of adopting and co-ordinating resources to the attainment of an objective.

Thus, strategy is the way of achieving the 'ends' or 'objectives' of a firm. It is a long-term vision of what the business is or is striving to be. It reflects on the firm's 'self and 'self-ideal' image. When translated in the context of promotion efforts, strategy will denote a long range view of what promotion will be and what it should be.

It is to be noted that marketing communication and promotional objectives stem out of the corporate objectives and marketing objectives. This relationship is shown in Fig. 11.4 below:

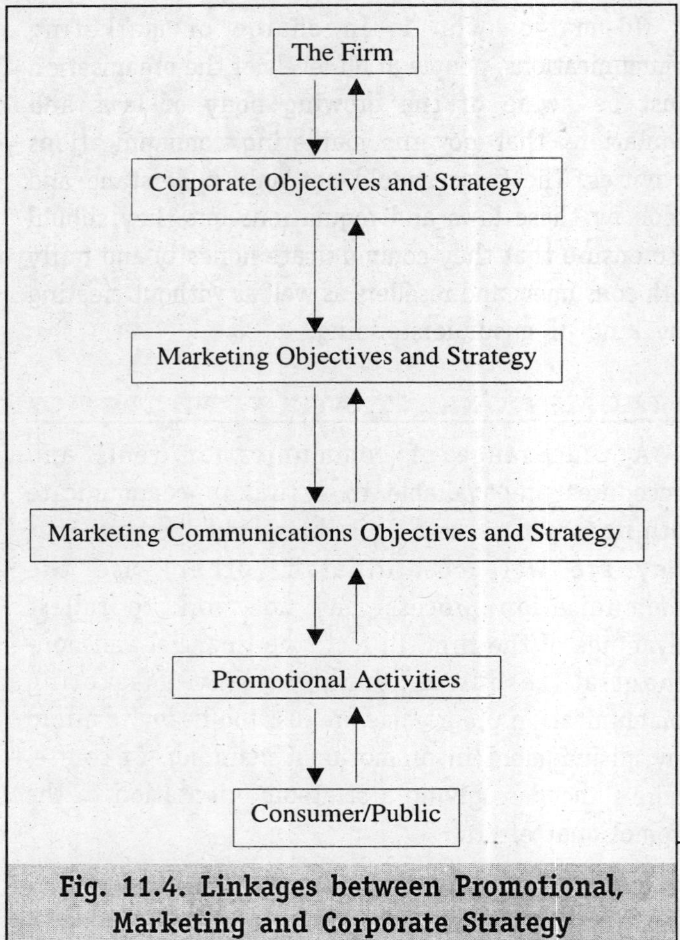

Fig. 11.4. Linkages between Promotional, Marketing and Corporate Strategy

It should be noted that 'tactics' are the ways for strategy application and involve a 'development of resources with a view to implement strategy objective'. This will be amply clear by an illustration of two marketing firms-called A and B. Supposing that firm 'A' has formulated a strategy of offering continuously new products in the market. Since new products take time in customer acceptance, marketing tactics for the firm would be to issue generous discount coupons to encourage first trial and repeat purchase rates. Similarly, if company 'B' has wished to introduce up-market products, it will have to use, *inter-alia,* tactics of attractive packaging and promotion of high-grade dealers.

Planning Framework of Promotional Strategy (Or Promotional Planning)

After a company has decided its promotional strategy and tactics, it turns its attention for evolving a framework of promotional planning. A typical approach for promotional planning comprises: situational analysis, setting up of objectives, allocation of funds, programming the elements of promotion, co-ordination and integration, measurement of effectiveness, and evaluation and follow up.

The various steps or stages or components in promotional planning process may be briefly described as follows:

1. Situational Analysis. The promotional planning begins along with an analysis of promotion environment. It includes and extends to both the external and internal environments.

Among the major external environmental variables, attention is focussed on market demand (including culture, attitudes, individual differences, and buyer decision process); definition and identification of target markets (including segmentation, and positioning); market competition; and legal constraints on promotional activities.

With regard to internal environment, focus will be on such aspects as personnel, financial and technological resources; established policies and procedures, and operational distinctive features.

2. Establishment of Promotional Objectives. Objectives are expressions of where a company would like to be in the future. These objectives will specify: relationship to market target, communication message objectives, and sales objectives. It may be noted here that promotional objectives are derived from corporate objectives and situation analysis. For example, the possible promotional objectives could be: specific conditions desired to be achieved in the minds of the consumers, including product knowledge, improving company image, and increasing brand awareness. Although the promotional objectives are normally for the direct utility for marketing managers only, it is advisable to have a macro view of these objectives so as to have a larger picture of promotional framework.

3. Setting the Total Promotion Budget (Allocation of Funds). The important question in this regard is: How does the company decide on the total promotion budget?

Budgeting for promotion is an area where a lot of subjectivity prevails regarding what is the right amount to be spent on the promotion function. However, all companies believe in one way or the other that: (i) incremental promotional expenditure yields incremental sales to a certain extent, and (ii) a minimum level of promotion activity must be taken up to have a meaningful effect — often such a minimum level of promotion is set by the competitor or more appropriately by an average firm of the industry.

It is not surprising to note that industries and companies very widely in how much they spend on promotion. Promotion spending may be 20% to 30% of sales in the cosmetics industry, and only 5% to 10% in the industrial machinery industry. Within a given industry, both low and high-spending companies can be found.

A company may decide on its promotion budget by using any one of the following methods or techniques:

(a) Arbitrary method. Under this method, the company arbitrarily decides the amount of promotion budget. For example, if the current year's promotion budget is Rs. 1,00,000 and the next year is expected to be a good year, the decision is taken to increase funds allocation by 10% to 15%. Thus, the allocation will stand between Rs. 1,10,000 and Rs. 1,15,000 for next year. This method is very simple to use. However, it is not rational and very much depends on the individual perception of future changes held by the decision maker.

(b) Percentage-of-sales method. This method views promotion budget determination by linking the appropriation to a fixed percentage of sales of the company products. Such sales may relate to the previous year, or an average of sales of the previous few years, or projected sale of the next year or years or an average of the previous few years' sales, as well as the projected sales of the next few years. For example, if the present promotion funds percentage is 10%, then for every sale worth Rs. 100, Rs. 10 is spent on promotion. Thus, if next year's sales are forecast to be Rs.l crore, the promotional budget will be fixed at Rs. 10 lakhs.

Automobile companies usually budget a fixed percentage for promotion based on the planned car price. Oil companies set the budget at some fraction of a rupee for each gallon of gasoline sold under their labels.

The percentage-of-sales method has a number of advantages: (i) Using this method means that promotion spending is likely to vary with what the company can afford. (ii) It also helps management think about the relationship between promotion spending, selling price, and profit per unit. (iii) This method supposedly creates competitive stability because competing firms tend to spend about the same percentage of their sales on promotion.

However, the percentage-of-sales method has certain demerits also: (i) It wrongly views sales as the 'cause' of promotion rather than as the 'result' (ii) The budget is based on availability of funds rather than on opportunities (iii) It may prevent the increased spending sometimes needed to turn around falling sales, (iv) Long-range planning is difficult because the budget varies with year-to-year sales, (v) It fails to account for the changing promotional costs (i.e., expenditure), and relating the 'appropriations made' to the 'product-market needs' (vi) The forcasted sales realisations remain uncertain, (vii) The method does to provide any basis for choosing a 'specific' percentage, except what has been done to the part or what competitors are doing.

(c) Fixed-sum per unit method. Very much like the percent-of-sales under this method the promotion budget is determined by allocating a fixed amount of money per physical unit of product for either past of future sales or a combination of the two. The only differentiating point of this method from the percent-of-sales method is that the base for budgeting, instead of being rupee sales, is the number of product units sold or targeted to be sold. This method, thus, has almost the same strengths and weaknesses as the ones associated with per cent-of-sales method, namely, simplicity in the determination but abitrariness in arriving at the percentage or per unit allocation.

(i) Affordable-funds method. Many companies set the promotion budget at the level they think the company can afford. For example, if a firm has a total marketing budget of Rs. 10 lakhs, out of which Rs. 5 lakhs are allocated for distribution, Rs. 4 lakhs for product testing, and Rs.30,000 for consumer surveys. then remaining amount of Rs. 70,000 is left for promotion tools.This method is based on management's view that promotion expenditure is one of those business costs which are desirable or avoidable as per the availability of residual funds.

This method of setting budget completely ignores the effect of promotion on sales volume. It leads to an uncertain annual promotion budget, which makes long-range promotion planning difficult. Although the affordable-funds method can result in overspending on promotion tools, it more often recalls in under spending.

(e) Competitive-parity method. Incorporating a measure of competitive-ness in planning, this method sets the promotion budget to match competitor's outlays. The company watches its competitors' advertising and other promotion tools or gets industry promotion-spending estimates from publications or trade associations, and then sets its budget based on the industry average.

The advantages claimed about this method are: (i) Competitors' budgets represent the collective wisdoms of the industry. Hence, the company gets benefit from them, (ii) Spending what competitors spend helps present promotion wars. However, there are some demerits in this method as follows: (i) There are no grounds believing that the competitors have a better idea of what a company should be spending on promotion than does the company itself, (ii) Companies differ greatly and each has its own special promotion needs which are ignored under this method, (iii) There is no evidence that budgets based on competitive-parity prevent promotion wars.

(f) Objective-and-task method. This is the most logical or scientific method of budget setting. Under this method, the company sets its promotion budgets based on what it wants to accomplish with promotion. Marketers develop their promotion budgets by (i) defining specific objectives, (ii) determining the task which must be performed to achieve these objectives, and (iii) estimating the costs of performing these tasks. The sum of these costs is the proposed promotion budget. The typical objectives for the next year might be: (i) to increase sales of the brand × by 5%, (ii) to introduce brand Y and attain recognition by 15% of the target market, and (iii) to improve positive rating of the company from 60% to 75%.

This method forces management to spell out its assumptions about the relationship between rupees spent and promotion results. However, it is alone the most difficult method to use. Often, it is hard to figure out which specific task will achieve specific objectives. For example, if BPL wants 90% awareness for its latest music system model during the five-month introductory period, then what specific advertising messages and media schedules would BPL need in order to attain this objective? How much would these messages and media schedules cost? BPL management must consider such questions, even though they are hard to answer. Moreover, there is another lacuna that this method presupposes that objectives set are realistic and promotion results can be measured precisely.

The practice. In practice most companies make use of more than one method for determining the promotion budget. The research into the practices of the companies in India in this regard revealed this finding. Among the individual methods used "affordable funds" method emerged as the most popular. There are, however, quite a few companies which have started using the approach of objective and task' in setting their promotion budget either exclusive or in combination with other methods. Most of such companies are dealing in consumer goods.

The practices of the companies using a combination of methods for determining promotion budget points to the efforts they are putting in together competitive promotion outlays and its apportioning to various promotion components.

4. Setting the Promotion Mix or Promotion Tools. The important question in this regard is: How does the company divide the total promotion budget among the major promotion tools, to create an appropriate promotion mix? After setting the total promotion budget, the company must divide it among the major promotion tools, i.e., advertising, personal selling, sales promotion, and public relations. It must blend the promotion tools carefully into a co-ordinated 'promotion mix' that will achieve its advertising and marketing objectives. Companies within the same industry differ greatly in how they design their promotion mixes. For example, some companies spend most of their promotion - funds on personal selling and catalogue marketing and the least of it on advertising. Whereas, some other firms spend heavily on consumer advertising. Yet some other companies sell most of their water purifiers and vacuum cleaners door to door, while some companies rely more on advertising.

It may be noted that companies always are looking for ways to improve promotion by replacing one promotion tool with another that will do the same job more economically. Many companies have replaced a portion of their field sales activities with telephone sales and direct mail. Other companies have increased their sales promotion spending in relation to advertising to gain quicker sales.

5. Co-ordination and Integration of Promotional Efforts. Past research has brought out what separate a successful strategy from a non-successful one. The major factor is effective coordination and integration of various efforts. The same is true for promotional strategy.

A promotion co-ordinator thus, has to ensure that unless otherwise required, advertising should not over-shadow personal selling for a given product or *vice-versa*. Similarly, a careful decision has to be taken for involving outsiders like advertisement agency, market research and media buying services in your promotional efforts. A proper balance is to be arrived at between management and outside experts thinking. Execution of promotion programme should be properly scheduled.

6. Measuring the Effectiveness of Promotion. It is widely recognised that part of a firm's promotional effort is ineffective. Measuring the effectiveness of promotional expenditures has become an extremely important research issue, particularly among advertisers. Studies aimed at this measurement dilemma face several major obstacles, one of them being the difficulty of isolating the effect of the promotional variable.

Most marketers prefer to use a 'direct-sales-results' test to measure the effectiveness of promotion. Such an approach would reveal the specific impact on sales revenues for each rupee of promotional spending. However, this type of technique has never been possible due to the marketer's inability to control for other variables operating in the market. For example, a firm may experience Rs. 1 crore in additional sales following a new Rs. 5 lakh advertising campaign. but the success may have resulted from price increases of competing products rather than from the advertising outlays.

As it is difficult to isolate the effects of promotion from the other marketing elements and outside environmental variables, many marketers have simply abandoned all attempts at measurement. However, others turn to indirect evaluation. These researchers concentrate on the factors that are quantifiable, such as 'recall' (i.e., how much is remembered about specific products or advertisements) and 'readership' (i.e., size and composition of the audience).The basic problem is the difficulty of relating these variables to sales. For example, does extensive readership lead to increased sales?

The frequently used assessment or measurement methods for determining promotional effectiveness include sales inquiries, and research studies aimed at determining changes in consumer attitudes toward the product and improvement in public knowledge and awareness.

It is to be noted that measuring promotion effectiveness in foreign markets can be especially challenging. In the United States, the technological innovation that has revolutionised evaluation of consumer advertising and sales promotion is the 'single-source' research system. It combines scanner-generated buying information at supermarkets with consumer demographics and the television advertising and in-store promotions to which those consumers are exposed. From this data, marketers can measure the effectiveness of that advertising and sales promotion, determine why or why not sales increase, discover which consumers respond to which promotions, and test the short and long-term profitability of advertising and sales promotion. With single-source data, marketers can avoid wasting money on ineffective communications.

7. Evaluation and Following up. At this stage, marketers have to evaluate implementation and efforts of the promotional strategy; identify the gaps between its objectives and results; and plan action for its follow up. This way, chances of making the same mistakes again and yet all over again, are reduced considerably. It also ensures that lessons are learnt from deficiencies. Finally, notwithstanding the presence of subjective perceptions in evaluation, accountability needs to be fixed for doing both right and wrong things in the promotion strategy. For this reason alone, the evaluation and follow up of promotional strategy is inescapable.

CHAPTER 12

ADVERTISING VIS-A-VIS COMMUNICATION

REACHING FOR THE SKYY

The last five years have been heady times for vodka as the product category has experienced strong growth and one wave of chic new brands has been followed by another. Consumption of vodka.has increased steadily since 1998, and the vodka category is double the size of the next distilled-spirits segment, rum. Ironically, a bland-tasting product that was best known for helping Russians make it through a cold, bleak winter has become a status symbol for many trendy 20- and 30-somethings in America. Marketers have been trying to capitalize on the growing popularity of vodka, and the growth of the "cocktail culture" that has brought more young adults to the spirits market, by creating a distinct image for their brands and getting consumers to think of them as cutting edge, edgy, and hip. While a myriad of new vodka brands have been introduced in recent years, none has been as successful at attracting the attention of consumers as Skyy. The brand has overtaken Stolichnaya as the number-two super-premium vodka in the United States, trailing only Absolut.

Skyy was founded in 1992 by Maurice Kanbar, who developed it as a premium brand for older connoisseurs, like himself, desirous of the perfect martini. Kanbar developed a four-stage distillation process that extracts many of the congers, which are natural impurities that remain in alcohol after distillation and may contribute to headaches, and created what he believed to be the purest of vodkas. The Skyy name came to him one day when he was looking out the window of his San Francisco apartment and viewing a brilliant blue sky. The additional "y" in the brand name was simply an addition to make the name less common and develop a trademark, while the cobalt-blue bottle was selected to connote a distinctive, daring product.

Much of Skyy's initial growth was driven by word of mouth. The company was successful in get-ting its eye-catching blue bottle into swanky Hollywood parties and nightclubs known for attracting a hip crowd. Skyy quickly generated a buzz on the nightclub circuit, where word spread that its quadruple-distilled formula reduced the likelihood of hangovers. The company also spent much of its limited marketing budget on sponsoring independent film festivals and producing artsy short films that were shown at these events. Skyy commissioned these short films by well-known independent film directors as part of its commitment to the independent film industry, which is one of Kanbar's passions. The directors are not asked to create an advertisement for Skyy, although each film does include "a cocktail moment." The Oscar-winning director of the film Europa has directed one of the films, and supermodel Claudia Schiffer has co-starred with Skyy in another cocktail moment. The company uses the internet to feature these films as a way of expanding its presence on the Web and also shows them as part of the festivals and movie premieres that it sponsors.

Advertising has also become an important part of Skyy's brand-building efforts. When the Lambesis agency took over the account in 1998, the challenge was to create a brand image that would generate buzz among young adults and create awareness and trial in a category already dominated by strong brands such as Absolut and Stolichnaya. The agency realized that it would be critical to establish an emotional connection with young adults, who were beginning to develop their brand loyalties, and set out to create image-based advertising that would distinguish the brand from competitors' more product-focused ads.

The "Skyy Cinema" campaign was launched in 1998 and targets 21-to 34-year-old urban, metro-consumers. To establish Skyy's brand platform, identifiable cinematic cocktail moments were created for the advertising. The high-impact ads do not contain any copy but, rather, rely on stylish, seductive visuals that set up various no/r-inspired story lines but leave the actual scenarios up to the mind of the viewer. Chad Farmer, the creative director for Lambesis, notes that all the ads establish Skyy's distinctive cobalt-blue bottle as the "star" and have made it an iconic symbol while showcasing the brand as a catalyst for a great cock-tail moment. To create a buzz about the campaign, a media plan was developed to reach style-conscious trendsetters through avant-garde publications such as Paper and Interview. As the buzz developed, more mainstream magazines were added to the media mix, such as Details, Spin, Vogue, Rolling Stone, InStyle, Movieline, and Entertainment Weekly, along with outdoor ads in key influential markets.

Skyy's former brand manager, Teresa Zepeda, notes that Skyy is all about style, innovation, and quality. She notes: "We have to be disciplined and be focused, and make an impact speaking to our target rather than speaking to every consumer just a little bit." Skyy has achieved its tremendous growth despite spending only a fraction of the media dollars of its big-spending competitors such as Absolut and Stolichnaya. Zepeda adds, "We look bigger than we actually are and that is the strength of our creative and focus behind the brand." Actually, Skyy is becoming quite big, its sales have jumped from 3,000 cases in 1993 to more than 1.3 million cases in 2002. The liquor trade has recognized Skyy as the "fasting-growth spirit of the decade," and it has received Impact magazine's Hot Brand Award in the spirits category for six consecutive years. It appears the sky may be the limit for this hot brand.

Sources: Kenneth Hein, "Strategy: Skyy Sets the Stage in Sultry Cinematic Scenes, Adweek, June 17, 2002; Melinda Fulmer, "Skyy Vodka Shoots for the Hip," Los Angeles Times, Apr. 17, 1999, pp. C1, 3; Theresa Howard, "Marketers of the Next Generation: Teresa Zepeda," Brandweek, Nov. 8, 1999, pp. 18-21.

In the present era of severe competition, companies are required not only to make good products but they must also inform consumers that they have made products with the features and benefits desired by the consumers, and must carefully position the products in consumers' minds. In other words, demand creation is almost as important as meeting the existing demand. Demand creation requires some kind of means to create awareness in the mind of the consumers about the availability, features, uses, and benefits of the product. Advertising is the most popular method to do so.

There are three elements of non-personal promotion: advertising, sales-promotion, and public relations and publicity. These are the mass communication tools available to marketers. As its name suggests, mass communication uses the same message for everyone in an audience. The mass communication has the advantage of reaching many people at a lower cost per person, especially in comparison to personal selling. However, mass communication is not made indiscriminately to all people. Advertisers always try to seek ways and means to present their message to well-defined target audiences or consumer. Because of its mass appeal, advertising is used not only by business organizations but also by many not-for-profit organizations, such as the governments, government agencies, educational institutions, recreational institutions, civic authorities, social organization environmental groups, consumer-right organization, and so on. These organizations confidently rely on advertising to make the public aware of their existence, objectives and activities. Advertising has become so popular among the masses that it is often regarded by them as synonymous with marketing, although advertising is just one element in the promotion mix which is, in turn, one element in the marketing mix. A master marketer can devise a competition-beating recipe through a creative and intelligent use of advertising. However, it is essential for him to know precisely the influencing stimuli that make the customer react positively to what is being offered.

In modern times, advertising prevails in all walks of human life. It has acquired the distinction of being the most visible and glamourous method of marketing communications. While listening to radio, or viewing television or a cricket match, or reading a newspaper/ magazine, or walking on a street, we come across a number of advertisements. These messages mostly appeal to buy certain products or services, or adopt certain ideas. Indeed, advertisements are used by companies to attract the attention of consumers towards their products which are claimed to serve consumers' needs and requirements, or which the consumer were desperately looking for. In modern industrial economies, business cannot grow and develop without the help of advertising. Some of the measures marketing and communication functions performed by advertising today include: to inform, entertain, persuade influence, remind, reassure, and add value to the product or service advertised.

ADVERTISING DEFINED

The word advertising has been derived from the Latin word "Advertere" which means to turn (the mind) to. Broadly speaking, advertising does turn the attention of people to a commodity or service. Simply stated, advertising involves dissemination or spreading of information concerning a product, service or idea to compel action on the part of the target people in accordance with the intent advertiser.

Advertising has been defined as follows:

Kotler and Armstrong. "Advertising is any form of non-personal presentation and promotion of ideas, goods, or service by an identified sponsor."

Boone & Kurtz. "Advertising is paid, non-personal communication through various media by business firms, non-profit organizations, and individuals who are identified in the advertising message and hope to inform or persuade members of a particular audience"

William Stanton & Other. "Advertising consists of all the activities involved in presenting to an audience, non-personal, sponsor- identified, paid-for message about a product or organization."

The American Marketing Association has also adopted the definition of marketing as given by Kotler & Armstrong.

Thus, advertising is paid, non-personal communication from an identified sponsor using mass media, resorted to persuade or influence audience.

Advertising has been defined by American marketing Association as:

"Any paid form of non-personal presentation of ideas, goods and services by an identified sponsor,

This definition falls short of incorporating the effects of advertising. Advertising not only "presents" ideas, goods and services, but must also persuade people to respond positively to the advertised massage. The definition can be refined of state:

"Advertising is any controlled form of non-personal presentation and promotion of ideas, goods and services by an identified sponsor, that is used to inform and persuade the selected market".

Advertising has become an integral part of our society. In has become embedded in our daily lives. We cannot go through a newspaper, listen to a radio of watch the television, without reading hearing and seeing some advertisement or commercial. We see them on billboards, on buses, in trains in magazines, on match boxes, on many novelty items, some message aimed at influencing us or making us aware of the advertisers product. Advertising is a forceful tool in mounding our attitudes and our behaviour towards our products and ideas and services. The word of mouth from friends and associates and our own direct experience with these goods and services further strengthen the effect of the advertising message of our minds.

Advertising is a vital marketing tool as well as powerful communication force. It is the action of calling something to attention of the people, especially by paid announcements. It is a message designed to make known what we have to sell or what we have to buy. By using various channels of information and persuasion, it can help to sell goods, services, images and ideas. In respect of public utility services also social advertisements can make people aware of the drug menace, the risk about other important problems like the need of promoting national integration.

One of the four major tools companies use to direct persuasive communications to target buyers and publics is advertising that consists of non personal forms of communication conducted though paid media under clear sponsorship.

Primarily a firm's marketing tool, advertising is used in all the countries across the world, including socialist countries. It is a cost effective way to disseminate messages, whether it is to build brand preference for Coca-Cola ore Pepsi or all over the world or to motivate a developing nation's consumers to drink milk or butter milk.

Basically this is because advertising goes into various media, magazine and newspaper space; radio and television; outdoor displays (posters, signs, skywriting); direct mail: novelties (matchboxes, blotters, calendars); cards (car, taxis, bus or what not); catalogues; directories, yellow pages and circulars, web, Internet etc.

Advertising has many uses; long-term buildup of the organization's image (institutional advertising), long-term buildup of a particular brand (brand advertising), information dissemination about a sale, service, product or event (classified advertising), announcement of a special sale (sale advertising) and advocacy of a particular cause (advocacy advertising).

Organizations obtain their advertising in different ways. In small companies, advertising is handled by someone in the sale department, who works with an advertising agency. Large companies set up their own advertising departments, whose managers report to the vice-presidents of marketing. The advertising department develops the total budget, approves advertising agency ads and campaigns and handles direct-mail advertising, dealer displays and other forms of advertising not ordinarily performed by the agency. Most companies use an outside advertising agency which offers several advantages.

NATURE/FEATURES OF ADVERTISING

1. Advertising is a paid from and hence is commercial in nature. Publicity is not paid for by the sponsor. Advertising is a paid from of publicity. Thus, any sponsored communication designed to influence buyer behaviours is advertising.

2. Advertising is non-personal, whatever the from of advertisement (visual, Spoken or written), it is directed at a mass audience and not directed at individual as in personal selling. Advertisements are identifiable with their sponsoring authority, which is not always the case with publicity.

All advertisements have the following features:

1. Form. There may be three forms of advertising: (a) verbal (Spoken), (b) Visual, or (c) Written.

2. Paid messages. For every advertisement, some money has to be paid to the medium, which carries the message. For instance, if the message is published in a magazine, payment must be made for printing and the space used in that magazine. If the matter is printed without any charge, it will not be treated as an advertisement.

This implies that all advertising messages have to be paid for, thus, involving a commercial transaction. Payment is made by the advertiser (sponsor) for buying space (if media like newspapers, magazines, journals or brochures, etc., are used) and time (if broadcast media such as TV or Radio are used).

3. Non-personal presentation. When a salesman directly talks to the customer about any product, it is personal presentation. If the message is communicated through mass media like radio, television, newspaper, magazine, direct mail, hoardings, etc., it is called non-personal presentation. In the case of advertising, the message is conveyed through non-personal media. In implies that message is presented to the customer by a salesman, it would not be treated as advertising.

4. Ideas, goods and services. This implies that advertising may be intended to help selling not only goods but also intangibles, such as ideas and services. For instance, banks, insurance companies, airlines, restaurants, dry cleaners, and similar organization advertise their services and ideas underlying the usefulness of savings, travelling, eating palatable food, etc., just as manufacturer of automobiles, soaps or hair oil advertise the usefulness of their products. Thus, the phrase ideas, goods and services explain that advertising is concerned with much more than the promotion of only tangible goods.

5. Identified sponsor. The sponsor of advertising is the advertiser.

The phrase 'identified sponsor' means that the producer or seller who advertises the product should be known through the advertised message. In other words, the receiver of the message should be able to identify both of source and purpose of the advertisement. If it is not sponsored by any individual or institution, it would not come under advertisement. This simply means that the originator or source of the advertising message must be identified. It states that advertising bears a signature in form of a company or brand name. In some cases the brand name and the company's name might be specified in the advertisement. For example, most "Godrej" and "Tata" products are advertised with brand name as well as company name whereas others such as Lux, Pears, etc., carry the brand name only. Any communication, using mass media not identified by a sponsor is not an advertisement. It is likely that some form of advertising has existed since the development of the exchange process. Most early advertising was vocal, done through criers and hawkers. (They advertise today also.) Later, development of printing press greatly expanded advertising's capabilities. The newspaper advertising started as back as the early 18th century in the United States. One identifying feature of advertising in the twentieth century is its concern for researching its target markets. Understanding consumer behaviour is now an important aspect of advertising strategy. Originally advertising research dealt primarily with media selection and the product. Then advertisers became increasingly concerned with determining the appropriate 'demographics', i.e., characteristics such as the age, sex and income level of potential buyers. Behavioural influences in purchase decisions, often called, 'psychographics' can be useful in describing potential markets for advertising appeals. These influences include factors such as lifestyle and personal attitudes. Increased information about consumer psychographics has led to improve advertising decisions.

PURPOSE AND IMPORTANCE OF ADVERTISING

Advertisement creates a demand for the goods and makes it possible for the introduction of mass production installation of up to date machinery and consequent reduction of the cost of the article. Advertising is beneficial not only to the manufacturer and the retailer but also to the consumer.

(A) Benefits to Manufacturer

The following are some of the benefits of advertising to the manufacturer.

1. The increase in demand caused by advertising makes possible the installation of latest plants and introduction of technological improvement. This results not only in improved quality of the product but in the reduction of the cost per unit.
2. Mass production needs mass selling. Advertising makes this possible.
3. Through advertising, the manufacturer can create a demand for his product and maintain it throughout the year and thereby reduce the seasonal slumps in the business.
4. Advertising also protects the manufacturer against unfair competition because the public learns to recognize the brand and the name of the manufacturer.
5. Advertising also creates pressure of the retailer to stock the goods which have a good demand, as otherwise he would run the risk of loosing his customers to the competitors.
6. Advertising tends to stabilize the selling price and this can create confidence in the public.
7. Pushing goods to the individual customer through the salesman is slow and expensive method and the number of calls is limited as considerable time is taken up in travelling, advertising provides a comparatively less expensive method.
8. In case of changes in the products, advertising helps in giving the necessary information very quickly to the customers.

(B) Benefits to Retailer

The following are some of the benefits of advertising to the retailer:

1. Advertising quickens the turnover, reduces risk on dead stock and can result in proportionate reduction of overhead expenses.
2. The retailer is generally afraid of fluctuations in prices. Advertising stabilize the price and thus unfair competition and 'price wars' are avoided.
3. The retailer can also easily anticipate the actual sales and plan his stock accordingly.
4. By creating new demands and including the public to spend more money on the foods, advertising increases the sales which benefits the retailer by reducing the percentage of overhead expenses.

5. By advertising, the retailer can himself inform the public of his existence and the product he sells.
6. The normal retailer has no salesmen who go out to get orders. Advertising goes out on his behalf right into the market and draws the customers towards his shop. Although attractive window display also helps. It can only attract those who pass by the shop.

(C) Benefits to Consumer

The following are some of the consumer benefits through advertising:

1. The manufacturer is compelled to maintain the quality of the goods advertised. Money spend on advertising being an investment, the manufacturer naturally expects returns on such investment. This interest will be forth coming as long as the manufacturer maintains the quality of the article, as the quality drops the sale of the article will also decline.
2. Well advertised goods are generally better in quality, thus justify advertising, although it can not be denied that certain firms may advertise worthless goods. In the letter case, however the advertising expense will be wasted in the long run.
3. Advertising also acts as an information service and educates the consumer. It enables to know exactly what he wants and where to get it.
4. Advertising stimulates production and reduces the cost per unit. This reduction in the cost is generally passed on to the consumer and that is why price of all advertised goods are found to be generally lower than other goods of the same quality which are not so well advertised.
5. Advertising also makes it possible to sell direct to the consumers by mail order business thus consumers in the out of the way areas can also enjoy the comforts and luxuries available only in the cities or towns. In this way advertising improves social welfare.
6. As manufacturer control the price of well advertised goods, price cutting is not available to the retailers and the shopkeeper tries to attract customers by giving better and more satisfactory service. This also is an additional benefit to the consumer brought about by advertising.

ACTIVITIES INCLUDED IN ADVERTISING

Advertising is a mass communication of information intended to persuade buyers to buy products with a view to maximizing a company's profits. The elements of the adverting are:

(i) It is a mass communication reaching a large group of consumers.
(ii) It is no personal communication, for it is not delivered by an actual person, nor it is addressed to a specific person.
(iii) It makes more production possible.
(iv) It is a commercial communication because it is used to help assure the advertiser of a long business life with profitable sales.
(v) Advertising can be economical, for it reaches long groups as people. This keeps the cost for message low.
(vi) The communication is speedy, permitting an advertiser to speak to millions of buyers in a matter of a few hours.
(vii) Advertising is identified communication. The advertiser sings his name to his advertisement for the purpose of publishing his identity.

The Chairman of American Express Company had once said "good advertising must have three effects: (i) increase sales, (ii) create news, and (iii) enhance the company's image." In a strictly commercial sense, these three elements would constitute the underlying purpose of all advertising must result in the interpretation of the above statement means that advertising must result in the growth of the company's business, create an impact and promote a favourable image of the company.

The objectives of advertising can broadly he divided into two types:

(a) Generalized objectives, and (b) Specific objectives.

(a) Generalized Objectives. Typically advertising has one or more of the three fundamental or basic objectives:

(i) **To inform target customers.** This information essentially deals with areas such as new products introduction, price changes or product improvement or modifications.

(ii) **To persuade** target audience, which includes functions such as building brand preference, encourage people to switch from one brand to the other, etc.

(iii) **To remind** target audience for keeping the brand name dominate.

Generalized advertising objectives fall under one or more of the following categories:

(1) To announce a new product or service. In a saturated market, the introduction of new products and brands can give the seller a tremendous opportunity of increasing his sales. In the case of innovative products (totally new to the market) such as FAX machines and Laptop Computers, a great deal of advertising has to be done over an extended period of time to make people aware of "What the product is" and "What it does" and "How the customer would find it useful". In addition, the advertisement also carries information about the availability of the product and facilities for demonstration/trial, etc. Similarly, new brands of existing product categories are also promoted quite aggressively. Two recent examples are the launching of "Ms" cigarettes for women, for the first time in India and the introduction of "Lehar Pepsi" soft drink.

(2) Expand the market to new buyers. Advertising can be used to tap a new segment of the market, hitherto left unexplored. For example, TV and Video Camera manufacturers who have been concentrating on domestic users and professional can direct their advertising to the government institutions and large organizations for closed circuit TV networks, security systems and educational purpose. Another way of expanding the consumer base is to promote new uses of the product. For example, Johnson's baby oil and baby cream were originally targeted to mothers. The same products have now been directed towards the adult market for their personal use. Similarly, Milkmaid was originally promoted as a substitute for milk. It is now being advertised as an ingredient for making sweet dishes and also as a sandwich spread for children, like Dabur Honey.

(3) Announce a product modification. For such advertising, generally, the term "new", "improved" etc., are used as prefixes to the brand name. For example, "The New Lux International" gives the impression of a new soap, although there may be no tangible difference between the earlier brand and the new one. Sometimes, a minor packaging change might be perceived by the coustomer as a modified product e.g., "a new refill pack for Nescafe".

(4) To make a special offer. On account of competition, slack season, declining sales, etc., advertising may be used to make a special offer. For example, noble house had announced 'three for the price of two' on their Soya milk drink 'Great Shake' to counter declining sales. We often come-across advertisements announcing "Rs. 2 off" on buying various quantities of products such as soaps, toothpastes, etc. Hotels offer special rates during off-season. Similarly, many products like room heaters, fans, air-conditioners, etc., offer season discounts to promote sales. In some cases, a free-gift item is given on the purchase of a company's product.

(5) To announce location of Stockiest and dealers. To support dealers, to encourage selling to stock, and to urge action on the part of readers, space may be taken to list the names and addresses of stockists, dealers, or distributers.

(6) To educate customers. Advertising of this type is "informative" rather than "persuasive". This technique can be used to show new users for a well-established product. It can also be used to educate the people about an improved product e.g., Pearl Pet odour free jars and bottles. Sometimes, societal advertising is used to educate people on the usefulness or harmful effects of certain products. For example, government sponsored advertising was directed at promoting the consumption of 'Eggs and Milk'. Similarly, advertisements discouraged the consumption of liquor and drugs. On the other hand, the advertisement shown in Figure-D encourages the people to get their children vaccinated.

(7) To remind users. This type of advertising is useful for products which have a high rate of 'repeat purchase' or those products which are bought frequently e.g., blades, cigarettes, soft drinks, etc. The advertisement is aimed at reminding the customer to ask for the same brand again.

(8) To please stockiest. A successful retail trader depends upon quick turnover so that his capital can be reused as many times as possible. Dealer support is critical, particularly for those who have limited shelf space for a wide variety of products. Advertisers send 'display' material to dealers for their shops, apart from helping the retailer with local advertising.

(9) To create brand preference. This type of advertising does two things:

(i) It creates a brand image or character by highlighting brand characteristics. (ii) It tells the target audience why brand X is better than brand Y.

In this type of advertisement the product or band acquires a 'personality' associated with the user, which gives the brand a distinctive 'image'. The second type of advertising also known as 'comparative advertising' takes the form of comparison between two brands and proves why one brand is superior.

(10) Inducing potential customers to buy. Another important objective of advertising is to induce potential customers to buy the product. Advertising is one of the best means by which the sale of an existing product can be increased. For this purpose, the advertisement should emphasize the usefulness of the product, its quality, price advantage, etc., so as to win over potential buyers and make them actual buyers. If the product is so advertised, traders expect sales to increase and keep larger stocks for sale. Thus, advertising leads to immediate buying action among customers as well as traders.

(11) To intimate customers about new uses of a product. Advertising is sometimes used to convey new uses of an existing product to the customers or to draw their attention to some new features of the product to the customers or to draw their attention to some new features of the product. The basic objective of advertising in this case is to convince the customers about the superiority of a product in comparison with other products in the same line.

(12) Other objectives. Advertising also helps to boots the morale of sales people in the company. It pleases sales people to see large advertisements of their company and its products, and they often boast it. Other uses of advertising could include recruiting staff and attracting investors through 'public issue' advertisements announcing the allotment of shares, etc. In some cases, the objective of the advertisement is to inform the customers in remote areas, which are not accessible to salesmen. Similarly, it is also aimed at informing customers in far off places or outside the country about the new product.

(B) Specific Objectives. From the advertiser's viewpoint, advertising objectives are defined in terms of: **(1)** Communication objectives, and **(2)** Sales Objectives.

(1) Communication Objectives of Advertising. Advertising is psychological process, which is designed to induce behaviour in an individual leading to a purchase. In other words, one of the major objectives of advertising is to change the person's attitude in a way that moves him or her closer to the product or service being advertised. But purchase behaviour is the result of a long process of consumer decision-making. It is important for the advertiser to know how to move the target customers from their present state to a higher state of readiness-to-buy.

We will look at advertising as a force, which moves people up a series of steps, as shown in Figure 12.1.

The Seven Steps (also known as the "Hierarchy of Effects") are described as follows:

(1) Brand ignorance. This stage includes potential buyers who are completely unaware of the product or service.

(2) Awareness. Target customers are aware of the existence of the product in the market.

(3) Knowledge. People know what the product has to offer.

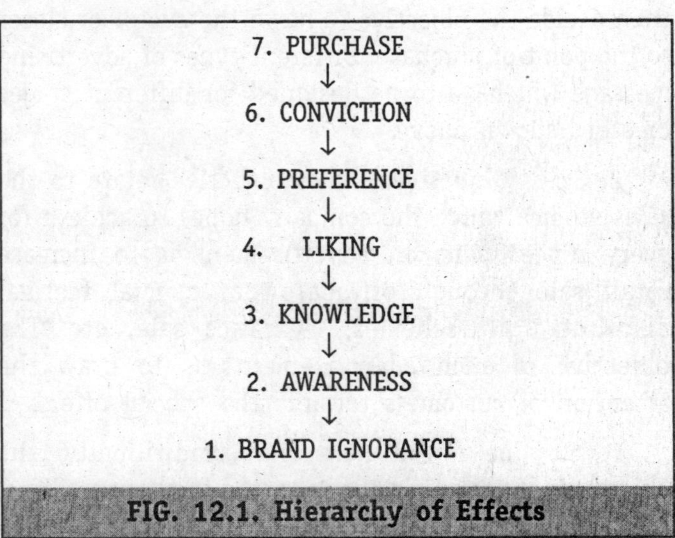

FIG. 12.1. Hierarchy of Effects

(4) Liking. People have favourable attitude towards the product-those who like the product.

(5) Preference. People's favorable attitude had developed to a point of preference of this brand over competitors' brand. Comparative advertising described earlier plays a very important role here.

(6) Conviction. Customers combine preference with a desire to buy and are also convinced that the purchase would be wise.

(7) Purchase. This is the step, which translates the attitude formed in step 6 into an actual purchase.

This model can be used for setting advertising objectives by a company. The advertiser must determine the proportion (percentage of the total target audience) of people who are at different stages mentioned above and then set the objectives accordingly.

For example, a company decides to launch a new brand of potato wafers (such as Binnies) for the first time. Obviously, the potential buyers will be unaware of the brand. Therefore, the advertising objective of the company would be to create awareness, with simple messages repeating the name. That is exactly what Binnies did.

Similarly, a company with a product, which has been in the market for some time, discovers that only a small percentage of the people are aware of the product. The advertising objective would be to increase awareness, say from the present 10% to 40% of the total target audience.

An important implication of this model is to determine the number of people at each stage and then decide the objective to move the customer closer to the point of purchase. Different types of advertising message will have to be designed for different stages or steps shown above.

2. **Sales Objectives.** Sales objective relate to the sales volume which the company hopes to achieve for every rupee spent on advertisement is to increase retail sale through off-season or special festival discounts, gift schemes, clearance sale, etc. The objective of such advertisements is to draw the attention of customers towards the special offers.

It may be noted here that traditionally, the objectives of advertising were stated in terms of direct sales goals. However, a more realistic approach is to view advertising as having communications objectives that seek to inform, persuade (i.e., create new demands), and remind potential customers about the product. Advertising attempts to condition the customer to adopt a favourable view point toward the promotional message. The goal is to improve the likelihood that the customer will buy a particular product or service. In this sense, advertising illustrates the close relationship between marketing communications and promotional strategy. Recent research findings have confirmed the ability of effective advertising to enhance consumer perceptions of quality in a product or service. The results of these quality perceptions are as follows. Stronger customer loyalty, more repeat purchases, and less vulnerability to price wars. In addition, perceived superiority pays off in the ability to raise prices without losing market share. Where personal selling is the primary component of a firm's marketing mix, advertising may be used in a support role, i.e., to assist salespeople.

An advertisement is either good or bad in its objectives. Though advertising is largely informative and persusive in nature, yet to do a good job, the objectives of each advertising campaigned to be clearly spelt out in measurable terms in order to focus clearly on one target audience and on the time period over which these are to be achieved.

Indian experience. The research on the practices of large-sized companies has pointed out that companies in India pursue a wide spectrum of advertising goals at different time periods and in relation to different products. Even similar companies placed in more or less similar market situation may pursue different advertising goals depending upon a host of factors like advertising philosophy, past experience, and the level of expertise existing in the company.

An analysis of advertising goals pursued revealed that these basically focused on moving the customer from one stage of the purchasing process to the other, expansion of the market, and creation of favourable image, besides the overall goal of improving sales. In general, the goals set lacked specific mention of the percent of target market to be reached and influenced.

It may be noted that some marketing experts prefer to group the functions of advertising under the following headings:

(a) Primary function- aspects relating to sales function.
(b) Secondary function- aspects relating to acts of help rendered to the firms.
(c) Economic function- economic advantage gained by consumers.
(d) Psychological function- persuasive efforts of advertising.
(e) Social function- societal gains.

ROLE OF ADVERTISING IN MODERN BUSINESS WORLD

The meaning and purpose of advertising have been explained in the introductory paragraphs of this chapter. The simplest definition of an advertisement is that it is a 'public announcement.' In earlier times, to 'advertise' meant merely to announce or to inform. Some advertisements today still do just that: provide information about 'birth," deaths," engagements,' with little or no intention to persuade. The majority of classified advertisements provide useful information about jobs, accommodation, sales of second-hand vehicles and furniture, etc., matrimonial advertisements, recruitment advertisements, and tenders, notices and similar types of public announcements also provide the public with valuable information, which would otherwise be difficult to obtain easily. The earliest advertisements in the first English newspaper published in India in the eighteenth century were little more than 'public announcements' about the arrival of ships and merchandise from abroad.

Before going into a serious study of the different facts of advertising. It is necessary that some the confusions and controversies raised about it are classified very often, we hear some are criticizing advertising as to wasteful, trying to manipulate people into buying the things they do not want. It has been blamed for exaggerating the benefits of the products and services advertised and concealing their limitations and drawbacks. Advertising in not truly informing this is the common complaints everyone makes. It creates a false impression on the minds of the buyers. May advertisement messages are silly, irrelevant and at times offensive. Advertising adds no utility to a product but only adds to its price: therefore, it is burdensome on the consuming society. Some cities have raised serious doubts about the useful role of advertising.

The role of advertising to inform people that a product or service exists has been well established. People do need such information, and this is passed on to them through advertising. It may be possible that some few persons may already have such information; but for many others, advertising conveys useful information and help them to make a choice from among the products or service offered to them.

It is well-known that advertisements are employed to communicate information about products and services. Most definitions neglect the use of advertising to promote ideas. The Posts and Telegraph Department advertising to promote the use of the PIN code for faster delivery of letters is an example of selling an idea for action. The Income-Tax Department advertising to persuade the income tax payers to pay their taxes before the due date to avoid default is another case of the application of advertising to ideas involving action.

Appointment ads by corporations and employment agencies, the seeking of donations by charitable institutions and political parties, and election candidates advertising to "sell" themselves to the public are striking examples of advertising being fruitfully employed for a persuasive communication of ideas for action. In fact, in the presidential election in America — a much-advertised and the most lengthy election in the world — candidates do employ ad agencies to sell "The President." This is not a product, nor a service, but an idea for action. In most social marketing, we advertise ideas for a social cause, may be family planning, prohibition, adult education, etc. The services of ads released by the Loss Prevention Association of India promoting the prevention of losses and the preservation of life are very relevant here. One such ad may highlight the hazards of fire-crackers during Diwali days which may take the lives of children who are some what careless. The headline may say: "This year, take that nagging fear out of Diwali days. Teach your children these simple rules of safety."

It has been charged that advertising really tells anything that is new, and that either it is an exaggeration or a misrepresentation of the influencing feature or benefits of the products and service.

Advertising are concerned only about gaining extra brand loyalty with a view to increasing their share of the market. Advertising is the marketing tool with which he faces competition to maintain his present market share or gaining an extra share of it.

In 1982-1983 the union finance ministry directed public enterprises and financial institution to reduce their advertising by 25 percent. This came on the heels of a similar 25 percent cut in 1981-1982. The decision of the finance minister proposing drastic cuts in advertising is evidently due to his view that it is easily dispensable and that it may be, to a good extent, wasteful. In our opinion, advertising *per se* is not wasteful, unless it really contains no information or tells the consumers something which they already know. But really speaking there cannot be an advertisement which has nothing to tell or which recreates no image in the minds of consumers that would influence them to choose a particular product or service.

Furthermore, advertising claim to have contributed to cost reduction to consumer in respect of a large number of products and services. This apparently does not sound convincing but is true. Why, otherwise should the brand advertised product cost less than the unadvertised? In addition, advertising contributes to new product developments and improvements in quality, and it offers freedom of choice to consumer from among the may available in order to satisfy their wants and needs. These rules of advertising have discussed earlier.

In the pursuit of its purpose, the economic and social effects of advertising have become the subjects of continuing debate. In the context of its role, advertising has been proved to be beneficial in many respects on one hand. However, on the other hand, it has been criticized by many for its demerits or limitations. Both these aspects of the role of advertising- benefits and criticisms- may be explained as follows:

Benefits or Significance of Advertising

The important of advertising is realized by many people. It has earned an indispensable place for itself in the marketing mix of a firm. It makes greater contribution in several situations concerning various groups as follows:

1. Benefits to Manufacturers. Advertising is beneficial to producers in the following respects:

(i) It leads to an increase in sales volume. The increase in sales volume leads to a higher rate of production, which in turn may lead to economies of scale resulting in a lower cost per unit. Further in the absence of advertising, the company would be spending more money on other expensive means of promotion such as personal selling and sales promotion.

(ii) Advertising helps in easy- introduction of products in the market.

(iii) It helps to establish direct contact between manufacturers and customers.

(iv) It helps to create an image and reputation not only of the product but also of the advertiser.

In summing up, we may point out that advertising cannot be said to be an economic waste. However, its gain and usefulness vary widely. In a monopoly market, in which a majority of Indian Public Enterprise are operating, the economic gains of advertising do not outweigh the advertising expenses put in. This may be a paint which influence the recent government decision to direct a further cut in the which influenced the recent government decision to direct a further cut in the advertising expenditures. However, there are cases at the others extreme, the gains of advertising are much more than expanses put in this fact strongly suggest that thee should be heavy advertising. We, therefore, conclude that advertising is economically gainful; but the extent of the again varies from one product to another and depends on the market situation, competition and the economic mailers. Whether advertising is done in a mixed economy, a market economy or a controlled economy.

Can we call an advertisement issued by a public utility industry, say , the State Electricity Board, engaged in the generation, transmission and distribution of electrical energy, justifying its impending tariff like, an economic waste? Such utility industry has absolute monopoly; and then if such an advertisement is not published. Its business and profitability are going to be unaffected for this advertisement would not bring extra business and profits. Even then in our opinion, such advertising has its usefulness.

The Electricity Board, in fact informs its consumers present and prospective and the public at large about the circumstances under which lit has been forced to revise its tariff. It expects consumers to appreciate these compulsion and prepares them psychological to welcome the hike Not only this, consumers should not be left with the feeling that they are being exploited. The idea is that the consumer should be convinced that the hike is reasonable and probably unavoidable.

He should not be left with the feeling that because of its monopoly the Electricity Board is exploiting the consumer, similar other arguments may be advanced in favour of advertising and its gainful role. Such advertisements are mainly institutional advertising, which builds up the corporate image, However, it may be interesting to note that the gains from such advertising would not be directly proportional to the advertising does if pursued beyond a particular level. The advertiser should eliminate advertising when it has become no longer informative for the audience at which it was aimed; for beyond this point, it may become a waste.

ADVERTISING A POWERFUL TOOL

Most of us feel that advertising is, after all, for the markets, a powerful persuasive tool for creating a demand for his product. Consumers apparently feel that they have nothing to gain from these advertisements. Most of us do not have cent percent faith in the correction of the advertising message. We have same sort of predetermined impression that advertisements are exaggeration highlight the benefits of the product which are not too important while concealing the drawbacks which are more important.

Some economic have argued that advertising creates products differentiation, as a result of which demand becomes increasingly inelastic that infect it does nothing but to replace price competition by advertising. It is possible that the gain in eliminating price competition by covering a market segment for the advertised product may be much more than the expenditure incurred on advertising.

Large firms have the power of huge money; the spend it on advertising, particularly when they introduce a product with a varying differentiation, which enables them to capture a substantial market. Not only is such prompting of a market possible; but such advertising has the power to create a barrier from new firms or a product to enter the market in competition. The result is that big companies continue to enjoy a large market share in a non elastic competitive situation, getting high prices and high profits which, again enable them to spend huge such on advertising. And so a vicious circle develops.

The power of advertising is so great that some author have even argued that it deprives consumers of the their discretion in the market place and makes it possible for suppliers to manage demand. John Kerneth Galbraith, in his monumental work the new industrial state, has observed.

Advertising is as old as man. There is a semblance of advertising in the many activities of a human being, especially those activities which influence others, either favorably or otherwise. A baby crying for its feed, a girl wooing the prince charming, a doting wife desirous of having a new sari are all aspects of advertising. They want to communicate, to persuade, to influence and to lead to some action. All this has been a part of human life almost from the time it took shape. We shall go a step further and state that the persuasive form of communication that is advertising pre-existed human life. Take, for instance, the dancing daffodils or sweet smelling roses which silently invited butterflies to achieve the objective of pollination. There were fruits, flora and fauna all advertising them selves even before man existed. Yes, but advertising informally is interwoven with nature and the evolution of the world. Padamsee, the ex-CEO of Lintas says: "when a man wears trouser-shirt instead of a dhoti, he is advertising he is westernized. When a woman wears lipstick, she is advertising that she wants to look beautiful. When a neta delivers a speech, he is advertising that he wants to be noticed. Ads are parts of human nature to be noticed." Perhaps, as a means of formal mass communication, advertising came to be practiced by royalty who sent drummers to make an announcement or communicate the will and desires of a monarch to his people.

Advertising, as we understand it today, was not used until about 200 years ago. The form of advertising for the transmission of information dates back to ancient Greece and Rome. Criers and signs were used to carry information for advertising goods and services well before the development of printing. Even during the middle Ages, advertising signs were very extensively used. These signs generally consisted of illustrations of symbols of the products advertised. The upsurge in advertising came after the development of printing. When printing techniques were perfected, and as this industry developed, the signs were replaced by written words or messages.

Advertising has evolved since the industrial revolution as a tool of marketing communication. It is an art as well as a science. It is a career for many, it is rapidly getting professionalized. Competition, growing marketing expenses, product failures, liberalization, emergence of new electronic media have given an impetus to advertising activity.

Advertising is the most visible marketing tool which seeks to transmit an effective message from the marketer to a group of individuals. The marketer pays for sponsoring the advertising activity. Advertising, unlike salesmanship which interacts with a buyer face-to face, is non-personal. It is directed at a mass audience; and not at an individual, as in personal selling.

Though marketers use advertising, basically it is a communication process. Here the advertiser is the source who transmits the message which passes through an appropriate medium like press, TV, radio or magazine. The message is decoded meaningfully. It is ultimately received by the target audience for whom the product/service is meant. The ultimate aim of advertising is to make the target audience favourably inclined towards the product or service. In that sense, advertising is not ordinary communication but marketing communication. Since it is received by a large number of people, through the mass media it is called 'mass communication.'

Advertising aims at drawing attention to a product. It seeks to create an awareness about the existence of advertised product. It passes on information about the product in such a way that interest is created in the mind of the prospective consumer about the product. Then are convincing arguments in favuor of the product. All this leads us to a buying inclination.

The central on management of demand is, in fact, a vast and rapidly growing industry in itself. It embraces a huge net work of communication a great array of merchandising and setting organizations'. Nearly the entire advertise industry, numerous ancillary research, training and other related services, and much more. In everyday parlance, this great machine and the demand and varied talents that it employee's are said to be engaged in selling goods. In his ambiguous language, it seems that it is engaged in the management of those who buy goods.

In this criticisms' of advertising economic assure that market response is directly proportional to the amount spent on advertising. The bigger the advertising budget, the greater is the market manipulative power available with the market. Another assumption is that advertising is too expensive not really with in the capacity of other medium and small size firms. The third assumption is that a company or firm takes the load, others are forbidden or cannot take away or snatch the market from it.

Let us examine these assumptions one by one. No doubt market respons has a relationship with the close of advertising; even so, advertising alone is not the only cause of the response. There are other equally important criteria which affect the buying decision. These are product quality prices, its availability and sales promotion. On a larger basis, firms cannot get away from competition, for others would step in and offer similar competitive products. Advertising them will again play its useful role in shifting brand loyalty. On a short term basis, therefore, advertising may be blamed for decreasing competition, but certainly not on a permanent basis. The assumption that advertising is too expensive cannot stand a critical analysis. Due to technological advancement and development of various media, advertising is economicaly used by manufacturers and marketers.

It is evident, therefore that though the criticism of advertising may be occasionally justified in the short period. It cannot be sustained on a regular basis. No doubt, advertising helps in building up the reputation of a particular brand, but it is not advertising alone. It is product performance that also matters. It influences the perception of consumers about the product and creates a desire to buy it. But it would happen only if consumers believe in the benefits promised in the advertisement of the product and its usage confirms their belief. This is the way advertising helps in value addition to a product or service.

Advertising: A tool for Consumer Welfare

Martin Mayer in his book Madison Avenue, U. S. A. has stated that advertising adds perceptional utility as manufacturing adds form utility. Transportation adds place utility and warehousing adds time utility.

Advertising is useful for buyer for both consumers and industry purchases. It provides them with news products, their new development research. It increases competition rather than reduces it as many critics claim. Above all, an advertising being a creative work brings out all work of the finest quality and design having enough aesthetic appeal to millions of eyes, though much advertising is routine and does not fall in this category.

Finally, talking about the social influence of advertising, we may observe that it cannot change values. It simply reflects the value system of a society. It does not create it. It simply responds to the prevailing value system. The advertiser has to know very minutely the attitudes, benefits and motive of the target audience. He then selects appropriate media, advertisement message, etc. Advertisers are keenly interested in favourable responses from the target audience; and these would be possible only when they offer, in the form of advertisement, product and services fully fitting into the value system of the audience.

Advertising promotes consumer welfare by encouraging competition and leading to improvement in product quality and reduction in price for him. In the words of Nail H. Bardan: "Advertising's out standing contribution to consumer welfare comes from its parts in promoting a dynamic expanding economy.

INDIAN ADVERTISING

In March 1980, the silver jubilee of the advertising club of Bombay was celebrated. An audio visual review workshop was arranged on 25 teams of Indian advertising; and the doniment feeling at that time was one of self congratulation with a certain amount of introspection. Indian advertising has grown to its maturity and become very professional. We have advertising clubs in each of the major metropolitan cities and name as many as about two hundred advertising agencies vying with each other in moving large accounts. The advertising contributing about 60 percent of the total billing of the advertising industry.

We have professional bodies represent the three parties concerned with advertising i.e., the advertiser, the advertising agency, and the medium of advertising — news paper, magazines and other publications and media. The ISA, the Indian Society of Advertiser is the sole representative body of advertiser. The AAAI the Advertising Agencies Association of India represents agencies in the industry which undertake advertising on behalf of advertising.

In less than 25 years, the gross billing of the advertising business has increased from Rs. 10 crores in 1955 to about Rs. 160 crores in 1978. This was possible because of the phenomenal growth of such media as television, radio and cinema, in addition to the large number of new products introduced as a result of the industrialization and economic development of the country. Advertising in India has played a vital role in the development process by locating a demand for consumer goods and raising the living standards of millions. It is not irrelevant or luxury oriented, as it has been made out to be. Further, advertising has a definite role to play in rural development and Indian advertising has made some progress in the direction as well. In this connection, the advertisement films of Hindustan Lever as cattle feed are noteworthy. Many other consumer goods manufacturers have successfully reached rural markets through appropriate advertising.

Indian advertising has no doubt registered a rapid growth and has acquired a certain amount of professional character. But by and large, it still appears to be in a sample, unable to attract the best managerial talent, apart from being administratively weak and unable to device a self-regulatory mechanism which is necessary if it is to register professional growth and play a useful role in the socio-economic development of the country.

Indian advertising has yet to shed its urban image and open up the vast rural market which, in per capita terms, may be poor but which is the aggregate in an important market segment to which advertising has not yet spread to the desired extent. Besides this, it has a great role to play in assisting in the eradication of poverty for 45 percent of our communicating the availability of goods, service and opportunities and is contributing to improvement in living standards.

The future of Indian advertising is bright, provided that those in the profession acknowledge the social responsibility of advertising and conduct themselves in such a way so to be seen as an important part of the economic development efforts of the country.

Development of Modern Advertising

Advertising in one form or another, has been with us for the past 5000 years. Early excavation in Babylonia uncovered inscriptions, which were interpreted by archaeologists as a form of advertising by an augment dealer and a show maker. Similar advertisement are found in the unions of pempiri, in Italy about 1000 B.C. Most of these signs were in symbolic form which were interpreted as advertisements for certain services. For example, a carpenter would be represented by a saw and a chisel.

Town carrier becomes a common form of advertising for events, new and even products by about the 12th century. They would blow a horn or beat the drums and when the crowds had gathered around them, they would make the announcements. Even now it is quite common in some villages in India, to use town cries to inform the public about some religious or political event.

The adventsement concept took a new dimension with the advent of the printing press. The Bible was the first book to be printed in 1450 A.D. the earliest newspaper advertisement dated back to 1591 in Germany.

The industrial revolution gave the biggest boost to advertising along with a geometrical growth in education and transportation facility. The mechanization and automation of industries changed the entire relationship between the maker and user of the goods standardization and specialization concept produced goods faster then they could be absorbed in the immediate region. Advertising thus provided a vehicle to promote the sale of these goods in other areas. This coincided with the rapid development of the transportation system, where advertising about the product as well as the product itself could be sent over long distances, much faster.

Until the electronic media appeared in the 20th century, newspaper, magazines and direct mail literature constituted the main channels of mass advertisements. More sophisticated printing technologies and compasing processes led to the boom in the newspaper and magazines in the western countries as also in the emerging nations of the third world and consequently to the sprout in printing ads. With the appearance of the electronic media and especially of TV a powerful audio visual mass media however, the situation has altered. This media has become the bulk carrier of ads.

The tough condition in marketing and promoting products also led to be establishment of advertising department in enterprises and the growth of independent advertising agencies. Today, advertising agencies are involved in planning, creating and executing advertising campaigns.

Advertising is a pervasive force in the American society and is becoming increasingly important in other nations throughout the world. Primarily becoming increasingly important a tool of business big and small, local and national in the never ending search for customer, advertising also can make significant contributions to non-business ventures.

Advertising can and should be viewed from both — a marketing and a communications perspective. It is under girded by two forms of mass communications mechanisms – the printing press and radio and television stations. The first was introduced in the fifteenth century, but advertising did not really start in the modern sense until the 1700's with true growth coming late in the nineteenth century, commercial broadcasting came in the early 1920's with the introduction of radio. Its universal success relies on a blend of printed and broad cast media.

Advertising is a well established institution today but before it could reach such status, a number of events had to pre-exit. A primary requisite is the industrialization of the economy, bringing a need for manufacturers to seek markets. This necessitates a means of communicating with prospects who know nothing of the maker's reputation. Advertising help of fill that void. Mass transportation facilities and well developed mass media are also essential. Before the development of broadcast media, a high rate of literacy was needed if advertising messages were to be understood.

Understanding of advertising and its role in modern society is one facet of being an informed person in today's world. Advertising provide information for better buyer behaviour. Furthermore, knowledge of advertising's functions techniques is vital to career success in such fields as journalism, public relations, television, commercial art, industrial design, marketing and business management.

The Process of Marketing Communication

The following diagram (Fig. 12.2) illustrates the marketing communication process as applied to promotional strategy.

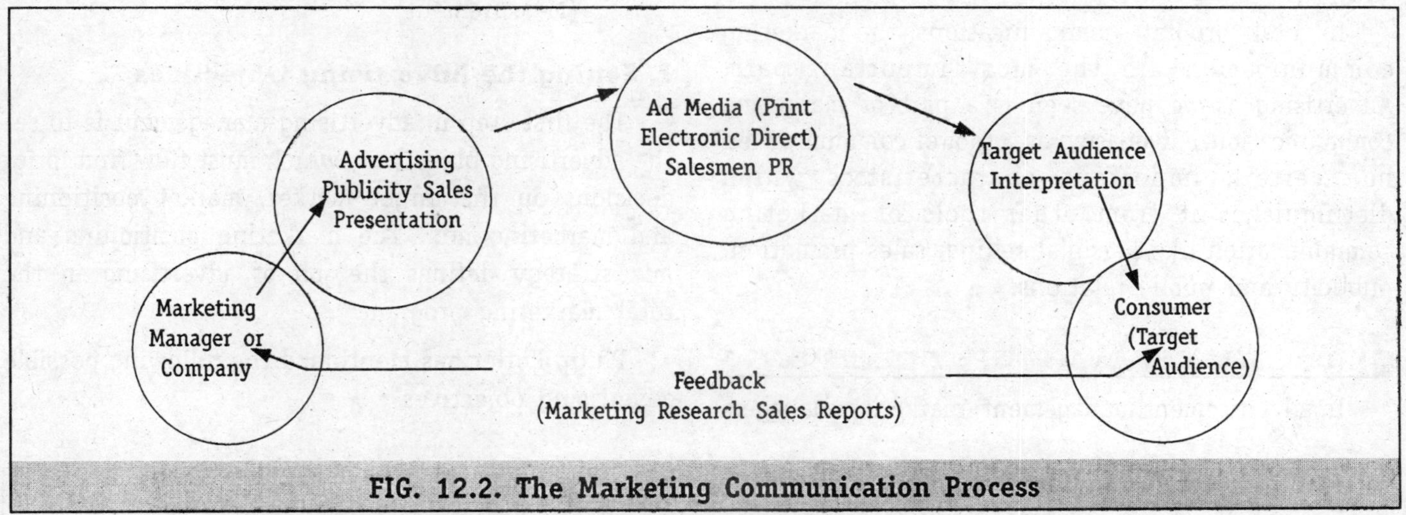

FIG. 12.2. The Marketing Communication Process

The marketing manager or the organization is the sender of the message. The message is encoded as advertising copy, publicity material, sales promotional displays or sales presentation by sales people. The media for delivering the message may be the print media like press and magazines or the electronic media like TV, radio and films or a salesman who makes a presentation. The decoding step involves the consumer's interpretation of the message. This is often the most challenging aspect of marketing communication as consumers may not always interpret the message the way the sender wants them to interpret. As seen previously, the fundamental difficulty in communication process occurs during encoding and decoding. This may happen because the meanings attached to various words and symbols may differ, depending upon the frames of reference and the field of experience between the sender and the receiver.

The overlapping of field of experience and frame of reference makes the communication possible. If there is no overlap, communication may be bad or

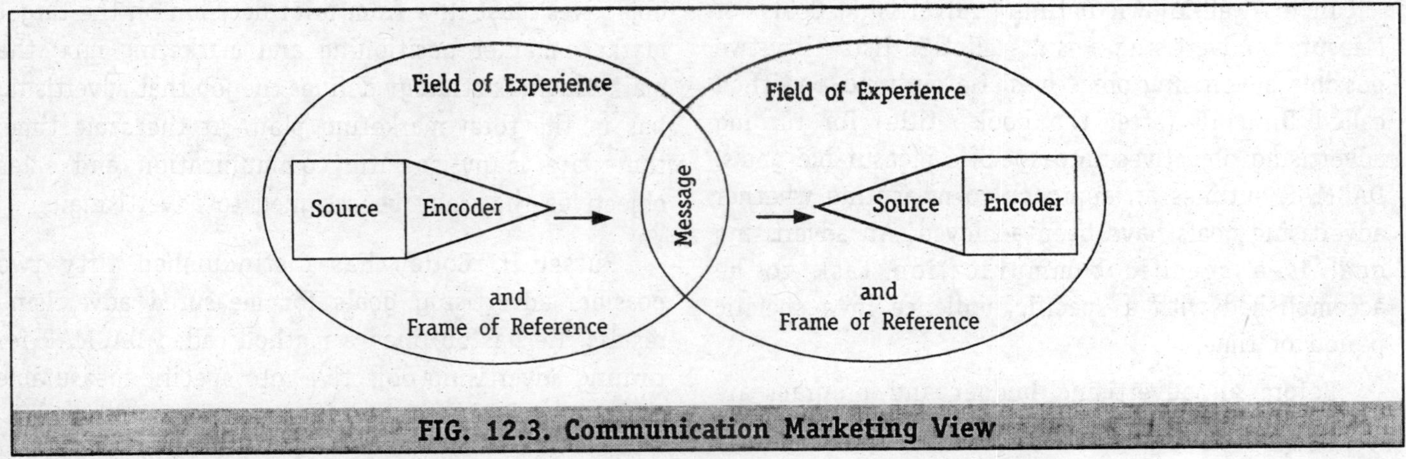

FIG. 12.3. Communication Marketing View

impossible. The consumer or audience response is known by undertaking a market research study or by analyzing the sales reports. The noise element is in the form of competitive promotional messages. There may be random noise factor like people fast forwarding a video cassette when advertisements are shown. Errors in communication may be minimized by knowing the relevant market dimensions, the needs and attitudes of potential buyers.

In total corporate communications, the marketing communication are the most important part. Advertising as we have seen is a part of marketing communication. Advertising as a tool of communication has certain important characteristics which distinguishes it from other tools of marketing communication like personal selling, sales promotion, publicity and public relations.

ADVERTING MANAGEMENT DECISIONS

In advertisement management, marketing managers make five decisions to develop an advertising program:

1. What are the advertising objectives? (Mission)
2. How much can be spent? (Money)
3. What message should be sent? (Message)
4. What media should be used? (Media)
5. How should the results be evaluated? (Measurement)

1. Setting the Advertising Objectives

The first step in advertising management is to set the advertising objectives, which must flow from prior decisions on the target market, market positioning and marketing mix. The marketing positioning and mix strategy defines the job of advertising in the total marketing program.

Philip Kotler has mentioned the following possible advertising objectives :

POSSIBLE ADVERTISING OBJECTIVES	
To inform :	
Telling the market about a new product	Describing available services
Suggesting new uses for a product	Correcting false impressions
Informing the market of a price change	Reducing consumer's fears
Explaining how the product works	Building a company image
To persuade :	
Building brand preference	Persuading customer to purchase now
Encouraging switching to your brand	Persuading customer to receive a sales call
Changing customer's perception of product attributes	
To remind :	
Reminding consumers that the product may be needed in the near future	Keeping it in their minds during off seasons
Reminding them where to buy it	Maintaining its top-of the mind awareness

In his well-known Defining Advertising Goals for Measured Advertising Results, Kotler lists fifty-two possible advertising objectives. He outlined a method called DAGMAR (after the book's title) for turning advertising objectives into specific measurable goals. DAGMAR outlines an approach to measuring whether advertising goals have been achieved. An advertising goal is a specific communication task to be accomplished with a specific audience in a specific period of time.

Before an advertising budget and program are developed, advertising objective must be set. These objectives must flow from prior decision on the target market, market positioning and marketing mix; the marketing mix strategy defines the job that advertising has in the total marketing plan. At the same time, there are many specific communication and sales objectives that may be assigned to advertising.

Russel H. Colley has distinguished fifty two possible advertising goals for measured advertising results. He has outlined a method called DAGMAR for turning advertising objective into specific measurable goals.

An advertising goal a specific communication task to be accomplished among a define audience in a given period of time. DAGMAR out lines a specific approach in measuring whether advertising goals have been achieved.

The development of operational objective usually starts with a consideration of the ultimate behavior that advertising is to influence. Is it to maintain the loyalty of existing customers, to attract new ones or to generate insights to a retailer operational objective provide criteria for decision making and standards against which to evaluate performance, and serve as a communication tool. Short run sales usually do not provide a basis for operational objectives for two reasons.

(i) Advertising is usually only one of many factors influencing sales and,

(ii) The impact of advertising often occur primarily over the long run.

Whatever the ultimate behaviour, it should be possible to conceptualize and perhaps estimate its value to the firm hopefully in terms of the profit stream over time. There may be behavioural measures For example, the number of new customers attracted that may provide the basis for advertising objective. However, it is usually helpful to consider the communication and decision process that will lead to the desired behaviour and to identify key intervening variable in that process. These intervening variables, such as brand awareness, image or attribute will then, either by themselves provide the basis of advertising objective. Further, to provide information for the development of objective, it is useful to study the market dynamics and to determine the various brand images and consumer attitude that prevail.

One possible target for advertising is made up of potential new customers. The number of people enticed into trying the brand may then form the basis for advertising objective. Often, However a process of learning and attitude development precedes the decision to try the brand, and advertising concentrates more profitably on this process. It may also attempt to increase or maintain the loyalty of existing customers. Advertising may also increase the product usage of existing customers. This approach to setting objective is a refinement and extenuation of DAGMAR's approach. DAGMAR defines advertising goal as a specific communication task, to be accomplished among a define audience in a given time period. Thus, a communication task is based on a hierarchy model of the communication process involving awareness, comprehension, conviction and action. The goal is specific, with a definite measure, a starting point, a define audience and a fixed time period. In defining the audience, a particularly useful segmentation scheme is based on the steps in the hierarchy model. Thus, it may be useful to direct a campaign to an audience that is not aware of the brand to aid those implementing the approach. DAGMAR suggest that the decision maker analyze the situation in terms of merchandise, markets, motives, messages, media and measurements.

By introducing the behavioral science theory into advertising management, DAGMAR provides the framework for the development of more operational objective. However, this has been challenged through the years on several fronts. Some critics are of the opinion that the only appropriate measure of advertising is to sell. Another objection is that it is difficult to select a hierarchy level on which to base objective and to know how to move people up the hierarchy.

Others believe that the approach is limited by measurement problems and noise in the system. By providing guidance to operating people, DAGMAR is said to inhibit the development of the great idea. The most fundamental attack is that the hierarchy model of the communication process is not appropriate. There is for example, empirical evidence that change in behaviour may precede and cause change in attitude in some situations.

Refinements of DAGMAR made an attempt to draw to improve the communication model on which DAGMAR was based. In which refinement emphasis, has to be determined in a given application. On late, more analytical models have been developed that make the link between intervening variable and behaviours.

An important question in many advertising campaign is to determine which intervening variable should be the focus of the campaign. One approach is to determine to those hierarchy levels that have not yet been reached by a large number of potential customers. An extension would not only consider the size of the segment but the difficulty and therefore the cost of moving them up the hierarchy, as well as the likelihood of their eventually making the desired decision once they have moved up.

To implement the DAGMAR approach people often need to be influenced about to particular intervening variable. For a durable product one method is to compare it with the brand image of other brands. Another method was given by Clay Camp and Liddy in their model, which made an attempt to specify the primary variable which determine the achievement of adequate levels of awareness and trial purchasing. A model test showed that advertising expenditure was important contribution to awareness if the advertising quality was high and that the awareness level in turn, contributed to trial purchasing.

DAGMAR was the study of Association of National Advertisers (ANA) that the goal of advertising is to achieve specialized objectives and it recognized that different advertisements can have a number of objectives.

"Advertising's job, purely and simply, is to communicate to a defined audience information and a frame of mind that stimulates action. Advertising succeeds or fails, depending on how well it communicates the desired information and attitudes to the right people, at the right time and at the right cost." Said **Russel H. Colley.**

The concept known as DAGMAR—Defining Advertising Goals For Measured Advertising Results.

Colley defined an advertising objective as a "specific communication task, to be accomplished. among a defined audience to a giver, degree in a given period of time".

DAGMAR Approach can be summarized in the following seven points:

(a) Advertising goals are virtually always communication goals: Colley pointed out that advertising is only one part of the marketing mix for all companies. He assumed that specific goal for advertising in virtually all situations would have to be represented in terms of some communication objective.

(b) Goals should be written down: The goals should be made very clear in the form of writing, so that every one understands what is being done.

(c) Advertising should be measured in terms of effects, not exposures: Colley pointed out that in reaching out to a certain number of potential consumers, no matter how astronomical that number seems to be, is meaningless unless there is some effect in terms of communication goals.

(d) Advertising operates through a hierarchy of communication effects: Colley was very specific as to the levels of this hierarchy and their relationship over time in response to advertising effort. His model suggests that there is a series of mental step through which a brand or objects must climb to gain acceptance. An individual start at some point by being of the brand's presence in the market. The initial task of the brand is to gain awareness to advance one step up in the hierarchy. The next step brand comprehension involves the audience member learning something about the brand. What are its specific characteristics and appeals including associated imaginary and feelings? In what way it differs from its competitors? Whom is it supposed to benefit? The next step is the attitude and conviction step and intervenes between comprehension and final action. The action phase involves some overt move on the part of the buyer like trying the brand for the first time, visiting a show room or requesting information.

(e) Creative planning considerations should come before media decisions in the advertising planning process : When media considerations come first, there is a tendency to be concerned about the amount of reach an advertising campaign can develop rather than the effects that are to be generated. The creative or message strategy decision is always intimately related to the communication effects that are intended. Therefore, the creative planning decision should occur first.

Advertising operates through a hierarchy of communication effects.

Suppose an automobile manufacturer is ready to bring out a new compact car which he has named, let us say "Venus". At the moment nobody has ever heard of Venus. His first communication job is therefore to make the consuming public aware of Venus. Next, he has certain information and menial impressions he wants to convey, Venus is light beauty a roomy, economical, compact. He wants comprehension of these features. Then he wants to create a favourable disposition (emotional or rational) towards the purchase of his product; he wants to develop public conviction about it. Finally, he wants to spur the consumer to action, which in this case, might mean persuading the consumer) to visit a dealer's show room and ask for a demonstration.

(f) Benchmark measurements should be: developed before the campaign is implemented: Colley suggested a particular research procedure for measuring advertising effectiveness. This involved developing a measurement of the level of an objective before the campaign and then measuring deviations from the measurement as an indicator of communication effect.

(g) Specific criteria must be developed: It's impossible to develop benchmarks unless the objectives are stated specifically in terms of some operational measurement. This means, that the advertising objective should state the specific target market segment, the marketing goal in some percentage terms, over some time period and the advertising goals, again in terms of a percentage attainment in a particular time period.

Colley identified 52 advertising tasks or advertising objectives that a firm can pursue. He still said that this list is still incomplete. These advertising objectives are:

- Perform the complete selling function (take the product through all the necessary steps toward a sale).
- Close sales to prospects already partly sold through past advertising effects ("ask for the order" or "clincher" advertising).
- Announce a special reason for "buying now" (price, premium, etc.).
- Remind people to buy.
- Stimulate impulse sales.
- Tie in with some special buying event.

Does the advertising aim at near term sales by moving the prospect step by step, close to a sale (so that when confronted with a buying situation the customer will ask for, reach for or accept the advertised brand)?

- Create 'brand image' or favourable emotional disposition towards the brand.
- Create awareness of existence of product or brand.
- Combat, or offset competitive claims.
- Implant information or attitude regarding benefits and superior features of the brand.
- Build familiarity and easy recognition of package or trademark.
- Correct false impressions, misinformation and other obstacles to sales.

Does the advertising aim at building a 'long range' customer franchise?

- Build customer demand which places company in stronger position in relation to its distribution (not at the "mercy of the market place").
- Build confidence in company and brand which is expected to pay off in years to come.
- Secure universal distribution.
- Place advertiser in position to select preferred distributors and dealers. Establish brand recognition and acceptance which will enable the company to open up new markets (geographic, price, age, sex).
- Establish a "reputation platform" for launching new brands or product lines.
- Specifically, how can advertising contribute toward increased sales?
- Hold present customers against the in-roads of competition.
- Cause people to specify advertiser's brand instead of asking for product by generic name.
- Convert competitive users to advertiser's brand.
- Make steady customers out of occasional or sporadic customers.
- Convert non-users of the product type to users of product and brand.

- **Example LADIES HOSIERY MARKET**

MARKETING GOALS	12 million women who customarily wear hosiery nearly every day Establish distribution in 1200 grade A retail outlet achieve sales volume of Rs. 15 million in three years.

ADVERTISING	**INTRODUCTORY:**
GOALS	1. Establish brand awareness among 60% of women in one year 2. Convey message : Anti-fatigue benefits plus sheer beauty to 30% in one year.
	ONCE ESTABLISHED :
	3. Maintain above levels of awareness and primary message registration 4. Increase registration of economy message from 10% to 30% in one year.

- **Example ELECTRICAL APPLIANCES**

MARKT	26 million logical prospects
MARKETING GOAL	Reduce excess year-end dealer inventories to normal level
ADVERTISING GOALS	Persuade 4,00,000 homemakers to visit 10,000 dealers (40 per dealer) in four weeks

- **Example TEA**

MARKET	All adult consumers
MARKETING SITUATION	Unfavourable image of tea as a beverage among large segment of the population
MARKETING GOAL	Increase tea consumption average of 5% per year
ADVERTISING GOAL	Raise favourable image of tea from 20% to 40% in five years.

Increase consumption among present users by:

- Persuading customers to buy larger sizes or multiple units.
- Advertising new uses of the product.
- Encouraging greater frequency or quantity of use.
- Reminding users to buy.

Does the advertising aim at some specific step which leads to a sale?

- Persuade prospect to visit a show room, ask for a demonstration.
- Induce prospect to sample the product (trial offer).
- Persuade prospect to write for descriptive literature, return a coupon, enter a contest.
- Aid salesman in getting preferred display space.
- Aid salesmen in opening new accounts.
- Aid salesmen in getting larger orders from wholesalers and retailers.
- Build morale of company sales force.
- Impress the trade causing recommendation to their customers and favourable treatment to salesmen.
- Give salesmen an entry.

Is it a task of advertising to impart information needed to consummate sales and build customer satisfaction?

- "How to use it" advertising.
- New prices.
- "Where to buy it" advertising.
- New models, features, package.
- New policies (guarantees, etc.).
- Special terms, trade in offers, etc.
- To what extent does the advertising aim at building confidence and goodwill for the corporation, among.
- The trade (distributors, dealers, retail sales people).
- Customers and potential customers.
- The financial community.
- Employees and potential employees.
- The public at large.
- Service.
- Product quality, dependability.
- Corporate citizenship.
- Growth, progressiveness, technical leadership.

Benefits of Specific Advertising Goals

Colley suggested the following benefits of the DAGMAR Process:

1. As the work of creating advertising is done by more specialists with narrow views beyond their own tasks, it becomes necessary for all involved to be able to see the common goal. The statement of objectives reduces wasted effort and keeps the advertising team on target by clearly showing what needs to be said.
2. People do better work when they have a clear toward what they are aiming. Specific goals

allow all who are involved with the process to deal with the appropriate issues.

3. Being specific allows measurement, which allows a better allocation of budgeted resources. The budget is aided in the short run of the current campaign and is also helped in the long run. By measuring success and failure, the firm gains insight for appropriate budgets in future campaigns.
4. Goals are critical because advertising is intangible and the resulting process is amorphous. Because advertising is so subjective, any opportunity to introduce objectivity must be used.

DAGMAR: Attacks & Counters

DAGMAR had enormous visibility and influence. Seven points given by Colley was accepted enthusiastically by a wide variety of scholars of advertising process and by advertising agency people as well as several large advertisers such as General Motors. The DAGMAR is criticized on the following points :

- Some people believe that any of the marketing communication elements should be measured in terms of its sales effectiveness rather than some intermediate goal.
- The objective focuses on many implementation difficulties inherent in the DAGMAR approach. In particular, the checklist falls short of providing sufficient details to implement the approach.
- Substantial conceptual and measurement problem underlie the DAGMAR approach.
- According to critics, the only relevant measure of advertising objectives is sales. But there are so many advertisements which are unable to increase sales but are able to achieve communication objectives. Advertising is seen as effective only if it induces consumers to make a purchase.
- The attack is that DAGMAR is applicable only to large organisations. It lacks practicability for small organisations. Colley's insistence on setting specific goals, writing them down and researching with benchmarks and specific measure criteria all suggest a very expensive and rigid managerial and research programme. The research that Colley suggested is quite expensive.

ADVERTISING AND PERSONAL SELLING

Advertising is communication with many consumers of products and services. To communicate with a large group, we put the advertising message through mass media like the press, magazines and T.V. Advertising is thus one from of mass communication. Advertising communication is non-personal. We communicate with the buyers through the media. There is no face-to-face conversation. Personal selling is personal communication were a salesman talk person to person with a prospect. Advertising aims at a group, i.e., mass while personal selling aims at individuals. Personal selling is not mass communication but individual communication. These days products are mass produced for mass communication it is not possible to contact each customer individually. Therefore, advertising a mass communication tool is a must for modern marketer. But industrial products and complex pieces of machineries can be sold better by personal selling where the salesman is in a position to explain the characteristic of the product to the buyer. Sales persons are in a position to tailor their messages according to unique characteristics of each prospect. In modern marketing, the marketing manager decides a judicious mix of advertising and personal selling. It is difficult to measure the effectiveness of advertising how sales persons receive immediate feedback during their interacting and can see how their messages are getting across. They may therefore, adjust the message or presentation quickly.

Personal selling is a very intense means of communication, people may skip an advertisement on T.V. but find it difficult to dismiss a salesperson. But this is its major weakness as well as strength. It is terribly inefficient for mass market producers, where advertising as a mass communication tool scores over it.

ADVERTISING AND SALES PROMOTION

Advertising predisposes a person favourably for a product /service/idea moving him towards its purchase. Sales promotion takes over at this point. It makes the consumer take a favourable purchase decision by providing one or other kind of direct inducement, e.g., discount, price off, gift, coupon etc. Mostly, advertising is indirectly concerned with sales. It either informs or persuades or reminds about a product or service. Most of the time, it is indirect in its approach and has a long term perspective, e.g., building up a company image or brand image. Sales promotion is a short-term approach, a direct approach and expects an immediate response in terms of sales. Sales promotion is adjunct to selling. Advertising is more frequent and repetitive then sales promotion. Sales promotion are non-recurrent selling efforts. They supplement the advertising and personal selling. Displays are effective method of sales promotion. Contests are also another effective method of sales promotion.

ADVERTISING AND PUBLICITY

Publicity is defined as non-personal stimulation of demand for a product/service/business unit by planting commercially significant news about it in a published medium or obtaining favourable presentation of it on radio, TV or stage that is not paid for by the sponsor. Two significant distinctions emerge. Publicity is not openly paid for. Secondly, presentation is not programmed.

Marketers have less control over publicity than they have over advertising. Publicity is left to the discretion of the media in terms of whether to present it or not, contents of presentation and the format of presentation. Publicity may be negative as well as positive.

ADVERTISING AND PUBLIC RELATIONS

The ultimate aim of public relations is to develop is to develop a favourable image in the eyes of the public. It refers to a company's communication and relationships with various sections of the public – customers, suppliers, shareholders, employees, governments, media, society at large. PR can be formal or informal. PR, unlike advertising, is personal.

Advertising is not the only form of persuasive communication. Very closely allied to advertising are sales promotion and public relations. In fact, both are important parts of advertising, and are often 'managed' by the same people or a agencies or departments. All three are vital to the 'marketing' of a product, service or idea.

While advertising is termed 'above – the –line' communication, sales promotion may be termed 'below-the-line' communication. The ultimate goal of all three is to sell products, services, and reputations, projects, and programmers, people, politicians, beliefs, ideas indeed every thing and anything.

The institute of Public Relations, London, defines Public Relations as 'the deliberate, planned and sustained effort to establish and maintain understanding between an organization and its public.' Public Relations is low-cost compared to advertising, for the publicity obtained, say in the press, though public relations is not directly paid for. Indirectly, the expenses involve keeping in close touch with people in the media through press visits and press releases. Besides, media persons have to be 'entertained' and some of them expect 'gifts' from companies.

According to Edward L. Bernays, the 'father' of Public Relations, and the author of 'Engineering of Consent,' the phrase Public Relations means, 'quite simply, the name of the engineering approach, i.e., action based on thorough knowledge of the situation and on the application of scientific principles and tried practices in the task of getting people to support ideas and programmers.'

There are four elements to the mechanics of PR:

1. The message to be transmitted
2. An 'independent' third party endorser to transmit the message
3. A target-audience that it is hoped will be motivated to buy whatever is being sold, and
4. A medium through which the message is transmitted.

Advertising and PR are different from the point of view of their objectives. Advertising is an aid to selling and it improves the bottom line of business.

PR, which is the business of image management, cannot replace advertising. Of course, PR can in some way push up sales because it changes the way consumers perceive the company and hence the product. Advertising and PR are complementary in most cases but sometimes advertising is not necessary. PR can do the job. If a new manufacturing facility is started by a company, it cannot be advertised. A PR effort is more effective.

PR no doubt is valuable. Edit space is far more important than paid ad space. Of course, what has been achieved by PR must be adequately supported by the product and service. If PR is professionally handled, it can achieve benefits for an organization at a fraction of a cost of advertising.

Advertising has a greater role when we are selling a tangible product. In a service industry, however, PR has a greater role, since the product is intangible.

Advertising and PR can't replace each other. By PR we create a good image. Advertising is necessary to take advantage of that good image for actual selling.

PR has higher degree of credibility since it is not paid for. Advertising, however, creates brand personality. Only advertisement can add value to a product.

PR has now slowly evolved into an integrated approach called corporate communications.

CORPORATE COMMUNICATIONS

There are papers on corporate communications in American Universities and there are departments of corporate communication in different companies including our Hindustan Lever. In the 90's, business seeks to communicate positively in terms of clarity of identity to a wide range of people – financiers, those in authority, the general public, among others. Corporate communications is not limited to mere PR. It includes crisis communication, e.g., corporate identity programmers, re-imaging, media relations, corporate advertising, sponsorship for image building, and communicating during takeover. Corporate communications is not restricted to image management but considers corporate philanthropy, media dealing and crisis management.

KINDS OF ADVERTISING OBJECTIVES

Advertising objectives can be classified as to whether their aim is to inform, persuade, or remind.

(i) To Inform-Informative advertising figures heavily in the pioneering stage of a product category, where the objective is to build primary demand. The yogurt industry initially had to inform consumers of yogurt's nutritional benefits and many uses.

(ii) To Persuade-Persuasive advertising is important in the competitive stage, where a company's objective is to build selective demand for a particular brand. Most advertising falls into this category.

(iii) To Compare-Comparison advertising seeks to establish the superiority of one brand through specific comparison with one or more other brands in the product class. Comparison advertising has been used in such product categories as deodorants, toothpastes, tyres and automobiles.

(iv) To Remind-Reminder advertising is highly important in the mature stage of the product to keep the consumer thinking about the product. Expensive four-colour Coca-Cola ads in magazines have the purpose of reminding people about Coca-Cola.

(v) To Reinforce-Reinforcement advertising, seeks to assure current purchasers that they have made the right choice. Automobile ads often depict satisfied customers enjoying some special feature of the car they bought.

COMMUNICATION AND ADVERTISING OBJECTIVES

The Chairman of American Express Company had once said "good advertising must have three effects: (i) increase sales, (ii) create news, and (iii) enhance the company's image." In a strictly commercial sense, these three elements would constitute the underlying purpose of all advertising must result in the interpretation of the above statement means that advertising must result in the growth of the company's business, create an impact and promote a favourable image of the company.

The objectives of advertising can broadly be divided into two types:

(a) Generalized objectives, and (b) Specific objectives.

(a) Generalized Objectives. Typically advertising has one or more of the three fundamental or basic objectives:

(i) **To inform target customers.** This information essentially deals with areas such as new products introduction, price changes or product improvement or modifications.

(ii) **To persuade** target audience, which includes functions such as building brand preference, encourage people to switch from one brand to the other, etc.

(iii) To remind target audience for keeping the brand name dominate.

Generalized advertising objectives fall under one or more of the following categories:

(1) To announce a new product or service. In a saturated market, the introduction of new products and brands can give the seller a tremendous opportunity of increasing his sales. In the case of innovative products, (totally new to the market) such as FAX machines and Laptop Computers, a great deal of advertising has to be done over an extended period of time to make people aware of "What the product is" and "What it does" and "How the customer would find it useful". In addition, the advertisement also carries information about the availability of the product and facilities for demonstration/trial, etc. Similarly, new brands of existing product categories are also promoted quite aggressively. Two recent examples are the launching of "Ms" cigarettes for women, for the first time in India and the introduction of "Lehar Pepsi" soft drink.

(2) Expand the market to new buyers. Advertising can be used to tap a new segment of the market, hitherto left unexplored. For example TV and Video Camera manufacturers who have been concentrating on domestic users and professional can direct their advertising to the government institutions and large organizations for closed circuit TV networks, security systems and educational purpose. Another way of expanding the sonsumer base is to promote new uses of the product. For example, Johnson's baby oil and baby cream were originally targeted to mothers. The same products have now been directed towards the adult market for their personal use. Similarly, Milkmaid was originally promoted as a substitute for milk. It is now being advertised as an ingredient for making sweet dishes and also as a sandwich spread for children, like Dabur Honey.

(3) Announce a product modification. For such advertising, generally, the term "new", "improved" etc., are used as prefixes to the brand name. For example, "The New Lux International" gives the impression of a new soap, although there may be no tangible difference between the earlier brand and the new one. Sometimes a minor packaging change might be perceived by the coustomer as a modified product e.g., "a new refill pack for Nescafe".

(4) To make a special offer. On account of competition, slack season, declining sales, etc., advertising may be used to make a special offer. For example, noble house had announced 'three for the price of two' on their Soya milk drink 'Great Shake' to counter declining sales. We often come-across advertisements announcing "Rs. 2 off" on buying various quantities of products such as soaps, toothpastes, etc. Hotels offer special rates during off-season. Similarly, many products like room heaters, fans, air-conditioners, etc., offer season discounts to promote sales. In some cases, a free-gift item is given on the purchase of company's product.

(5) To announce location of Stockiest and dealers. To support dealers, to encourage selling to stock, and to urge action on the part of readers, space may be taken to list the names and addresses of stockiest, dealers, or distributes.

(6) To educate customers. Advertising of this type is "informative" rather than "persuasive". This technique can be used to show new users for a well-established product. It can also be used to educate the people about an improved product e.g., Pearl Pet odour free jars and bottles. Sometimes societal advertising is used to educate people on the usefulness or harmful effects of certain products. For example, government sponsored advertising was directed at promoting the consumption of 'Eggs and Milk'. Similarly, advertisements discouraged the consumption of liquor and drugs. On the other hand, the advertisement shown in Figure-D encourages the people to get their children vaccinated.

(7) To remind users. This type of advertising is useful for products which have a high rate of 'repeat purchase' or those products which are bought frequently e. g., blades, cigarettes, soft drinks, etc. The advertisement is aimed at reminding the customer to ask for the same brand again.

(8) To please stockiest. A successful retail trader depends upon quick turnover so that his capital can be reused as many times as possible. Dealer support is critical, particularly for those who have limited shelf space for a wide variety of products. Advertisers send 'display' material to dealers for their shops, apart from helping the retailer with local advertising.

(9) To create brand preference. This type of advertising does two things:

(i) It creates a brand image or character by highlighting brand characteristics. (ii) It tells the target audience why brand X is better than brand Y.

In this type of advertisement the product or band acquires a 'personality' associated with the user, which gives the brand a distinctive 'image'. The second type of advertising also known as 'comparative advertising' takes the form of comparison between two brands and proves why one brand is superior.

(10) Inducing potential customers to buy. Another important objective of advertising is to induce potential customers to buy the product. Advertising is one of the best means by which the sale of an existing product can be increased. For this purpose, the advertisement should emphasize the usefulness of the product, its quality, price advantage, etc., so as to win over potential buyers and make them actual buyers. If the product is so advertised, traders expect sales to increase and keep larger stocks for sale. Thus, advertising leads to immediate buying action among customers as well as traders.

(11) To intimate customers about new uses of a product. Advertising is sometimes used to convey new uses of an existing product to the customers or to draw their attention to some new features of the product to the customers or to draw their attention to some new features of the product. The basic objective of advertising in this case is to convince the customers about the superiority of a product in comparison with other products in the same line.

(12) Other objectives. Advertising also helps to boots the morale of sales people in the company. It pleases sales people to see large advertisements of their company and its products, and they often boast it. Other uses of advertising could include recruiting staff and attracting investors through 'public Issue' advertisements announcing the allotment of shares, etc. In some cases the objective of the advertisement is to inform the customers in remote areas, which are not accessible to salesmen. Similarly, it is also aimed at informing customers in far off places or outside the country about new product.

(B) Specific Objectives. From the advertiser's viewpoint, advertising objectives are defined in terms of: **(1)** Communication objectives, and **(2)** Sales Objectives.

(1) Communication Objectives of Advertising. Advertising is psychological process, which is designed to induce behaviour in an individual leading to a purchase. In other words, one of the major objectives of advertising is to change the person's attitude in a way that moves him or her closer to the product or service being advertised. But purchase behaviour is the result of a long process of consumer decision-making. It is important for the advertiser to know how to move the target customers from their present state to a higher state of readiness-to-buy.

IMPORTANCE AND VALUE OF OBJECTIVES

Perhaps one reason many companies fail to set specific objectives for their promotional communication programme is that they do not recognize the value of planning & setting of objectives. Communication objectives should be well derived and communicated at the right time. These objectives are needed for several reasons:

- Specific promotional objectives guide development of the integrated marketing communication plan. Good promotional strategy should be based on established objectives. Specific and meaningful objectives are useful as a guide for decision making. The evaluation of alternatives and the selection should be made based on how well a particular strategy matches the firm's promotional objectives.
- Well defined objectives facilitate co-ordination of the various groups working on the campaign. The advertising and promotional programme must be coordinated within both the company and the advertising agency as well as between the two. Many problems can be avoided if all parties have written, approved objectives to guide their actions and serve as a common base for discussing issues related to promotional programme.
- The most important aspect of objective setting is that they provide a bench mark against which the success or failure of the promotion

campaign can be measured. The objective are necessary for control purpose. Most organisations are concerned about the return on their promotional investment and comparing actual performance against measurable objectives is the best way to determine if the return justifies the expense.

The basic objectives of advertising program include :

1. To stimulate sales amongst present former and future consumers. It involves decision regarding the media, e.g., rather than print.
2. To communicate with consumers. This involves decision regarding copy.
3. To retain the loyalty of present and former consumers. Advertising may be used to reassure buyers that they have made the best purchase, thus building loyalty to the brand name or the firm.
4. To increase support, Advertising blusters the morale of the sales force and of distributors, wholesalers and retailers. It thus contributes to enthusiasm and confidence attitude in the organization.
5. To project an image. Advertising is used to promote and overall image, respect and trust for an organization. This message is aimed not only at consumers, but also at the government, share holders and the general public.

Each advertisement is a specific communication that must be effective, not just for one consumer, but for many target buyers. This means that specific objectives should be set for each particular advertisement, as well as whole advertising campaign.

These agencies are comparatively well organized and staffed to offer the following services to the clients.

1. Creating the Message. As the content and the strength of the message is the most important part of the advertising process is promoting a product or a service, a major share of agency personnel and budget is committed to designing, preparing and recommending the format and the method of presentation of advertisement.

2. Selection of Media. The purpose of selecting proper media is to target the maximum of the target market while minimizing the cost factor. it involves analysis the target market so as to reach the desired potential buyers and consumer and then preparing strategies and media scheduling to accomplish these objective. The media is selected by the agency on behalf of the advertiser or client.

3. Auxiliary Service. Advertising agencies offer some specialized support service to the client. Among others, these include consumer and market research and sales training. These agencies have well organized creativity and media planning department. The other major service provided is credit facilities.

4. Co-ordination. Co-ordination of plans and activities between the advertising agency and the advertiser of the product is highly desirable. The ideas of the agency may be approved by the advertiser since the ultimate responsibility lies with the advertiser and the enterprises that he is representing. The advertising agency must often has to consider the needs and requirements of the clients sales force as well as those of his distribution and retailers. The optimum effect of advertising can be achieved best when all concerned parties join in the effort.

PROBLEMS WITH COMMUNICATION OBJECTIVES

It is very easy to say that objectives should be specific but in practical sense it is very difficult to translate a sales goal into a specific communication objectives. But at some point, a sales must be transformed into communication objective. The possible communication objectives include:

- Increasing the number of consumers in the target audience who prefer our product over the competitors.
- Encouraging consumers who have never used our brand to try it.
- Increasing the percentage of consumers in the target market who associate specific features, benefit, and advantages with our brand.

Encouraging current users of the product to use it more frequently or in more situations.

In the attempting to translate sales goals into specific communication objectives , promotional manager are not sure what constitutes adequate levels of awareness, knowledge , liking , preference or conviction. There is no formulas to provide this information. The promotional manager has to use personal experience , the marketing history etc.

APPROACHES TO OBJECTIVE SETTING

(A) Management by Objectives

The management by objectives concept was first presented by Peter Drucker in 1954. MBO was designed to help management establish clear and measurable goals with time component to constrain the period in which the objective is to be met. These clear & specific objectives are then compared with the actual achieved results to know how far the objectives are met and what are the limitations in achievement.

Another key aspect of MBO encompasses the relation between the superior and the subordinate persons in the management hierarchy. This aspect is very important in relation to advertising because goals are often set by the client and given then to the agency. It is not a fruitful exercise. If both client and the agency comes to the mutual benefit and optimum results in the long run, the results can be achieved in much better way.

Etzel and Ivancevieh have written about the application of MBO concept in marketing and derived seven potential benefits:

1. MBO can provide subordinates with the latitude and freedom to reach decisions without always checking for approval.
2. MBO can produce a shift from control over people to control over operations. Managers are evaluted on how well they manage the operation.
3. MBO can point out where greater co-ordination between managers are required. For example one marketing unit may have to cut down its request for budget money beacuse another unit needs the money more.
4. MBO can generate a more immediate- response to deviations from standards because the manager knows the objectives and their priorities.
5. Concrete objectives can direct performance, reduce uncertainty, and serve as an instrument of communication.
6. MBO can remove performance appraisal from the realm of a superior acting as a judge evaluating subordinates, to a role of counsellor and
7. MBO can lead in improved planning, the manager knows what his objectives are, as well as the expectations of superiors.

In order for MBO to work well, the objectives must become more specific, as one moves down in the organisation. This relationship can be explained by the Fig. 12.4.

In reference to the Fig. 12.4, in relation to time dimension, the top management objectives the longest time horizon and the advertising account executives and brand managers have the shortest horizon. The figure states that the advertising objectives must fit within the broader corporate and marketing objectives.

The MBO process (Fig. 12.5) reveal? the following aspects :

1. There are contracts for performance based on objectives,
2. Organisational objectives give direction to more specific group or division objectives.
3. The evaluation serves as input to the next time period's objective. This last issue is important because it ties directly to a similar proposed ordering of events in the decision sequence framework.
4. There is an evaluation of performance.

Multiple Communication Objectives

Objectives are multiple in nature. As there is hierarchy of positions, in the same way the objectives also have hierarchy. One set of objective is insufficient. Different objectives may be needed at different points of time of the year. This is most likely to occur in the fast changing world of a new product introduction or for products with severe seasonality.

For example, for a new convenience good introduction, the goal for the first three months may. be to generate awareness, the goal of the next three months may be to generate trial, and the goal for the final six months of the first year may be to ensure repeat purchases and the development of loyalty.

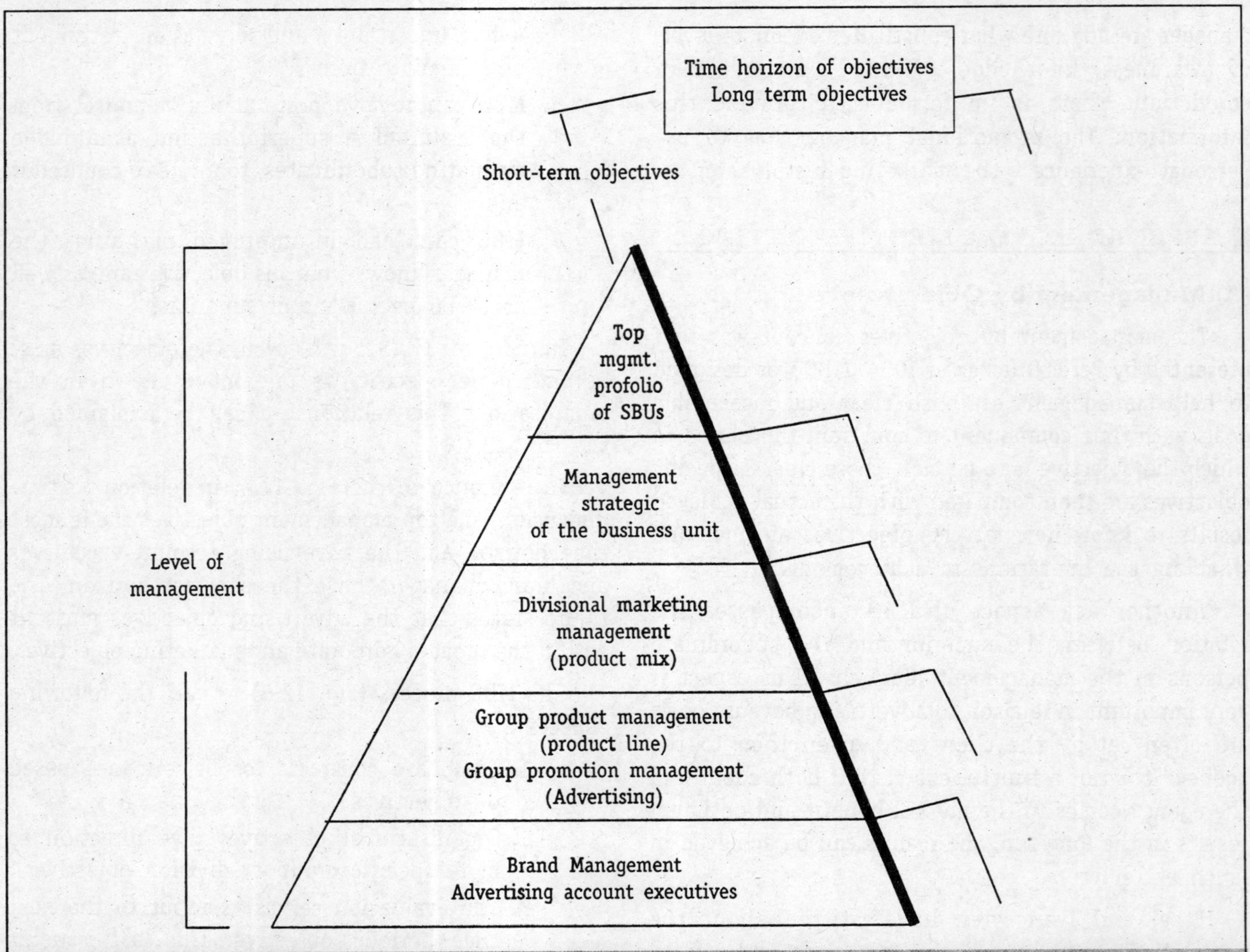

Time horizon of objectives
Long term objectives
Short-term objectives
Level of management
Top mgmt. profolio of SBUs
Management strategic of the business unit
Divisional marketing management (product mix)
Group product management (product line)
Group promotion management (Advertising)
Brand Management
Advertising account executives

FIG. 12.4. Levels of Objectives and Relevant Time Horizon

1
Organizational objectives set
2
Organizational objectives translated into group or division objectives
3
Superior subordinate at each level set objectives
4
Intermediate progress review
5
Evaluation process
Performancee
Salary

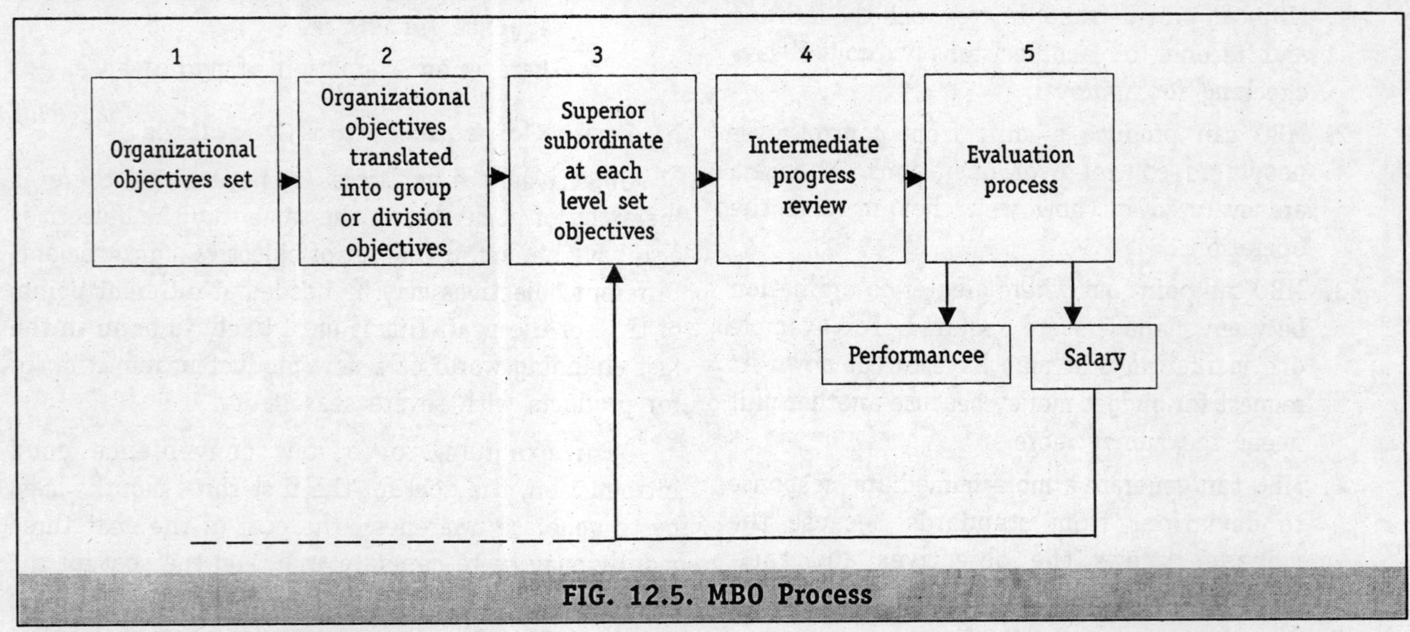

FIG. 12.5. MBO Process

Because most advertising plans cover a one year period, it will be necessary to set goals to cover that entire year. It is easy to see that this may mean multiple objectives.

With the goals of the previous paragraph established for the first year, there might be a very heavy advertising campaign during the first quarter. In the second quarter, the strategy might show lighter advertising but heavy promotion geared to trial usage (such as samples and print or mail delivered coupons). The third and fourth quarters would probably show promotions geared to repeat usage such as in pack coupons and multiple purchase refund offers. In this way, the strategies would be consistent with the objectives and the introduction would proceed smoothly while moving consumers through the hierarchy from unawareness to awareness to trial to repeat usage.

STEPS IN DECIDING ON THE MESSAGE

Many studies of the sales effect of advertising expenditures neglect the message creativity factor. Some analysts argue that large advertising agencies are equally creative and therefore differences in individual campaigns "wash out". Advertisers seek the differences in individual campaigns. By leaving out the creative factor, a substantial part of the market-share movement is unexplained. One study that includes the creativity factor found that a campaign's quality is more important than the number of dollars spent. There is little doubt that differences in creative strategy are very important in advertising success.

Advertisers go through the following steps to develop a creative strategy: message generation, message evaluation and selection and message execution.

1. Message Generation-Many things can be said about any product. No ad should say more than a few things and a case could even be made that to gain distinctiveness, an ad should emphasize one thing. It should generate some-alternative messages and pretest them a find the best one.

(i) Inductive Method-To carry out the advertising objectives creative people use different methods to generate advertising ideas. Some proceed inductively by talking to consumes, dealers, experts and competitors. Consumers are the most important sources of good ideas. Their feelings about the strengths and shortcomings of existing brands provide important clues to creative strategy.

(ii) Deductive Method-Some creative people use a deductive framework for generating advertising messages. John C. Maloney proposed following framework. He saw buyers as expecting one of four types of reward from a product: rational, sensory, social, or dissatisfaction and buyers may visualize these rewards from results of-use experience, product-in-use experience, or incidental-to-use experience. Crossing the four types of rewards with the three types of

	Types of Potentially Rewarding Experience with a Product	*Results-of-Use Experience*	*Product-in-Use Experience*	*Incidental-to-Use Experience*
Potential type of reward	**Rational**	1. Get clothes Cleaner	5. The flour that needs no sifting	9. The plastic pack keeps the cigarette fresh
	Sensory	2. Settles stomach upset completely	6. Real gusto in a great light beer	10. The portable television that's lighter in weight, easier to lift
	Social	3. When you care enough to serve the best	7. A deodorant to guarantee social acceptance	11. The furniture that identifies the home of modern people
	Ego	4. For the skin you deserve to have	8. The shoe for the young executive	12. Stereo for the man with discriminating

Fig. 12.6. Examples of Twelve Types of Appeals

experience generates twelve types of advertising messages.

The advertiser can generate a theme for each of the twelve cells as possible messages for his product. For example, the appeal "gets clothes cleaner" is rational-reward promise following results-of-use experience and the phrase "real gusto in a great light beer" is a sensory-reward promise connected with product-in-use experience.

The more ads created, the higher the probability that the agency will find a first-rate one. Yet the more time it spends creating ads, the higher the costs. There must be some optimal number of alternative ads that an agency should create and test for the client. Under the present commission system, the agency does not like to go to the expense of creating and pre-testing many ads. In an ingenious study, Irwin Gross concluded the agencies generally create too few advertisement alternatives for their clients. He estimates that advertising agencies spend from 3 to 5 percent of their media income on creating and testing advertising, whereas he estimates they should spend closer to 15 percent. He thinks agencies should devote a larger part of their budgets to finding the best ad and somewhat less to buying media. He proposes that a company should hire several creative agencies to create advertisements, from which the best one is selected.

Message Evaluation and Selection-The advertiser needs to evaluate the possible messages. Dik Warren Twedt suggested that messages should be rated on desirability, exclusiveness and believability. The message must first say something desirable or interesting about the product. It must also say something exclusive or distinctive that does not apply to every brand in the product category. Finally, the message must be believable or provable.

Though consumer ratings of ad appeals are not that reliable, however, they reflect opinion and not necessarily behaviour. The advertiser should employ some pretest to determine which appeal is the strongest.

Message Execution-The messages impact depends not only upon what is said but also on how it is said. Message execution can be decisive for those products that are highly similar, such as detergents, cigarettes, coffee and beer. The advertiser has to put the message across in a way that wins the target audience's attention and interest. Execution is also important for some industrial products that are undifferentiated, such as Pharmaceuticals in certain mature categories {antibiotics, and so on). Companies like Pfizer have launched aggressive campaigns designed to promote product image as well as quality. Describing the objective, content, support, and tone of the desired ad, the advertiser usually prepares a copy strategy statement.

(i) Creative people must now find a style, tone, words, headlines and format for executing the message.

(ii) Execution styles-According to Philip Kotler any message can be presented in the following execution styles:

- **(a) Slice-of-life-**It shows one or more persons using the product in a normal setting. A family seated at the dinner table might express satisfaction with a new biscuit brand.
- **(b) Lifestyle-**It emphasizes how a product fits in with a lifestyle. A Scotch ad shows a handsome middle-aged man holding a glass of Scotch in one hand and steering his yacht with the other.
- **(c) Fantasy-**This creates a fantasy around the product or its use. Revlon's ad for Jontue features a barefoot woman wearing a chiffon dress coming out of an old French barn, crossing a meadow, and confronting a handsome young man on a white steed, who carries her away.
- **(d) Mood or Image-**This builds an evocative mood or image around the product, such as beauty, love or serenity. No claim is made about the product except through suggestion. Many cigarette ads, such as those for Salem and Newport cigarettes create moods.
- **(e) Musical-**This shows one or more persons or cartoon characters singing a song involving the product. Many cola ads have used this format.
- **(f) Personality Symbol-**This creates a character that personifies the product. The character might be animated (Green Giant, Capon Crunch, Mr. Clean) or real (Marlboro man, Moires the Cat).

(g) **Technical Expertise**-This shows the company's expertise and experience in making the product. Thus Hills Brothers shows one of its buyers carefully selecting the coffee beans, and Italian Swiss Colony emphasizes its many years of experience in wine making.

(h) **Scientific Evidence**-This presents survey or scientific evidence that the brand is preferred to or outperforms one or more other brands. For years Crest toothpaste has featured scientific evidence toothpaste of Crest's superior activity-fighting properties.

(i) **Testimonial Evidence**-This features a highly credible or likable source endorsing the product. It could be a celebrity like O. J. Simpson (Hertz Rent-a-Car) or ordinary people saying how much they like the product.

(j) **Tone**-The communicator must choose an appropriate tone for the ad. Ads of Procter & Gamble say something superlatively positive about the product. Humour is avoided so as not to take attention away from the message.

(iii) Words-Memorable and attention-getting words must be found. Without the creative phrasing on the right themes listed below on the left would have had much less impact.

Theme	*Creative Copy*
7-up is not a cola.	"The Un –Cola"
Let us drive you in our bus instead of driving your car.	"Take the bus, and leave the driving to us."
Shop by turning the pages of the telephone directory.	"Let your fingers do the walking."
If you drink a beer, Kingfisher is a good beer to drink.	"The beer to have when you're having more than one."
We don't rent as many cars, so we have to do more for our customers,	"We try harder."

(iv) Headlines-Creativity is especially required for headlines. There are six basic types of headlines:

(a) **News** ("New Boom and More Inflation Ahead.......and what You Can Do About It")

(b) **Question** ("Have You Had It Lately?")

(c) **Narrative** ("They Laughed When I Sat Down at the Piano, but When I Started to Play!")

(d) **Command** ("Don't Buy Until You Try All Three"); 1-2-3.

(e) **Ways** ("12 Ways to Save on Your Income Tax");

(f) **How-What-Why** ("Why They Can't Stop Buying").

(v) Format-Format elements such as ad size, colour and illustration make a difference in an ad's impact as well as its cost. A minor arrangement of mechanical elements within the ad can improve its attention-gaining power by several points. Larger-size ads gain more attention though not necessarily by as much as their difference in cost. Instead of black and white four-colour illustrations increase ad effectiveness and cost.

In 1982, an industry study by David Ogilvy and Joel Raphaelson about television and print advertising's ability to change brand preference listed the following characteristics for ads that scored above average in recall and recognition: innovation (new product or new uses), "story appeal" (as an attention-getting device), before-and-after illustration, demonstrations, problem solution and the inclusion of relevant characters that become, "brand (these may be cartoon figures such as the Jolly Green Gaint or actual people, who may or may not be celebrities).

STEPS IN DECIDING ON THE MEDIA

In the task to choose advertising media to carry the advertising message, the steps are deciding on the desired reach, frequency and impact choosing among major media types; selecting specific media vehicles and according on media timing.

1. Deciding on Reach, Frequency and Impact-Media selections is the problem of finding the most cost-effective way to deliver the desired number of exposures to the target audience. The next task is to find out how many exposures, will produce a level of audience awareness. The effect of exposures on audience awareness depends on the exposures' reach, frequency and impact:

(i) **Reach (R)-**The number of different persons or households exposed to particular media schedule at least once during a specified time period.

(ii) **Frequency (F)-**The number of times within the specified time period that an average person or household is exposed to the message.

(iii) **Impact (I)-**The qualitative value of an exposure through a given medium.

The media planning challenge is as follows:

Suppose the media planner is willing to use average-impact media. This leaves the task of deciding how many people to reach with what frequency. It would make sense to settle the issue of frequency first. Once this target frequency is decided, then reach will fall into place. Many advertisers believe that the target audience needs a large number of exposures for the advertising to work. Too few repetitions may be a waste. According to Darrell B. Lucas and Stauart Henderson Britt, "It can be reasoned that introductory advertisements make too weak an impression to initiate much interest in buying. Succeeding advertisements may sometimes be more effective by building up already established weak impressions to the action level". Other advertising researchers doubt the value of many exposures. They feel that after people see the same ad a few times, they act on it, get irritated by it, or notice it. According to Krugman, three exposures may be enough. His thesis has to be qualified. He is using exposures to mean actual attention episodes on the part of the target audience. The advertiser would have to buy more exposures than three to insure that the audience actually sees three ads. There is also forgetting factor that operates. The job of advertising repetition is partly to put the message back into memory. The higher the forgetting rate associated with that brand, product category, the higher the warranted level of repetition.

Choosing Among Major Media Types-The media planner has to know the capacity of the major media types to deliver reach, frequency and impact. The major media types, in order of their advertising volume, are newspapers, television, direct mail, radio, magazines and outdoor. Each medium has certain advantages and limitations as shown below :

ADVANTAGES AND DISADVANTAGES

1. NEWSPAPERS

Advantages-Flexibility, timeliness; good local market coverage; broad acceptance; high believability.

Limitations-Short life; poor reproduction quality; small "pass-along" audience.

2. TELEVISION

Advantages-Combines sight, sound and motion; appealing to the senses; high attention, high reach.

Limitations-High absolute cost; high clutter; fleeting exposure; less audience selectivity.

3. DIRECT MAIL

Advantages-Audience selectivity, flexibility; no ad competition within the same medium: personalization.

Limitations-Relatively high cost; "junk mail" image.

4. RADIO

Advantages-Mass use; high geographic and demographic selectivity; low cost.

Limitations-Audio presentation only; lower attention than television; non-standardized rate structures; rate structures; fleeting exposure.

5. MAGAZINES

Advantages-High geographic and demographic selectivity; credibility and prestige; high-quality reproduction; long life; good pass-along readership.

Limitations-Long ad purchase lead time; some waste circulation; no guarantee of position.

6. OUTDOOR

Advantages-Flexibility; high repeat exposure; low cost; low competition.

Limitations-No audience selectivity; creative limitations.

VARIABLES OF CHOICE

Media planners make their choice among these media categories by considering several variables.

1. Target-audience Media Habits-For example, radio and television are the most effective media for reaching teenagers.

2. Product-Women's dresses are best shown in colour magazines. Polaroid cameras are best demonstrated on television. Media types have different potentials for demonstration, visualization, explanation, believability and colour,

3. Message-A message announcing a major sale tomorrow will require radio or newspapers. A message containing a great deal of technical data might require specialized magazines or mailings.

4. Cost-Television is very expensive, while newspaper advertising in inexpensive. What counts, of course, is the cost-per-thousand exposures rather than the total cost.

Ideas about media impact and cost must be re-examined regularly. Television enjoyed the dominant position in the media mix for a long time. While other media were neglected, then due to increased commercial clutter media researchers began to notice television's reduced effectiveness. Advertisers beamed shorter and more numerous commercials at the television audience, resulting in poorer attention and impact. Television advertising costs rose faster than other media costs. A combination of print ads and television commercials often did a better job than television commercials alone. Thus, advertisers must* periodically review the different media to determine their best buys. The media planner must decide on how to allocate the budget to the major media types.

Selecting Specific Media Vehicles-Now if the media planner chooses the specific media vehicles that would be most cost effective, he turns to several magazines that provide circulation and costs for different ad sizes, colour options, ad positions and quantities of insertions in different magazines. He evaluates the magazines on qualities and characteristics such as credibility, prestige, geographical detaining, occupational auditioning, reproduction quality, editorial climate, lead time and psychological impact. He decides which specific vehicles deliver the best reach, frequency and impact for the money. He calculates the cost per thousand persons reached by a particular vehicle.

Several adjustments have to be applied to this initial measure:

(a) The measure should be adjusted for audience quality. For a baby lotion advertisement, a magazine read by one million, young mothers would have an exposure value of one million, but if read by one million old men would have a zero exposure value.

(b) The exposure value should be adjusted for the audience attention probability. Readers of one imagazine, pay more attention to ads than readers of another magazines.

(c) The exposure value should be adjusted for the editorial quality (prestige and believability) that one magazine might have over another.

(d) The exposure value should be adjusted for the magazine's ad placement policies and extra services.

For arriving at the best media mix, media planners are increasingly using more sophisticated measures of media effectiveness and employing them in mathematical models. Many advertising agencies use a computer program to select the initial media and then make further improvements based on subjective factors omitted in the model.

Deciding on Media Timing-In this step, the advertiser faces a macro scheduling problem and a micro scheduling problem.

(i) Macro-scheduling Problem-The advertiser has to decide how to schedule the advertising over the year in relation to seasonality and expected economic development. Suppose a product's sales peak in December and wane in March. The seller has three options. The firm can vary its advertising expenditures to follow the seasonal pattern, to oppose the seasonal pattern, or to be constant throughout the year. Most firms pursue a policy of seasonal advertising. Even here the firm has to decide whether its advertising expenditures should lead or coincide with seasonal sales. It also has to decide whether its advertising expenditures should be more intense, proportional, or less intense than the seasonal amplitude of sales.

(a) Forrester Model-Jay W. Forrester has proposed his "industrial dynamics" methodology to test seasonal advertising policies. He sees advertising as having a lagged impact on consumer awareness. Awareness has a lagged impact on factory sales; and factory sales have a lagged impact on advertising expenditures. These time relationships can be studied and formulated mathematically into a computer-simulation model. Alternative timing strategies would be simulated to assess their varying impact on company sales, costs and profits.

(b) Kuehn Model- Kuehn developed a model to explore how advertising should be timed for frequently purchases, highly seasonal, low-cost products. He showed that the appropriate timing pattern depends upon the degree of advertising carryover and the amount of habitual behaviour in customer brand choice. Carryover refers to the rate at which the effect of an advertising expenditure decays with the passage of time. A carryover of 0.75 per month means that the current effect of a past advertising expenditure is 75% of its level last month. A carryover of 0.10 per month means that 10 percent of last month's effects is carried over. Habitual behaviour indicates how much brand holdover occurs independently of the level of advertising. High habitual purchasing, say 0.90, means that 90 percent of the buyers repeat their purchase of the brand regardless of the marketing stimuli.

Kuehn found that the decision maker is justified in using a percentage-of-sales rule to budget advertising when there is no advertising carryover or habitual purchasing. The optimal timing pattern for advertising expenditures coincides with the expected seasonal pattern of industry sales. But the percentage-of-sales budgeting method is not optimal if there is advertising carryover and/or habitual purchasing. It would be better to time advertising to lead the sales curve. The peak in advertising expenditures should come before the expected peak in sales. The trough in advertising expenditures should come before the trough in sales. Lead time should be greater, the higher the carryover. The advertising expenditures should be steadier, the greater the extent of habitual purchasing.

(ii) Micro-scheduling Problem-The micro scheduling problem calls for allocating a set of advertising exposures over a short-period of time to obtain the maximum impact. The most effective depends upon the advertising communication objectives in relation to the nature of the product, target customers, distribution channels, and other marketing factors. For example, a retailer wants to announce a pre-season sale of skiing equipment. She recognizes that only certain people will be interested in the message. She thinks that the target buyers need to hear the message only once or twice. Her objective is to maximize the reach of the message, not the repetition. She decides to concentrate the messages on the days of the sale at a level rate.

(a) Timing Pattern-The timing pattern should consider three factors:

(i) **Buyer turnover-**It expresses the rate at which new buyers appear in the market; the higher his rate, the more continuous the advertising should be.

(ii) **Purchase frequency-**It is the number of times during the period that the average buyer buys the product; the higher the purchase frequency, the more continuous the advertising should be.

(iii) **The forgetting Rate-**It is the rate at which the buyer forgets the brand. The higher the forgetting rate, the more continuous should be the advertising.

(b) Launching-In launching a new product, the advertiser has to choose between ad continuity and ad pulsing. Continuity is achieved by scheduling exposures evenly within a given period. Pulsing refers to scheduling exposures unevenly over the same time period. Those who favour pulsing feel that the audience will learn the message more thoroughly and money could be saved.

Advertising is a pervasive force in the American society and is becoming increasingly important in other nations is throughout the world. Primarily becoming increasingly important a tool of business big and small, local and national in the never ending search for customer, advertising also can make significant contributions to non-business ventures.

Advertising can and should be viewed from both a marketing and a communications perspective. It is under girded by two forms of mass communications mechanisms – the printing press and radio and television stations. The first was introduced in the fifteenth century, but advertising did not really start in the modern sense until the 1700's, with true growth coming late in the nineteenth century, commercial broadcasting come in the early 1920's, with the introduction of radio. Its universal success relied on a blend of printed and broad cast, media.

Advertising is a well established institution today but before it could reach such status a number of events had to pre-exit. A primary requisite is the industrialization of the economy, bringing a need for manufacturers to seek markets. This necessitates a means of communicating with prospects who know nothing of the maker's reputation. Advertising help of fill that void. Mass transportation facilities and well developed mass media also are essential. Before the development of broadcast media, a high rate of literacy was needed if advertising messages were to be understood.

Understanding of advertising and its role in modern society is one facet of being an informed person in today's world. Advertising provider information for better buyer behaviour. Furthermore, knowledge of advertising's functions techniques is vital to career success in such fields as journalism, public relations, television, commercial art, industrial design, marketing and business management.

The following points are to be kept in mind while communicating with an audience:

1. Instead of building a wall around the product, the message should create a bridge to the target audience by being persuasive.
2. Arouse the audience, and give it a reason for listening to you.
3. Make use of questions to involve the audience.
4. Use familiar words and build up points of interest.
5. Use specific and concrete words.
6. Repeat key points.
7. Convince the audience by sticking to facts.
8. Empathise with your audience.
9. Use rhyme and rhythm, for instance when Waterbury's compound is advertised they say 'when vitality is low, Waterbury's brings back the glow.'
10. Make use of Zeigarnnik effect; i.e., leave the message incomplete, where the audience is provoked to complete and close it by pondering over it.
11. Ask the audience to draw conclusions.
12. Let them know the implications of these conclusions.

In the pursuit of its purpose, the economic and social effects of advertising have become the subjects of continuing debate. In the context of its role, advertising has been proved to be beneficial in many respects on one hand. However, on the other hand, it has been criticized by many for its demerits or limitations. Both these aspects of the role of advertising- benefits and criticisms- may be explained as follows:

Benefits or Significance of Advertising

The important of advertising is realized by many people. It has earned an indispensable place for itself in the marketing mix of a firm. It makes greater contribution in several situations concerning various groups as follows:

Benefits to Manufacturers. Advertising is beneficial to producers in the following respects:

(i) It leads to an increase in sales volume. The increase in sales volume leads to a higher rate of production, which in turn may lead to economies of scale resulting in a lower cost per unit. Further in the absence of advertising, the company would be spending more money on other expensive means of promotion such as personal selling and sales promotion.

(ii) Advertising helps in easy- introduction of products in the market.

(iii) It helps to establish direct contact between manufacturers and customers.

(iv) It helps to create an image and reputation not only of the product but also of the advertiser.

Indian experience. The research on the practices of large-sized companies has pointed out that companies in India pursue a wide spectrum of advertising goals at different time periods and in relation to different products. Even similar companies placed in more or less similar market situation may pursue different advertising goals depending upon a host of factors like advertising philosophy, past experience, and the level of expertise existing in the company.

An analysis of advertising goals pursued revealed that these basically focused on moving the customer from one stage of the purchasing process to the other, expansion of the market, and creation of favorable image, besides the overall goal of improving sales. In general, the goals set lacked specific mention of the percent of target market to be reached and influenced.

It may be noted that some marketing experts prefer to group the functions of advertising under the following headings:

(a) Primary function- aspects relating to sales function.
(b) Secondary function- aspects relating to acts of help rendered to the firms.
(c) Economic function- economic advantage gained by consumers.
(d) Psychological function- persuasive efforts of advertising.
(e) Social function- societal gains.

Advertising a Mirror of Society

Advertising is a social institution. An examination of current advertising provides a realistic glimpse of the life and values of the period. The products and services advertised indicate to a large extent how people live and aspire to live. The style of the period's advertisements like there style in any other period suggests much about the vocabulary of the time as well as sometime about general interests and opinion. The basic task of advertising being to communicate information efficiently to groups of individuals that could number in the hundreds or millions. It helps audience members mark better economic decision by informing them about products and services. Advertising can thus be considered a mirror of society. Advertising by its very nature receives wide exposure. Because of this exposure and because of its role as persuasive vehicle, it has impact on the values and life styles of society.

Economic Role of advertising the Future

The prediction for future is not always easy to make, still every one is curious to know about the future for an individual and society to which one belongs. Calculation may fail as desired but events added to meaningful results.

Advertisements should adapt to changes in life. Hence, advertisers should know the political, economic and social forces by which changes are seen. We have seen the changes since independence. The changes before 1947 were of other faces but later on we have the problems of minorities, languages, women's movement, economic growth also influenced people to a great extent. These were demographic, economic, social, political, and technological change. Hence, advertising must change its style through times. Future may bring vast changes in marketing also. Advertising is dynamic activity, which changes to the tastes of people. Advertising is considered as:

(a) An economic force.
(b) A social institution.
(c) A communicative art.

Economic changes. These are going on very fast with the changes in technology. Industries now produce goods on a mass scale. This brings about advertisement with which the goods cannot be sold. Specialization of labour spread in distribution of business and marketing of product is taken by intermediaries. Consumers can not reach the producers to ask for the qualities of goods. Intermediaries and producers should have a communication process. This job is done by advertising. Hence, advertising fills this blank space between the producers and consumers also to intensify the separation. Other changes have also shared to the development of advertising.

Mass Consumption. A new economic order has emerged. Markets are full of people with enough purchasing power and also-willingness to spent it. The present society which is the result of gradual but study development is a mass consumption society. It has three important characteristics:

(a) Affluence of the population.
(b) Consumer power over the growth of the economy.
(c) Increasing importance of consumer psychology.

Thus, present society gives majority of families having discretionary purchasing power and constantly replace and enlarge their stock of consumer goods as has been said by George Katona.

Population Trends. As a population increased demand for many products and services came almost automatically. Still a break to early marriages and ideal family system of two or three children acts as checks. But the decline in death rates coupled with immigration trends is still alarming with the formation of new families. Consumer durables are purchased, new homes are furnished, children are born and all these lead to new purchases every time. Here advertising informs the buyers and if not available persuade consumers for alternatives to satisfy their needs if they have enough money with them.

Family Income Trends. With the advent of five year plans family income increased. Increases in disposable income which was money left after tax deductions and indiscretion any income i.e. money left over after the purchase of necessaries are important factors to the demand for products and services. As is seen in the underdeveloped or undeveloped countries. Population increase does not create sufficient demand to bring about national prosperity. Hence, advertising should play a significant role for businesses.

Then there is willingness to buy as an opportunity area for the advertising. Advertising serves as a means of instigating people to buy. Advertising provides an essential communication system for business firms wishing to participate in the larger markets resulting from more people with more money.

Socio-Economic Trends. Education plays its role. More education means greater earning capacity. It means also different taste for different products and changing levels of aspiration. Advertising helps people who are seeking to learn value systems of their new staion in life. When consumers have greater education and higher income levels, market tend to be more fragmental than was the case of the old style mass environments. Different advertising approaches should be used if the seller is to tap the full market potential. Mobility also influences. The population changed places of residence from villages to cities. After independence urbanization has started with the rapid development of industries. People more from the villages in search of employment. People have access to move retail stores. The changes bring about a need for a different kind of advertising. While consumer comes to a new place, he looks for new retail stores and hence seeks new and useful information. They get clues from advertisements about the shops where he is to get the things of his requirements. Working women help to expand the markets in future. Their income level is also going up. This change was possible by new attitudes concerning the role of women in our society and by legislation, which opened up employment opportunities. Better educational facilities and the movement for women's liberty have contributed in bringing about revolutionary changes in the ideas and attitudes of the women in society. The old customs like purda-system are not rigidly followed now and the economic pressures have forced the fair sex to compete with men folk in every walk of life. Family income increases when two earners are in the same home. The women's traditional role as the house hold purchasing agent is changed. Male and children are most responsible for family purchases. Women still perform the shopping function but differently. Advertising gives information more about products and prices and this save-time. Product reputation is created by advertising. Advertising has also increased the market for prepackaged prepared foods and other items with time saving features. Advertising plays the job of explaining these products and their availability to working women.

Changes on the Business Scene. Advertising has been influenced by other forces as well. Some of these forces are as follows:

(1) New Products and Advertising. With the increased income, new products flow in the market and they need advertising. The innovator must tell the potential users about the existence of a thing. The successful launching of new consumer products is heavily dependent upon larger than average expenditure for advertising. Companies look for growth through new products, they need for advertising designed to inform consumers of the products availability in the market place.

(2) Mergers and Conglomerates. We find that business consolidates into the fewer produces with the increased diversification in the products marketed by produces. This changing trend has made business trend to go ahead with advertising. Advertising acts as a link whereby large producers can communicate with customers. Without this they depend more on intermediaries. Many businesses blend together and thus merge in one group though they are not related to product line. The buyer knows through advertising. As has been said by Martis Mayer: "Advertising appropriations grow as company prospers." Harry G. Johnson has also expressed the same idea in the following words:

"Advertising is a form of insurance for the co-operation against the risks of managerial mortality."

Gross National Product and Advertising

Advertising expenses should be related to the gross national product. Rising costs of advertising and the grater efficiency of advertising prohibit it. In the opinion of Leo Bagart:

"It is fair to state, however, that advertising now represents a declining part of the consumer sector of the economy and that advertising to sales ratios are diminishing for national manufacturing companies, especially in the packaged field." Again he says "This may reflect the fact that we are approaching the limits of consumer's capacity to absorb additional advertising communication and that it may mean a shift in the balance of advertising and other forms of sales promotion." Advertising is an important element in the marketing mix for most firms as put by Peter Druker:

"Wherever conditions do not resemble.............extreme scarcity....... ; new technology needs above all effective marketing. It needs understanding of market and its dynamics. Hence, this is necessary to direct the technological efforts.......... It takes innovative marketing to create the new perception for the consumer so that he can use the new to expand his horizon, to raise his expectations and aspirations and to derive new satisfactions. Economic advance is not greater satisfaction of old needs and wants. It is new choice, it is the widening of the horizon of expectations and aspirations. This is largely a function of marketing which, therefore, is needed to make the technological change economically productive, that is, result in the satisfaction of human needs and 'wants'.

Economic Forces Decreasing Demand for Advertising

If consumers spend less, there is less need of advertising. The more family income is spent on transportation and fuel costs. Consumers continue to improve their economic condition and this definitely affects buying habits. Consumerism as described by Philip Kotler: "It is social movement seeking to augment the rights and power of buyers in relation to sellers." Advertising has been put to government taxation like sales tax. Consumerists desire that the content of the advertising message be informational and not persuasive. The advertising industry should build communication with consumer leaders and adopt to their needs when feasible. The need to avoid deception in advertising is well recognized by both industry and government. All unfair methods of competition in commerce or deceptive actions or practices should be checked strictly and the interests of the consumers be safeguarded. The advertising industry has developed an ambitious programme of self-regulation, which rests largely on the support of the industry itself. The industry needs to be committed to the concept that improvement in advertising is desirable because it is right, as the credibility of all advertising will there by be enhanced.

Feature of Advertising as a Social Institution

Advertising is mass communication involving an identified sponsor, the advertiser who normally pays a media organization such as a television network to run an advertisement that has usually been created by an advertising agency. Advertising can be considered a great institution. An examination of advertisements at the turn of the century provides a realistic glimpse of the life and values of that period. The products and services advertised indicate to a large extent how people lived and aspired to live. The style of this period's advertisements like their style in any other perod since then, suggests much about the vocabulary of the times as well as something about general interests and opinions. Advertising can thus be considered a mirror of society. It is also an influence on the times. Advertising performs an important economic function for both the advertiser and the audience. It helps audience members make better economic decisions by informing them about products and services. It provides the advertiser with a mechanism for communicating economically with his audiences. Of special significance is the economic role that advertising plays in new products. It many cases the introduction of new products should be economically feasible if advertising were not available to inform people about them.

As a social institution advertising involves – the advertiser, the advertising agency and the media. There is a wide variety of advertisers – the national advertisers and the local advertisers. The advertising agency actually creates the advertisements. An advertising agency creates the advertisements and makes the media allocation. Media developments have dramatically influenced the thrust of advertising through the years. The printing press made possible newspapers and magazines, the major media before the advent of the broadcast media television and radio. Radio in 1922 and television in 1948 provided a new dimension to advertising and sparked a period of growth. Despite the competition of the broadcast media, newspapers continue to be the largest medium.

Advertising influences social behaviour in our society. It controls the society and economy as a whole. But it has been criticized for its social function. Criticisms are based upon:

(a) It is dishonest.

(b) It corrupts the society.

(c) It debases the public mind and spirit.

The argument that advertising manipulates consumers takes several forms. First there is concern that advertises using subconscious motives uncovered by motivation research can manipulate an unwilling consumer. Although it is now recognized by professionals that the power of motivation research is limited. Some ethical questions about its use still remain. Secondly, there is concern with the use of "Emotional appeals". The key issue is whether a product is an entity with one or more primary functions or does it involve any dimension relevant to the consumer when he makes his purchase decision. Finally, there is the more general concern with the power represented by the volume of advertising and the skill of the people who create it.

Some advertising is criticized on the basis of taste – that it uses appeals that are offensive that the content is annoying or that is simply too intrusive. Some critics object to use of sex, especially when children may be exposed to it. Others are concerned with the use of fear appeals.

Advertising has also a negative impact on values and life styles of society. It is unreasonable to separate the economic and social impact of advertising. Advertising is basically an economic institution and any overall appraisal of advertising should include an analysis of its economic impact. Advertising should include an analysis of its economic impact. Advertising provides economic value to society in many ways. It enhances buyer decision making by providing information and by supporting brand names. It provides an efficient means for firms to communicate with their customers. Such a function is particularly important in the introduction of new products. By generating various product associations, advertising can add to the utility a buyer receives from a product. It supports the various media and has the largely unrealized potential to reduce extremes in the levels consumer buying.

Impact of Advertising on Competition. Heavy advertising expenditures in some industries generate product differentiation among products that are essentially identical. This product differentiation provides the basis for brand loyalties that represent a significant barrier to potential competitors. It is also hypothesized that in these industries heavy advertising expenditure are heeded for successful competition. Such large expenditure levels represent another barrier to entry of new competitors. With the entry of new competitors inhibited there is a tendency for industries to become more concentrated over time to have fewer competitors. The result is a reduction in vigorous competition, higher price and excessive profits. Advertising is such industries is regarded as non-informative; its role is to shift buyers around among "identical" products and is thus largely an economic waste. The evidence of association between advertising and probability was somewhat stronger.

Truth in Advertising. Everywhere dishonesty is found, hence advertising cannot be blamed for it. Hence, the consumers should be educated and should know the laws. Everyone tries to put his item in the best possible way for sale. A clergyman said, Truth be the sole basic moral criterion in advertising. Law should punish the untruthful advertising.

Advertisement as Corrupter. Advertising is in bad taste. Some advertisements deal with offensive or deligate subjects and regular subject matter is featured. Crime, violence or sex is introduced in their themes. This has been put by Leo Rosten in these words:

"Most intellectuals do not understand the inherent nature of the mass media........They project their own tastes, yearnings and values upon the masses – Who do not fortunately share them." Advertising persuades people to want things they do not need or should not have. However, the accusations that advertising is dishonest and a corrupting influence are outweighted by its overall and its influence for the general good.

Materalism. Materialism is defined as the tendency to give undue-importance to material interests. Presumably there is a corresponding lessening of importance to not-material interest such as love, freedom and intellectual pursuits. Advertising raises the expectations of economically deprived segments of our society to their disadvantage. The conscious appeal in the television commercial is essentially materialistic. Central to the message of the radio or television commercial is the premise that it is the acquisition of things, which will gratify our basic and inner need and aspirations. It is the message of the commercial that all of the major problems confronting an individual can be instantly eliminated by the application of some external force – the use of a particular product. Externally desired solutions are thus made the prescription for life's difficulties. Television gives recognition to the individual's essential responsibility for at least a part of his own capacity to deal with life's problem. In the world of television commercial all of life's problems and difficulties, all of our individual yearnings hopes and fears can yield instantly to a material solution and one which can work instantly without any effort, skill or trouble on our part. Advertising has a negative impact on values and life styles of society.

The Future of Advertising as Communication

Advertising is used not only in the commercial world. Most advertising effort and expenditure is now done on political, social, philanthropic, Government and non-profit organization advertising. There is growing more and more emphasis on scientific methods. Methods of advertising are improving. The scope of advertising is widening everyday. The world nations have become independent and they have mutual trade relations. International advertising is already important on the world business scene and appears destined to grow in magnitude and significance.

A competition for international markets increased with productive capacities and improved marketing techniques, every nation expanded their oversea's advertising efforts. They established branches in the world, many took to agency services while few had partnerships.

Advertising is gaining prestige throughout the world with advertising expenses. It has also touched non-business fields. The scope of advertising effort is widening rapidly. Besides commercial advertising, it has already extended to other fields like, political, social and non-profit organization advertising. The representatives are allowed to make speeches before audiences to collect vote in their favour. They are even allowed to use radios and televisions for this purpose. This is political advertising. In the same way social cause include securing of public support for war, flood or blood donations through advertising. Tourists and industries are attracted by government to visit their states. This is an example of government organization advertising. Advertising is thus applicable to non-business purposes also. Philip Kotler divides them into five groups:

(a) Political Advertising.

(b) Social cause advertising.

(c) Philanthropic organization advertising.

(d) Government organization advertising.

(e) Private non-profit organization advertising.

CHAPTER

13 ADVERTISING COMMUNICATION

MILLER LITE SEARCHES FOR THE RIGHT CAMPAIGN THEME

One of the most memorable and successful advertising campaigns of all times was the "Tastes Great, Less Filling" theme for Miller Lite beer, which began in 1974. The campaign used humorous commercials featuring famous (and not-so-famous) ex-athletes and other celebrities arguing over whether the brand's main appeal was its great taste or the fact that it contained fewer calories than regular beer and was less filling. The campaign ran for 17 years and helped make Miller Lite the second-best-selling beer in the United States for many years, as well as making light beer a legitimate segment of the beer market.

In the late 80s, Miller began taking the campaign in a new direction, and the ads began moving away from the use of ex-athletes. Although the tagline was still being used, the executions started using rock bands, old movie and party scenes, the Miller Lite girls, and other images in order to appeal to a broader and younger market. Miller Lite was also facing strong competition in the light-beer market from other brands such as Bud Light and Coors Light. Despite not entering the market until 1982, Anheuser-Busch had developed Bud Light into a strong brand and Coors Light had replaced the flagship brand as the company's best-selling product. By the early 90s, Miller Lite was continuing to lose market share and the company decided to drop the "Tastes great, Less Filling" campaign. What followed was a six-year odyssey of advertising flip-flops that included adolescent humour and far-out wit to chase young male beer drinkers. Spots featuring cow-boys singing good-bye to their beer on the way to the bathroom didn't help sell a lot of Miller Lite.

In early 1999, Miller dusted off the 24-year-old formula of having people debate the merits of the brand. The new ad theme, "The Great Taste of a True Pilsner Beer," pitted celebrities against one another in mock arguments over whether Miller Lite tastes great because its smooth or because of its choice hops. Miller marketing people felt the celebrity-bickering approach would work a second time because the new campaign was different from the original ads. In the new campaign, there was no more talk about "less filling," since this claim had lost its uniqueness as other light beers appeared. The ads focused on Miller Lite's taste and ingredients, which is what the company felt really mattered to beer drinkers. This campaign lasted less than a year: Miller switched agencies as well as ad themes and revived the 30-year-old "Miller Time" tagline that was used in the 1970s for the Miller High Life brand. The new ads, from the Ogilvy & Mather agency, modified the theme to "Grab a Miller Lite. It's Miller Time" and featured guys bonding over beer, sexy women, and humorous vignettes. They showed friends doing things and enjoying their time together and focused on the ritual and camaraderie of having a beer. The agency's creative director noted: "When we get down to the heart and soul of the brand, it's always been about the occasion and the time guys spend together-the banter and the real talk."

In 2002, the agency took the bonding concept in a slightly different direction with a new campaign for Miller Lite featuring ads that focus on real consumer insights and storytelling. The commercials open with a flashback to an embarrassing moment and end showing the embarrassed person telling the story. For example, one of the ads begins with a couple in a car, each with something he or she wants to discuss. The young man talks first, telling the woman he doesn't want to marry her. She then tells him that she won millions in the lottery. The commercial ends with the man telling the story to friends while playing pool and, afterward, one of the friends sneaking off to phone the woman for a date. Each ad closes with the slogan "Life is best told over a great-tasting Miller Lite at a place called Miller Time." Print executions also focus on the theme of friends getting together to enjoy a Miller Lite.

The new Miller Lite ads have been received very favourably by Miller beer distributors and by consumers. Some critics have argued that, with the storyteller ads, Miller has created one of its most popular campaigns since "Tastes Great, Less Filling." A Miller executive notes: "This whole storytelling metaphor is very powerful. Consumers tell us, 'This is how I drink beer with my friends.' " Of course, the company hopes that the new ads ensure that Miller Lite is the brand consumers are drinking when they get together with their friends.

Sources: Michael McCarthy, "Milter Turns to Classic Strategy," USA TODAY, Aug, 5,2002, p. 2B; Sally Beatty, "Philip Morris Taps Old Formula to Help Boost Miller Lite Brand," The Wall Street Journal, Mar. 15, 1999, p.B5.

Advertising communications is basically concerned with the process of sharing a paid message, either by a company or a store, by way of mass media with their existing and potential consumers. There is a marked difference between the study of advertising and advertising communication. Among the various aspects of advertising it includes study of advertising agencies, advertising departments and advertising budget. Therefore, we can say that advertising communication is a sub - set of advertising. Advertising communication focuses its attention to achieve a desired set of response within a specific market segment of consumers.

WHY ADVERTISING COMMUNICATIONS?

Advertising has become an integral part of our society. In a way, it has become embedded in our daily lives. We cannot go through a newspaper, listen to a radio or watch the television, without reading hearing and seeing same advertisement of commercial. We see them on billboards, on buses, in trains, in magazines, on match boxes, on many novelty items, some message aimed at influencing us or making us aware of the advertisers product. Advertising is a forceful tool in moulding our attitudes and our behaviour towards products, ideas and services. The word of mouth from friends and associates and our own direct experience with these goods and services further strengthen the effect of the advertising message of our minds.

Everyone wants to be cleverer, think faster, and remember more. Thus, the endless appeal of advertisements that promises to boost your brainpower and provide total recall.

Advertising can be defined as communication which promotes the purchase of products and services, and advertisements are pervasive in the culture. Ads are sandwiched between programs on television, interspersed with popular songs on the radio, and scattered among news features in the daily paper. While advertisements may distract from a TV program or a newspaper's other messages, might they also, serve a more positive purpose? Can advertising advance consumer knowledge? At the same time, can consumer education help people become more knowledgeable and critical about the goals of advertising?

Advertising is a vital marketing tool as well as powerful communication force. It is the action of calling something to attention of the people especially by paid announcements. It is a message designed to make known what we have to sell or what we have to buy. By using various channels of information and persuasion it can help to sell goods services images and ideas. In respect of public utility services also social advertisements can make people aware of the drug menace, the risk about other important problems like the need of promoting national integration.

Marketing men have long recognised that if a product does not sell without advertising, it will not sell with advertising. For a product to sell at all with or without advertising it must appeal to and satisfy, some needs and wants for some consumers at least as well as competing items. An advertising appeal refers to the approach used to attract the attention of consumers and/or to influence their feelings toward the product, service, or cause. It's something that moves people, speaks to their wants or need, and excites their interest. Often it is the underlying content of the advertisement; think of it as a "movie script". Advertising in other words, possesses no magic capable of causing people to buy things they do not need or want: however, it may help them to rationalise purchases of product they want but do not need in the strict economic sense. Who 'Needs' custom-made shirts at double the price of ready-made shirts? Only a small percentage of men of unusual sizes actually need custom made shirts; but many men want them for prestigious reasons. Appeals to these other wants help consumers to rationalise uneconomic but satisfying wants. In appraising a product with regard to advertising opportunity, the really important questions to ask are: 'Do potential buyers have needs or wants that this product or brand is capable of satisfying?' And how important, or how strong, are these needs or wants? If there are strong needs or wants for the product the chances for its sale exist. If the product is capable of satisfying only the comparatively weak and less basic needs or wants there is not nearly so much advertising opportunity. The extent of the advertising opportunity varies with the strength of basic underlying needs or wants that are satisfied by the product or brand.

Advertisers do not operate in secret; if their advertising remains hidden, then all is a waste. The advertiser's identity and his objectives are both known to buyers. Unless communication is received and accepted by the audience for which it was intended the communicator has failed. The advertising which insults the intelligence of intellectuals may not have been created to be sent to them; it may however be exactly the advertising necessary to communicate to the advertiser's intended audience. Advertising does not impose a scale of values or a set of motives on individuals.

The great majority of Indian consumers believes that each person should expend his needs and then gratify them. Parents want their children to enjoy more material comforts than the parents did. They want more material comforts for themselves too. Advertising should not be blamed because our society actively seeks more and better physical possessions. Materialism should not be an end — it should be a means to even better ends. Clearly, the purpose of advertising is to make ultimate consumers want to consume more. Persuasion and influence here are just as ethical as in politics, religion or education. The ultimate consumers want more than just as individualistic as he prefers. There are enough different goods and services to afford a wide range of choice. Public service advertising is significant both in impact and in volume in our country.

Advertising is a form of communication whose purpose is to inform potential customers about products and services and how to obtain and use them. Many advertisements are also designed to generate increased consumption of those products and services through the creation and reinforcement of brand image and brand loyalty. For these purposes, advertisements often contain both factual information and persuasive messages. Every major medium is used to deliver these messages, including: television, radio, movies, magazines, newspapers, video games, the Internet, and billboards. Advertising is often placed by an advertising agency on behalf of a company.

Advertisements can also be seen on the seats of grocery carts, on the walls of an airport walkway, on the sides of buses, heard in telephone hold messages and in-store public address systems. Advertisements are usually placed anywhere an audience can easily and/or frequently access visuals and/or audio and print.

Organizations which frequently spend large sums of money on advertising but do not strictly sell a product or service to the general public include: political parties, interest groups, religion-supporting organizations, and militaries looking for new recruits. Additionally, some non-profit organizations are not typical advertising clients and rely upon free channels, such as public service announcements.

Advertising spending has increased dramatically in recent years. In the United States alone in 2006, spending on advertising reached $155 billion, reported TNS Media Intelligence. That same year, according to a report titled Global Entertainment and Media Outlook: 2006-2010 issued by global accounting firm PricewaterhouseCoopers, worldwide advertising spending was $385 billion. The accounting firm's report projected worldwide advertisement spending to exceed half-a-trillion dollars by 2010.

While advertising can be seen as necessary for economic growth, it is not without social costs. Unsolicited Commercial Email and other forms of spam have become so prevalent as to have become a major nuisance to users of these services, as well as being a financial burden on internet service providers. Advertising is increasingly invading public spaces, such as schools, which some critics argue is a form of child exploitation.

The History of Advertising in India

"Advertising, a form of commercial mass communication designed to promote the sale of a product or service, or a message on behalf of an institution, organization, or candidate for political office."

Advertising can be looked at from various perspectives. As the quote above states, its purpose is to increase the number of articles or products sold. These are not only things we can buy in different stores, for example clothing or supplies for our daily life, but also such simple things as a message placed by an institition or organization asking for attention of the public to raise money or to make them aware of a problem, such as anti-smoking ads. Even political parties use advertisements and commercials to state the opinion of their candidate.

Advertising became big business in the 20th century, offering many different jobs in advertising agencies and the marketing section. The use of the media, like newspapers, television, direct mail, radio, magazines, outdoor signs and of course the Internet made this growth possible. It is a form of transporting information to the consumer, but which does not only have positive sides. There are many critical aspects about it, like persuading people to doing unhealthy things, like smoking, or producing special stereotypes everybody tries to follow. Nevertheless, advertising has become international, since producers and companies try to sell their products on a globalized market in almost every corner of the world.

A sophisticated & professional industry called Indian Advertising started with the hawkers calling out their wares right from the days when cities and markets first began Shop front signages, from street side sellers to press ads.

Concrete advertising history began with classified advertising in 18th Century in India. Ads appeared for the first time in print in Hickey's Bengal Gazette. India's first newspaper (weekly).

Studios mark the beginning of advertising created in India (as opposed to imported from England) The first brand as we know them today were a category of advertisers. Horlicks becomes the first 'malted milk' to be patented on 5th June 1883 (No. 278967).

A chronological significant events in the advertising history in India is given below:

The 1900s

1905	—	B Dattaram & Co. claims to be the oldest existing Indian agency in Girgaum in Bombay
1912	—	ITC (then Imperial Tobacco Co. Ltd.) launches Gold Flake
1920s	—	Enter the first foreign owned ad agencies - Gujarat Advertising and Indian Advertising set up
	—	Expatriate agencies emerge: Alliance Advertising, Tata Publicity
	—	L.A. Stronach's merges into today's Norvicson Advertising
	—	D. J. Keymer gives rise to Ogilvy & Mather and Clarion
1925	—	L.R. Swami & Co, Madras
1926	—	L.A. Stronach & Co, (India) Pr. Ltd, Bombay starts
	—	Agency called National set up for American rather than British advertisers
	—	American importers hire Jagan Nath Jaini, then advertising manager of Civil and Military Gazette, Lahore. National today is still run by Jaini's family
	—	Beginning of multinational agencies
	—	J Walter Thompson (JWT) opened to service General Motors business
1928	—	BOMAS Ltd (Formerly D.J. Keymer & Co. Ltd.) set up
1929	—	J. Walter Thompson Co. Pr. Ltd. formed

Indian agencies, foreign advertising in the thirties

1931	—	National Advertising Service Pr. Ltd. Bombay set up - Universal Publicity Co. Calcutta formed

1934 — Venkatrao Sista opens Sista Advertising and Publicity Services as first full service Indian agency

1935 — Indian Publicity Bureau Pr. Ltd. Calcutta established

1936 — Krishna Publicity Co Pr. Ltd. Kanpur begins operations

— Studio Ratan Batra Pr. Ltd. Bombay established

Indian Broadcasting Company becomes All India Radio (AIR)

1938 — Jayendra Publicity, Kolhapur started

1939 — Lever's advertising department launches Dalda - the first major example of a brand and a marketing campaign specifically developed for India - The Press Syndicate Ltd. Bombay set up

Indianising advertisements in the forties

1940 — Navanitlal & Co., Ahmedabad set up

1941 — Lux signs Leela Chitnis as the first Indian film actress to endorse the product

— Hindustan Thompson Associates (HTA), the current incarnation of JWT, coins the Balanced Nourishment concept to make Horlicks more relevant to India

— Green's Advertising Service Agents, Bombay formed

1943 — Advertising & Sales Promotion Co. (ASP), Calcutta established

1944 — Dazzal, Bombay comes into existence

— Ranjit Sales & Publicity Pr. Ltd., Bombay started

1945 — Efficient Publicities Pr. Ltd. Madras set up

— Tom & Bay (Advertising) Pr. Ltd., Poona begins operations in India

1946 — Eastern Psychograph Pr. Ltd., Bombay set up

— Everest Advertising Pr. Ltd., Bombay established

1947 — Grant Advertising Inc. Bombay formed

— Swami Advertising Bureau, Sholapur started

1948 — RC Advertising Co. Bombay set up -Phoenix Advertising Pr. Ltd., Calcutta formed

Corporate advertising in the fifties

1950s — Radio Ceylon and Radio Goa become the media option

1951 — Vicks VapoRub: a rub for colds, causes ripples with its entry in the balm market

1952 — Shantilal G. Shah & Co, Bombay

1954 — Advertising Club, Bombay set up

— Express Advertising Agency, Bombay

— India Publicity Co. Pr. Ltd., Calcutta

1956 — Aiyars Advertising & Marketing, Bombay

— Clarion Advertising Services Pr. Ltd, Calcutta

1957 — Vividh Bharati kicks off

1958 — Shree Advertising Agency, Bombay

1959 — Associated Publicity, Cuttack

Creative revolution in the sixties

1960 — Advertising Accessories, Trichur started

— Marketing Advertising Associates, Bombay set up

1961 — Industrial Advertising Agency, Bombay comes into existence

— Bal Mundkur quits BOMAS to set up Ulka the same year

1962 — India's television's first soap opera—*Teesra Rasta* enthralls viewers

1963 — BOMAS changes names to S.H. Benson's

— Stronach's absorbed into Norvicson

— Lintas heading for uncertainty

— Levers toying with giving its brands to other agencies

— Nargis Wadia sets up Interpub

— Wills Filter Tipped cigarettes launched and positioned as made for each other, filter and tobacco match

1965 — Kersey Katrak sets up Mass Communication and Marketing (MCM)

1966 — Government persuaded to open up the broadcast media

— Ayaz Peerbhoy sets up Marketing and Advertising Associates (MAA)

1967 — First commercial appears on Vividh Bharati

1968 — Nari Hira sets up Creative Unit - India wins the bid for the Asian Advertising Congress

1969 — Sylvester daCunha left Stronach's to run ASP; later sets up daCunha Associates

1970 — Frank Simoes sets up Frank Simoes Associates

The problematic seventies

1970,
1978 — National Readership Studies provided relevant data on consumers' reading habits

1970 — Concept of commercial programming accepted by All India Radio
— Hasan Rezavi gives the very first spot on Radio Ceylon
1971 — Benson's undergo change in name to Ogilvy, Benson & Mather
1972 — Western Outdoor Advertising Pvt. Ltd. (WOAPL) introduces first closed circuit TV (CCT) in the country at the race course in Bombay
1973 — R.K. Swamy. BBDO established
1974 — MCM goes out of business
— Arun Nanda & Ajit Balakrishnan set up Rediffusion
1975 — Ravi Gupta sets up Trikaya Grey
1976 — Commercial Television initiated
1978 — First television commercial seen
1979 — Ogilvy, Benson & Mather's name changes to Ogilvy & Mather

Glued to the television in the eighties

1980 — Mudra Communications Ltd. set up
— King-sized Virginia filter cigarette enters market with brand name of 'Charms'
1981 — Network, associate of UTV, pioneers cable television in India
1982 — The biggest milestone in television was the Asiad '82 when television turned to colour transmission
— Bombay Dyeing becomes the first colour TV ad
— 13th Asian Advertising Congress in New Delhi
— Media planning gets a boost
1983 — Maggi Noodles launched to become an overnight success
— Canco Advertising Pvt. Ltd. founded
— Manohar Shyam Joshi's *Hum Log* makes commercial television come alive
— Mudra sponsors first commercial telecast of a major sporting event with the India-West Indies series
1984 — *Hum Log*, Doordarshan's first soap opera in the colour era is born
— Viewers still remember the sponsor (Vicco) of *Yeh Jo Hai Zindagi!*
1985 — Mudra makes India's first telefilm, *Janam*
1985-86 — 915 new brands of products and services appearing on the Indian market
1986 — *Sananda* is born on July 31. The Bengali magazine stupefies India by selling 75,000 copies within three hours of appearing on the news-stands.
— Mudra Communications creates India's first folk-history TV serial *Buniyaad*. Shown on DD, it becomes the first of the mega soaps
— Price quality positioning of Nirma detergent cakes boost sales
1988 — AAAI's Premnarayan Award instituted
1989 — Advertising Club Bombay begins a biennial seminar called 'Advertising that Works'
— *Advertising & Marketing* (A&M) magazine launched Tech savvy in the nineties
1990 — Marks the beginning of new medium Internet
— Agencies open new media shops; go virtual with websites and Internet advertising
— *Brand Equity* (magazine) of *The Economic Times* is born
1991 — First India-targetted satellite channel, Zee TV starts broadcast
— Close on the throes of the Gulf War enters STAR (Satellite Transmission for Asia Region)
1992 — Spectrum, publisher of A&M, constitutes its own award known as 'A&M Awards'
— Scribes and media planners credit *The Bold And The Beautiful* serial on STAR Plus channel as a soap that started the cultural invasion
1993 — India's only advertising school, MICA (Mudra Institute of Communications Ahmedabad), is born
— *Tara* on Zee TV becomes India's first female-centric soap
1995 — Advertising Club of Bombay calls its awards as Abby
— Country's first brand consulting firm, SABRE (Strategic Advantage for Brand Equity) begins operations
1996 — The ad fraternity hits big time for the first time by bagging three awards at the 43rd International Advertising Festival, Cannes Sun TV becomes the first regional TV channel to go live 24 hours - a day on all days of the week
1997 — Media boom with the growth of cable and satellite; print medium sees an increase in titles, especially in specialised areas
— Government turns towards professional

advertising in the private sector for its VDIS campaigns
— Army resorts to the services of private sector agencies
— Advertising on the Internet gains popularity
— Equitor Consulting becomes the only independent brand consultancy company in the country
— Several exercises in changing corporate identity
— For the first time ever, Indians stand the chance of winning the $ 1 million booty being offered by Gillette as part of its Football World Cup promo 1998
— Events assume important role in marketing mix
— Rise of software TV producers banking on ad industry talent
— Reinventing of cinema -advertising through cinema begins

1998 — Lintas becomes Ammirati Puri Lintas (APL)

1999 — B2B site agencyfaqs.com launched on September 28,

1999 — The Advertising Club Bombay announces the AdWorks Trophy

In the new millennium

2000 — Mudra launches magindia.com
— India's first advertising and marketing gallery
— Lintas merges with Lowe Group to become Lowe Lintas and Partners (LLP)
— bigideasunlimited.com
— a portal offering free and fee ideas for money launched by Alyque Padamsee and Sam Mathews
— Game shows like *Kaun Banega Crorepati* become a rage; media buying industry is bullish on KBC
— *Kyunki Saas Bhi Kabhi Bahu Thi* marks the return of family—oriented soap on TV
— French advertising major Publicis acquires Maadhyam

2001 — Trikaya Grey becomes Grey Worldwide
— Bharti's Rs. 2.75-crore corporate TV commercial, where a baby girl is born in a football stadium, becomes the most expensive campaign of the year

2002 — Lowe Lintas & Partners rechristened Lowe Worldwide
— For the first time in the history of HTA, a new post of president is created. Kamal Oberoi is appointed as the first president of HTA.

GROWTH OF INDIAN ADVERTISING HISTORY

If the product is good, what do they need to advertise it for?" Is the dour sort of question most of us grew up hearing from our elders at home. Regardless of the offence it gave the older generation's socialist sensibilities, and despite the nationalisation of private entities, advertising in India continued nonetheless to thrive, just as it had done ever since the Irishman James Augustus Hickey published Hickey's Bengal Gazette, two-and-a-quarter centuries ago. As a six-year-old pouring over Indrajal comics, there's no way I could have known, or cared, what ads were doing to help keep the price of Phantom, Bahadur and Mandrake in reach. Today, of course, I know better. Advertising gives me free-to-air channels, helps me run a personal space on the Internet for free, provides me with instant e-communication at no explicit cost and gets me newspapers at a price so low I can get a substantial part of it repaid by the raddiwallah.

Unabashedly, I am one of those people who hordes old magazines and newspaper clippings; under my bed hibernate cartons of half-century-old printed pulp, fraying edges providing tell-tale evidence of well-fed silverfish. Flipping through them, it's the ads that still arrest: quaint, even rudimentary by today's glossy standards, yet their appeal not just intact but enhanced by nostalgia's natural preservatives. Ads, after all, tell stories, history tellers might not have thought worth picking up on. In the early years of Indian advertising, till the 1930s, foreign manufacturers used the same advertising here as they did in their home countries. The first Lux-loving Indian film star was featured in 1941 (Leela Chitnis). The Hinglish that purists so despise had made its incursions into advertising lingo by the last quarter of the 19th century. Colour ads entered The Times of India in 1910. Kodak's revolutionary, "You press the button. We do the rest" inspired this chilling spin-off from G. Edward's & Co, a Calcutta-based taxidermist: "You shoot!! We do the rest," to the near-extinction of the national animal.

Baby appeal has always worked for Pears'; as seen in 1910

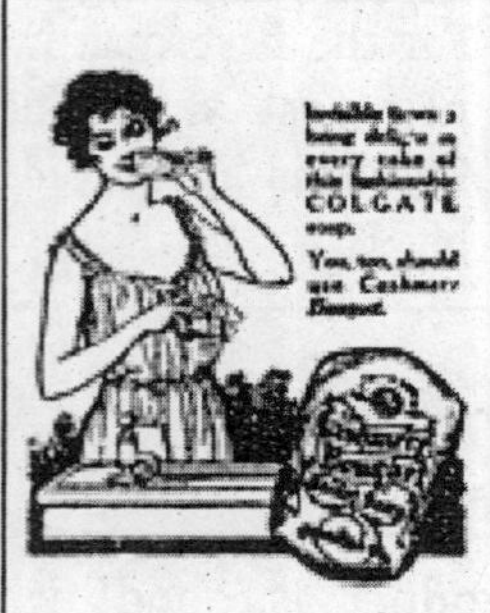

Colgate peddling flower power in 1925

Nanda in a less celebrity-driven age; in small print, 'Star of Teen Deviyan'

Sometimes resemble tracts; copywriters in 1965 expected to be read Ads could

Campa didn't survive the MNC deluge

The decades after Independence were no time for innuendo; everything had to be self-explanatory.

In the 1950s, in a nascent republic of young hope, advertisements told of how much Indian industry believed in the new India. Text and images conveyed impressions of progress. Escorts was making medical equipment from the time when Faridabad used to be part of Punjab and plastic - ware entered kitchens before my mom did. It was also not the time for people to comprehend hidden meanings; everything had to be self-explanatory. Today's "Daag acche lagte hain" Surf theme wouldn't have worked back when black-and-white was all there was. A stain was dirty and couldn't possibly make you feel good. Surf continued "washing the whitest" for decades, until someone realised that white was not the only colour in the wardrobe.

In 1964, the Surgeon General of the United States, Luther Leonidas Terry, submitted a report connecting cigarette smoking with lung cancer; in 1965, the Bank of India's general manager, T.D. Kansara, started saving his 'smoke money' with the bank at 4 percent per annum, or so their ad claims. Contrary to this, a swadeshi-sounding ad by John Petrino & Co. asked readers to "Support the Indian industry by smoking guaranteed Indian-made Nizam, Vazeer & Gold Tipped Nizam."

The waterfall was Indian advertising's watershed, when former Air-India hostess Karen Lunel appeared in a green two-piece bikini for Liril. The first in a series that later also brought us Preity Zinta, Liril gave Indian advertising the sex appeal of the semi-clad feminine form, which it has used ever since to sell aftershaves, cars, clothing and condoms. Believe it or not, in the 1970s and 80s, patently unfit male models featured in sanitary ware ads, now exclusively a female domain. The only thing with well-formed muscles back then was the MRF man.

Somewhere down the line, creative directors also discovered that laughter is the best medicine and humour entered the world of advertising, most

The 60s Pond's Dreamgirl: 'traditional' meets 'modern

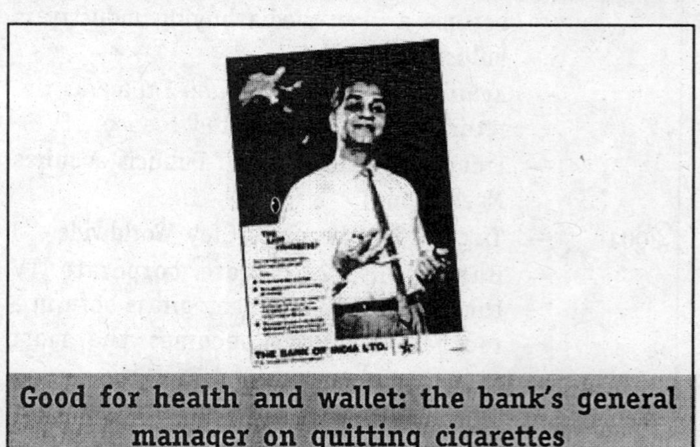

Good for health and wallet: the bank's general manager on quitting cigarettes

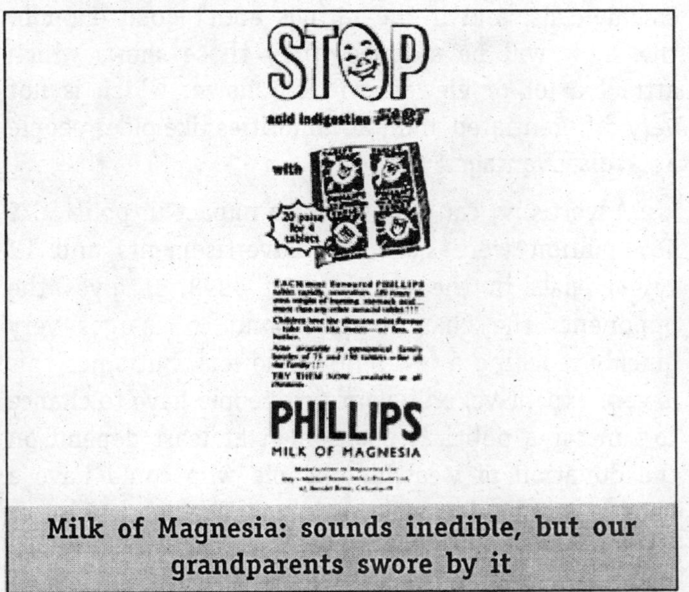

Milk of Magnesia: sounds inedible, but our grandparents swore by it

consistently through the Amul moppet who made her debut in the summer of 1967. When the country's burgeoning population rates brought on a slew of government-sponsored family planning ads, Sylvester da Cunha and the team behind the Amul campaign took a shot at the forced sterilisations of the 1970s. The Hinglish that purists so despise had made its incursions into advertising lingo by the last quarter of the 19th century.

With the arrival of the Pooja Bedi supernova, courtesy KamaSutra, a series of clothes shedding (matched only by summertime load shedding) commenced. So much skin show called for lighter shades; Fair & Lovely, for years a feminine preserve, now has its masculine version in Fair & Handsome.

Older ads also point to the leisureliness of times past. Copywriters expected readers to pore over hundreds of words of grey matter — and readers did. The celebrity quotient was much lower as well. You did have an occasional Farukh Engineer applying Brylcreem or Kapil Dev with his "Palmolive da jawab nahin". But in the main, actors and sportsmen were kept to what they did best, allowing professional models to earn a livelihood.

Pop memorabilia, as every culture studies department knows, holds an invaluable reflection of a society's image of itself. Our advertising history isn't on university syllabi yet, but when it makes it, I'll be first to sign up for the course.

Duckback has weathered generations of school-goers

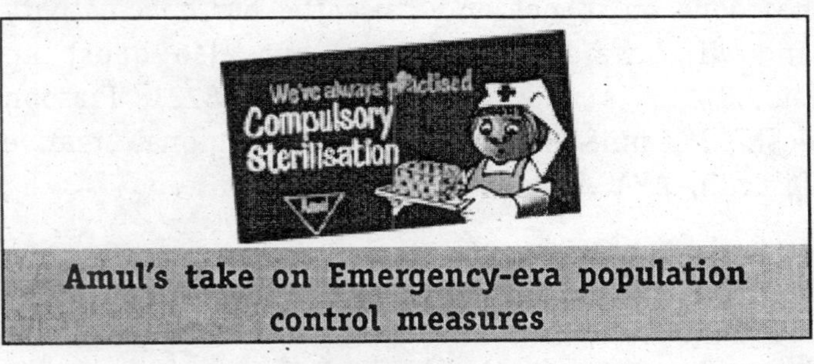

Amul's take on Emergency-era population control measures

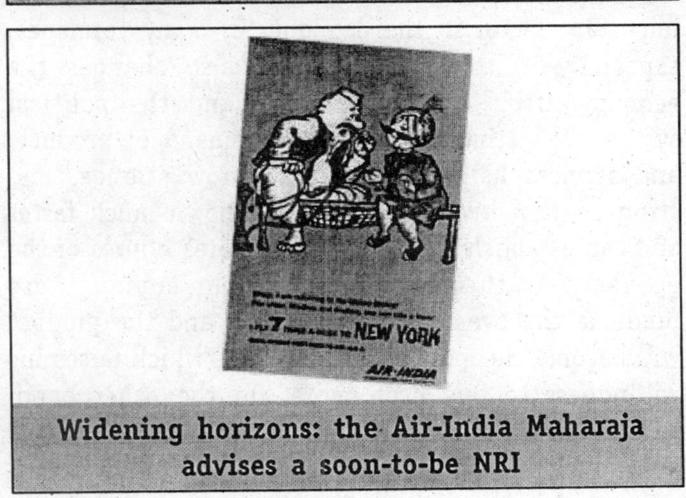

Widening horizons: the Air-India Maharaja advises a soon-to-be NRI

Happydent TVC Brings Laurels to India

India catapulting to the 15 position in 2007 (from the 21st rank) in the coveted Gunn Report is by no means a small feat. A significant role which was played by McCann India.

With its celebrated Happydent palace commercial making it to the Top 10 list of the Most Awarded Commercials Worldwide, McCann has helped Indian billing move up the ranks.

This is the first time in Advertising history that an Indian ad has made it to the top 10 most awarded list of the Gunn Report.

Gunn Report is an annual rating of creative work based on awards won by Advertising agencies worldwide in nearly 60 varied award shows and is the prestigious list which agency professional’s across the globe eagerly await.

The Gunn Report positions McCann India at no. 22 worldwide and O&M India at no. 45 with its adoption campaign garnering the 12th spot. & #8220;I am happy that apart from making a more than positive impact on the sales of the product, the happydent commercial has gone on to not only raise the bar on creativity and win awards for McCann but also boost up India’s ranking as a whole.” Prasoon Joshi, McCann’s Chairman & Regional Creative Director, APAC, said.

THE IMPACT OF ADVERTISING

The advertising business has become such an important factor in the economy in many countries, especially in the India, that it also changes the economy itself, society, culture, and the political system. The stimulation for the demand of products and services helps the economy grow stronger and stronger. New inventions become known much faster and can establish their spot in the sales figures of the economy. If there are more people buying these products the overall costs will drop and the product will become cheaper for the customer which raises his willingness to buy even more. On the other hand, advertisements are very expensive and some economists believe that these costs are put on top of the actual price paid by the customer.

Critics argue that advertising can also have a huge influence on society. It tells the consumers that only purchasing products makes you happy and therefore people compare each other on their belongings. Women also compare themselves with the beautiful and very skinny models they see on commercials and ads. This sometimes results in eating disorders and a low self-esteem of women who don't look like these models. Another bad effect is, that minority groups, especially in India are portrait in a subordinate position, which settles in the minds of people. Commercials are also an important part of the income of a TV station which leads to the suspicion that a news channel might not report on an incident about a company they depend on. A lot of TV shows are also based on these commercials, and if the ratings aren't good enough, the show will be stopped. Only those shows which attract a lot of viewers will be shown, which is not very differentiated and put minorities like older people at a disadvantage.

Advertising can also have an impact in politics. $ 467 million were spent on advertisements and TV commercials in the elections of 1998. It gives the opponents the chance to respond to charges very quickly reaching a few million viewers. But since this is very expensive, only very rich people have to chance to run for a political position or at least depend on the donation of wealthier people who could have a huge impact on democracy this way. The political issues talked about in an election are also very much simplified because the spots are only about 30 seconds long, and you can't really discuss a lot in such a short period of time.

There is finally the impact advertising can have on the culture of a country. The globalized economy uses the same commercials in a lot of different countries, which leads to a break down in the differences of these societies. Children will grow up not knowing how their culture has been before in their country. It can also lead to a lot of discussion about moral values if we just think about the very controversial ads of Benetton.

ADS ARE EVERYWHERE

People sometimes complain about the perceived overabundance of advertising in daily life. While consumers are accustomed to ads on television and in magazines, commercial promotion appears to be cropping up in more and more places. A proposed cable TV channel (Channel One) for use in schools faltered when it was learned that the channel would carry commercials aimed at the students, but it now appears to be heading for success, even though school administrators are divided on its merits (Rist, 1989). A profile of Channel One founder, Chris Whittle, in "The New York Times" reported that, while many teachers and administrators extol the value of the newscast which Channel One presents, others will never accept the infusion of commercialism in the schools. Whittle, however, has already signed up the 8600 schools he needed to cover his capital costs and achieve the audience size he felt would interest advertisers (Kleinfield, 1991).

Advertising is also found in some of the free curriculum materials which businesses supply to schools. A content analysis of materials within the areas of nutrition, energy, and economics education revealed that business-sponsored materials were found to contain significantly more advertising statements than did non-business-sponsored materials. Additionally, sponsored materials contained significantly more references to brand names/models and more company/brand logos and names than did non-sponsored materials. Many educators believe that the value of these materials is suspect, because of the preponderance of the commercial message over the informational content (Rudd 1986).

RECOGNIZING ADVERTISING

Advertising serves some very important purposes. It promotes competition among producers of products and services, keeps prices low through the development of mass markets, encourages store owners to stock a variety of items, supports free expression by funding media sources, and spurs invention. In theory, access to all available information on a given product should promote all of these ends and allow a consumer to make the most intelligent possible product purchase decisions. In practice, no one takes the time to gather that many facts. The amount of information needed to make a knowledgeable product purchase depends on such considerations as the cost of the product and the difficulty of obtaining further data. At some point, the cost of the additional information will exceed the value of the product. Intelligent consumers learn to balance these factors, and students can cultivate this skill through appropriate learning exercises (South Carolina 1983).

The average person is exposed to dozens of advertisements every day. A student may not appreciate just how influential advertising is until confronted with large numbers of familiar slogans, logos, and characters taken directly from the ads. Teachers can encourage students to identify advertisements and examine their content. Students must learn to separate facts from images, and to tell the difference between what the ads imply and what they actually say (Hawaii 1982). It is possible to identify many kinds of advertising appeals (snob appeal, statistics, humour, etc.), and even elementary school children can learn to recognize these. The students can gain an appreciation of the diversity of advertising appeals through discussion, analysis of commercial messages, creation of advertisements for imaginary products, and other classroom activities (Dianna 1983; Garrahy 1982).

Unscrupulous advertisers will sometimes advertise products that are just too good to be true.

The Latin maxim, *"caveat emptor,"* which means "let the buyer beware," is an important phrase to keep in mind when making consumer purchases. A child can learn that purchasers do not ordinarily get something for nothing. It is preferable if the child grasps this lesson before getting cheated, rather than afterwards. Teachers should encourage students to scan the daily newspaper or television for ads that do not ring true (Greenup 1983). The more exposure a child has to the motivations that lie behind questionable advertising methods, the less likely it will be that the child will be fooled by such tactics.

The relationship between advertising and consumer knowledge has been the subject of much study. Interestingly, there does not appear to be a necessary connection between the amount of advertising to which a child is exposed and that child's consumer knowledge. In fact, one study indicates that the viewing of television advertising may render an adolescent more susceptible to inflated advertising claims. At the same time, consumer education courses appear to increase student dissatisfaction with the marketplace, suggesting that such courses increase awareness of unfair business practices (Moschis 1983).

TRUTH IN FINANCIAL ADVERTISING

Consumer vulnerability to deceptive advertising is particularly acute in the area of financial services. Individuals often have little knowledge of the workings of credit, leases, security agreements, and so on. It is sometimes difficult to obtain information on such subjects that would be meaningful to the average consumer, so it is especially important that consumers be on guard against misleading or fraudulent advertisement. Because of the great inequality of bargaining power in this area, the government often backs up the consumer with protective laws.

The desire for accurate information regarding consumer borrowing has been the driving force behind a great deal of legislation in Congress and in the legislatures of the 50 states. Regulations such as the Federal Truth in Lending Law are designed to protect individuals from misleading practices by loan institutions. An important portion of the law provides that if one feature of a credit arrangement is mentioned in advertising, other important loan terms must also be explained. Similar provisions in the Consumer Leasing Act protect consumers who enter into lease agreements. The intent of these laws is to extend the government's help to the making of informed decisions on difficult financial matters (Fed. Res. 1981, 1983).

One way in which fallacious arguments are constructed is by trying to elicit an emotional reaction from people and then using that reaction to get them to agree to the conclusion. When this occurs, the arguer is committing the fallacy of an Appeal to Emotion.

This sort of fallacy is a type of 'Fallacy of Relevance', because your emotional reaction does not necessarily have any bearing on the truth or falsity of a conclusion. You might, for example, be on a jury and hear all sorts of things about how the defendant is a nasty person - but no matter how much you are led to despise that person, that doesn't necessarily make them guilty of the crime they are being tried for.

Although we find this fallacy being used by lawyers, the most common place we are likely to find it is in advertising. Almost all effective advertisements appeal to our emotions in some fashion by evoking either good feelings for the product being sold, or bad feelings for some situation that the product is supposed to alleviate.

Soft drink advertisements are a good place to look for such appeals. There is very little marketing that can be done for soft drinks based upon facts alone. If they were advertised solely on facts, we'd hear that they are sweet and carbonated and that's about it. That doesn't make you want to run out and buy any, does it?

So, marketers create much more interesting advertisements by linking the drinks to comforting images or home and family, or to sports and recreation. The implication is, you can enjoy similar feelings in reality by consuming their product.

One common way the Appeal to Emotion is created is by appealing to an audience's prejudices or desires. When this occurs, the person is committing the fallacy of appeal to desire. This is also a type of Fallacy of Relevance, because what we want to be true isn't relevant when trying to determine what is true.

I may want to win the lottery, but that desire has no effect on whether or not I actually will win. I may want to have the nicest house in the neighbourhood, but merely wishing it won't accomplish anything - and certainly won't convince anyone to conclude that my house is indeed the best.

Usually, such an appeal is not made openly or obviously. Instead, the appeal is made to a person's prejudices through subtle suggestions that certain ideas or facts have more inherent worth than others. Once again, we find this quite a lot in advertising - for example, when the newest things are promoted as having more worth simply because they are new.

Advertising is the primary way that companies convince you to buy their products and services. Advertising serves two purposes. First, a successful advertisement educates you about the product. Why would you buy a product, if you don't know what it does? Second, advertisements appeal to your interests, insecurities, and desire to convince you that the product is not only useful, but necessary.

Characteristics of Advertising Communication

Advertising communication has a set of characteristics which differentiates it from other marketing communication activities:[1]

1. Public presentation: As compared to personal selling advertising communication is massive and public in nature. It is out where everyone can see it. Because it is public — it tells your friends, neighbours, and relatives about the product and therefore enhances your prestige in owning it. Whatever symbolic content the product derives from advertising communications is automatically conferred upon its owners.

2. Pervasiveness: Advertising communications seems to be everywhere all the time. Due to its pervasive nature advertising communications allows consumers to take considerable time to think over their purchase decisions. This period includes time to compare at length one brand against many others and through repetition affords consumers an opportunity to learn the features and benefits of the various alternatives.

3. Amplified expressiveness: Through its utilisation of music, dramatic visualisations and creative expressiveness, advertising communications can dramatise and exaggerate a company's product offering. The degree of amplification, however, must be considered carefully. On one hand, the intense dramatisation feature can provide consumers with pleasurable entertainment and can thereby aid in the achievement of certain communications objectives such as increased awareness and recall. But an overly intense and dramatised message can detract from the main selling points of the message.

4. Impersonality: As compared to personal selling advertising communications is impersonal. Because of its impersonal nature, advertising communications has certain advantages and disadvantages relative to personal selling. One disadvantage is that advertising communications lacks immediate feedback from consumers. Further, the company (or advertiser) is not sure who is actually receiving its message. On the other hand the impersonality of advertising communications does not obligate the consumer to respond in any particular fashion. The receiver, therefore does not feel the pressure which is often associated with the personal selling situation. The lack of pressure allows the consumer to leisurely attend to and think about the advertising message.

Role of Advertising Communications

As advertising can be said to be a controlled form of non-personal presentation and promotion of ideas, goods, services and messages with the object to persuade people to respond in a favourable manner to the communicated/advertised message in a selected market and advertising communication being a sub set, it has several important roles. These various roles of advertising communications can be seen as (1) informer (2) entertainer (3) persuader (influencer) (4) reminder (5) reassure (6) providing assistance in marketing functions and activities and (7) value adder to a product.

Informing

As an informer advertising communication has a varied function. It tells the market as well the consumers about a new product besides existing products and brands. Tells them from where to obtain these products and at what price. Further, it educates its existing and potential consumers about the various uses, benefits and features of the product besides helping in correcting the false impression and building a company image. As advertising is capable of reaching mass audiences at a relatively low cost per contact, it is an efficient form of communicating with consumers and increasing demand.

By providing this information, advertising communications provides a valuable service to consumers by helping them to spend considerable time, money and effort to obtain the information necessary to make their purchase decisions. Otherwise they would have to make these decisions 'on a less informed basis.[2]

Entertainment

Advertising communication often includes pleasant backgrounds and pleasant associations with its basic selling message. This entertaining quality often serves to increase consumer attention comprehension and learning of the primary message. Entertainment in advertising is usually in the form of human, aesthetic scenes and imagery. It is used to create a pleasant environment around the advertised brand. In every case it is intended to accomplish certain basic communications objectives and frequently is designed to create a favourable image for the product.

Persuading

Advertising communications helps in gaining consumer awareness and facilitating comprehension of various benefits and features of a product. It also predisposes the prospective consumer to purchase the brand at least on a trial basis by creation of favourable impression and an intention to buy. Quite often this persuasion is in the form of influencing primary demand for a product. More frequently it attempts to build secondary demand of selective demand for example, creating the demand for a specific brand of a company's product. Even persuasion advertising has switched over to comparison advertising which seeks to establish the superiority of one brand through specific comparison with one brand or more other brands in the product class. Recall the advertising communications of Bajaj Auto Ltd. and L.M.L. for their scooters, Videocon's washing machines, Colour TVs, and refrigerators, Hero Honda and TVS for their mobikes and J.K.Tyres.

Reminding

Because of its repetitive nature advertising communications continually reminds both present and potential users of a company's brand and its benefits. The major purpose of reminder advertising is to keep the company's brand at the 'top' of the consumer's memory so that when a need which this product can satisfy does arise the consumer will give consideration to the company's brand. As we discussed earlier, familiarity tends to result in liking. Therefore, the more familiar the brand is to consumers the more likely they are to respond positively toward the heavily advertised brand. Moreover, consumers tend to develop some degree of confidence in heavily advertised brands over those with which they are less familiar.

Be it a Zen, a Sierra or a Mercedes, all top models enjoy close proximity with us. in fact, our tyres are the most preferred original equipment in the automobile industry. And if you think we are just flattering ourselves, consider the facts given below.

COMPARISON CHART

	JK Tyre	Ceat	MRF	Dunlop	Goodyear	Modi	Modistone	Apollo
Mercedes	✓	–	–	–	–	–	–	–
Armada	✓	✓	–	–	–	–	–	–
Cielo	✓	–	✓	–	–	–	–	–
Peugeot	✓	✓	✓	–	–	–	–	–
Sierra	✓	–	–	–	–	–	–	–
Zen	✓	✓	✓	–	–	–	–	–
Tata Estate	✓	✓	–	–	–	–	–	–
Contessa	✓	✓	–	–	✓	–	–	–
Esteem	✓	✓	✓	✓	✓	–	–	–
Maruti 800	✓	✓	✓	✓	✓	✓	✓	–
Ambassador	✓	✓	✓	✓	✓	✓	✓	–

JK TYRE
High Performance Steel Radials

INDIA'S LARGEST OE SUPPLIER OF STEEL RADIALS TO CAR MANUFACTURERS.

FIG. 13.1. Comparison Advertising

Reassuring

For consumers who use a certain brand, continual reassurance is essential for keeping present consumers and helping them to reduce dissonance which they may suffer after their initial purchase. Consumers need to realise that they have made a wise purchase decision. Reassurance is necessary for development of brand loyally and continued sales. This aspect of advertising is also known as reinforcement advertising, because it seeks to assure current purchasers that they have made the right selection of the product. Recall the famous ad, 'Yehi Hai Right Choice Baby' of Lehar Pepsi. The sole object is not of persuading or informing but reinforcing that Pepsi is the right soft drink for all occasions.

Assisting Other Efforts

Advertising communication plays the role of 'assister' like a technician during the surgical operation. The success of a doctor and his surgery heavily depends upon his team of technicians associated with him. So is advertising communication, it facilitates the various efforts of a company in marketing communications. It is a vehicle for delivering sales promotion. For example, often ads include discount coupons and further information request coupons. Such advertisements help companies to identify genuinely interested people in turn saving a lot of time, efforts and money.

Advertising communication being an important member of the promotion team also plays an important role by providing assistance to sales representatives. In practice, it pre — sells a product, makes the prospects pre knowledgeable and thus when sales representative approach the prospective consumer, they have to spend much less time and effort in convincing them. It is said advertising legitimises and makes more credible the sales representatives' claim about the product, but one study suggests that there exists no co-ordinated effort between advertising and personal selling as a one way flow from advertising to personal selling. Rather this study has demonstrated a reverse phenomenon, i.e., quite often personal sales calls by sales representatives pave the way for advertising.[3]

Besides supporting the efforts of sales representatives advertising communications enhances other marketing communications efforts. Because of the firm's advertising communications consumers more easily identify product packages in the store and recognise the 'value' of a product thereby justifying the price. Also the image and reputation of the stores carrying the product are enhanced.

Value Addition

The old belief that the sole purpose of advertising communications is informing consumers about a product does not stand any more. Advertising communications have a substantial role in value addition of products by greatly influencing the customers' perception of a product. It is only because of this reason people's perceive some product as more stylish, elegant, durable, delicate, prestigious and more superior than to their competitor's product.

A multiplicity of methods are employed to add value to a product. For example, normally models are depicted in ads, using a certain product. Result — though the people have no direct or personal experience of the product they can imagine through the experience of others. This attempts to influence consumer perception by having them observe the actions of others (for examples, models in advertisements) and the consequences of the model's behaviour.[4] For example, in an effort to increase overseas call through its 'Namaskar Sewa' in India AT&T portrayed a touching personal situations reuniting people through phones. One of their advertisements shows 'Whisper in the ear again. Call U.S.A. at the cost of one local call.' A.T.&T's campaign is directed to encourage the people to renew their old friendship or relations with their people who live abroad through the use of their Namaskar Sewa at a very little cost. The advertisements of Reliance, Idea, Airtel and BSNL are also worth remembering in this context.

The basic rationale for this idea is based on behavioural theories.[5] In terms of communication's language a product is referred as a significate. A significate refers to the object itself. A stimulus which is responsible for evoking a thought or idea of a significate is referred to as a sign. Thus, the brand name for example, 'Close-up' is a sign which represents a particular kind of a tooth paste, the object. This might only evoke an idea of a tooth cleaner, but through marketing communications, particularly advertising communications. Close-up evokes a number of ideas in the mind of consumers such as a complete mouth wash and protection against tooth decay like the ads of Pepsodent or Anchor White toothpaste.

To understand how this process works it is necessary to introduce two new concepts. The first concept that we need to understand is that of sign — relevant significates. These significates are ones for which the sign evokes meanings which are inherent in the product (or object). Water for example has the intrinsic quality of satisfying thirst. Thus, the word 'water' evokes a thirst quenching quality inherent to the significate water.

The other concept is that of arbitrary significates. These arbitrary significates are ones which are not inherent characteristics of a sign. They are the ones which become associated with a sign because of the learning process. For example, masculinity is associated with Panama Cigarettes. This association is arbitrary

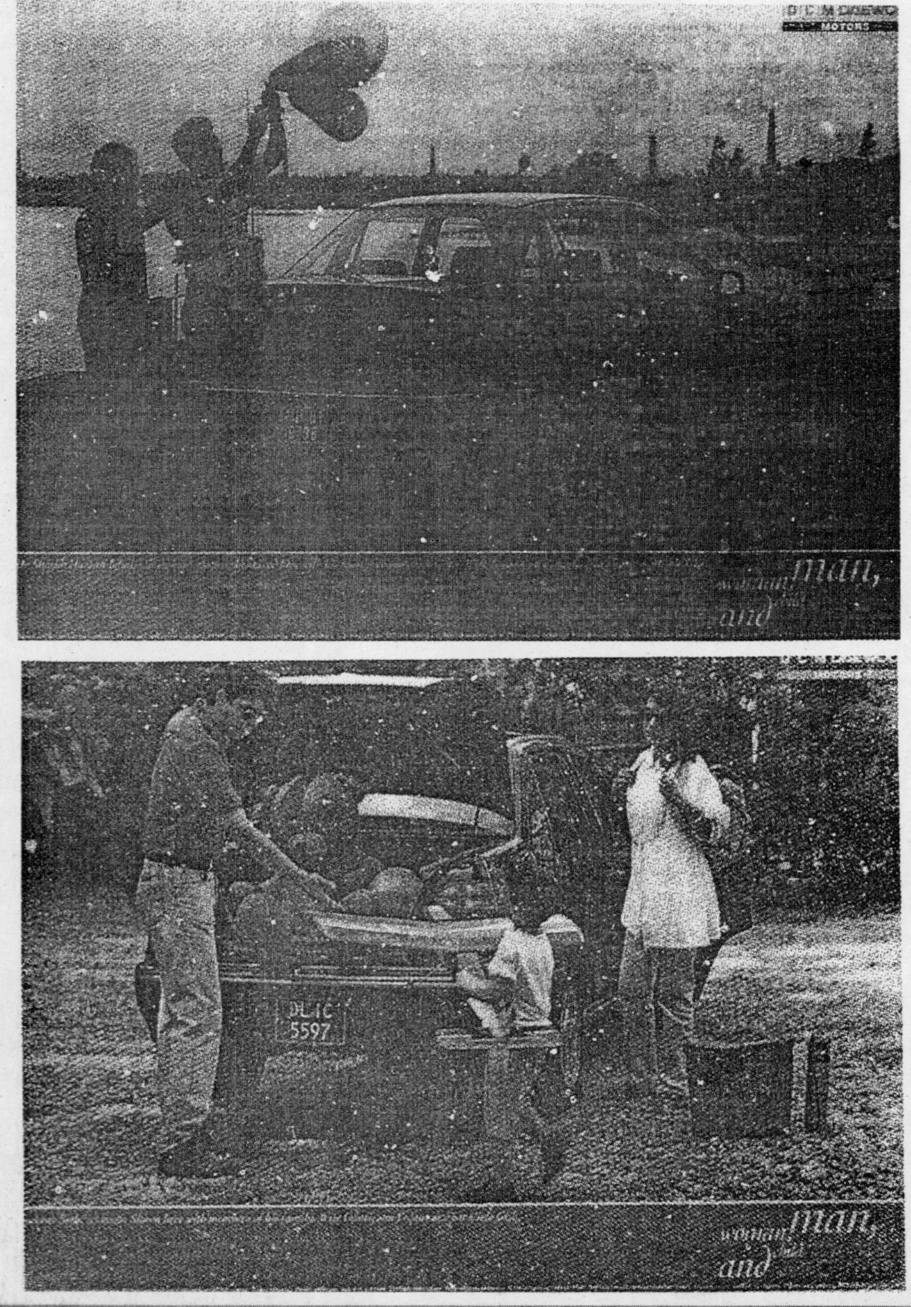

FIG. 13.2(A). Communicative Social Significance

FIG. 13.2(B). Communicative Social Significance

because it is learned and not an inherent characteristics of the brand. These arbitrary significates can go either external or internal. Arbitrary external significates are those which are known or familiar to a large segment of people in the society, whereas internal significates are those which are able to evoke feelings and are confined to an individual only. Both of them are associated arbitrarily with the object, i.e., a product.

Arbitrary external significates arise from the sanctions of groups. An object which possesses status has that status because 'others' say it does. That is it is socially affirmed as having status. An automobile is an object which moves people and things from point A to point B. Advertisers, however do not emphasise the transportation function of an automobile. Instead, most advertisers have concentrated on the social significance their cars have for their owners. The car is not only a mode of transportation, but a social symbol.

Arbitrary internal significates result from inner personal meanings and feelings which a sign evokes. Various personality traits can account for the differences in the meanings a sign holds for people. Thus, people with different personalities and needs may have different meanings for brands and, therefore, different preferences. When instant coffee first appeared, women shunned it through guilt feelings over not doing a full share of work in the kitchen. They continued using regular coffee until persuaded otherwise by advertising.[6]

Therefore, advertising communication employs both types of arbitrary significates in order to enhance the value of the products. People arbitrarily assign meaning and associate themselves with a product which are extrinsic to it. Therefore, 'Wills' is made for each other, 'India Kings' Cigarettes are prestigious, 'Lifebuoy' soap for health and 'Liril' refreshes naturally. Thus, a value is added to the meanings of the product already inherent in it by associating external and internal significates.

How well the advertisers try to blend all the above characteristics was noticed in the advertisement war during Wills World Cup.

Fever seems too mild a word to describe the hysteria generated by the Wills World Cup. Millions of cricket lovers hooked on to this mother of all sporting events remained glued to the TV set mornings, afternoons and evenings. Exasperating those few misguided souls who do not start frothing at the mouth with excitement when the world cricket is mentioned but also equally delighting ad agencies who see in the World Cup and ultimate opportunity to advertise their products. The result? A plethora of television commercials specially focused on cricket and even more specially — The World Cup. Whether they are selling a soft drink, a jeep or a dress material. They have all basically cashed in on the cricket craze sweeping the entire sub-continent, if not the entire globe by riding piggy back on the Wills World Cup.

Undoubtedly the two biggest advertisers were Coca Cola and Pepsi, the former by virtue of being the official drink of the cup. Of the series of ads unleashed by each of them Coca Cola definitely had the more unusual ads. Pepsi had the more peppy fun kind. Coca Cola's red black white animation ads showing a bowler delivering a ball to the batsman with the trademark Coke wave in the background was off the beaten track. The full thwarted yet muted 'Mast Kalandar' refrain in the background coupled with the magnificently strung images of urchins playing cricket in the shadow of the Taj Mahal in little alleys and gallis with a splash of the colour red in every frame whether it is rows of red chillies drying in the sun or a woman throwing a fistful of red gulal in the air or the red of a gas cylinder evoking the colour of Coke, combine to make the entire commercial truly memorable. Compared to this commercial the Pepsi commercial with the punch line, 'There's nothing official about it', seems almost trivial. Petulant a case of sour grapes. But there are so many of them and all the commercials have been made so well that they nevertheless work. The main ad outlining the various official attributes of the game. A game that is played in whites (lots of aggression on the cricket field) culminating in the cricketers making disgusted faces when confronted with the official drink, but brightening up when faced with chilled Pepsi says thing unequivocally.

But in a sense the whole campaign is a negative one trying to bring down Coke rather than trying to plug Pepsi on its own (And it must be noted that Coca Cola has with dignity refrained from any reprisals of this kind). The other ads on the same theme, which feature individual cricketers Sachin Tendulkar, Mohammed Azharuddin, Courtney Walsh, lan Bishop are nice enough in their own way, but definitely satellite ads to the main commercial. The best of this lot is the one which features Sachin Tendulkar breaks a windshield and then attempts to hide from an irate Sardarji who when he finally catches Tendulkar beams at him, and heartily urges him to have a Pepsi, heavy Punjabi accent and all and then Sachin Tendulkar India's one man army on the cricket field grabs a Pepsi and reminds viewers that there's nothing official about it.

In the ad featuring Mohammed Azharuddin the Indian captain wearing casual clothes leaps about eventually snatching a bottle of Pepsi from someone else and then giving us the same line.

As for the West Indian cricketers, Courtney Walsh is exotically perched on a bulldozer while lan Bishop is very prosaic perched on something as mundane as the ground though perched is a wrong word as he is actually dancing with gay Caribbean, abandon needless to say Calypso magic surfaces in the Kingfisher commercial too. The king of one dayers, the king of all shots, the king of all catches as the West Indian cricketers dance, drink beer and generally make merry. And the final Pepsi ad with Dickie Bird is also more of the same.

All the other World Cup special ads do pale into relative insignificance when compared to the commercials of these two giant soft drink manufacturers official and unofficial. But the Wills ads are quite charming. Celebrating the spirit of partnership, celebrating team spirit, each line is illustrated by a quote from a famous cricketer (Sunil Gavaskar, Ajit Wadekar) though the images are of a romantic young couple sharing tender moments together.

The 'Vimal' commercial that celebrates the spirit of winning is also excellent. Stirring cricketing images flash by, including a stadium aflame with enthusiastic spectators, even as a slot machine display clatters to a perfect, winning combination. The 'Four Square' ad with the punch line you never know what you can become is good too. Vinod Kambli's batting statistics flash across the screen, even as he is shown trying to keep wickets.

The official chewing gum of the World Cup 'Center fresh' has a commercial of a batsman facing Australian bowler Craig MacDermott with some nervousness but then hitting a boundary. Tame stuff.

The commercial for 'Mahindra Armada', the jeep, features Kapil Dev and shows the jeep cruising along all sorts of terrain. With an excited cricket style commentary in the background. As the jeep skids close to a mountain edge, the frenzied voice in the background talks of it as going close to the boundary when the jeep finally stops at a porch, a formally dressed Kapil Dev steps out, adjusts his bow tie discreetly, taps the jeep with a proprietarial air, nods and smiles into the camera and then disappears. 'Humdrum'.

Phillips who also features Sachin Tendulkar as a batsman who as he plays cricket starts seeing the cricket ball clearer and clearer, till he sees it as clearly as a football. The idea is that when you watch a Phillips TV you too will see things as clearly as that good special effects. Tendulkar also starts in another ad a fairly straightforward neat commercial for visa card. Cricket enthusiasts are shown buying World Cup tickets with the card, even as Tendulkar holds up a 'Visa Card' saying, 'I have the power.'

Probably the most disappointing ad is the rather boring black and white 'Onida' ad which shows the backs of two cricketers as they talk of individual achievement as opposed to team spirit. The ad ends with one of them rather pompously reiterating that it is the team spirit that counts, that is what cricket is. As the Americans would say give me a break.

Most of the ads rather predictably rely heavily on the concepts of winning sportsmanship, team spirit and the like. Appropriate and fitting yes but also a trifle unimaginative. Which is why the Coca Cola commercial passion has a colour so superb. It transcends all these very usual images and ideas to capture the universal mesmerising appeal that cricket has on the sub-continent creating a commercial that has an arresting even moving quality.

PTV (Pakistan TV) is almost as full of cricket World Cup commercials as the Star network. While most of the ads are the familiar Coke and Pepsi ads the two soft drink companies have also collaborated with PTV to make what can only be described as 'rah rah films' for the Pakistani cricket team. One of the films replete with images of the aggressive ambitious cricketers of Pakistan all set to demolish the competition is set to a song which appears to have just two words in it 'Hum jeetenge', talk of overflowing confidence. If the Pakistanis do not win the World Cup, the entire nation will probably go into mourning. And Pepsi could very well add, 'There's nothing official about it.'

Getting Desired Response

The sequence of psychological responses that the consumer makes toward an advertising message has to be understood if we want to know how advertising communications works to get the desired response. The psychological responses from the set of goals that the communicator attempts to achieve and they can be as follows:

1. To stimulate consumer attention to the advertised brand
2. To influence favourably the consumer's perception of the advertised brand
3. To facilitate consumer retention of the advertised brand
4. To gain conviction (create favourable attitudes) toward the advertised brand
5. To generate a favourable action (e.g., search and purchase behaviour) towards the advertised brand
6. To effect favourable postpurchase behaviour (e.g., reduction of postpurchae dissonance, towards the advertised brand.

Stimulating Attention

On an average an individual is exposed to number of commercial messages each day, perhaps thousands of messages. Out of these only a few of them are capable to attract his attention, and still a lessor number maintain attention for such a period of time to communicate the basic selling proposition. Therefore, an advertising communicator is confronted with two major problems (*i*) attracting and (*ii*) holding consumer attention.

To attract and hold attention, the advertising communicator has at his disposal a number of useful concepts. These concepts can be classified into two sets — those which relate to the physical features of the advertisement and those which concern the message appeal.

The technical or physical features of the advertisement refer to such things as size, colour, and sound effects. Part 1 of Table 13.1 provides some useful generalisations concerning ways in which the physical attributes of an advertisement can capture a consumer's attention.

The message appeal used in an advertisement can also attract attention. Consumers ordinarily selectively attend to advertisements which are of interest to them or which are relevant to their particular needs and problems. Part 2 of Table 1 provides some useful generalisations concerning message appeals. Specific appeals are discussed later in this chapter.

TABLE 13.1

Guidelines for Stimulating Attention in Advertising

1. Physical characteristics of the advertisement (Part 1)

In general:

(*a*) Larger ads attract more attention than smaller ones.
(*b*) Movement or the illusion of movement in ads attract greater attention than ads which are static.
(*c*) The more intense an ad is (e.g., loud sounds), the more attention it will gain (up to some point).
(*d*) Ads which are unusual or novel attract attention.
(*e*) The use of contrast in ads attracts attention.
(*f*) Colour ads attract more attention than black-and-white ads.
(*g*) The shape of an ad affects attention. Taller-than-wide ads attract more attention than wider-than-tall ads.
(*h*) An object which appears in isolation in an ad attracts attention.
(*i*) Advertisements which stimulate more than one sense mode are effective in gaining attention (e.g., combined use of sight and sound).

2. Characteristics of message appeals which attract and hold attention (Part 2)

In general:

(*a*) Ads which appeal to consumers' permanent interests or their immediate concerns attract and hold attention.
(*b*) Ads which are supportive of consumers' presently held attitudes and opinions attract and hold attention.
(*c*) Ads which permit consumers to naturally fluctuate their attention hold attention.

In summary, the physical features of an advertisement are primarily useful in attracting attention, whereas, the message appeal is not only helpful in attracting attention, but also important in maintaining attention as well. It should be noted that the technique(s) used to attract attention should never offend the consumer or hinder the basic selling purpose of a message.

Influencing Perception

Perception involves the mental process of constructing pictures of the numerous objects we see, around us in the environment. In previous chapters, we have discussed the various factors responsible of creating the image of a product in our mind.

The interest which marketing communicators have in the human perceptual process is in its relevance to image formation. In particular, marketing communicators are interested in how they can influence consumers' images of their brands, corporations and retail stores. Marketeres have come to realise the importance of brand image in their efforts to influence consumer choice behaviour. 'People buy things not only for what they do, but also for what they mean.'[7] A brand's image may evoke several meanings. A brand of beer, for example, may evoke meanings of sociability, prestige, hospitality, relaxation, and so on.

Given that brand images are important to consumer purchase decisions, how do marketers determine what their brand's image should be? Research in this area suggests that consumers purchase some products on the basis of how congruent a brand's image is with the consumer's self-and-self-ideal images.[8] The notion is advanced that by studying consumer self-images, marketers can design communications programs based on the 'blueprints' derived from self image research to 'fit' the images consumers' have or desire to have of themselves.

It should be noted that a brand's image is what consumers see the brand as, not how a company sees the brand or intends for it to be seen by consumers. An example of the failure of a company to evoke the intended image in its consumers is cited by Buriegh

Gardner.[9] The company's ad depicted a famous orchestra conductor, dressed in tails, a beer in hand, talking to women dressed elegantly in evening gowns. The purpose of the ad was to evoke an image of status for the advertised beer and suggest to beer drinkers that they too could enjoy this status by drinking this beer. Research indicated, however that consumers had negative and even hostile reactions to the advertised beer because they were unfamiliar with the conductor and he held no meaning for them. Determining the 'right' image for consumers is one thing, having the intended image evoked in the minds of consumers is still another.

Consider the case of Pond's advertising campaign of its Dream Flower Talc (DFT). Pond's Dreamflower Talc is a well-established brand and the market leader in the talcum-powder market. The market is divided into four major segments and Pond's DFT was positioned in the premium category.

Prior to 1972, only one campaign ran in the process in both metropolis and non-metropolis cities and towns. This was, however, considered old fashioned, considering the model used as well as the design of the mnemonic adjacent to the illustration on the Pond's talc in Fig. 13.3 A.

Fig. 13.3(A). A 1972 campaign

In the metropolis campaign, a top model, Ayesha, was used in a relatively sophisticated situation and the mnemonic alongside the Pond's powder box eliminated. The visuals, in small illustrations, were those of fashion shows and 'time for a date'. A distinctive feature of the main illustration was a cone-piece telephone, apart from the mod appeal of the model. The non-metropolis ad showed a less sophisticated slim model and the mnemonic was included. The only other change was a larger size of the talc container. The consumer research studies carried out in 1971-72, through the Advertising and Marketing planning Index, indicated that high priority should be given to the following two aspects: Freshness and fragrance.

A new campaign was developed in 1975. This advertisement emphasized the fragrance aspect by bringing 'Dreamflower' in the headline. The model was changed. No attempt was made to modernize the brand image. Fig. 13.3 B.

The following aspects were taken into account in developing the campaign which was introduced in 1977.

Fig. 13.3(B). A New Campaign Developed in 1975

1. An attempt was made at integrating the so called sophisticated and unsophisticated segments of consumers.
2. The decision-making unit was considered to be the family as a whole, especially a young family. Only females were used as models in the previous campaigns.
3. The fragrance aspect was kept in the fore-front.

The above considerations went into the making of the new campaign featuring the husband, an attractive wife and a little girl behind a large 'Dreamflower' talcum powder tin. See Fig. 13.3 C.

One leading advertising agency executive believes that once an image is chosen it should be considered a long-term investment in the brand. To change every six months confuses consumers and the brand never establishes a consistent image in the consumer's mind. As examples of brands which have established a consistent image over the years Ogilvy cites the successes of Betty Crocker and Campbell Soup among others.[10]

It should be recognised that advertising communications is not the sole contributor to a brand's image. Other marketing communications variables play roles in varying degrees to establish and reinforce a brand's image. Some product categories do however rely on advertising communications more than do other product categories. Companies whose products are relatively homogeneous physically, such as, beer, cigarettes, colas and liquor rely heavily upon advertising communications to create product differences in the minds of their consumers. Advertising communicators generally create this kind of 'product differentiation' by associating emotional or social connotations with the advertised brand; whereas for products with obvious physical and functional differences advertisers ordinarily emphasise the advantages of these features over those of competing brands. Obviously, there is a continuum along which products lie from highly homogeneous to highly heterogeneous. Products such as automobiles advertisers may find it advantageous to emphasise both functional and psychological differences in creating a brand image.

Facilitating Retention

Learning is the process which reinforces the behaviour and facilitate retention power of an

Fig. 13.3(C). Campaign introduced in 1977

individual. In the chapter relating to learning, we have discussed the importance of learning in marketing communications. Some of these principles discussed earlier and also applicable to advertising communications have been summarised in Table 13.2 below.

TABLE 13.2

Facilitating Retention: An Application of Learning Theory to Advertising Communications

In advertising:

1. Unpleasant messages are learned as easily as pleasant messages.
2. Meaningful messages are learned more easily than unmeaningful messages.
3. Ideational learning is faster if massive advertising is followed by distributed advertising.
4. Products requiring mechanical skills are learned best if demonstrated in the ad as though the consumers were doing the task themselves.
5. Products benefits are learned best when presented at the beginning and end of a message.
6. Messages which are unique or unusual are better remembered than commonplace advertisements.
7. Rewarding the consumer who attends to a message enhances learning of the message.
8. Learning by consumers is enhanced when they are told the benefits they will receive from using the product.
9. Active participation in the message enhances learning.
10. Messages learning is faster if previous or following messages do not interfere.
11. Repetition increases the strength of an older idea more than a newer idea.
12. Messages presented closer in time to an intense need are learned faster than those which are presented when the need is weaker.
13. The greater reward a consumer perceives from viewing (or listening) to an ad message, the faster his learning of the message.
14. The less effort required to respond to an ad, the faster learning occurs.
15. The more complex an ad message is, the more difficult it is to learn.

Gaining Conviction

Gaining conviction we mean that positive attitudes and opinions are formed by an individual toward the advertised product. This is somewhat same as principles of persuasion. Therefore, gaining conviction and persuasion may be looked as complementary to each other. Table 13.3. summarises principles of persuasion applicable to gaining conviction. All These factors are primarily responsible to influence consumers' attitude towards a brand and thus gaining conviction.

TABLE 13.3

Gaining Conviction: Guidelines for Persuasive Advertising Communications

In general, the source of an advertising message is more persuasive on consumer attitudes and opinions of the consumer:

1. Is perceived by his audience as highly credible (prestigious, expert, honest, etc.)
2. Initially expresses some views held by his audience, then presents his appeal.
3. Is perceived by his audience as similar to themselves.
4. Is perceived as powerful or attractive to his audience.
5. Is low in credibility, but argues against his own self-interest.
6. Has no perceived intention to manipulate his audience or has nothing to gain from what he advocates

In general, as advertising message is more effective in creating or changing consumer attitudes and opinions in the desired direction if the message:

1. Is one sided and is presented to consumers who (*a*) initially agree with the position advocated in the message, (*b*) are poorly educated, and (*c*) are not expected to see or hear subsequent counter arguments.

2. Is two sided and is presented to consumers who (*a*) initially disagree with the position advocated in the message, (*b*) are well educated, and (*c*) are likely to hear counter arguments.
3. Uses the anticlimax order for consumers who have a low level of interest in the product.
4. Uses the climax order for consumers who have a high level of interest in the product.
5. Uses a primacy order for controversial, interesting, and highly familiar product.
6. Uses a recency order for uninteresting or moderately unfamiliar product.
7. Arouses a need first, then offers the product as a means of satisfying the need.
8. Draws a conclusion by suggesting the correct action to take.
9. Uses strong fear appeals when they pose a threat to the consumer's loved ones, or are presented by a highly credible source, or concern topics somewhat unfamiliar to the consumer or are directed at consumers high in self-esteem.
10. Actively involves the audience in the advertisement.
11. Uses highly effective language to describe the product.

FIG. 13.4. Facilitating Retention through Negative Appeal

12. Associates the product with popular ideas.
13. Arouses feelings of aggression, followed by suggestions of how the product can reduce those aggressive feelings.
14. Associates highly desirable ideas or feelings with the product.
15. Uses non-verbal communications to enhance the product's meanings, especially non-verbal cues which elicit positive consumer feelings and emotions.

Consumers exhibiting certain personality traits are more persuasible than others. In general, consumers who would be expected to be more easily persuasible are those who:

1. Are low in self-esteem and require social approval for their behaviour.
2. Exhibit social withdrawal tendencies.
3. Inhibit aggressive feelings.
4. Are low in anxiety.
5. Are high in rich imagery and fantasy.
6. Are women (in our society).

The persuasibility of certain consumer personality types depends upon the characteristics of the message and the message source. In general, it would be expected that:

1. Consumers who have authoritarian personalities are more susceptible to messages attributed to anonymous sources than those attributed to authority figures.
2. Consumers who have non-authoritarian personalities are more susceptible to messages attributed to anonymous sources than those attributed to authority figures.
3. Consumers who have highly dogmatic personalities are more likely to be persuaded by authority figures whom they trust than by authority figures whom they do not trust.
4. Consumers who are open-mind are persuaded more by the merits of the advertising message than by who delivers the message.
5. Consumers who have the ability to draw valid inferences are influenced more by logical argumentation than by a message based on irrelevant and unsupported generalities.

Consumers also possess characteristics which make them resistant to persuasion. In general, consumers are resistant to the persuasive attempts of an advertising message which:

1. Attacks one of a consumer's centrally held beliefs.
2. Attacks one of a consumer's 'derived' beliefs (i.e., those tied to centrally held beliefs.)
3. Attacks a belief to which a consumer is strongly committed.
4. It is contrary to the norms of the group to which a popular prestigious person belongs.

FIG. 13.5. Gaining Conviction through arousing a need

Consumers are influenced in their purchase decisions by the groups to which they belong. Some useful principles of persuasion in advertising communications are the following:

1. Advertising communications which appeal to culturally learned behaviour are more persuasive than those which run counter to such behaviour.
2. Advertising communicators are more likely to be successful when appealing to specific sub-cultural group attitudes and norms than when appealing to broad-based cultural attitudes and norms.
3. Because the vast majority of family income is lower-income groups in for routine household purchases, advertising messages directed towards these groups should be aimed toward the wife.
4. Marketers who define their target market as young married should design and direct their advertising messages forward both husband and wife. (They exhibit more joint-purchase decision-making).
5. Advertising messages which emphasise instrumental functions of a product should be directed toward the husband in a family, whereas those emphasising the aesthetic features should be directed toward the wife.
6. Product advertising directed toward family purchase should consider the family's stage in the life cycle.
7. When product or brand purchase decision are not influenced strongly by reference groups, the advertising message should emphasise brand features, intrinsic qualities, and benefits over competing brands.

8. When a reference group influences consumer purchase decisions, the advertising message should emphasise the kind of people who use the brand and reinforce these stereotypes in the minds of consumers.
9. For new products, advertising communications should stress the relative advantages of the new brand over existing brands, show how it fits into consumer's present ways of doing things (i.e., reduce perceived complexity), and show the results of using the product (observability).
10. Some advertising messages should be designed to help consumers reduce post purchase doubt. This task can be accomplished by (*a*) providing the consumer with a way to rationalise his decision and (*b*) providing the consumer with additional evidence to support the wisdom of his decision.
11. Where opinion leaders for a product can be identified and for whom media habits are somewhat homogeneous, the advertising communicator should direct a substantial portion of his communications effort toward this group, so that they might in turn, favourably influence their followers.

Advertising Changes with Time — So The Maharajah Changes with Time

'We call him a Maharajah for want of a better description. But his blood isn't blue. He may look like royalty, but he isn't royal.' These are the words of Bobby Kooka, the man who conceived the Maharajah, the mascot of Air India and a benchmark of those days. Air India's legacy mascot is given a boost...out of the door. Let us see how this once a legend mascot changed with the passage of time. The Maharaja takes a final bow.

This once familiar lovable figure first made his appearance in Air India way back in 1946, when Bobby Kooka as Air India's Commercial Director and Umesh Rao, an artist with J.Walter Thompson Ltd., Mumbai, together created the Maharajah. Born in 1946 - with all credit of his ideation going to the late Bobby Kooka (the then Commercial Director of Air India) - this royal ruler stole all eyes, proudly donning a fresh avatar each time he was happily placed on the government air-line's towering bill-boards of the 50s, 60s, 70s, 80s and right within the churning 90s too.

The Maharajah began merely as a rich Indian potentate, symbolizing graciousness and high living. And somewhere along the line his creators gave him a distinctive personality: his outsized moustache, the striped turban and his aquiline nose. What began as an attempt as a design for an inflight memo pad grew to take Air India's sales and promotional messages to millions of travellers across the world. Today, this naughty diminutive Maharajah of Air India has become a world figure. He can be a lover boy in Paris, a sumo wrestler in Tokyo, a pavement artist, a Red Indian, a monk... he can effortlessly flirt with the beauties of the world and most importantly, he can get away with it all. Simply because he is the Maharajah!

He has completed more than 60 years and become the most recognizable mascot the world over. His antics, his expressions, his puns have allowed Air India to promote its services with a unique panache and an unmatched sense of subtle humour. In fact, he has won numerous national and international awards for Air India for humour and originality in publicity.

His attire, persona and communique - sometimes dressed as a sumo-wrestler; sometimes playing the snake charmer and some other times, be-coming a part of Moscow's popular chess board - all combined to make him perhaps the most recalled brand of us Indians through the latter part of the last century! When 4Ps B&M caught up with the effervescent J. Bharghav, Head, Corporate Communication, Air India, he expectably and quite succinctly agreed on the un-beaten popularity of the Maharaja, 'Around 30-40 years ago, the advertising of Air India was purely conservative as Air India spent most of its advertising budgets on hoardings based on current affairs fancying the Indians at large with the Maharaja as the spokesperson.'

But we wanted more dope; and dope was what we got when we found that it was J. Walter Thompson that was the agency credited to have co-ordinated with Bobby Kooka to create the Maharaja! We scurried out Ivan Arthur, former National Creative Director, JWT and current Vice Chairman, Aicar, who gave some eye-openers, 'One day, simply looking for an interesting letterhead, Bobby Kooka phoned the agency and promptly received a number of designs, all done by this talented young JWT Art Director named Umesh Rao. One of these designs had a neat line-drawing of some Maharaja bowing in a gracious welcome. Kooka liked it a lot and the letterhead was finalised.'

But remaining confined to the letterheads wasn't supposed to be the fate of our prince, there was more to come. Initially introduced merely to ornament the Air India letterhead. As Arthur reveals, 'Sometime later, the ever-inventive mind of Bobby Kooka asked why that cute little drawing could not step out of the letterhead and be used in the advertising as an add-on. 'But of course, it could', said the agency and the next advertisement had the little bowing Maharaja signing off above the Air-India International logo. (The airline was called Air-India International then). Kooka was pleased. And the Maharaja con-tinued to sign off on some of Air-India International's advertisements, till on another inventive day, Kooka asked why the little fellow could not grow bigger and actually take centerstage? He did. And so was born the Maharaja as mascot.'

Soon the Maharaja won many hearts and became one of the most important members of the Air India family. And since then, he, was seen in all their advertisement campaigns; and for over sixty years, he continued to remain Air-India's surrogate sales-man, selling tickets not by hawking but by being charming. Rohit Manchanda, CEO, Planman Life, comments, 'The Maharaja usage was the first example of non-advertising icons used as advertising, in the Indian ad industry. A breakthrough!'

Could anyone have then imagined that this royal ad-king would subsequently gel not only with Indians, but most brilliantly with foreigners as well? Ergo, it seems more surprising that such an emblazoned iconic creation's dominance has now ended, and that too because of competition. Bharghav diplomatically explains, 'No doubt, Air India has been a conservative advertiser in the past; but now, as the environment has changed to become much more competitive... the need of the hour is to move on...'

And as with all great men, he too has had his critics. But the millions of travellers whose lives he has touched far outnumber them. In fact, to them, the Maharajah with his inimitable style, charm and wit is a very real person. He's almost like a friend to every Air India traveller. A friend who reaches out with warmth and hospitality, even to the farthest corners of the world.

'At a time when the competition was the likes of BOAC and Pan Am, the Maharaja did with a chuckle what they found hard with their dollars. And with so much more competition today, the Maharaja is even more useful now; only, we must know how to make him relevant, meaningful and today. Arthur claims that in the absence of anything else to set the airline or its communication apart, Air-India today is merely a product, not a brand! But really, can a yesteryear champion speak to a global audience in different contemporary languages without losing his identity?

Bharghav gives his take, 'Now, advertising is making use of all media channels, and leaving not even a single medium untouched. There are highly acclaimed ads and a total departure from the past, as market scenario has changed. We need to reach out to the customer for him to understand the product to be used. So luring and incentivising is our mantra.' And not the Maharaja! Quoting examples, Bharghav elaborates on his recent advertising strategies, 'USP changes overtime. You have to keep changing according to the environment. For non-stop flights, it's been comfort, high degree of punctuality and luxurious seats. But it's different for the limited-budget or the price-sensitive consumer; we offer good deals to them. Earlier in the 60s and 70s, we had a limited budget so we did it via our mascot cum spokesperson-Maharaja, but advertising today is much superior.' Issues like Air India's on-going future alliance with Star Alliance - that gives the company a global touch - become more pristine selling points than the Maharaja.

Clearly, times are changing, during those times, the post-independence Indian aspired to be... and experience, royalty! The Maharaja was a classic metaphor for that! But today's Indian identifies more with the Bills and the Gates than with the heirs and the fiefdoms. Today's Indian aspires more for the Virgin than the Prince! The King is no more! Long live the King of Moustaches... Maharaja!

'As the environment has become competitive, it's time to move on,' J. Bhargav, Head, Corp-Comm, Air India asserted.

Advertising Communications Economic Function

There are two views regarding advertising communications economic function. One school of thought is based on the assumption that it is equal to market power. The other school of thought views advertising communication as information function. Both of the two perspectives have been summarised in Table 13.4.

FIG. 13.6. Changing Mascot with time

FIG. 13.7. New Ad of Air India

TABLE 13.4
Two Schools of thought on Advertising's Functions

Advertising	*Advertising = Market Power*	*Advertising = Information*
Consumer-Buying Behaviour	Advertising affects consumer preferences and tastes, changes product attributes and differentiates the product from competitive offerings.	Advertising Informs consumers about product attributes and does not change the way they value those attributes.
Barriers to Entry and Market Power	Consumers become brand loyal, less price sensitive, and perceive fewer substitutes for advertised brands.	Consumers become more price sensitive and buy best 'value.' Only the relationship between price and quality affects elasticity for a given product.
Industry Structure	Potential entrants must overcome established brand loyalty and spend relatively more on advertising.	Advertising makes entry possible for new brands because it can communicate Product attributes to consumers.
Market Conduct	Films are insulated from market competition and otential rivals; concentration increases, leaving firms with more discretionary power.	Consumers can compare competitive offerings easily and competitive rivalry is increased. Efficient firms remain and as the inefficient leave, new entrants appear; the ambiguous.
Market Performance	Firms can charge higher prices and are not as likely to compete on quality or price dimensions. Innovation may be reduced. High prices and excessive profits accrue to advertisers and give them even more incentive to advertise their products. Output is restricted conditions of perfect competition.	More-informed consumers put pressures on firms to lower prices and improve quality. Innovation is facilitated via new entrants. Industry prices are decreased. The effect on profits due to increased competition efficiency compared to is ambiguous.

Source : Paul W. Farris and Mark S. Albion, 'The Impact of Advertising on the Price of Consumer Products,' *Journal of Marketing*, Vol. 44, Summer 1980, p. 18.

The first school of thought which views advertising as market power is based on the fact that advertising is able to differentiate homogeneous products. Advertising is in a position to faster brand loyalty, thus encourages customers to be less sensitive to price, than they would be in the absence of advertising. Therefore, entry barriers are increased. In order to make an entry in the market, more expenditure on advertising has to be done for new products than established products to overcome existing brand loyalty. Because of advertising communication, products can be isolated from their rivals and in return get discretionary power to increase prices of their product and influence the market in other ways. According to this view, who look at advertising as equal to market power companies are in a position to charge higher prices than they could in the absence of advertising and ultimately are able to make excessive profits.

An anti thesis to the market power view point is given by the second school of thought that view advertising as information. They argue that by giving information to the customers about product's features, benefits and other attributes, price sensitivity of consumers is enhanced. Once the consumers' price sensitivity is increased, their ability to obtain the best value of the money they spend on a product purchase is a natural process. Barriers to entry for prospective new products are considerably reduced because advertising enables these new entrants to communicate product attributes and their benefits to consumers.

According to this information perspective, because of advertising consumers are in a better position to compare prices of the similar products and thus there is a increased competition rivalry as evident in Coke *vs.* Pepsi case. However, product innovation is easy through new entrants and quality is improved. Further, prices are slashed and lucrative offers are given along with the product like 25% extra or two at the cost of one, because consumers exert pressure of companies to lower prices, being well informed through competitor's advertising.

Both the views expressed above regarding advertising communications economic function cannot be said to be entirely correct or adequate by itself. Both views are debatable as the exact role varies from situation to situation. Therefore, no generalisation is desirable.

Critics of the advertising = market power view content that a number of factors other than advertising (e.g., superior product quality, better packaging, and better distribution) also account for brand loyalty and price insensitivity.[11] Advertising is not the sole marketing force responsible for a firm's market power.

Similarly, advertising does not possess all the virtues that advocates of the advertising = information school would lead us to believe. Critics of this view contend that advertising goes beyond merely providing consumers with information in fact, it influences consumers relative preferences for different products attributes. It follows from this contention that advertising may create the same undesirable consequences (i.e., market concentration, price insensitivity, entry barriers, etc.) claimed by the advertising = market power proponents.[12]

Therefore, advertising's macroeconomic aspect can be referred as both good and bad. It has negative economic effects as claimed by the market-power school to the limited extent that only one or a few advertisers in a given product market situation possess differential advantages over competitors in terms of competitors advertising spending power or effectiveness. However, when any one competitor's advertising efforts can be countervailed by other advertising, the positive economic effects of advertising, as claimed by the information school, outweigh the negative.[13]

The Indian advertising industry is talking business today. It has evolved from being a small-scale business to a full-fledged industry. It has emerged as one of the major industries and tertiary sectors and has broadened its horizons be it the creative aspect, the capital employed or the number of personnel involved. Indian advertising industry in very little time has carved a niche for itself and placed itself on the global map.

Indian advertising industry with an estimated value of es13, 200-crore has made jaws drop and set eyeballs gazing with some astonishing pieces of work that it has given in the recent past. The creative minds that the Indian advertising industry incorporates have come up with some mind-boggling concepts and work that can be termed as masterpieces in the field of advertising.

Advertising agencies in the country too have taken a leap. They have come a long way from being small and medium sized industries to becoming well known brands in the business. Mudra, Ogilvy and Mathew (O&M), Mccann Ericsonn, Rediffussion, Leo Burnett are some of the top agencies of the country.

Indian economy is on a boom and the market is on a continuous trail of expansion. With the market gaining grounds Indian advertising has every reason to celebrate. Businesses are looking up to advertising as a tool to cash in on lucrative business opportunities. Growth in business has lead to a consecutive boom in the advertising industry as well.

The Indian advertising today handles both national and international projects. This is primarily because of the reason that the industry offers a host of functions to its clients that include everything from start to finish that include client servicing, media planning, media buying, creative conceptualization, pre and post campaign analysis, market research, marketing, branding, and public relation services.

Keeping in mind the current pace at which the Indian advertising industry is moving the industry is expected to witness a major boom in the times ahead. If the experts are to be believed then the industry in the coming times will form a major contribution to the GDP. With all this, there is definitely no looking back for the Indian advertising industry that is all set to win accolades from the world over.

REFERENCES

1. Sidney J. Levy, 'Promotional Behaviour', Scott, Foreman and Company, Glenview, III, 1971, pp. 64-65.
2. Herbert Stein, 'Advertising is Worth Advertising,' *Advertising Age,* November 21, 1973, p. 5.

3. William R. Swinyard and Michael L. Ray, 'Advertising Selling Interactions: An Attribution Theory Experiment,' *Journal of Marketing Research*, Vol. 14, November, 1977, pp. 509-516.
4. Walter R. Nord and J. Paul Peter, 'A Behaviour Modification Perspective in Marketing,' *Journal of Marketing*, Vol. 44, Spring 1980, pp. 36-47.
5. Much of this discussion is based on Ivan L. Preston, 'Theories of Behaviour and the Concept of Rationality in Advertising,' *Journal of Communication*, Vol. 17, No. 3, pp. 211-222, September 1967, and Charles Osgood, George Suci, and Percy Tannenbaum, The Measurement of Meaning (Urbana The University of Illinois Press, 1957), chap.1.
6. Preston, *Ibid.*, p.217.
7. Sidney J. Levy, 'Symbols for Sale,' *Harvard Business Review*, Vol. 37, pp. 117-124, July-August 1959, in Harold H. Kassarjian and Thomas S. Robertson (eds.) Perspectives in Consumer Behaviour (Glenview, Ill: Scott, Foresman and Company, 1968), 212.
8. Wayne De Lozier and Rollie Tillman, 'Self Image Concepts — Can They Be Used to Design Marketing Programs?' *The Southern Journal of Business*, Vol. 7, No. 4, November 1972, pp. 8-15, Edward Gregg and Gregg Hupp, Perceptions of Self Generalised Stereotypes and Brand Selection,' *Journal of Marketing Research*, Vol. 5, pp. 58-63, February 1968 and Ira Dolich, 'Congruence Relationships between Self Images and Product Brands,' *Journal of Marketing Research*, Vol. 6, pp. 80-84, February 1969.
9. Burleigh Gardner, 'Symbols and Meaning in Advertising,' in C.H.Sandage (Ed.), The Promise of Advertising (Homewood, I. ll.,: Richard D. Irwin, Inc., 1961).
10. David Ogilvy, 'Confessions of an Advertising Man' (New York : Atheneum Publishers, 1963), pp. 100-103.
11. Paul W. Farris and Mark. S. Albion, 'The Impact of Advertising on the Price of Consumer Products,' *Journal of Marketing*, Vol.44, Summer, 1980, pp. 17-35.
12. *Ibid.*, p. 20.
13. Kent M. Lancaster and Gordon E.Miracle, 'How Advertising Can Have Largely Anti Competitive Effects in One Sector But Largely Pro Competitive Effects in Another,' University of Illinois Working Paper No. 7, Urbana, IL, November, 1979.

CHAPTER 14

ADVERTISING BUDGET

DOES IT REALLY MATTER WHAT WE SPEND ON ADVERTISING?

As you can imagine, marketers have probably always wondered whether their advertising dollars have an impact. This is particularly true now, as advertising budgets are being slashed in virtually every industry due to the downturn in the U.S. economy. Simply put, marketers want to know whether it is worth advertising their brand, and how much they should be spending if it is.

There are some out there who think that the amount spent on media has little or no impact— at least as it relates to consumers' perceptions of the brand's quality. In a study commissioned by Brandweek magazine, a Princeton-based research company concluded: "Consumer opinions pertaining to quality bear little correlation to the amount of time and money companies spend advertising their wares on Friends, FM radio or Foxsports.com." According to Total Research Corp., none of the 10 brands most heavily advertised in the United States were recognized as among the top 100 "quality" brands—even though they accounted for over $3.5 billion in expenditures. On the other hand, the brands considered in the top 10 spent only approximately $150 million. The top three media spenders-McDonald's, Burger King, and Circuit City—didn't make the top 100 list! {List numbers 1 to 3 were Waterford Crystal, Craftsman tools, and the Discovery Channel.)

When asked why, this might be the case, some consultants noted that advertising may be less effective than initially thought or that it lacked credibility in general. Others argued that advertising is too weak to establish a brand and that word of mouth or customer experience is far more valuable in establishing quality.

But not everyone is ready to dismiss advertising as ineffective. Even those that conclude that advertising is not effective in creating a quality image are not yet ready to recommend that companies stop advertising. They agree that while advertising may be weak for this objective, it is (if well designed and placed) quite effective, particularly when it comes to creating awareness and reinforcing the product's message. Further, Robert Passikoff, President of the Brand Keys consulting agency, notes that advertising has different objectives depending on the product category. He notes that "quality is less important in hamburgers than in crystal" and if the list was about fun, "Waterford would be down at the bottom."

Others agree with Passikoff, contending that stressing quality may be only one objective of advertising and that many companies do not use metrics to measure the ROI on advertising expenditures or—if they do—use the wrong ones. The result is that these expenditures are easy to cut, even when they should not be. As noted by Keith Woodward, VP of finance at General Mills, Inc., most managers want to see the direct returns to volume or revenue, and "you can't do that with advertising." He suggests the consideration of new forms of metrics.

Woodward notes that brand value is important but investments must consider other objectives as well. Factors such as opportunity for growth, historical performance, growth versus the competition, and previous advertising effectiveness metrics must also be taken into consideration. Once the campaign is launched, revenue, market data, and other proprietary data are considered. Woodward notes that while there is no absolute metric for advertising ROI, he feels that General Mills has some good insights and that advertising does work.

Carol Gee of Du Pont (Lycra, Cordura, and other brands) agrees. As global director of brands, Gee notes that it is difficult to track the effectiveness of advertising on the end consumer, "but if we just advertised to our direct (OEM) customers we would be a commodity overnight." While most consul-tants and experts agree that creating awareness and reinforcing the brand's image are both necessary and measurable, most do not agree on what other factors should be considered in computing ROI. Brand revenues, sales, and even contributions to stock values have been suggested—though there are certainly some limitations to each.

For their part, advertising agencies are also offering their opinions. In addition to awareness, factors such as valuation, ability of the campaign to differentiate the brand name, and other "response components" are suggested. Getting the ad to prompt the consumer to call a toll-free number, visit a website, or request additional information about the brand is also a valuable objective, they contend.

While the experts and consultants may disagree as to the real value of advertising—and perhaps even the real objectives—they do agree on a couple of things. First, it is hard to measure the direct impact of advertising. Second, a variety of objectives might be used in the evaluation process. And third, so far as determining the ability of advertising to demonstrate positive ROI, we aren't exactly there yet.

Sources: Kris Frieswick, "New Brand Day," CFO, November 2001, pp. 97-99; Kenneth Hein, "Can't Buy Me Love," Brandweek, June 4,2001,pp.S20-S22.

The advertising budget is fixed under a plan. Questions relating to the amount of money to be expended on the total planning process and how much expenditure should be incurred on each step of the action and process are decided by the planner. The total amount of expenditure and the expenditure on each process are decided for a particular period. The production costs of advertising in each medium for a specified period are laid down in the beginning. The total expenditure to be made in future is logically decided. Administrative expenses and reserves for unanticipated situations are determined when formulating advertising plans.

Estimated to meet the financial requirement of advertising plans so that advertising objectives with planned strategies may be realised within a given time. The advertising budget is a statement of proposed advertising expenditure; a guideline for allocating the available funds to the various functions and activities of advertising.

It is important to budget advertising expenditure carefully to ensure that it is made wisely. The budget is prepared to control the use of funds in several departments. It is a plan for allocating the amount to each department. The advertising appropriation, *i.e.*, the total amount allocated to advertising, is first decided. The budget for each medium, product, message, geographic or consumer market is decided for different periods of time after estimating the advertising costs under each head and sub-head.

The budget is an expression of the expenditure plan. In the advertising campaign the advertising budget is a plan of expenditure to be incurred to meet the present as well as future expenditure. Budget decisions explain the budget strategies and programmes. Its appropriation is the total amount of the expenditure to be incurred on budgeting. It is a limiting factor which determines the size of the advertising campaign. The selection of media and messages also depends on it. A moderate budget is neither too little nor too big in terms of money spent on advertising. By framing a precise message and determining the colour, space and time to be used without hampering the total advertising plan the budget may be curtailed.

The budget is merely a plan of expenditure. This financial plan, *i.e.*, the budget, is reviewed from time to time in the light of changing marketing situations.

Changes in distribution patterns, production capacity, competition and other elements in the marketing situation should be constantly reviewed to find out changes in advertising objectives and strategies and consequent adjustments in the advertising budget are required. Flexibility should be regarded as the key element in the budget. Contingency funds should also be provided in the advertising budget.

The key factors in determining the optimum size of an advertising fund are the experience and judgment of marketing management. The budget is not merely current expenditure but capital expenditure on build-ing image and reputation. It is more than an instrument of stimulating immediate sales. It is a capital investment, therefore, it should incorporate current expenditure as well as capital investment for the future development of goodwill, image and reputation.

ADVERTISING AS AN INVESTMENT

Advertising budget seeks to build the image and reputation of the organisation. Its achievement is observed over a long period. Sometimes, the revenue expenditure on advertising is successful in attracting customers immediately. They buy the product when they listen to or view the advertising message. The effects of expenditure incurred on building are creating the image and reputation. These are realised gradually over a long period. This is capita! expenditure or investment. The income-tax authorities accept the expenditure on advertising as revenue expenditure. The marketing manager is authorised to control and spend the money assigned to him for advertising purposes. The appropriation is determined by using several formulas, such as affordable approach, sales approach, competition approach etc. Thus, the advertising appropriation takes into account the factors influencing appropriation and determination of appropriation.

Another Perspective

Cutting Budgets When Times Get Tough – Wise Strategy or Potential Pitfall?

A downturn in the U.S. economy led a number of companies to slash their advertising budgets significantly in 200I and 2002. Even the top spenders cut deeply, with GM cutting the budget by 24 percent and the top 10 overall spending 7 percent less on the average. The companies seemed to be saying that since sales are down, advertising expenditures should go down. But is this the right thing to do? A lot of companies don't think so.

For example, not all of the top 10 advertisers slashed budgets (though 7 of them did). Some like AOL and AT&T actually increased expenditures. For these companies, the downturn is viewed as an opportunity rather than a threat. They take a "spend now, win later" approach, viewing such expenditures as an investment rather than a cost. Take Monster.com as an example. While many dot-coms announced advertising cuts for 2002, Monster indicated that it would maintain its advertising expenditures and number of ads constant. Not only that, but it announced that it would spend additional promotional dollars in other areas. In the first quarter of 2001, Monster invested $37.4 million in measured media, as opposed to $28.7 in the same period for 2000. The same amount was budgeted for 2002. fn addition, Monster paid more than $10 million to be part of the Winter Olympics in Salt Lake City. The company is also negotiating for advertising on the 20, 03 Super Bowl. Monster has also kept its print budget the same, though it is increasing expenditures online.

What does Monster know that others do not? The goal of the new Monster campaign is to raise brand awareness. The company believes that in a time when the economy is down and layoffs may occur, a job placement firm has a golden opportunity to gain by increased investing. Jim Dietz, president of Andover Franchising, Inc., agrees with this philosophy. As Dietz notes, "Pink slips can help us. When downsizing is in the headlines, more folks are willing to look at making an investment in themselves." Andover has increased its expenditures, as well as its media options. Primarily an online advertiser, its 2002 plan included print ads in Entrepreneur and Franchise Times magazines.

To encourage advertisers to consider ad dollars as an investment rather than an expense, the American Advertising Federation (AAF) has initiated a "Great Brands" campaign, debuting with two 15-second TV spots and a number of print ads encouraging marketers not to neglect market spending during the slump. Wally Snyder, CEO of the AAF, notes: "The companies behind leading global brands ... recognize that advertising dollars translate into increased market share." The first two companies featured in the campaign are Intel and Coca-Cola.

Thus, while some companies cut, others increase expenditures in a down economy. Much of the reason for this is rooted in the underlying philosophy as to what advertising is all about—an investment or a cost of doing business.

Sources: Erin Strout, "Spend Now, Win Later" Sales & Marketing Management, April 2002, pp. 65-66; Hillary Chura,"Monster.com Beefs Up Ad Plans," www.Adage.com, Dec. 3,2001, pp. 1-2; Vanessa O'Connell,"Ad Spending in All Media Is Slashed 5.2%," The Wall Street Journal, June 8,2001,p. B6.

CAPITAL INVESTMENT

Advertising expenditure is a capital investment as it is incurred to build the image; goodwill and reputation of product and company. This results in a gradual increase in the sales. In the accounting entry it is considered as revenue expenditure. It is an expenditure made today to achieve benefits in future. Although it is assigned under the revenue budget it is known as capital investment.

Depending on a particular situation the advertising expenditure may be increased or decreased. If advertising is not yielding satisfactory results, the expenditure is curtailed or not incurred at all thereafter. To ensure that the budgeted money has been rationally and economically spent, the costs and benefits of advertising are evaluated periodically. The present returns is not a guideline to advertising expenses. The future returns and inflows are properly evaluated to suspend or reject the expenditure. During a recession a cut in the advertising budget may result in the maximum shortfall in sales in subsequent years. Although the present returns may be nominal, higher expenditure during recovery may give higher returns in future. The expenditure on advertising is made for the present as well as the future returns, incurred to stimulate future sales as well as to retain the present market share of the product. Building consumer franchise, advertising expenditure is a long-term investment for the building of the image of brands, products and the company.

STEPS IN PREPARING ADVERTISING BUDGET

In financial terms the advertising budget is a statement of the advertising plan. After determining the total funds available for advertising purposes during a specified period, it is the allocation of available funds to various advertising functions. The budgetary process involves the steps of preparation, presentation, execution and control.

1. Preparation - The total expenditure on advertising is estimated on the basis of the information of markets, product, pricing, image, message and media.

(i) Budget Appropriation - The first step in budgeting is known as budget appropriation. It is the determination of the total funds. The determination of advertising appropriation depends on the existing sales, the unit of sales, the expenditure on advertising and affordable capacity.

(ii) Specification of Expenditure - After determining the appropriation, the next step is to specify the expenditure to be incurred on each function of advertising. The allocation of appropriation to different advertising activities in made on the basis of their contribution to advertising and the attitude of the management. The total budget is divided into" small budgets for each advertising function. Advertising budgets are prepared for each market segment, time and geographic area.

2. Presentation - Prepared by the advertising manager the budget is presented to the marketing manager. He decides the rationale and the contribution of the budget components. It is modified on the basis of the prevailing marketing conditions and management requirements. The top executive may fix the budget and budget components, after consulting the financial manager. The budget is modified in the fight of sales forecast, sales opportunities and the role of advertising in capturing the market share. Now, the advertising plan is formulated for the final budget.

3. Budget Execution - The execution of the budget is done through routine activities. It considers the cost of advertising, production, purchase of advertising time and space and other functions. Constant surveillance and periodic checks determine whether the advertising norms are implemented and budgets properly utilised. The budgets are prepared in the light of the normal marketing conditions. If the conditions change, they are changed accordingly. Contingency funds provided in the beginning, are used during times of need.

4. Control of Budget - The size of the advertising budget should not be less than the advertising expenditure. The expenditure is compared with the provision in the advertising plan. Unless the advertiser is constrained to do so in the light of existing conditions, larger amount should not be spent. Both the planned expenditure and the actual expenditure should be on parallel lines. Since sales promotions include several functions other than the advertising function, the advertising budget should be used only for the advertising purposes and not for other sales promotion strategies such as personal selling, merchandising, packaging, public relations, etc. There should be a separate budget for each sales promotion strategy. The phenomenon when the budget is exhausted by other functions is known as budget irritation. This should be avoided. Some combined expenditures on sales promotion may be drawn from the advertising budget.

ADVERTISING APPROPRIATION

Pointing to the total sum of money allocated to advertising during a Specified time, the term advertising appropriation is the way in which this sum of money is allotted, during this period, the different advertising activities. The different budget includes advertising appropriation and allocation etc. As the appropriation is determined by using several formulas — such as affordable approach, sales approach, competition approach and so on, it takes into account the factors influencing and determining appropriation.

FACTORS INFLUENCING APPROPRIATION

The factors influencing budget appropriation are advertising plans, marketing opportunities, competition, product life cycle, cost of advertising, type of the product and importance of the retailer.

1. Advertising Plans -The advertising objectives, strategies and programmes determine the total amount of expenditure to be incurred for advertising purposes by the company. The internal as well as external opportunities are evaluated for the appropriation.

(i) **Objectives** - The objectives refer to advertising opportunities which can be exploited by the company.

(ii) **Strategies -** Depressed economic climate and intense competitive activity call for a larger outlay on advertising. The implementation of sophisticated strategies requires more money for the purpose.

(iii) **Programmes** - The implementation of sophisticated strategies requires more money for the purpose. Adequate money should be provided for the implementation of the routine programme of advertising.

2. Marketing Opportunities - Advertising should exploit the potential of the market. Marketing opportunities determine the amount of appropriation. The characteristics of consumers and their requirements suggest the total amount of funds to be utilised by the company. As marketing opportunities are different in different markets, so the quantum of advertising appropriation has to be differently determined to arrive at the total amount to be budgeted, Seasonal demand advertising triggers a longer expenditure than the off-season demands. The market may be regularised by off-season discounts and sales promotion for which advertisements are given in newspapers, television, radio, etc. While determining market opportunities, product opportunities are also taken into account. The strategies of emotional appeal, fear appeal and other factors to exploit existing as well as potential marketing opportunities determine the size of the funds to be allocated.

3. Competition - The nature and pressure of competition influence the size of the appropriation. Competitive advertising helps expand demand. A greater intensity of competition may call for larger funds for advertising. Domination of media or markets by the competition may call for larger funds. The cost and efficiency of each medium determine the size of the appropriation. Competitive advertising is used to meet competition. An imaginative advertising theme with a unique selling proposition may perform suitable jobs for competitive advertising.

4. Product Life Cycle - The product life cycle is an important determinant of the size of the total budget. Knowledge of the life cycle of several products of the company is helpful in determining the size of the appropriation and the budget. Consumer awareness and increased usage are taken into account to determine the level of advertising and costs. As the age of the product increases the need for advertising decreases. One may rejuvenate the product by injecting more funds to build its image. Efforts should be made to know which life cycle demands how much funds for advertising so that the total appropriation may be finally approved by the management.

5. Costs of Advertising - The total costs of advertising decided for appropriation, include the expenses incurred on developing and preparing advertisements, designing the message and selecting the media. The fees for action, direction, the costs of building sets and travelling to locations, tape recording and visual cassette recording, expenses on print media and broadcast media, etc. are included in the costs of advertising. It also includes administrative expenses, salaries, costs of resources used, fees to outside bodies and institutions and contingency funds.

6. Type of Product - The type of product to be marketed determines the size of the appropriation. Consumer products require a large advertising budget than industrial products. If the opportunities for product differentiation are substantial, the returns on advertising will be higher than those on undifferentiated products. In the selection of the media, the hidden qualities of the product and brand are the guiding factors. The absence of price competition may reduce advertising costs people pay a higher price for a brand.

Disadvantages

(i) The disadvantages of the percentage sales approach are also the disadvantages of the unit-of-sale approach.

(ii) It is inflexible and illogical.

Objectives and Task Approach - This approach refers to the cost of achieving the objectives by applying the appropriate task. The advertising objectives are established. After selecting the media the number of insertions needed for achieving the objectives is estimated and the cost of the media programme is calculated. The cost per medium is estimated to arrive at the total cost of advertising. The relationship between costs and objectives is determined. The cost are examined on the affordable and benefits grounds. The costs of advertising are estimated accordingly.

The objectives of advertising are determined after a thorough evaluation of the internal and external environment. After defining the objectives in terms of sales, profits, and promotion, the cost of achieving them are estimated. If the cost of advertising works out to be higher than the affordable funds, the cost is curtailed or the objectives lowered. If the percentage-of-sales method is used for cost determination in advertising, the sale is a specification of objectives. It is suggested that sufficient advertising should be done for two or three years to produce an adequate sales-return.

Marginal Approach - While the cost-and-benefit analysis offers the basis of budgeting and the costs of advertising, the marginal contribution of each unit of each media is a guiding factor in estimating the cost per unit, the aggregation of these costs of units is taken as the total cost of advertising. The cost of advertising should be at least equal to its benefits. An economic and marginal analysis is made to arrive at the optimum level. The marginal costs and marginal benefits should be equal in determining the optimum level of advertising. The total cost is decided at that point. Benefits are determined on the basis of sales. This approach may provide a regional solution not only for determining the size of the appropriation, but also for the allocation of funds in the budget.

Mathematical Models of Advertising Budget

Successful for determining the size of the advertising appropriation, these models have been developed for advertising appropriations to attain the objectives and tasks of advertising and to measure the level of success that has been achieved by the advertiser. The advertising objectives are set within the periphery of marketing objectives. The tasks to achieve the advertising objectives are determined on that basis. The appropriation is fixed to attain them effectively and economically. When the total cost of advertising does not exceed the additional profit derived from it an optimal budget is developed.

Mathematical model is used to arrive at the total amount required for advertising purposes. Important mathematical models are sales response and decay models, communication-stage models, adaptive-control models and competitive-share models.

1. Sales Response and Decay Models - This model was developed by Vidale and Wolfe. In this model, the change in the rate of sales at a time is a functions of four factors: the advertising budget, the sales-response constant, the saturation level of sales, and the sales-decay constant. This models set out a measure to shape the advertising sales-response function order to determine mathematically how much advertising is needed for profit. It establishes a relationship between advertising expenditure and sales. The future budget is determined on the basis of this relationship. To find out the relationship at a particular point, the sales-response to advertising is developed in the form of a curve. The relationship indicates three stages; sales response constant, sales decay constant and the saturation level of sales.

(i) Sales Response Constant Relationship - It represents the sales revenue generated by one unit of advertising expenditure when sales are zero. For example, if a firm having no sales spends Rs. 1,000 on advertising in one month and if this results in sales of Rs. 5,000, the sales response constant will be 5, i.e., Rs. 1.0 spent on advertising yields a sale of Rs. 5.00.

(ii) The Sales decay Constant Relationship - It is used to describe the behaviour of sales revenue in the absence of advertising. If a company stops advertising, the sales will decline. The competitors will lure away all the customers of the company. Gradually, consumers will forget the brand and sale may go down to a very low level.

(iii) The Saturation Level of Sales - It represents the level of sales which is unlikely to be surpassed, irrespective of the level of advertising. This level gives the following relationship.

$$\frac{\lambda_s}{\lambda_t} = rA \; \frac{(M - S)}{M} - \lambda S$$

where

λ_s stands for change in sale.

λ_t stands for change in time.

r stands for the sales response constant, *i.e.*, the proportion of sales generated per advertising at zero level of sale.

A stands for the rate of advertising expenditure at the time.

M stands for the saturation level of sales, i.e., the maximum that can profitably be achieved by means of the advertising campaign.

S stands for the rate of sales at the time.

λ stand for the sales decay constant, i.e., the proportion of sales lost in each time period when advertising is reduced to zero.

The equation says that the-rate of sales increase will be higher, the higher the sales response constant, the higher the advertising expenditure, the higher the untapped sales potential, and the lower the decay constant. Suppose the sales response to advertising dollars is estimated at 4, current sales are Rs.40,000, saturation-level sales are Rs. 100,00 and the company loses 1 of its sales per period if no advertising expenditure is made. In this case, by spending Rs. 100,00 in advertising the company can hope to achieve an additional Rs.52,000 of sales.

λ s/dt = 4(10,000) 100,000 – 40,000 / 100,000 – 1(40,000 = Rs.20,000)

If the profit margin on Rs.20,000 is better than 50 percent, it pays to spend the Rs.10,000 on advertising.

The Vidale-Wolfe model can be used to estimate the profit consequences of alternative advertising-budgeting strategies. It brings and inter relates three useful concepts for determining the advertising budget.

Advantages

(i) This model suggests that the change in the rate of sales in time will be the effect of advertising, sales response constant and the sales decay constant. Larger advertising is required, to achieve a high sales rate, provided that the sales response and sales decay are constant. The advertising effect will also very with the change in the saturation level of sales, response constant and sales decay constant.

(ii) This is also used to determine the amount of advertising required to achieve a specified rate of growth in sates.

Disadvantages

The sales response constant, the sales decay constant and saturation level are difficult to calculate. The company's sales response to advertising is a function of six factors, i.e., percentage of loyal consumers; no loyal consumers; relative roles of price, distribution, advertising and product characteristics; the relative roles of the interaction of the product and advertising; the relative amount and value of the company's advertising appropriation and the size of market.

2. Communication Stage Models - In these models the logic is the money spent on advertising media process, the gross impressions on a target market which results in awareness, interest and desire leading ultimately to sale. By observing the effects of the budget on the variables that link advertising expenditure to sales, it arrives at the appropriation. The market-share goal is developed first to calculate the size of the market that might reasonably be expected to be reached by advertising. The size of the market of the product is calculated to estimate the number of advertising per exposure or trial. The gross rating points (GRP) are calculated to estimate the appropriation necessary on the basis of the average cost per GRP.

Evaluation

The communication stage model incorporates the objectives and tasks to be realised. The calculation at every stage is a difficult task.

3. Adaptive-Control Models -These models assume that the advertising sales-response function is not sufficiently stable over a function. It is influenced by such factors as economic conditions, product design, competitive activity and advertising copy.

Evaluation

This model experiments with each factor for a period. The advertiser can get estimates of sales response for each stage and update his advertising budget accordingly. The cost for influencing these factors are estimated to arrive at the size of the appropriation.

This advertising-budgeting model assumes that the advertising sales-response function is not stable but changes through time. If it was stable, the company should make one large effort to measure it and the benefits would extend far into the future. But because of changing competitive activity, advertising copy, product design, and economic climate the parameters are not stable. It would not pay to invest heavily in researching the parameters of the current sales-response function. If the parameters change through time, it would pay to collect new information each period and combine it with the old information to produce new estimated parameters for the sales-response function on which to base the new advertising budget.

John D. C. Little proposed the adaptive control method for setting advertising expenditures. Suppose the company has set its advertising expenditure rate for the coming period based on its most current information on the sales-response function. It spends this rate in all markets except in subset of In Markets randomly drawn. In n of the test markets the company spends at a lower rate and in the other n it spends at a higher rate. This will yield information on the average sales created by low, medium and high rates of advertising that can be used to update the parameters of the sales-response function. The updated function is used to determine the best advertising expenditure rate for the next period. If this side experiment is carried out each period, advertising expenditures will closely track optimal advertising expenditures.

4. Competitive - Share Model – This model takes competitor's expenditures into account. While there are many competitors, none of whom is large; or where it is difficult to know what competitors are spending for advertising in many situations, firms know their competitors' expenditures and try to maintain competitive parity. In these situations, a firm must consider competitive reactions in determining its advertising appropriation.

Lawrence Friedman has developed some models to show how industrialists should allocate advertising budgets to different territories, to take maximum advantage of the other's mistakes. He distinguishes two situations; where company sales are proportional to the company's share of total advertising expenditures and where the company with 50-pius percent of the total advertising takes the whole market as when a single customer is at stake.

The competitor's activities and market share are plugged into a decision situation. The competitors' reactions are calculated to determine the size of the appropriation. The probable reactions of competitors are evaluated. The principle of the game theory is used to evaluate competitive reactions and strategies.

Advantages

(i) The model is straightforward and requires a matrix with the strategies open to the producer, on the one hand and the possible sections of the competitor, on the other. Probabilities of outcome are assigned to each combination of strategies. The producer takes advantage of the weaknesses of the competitor.

(ii) The game theory is the fundamental theorem of market-share determination. According to it, an equivalent share of profit is to be spent to acquire a similar market-share. Competitive share determination and interaction are a very dynamic phenomenon. The actions and reactions of competitors are recorded at each stage of the advertising campaign. The competitor may retaliate by maintaining his expenditure on advertising at a constant level, increasing the size of the sales force, reducing the price and engaging in an intensive sales promotion campaign.

DETERMINANTS OF ALLOCATING ADVERTISING BUDGET

In the allocation of appropriation to different tasks and media of advertising in fixing the advertising budget, the avenues of budget-utilization are determined for an effective and economical use of the expenditure. The advertising process is broken into several units. Each unit is assigned adequate, funds for completion of the task. The size of the allocated funds is revised from time to time to find out their effectiveness. The revision process begins at the bottom of the activity to find out whether the size of the budget is adequate or inadequate. The advertising budget is allocated according to the objectives, the media used, the message transmitted and the geographic regions to be covered.

1. Allocation by Objectives - Useful guidelines to the allocation of funds, the advertising objectives are broken down into campaign objectives. The month, year and other time factors are the basis of campaign objectives. Funds are allocated to meet each campaign objective. The length of the campaign determines the amount of funds required. Media goals and other short-term functions are determined.

The results of previous advertising objectives determine the level of funds required for the purpose. The objectives of media, message and competitive approach determine the size of the appropriate funds required to meet the tasks. The advertising objectives are revised and supporting budgets are allocated for each component of the objective. Appropriate and experimental campaigns are formulated and the cost per campaign is determined. Some contingency reserve funds are set apart to meet any unforeseen requirements of the campaign. The campaigns with budgeted funds are submitted to the marketing management which determines the size of the budget for each campaign. If, in its opinion, the budget is higher, it is pruned for each campaign or the campaign itself is curtailed by the management. The allocation process continues to determine the budget for each component of the objectives of the advertiser.

2. Allocation by Media - According to their contribution, the administrative overhead, media copy development and reproduction, and research, the budget appropriation is allocated amongst the different media. The media require significant funds for coverage. Generally, 80 percent of the total budget is allocated to the media. Of the several media, television accounts for about 60 percent of the total budget. Small firms spend about 90 percent of their budget on the print media the newspaper and magazine advertising. Some tiny industries may spend 100 percent on vehicles and loudspeaker announcements. The allocation depends on the industry, the size, needs and objectives of each firms. Reach, frequency and continuity also determine the size of the funds required. Media objectives are met with the allocation process.

3. Allocation by Message - The budget is allocated according to the message developed for each media. The copy development and research functions require specific amounts. Message development is divided into layout, design and illustration. The marginal contribution of each message and copy determines the maximum amount of expenditure to be incurred on them. The probability of expenditure and the contribution of each copy are compared to determine the actual amount of budget for each copy. A comparison of several years' budgets shows how much is to be spent and how much expenditure should be curtailed with a view to economical and effective utilizations of funds. The budget becomes the control mechanism of expenditure.

4. Market Segments - The market is divided into several segments whose development requires allocation of funds. The management decides how much money should be spent on a particular market segment. The push or pull theory is used for distribution purposes.

(i) The Push Theory - According to the push theory, the development of middlemen in the channel of distribution is essential. The longer the distribution-channel, the higher the cost of advertising. The contribution of each component of the channel is assessed before advertising at the cost-and-budget decision.

(ii) The Pull Theory - It lays emphasis on the need for communication with the final user of the product. The users may be heavy users, light users, opinion leaders, innovators, followers and late adopters. Each product stage is identified and an adequate amount of budget is allocated for success at every stage. The contribution of every component of the channel determines the amount of appropriation to be allocated to each.

5. Allocation by Products - Generally, the budget is allocated on the basis of the sales of each product line. If the manufacturer is producing different articles, the budget is allocated on the basis of the value of sales of each article. The stage of product life cycle, the amount of competition, the product and the role of advertising for their development, are the deciding factors in budget allocation: "A product contributing a significantly higher share of the profit is allocated larger funds. A product in the initial stage of marketing requires a larger advertising budget than the product in its maturity stage.

6. Allocation by Geographical Area - Budget is allocated according to the geographical area covered by advertising. Larger budgeted funds are assigned to some areas to harness the potential marketing opportunities. To exploit the local marketing opportunities advertising in local newspapers and magazines receives larger funds than advertising in the national print media. In some markets, sustained spending is essential to prevent deterioration in the brand's competitive position. While larger fund are allocated to develop a poor market and a smaller amount is allocated to highly developed markets, a smaller budget is required for advertising purposes if trading is controlled by middlemen and retailers.

ALLOCATING ADVERTISING BUDGET – OTHER METHODS

The appropriation for advertising may be determined on the basis of the affordable approach, competitive parity, percentage of sales, unit of sales, and various other methods as discussed above also.

(a) Affordable Approach: Affordable approach means that advertising will be appropriated after all the other unavoidable investments and expenses have been allocated. The appropriation is set simply on the basis of an assessment of what the company can afford for advertising purposes during the period of the operation of the budget. It is an arbitrary method, but it limits the maximum expenditure to be incurred on advertising. This is the decision of the management, which is based on past experience. The goals and aggressive methods of advertising are considered for appropriation purposes. The management may decide to spend 20 per cent or 10 per cent of liquid assets for advertising purposes. If it is very conservative, the budget may be low. Some managers use the go-for-broke method, whereby every month, the advertising budget is expanded by a certain percentage or amount. For example, if it is decided that Rs.5000 should be added every month to the basic advertisement expenditure of Rs.1,00,000, this would be an acceptable proportion if the sales are increased by Rs. 5,000 or more per month. If the sales do not increase proportionately, the additional expenditure should not be incurred at all.

The affordable approach does not encourage long-term planning. The affordable amount cannot be predicted easily. The short-term objectives are overlooked. If the sales decline, the size of the budget may be reduced. This may not prevent the emergence of the laggard situation, it is, therefore, not a logical or quantifiable approach. However, the affordable approach on the basis of the experiences of the management is often adopted by the planner.

(b) Competitive Parity: The producer tries to establish parity with the competitors. So he formulates such types of budget as would be equal to the budgets of the competitors. The competitive parity method has the advantage of recognising the importance of competition in advertising. Imitating the competitor's budget is not productive because it ignores the objectives, strategies and programmes of the producers. The level of production and marketing have a significant bearing on the budgeting process, but the competitive parity ignores it. The competitive parity is used to maintain the collective wisdom of the industry. It minimises aggressive action and advertising wars. This approach is acceptable as rational because the budget is decided in the same market conditions, for the same opportunities, pursuing the same goals, having the same reputation, allocating the funds in the same way in the same media, and because the company is operating in the same manner. It is not always feasible because competitors keep their plans secret. There may be an unwise allocation of money. The imitator may be unable to afford the budget of the competitors.

(c) Percentage of Sales: The percentage-of-sales method is more popular than the other methods. A pre-determined percentage of sales value is earmarked for advertising purposes. The percentage remains constant. The previous year's sales are taken as the yardstick for the allocation of the budget.

The main advantage of this method is its simplicity. The budget varies with what the firm can afford on the basis of its sales. Suppose, it is decided that one per cent of the sales will be allocated to advertising; the advertising budget will then increase or decrease in proportion to the rise or fall in sales. The quantum of sales determines the financial capacity of the firm. Competitive stability may also emerge, for the expenditure is directly related to the funds available on the basis of sales.

The procedure is illogical because it assumes that advertising is a result of sales rather than a cause. It is not very flexible because it does not allow for extensive advertising when the need for advertising increases because of a fall in sales. The company does not take advantage of sales opportunities. The sales may increase rapidly if advertising is adequate during the innovation-stage or rising potential. But there is a large variation in the productivity of advertising at different levels of sales. The return on advertising may diminish after a certain stage, although this approach permits a bigger size of the budget at higher sales. The company may, therefore, under spend when the potential is great and overspend when the potential is low. Since the funds made available will vary in proportion to sales, there is a limited scope for long-term planning of advertising expenditure. Moreover, it does not take into account the chang-ing goals of the company and the market conditions. Short-term and long-term opportunities are overlooked.

The size of the budged may be determined on the basis of opportunities, i.e., anticipated future sales. This is also logical because the budgeting process precedes the sales. Advertising is not the only factor stimulating the sales. The sales forecast technique is used for the purpose of evaluating future sales opportunities. The economic and market conditions are evaluated to forecast these opportunities. The past and future sales are averaged to stabilise this approach.

(d) Unit of Sale: The unit of sale determines the size of budget. A fixed amount per unit is allocated for advertising purposes. If Rs. 1,000 per vehicle is assigned to advertising, the budgeted amount will be Rs 100,000 for 100 vehicles. The unit of sale is the basis of budgeting for durable goods and industrial goods. The units of forecast sales are the basis of appropriation.

The unit-of-sale method is applied easily and for a sufficiently long period. It can give the advertiser reasonably accurate predictions of the advertising-to-sales ratios. The advantages and disadvantages of the per-centage sales approach are also the advantages and disadvantages of the unit-of-sale approach. It is, therefore, inflexible and illogical.

WHAT IS RETAIL ADVERTISING BUDGET?

The advertising budget prepared by a retail store is called the retail advertising budget. The problems and the process of budgeting of the retail store are the same as those of the manufacturer. The head of the retail store is involved intimately in budgetary matters of all kinds. The difference between a retail advertising budget and the manufacturer's advertising budget is only of size. Advertising plays the same role in a retail store as in a manufacturing concern. However, efficient handling of advertising funds is mere crucial in retail budgeting. Many retailers use advertising for sales expansion.

The retail advertising budget is a part of publicity budget in a retail store. Publicity for retail store includes advertising, point-of-purchase, display, etc. Retail advertising is divided into institutional advertising and promotional advertising. Institutional advertising is designed to establish the store as a place of selling. Promotional advertising appeals for direct action. Pricing is important for promotional purposes. Institutional advertising is concerned with the reputation of the store, with style leadership, quality merchandise and services. The retail store decides how much institutional and how much promotional advertising will be effective for its purpose. The retail advertising budget covers display, point-of-purchase, reputation, publicity expenditure, services and quality merchandise.

FACTORS INFLUENCING RETAIL BUDGETING

The factors influencing retail budgeting are those which influence the budgeting process of the manufacturer. They may relate to age, location, merchandising, competition, media, area, type of product and support from the manufacturer. To win the confidence of customers, a new store spends more on advertising than an established store. 'A store located in the centre of the market place needs more advertising to attract people. Promotional stores depend on price cutting. Fashion and dress notes undertake more advertising to attract customers. Retailers need more advertising. A multi-media town draws a larger public. Advertising is essential for furniture and jewellery stores. There will be need of retail advertising if a retailer is an exclusive dealer for one or more brands and if the brand advertisers promote it. The manufacturers help retailers in advertising their product. If advertisement facilities are available to the retailer, he may not undertake extensive advertising.

RETAIL BUDGET-MAKING PROCESS

Under the retail budget, sales goals are set, the quality and extent of advertising are determined for promotional purposes and a schedule is proposed for day-to-day advertising*.

1. Seting the Goals and Tasks of Advertising - It is the starting point of the advertising programme. Each task or objective is expressed in terms of sales volume. The retailer is urged to start with the previous year's sales. Store expansion, increased population, higher income, greater employment, competitive activities, product diversification, etc., are the factors considered in retail advertising. To arrive at the final amount of the budget for retail advertising the amount of expenditure on each task and objective is decided and aggregated.

2. Amount of Advertising -The amount of advertising is fixed to fit the sales goals. Competitive advertising should be taken as the base of retail advertising. The retailer may fix the amount of the budget as a percentage of his sales. Several other factors influence the quantity of advertising and the outlay on it such as store location, length of time, local reputation, competition, etc.

3. Promotional Avenue - The total budget is divided into various departmental budgets. The retailer predicts the requirements and needs of the customers. He organises advertising in the light of consumer behaviour. Sales opportunities are evaluated, and advertising campaigns are developed accordingly.

4. Budget Schedule - The advertising budget is scheduled according to the time available and the market season. A monthly schedule may be proposed for an effective utilisation on the budget. A step-by-step advertising budget is framed and used to popularize the products.

FACTORS BEARING ON BUDGET SIZE

Among the more important factors bearing on budget size are (1) size and extent of the market, (2) role of advertising in the marketing mix, (3) stage in the product life cycle, (4) product differentiation, (5) profit margins and volume, (6) competitive spending, and (7) financial resources. Each of these factors is considered one at a time on the basis of "other things being equal", which is never the case in reality. As such factors are interdependent, interrelated and changing, these must be considered simultaneously in the actual budget setting situation.

1. Size of the Market - The size of the budget is a function of how many people are to be reaches. It costs more to reach large, widely dispersed, national markets than small, highly concentrated, local markets. A single 30-second commercial on permitting network television, costs Rs. 70,000 to Rs. 1,00,000. Only advertisers with sufficiently large and widespread markets can justify budgets calling for such large expenditures. For established nationally distributed products the size of the market is given. However, the size of the market must be determined when introducing a new product or when considering market expansion. Relatively few advertisers can afford to introduce market by market or region by region. It is better strategy to spend enough on a smaller scale than to spread a large amount on it.

2. Extent of the Market - In demographic terms it costs more to reach broad heterogeneous markets than one or two well-defined market segments. To reach heterogeneous markets requires costly television, general magazines, and newspapers- To reach smaller, well-defined segments requires less costly specialized magazines and local radio involving less wasted coverage. While the big spenders usually have the advantage of lower CPMS, the availability of local and selective media makes it possible to reach particular market segments with minimum wasted coverage.

3. Role of Advertising in the Marketing Communication Mix - The greater the role of advertising in generating sales, the larger the advertising budget is likely to be. The full burden of selling manufacturer's brands to consumers in self-service supermarkets in carried by advertising. On the other hand personal selling is relied upon to sell industrial equipment such as metalworking machinery. There fore the advertising budget is higher for the former than for the latter. Manufacturers of competing brands in the consumer goods market find it necessary to presell their brands by building brands awareness and preference before buyers enter the retail outlet. Dependence on advertising to do this preselling is reflected in larger budgets. Where there are fewer customers who are more easily reached directly, advertising plays a supporting role to personal selling and the budgets are smaller, in the marketing of industrial goods. In practice, some industrial marketers spend large sums on advertising. However, as a percentage of sales the figure is smaller than for most consumer goods. Budgets are increased to pay for such corporate advertising to the extent that major firms find it useful to talk to the public about controversial or public policy issues affecting their interests.

4. Amount to be spent on Promotions - In the marketing mix a major factor that directly affects the amount to be spent on advertising is the amount to be spent on promotions, both to consumers and to die trade. To induce trail of a new product through sampling, cooping, trade allowances, and so forth, it is common to spend more on promotions than on advertising in an introductory year. Some product categories follow rather well-established expenditures. For products such as coffee, frozen pizza, paper products and flour the trade allowances are high. The media expenditures may represent no more than 10 percent to 15 percent of the total promotional budget. On the other hand, health and beauty aids, cigarettes, and soft drink use a high percentage of media advertising with trade allowances being as small as 20 percent of the total. Trade allowances do little or nothing to build a brand franchise and, therefore, should not be allowed to siphon off funds from advertising.

5. Stages in Product Life Cycle - The cost of launching a new brand in a highly competitive field generally requires heavier advertising. It may wipe out gross profit for the first year. Building brand awareness, inducing trail, and gaining retail distribution require heavy initial advertising and promotion expenditures.

STRATEGIES

Once a new brand is successfully launched, i.e., it meets or exceeds the firm's objectives in sales volume, market share, return on investment (ROI), etc., the firm might pursue one of three strategies - (i) building strategy, (ii) holding strategy, or (iii) harvesting strategy.

(i) **A Building Strategy -** It calls for substantial increases in advertising accompanied by lower short-term earning to exploit an opportunity the brand offers to attain a higher market share.

(ii) **Holding Strategy -** For established brands in mature markets, which is true of most brands, a holding strategy calls for continued advertising from year to year at about the same relative weight.

(iii) **Harvesting Strategy -** It is designed to gain higher short-term earnings and cash flow by reducing advertising expenditures and permitting market share to decline.

Product Differentiations - When the product offers a unique benefit that the buyer can readily perceive when using it, the amount of advertising needed tends to be less than when no such clear differentiation exists. A discernable difference can be simply portrayed or demonstrated, the Polaroid camera's uniqueness, for example. Such a product's demonstrated performance is the message which is clearly understood, believed, and acted upon, thereby requiring less complicated copy and less repetition. Fewer and shorter messages cost less and this would be reflected in a smaller budget. on the. Other hand, when there are no apparent differences among competing brands, the budget should allow for investment spending to build a long-term capital asset in the brand image.

Profit Margin of Sales - Profit margin per unit and volume of sales are inseparable considerations. If the margin is substantial there is considerable leeway in establishing the size of the budget. For cosmetics, health and beauty aids, the margin available for advertising, promotion, and profit is typically 40 to 50 percent of the retail price. Hence, most advertisers in those product categories are big spenders.

A small margin per unit may be made up for by a large volume. Cigarettes, soap, and detergents are heavily advertised as their volume of sales is so high. A study by Paul W. Farris and David Reibstein found that brands supported by relatively higher advertising budgets also charged higher price than other brands in the same product category. This raises an interesting question. Do consumers pay higher prices for more heavily advertised brands or do marketers advertise more when gross profit margins are higher? The answer is both. Advertising adds value to the brands enabling the marketer to charge a higher price which, in turn, supports a larger advertising budget. Of course, the price-elasticity of demand and competition tend to keep the spiral in bounds.

Competitive Spending - A comparison of brand shares of total sales and brand shares of total advertising in a product category generally reveals a high correlation. Thus, a brand's share of sales is likely to be close to its share of advertising. Share of sales is related to the share of mind that results from share of advertising (share of voice). This relationship may be a self-fulfilling prophecy: the greater the sales, the more we spend on advertising. Thus, a brand's anticipated share of market suggests an approximate advertising budget level when total category spending in considered.

Spending, in and of itself, does not determine advertising success, and how much competitors spend should not be the only deciding factor. However, to the extent, what competition for share of mind is related to share of market this factor should be taken into account.

Financial Resources - The most obvious limitation on budget size is the amount of funds available. The advertising cost to enter the national market in many product categories is prohibitive except for relatively few firms who have tremendous financial resources. Relatively small firms with limited funds that have a superior product or service can start on a small scale and generate more dollars for advertising on an pay-as-you-go basis as sales increase. The scale of advertising, like the scale of manufacturing, must be adapted to funds available.

PROCEDURES FOR SETTING BUDGET SIZE

The practice generally is to use a combination of approaches from the following. Several procedures are followed in setting the budget. (1) Ratios to sales, (2) Objective and task, (3) Communication/buyer behaviour models, and (4) Payout planning.

1. Ratios to Sales - The most frequently used ratio is the advertising to sales "percentage :

$$\frac{\text{Advertising in Rupees}}{\text{Sales in Rupees}} \times 100$$

The A/s ratio in itself is not a determing factor; it is an expression of relationship between two variables.

The A/s ratio can be derived historically. What has it been in previous years? Continuing to use the same ratio assumes that an optimum relationship has been achieved. Increasing or decreasing the ratio assumes a need to spend more or less on advertising in order to achieve a projected level of sales. Using this approach a decision market is likely to look at competitors' A/s ratios as well as the average ratio in the product category. The person then decides whether to spend more, less, or the same amount.

Once a ratio is accepted, the key decision is to forecast the product's sales for the coming year. This requires a forecast of the total industry's sales. Both forecasts can be made rather arbitrarily by extending the trend, or more precisely by examining all internal variables of control label by the firm and external variables beyond the firm's control. Controllable internal variables include production capacity, product improvement, pricing and promotion. External variables include state of the economy, consumer attitudes, competitors moves, and media costs. In recent years, due to rising media costs advertisers have had to increase their budgets sharply just to buy the same amount of advertising space and time. The more sophisticated forecasts of sales are likely to be made by the firm's economists and marketing planners.

Another way of expressing the advertising-to-sales ratio is to state it in terms of rupees per unit. This is a common practice in several industries including automobiles, beer, and cigarettes. Thus, the ratio would be rupees per car, cents per barrel, or cents per carton. The decision maker still must set the ratio and forecast sales in much the same manner as above. When based on units produced, the advertising budget can readily be adjusted to fit fluctuations in sales and output.

To relate competition, advertising, and sales in a single ratio, advertising spending per share point is used. Spending per share point incorporates competitor's performance inasmuch as each firm's share is affected by every other firm's. This ratio is useful for comparing each firm's advertising efficiency. The firm spending less per share point is assumed to be advertising more efficiently.

2. Objective and Task - Advertising to sales ratios are convenient to use and easy to understand. Their use acknowledges the fact that advertising expenditures are both a cause and an effect of sales. However, using such ratios may obscure the dynamics of the marketplace, the changes that occur from year to year, from market to market and from brand to brand. Neither the market nor the competition stands still. A firm's total sales are the result of different responses from different market segments in different areas under different competitive circumstances. Sales forecasts should take these various factors into account but applying an arbitrary ratio may overlook the extent to which advertising can or cannot be used to exploit specific opportunities.

The objective and task approach focuses on specific objectives to be achieved and the role to be played by advertising. It is a multifaceted process. For example, a competitor's local or regional brand may be so well entrenched that a national advertiser may be well advised to follow a holding strategy and restrict spending in that area. Alternatively, an advertiser may discover that a new creative strategy is working so well that he should give it a chance to work harder by spending more on it.

Particular market segments offer greater opportunities than others. For budgeting purposes it is useful to quantify these differences.

3. Communication/Buyer Behaviour Model - As advertising functions as communication intended to induce consumer responses leading to regular purchase of the advertised product, various models have been developed to trace and quantify these responses. Such models are especially useful in planning the advertising and promotion budget for introducing a new product. The response stages most frequently used are awareness, trail repurchase, and rate of purchase. To achieve a planned volume of sales there must be a sufficient number of consumers, each buying a sufficient number off units per year and paying an adequate price per unit. Building such a user base for a new product in its first year starts with achieving a level of awareness (number of people who have seen, heard about, or know of the brand), inducing trail (number who try through either initial purchase of free sample), gaining repurchase (number who buy again and become regular purchasers), and sustaining a rate of purchase (number of units purchased per average buyer per year). The number of respondents decreases from one stage to the next. Therefore, to achieve a certain level of regular users requires starting with much higher level of awareness.

Lacking precise data for predicting the level of awareness required to get the level of trial required to get the level of repurchase required, the planner must use considerable judgment in arriving at these figures. However, starting with the number of customers required and thinking through the numbers at each response level injects a useful discipline in the budget-setting process. It focuses on people and their behaviour, not on dollars and how they are to be spent.

Once the required levels of awareness, trial, and repurchase are decided upon, the required reach and frequency are determined, the media plan is worked out, the cost of the plan is estimated, and the budget is thus set. Building a user base through response stages is only one approach and is best used in combination with others.

4. Payout Planning - To launch a new packaged-good item on a national scale requires heavy spending on advertising and promotion at the national level. Sufficient. momentum is needed in the early months to generate enough sales quickly enough to attain a profitable operation. An appropriate analogy is a jet aircraft taking off and climbing to cruising altitude. It takes a lot more fuel to take off and climb than it does to sustain flight once the cruising attitude-is reached. It takes a lot more advertising and promotion to build awareness and trial than it does to sustain a high volume of sales amount for regular users. The heavy spending initially when sales are climbing from zero typically results in the operating loss in the first year. This loss may even extend into the second and third years until sales reach a high enough volume to yield sufficient gross profit to cover ongoing expenses and recover the earlier loss. Spending at such a high rate, "up front" is referred to as investment spending. The term implies that initial expenditure on advertising, like investments in capital goods, yield a return over subsequent years. A budget that shows why and how an early loss is incurred as well as when and how it will be recovered is called a payout plan.

ESTIMATES AND CALCULATIONS COMPRISING A PAY OUT PLAN

Size of market	Forecast of total sales in category based on past sales and predicted growth.
Share goal Estimated	End of year is higher than average during first and second years, reflecting early growth of sales.
Consumer movement	Average share × total market.
Pipeline	Estimated shipments required to load the trade (retailers and wholesalers) with adequate inventory. Loading the "pipe" tapers off as going-year volume is achieved. Once it is loaded, the pipeline requires no further additions.
Total shipments	Consumer movement plums pipeline:
Factory income Costs	Total shipments × cost per case.
Available for profit, advertising, and promotion	Income minus cost.
Spending	Estimated advertising and promotion expenditures deemed necessary to achieve volume goals in specified time.
Profit (loss) Annual Cumulative	Profit or loss for the year.
Cumulative	Accumulated profit and loss.

To illustrate three types of payout plans, assume the following for Brand X:

	Per Case
Factory sales price	Rs. 9
Cost of Goods, overhead, and sales	Rs. 5
Available for profit, advertising, and promotion	Rs. 4
Normal profit	Rs. 2
Normal advertising and promotion spending	Rs. 2

When the stakes are high and achievement of sales and profit goals is much less than certain, which usually is the case, it makes sense to execute the plan in the test markets. Through testing the plan in few relatively small market areas it is possible to find out if the proposed marketing mix including the advertising budget is the predicted volume. Test marketing also offers the opportunity to experiment with alternative budgets but spending at a higher level in some markets, at a lower level in others, and comparing the results.

EVALUATING ADVERTISING EFFECTIVENESS

Good planning and control of advertising depend on measures of advertising effectiveness. However, the amount spent on fundamental research on advertising effectiveness is appealingly small. Most of the measurement of advertising effectiveness is of an applied nature, dealing with specific ads and campaigns. Most of the money is spent by agencies on pretesting the given ad while much less is spent on postulation of its effects.

Most advertisers try to measure the communication effect of an ad, that is, its effect on awareness, knowledge or preference. They would like to measure the sales effect which is too difficult to measure. Yet both can be researched.

1. Communication-Effect Research - It seeks to determine whether an ad is communicating effectively. Called copy testing, it can be done before an ad is put into actual media and after it is printed or broadcast.

(i) Methods of ad Pretesting

(a) Direct Ratings-Here a panel of consumers or advertising are exposed to alternative ads and asked to rate them. The question might be "Which ad do you think would influence you to buy the product?" Or a form with rating scales may be used, such as the one shown in following Figure 14.1 given by Philip Kotler. Here assigning a number of points up to a maximum in each case the person evaluates the ad's attention strength, read-through strength, cognitive strength, affective strength and behavioural strength. An ad must score high on all of these if it is to stimulate buying action. Too often ads are evaluated only on their attention- or comprehension-creating abilities. Direct ratings are less reliable than hard evidence of an ad's actual impact, but they help to screen out poor ads.

Attention : How well does the ad catch the reader's attention ? - (20)

Read-through strength : How well does the ad lead the reader to read further ? - (20)

Cognitive strength : How clear is the central message or benefit ? - (20)

Affective strength : How effective is the particular appeal ? - (20)

Behavioural strength: How well does the add suggest follow-through action ? - (20)

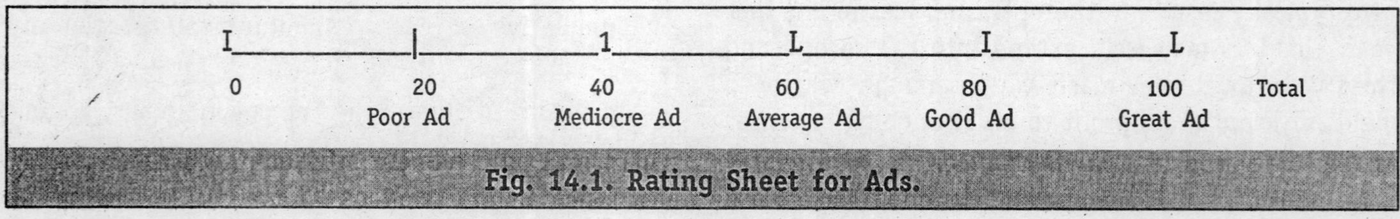

Fig. 14.1. Rating Sheet for Ads.

(b) Portfolio Tests-Here consumers are asked to look over a portfolio of ads, taking as much time as they want. The respondents are then asked to recall all the and as much of their content as they remember-unaided or aided by the interviewer. The results indicate an ad's ability to stand out and its message to be understood and remembered.

(c) Laboratory Tests-Some researchers use equipment to measure consumer's physiological reactions to an ad such as heartbeat, blood pressure, pupil dilation, perspiration etc. These tests measure attention-getting power rather than attitudes or intentions.

(ii) Methods of ad Post-testing-

(a) Recall Tests-The researcher asks people who have been exposed to the media vehicle to recall advertisers and products contained in the last issue or installment. They are asked to play back everything they can remember. Recall scores indicate the ad's power to be notice and remembered.

(b) Recognition Tests-Here readers of a given issue of a magazine, are asked to point out what they recognize as having seen before. For each ad, three different Starch readership scores (named after Daniel Starch, who provides the leading service) are prepared: (a) noted, the percentage of readers who say they previously saw the ad in the magazine; (b) seen/ associated, the percentage who correctly identify the product and advertiser with the ad; and (c) read most, the percentage who say they read more than half of the written material in the ad. Starch also furnishes adnorms showing the average scores for each product class for the year, and separately for men and women for each magazine, to enable advertisers to compare their ad's impact to competitors' ads. A 1981 study examined the accuracy of Starch score predictors in testing "ad and brand recognition. The relative importance of "noted" (ad recognition), "associated' (brand recognition via the ad), and "read most" in determining communication effectiveness was related to the consumer decision process. For low-involvement decisions, brand recognition ("associated"), may be sufficient, whereas actual readership is probably necessary in high involvement cases.

2. Sales-Effect Research-The sales effect of advertising is harder to measure than the communication effect. Sales are influenced by many factors besides advertising, such as the product's features, price, availability and competitors' action. The fewer or more controllable these other factors, the easier it is to measure advertising's impact on sales. The sales impact is easiest to measure in mail-order situations and hardest to measure in brand or corporate-image-building advertising. Researchers try to measure the sales impact either through historical or experimental analysis.

(i) The Historical Approach-It involves correlating past sales to past advertising expenditures on a current or lagged basis using advanced statistical techniques.

Montgomery and Silk estimated the sales effectiveness of three communication tools used in the pharmaceutical industry in USA. A drug company spent 38 percent of its communication budget on direct mail, 32 percent on samples and literature, and 29 percent on journal advertising. Yet the sales-effects research indicated that journal advertising, the least used communication tool, had the highest long-run advertising elasticity. They concluded that the company spent too much on direct mail and too little on journal advertising. At the same time, the results from historical analysis must be carefully interpreted because of problems of high inter-correlation among the explanatory elements, insufficient number of years of sales data and other problems.

(ii) Experimental Analysis-Other researchers use experimental design to measure the sales impact of advertising. In USA, Du Pont was one of the first companies to design advertising experiments. Its paint division divided fifty-six sales territories into high, average, and low market-share territories. The company spent the normal amount for advertising in one-third of the group; in another third, two and one-half times the normal amount; and in the remaining third, four times the normal amount. At the end of the experiment, Du Pont estimated how much extra sales was created by higher levels of advertising expenditure. They found that higher advertising expenditure increased sales at a diminishing rate, and that the sales increase was weaker in their high market-share territories.

Today, a growing number of companies are striving to measure the sales effect of advertising expenditure instead of settling for lower-order approaches such as testing ad recall or noting scores.

CHAPTER 15

ADVERTISING AGENCY

MADISON AVENUE GOES HOLLYWOOD

In the spring of 2000, the creative group at the Fallon Worldwide agency assigned to the BMW North America account was in the process of developing a new branding campaign for the German automaker. Both the BMW and Fallon people were becoming increasingly concerned with their ability to reach their core market of overachieving, hard-working consumers via traditional methods such as network television. BMW had done three different campaigns recently emphasizing responsive performance with product-focused ads designed to show what it's like behind the wheel of a BMW. However, from the perspective of both the client and the agency, the look and feel of the ads had begun to be copied by competitors and wannabes, making them less distinctive than before. Meanwhile, their research indicated that many Bimmer buyers were tech-savvy and had fast, reliable access to the Internet; most importantly, 85 percent of them had researched their car purchase on the Web before stepping into a dealer showroom.

As the creative team worked to develop a new branding campaign for BMW, concern over the effectiveness of traditional media advertising and curiosity over how to exploit the popularity of the Internet among car buyers were two key factors they were considering. Another creative team at Fallon had recently completed a campaign for Timex that incorporated an internet element by featuring short video clips developed specifically for the Web. So the idea emerged of doing something for the Web that would be not only entertaining but also cinematic. However, the associative creative director for the BMW group at Fallon noted that the goal was to do a different level of web film—one that by its very nature would call attention to itself and could be promoted like regular films. The agency took the web film concept to Anonymous Content, a Hollywood production company, where director David Fincher is a partner. Fincher took the original concept for a longer film that would be shot in segments and suggested instead a series of stand-alone shorts, each directed by a marquee name. He also came up with the idea for a central character, the Driver, played by young British actor Clive Owen, who appears in all the films as a James Bond-type driver who takes such co-stars as Madonna, Mickey Rourke, and Stellan Skarsgaard for the ride of their lives in a BMW.

The series of five to seven-minute films created by Fallon and Anonymous Content is called "The Hire," and the films have been directed by big names such as Ang Lee, John Franeheimer, and Guy Ritchie. The most popular film in the series was Ritchie's seven-minute short called "Star," which starred his wife, Madonna, portraying a spoiled pop diva who is taken on a wild ride to her hotel in a BMW 540 by the hired driver. Each film shows a different BMW model pushing the envelope of performance by showing what the car can do. In extreme conditions and situations that could never be conveyed in a traditional TV commercial.

A special website, BMWFilms.com, was created to show the five films in "The Hire" series. The site also includes five "sub stories," which are two-minute vignettes that introduce additional characters, as well as a behind-the-scenes look at how the films were made, interviews with the stunt drivers, and commentaries by the directors on their individual shoots. Fallon also created an integrated campaign to drive consumers to the website that included television, print and Internet ads, viral marketing efforts, and an aggressive public relations effort. "The Hire" film series has been singled out as the first high-profile, big-budget, celebrity-laden marriage of advertising and entertainment. Since its launch in April 2001, more than 13 million people have logged on to BMWFilms.com to view the five films in the series, and its success prompted BMW to commission three new films, which debuted in Fall 2002.

BMW Films was awarded the Super Reggie Award in 2002 by the Promotion Marketing Association (PMA) for the best promotional campaign. The PMA director noted: "BMW Films has truly established a creative benchmark in integrated and interactive promotions, allowing consumers to interact with the BMW name on their own terms. The promotion helped drive increases in brand measures and dealership visits as well as vehicle sales numbers." The film series also won the Cyber Grand Prix award at the 2002 Cannes Advertising Festival for the best online marketing campaign.

BMW is not the only marketer that has turned to the advertainment genre to promote its products. Skyy Vodka, which has a history of support for independent filmmakers and film festivals, was one of the first companies to use the genre, with its "Skyy Short Film Series." The three short films, which were created by the company's ad agency Lambesis, also used top directors and talent including model-actress Claudia Schiffer and Dian Merrill. The short films, which are featured on the "Skyy Cinema" section of the company's website, are seen as a way to build its brand image with its primary target audience of young, technologically savvy adults. Bartle Bogle Hegarty, a London agency, has also created short films for several clients including Levi's jeans and Microsoft's Xbox video game. The long-form ad for the Xbox, called "Champagne," shows a baby being shot out of a window at birth and morphing into old age and has been downloaded more than 4 million times.

Experts note that these digital short films signal the way toward the long-awaited convergence of television and the personal computer. They note that other technological developments such as the personal video recorder, digital cable, and satellite TV will allow consumers to watch what they want when they want to and this will change how they relate to advertisers. Thus, advertisers and their agencies will continue to use the short-film advertainments as a way to make their messages more compelling and to encourage consumers to actually choose to view their ads rather than avoid them.

Sources: Michael McCarthy, "Ads Go Hollywood with Short Films/' USA Today, June 20, 2002, p. 3b; Anthony Vagnoi, "Behind the Wheel" Advertising Age, July 23, 2001, pp. 10, 12; Benny Evangelista, "Marketers Turn to Web Films to Push Their Products," San Francisco Chronicle, July 23, 2001, p. E2.

Whatever else we may be, all of us are certainly consumers. In this common role, we generally do not give much thought to the individuals and organisations involved in the detailed and complex process that leads to the creation of clever advertisements that capture our attention and influence our choices. Some important players in the system are clients or advertisers, advertising agency, media organisations, marketing communication specialist organisations and providers of collateral services.

Advertisers i.e., clients are the key participants in this process. They are the ones who want to communicate with the target audience about their products, services, ideas, or causes with a persuasive intent. They also provide the necessary funds that go into media buying and creating the advertisements. Clients have the major responsibility of developing the marketing programme and making the final decisions regarding advertising and other promotional aspects. Any company may handle most of these functions through its advertising department or by setting up an in-house advertising agency.

Advertising agency is an independent organisation that provides one or more specialised advertising and promotion related services to assist companies in developing, preparing and executing their advertising and other promotion programmes. Most large and medium-sized companies usually use an advertising agency.

For most companies, advertising planning and execution is handled by an outside advertising agency. The American Association of Advertising Agencies (AAAA, or the 4As) has given the following definition to advertising agencies:

"Advertising agency is an independent business, composed of creative and business people who develop, prepare and place advertising in advertising media for sellers seeking to find customers for their goods or services." In the present scenario, more and more advertising agencies are acting as partners with clients and assuming more responsibility for developing the marketing and promotional programmes.

How Advertising Agencies Developed

According to James Melvin Lee "William Bradford, publisher of the first Colonial weekly in New York, made an arrangement with Richard Nichols, post master in 1727, whereby the later accepted advertisements for the New York Gazette at regular rates."(James Melvin Lee, History of American Journalism, rev.ed., Boston: Houghton Mifflin, 1933)

Volney B. Palmer (1840) is the first known person who worked on a commission basis to sell space in newspapers. During the 1850s, in Philadelphia, George P. Rowell bought large blocks of space from publishers at quite low rates and, after deducting the agent's commission, paid them in cash. He published a directory of newspapers in 1869 with their rates for ad space and his own estimates of their circulation.

Charles Austin, (early 1870s) began writing ads for anyone who wanted them. Two of his employees, Earnest Elmo Calkins and Ralph Holden, founded their own agency in the 1890s and brought together planning, copy and art to set a trend of combining all three into effective advertising. Their agency was one of the most successful for nearly half a century. The influence of their work helped establish the concept of an advertising agency.

In 1917, newspaper publishers set 15 per cent as the standard agency commission. Since then, the nature of advertising agency has changed in many ways, however, the basic method of compensation has remained the same and agencies still receive media commissions for space that they buy for clients.

The major changes in the structure, functioning and the range of services provided by advertising agencies evolved mainly in the later part of the 20th century. Over 400 advertising agencies are accredited to the Indian and Eastern Newspapers Society (IENS), besides many unaccredited agencies.

During the 1980s, there was a wave of acquisitions and mergers of ad agencies and support organisations to form super-agencies. These large organisations were formed so that they could provide their clients integrated marketing services worldwide. Some clients became disillusioned with these very large agencies and moved their accounts to smaller, more flexible, and responsive agencies. Another wave of consolidation hit the agency business in the mid-1990s, resulting in acquisition of a number of the mid-sized agencies by large agency groups. According to Sally Goll Beatty, many companies want an agency with international advertising capabilities and select large groups that have an agency network around the world.

Probably the main reason why companies use outside ad agencies is because they provide their clients with services of highly skilled specialists in their chosen fields. An advertising agency may have personnel that include writers, artists, media specialists, market research specialists and others with specific knowledge, skills and experience to help clients, marketing their products and services. Some agencies distinguish themselves in providing specialised services for companies in a particular industry, or market, such as the healthcare industry, or rural markets. The size of an ad agency may vary from few persons in a small agency to over a thousand employees in large organisations. The services offered and functions performed by agencies vary. We have already discussed how some companies handle advertising and other promotion related functions within the company.

Media organisations perform a vital function in the advertising communication process by providing information or entertainment to their audiences and thereby provide the right platform for the advertiser's message. The chosen media must possess those attributes that attract audiences so that clients and their advertising agencies want to buy space or time with them to reach their target markets with the ad message in a cost effective manner.

Another important group of participants includes various service specialists and providers of collateral services. They include direct response agencies, sales promotion agencies, marketing research providers, package design specialists, video production houses, printers, photographers, etc.

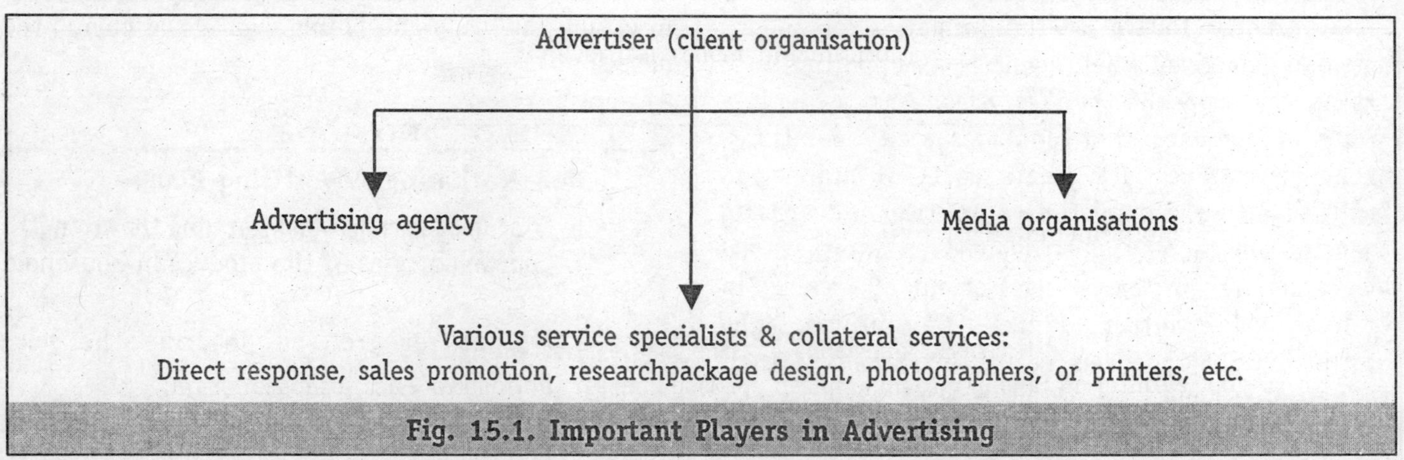

Fig. 15.1. Important Players in Advertising

Advertising agency represents the core of the advertising profession, "Madison Avenue," an area in New York, USA where several large agencies are located, has become a symbol of advertising to the world. Planning and executing successful advertising campaigns require persons with specialized knowledge and skills. They should be well informed in all aspects of marketing and consumer behaviour. They should be sensitive to people and communication. They should know the media and markets. They should be skilled writers, artists, television producers, researchers and managers. Advertising agency is the organisation that brings such people together in a single business enterprise. Various specialists interrelate and combine their talents to create effective advertising for the agency's individual clients.

ADVERTISING OF AD AGENCY

The advertising agency offers a quality and range of service much better than any single advertiser could afford or would need to employ. Operating outside the advertiser's own organization it is in a position to draw on the broad experience it gains while handling the diverse problems of different clients. As an outsider it can approach the advertiser's problems from an objective point of view.

CLIENT OR ADVERTISER'S ROLE IN ORGANISING FOR ADVERTISING

The manner in which a company organises for advertising and other promotional elements depends on several factors such as company size, number of products, role of advertising in promotion-mix, the budget and structure of its marketing organisation. Advertising function is an intimate part of the marketing department. Many marketing personnel often provide inputs in campaign planning, agency selection and evaluation of proposed programmes. Many companies have an advertising department, headed by a manager. In multi-product companies, with decentralised marketing, product management or brand management system operates. Some large organisations form a separate in-house agency responsible for advertising and other promotional activities.

KINDS OF AD AGENCY

The advertising agency's primary asset is people. Typically, 65 percent of gross income goes for salaries, employee benefits and retirement plans. The advertisement agencies can be classified as follow:

1. Large Agencies—These serve large advertisers who are concentrated in relatively few product categories, food and beverages, drugs and cosmetics, automobiles, tobacco, soap and detergents. With the exception of automobiles, all the above categories are packaged goods, which have high volumes of sales, are purchased frequently and are sold primarily in self-services stores. The manufacturers advertise nationally to presell consumers and build preference for their particular brands. As advertising is the dominant element in their marketing mix, therefore the business of large agencies is concentrated in these same product categories.

2. Small Agencies—There are not able to offer the same breadth of service as large agencies. However the large agency seldom makes its services available to small advertisers, who are industrial, trade profession and retail advertisers.

3. Agency Network—The formation of agency networks has given small agencies an opportunity to extend the scope of their services. A network is a group of agencies that pool research operations, exchange market data, share costs of production facilities and set administrative practices. Advertising agencies are increasingly involved in international marketing. The increased involvement of agencies in international advertising is likely to continue. Many of the top U.S. agencies get at least half of their advertising volume from abroad. Most of these agencies get even a higher percentage of their profits from foreign billings. The 10 largest U.S. agencies in 1981 derived 47 percent of their total billings outside the United States. Of the 40 agencies in the U.S. today, 29 have billings in foreign countries. Many companies whose products are distributed internationally prefer to use the same agency throughout the world.

FUNCTIONS OF ADVERTISING AGENCIES

Advertising agencies range in size from a one-person firm to a large organization employing more than 2,000 people. All agencies are engaged in planning, preparing and placing advertising. The range and depth of their services, however, differ considerably. The volume of business is concentrated in the larger agencies, generally referred to as "full service" agencies.

CENTRAL FUNCTIONS

The central function of ad agencies is to create advertising. It is their specialty, their reason for existing. However these advertisements are end products of a complicated problem-solving process requiring consideration of all elements in the client's marketing mix.

1. Planning Functions —These include researching the consumer, the product, and the market; developing creative and media strategies and budgeting expenditures.

2. Preparing Functions —These include writing, designing and producing the ads.

3. Placing Functions —These include contracting for media time and space, delivering the ads in appropriate form to the media, checking and verifying insertions, auditing and billing clients and paying the media.

PLANNING FUNCTIONS

1. New Marketing/Advertising Plan—

1. Consumer research to determine the strengths and weaknesses of the product in household use.
2. Market research to describe the best prospects.
3. Development of marketing strategy and budget.
4. Help in naming and packaging.
5. Development and pretesting of the creative concept.
6. Media planning to reach target markets efficiently.
7. A plan for launching the product of the trade.
8. Application of the creative concept to promotion and point-of-sale material.
9. Publicity plan for exploiting the product's news.
10. A plan for generating enthusiasm within the sales force.

All these elements have a bearing on one another in an effectively integrated plan. Progress in one area needs to be communicated to people working in the other areas. The major responsibility for this communication and co-ordination is borne by the agency.

2. Preparing Plan for an Established Brand—This may or may not require a new creative strategy. The agency performs similar functions. There is a planning cycle, usually a year, for every brand. The cycle begins with an analysis of the brand's performance, knowledge of how it is faring against competing brands, research on consumer usage and perceptions of the brands in the product category and development of strategy and tactics for the next year. As soon as one series of problems is solved, there a another series to be tackled.

OTHER FUNCTIONS

Full service agencies offer their clients services in fields other than advertising, such as public relations, consumer and trade promotions, merchandising, Sales literature and sales meetings. Their range of expertise embraces the entire field of communication. These might be called "communication agencies."

GUIDING PHILOSOPHY

While most agencies offer the same services they do differ considerably in their style of operation. Some agencies proclaim their guiding philosophy to set the tone for their own employees and set themselves apart in the eyes of their clients. For example Benton & Bowles says, "We have a strong point of view about the best way to create advertising. We are convinced that the road to successful advertising lies in single-mindedness. We build every campaign, every advertisement, every commercial around a single idea. We distill the creative strategy into one simple, relevant idea that we want to communicate to the target audience".

There is no Benton & Bowles "formula" for advertising execution. We believe that each product or service demands its own tone of voice and method of presentation. Each of our clients is different, each needs his own style of advertising. Thus, the kind of advertising executions we do for Texaco are very different from those for Crest.

Most of all, we feel a deep sense of responsibility for the productivity of the advertising we create. Advertising is a serious—and expensive— business tool. It is not an entertainment medium. Its purpose is not merely to attract attention, but to persuade and sell. This is why we say "It's not creative unless it sells."

AGENCY ORGANIZATION

Agencies organize themselves in different ways. The large agencies group their various specialists into departments with defined areas of responsibility. A typical organization chart is illustrated in Figure 15.2.

The four functional groupings are (1) creative services, (2) account services, (3) marketing services and (4) administrative services. Though this, chart locates the specialists it does not show how, they work together. They work in account groups composed of individuals from each area; creativity, research, media, and account, management. The account group

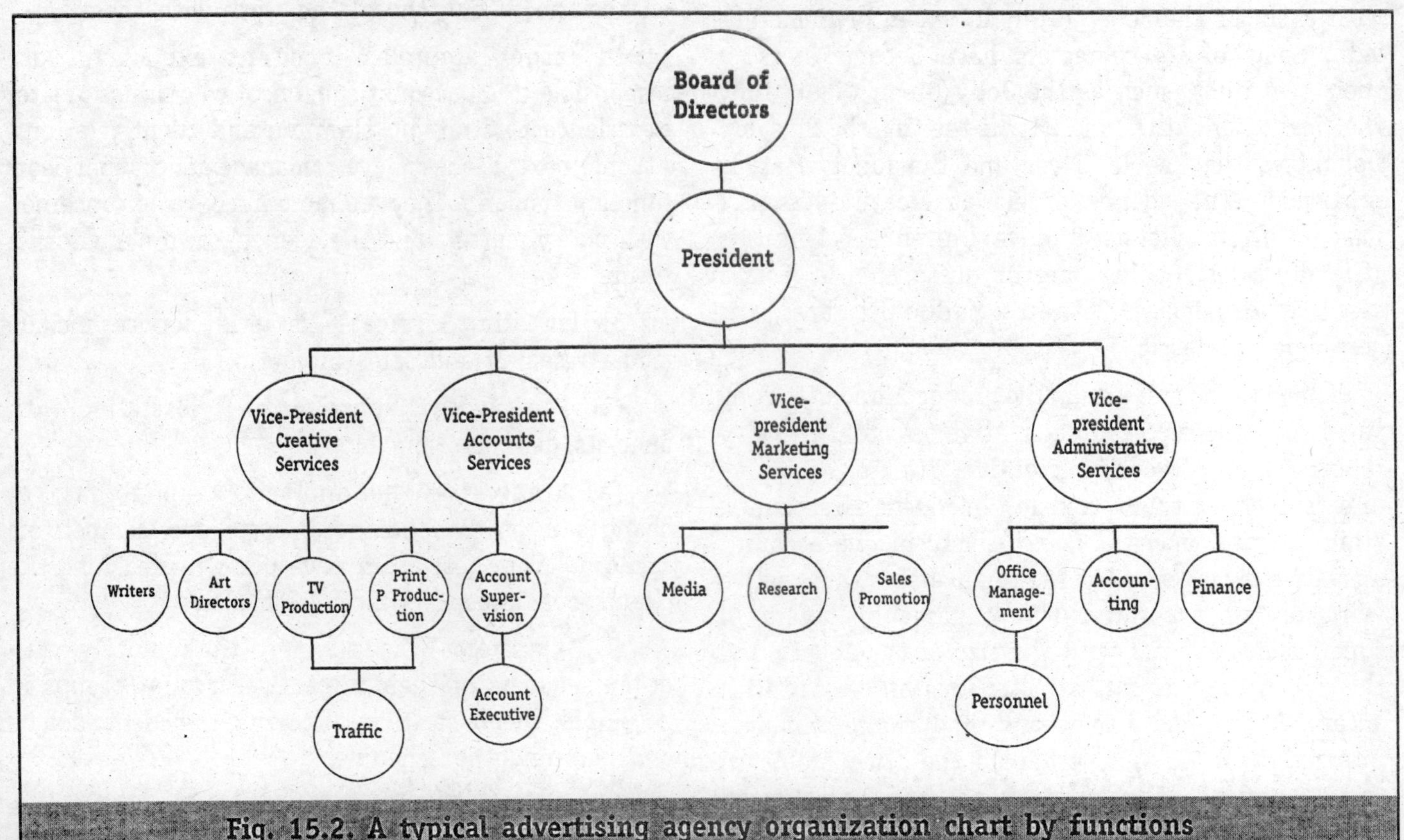

Fig. 15.2. A typical advertising agency organization chart by functions

works as a team for a particular client, ltd plans are reviewed and approved within the agency by a group of senior managers variously referred to as a plans board, a strategy review board, or a creative review committee. The plans must be approved by the client. After the plans are confirmed, the process of producing the ads gets under way.

1. Creative Services—According to David Ogilvy "The creative function is the most important of all. The heads of out offices should not relegate their key creative people to positions below their salt. They should pay them, house them, and respect them as individual stars." The copywriters, artists, art directors and graphics specialists are creative people. These people are directly involved in creating the advertising messages, though they have no monopoly on creativity. Account managers, media planners, and researchers also work creatively in their own areas.

Agencies pride themselves on their creative work. While some set forth a philosophy or guidelines to be adhered to others develop a style reflected in the ads they do. A 1977 Wall Street Journal article thus commented on the creative work done by the Leo Burnett Company. "Burnett's ads personify products with a single character, often in a gently humorous vein. Some of its characters have become stars in their own right, such as the Jolly Green Giant, Tony the Tiger, Charlie the Tuna, Morris the Cat, the Pillsbury Doughboy, the Keebler Elves and the lonely Matyag repairman. The agency excels at creating distinct images for its clients. It gave United Air Lines its "friendly skies" Schlitz beer its gusto, and RC Cola a sassy country image. Burnett's Marlboro campaign is considered a classic.

Copywriters are; generally grouped under a copy supervisor who reports to a creative director, who may report to an executive creative director. Creative directors spread their attention over several accounts. While a writer may work exclusively in one account, a creative review board at the top oversees the creative work on all accounts. The number of layers of supervision increases with the size of the agency and the size of the account. A writer is often teamed with an art director and a television producer to stimulate interaction. Working together on the same problems, they experience the enterprising spirit of a small agency.

2. Account Services—People with titles such as account executives, account supervisors or management supervisors handled account management. Account executives are closest to the client in terms of day-to-day contact. They are assigned full time to one of the client's brands. They represent the agency to the client and represent the client within the agency. They must be competent in both worlds. They must have a thorough knowledge of their client's business. They must understand all operations within the agency. From initial planning to final executions they organize and control the flow of work on the account through all stages. They assemble all relevant facts bearing on the brand, analyses and interpret them, develop strategy, present the agency's plans including creative work to the client, obtain ail necessary approvals, oversee the execution of those plans, and monitor the results.

To do all this they have to build good business relations with in the agency and a good rapport with the client. They must be able to get co-operation. They must be able to synthesize the thoughts of all involved and communicate them well to others. As leaders, they must take the initiative and generate enthusiasm among those who work with them.

In larger agencies, account executives are responsible to an account supervisor who brings greater experience to strategic planning and client relations. At the next highest level, management supervisors function similarly. They are more likely to be concerned with policy matters and the agency's own plans for its future.

3. Marketing Services—Marketing services include media research and sales promotion.

(i) The Media Department—It is staffed with analysts, planners and buyers.

(a) Analysts—The analysts keep abreast of changes in media audiences, costs and competitors spending. They test alternative plans for reaching the clients best prospects most efficiently.

(b) Planners—The planners work closely with other members of their respective account groups in developing media strategy, allocating the clients dollars and planning the schedule.

(c) Buyers—The buyers execute the plan. Those who buy spot television and radio time look for the best rates and place the orders. A detailed knowledge of the media situation in each market area can be of much advantage. Therefore, television and radio spot buyers in some agencies are assigned particular markets and buy time in those markets for all of the agency's clients. In other agencies, these buyers concentrate on assigned clients and buy for those clients in all markets. Due to the large investment involved when buying network television time, most agencies assign that responsibility to a person who specializes in negotiating with the networks. Other buyers specialize in the print media—magazines, newspapers and outdoor.

(ii) The Research Department—It is involved in all phases of agency planning—testing product concepts, defining market targets, developing marketing and test marketing and measuring results. Research requires specialists in questionnaire construction, sampling, focus-group interviewing, statistical analysis and experimental design. Assigned to particular clients research supervisors serve as the department's representatives on those account groups. They focus on the problems to be solved. They marshal the resources of the research department to help solve those problems. People in the research department design the projects, interpret the data, and present the findings. Field work, including large-scale interviewing and data collection and tabulating, is framed out to outside firms specializing in those operations.

In the marketing of packaged goods sales promotions directed to consumers and the trade are highly important. Hence, large agencies have specialists in planning and managing promotions. Typical consumer promotions include sampling, couponing premiums, contests and sweepstakes. Trade promotions include trade allowances, co-operative advertising and point of purchase displays.

4. Administrative Services—To earn a profit, advertising agencies like any other Successful business, must be well managed. In addition to be bookkeeping functions now largely performed by the computer, there should be people who plan and control the agency's financial future, budget revenues and expenses, set operating policies, and function as administrators from the president of chief executive officer to the various department heads. As agency is a people business, its success largely depends on its personnel practices, on how well it hires, trains, inspires and rewards its people. Strong leadership at the top is often the key. David Ogilvy chairman of Ogilvy & Mather International USA said, "I want all our people to believe that they are working in the best agency in the world. A sense of pride works wonders.

The best way to "install a generator" in a man is to give him to greatest possible responsibility. Our management should devote more time to this than routine salary reviews.

Of course salaries must be reviewed at regular intervals and "routine" raises must be given out, they are expected.

But the most effective way to use money is to give outstanding performers spectacular rewards at rare intervals. Nothing is too good for our make-or-break individuals.

It is virtually important to encourage free communication upward. Encourage your people to be candied with you. Ask their advice—listen to it.

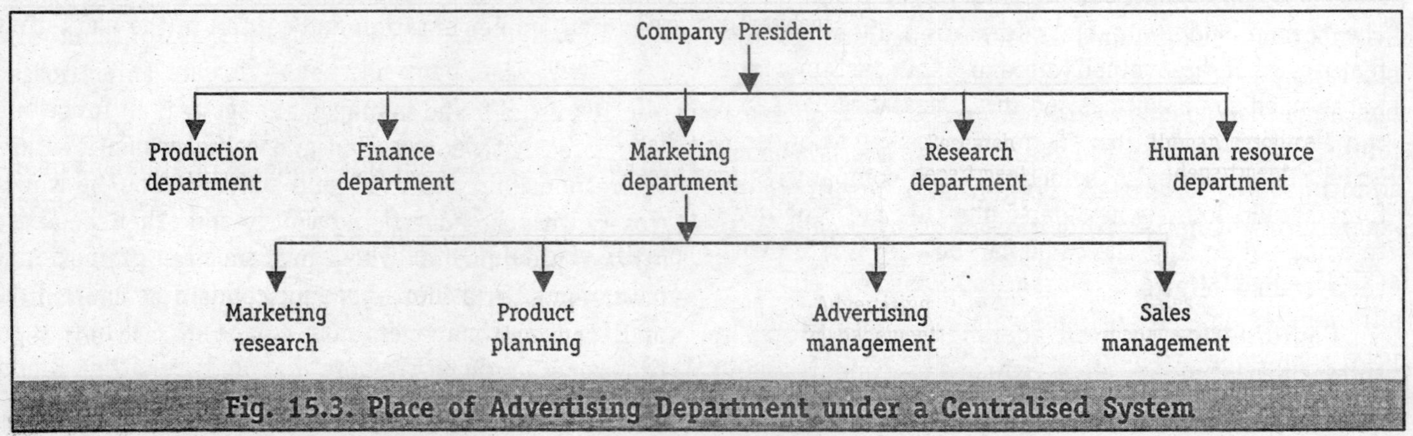

Fig. 15.3. Place of Advertising Department under a Centralised System

Ogilvy and Mather offices should not be structured like an army, with over privileged officers and underprivledged subordinates. We are all fellow-professionals, dedicated to the service of our clients.

The Centralised System

Marketing activities, in some companies, are divided along functional lines such as advertising, sales, marketing research, product planning, etc. The advertising manager looks after all promotional activities concerned with the company's products and services, including budgeting, creation of ads and their production, media schedules and sales promotions, but excluding sales management.

Following are the basic functions performed by the advertising department under the centralised system.

Planning and budgeting: Its foremost responsibility is to develop advertising and other promotional plans in line with the marketing objectives, strategies and budget of the company and get it approved by the higher management. Even though the advertising department prepares the budget, the top management makes the final decision regarding it.

Administration and execution: The advertising manager is responsible for the organisation, supervision and control of the advertising department. She/he supervises the plan execution by subordinates and the advertising agency. This needs working closely with production, media, copy, art and sales promotion. In case an outside ad agency is hired, the advertising manager reviews and approves the prepared advertising plans.

Coordination within the company: Advertising manager has to coordinate with other marketing functions, particularly marketing research and sales. They can provide valuable information about product features that are valued more by the customer and hence need to be emphasised in ad messages. Research can also furnish profiles of product user and non-user, which help in media selection. The company sales force should know when particular ads are scheduled to come out so that the same can be coordinated with their selling efforts.

Coordination with ad agencies and services; In spite of having an advertising department, many companies use outside advertising agencies and their services. The ads may be developed in-house and the services of media buying agencies may be used to place the ads in suitable media. The department may use the services of collateral agencies to develop brochures and point-of-purchase (POP) ad materials, etc. The advertising manager closely co-ordinates with the personnel of outside advertising agency and also determines which service providers to use.

Usually, companies that do not have many divisions, products or service lines, or brands often use a centralised system. Having a centralised advertising department makes it easier for the top management to participate in decision making Since fewer people are involved in deciding the programmes in a centralised system, better operational efficiency is ensured.

On the negative side, it is often difficult for the advertising department to fully comprehend the overall strategy for the brand and the response to specific problems faced by the brand may be slow. When companies grow in size beyond a point, centralised advertising department may be unsuitable and impractical.

The Decentralised System

A decentralised system is followed in large corporations with many product lines and brands. Typically, the company has many strategic business units, or divisions, with separate manufacturing, research and development, marketing, sales, product or brand management departments. Each brand is assigned to a brand manager (also termed as product manager) who is totally responsible for managing the brand, including planning, budgeting, sales and its profit performance. The brand manager often has one or more assistant brand managers to help in the planning, implementation and control of the marketing programme.

Under the brand management system, all functions associated with advertising and other promotions are the responsibility of the brand manager. She/he works closely with the advertising agency and other specialist service providers as they prepare the promotional programme. In a multi-product company such as P&G or HLL, brand managers may compete with brands in the same product category handled by other brand managers within the company and not just outside

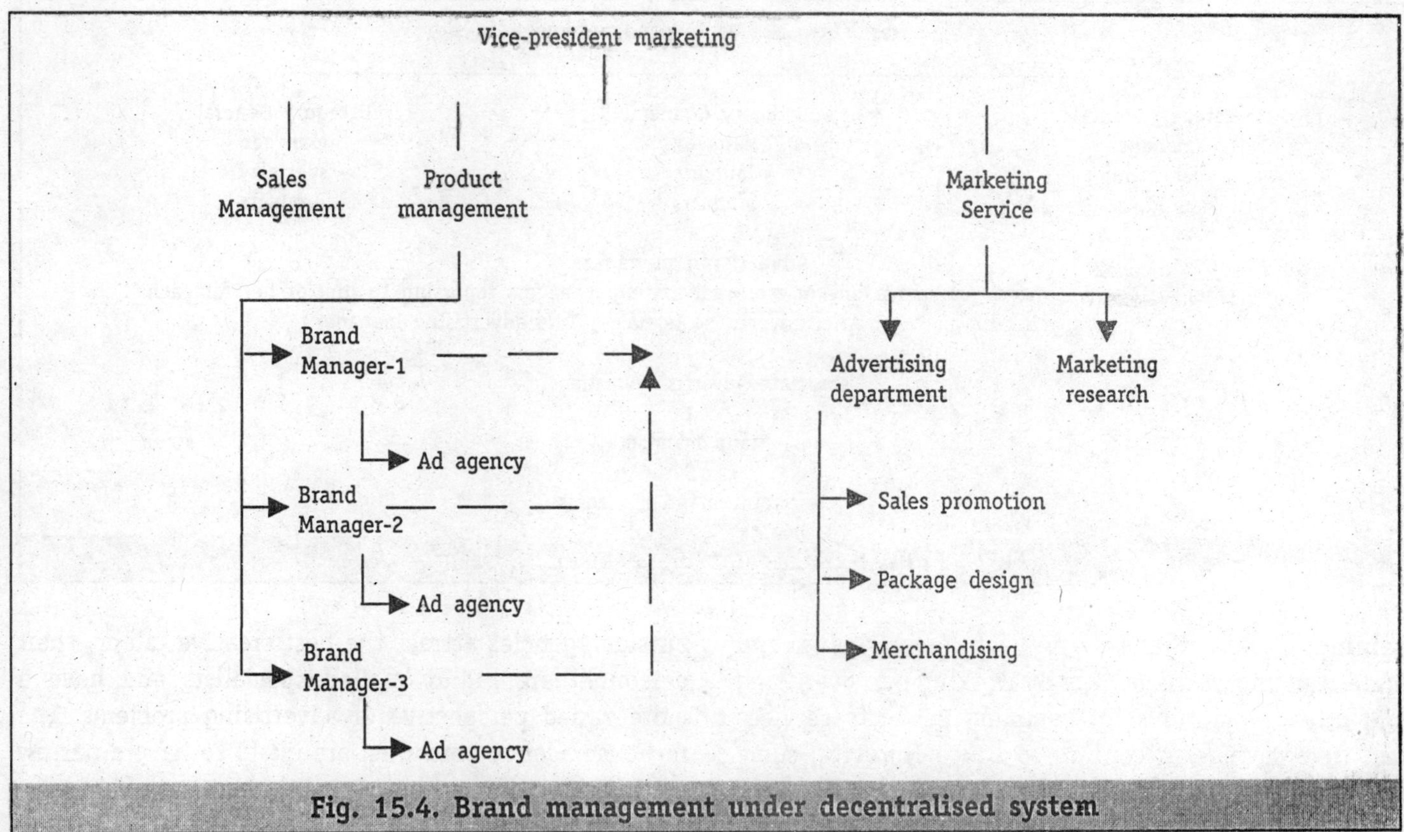

Fig. 15.4. Brand management under decentralised system

competitors. P&Gs detergent brands Ariel and Tide compete with each other for market share. Likewise, HLLs different brands of toilet soaps compete against each other.

There are some disadvantages in the decentralised system. Brand managers, often lacking in training and experience, may develop a brand strategy without a deeper understanding of what the advertising and other promotions can or cannot accomplish, and how each should be used. Because of pressures to show profits, their focus is more on short-term gains rather than developing long-term programmes for the brand.

In this system, brand managers are often involved in competition among themselves to gain top management attention for more budget allocation, leading to undesirable rivalries and, sometimes, even disproportionate fund allocation. Individual brand manager's successful persuasion may often influence budget allocation rather than the future profit potential of the brands. P&G considered these problems as serious and switched to the category management system.

According to Victor P. Buell, a flaw of the brand management system is that brand managers have responsibilities but are not provided with matching authority over functions necessary to implement and control the plans that they prepare.

In-house Advertising Agency

For companies with their own in-house advertising agencies, the major consideration is to decrease advertising and other promotional costs by exercising greater control over their activities. The in-house agency is set-up and given an identity of its own. It is owned and operated by the advertiser and handles large sums of advertising money. The substantial advertising money paid to outside agencies in the form of media commissions goes to the in-house agency. Large advertisers, such as Calvin Klein and Benetton, use in-house agencies. Some companies exclusively use in-house agencies while others are flexible and combine in-house agency efforts with those of independent outside advertising agencies. In some companies, the status of an in-house agency is little more than that of an advertising department.

Other reasons for using in-house agency include advertisers' bad experience with outside agencies,

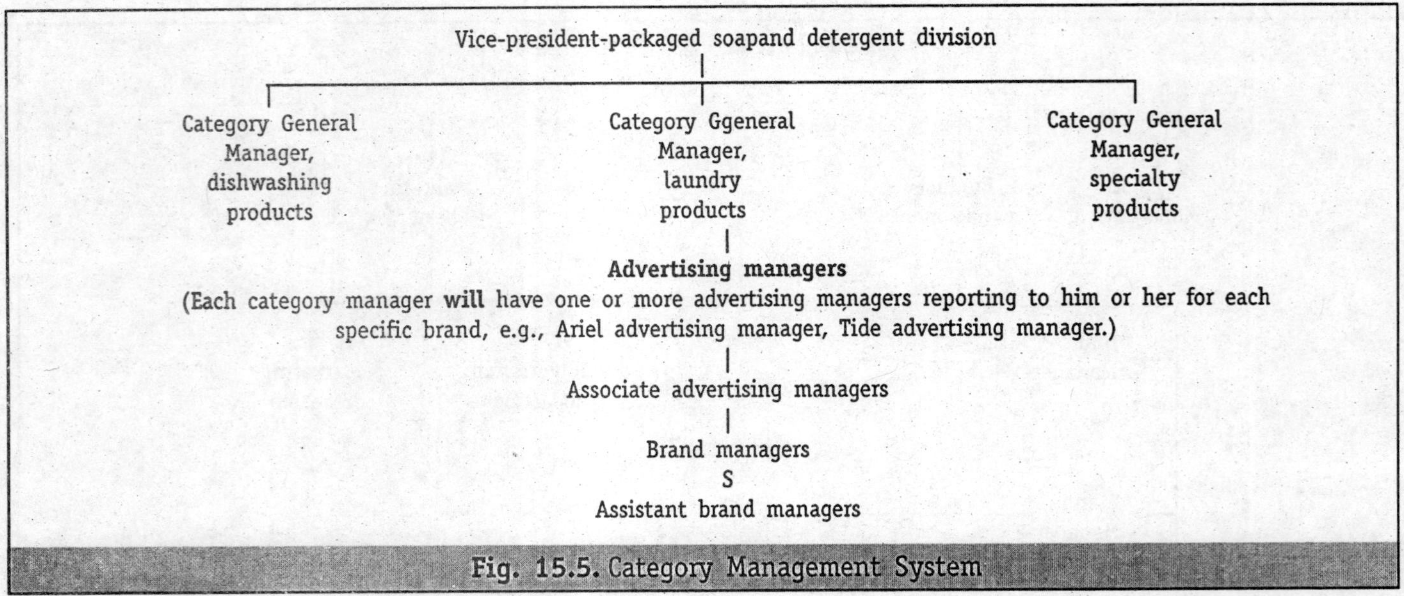

Fig. 15.5. Category Management System

gaining increased and very useful knowledge and understanding of the market by working on advertising and other promotions for company products/services and time savings. According to Bruce Horovitz, some companies use an in-house advertising agency simply because of their belief that the same can do a better job than an outside agency ever could.

Critics of in-house agency system say that the advertiser's in-house agency efforts cannot match the exposure, experience and objectivity of outside ad agencies and also the range of services provided by them. The arguments to support this view are that outside agencies attract the best creative talent, their personnel are highly skilled specialists and have a more varied perspective of advertising problems. The in-house agency personnel are likely to have a narrow perspective and may become stale because of working on the same products or services, while the outside agencies may have different people with varied backgrounds and ideas to work on the accounts. The advertiser can change the ad agency if not satisfied but changes in an in-house agency can be accomplished rather slowly and could prove to be more disruptive.

TABLE 15.1
Different advertising organisation systems

System	*Advantages*	*Disadvantages*
Centralised	• More efficient communications • Requires fewer personnel • Continuity of staff • More involvement of top management possible.	• Less involvement and understanding of overall marketing goals. • Longer response time • Limited ability to handle many product lines.
Decentralised	• Concentrated, individual manager's attention • Rapid response to problems and emerging opportunities • Increased flexibility.	• Less effective decision making • Unhealthy internal conflicts • Misallocation of funds • Managers lack sufficient authority.
In-house ad agencies	• Cost savings • More control on activities and costs • Increased co-ordination.	• Less experience • Less objectivity • Less flexibility.

The choice of how to organise for advertising depends on whether the company's marketing success critically depends on high quality advertising. This factor should be very critically evaluated against cost savings and serve as an important parameter in making the decision. Some companies, according to Bruce Horovitz, moved their in-house work to outside agencies as they felt the need for a "fresh look" and objectivity, noting that the management gets too close to the product to generate new and different creative ideas.

Full-service Agencies

Even a relatively small agency may meet the qualifying criteria of a full-service agency. Above all else, the function of an advertising agency is to see that its client's advertising leads to greater profits in the long run than could not be achieved without the help of the agency. Most such agencies are usually large in size and offer their clients a full range of services in the area of marketing, communications and promotions. These services also include planning, creating and producing the advertising; media selection; and research. A thorough knowledge of the company's products, their strong and weak points as compared to the competition, how the advertiser wishes to position the product in the consumers' mind, past advertising background and present market conditions are all important to do an effective job. Other services offered by the ad agency to the advertiser may include strategic marketing planning; sales training; package design; sales promotions; event management, trade shows; publicity and public relations.

The fall-service agency is composed of various departments, each responsible for providing inputs needed for performing various functions to serve the client. Such an agency often tends to have five functional areas: account management, creative, media and support services, and finance and administration. A typical organisational structure of a full-service agency is shown in figure 15.6.

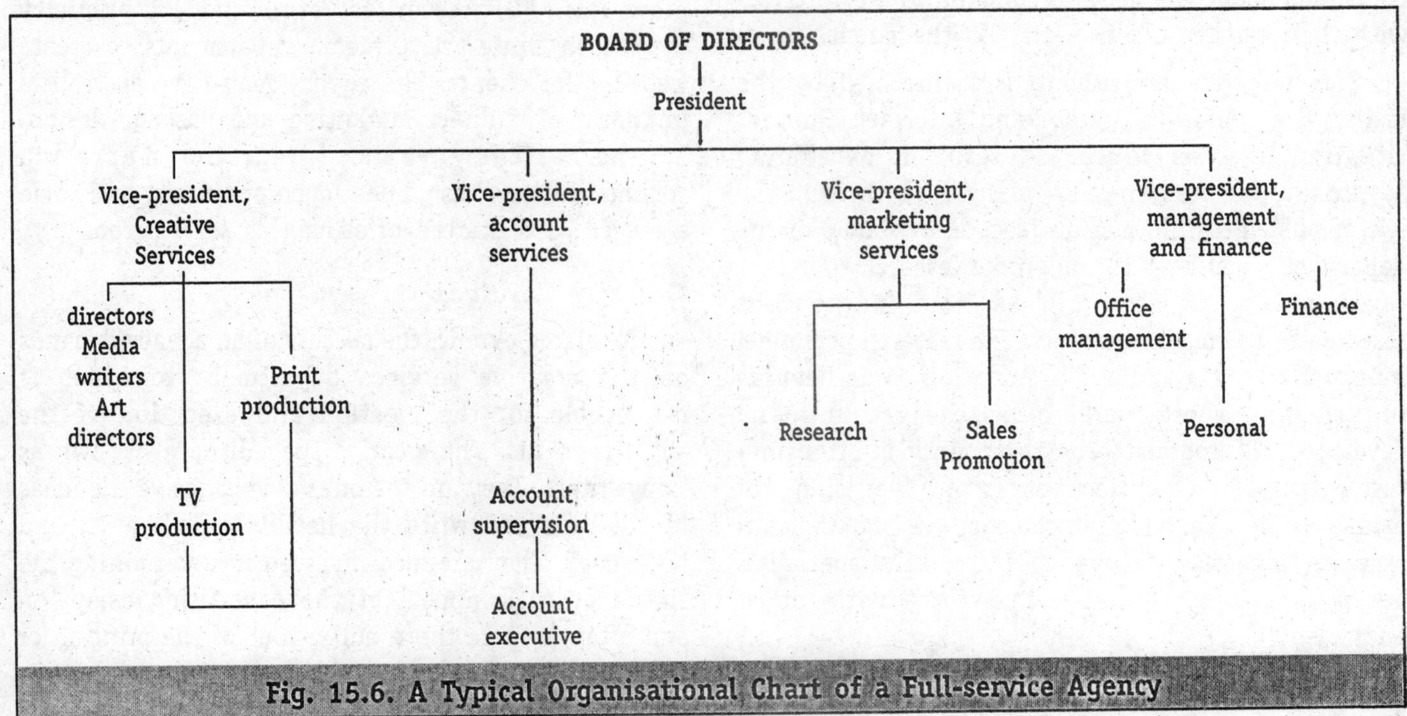

Fig. 15.6. A Typical Organisational Chart of a Full-service Agency

Account Services

Account services or account management is responsible for the relationship between the agency and the client. One or more account executives are assigned to serve as liaison, depending on the client's size and the advertising budget. The account executive's job requires a high degree of diplomacy and tact as misunderstandings may lead to loss of account. She/he represents the client by explaining the firm's point of view to all the agency personnel working on the account and also presents the agency point of view to the client. The account executive is responsible for acquiring knowledge about the client's business, profit goals, marketing problems and advertising objectives. The ideal account executive has a strong marketing background and a deep understanding of all aspects of the advertising process.

The account executive is responsible to help formulate the basic advertising strategy recommended by the agency and obtain client approval for media schedules, budget and rough ads or storyboards. The next task is to make sure that the agency personnel produce the advertising to the client's satisfaction. The biggest contribution of the account executive is keeping the agency ahead of its client's needs through follow-up and effective communication.

Marketing Services

The use of marketing services has dramatically increased in the last couple of decades. Research has gained increased attention because agencies are most concerned about the need to communicate effectively with their target audience, that is the client.

The 'research department' is maintained by the full-service agency to gather and interpret data for situation analysis which is useful in developing advertising for their clients. This is done through the use of published information (secondary data), or the department may have to undertake research to gather primary data, or acquire data from independent research firms, and consultants. The research personnel interpret the data and the information so gathered is furnished to those working on the account. The developed ad programme by the agency is often pre-tested to assess the effectiveness of advertising. For example, the agency conducts copy testing to learn how the messages developed by the creative specialists are likely to be interpreted and perceived by the target audience.

The responsibility of the agency's 'media department' is to develop a media plan which can reach the target audience effectively in a cost effective manner. The staff analyses, selects and contracts for media time or space that will be used to deliver the ad message. This is one of the more important decision areas as a significantly large part of the client's budget is spent on media time and/or space. Media specialists must consider the reach and frequency of the chosen media, their rates and how well the media matches the target audiences' media preferences and habits before actually purchasing the time and space.

The media department has acquired increasing importance in an agency's business as large advertisers seem more inclined to consolidate media buying with one or a few agencies thereby saving money and improving media efficiency. Bradley Johnson has reported that Nestle was using 11 agencies to purchase media worth $250 to $300 million before subsequently consolidating media buying into one agency. This gave Nestle increased clout in the media market and the company saved considerable amount of money. Similarly, as reported by Sally Goll Beatty and Kevin Goldman, Coca-Cola and General Motors are other large spenders on media who have consolidated their media buying with one or two agencies.

Some full-service agencies offer additional marketing services and have departments such as sales promotion department that specialises in contests, premiums, POP materials, etc., and PR/publicity department, interactive media departments to create websites for clients. The agency may have specialists in the area of direct marketing and package design. In the last few years, integrated marketing communications has gained much popularity and some agencies have started offering this service too.

Creative Services

To a large extent, the success of an agency depends on the creative services department to which is responsible for the creation and execution of the advertisements. The creative specialists are known as 'copywriters'. They are the ones who conceive the ideas for the ads and write the headlines, subheads, and body copy. They are also involved in determining the theme or basic appeal of the advertising campaign and often prepare the rough layout of the print ad or storyboard for TV commercials.

Creation of ad message is the responsibility of copywriters and the art department decides how the ad should look. The art director and the graphic designers coordinate their work and prepare the layouts for a print ad. These sketches or drawings of the ad show what it will look like when fully completed. The layout prepared for a TV commercial is a sequence of

BOX 1. Creating by computers

Computers have become as indispensable to advertising agencies as they are to other businesses, fn a 1990 survey conducted by Adweek magazine, 97 per cent of the agencies polled had bought or leased computers, using them at the rate of one for every two employees. AH of the agencies with computers were using them for word processing, and most of them also relied on computers to create spreadsheets, analyse income, and keep records of billings. Over half of the agencies were gathering information with computers, and in about one-third of the agencies, people were communicating through electronic mail.The last bastion of pencil-and-paper work in most agencies is the art department, and even the creative artists are beginning to lose their fear of computers. As one agency creative director puts it, "if you treat (the computer) as competition ... you feel hesitation. But if you treat it as a tool, it's on your side."More art departments are seeing that computers are on their side as the software. Becomes more user-friendly and the tools themselves become better adapted to the artist's need. One big step for many artists was the perfection of scanners which can "read" anything on the page - a pencil drawing, for instance, or a photograph - and transfer it into the computer. Once in the computer, the drawing can be altered, enlarged, manipulated, or integrated with other art or copy.The most advanced agencies do everything on the computer, producing camera-ready ads: Many of the ads they create would be impossible or prohibitively expensive to produce any other way.

Source: Betsy Sharkey, "The Art Department Timidly Turns to Computer Science," Adweek (February 29,1988).

frames showing the commercial in still form and is called a storyboard.

The agency's creative director is responsible for all the advertising produced by the agency and supervises the work of copywriters and artists. The creative director sets the creative philosophy of the agency and its artistic standards and generates a stimulating environment that attracts the best talent to the agency.

After completion and approval of the copy, layout, illustrations and mechanical specifications, the ad is handed over to the 'production department'. Generally, agencies do not actually produce finished ads; instead they hire printers, photographers, engravers, typographers and others to complete the finished ad. For the production of approved TV commercial, the production department may supervise the casting of actors to appear in the ad, the settings for the scenes, and selecting an independent production studio. The production department sometimes hires an outside director to transform the creative concept into a commercial.

Creation of an ad often takes several months and may involve many people. A major problem with large agencies handling many accounts is co-ordinating the creative and production processes. The responsibility of 'traffic department' is to co-ordinate all phases of production and ensure that the ads are completed on time to meet the media deadlines.

Management and Finance

An advertising agency is in the business of providing services and must be managed that way. There is an administrative head who takes charge of functions such as finance, accounting, human resource and office management.

Agency Structures

Popular among medium and large sized agencies are two types of structures: departmental system and a group system. The full-service agency structure shown in Figure 15.6 is an example of departmental system. Departments are grouped around functions and, as per the need, a specific department is called upon to serve all of the agency's clients. For example, creative services department is called upon for ad layout, writing and production services for all the clients. This type of organisational structure is preferred by some agencies because it provides employees with the opportunity to develop expertise in servicing different types of clients.

Many large full-service agencies use group system to form their organisational structure. Individuals are drawn from different functional areas and work as groups to serve particular clients.

Each group is headed by an account executive. Agencies using the group system believe that employees become very knowledgeable about particular clients' business and thus are able to ensure continuity in servicing the account.

Other Types of Agencies

A number of advertisers, including heavy spenders, look for specific high quality service agencies and do not want to contract a full-service agency.

Media Buying Services

These are independent agencies specialising in media buying services and have been experiencing strong growth. The advertising media buying has become complex with the increase in specialised media. Clients and ad agencies generally develop their own media strategies and contract media buying services to execute them. Agencies offering this service buy large chunks of space and time, thus receiving large discounts, and save money for clients and small ad agencies on media purchases. For the service rendered, they are paid a commission or fee by the agency or the advertiser.

Creative Boutiques

Such an agency provides only creative services. These creative boutiques have grown in response to advertisers' desire to use only the high quality creative talent of an outside service provider and rest of the functions are completed within the advertiser's organisation.

Many full-service agencies too sub-contract work to creative boutiques when they want to avoid increasing full-time employees or are very busy. These boutiques usually work on an agreed fee basis. Creative department people on leaving big agencies start such boutiques and carry with them some of the agency's clients who want to retain their creative talent.

THE AGENCY CLIENT RELATIONSHIP

The First AD Agent

The early agents worked for and were paid by the media. The first agent on record was Volney B. Palmer of USA in 1841 he organized a newspaper advertising and subscription agency. By 1849 he had established offices in New York, Boston, Baltimore, and Philadelphia. At this early date, there were no directories of newspapers and no published rates. Operating as an independent salesperson. Palmer sold space in the newspapers he represented to advertisers who wanted to reach those newspapers readers. The. publishers paid him a commission of 25 percent on his sales. The publishers found this method of selling more efficient than selling direct through their own sales representatives. Advertisers wishing to reach people in several cities found value in such service.

In 1865, George. P.. Rowell opened an agency that started the practice of wholesaling space. He contracted with 100 newspapers to sell him a column of space each week for a year. He received a discounted price plus the 25 percent agency commission for such quantity purchases. He resold space to advertisers in one-inch units at prices much higher than he paid.

N. W. AYER & SON

In 1876, was founded N. W. Ayer & Son, an Ad agency, they changed from space selling for publishers to space buying for advertisers;. Ayer bunched on open-contract-plus-commission plan in which he would act for advertisers, trying to get the lowest possible rates from media, then add a commission for its services. His commission ranged from 8 to 15 percent. In establishing the agency as servant to advertisers he started the agency function of planning, preparing and placing advertising.

AD AGENCY, TODAY

The main difference between the early Ayer organization and today's agencies is in the range of quality of services that have increased with the development of new media and expanding markets. There is an important difference between this type of agency-client relationship and the traditional agency-client relationship such as exists between lawyers and their clients. In its classical definition an "agent" acts on behalf of a principal. However, the advertising agency contract with media contains a waiver which holds the agency solely responsible for the payment for the space or time despite the fact that the advertiser may default on payment to the agency for any reason.

THE FORMAL AD CONTRACT

The formal contract between advertiser and agency specifies what the agency is expected to do: media, creative research, billing, etc. It details the compensation arrangement between the parties. It discusses ownership of material provided by the agency.

It spells out the basis upon which the agreement can be terminated. In this book, Auditing Productivity, William Weilbacher notes "although the purpose of the contract is to spell out the legal relationship, it rarely specifies the exact way in which the relationship is to be implemented. Nor should it, since its purpose is to define the legal relationship between the parties rather than professional relationship which the legal relationship, envisions and permits."

The advertising ad agency places for its client is the property of the client. It is copyrighted in the client's name. However, the agency is jointly liable. It must defend itself against claims for libel, slander, copyright infringement, idea, piracy, plagiarism violations of the right of privacy deceptive advertising, and unfair practices. Hence, most agencies carry liability insurance against such claims.

OWNERSHIP OF CREATIVE IDEAS

A prospective client invites a number of agencies to present creative ideas on how they would handle the account, It he pays the agencies for making their presentations as hallmark did in 1982, the client is likely to retain the ideas. Whether payment is offered or not the agency should have a clear understanding with me client about who will own the ideas before making a speculative presentation.

Most firms are too small to hire such a pool of talent as employees. However, even large firms that can afford to hire top-flight people to do their own advertising and buy direct from the media do hot do so. Most of the firms prefer to use advertising agencies. This is due to the following reasons :

1. The advertising agency works for several clients. Though it is responsible to each client, it is not exclusively so. Though it aims to render the best of service to each client, it is subservient to none. An independent agency is in a stronger position to bring an outside point of view and objective judgment to the client's problems. It is freer to follow its own standards in producing effective advertising. It is less likely to succumb to the whims of senior officers in the client organization.

2. Agency people get breadth of knowledge and experience from working on different accounts. The knowledge gained in one industry often 'proves helpful to advertisers in other industries.

3. The best professionals, in the business are concentrated in the agencies. Even the largest clients find it advantageous to share the pool of talent with others.

4. Whatever savings the client might gain from operating a house agency, have generally been considered less than the value of the superior service they lose by not using independent agencies.

HOW DO AGENCIES GET PAID? AGENCY COMPENSATION

1. The Commission System—It is a carry-over from the early days when the agency sold space for the media. They were paid a commission on their sales. Even though agencies now work for advertisers and buy space and time from the media, the, old system persists. It works like this. An agency places a full-page advertisement for one of its clients in a magazine. The rate, for a full page in the magazine is Rs. 30,000. After the ad has run, the magazine bills the agency for Rs. 15,500 (30,000 less 15 percent or Rs. 4,500). The agency which bills the client the full amount of Rs. 30,000 pays the magazine Rs. 25,500 and keeps Rs. 4,500 which becomes part of the agency's gross income. Out of gross income the agency pays the costs of planning, preparing, and placing the ad, leaving a contribution to overhead expenses and profit. If the agency pays within 10 days of the billing date most media grant a 2 percent cash discount. The discount usually is passed along that pay promptly.

The most traditional method for compensating advertising agencies for their services is through a 'commission system'. The agency is paid a fixed commission (usually it is 15%) from the media on any advertising space or time purchased for the advertiser. The rates for outdoor media are slightly higher (usually 16.66%). This is a simple system to determine the amount of commission.

For example, the agency places the order to purchase a full-page in a particular monthly magazine costing Rs.30,000. The magazine will bill the agency for Rs 30,000, less 15 per cent (Rs. 4,500) commission, after the ad is run. The media also offers a 2 per cent cash discount for early payment, which the agency may pass along to the client. The agency will bill the client for Rs. 30,000 less 2 per cent cash discount (Rs.

29,400). In this example, the agency earns Rs 4,500 as compensation for its services.

The commission system, to compensate agencies, has been under a cloud of controversy for many years. The major question raised by critics is whether the 15% commission represents an equitable compensation for services rendered by the agency. To produce an ad, two agencies may put in the same amount of effort, however, one client spends Rs. 500,000 on media and the other spends Rs. 10,00,000. The agency serving the first client would get paid only Rs. 75,000, while the other agency would get Rs 150,000 in commissions. The critics say that this system encourages agencies to recommend higher media expenditures to increase their earnings. The clients say that in periods of media cost inflation, the agencies earn disproportionate amounts as commissions. Still others point out that agencies avoid media where there is no commission, such as direct mail, or advertising specialities, unless specifically requested for by the client.

Those who favour the commission system say that not only is it easy, but it also encourages competition among agencies on factors other than price, such as quality of the advertising produced. They further argue that agencies have to devote more time and effort to large accounts and often perform other services for them, so the accounts generate proportionately higher revenues for the agency.

The commission system of compensation has become a fiercely debated topic in advertising circles. The present system may not be the best, but there seem to be no better alternatives. The media spend is an indicator of the value that the client attaches to the agency's idea.

FUNCTIONAL DISCOUNT

The 15 percent commission operates as a functional discount granted to agencies for performing functions that benefit media. Agencies promote advertising as a marketing instrument; develop new business, increase the productivity of advertising, centralize the servicing of many accounts, reduce the media's cost in mechanical preparation and reduce the media's credit risk.

COMMISSION RATE

Prior to 1956, media granted commissions to only "recognized agencies" in USA, those that met certain standard qualifications set by the various media trade associations. On May 12, 1955 the Department of Justice USA, filed a facial antitrust suit challenging the recognition procedure, with particular reference to the uniform standards for recognition, the withholding of commissions from agencies not recognized, the charging of gross rates to direct advertisers and the fixing of the commission at 15 percent of the gross rate, In 1956, the 4 A's and the media trade associations agreed to stop the practice. Today, agencies have to meet the usual credit standards required by one firm doing business with another to qualify for the 15 percent commission.

The media do not pay agencies. The money which the agencies deduct from advertisers payments is never in the hands of a medium who simply allows the agency to make the deduction. In fact, the advertiser pays the agency.

Agencies paid on the commission also receive direct payments from their clients for materials and outside production services, such as engravings, finished art, television story boards, and television production. Usually, the agency bills the client the cost plus 17.65 percent for these materials and sense services.

NEGOTIATED FEE

A number of agencies and their clients negotiate some type of fee system or cost-plus arrangement for compensation. Some use an incentive-based compensation system combining a fee and commission system. Agency executives sometimes feel that 15 per cent commission is inadequate for the services rendered to the client. In an arrangement of 'fixed-fee method', the agency charges a fixed monthly fee based on the work being done. This would apply to all the services provided and the agency passes on to the client any media commissions earned. The fee system is used in TV advertising where once the commercial is created it may be used over a long period of time. Without an agreed fee system, the agency would receive 15 per cent commission on media time, every time the commercial is run.

Sometimes, the agency is paid through a combination of fee and commission method. The media commissions received by the agency are adjusted against the agreed fee. If the received commissions are less than the agreed upon figure, the client has to make up for the difference.

The agency should carefully assess the costs of serving the client for the specific project, or the specified time period, and what profit margins are desired. Such a fee arrangement should specify exactly what services the agency has to perform for the client. This would help avoid the possibility of any unpleasant disagreements between the two.

Under the 'cost-plus system', the client agrees to pay a fee based on the cost of work the agency performs, plus some mutually agreed margin of profit for the agency. The agency is required to keep detailed records of the costs incurred in performing the desired services for the client.

The fee system can be advantageous to both the client and the agency. Many clients prefer, and are more satisfied with, the fee or cost-plus system because they receive a detailed breakup of expenditures of their advertising money. The procedure is cumbersome for the agencies and the agencies also feel reluctant to let the clients see their internal records of costs.

Some companies spend large sums of money on advertising and have started demanding more accountability from their agencies. They use some type of 'incentive-based system' to compensate agencies for their performance. The basic idea rests on how well the agency meets its predetermined goals set by the advertiser and agreed upon by the agency. Performance criteria may relate to sales or market share and/or the quality of the agency's creative work. Under this arrangement, the agency is compensated through media commissions, fees, bonuses, or some combination of these methods. In a sliding scale approach, the agency's base compensation is less than 15 per cent commission, but the agency can earn a bonus on how well it meets the sales or other performance criteria.

PERCENTAGE CHARGES

When the agency purchases various services from outside providers, they do not allow the agency a commission and to cover up administrative costs and a reasonable profit for the agency's efforts, a mark-up of 'percentage charges' for such services is added to the bill. These services may include market research, artwork, photography, printing and other services. The percentage charges range between 17.65 per cent and 20 per cent. For example, if the agency pays Rs. 1,00,000 for research, 17.65 per cent of this figure is added to reach a total of Rs. 1,17,650. The agency adds 17.65 per cent of this total in its overall bill. Approximately this yields 15 per cent commission (17.65 per cent of Rs. 1,17,650 = 17,647.50 and equals to 15 per cent of Rs. 1,17,650).

There is no one method to compensate agencies to which every advertiser agrees. Most agencies favour the commission system while some others think the system is outdated. Some advertisers are quite critical and argue against the traditional commission system and are trying to reduce agency compensation. However, most recognise the importance of profitability of their account for the agency to get the quality work. According to Laurel Wentz, two of the largest global consumer product marketers, Nestle and Unilever, revised their compensation policies to ensure that their agencies get a reasonable profit and the firms get the best results from their agencies.

ARGUMENT AGAINST

(i) A Fixed Percentage of Media Costs—A fixed percentage of the cost of space and time provides the agency with compensation that may not be related to the cost of services performed. The agency's cost of producing an advertisement to appear in space costing Rs. 40,000 would probably not be 10 times the cost of producing an ad to appear in space costing Rs. 4,000. Yet, the agency's compensation would be 10 times greater for the former than for the latter. On a fixed percentage basis, the more the client spends, the more the agency makes. This creates the suspicion that the agency has no incentive to hold down the cost of advertising.

(ii) The Client's Lack of Control Over Services Paid for Through the Commission—Lacking control over the services covered by the commission, advertisers are compelled lo negotiate for so-called free services, Many advertisers feel that they do not play a large enough part in planning what the agency is to do for the commission it receives.

ARGUMENTS FOR

(i) Supporters of the commission system argue that it is a means of rewarding agencies in direct proportion to the use that is made of their creative work. A box office approach to determining the value of an agency's service it assumes that the value of an advertisement depends on the size of the audience it reaches, not on the cost of producing it. However, most agencies point out that they allocate more time and higher-salaried creative people to producing advertisements for big audiences than for small audiences, adopting the cost of production to the size of the audiences to be reached. Agencies generally include more free services on big billings than on small billings to further reduce possible inequities arising from a fixed commission on media expenditures.

(ii) The commission system places agency competition on a creative service basis instead of a price basis.

(iii) It has worked satisfactorily though imperfectly, through the years.

(iv) It will have to do until a better system comes along.

2. The Fee System—In it the agency estimates the total cost of handing the client's advertising for a year and collects the fee in equal monthly installments. They agency estimates the total number of hours of services that will be required in all the various departments—creative, media account handling, and so on. It now multiplies the hours by average hourly rates and adds 25 percent to cover overhead and profit. Commissionable media purchased by the agency are billed to the client at the published rates minus 15 percent. Costs of materials and services from outside suppliers are billed to the client at actual cost. During the course of the year or at the year's end; the fee is adjusted to compensate for any difference between estimated and actual cost. Another kind of fee system is the monthly fee. The hourly charges for all time-reporting employees working on the account are totalled monthly, a percentage of 25 percent is added to cover overhead and profit, commissions are credited to the account and the resulting amount is billed to the client each month.

Advantages

(i) The agency tailors its services to fit the client's needs.

(ii) Each fee account pays its own way with none being subsidized by others.

(iii) The client has greater assurance of getting what has been paid for.

(iv) The agency is less likely to be biased in favour of commissionable media.

(v) The agency's income is more stable throughout the year.

(vi) A more professional relationship between agency and client is attained.

Disadvantages

(i) Agencies might be tempted to compete on the basis of price instead of quality.

(ii) The client might become too involved in the agency's internal operations; and

(iii) The agency might over service by doing more work for the client than is needed.

While most agencies use both commission and fee systems the trend is moving toward greater use of fees.

FUTURE OF THE FULL-SERVICE AGENCY

Recently smaller organizations specializing in a single function have challenged the full-service agencies. By concentrating at first on spot television ads independent media buying services were able to negotiate lower prices and get better buys. They charged a 5 percent fee for their service. Gradually, they expanded to include all media. Some clients turned to these services because they did not care who did the buying as long as it was done well at reduced costs. Full-services agencies responded by increasing the efficiency of their own media buying by having their own buyers socialize in particular media and markets.

CREATIVE BOUTIQUES

Closely related to the development of independent media buying services there has been the emergence of specialists in the creative function— "creative boutiques." These organizations limit their client services to creative planning and execution. Creative-

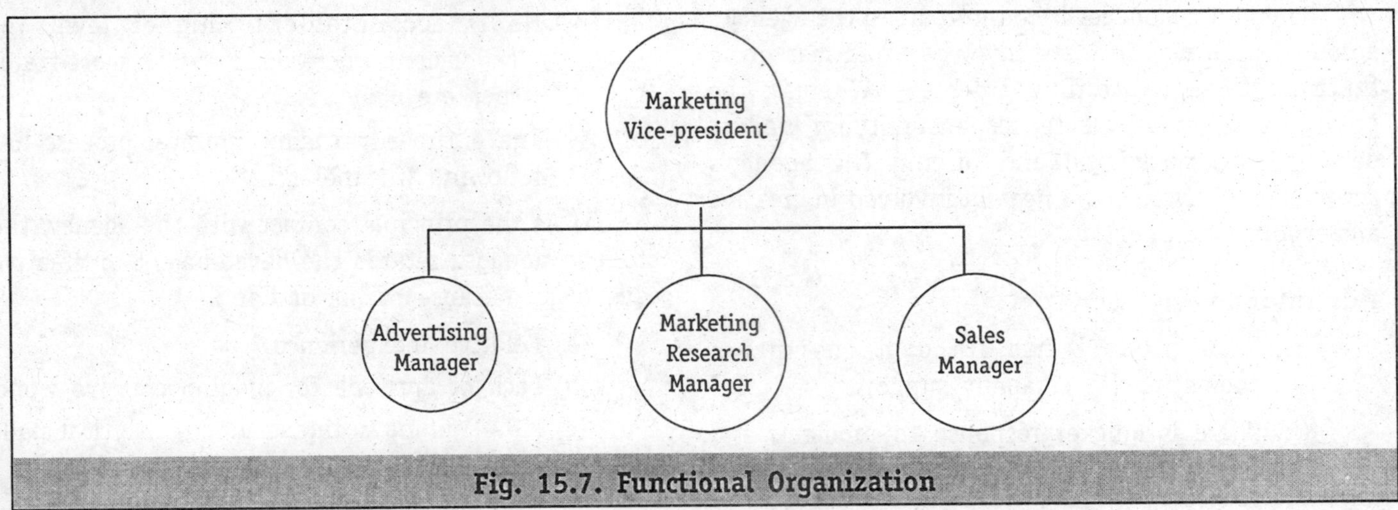

Fig. 15.7. Functional Organization

only agencies got their start because it was assumed that a few creative people could do better work if they were isolated from the day-to-day routines and diversions of the full-service agency. In their splendid isolation they would interact and concentrate on the creative problem and come up with a better solution. Some clients wanted professional creative work without having to pay for other agency services. They could get the work done faster and have a better chance of getting the big creative idea. Such specialized services continue to have a place although they remain small in scale.

Due to the growth of media buying services, creative boutiques and specialized research services full-service agencies have strengthened their services within the conventional organization or have modified their organization to offer clients service on an carte or "modular" basis. To add to their roster firms specializing in public relations, sales promotion, retail advertising and corporate communications. Other agencies have expanded through mergers and acquisitions.

TYPES OF ADVERTISER ORGANIZATION

1. Functional Organization—The larger the advertiser, the greater the need for an organizational structure that delineates the tasks of the people responsible for the firm's advertising. As shown in Figure 15.7, in a functional organization the various marketing specialists hold the titles: advertising managers, sales managers and research managers. They report to the marketing vice president who coordinates their activities. Functional organization is appropriated for companies that have a relatively simple product line with only a few items sold to relatively few markets. To plan and execute advertising strategy in conjunction with the company's agency advertising managers have line authority. They communicate the company's objectives, provide relevant information, participate in the planning process and review and approve the agency's recommendations. If collateral materials such as catalogues, sales literature and point-of-purchase displays are prepared internally, the advertising managers supervise their preparation.

A functional organization has the advantage of simplicity. However, as a company grows and adds new products, a point is reached at which a single marketing director and a single advertising manager cannot effectively supervise the entire line.

2. Product Manager Organization—Most packaged-goods manufactures have adopted the product manager system also called a brand management system to concentrate managerial attention on each product or brand. Each product has its own manager. The product manager has line responsibility for planning strategy, working with the agency to develop advertising and promotions, stimulating support of the company's salespeople, and monitoring the product's performance. The advertising manager assumes a staff or advisory role to the product managers. Large manufacturers marketing several brands in several product categories place several brand managers under a group manager.

The product manager is counterpart to the agency's account executive. Both are involved in all marketing functions though to differing degrees. Whereas, the product manager has greater responsibility for product development, packaging and pricing the agency's account executive is more heavily involved in creative and media planning.

Advantages

(i) Each product has its own champaign competing for company support.

(ii) There is quicker response to problems and opportunities as they arise.

(iii) Lines of communication between client and agency are shorter.

(iv) The wide range of product manager's responsibilities offers excellent training for future executives.

Disadvantages

(i) The product manager is given responsibility without authority.

(ii) He does not have control over essential support functions including product design, manufacturing, pricing and selling.

(iii) He is accountable to higher levels of management where decisions on most major issues are made.

(iv) The entire advertising approval process has following. weakness :

(i) As the principal contact with the agency, the product manager retards the development of creative advertising because of his or her :

(a) Relative inexperience.

(b) Lack of aptitude for judging creative work.

(c) MBA training in financial and analytical skills but little or no training in advertising.

(d) Over reliance on copy testing.

(e) Personal insecurity with respect to advertising, which leads to selection of safe rather than creative approaches.

(f) Nitpicking, resulting in rework of ads, slowdown of the development process and added costs.

(ii) High turnover, which places emphasis on short-term results and deemphasis on long term solid building of market position.

(iii) The hierarchy of decision levels beginning with the product manager which :

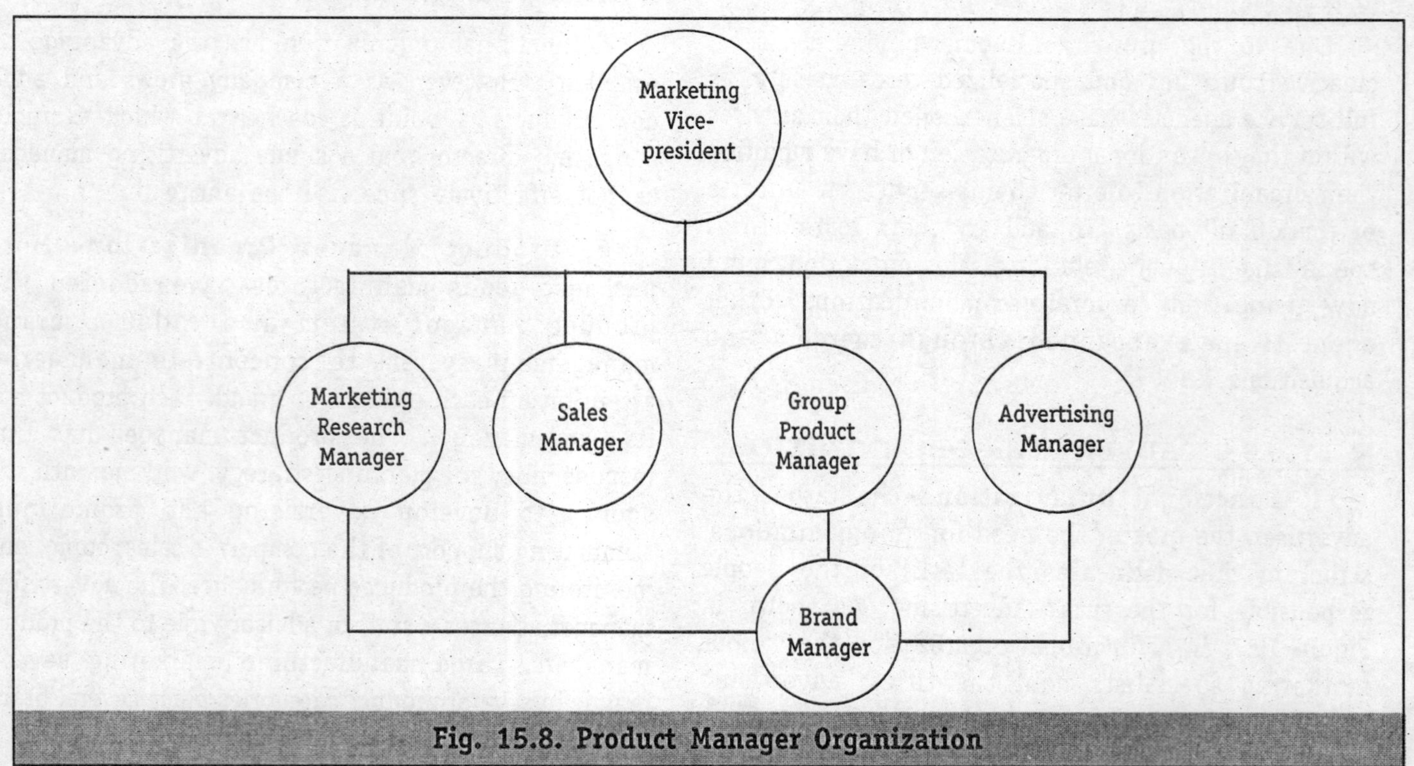

Fig. 15.8. Product Manager Organization

(a) Slows down the approval process.
(b) Results in so many changes that the effect of the original creative proposal is lost.

(iv) As managers with MBA training are promoted, management's ranks become filled with executives who, while they have gained experience, do not necessarily become good judges of advertising.

AMENDMENTS

In order to overcome these weaknesses the product manager's role has been redefined to play down the role of advertising decision maker and emphasize the role of product and co-ordinator. In developing effective advertising with the decisions being made at higher levels the manager assists the agency and higher management. To speed up decision making and to reduce the risk of tampering with the agency's creative work, agency submissions are often made to two or three management levels including the product manager at the same time.

The types of advertising decisions made by management level in a division of a major packaged goods company.

CRITERIA FOR SELECTING AD AGENCY

While there is no standard procedure for selecting the agency to handle an account, the advertisers establish criteria for evaluating the candidates. The General Electric Company uses the following criteria :

1. Growth—Have growth and billings been sound and consistent or have billings been up one year and down the next ? Why ?

2. Experience—In what fields of industry do its accounts lie? Has it demonstrated extreme versatility in all product areas or does it have particular strength in an individual product classification area?

3. Account History—What is its average age of service to its clients; what has been its account turnover?

4. Man Power—Here we look at the depth of experience and the number of people on second and third levels as well as the top level; here, too, we look at turnover.

5. Marketing Concept—Here we ask for the agency's philosophy of business operation. Is it progressive or conservative? Does it treat each problem individually or does it stick pretty close to a rigid formula? Does it reveal a keen appreciation of the place of business in its economic, social and political environment?

6. Campaign Planning—Here we judge the ability of the agency to secure, analyse and interpret all the facts and conditions affecting the marketing problem and their ability to develop advertising objectives and competitive strategy that form the essence of the campaign.

7. Creative—This is the judgement of the agency's ability to create essentially goods ideas—applying imagination to the problem and developing sound ideas of unique value with great competitive impact.

8. Media—Here we are judging the evidence of thoroughness and soundness in media research, the preliminary media recommendations, relative cost compared to budget and so on.

9. Sales Promotion—As used in this appraisal, this is that part of the campaign plan designed to stimulate, and persuade, men from all people who sell the product department salesmen, wholesalers and their salesmen, retailers and their salesmen.

10. Research—This means primarily evaluating the resources to collect and interpret facts for a campaign plan that will determine and achieve the sales and advertising objectives. Here we evaluate the abilities of the agency in the way of research such as copy research, motivation research, product planning research, package research, and others.

11. Merchandising—This is an evaluation of the ideas and materials that an agency can provide to make all forms of selling pay off at the point of purchase.

12. Product Publicity—This service need not necessarily be performed by any agency especially if other means for clearing news of company operations is maintained.

13. Production—This is an evaluation of the agency's resources to produce or supervise production of all types of advertising, promotional and merchandising material. This will include slide films, motion pictures, radio and television programmes and commercials, if they should be an essential part of the advertising campaign.

14. Personnel—This is the number and quality of the people who will be assigned full time to the account—the most important factor in agency service. In a sense, we want to regard these people as being a part of our organization and thus, their personalities and attitudes, as well as their planning and creative abilities, should be of a nature that will work well in harness with our people.

15. Technique—Here we evaluate the mechanics of getting a job done. Who does what, when and how, must be planned, controlled and communicated to all who are affected both within the client's organization and that of the agency.

16. Contact—This means the availability of agency personnel for personal contact with the frequency desired; the convenience and speed of contact for both regular and emergency purposes.

ADVERTISER-AGENCY RELATIONSHIP

COMPLICATING FACTORS

1. The division of function and responsibilities between the two parties is seldom, if ever clearly defined.

2. Advertising is an intangible product. Predicting and measuring if productivity is highly subjective. The contributions of the various people on each side of the relationship have different commitments.

3. Advertising is not the only thing on the client's mind and a single client's advertising is not the only thing on the agency person's mind, Approval of advertising plans on both the client's and the agency's sides takes place at several levels with the attendant possibility of contradiction from one level to another.

HINDERING FACTORS

Weilbacher's recent study of advertiser-agency productivity, listed the following factors that hinder a productive relationship.

1. Quality of Staff Factors

(i) Too many unproductive/unnecessary meetings.

(ii) Doesn't give agency enough lead time.

(iii) Inability to plan ahead.

(iv) Unwilling to experiment/take risks.

(v) Inability to adhere to schedules.

(vi) Company unfamiliar with agency cost constraints.

(vii) Too much reliance on research/not enough use of judgment.

(viii) Company, unwillingness to take a position.

(ix) Unwillingness to listen to other points of view.

(x) Too much "change for change's sake".

(xi) Lack of candor.

(xii) Failure to show initiative.

(xiii) Failure to ask the right questions.

(xiv) Unable or unwilling to set priorities.

(xv) Failure to operate with agreed-upon strategy.

(xvi) Too many "make work" projects.

2. Organization Factors

(i) Company has too many levels of approval.

(ii) Too many important decisions made by "juniors".

(iii) Unnecessary duplication of agency work at company.

3. Management Participation Factors

(i) Client unwilling to commit sufficient funds.

(ii) Too much personnel turnover.

(iii) Not enough senior management involvement.

4. Communication Factor

Failure to follow established lines of communication.

RECOMMENDATION

To provide a more productive relationship the same study recommended that advertisers periodically review and evaluate the agency's performance across abroad spectrum including :

1. Does the agency organize itself effectively to work with the advertiser?
2. Does it staff the account with compatible, productive people ?

3. Does the advertising process with its attendant work flow more smoothly ahead ?
4. Does the agency remove irritants in the relationships as they appear?
5. Is there evidence of agency involvement in and powerful thinking about the client's business ?
6. Does the agency's creative and media work respond to the needs and perceptions of the client organization ?
7. Does creative and media work proceed smoothly through advertiser review processes, or is there continual bickering about and acerbity in the presentation of the agency's work ?
8. Do all of the agency's departments make a distinct contribution to the advertiser, or are some departments inept or ineffective ?

RETAIL ADVERTISERS

SMALL AND LARGE RETAILERS

For help in planning and preparing their advertisements small retailers turn to the local media, the newspapers, television, and radio stations. Large retailers particularly the major departments stores operating several branches in metropolitan areas, have their own advertising departments with a full complement of skilled professionals—such as writers, artists, media buyers, and promotion planners.

FUNCTIONS OF RETAIL ADVERTISING

The retailer is the last link in the channels of distribution. He is closest to the consumer. He is sensitive to the changes in consumer needs and wants. He must offer the kinds of merchandise in the assortments and at prices the customers want.

1. The primary function of retail advertising is to keep the store's customers informed about the various items currently featured.

2. From the consumer's viewpoint, retail advertising functions as a shopping guide telling where to go to get the best buys.

3. To recover the cost of advertising and make a profit and also advertises items that build traffic the retailer advertises those items that are expected to see in sufficient volume. These would include special purchases offered at sharply reduced prices, regular sales events, seasonal items, and new fashions.

4. Item and price advertising accounts for nearly all of the advertising of supermarkets, mass merchandisers, and drug chains.

5. Department stores and specialty shops have a dual advertising job to do. They must not only sell specific items, but also sell the store as an attractive place to shop. The store's location, its architecture, fixtures, interior design and displays communicate much about its character, The store's advertising should project its character (image) to current and potential customers. Through the use of white space, style of art, language, graphics and tone, newspaper ads can clearly say that the advertiser is an elegant, exclusive top-of-the-line store, where one does not expect to find anything but the very best, at substantial prices or that the advertiser offers middle-of-the line merchandise at modest prices for people who must stretch their shopping dollars.

KINDS OF RETAIL ADVERTISING

1. Co-operative Advertising—Co-operative advertising does what an individual retailer cannot do individually.

(i) Horizontal Co-operative Advertising—It is the joint effort of independent retailers in the same category, such as hardware stores and realtors. Auto dealers selling the same make of cars form dealer associations and advertise as one within metropolitan areas. Individual retailers get the benefits of professional agency service through such co-operative ventures. They also get exposure to the larger media audiences of metropolitan newspapers, television and radio stations at a cost they could not otherwise afford. A significant extension of this kind of co-operation is the advertising done by and for franchise outlets.

(ii) Vertical Co-operative Advertising—It is a joint venture between manufacturer and retailer. The manufacturer offers the retailer an allowance front the full cost of the brand's space to 50-50 for advertising the manufacturer's brand in the store's advertising. The manufacturer may or may not require proof of performance in the form of a tear sheet to prove that the ad that was paid for actually ran. As the retailer gets a lower rate than the manufacturer gets from the local media both parties gain; both benefit from the ad while sharing the cost.

Limitations

The co-op advertising allowance has become part of a more general promotional allowance. The manufacturer offers retailers an allowance of so much per case (case allowance) to be used in a variety of ways—end of aisle display, shelf talker, more facings, cents-off retail price co-op advertising and others. The retailers may or may not advertise the manufacturer's brand but use the allowance simply to augment, their gross margins. With the greater margins, they may order cases and do some form of promotion to increase volume and total profit. The manufacturer, benefits from the extra volume, although at a lower profit per case, which he is willing to endure because it helps build goodwill with the dealers who probably have come to expect the allowance anyway because it has become a practice of the trade.

2. Agency Advertisement—Retailers generally do not use advertising agencies. Their scale of operation is too small. Their day-to-day selling activities require more quick-changing tactical maneuvers than long-range strategic planning. The small or medium-sized store does not generate enough billings from commissionable media to become a profitable client for an agency. Billings of Rs. 1,00,000 would gross only Rs. 15,000 a year in commissions, which would hardly be enough to cover the agency's cost of 'preparing the many ads required throughout the year. If paid on a fee basis, the agency would have to charge more than such retailers would be willing or able to pay.

The giant retailers operate as both national and retail advertisers. They have their own brands and institutional advertising. Most of their day-to-day store advertising is handled internally. Though agencies have not been a dominant factor in the retail field, there, is considerable evidence that they will grow in importance. With greater funds in their hands, more retailers will be attractive clients for Ad agencies, .The renewed emphasis on local promotions gives smaller ad agencies with specialized knowledge of a market or an industry or a local area, a decided advantage. The larger Ad agencies have bought into smaller shops to gain this local expertise.

Agency Evaluation

The process of agency evaluation involves regular assessment of two aspects of performance area-financial and qualitative. The financial assessment focuses on how the agency conducts its business *vis-a-vis* costs and expenses, the number of personnel hours charged to an account and what payments are made to media and other outside service suppliers. Qualitative assessment explores the agency's efforts devoted to planning, developing and implementing the client company's advertising campaign and an assessment of the achievements.

Depending on the importance of advertising in a company's marketing programme, both informal and formal methods of assessment are used by different companies. Some companies develop a formal and systematic evaluation method that uses a ranking scale for creative and media services, such as 'poor/average/excellent' on a scale of 1 to 10. Brand or promotion managers complete the advertising agency performance evaluation, usually once a year. These reports are reviewed with the agency at each annual meeting.

The results of the evaluation may or may not be favourable to the agency. Mark Gleason has reported a survey of 1996, conducted by the American Association of Advertising Agencies. According to the survey report, the average tenure of client-agency relationships has declined from 7.2 years to 5.3 years since 1984. Gleason has mentioned some of the most valuable brands with long-term agency relationship.

Role of an Advertising Agency

Advertising is a large and highly competitive industry occupying a very important position in most developing and developed economies. With a plethora of brands on offer, the need to inform, persuade and convince the customer is becoming increasingly

TABLE 15.2.

Some of the world's most valuable brands with long-term agency relationship

Brand	*Age of brand*	*Agency name*	*Years of relationship*
Marlboro	43 years	Leo Burnett Co.	43 years
McDonald's	42 "	DDB Needham Worldwide	27 "
Kodak	105 "	J. Walter Thompson Co.	67 "
Kellogg's	91 "	J. Walter Thompson Co.	67 "
Gillette	94 "	BBDO Worldwide	31 "
General Electric	101 "	BBDO Worldwide	77 "
Pepsi-Cola	99 "	BBDO Worldwide	37 "
Frito-Lay	65 "	DDB Needham	43 "
Levi's	145 "	Foote, Cone & Belding	67 "

Source: Mark Gleason, "MIA on Madison Avenue: Agency, Client Loyalty," Advertising Age, January 1997.

important. And this is where the tools of Advertising and Advertising Agencies that use this tool step in!

What is an Advertising Agency? An Advertising Agency or ad agency is a service provider that works for clients to create an effective and goal oriented advertising campaign aimed at representing the company positively in the eyes of its target customers.

Businesses hire advertising agencies to connect with their target customers. In the face of stiff competition, every Co. / brand wants to break through this clutter and create a favourable space for itself. Ad agencies help clients to do just this by creating attention grabbing, persuasive and unique ad campaigns that make the brand stand out in the minds of customers.

What does an Advertising Agency Do?

A plethora of businesses, corporations, government organizations and non-profit set-ups hire advertising agencies to advertise their products, brands and services to present and prospective customers.

- **Understand the Product / Company:** An advertising agency begins by getting well acquainted with the client's goals, products & target audience. This knowledge proves beneficial in planning and creating an effective advertising campaign.
- **Plan & Create an Advertising Campaign:** Once an advertising agency understands its clients' needs, the process of brainstorming and planning begins. Keeping in mind the client's goals which can range from pushing sales of its products and services introducing new products in the market reiterating its brand's benefits attracting new customers or keeping in touch with old ones the advertising executives work towards creating an effective advertising campaign (a single or a series of attention grabbing and unique ads) which is within the client's marketing goals and budget. This includes creating interesting slogans, attractive jingles and attention grabbing body copy for advertisements. The client has the final word and may ask for rework.
- **Strategize:** Some companies like to outsource their overall marketing responsibilities to advertising agencies. In such a case, the ad agency takes over the process of brand building, strategizing and pushing sales through other promotion techniques like sales promotions etc.

Advertising agencies vary in size in India & abroad - from a couple of people handling all responsibilities to a medium or large sized agency that hires specialized professionals to function each department. It has been generally seen that Full Service Ad Agencies are well equipped to plan and create advertising campaigns for a range of media including TV commercials, Radio jingles, print advertisements etc. Depending on the budget, client's select their agency.

Indian Advertising Agencies

In today's modern world of cutthroat competition and survival for fittest, one can hardly imagine the survival of a brand without advertisement. This is where advertisement agencies in India come into the picture. From building a brand to promoting it, advertisement agencies in India have been providing its services to its clients all over. Going ahead, advertisement agencies in India have a bright future considering the ever expanding Indian market and its dependence on advertisement.

Advertising agencies in India service their client by preparing slogans, brochure and logos in a way that the brand connects well with the consumers and attracts their attention. They come up with descriptive copy for sales materials. Apart from these activities, they also issue press releases for upcoming programs, events, as well as products.

With increasing competition in the market, technological changes, advertising agencies in India is undergoing many changes. One such trend is the extensive market services , studies and research conducted by these agencies. The broad scope this marketing research includes quantity and quality, international marketing and ethical issues.

These include a redefinition of the marketing researcher, the on-going nature of marketing research, qualitative research, quantitative research, international marketing research, Internet marketing research, and ethical issues in marketing research. Based on their findings, they advise the manufactures.

Another visible trend is the increasing use of television as an advertising medium. With cable television reaching to millions of homes, and with an increasing number of channels, television is clearly the favourite medium among advertising agencies and their clients. With its advantage of creating visual and emotional appeal, more than 40 percent of total money spend on advertising is consumed by this medium.

The use of Internet for advertising is yet another trend. With about 25 million users, Internet advertising in India is increasingly on the rise. This may well explain the growth of Graphic Design & Advertising Agencies servicing their clients with high quality professional graphics, advertising material. With mobile phones and FM climbing the popularity chart, telecom firms and FM radios have joined hands with advertising agencies in India. Likewise outdoor advertising like billboards, hoarding have also become a reckoning force.

Role of Advertising Agency in the 21st Century

In the beginning of the 21st century Advertising Agencies are playing a very important role in the business of advertising. A lot of water has flown past the Ganges during the last 5 decades since the foundation of the first professional agency in India in 1950's by J.W. Thompson & D.J. Keeymer.

Gone are those days when advertising agencies were only playing a vital role in Planning the campaign for their clients, preparing the campaign and placing it in suitable media on behalf of their clients. In today's competitive situation it is evident that reputed ad agencies are not restricting themselves to the above services but are also willing to offer something extra to their clients in the areas of marketing research, sales promotion & merchandising activities and public relation oriented services.

National and reputed advertising agencies are increasingly going for 360 degree approach in their communications and are prepared to walk the extra yard to understand their client's business in a better manner in order to communicate with the target audience effectively and efficiently.

Reputed agencies like O and M, Mudra Communications, JWT and others preferred to be treated as 'PARTNERS' in their client's business and are always trying to suggest the best and cost effective communication strategy to reach the target audience.

With the passage of time along with the concept of 'FULL SERVICE AGENCY', specialized MEDIA AGENCIES like, Madison; Carat etc., have come up to take care of the client's special media requirements. We also see CREATIVE BOUTIQUES like Aloke Nanda Communications, Vyas G. Creative etc., just offering creative service to their clients.

Advertising agencies being prime facilitator in the business of advertising have rightly understood the need of the hour and are playing a key role in the business of advertising.

Today, there is enough recognition for the advertising agency's contribution to brand building.

Today, more and more companies report their brand's value in the balance sheet. Not because they have to; but because they want to. Today it is common knowledge that a brand's value has nothing to do with the physical assets owned by the company. And if brand Coca-Cola has been valued at billions of dollars then, clearly the advertising agency's role in this is being accepted, if grudgingly. Categories like soft drinks are dependent and driven by advertising. Advertising agencies can and will give an arm and a leg to handle a soft drinks major. Pitches to handle accounts like these are high profile ones with inputs and support from the agency's global network. The media keeps a close watch reporting the agencies that are in the short-list and predicting who is in front. When the account is gained, the agency goes to town and the whole world knows. Agencies have also used their portfolios to acquire visibility, awards and more business. The world knows that JWT has been behind Pepsi's visibility in India , O&M behind Cadburys, Lowe behind Surf Excel, Mudra behind Vimal and Rasna and so on. All these brands are dependent on advertising. Rightly so, but there are many technology, business-to-business and corporate brands who do not have the luxury of huge advertising budgets and a global agency network at their beck and call. They depend on public relations agencies to provide them visibility and build their brands and here lies the difference. Who really knows which is the public relations agency behind some of India 's most visible brands? And how often do clients go on stage to acknowledge the role of the PR agency as contributing to their brand's success.

CHAPTER

16 CREATIVE STRATEGY

NIKE TARGETS WOMEN

Perhaps, no company in the world has been as successful in capitalizing on the fitness boom of the past few decades as Nike. Since its inception, Nike has been a leader in the high-performance athletic-shoe market and has become one of the world's great brand names. The company ran past all its competitors to become the largest seller of athletic footwear and apparel in the world, with sales of nearly $10 billion in 2002. The Nike ethos of pure, brash performance is captured in the "Just Do It" slogan, which has become a catchphrase for the sports world and has been personified in advertising featuring some of the world's greatest athletes.

Nike is the overall leader in the $15.6 billion market for athletic shoes and apparel in the United States. However, the industry has been stagnant for years, and Nike, along with its competitors, is looking for new growth opportunities and areas where the company can gain market share and attract first-time customers. One of the areas Nike is targeting is the women's market, which has been experiencing strong sales growth but has been the company's Achilles' heel. Women's athletic footwear accounts for one-third of the total industry sales and apparel for more than 50 percent, but women's products account for only 20 percent of Nike's revenue. Although the company has been selling shoes and apparel to women for years, Nike has been better known as a brand catering to male athletes and building its image around superstars such as Michael Jordan, Pete Sampras, Lance Armstrong, and Tiger Woods. These efforts have resulted in Nike's dominance of the male market, where the company has a 50 percent market share.

For much of its 30-year history, Nike has been about men and either treated women like men or didn't give them much attention. However, sometimes Nike did get it right in communicating with women. In 1995, the company ran a campaign titled "If You Let Me Play" that struck a responsive chord with many women. The campaign featured ads showing female athletes talking about how sports could change women's lives, from reducing teen pregnancy to increasing the chances of getting a college education. The campaign, along with subsequent ads featuring top female athletes such as sprinter Marion Jones, helped make Nike the market leader, but it was focused primarily on the high-performance segment of the female market.

In 2001, Nike launched a new strategic initiative termed "Nike Goddess," which is a companywide, grassroots effort that has the goal of changing how the company does business with women. The new strategy appeals to a broader segment of the female market and is designed to take advantage of the differences between women and men in how they conceive of sport, how they shop for clothing and shoes, and even how they view celebrity athletes. Nike wants to appeal more to women's desire for an active lifestyle than to any image they have of themselves as hard-core athletes.

Nike began its new women's movement by spending time listening to women and learning how they balance their lives, what they like to wear, where and how they shop, and what moves them. Nike designers and researchers spent time scouring trendy workout spots like London's Third Space to pick up on new fitness trends. One key insight that emerged from the research is that for most women, high performance isn't about sports; it's about fitness fitting in with their active lifestyles. Nike stepped up its product development and introduced flashier shoe designs such as the Air Max Craze, which has a strap for a heel and a zipper over the lace. Another new line, the Air Visi Havoc, features materials not normally seen on a playing field, such as a faux snakeskin look, baby-blue satin and red mesh.

Nike Goddess also includes new ways to reach women and communicate better with them. A new ad campaign takes a different look at women and sports and veers away from Nike's traditional strategy of relying on big-name endorsers and producing product lines named after them. Jackie Thomas, Nike's U.S. brand marketing director for women, notes: "Women love that Nike is aggressive, that it is competitive. The difference between women and men is that women don't treat athletes like heroes. No woman thinks that she'll be able to run like Marion Jones because she wears shoes that are named after her." Rather than dwell on superstars, the new advertising campaign consists of print and TV ads that show ordinary women taking part in sport—from a swimmer to a young fencer to the "Yogini," a yoga instructor who stands on her hands on a hardwood floor and arches her back until her feet touch her head.

Nike has also launched a new website for women: nikegoddess.com. The site offers profiles of both famous athletes and everyday women who are trying to meet the challenges of balancing their hectic lives. It includes product information, health and fitness tips, city profiles to help women find fitness and fun when they are traveling, links to other sites, and online shopping for Nike products. Nike also launched NikeGoddess, the company's first "magalog" (a cross between a magazine and a catalog), to help roll out the name and communicate with today's active women.

One analyst noted that for many years, even within Nike there was a "general sense that it's by guys for guys." However, if Nike is to continue to grow, a company built on brash ads and male athletic fantasies is going to have to connect with female customers as well. The goal for the Nike Goddess initiative is to double Nike's sales to women by mid-decade. This will require that Nike change the way it sells to, designs for, and communicates with women. However, it appears that Nike is rising to the challenge. And lest anyone forget, Nike is named after a woman—the Greek goddess of victory.

Sources: Fara Warner, "Nike's Women's Movement," Fast Company, August 2002, pp. 70-75; Edward Wong, "Nike Trying New Strategies for Women," The New York Times, June 19, 2001, p. C1; Hillary Cassidy, "Hail the Goddess," Brandweek, Feb. 5, 2001, p. 42.

Suppose you are advertising mutual funds to individual investors. Is it better to use the likable Peanuts characters to talk about your funds (which is what MetLife did for its funds), or quote comparative performance statistics from a fund-rating service like Morningstar (which is what AIM Value Funds did)?

Suppose you want to compare yourself with a competitive brand in your advertising. Is it better to name and show your competitor (as Alfa Romeo did in comparing itself to the BMW), or merely to show (but not name) the comparison brand (which is what BMW did in comparing itself to the Lexus)? In fact, should a leader like BMW compare itself to the newer Lexus at all?

One of the most important components of an integrated marketing communication programme in advertising message is to communicate information, it does much more. The commercials, watch on TV hear on radio and see the print ad, we see in magazines and newspapers are a source of entertainment, motivation, fascination, fantasy, and sometimes irritation as well as information. Ads and commercials appeal to, and often create or shape, consumer's problems, desires and goals. From the marketer's perspective, the advertising message is a way. to tell consumers how the product or service can solve a problem or help satisfy desires or achieve goals. Advertising can also be used to create images or associations and position a brand in the consumer's mind as well as transform the experience of buying and using product or service.

We listen or view hundreds of messages daily. Underlying all these messages however are a creative strategy that involves determining what the advertising message will say or communicate and creative tactics dealing with how the message strategy will be executed. Today, the creative writers and executors are finding out various approaches to determine the big idea that will be used as a central theme of the advertising campaign and translate into attention getting, distinctive and memorable messages. Creative specialists are finding it more and more difficult to come up with big ideas that will break through the clutter and still satisfy the concerns of their clients are continually challenging them to the creative message that will strike a response from their target audience.

The present genre of advertising is significantly different from the traditional approaches of the past. Quite a good number of present day commercials seem to be totally unrelated to selling any particular product at all. There seems to be an obsession with images and feelings in the ads and an almost complete absence of any concrete claims about the product, or any "reason why" approach to convince the consumer to buy it. The Thumps Up commercial says, "I want my thunder." There are no claims, no product features and no reasons to convince the consumer to buy it. The ad simply attempts to communicate certain types of feelings and uses imagery. Ads of Nike say little, if anything, about athletic shoes but are rather based on concepts such as winning, unimportance of age and the unifying spirit of sports. The famous commercial "one black coffee please" of Ericsson mobile phone says nothing about the product, only portrays fantasy, and humour. At the heart of the old faith of advertising was "unique selling proposition" (USP), an approach advocated and popularised by the legendary advertising personality, Rosser Reeves. The comments by the director of brand planning at the J. Walter Thompson agency sum up the present advertising situation.

"USP is a great theory, but what do you do when most products come to the market without a visible point of difference? We are communicating a different type of information today - a feeling of what the world is like, and if you identify with that feeling, may be you identify with the advertised brand."

A major present day communication problem is "time famine". There is an ever-growing mass of ad messages directed at consumers who not only have less time to listen to advertisers messages but also less inclination.

The most basic role of an advertising message is to communicate information. While attempting to accomplish this, advertising does much more. The commercials that people watch on TV, hear on radio, or see and read in newspapers and magazines can be a source of information, entertainment, fantasy fascination, motivation and, sometimes, a cause of boredom or even irritation. Advertising message appeals should help create, or shape, "consumers" problems, goals and desires. They should tell consumers how the product or service can solve a problem, or help satisfy their desires or accomplish goals. Advertising can create associations or images and may position a brand in the consumers" mind. Advertising may also help transform the consumers" experience of buying or using a particular product or service. Many of us feel good about sending Hallmark greeting cards to our loved ones because of the company's advertising theme "when you care enough to send the very best." The ad theme of BMW "the ultimate driving machine" is perceived as real even by those who have never driven one.

Most of us have seen ads and commercials we like or even love and there are also many of those ads that we probably dislike or even hate. The ads we love, we refer to as "great". A great print ad has compelling attraction and a great commercial is a joy to see and often an epic to create as often the cost of producing a TV commercial can run into several lakh rupees. Most companies consider this as money well spent because the manner in which the advertising message is developed and executed is critical to the success of the advertising campaign. Hindustan Lever, Procter & Gamble, Coke, Pepsi, McDonald, Nestle, Dabur, ITC, Wipro, Colgate-Palmolive and many other companies spend huge sums of money on advertising each year and realise that creative advertising is an important part of their marketing success.

After an advertiser decides on the content of an ad-the "what to say" decision, the task of creating the ad itself is usually handed off to the creative people at the ad agency. Before these writers and art directors proceed to conceptualizing and creating the ad, however, it is usually a good idea to give some thought to the broad framework within which the ad should be created: What kind of appeal should the ad utilize? For instance, should the ad attempt a competitive comparison (a "rational") approach? Or, should it use some type of emotional appeal, such as fear, or humour? Should it use an endorser, and if so, what kind of endorser-an expert in that product category, or a likable celebrity?

While decisions of this sort are not always part of the advertising planning process at either the client or the agency (because of a desire not to limit the flexibility of the creative, or because of ignorance), the ad creation process could un-doubtedly benefit from the accumulated knowledge on when each of these creative approaches is most appropriate, and how each can be implemented most effectively. This chapter will thus present some material on various creative approaches (such as the use of endorsers, or of comparisons), focusing both on when each approach is most appropriate, as well as how it-is best implemented.

ADVERTISING STRATEGY

Most recent research indicates that "ad liking" has a tremendous impact on "ad success". However, just because an ad attracts attention, captures everyone's imagination and is liked, does not guarantee success. Many ads have won awards for creativity but failed to increase sales or reverse the fortunes of a declining brand. Some advertising and marketing people believe that advertising must ultimately motivate the consumer to purchase the product or service. Great ads give advertisers more advertising effectiveness per unit of money spent. The reality is that many ads are not great and arc a terrible waste of promotional money. Great advertising results by creating a combination of "ad liking" and its "strategic relevance". While the text and the visuals carry the ad message, behind the creative team's choice of tone, words and ideas, lies an advertising strategy. When the ad is completed it must have relevance to the sponsor's strategy, otherwise it will fail. It may turn out to be great entertainment but not great advertising. Great advertising always has a strategic mission to accomplish and is the key element that serves as a guide to great creative work.

BOX 1. Great advertising elements

The Creative Council of David Ogilvy & Mather Worldwide found that examples of great advertising have certain elements in common:

- ***Potent strategy.*** The strategy is the heart of advertising. It is impossible to do great advertising if the strategy is weak or does not exist at all.
- ***A strong selling idea.*** Great advertising promises a benefit to the consumer. The idea must be simple and it must be clear. The brand must be integrated into the selling idea.
- ***Stands out.*** A great ad is memorable, even when competing for attention with news and entertainment.
- ***Always relevant.*** Prospects can always relate the advertising to their experience and to the role of the product in their lives.
- ***Can be built into campaign.*** No matter how clever an idea may be, if you cannot make it into a campaign, it is not a great idea.

Source: Luis Basser, "Creative Paths to Great Advertising." Viewpoints, September/October 1991, pp 23-24.

Advertising or creative strategy blends the elements of creative mix. Four elements, the target audience, the product and its positioning, the communications media, and the advertising message constitute the creative mix. As pointed out earlier, advertising objectives say where the advertiser wants to be with respect to consumer awareness, attitude and preference. The advertising strategy (also called creative strategy) describes how to get there. One simply needs to watch TV commercials or scan a few magazines to appreciate numerous different ways of conveying advertising messages. Underlying all these messages are creative strategy and tactics to address target audiences to effectively communicate the product positioning through selected media.

- **The target audience:** The specific audience that the advertising is intended to focus upon will typically be larger than the target market. Advertisers need to know who the actual end user of the product or service is, who is involved in influencing and making the purchase decision and who makes the purchase. Various family members, friends and others may be involved in purchase decision making. Research shows that brand popularity cuts across all levels of purchasing frequency which means that while the company may target heavy users of a product, many light users and non-users of the product are also exposed to advertising. The dominant brands are purchased the most by both heavy and light users because advertising helps make them popular.

• **The product and it's positioning:** The product is a "bundle of values" offered to the consumer and is made known to the consumers through their creative designed ads.. Dabur Chayavanprash is meant for the entire family, while Baidyanath Chayavanprash is positioned for growing children. While writing the advertising plan, the concerned manager must develop a simple statement describing the product and it's positioning - how the advertising will present the product to the audiences.

Foote, Cone and Belding Model, Rossiter and Percy Grid and Kim and Lord Grid have shown how different kinds of products (high and low-involvement) typically give rise to different levels and types of consumer involvement. These models help in determining which type of advertising would be most appropriate for different types of products or services, keeping in view the level of involvement and the type of consumer motivation.

• **The communications media**: Communications media involve all the media vehicles that might carry the marketer's advertising message and include TV, radio, newspapers, magazines, billboards, Internet and others.

• **The advertising message**: It involves everything that the marketer plans to say in its ads and how it plans to say the same, both verbally and non-verbally.

Both, the advertising agency and the client team must understand and agree to these four elements of advertising strategy before beginning any creative work. In most advertising agencies, the account management is responsible for developing the strategy. In some agencies, depending on the necessity, account planners first research the market. Then they prepare the advertising strategy in consultation with account management personnel and their final approval. After completing the task of strategy development, account department prepares a creative brief (often referred as copy platform, a work plan, copy or creative strategy document) to communicate the strategy to the creative team. It is a simple written statement of the most significant issues to consider and guide the team in the development of an advertisement or campaign. The statement addresses the following issues

• Who? Who is the potential customer in terms of geographic, demographic, behaviouristic and psychographics qualities? What is the personality profile of a typical prospect?

• Why? Does the consumer have specific needs and wants that the ad message should focus upon and appeal to? There are two broad categories of appeals. Rational appeals are directed at the consumer's practical, functional need for the product or service, whereas the emotional appeals aim at the consumer's psychological, social, and symbolic needs. (See Table 16.1).

• What? Are there any special features of the product or service to satisfy the consumer's needs? What factors support the product claim? Know is the product positioned? What image or personality of the brand can be created or has been created? What perceived strengths or weaknesses of the brand need to be addressed?

• **Where, when, and how?** In which market area, what time of the year and through what medium will these messages be delivered?

• **What style, approach, or tone will the campaign use?** Generally, what will the copy say?

Creative brief only identifies the benefits to be presented to the consumers but how these benefits will be presented is the domain of creative specialists. A typical creative brief may include the following:

• **An objective statement**: A specific, concise statement of what the advertising is expected to achieve or what problem is it supposed to solve. The statement also includes the name of the brand and a specific but brief description of the target audience.

• **A support statement**: A brief statement of the evidence that backs up the product promise.

• **A tone or brand character statement:** A brief description of the tone of advertising or the long-term brand character. Tone statements refer to short-term emotional description of the advertising strategy (tone may convey quality, beauty, sophistication, etc.). Brand character statements relate to long-term descriptions of the brand's values (finest material, patented technology, hand crafted, etc.).

TABLE 16.1

Maslow's Need-Hierarchy and Selected Advertising Appeals

	Rational approach	*Emotional approach*	
Self-actualisation Needs	Opportunity for more leisure	Ambition Avoidance of physical Labour Curiosity Entertainment	Pleasure of reaction Simplicity Games and sports, physical activity
Esteem Needs	Dependable quality Dependability in use Enhancement of earnings Variety of selection	Pride of personal appearance Pride of possession	Style/beauty Taste
Social Needs	Cleanliness Economy in attraction	Co-operation Devotion to others Guilt, shame Humour Home comfort	Romance Sexual Social achievement Social approval Sympathy
Safety Needs	Durability Safety	Fear, health	Security
Physiological Needs	Protection of others rest, seep	Appetite	Personal comfort.

After developing the advertising strategy, the next step is the creative process. The creative team develops a message strategy and the search begins for the big idea. The message strategy may be developed before, during, or after the creative process of searching for the big idea.

The message strategy is a brief description and explanation of the overall creative approach of an ad campaign. It is composed of three elements

- **Verbal element:** This furnishes guidelines for what the advertising message should say. It includes the considerations that affect the choice of words and the relationship of copy approach to the medium.
- **Non-verbal element:** This point to the overall nature of graphics and any visuals that must be incorporated and their relationship to the media that will be used for the ad.
- **Technical element:** This refers to the preferred way of execution and mechanical outcome, budget and scheduling limitations as a result of chosen media and any specific requirements for each ad such as logos, slogans or the address.

Though, in most advertising campaigns, the starting points of message strategy are the verbal elements, yet the nature of these elements is such that they are all intertwined and evolve simultaneously. For example, language and imagery can influence each other quite significantly. The message strategy must conform to the advertising strategy outlined in the creative brief.

What is Creativity?

Creativity is probably one of the most frequently used terms in advertising circles. Perhaps so much attention to creativity is given because people consider the specific challenge of developing an advertising message as the domain of creative people. Individuals and advertising agencies often build up reputations for their creativity.

Some people exhibit more creativity than others

but some of it, is present within all of us. It is the creativity that helped humans to discover and harness fire, domesticate animals and cultivate fields. Without creativity, the human race probably would not have survived.

The word "create" denotes originating, or conceiving an idea or a thing that did not exist before. Typically, though, creativity involves combining previously unconnected ideas or objects into something new. There is a general belief that creativity emerges directly from human intuition, but the reality is that creativity can be learned and used to generate original ideas.

Creativity is probably one of the most commonly used terms in advertising ads. The people who develops ads and commercials are known as creative professionals. And advertising agencies develop reputations for their creativity. Perhaps so much attention is focused on the concept of creativity because many people view the specific challenge given to those who develop an advertising message as being creative. It is their job to turn all of the information regarding product features and benefits, marketing plans consumer research and communication objectives into a creative concept that will bring the advertising message to life. This begs the question: What is meant by creativity in advertising?

Creativity is generally defined in aesthetic terms: The ability to produce new, useful ideas; originality, imagination or the capacity for joining two or more elements to form a new unity or purpose. However, each definition leaves out the utilization or productive function of creativity which applies to advertising.

An individual creates an environment which affects the extent and manner of his creativity. What emerges is not only an expression of the inner state of the creator; it is also designed to meet externally defined needs and goals. Creativity in advertising is an example of a combination of both aesthetics and problem solving.

There are differences of opinion on what constitutes advertising creativity. There are those who are of the view that advertising is creative only if it sells the advertised product or service. The ad message's positive impact on sales is viewed as more important than whether it is innovative or wins awards. On the other extreme are those who judge an advertisement's creativity in terms of its originality and artistic or aesthetic value. They argue that creative ads can break through the advertising clutter, capture the audience attention and produce some impact. Elizabeth Hirschman's study examined the perceptions of individuals involved in the creation and production of TV commercials such as brand managers, account executives, art director, copywriter, commercial director and producer. She observed that product managers and account executives believe that a commercial should be evaluated in terms of whether it accomplishes the client's marketing and communications objectives. Those on the creative side had a more self-serving perspective.

She noted: "In direct contrast to this client orientation, the art director, copywriter and commercial director viewed the advertisement as a communication vehicle for promoting their own aesthetic viewpoints and personal career objectives. Both the copywriter and art director made this point explicitly, noting that a desirable commercial from their standpoint was one which communicated their unique creative talents and thereby permitted them to obtain "better" jobs at an increased salary."

Perspective on what constitutes creativity in advertising vary. At one extreme are those who argue that advertising is creative only if it sells the product. An advertising message or campaign's impact on sales counts more than whether it is innovative or wins awards. At the other end of the continuum are those who judge the creativity of an ad in terms of its artistic or aesthetic value and originality. They contend creative ads can break through the competitive clutter, grab the consumer's attention, and have some impact

What constitutes creativity in advertising is probably some where between the two extremes. Tb break through the clutter and make an impression on the target audience, an ad often must be unique and entertaining. Research has shown that a major determinant of whether a commercial will be successful in changing brand preferences is its "likeability" or the viewer's over all reaction. Television commercials and print ads that are well designed and executed and generate emotional responses can create positive feelings that are transferred to the product or service being advertised. Many creative people believe this type of advertising can come out only if they are given considerable latitude in developing advertising messages. But ads that are creative only for the sake of being creative, often fall to communicate a relevant or meaningful message that will lead consumers to purchase a product or service.

Every one involved in planning and developing an advertising campaign must understand the importance of balancing the 'it's not creative unless it sells' perspective with the novelty/uniqueness and impact position. Marketing and product managers or account executives must recognise that imposing to many sales - and marketing oriented communication objective on the creative team can result in mediocre advertising which is often ineffective in today's competitive, cluttered media environment. At the same time, the creative specialists must recognise that the goal of advertising is to assist in selling the product or service and good advertising must communicate in manner that helps the client achieve this goal.

Advertising creativity is the ability to generate fresh, unique, and appropriate ideas that can be used as solutions to communication problems. To be appropriate and effective, a creative idea must be relevant to the target audience. Many ad agencies recognise the importance of developing advertising that is creative and different yet communicates relevant information to the target audience. The agency views a creative advertising message as one built around a creative core or power idea and using excellent design and execution to communicate information that interests the target audience.

Advertising creativity is not the exclusive domain of those who work on the creative side of advertising. The nature of business requires creative thinking from every one involved in the promotional planning process. Individuals in the agency, such as account executives, media planners, researchers and attorneys, as well as those on the client side, such as marketing and brand managers must all seek creative solutions to problems encountered in planning, developing and executing an advertising campaign.

Where of creative writers such as poets or novelists are concerned, their purpose is self-expression-enjoying pure freedom of imagination. Advertising creativity is disciplined and purposeful to meet certain business demands and lies probably somewhere between the two extremes. To break through the advertising clutter and make an impression on the target audience, an ad must have the quality of being unique and entertaining. Well-designed and executed print ads or TV commercials evoke emotional responses and can create positive feelings and images. These feelings and images often get transferred to the advertised product or service. Many creative people are of the opinion that this type of advertising is possible only if they are given considerable latitude in creating advertising messages. But advertising creativity for the sake of being only creative often fails to deliver a meaningful, relevant and persuasive message that will lead the consumers to purchase the advertised product or service.

Creative use of visuals helps capture attention

Advertising creativity is the ability to come up with fresh, perhaps unconventional, unique, appropriate and effective ideas that can be used as solutions to an advertiser's communications problems. A creative idea can be appropriate and effective only when it is relevant to the target audience's needs, wants, or aspirations. Probably this is the reason why some ads are successful in winning awards for creativity but fail to help the client in accomplishing the desired goal, as they are not relevant to the target audience. The creative specialists must recognise that the purpose of adverting is to assist in selling the product or service and good advertising must communicate in a manner that helps the client achieve this goal. The agency, D'Arcy, Masius Benton & Bowles have developed nine principles to guide its creative efforts. The agency calls them DMB &B's universal advertising standards. The nine principles are :

1. Does this advertising position the product simply and with unmistakable clarity?

The target audience for the advertised product or service must be able to see and sense in a flash what the product is for, whom it is for, and why they should be interested in it. Creating this clear vision of how the product or service fits into their lives is the first job of advertising. Without a simple, clear, focused positioning, no creative work can begin.

2. Does this advertising bolt the brand to a clinching benefit?

Our advertising should be built on the most compelling and persuasive consumer benefit-not some unique-but-insignificant peripheral feature. Before you worry about how to say it, you must be sure you are saying the right thing. If you don't know what the most compelling benefit is, you have got to find out before you do anything.

3. Does the advertising contain a 'power idea'?

The power idea is the vehicle that transforms the strategy into a dynamic, creative communications concept. It is the core creative idea that sets the stage for brilliant executions to come. The ideal power idea should.

- Be describable in a simple word, phrase, or sentence without reference to any final execution
- Be likely to attract the prospect's attention
- Revolve around the clinching benefit
- Allow you to brand the advertising
- Make it easy for the prospect to vividly experience our client's product or service.

4. Does this advertising design in brand personality?

The great brands tend to have something in common: the extra edge of having a brand personality. This is something beyond merely identifying what the brand does for the consumer; all brands do something. A brand can be whatever its designers want it to be - and it can be so from day one.

5. Is the advertising unexpected?

Why should our clients pay good money to wind up with advertising that looks and sounds like everybody else's in the category? They shouldn't. We must dare to be different, because sameness is suicide. We can't be outstanding unless we first stand out. The thing is not to emulate the competition but to annihilate them.

6. Is the advertising single-minded?

If you have determined the right thing to say and have created a way to say it uncommonly well, why waste time saying anything else? If we want people to remember one big thing from a given piece of advertising, let's not make it more difficult than it already is in an over-communicated world. The advertising should be all about that one big thing.

7. Does this advertising reward the prospect?

Lets give our audience something that makes it easy - even, pleasurable - for our message to penetrate: a tear, a smile, a laugh. An emotional stimulus is that special something that mate them want to see the advertising again and again.

8. Is the advertising visually arresting?

Great advertising you remember - and can play back in your mind - is unusual to look at: compelling a nourishing feast for the eyes. If you need a reason to strive for arresting work, go on further than Webster: "Catching or holding the attention, thought, or feelings; Gripping, Striking, Interesting."

9. Does this advertising exhibit painstaking craftsmanship?

You want writing that is really written. 'Visuals' that are designed but 'Music' that is composed. Lighting casting, wardrobe, direction - all the components of the art of advertising are every as important as the science of it. It is a sin to nickel-and a great advertising idea to death. Why settle for good, when there's great? We should go for the absolute best in concept, design and execution. This is our craft - the work should sparkle.

"Our creative standards are not a gimmick," Steve emphasizes. "They're not even revolutionary. Instead they are an explicit articulation of a fundamental refocusing on our company's only reason for being. DMB & B's universal advertising standards are the operating link between our vision today and its coming reality."

Styles of Thinking

Max Weber, the German sociologist, determined that people think in two ways: an objective, rational, fact-based manner and a qualitative, value-based manner. We use a fact-based style of thinking while preparing for a test but when we buy a dress, we call on taste, intuition and knowledge to make a qualitative value judgement of the styling, colour, looks and the price.

In the 1980s, social scientists Allen Harrison and Robert Bramson defined five categories of thinking: the synthesis, the idealist, the pragmatist, the analyst and the realist. They concluded that the analyst and realist fit Weber's fact-based thinking type and the synthesis and idealist fit his value-based thinking type.

Roger Von Oech defined this division of two types as hard thinking and soft thinking. Hard thinking refers to concepts like logic, reason, precision, consistency, work, reality, analysis and specificity. Soft thinking refers to less tangible concepts such as, metaphor, dream, humour, ambiguity, play, fantasy and hunch. On the hard thinking side, things either are right or wrong, black or white. On the soft thinking side, there may be many right answers and many shades of grey between black and white.

Alessandra, Cathcart and Wexler developed a model featuring four types of personalities and relationship behaviours based on assertiveness and responsiveness factors. They are called the relater, the socialiser, the director, and the thinker. The relater and the socialiser exhibit value-based traits and the director and the thinker display fact-based traits.

People who predominantly use fact-based thinking style tend to sort out concepts into components and to analyse situations to separate out one best solution. They can be creative but generally tend to think in a linear manner and prefer hard data that they can analyse and control. They feel uncomfortable with ambiguous situations like logic, structure and efficiency. In sharp contrast, people whose preferred thinking style is value-based, make decisions based on intuition, values and ethical judgments. They are more adept to accepting and embracing change, paradox and conflict. Value-based thinking style fundamentally takes advantage of blending or merging and these people attempt to integrate the divergent ideas in a manner that lets everybody win. They are bright at using their imagination to generate new ideas and blending existing concepts to create something novel.

Creative people are more inclined to use value-based thinking and prefer ads that are intuitive, soft, subtle and metaphorical. As long as this is in tune with the client's preference, it is fine.

Those clients, who prefer fact-based thinking style, generally seek ad agencies that are known to produce practical, simple, straightforward layouts with rational appeals and lots of hard data. Value-based ads might even make such clients uncomfortable.

In some market segments, such as high-tech products, or fashion and beauty products, the customers may tend to use one style of thinking over another. The nature of the product and the personality profile of the typical prospect could influence the style of thinking. The best art directors and copywriters use both styles at the right place. For instance, in the creative work they use their imagination, intuition, etc., (value-based thinking) to accomplish the task and generate a number of different ideas. But to choose the most suitable alternative and get the job done, they probably use fact-based style of thinking.

THE CREATIVE INDIVIDUAL

In past years a number of studies have tried to isolate the distinguishing characteristics of highly creative and original people. Although the studies are not directly comparable or additive, there are some generalisations that seem to be emerging:

1. Highly creative people are more likely than others to view authority as conventional rather than absolute; to make fewer black and white distinctions; to have a less domatic and more relatilistics view of life; to show more independence of judgment and less conventionality and confirmity, both intellectual and social; to be more willing to entertain, and sometimes express, their own "irrational" impulses; to place a greater value humour and, in fact to have a better sense of humour; in short to be some what freer and less rigidly controlled.
2. Creativity is not simply a matter of intelligence. A high IQ is necessary for creativity in some fields like nuclear physics, not necessary in others like graphic arts, and is never sufficient. Highly intelligent subjects are found in low creativity groups in virtually every study.
3. In general, highly creative work is produced relatively early in the artistic, scientific or scholarly career typically from a person in his thirties.
4. Creative people may have a particular cognitive style. Cognitive style refers to recurrent pattern

in the way a person approaches problems or processes information, Some patterns of thinking promote creativity-for example, the problem solving approach to tasks. Creative people are more reluctant to judge what ever they encounter, while less creative people seem prone to evaluate quickly and turn to other matters. Creative people have a tendency to think in terms of opposites or contraries and unite them in inventive ways.

5. Highly creative people show a preference for, and interest in, complexity and novelty. They have intrinsic interest in situations that require some resolution, rather than those that are cut and dried.
6. The highly creative person has more ability to associate research data into problem - solving advertising communication.
7. The highly creative person suffers less from functional fixedness and is more flexible. This characteristic has led to the development of creative tests composed of questions intended to measure flexibility such as "How many uses can you find for a bicycle tyre".

Planning Creative Strategy

The work of creative people in advertising business is challenging. They must take all the inputs such as research findings, creative briefs, strategy statements and the communications objectives to convert them into a suitable advertising message to effectively communicate the central theme of the ad campaign. The ad message must be put into a form that will get the audience interested and make the ad memorable.

Advertising situations in each case are different. Each individual advertisement or an ad campaign needs a totally different creative approach. Over the years, numerous approaches and guidelines have been developed for creating effective advertising, but there is no magic formula in this trade. In his book, Advertising Pure and Simple, copywriter Hank Sneiden writes:

"Rules lead to dull stereotyped advertising, and they stifle creativity, inspiration initiative, and progress. The only hard and fast rule that I know of in advertising is that there are no rules. No formulas. No right way. Given the same problem, a dozen creative talents would solve it a dozen different ways. If there were a sure-fire formula for successful advertising, everyone would use it. Then there would be no need for creative people. We would simply programme robots to create our ads and commercials and they'd sell loads of product - to other robots."

A number of creative people believe in safety and follow proven approaches to creating ads. As mentioned earlier, because of their thinking style, many clients feel uneasy with advertising that is strikingly different. Many creative people are of the opinion that it is important for clients to take some risks if they really desire outstanding advertising that captures attention and is remembered. According to Jeff Jensen, Weiden & Kennedy agency's (it has worked for Microsoft and Nike) founders believe that a key factor to their success has been a firm belief in taking risks when most agencies and their clients have become more conservative in their approach to advertising. This agency gives more importance to creative work than the client-agency relationship. There are instances when this agency has terminated relationships with large clients when they interfered too much with the creative process.

Of course, all companies and advertising agencies do not agree that advertising has to be risky to be effective. Many marketing executives feel that they invest huge amounts of money in advertising to sell the product and not to finance the whims and fancies of their advertising agency's creative staff. They feel more at ease with advertising that simply communicates the features and benefits of a product or service, and gives the consumer a reason to buy.

The most important product ingredient that an agency offers is creativity and this is the major component on which most agencies thrive. For this reason, the agencies must create an environment that encourages creative thinking and creative advertising. Though the client has the final authority to accept or reject the advertising, clients must appreciate the differences between the perspectives of the creative specialists and the marketing personnel. The opinions of creative specialists must be accorded due consideration while evaluating the ideas and content.

The Creative Process

Creativity in advertising does not exist in a vacuum. Productive originality and imagination are useful in all areas, even those that relate to such typically managerial tasks as the planning and organisation of advertising departments, and the establishment of controls. In a recent survey of top managers in large corporation the lacks of innovative thinking in promotion was identified as a major concern. Specifically there appeared to be general unwillingness to take necessary risks, as well as inability to define new methods for promoting products to customers in the face of major increase in the cost of media advertising and personal selling.

The creative process is not a scientific process; rather it evolves from insight or inspiration. Nonetheless creativity in advertising must not only produce unique and interesting results, it must also produce useful solutions to real problems. Baker describes the concept of creativity as a pyramid divided into three parts. Advertising creativity frequently takes off from a base of a systematic accumulation of facts and analysis. The second phase represents processing, or analysis, and the third part — the idea — is the culmination of creative efforts.

English sociologist Graham Walls outlined the four steps in creative process as follows (Fig. 16.1):

STEP-I

Preparation : Gathering background information needed to solve the problem through research and study.

STEP-II

Incubation : Getting away and letting ideas develop.

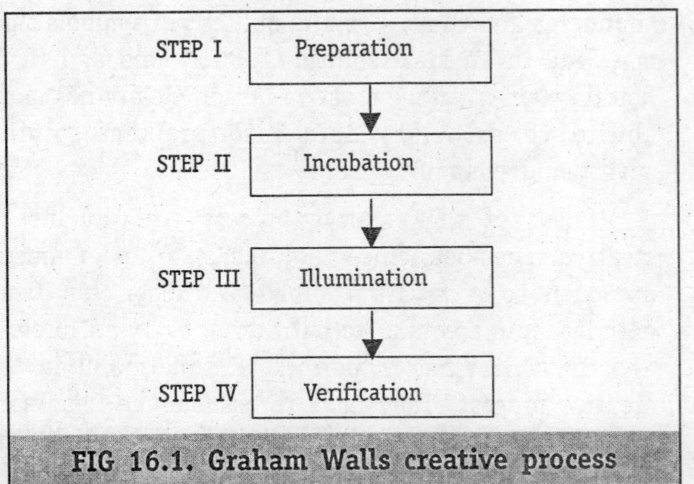

FIG 16.1. Graham Walls creative process

STEP-III

Illumination : Seeing the light or solution.

STEP-IV

Verification : Refining and polishing the idea and seeing if it is an appropriate solution.

James Web Young, a former Vice President at J. Walter Thompson, developed one of the most popular approaches to creativity in advertising. He developed a five-step model of the creative process and said "The production of ideas is just as definite a process as the production of Fords; the production of ideas, too, runs an assembly line; in this production the mind follows an operative technique which can be learned and controlled; and that its effective use is just as much a matter of practice in the technique as in the effective use of any tool."

One of the most popular approaches to creativity in advertising was developed by James Webb Young, a former creative vice president at the J. Walter Thompson agency. Young said that "the production of ideas in just as definite a process as the production of Fords; that the production of ideas, too, runs an assembly line; that in this production the mind follows an operative technique which can be learned and controlled; and that its effective use is just as much as a matter of practice, in the technique as in the effective use of any tool". Young's model of the creative process contain five steps (Fig. 16.2):

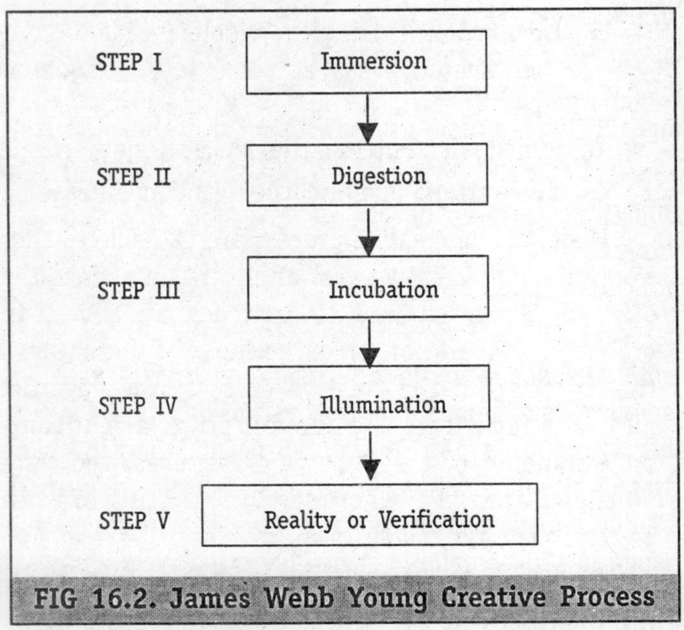

FIG 16.2. James Webb Young Creative Process

STEP-I

Immersion : Gathering raw material and information through background research and immersing yourself in the problem.

STEP-II

Digestion : Taking information, working it over, and wrestling with it in the mind.

STEP-III

Incubation : Putting the problems out of your conscious mind and turning the information over to subconscious to do the work.

STEP-IV

Illumination : The birth of an idea-The "Eureka! I have it" phenomenon.

STEP-V

Reality or verification : Studying the idea to see if it still looks good or solves the problem, then shaping the idea to practical usefulness.

According to Alex F. Osborn, former head of BBDO agency, who established the Creative Education Foundation, the creative process involves the following seven steps:

1. **Orientation:** Pointing out the problem
2. **Preparation:** Gathering pertinent data
3. **Analysis:** Breaking down the relevant material
4. **Ideation:** Piling up alternative ideas
5. **Incubation:** Putting the problem aside to invite spontaneous ideas at some later, unguarded time.
6. **Synthesis:** Putting the pieces together, and
7. **Evaluation:** Judging the resulting ideas.

Model of the creative process are valuable to those working in the creative area of advertising, since they offer an organised way to approach an advertising problem. Preparation or gathering of information is the first step in the creative process. The advertiser and agency start by developing a thorough understanding of the product or services, the target market, and the competition. Attention and promotional programme.

These models do not say much about how this information will be synthesized and used by the creative specialist because this part of the process is unique to the individual. In many ways, it is what sets apart the great creative minds and strategists in advertising.

Most ads are the result of much sweat, tears and persistence. Many advertising professionals are of the opinion that creativity in advertising can best be viewed as a process and that creative success is mostly achieved by following an organised approach. There is "though" no infallible formula that guarantees the creation of effective advertising. As mentioned earlier, many advertising professionals reject attempts to standardise creativity or develop any rules.

No one really knows why one person can consistently create successful ads and why the other person meets repeated failures. A creative individual is most likely to be one—

- Who can produce a large number of ideas quickly (conceptual fluency)
- Is original
- Is capable of separating source from content in evaluating information
- Suspends judgement and avoids early commitment
- Is inclined to be less authoritative
- Accepts personal impulses
- Is capable of judging independently and
- Possesses a rich, bizarre fantasy life.

Hanley Norins is of the opinion that there is only one distinctive trait in a highly creative person-the ability to associate. Given a particular problem, this individual can immediately begin to associate "hundreds and thousands and millions of symbols that may lead to an ideal solution." L. N. Reid and H. J. Rotfeld claim that the creative person clearly has more ability to associate data into problem solving advertising communication.

Models of the creative process are valuable to creative specialists since they facilitate an organised approach to advertising problems. Roger von Oech describes four essential activities that every art director and copywriter has to perform at some point in the creative process. They have to assume the imaginary roles of the explorer, the artist, the judge, and the warrior[7].

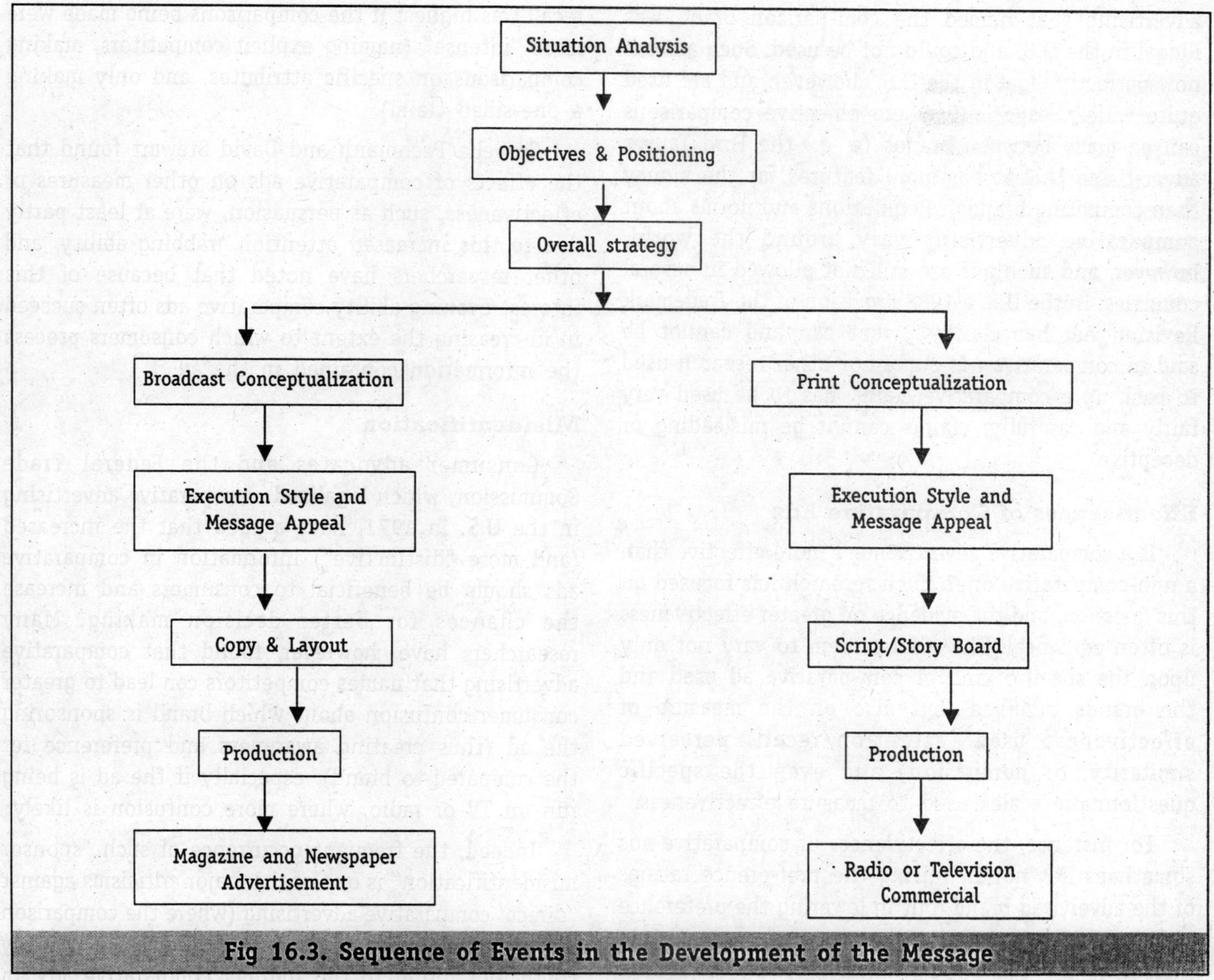

Fig 16.3. Sequence of Events in the Development of the Message

- The explorer gathers new information and looks for any unusual patterns.
- The artist considers many different approaches to come up with an original idea.
- The judge evaluates the results of these approaches and selects the most practical one.
- The warrior overcomes hurdles and idea killers to bring a creative concept to reality.

RATIONAL CREATIVE APPROACHES

Comparative Advertising

Comparative advertising is a form of advertising in which two or more named or recognizable brands of the same product class are compared and the comparison is made in terms of one or more product attributes.' The comparisons can be implicit (brands implied but not named), or explicit (brands named); the comparisons can be verbal or visual; and the claims can be of complete superiority, of superiority on some attributes but not on others, or of parity; and the advertised brand can have a market share smaller than, roughly equal to, or greater than the comparison brand. Obviously, not all types of comparative ads are equally effective, and we will discuss below what is currently known about which types work best.

Different studies conducted in recent years have found that comparative ads often form about 20 to 30 percent of all the ads being run. It is interesting to note, however, that prior to about 1970, comparative advertising that named the com-parison brand was illegal in the U.S. and could not be used. Such ads are now perfectly legal in the U.S., however, and are used quite widely, especially where objective comparisons can be made between brands (e. g., the Ford Taurus adver-tising that it has more features for the money than competing brands). Regulations and norms about comparative advertising vary around the world, however, and such ads are still not allowed in several countries. In the U.S. a 1988 provision of the Trademark Revision Act has clarified what can and cannot be said in comparative ads-survey or other research used to back up a comparative claim. has to be used very fairly and carefully; claims cannot be misleading or deceptive.

Effectiveness of Comparative Ads

Is a comparative advertisement more effective than a non-comparative one? Much research has focused on this question, and the evidence on greater effectiveness is often equivocal. The results seem to vary not only upon the specific kind of com-parative ad used and the brands involved, but also on the measure of effectiveness used (attention/recall, perceived similarity, or persuasion) and even the specific questionnaire scales used to measure effectiveness.

For instance, the effectiveness of comparative ads sometimes lies not in raising the pref-erence ratings of the advertised brand, but in lowering the preference ratings of the comparison brands, or even in simply increasing the perceived similarity of the advertised and comparison brands without affecting any preference measures at all.' It is thus important, in copy testing or tracking the effectiveness of comparative ads, to measure beliefs and preferences not only toward the advertised brand but also toward competition, as well as measure perceived similarities among these brands.

If attention and recall are used as the measures of ad effectiveness, various studies have shown that comparative ads do usually get more attention and higher recall than non-comparative ads. Pontiac used comparative advertising for its Grand Am in 1992, comparing it to the Toyota Camry and Honda Accord, because they found focus groups reacted more strongly to comparisons with specific com-petitors than to unnamed imports. Naveen Donthu found the gain in recall was highest if the comparisons being made were more "intense" (naming explicit competitors, making comparisons on specific attributes, and only making a one-sided claim).

Cornelia Pechmann and David Stewart found that the effects of comparative ads on other measures of effectiveness, such as persuasion, were at least partly due to this increased attention-grabbing ability, and other researchers have noted that because of this interest-evoking ability comparative ads often succeed in in-creasing the extent to which consumers process the information contained in the ad.

Misidentification

Consumer advocates and the Federal Trade Commission, which legalized com-parative advertising in the U.S. in 1971, have argued that the increased (and more "distinctive") information in comparative ads should be beneficial to consumers and increase the chances for better decision making. Many researchers have, how-ever, found that comparative advertising that names competitors can lead to greater consumer confusion about which brand is sponsoring the ad (thus creating awareness and preference for the compared-to brand), especially if the ad is being run on TV or radio, where more confusion is likely.

Indeed, the frequent occurrence of such "sponsor misidentification" is one of the major criticisms against "direct" comparative advertising (where the comparison brand is explicitly named), it is one reason why many companies prefer to run indirect comparative ads, in which they do not name comparison brands directly but imply them by showing packaging colors or shapes (such as Folgers coffee not naming Maxwell House but showing the other brand packaged in the latter's blue can).

Leaders versus Followers

Interestingly, research supports the logic that a direct comparative ad from a small-share market follower is least likely to lead to higher awareness for the compared-to market leader (because the market leader already has high awareness), whereas a market-leading high-share brand has the most to lose from a direct comparative ad (by creating "free" awareness for the compared-to smaller brand). This leads to the conclusion that while low-share brands ought to use direct comparative ads, market leaders perhaps ought to use non-comparative or indirectly comparative ads (those that don't name competitors). This suggests that while VISA credit cards might gain by comparing itself to American Express (which has more prestige), American Express might not gain by comparing itself in its ads with VISA. (Both companies ran such comparative ads, comparing themselves with each other, in 1993 and 1994.)

Smaller-share market follower brands also stand to gain more from direct comparative ads in another way; such ads have the effect of getting consumers to put both the advertised and the comparison brand in the same "consideration set," by increasing the degree to which they are perceived as similar to each other. Gerald Corn and Charles Weinberg point out that a leading brand might therefore not want to engage in comparative advertising, whereas a challenger brand might gain from associating itself with the leader. Their study found that comparative advertising was much more effective than non-comparative advertising in increasing the perceived similarity of the challenger and leader brands, particularly when the leading brand was explicitly named in the ad. Research by Michael Johnson and David Home also shows that comparative ads promote the consumer perception that the brands being compared are similar to each other.

These studies thus lend support to the idea that comparative advertising by new brands or challenger brands makes sense as an excellent positioning tool. For example, the Subaru ad in which Subaru claims a safety record as good as Volvo's, will clearly help to position Subaru as a "safety car' in the same league as Volvo. By the same token, market leaders might be better off not comparing themselves to market followers, for fear of giving them legitimacy. As one senior marketing executive puts it, "Comparative ads are good when you're new, but when you're the standard, it just gives a lot of free publicity to your competitors."

This similarity-increasing effect, however, seems to depend on the nature of the attributes used: one study suggests that direct comparative ads increase the similarity of the advertised and compared-to brand on attributes not featured in the ad. However, they simultaneously differentiate the brands by lowering consumer perceptions of the compared-to brand on the specific attribute used in the comparison.

Effects on Persuasion

Thus far, we have talked about how a comparative ad might help the advertised brand by gaining it "extra" attention and by bringing it perceptually "closer" to the comparison brand. Do these gains necessarily also translate into increased preference for the advertised brand? Not always. Gorn and Weinberg, whose study was cited earlier, found that while while a comparative did bridge the perceived "distance"

MCI Math, Part II

40% = 13%

40% = The discount on calls to MCI customers
In your friends & Family II calling circle

13% =The average discount that shows up on your
MCI friends & Family II Basic bill

Friends & Family II. Big claims. Big disappointments.

Friends & Family II advertises 40% off on calls to other MCI customers in your calling circle But on calls to non-MCI customers in your circle, the savings is only 20%. And on calls to numbers outside your calling circle-that's any number you don't give them in advance-the savings is a nice round 0%.

Then there's the small matter of the $36 a year in monthly fees. In the end, the total Friends & Family If discount is a far ay from the 40% you might expect. It's more like 13%.* No wonder 4 out of 5 Friends & Family II Basic customers will save more with...

❖ Discount off MCI basic rates AT&Ts and MCT's basic rates are about the same

Fig. 16.4. AT&Ts Ad Comparing itself to MCI

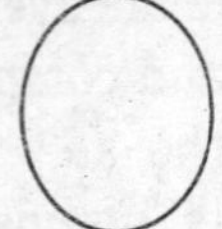

Fig. 16.5.

between the "leader" and the "challenger" brand, it did not significantly raise the attitude toward the advertised brand. Many other studies have also failed to find such attitude-enhancing effects.

These failures could be due, in part, to the fact that these studies often failed to measure (and could not therefore find) possible decreases in consumers' attitudes toward the comparison brand. It has also been shown, however, that comparative ads often fail to sway attitudes and preferences because, while people may indeed notice them more, they nonetheless may consider a comparative ad offen sive, less credible, and less informative (especially if they happen to like the brand being shown in a negative light). In fact, there is some evidence that consumers' liking for comparative ads goes up with the "intensity" of the comparative ad, but only up to a point-ads that are "too intense" appear to be disliked. Thus, while AT&T's ad comparing itself to MCI might rate high in persuasion because of its use of specific, persuasive statistics, MCPs response (which was more vitriolic) might to many appear too intense and therefore less persuasive.

Many studies have shown that comparative ads often evoke such an unfa-vorable attitudinal reaction because they stimulate more counter arguing by consumers, often because they are perceived as less truthful. Obviously, therefore, comparative ads ought to be designed in ways that try to reduce such counter arguing. Message content that tries to stay as factual and "objective" as possible can reduce such counter argumentation. It helps to include a credible source, and to get the target audience involved in the ad, so they are motivated to actually make the invited comparison, rather than dismissing it out of hand. It also helps to make the comparison in as "positive" a manner as possible: rather than derogate the comparison brand, it is better to claim superiority over the comparison brand in a non derogatory manner.

Two-Sided versus One-Sided Comparative Ads

William Swinyard, Michael Edgar and Stephen Goodwin, and others have also ar-gued that there is more counterarguing if the message is one-sided instead of two-sided. (A message is one-sided if it presents only positive arguments or attributes and two-sided if a few qualifications, usually about relatively minor attributes, are presented.) Two-sided ads are seen as more credible, because they admit that the advertised brands have some shortcomings.

However, not all two-sided ads beat one-sided ads in credibility: research has shown that two-sided ads are especially credible when the attribute on which the weakness is admitted is (a) relatively unimportant, but not trivial, to consumers; (b) perceived to be negatively correlated with the attribute on which superiority is claimed (e.g., "we are more expensive (weakness), but only because we give you higher quality"); (c) one that would not otherwise be known to consumers prior to purchase, so that the advertiser gains some "brownie points" for honesty.

Other research has also shown the general superiority of two-sided appeals, especially with more educated audiences, and with those consumers initially opposed to the brand making the claims, and on attitudes rather than purchase intentions. These results suggest that comparative ads are more likely to be persuasive in changing brand attitudes if they are two-sided rather than one-sided.

Open-Ended versus Close-Ended Comparisons

Another relevant issue is whether conclusions and arguments should be spelled out explicitly in a comparative advertisement or whether the receiver should be left to draw his or her own conclusions about the superiority of the brand spon-soring the comparison. It is often advantageous to leave something out of a message: the closure principle comes in here. Leaving something out can stimulate curiosity and motivation to seek additional information about the brand and lead to a consumer-generated belief that is relatively more powerful than a belief created by an explicit statement in the ad. This would argue for not making explicit claims of the sponsoring brand's superiority.

However, there is some risk in assuming that a receiver will "draw his own conclusions." Research suggests that conclusions should be stated explicitly when there is a significant chance that the audience will not be motivated or unable to draw their own conclusions, or when there are real risks of having them draw the wrong conclusions. Alan Sawyer and Daniel Howard found that if the audience is involved in the message, and if the message is one where a conclusion can be eas-ily drawn, an open-ended message (where no explicit conclusion was drawn) led to greater brand attitudes, intentions, and choice than a close-ended message (there was no difference for an uninvolved audience).

Consistent with this finding, Mita Sujan and Christine Dekleva have found that comparative ads gain in relative effectiveness when aimed at more expert consumers and when they make comparisons with specific, well-known brands (rather than types of brands), because the comparative ad can be interpreted more unambiguously under these conditions.

Inoculative Advertising: Building Resistant Attitudes

Can a person be made to resist attempts by competitors or outside influences to change his or her attitudes? How can AT&T prevent residential telephone service consumers from being swayed by a subsequent MCI marketing effort-or *vice versa*?

A great deal of advertising activity is associated with this goal of "defensive" marketing. Given that we have developed favorable patronage-have a good share of market, for example-how can it be sustained? In attitude theory terms, how can we induce those currently loyal to our brand to remain loyal?

A consumer can be made more resistant to competitive appeals either by at-tempting to make a brand offering more attractive, or by attempting to train the consumer to withstand the persuasive efforts of competitors. From the first view-point, for example, one strategy would be to anchor beliefs about the brand to other beliefs that the consumer values highly. The brand might be shown to be significant in maintaining one's self-esteem or in otherwise enhancing the ego in various ways.

The alternative, of attempting to train a consumer to withstand competitive attacks, has been the subject of some empirical work in marketing. The diffusion of advertising messages can be thought of as similar to the diffusion of germs in the spread of a disease through a population. If individuals are given weakened doses of the germs, they can build defenses to withstand the more potent ones, and thus be made resistant to the disease when exposed to it. The medical or biological analogy is, of course, the notion of inoculating an individual with a weakened dosage, and for this reason it has been called the inoculation approach.

In the advertising context, it has been demonstrated that preexposure to weakened forms of counterargument (arguments counter to the position or object being defended) is more effective in building up resistance to strong subsequent attacks than is a simple repetition of supportive arguments. Other research has also shown that a refutational appeal provides a greater resistance to attack than a standard supportive appeal

Back to the telephone service example: A 1990 ad campaign utilizing this in-oculation approach was that of AT&T's, warning consumers not to switch to a rival long-distance telephone service on the basis of a telemarketing call promising big savings in monthly phone bills. One newspaper ad said: "Another long distance company might be calling soon. They'll tell how you can save big over AT&T. With quality better than AT&T. How you have nothing to lose by switching now. But you do. If you don't get their pitch in writing. Because there are lots of things they may not tell you.....Don't get taken in by big claims. Get the facts."

MCl, in turn, tried its own form of inoculation. In 1993. consumers signing on with MCI were sent a direct-mail warning that "AT&T may call and attempt to switch you from MCI. If they do, we hope you ask AT&T these tough questions .. ."followed by five questions'. The fifth question said, for example: "Why does AT&T declare that MCI's savings are only "a penny per minute"-when those pennies multiplied by many minutes can really add up? The fact is, month after month, MCI adds up to real savings." Note here how the MCI customer is being inoculated to AT&T's claim that MCI's savings are only "a penny per minute."

Refutational Advertising

Another term closely related to inoculation is refutation. It refers to the process of explicitly or implicitly stating competitive appeals (or consumer beliefs) and then refuting them, instead of dealing exclusively with brand benefits (supportive advertising). Hertz and Avis advertising are examples of both refutational and supportive advertising. For many years, Hertz used a supportive approach, emphasizing the many benefits of renting a Hertz car. Avis, on the other hand, refuted the implicit claim that "No. 1 equals the best" by suggesting that "No. 2 tries harder."

Another example of a refutational automotive ad is the one for Nissan, in which Nissan tries to refute the perception that Honda and Toyota are the better-quality Japanese imports. In the headache-remedy market, Bayer re-futes the claim that various products are stronger or better than aspirin as follows: "Does buffering it, squaring it, squeezing it, fizzing it, flavouring it, flattening it, gumming it or-adding to it improve aspirin?"

Ray cites three reasons why refutational messages appear to work:

1. They are more stimulating than supportive messages. They underline conflict and get people concerned about an area. This motivating factor alone can be quite effective, since refutational defenses can work even if they deal with claims other than those that appear in subsequent attacks.
2. They refute counterclaims and thus make the competitive attacks appear less credible when they appear. This refutation is probably quite satisfying, statements of counterclaims can arouse dissonance or imbalance. The refutation can restore balance.
3. Refutational messages do contain some supportive information, even though less than supportive messages.

Other research by Michael Kamins and Henry Assael has also shown that refutational ads lead consumers to generate more support-arguments and fewer source derogations than ads with only supportive information. One disadvantage of refutational messages is that they provide a viewer with information about a competitor's product and thus might enhance rather than defend against competitive alternatives. It is, nevertheless, a preferred approach to market situations in which the goal of an advertiser is to build resistance to attitude change and defend against competitive attack.

As mentioned earlier, a refutational approach can be useful not only against a competitive claim but also against a prior consumer belief that is negative. The famous ad for Life cereal that featured the little boy called Mikey is an example of refutational advertising. Here, the challenge was to convince mothers that their kids would actually like Life cereal, despite the fact that it was "healthy" cereal.

The TV spot showed two other boys watch Mikey eat Life cereal, betting that he wouldn't like it and then watching with amazement when he ate it up.

As another application, if a certain segment of American consumers believe that Japanese cars are superior in quality, an ad by an American auto manufacturer aimed at this segment might be more successful in credibly communicating the actually high quality of American cars by first acknowledging this belief about poor quality and then refuting it with evidence (instead of making no reference to that prior belief about lower quality).

A refutational ad in such a situation might gain even more credibility if it were two sided-conceding that quality in prior years was, in fact, poor but then going on to argue that it has since improved substantially. Thus, continuing with the auto example above, General Motors ran a campaign in 1992 headlined "If you've been away from American cars and trucks for a while ... the people of General Motors have something to show you," following up with quotes from favorable reviews about its new models, and concluding "... (in the last six years) 96 percent of our cars and 60 percent of our trucks have been redesigned..." A 1993 General Motors campaign in California featured an automotive scrap-yard operator describing how he made a good living over the years scrapping GM vehicles, but then noting that GM's quality now seems to be improving, so that "there's a trend here. It's not good for my business!"

Another example of this creative approach is an ad run by USAir in August 1990 in The Wall Street Journal, which highlighted the on-time arrival record of its flights. The ad spanned two bottom half-pages, starting with the headline "It was the worst of times." and ending with "It was the best of times." Under the first head-line was a panel of on-time performance statistics from January 1990, showing US-Air in sixth place among major airlines. Four other monthly panels followed, showing USAir in second place, followed by the last panel for June 1990 showing that USAir was now number 1. The headline at the bottom of the second page said it all: "USAir now leads the six largest U.S. airlines in on-time arrivals. My, how times have changed."

EMOTIONAL CREATIVE APPROACHES

The creative approaches discussed thus far are "rational" in the sense that they rely for their persuasive power on arguments, or reasons, about brand attributes. For instance, a comparative approach attempts to show, based on reasons, why the sponsoring brand is superior to competition. There is, of course, the whole category of creative approaches that rely on emotions or feelings for their effectiveness, such as the attempted evocation of warmth and affection, or surgency and excitement, or the use of humour, or of fear.

Emotion-evoking creative ap-proaches are most suitable when the product category is one where, typically, consumers buy the product because of a "feeling" benefit-either the low-involvement "small pleasures" of candy or soda pop or the highly involving feelings associated with fragrances, sports cars, and jewellery. Emotion-evoking creative approaches do not appear to be very successful in "high-involvement, thinking" situations.

USING AN ENDORSER

Advertisers often use endorsers for their products or services-and this makes many endorsers very rich. Basketball star Michael Jordan reportedly earned $36 million per year in endorsement fees when he retired in 1993 ($18 million from Nike, which created its Air Jordan line of basketball shoes around him; $3 million from McDonald's, which created a McJordan hamburger named after him; $2 mil-lion from Gatorade, which urged consumers to drink Gatorade to "Be Like Mike;" $3 to $4 million from Sara Lee/Hanes, $2 to $3 million from Wheaties, and others).

Other Sports stars, including top golfers like Arnold Palmer, Jack Nicklaus, and Greg Norman, football quarterbacks like Joe Montana, ice hockey star Wayne Gretzky, and tennis champ Andre Agassi also earn millions of dollars every year from advertising endorsements. Star entertainers get rich too: Michael Jackson is reported to have received $5.5 million in 1984 and Madonna $5.0 million in 1989 for appearing in Pepsi's commercials.[32] The question therefore arises: what did these advertisers get in return? When should endorsers be used, and how and when do they help a brand?

In brief, research and commonsense suggest three types of benefits. First, endorsers enhance advertising readership (or viewership or listenership) scores. Second, endorsers can induce positive attitude change toward a company and its products. In general, the more credible a source, the more persuasive that source is likely to be. Third, the personality characteristics of the endorser can get associated with a brand's imagery. These benefits are not automatic, however and obtaining them requires a careful consideration of a brand's marketing or advertising needs, and an endorser's characteristics.

There are two ways of thinking about an endorser's characteristics. The tra-ditional way is to think of an endorser is a "source" of the information in the ad, contributing to the acceptability of the content of (arguments in) the message because of the source's credibility or attractiveness. We shall say more about this way of thinking below. The second, more recent, way is to think of the endorser as possessing some symbolic properties, which are transferred from the endorser to the endorsed brand (through advertising) and then from the brand to the consumer (through the acts of purchasing and consuming or owning the brand).

According to this meaning transfer model popularized by McCracken, brands benefit from associations with endorsers because endorsers acquire or possess particular configurations of cultural meanings that cannot be found elsewhere. Thus, for instance, the symbolic cultural meanings linked to Michael Jackson and Madonna-presumably their anti-establishment, "bad" images-were what Pepsi wanted and obtained for itself through their endorsements, which then helped Pepsi attract the youths and teenagers who form the crucial part of the soft-drink market. Similarly, Coca-Cola hoped that ads featuring pop star George Michael might improve Coke's image as being "young" and "modern."

PRINCIPLES OF ADVERTISING STRATEGY

As all advertising process begin with an advertising strategy. Advertising strategy is the formulation of advertising message that communicate the benefit or problem solution characteristics of the product or service to the market. The message must be consumer oriented in meeting consumer needs or wants and must offer the desired consumer benefit, otherwise even a brilliant advertising strategy will not succeed. Hence, the advertising message must be the right one which when projected to the right audience at the right time, will bring the desired results. Following principles (guide lines) are to be kept in mind while formulating the advertising strategy :

(a) The consumer benefit must be directly related to the specific features of the product. This strategy would differentiate the product from the competitors. Then the consumer need or want associated with a particular brand reduces the competitor's edge.

(b) Right type of media should be chosen for the product /service advertising for the proper and effective communication.

(c) The benefit offered to the consumer must be wanted by the consumers. The product features offered must be what the consumer actually wants and not what the manufacturer thinks that the consumer wants.

(d) The advertising message must be clear that the product offered will solve a consumer problem and fulfill a consumer need or offer a consumer benefit. The benefit must be clearly communicated.

Gathering Information

The creative personnel review the creative brief, including the marketing and advertising plan. They make themselves thoroughly familiar with the market, the product, and the competition. They may also seek additional information from the account executives and from the client company's marketing, product, sales, or research departments to learn about the nature of the company, its products, its marketing history, its competitors and the competitor's advertising styles.

According to Sandra E. Moriarty, creative specialists can acquire background information in many ways. Some informal fact finding techniques can be[8]:

- Reading anything related to the product or market - books, trade publications, general interest articles, research reports, and the like.
- Asking everyone involved with the product for information - designers, engineers, salespeople and consumers.

- Listening to what people are talking about. Visits to stores, malls, restaurants and even the agency cafeteria can be informative. Listening to the client can be particularly valuable, since he or she often knows the product and its market the best.
- Using the product or service and becoming familiar with it. The more you use a product, the more you know and can say about it.
- Working in and learning about the client's business to better understand the people you are trying to reach.

It is important for creative personnel to get off the beaten path to look in new and uncommon places to discover new ideas and to identify new patterns. They must have a positive belief that good information is available and that they have the skills to find and use it in an effective manner. This requires opening up to the outside world by adopting an "insight outlook" to receive new knowledge. Ideas are everywhere. When one thinks about the colour red and looks around, it suddenly jumps out at the person looking for it. But if the person were not looking for it, she/he probably would not notice it.

The creative brief is so important because it helps define what the creative specialists are looking for and as the philosopher John Dewey said, "A problem well-stated is a problem half solved."

In an attempt to assist the creative people in the preparation, incubation and illumination stages, a number of agencies provide general and specific preplanning inputs which can include books, periodicals, trade publications, journals, pictures, newspaper and magazine articles on the product, the market, the competition and its advertisements. Product or service-specific inputs may include specific studies conducted on the product or service, target audience studies such as attitude surveys, positioning studies such as perceptual mapping and life-style research, focus group interviews, demographic and psychographics profiles of the product, service, or brand users.

In-depth interviews of prospects and consumers, or focus groups, can furnish the creative team with valuable insight at the early stages of the creative process. "Focus groups" are an important research technique whereby 10 to 12 consumers from the target market are invited to discuss a given topic. This method helps marketers to gain insight as to why consumers use a particular product or service, their criteria in choosing a particular brand, what they like or don't like about the products or services being discussed and any specific needs that they have which are not being fulfilled. The group may also be used to evaluate different advertising appeals or the advertising of competitors. Listening to a focus group helps art directors, copywriters and other creative specialists to develop a more focused sense of who the target audience is and what is it like and what they need to write and design in creating an effective ad message.

After all the collected information has been digested, "idea generation" is the next critical step in die creative process. It is important to generate a large number of ideas to have more alternatives to choose from.

One technique used for idea generation is termed "brainstorming" (developed by Alex F Osborn). A group of six to ten people get together to focus on a problem to generate new ideas. A brainstorming session is often a source of sudden inspirations. For this technique to worked couple of rules have to be followed. No idea is "wrong" and all criticism is prohibited. All ideas are written down for later review. The purpose is to record any inspiration that comes to mind. Psychologists term this "free association" as it allows each new idea an opportunity to stimulate another. The participants are encouraged to build on ideas that emerge. The atmosphere is positive and the objective is to have a large quantity of ideas.

Several techniques can be helpful in generating new ideas.

- **Adapt:** Ask yourself what other ideas the product or service suggests besides the obvious. Epson Ink cartridge ad says "No side effects."
- **Put to other uses:** Is there any new way to use it? Other uses if modified? Milkmaid to prepare sweets and desserts.
- **Modify:** Give a new twist. Change meanings; reduce size, change colour, motion, odour, form, shape, or any other changes. Apple computers introduced a new computer design and looks in its iMac models.

- **Imagine:** Let the imagination fly. What if animals stayed in hotels? What if people watch TV while asleep? What if human beings were to have a third eye?
- **Reverse:** Transpose positive and negative? Sometimes opposite of what is expected great impact and enhances recall. A wrinkle removing cream ad can boldly say, "Introduce your husband to a younger woman."
- **Connect:** Join two unrelated ideas or objects together. Combine appeals. Combine Nizoral Blue shampoo ad showed a man with hair shaved off from his head.
- **Eliminate:** Break the rules. Eliminate something. Don't do things the way they are 7Up became the "Uncola" and an alternative to all colas.
- **Creative strategy development:** Depending on the advertising objectives, the creative aims at what must be communicated to the target audience and serves as a guide to developing all the messages to be used in an ad campaign. The creative aspect takes into account target audience; the basic problem, issue, or the opportunity that the advertising must address the big idea or the key selling proposition the ad must communicate; and other importa information that needs to be part of the co After determining these factors, the creativ strategy statement should describe the ad appeal and execution style to be used.
- **Copy platform (creative brief):** The basic components of creative strategy are specified in the written copy - platform prepared by the account executive. Other names given to platform are creative platform, creative blueprint, work plan, or creative contract, copy platform gets the final approval from the client firm's marketing or brand manager or the advertising manager. A typical copy platform outline is shown in the following box

BOX 2. Outline of a Typical Copy Platform

1. Basic problem or issue the advertising must tackle.
2. Advertisting objectives and communication objectives.
3. Precise description of the target audience.
4. Major selling idea or the key consumer benefits to communicate.
5. Creative strategy statement specifying campaign theme, appeal and execution technique to be used.
6. Any supporting information and requirements.

The two components of the copy platform-development of the major selling idea and the creative strategy development are the responsibility of the creative specialists and form the basis of the advertising campaign.

QUESTIONS IMPORTANT IN ADVERTISING STRATEGY FORMULATION

Before an advertising strategy can be developed, it is important to look at the number of factors and considerations including advertising objectives. In developing the advertising strategy, consumer interest must be kept at the top of the list. A strategy must identify clearly, the benefit to the consumer or solution to the given problem otherwise the strategy is not an effective one or even a workable strategy. The following questions are to be answered while developing the successful advertising strategy:

(a) What are we really selling?	Product/Service
(b) Who are our customers?	Customers
(c) What is our prospect's problem?	Need/Wants
(d) Is our sale generic or competitive?	Primary/ Selective demand
(e) Personality of the advertisement?	Aggressive/ Contemporary
(f) What other selling points can be developed?	Additional benefits
(g) What do we want our prospects to do?	Feedback

CREATIVE STRATEGY DEVELOPMENT

Like any other area of marketing and promotional process, the creative aspect of advertising is guided by specific goals and objectives. A creative strategy 'hat focusses on what must be communicated will 'uide the development of all messages used in the ad :ampaign. Creative strategy is based on several factors, including the identification of the target audience; the basic problem, issue, or opportunity the advertising must address; the major selling idea or key benefit the message needs to communicate; and any supportive information that needs to be included in the advertisement. Once these factors are determined, a creative strategy statement should describe the message appeal and execution style that will be used in the ad. Many advertising agencies outline these elements in a document known as the copy or creative platform.

EXHIBIT 1. Copy platform outline

- Target audience.
- Creative strategy statements (campaign theme, appeal and execution technique to be used).
- Basic problem or issue the advertising must address.
- Supportive information and requirements
- Advertising and communication objectives.
- Major selling idea or key benefits to communicate.

(a) Preparing Copy Platform : The written copy platform specifies the basic elements of the creative strategy. Different agencies may call this document a creative platform or work plan, creative blue print, or a creative contract. The account representatives or manager assigned to the account usually prepare the copy platform. In larger agencies, an individual from research or the strategic planning department may write the copy platform. Individuals from the agency team or group assigned to the account, including creative personnel as well as representatives from media and research, have input into this document. The advertising manager or the marketing and product managers from the client side ultimately approve the copy platform. Just as there are different names for the copy platform, there are variations in the outline and format used and in the level of details included.

(b) Searching for the Major Selling Idea: An important part of creative strategy is determing the central theme that will become the major selling idea of the ad campaign. Some advertising experts argue that for an advertising campaign to be effective it must contain the big idea that attracts the consumer's attention. Gets a reaction, and sets the advertiser's product or service apart from the competitor's. Well known ad man John O' Toole describes the big idea as "that flash of insight that synthesizes the purpose of the strategy, joins the product benefit with consumer desire in a fresh, involving way, brings the subject to life and makes the reader to audience stop, look and listen.

Jerome Jeweler in his book creative strategy in Advertising stated :

"The major selling idea should emerge as the strongest singular thing you can say about your product or service. This should be the claim with the broadest and most meaningful appeal to your target audience. Once you determine this message, the certain you can live with it; be sure it stands strong enough to remain the central issue in every ad and commercial in the campaign".

U.S.P. - Essence of Today's Advertising

On the age of product positioning and competitive advantage, the markets and advertisers are coming to a veritable reality in advertising. Rossers Reeves, chief of the Ted Bates &Co., one of the world's leading advertising agencies wrote a book titled "Reality in Advertising" in 1970 which was based on nearly 20 years of intensive research. In his book he highlighted the concept of USP and the USP concept stormed the advertising world. A campaign with a USP tells something about that product which pulls over the most customers.

There are hundreds of examples of advertising campaigns which have that unique selling preposition and have succeeded in the market in the intense competition. For example Promise Toothpaste, which came no where to occupy the second position in the market in 1980 dominated by the foreign brands. The USP was "The unique Toothpaste with time tested clove oil". As we know most toothpaste have clove oil but only Promise made in USP. The maggie noodles by Nestle with the USP just two minute wrote the success story.

Lifebouy soap made the advertising history with the slogan "Stops BO". All soaps stop body odour but nobody made this as USP. Competitors were busy in highlighting the cooling effect of bath soaps by fresh, fragrant & fancy features.

Colgate dental Cream came with USP 'Cleans your breath, while it cleans your teeth'.

Surf Communicated its USP by personification-Lalita Ji-"Surf Kee Kharidna Ma He Samajhdari Hai".

Hero Honda USP-Fill it, shut it, forget it.

Hero Honda USP-Environmental friendly Bike-highlighting the features of bike in connection with the Government's is anti pollution norms

Maggie Sauce USP-It is different

Surf Ultra USP-Doondta Reh Jao ge.

Rooser Reeves, whose ad agency Ted Bates pioneered USP since 1940, raised its billing from just S 4 million to $150 million with in two years without losing a client.

One of the old advertising truisms is, "It is a good campaign if Sales go up" and *vice versa*. In all the cases when the right USP has been identified, before the competitor did, the product has been tremendrously successful. It is all time reality in advertising.

The concept of unique selling preposition (USP) was developed by Rosser Reeves, former chair of the Ted Bates agency, and is described in his influential book Reality in Advertising. Reeves noted three characteristics of unique selling proposition :

1. Each advertising must make a proposition to the consumer not just words, not just product puffery, not just show window advertising. Each advertisement must say to each reader : "Buy this product and you will get this benefit".
2. The proposition must be one that the competition either cannot or does not offer. It must be unique either in the brand or in the claim.
3. The proposition must be strong enough to move the mass millions, that is, pull over new customers to your brand.

Reeves said the attribute claim or benefit that formed the basis of the USP should dominate the ad and be emphasized through repetitive advertising. According to Reeves, there must be a truly unique product or service attribute, benefit or inherent advantage that can be used in the claim. This may require considerable research on the product and consumers not only to determine the USP but also to, document to claim. Advertisers must also consider whether the unique selling preposition affords them a sustainable competitive advantage that cannot easily be copied by the competitors.

According to Reeves, much of advertising was smoke and mirrors. What a campaign required was an effective USP to move merchandise off shelves same thing he did successfully for companies such as Colgate Palmoliva. To him all successful advertising should make a proposition-or Promise-which makes the product worth buying mid is different from what's offered by others in the same category.

To Reeves, the proposition 'Fights bad breath and tooth decay' was a strong Colgate USP, Just as was that of LUX – the beauty soap of film stars'. He reasoned that if this was done consistently, consumers would not only perceive a brand as unique but would also buy it because of the selling proposition in its advertising.

The Search for Major Selling Idea

President of the American Association of Advertising Agencies, John O. Toole, describes the big idea as a "flash of insight that synthesizes the purpose of the strategy, joins the product benefit with desire in afresh, involving way, brings the subject to life, and makes the reader or the audience stop, look, and listen."

This description of "big idea" presumably refers to the creative specialist's experience in generating the idea, which links the product or service benefit to a relevant purchase situation and clearly refers to the processing step in the consumer response process.

A. Jerome Jeweler writes in his book, Creative Strategy in Advertising.

"The major selling idea should emerge as the strongest singular thing you can say about your product or service. This should be the claim with the broadest and most meaningful appeal to your target audience. Once you determine the message, be certain you can live with it; be sure it stands strong enough to remain the central issue in every ad and commercial in the campaign."

The opinion of some advertising specialists is that for an ad campaign to be effective, it must have a big idea that captures the consumer's attention, elicits a response and makes the advertiser's product or service distinct from that of the competitor's.

The real challenge to the creative specialists is to .come up with the big idea to use in the ad. More and more products and services in their category are perceived as similar and unable to offer anything unique. In most situations it is difficult to find something really interesting to say. In this respect David Ogilvy, generally considered as one of the most creative copywriters ever to work in the advertising business, has said

"I doubt if more than one campaign in a hundred contains a big idea. I am supposed to be one of the more fertile inventors of big ideas, but in my long career as a copywriter, I have not had more that 20, of that."

It is very difficult to come up with great ideas in advertising, yet there are examples of some famous big ideas that have been used to build successful ad campaigns. Some examples are "We try harder" (Avis car rental company), "just do it" (Nike), "Pepsi generation" and "the taste of new generation (Pepsi), "ultimate driving machine" (BMW), "made for each other" (Wills cigarettes), "Suraksha Chakra" (Colgate toothpaste), "Taste of India" (Amul), and a more recent "Intel Inside" (Intel's computer microprocessors).

Some Approaches Suggested by Well-known Names in Advertising

Several approaches have been suggested to guide the creative people to kindle the inspiration and generate major creative ideas to develop effective advertising. Some of the best known creative approaches used are attributed to David Ogilvy, William Bernbach, Rosser Reeves, Leo Burnett and Jack Trout and Al Ries.

David Ogilvy

Increasing numbers of competing brands in many product and service category do not seem to offer anything unique in terms of features or benefits. They all seem to be almost similar and difficult to differentiate on a functional or performance basis. To find or create a unique benefit or feature as a major selling idea for them is very difficult. The creative strategy in such situations is based on the development of a strong brand identity by emphasising on a psychological meaning or symbolic association with certain values, life-styles, etc. This type of advertising is referred as image advertising.

In his famous book, David Ogilvy, Confessions of an Advertising Man, popularised the idea of "brand image". He argued that the brand's image or personality is particularly important when competing brands are similar. He said[12]

"Every advertisement should be thought of as a contribution to the complex symbol which is the brand image. If you take that long view, a great many day-to-day problems solve themselves."

David Ogilvy has further argued that in the long run it pays to protect a favourable image even if some appealing short run programmes (sales promotions) are sacrificed in the process, He goes on to say.

"The greater the similarity between brands, the less part reason plays in brand selection. There isn't any significant difference between the various brands of whiskey, or cigarettes, or beer. They are all about the same and so are the cake-mixes and the detergents, and the margarines. The manufacturer who dedicates his advertising to building the most sharply defined personality for his brand will get the largest share of the market at the highest profit. By the same token, the manufacturers who will find themselves up the creek are those shortsighted opportunists who siphon off their advertising funds for promotions."

Creating Brand Personality via Famous Movie Atar

Ogilvy used prestigious individuals to convey the desired image for the product in : his most well known campaigns and, when possible, he would use testimonials from celebrities even used Queen Elizabeth, Winston Churchill and Mrs. Roosevelt as endorsers. He put the following eleven commandments for creating advertising campaigns in Confessions of an Advertising Man:

1. What you say is more important than how you say it.
2. Unless your campaign is built around a great idea, it will flop.
3. Give the facts. The consumer isn't a moron; she is your wife. You insult her intelligence if you assume that a mere slogan and a few vapid adjectives will persuade her to buy anything. She wants all the information you can give her.
4. You cannot bore people into buying. We make advertisements that people want to read, can't save souls in an empty church.
5. Be well mannered, but don't clown.
6. Make your advertising contemporary.
7. Committees can criticise advertisements, but they cannot write them.
8. If you are lucky enough to write a good advertisement, repeat it until it stops pulling.
9. Never write an advertisement which you wouldn't want your family to read. Good products can be sold by honest advertising. If you don't think the product is good, you have no business to be advertising it. If you tell lies, or weasel, you do your client a disservice increase your load of guilt, and you fan the flames of public resentment against the business of advertising.
10. The image and the brand: it is the total personality of a brand rather than any trivial product difference, which decides its ultimate position in the market.
11. Don't be a copycat. Nobody has ever built a brand by imitating somebody else in advertising.

In many product categories and services, image adverting has become increasingly and is used as the main selling idea. For example, image advertising is used for soft perfumes, watches, cigarettes, two and four wheeler autos, ready-to-wear clothing, beauty care services, airlines, etc.

William Bernbach: The primary function of an advertisement is to communicate message and David Ogilvy's prescription for copywriters is "what you say is more important how you say it." William Bernbach had a radically different approach and said "execution become content, it can be just as important as what you say." He emphasised the ad execution elements. His ads communicated a feeling that the consumer is bright enough to understand the advertising is saying. The copy was honest and any heavy repetitions were avoided. The message approach was clean and direct. He believed that one should be as simple, as penetrating as possible, and the advertisement should stand out from others and show character. In his own words:

"Why should anyone look at your ad? The reader doesn't buy his magazine or tune in his rod TV to see and hear what you have to say.....What is the use of saying all the right things in the world if nobody is going to read them? And, believe me, nobody is going to read them if At said with freshness, originality and imagination..-.If they are. not, if you will, different.

Bernbach frequently used humour in advertising to gain attention ignoring otter rule that humour does not sell. He believed in rewarding the reader positively through humour. A copywriter of Doyle Dane Bernbach now DDB Needham part of the Omnicom group Fine said:

"We recognise that an advertisement is an intrusion. People don't necessarily like advertisements, and avoid them if possible. Therefore, to do a good advertisement you're obligated, realty to reward the reader for his time and patience in allowing to interrupt the editorial content, which is what he bought the magazine for in the first place. This is not defensive. It just takes into account the fact that an advertisement pushes its way uninvited into somebodys mind. So entertainment is sort of repayment."

Bernbach was not a believer in research and expressed his views in these words :

"One of the disadvantages of doing things mathematically, by research, is that after a while, everybody does it the same way..... If you take the attitude that once you have found out what to say, your job is done, then what you are doing is saying it the same way as everybody is saying it, and you have lost your impact completely.[15]"

Doyle Dane Bernbach agency created the new classic and frequently quoted ad campaign of Avis, "We are No.2. We try harder." The campaign daringly admitted that Avis was not the leader in car rental, but in the second place. This fact was turned to advantage with a clever twist that a customer could expect better service from No.2 because "We try harder" to serve and please the customer. This is a perfect example of a two-sided message that accepts the weak position and then refutes it.

The ad position the car as "small" in consumers" mind

Ads created by Doyle Dane Bernbach agency almost always had a large photograph of the product in a setting with a headline and copy below. The headlines used were usually quite provocative and generated a temptation in the readers to continue to the body copy. Some adds of Volkswagen, viewed as classic, had headlines "Ugly is only skin deep," "Think small," and "Lemon". The ads were well accepted and read by large numbers. Common people talked about these adds. The ads were also picked for many creative awards.

Rosser Reeves: Rosser Reeves of Ted Bates agency (now part of Saatchi group developed the concept of Unique Selling Proposition (USP). His book, Reality in Advertising, is considered an important contribution and has significantly influenced advertising. His approach was to create sales rather than for aesthetic appeal. He was particularly critical of such approaches in which the copy is so cleverly written that it distracts the audience from the ad message . He mentioned three characteristics of USP —

1. Each advertisement must make a proposition to the consumer. Not just words, not just product puffery, not just show window advertising. Each advertisement must say to reach the reader: "Buy this product and you will get this benefit."
2. The proposition must be one that the competition either cannot or does not offer. It has to be unique either in the brand or in the claim.
3. The proposition must be strong enough to move the mass millions, that is, pull over new customers to your brand.[16]

Reeves proposed that each product develop its own USP, which should dominate the ad and be emphasised through whatever repetition is necessary" to communicate the Unique Selling Proposition to the target audience. Reeves relied heavily on product research to develop and support USP. He believed that once an effective USP is found, it must be retained for as long as possible.

Reeves approach of USP was undoubtedly successful, but this requires finding out a truly unique product or service attribute, benefit, or inherent advantage that can be used in developing the claim. Another aspect that advertisers must consider is whether the USP offers them a "sustainable competitive advantage" that cannot be copied easily. In many product categories, companies can quickly match a brand feature for feature and this makes the USP approach somewhat obsolete. USP is a good theory as long as one can really find a unique and persuasive, but sustainable claim.

Leo Burnett: He was the founder of Leo Burnett agency in Chicago. His approach to determining the major selling idea is termed as "inherent drama". This approach focuses on finding out the product characteristic that made the manufacturer make it and the product benefit that motivates the consumer to purchase it. Burnett believed that the inherent drama "is often hard to find but it is always there, and once found it is the most interesting and believable of all advertising appeals."

He believed that the foundation or advertising should be based on consumer benefits with an emphasis on the dramatic element in communicating these benefits. He reflected 'common touch' in advertising, using plain ordinary people. His approach vividly contrasted that of David Ogilvy. Who used prestigious personalities to convey the desired brand image. Leo Burnett said in a speech given before the Chicago Copywriters Club.

"Not only is great copy "deceptively simple" - but so are great ideas. And if it takes a rational to explain an ad or a commercial - then it's too complicated for that "dumb" public to understand.

I am afraid too many advertising people blame the public's inability to sort out commercial message in magazines on stupidity. What a lousy stupid attitude to have! I believe the public is unable to sort out messages, not just because of the sheer flood of messages assaulting it every day but because of sheer boredom! If the public is bored today - then let's blame it on the fact that it is being handed boring messages created by bored advertising people, in a world every where no body seems to know what's going to happen next, the only thing to do to keep from going compelitly from frustration is plain old-fashioned work! Having worked many, many years for peanuts and in obscurity, I think I know how a lot of writers feel today and I sympathise with them but I also wonder if a lot of writers are not downright spoiled."

BOX 3. Twelve Tested Creative Hot Buttons

To answer the question, what makes a creative message effective, here are twelve qualities found in most safes effective advertising as measured by research firm Spielman Worldwide.

1. Brand rewards/benefits are highly visible through demonstration, dramatisation, feelings, or analogy.
2. The brand is the major player in the experience (the brand makes the good times better).
3. The link between the brand and execution is clear (the scenario revolves around and highlights the brand).
4. The execution has a focus (there is a limit to how many images and vignettes he can process).
5. Feelings (emotional connectives) are anchored to the needs and aspirations of the consumer.
6. Striking, dynamic imagery is a characteristic of many successful executions, their ability to break out of the clutter.
7. An original, creative signature or mystique exists in many of the best commercials v. the consumer to the brand and give it a unique personality.
8. In food and beverage advertising, high taste appeal is almost always essential.
9. The best creative ideas for mature brands often use fresh new ways of revitalising the message.
10. Music (memorable, bonded tunes and lyrics) is often a key to successful execution of many brands.
11. When humour is used, it is relevant, with a clear product purpose.
12. When celebrities are used, they are well matched to brands and have credibility as user/ endorsers and their delivery is believably enthusiastic.

Burnett belived that the best copywriters have a natural ability to do things in any way. In his own words:

"a fair for expression, putting known and believable things into new relationships. ..We try to be more straightforward without being flatfooted. We try to be warm without being mawkish.[18]"

Some of the famous ads created by Burnett's agency using "inherent drama" approach are for McDonalds, Hallmark cards, Kellogg's cereals, etc.

BOX 4. Example of a Copy Platform or Creative Brief

Product: ROMINS

Key Fact

Romins India is a 40-year old New Delhi based cosmetic company. In 2001, Romins introduced a new line of premium perfumes to be distributed nationally.

Problem the Advertising Must Solve

Currently there is no awareness of the Romins product among potential customers.

Advertising Objective

To achieve 75% awareness of the product at the end of year one. To communicate the exclusiveness and long lasting fragrance of the perfume.

Creative Strategy Prospect Definition

Women 18-35, urban, educated, with household incomes 6 lakh plus. Psychographically, they are active, social, party goers, seek variety and excitement, avid consumers and spenders.

Principal Competition
Medium to expensive perfume brands from multinationals.
Key Promise
Irresistible personality and high society image.
Reason Why
Premium and exclusive perfume.
Supporting Requirements
Must use logo, show package.

Al Ries and Jack Trout: In early 1970s, Al Ries and Jack Trout introduced the concept of "positioning". Positioning theory acknowledges the importance of product features and images but insists that what is really important is how the brand is perceived and ranked against the competition in the consumer's mind. Positioning approach became a popular basis of creative strategy development.

Using cola as a frame of reference, Al Ries and Jack Trout say

"To find a unique position, you must ignore conventional logic. Conventional logic says you find your concept inside yourself or inside the product.

Not true. What you must do is look inside the prospect's mind.

You won't find an "uncola" idea inside a 7-Up can. You find it inside the Cola drinkers bead."

BOX 5. Some Successful Long-running Ad Campaigns

Company/Brand	*Ad campaign theme*
Amul	"Taste of India."
De Beers	"A diamond is forever.
BMW	"The ultimate driving machine."
Nike	"Just do it."
Hallmark cards	"When you care enough to send the very best"
Timex watches	It takes a licking and keeps on ticking."
Wills cigarettes	"Made for each other."
Videocon	"Bring home the leader."
Philips	"Let's make things better."
BPL	"Believe in the best."
Femina magazine	"For the woman of substance"
Woodland shoes	"Leather that weathers."
Citibank	"Unfixed deposit."
Maggi	"2-Minute noodles."

Products or services can be positioned on the basis of attributes, price/quality, usage or application, users, or product class. Any of these can kindle a novel selling idea that becomes the basis of the creative strategy. The creative outcome may help the brand occupy a particular position in the minds of the target audience.

Some Others

Some of the more recent advertising personalities who have had significant influence on contemporary advertising include Hal Riney (Hall Riney & Partners), Lee Clow and Jay Chiat (TBWA/Chiat/Day), Dan Weiden (VCeiden & Kennedy), and Jeff Goodby and Rich

Silverstein (Goodby, Silverstein & Partners. Anthony Vagnoni writes. "The modern creative kings don't write books, rarely give interviews or lay out their theories on advertising. They have endorsed no set of miss, professed no simple maxim like Mr. David Ogilvy's famous "When you don't have anything to say, sing it. " If pronouncements and hooks are out the window, what has replaced them is a conscious desire to lift the intelligence level of advertising. Today's leaders see advertising as an uplifting social force, as a way to inspire and entertain."

Goodby and Silverstein describe their creative formula as doing intelligent work that the public likes to see and that has a sales pitch.

"Advertising works best when it sneaks into people's lives, when it doesn't look or feel like advertising. It's about treating people at their best, as opposed to dealing with them at their lowest common denominator."

Lee Clow says

"No rulebook will tell you how to target the masses anymore. The best of understand the socio-cultural realities of people and how they interact with the media. If we didn't, we couldn't make the kinds of messages that people would be able to connect with."

The brand image (David Ogilvy), ad execution (William Bernbach), USP (Rosser Reeves), inherent drama or common touch (Leo Burnett), and positioning (Al Ries and Jack Trout) approaches have become associated with some of the most successful and creative minds in advertising, Creative professionals often use these approaches as the basis of developing creative strategy for ad campaigns. However, these approaches are not the only ones. Many other approaches are available and individual agencies are not limited to any particular creative approach are real challenge to the creative specialists is to find the "big idea" and use it in developing an effective creative strategy.

Therefore, to a large extent, in many present day ads, there seems to be an obsession with images and feelings and ads appear to be unrelated to selling any particular product or service. There is often complete absence of any concrete claims related to the advertised item.

Research indicates that ad liking influences the success of advertisements. But it is important to appreciate that just ad liking is not sufficient. The ad must be relevant to its target audience; the message must effectively communicate the product positioning through selected media.

In most situations, agency people prepare the advertising strategy in consultation with the client's personnel and their final approval. Subsequently, the account management prepares a creative brief. It, is a simple written statement of the most significant issues to consider and guide the agency team in the development of a single ad or an ad campaign.

Creativity is present within all of us. However, some individuals exhibit more creativity than others. Advertising creativity is the ability to generate fresh, unique, appropriate and effective ideas that can be used to solve marketing communications problems. Advertising creativity is disciplined and focused. Well-designed ads or commercials evoke emotional responses and can create positive feelings about the advertised product or service.

The work of creative people in advertising is challenging. They must take into consideration inputs from research findings, creative brief, strategy statement, communications objectives, etc., to create an ad message to effectively communicate the main theme of the ad campaign.

Many advertising professionals believe that creativity can best be viewed as a process and can be achieved by following an organised approach but there is no infallible formula to guarantee the creation of successful advertising. Some experts have suggested various sequential steps to come up with creative ideas. Such models are valuable as they facilitate an organised approach to come up with solutions to advertising problems.

Some of the best creative approaches used are attributed to David Ogilvy, William BernBach, Reeves, Leo Burnett, and Al Ries and Jack Trout.

A Model of Source Factors in Advertising

Returning to the source model, Figure 16.5 shows various factors of source on which research has focused. The central idea is that consumers view the information in ads as coming from a source, with sources varying in "credibility" (The term credibility should not be interpreted literally, and is explained further below.) According to this model, the more credible the source, the more persuasive he or she is likely to be in getting the audience to accept the ad's message.

Shown to the right in Figure 16.5 are various source components of advertising copy. At the centre is the object of the advertising, such as the brand, product, service, idea, political candidate, corporation, and so on. The model shows the credibility of this object to depend on the sponsor, the endorser, the media vehicle, etc.

The sponsor could be the company itself. A famous study by Theodore Levitt, for example, tested whether the effects of salespeople representing a prestigious company (Monsanto Chemical), a medium-credible company (Denver Chemical), and an anonymous company had a differential impact on purchasing agents. It was found that the better the company's reputation, the better were the salespeople's chances of getting a first hearing for a new product and early adoption of the product. Company source effect declined, however, with the riskiness of the decision. For high-risk decisions, the nature of the sales presentation and other factors were more important than the source effect. Another recent study found that an advertiser could successfully make a more extreme (stronger) claim in an ad if it already had a very positive reputation; a firm with a negative prior reputation could not successfully make the same claims, because it lacked the necessary credibility.

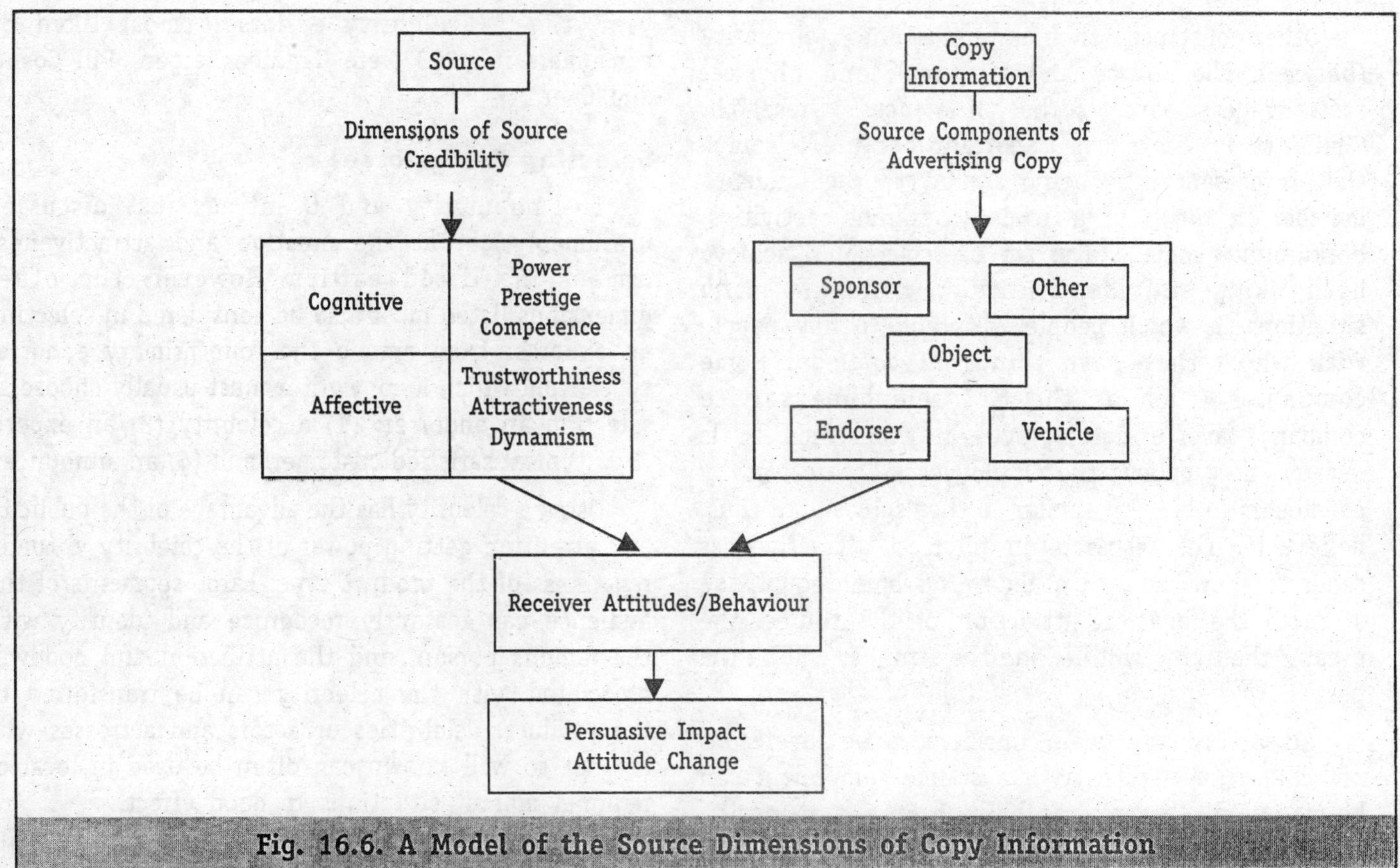

Fig. 16.6. A Model of the Source Dimensions of Copy Information

A key source component, our focus here, is the endorser. The endorser in an advertisement is the person, celebrity, spokesman, announcer, and so on who endorses or who demonstrates the product. Not all advertisements have an endorser as a copy component, but many of them do. Most of the work on source credibility in advertising has focused on this component, and we shall discuss findings and implications later.

Another aspect is the credibility of the media vehicle itself. The same advertisement appearing in The Ladies Home Journal, for example, can have a different impact than if it appeared in Playboy. We will discuss this source component further in later chapters dealing with media decisions, but you should recognize here that it is also an important source factor in advertising.

DIMENSIONS OF A SOURCE

What exactly is meant by the credibility of a source? As shown on the left of Figure 16.5, researchers have recognized that some judgments about a source concern a cognitive dimension and others an affective dimension. The cognitive dimension includes judgments about the power, prestige (from past achievements, reputation, wealth, political power, or visibility), and competence (expertise) of the source. The affective dimension includes judgments about trustworthiness, attractiveness, and dynamism.

Other constructs, such as unbiasedness, similarity (between the source and receiver), and physical attractiveness, have also been the focus of research. Similarity is sometimes important because a source that is presented as being similar to the audience member in terms of attitudes, opinions, activities, background, social status, or lifestyle could achieve both liking and identification: there are many situations in which people will tend to like people with whom they have things in common. Some companies (such as the MCI telephone service company) favor using employees in their commercials because they believe the employees are perceived by consumers to be very similar to themselves and, thus, believable. The research on physical attractiveness tends to show that, all other things being equal, the stronger the physical attraction of the source, the greater the liking will be, and the stronger will be the persuasive impact.

All such constructs are considered to be dimensions on which the credibility of a source component can be measured. A source can be high on one dimension and low on another. Consider the competence and unbiasedness dimensions. A doctor could be regarded as very competent (an expert) in recommending a drug product, but he or she would have less persuasive influence if listeners or viewers considered the recommendations to be biased by money payments given the doctor for making the commercial. Similarly, many politicians, although regarded as expert in their field, are also considered biased in their viewpoints.

A research firm, Marketing Evaluations, annually determines a familiarity and likability rating of top male and female personalities (and cartoon characters) based on a mail questionnaire survey of television viewers. The basic rating, called a Q rating, is obtained by dividing the number who rated the personality as "one of my favourites" by those who indicated that they were "totally familiar" with the personality. The survey is widely used by marketers and agencies to select celebrity endorsers and is used by TV networks and Hollywood producers to cast their shows and movies. The top personalities overall in August 1992 included Bill Cosby, Jimmy Stewart, Clint Eastwood; Michael Jordan ranked number 1 among teens. According to another company, Video Storyboard Tests, which surveys 3,000 people by phone and mail every year, the TV celebrity endorsers most liked by consumers in 1993 were Candice Bergen, Bill Cosby, and Cher.

Selecting An Endorser

The popularity and Q ratings just discussed presumably get at the prestige and attractiveness dimensions listed earlier. However, the other dimensions listed must also be considered in selecting an endorser from among the four primary endorser types from which a copywriter must usually choose in selecting an endorser: (1) a celebrity (2) an expert, (3) a typical satisfied customer, and (4) an announcer.

Using a celebrity has the advantage of the publicity and attention-getting power of the celebrity virtually regardless of the product type. Large segments of the audience can instantly recognize and identify with the famous person, and the attraction and goodwill associated with the celebrity can be transferred to the product. Celebrities or actors and actresses who are not so well known can often be used in local or regional market situations to good effect.

On the negative side, celebrities aren't usually considered experts, although celebrities can also be experts in some situations. Thus, Michael Jordan is not just a celebrity but an expert in basketball shoes, and a celebrity like TV talk-show host Oprah Winfrey was also an "expert" when she announced to the world in 1988 that she had lost 67 pounds when using a weight-loss product called Optifast (she had been visibly overweight before). As a result of her endorsement, sales of diet products soared in the following two years.[44] It is very easy, however, to use a celebrity mistakenly for a high-involvement product, a situation in which the consumer is looking for credible information from an expert, For instance, a copier company recently used a basketball and football coach to endorse the reliability of its products.

Furthermore, celebrities not only cost a lot but are hard to get, and if they are already being used by other advertisers, they may be losing credibility at the time they are chosen. Endorsers are usually contractually prohibited from endorsing similar or competing products through exclusivity clauses in contracts, but they may still be overexposed. Very importantly, if some event happens to reduce the popularity of the celebrity with the public, the publicity could backfire on the associated brand as well. Recent examples include the child molestation charges against Michael Jackson, the divorce of Burt Reynolds, Magic Johnson disclosing he had AIDS, the controversy over Madonna's music videos, and the retirement of Michael Jordan.

Research by Michael Kamins suggests that the credibility of celebrity endorsers can be raised if they say things that are not only in favour of the brand but also a few things that are mildly critical of it—that is, a two-sided ad with a celebrity endorser works better than a one-sided ad with a celebrity endorser. And, as noted below, in cases in which the audience is already very supportive of the product, a highly credible source might result in less persuasive impact than an endorser which has lesser power and prestige. There is also the very real danger that while the consumer may find the ad with the celebrity entertaining, very little benefit may actually accrue to the brand being advertised. This distraction effect is discussed further below.

An expert is likely to be the best choice when the product is technical or consumers need to be reassured that the product is safe to consume (high-involvement decisions). An expert can allay fears in the audience concerning the product whether those fears arise from not knowing how something works, concern about side effects, concern about fulfilling a role such as father, mother, housewife, and so on, or health-related concerns about product use. Doctors, dentists, lawyers, engineers, and other kinds of experts can be chosen and at considerably less cost than a national celebrity.

Atypical satisfied consumer is often the best choice when it can be anticipated that there will be strong audience identification with the role involved, the person is "like" many members of the audience, and attributes of sincerity and trustworthiness are likely to come through. To maximize the naturalness of the situation, it is often useful to use a hidden camera and capture the consumer's real-world reactions to using the product in a situation with which the audience can identify. The choice might be a child rather than an adult, or an animal, such as an enthusiastic dog for a dog food commercial.

The national or local talk show in television, and a great deal of local radio advertising, typifies the choice of the announcer format. Local radio disk jockeys are classic examples of using an announcer spokesperson as the essential source component. Announcers are more like celebrities than experts, in that they confer some notoriety to the brand, with the likely advantage of some trustworthiness. The actual copy generation process is often less expensive because only the script and, in television, some simple props must be provided. This does not imply that the media buy will be less expensive, but the trade-off is really deciding to put more money into the media buy than into copy production. The addition of props or ways to have the announcer do more than simply sit behind a desk and talk about the product can often enhance the persuasive impact considerably.

As we said earlier, the key criterion in selecting an endorser must be the appropriateness of the "match" or "fit" between the needs of the brand and the characteristics of the endorser. Research shows that the effectiveness of an endorser is related to the type of product being endorsed. In an experiment comparing the impact of using an expert rather than a typical consumer or celebrity in advertising a low-priced but fairly technical product (electronic calculator), it was found that the expert was more effective than either a typical consumer or a celebrity. In con-trast, celebrities are often more effective in situations where the product has a high element of psychological and "social" risk (e.g., costume jewellry). Good reviews of the source credibility literature are available.

In general, when the purchase is based most strongly on a brand's awareness and or likability (such as in many low-involvement purchase decisions), the more appropriate a celebrity endorser is likely to be. A celebrity endorser may also be very useful when the cultural meanings desired for the brand's imagery are linked to the celebrity endorser, and/or when consumers aspire to the lifestyle or reference group associated with that celebrity endorser. Lynn Kahle and Pamela Homer, and Michael Kamins, have also shown that when the product being advertised has improved physical attractiveness as its major benefit, ad effectiveness is usually enhanced to the degree that there is a congruence between the product image and the celebrity image. Thus, an attractive celebrity like Tom Selleck is superior to an unattractive one like Telly Savalas for a luxury car, which promises social appeal, but not for a computer.

In contrast, experts and not celebrities are likely to be more appropriate for more rational and highly involved purchase decisions. If the purchase is driven by logical reasons why a brand is better, then a celebrity may be a waste of money: a non-celebrity might be equally effective, and a lot cheaper. Thus, returning to our chapter-opening example, mutual funds are probably better associated with an expert fund-rating group than with cartoon characters like the Peanuts, however likable they may be. Note that Bill Cosby, despite his top-notch popularity and liking ratings, was a failure when he endorsed the brokerage firm E. F. Hutton in the mid-1980s. Presumably, the selection of a brokerage firm requires an expert endorser more than it does a likable entertainer, it has also been shown that consumers are most skeptical of advertising claims and thus might benefit most from a credible and expert endorser, when the claims involved are subjective rather than objective. Considering the large sums of money involved, it is always appropriate to pre-test an endorser's attractiveness and expertise ratings before deciding to use one.

Additionally, one other key aspect that should be copy-tested when an advertisement uses endorsers is whether the endorser's presence, while possibly raising awareness of the ad and/or brand, is also detracting from communication of the main copy points. Research shows that this often does happen: an ad with an endorser, compared to an ad without one, often has higher awareness but com-municates less about the brand's characteristics or advantages, which can hurt the ability of the ad to create the attitude change or persuasion necessary in many high involvement situations. For instance, though the fictitious endorser Joe Isuzu raised the brand awareness of Isuzu cars, he failed to convince car buyers to visit Isuzu dealerships to check out Isuzu cars in large enough numbers and was subsequently dropped as an endorser. This typically happens because the endorser's presence distracts the consumer from the main message in the ad about the brand. Since distraction effects are often of interest in advertising, we will be discussing them more thoroughly later.

It has been suggested that an endorser can be used to attract attention even if there is high risk of the perceived credibility of the source being low. The reason is called the sleeper effect. The sleeper effect refers to the case in which the persuasive impact of a message actually increases rather than decreases over time. One hypothesis of why persuasive impact increases is that although the effect of the source is negative (it is not liked or not credible) at the time of viewing or reading, with the passage of time, the association of this negative cue with the message breaks down. The result is an increase in the overall impact of the message over time. Although the idea is intuitively appealing, there are surprisingly few studies that have demonstrated the presence of a sleeper effect, even though dozens of experiments have been done on the subject.

Consistency Theories

Why should a credible source (endorser, company, media vehicle, whatever) raise attitudes toward the advertised brand? The effects of an endorser on the attitudes toward the advertised brand can be understood using consistency theories of attitude. This important group of attitude-change theories rests on the assumption that attitude change results by exploiting a person's drive for consistency among the facts associated with an object. For example, an audience member may have a negative opinion about a brand but a positive opinion about a person who is endorsing the brand in an advertisement. This inconsistency should create a tension and a drive to reduce that tension.

There are three obvious routes to the reduction of tension in this context. First, it can be assumed by the consumer that the endorser is not really enthusiastic about the brand. Second, the positive opinion of the endorser can be altered to one less positive. Third, the attitude toward the brand can be changed to one more positive. If the advertising can select an endorser for which audiences have strong positive attitudes and link the endorser strongly to the brand, there will be a ten-dency to engage in brand-attitude change. To maximize the likelihood of attitude change, it is useful for the source not only to be well liked but also relevant and credible with respect to the product class involved. Otherwise, the audience member can resolve the inconsistency by observing that the endorser's opinion about the product is not relevant because the endorser is not knowledgeable about the product or that the endorser's experience will not apply to others.

here are several types of consistency theories, including balance theory (which emphasizes the role of an endorser), congruity theory (which predicts the size of attitude change knowing the strengths of existing attitudes and the size of the advocated change), and dissonance theory (which considers the drive to make attitudes consistent with behaviour). They all focus attention on tension created by cognitive inconsistency that can be resolved by changing beliefs and attitudes.

In the Jell-O campaign, for example, in which Bill Cosby is shown with little children expounding the benefits of Jell-O, the congruity theory explanation is that people who like Cosby may shift their liking for Jell-O because the Jell-O-Cosby link is so strong and positive. Of course, the reverse is true for people who do not like Cosby. The theory offers predictions of the overall attitude effect for conditions such as dislike Cosby-like Jell-O, like Cosby-dislike Jell-O, and so on. However, the proposition that highly credible sources (Cosby) will always lead to an increase in positive attitude for the object (Jell-O) must be qualified somewhat. The theory predicts that although a low-credibility product should gain from the association with a high-credibility source, the source will tend to lose some credibility from the association as well. The predictions of relative gains and losses of each component are functions of the initial credibility positions of each before the association occurs.

Conditions under which the basic proposition that "high-credibility sources lead to higher persuasion" breaks down have been the focus of some studies. There are situations in which a low-credibility source is about equal in effectiveness to a high-credibility source. Even more interesting are those situations in which a low-credibility source is more effective than a high one.

First, it has been found that when receivers feel their behaviour is being con-trolled, negative reactions-such as "this endorser must have been paid to say this"-can be increased if the source is highly credible. According to psychological theories of attribution, we are more likely to believe that another person really believes what he says if we cannot easily find another reason (such as financial inducements) why he might have said what have did. That is why so-called "hidden camera" ads that show ordinary people saying nice things about the advertised brand can often be very effective-since the ordinary "people on the street" are not being paid to say what they are saying, they must believe it.

The second case occurs in situations in which receivers have a strong initial positive attitude about the brand or product. Such people tend to generate more support arguments during exposure if the source has low credibility rather than high. The reason is that they are more highly motivated to assure themselves that the position with which they agree is the right one, when the endorser is of low credibility rather than high credibility.

The choice of a source to be included in an advertisement must therefore be done very carefully. If the strategy is to try to increase positive attitudes, high-credibility sources should be used. However, if the strategy is to induce behaviour such as product trial directly, it is possible that using a highly credible source can undermine the formation of "real" positive attitudes (internal to the consumer) and thus reduce the incidence of future repeat purchases and brand loyalty.

DISTRACTION EFFECTS

Probably the most useful research finding supported by numerous studies is that distraction (e.g., from elements of the ad execution such as endorsers or music) can affect the number of support arguments and counter-arguments evoked by an ad. In some situations, this can enhance persuasion: negatively predisposed audience members who would otherwise have generated counter-arguments can be distracted from counter-arguing, so that the communication will be more effective. For example, in a study by L. Festinger and N. Maccoby, a strong, persuasive tape-recorded message opposing fraternities was more effective at changing attitudes among fraternity men when a silent film on modern painting was shown rather than pictures of fraternity scenes in general, distracter tasks that involve cognitive activity result in more distraction than do tasks that simply provide visual distraction or manual skills.

An advertiser interested in using distraction to break down resistance to her or his arguments is faced with the delicate task of devising something that will interfere with counter-arguing but not, at the same time, interfere with the reception or learning of the message. This is a formidable task that must take into consideration all aspects of the communication and the audience. As David Gardner explains, the critical question in defining distraction seems to be whether the process of counterarguing is interfered with. If attitude change is more apt to be induced due to interference with counter-argument, then this is defined as distraction. Based on this definition, distraction takes on many dimensions. If an element in the communication is designed to add support to the message-that is, mood music or artwork — this cannot be defined as distraction because it does not interfere with the counter-arguing process; what is support in one communication could be distraction in another due to products, audiences, channels of communication, or a host of unique factors.

A good example of the use of distractors in trying to communicate with a hostile audience is a campaign developed by the Standard Oil Company of California for its Chevron brand.[56] At the time, many consumers were very hostile to oil companies generally; the oil company image as a good corporate citizen was considerably tarnished. One of the first campaigns involved on-the-scene stories, showing tankers being built, explorations, and other activities. Although reasonably successful, the company subsequently developed a whimsical campaign around the theme "We're running out of dinosaurs" to encourage energy conservation. The campaign not only proved effective in educating consumers about the energy situation, but most important, resulted in a significant shift in favourable attitudes for Standard Oil.

Before ads are handed off to the advertising agency and actual creative work begins, it is important to consider the broad framework and creative approaches open to copywriters and art directors. This chapter reviews several rational and emotional approaches and some of the research that has been done on each.

The chapter is organized around a discussion of the rational approaches such as comparative advertising, inoculative advertising, and refutational approaches, emotional approaches, using endorsers, and the use of distraction in advertising. Comparative advertising is advertising in which two or more specifically named brands of the same product are compared in terms of one or more attributes. It is now widely used, even though it was illegal prior to 1970. The research on comparative advertising presents a mixed picture of it being more or less effective than noncomparative advertising depending on counter-arguing and other information processing mechanisms which come into play. From a strategic viewpoint, comparative advertising is more appropriate for follower brands than for leader brands.

Inoculative advertising utilizes the principles of inoculation in medicine. The objective is to inoculate the audience with small doses of the offending campaign (competitor arguments) so that when the full campaign hits they will be less susceptible and resistant to those arguments. It has been demonstrated that pre-exposure to weakened forms of counterargument is more effective in building resistance than prior presentation of supportive arguments. AT&T's famous campaign to counter MCI inroads is a good example.

Refutational advertising involves explicitly stating competitive claims and then refuting them. It is often contrasted to supportive advertising which focuses on a one-sided presentation of brand benefits only. USAir's "Best of times, Worst of times," campaign is an example.

There is a whole category of approaches that rely on emotions or feelings and pathos as the essential ingredient. Emotion-evoking approaches are most suitable when the product category is one where buying is based on a "feeling" benefit-either the low-involvement small pleasures of candy or soda pop or the highly involving feelings associated with products like perfume, sports cars, or jewellry.

Endorsers are often used in testimonial advertising and are examples of source-oriented approaches. There are many types of sources in advertising and a model of source factors shows the range of source components and the cognitive and affective ways in which the credibility of any of the components can be assessed. Consistency theories encompass a range of theories of attitude change (balance, dissonance, and congruity) that explain endorser and source effects. Research on source credibility has shown that, in some cases, a low-credibility source can be more effective than a high-credibility source. In advertising, three di-mensions of course credibility-prestige, similarity, and physical attractiveness are particularly important.

A final approach is called distraction and involves trying to distract the audience from counter-arguing during the viewing or listening process. The Chevron dinosaur campaign, "We're running out of dinosaurs," designed to divert and dissipate some of the audience hostility against oil companies during the energy crisis, is an example.

REFERENCES

1. Elizabeth C. Hirschman, "Role-based Models of Advertising Creation and Production, Journal of Advertising 1989.
2. Hank Sneiden, Advertising Pure and Simple, 1977.
3. Hanley Norins,The Complete Copywriter, McGraw-Hill, 1966.
4. L. N. Reid and H. J. Rotfeld, "Toward an Associative Model of Advertisin Creativity," Journal of Advertising 1976.
5. Alex F. Osborn, Applied Imagination, Charles Scribner & Sons, 1953.
6. James Web Young, A Technique for Producing Idea, 3rd ed. Chicago: Crain Books, 1975, p.42.
7. Roger Von Oech, A Kick in the Seat of the Pants, New York: Harper-Perennial, 1986.
8. Sandra E. Moriarty, Creative Advertising: Theory and Practice, Prentice-Hall, 1986.
9. John O. Toole, The Trouble with Advertising, 2nd ed., New York: Random House, 1985.
10. A. Jerome Jeweler, Creative Strategy in Advertising, Belmont, CA: Wadsworth, 1981.
11. David Ogilvy, Ogilvy on Advertising, New York: Crown 1983.
12. David Ogilvy, Confessions of an Advertising Man, New York: Atheneum Publishers, 1963.
13. Martin Mayer, Madison Avenue, USA, New York: Pocket Books, 1958.
14. Frank Rowsome, Jr., Think Small, New York: Balfanttne Books, 1970.
15. Rosser Reeves, Reality in Advertising, New York; Knopf, 1961.
16. Leo Burnett "Keep Listening to That wee small voice," in Communications of an Advertising Man, 1961.
17. Dennis Higgins, ed., The Art of Writing Advertising, Crain Books, 1965.
18. Al Ries and Jack Trout, Positioning: The Battle for Your Mind, Warner Book by arrangement with McGraw-Hill Book Company, 1986.
19. Anthony Vagnoni, "The Might Be Giants. Advertising Age, April 1998.
20. Anthony Vagnoni, "Goodby; Silverstein Do" intelligent Work" with a seals pitch,"Advertising Age, April 1998.
21. Anthony Vagnoni, "Having Ad Bosses Focus on the Work Key to Cult Of Clow,"
22. Advertising Age, April 1998.
23. William L. Wilkie and Paul Farris, "Comparison Advertising: Problems and Potential," Journal of Marketing, 39 (October 1975), pp. 7-15.
24. Thomas E. Barry, "Comparative Advertising: What Have we Learned in Two Decades?" Journal of Advertising Research, 33, no. 2 (March/April 1993), pp. 19-29.
25. Adweek's Marketing Week, June 12, 1989, p. 17.
26. Kathy L. Pettit-O'Malley and Mark S. Johnson, "Differentiative Comparative Advertising: Some Positive Results Revealed by Measurement of Simultaneous Effects on the Ad-Sponsoring and Comparison Brands," Journal of Current Issues and Research in Advertising, 14, no. 1 (Spring 1992), pp. 35-44.
27. "Comparison Ads Rev Up," Advertising Age, January 20, 1992, p. 3.
28. Naveen Donthu, "Comparative Advertising Intensity," Journal of Advertising Research, 32, no. 6 (November/December 1992), pp. 53-58.
29. Cornelia Pechmann and David W. Stewart, "How Direct Comparative Ads and Market Share Affect Brand

Choice," Journal of Advertising Research, 31, no. 6 (December 1991), pp. 47-55.

30. Cornelia Pechmann and David W. Stewart, "The Effects of Comparative Advertising on Attention, Memory, and Purchase Intention," Journal of Consumer Research, 17 (September 1990), pp. 180-191.
31. The Wall Street Journal, October 18, 1994, p. B1.
32. Gerald J. Corn and Charles B. Weinberg, "The Impact of Comparative Advertising on Perception and Attitude: Some Positive Findings." Journal of Consumer Research, 11 (September 1984), pp. 719-727.
33. Michael D. Johnson and David A. Home, "The Contrast Mode! of Similarity and Comparative Advertising," Psychology and Marketing (Fall 1988), pp. 211-232.
34. "Creating a Mass Market for Wine," Business Week, March 15, 1982, pp. 102-118.
35. Cornelia Pechmann and S. Ratneshwar. 'The Use of Comparative Advertising for Brand Positioning: Association versus Differentiation," Journal of Consumer Research, 18 (September 1991), 145-160.
36. The Wall Street Journal, December 20, 1994, p. B7.
37. George E. Belch, "An Examination of Comparative and Non-comparative Television Commercials: The Effects of Claim Variation and Repetition on Cognitive Response and Message Acceptance," Journal of Marketing Research, 18 (August 1981), pp. 333-349. For a listing of some other studies, see Barry (1993), cited earlier.
38. Easwar S. Iyer, "The Influence of Verbal Content and Relative Newness on the Effectiveness of Comparative Advertising," Journal of Advertising, 17 (3), 1988, pp. 15-21.
39. Jerry B. Gotlieb and Dan Sarel, "Comparative Advertising Effectiveness: The Role of Involvement and Source Credibility," Journal of Advertising, 20, no. 1 (1991), pp. 38-45.
40. Shailendra P. Jain, "Positive versus Negative Comparative Advertising," Marketing Letters, 4, no.4 (1993), pp. 309-320.
41. William R. Swinyard, "The Interaction Between Comparative Advertising and Copy Claim Variation," Journal of Marketing Research, 18 (May 1981), pp. 175-186.
42. Michael Edgar and Stephen A. Goodwin, "One-Sided Versus Two-Sided Comparative Message Appeals for New Brand Introductions," Journal of Consumer Research, 8 (March 1982), pp. 460-465.
43. Cornelia Pechmann, "Predicting When Two-Sided Ads Will Be More Effective Than One-Sided Ads: The Role of Correlational and Correspondent Inferences," Journal of Marketing Research, 29 (November 1992), pp. 441-453.
44. Alan G. Sawyer and Daniel J. Howard, "Effects of Omitting Conclusions in Advertisements to Involved and Uninvolved Audiences, Journal of Marketing Research, 28 (November 1991), pp. 467-474.
45. Mita Sujan and Christine Dekleva, "Product Categorization and Inference Making: Some Implications for Comparative Advertising," Journal of Consumer Research, 14 (December 1987), pp. 372-378.
46. William J. McGuire, "The Nature of Attitude and Attitude Change," in G. Lindzey and E. Aronson, eds., The Handbook of Social Psychology, Vol. 3 (Reading, MA: Addison-Wesley, 1969), p. 263.
47. Stewart W. Bither, Ira J. Dolich, and Elaine B. Nell, "The Application of Attitude Immunization Techniques in Marketing." Journal of Marketing Research, 8 (February 1971), pp. 56-61.
48. Michael A. Kamins and Henry Assael, "Two-Sided Versus One-Sided Appeals: A Cognitive Perspective on Argumentation, Source Derogation, and the Effect of Discontinuing Trial on Belief Change," Journal of Marketing Research, 24 (February 1987), pp. 29-39.
49. "GM Ad Blitz Aima at Californians, Touts a New Image," The Wall Street Journal, September 24, 1993, p. B5A.
50. "Is There Life After Basketball? Firms that use Jordan Are About to Find Out," The Wall Street Journal, October 7, 1993, p. B1.
51. The New York Times, March 27, 1989, p. 30.
52. W. Freeman, The Big Name (New York: Printer's Ink, 1957), and H. Rudolph, Attention and Interest Factors in Advertising (New York: Printer's Ink, 1947).
53. R. B. Fireworker and H. H. Friedman, "The Effects of Endorsements on Product Evaluation," Decision Sciences, 8 (1977). pp. 576-583, and Joseph M. Kamen *et al.*, "What a Spokesman Does for a Sponsor," Journal of Advertising Research, 15 (1975), pp. 17-24.
54. Grant McCracken, "Who Is the Celebrity Endorser? Cultural Foundations of the Endorsement Process," Journal of Consumer Research, 16 (December 1989), pp. 310-321.
55. Joanne M. Klebba and Lynette S. Unger, "The Impact of Negative and Positive Information on Source Credibility in Field Settings," in Richard P. Bagozzi and Alice M. Tybout, eds., Advances in Consumer Research, Vol. 10 (Ann Arbor, MI: Association for Consumer Research, 1982), pp. 11-16.
56. Theodore Levitt, Industrial Purchasing Behaviour (Boston: Harvard University Graduate School of Business Administration, 1965).

57. Marvin E. Goldberg and Jon Hartwick, "The Effects of Advertiser Reputation and Ei tremity of Advertising Claim on Advertising Effectiveness," Journal of Consumer fc search, 17 (September 1990), pp. 172-179
58. Galen R. Rarick, "Effects of Two Components of Communicator Prestige." Unpublished doctoral dissertation, Stanford University, Palo Alto, California, 1963.
59. "Candice Bergen Leads the List of Top Celebrity Endorsers," The Wall Street Journal, September 17, 1993, p.B1.
60. "Stewart, Cosby Top Q Ratings; Where's Mike?" Advertising Age, August 31, 1992, p. 3.
61. Business Week, April 16, 1990, p. 86.
62. "Marketers Tally the Price of Michael Jackson's Fame," The New York Times, November 16, 1993, p. Cl.
63. Michael A. Kamins, "Celebrity and Non-celebrity Advertising in a Two-Sided Context," Journal of Advertising Research (June/July 1989), pp. 34-42.
64. Hershey H. Friedman and Linda Friedman, "Endorser Effectiveness by Product Type," Journal of Advertising Research, 19 (October 1979), pp. 63-71. For reviews of literature.
65. W. Benoy Joseph, "The Credibility of Physically Attractive Communicators: A Review," Journal of Advertising, 11 (1982), 15-24.
66. Brian Sternthal, Lynn W. Phillips, and Ruby Dholakia, "The Persuasive Effect of Source Credibility: A Situational Analysis," Public Opinion Quarterly, 42 (Fall 1978), pp. 285-314.
67. Lynn Kahle and Pamela Homer, "Physical Attractiveness of the Celebrity Endorser: A Social Adaptation Perspective," Journal of Consumer Research, 26, no. 1 (1985), pp. 954-960.
68. Michael Kamins, "An Investigation into the "Match-Up" Hypothesis in Celebrity Advertising: When Beauty May be Only Skin Deep," Journal of Advertising, 19, no. 1 (1990), pp. 4-13.
69. "Best Ads Don't Rely on Celebrities," Advertising Age, May 25, 1992, p. 20.
70. Gary T. Ford, Darlene B. Smith, and John L. Swasy, "Consumer Skepticism of Advertising Claims: Testing Hypotheses from Economics of Information," Journal of Consumer Research, 16 (March 1990), pp. 433-441.
71. Darlene B. Hannah and Brian Sternthal, "Detecting and Explaining the Sleeper Effect" Journal of Consumer Research, 11 (September 1984), pp. 632-642.
72. Ruby Roy Dholakia and Brian Sternthal, "Highly Credible Sources: Persuasive Facilitators or Persuasive Liabilities?" Journal of Consumer Research, 3 (March 1977), pp. 223-232.
73. Brian Sternthal, Ruby Dholakia, and Clark Leavitt, "The Persuasive Effect of Source Credibility: Tests of Cognitive Response," Journal of Consumer Research 4 (March 1978), 252-260.
74. Edward E. Jones and Keith E. Davis, "From Acts to Dispositons," in Leonard Berkowitz, ed., Advances in Experimental Social Psychology, 2nd ed. (New York: Academic Press, 1965).
75. L. Festinger and N. Maccoby, "On Resistance to Persuasive Communications," Journal of Abnormal and Social Psychology, 68 (1964), pp. 359-367.
76. David M. Gardner, "The Distraction Hypothesis in Marketing," Journal of Marketing Research, 10 (December 1970), pp. 25-30.
77. Lewis C. Winters, "Should You Advertise to Hostile Audiences?" Journal of Advertising Research, 17 (June 1977), pp. 7-15.

CHAPTER

17

COPY WRITING

AGENCIES LEARN THAT IT'S ABOUT MORE THAN ADVERTISING

During the late 1980s, many of the world's largest advertising agencies recognized that their clients were shifting more and more of their promotional budgets away from traditional media advertising to other areas of marketing communication such as direct marketing, public relations, sales promotion, and event sponsorship. In response to this trend, many of these agencies began acquiring companies that were specialists in these areas and ended up turning them into profit-centred departments or subsidiaries that often ended up battling one another for a piece of their client's promotional budget. While the agencies could point to these specialists when touting their IMC capabilities, there was really little emphasis on integrating the various communication functions.

During the 90's some agencies began taking steps to place more of an emphasis on IMC by truly integrating it into all aspects of their operations. For example, the Leo Burnett agency brought in direct-marketing, sales promotion, event marketing, and public relations professionals and dispersed them throughout the agency. Burnetters were expected to interact with clients not as advertising specialists who happened to know about sales promotion, direct marketing, or public relations, but as generalists able to work with a variety of integrated marketing tools. Another agency that embraced IMC was Fallon McElligott, which hired a president of integrated marketing and expanded its capabilities in areas such as PR, events, and interactive advertising.

As we begin the new millennium, the shift toward IMC is taking place at a number of major ad agencies that are recognizing they must embrace a way of doing business that doesn't always involve advertising. Many companies are developing campaigns and strategies using event marketing, sponsorships, direct marketing, targeted radio, and the Internet with only peripheral use of print and TV advertising. The Internet poses a particular threat to traditional agencies as it is not well understood by many agency veterans and is taking yet another slice from the marketing communications budget pie.

Foote, Cone & Belding is remaking itself as a New Economy ad agency by building up its capabilities in areas such as direct marketing, interactive, customer relationship, management/database, event marketing, and sports marketing. FCB touts its ability to offer clients a broad spectrum of integrated marketing communications services through its "Model of One," which ensures that all these services are seamlessly integrated and unified. All efforts are managed under one team and based on one strategy and one broad creative idea.

At J. Walter Thompson, the agency's CEO, Chris Jones, has championed a program called Thompson Total Branding (TTB) that makes JWT the manager of a client's brand. TTB involves taking what the agency calls a "Branding Idea" and developing a total communications plan that helps decide which integrated marketing tools can most powerfully and persuasively communicate it. One of the company executives notes, "Agencies are finally realizing that our job is creating branding solutions and, while those may involve advertising, it's not necessarily about advertising. That's a fundamental change in the way we operate." The ability to use various IMC tools has helped the agency secure new accounts and strengthens relationships with existing clients.

While traditional agencies have been preaching integrated marketing for years, many have not been really practicing it. However, these agencies are realizing they must alter their course if they plan to be competitive in the future. They are retraining their staffers in the use and best practices of various IMC tools and getting them, at Song last, to focus on total communications solutions to their clients' businesses. The move toward integrated marketing communications appears to be for real this time around.

Sources: Laura Q. Hughes, "Measuring Up," Advertising Age, Feb. 5, 200I, pp-1, 34; Kathryn Kranhold," FCB Makes Itself a New Economy Shop" The Wall Street Journal, June 14,2000, p. B8; Ellen New borne/'Mad Ave: A Star Is Reborn," BusinessWeek, July 26, 1999, pp. 54-64.

Advertisements are needed not only to introduce new products but also to boost the sales of the ones already in the market. With limited funds at a customer's disposal, his buying capacity is also limited. He can not buy everything available to him. And the one thing he decides to buy is available in so many brands that he again finds himself in a sort of dilemma which particular brand to buy? So advertisements are designed to persuade a customer into the belief that the article being advertised will give him greater satisfaction than the money in his pocket or any other item available to him, or even a similar item of a different brand. A successful advertisement tries to convince a person that he just cannot live without the particular item being advertised. In fact, advertisement has been defined as some thing which makes one think he has longed all his life for a thing he never heard of before'. And the tenacity with which advertisements impose themselves upon us prompted a writer to present the advertising man as 'Yes Sir, No Sir' man..

There was a time when advertising has enough to sell the goods being produced by one producing unit. But with large scale production, manufacturers aim at capturing much wider markets. The 'Necessitates' massive publicity campaigns, and big industrial houses allocate huge amounts on this item. Hindustan Lever spends much above Rs. two crore a year on their promotional campaigns' and ITC, are not for behind. Comparing it with above Rs. 150 crore a year being spent by General Motors, America or about Rs. 100 Crore by Colgate-Palmolive, America, and the advertisement expenses of our manufacturing units will start looking very little. When such astronomical figures are involved, advertisers would naturally like to ensure that the money being spent by them brings them adequate returns as well. That is what makes the job of a copy writer for advertisements so important.

But it is not just the money being spent that matters, the number of advertisements meeting our eye or assailing our ear in so large that a casually produced advertisement will have absolutely no effect on customer's mind. A few years back a survey was conducted to ascertain how many of the commercial manager broadcast over the Vividh Bharti Programme of the Akashvani really went home and it was revealed that only 2% messages were remembered by over 20% of the radio listeners. About 70% of the messages were remembered on an average by less than 5 percent listeners. Other messages fell in between. A similar survey undertaken in the United States of America showed that of about 1,500 advertising messages presented to the American consumer everyday, only 76 ads (in newspaper;, magazines, radio and TV) are noticed by him, and of these 76, only 12 or 13 create some king of impression on him beyond mere noticing. If these facts are put by the side of over 20,000 million dollars being annually spent on advertisement in that country, it is easy to realise how hard the advertisers must be trying to fall among the lucky 76, if not among the extra lucky 12 or 13.

Each year there is a different objective set for a company's advertising. As the days go by, the company's competitive position changes, customer requirements wax and wane, and economic conditions vary. The more dynamic these changes are, the less reliance can be placed on the application of conventional or traditional objectives and expense ratios to be advertising programme. There must be naturally, long -run advertising objectives. Well -known brand names are the result of advertising used continuously over a period of years. On the other hand, sometimes the advertiser must strike fast to meet situations unforeseen during any planning period. For instance, inventories may have accumulated because of an unexpected slump in consumer buying, or competitors may have launched new products with extensive promotion. The sudden announcement of a decay inhibitor in toothpaste, or an additive in gasoline, can throw competitors into alarm, into defensive promotion, and into the speeding-up of their own new product introduction plans. In such situations, advertising effort may be thrust into high gear with the objective of obtaining immediate sales in order to block competitive gains. Usually, advertising is intended to help make a sale. Some recent writers have suggested the value of advertisers' addressing themselves to reassuring purchases after the sale is made.

For example, the owner of a new automobile may realize that other makes are superior in important ways to the one he has purchased. Knowledge of these foregone advantages may place him in a state of anxiety called "cognitive dissonance." The proposed solution is to use advertising to help create satisfied purchasers by specifically aiming advertising at recent purchasers.

Qualities of Good Advertisements

1. Advertisements must accord to the latest fashion trends.
2. They must be brief.
3. Advertisement must cater to the consumer psychology.
4. There should be both repetition and variation in advertisements.
5. Advertisements must have a visual or auditory effect.
6. Advertisements must make the products look unique.

1. Advertisements must accord to the latest fashion trends: Advertisements must also keep abreast of changing fashions. Big business houses are always conducting sample studies to discover why people would like to buy a particular object, and they devise their messages accordingly. Once a questionnaire was circulated among a group of ladies to find out the reasons for which they would buy a face cream.

Cleans deep into pores	prevents dryness
Is a complete beauty treatment	recommended by skin doctors
Makes skin look younger	prevents make-up caking
Contains estrogenic hormones	posteurised for purity
Prevents skin from aging	smooths and wrinkles.

Majority of women said they would like to buy a cream that cleans deep into the pores. So they perceived their cream as a deep cleanser and it sold.

Similarly, one can buy a tooth paste for various reasons:

- It whitens the teeth;
- It fights tooth decay;
- It takes care of gums;
- It refreshes breath;

As a matter of fact, a good tooth paste should possess all these qualities. But today when dating is so popular, it is the effectiveness of toothpaste; as a deodorant that is most emphasised.

2. They must be brief: Commercial messages must be as brief as possible. Brevity is now Where better appreciated than in an advertisement. Nobody cares to read long messages. So either totally avoid long messages or give short, catchy captions that may compel a person to read on a long one.

A double page advertisement for JCT fabrics in 'India Today' shows a gorgeously dressed couple sitting closingly together on a luxurious sofa. Luxury is, in fact, the key note of the environment surrounding them. The dresses worn by the couple look very elegant and expensive and the only message the advertisement carries is:

It's got to be JCT.

Another advertisement for a tooth brand shows a glamorous, gorgeous American lady with her mouth open but teeth missing and a brief message boldly staring at us:

What would happen if American didn't import Royal tooth brushes?

Needless to say those such brief messages have a better chance of sticking to one's memory than long messages containing unnecessary details.

3. Advertisements must cater to the consumer psychology: Effective advertisements are always designed in the light of consumer psychology. The first important factor to ascertain before finalising a commercial message is the class of people that constitute the prospective buyers—are they man or women?—Young or old?—rich, not-so-rich or poor? — office goers, businessmen, professionals or college or university students?- Connoisseurs or laymen? All these customers will have different considerations while going in for a product. Women would willingly part with the last penny they had if same beauty aid could help them to look more adorable, or if some new product was in fashion, or if some kitchen gadget could enable them to escape the drudgery of household work. Men would prefer something to enhance their masculinity and give their personality a touch of the rugged. Young boys and girls go in for glamour and ostentatious and they prefer to look adventurous and unconventional. Durability and inexpensiveness of goods appeal to the old and the middle class people. Middle classes would also like to buy something inexpensive that could enhance their prestige and raise their social status. University and College students would swear by the 'in things' —pop music, jeans, elevators, etc. Connoisseurs would like to show they care for class.

Now analyzing the advertisements appearing in the magazines and newspapers. Most of the ads for gents suiting and make the male figure look more assertive and forceful, Digjam Suitings have "dashing designs" Old Spice is the "mark of man" Raymonds for the best dressed man from generations. An advertisement for Dinesh Suitings shows a macho man (with very prominent moustaches to underline the macho image), immaculately dressed in a suit (obviously stitched from Dinesh suitings), sitting at a table in a restaurant next to an awesome lion. VIP Frenchie (briefs for men) advertisement shows an envelope addressed to:

All those big boys
Knocking at the
doors of adulthood
India

And in place of the sender's name, it is written:

From:

VIP Frenchie
A tribute to the Indian male.

Another advertisement for HMT watches shows a bride facing a problem—which particular watch to choose for the bridegroom, for one is "Superbly Masculine". While the other is "a personification of virility."

The first thing that women dread is aging. So they would love to buy anything that would perpetuate their youth or at least prolong it as much as possible. That is why the makers of the Pears soap say:

Some Complexions Just never grow up and the message at the bottom says:

Pears Keeps your skin

Young, innocent

or, Satin doll Shampoo is for gorgeous dolls like you! And the Shampoo bottle shows a beautiful doll alongside—sufficient to appease the vanity of any young lady.

4. There should be both repetition and variation in advertisements: Advertisements have to be repetitive without being monotonous. If an advertisement is not repeated at regular intervals, its message fails to get properly registered. But if the same message is constantly hammered, soon it stops drawing attention. In fact, a stale message evokes revulsion. So an advertisement must combine in it the qualities of repetition and variation. Very often a slogan or a trade mark is made a permanent feature of a product, while subtle variations are introduced into the body of the advertisement.

Philips advertisements carry the slogan 'Let's make things better'. The advertisements present a variety of products and a variety of situations, but the slogan-Let's makes things better-remains the common denominator in all of them. Some other advertisements with such slogans are:

Ford Escorts (Car) : winning the world over

Cielo (Car) : It's not just a car; it in Care

Motorola (Pager) : What you never thought possible

Compac (Computer) : Has it changed your life yet.

Bajaj (Scooter) : Hamara Bajaj

Though the Pepsi campaign undertaken during the World Cup matches in 1996 has long been withdrawn, words to a Sikh taxi driver offering a Pepsi - Nothing official about it.

One of the best examples of using repetition and variation in the television advertisement is for Maggi Hot and Sweet Sauce. (It is a little old now). It made use of two renowned artists of the small screen—Pankaj Kapoor and Javed Jaffery-engaged in hilarious situations with Pankaj Kapoor always repeating the same slogan at the end—It's different. "Rasna" advertisements are also structured on the same principle. They deal with different situations with a lovable child giving the slogan at the end- 'I love you Rasna'.

5. Advertisements must have a visual or auditory effect: All good advertisements have a visual or auditory effect. They are either attractively displayed in magazines or newspapers, or if broadcast over the radio they sound pleasant. Advertisements flashed on the TV or the cinema screen combine in them both these qualities and are therefore quite easily remembered. In fact, many television addicts, kids in particular, get hooked to these advertisements and can reproduce them verbatim.

6. Advertisements must make the products look unique: Markets are often flooded with different brands of the same product. If all advertisements emphasize the same qualities, they will not prove effective. Therefore, discreet advertisers take pains to make their product to look unique. Take, for example, the following advertise-ments of toothpastes:

For Cleaner, Fresher breath and Whiter teeth (Colgate), Only a dentist can give her better dental care (Colgate), Toothpaste for total mouth protection (Cibaca Top). The toothpaste created by a dentist (Forhans), India's No. 1 gum health toothpaste (Pepsodent). Different people can buy different brands according to the quality that appeals to them.

Or look at the advertisements of some cigarettes.

The Four Square people say:

Live Life King Size

Four Square Kings

The one with length and strength

(emphasis on length and strength)

The Gold Flake advertisement says:

The world of Gold Flake Always smooth,

Always Mellow (emphasis on smoothness and mellowness)

And for Wills, it is

Filter and tobacco perfectly matched (with the famous slogan-made for each other)

Rothmans, perhaps, want to cash in on their reputation:

The great name in cigarettes - Rothmans. Be sure that if an advertisement cannot make a product look unique, it will not be able to sell it.

A first step in advertising a product is to determine what is to be said about it. A good deal has been written, continues to be written, and will probably always be written on the question of how to write advertising copy. Market-ing trade journals are replete with articles on how to write advertising copy. Marketing trade journals are replete with article on how to write good copy. Usually there are 5, 10, or 20 points given to bear in mind in preparing copy. There are many skills involved; and while almost any literate person might lean how to write good advertising copy, there are undoubtedly those who have a flair for this type of work. There are a few simple rules, however, which would help anyone. In the first place, the copy-writer must have a clear idea of the audience for whom he is writing. Second, there is the need for having a clear understanding as to what is going to be said. Finally, there is the importance of saying what must be said in the briefest, most interesting and forceful manner.

The second need that has been suggested knows what to say. Therefore, in copy writing is for the writer to have an easy working familiarity with the product: what it is, how it is made, and what it is supposed to do for the buyer. Although the copywriter must start with a study of factual matter matters, he often faces interesting problems in presenting these facts to the buyer in terms meaningful to the latter. Product facts can often be meaningless to the buyer. To exaggerate in order to make the point, consider colours as an example. Paint manufacturers, fabric and garment products, interior decorators, and others, frequently use such colourful terms as Moroccan Sand, Caribbean Blue, Shocking Pink. Now each of these colours has a wavelength somewhere in the visible spectrum, and the most factual way to describe these colours would be in terms of wavelengths. No consumer, however, would get any psychic satisfaction from saying she had done the library over in a wave-length of 578 thousandths of a millimeter (green). If the colour were advertised to her as such, she certainly would have no concept of what was being talked about in the advertisement The problem, therefore, is to translate the product's features into the consumer's needs.

With regard to the brevity, most people take too long to say what is on their minds and then usually enlarge on matters that have never in any real sense entered their minds. The good copywriter is trained to say what needs to be said briefly and then stop.

Instances with regard to the audience's ability to perceive and interpret an advertisement are: (1) the more trustworthy the communicator is seen to be, the greater is the tendency to accept his conclusion; (2) when the trustworthiness of the communicator is not known, the audience decides by relating the message content to their predispositions (3) if the message is attributed to "majority opinion" of a group respected by the audience, this contributes to changing attitudes; (4) "majority opinion" is more effective than "expert opinion."

Other examples can be given with regard to the effect of different communications: (1) there is no clear-cut evidence with regard to the effectiveness of rational or emotional appeals, probably because human behaviour is such a mixture of the two; (2) there is a point beyond which communication aimed at arousing fear and concern in the individual arouses so much attention that he seeks to avoid the communication; (3) after people make decisions on controversial matters, they will seek communications confirming their decisions; (4) mass media exert an important influence through opinion leaders who are "models" for opinion within their group; (5) word-of-mouth communication from a close and trusted source is more effective than media communication from a distant and trusted source; (6) arousing audience interest early in a message encourages retention of the message; (7) placing a major argument first is probably better where the subject is unfamiliar or the audience uninterested; (8) placing the major argument last is probably more effective where the subject is familiar and the audience concerned; (9) a two-sided argument is more effective when the audience is initially opposed to the communicators position, the audience is better educated regardless of its initial position, and the audience will be exposed to subsequent counter-communication regardless of its initial position. On the other hand, the two-sided argument is less effective when the audience is initially in favour of the communicator's position and will not be exposed to later counter communication.

Characteristics of good Advertisements

- Conform to the latest fashions—it is useless highlighting things nobody cares for.
- Should have both repetition and variation—repetition for continuity and as a valuable recall aid, variation to same the advertisement from monotony.
- Have, a visual or /auditory effect—Advertisements in print media should carry attractive visuals; advertisements in electronic media should have jingles or catchy dialogues.
- Should explain how the product is unique and why it should be preferred to others?
- Appeal to the psychology of the target group — The same advertisement cannot appeal equally to the man and the woman, the old, the young and the kids, the rich and the poor.
- Should be as brief as possible.

Making the advertisements attractive & effective:

1. Give catchy captions.
2. Give statistics to prove your point.
3. Enumerate your achievements.
4. Make an effective, discreet use of sex appeal.
5. Use anecdotes.
6. Make use of crazy slogans.

1. Give Catchy Captions: Catchy captions prove really effective. A caption should be dramatic so that it can immediately arrest the attention of the reader and force him to read on. See how interesting is the following advertisement for a brand of cigarettes called Abdullah:

(This is an advertisement in the no-smoker compartment of a London Transport System). & NO SMOKING NOT EVEN ABDULLAH!

'Another very interesting advertisement for Black and White Scotch Whisky appeared in Life. This advertisement shows a bottle of Black and White Scotch Whisky with the accompanying caption:

WE PROMISE NOT TO IMPROVE IT.

And at the bottom there is a brief rejoinder.

AS IF WE COULD!

A third advertisement carried the caption:

SOMETHING SPECIAL IS COMING YOUR WAY

The picture that follows shows a bewitchingly beautiful young lady climbing up the stairs and approaching the door of a room. This photograph is followed by the question.

Did you Cherry Blossom your shoes today?

2. Give Statistics to prove your point: Sometimes, statistics can be very effective provided they are depicted in a visual form, say in the form of pictograph or a pie chart.

3. Enumerate your advertisement: It is like giving statistics to prove your point an advertisement from the Khodiyar Pottery Works Ltd. (Gujarat) shows their medals lying in a row and a large sized trophy below. With an accompanying slogan: A tribute to excellence.

And the advertisement explains that after the hat-trick of council awards, the Kodiyars have now bagged a special export award. The atlas cycles proudly announced the fact that their production had crossed the one million mark. The best sellers often till you how many copies of the book have been sold and that is an inducement strong enough to make you buy it.

4. Make an effective discreet use of sex appeal: There are various kinds of misconceptions among people about the use of the female form and sex in advertisements. While some people feel that the female form can sell anything, others dismiss it as some thing cheap and vulgar, and still others feel that it proves more a distraction than an aid. A scantily clad girl showing her smooth, velvety skin may be very good for advertising a hair removing cream or a cleansing milk but we can not use the face of a beautiful girl or her curvaceous body to sell shock absorbers, unless our imagination is so fantastic that we can justify her presence in the advertisement. In advertisement from Liberty people, sex has been used with subtle wit.

The picture shows a couple embracing with only the face of the girl and the back of the man majestically covered with a liberty shirt visible, and the writing below says:

For one glorious minute they stood unmoving.

Then .... "Darling", she said,

"I can't stand on one foot the entire evening, besides my shoe is ruining (the lady has one shoe in her hand touching his shirt)

Your perfectly beautiful Liberty Shirt."

His big bold liberty plaid

made him feel devastatingly male.

"You got a choice kid", he said,

"Off with my shirt or you take off

Your other shoe. "Such a thrilling decision.

'Pet', She said, "let's compromise."

And a golden Evening began.......rhyme.

Later much later, she remembered a Nursery a

"one too, If you unbuckle your Shoe-

three, four, he'll shut the door."

And of Course, got it all wrong.

His shirt from Liberty's all new summer collection. Brilliantly designed stripes, checks, coloured, cottons, blends and pure synthetics. From Rs. 150 to Rs. 300 and over.

5. Use anecdotes: Insurance people have very often used stories and anecdotes to sell insurance ideas. These stories often describe how insurance was able to save a family from total disaster or how if the head of the family had been wise enough to provide for insurance, his family would not have suffered as it is suffering today. Similar advertisements can be used to popularise prohibition, but they tend to be long and hackneyed, so they should be used sparingly.

6. Use of Crazy Slogans: Crazy Slogan immediately draw the attention of the readers by virtue of their being so different, so original and so refreshing. Limca advertisements have been using very interesting slogans :

LIMCA IS 'VERI VERI LIME N' LEMONI'

Another advertisement show a child sipping Limca and the message says :

THIRST EXPERIENCE (Pun on first)

or the advertisement shows a crate of Limica bottles beautifully photographed with the message saying :

THIRST AID BOX (Pun on 'first aid box').

The producers of Amul butter and cheese have also been using such interesting slogans and their slogans are always structured around situations of topical interest. The very famous punch line from Amul - 'Utterly - Butterly - Delicious - Amul'.

While drafting the copy for presentation through print, the attention of buyers must first be gained so that they can be informed. Hence, an attractive design is the first virtue of a copy. Information about the product or service must be made eye or ear catching (and perhaps nose catching), and certainly interesting enough that the desire to purchase is aroused.

Advertising normally attempts to sell merchandise by explaining and often by exaggerating or "puffing" product characteristics or performance. Occasionally, unusual effectiveness is achieved by a judicious use of the opposite of puffing" when well-combined with humour. One entertainer's presentation on a television programme of frozen desert mix, illustrates this approach— "This mix," said he in substance, "tastes just like ice cream—why not buy ice cream?" One can speculate as to the mental processes which this commercial sets in motion in the minds of those buyers who then go out to buy the mix. Such speculation might be verified by research, of course, but in the interim period at least we can say that it is not always necessary to disparage the virtues of a product in order to induce sales.

Your advertisement is as much a selling approach to your customer as the visit of your representative. Therefore, it must be well 'spoken', 'well dressed' and create as favourable an impact as that of your successful salesman.

Advertisement 'copy' can be compared to sales talk 'layout', personality and appearance. The copyw[illegible] must project himself into the mind of the reader of the advertisement. He must anticipate any possible negative reaction to any aspect of the copy—for example, the price factor (if it is higher than the average), and by logical argument, which causes repulsion. Indeed, attack being the best form of defence, it may be used as a principal selling point, like it pays to pay for quality'. The copywriter must tell as much of the story as he feels will interest the reader but tell it concisely and in as few a words as possible. This is a general rule but like all other rules, it has its exceptions and the copywriter whose subject is suitable and who possesses the ability to hold the attention of the reader may practise his are in less condensed form—provided always that he has the advertising space at his disposal. The motorist is prepared to read lengthy copy about the car he proposes to purchase, the average woman about the fashion and beauty and so forth.

Types of Advertising Copy:

1. Narrative or story copy
2. Expository copy
3. Straight-selling copy
4. Suggestive copy
5. Institutional copy
6. Educative copy
7. Comic or humorous copy.

1. Narrative or Story Copy: This kind of advertisement narrates a story or an incident with the help of the product presented. The customer is expected to react sympathetically to the narration and be tempted to buy and try the product or service.

2. Expository Copy: If a copy tells openly and directly all the features of a product or a service in addition to using a suitable picture to impress a customer, it is called an expository copy. Services like hotels and airlines usually adopt this type in order to give a picturesque description of the service.

3. Straight Selling Copy: A copy which tells us why a particular brand of a certain product should be used is known as a straight selling copy or a reason why copy? The purpose of using the product and how best this purpose is served by the brand advertised are clearly explained. Any questions that might arise in the buyer's mind are anticipated and answered in the advertisement itself. The reasons for buying the product may relate to health, economy, fashion etc.

4. Suggestive Copy: This type of copy says something about a product or service but does not directly place an appeal to the customer's mind. It simply suggests that if the customer were to buy the product, he would certainly be benefited by it.

5. Institutional Copy: An institutional copy is one which tries to advertise on the strength of the the manufacturer's reputation, It tries to emphasise the fact that the manufacturer is not only well known but established enough to give the prospects the right goods. Advertisements for Khaitan fans often say: Khaitan- the name is enough. The Bajaj people also lay stress on the name Bajaj while advertising their scooters.

6. Educative Copy: Sometimes, when a particular class of buyers is to be approached the advertiser may include valuable scientific or technological information of interest to the class. Such a copy may be described as educative.

7. Comic or humorous Copy: Some humour may also be introduced into advertising copies to effectively exploit the predicament of a prospect. A humorous touch may be given through exaggeration or through caricature.

SUCCESSFUL CREATIVE STRATEGY-ONIDA

The advertising campaign for ONIDA TV will remain in the history of Indian advertising as a brilliant piece of creative work. It transgressed several rules of successful advertising and still came through as a winner. It was daring and refreshingly different—it challenged the unwritten advertising rule that advertisements had to be pleasing. Its tremendous success the product into the big league in a highly competitive market.

Onida was launched in July 1984, at a time when the transmission network in India was being rapidly expanded. At the time of Onida's entry, there were already more than 20 brands of colour television of national repute. As Onida was positioned at the upper segment of the market, the advertising campaign had to project an exclusive image for the brand. During the time of advertising development for the brand, the company felt that inspite of the product's superior quality, a feature based campaign would not work. The logic was that most of the leading competitors were already bombarding the public with such messages, inspite of which most consumers were ignorant about the finer differences in technology. The initial communication, therefore, had to be different. Hence, the advertisements carried the headline— "The boss is not late. It's the others who arrived in a hurry". The message obviously was not though Onida was a late entrant on the scene, it was the best of the lot. This advertisement was appreciated by consumers and their reactions confirmed that the message had been given home.

After the brand had been in the market for a year, the advertising message was revamped. As television sets were fast emerging as status symbols, the new ad needed to position the product at the very top. The advertisement had to serve another purpose: a colour television in India is a once-in-a-life-time purchase and people decide on a brand only after a lot of deliberation and careful search. The advertising campaign needed to persuade potential buyers to include Onida in their short list of brands. The other point to be kept in mind, of course, that was that the advertisements had to be eye catching. They had to stand out from the clutter of advertising for television sets done at that time. The advertisements created now transgressed several established rules of successful advertising. The headline proclaimed: "The most envied colour TV within a stones, throw!" and the advertisement displayed a television set with a smashed screen. The advertisement, apart from showing the product in such a poor light (i.e., with a broken screen), neither conveyed any apparent consumer benefit nor did it show a happy family scene as was the norm. Surprisingly, the public reaction was positive. After the release of the advertisement, many potential customers began trooping into dealer shops wanting to see the 'toota' (broken) television.

The 'toota' television advertisement campaign was run for a year. Therefore, it was felt that a new angle was once again needed to draw attention to the brand. The creative strategy, associating a symbolic analogy of the product with the concept of the devil, though one that is better grasped in Christian societies, was nevertheless understood by the target audience. Which was upper class? there after the devil became the spokesman for the brand. The devil made his appearance on an intact television screen in March

1986, but by then, the shattered television set has become so well recognized that the Onida dealers insisted on its revival.Three months later, the advertisement was altered accordingly to show the devil in a broken television set.

At the end of 1986, another unusal decision was taken—to advertise on television. Theoretically, this did not seem logical. Since the message would reach the homes of people who already owned television sets. But there were several good reasons for this step. It would be seen by millions of homes with black and white sets whose people aspired to own coloured television sets and also, by the millions who watched television in other's homes. Even among colour television owners, it was felt that the advertisement would become a talking point. For nearly a year, Onida got excellent mileage on TV, as no other manufacturer thought it worth while to use this medium. Latter, of course, a number of other manufacturers realised the utility of this medium.

The 21-inch Onida model advertised with the question; should the new Onida be banned is a logical extension of what the brand has stood for. Its provocative advertising has increased its sales.

Onida televisions are today among the three largest selling colour televisions in the country. The unique and memorable advertising has given them a secure nich in the Indian market The Onida campaign was indeed one of innovation and creativity with a lot of rink; yet it succeeded.

The copywriter must be intimately conversant with all competitive lines whether advertised or not (information supplied to him by the market research section), as well as all competitive advertising, being careful to avoid any idea or statement, which should constitute plagiarism or could be regarded as 'knocking' copy. He must be quite conversant with the various Codes of Standards and Merchandising Acts etc., where highly technical copy is concerned the 'specialist' copywriter is employed.

In the preparation of the layout, many factors have to be taken into account and carefully balanced. Should the advertisement be illustrated or not, and if illustrated, what should be the nature of the picture? Should it be of the product of some extraneous eye-catching device or both? Sometimes, the nature of the copy and the caption may have already pre-determined this point and in any case the visualiser and the copywriter co-operate.

ADVERTISING CAMPAIGN OF 'MARLBORO CIGARETTES'

In 1954, in USA there were only six filter cigarettes and together they added up to only 10% of the market and remaining market share was constituted by non filter cigarettes because of smoking had not yet hit the headlines and filters were regarded on the sissy side. Marlboro was known as women's cigarette — it had even the red tip to mask lipstick smears and its market share was 0.25%.

Philip Morris, owner of the brand commissioned the research to find out the reason of the dismal performance of the Marlboro cigarette. Research findings called for the masculine image and cowboy was regarded as the sign of masculinity.

The research findings were incorporated and the advertisement released (Ad 21.4) showed this using a cowboy to show the masculine image in 1955.

This positioning led to the spectacular change in the Marlboro cigarette from the women cigarette to the virile and masculine position represented by the cowboy.

To match this positioning change, the cigarette itself was given a more aromatic blend of tobacco and the pack design was modified.

Later on, the campaign was made like this, "come to where the flavour is, come to Marlboro country" and according to Robert Glatzer in his book The New Advertising called this campaign of Marlboro cigarette as the one of the most beautifully photographed series of television commercials and print ads ever done in the country.

No doubt that the filter tip of Marlboro cigarette also added the feminine image but it was made an positive attribute as the cowboy ad said "you get a lot to like in Marlboro - Filter, flavour, flip top box". Today, Marlboro cigarette is the largest selling brand of cigarette in the world.

Epilogue: The Marlboro example illustrates a situation where instead of changing the product attribute, the brand's position and perception was alerted and the given attributes were communicated in such away that its perception by the consumers was radically altered.

Philip Kotler described this exercise as the most successful cigarette brand in the history.

COPY WRITING

Copy writing is a specialized form of communicating ideas that are meant to serve the requirement of modern, marketing. The purpose is to inform or persuade or remind or collective/But before copy writing the objective of the copy should be well defined.

The copy writer must be totally familiar with the marketing goals of the advertiser and specific advertising objective. Copy writing skills require command over language and on intellectual and creative mentality.

Copywriting, illustrating, and layout are different activities associated with the creative stage of advertising development and are usually done by different people who specialize in one or the other. Copywriting in print is the activity of actually putting words to paper, particularly those contained in the main body of the text (the main arguments and appeals used), but also including attendant bylines and headlines. In broadcast, the copywriter is, in effect, a script writer who develops the scenario or script to be used in a radio or television medium; writing a jingle, or the lyrics for music, may also be involved. Illustrating is usually the work of an artist in the case of television. Layout generally refers to the activity of bringing all the pieces together and, as will be seen, differs in the case of print and broadcast.

How does one write good copy? John Caples is a member of the Advertising Hall of Fame, and his wisdom is worth reading. He retired in 1981 after fifty-four years at Batten, Barton, Durstine & Osborn, the last four decades as Vice President. Caples was one of the giants contributing to the success of BBDO. Caples states that the best ads are "written from the heart." "Write down every idea that comes into your head, every selling phrase, and every key word. Write down the good ideas and the wild ideas. Don't try to edit your ideas at the start. Don't put a brake on your imagination." In his book, he develops a checklist of important guidelines for copywriting:

1. Cash in on your personal experience
2. Organize your experience
3. Write from the heart
4. Learn from the experience of others
5. Talk with the manufacturer
6. Study the product
7. Review previous advertising for the product
8. Study competitors, ads
9. Study testimonials from customers
10. Solve the prospect's problem
11. Put your subconscious mind to work
12. "Ring the changes" on a successful idea.

Following these rules is good advice in creating copy. The idea of "ring the changes" is particular use full and interesting. Once a successful idea has been found, it should be used repeatedly with variations on the central theme. For example, an insurance company found that ads featuring retirement annuities brought the most coupon replies. So all its ad headlines featured retirement. However, the appearance of the ads was varied by using different illustrations such as a man fishing ...a couple sitting on the beach under a palm tree ... an elderly couple embarking on a cruise ship. As Caples says:

"Once you have found a winning sales idea, don't change it. Your client may be tired of it after a year or two. He sees all the ads from layout stage to proof stage to publication stage. Explain to him that whence is tired of the campaign, it is just beginning to take hold of the public".

Copywriting obviously becomes more important in the case of long copy and less important in the case where few words are included. Copy should be only as long as necessary to complete the sales job—this means that long copy is often appropriate only for the highly interested reader (such as people contemplating car purchases).

Steps in Copy Writing

Creativity is of paramount importance initiating the process of writing a copy. Creative ardour has to be combined with purposeful thinking. According to Clarke, there are following steps (Fig. 17.1) in copy writing:

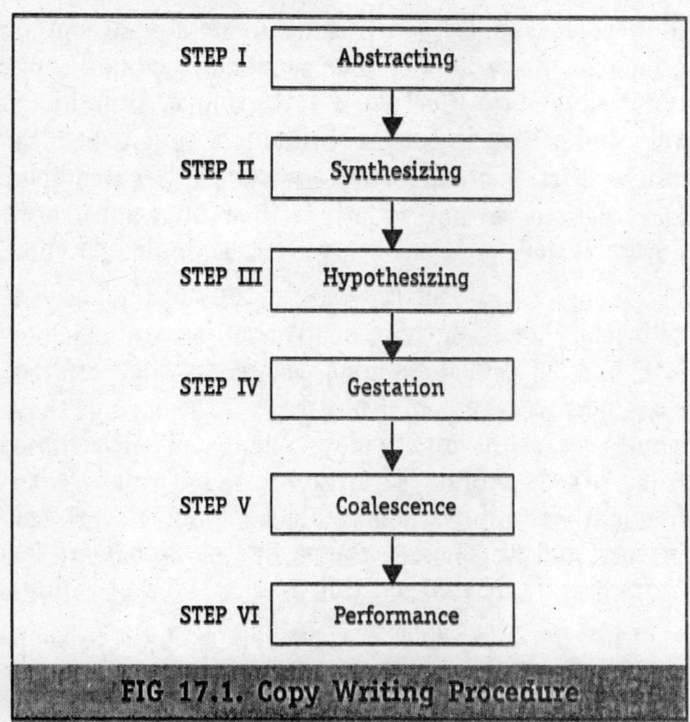

FIG 17.1. Copy Writing Procedure

STEP-I

Abstracting: Relevant data are obtained from the market situation, prospects and relevant media.

STEP-II

Synthesizing: Elements are blended and combined, ideas and approaches accepted, rejected, revised etc.

STEP-III

Hypothesizing: Ideas formulated into experimental patterns culminating in a working statement.

STEP-IV

Gestation: Objection and difficulties resolved may involve discussion with others or reference to sources of information.

STEP-V

Coalesence: Decisions are made for transferee of ideation to physical expression; U-writing.

STEP-VI

Performance: Action is taken in the form of actual writing.

COPY STRUCTURE

The total advertising copy can be classified into:

(a) Headline
(b) Body copy
(c) Close of the copy.

(a) **Head line:** The head line is that part of the copy which has been made to stand out in the advertisement by the size or style of type in which it has been set. The function of a head line is to attract the favourable attention of prospective purchasers and to interest them so that they will read the advertisement. The head line style and content will vary according to the product and purpose may be presented in the following way :

1. An indirect head line that arouse the curiosity of the reader
2. State benefit to the customer
3. A questioning approach
4. News oriented head line
5. Address to buyer directly.

(b) **Body copy:** Body copy is the middle part of advertisement which includes the text of the advertisement. A copy should do the following things in order to produce results:

1. Involve the reader
2. Help the reader
3. Conviction
4. Inducing a response
5. Inform
6. Persuade
7. Create interest.

(c) **Close of the copy:** Close of the copy calls for action. A copy may be concluded by a specific selling approach i.e., hard sell or soft sell. Hard sell calls for instant action like 'one day sale', 'limited quantity', 'offer valid till stock lasts ', 'first come first serve'. In hard sell, copy is pushy. Soft sell calls for persuasion in the phased manner but does not call for instant purchase.

Copy Elements:

(a) Headline
(b) The sub-head
(c) The body copy
(d) Captions
Hypothesizing

(e) The blurb or balloon
(f) Boxes & panels
(g) Slogan, logo types & signature.

(a) **Head line:** Presents the selling idea. Primary function is to catch the eye of the reader. Head line need not always contain special message. Company or brand name could be used as a head line.

(b) **The sub-head:** Important facts may be conveyed require more space than the head line. All advertisements do not require sub-heads.

(c) **The body copy:** Refers to the text in the advertisement. Contains details regarding the functions of the product/service and its benefits. Body copy can be short or long.

(d) **Captions:** Are small units of type used with illustrations, coupons and special offers. It can be in the form of picture option.

(e) **The blurb or balloon:** Display arrangement where words appear from the mouth.

(f) **Boxes and panels:** Special display positions to get greater attention.

(g) **Slogan, logotypes & signatures:** Logotype—company name, seal or trade mark also refer to signature. Logotype is an important aid in quick recognition.

Characteristics of Effective copy

A good copy should have the following characteristics:

1. It should be concise
2. It should have air to sell
3. It should be addressed according to the type of audience
4. It should influence the reader's thoughts and/or action
5. It should inspire confidence
6. It should be precise
7. It should be sincere
8. It should create desire
9. It should stimulate interest
10. It should aim to sell.

General Copy Principles

While there are no (and should never be any) "rules" for what makes for good copy, it is worthwhile to become familiar with some generally accepted principles. Regardless of the specific ad medium, copy is usually more effective if it is simple, containing only one or two key ideas; contains a benefit or idea unique to the brand being advertised; is extendible (can lead to several variations in a campaign); and flows naturally and smoothly from beginning to end.

Good ads are specific, using facts and figures and believable details instead of generalities. An example is the 1993 MCI telephone campaign that offered customers written "proof positive" of the savings they would get every ninety days, compared with those from other phone carriers. Another "rule" is to frequently mention the brand name and key consumer benefit; and to conclude the ad by linking back to its beginning, with a strong call to some kind of action.

One overriding rule for developing copy is to keep the format simple, uncluttered, and straightforward. Whether in print or in broadcast, the tendency for including too much information or for complicating the television commercial with too many scene changes, or scenes that are not well integrated, should be avoided. This principle of simplicity extends to the language used as well. Like cluttered format, complicated language is unlikely to induce people to spend the time to "figure it out." The message should always be true to the product. Claims should be sub satiable, and the style should not be radically altered over the life cycle of the product.

Print Copy Principles

For print ads, one of the key elements is the headline, which must flag down the target reader and pull him or her into the body copy, offering a reward for reading on. This is best achieved by headlines that appeal to the reader's self-interest (e.g., by offering free, useful information), are newsy, offer new twists on familiar sayings, and/or evoke curiosity (e.g., by asking a quiz like question).

Since most people reading print ads never go beyond the headline, it is also extremely important that the headline and visual complement each other so well and "tell the story" so easily, that a reader who only looks at the headline and main visual can "get the message" without having to read a word of the body copy.

As for the body copy itself, it should be detailed and specific, support the headline, and be readable and interesting. Story appeal is another effective copy device. Copy should be only as long as needed to do the selling task (high-involvement purchases may call for detailed copy), but body copy can be made readable by the use of sub-heads and captions.

Research by Michael Houston, Terry Childers and Susan Heckler has shown that attribute information is recalled better when it is presented both as a picture and in words (for example, a teddy bear to depict softness in a fabric softener ad) than when it was presented only as words with a different attribute conveyed in the picture. However, this extra recall effect of pictures that exemplify verbal product attribute information appears to occur only when the verbal information is itself of low imagery (does not involve visualization of a concept or relationship). Such imagery or visualization occurs more easily if the ad uses concrete rather than abstract words, if the ad is believable, and if the ad does seem to create more liking for the ad and the brand. The message of the ad is also more memorable if its various parts are consistent rather than inconsistent, for example an ad for ICY Vodka from Iceland, showing a bottle apparently made out of ice and using copy reading "Smooth as Ice ... Icy cold, Icy clear..."

Other research has discovered that more imagery is evoked if the picture makes it easy for the consumer to plausibly imagine himself or herself in engaging in that behaviour. The effects of an ad's pictures on brand attitudes (liking) seem to increase if they contain product-relevant information, especially for highly involved consumers.

THEMATIC CLASSIFICATION

The central theme of the advertisement runs through the entire advertisement. Advertising themes can be classified an under:

(a) Utilitarian
(b) Focussed
(c) Informative
(d) Non-specific
(e) Achievement orientation
(f) Descriptive and projective
(g) New product service, scheme or idea.

(a) Utilitarian: The emphasis on the value-(benefit) of the product/service.

(b) Focused: Are appeal to specific market/ audience segment.

(c) Informative: Consists primarily of imparting information about the product/service.

(d) Non-specific: Theme which is vague and diffuse.

(e) Achievement orientation: Advertise the achievement of the advertiser as increase in turnover, winning an award etc.

(f) Descriptive and projective: Combination of information and achievement orientation themes.

(g) New product service, scheme or idea: Advertising for launching a new product, service schemes or propagating a new idea.

ADVERTISING CREATIVE STRATEGY EVALUATION

- The end product advertising planning and creative strategy. And its execution, is the form in which an advertisement appears.
- There are variations according to the media used.
- The creation of an advertising message commences with the overall marketing and advertising goals.
- Setting of advertising budget provides boundary parameters so that the formulation of the message may be trimmed down accordingly.
- the seeds of advertising message are to be found in the purchase preposition.
- The success or failure of the message, as measured by the reception by the audience depends a great deal on what the advertiser has to offer, not merely in terms of product quality and characteristics but more as to their relevance to the prospect's requirements and mental make up.
- The entire copy should be structured along the AIDA line.

ADVERTISEMENT LAYOUT

In the initial stages of an ad's development either the copy writer or the art director forms a mental image of the ad. The copy writer may use rough sketches to develop the theme and to convey ideas to the artist. The artist will visualize the thought sketch and provide a pictorial representation of it.

Visualisation is often confused with the terms illustration and layout. Visualisation precedes both the illustration and layout and is the process of forming a mental image, picture or representation of an object or idea. The layout is the physical arrangement of the elements in an advertisement so that this mental idea may be effectively presented. The picture portion of the layout is generally referred to as the illustration.

Much of the creativity in advertising evolves from the process of visualisation and the countless ways in which mental images can be made to represent ideas. Impending danger is vividly and graphically presented by an onrushing train over an old trestle, a child retrieving a ball in a street, or a flashing red light. Effective advertising requires that these images be consistent with a advertiser's message, which is concerned with the need or desire the product fulfills.

It is the job of the layout artist to combine all the elements in the idea into a single, effective communication. This requires adding to the idea a head line, illustration, body text, logotype and occasionally a sub-head line, picture caption trade mark, coupons or seal of approval.

The layout is the arrangement of the entire verbal copy element plus the art work (drawing, photography, logo types) on the paper. The layout shows the rough composition of the design of a print ad so that all of those concerned with the ad can evaluate it and so that those who need to produce the ad will have the blue print to follow.

Purposes and Function of Layout

There are following reasons for making a layout:

1. The layout provides a working blending of the creative abilities of all personnel involved in the preparation of the advertisement.
2. It provides a blur print in meet the mechanical requirements of engravers, typographers, and others, as well as giving specifications for estimating costs.
3. A layout shows how an ad is look and, therefore, must contain all the necessary elements.
4. It permits all interested parties particularly the client, to see the advertisement before final stops air taken in put it in print.
5. The layout also serves as gauge to determine if all the materials that will go into the advertisement will fit into a given space.

Layout Procedure

Layout procedure is a logical progression from the visualization to the completed arrangement. Layout procedures involves the following steps (Fig. 17.2).

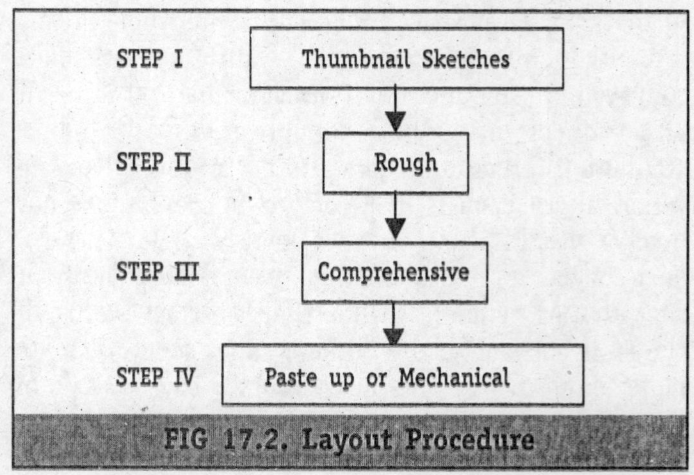

FIG 17.2. Layout Procedure

STEP-I

Thumbnail sketches: Frequently layout starts with thumbnail sketches, simple drawings that contain an ad's basic elements. These small sketches are generally drawn in the experimental stage to show the different ways of arranging the elements. Not every designer uses a thumbnail sketch, however, some skip this step altogether and begin with the rough.

STEP-II

Rough: The rough, or visual, evolves from the acceptable thumbnail and although it is still some what sketchy, it begins to present more detail. The purpose of the rough is to convey the idea to agency personnel. It is the same size as the future advertisement, but the illustrations are roughed in, the headlines are lettered hastily, and the copy blocks are represented by horizontal parallel lines. Despite the hasty sketching and lack of detail, tonal values are clearly apparent, as is the spacing of the elements. The rough is good for analysis and criticism and a number of roughs may be completed before the final one is accepted.

Many agencies feel that roughs are fresher and have more spontaneity than the comprehensives which is the next steps. Therefore, they use roughs exclusively to show to clients. The philosophy behind this is that the required to judge the idea, not its execution. Roughs are also less expensive.

STEP-III

Comprehensive: A comprehensive usually on heavy paper or card board and provides further refinement of the rough. The art work is shown in approximately its final form or, when a photograph in used, the photograph or a carefully prepared postal representing it, will be pasted into position. Headlines are carefully traced or reproduced by other means. Typed matter is shown by ruled lines and careful lettering is shown in its exact hue and value to indicate tone and colour.

Comprehensives are expensive. They are frequently prepared by a freelance artist or art studio and used to help the client judge the effect of the finished advertisement. Payment for the art work is subject to negotiation when an agency is hired. Generally, advertising agencies absorb the cost of finished layouts in commissions they receive from media, but the client may be billed for the additional expense of a comprehensive layout when a comprehensive is not prepared the finished layout, which is more carefully executed than the rough, may be submitted to the client for approval.

STEP-IV

Paste up or mechanical: The paste up or mechanical, is actually a step beyond layout, but is so closely allied that it is frequently considered as part of the process. To determine the size for the paste up, the designer can refer to a publication rate card or standard rate and data service which offers such information for various media.

The paste up contains all the elements of a layout. Often the type is photographed in place but, the art elements are photographed separately. Then all parts are "stripped" in and made into a final film-from which plates are made.

Principles of Effective Layout

Fundamentally a good layout should attract attention and interest and should provide some control over the manner in which the advertisement is read. The message to be communicated may be sincere, relevant and important to the consumer, but because of the competitive noise in the communication channel, the opportunity to be heard depends upon the effectiveness of the layout. In alteration to the attracting attention, the other requisite for the effective layout includes:

(a) Space division and balance
(b) Proportion
(c) Movement
(d) Unity
(e) Emphasis
(f) Clarity and simplicity.

(a) Space division and balance: While it is difficult to give an exact definition for the division of space, it is, however, this proper dividing of space that satisfies an inner sense of proportion and causes the reader to be pleased with the harmonious structure of the advertisement.

The division of space leads in to a wide variety of complicated designs or patterns. However, at present it is more important to consider the fundamental divisions and their comparative values in order that the different units (illustration, headlines, copy, trade mark, signature, and so on) may be placed and divided effectively.

Fig. 17.3 illustrates the various space divisions. Illustration 3 in divided at the centre by a vertical dotted line. Number 2 is divided into a equal parts by a horizontal line. Both spaces have been cut exactly in half, leaving two equal divisions for space. This is the least complex of any possible division. Such divisions which are equal have a tendency to be uninteresting & monotonous. Monotony many result from equality or uniformity. Thus, to avoid monotony, it is usually better not to divide the space into equal parts.

Illustration 3 & 4 depicts inequality. It illustrates a dramatic, unequal, interesting situation. These situations are the kinds that attract attention.

Illustration 5 & 6 are similar to 3 & 4 except that each one has divided into 3 spaces instead of two. These divisions give dramatic situation which for attracting interest are probably greater than those found in 3 & 4.

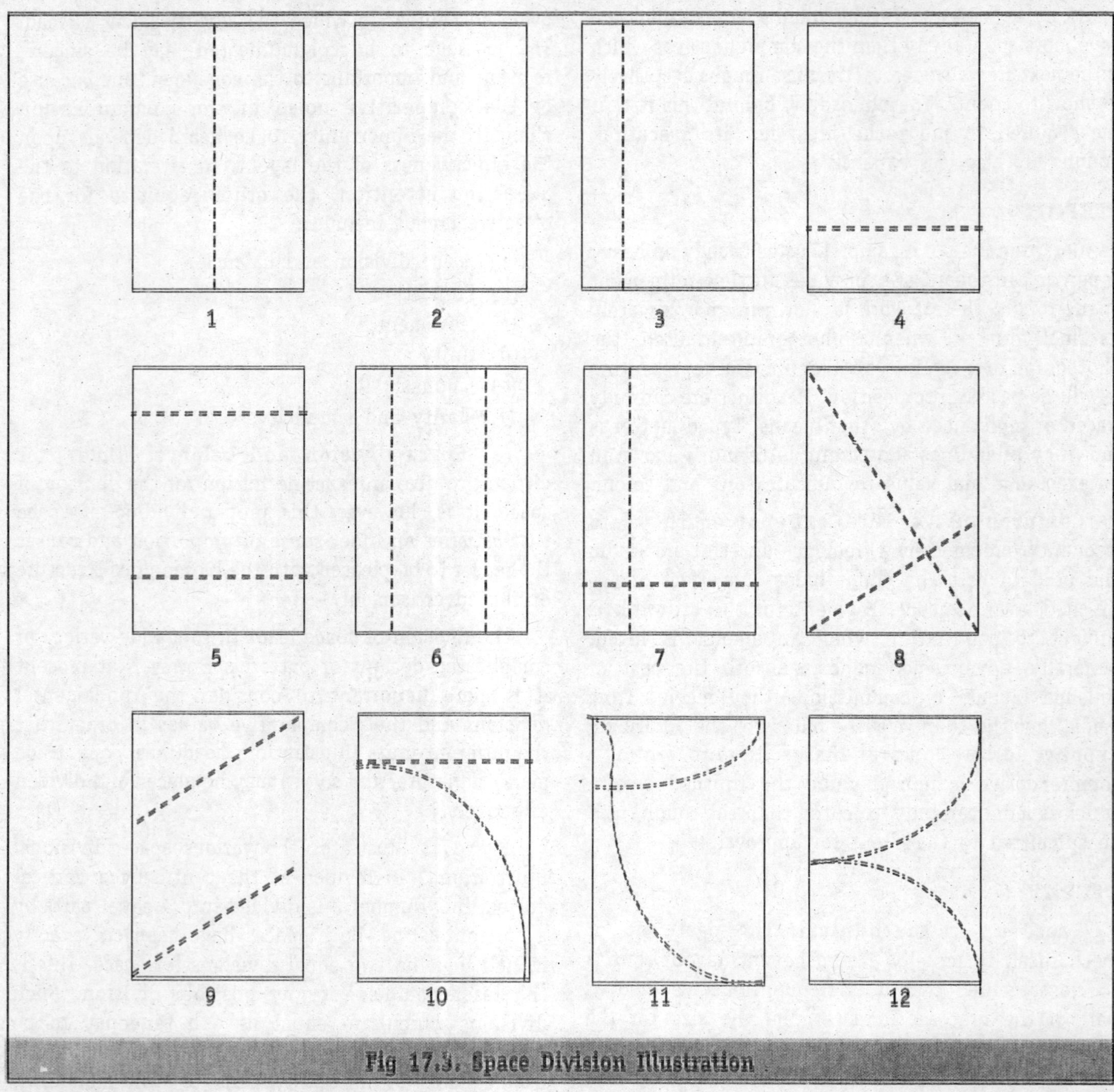

Fig 17.3. Space Division Illustration

Illustration 7 gives a more complex division of space. None of the four spaces is equal in area. It broadens even further the possible fields of activity which enable a layout man to produce greater variety. It has the advantage of oblongs, both horizontal and vertical. The intersecting point of the two divisional lines also results in an "X". This provides another device for attracting attention.

Illustration 8 provides a space divided into 4 unequal parts, three of them forming triangles of different sizes. The division is brought about by two diagonal lines crossing each other, producing the "X". The crossing of opposed diagonal lines is symbolic of crossed swords, and creates the atmosphere, of duels, battle the like. This dramatic attraction attracts attention and creates interests.

Illustration 9 is another of the many possible uses of diagonals. This is similar to illustration 5, but possesses an appeal with gets the feeling of the power required to pull some thing effect of cosign down at a high rate of speed.

Illustration 10 portrays a combination of straight and circular lines bringing about two curved space divisions, curves create soft fluid designs, lacking in force and directness when compared to straight lines, but making up for this deficiency in beauty.

Illustration 11 and 12, the divisional lines are curved. It is the opinion of many artists that straight lines are masculine in fouling and curved lines are feminine. Men usually are attracted by advertisements that go straight to the facts in a logical manner. Beauty in advertising is not as important to man as it is to women. Women are usually attracted by advertisements that tend toward the artistic and consider logic and facts as secondary. It should not be overlooked, however, that curved divisions of space made by straight lines create a feeling of power, speed and excitement.

(b) Proportion: Proportion helps develop order and creates a pleasing impression. It is related to balance but is concerned primarily with the division of space and the emphasis is to be accorded each element. Proportion, to the advertising designer, is the relationship between the size of one element in the ad to another, the amount of space between elements, as well as the width of the total ad to its depth. Proportion also involves the tone of the ad, the amount of light area in relation to dark area and the amount of colour and non-colour.

As a general rule unequal dimensions and distances make the most lively design in advertising. The designer also places the elements on the page so that each element is given space and position in proportion to its importance in the total advertisement and does not look like it stands alone.

(c) Movement: If an advertisement is to appear dynamic rather than static, it must contain some movement. Movement (also called sequence) provides the directional flow for the advertisement, gives it its follow through, and provides coherence. It guides the reader's eye from one element to another and makes sure he does not miss anything.

Motion in layout is generally from left to right and from top to bottom — the direction established through the reading habits of speakers of Western language. The directional impetus should not disturb the natural visual flow but should favour the elements to be stressed, while care should be taken not to direct the reader's eye out of the advertisement.

(d) Unity: Another important design principle is the unification of the layout. Although an advertisement is made up of many elements, all of these should be welded into a compact composition. Unity is achieved when the elements tie into one another by using the same basic shapes, sizes, textures, colours and mood. In addition, the type should home the same character as the art.

A border surrounding an ad provides a method of achieving unity. Sets of borders may occur within an ad, and, when they are similar in thickness and tone, they provide a sense of unity. Effective use of white space can help to establish unity, white space in defined as that part of advertising space which is not occupied by any other elements in this definition. White space is not always white in colour. White space may be used to feature an important element by setting it off, or to imply luxury and prestige by preventing a crowded appearance. It may be used to direct and control the reader's attention by tying elements together. If white space is used incorrectly, it may cause separation of the elements mid create difficulty in viewing the advertisement as a whole.

(e) Emphasis: Although varying degrees of emphasis may be given to different elements, one unit should dominate. It is the designer's responsibility to determine how much emphasis is necessary, as well as how it is to be achieved. The important element may be placed in the optical center or removed from the clutter of other elements. Emphasis may also be achieved by contrasts in size, shape and colour, or the use of white space.

(f) Clarity and simplicity: The good art director does not permit a layout to become too complicated or tricky. An advertisement should retain its clarity and be easy to read and easy to understand. The reader tends to see the total image of advertisement; thus it should not appear fussy, contrived or confusing. Colour contrasts, including tones of grey, should be strong enough to be easily interpreted, and the various units should be clear and easy to understand. Type size and design should be selected for ease of reading, and lines of type should be a comfortable reading length. Too many units in an advertisement are distracting; therefore, any element that can be eliminated without destroying the message should be done in a way in which clarity can be achieved is by combining the logo, trade mark, tag line, and company name into one compact group.

Since a large amount of money is risked in advertising, pre-testing of advertisements before use is common. The problem is to present the advertisements in a normal setting. To do this the respondents should be representative or the readers and viewers of, or listeners to, the medium in which the advertisement will appear. Second, the respondent should give as much and no more attention to the advertisement in the test setting than in the normal setting. Third, the test advertisement must be presented in a medium identical to that in which it will be used and in the same form. Unfortunately, it is not always possible to meet these conditions. First, it is often difficult to define the universe of potential customers interested in the product so that a probability sample can be drawn. Second, the respondent in, most situations is either told or can infer that his opinions on advertisements are sought, and consequently he does not behave normally. And third, unless the advertisement is actually used in a test market, the medium and the advertisement under test conditions will not match actual conditions.

There are three basic techniques for comparing advertisements. The first is termed monadic in that the' respondent is shown only one advertisement. Since only one advertisement is used, it is believed that the respondent does not become overly pre-occupied with evaluation and that his responses may be more natural. The difficulties with this method are that it is costly, because different groups are required for each advertisement, and in addition, there are problems in matching test groups. A second method is that of paired comparison, where the respondent is shown no more than two advertisements simultaneously or serially. Use of more than two advertisements is thought to confuse the respondent. The advantage of this approach is that it presents a readily understandable choice, and the need for choice facilitates making detailed comparisons. The disadvantage is that while a choice is made, one doesn't know how good or bad the advertisement is. A third method is that of order of merit or rank order designs. Here the respondent ranks three or more advertisements or their components against pre-chosen criteria. One can see that the paired-comparison and order-of-merit methods may be combined by taking a winning advertisement from the former method and comparing it with a third advertisement. Opinion is divided as to whether using three or more advertisements facilitates or complicates comparisons.

RADIO AND TELEVISION COMMERCIALS

Radio and television stations, unlike the print media rely on waves passing through the air and ground around us to carry their messages.

Listeners and viewers turn to radio and television for a multitude of reasons but the primary purposes are to be entertained or informed. Beyond those reasons, there is the widely accepted idea that many listeners or viewers employ radio and television for background melody when engaged in day-to-day activities. They value these media simply for their presence. When at home many people use broadcasting simply for company; students and office workers often use it as a backdrop, for other mental activity.

Unlike most printed publications, broadcasting appears to the listening and viewing publics to be free. But this is a misconception. About 10 crores of rupees are spent for radio and television sets each year, not to mention the cost of electricity used for running those receivers. Broadcasting and telecasting stations even when publicly owned are subsidized by tax monies, and income from programmes sponsored by business houses for publicity of their products. This brings in the contributions to keep these stations airborne. The advertising money that supports commercial broadcasting is ultimately paid by the buyers of advertised products.

Radio Copy Principles

For radio ads, a key principle usually is to write copy that "creates a picture in the mind's eye" of the listener. The radio ad must pull the listener in from whatever is being done when the ad comes on, into an imagined situation, through use of the human voice, sound effects, humour, and music. Research shows that sound effects increase imagery activity and, through that, the evocation of feelings that are not verbally described in the ad. Though it can occasionally be distracting, product related imagery usually increases the ad's liability and the recall and recognition of ad claims.

It is usually also important in radio to mention the brand name and the key selling benefit early and often. Short words and short sentences are usually easier to understand on the radio. Obviously, radio ads can use various creative tools, and a typology of different kinds of radio ads has been developed.

Television Copy Principles

Television scripts must usually be written to take advantage of the visual nature of the medium, by using demonstrations, pack close-ups, and the like. The message contained in the pictures is especially important now that many consumers pay only limited attentions to advertisements. Since TV ads are fleeting and cannot usually easily communicate much information, simplicity (and frequent and early mention of the brand name and key idea) are strongly recommended. TV ads get higher recall scores if they contain more frequent visual representations of the brand name, package, and key product attributes.

TV ads also get higher persuasion scores if the shots in the ad are more "connected" and better-linked to each other. While there seems to exist a belief that TV ads should use more shots because viewer attention spans are getting shorter—the average number of shots per ad is up from eight in 1978 to thirteen in 1991—research has actually found that as the number of shots per ad goes up, the ad's recall and persuasion scores go down, even among young viewers. Amazingly, it has been found that if the camera angle is such that the product or person appears bigger, stronger or bolder, the ad is evaluated more favorably, though this happens mostly for consumers processing the TV ad in a low-involvement fashion. It bears repeating, however, that the key factor making for a persuasive TV ad is as simple as the presence of a strong brand-differentiating benefit. While the creative execution is certainly important, if you want a persuasive ad, make sure you've got the right (strong and convincing) message.

Types of Broadcast Advertising: A national advertiser who decides to embark on an advertising campaign using the broadcast media has a number of decisions to make beyond simply selecting radio or television or a combination of the two. This section deals with the major alternatives and some of the criteria used in determining how to approach campaign.

1. **The Network Approach:** Advertisers often turn to the radio or TV networks to carry their advertising message when they wish to cover the entire country or a very large geographical section there of. It is better in its coverage to even advertising in a large national magazine. There are many different reasons for choosing the network to carry advertising messages, some of the most important of which are:

1. Networks offer an opportunity to air an advertising message through hundreds of local stations at a lower cost than buying the same stations individually.
2. Advertisers have better control over the presentation of their commercials through network broadcasting.
3. Networks provide a single billing for all stations covered.
4. Networks can offer simultaneous coverage with excellent control over time and location of commercials within the network's own programming.

2. **The Spot Broadcasting Approach:** Geographical flexibility is provided to the national radio or TV advertiser through the spot broadcasting device. There is often some confusion about the term spot because it is used in two different ways. Most people think of a broadcast commercial as a spot, and it is common to hear advertising professionals apply the same term as a slang expression for a short announcement or commercial. But lay people think to realize that the expression is also used by advertising people in a second sense. Spot broadcasting is the selection of specific markets and specific stations within those markets. It is an alternative to networks to achieve national advertising objectives; in short it is non-network national broadcast advertising. Spot broadcasting is particularly suitable for advertisers who have incomplete national product distribution limited advertising budgets that preclude the use of networks, of fluctuating regional sales patterns.

Spot television has been described by its promoters as a method of approaching TV advertising that delivers infinitely varying kinds and varying amounts of advertising pressure anywhere as the advertiser requires it.

It always originates from and is controlled in, the individual market where it is released. Commercials are not "piped through" local stations from the networks. They are originated from each station participating in a campaign.

3. Programme Sponsorship Approach: Most adults think of television broadcasting in terms of specific programme and the sponsors of those programmes. We have already stated, however, that radio programme sponsorship as such disappeared when television swept the country.

4. Participation Shows: In the natural evolution of things, the participation programme has replaced the fully sponsored show on network television. A participation show is one in which a variety of sponsors place commercials within the body of the programme that is after the first introduction of the programme, during breaks, and at the program's conclusion. Contrary to a popularly held idea, the expression "participation" has nothing to do with whether or not members of the studio audience participate in contests or exchange pattern with the master of ceremonies.

The term "participation" as we employ it here refers to advertisers participating in paying for the programme as though they were actually sponsors when in fact; they have nothing to do with the production of the show itself. This has been a growing trend in network television for many years and has been referred to as the "magazine concept".

In this regard, advertisers buy into a network programme as they would buy into a magazine. They place their commercials in an appropriate programme with no responsibility for the details of the program (editorial) content.

5. Announcement Campaigns: Announcement campaigns are a form of local advertising or spot broadcasting. The fundamental difference between these commercials and those within network programme is that these commercial announcements are sold only by local stations (these are privately owned in some countries) or their representatives and are aired between regular programs, rather than within them. There is little opportunity for the advertiser to identify a product with the shown in as much as the commercial announcements placed between shows are isolated from the shows themselves. This is viewed by some as a disadvantage.

There is the additional disadvantage inherent in the fact that the break between programmes is often a relatively long one with many commercials, station identification breaks, promotional spots for coming programme etc. It is a fine time for viewers to remove themselves from the television set for a visit to the bathroom or kitchen, or to catch up on a little reading. Lastly, many people are great deal switchers and it is possible that the announcement will be aired at the moment when thousands of viewers are flipping from one channel to another.

6. Radio and T.V. Advertising in India: In India radio and T V advertising has come to possess vast potentiality. Vividh Bharti programmes of Delhi, Mumbai Kolkata and Channai have their Commercial Services - To make them attractive, the programmes usually comprise light music of regional taste with commercial message broadcast in between the songs. The four Commercial Service Programmes cover the entire country in respect of their respective regions - Northern, Eastern, Western and Southern.

Most of the progressive firms find it profitable to relay their messages in the Commercial Publicity programmes. Any good manager is supposed to be aware of the procedures involved in issuing out the business messages and to give maximum publicity in minimum possible words. There are professional organisations mainly located in Delhi and Bombay undertaking to tape the messages with the help of sound models.

As for TV advertising there are video producers who film dynamic shots both spot and sponsored with the help of beautiful models trained for display in attractive colors, coupled with stereo audio systems and tape recorders.

7. The Photograph Approach:

Uses of Photographs: The use of photography in public relations deserves special attention as many people do not realize the full potentialities of photographs. The first point to appreciate is that photographs always lend authenticity. Everyone knows that photographs can be as misleading as statistics, but nevertheless they are accepted, by and large, as authentic proof of facts or events.

Good photographs have a compelling appeal that is absent from printed matter, however well laid out and displayed. Few publications are found these days in which photographs and other types of illustrations are absent for it has become generally accepted that photographs add to the interest and stimulate close attention. This is now true even of such publications as company's annual reports which were formerly austere documents but are now often illustrated.

Photographs may be required for the following reasons:-

1. To illustrate news stories, for newspapers or technical press
2. To illustrate reports, booklets, house journals, etc.
3. For record purposes
4. For use in advertisements or posters
5. For training and research.

There are seven main points to watch for securing the best results from photography.

1. Secure the best photographer for the particular type of assignment. It is more useful to have a few photography by an expert than many by a less brilliant exponent.
2. Give the photographer a careful briefing on the type of photographs required. It is necessary to tell him what shots to take.
3. Unless the photographer secures friendly and willing co-operation from those with whom he is dealing, his job is almost impossible of accomplishment.
4. Ensure that all prints and negatives are adequately housed and catalogued for easy reference.
5. When using photographs for block-making take considerable trouble to ensure the best result by "cropping" the print.
6. Carefully examine prints before blocks are made in order to make sure that there are no old tin cans, trailing wires or other accidental and unwanted extras in the picture.
7. Choose the best screen for block-making, having regard to the type of printing paper to be used and the quality and contrast of the print.

8. **Film as an Advertising Medium**: Documentary films are a very powerful medium of publicity. India can rightly claim to be the producer of good documentary films and many extremely good ones are always being made. Films play an important part in teaching, education, training, research and in many aspects of society, science but it is their use in public relations that will be considered here. Before embarking on film making, it is essential to consider three fundamental points:

1. What is the object of the film?
2. For what audience is the film intended and can this audience be reached successfully?
3. How much money can be spent to better advantage in other ways?

   It is on these basic questions that advertisement departments should be competent to advise.

A film should be conceived in a very precise way. It must be aimed at a specific audience, with the intention of imparting information out putting over a particular point of view. Film has the power, shared only by television of bringing audiences into direct communication with facts and ideas through the senses—sight and hearing—and the emotions. It is only worth making a film if the intended audience can be defined and it there is a reasonable prospect of being able to reach it. A small influential audience may sometimes justify the total expense of the film but it is a true anomaly that films made specifically for a particular audience often have a surprising success with a much wider public. This possibility does not excuse the need to define audiences in advance. The audience to be reached is either the general public through the commercial cinema or television (the "theatrical audience") or other audiences which are classified as "non-theatrical audiences"). These audiences may be home and/or overseas. These two groups of audiences will react better to different methods of approach and often require different techniques in film production.

Cinema audiences are reached either by advertising films or by general interest films which are shown for their entertainment value. Such films must be of high quality and artistic standards, and because the film must avoid advertising it is more likely to be made by an industry than an individual company. In fact, it is seldom worthwhile for a company to make a film for theatrical distribution alone, since the message must be so indirect. An exception to this general rule is when the product is of national interest such as motor cars, steel, oil, gas or electricity; or when the film is made for showing in a town which is dominated by the firm's own employees.

An Industrial Film: The making of an industrial film for cinema distribution is always something of a gamble and the possibilities should be discussed with the producer at an early stage. It is desirable to endeavour to get a film renter to agree that the script is agreeable to him before production commences, but it is unusual for a renter to agree to distribute a short film theatrically until he has seen the finished film. If cinema distribution is considered to be very important, it is wise to engage the services of a film company with a good record of achieving such distribution for its films. Films may achieve TV showing as well as cinema distribution, very seldom both.

Making the Film: In making a film it is wise to use the services of an established film company unless specialist knowledge is available within one's own organisation. It is possible to make good films oneself, using free-lance producers and camera-men, and it works out much cheaper but this is a course to be adopted with great caution. In general, one gets the film one pays for and it is unwise to draw up too parsimonious a film budget as it will probably be reflected in the result.

The established film companies charge considerably more than some private producers, but the sponsor can usually expect a much higher standard of production if he deals with a well -established company, fully equipped and employing a regular staff of high-grade technicians.

It is important to choose a producer with whom the sponsor will be able to work harmoniously and who inspires confidence. Before any production company is approached direct, it is a good idea to contact both the Association of Specialised Film Producer Ltd., which will furnish a list of its members, and any people who have made film of a somewhat similar nature and are willing to pass on the benefit of their experience.

Thus most valuable guide to the ability of a producer is to see some of his recent films. A producer should be pleased to arrange such a show and it will permit an assessment of the technical standard of the films and give an idea of the producer's method of tackling different subjects. The producer should also be willing to give some idea of the cost of the films shown. This will provide an approximate idea of the likely cost of the film in prospect.

The Production: In order of their, appearance on the scene it will consist of the producer, writer, director, cameraman and editor. This is the creative team but behind them come the laboratory processing facilities and the recording technicians staffing the studio.

The Producer: The producer will conduct most of the preliminary negotiations with the sponsor. His duty is to conceive the way in which the sponsor's objects can be achieved through the medium film and to interpret this to his creative team. Every film bears the clear imprint of its producer, and he is responsible at all times for the production of the film and the selection of his team working on it. A producer, however, may have several films in production at the same time, and so it is important that he should have at his disposal skilled directors and cameramen who can deal with the actual shooting of the film.

The Writer: The writer's job is to prepare the "treatment" which is the working draft giving a general outline of the film. He, or possibly another commissioned by the producer specifically to deal with a very specialized subject, also writes the completed script, or shooting script, which gives the dialogue or commentary of the film and the shots appropriate to the text. The producer sometimes writes the script himself but often he prefers to be able to criticize the film objectively and so takes no part in the writing or direction. The writer naturally works closely with the producer at all stages of production and accompanies him during the "investigation" when the producer makes his preliminary study of the subject of the film.

The Director: The shooting script is interpreted in film form by the director. In certain cases he may have Written the shooting script himself. Directors are often particularly good at certain types of film and it is the producer's responsibility to select a director who is suited both technically and temperamentally to the film in question. A good director is a skilled and highly paid man for he requires a complete knowledge of all the camera techniques available to him and the artistry to present picture and sound to achieve the maximum effect from the script.

Cameramen: In a major film there are usually both the lighting cameraman and the camera operator. The lighting cameraman creates a picture in light and shade, by his sitting of the camera in relation to the lighting. The success of the visual element of the film will depend largely on his skill. The camera operator operates the camera and is responsible for the techniques which record the picture successfully on film. In many instances, the lighting cameraman does both jobs with' the aid of an assistant.

The Editor: The editor's job is a most important one, for by cutting and arrangement he turns a number of isolated sequences into a finished film. This is not a mechanical task; for example, it is his job to evaluate the emphasis to be given to each shot by regulating the length of time it appears on the screen. The editor must work closely with the producer in order to achieve the desired result from the film.

9. The Sequence of Operations: Once a producer has been chosen it is necessary to furnish him with a statement of the policy on the film, which is known as a brief. The brief will normally include information on nine headings.

1. **The Object of the Film:** This should state clearly what it hoped to achieve by the use of the film. This statement will be the producer's main guide through his subsequent work on the film.

2. **Audience:** It is important that the producer should be given a clear indication of the types of audience for which the film is intended.

3. **Content:** This should list all the material which it is hoped can be included in the film. The relative importance of the items should be given as a guide to the producer and editor on the intended emphasis of the film.

4. **Length:** This must be stated but it will be influenced by the cost of the film.

5. **Facilities:** Details should be given of the facilities that will be available during the production of the film. These may include library information, use of factory staff or technicians, etc.

6. **Time Factor**: It is desirable to state the date when the finished film is required for Radio & Television Commercials.

7. **Distribution:** The producer needs to know the methods of distribution by which it is planned to reach the principal audience. This will help the producer to decide the techniques he should use in the actual making. of the film.

8. **Cost:** It is necessary to give the producer some idea of the amount of money available in order that he may suggest the appropriate type of film that can be made within the budget. In arriving at these figures, it is necessary to allot sufficient money to cover the costs of distribution.

9. **Liaisons**: The contact between producer and sponsor will normally be through the public relations staff. It may be desirable in certain cases, however, to appoint a special liaison officer who will be able to ensure that the producer and film director will receive full co-operation and all the facilities they may need. The producer will study this complete brief and will, in due course, present: proposals for making the film. There should be very full discussion at this point as this is the best time to make sure that the producer has the right idea of what the sponsor wants to achieve from the film.

The next stage is the investigation. This is the period of study by the producer and the writer in which they assimilate the necessary knowledge and background to plan the film. They visit any factories or installations to be filmed and meet the people involved, working in close co-operation with the liaison officer, and the technical adviser where the theme of the film merits it.

From the investigation, the writer prepares the treatment. This is the written presentation of the film, presented in such a way as to give a clear picture of the proposed shape and contents. The presentation of the treatment is the first approval stage and all members of the sponsor's organisation who will have to approve the film should study the treatment, criticizing it on its general approach, content, and method of presentation.

The producer should now be able to give a fairly accurate indication of the cost of making the proposed film and the sponsor has thus the first real indication of the ultimate cost. At this stage it is possible to cancel the film by paying a previously agreed fee for the investigation and treatment.

Assuming that it has been agreed to proceed on the basis of the submitted treatment, the next step is the preparation of the shooting script. A number of technical questions have to be discussed relating to such points as colour, music, and use of commentary or dialogue.

The Shooting Script: It is the blueprint of the film. It is usually laid out in two columns. On one side, the visuals are set out shot by shot and in the other column, the appropriate sounds (words, music, effects, etc.) are set out opposite the visual shots to which they apply. This is a very detailed document and will form the basis for the contract which will cover the making of the film. It is essential that this shooting script should be scrutinised very closely and any queries discussed with the producer.

When the shooting script is received it should be accompanied by a film quotation for the production of the film with details of how the prices are arrived at. This quotation will be covered by contract and provided there' are no major alterations at a later date this should be the final cost of the film.

Shooting the Film: If there is no extended traveling involved, the actual shooting of a typical public relations film may take between three weeks and two months. In order to work efficiently, pre-planning is necessary as the camera team will not shoot the film according to the shooting the script but in the most convenient and economic manner. For example, all the shots in a particular location will be taken on one visit if possible, on outdoor locations, the weather may be a great hindrance to the maintenance of the programme.

It is advisable to ask that a number of still pictures should be taken during shooting as these often prove very useful later on for publicity purposes. Enlarged prints from the actual 16-mm or 35-mm film are seldom entirely satisfactory.

The Rough Cut: When the shooting as set out in the shooting script has been completed, the editor arranges the various shots in their correct sequences as envisaged by the script and producers what is known as the rough cut. This is the first version of the film and visually it is fairly rough. The visual tricks, called opticals, which are used to transport the viewer from one scene to the next, are not inserted. The commentary has not been recorded and the rough cut is thus projected silent. It is usually shown in black and white, but when a colour film is being made some pilot colour shots are usually included.

This is the most important approval stage. The sponsor can suggest the deletion of scenes or the alteration of the length of shots where it is considered advisable in order to influence the emphasis of the film. Any basic alterations or new scenes demanded at this stage will probably be the cause of extra cost but this should not be shirked if any re-thinking is essential.

Assuming the rough cut has been agreed, the length of the commentary or dialogue can be considered to accommodate the commentary. It is a poor film, however, that relies too heavily on the commentary.

The Fine Cut: When the rough cut has been approved, the editor and other technical staff proceed to the preparation of the fine cut. Opticals are added and the film can be shown in its final form for approval. The music, sound effects and commentary are now recorded and the picture and sound tracks are married. The show prints can be made and the film is complete.

Sound; Few films can be made without the use of synchronous sound but it does of course add considerably to the cost of production. If the sound is to be shot on location, a sound-recording crew and equipment have to be taken to the site, and if it is shot in studios, this involves the usual studio costs of sets, actors, etc. It is often difficult to get amateurs to speak convincingly even when they are talking about their own jobs and it is often necessary to use trained actors.

In making public relations films it is usual to use recorded music. If the film relies on its musical accompaniment to a marked degree, however, it is well worth considering the commissioning of a specially composed musical score. This may cost an extra few thousand but where the type of film merits it, the money is well spent.

If the film is to include a commentary, this is recorded when the film has been completed, and dubbed on to the sound track. The costs involved are moderate. If a film with a commentary is intended, for distribution in non-English speaking countries, this should be made known to the producer from the outset-Foreign language prints will have to be made, and the film will be made with two sound tracks, one carrying music and effects and the other the commentary. For between $ l00 and $ 200 this second sound track can be replaced by a track carrying the commentary in a foreign language. However, if the producer was not warned beforehand, music effects and commentary may all printed on the same track, and if a foreign language version is required, the music and effects will have to be recorded again, thus involving unnecessary extra expense. Another point that has to be watched is that some of the foreign language commentaries may require more screen time than the original English version.

The importance of careful pre-planning is emphasized by the fact that when sound and picture are finally married, sound is printed many frames ahead of the appropriate picture, and if an alteration in the film is demanded at a later stage, the taking out of a length of film and the insertion of a new shot becomes a difficult and costly business.

Animation: Certain types of films are more effective if they are made partly or wholly in the medium of cartoons or puppets but this process is very expensive. This medium is very effective for dealing with detailed explanations of technical processes and it is also used to get over the difficulty of language or for conveying abstract ideas. For one minute's showing, a cartoon film needs 1,400 separate drawings each done by hand and so a twenty minutes' cartoon film in Eastman Colour is likely to cost at least $ 15,000. Similarly, film puppets are not worked by strings or any mechanical means; they are made of plastic or some similar material and each puppet is moved by hand to a new position for every frame of film, and so for one minute of puppet filming, the puppets must be moved 1,400 times.

Lighting: The cost of lighting is very variable. If the shooting takes place in a studio which the producer has at his disposal the cost of lighting may be small. If however electricians and lamps must be hired and taken to several locations, the cost may be heavy.

Location: It is naturally more economical to shoot the complete film in one central place but the subject may demand shooting in a number of different locations. This may involve a substantial cost for travelling and subsistence.

Using Film as Exhibitions: Films can reach a specialized audience at exhibitions. Exhibitors can show their films on a section of their stand or in some cases can hire a suitable room elsewhere on the exhibition premises.

When exhibitors show films on their known stand it may be in order to have an eye-catching focus of interest or to tell a story that is not easy to portray in ordinary exhibition display techniques. A number of visitors to the stand can be addressed more efficiently and expeditiously by a film than could be done individually by the stand staff. It is also possible to offer the commentary in a number of different languages to the audiences by using earphones. This technique has been used very effectively by the United Kingdom Atomic Energy Authority at a number of overseas exhibitions. They use four 35-mm cinema projectors coupled together. One shows the film with the sound track in English, the local dialect. The other three projectors do not project a picture but merely have a sound track in the chosen language.

There is a choice of two methods of showing films on exhibition stands either by the provision of a small auditorium is on the stand—preferably with suitable seating—or by one use of an endless film loop projected automatically and continuously from a special self-contained unit. Both these methods use "back projection". The picture is thrown on the back of a semi-translucent screen and viewed from the front, thus, leaving the viewing area unencumbered by the projection equipment Naturally, only small audiences can be reached by these methods and the level must be kept low enough to avoid interference with normal conversation on other parts of the stand or on neighbouring stands. If films are to be shown elsewhere in the exhibition, it is advisable to check that the equipment is satisfactory. It is desirable to have fixed times of showing and to publicize these adequately on the stand. A ticket system may also be desirable in order to avoid overcrowding and possible disappoint-ment to visitors. The acoustics of the room may mar the shows. Some of the "spare" rooms at exhibition halls are completely bare and so resonant that recorded speech becomes difficult to follow.

At some exhibitions the organizers arrange film shows as one of the attractions for visitors. The programme is made up by the organizers from films available and exhibitors are able to offer films for inclusion.

TYPES OF TELEVISION COMMERCIALS

Audio and visual elements can be combined to produce several types of television commercials, just as a story can be told in many different ways. Emphasis can be placed on the story itself, on the problem to be solved, on the central character such as in a testimonial, or on special human emotions or storytelling techniques such as satire, humour, fantasy, and so on. Albert Book and Norman Cary provide a useful classification of the possible alternatives, based on the point of emphasis, focus, or style adopted. Each is referred to as a particular kind of commercial structure to emphasize that a commercial is other than an unrelated jumble of ideas and techniques. The thirteen types of structure identified by them are as follows:

1. **Storyline:** a commercial that tells a story; a clear, step-by-step unfolding of a message that has a definite beginning, middle, and end.
2. **Problem-solution:** This presents the viewer with a problem to be solved and the sponsor's product as the solution to that problem, probably the most widely used and generally accepted example of a TV commercial.
3. **Chronology:** It delivers the message through a series of related scenes, each one growing out of the one before. Facts and events are presented sequentially as they occurred.
4. **Special effects:** These are no strong structural pattern; strives for and often achieves memorability through the use of some striking device, for example, an unusual musical sound or pictorial technique.
5. **Testimonial:** also called word-of-mouth advertising; it uses well-known figures or an unknown "man in the street" to provide product testimonials.
6. **Satire:** A commercial that uses sophisticated wit to point out human foibles, generally produced in an exaggerated style; parodies on James Bond movies, Bonnie and Clyde, Hair, and the like.
7. **Spokesperson:** The use of an on-camera announcer who, basically, "talks." Talk may be fast and hard sell or more personal, intimate sell.
8. **Demonstration:** It uses some physical apparatus to demonstrate a product's effectiveness. Analgesic, watch, and tire commercials employ this approach heavily.
9. **Suspense:** It is somewhat similar to story-line or problem-solution structures, but the buildup of curiosity and suspense to the final resolution is given a heightened sense of drama.
10. **Slice-of-life:** A variation on problem solution; begins with a person at the point of, and just before the discovery of an answer to a problem. This approach is heavily used by detergent manufacturers.
11. **Analogy:** It offers an extraneous example, then attempts to relate it to the product message. Instead of delivering a message simply and directly, an analogy uses one example to explain another by comparison or implication: "Just as vitamins tone up your body, our product tones up your car's engine."
12. **Fantasy:** It uses caricatures or special effects to create fantasy surrounding product and product use: Jolly Green Giant, White Knight, White Tornado, the washing machine that becomes 10 feet tall.
13. **Personality:** A technical variation of the spokesperson or announcer on camera, straight-sell structure relies on an actor or actress rather than an announcer to deliver the message. Uses a setting rather than the background of

a studio. The actor plays a character who talks about the product, reacts to its use, or demonstrates its use or enjoyment directly to the camera.

These structures are, of course, not mutually exclusive, but rather serve to provide points of focus for analysis, copy production, and research. For example, in testimonials and, perhaps, in spokesperson and demonstration commercials, the credibility of source and/or the mode of presentation are likely to be most important. Customer reactions to source could receive special attention, utilizing the ideas on source credibility given earlier in Chapter 12. In story-line, problem solution, and perhaps the chronology and analogy structures, focus would tend to centre more on-the type of argument (for example, one- versus two-sided or refutation) or the order of argument (primacy-recency, stating a conclusion) dimensions. Each of these seven types of commercials also tends to be more factual in orientation.

The remaining six types all are more emotional in orientation and can be distinguished on the basis of whether the emotion-arousing capacity or the characterization being used relates to source or message. The personality and slice of life structures, for example, are likely to be more source oriented. The choice of the personality to be used or the characters who will play the role in the slice-of life situation are emphasized. The special effects, fantasy, satire, and suspense structures are all fundamentally emotional in orientation. Special effects, for example, might be used to arouse emotions with respect to fear, sex, or status. The principal objective would be emotional arousal, and interest would centre on whether the particular emotion was evoked in the target consumer.

A slightly different typology has been developed by Henry Laskey, Ellen Day, and Melvin Crask. They divide TV ads into two main types of Informational versus Transformational. Informational commercials are then sub-divided into comparative; those using a unique selling proposition; "preemptive"; generic/ product class; and those using hyperbole. Transformational ads are classified as either generic; based on the use occasion; using brand image; or communicating user image.

Exhibitions and Trade Fairs: The modern exhibitions and trade fairs have become an accepted medium of public relations and trade promotion. There is no clear demarcation between an exhibition and a trade fair and these terms are often inter-changed freely. A trade fair, however, as its name implies, is staged for the purpose of selling goods or demonstrating new ideas and techniques. An exhibition, on the other hand, may range from a prestige international show like. National or International World Fair held at Pragati Maidan in New Delhi or at the local levels in villages or towns. In most organisations the public relations departments are responsible for all types of exhibitions. Participation in an exhibition breaks down into three parts:

1. Deciding which exhibitions to support and to what degree.
2. Preparing a brief and organizing the construction of the stand.
3. Staffing and controlling the stand during the duration of the exhibition. This will include the period prior to the opening and during the dismantling.

Mobile Exhibits: The usual procedure in exhibition work is for the contractor to construct the stand, lending the materials for the duration of the show and then returning all usable parts to his general store. This does not apply to models, photographs, transparencies etc., which can be used again possibly at future exhibitions. This method of construction is accepted by experts as being the most satisfactory way of working but laymen on committees constantly query the idea the popular idea is that it should be possible to design and construct an exhibition stand which can then be used over and over again at different shows. This would be a practical proposition if all stands were of the same shape and size. Furthermore, stands are usually built of fairly lightweight materials which stand up to a short life but would not survive removal to other sites without extensive repair and renovation. Few organisations, too, have the storage space necessary and if storage is hired it has to be paid for. The ideal is that each stand should be designed to fit the actual site and to take advantage of all the circumstances. A mobile stand would not be so adaptable and would have to be built for stouter materials in the first place. In short, the snags usually outweigh the possible advantages. It is, of course, quite practical to make sections of a stand that can be used at different exhibitions, but it is not a good idea to try to transport the whole stand or the major part of it. The one exception is when a small travelling exhibition is planned. Such a show will usually be staged in an empty room or hall and it is possible to design a series of displays which can be erected to form an exhibition of different size and shape according to the venue.

Travelling exhibitions will fail unless they are simple to erect and do not require the services of a dozen men and a team of electricians. The components of the exhibition must be strong enough to stand upto the rigours of frequent transport but light enough to avoid heavy carriage and labour costs.

Exhibition techniques are most successful when they are used to portray solid objects or ideas which lend themselves to three-dimensional representation. Photographs, diagrams, illustrations and text can be used effectively to support a three-dimensional presentation but they lack sufficient interest-catching ability if used alone. Models are used a great deal now-a-days and some of them are very fine works with every part moving. A stand that is entirely made up of models, however may give an impression of miniaturization and where models are employed it is desirable to have some objects that are life size to give the right idea of scale. Another possible weakness is when models are made of different scales. It is a good plan to work to a common scale, of, say, half an inch to a foot when a number of models are likely to be used together on one stand.

Animated flow of diagrams, recorded sound, telephones giving messages in a number of languages, murals, sculptures and many other novelties are used by designers to give exhibition stands that "little extra something the others haven't got". These cannot make an exhibit successful, however, if there is not an idea to put over which leads to three-dimensional treatment.

When the stand is a large of complicated one, it is a good idea to ask the designer to supply a small scale model. This will give a clear impression of the details of the finished stand and will be very useful when discussing the stand with members of the organisation unaccustomed to visualizing drawings in terms of three-dimensional display.

Organisations which exhibit frequently will probably have an exhibition department as a sub-section of the public relations department. Where this does not apply, it is essential that one man, or women, should be given the responsibility for organizing and progressing the many details involved in exhibiting. One of the main duties will be keeping in close touch with the designer and the contractor. However capable and experienced the designer, it is wise for the representative of the client to take a careful and close interest throughout and not to be afraid of expressing an opinion.

The designer, or his assistants, will be on site during the erection and will ensure that the stand is completed in accordance with the specification, and in time for the opening.

The type of exhibition will determine the advisability of preparing special literature for distribution and whether it should be given out freely or only to selected visitors to the stand. Often a thin leaflet is prepared for a wide distribution and a more detailed booklet for restricted issue. The utmost care should be taken to ensure the accuracy of any foreign language texts used.

The Exhibition Catalogue: It is usual for exhibitors to be offered a free entry in the exhibition catalogue but the copy is often required several months ahead. In addition, it is often possible to have further entries on payment, or to take displayed advertisements in the catalogue. This question should receive proper attention as entries in the appropriate sections of the catalogue are very helpful.

Advertising on the Internet

Today, advertisers have begin to advertise on the Internet, the worldwide web of computer networks that promises to become another avenue of electronic commerce. Advertisers set up "home pages" that can be accessed by "web browser" software, and occupy "storefronts" in "on-line malls." It is far too early to tell how advertising will evolve on the Internet, but according to Ogilvy and Mather Direct, one of several agencies venturing in this medium, Internet advertising should not be intrusive, should take place only in designated newsgroups and list servers, should offer full disclosure of what is being sold and under what terms, should only perform consumer research with the consumer's consent, and should not resell consumer data without express user permission. Various classifications have been developed for print ad layout styles. These include:

1. Picture window (also called Ayer #1): a large picture or illustration with tightly edited copy fitting into the small space allotted to it.
2. Mondrian/grid: named after the Dutch painter, these break out space into a series of severely demarcated rectangles or even-sized boxes.
3. Type-specimen: these exhibit large type size with no illustration at all.
4. Copy-heavy: no illustration, or only a small visual, rely mostly on words.
5. Frame: artwork or illustrative material framing the copy (or *vice versa*).
6. Silhouette: the elements form an overall silhouette, or shape, against the background; for example, white space pushed toward the edges of the ad.
7. Multipanel: these look like comic-strips.
8. Circus: like multipanel, with even more components (e.g., grocery store ads).
9. Rebus: photographs, illustrations or diagrams are inserted into the copy, which is usually quite long.

Some research by Chris Janiszewski has shown that the arrangement of ad elements on a page also determines which of the brain's hemispheres processes which element of the ad. Usually, the right hemisphere is better suited for the processing of pictures, and these are better placed on the left side of the page in order to be processed by the right hemisphere. The opposite applies for words. He recommends that if the key information in the ad consists of certain verbal claims, the ad will be more effective if the pictorial attention-grabbers are placed to the right of those key verbal claims, and verbal attention grabbers are placed to the left of those key verbal claims. Such an arrangement will lead to less interference in the processing of the key verbal claims, because each of the attention-grabbing kind of information will be sent to the inappropriate hemisphere (pictures to the left hemisphere instead of the right, words to the right instead of the left).

The layout of a television commercial is the storyboard. Here, again, it can be generated in a relatively primitive form, in which only artist sketches and suggestive copy are included, or in a more comprehensive form that details more precisely what actors are to say, how scenes will blend in, and the precise location of identification marks, background music, special effects, and so on. The copy/art team creating a TV commercial will indicate the nature of the camera shots and camera movements, the level and type of music, and so on. Of course, much will change as the commercial is actually shot and then edited, by the director selected for the commercial.

Outdoor Advertising: Outdoor Advertising is one of the many ways of advertising that are available to the manufacturer who wishes to make, through advertising, direct contact with his potential customers. All advertising media are complementary is each other and each has its special contribution to make to the build-up of an advertising campaign. The advertiser and his agent must by skill select the most penetrating and economical means for the conveyance of the selling message and, therefore, the correct selection of advertising media is of the highest importance and forms one of the corner-stones on which a good advertising campaign is built.

Today, in this world of competitive branded goods there are two main divisions of the selling arguments:

1. By the reasoned selling argument and informative advertising —why he, or she will be better off in some way or other;
2. By ensuring that the brand name is repeatedly impressed on the potential customer so that having once bought the product—and found it good, the name becomes fully associated with the need.

From this basic study of the advertising media available shows that they can be broadly divided into two groups which fit into the selling pattern outlined.

First, there is indoor advertising, comprising the Press—periodicals, films, radio, television and direct mail. These media provide the best opportunity of putting over a reasoned selling argument. The advertisements are addressed to the reader, listener, or viewer at a time of leisure, when he or she can absorb the message.

Secondly, there is outdoor advertising, comprising posters, transportation advertising and signs. These media provide a frequency of repetition, unobtainable by any other means of a simple selling message, a brand name and an illustration of a package. Outdoor advertising, therefore, provides the best means of ensuring brand familiarity.

Most advertising campaigns should, therefore, be a combination of these two methods of persuasion and a balanced use of these two groups of media.

A simple illustration on a poster may provide ail the arguments needed for selling a product to the mass market. The bulk of the advertising appropriation would then be spent on outdoor advertising. Again, the use of the product may be so well known that poster advertising alone will do all that is necessary to ensure brand familiarity and that the name becomes fully associated with the need.

Poster Campaign: A poster campaign should be built up like a Press schedule. Different newspapers are selected for the Press schedule because of their different readerships, so different poster sites are selected for the same reason. However, it is the location of a poster site which determines its readerships.

There are no set displays, though within certain limits there are accepted figures for what constitutes a full-weight campaign for a town or region. These figures are based on the use of a 16-sht. double crown posters only, and it is by the use of 16-sht double posters, spread as evenly as possible throughout the area to be covered that the real strength of poster advertising is developed and figures of coverage and frequency, as mentioned earlier, are obtainable.

There are four main questions to be answered:

1. How many different people in a town have the opportunity to see the posters of a campaign?
2. What proportion of the town's population do they represent?
3. How may times each week, on an average, does each member of the audience see the posters of the campaign?
4. How do these figures vary for different campaigns?

First, the number of people in the sample who pass typical campaigns is found and how often they pass. These figures provide the answers to the first three questions. The fourth answer comes when data from all towns has been compared.

It is found that for campaigns accepted today as standard, the audience that is the number of different people who have an opportunity of seeing the advertising in one week is 80% to 85% or even 90% of the town population. Also, it is found that each different person has on an average 20 to 30 and in some cases as much as W opportunities per week of seeing the advertising. These figures, of course, vary with the weight of the campaign, but it is relatively easy to reach approximately 8.0% coverage; additional sites then only add small increments to the cover, but add considerably to the repetition factor. For example, in a town with a population of 100,000 a campaign using sixteen 16-sht double crown posters will reach 80% of the population and the repetition factor will be 20, and a campaign using twenty five 16-sht double crown posters will reach 87% of the population, with an increase in repetition, with an increase in repetition value to 30. Twenty five 16-sht double crown posters would be considered reasonable weight campaign for a town with a population of 1,00,000 for a household product sold frequently.

Outdoor advertising and in particular posters, is a medium of repetition - repetition that adds the brand familiarity. It is a most flexible medium and one in which campaigns can be built to meet the particular needs of the advertiser. There is, thus, no simple rule for the advertiser to follow when planning and executing an outdoor advertising campaign. Its final advice is to employ the specialist advertising agent or one of the poster contractors themselves to advise on the plan and execution of an outdoor advertising campaign.

Outdoor Copy Principles

For outdoor ads, where the message must be communicated in a few seconds, the copy and visual (such as a large pack shot) must be extremely short, simple, strong, and obvious—there is no time for subtlety. Outdoor ads are recalled more if they have fewer words, are about more involving products, are creatively more distinct, and are on the right-hand side of highways than on the left-hand side (from the drivers, perspective).

Retail Copy Principles

Retail ads usually must contain specifics about the merchandise being offered (such as exact sizes, colors, and prices) in order to stimulate immediate buying action. Yet they must also be created in a manner consistent with (and must strive to reinforce) the image of the store.

Business-to-Business Ads

Since business-to-business ads are usually written to an audience seeking problem solving or profit improving information, they should usually be in formative and offer specifics, serious (but not boring), and (ideally) offer case histories of how the advertised brand helped someone else in a similar situation. The software company Lotus, for example, in advertising its Notes product to corporate users, ran ads in September 1993 citing successful adoption by twelve different companies, each named explicitly, with a paragraph describing each specific case.

Long copy ads are good, but they should focus on a. single benefit, and it helps if they have a single dramatic image. While the ads need to be factual and informative, they should nonetheless contain some drama or human interest, according to a study by Roper Starch Worldwide. A coupon or phone number can be used to provide moredetailed information and generate a lead for a subsequent sales call, either in person or via the telephone.

Advertising and publicity: It may be considered advisable to advertise the company's participation in an exhibition in the trade Press, the national Press, by posters or by direct mail. Details of the stand should be sent, of course, to appropriate sections of the Press in the hope of securing editorial mention.

Press Conferences: Exhibition organizers usually invite the Press to attend on the first morning, or on the previous day, and it is essential to be ready to receive the Press on the stand on such occasions. In addition, it may be considered desirable to hold an individual Press conference at an earlier date to give information about the stand. This is only worthwhile when the stand is a very special one or there are circumstances which warrant it. At most exhibitions there is a Press office where exhibitors can place Press releases and other publicity material for visiting journalists to collect. Care should be taken to replace stocks each day that the exhibition is open as the exhibition Press staff cannot be expected to do this. Control of the stand must be vested in one person, with a reliable deputy. This person may be the same individual who has acted as the organizer of the exhibit and this has the advantage that he or she will be familiar with every detail. It may not be possible if the organisation has stands at other exhibitions at the same time, and then it may be wise to choose the most reliable member of the stand staff. It is essential that this stand manager should be briefed in every detail and should be competent to control the behaviour of the other stand staff. One of the jobs will be to prepare a staff roster and to see that punctuality is observed. Another obvious duty is to inspect the stand frequently for cleanliness and orderliness and to take immediate action to remedy any damage or interference with the lighting or working models.

Dealing with inquiries: Everything possible should be done to make it easy for visitors to ask questions. Some stands are designed in such a way that the visitor has to make a positive effort to enter the stand—by stepping up on to a high platform or by finding the right part of the stand to enter. Anything of this kind may reduce the likelihood of inquiries. When inquiries are made they should be answered as fully as possible and details recorded so that in suitable cases the inquiry can be followed up from headquarters. A visitors' book for V.I.P.s is also a desirable adjunct to a stand. People are usually flattered at being asked to sign the book and it provides a useful reference for follow-up activities.

Some points to watch:

1. In many exhibition halls the general lighting is poor and it is therefore desirable to make sure that the stand illumination is adequate, many fine stand designs are spoilt by lack of light.

2. It is generally accepted that an exhibition stand must tell its story three dimensionally and that the text should be kept to a minimum. Unfortunately, some designers go further and always keep the size of the type to a minimum. Apart from the fact that

visitors are unlikely to bother to read very small type, there may be many whose vision is inadequate.

3. Some stands are designed without any thought to storage space or room for hats and coats. It is always possible to make some suitable provision for this at the design stage but not so easy when the stand has been completed.

4. Even when a stand is in a shell scheme it can be made to stand out by good design. Illumination and the wise use of colour can prevent that box-like appearance that is also often a failing of shell schemes.

5. A good stand is wasted if it is not visited. It is necessary, therefore, to devote considerable thought to methods of securing the attendance of those likely to be interested. The promoters of the exhibition will publicize it is general terms and this should be backed up by sending invitations to suitable people, not forgetting universities and technical colleges, women's organisations, and similar sources of likely visitors.

6. If a stand is on the ground floor and is visible from the balcony care should be taken to see that the appearance of the top of the stand is not untidy, as it can make a very bad impression.

7. It is usually necessary to obtain permission from the organi-zers for any flashing signs, noisy machinery and any other exhibits that may interfere with the comfort of nearby exhibitors. It is always wise to contact, at an early stage, the exhibitors who have the adjacent stands in order to ensure that neighbouring stands do not clash unduly in style or colour.

8. Photographs of the stand are useful for publicity and record purposes. It is usually rather difficult to get really good photographs of an exhibition stand and it is, therefore, wise to use a specialist photographer in preference to a Press or agency photographer. Photographs of stands are often taken at night as it may be impracticable to photograph the completed stand before the exhibition opens and it is likely to be difficult for the photographer to work properly while the exhibition is open. In addition to photographs of the stand, it is desirable to make arrangements for news pictures to be taken when V.I.Ps. visit the stand.

9. Pilfering is always a problem at public exhibitions but the most dangerous time is after the exhibition finishes and before dismantling actually commences. There have been cases when a large and valuable carpet has been stolen even though the actual stand was on top of it.

10. It is essential to do nothing at Earls Court or Olympia which conflicts with union regulations as any infringement may cause a strike of the whole labour force in the exhibition.

11. If it is intended to dispense hospitality on the stand, it is necessary to see that proper facilities for this are included in the design. It is desirable that the bar and entertaining area should be shut off from public view.

12. The electrical wiring plan for the stand should cover all likely needs, not forgetting a point for the vacuum cleaner if the stand is carpeted.

CREATIVE STYLES

As has already been suggested, creating advertising is a little like creating art. Two artists viewing the same scene may paint it quite differently, but both can produce high-quality .paintings and "effective" products. In this portion of the chapter, several of the creative giants of advertising and examples of their work are presented. An important factor that tends to distinguish them is the nature of the product or market situation. As will be seen, however, there are points of emphasis and style that tend to characterize the approach and make it recognizable.

Just as an art critic can distinguish a Picasso from a Monet, so an experienced copy director can distinguish the work of a David Ogilvy from that of a Leo Burnett. The styles of creative giants in advertising have, over time, become exaggerated to the point of caricature. Furthermore, right or wrong, their approaches become associated with a considerable amount of advertising of the agency with which they are associated. Thus, any description of their creative style may tend to be exaggerated. Such an exaggeration is useful for our purposes, however, because it helps to illustrate the diversity among creative teams in the advertising profession.

The first set of examples profiles the works of David Ogilvy, William BernBach, Rosser Reeves, and Leo Burnett. These creative giants have had major impacts on advertising over the years, and it is useful to study their styles and classic examples of their work. This is followed by three copy directors who have achieved prominence and recognition in recent years: Philip Dusenberry, Lee Clow, and Hal Riney. Each has had a major impact on the creative output of the ad-one a "bad" ad. Then write a one-page assessment on each, justifying your assessment.

2. Repeat the exercise in question 1 for a pair of radio ads, a pair of television ads, a pair of retail ads, and a pair of business-to-business ads.

3. Take a marketing positioning statement, based en a situation analysis for a brand and product category that you may have worked on for some marketing project and attempt to come up with five creative ideas that could be used in creating advertising for the selected brand.

4. Now select one of these creative ideas for further development and create rough or mock ads (a print ad, a television storyboard, and a radio script) that build off that creative idea.

5. Ogilvy, Bernbach, Reeves, and Burnett are all creative giants in advertising who have retired or passed on. Compare and contrast their styles with those of Dusenberry, Clow, and Riney, who are current leaders in the field. Who is more like whom? Why?

6. The creative styles of Bernbach and Reeves are probably two ends of a continuum, yet both are associated with highly successful agencies and campaigns. One could conclude that creative style makes no difference. Do you agree or disagree? Why or why not?

7. Suppose that you were chairperson of a billion-dollar agency and were having to choose among three candidates for the position of creative director. Discuss the qualities you would look for in filling the position. What are the characteristics of a top-quality creative person?

THE DESIGNING OF ADVERTISEMENTS

1. Layout: A layout is an arrangement of headlines, copy blocks, photographs, works of art, logotypes, borders and other typographic devices that serves as a preview for the client and **a** guide for the illustrator, lettering artist, engraver, typesetter and printer. To layout (two words) an ad is to engage in activity that will produce a layout (one word). When principles of design are followed in doing the layout, the advertisement becomes a more pleasing visual experience for the viewer. The advertisement then is said to be "designed" not merely "laid out". We associate the word "design" ordinarily with the handsome ads those meant to stand for a period of months or years. An ad for a department store appearing in a newspaper ordinarily would be "laid out"; a package or trademark would be "designed".

No layout artist should be ashamed to study the patterns and arrangements and designs of other layout artists and, when appropriate, to borrow parts of these, combine them with others, and apply them to his own layouts. Every artist maintains what he calls, without apology, his "swipe file"- his collection of clippings of ads and other works that appeal to him visually, and although he does not make the mistake of rushing to that file for help each time he faces a new job, the very fact that he has noted the work and filed it has left an impression on his subconscious. A design solution that works once has a tendency to appear and reappear in the layouts of many artists, few of whom regard themselves as plagiarists.

Dr. Irving A. Taylor a social psychologist identifies five levels of human creativity.

1. **Expressive creativity**—where skills are not important, as in the drawings of children. The artist allows his mind to wander, unrestricted.
2. **Productive creativity—**where the artist achieves proficiency but only in "heightened realism."
3. **Inventive creativity**—where the artist-as-inventor uses old parts in new ways. No new, basic ideas are evident; the ingenuity lies in the skilful use of tools.
4. **Innovative creativity** —where the artist exhibits a skill for abstracting. He gets away from realism. He is probably a follower of some new school of design.
5. **Emergentive creativity**—where the artist works with entirely new principles (or what appear to be entirely new principles). Such an artist, highly skilled in the art of abstraction, may start a new school.

2. **Sequence in Creativity:** The designer of ads engages in expressive creativity as he works on his first crude sketches or doodles. As he polishes his

doodles, making them more readable to people he works with, he engage in productive creativity. In most cases, this is as far as his creativity takes him. Only the most talented designers carry their art to the innovative and emergentive levels, nor can brainstorming function effectively at the two highest levels.

At none of the levels does high intelligence play an important role, Nor does logic necessarily help. In fact, "The rules of traditional logic are essentially a psychological straight-jacket for creative thought which suppress rich and free fantasy associations and the necessary relaxation for unconscious play so essential for creative insight, the 'sublimal uprush' says Dr. Taylor.

The artist solving a design problem theoretically goes through four stages of creativity, at whatever level he works. First, he studies the client, the product, the medium, the audience, other design solutions—anything to prepare himself to handle the assignment better. This is the exposure stage. Second, he turns away from the assignment for a time, allowing his sub-conscious to work on the material he has assimilated. This is the incubation stage. Third, he finds his solution, perhaps accidentally. There may come a flash of inspiration. This is the illumination stage. Finally, he goes into action, working swiftly, trying not to lose any of the spontaneity any of the quality of his idea in the translation from brain to hand. Now he is communicating. This is the execution stage.

3. **The Printing Processes.** The printer does today what the scribe did in medieval times; he makes copies of an original manu-script. But, using machines, he does it with more speed and, consi-dering the great volume of work, with fewer errors and he freely and accurately reproduces pictures.

In the early days of printing, the printer did his own designing. He drew and cut his own types and did the arranging of elements to be printed. Later, specialists moved in. Today, designers on the outside make decisions regarding type faces and do the arranging of elements, the printer follows a plan submitted to him.

While the designer himself does not touch the type (the union forbids it) or operate the presses or even fully understand them, he does have a basic knowledge of processes so that what he turns out can actually be produced.

Each of the printing processes, for instance, has limitations and advantages that should be considered. What is designed for one of the processes may not work for another.

4. **The Letterpress:** In the letterpress operation, the printer uses a raised surface to make his impression. The material which will do the printing (it usually is unyielding, tough metal) is "type-high" (something slightly under an inch); that which is not to print is lesser than the "type-high".

Letterpress, the grandfather of printing processes and still vital in some countries can make immediate use of typeset by hand or machine. No photographing is necessary. Most advertising men and printers agree that ordinary advertisements call for letterpress printing. But letterpress, with its sharpness and harshness and harshness of impression, does an excellent job of printing pictures, too. No process does better by line drawings and halftones, provided the screen is fine enough and the paper smooth enough, are at their best in letterpress impression. They should be square or rectangular, however. The hard edges of letterpress have a tendency to "fill in" on vignettes highlight halftones.

The cost-conscious designer should understand that, good as pictures can look in letter-press, they do cost more in this process than in offset lithography.

The printer if not the designer regards letterpress as the flexible process. He can make last-minute changes easily, even to the point of stopping the presses. More readily than other printers, the letterpress printer makes proofs available at any stage for checking by the designer and client.

For long runs in letterpress and for all runs on rotary presses (not all letterpress presses are rotary) the printer makes mats or moulds of the pages from which he casts durable plates. Plates used for rotary presses have to be rounded to fit the cylinder. For short runs (a few thousand) on non-rotary presses, the printer uses the type and engravings as provided.

For ads appearing in letterpress publications, the advertising, designer working for other than retail clients usually does a "paste -up" of the type proofs and art, and the production director at the agency orders photoe-ngraving or a master plate for making stereotype mats or electrotypes to send to the media for insertion in contracted space. Or the production director sends mats of the plate from which the media will cast their own plates. Either way, the designer keeps complete control of the placement of elements in his ad.

Our daily newspapers and most of our general circulation magazines use the letterpress process. If the quality of newspaper printing does not seem to measure up, it is because of necessary economies adopted by publishers—principally the relatively inexpensive paper (newsprint) used and the newspapers' use of stereo-types for art instead of higher quality electrotypes.

5. Offset Lithography: Offset lithography, as a printing process, is based on an art from: stone lithography.

Interestingly, the image on the plate is flat, you can't feel it as you rub your hands over it, how, then can it print?

Chemistry provides the answer: oil or grease and water don't mix. The image is grease-based, in the printing both water with glycerin and an ink are applied to the plate. The water stays away from the impression areas; the ink stays away from the damp or watered areas and sticks to the impression areas.

In regular stone lithography, the artist draws on his flat plate with a grease-base crayon; he applies the water and ink, then places his paper down on the plate. What he gets is an impression in mirror reverse a head facing right, for instance, would be facing left in the printing. In offset lithography, the "wrong facing" takes place on the rubber-covered cylinder; when the impression is then made on the paper, the facing is right again.

Offset provides a softer image than letterpress because of that rubber-covered cylinder. Inexpensive offset printing often produces halftones that are gray and washed-out looking. But good quality offset can reproduce halftones that are as sharp as letterpress halftones and at a considerable savings. In offset, continuoustone art work has to be screened and photographed separately from type images and line art work, but this process is far less expensive than making photo engravings for letterpress printing.

In offset, everything has to be photographed. Negatives are used to make thin metal plates that are wrapped around press cylinders for printing.

Somewhere along the line, somebody has to make a paste up for the camera. Line artwork and reproduction proofs of type are rubber-cemented in position exactly as they are to appear in the final printed version of the job. Photographs and other continuous-tone art are usually submitted separately to the cameraman. He photographs them through a screen and "strips" the negatives into position with the line negatives. The stripped-in negatives—they are called flats—are used then to make the plates. If original line artwork is oversize (or under size) it is shot separately and reduced or enlarged to the correct size and stripped into place.

Because everything on the page has to be photographed anyway. You can use all the line artwork you want (provided it is done to size) and it costs you nothing extra. Furthermore, in offset lithography it is possible to use typewriter copy and other "cold type" composition, cutting type costs by half and more. Of course, with most cold types you do this with some sacrifice in typographic quality.

The Multilith Machine: It makes use of metal plates made like regular offset plates, but it can also use paper plates, on which the advertiser's message has been typed on typewriters with special ribbons and his art drawn with lithographic pencils, thus by passing the photography phase. It is the old stone lithography process all over again, but this time the image can be drawn as it is to appear in printing. There will be no "flopping" of image because the "flopping" takes place on the rubber-covered cylinder. The image reverts to its original facing as it leaves the blanket and registers on the paper.

Cost cutting has endeared the offset process to marginal advertisers and encouraged their venturing into a field formerly dominated by the giants. It has also resulted in much low quality work. But in proper hands, designing for offset, even the small Multilith press can be on the same high plane as for letterpress. Countless brochures, booklets, and other direct mail pieces and company and specialized magazines publications with lots of art and comparatively small circulations—bespeak the quality that is inherent in the medium. Like stencil printing, offset can leave its imprint on almost any material or surface. Rough textured papers present no challenge to the offset printer.

6. **Gravure:** The professor, standing there blotting the blood from the scratches in his face (his wife found the handkerchief) in a way now demonstrates the principle of gravure printing. Most people call it "rotogravure" a term that is not inclusive enough. Some gravure is sheet fed; that is, it makes use of sheets of paper rather than rolls. A few call it "intaglio".

"Intaglio", means a design carved or engraved below the surface, and that's what gravure is. Everything that is to print is incised, in tiny wells of varying depths, on the printing plate. That includes the type. The ink is deposited in these wells (excess ink is wiped from the plate by the "doctor blade") moving from them to the paper. Everything that is to print then, has been screened. You don't notice the screen because it is 150-line or finer; and the small dost are further minimized as the ink is sucked mil of the wells and onto the slightly absorbent paper. The type, though, even to the naked eye, is often fuzzy. Obviously, this is no process for reproducing column after column of type.

It is a great process, however, for reproducing-photographs, or My continuous-tone art. The gradations of tones in gravure, thanks to the fine screen, are almost as numerous as in the continuous-tone original. Great tone subtlety is possible in this process.

Reproducing the Pictures: Cartoons, paintings, wash drawings, scratch board drawings, photographs. These are the kinds of art, the advertising designer works with. But from the printer's standpoint the list boils down to two items, line drawings and halftones. Put another way, the printer can reproduce art including photographs in one of these two ways.

7. Line Reproduction: Artwork done in black ink on white paper in lines and solid areas of black call for line reproduction. In making his plate, the printer (more correctly; the engraver or offset cameraman) takes a picture of the art, using high contrast film. He uses the film then to expose a sensitized plate, as photographer in his darkroom exposes a sensitized sheet of paper. The plate—for letterpress printing—goes through the etching process by which parts that are not to print are in effect, eaten away and parts that are to print are left standing. This is photoen-graving. For offset lithography a different kind of plate—thinner, for one thing—is used; it does not have to be etched. The term "photo-engraving" does not apply.

Artists and printers work constantly to devise ways of adding tone to line drawings to give them the effect of halftones or more pattern and texture. The original system for adding tone to line drawings was developed by Benjamin Day in the nineteenth century. Still in use today, it involves the affixing of a pattern in certain areas of either the negative or the plate by the printer or engraver. The artist directs placement by shading-in those areas with a light blue pencil or water colour tone (the engraver's camera does not pick up the light blue). More recent developments allow the artist to place the tone directly onto the drawing, through use of sheet of transparent paper on which a pattern is printed, drawing paper with built-in patterns that can be brought out with chemicals or with pencils and shading sheets from which patterns that can be rubbed off onto the original art work.

The tone, of course, is an optical illusion; it is formed by closely placed black dots or lines that merge into middle values as the eye recedes from them. Under a magnifying glass they show up for what they are; line art, ready for camera.

Line art can be patched, scratched and retouched; the printer has no trouble keeping resulting shadows and slight differences in tone from registering on the plate. Often line art is reduced, to remove slight imperfections in the drawing. Reproduction proofs of type if they are to be used would be short as line art.

8. **Halftone Reproduction;** When the designer wants to use a photograph or a piece of artwork that has a continuous-tone that moves subtly up and down the tonal value scale (a wash drawing, fine pencil drawing or painting), in ordinary circumstances he will want to order halftone reproduction. (That's not a very good term: "halftone". Many tones are involved; light, middle and dark. It is more than a matter of having tones that are halfway between white and black. But "half-tone is the term we're stuck with.)

To hold onto the may tones of the original, the engraver (or offset cameraman) inserts a screen between the lens and the film. The standard screen is a two-ply piece of glass; one piece has lines cut perpendicular to the first lines, forming a cross-hatching (the lines are filled in with an opaque material). The resulting small squares act as individual lenses, breaking up the light into dots of various sizes, depending, upon how much is reflected from the subject being photographed. From then on, the negative is used as it would be in making a line reproduction.

A halftone, then, has small dots over the entire area of the print, even if some of the area is meant to be white. With special handling, the printer's cameraman can work some blank areas—pure white—into the artwork where it is needed. Such halftones are called "highlight" or "dropout", halftones.

The student must understand that whatever system of printing is used where continuous-tone: artwork must be reproduced screen-ing is necessary. Printers do not print ordinarily in shades of gray., they print in black. The effect of gray must be achieved through optical illusion. Stepping back from a halftone printed in a publication, you see it as tones of gray, from light to dark. Looking at it closely, you see the dots—and nothing but black ink. Pinpoint dots cover and define the lighter areas, larger dots the darker area.

For pictures in colour, separate plates and printings must be made for each colour used. Through judicious use of the plates for black, yellow, red and blue inks, the printer is able to achieve the illusion of full colour. If the colour picture is a halftone, each of the plates will be made up of dots.

As: artists and printers work to make line art look like halftone art, they also work to make halftone art look like line art. Eastman Kodak Co. introduced in 1953 the Tone-Line process by which continuous tone art—photographs, primarily—are changed into line art with unusual texture. They are then ready for line reproduction. Most people, looking at one of the prints, would conclude it was a drawing of some kind. A similar effect can be had simply by ordering line reproduction for a continuous -tone original. What happens is this: the tones darker than 50 per cent fill in as solids, the tones lighter than 50 per cent drop out altogether. It is as though an artist had drawn a picture using no lines, only shadows.

Plates for printing pictures continue to demand large expenditure from advertisers. It was to alleviate some of these costs that offset lithography was developed. Letterpress's answer to inexpensive line and halftone reproduction has been electronic engraving-with the Fairchik machine or the Photola but at some sacrifice in quality.

9. Setting the type: Printers call the setting of type "composing" and the type itself "composition". They work with two basic kinds of composition: hot type and cold type.

Hot type: Somewhere in the manufacturing process, the type is hot. Molten metal pours into moulds or mats as type is cast. But printers refer to such type simple as type—as though there were no other. They bring in the adjective—"cold"—when they refer to the other and newer kind of type, to distinguish it from the original.

The first method of setting type—hand setting—remains in use today, some 500 years after Johann Gutenberg developed it. Nor has the system changed much. To set such type—called foundry type—the printer or compositor picks up the already manufactured pieces of type one by one (by this time, they have cooled down) and places them in a composing stick, a tray with three sides, one of which may be adjusted for the line-length desired. As in any hand operation, an extra touch of quality is possible—in this case, better spacing. And because an assortment of foundry type in a specified style and size is relatively inexpensive most of the new types come out first in foundry and are then readily available from the firms that specialize in type setting. Many headlines for advertisements, especially in the magazines are set in foundry type. But foundry type, from the client's standpoint, because of the labour involved, is more expensive than other methods of setting type when large blocks of copy are needed.

The second method of setting type (we're still dealing with hot type) is by line casting machines. You know it as Linotype composition; but Linotype is a trade name and technically should not be used as the generic name for this process any more than Frigidaire should be used as the generic name for refrigerators. At least one other brand name is involved here: Intertype. Printers call this process for setting type the "line casting system" because the product of the Linotype or Intertype machine is a line o' type cast as one unit on a metal slug. Such composition is cast line by line; the lines or slugs are gathered in a tray or galley and then "proofed" for client inspection. (Proofing for all hot type composition involves making a first printing from the type on long, narrow sheets of paper, using a proof press that is usually hand-operated.

In machine composition, what is assembled are not pieces of type but matrices, or mats (or molds) of individual letters from which the lines are cast. In other words, the type of manufactured right there on the scene.

Essentially, the Linotype and the Intertype machines have four basic sections; the magazine, which houses the mats, the keyboard, which releases the mats from the magazine and causes them to assemble in lines, the casting mechanism, which does the manufacturing; and the distribution system, which, Rube Goldberg-like, causes each mat to return to its compartment in the magazine.

Line casting machine composition is used for small sizes of type— for columns of copy, but it can also produce type as large as half an inch high. The copy you are now reading was set on a Linotype machine.

The third method of setting type involves the Ludlow process. Ludlow composition is in one way related to the foundry operation, in one way related to line casting composition. The letters assembled in Ludlow are assembled by hand; but these items are' not in individual pieces of type, they are matrices, or mats, from which the type will be cast.

The Ludlow mats are kept in cases or drawers, as type is kept for the foundry operation. After the mats are assembled in the compositor's stick, they are put into the casting device and the line of type emerges almost at once. Like type in the foundary operation, the mats have to be redistributed by hand for further use.

Ludlow, its slugs T-shaped, is especially useful for setting large-size types; types for headlines in newspapers and in ads. The fourth method of setting type involves the Monotype process, an English invention. Monotype consists of two machines, one with a key-board to punch a tape or ribbon, the other with a casting mechanism that receives the tape and automatically casts type from a matrix case. The final product is more like the product of the foundry operation than Linotype setting; individual pieces of type are produced. This system makes possible careful fitting of type and easy corrections, especially in tabular work. The designer who wants exceptional quality in his typography specifies, when he can, **Monotype.** Newspaper advertising at least in the United States, makes little use of Monotype composition.

Type specimen books published by printers and typesetting houses for their clients usually indicate how each of the types shown are set; whether by hand, by machine, by Ludlow or by Monotype.

Cold Types. No question about it no matter the typesetting system used the product costs dearly. In the years since the systems were invented, printers have been able to perfect precious few changes. One exception, line casting machines that can now be activated with types typed by lowly typists, thus doing away with the high-salaried operators another computerized justification of the right-hand margin when type is used. The big progress in type setting, has been made through substitute methods which have come about as a result of that relatively new system of printing called offset lithography. "Cold-type composition", as a term, sometimes gets confused with "photocomposition". The first term is the broad heading; the second term is simply a form of cold-type composition.

You can count five different methods of cold-type composition. The first three produce large-size letters, the last two small letters or body copy.

First, hand-lettering. In the hands of a professional, lettering surpasses types for beauty and effectiveness. In the hands of an amateur, nothing could be worse aesthetically.

Second, hand-setting of letters printed on paper. The letters may be in tablet form, one letter or each small page, or on sheets of transparent paper.

Third, photo-lettering, Machines from several manufacturers make use of negative of complete alphabets that are dialed or otherwise put into proper position for light to shine through the desired letter onto sensitized paper. Such machines release strips of paper which carry photographical produced headlines.

Fourth, typewriting. The typewriter can be an ordinary office machine; an electric machine, like IBM, a special use-once ribbon and type in several widths and designed to resemble regular type; or a more sophisticated machine like the Vari-Typer, that can offer several type faces in a single setting, or the Just to writer, which is tape -operated and automatically justified the right-hand margin.

Fifth, photo-typesetting, Keyboard machines have now been fitted with negatives or negative grid fonts in place of mats; when the operator hits the keys of the keyboard, these negatives move into position and line-by-line allow light through to sensitized galley paper. Here you have columns of type produced photographically-type as good as though it were produced in the standard way by the original machines. Designers still prefer hot-type composition for quality. Hot type basically is for letter-press printing, but the offset lithographer, getting a perfect proof or first printing from the types can photograph it and make his plates. Cold type is useful mainly in offset; its product can only be photographed. But, with recent developments, the printer can use photo-type setting negatives to make exposures directly onto plates, thus by passing the photographing of prints.

Laser Typesetting: The latest arrival in typesetting processes is the laser which is operated by a computer with key board as in prototype setting machine. Laser typesetting enables not only speedy composing of subject matter but also decorative make-up of pages with borders, screens and page numbering. Some of the laser machines are also capable of reproducing designs in geometrical shapes. This is fast replacing the letter-press and photo-typesetting processes and revolutioning the publishing and printing businesses.

10. Production and Designing: The designer familiar with the terminology can communicate with the printer. The printer will have more respect for the designer, will know he can't so easily put things over on him. The printer's "It can't be done" will be fewer. On the other hand, the designer will no longer make impossible requests of his printer.

The designer will be able to take advantage of the economies each process offers. He will design his advertisement "to fit" when he can't work directly with the printer, as for an ad going into a national magazine, he can consult the appropriate Standard Rate & Data Column covering that medium and see at once what the mechanical requirements are for the medium. Without an understanding of production, the designer will not even be able to read SRDS.

The designer can prepare his materials so that they will reproduce at their best. Knowing, for instance, that the halftone process picks up all tones, he will avoid making any marks on photographs, even on the back, for fear they might be picked up as shadows and' reproduced as lines or blotches.

He will know what kinds of type show up best in the various processes. Through experience he'll learn, for instance, that some of the Bodoni faces, with their very thin lines contrasting with thicker ones, drop out some of their parts in offset printing, making text matter unreadable. He'll learn what types can be reversed—shown in white—in gray areas of photographs. Knowing that type is not made of rubber, he'll pick the right size to fit a given space.

Appreciating the fact that a printer can hardly be expected to improve the quality of a photograph in printing (the printer's cameraman after all, copies a copy from a negative), he will insist that the starting photograph has enough quality to hold up in copying.

REFERENCES

1. Raymond R. Burke, Arvind Rangaswamy, Jerry Wind and Jehoshua Eliashberg "A Knowledge-Based System for Advertising Design," Marketing Science, 9, no. 3 (Summer 1990), pp. 212-229.
2. Alex F. Osborn, Applied Imagination, 3rd ed. (New York: Scribner's, 1963), p. 11.
3. Leo Burnett, "Keep Listening to That Wee, Small Voice," in Communications of an Advertising Man, © 1961 by Leo Burnett Compnay, Inc.; from a speech given before the Chicago Copywriters Club, October 4, 1960, p. 160.

4. Denis Higgens, ed., The Art of Writing Advertising (Chicago: Crain Books, 1965), p. 43.
5. Alex F. Osborn, Your Creative Power (New York: Deli, 1948), p. 135.
6. Edward M. Tauber, "HIT: Heuristic Ideation Technique—A Systematic Procedure for New Product Search," Journal of Marketing, 36 (January 1972), pp. 58-61.
7. Osborn, Your Creative Power, p. 294.
8. Discussed in Philip Kotler, Marketing Management: Analysis, Planning, and Control (Englewood Cliffs, NJ: Prentice Hall, 1967;, p. 256.
9. John M. Keil, The Creative Mystique: How to Manage It, Nurture It, and Make It Pay (New York: John Wiley,1985). See also "Popular Myths About Creativity Debunked." Advertising Age, May 6, 1985, p. 48.
10. John Caples, How to Make Your Advertising Make Money (Englewood Cliffs, NJ: Prentice Hall,1983).
11. John Caples, "A Dozen Ways to Develop Advertising Ideas" Advertising Age, November 14, 1983, pp. M-4ff.
12. William H. Motes, Chadwick B. Hilton, and John S. Fielden. "Language. Sentence, and Structural Variations in Print Advertising," Journal of Advertising Research, 32, No. 5 (Sep./Oct. 1992), pp. 63-77.
13. Richard F. Beltramini and Vincent J. Blasko, "An Analysis of Award Winning Advertising Headlines," Journal of Adoetising Research (April/May 1986), pp. 48-52.
14. H. Rao Unnava and Robert E. Burnkrant, " An Imagery-Processing View of the Role of Pictures in Print Advertisements," Journal of Marketing Research, 28 (May 1991), pp. 226-231; Michael J. Houston, Terry L. Childers, and Susan E. Heckler, "Picture-Word Consistency and the Elaborative Processing of Advertisements," Journal of Marketing Research, 1987, 24 (December), pp. 359-369.
15. Alvin C. Burns, Abhijit Biswas and Laurie A. Babin, The Operation of Visual Imagery as a Mediator of Advertising Effects," Journal of Advertising, 22, No. 2 (June 1993), pp. 71-85.
16. Bernd H. Schmitt, Nader T. Tavassoli, and Robert T. Millard, "Memory for Print Ads: Understanding Relations Among Brand Name, Copy, and Picture," Journal of Consumer Psy-chology, 2, No. 1 (1993), pp. 55-81.
17. Paula F. Bone and Pam S.: Ellen, "The Generation and Consequences of Communication-evoked Imagery," Journal of Consumer Research, 19 (June 1992), 93-104, and Kathleen Debevec and Jean B. Romeo, "Self-Referent Processing in Perceptions of Verbal and Visual Commercial Information," Journal of Consumer Psychology, I, No. 1 (1992), pp. 83-102.
18. Paul W. Miniard *et al,* "Picture-based Persuasion Processes and the Moderating Role of Involvement," Journal of Consumer Research, 18(June 1991), pp. 92-107.
19. Wendy J. Bryce and Richard F. Yalch, "Hearing versus Seeing: A Comparison of Consumer Learning of Spoken and Pictorial Information in Television Advertising," Journal of Current Issues and Research in Advertising, 15, No. 1 (Spring 1993), pp. 1-20.
20. Charles E. Young and Michael Robinson, "Visual Connectedness and Persuasion," Journal of Advertising Research, 32, No. 2 (March/April 1992), pp. 51-55.
21. James MacLachlan and Michael Logan, "Camera Shot Length in TV Commercials and their Memorability and Persuasiveness," Journal of Advertising Research, 33, No. 2 (March/April 1992), pp. 57-61.
22. Joan Meyers-Levy and Laura Peracchio, "Getting an Angle in Advertising: The Effect of Camera Angle on Product Evaluations," Journal of Marketing Research, 29 (November 1992), pp. 454-461.
23. David W. Stewart and David F. Furse, Effective Television Advertising: A Study of 1000 Commercials (Lexington, MA: Lexington Books, 1986),
24. Daryl W. Miller and Lawrence J. Marks, "Mental Imagery and Sound Effects in Radio Commercials," Journal of Advertising, 21, No. 4 (December 1992), pp. 83-97.
25. Avery M. Abernathy, James I. Gray, and Herbert J. Rotfield, "Combinations of Creative Elements in Radio Advertising," Journal of Current Issues and Research in Advertising, 15, No. 1 (Spring 1993), pp. 87-98.
26. Naveen Donthu, Joseph Cherian, and Mukesh Bhargava, "Factors Influencing Recall of Outdoor Advertising," Journal of Advertising Research, 33, No. 3 (May-June 1993), pp. 64-80.
27. Robert Chamblee and Dennis M. Sandier, "Business-to-Business Advertising: Which Layout Style Works Best?" Journal of Advertising Research, 32, No. 6 (Nov. Dec. 1992), pp. 39-48.
28. Wall Street Week, October 1, 1993, p. B6.
29. Martin Nisenholtz, "How to Market on the Net," Advertising Age, July 11, 1994, p. 28.
30. Lester Guest, "Status Enhancement as a Function of Colour in Advertising," Journal of Advertising Research, 6 (June 1966), pp. 40-44.
31. Stephen Baker, Advertising Layout and Art Direction (New York: McGraw-Hill, 1959), p. 3.
32. Florence G. Feasley and Elnora W. Stuart, "Magazine Advertising Layout and Design: 1932-1982," Journal of Advertising, 16, No. 2 (1987), pp. 20-25; Chamblee and Sandier, 1992.

33. Chris Janiszewski, "The Influence of Nonattended Material on the Processing of Advertising Claims," Journal of Marketing Research, 27 (August 1990), pp. 263-278.
34. Michael J. Arlen. Thirty Seconds (New York: Farrar. Straus & Giroux, 1980).
35. Albert C. Book and Norman D. Cary, The Television Commercial: Creativity and Craftsmanship (New York: Decker Communication, 1970).
36. Henry A. Laskey, Ellen Day, and Melvin R. Crask, "Typology of Main Message Strategies for Television Commercials," Journal of Advertising, 18, No. 1 (1989), pp. 36-41.
37. David Ogilvy, Confessions of an Advertising Man (New York: Atheneum, 1964), pp. 100-102.
38. Martin Mayer, Madison Avenue, U.S.A. (New York: Pocket Books, 1958), p. 64.
39. Jerry Della Femina, with Charles Spokin, ed., From Those Wonderful Folks Who Gave You Pearl Harbor (New York: Simon & Schuster, 1970), p. 29.
40. Higgens, The Art of Writing Advertising, pp. 117-118.
41. Mayer, Madison Avenue, U.S.A., p. 66.
42. Frank Rowsome, Jr., Think Small (New York: Ballantine Books, 197J3), p. 81.
43. Mayer, Madison Avenue, U.S.A., p. 65.
44. For an interpretation of this campaign from which these comments were drawn, see Della Femina, From Those Wonderful Folks, pp. 38-39..
45. Rowsome, Think Small, p. 116.
46. Higgens, The Art of Writing Advertising, p. 120.
47. Mayer, Madison Avenue, U.S.A., pp. 59-61.
48. Higgens, The Art of Writing Advertising, p. 124.
49. Described in Mayer, Madison Avenue, U.S.A., p. 300.
50. Burnett, "Keep Listening to That Wee, Small Voice."
51. Higgens, The Art of Writing Advertising, p. 17.
52. Burnett, "Keep Listening," p. 154.
53. Mayer, Madison Avenue, U.S.A., p. 70.
54. Higgens, The Art of Writing Advertising, p. 45.
55. Della Femina, From Those Wonderful Folks, p. 141.
56. The New York Times, November 16, 1990, p. F29.
57. Stewart Altr, "Ad Age Honors BBDO as Agency of Year," Advertising Age, March 28, 1985, pp. 3ff.
58. Jennifer Pendleton, "Bringing New Clown-T to Ads, Chiats Unlikely Creative," Advertising Age, February 7, 1985, pp. 1 ff.
59. Insight, September 14, 1987, pp. 38-40.
60. The New York Times Magazine, December 14, 1986, pp. 52-74.
61. David W. Stewart and David F. Furse, Effective Television Advertising: A Study of W00 Commercials (Lexington, MA: Lexington Books, 1986).
62. Advertising Age, July 5, 1993, p. 27.

CHAPTER 18

ADVERTISING COMMUNICATION RESEARCH

GATEWAY SEARCHES FOR THE RIGHT AD AGENCY

While some companies have long-lasting relationships with their advertising agencies, others often find themselves changing agencies more frequently. Decisions to switch ad agencies can be driven by a variety of factors including increases in the client's size, changes in the markets it serves, reorganizations that lead to changes in top management, and/or changes in its advertising strategy or philosophy. One company that found itself changing agencies quite frequently during the past 10 years is Gateway, which is one of the world's largest computer companies.

Founded in 1985, Gateway was a pioneer in the build-to-order, direct-marketing segment of the personal computer business. The company's chairman and CEO, Ted Waitt, started Gateway on his family's cattle farm in Iowa and built it into a multibillion-dollar company. The Holstein dairy cows on the Waitt farm inspired the company's distinctive and nationally recognized logo and the cow-spot patterns on its boxes. The spots serve as a constant reminder of Gateway's midwestern roots and the company's values: hard work, honesty, friendliness, quality-and putting people first.

Until 1993, Gateway relied solely on print advertising that was produced in-house. However, as the company's rapid growth continued, it decided to add television ads to the media mix and to retain the services of an outside agency to work with its in-house advertising department. The agency, Carmichael Lynch of Minneapolis, hired a New York commercial director and filmmaker, Henry Corra to direct the first Gateway commercials. Ted Waitt liked the unscripted, folksy ads that Corra was shooting, with their emphasis on "real people," and the visionary entrepreneur and artist developed a strong personal relationship.

As Gateway grew and its international sales increased, the company decided it needed a global agency. In 1997, the company moved its account to D'Arcy Masius Benton & Bowles. However, Waitt quickly became dissatisfied with DMB& B's traditional campaigns and dropped the agency after a year. He brought back Henry Corra to work on Gateway's advertising with a new agency, DiMassimo Brand Advertising, a small but aggressive creative boutique. Corra and the new agency produced a number of unscripted TV commercials throughout 1998. However, that some year Jeff Weitzen, a former AT&T executive, was brought in to run Gateway, when Waitt decided to step back from the day-to-day operations of the company. The new CEO quickly moved the entire Gateway account again—this time to McCann-Erickson, one of the largest agencies in the world.

McCann worked on the Gateway account for three years and developed the "People Rule" campaign, which included actor Michael J. Fox as a spokesperson and also featured Waitt touting the company's services for small businesses. However, in January 2001, Weitzen resigned as CEO and Waitt once again took the helm. A few days after Waitt resumed control of the company, Gateway dismissed McCann-Erickson as its agency. A Gateway spokesman described the parting as "amicable," while McCann viewed the dismissal as part of the wholesale changes and management shake-up that accompanied Ted Waitt's return.

A few days later, several agencies made presentations to Waitt and the Vice President of advertising for Gateway's consumer business, including former agency DiMassimo Brand Advertising; Fallon, Minneapolis; and Siltanen / Keehn. However, Gateway decided to move its advertising back in-house. Once again, Ted Waitt turned to his friend Henry Corra to direct the company's commercials. While Corra continued to direct and shoot the TV commercials for Gate-way, the company also began working with yet another agency, Siltanen/Keehn, whose founders worked on Apple Computer's "Think Different" campaign at TBWA/Chiat/Day. After working with Gateway on a project basis for five months, Siltanen/Keehn became the company's agency of record for print and broad-cast advertising in early 2002.

The relationship with Siltanen / Keehn was also short -lived as Gateway parted ways with the agency after only 10 months and moved its account to the Arnell Group, New York. The change was part of Gateway's decision to move aw y from the folksy, rural image and brand itself as a more modern and hip company. The new advertising tagline is "Gateway a better way" and the ads show computer users in a series of vignettes with an urban look and feel. Gateway is also touting a new logo as the old one, which featured a cow-spotted shipping box, has been replaced. The new logo is a computer power button rotated on its side to form a stylized "G" but still retains a hint of a cow spot. However, the talking cow has been retired and Gateway feels that it has found the right image for the future as well as the right agency. Hopefully, the company will no longer have to keep looking for an udder agency.

Sources: Bruce V. Bigelow, "How now Gateway cow?," The San Diego Union Tribune, December 8,2002,pp. Hi, 10; Richard Linnett, "Regarding Henry," Advertising Age, Mar. 26,200l,pp. 1,37,41; Tobi Elkin, "Troubled Gateway Turns to New Shop as Earnings Fall," Advertising Age, Feb. 12,2001, p. 4.

A famous company President once said, "advertising to me is really one of the mysteries of American business..., I can figure my taxes, estimate my depreciation, determine my met, sales cost, derive return per share. Yet there are times when I spend as much as $ 18,000,000 a year on advertising and have no idea what I am really getting for my money."

ROSSER REEVES

All advertising efforts are directed mainly towards the achievement of business, marketing and advertising objectives i.e., to increase the sales turnover and thus to market the maximum profit. The advertiser spends lakhs of rupees in to this advertising activity. In the background of all these efforts, is an attempt to attract the customer towards the product through advertising.

In recent years the investment in all forms of advertising has increased dramatically. Advertising Industry in India is increasing at the growth rate of 40% approximately though the growth rate has come down to 30% in the last two years. This testify the fact that advertisers have found advertising a powerful selling tool. Yet those who use advertising have learned to their sorrow that it does not produce the expected results. Some advertisements and some advertising campaigns turn out to be flops and others may be only fair producers and many are very successful.

How can advertiser weed out the poor advertisements and pick the good ones? This is a very important question and the advertisers turn to advertising research for the answer. They can no longer afford the luxury of hoping or of guessing about the effectiveness of their advertising. The stakes are too high, the competition is too stiff and failure is too expensive.

Advertisers have actively and continuously sought new methods which would help them to better evaluate the effectiveness of their advertising with the aim to eliminate waste increase the effectiveness of their advertising. Measurement of advertising effectiveness helps management to maximize the contribution that advertising can make. For most advertising, the eventual measure of effectiveness is frequently tied to sales per rupee spent. Hoi before advertising can make its contribution certain communication objectives must be met. The eventual buyer must have been exposed to advertising, it must have communicated a message, and it must have motivated or conditioned the buyer, either consciously or unconsciously to want to purchase. The effectiveness of the advertising in achieving these communication objectives will regulate its sales effectiveness. Measurements of effectiveness may be based on a single advertisement, on a campaign, or on a sequence of campaign may be taken at a single point in time or compiled over short or extended periods of time.

NEED OF MEASURING ADVERTISING EFFECTIVENESS

After a campaign has been launched, it is essential to know how far the advertising plans, strategies and programmes have been successful achieving the objectives so that they may be modified and redesigned for better performance and higher achievement in subsequent years. The results of an advertising campaign are measured to find out its effectiveness in the light of established objectives. Strategies and programmes are developed to attain the objectives.

Advertising measurement is adopted both before and after an advertising campaign is launched. The advertiser and the producer must know the extent of the success that has been achieved, while the advertising plans are being implemented. The competitor's success, the producer's objectives, the tasks given to distributors, price policy, etc., are considered while measuring advertising effectiveness. The methods of measuring this effectiveness may be explained in the light of objectives, the measuring of sales communication performance, the time of measurement, methods of measuring and advertising audit etc.

Some advertising may benefit the competitors. It is productive advertising while may be extensive but ineffective in approach. An unnecessarily large amount is sometimes spent without any reward. An improper display may tarnish the image of the product. The media, message, presentation, approach, production, competition, etc., influence the sales of advertised products. Producers and advertisers should be aware of the effectiveness of advertising. Because of these factors, advertising effectiveness is evaluated and suggestions for improvements are incorporated in subsequent advertising campaigns.

OBJECTIVES OF MEASURING ADVERTISING

1. Assessment for Future Use— Some advertisers expect that the sales will ultimately increase by reason of advertising. They do not bother to measure advertising effectiveness. Recently, however, advertisers have been forced to measure effectiveness. Because they incur a sizeable amount of expenditure on advertising the producers themselves adopt a measuring device. Problems and difficulties compel them to measure advertising effectiveness. The effectiveness of media and message are assessed for their use in future.

2. Testing Advertising Campaign—The same amount of advertising budget is not necessarily effective to the same extent. Their results vary for several reasons. The measuring of advertising effectiveness shows how effective and successful **a** particular campaign has been. Adequate measuring techniques are developed to measure effectiveness at every stage. The copy media and other advertising components have been tested.

3. Achieving Maximum Sales—The ultimate purpose of advertising is to achieve optimum sales. Therefore, positive relationships are established between these factors and sales. Copy testing before and after use is done with reference to customers. The best read and highly rated advertisements are determined by consumers through an advertising research programme. There are different methods of measuring audience response, the advertisers generally want from their promotional effort an increase in marketing performance parameters such as sales, market share, profits, etc.

There should not be any mistake in setting the ad objective. Lack of clarity in setting advertising objectives may arise due to the following factors:

1. Apparent failure in realising that results of advertising cannot generally be measured in terms of sales.
2. Inadequate information about media, its qualitative focus and reach.
3. Problems in stating objectives in quantifiable terms.
4. Inability in identifying the target audience.

The overall purpose of advertising in any situation must be defined first and then broken down in various stages.

We allocate a huge budget to our advertising activity. The main objective of this allocation is to increase sales and profits of the firm. The multivariable forces influencing sales make it almost impossible to measure with high precision the sales effect of advertising. Consequently, to most advertising research measures the characteristics of an advertisement such as exposure, the ability of receiver to comprehend, retain and believe in advertisement. If all of these characteristics are present in an advertisement, it can be inferred that the advertisement is effective in generating sales. Measuring, the effectiveness, however, is not an easy task, it is still a complex problem and no scientific method can be applied precisely particularly, in Indian conditions in which the advertising industry is growing because its problems are closely related to the economic and cultural problems of the country.

Importance of Measuring the Effectiveness of Advertising

Why do we measure the worth of advertising? There are a number of answers of this question :

(1) **To Get the Cost Benefit of Advertising.** The cost of adverting is mounting day-by-day and consequently profits are being squeezed. So, the top management should be concerned about the cost benefit of advertising in the various items of expenditure in the balance-sheet of the company, the contribution of which cannot be measured in terms of sales or profitability. Its contribution in terms of sales or profitability can only be estimated to a reasonable extent. Due to high costs of materials and wages, strangulated by higher over-heads and taxes, the management is reasonable in not approving any expenditure on advertisement which is not likely to bring in additional sale, resulting in additional profits. The main concept is that additional cost of advertising must produce additional profit and, therefore, the advertising should prove its contribution in total marketing efforts like any other allocation of corporate resources or else the advertising expenditure will be set arbitrarily or be slashed drastically. So, if the management measures the effectiveness of the advertising campaign, it should compare the cost with the contribution received. The cost must be linked with the benefits derived. If contribution of any advertising campaign is higher, it means the cost benefit is higher and the advertisement is effective.

(2) To Justify the Investment in Advertising— The expenditure on advertisements is considered to be an investment. In an investment decision planning, there is always a statement of objectives which are spelt out in detail, together with the nature and size of the returns expected on investment. The case of investment in advertising is no more different. Advertising is a marketing investment and its objectives should be spelt out in a similar manner, clearly indicating the results expected from the campaign. The rate and size of return should be determined in advance. If the expected rate of return is achieved in terms of additional profits, the advertisement can be considered an effective one. In order to justify the investment in advertising, the management makes an attempt to measure the effectiveness of the advertisement.

(3) To Compare the Results with the Objectives and Goals—advertising objectives and goals and two distinct terms must be distinguished. An objective is a broad aim; a goal is specific and quantified objective. The objective is not measurable whereas the goal is. Generally, the objectives of advertising are warded vaguely in general terms such as 'to increase sales or profits' or 'to expand our share of market', or 'to maintain a favourable attitude of the company and its product. Evaluation of these objectives is not possible. If these objectives are stated in terms of the quantity or the amount of sales or percentage of total market shares these are measurable in these terms and effectiveness can be measured. If the goal have been achieved the advertising may be said to be effective. The results (actual sales) are compared with the goals and if the actual performance is better, the advertising is effective otherwise, it is ineffective.

(4) To Know the Communication Effect—The effectiveness of the advertisements can be measured in terms of their communication effects on the target consumers or audience. The main purpose of 'advertising is communicate the general public, and existing and: prospective consumers, various information about the product and the company. It is, therefore, desirable to seek post measurements of advertising in order to determine whether advertisements have been seen or heard or in other words whether they have communicated the theme, message or appeal of the advertising. Clearly, if advertisements are not seen or heard or are low in communication ability relative to advertisements, "for comparable products, then the advertising probably is ineffective and change is called for. It is not enough that advertising is seen or heard, the advertiser needs also to know the degree to which prospects retain messages and have been induced to develop favourable attitudes towards the product advertised. Thus, if the advertisements succeed in communicating the desired information and developing the favourable attitude, the advertising is effective.

(5) Compare Two Markets—Advertisers frequently seek to evaluate alternative types and amounts of advertising by experimentation in so-called test markets. Under this procedure, advertising is published is test markets and results are contrasted with other markets—so called control markets—which have had the regular advertising programme. The measurements made to determine results may be measurements of change in sales, change in consumes altitudes, changes in dealer display, and so on depending upon the objectives sought by the advertiser. Although experimentation in test markets provides an excellent means for testing alternative advertising approaches to see if they are effective in actual operations, the measurement made are actually measurements of the effectiveness of the sales promotional programme as a whole rather than measurement of the effectiveness of the advertising itself.

(6) Basis for Planning—Measuring the effectiveness of the advertising is done with a view to improve the advertising plan by paving a comparative view of the objectives set out in the plan and the objectives or goals achieved during the course of execution of the plan. If achievement is higher an attempt should he made to maintain the position and if there is an unfavourable attitude, this should be avoided by making the necessary adjustments, in the goals or by improving the functioning of the various activities, these variations—favourable or unfavourable may form the basis of the new advertising plan. Variation is a must and it should be located properly and then corrective steps should be taken. Thus, measuring the effectiveness is necessary for the planning.

Thus, measurement of effectiveness of advertising is necessary otherwise the whole planning process will be disturbed. For this purpose, many tests and surveys are conducted, necessary data are collected and are used extensively in the decision making process. On the basis of the information collected during the course of surveys, management confirms the standards and improves them wherever necessary, so that it may fetch the maximum out of its limited resources.

The type of copy used in the advertisement is clearly influenced by the medium in which in is to be used. Hence both the selection of the copy to be used and the medium or media to be used call for research to determine the best copy and the best medium and to the best medium and to attempt to measure the effectiveness of the advertising.

Because of the large sums of money invested in advertising today and the highly competitive nature of today's market, advertisers, media owners, and advertising agencies are all vitally, interesting in determining the effectiveness of advertising.

Because of the complexities of testing advertising effectiveness, many advertisements are not tested. That is, some people engaged in advertising doubt the validity of tests designed to measure advertising effectiveness or they feel the qualities of advertising that can be tested do not truly measure the value of the advertisement to achieve its ultimate goal—the sale of the product or service — and so it is not worthwhile to test.

However, the use of testing and measuring of advertising effectiveness has increased in recent years due to several factors. One factor is that the increased interest by top executives in getting the best possible results with the larger advertising appropriations required today causes them to support expenditures for testing. The development of scientific methods of testing has also helped convince more agencies and advertisers to budget sufficient funds for the proper testing of their advertising.

Most advertising professionals agree that it is wise to make judicious use of testing. They would also agree that all methods of testing do have certain limitations. However, they believe that careful and adequate use of testing can be real aid to design better advertisements and advertising. Generally speaking, it is not always possible to measure the effect of an advertisement or advertising on sales and profits of a company. Hence it is usually necessary to establish other criteria of effectiveness for advertising and to test these. Other objectives may be established for advertising, and tests are devised to measure the effectiveness of advertising in achieving these more specific and narrower objectives such as readership, understanding, believability, and so on.

ADVERTISING EFFECTIVENESS MEASUREMENT

How can advertising manager evaluate the effectiveness of a firm's advertising? Advertising is aimed at improving the sales volume of a concern, so its effectiveness can be evaluated by its impact on sales. Most of the managers believe that the advertisement directly affects the sales volume and hence they evaluate the effectiveness of the advertising campaign by the increase in the sales volume. Although, it is not correct to anticipate that the advertisement is the only factor to influence sale. There are many other influences to sales in addition to that of advertising. Though sales volume is not the valid measure of advertising effectiveness, yet, it is a good measure where the management believes that advertising is the sole, or at least, the most important influence on sales. However, where advertising objectives are defined in terms of sales, it is desirable to measure the effective. of advertising campaign on sales.

The advertising effectiveness is measured in the light of sales and communication objectives. These are the two important kinds of measurements.

1. Measuring Sales- Sales measurement makes a realistic approach to the assessment of advertising effectiveness. Where advertising is the predominant contribution to sales, when the sales response is immediate and when internal and external factors affecting sales are held constant or are ineffective sales measurement is a useful tool. But advertising is not the only contributory factor to sales. Therefore, measuring its effectiveness in terms of sales only is not very logical or scientific though, this is the only realistic approach to the measurement of the effectiveness of advertising.

Though some models can be built between advertising expenditure and sales, there are certain difficulties in building such models. A non-linear relationship exists between advertising and sales. There are carry-over effects of advertising for a long period. The advertising effect is not always immediate there are the adverse effects of competition. Sales are greatly affected by internal and external factors. While measuring the advertising with the yardstick of sales, these factors may be constant or ineffective. If the controllable and uncontrollable factors are taken as constant, the measurement of advertising effectiveness becomes easy.

2. Measuring Communication Effects- As advertising is a communication process the effectiveness of advertising can be measured by the effect of the communication process or its usefulness in motivating consumers. This method is more economical and easy. Communication effects can be measured by research, opinion, mathematical model, etc. The communication objectives such as establishing brand awareness, improving recall, increasing brand recognition, bringing about an attitude change, etc., can be measured.

In this method the advertising effectiveness is measured by its direct and immediate impact on consumer behaviour. As the advertising objectives ate to create awareness, the measurement of attitude is not logical. If image building is the objective of advertising, its effectiveness should be measured in terms of image building and not in terms of the attainment of any other communication objectives.

There may be two types of measures (i) Direct measures; and (ii) Indirect measures—

(i) Direct Measures of Advertising Effectiveness.

Under direct measures, a relationship between advertising and sales is established. A comparison of sales of two periods or two markets may be done and the corresponding changes may be noted. 'The following are some of the methods that are generally used in measuring the advertising effects —

(a) Historical Sales Method. Some insights into the effectiveness of past advertising may be obtained by measuring the relationship between the advertising expenditure and the total sales of the product. A multiple regression I analysis of advertising expenditure and sales over several time periods may be calculated. It would show how the changes in adver-tising expenditure have a corresponding charges in sales volume. This technique estimates the contribution that advertising has made to explaining in a correlation manner rather than a casual sales, the variation in sales over the time periods covered in the study. The data required for this analysis are periodic advertising expenditure which can be attained from the company's advertising budgeting records and the product.or brand sales figures, from sources like the audit records. Where house shipments or other sales records maintained by the company. If it has a positive correlation the expendi-ture on budgeting will show an effective relationship.

However, the historical sales analysis method is only a post-test measure of advertising effectiveness and is net applicable to pre-testing. It means that in this analysis, advertising effectiveness can be measured only when sales are effected and not earlier.

(b) Experimental Control. The other measure of advertising effectiveness is the method of experimental control where a casual relationship between advertising and sales is established. This method is quite expensive when related to other advertising effectiveness measures, yet it is possible to isolate advertising contribution to sales. Moreover, this can be done as a pre-test to aid advertising in choosing between alternative creative designs, media schedules, expenditure levels or some combination of these advertising decision areas.

One experimental approach to measuring the sales effectiveness of advertising is test marketing.

(i) Before-after with Control Group Design. This classic design uses several test and control cities (Fig. 18.1) In this design two types of cities are selected. Cities in which adver-tising campaigns are affected may be named as test cities and other cities may be called cities.

First of ail the normal sales level is calculated for both types of cities prior to advertising campaign, and then the advertising campaign is presented to be test cities and not the central cities. The effect of advertising campaign, can then be measured by subtracting the amount of post- campaign figure of sale from the pre-campaign sale figures in test cities.

A Before-after with Control Group Design for Measuring the Effectiveness of Advertising Campaigns

	Test cities	*Control cities*
Pre-campaign measure of sales	Yes	Yes
Advertising campaign	Yes	Yes
Post-Campaign measure of Sales	Yes	Yes

Fig 18.1.

The difference of post and pie campaign sales in cities is the result of advertising and all other factors that affect the sales. In control cities, the difference of these two sales shows the affect of other factors except advertising. By subtracting the sales differences in control cities from those in test cities, a tolerably accurate estimate can be gathered of the effect of advertising only on sales provided that the test and the control cities are reasonably comparable.

(ii) Multivariable Experimental Designs. While the experimental design discussed above yields a reasonably accurate estimate of the effects of the advertising on sales, it is not successful in explaining the success or failure of the campaign itself. Multivariable designs produce these explanations and are, therefore used by some very large firms because of their diagnostic value. Fig. 18.2 shows the multivariable design—

A Multivariable Experiment for Measuring the Effectiveness of Advertising Campaigns

	No Newspaper				Newspapers			
	No Radio		Radio		No Radio		Radio	
	No. T.V.	T.V.	No. T.V.	T.V.	No. T.V.	T.V.	No. T.V.	T.V.
No. outdoor	(1)	(2)	(3)	(4)	(5)	(6)	(7)	(8)
Outdooor	(9)	(10)	(11)	(12)	(13)	(14)	(15)	(16)

Fig. 18.2.
(The figure shown in brackets shows the area number)

The power of this multivariable factorial design is explained by G.H. Brown, former Fords Director of Marketing & Research. For single medium, eight possible geographic areas have been exposed and eight have not been exposed. Thus, in this experimental model, it is possible to evaluate how each individual medium behaves alone and in all possible combinations with ether media.

Mr. Brown has explained the functioning of this model as follows :

If identical dollar expenditures (at national rates) are established for each medium, area 1 will share no advertising expenditures; area 2, 3, 5, and 9 will receive advertising expenditure at the same par rates : areas 4, 6, 7, 10,11 and 13 will receive advertisi at twice this dollar rate; areas 8,12, 14 and 15 at three times the dollar rate; and area 16 at four times this dollar expenditure. (G.H. Brown "Measuring the Sales Effectiveness of Alternative Media" Proceedings of the 17th Annual Conference (N.Y. Advertising Research foundation) pp. 43-47.)

This type of factorial design is capable of measuring the effectiveness of all combinations of media used, as well as four different level, of advertising expenditures. For these reasons, it is a very efficient design. However, the complexities and the costs involved make it impractical for all except very big advertiser.

(ii) Indirect Measures

As it is very difficult to measure the direct effect of advertising on company's profits or sales, most firms rely heavily on indirect measures. These measures do not evaluate the effects of advertisements directing on sales or profits but all other factors such as customer awareness or attitude or customer recall of advertising message affect the sales or profits or goals of the business indirectly. The assumption of these measures is that favourable change in customer awareness, attitude and recall will lead in some way or the other to the attainment of greater sales and profits or whatever is the primary object of the marketing and corporate strategy. This assumption, in turn, is based upon universal human behaviour that is by no means firmly established. It is quite obvious if we make a housewife aware of the brand, she will not necessarily go for the purchase of the brand immediately. If she buys the brand, it may not be due to the advertisement. There may be certain other factors that instigate her to buy the product.

Despite the uncertainties about the relationship between the intermediate effects of advertising and the ultimate results, there is no other alternative but to use indirect measures. The most commonly used measures are:

(1) Exposure to Advertisement : In order to be effective, the advertisement must gain exposure. The management is concerned about the number of target audience; who see or hear the organisation message set in the advertisement. Without exposure, advertisement is bound to failure.

Marketers or advertisers may obtain an idea, of exposure generated by the medium by examining its circulation or audience data which reveal the number of copies of the magazine, newspaper or journal sold, the number of persons passing the billboards or riding in transit facilities, or the number of persons living in the televiewing or radio listening area, and the number of persons switching on their T.V. and radio sets at various points of time. This number can be estimated by interviewing the numbers of the audience for different media.

The audience and circulation data, as collected by the advertiser, may be further classified by such variables as the age, income, occupation, and areas of residence of the audience or reader population and the advertiser can estimate the approximate number of target consumers that are exposed to advertising messages. Another means of gauging exposure is readership or listener surveys in which interviewers ask the listeners or readers whether they have read or viewed the advertisements.

(2) Attention or Recall of Advertising Message Content : This is one of the widely used measures of advertising results. Under this measure, a recall of the message content among a specified group or groups of prospective customers is measured within 24 hours of the exposure of the advertisement.

Attention value is the chief quality of the advertising copy the advertisements cannot be said to be effective unless they attract the attention of the target consumers. There are two methods for evaluating the-attention getting value of the advertisements. One is pre-test and the other is post-test.

In a pre-test evaluation, the consumers are asked to indicate the extent to which they recognise or recall the advertisement, they have already seen. This test is conducted in the laboratory setting. Here consumers read, hear or listen to the advertisement and then researchers ask question regarding the advertisement just to test the recall and then evaluate it.

In post-test method, the consumers are asked questions about the indication of recognition or recall after the advertisement has been run.

These measures assume that customers can recall or recognise what they have viewed or listened to.

Various mechanical devices are being used in the western countries which provide indices of attention such as eye-camera etc.

(3) Brand Awareness : The marketers who rely heavily on advertising often appraise its effectiveness by measuring the customer's awareness about the particular product or brand. The assumption of this type of measure is that there is a direct relationship between the advertisement and the awareness. This type of measure is also subject to the same criticisms as is applicable to direct measures of effectiveness of sales measures because awareness is also not the direct result of the advertisement. It is also effected by many other factors. But for new products, changes in awareness can often be attributed to the influences of advertising.

(4) Comprehension : Consumers generally use advertisements as a means of obtaining information about the product, brand or the manufacturer. They cannot be informed unless they comprehend the message (grasp the message mentally and understand it fully). Various tests for valuating comprehension are available.

One is recall tests —an indicator of comprehension because it is evident that consumers recall what they comprehend. Another measure of this variable is to ask questions about subjects how much they have comprehended a message they have recently heard or seen. One may employ somewhat imprecise test of the comprehension of a newspaper arid radio advertisement. One may ask typical, target consumers from time to time such questions like 'what did you think of our new commercial ?' and Did it get the message across'? The answers of these questions will provide sufficient insight into advertising decision making.

(5) Attitude Change : Since advertising is considered to be one way of influencing the state of the mind of the audience towards a product, service or organisation, the results are very often measured in terms of attitudes among groups exposed to advertising communication. Several measures are used ranging from asking the questions about willingness to buy the likelihood of buying to the measurement of the extent to which specific attributes (such as modern or new) are associated with a product.

This involves the measurement of attitude of the customers towards the product, service or organisation in question both before and after the appearance of the advertisement. This may be a pre-test or post test efforts. For gauging the attitude change, attitude scales are used. A typical scale contains questions like:—

NIRMA Detergent is :—

Expensive———Inexpensive
Strong———weak
A good brand———A poor brand

The measuring instrument normally contains 15-20 scales (such as three set forth above). This technique (called a semontic technique) provide a useful means of measuring attitudes in a short period of time.

Other methods of measuring attitude change are recall and enquiries. The assumption underlying these methods is that consumers generally recall or inquire about what they prefer or to which they have a favourable attitude.

(6) Action : One objective of advertisement may be assumed to be to stimulate action or behaviour. The action or intention to take an action may be measured on the intention to buy measuring instrument. Under this type of measure, consumers are asked to respond why they are interested in purchasing the product or brand. Their responses may include such points as the following regarding the product under consideration—

(a) I already own it.
(b) I have no intention to buy the product.
(c) I hope to buy it soon or within a year.
(d) I will probably buy it sometime in the future.
(e) I am sure, I will never buy it.

The classification and analysis of such responses will show the extent of the intention of consumer towards the action they had in mind about the product and are indicative of expected future purchasing activities.

One type of action that advertisers attempt to induce is buying behaviour. The assumption is that if an increase in sales follows a decrease in advertising expenditure, the change in sales levels are good indicators of the effectiveness of advertising. Logic suggests that measurement of sales are preferable to other measurements.

Thus, these above measures (direct or indirect) are used to evaluate the effectiveness of the advertisements. It seems from the analysis of the above methods of measuring effectiveness that directly or indirectly changes in sales or profits are taken as the measuring rod of the effectiveness of the advertising. After all, however, advertisement is done either to increase or maintain sales either directly or indirectly.

Advertisement Copy Testing

Almost every firm spends thousands of rupees on advertising every year, it is very much pertinent to know the effectiveness of the advertisement copy. The main purpose of every advertising is to arouse the interests of the people in the firm's product can everyone be perused by the same advertisement? Or will the same advertisement satisfy all types of people? The simple answer is an negative because people differ so greatly in their wants, in the economic and other motives which actuate them, and in the various ways by which their interest is aroused. The amount is spent on advertising not only because the advertisement does not get to the right people but because it carries an appeal which does not interest those to whom it goes. An often quoted remark about advertisement is that half the money spent on advertising is wasted; but no one knows which half.

Everyone in the business (government and non-government) heavily rely upon the advertisement to influence the mind emotions and actions of the people favourably towards the product or brand or an idea. Though advertising is expensive yet it is vital to every business for its success. The advertiser wants that the audience should see or read his advertisement with interest so that it may arouse their demand, desire and action.

For this purpose, advertising copy research is done to see how will an advertisement succeeds in attracting the attention and stimulating the desire and action of the people for whom it is made and how will it delivers the intended message about a product or an idea. Advertisement copy is done to be sure of its effectiveness.

What is Copy Testing

Copy testing is a tool involving a procedure where the effectiveness of an advertisement is measured before it appears in its final form, during and after its exposure to the audience to determine whether and to what extent, it has accomplished its assigned task. In this way, the copy testing is a method used to control the effectiveness of future advertising. It addresses the following questions —

(a) Will a proposed copy theme be effective at achieving advertising objectives?
(b) Does the set of advertisings that makes up an advertising campaign create the desired interest level and image ?; and
(c) Will an individual advertisement attract the attention of the audience?

Copy testing is an important part of advertising management and also an interesting subject from the professional and scientific points of view. Professionally, there are a number of ton that after such services of assessing the effectiveness of print advertisements and broadcast commercials. It has developed as an industry in the United States and in other country. From the scientific point of view, advertising research reflects the application of theories and methodologies that derive from psychology, sociology, and economics and more specifically, from various brand of each of these disciplines.

The term 'copy tests' rather than copy research or any other term is used to emphasise that consumers reactions are sought concerning the copy and to highlight that such tests usually focus on relative rather than absolute measures or effectiveness. In many cases, for example, the advertiser wants to know whether one alternative is relatively more effective than another, rather than had many sales, a piece of copy will generate in an absolute sense.

Types of Tests

Copy Tests can be grouped as pre-tests and post tests. Pre-tests are made before an advertisement has been run. It can be done at three stages—(i) at the beginning of the creation process, (ii) at the end of the creation process, and (iii) at the end of the production stage. The main purposes of such testing is to measure the effectiveness of different presentations of the message inducing alternative presentations of the single theme. Such tests help one to choose the best form of advertisement before incurring the expenses and the risk of presenting it on a full scale run. They are intended to discover the plus and minus points of an advertising campaign of the individual advertisement.

The tests which are made after the campaign has been launched are generally known as post-tests. These tests are conduced to determine the effectiveness of an advertisement after it is published. Post-tests measure the impact of the message. They seek to discover which advertisements and what elements of various advertisement get the best response, what position produces better results, what medium or issue of a medium pulls better or how well a whole advertising campaign is processing. Such tests provide information about whether a brand name or the selling theme of a given advertisement or advertising campaign penetrated the reader's mind and the extent of its penetration.

Fig. 18.3 represents the tests that are desired to test the effectiveness of advertising communication:

Pretesting

Advertising effectiveness is measured by pre-testing and post testing. Pre-testing is preferred. It enables one to know how effective an advertisement in likely to be, before spending the budget and adopting advertising actions. Pre-testing methods are employed to examine the effectiveness of each campaign. The advertiser should use only those messages and media which prove to be the strongest in producing the desired results. He should adopt corrective methods against mistakes. Pre-testing may involve a consumer jury, storyboard tests, laboratory tests, tachistocope, psychogalvanometer, eye camera, pupil dilation attitude test, and depth interviewing.

Pretesting is used more commonly than posttesting, since it is much more important to measure advertising effectiveness before an advertisement has been run than afterwards. Therefore, pretesting should be viewed as a means of saving money, whereas post-testing is often devoted to finding out what went wrong. Many of the techniques used in pre-testing may also be used in posttesting, and *vice-versa*. Two of the most common pretesting techniques are consumer jury tests and laboratory tests.

Pretesting is desireable to be conducted in the following situations:

1. To introduce a product or a brand
2. When there are uncertainties or contradictory views expressed about the content of an advertisement

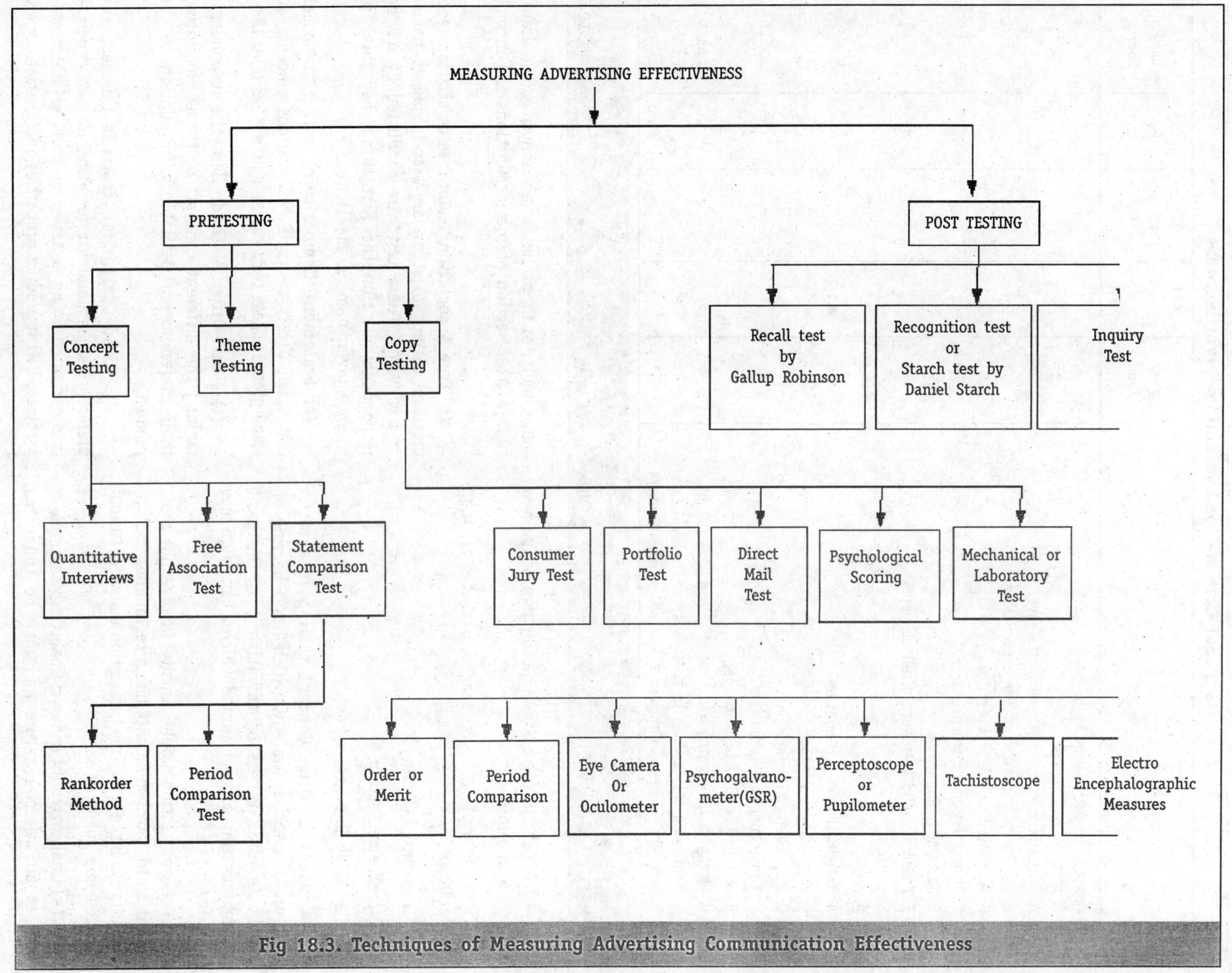

Fig 18.3. Techniques of Measuring Advertising Communication Effectiveness

General Criteria for Evaluating Advertisement					
	(5) Very Good	*(4) +*	*(3) Average 0*	*(2) –*	*(1) Very Poor - -*
I. Concept of Ad or Campaign Is it.... A. In harmony with objectives? strategy? B. A clear presentation of one central idea? C. Addressed to the prospect? D. Distinctive in approach? E. Tasteful in its appeal? F. Based on solid teamwork of all elements? **II. Execution** Is it... A. Imaginative in presentation? B. Emphatic on product/benefits? C. Esthetically pleasing? D. Convincing in its argument? E. Simple and clear in language? F. Strong in its opening and closing? G. Employing the medium to its fullest? H. A tie-in to, or development of, a continuing theme?					

Fig. 18.4

Source : Charles F. Frazer, "Foward Some Criteria for Exaluating Advertisements." Proceedings, American Academy of Advertising.

3. To substitute an ongoing campaign with a new campaign.

Pretesting of an advertisement is routed through the following:

1. Concept Testing
2. Theme Testing
3. Copy Research.

Concept Testing: Concept testing is a major feature of creative strategy, which has a bearing on ultimate effectiveness of advertising, is the basic communication concept around which a campaign may be developed.

Concept testing would usually involve not more than 50 to 100 respondents using techniques such as qualitative interviews, free association tests and various statements comparision tests.

(a) Qualitative Interviews: Quantitative interviews are of an informal nature and may be conducted indivigually, or in groups from amongst people drawn from a cross section of age, occupations and income levels.

(b) Free Association Tests: Free association tests are used to pick to secondary associations to names or key words. These tests are conducted by having respondents mention the first thing they think of when a given name is mentioned.

(c) Statement Comparision Tests : Statement comparision tests are used while various concepts on small groups. These tests can be classified as (Fig. 18.5)

(i) Rank Order Method: Here the respondents ranking the different concepts or themes indicating their preference or desirability in relation to the product.

(ii) Paired Comparison Tests: In this test, the preference of respondents for either of two concepts is determined using a series of pairs of statements associated with product properties and characteristics,

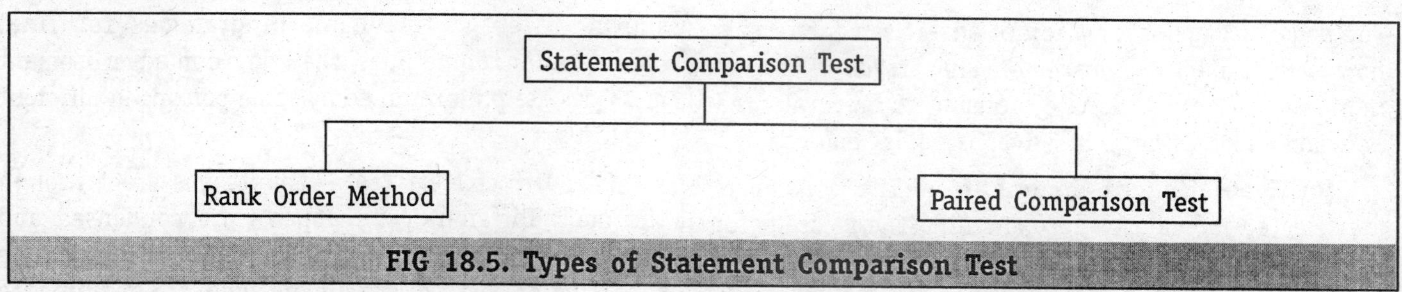

FIG 18.5. Types of Statement Comparison Test

(b) Theme Testing: No specific guidelines are avail-able for classifying themes for the purpose of analysis and research. In general, the themes can be classified as under:

(i) Utilitarian
(ii) Focussed
(iii) Informative
(iv) Non-specific
(v) Achievement orientation
(vi) Descriptive & projective
(vii) New product, service scheme or idea.

(c) Copy Research: The basic purpose of copy research is to establish whether the message content and presentation are likely to perform their allocated task efficiently and what changes and improvements may be helpful. Copy research involves the following tests :

(i) Consumer jury test
(ii) Direct mail test
(iii) Portfolio test
(iv) Psychological scoring
(v) Mechanical or laboratory test.

(i) Consumer Jury Test: Consumer jury tests are useful method for evaluating an advertisement's effectiveness, before it is run. A "Jury" composed of hyperthetical customers is asked to evaluate an advertisement. The number of prospective customers on the jury may range from a dozen to several hundred. The test may take a number of forms. Jurys may evaluate one advertisement or many. They may view advertisements individually or correctively and the evaluation process may take place at home in controlled conditions.

Both television commercials and print advertisements may be evaluated by the use of consumer jury testing method. In either case, the normal method is to have jurys look at several advertisements in order to determine which receives the best rating.

It involves persons most likely to be exposed to the advertisement. As consumer reactions have greater validity than the reactions of non-consumers, consumers can provide true information on reaction to and adoptability of products following an advertising campaign. Non-consumer persons may underestimate or overestimate the reactions to and acceptability of advertising. The consumers concerned with the product layout, etc., may see the copy, illustrations, filming techniques. The print media's message should be evaluated before its publication. The other media's message should be evaluated before their presentation. The consumer jury technique is adopted for print media, broadcast media and direct mail.

(i) Print Media – The consumer selected to test the message for print media are asked either to evaluate an advertisement or rate two or more advertisement by their attention-getting power and believability.

(a) Rating by Jury – The consumer-jury or well-known respondents are asked to rank each print message. Each respondent is asked to express his preferred for each advertisement. The most common method is to insert a questionnaire in the advertisement and request the readers to indicate their preferences on the from and return it to the advertiser or the producer. Aided an denuded recall techniques may be used for this purpose.

(b) Reaction to AD Copy – Almost all copywriters test their creations on consumers. Some newspaper advertisers invite consumers or prospective consumer to their office and ask reaction to the advertising copy. Copies of magazines are sent to some selected panels of consumers to find out how and why the advertisements placed therein have their attention.

The page by page observation of advertisement reveals how a particular advertisement has made a lasting impression. The reactions of consumers are evaluated and any inconsistency in advertising is removed.

(c) Evaluation of Comments – The consumers are selected judiciously for examining the message for print media, the comments are then evaluated. The rating scale, predisposition-to-buy scale, the constant-sum scale, paired comparisons; forced switching techniques are used to judge the effectiveness of the advertising message. Consumers may adopt a particular method desired by the advertiser. They are generally to show their first and second choices of the image of the message. They are asked to show which brand they would buy and why. Their awareness must be recorded. To improve the message and presentation, the advertiser may ask for some diagnostic information.

Advantages

(a) The major advantage of the consumer opinion of ads in the print media is that they separate out the weak advertisement from the strong at a low cost and high speed.

(b) The actual consumers are contacted who may suggest improvements and modifications.

(c) The consumers-jury method is flexible and can be moulded at any time in accordance with need.

Limitations

(a) Consumers are asked to indicate which was the best liked message or picture, although they may have not liked them at all.

(b) The ratings are based on unimportant details.

(c) Only conscious ratings are evaluated, while sub-conscious ratings are ignored.

(d) The consumers on a panel may reply to the questions in a very conscious manner, which do not give a correct impression of advertisements.

(ii) Broadcast Media – The juries are selected at random or from among specific consumer groups with a view to testing specific types of advertisement. The consumer-jury has been used for presetting a broadcasting media campaign. Consumers are sometimes asked to come to the television studio where they are shown different television programmes for final consideration. Sometimes, the television advertisement messages are pre-examined by some persons in different localities.

(iii) Direct Mail Test – this test is used through the mail. Different copy appeals are condensed and printed on reply-paid post cards. These post cards are sent free-of-cost to consumers who are required to indicate how they evaluate the direct mail copy.

(iv) Storyboard Tests – Prepared for television advertising the storyboard is tested before it is used. The storyboard pictures are transferred to a filmstrip and the audio section onto a tape. Vision and sound are synchronized and shown to an audience for evaluation. By reducing the unnecessary part of the storyboard the costs involved can be cut. This test uncovers the unnecessary part for deletion. The important part of advertising is accepted for telecasting. Care is taken to house storyboard advertising in a finished and economical form for visualizing a television commercial. If the mood of the audience is important this should be done by way of testing. The anteroom trailer method is used to test the commercial. The anteroom contains magazines, newspapers, distractions and television recorded programmes. After the commercial has been shown, the audience is taken to another room for an interview and assessment.

The two main procedures for evaluation are:

1. Order of merit
2. Paired comparisons.

Order of merit: Involves having each respondent rank several advertisements in order of preference. It is usually unadvisable to ask respondents to rank more than six advertisements at once. Since the average consumer can rarely work with more than six with any degree of accuracy.

The Paired comparison method: This is especially advantageous when the researcher wishes to have jurors evaluate more than six advertisements. In this method, respondents compare two advertisements at a time, so that only two are being considered at any one time. Each advertisement is compared with every other advertisement in the group. The winner in each comparison is noted on a score card and at the end, the number of times each ad "won" is to tatted.

A major advantage of the paired comparison method over the order of merit method is that it enables the researcher to obtain advertisement ratings of greater consistency and accuracy. It also allows the evaluation of a larger number of advertisements. However, this advantage disappear if the number of advertisements evaluated becomes too large. The number of advertisements being evaluated should not exceed ten, otherwise, the procedure becomes too tedious.

Total number of comparisons = n(n-1)/ 2

Here n equals the number of advertisements being evaluated. For example, in case where respondents were asked to rank eight advertisements by paired comparison method, a total § of twenty eight comparisons would be involved.

$$\frac{N\ (n-1)}{2} = \frac{8\ (8-1)}{2} = \frac{8(7)}{2} = \frac{56}{2} = 28$$

Evaluation of consumer jury tests: Though jury tests are useful and have wide application, here are certain fundamental difficulties inherent in their usage, which include:

1. Sample selection problems: Here the difficulty lies in getting that accurately reflects the market.

2. Measurement criteria problems: On what basis is the advertisement being evaluated? What is the definition of "effective"? Does "effective" mean respondents like the ad best, find it most believable, think it as most interesting one?

3. Respondent control problems: Unless respondents evaluate advertisements under controlled conditions, there is no guarantee that evaluation process is being done properly. In group evaluations the respondents may influence others,

4. Artificial nature of the test: The most serious weakness of the consumer jury test is that it tends to be unrealistic. Since it is only a test, the conditions are not what they would be in the actual market place, and jurors' answers are only hypothetical.

Despite these weaknesses, the jury test remains a popular method for pretesting advertisements. This method allows the researcher to get the evaluation in a relatively brief period of time than if the advertisement has been run through the mass media.

(ii) Direct mail test: Also called as Post card test. In this test different copy appeals are condensed and printed on post cards. Each card makes some sort of free offer, the same on all cards. The post cards are sent to a large and representative sample of consumers of the product involved. The per cent of people who write in to take advantage of the offer is regarded as an indication of the effectiveness of the appeal. Instead of a post card, a letter, booklet, or other promotional literature may be mailed to prospects.

The principle advantage of this test is that it measures action rather than opinion. respondents take a positive action, presumably as a result of advertisement. Also it minimizes variables, because every one receives the message under much the same conditions. Obviously, it is relatively inexpensive.

One limitation is that this method can never test more than general appeal. It does not necessarily follow that the most effective appeal in mail promotion will also be best for the mass media. It would probably not be valid test of an advertisement designed to build images rather to stimulate direct action.

(iii) Portfolio test : A portfolio of different advertisements is prepared and is given to selected group of individuals who are asked to go through this portfolio and can take as much time as they wish. The portfolios are then taken back and respondents are asked to recall the advertisements. Some may also by aided in recalling. The opinion of the respondents are taken and conclusions drawn as to the extent that a message stands out or is understood.

While portfolio tests offer the opportunity to compare alternative ads, directly, a number of weaknesses limit their applicability,

(i) Recall may not be the best test. Some researchers argue that for certain types of products—those of low involvement—ability to recognise the ad when shown may be a better measure than recall.

(ii) Factors other than advertising creativity and presentation may affect recall. Interest in the product or product category, the fact that respondents know they are participating in a test or interviewer instructions (among others) may account for more differences than the ad itself.

One way to determine the validity of the portfolio method is to correlate its results with readership scores once the product is placed in the field. Whether such validity tests are being conducted or not is not readily known, although the portfolio method continues to remain popular in the industry.

(iv) Psychological scoring: Under this semantic differential is a rating scale that has been used extinsely in advertising measurement. Under this method, respondents are asked to mark on a seven point bipolar scale, their "feelings" toward a particular advertisement. In a way, various ad treatments can be measured in terms of consumer reaction. Fig. 18.6 shows the profile of three alternative advertisements.

Some advertising specialists feel that scales serve more as preliminary checklists for creative people than as research tools. Actually almost all copy writers devise some sort of checklist of the qualities to include in every advertisement and those to avoid. Most checklists are based on some research evidence. For example, a checklist devised by Richard Manville is based primarily on the ability of certain ads to produce inquiries. The Thompson - luce method is based on the correlation between readership and certain elements. A much publicized checklist of judging "advertising effectiveness" was devised by the Town send brothers in 1938. For several years it was much used by advertisers and agencies. Today's more sophisticated advertising people are not inclined to accept any thing so rigid.

A variety of so called motivational research techniques are used in pretesting advertisements, such as depth interviewing, the Rorschach (inkblot) test, Thematic Apperception Test (T.A.T.), Word Association, and Role Playing. These methods seek to ascertain whether a particular advertisement or commercial conveys the intended meaning to consumers or not.

(v) Mechanical or laboratory tests: These are used for pre-testing of advertisements. Laboratory conditions offer a controlled environment that excludes the variables, which may indicate the test. The respondents' responses are recorded. Special laboratory tests are conducted to examine the effect of the advertisements. Important means are developed to measure the stimuli. The laboratory test is used to measure awareness, attention, desire, retention, etc. The respondents are placed in laboratory situations

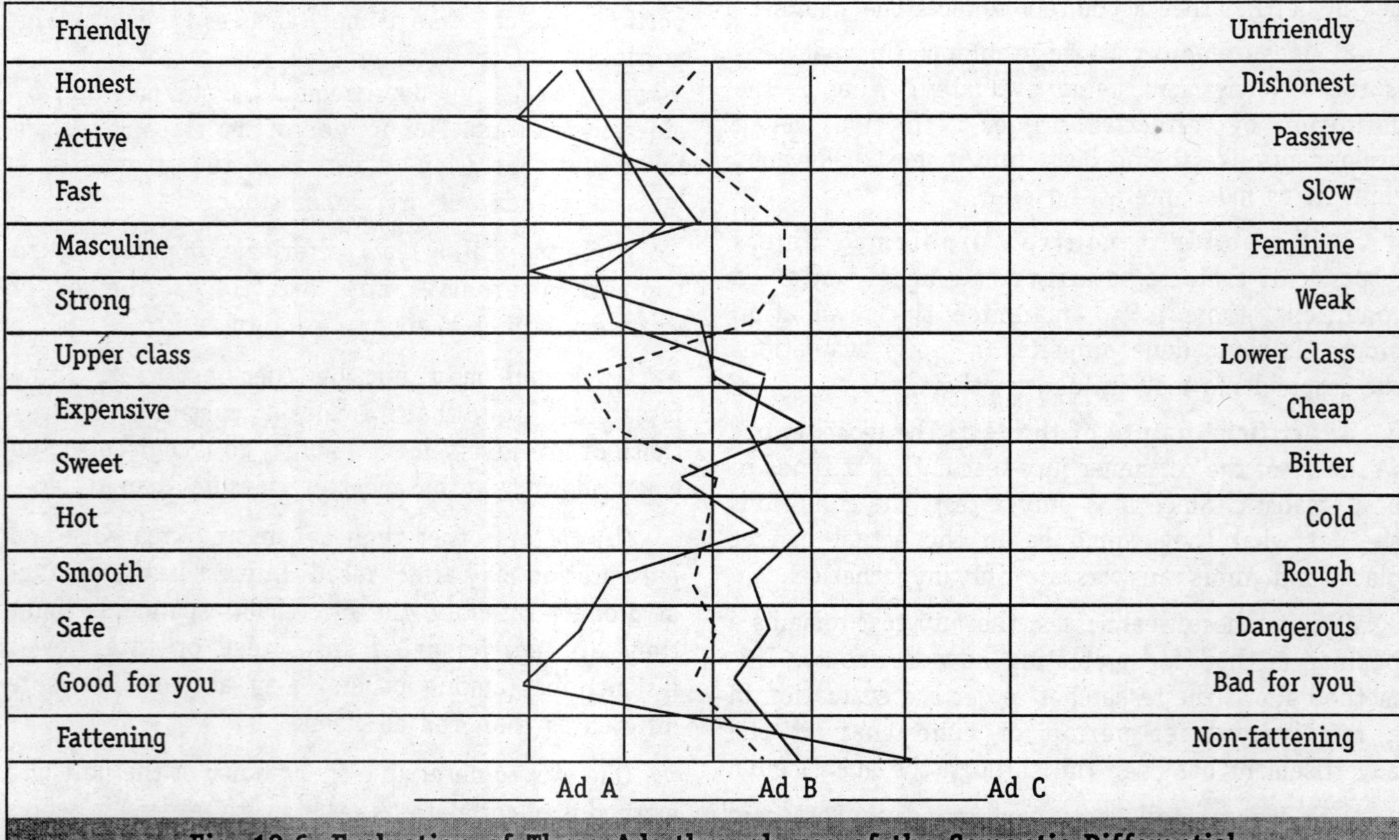

Fig. 18.6. Evaluation of Three Ads through use of the Semantic Differential

and are asked to explain the measurements regarding the effectiveness of the advertisement. The laboratory environment is artificial. The respondents reply under conditions, which are less than normal. For example, they are taken to a theatre, mock-up supermarkets or some other place for experimental purposes. Mechanical devices have not been very useful for recording attention. The size of the sample for laboratory test is a critical matter.

These are designed to measure the psychological reaction of respondents to an advertisements. These tests are conducted in laboratory by using various mechanical and electronic equipment. These are primarily designed to test the attention getting power of the advertisement and do not measure other attributes.

The principal measuring devices used in such testing include :

- Eye camera or Oculometer
- Psychogulvanometer (GKS or GSK. Test)
- Perceptoscope or pupilometer
- Tachistoscope
- Electro encephalographic measures (EEG) Brain waves measures.

Eye camera or Oculometer

It was first developed about in 1890, but it was not used in advertising research until 1938, when results of its use were reported by Look magazine. In an eye camera test the respondent views an advertisement while the camera records how long and on what area of the advertisement the reader's attention is focussed. Though the eye camera has two advantages of accurately measuring what part of the advertisements the respondent's eye focussed on. It does not measure interest in the advertisement. It is an instrument of questionable usefulness, despite its objectives.

Perception Research Services, a subsidary of the Inter Public Group, uses eye movement cameras to measure respondent interest to each part of an advertisement. Interviewers then question respondents further about both the advertisement and the product. The firm thas found his research most useful when creative work is still in process.

Psychogalvanometer: (GSR Test) is another mechanical device used for pretesting advertisements under laboratory conditions. This instrument is similar to a lie detector, has been used by psychologists to measure respondent reactions and emotions. Emotional changes in respondents are recorded by measuring, through electronic impulses. Perspiration changes in the palm of the hand. Presumably, an increase in perspiration indicates a reaction to a given advertisement. However, left unanswered is the question whether a favourable or an unfavourable reaction is being recorded. The measurement of galvanic skin responses is an extremely questionable technique in advertising research. It is useful mainly for advertisements of sensitive nature.

Perceptoscope or Pupilometer: A third laboratory measuring device is also intended to measure respondent arousal or interest in a particular advertisement. This instrument records changes in the pupil size of the respondent's eye. The principle involved is that pupil dilation is indicative of interest and pupil contraction indicative of lack of interest in what is being viewed. Though the perceptoscope is an instrument of great potential for measuring respondent's interest in advertisements, it does not directly measure advertising effectiveness.

These laboratory testing devices remain instruments of limited utility to the advertising researcher however, with proper use by qualified experts, such devices can play a worth-while role as aids in the pretesting process.

Eye Camera – It measures the viewing behaviour of the audience. It records the activity of the eye by its movements. While being unaware, that their eye actions are being photographed the audience is asked to look at a series of pictures on a screen. The eye movements are recorded by a video camera, which shows what the respondent sees. If a commercial is interesting and if one is attracted by it, his eye will be fixed on that. The eye camera can be used to measure the print media advertisements, too. It shows the path taken by the eye over an advertisement and discovers which part produced the initial attention. The respondents may be asked some questions about the advertisement.

Pupil Dilation – The change in the pupil of the eye follows different advertising stimuli. The size of the pupil changes as people see different things. As greater interest is aroused it becomes wider. The pupil shrinks if the eye is not interested. A pupil meter is used to measure the size of the pupil. It records the involuntary dilation, which measures the interest shown by the respondent.

Tachistoscope: It is a mechanical device to measure the amount of perspiration in a respondent supposedly indicative of a change of emotional reaction. It measures a respondent's reactions to new records and slogans. Electrodes are attached to his palms to detect changes in electrical resistance arising from perspiration. If the machine registers lower electrical resistance, it is believed that a tension exists as a result of advertisement. It is assumed that the body response is the outcome of product advertisement. The main objective of an advertisement is to attract attention to the product reflected by the galvanic skin response. However, greater tension does not always reflect a greater success of the advertisement.

One or several advertisements are flashed on the screen for a fraction of second each and the subjects are asked to comment on what they have seen. This text measures the extent of perception of the message on the part of the receiver.

Electro Encephalographic Measures (EEG) Brain Waves Measures: EEG measures can be taken from the skill to determine electrical frequencies in the brain. These electrical impulses are used in two areas of research: Alpha waves and Hemispheric laterlization.

Alpha activity: It refers to the degree of brain activation. People are in an alpha state when they are inactive, resting or sleeping. The theory is that a person in an alpha state is less likely to be processing information (recall correlates negatively with alpha levels) and that attention and processing require moving from this state. By measuring a subject's alpha level while viewing a commercial, researchers can assess the degree to which attention and processing are likely to occur.

Attitude Test – Several psychological techniques are used for measuring the attitudes of respondents.

(i) The Semantic Differential – It is a rating scale which has been used extensively to measure advertising effectiveness. Respondents are asked the questions to be answered on a seven-point bipolar scale about their feelings about a particular advertisement. The various advertising treatments can be measured in terms of consumer reactions.

(ii) Checklist – Advertisers devise some sort of checklist of the qualities to be included in advertising. The checklist is based primarily on the quality of an advertisement, which is capable of generating inquiries. Some relationships are developed and are measured on this scale.

The attitude is closely related to advertising effectiveness. The psychological technique is characterized by a predisposition or state of readiness to act or react in a particular way to some stimuli. If the attitudes of potential customers toward the products are changed the advertisement is considered effective. An advertising campaign lays emphasis on image building and attitude change toward the product. If attitudes can be measured, the effectiveness of advertising campaign can also bemeasured.

ATTITUDE SCALE

The attitude of potential customers or respondents can be measured accurately on the attitude scale. The test is applied without letting the respondents know the objectives of the inquiry. The attitude scale measures the position of the consumers' attitudes on a continuum, varying from favourable at one end and to unfavourable at the other end with the neutral point in the middle. The degrees of variation on the left side and the right side of the neutral point indicate the favourable and unfavourable attitudes respectively. Attitude scale is applied before the use of the advertising media, message and campaign to find out far they would influence consumer attitudes.

Depth Interviewing – This technique is useful for exploratory research for ideas and suggestions are sought for further improvements in the advertising campaign. It is concerned with getting the respondent to react freely to the brand, organization and product. The interviewer brings out resentments and unconscious reactions to the surface by suitable questions. To bring out the facts for the advertiser the reactions to communication stimuli are noted. Depth interviewing involves non-structured questions. The flexibility and intelligence of the interviewer identify the significant points made in the interview and achieve meaningful results. The sentence-completion test, the thematic appreciation test (TAT), and expressive techniques are used the pretest the advertising effectiveness.

The interviewer must ask provocative questions in original atmosphere. He should be polite, rational and helpful. Consumer attitudes are indirectly ascertained. No direct questions are attempted about confidential matters.

POST TESTING

If advertising pretesting were an established science of great precision, there would be little need for posttesting advertisements. Unfortunately, pretesting is primarily a screening device, which, it is hoped to enable the researcher to eliminate the least effective advertisements.

Posttesting is designed not only to measure effectiveness (or lack effectiveness) of advertisements after they have already been run, but to find out the reasons why an advertisement was effective or ineffective.

Since it is generally assumed that one significant and measurable factor is respondent's memory of an advertisement, post-testing techniques often concerned with measuring what (if any thing) the respondent remembers about the advertisement. Two standard techniques' used in testing are :

(a) Recall test by Gallup Robinson

(b) Recognition test or Starch test by Daniel Starch

(c) Inquiry test.

(a) Recall test: The recall type of test, like the recognition test, is based on the memory of the respondent and is designed to measure the positive impression created by the advertisement on the person being interviewed. Probably the best known of the recall tests are the impact studies of magazine and television advertisements done by Gallup-Robinson.

The interviewer first ascertain that the respondents have seen the issue of the magazine being studied by showing them the cover of the magazine but not opening it and then asks the respondents to name all the advertisements they can recall having seen in the magazine. If the respondents have seen or can correctly identify at least one item in the magazine, they are handed a set of cards carrying the names of advertisers or brands appearing in the issue, and are asked how many of these they remember having seen and then asked to tell the interviewer every thing they can remember about each of the advertisements they can identify—including the appearance of the advertisement, what it said about the product, and the main message of the advertisement. There are three main types of recall test :

"Unaided recall"—in which the respondent is given no help whatsoever by the interviewer. Respondents are asked whether the advertisement included a particular picture of message. The name of the product is not given to the audience; they have to recall it themselves. If they do remember, it is established that there was some impact of the advertisement. The impact may be probed to find out the attitude of the audience to product.

"Aided recall" in which the respondent is given cues: and the triple associate test in which the interviewer seeks to measure respondent's recall in associating product brand name, copy theme. It is used to measure the reading memory of magazine advertising impressions. It has a high degree of objectivity arising from the respondents attempting to perform at the maximum level of recall without subjectively screening out the response. It is necessary to use a large sample size for statistical reliability. Used mainly to measure television advertising, the aided test makes it easy to determine when a commercial, advertising appeared on the television screen. To find out something about their recall of the commercial the interviewer may approach the respondents over the telephone or in person. A radio advertisement may be given the aided recall test followed by an unaided question. For example, "What products have been advertised during the last two days?" Then for recall aid is provided by asking: "Have your heard the advertisements of brand Y?" The recall test may be administered immediately or two or three days after the exposure. The triple associate test is useful when the researcher wishes to find out if an advertising campaign is successful in promoting consumer awareness of a product through the brand name and copy theme. The scores reflect the advertiser's ability to register the sponsors name and to deliver a meaningful message to the consumer. However, a high recall score does not necessarily mean that consumers will buy the product; it means only that consumers remember the advertisement.

Combined Recall Tests – These include aided as well as unaided recall tests. Developed by Gallup and Robinson they were designed to test the impact of an advertisement. Respondents were asked whether they have read the magazine or newspaper, or listened to the radio or watched television. This technique involves five steps :

(a) The respondent should recall and describe correctly at least one editorial feature in the magazine or newspaper.

(b) They are handed a group of cards on which are printed the names of brands advertised in the issue.

(c) The respondents are questioned in depth to evaluate the accuracy of their recall.

(d) A copy of the magazine is given to the respondents. They are asked whether they have seen the advertisement for the first time or seen it a second or third time.

(e) The reply that they have seen it a second time or more often is discarded from the real test because they are included under the proven name registration (PNR). The information on age, sex, education, occupation, etc., may establish a relationship between these factors and recall. This method measures the recall of. qualified readers to assess the depth of penetration achieved by the advertised message. The respondents may be asked whether they are representative buyers of the product.

Advantages

(a) This test is known as the impact method designed to measure the depth of impression an advertisement has made on the readers.

(b) The impressions may be proven name registration, idea penetration or conviction which determine the extent of brand name recognition as well as various selling points.

(c) Recall tests provide guidance for penetration of copy, indication of the audience's language and frame of reference.

Limitation

(a) The tests suffer from a heavy cost of a good study.

(b) They are limited by usual variation in human memory. Some people have better memories than others. Some people can express what they recall in a very effective manner. The audience may recall because it has seen the previous advertisements of the product.

(c) The inconsistency in the message may cause desertion.

The recall test cannot effectively test the success or failure of symbolic association.

(b) Recognition test: Also known as readership test are designed to find out which advertisements respondents have read. Accordingly, recognition test measures market penetration. The best known and widely used recognition tests are the Starch Advertisement Readership Ratings which have been conducted by Daniel Starch Organisation since 1932. In the Starch Readership test the respondents are shown issues of magazines that they claim to have read. Then the respondent is asked to go through the magazine page by page by the interviewer and to indicate which of the advertisements he has observed or seen and how much of the copy was read. Various influencing conditions such as order of going through the magazine are controlled by the interviewer. This test of the number seeing and reading the advertisement is not so significant from the stand point of the actual score made by the particular advertisement as it is from a comparative stand point—that is, for comparing the figures with those for advertisements run in the magazine over a period of time and with the figures of similar advertisements for the same category of product run in the same issue of the magazine.

While these were developed by Daniel Starch to measure the readership of printed advertisement, George Gallup supported his views. Starch and Gallup pointed out that the mere presence of advertisements in some publication had no meaning unless they were read by some person. Hence, the recognition test is also called the readership test. Researchers organized research activities to find out how many readers went through printed magazine advertisements. A particular advertisement is examined by sending the readers the whole newspaper or magazine where in it is published. After a few days, readers are approached to find out whether they have read the advertisements or not. Those who read the advertisements are counted from among the total number of persons given the advertised publication. The percentage of readership is calculated accordingly. Half-page advertisements are examined by way of illustration. Only one advertisement copy was examined at a time. The readership tests provide information regarding the percentage of readers who have seen the advertisement and remember it, who identifying the product and brand recall seeing or reading any part of it, and who report reading at least one half of the advertisement. Recognition tests have been helpful in determining the actual percentage of persons who "recognized" the advertisement. The number of readers attracted by the advertisement for each rupee of space is also found out by this test. The relationship between readers per rupee and the medium readers per rupee can be established by this test. The validity of readership test has been recognized by many persons; though it also has been criticized by others. In fact, a recognition test is based on the assumption that there is a high correlation between the readings of the advertisement and the purchase of the product. This relationship has been established by researches. Non-readers were not affected, while readers who did not read advertisements did purchase the product.

Advantages

(i) The recognition test measures something, which has been realized under normal conditions. The bringing-out of attention and interest by an advertisement is an important reading behaviour. It is objective and logical.

(iii) The sampling estimate of readership can be used as a final estimate of the recognition of advisements.

(iv) Co-operative achievements can also be estimated with this test.

(v) The recognition tests show the importance of each type of advertisement on the basis of the readership.

(vi) It is a simple test and does no require any specialized knowledge.

Disadvantages

(i) This test is irrelevant to purchasing readership and recognition of the product. Readers do not necessarily purchase a product, nor do non-readers shy away from it. A trick picture can attract a large number of readers without achieving any sale. It does not necessarily follow that the advertisement has a solid motivating force.

(ii) As readers are confused about magazines so by examining readership of one magazine, one may not get an accurate picture of the actual readers.

(iii) Some readers may reply in the affirmative to please the interviewer, although they may not have read the advertisement.

(iv) Bias and recklessness may take place under this test.

(v) Distorted figures about readership may be provided by research.

This is an uncontrolled interview and suffers from the problems of uncontrolled interview and suffers from the problems of uncontrolled techniques of examination.

Results of the test are tabulated for three categories of readership :

1. Noted (N)
2. Seen-Associated (A)
3. Read Most (RM)

Noted means the percentage of readers having seen the advertisement.

Seen Associated means the percentage of readers associating the advertisement with the product or the advertiser.

Read Most means the percentage of readers having read over half the advertisement.

From these data, a calculation of readers per rupee can be determined, using the following formula:

Readers per rupee = Percent noted Magazine's primary readers / Space cost

Readership tests provide information regarding:

1. The percentage of readers who reported reading at least one half of the advertisement.
2. The numerical ordering of readers for all advertisements.
3. The number of readers attracted, by the advertisement for each rupee invested in space.
4. The percentage of readers who remember seeing the advertisement.
5. The relationship between readers per rupee and the medium readers per rupee for all half page or larger advertisements in the issue.
6. The percentage of readers who recall seeing or reading any part of the advertisement identifying the product or brand.

Starch test is helpful to the advertiser in the following manner :

1. The effectiveness of competitor's ads can be compared through the norms provided.
2. Readership scores are a useful indication of consumers involvement in the ad or campaign.
3. The pulling power of various aspects of the ad can be assessed through the control offered, and
4. Alternative ad executions can be tested.

Despite its above stated usefulness, many researchers have criticized the Starch Recognition method on the following grounds:

(i) Interviewer sensitivities: Any time research involves interviewers, there is a potential for bias. Respondents may want to impress the interviewer or fear looking unknowledgeable if they continually claim not to recognise an ad. There may also be variances associated with interviewer instructions, recordings and so on, regardless of the amount of training and sophistication involved.

(ii) Reliability of recognition scores: Starch admitted that the reliability and validity of its readership scores increase with the number of insertions tested, which essentially means that to test just one ad on a single exposure may not produce valid or reliable results.

(iii) False claiming: Research shows that in recognition tests, respondents may claim to have seen an ad when they did not. False claim may be a result of having seen similar ads elsewhere, expecting that such an ad would appear in the medium, or wanting to please the questioner. Interest in the product category also increases reporting of ad readership. Whether this false claiming is deliberate or not, it leads to an over reporting of effectiveness. On the flip side factors such as interview fatique may lead to an under reporting bias— that is respondents not reporting an ad they did see.

(c) Inquiry test: These tests are designed to measure advertising effectiveness on the basis of inquiries generated from advertisements appearing in various print media and is used both consumer and business to business market testing. This inquiry may take the form of the number of coupons returned, the number of phone calls generated, or direct inquiries through reader cards. For example if we called in response to an ad in a local medium recently, perhaps we were asked how we found out about the company or product or where we saw the ad. This is a very simple measure of the ad's or medium's effectiveness.

Most complex methods of measuring effectiveness through inquiries may involve.

1. Running the ad in successive issues of the same medium,
2. Running split run tests, in which variations of the ad appear in alternate copies of the same newspaper or magazine and
3. Running the same ad in different media. Each of these methods will yield information of different aspects of the strategy. The first measures the cumulative effects of the campaign; the second examines specific elements of the ad or variations of it. In the final method, the medium rather than the ad itself, is the focus of the effectiveness measure.

While inquiry tests may yield useful information, weaknesses in this methodology limit its effectiveness. For example, inquiries may not be a true measure of the attention getting or information providing aspects of the ad. The reader may be attracted to an ad, read it, and even store the information but not be motivated to inquire at that particular time. Time constraints, lack of a need for the product or service at that time the ad is run, and other factors may limit the number of inquiries. They may conclude that the ad was not effective may be erroneous. Attention, attitude change, awareness and recall of copy points may all have been achieved without being reflected in inquiries. At the other extreme, a person with a particular need for the product may respond to any ad for it, regardless of specific qualities of the ad.

Major advantages of inquiry test are that they are inexpensive to implement and they provide some feedback with respect to the general effectiveness of the ad or medium used. But they are usually not very effective for comparing alternative versions or specific creative aspects of an ad.

(d) Attitude Change Measurement – These tests measure advertising effectiveness by measuring the extent to which favourable opinions have been created about the product, image and company. Loyalty, acceptance, preference, intent, etc., are measured with this technique. Techniques for the include the semantic differential, the Likert scale, the ranking technique and the projective technique.

(i) Semantic Differential Technique – Used to measure attitude in the field of marketing and advertising research it uses a bi-polar (opposite) adjective statement about the subject of evaluation. The attitude is measured in the light of some objectives but the salient features of an attitude cannot be measured. The two-way is used for the purpose. The neutral is mid-point, while the three points on both the sides of the neutral point, on the same scale provide the degree of favourable and unfavourable characteristics. The semantic differential is illustrated in Fig. 18.7.

Known	....	Unknown
Informative	....	Uninformative
Realistic	....	Unrealistic
Persuasive	....	Not persuasive
Instructive	....	Destructive
Effective	....	Ineffective
Useful	....	Useless

Fig. 18.7. Semantic Differential

This technique may be used to determine how far the advertising of a particular brand has been effective. It can be more than the number of points referred to in Fig. 18.1. depending upon the characteristics and features of an advertisement.

Advantages

(a) The attitude change is closer to the purchaser than a mere recall and recognition.

(b) This tests relatively cheap and easy to administer.

(ii) The Likert Scale – Used to measure audience attitude to advertisements a series of statements are described in the Likert scale to measure the attributes of the advertisement. Only the relevant statements are used for the purpose. Each statement is measured on a five-point scale as given in the following example.

Similar scales may be developed to evaluate the effectiveness of advertisements of products in measuring attitudes to brads.

(iii) Ranking Techniques – In these the preferences to several types of advertisements are ranked to find out the place of particular advertisement among the several advertisements. In the paired comparison approach adopted for this purpose an advertisement of one product can be measured with the advertisements of other products taken together. The measurement with the competitive products is done to find out the effectiveness of the advertisements in competitive atmosphere. The winner may be given rank I while the loser is given rank 5. The other four advertising copies are also included to determine the comparative figure. For example, the advertisements of Lux may be compared with the advertisements of Hamam, Margo, Pears and other soaps. The ranking is based on several grounds, such as awareness, interest, attitude change, attractiveness, usefulness, entertaining respect, effectiveness, action following experiment to advertisements, etc. A sufficient number of consumers are selected for a sample survey. The overall rank is summed up to determine the final rank of the advertisement of the brand. The puzzle games of the advertised copies are used to evaluate the attention-getting attributes of the advertising and get attitude measurements.

(iv) Projective Techniques – Used to measure attitude change the projective techniques include association techniques, completion techniques construction techniques and expressive techniques to measure the change in attitude.

(a) Association Techniques – These require the respondents to a given stimulus to give their first

1. TV advertising has seen been seen by: a majority of the population.

Strongly Agree	Agree	Uncertain	Disagree	Strongly Disagree

2. Lux advertisement has appealed to people who have accepted it.

Strongly Agree	Agree	Uncertain	Disagree	Strongly Disagree

3. Repetition of advertisement has reminded people about the product.

Strongly Agree	Agree	Uncertain	Disagree	Strongly Disagree

Fig. 18.8. The Likert Scale

thought of idea that comes to their minds. The first thought that comes to the mind is recorded. Similarly, for other stimuli the words or ideas are recorded. Finally, their attitude to the brand is noted.

(b) Story-Telling and Sentence-Completion – These give some impression about the brand and attitude.

(c) The Expressive Techniques – These may also be used to find out the attitude to the respondents, though the enquiry is made in the third person's voice. The attitude-measurement with the above techniques requires skill and professional competence. Cartoons, third person's picture-response, etc., may be used in attitude measurements with caution.

4. Sales Tests – Designed to evaluate the effects of advertising on the purchase behaviour of the consumer, these tests produce sales after creating an image of and interest in the product. Although there are a larger number of variable that affect sales, advertising and sales functions are correlated. It is possible to evaluate the effects of advertising on sales with the help of sales audit and audience response. Sales tests have been successfully applied to examine the consumer behaviour to advertisement of consumption goods. Sales techniques are of three types : measure of past sales, field experiments and matched samples.

(i) Measure of Past Sales – Advertising and sales are correlated by using the past sales data. Brand wise data are collected and tabulated. The product, brand and company sales in the past ten years as well as the advertising expenses establish the correlation between the sales volume and advertising expenses establish the correlation between the sales volume and advertising expenses. All other factors influencing sales are also correlated with the sales. Multi-correlation shows the degree of correlation between advertisements and sales. The past data on sales are diversified. Their advertising expenses are correlated to establish their relationship. The differences between their correlation show the importance of each individual factor influencing sales.

(ii) Field Experiments – Done by advertisers, producers, wholesalers, retailers and researchers field experiments may show the extent to which a particular advertising campaign has affected sales. After the whole market may be divided into test and control areas one treatment may be randomly administered to each area. Showing how a particular factor has influenced the sales in that area, the different treatments with the same experimental subjects may eliminate irrelevant variables. The results of each variable are recorded for different periods. The early figures give the total impact of advertising on sales.

(iii) Matched Samples – In this technique, the respondents selected for comparison of advertising effectiveness are of the same age, educational status, occupation, sex, etc., matched in every respect but not for the test treatments. One group has seen the advertisements while the other group has not seen them. The sales of the treated group compared with those of the not-treated group would show the difference between the sale of the advertised and of the non-advertised products.

5. Inquiry Tests – In these, the effectiveness of

advertisement is measured through inquiries. Respondents are offered certain inducements, a booklet, a sample of the product, a diary, a calendar to reply to questions. This method is employed to check the effects of media as well as individual advertising. The effectiveness of different media is tested by asking people about their effectiveness. Only one factor of advertisement is examined at a time through several media.

SPLIT RUN TEST

The split-run test is used to assess effectiveness. Two or more versions of an advertisement are published in the same issue, with some differences between the two copies. The audience is asked to mention the difference between the two copies. Their impact on interest, attitude and sales are examined by the same groups of respondents. The effectiveness of media is examined by administering the same copy to them to determine effectiveness.

AN IDEAL COPY TESTING PROCEDURE : PACT

The reliability and validity of any copy testing procedure need to be demonstrated. Reliability means that the procedure is free of random error. That is, the measure is consistent and accurate. Validity refers to the procedure being free of both random and systematic error. Validity addresses the question of bias, and deals with the question; are we measuring what we think we are measuring? Thus, a reliable test would provide consistent results every time an ad is tested? A valid test would provide predictive power to the performance of the ad in the market.

Unfortunately, all too many suppliers of copy testing services do not provide measures concerning these issues. Twenty one of the united states largest advertising agencies endorsed a set of principles aimed at improving copy testing. These principles are called PACT (Positioning Advertising Copy Testing).

These nine principles state a "good" copy testing system.

1. Provides measurements which are relevant to the objectives of the advertising.
2. Requires agreement about how the results will be used in advance of each specific test.
3. Provides multiple measurements, because single measurements are generally inadequate to assess the performance of an ad.
4. Is based on a model of human response to communication, the reception of stimulus, the comprehension of the stimulus, and the response to the stimulus.
5. Allows for consideration of whether the advertising stimulus should be exposed more than once.
6. Recognizes that the more finished a piece of copy is, the more soundly it can be evaluated and requires, as a minimum, that alternative executions be tested in the same degree of finish.
7. Provides controls to avoid the biasing effects of the exposure context.
8. Takes into account basic considerations of sample definition.
9. Demonstrates reliability and validity empirically.

These are important recommendations that should be followed. In doing so, the reliability and validity of copy testing would improve greatly.

GUIDELINES FOR FACILITATING RETENTION

1. Message learning is fast if it is not lost within the previous and the following messages.
2. If the message is pleasant and the content and presentation appealing, then it is likely that the message will be retained by the consumer in positive terms. Research has however shown that unpleasant messages are equally likely to be remembered, although perhaps, in a negative way.
3. If products that require mechanical skills are advertised, then they are most effective if the machines are demonstrated and the ease of operations emphasized.
4. If messages are unique or unusual then they are better remembered than common place ones.
5. The simpler the message, the easier it would be to retain.
6. Repetitive messages enhance the learning

process to some degree. Repetition should not be monotonous.

7. If the benefits of the product are demonstrated and the consumer perceives them as great or even adequate then the message will be learned faster.
8. Messages presented at a time when the need of the consumer is intense, are learned faster than those which are presented at a time when the needs are weaker.

TIME OF MEASUREMENT

The measurement of advertising effectiveness can be done at any time for planning to final action. The planning process is also examined to find out the feasible and most effective plans. If an advertising campaign is tested before it is run, it is known as pre-testing. It assists in the development of more effective communication and exercises control over costs. Exhaustive tests are used to pre-test advertising effectiveness and other components of the marketing mix pre-testing involves simulated and laboratory experiments. The effectiveness of advertising activities is generally examined when the campaign has been run and advertising functions have been performed. This is known as posttesting because the effectiveness is measured after the final stage of the campaign has been reached. The advertising effectiveness can also be tested when the campaign is under way with a view to modifying it, if necessary. The testing involves costs. So while adopting a particular test, the cost of testing should be borne in mind. Specially, there are three occasions when testing can be done, *viz.*, pre-testing, post-testing, and mis-testing. Pre-testing is adopted to measure the effectiveness and accuracy of an advertising plan before its implementation. Posttesting is done after the advertising activities have been completed to examine the effectiveness of these advertising activities. A mid-test involves a test before the completion of advertising functions and after the implementation of the advertising plan. This is also known as intermediary testing, for it takes place after the date of the first function of advertising but before its final action is performed. It may be adopted at any time during this time.

Communication Effects of an Advertisement

The management should attempt to evaluate the effectiveness of the advertising campaign if the firm's advertising goals are to be achieved and the ad effectiveness is to be increased. By regular evaluation of the effectiveness, the short comings and the plus points should be revealed and the management would be able to improve the campaign by negating the shortcomings and retaining the favourable point. For this purpose, it is very necessary to know how advertising affects the buyer's behaviours. But this is very difficult because measurements are imperfect and imprecise.

The effectiveness of advertising can be measured by the extent, to which it achieves the objectives set for it. If it succeeds in maintaining the objectives, advertising can be said to be effective otherwise it will be a waste of money and time. In this sense, advertising can be recognised as a business activity like other activities.

In a very real sense, the integrity of promotional activities rests on how well those activities work. An advertising budget that is spent on some poorly defined task or on undefined tasks, may be in regarded as an economic waste as compared to that spent to achieve the well defined objectives for which the results can be measure Any social institution upon which a significant portion of our to the productive efforts is expanded should be able to point to its special accomplishments. Indeed, it is a source of discomfort that special results of advertising activities have not always been subject to precise measurement. Both practitioners and critics feel that promotional activities should only be accepted as socio-economic-institution' with fall rights and privileges "when the means exist to prove that advertising super are productive rupees". It is undoubtedly source of embarrassment that we cannot exactly measure the effectiveness of advertising in definitive terms.

The exact result of advertising expenditure is very difficult to predict because:—

a. The reactions of consumer-buyers to the advertising effort cannot be known in advance :
b. The reaction of competitors in the field cannot be guess in anticipation ; and

c. The unexpected events (such as change in social and economic environment and the government policies etc.) cannot be accurately anticipated. Such events may influenced the results of the advertising efforts.

If we take a hypothetical case of a retailer who contract to spent Rs. 5,000 on advertisement with a local newspaper for a special sales event. The advertisement is seen and the response is much greater than it is anticipated. What caused the success of sale? There may be a number of reasons to be attributed to the success. The message, theme, colour etc., of the advertisement or the low prices quoted during the sale of the superior quality of the product or absence of competition in the market on the day or the favourable weather conditions or the goodwill of the firm etc. The overwhelming success of the sale is the joint result of all the above variable and it is quite impossible to isolate the role of any one variable. It is so because the cause and effect-relationship cannot be established in advance when a multitude of variable impinge upon a particular event. It is entirely possible that a poor advertising support may push up the sale because everything else falls into its proper place of the reverse may be possible. But it does not mean that we cannot measure the effects of particular advertising effort.

The advertising executives are much concerned about the assessment of the effectiveness of the advertising efforts. For this purpose, the management needs answers to such questions as : Was the advertising campaign really successful in attaining the advertising goals? 'Were our T.V. commercials as good as those of our competitors? 'Will the print advertisement, which we have designed, make consumers aware of our new product? To get the answers of these questions, various tests of effectiveness (Pre-tests and Post-tests) are needed to determine whether proposed advertisements should be used, and if they are not satisfactory, how they might be improved and whether on going campaign should be stopped, continued or changed. Pre-tests are conducted before exposing target consumers to the advertisements and post tests after consumers have been exposed to them.

As indicated earlier, the advertisers are interested in knowing what they are getting for their advertising rupees. So they test the Proposed advertisement with pretest, and measure the actual results with a post test. In the past, pretesting was done by the advertising agencies but now the advertisers have been taking an increasingly active role in pretesting process. Pretest may be done either before an advertisement has been designed and executed, after it is ready for public distribution or at both points.

During pre-testing, there is often research on three vital questions :

1. Do consumers feel that the advertisement communicate something desirable about the product ?
2. Does the message have an exclusive appeal that differentiate the product from that of the competitors?
3. Is the advertisement believable?

Although a lot of money is spent on pretesting yet the adver-tisers like to confirm the results by post-testing of their promotional campaigns due to the following reasons:

1. There is a need to produce more effective advertising by retaining the good and removing the bad;
2. The advertising executives can prove to the satisfaction of the management that a higher advertising budget will benefit the firm ;
3. There is a need for measuring the results to determine the level of expenditure that is most promising.

Most research focusses on the communication effect rather than sales effect because it is a long run process. In the short run, however, sales may be slight and important but in the long run, its effects on brands and companies may be of great importance. Indirectly, it will affect the sales in the long run, by changing the consumer awareness and attitude. The advertisers are, therefore, concerned with their impact on consumer awareness and attitude. The communication effect on sales may be presented in the following figure 18.9.

Awarenes builds a favourable or at least a curious attitude towards the product which leads to experimentation. If consumer is satisfied with the trial, he may decide to purchase the product.

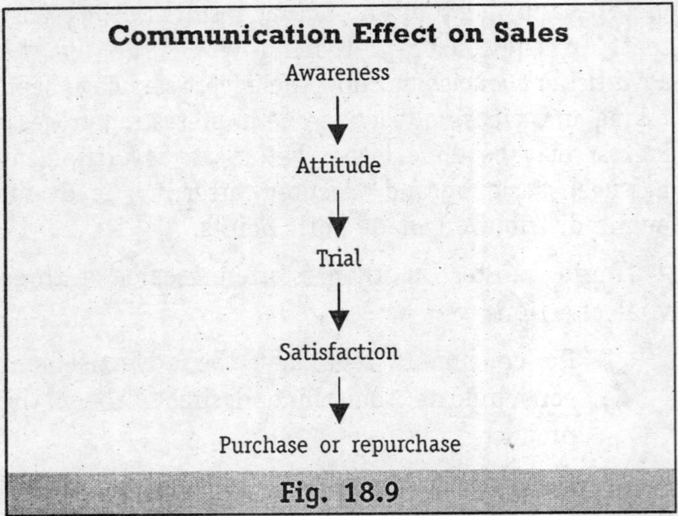

Fig. 18.9

There are many critical and unresolved issues in determining hew to test the communication effects of advertising. Among these are :—

(1) Exposure Conditions. Should advertising be tested under realistic conditions or under more controlled laboratory conditions?

(2) Execution. Pretesting a finished advertisement as an expensive and time consuming. Does pretesting a preliminary execution produce accurate and useful data ?

(3) Quality Vs. Quantity Data. Quantitative data are the easiest and the most precise measurement. But qualitative data collected through interviews may provide information that short answer questions never can.

It is easier to assess the communication effect than the sales effect of advertising :

It is easier to assess the communication effect of advertising than the sales effect. Many firms try to measure the effectiveness of advertising in terms of sales results but this practice is always mis-leading. Since, the sales effect is the result of so many variables, a distinct effect of advertising on sales cannot be correctly measured, although there may be some exceptions. For example, direct mail advertising can effectively be measured by the inquiries received. But in many situations, the relationship between advertising activity and sales cannot be established satisfactorily.

We can correctly assume that some sales will occur even though there is no advertising or little advertising or conversely, there will be no increase in sales after the point of saturation is reached or it may be that sales will show a decreasing trend at this point inspite of a large amount of expenditure on advertising is done. It is so because advertising is not the only variable that, effect the sales.

Thus, we may conclude that sales-effect of advertising is difficult to measure because a number of variables affect the quantum of sales and the contribution of advertisement cannot be measured parately unless all other variables are presumed to be constant, his situation is quite hypothetical and almost non-existent. Added to this is the fact that advertisement itself is made of a variety of gables such as media, messages, colours, page or time of the day, locations, the size of the headline and the appeals used. Thus, even if the advertising variable is separated this would still not answer the question about the effectiveness of the individual components of the advertising campaign. So, advertisers try to measure the communication effect of the advertising.

ADVERTISING AUDIT

Advertising audit is a management tool assisting the advertising manager to arrive at interrelated decisions. Like the accounting audit it is a control procedure enabling the advertising manager to assess the success of various advertising campaigns and how functions have been performed to avoid failure and promote success in implementing advertising strategies and programmes. It is a sequence of decision-steps for an analysis of resources, opportunities, objectives and strategies. The product, market, consumers, etc., offer opportunities to be exploited by formulation suitable advertising strategies and programming. Advertising audit may be carried on into three parts internal resource audit, advertising agency audit and decision process audit.

(i) Internal Resource Audit (IRA) – Its objectives are to determine the capability of the advertising manager to develop an advertising programming without the help of any advertising. It considers three dimensions of the advertiser's organization—people, money and time. It uses the expertise and objectivity of the internal people, money and time. Product marketing and consumer factors are used to attain the objectives with the resources available with the company. It explores the research and creative capability of the company, analyses the media and message capability of the firm and evaluates with a view to determining objectives and efficiently utilizing resources. The advertising people enlist the assistance of marketing managers and executives.

(ii) Advertising Agency Audit (AAA) – Marketing managers need the assistance of an outside advertising agency that can assist them in accomplishing the marketing and advertising objectives of the company. The advertising agency audit has been devised to evaluate the capability of an advertising agency, its size and the number of employees the agency would employ for the job. Advertising audit revalues compensation plans, the attitude of the advertising agency toward the management, the services to be offered by agency and its basic creative approach. The management also evaluates to the media capability of the agency and its approaches to the problem-solving decisions and its capability to take up advertising takes.

(iii) Decision Process Audit (DPA) – An audit of all the management decisions is necessary for the analysis, implementation and measurement of an advertising programme, DPA may include communication audit, marketing analysis audit, advertising objectives audit, advertising expenditure audit, marketing strategy audit, media strategy audit, and message audit separately performed to develop an effective decision process for the attainment of the objectives of advertising.

While the marketing analysis audit analyses markets, customers, product, competition, etc., the advertising objectives audit includes an analysis of planning hierarchy, corporate objectives, production audit and measurement audit. Under the integration audit are analysed the congruence with responsibilities, sales, production, etc.

Most measures of advertising effectiveness are superficial such as the size of the audience, programme rating, advertisements noted and remembered by the reader or audience, and the number of orders received. Although such causes are useful in determining the extent to which the advertiser's message in reaching the market, they do not serve as "real" measures of advertising success, which can only be measured in terms of added sales and profits. No superficial measure of advertising effectiveness can substitute the real measures – sales and net profits.

LIMITS OF MEASUREMENT

The range of measurements or types of evaluation are not unlimited. It is not possible to measure the precise co-relation between advertising and sales, for advertising rarely contributes to sales in a direct way or in a way that can be assessed in quantitative terms.

1. Role of Other Factors – Advertising rarely works in isolation. Distribution, price, packing, promotion and many other factors are instrumental in producing sales. To predict the sales effectiveness of advertising alone would mean isolating the partial effect that advertising has on sales from the multiple and interrelated effects of all the other elements in the marketing mix. Such an attempt would require a great deal of time and money. It is also doubtful whether a reasonably precise prediction can ever be achieved: the mathematical models that have been used to assess profit are purely of academic significance. They have not yet been tested empirically or put into practice. At the moment, there is no entirely acceptable method of measuring advertising effectiveness precisely or directly in terms of sales.

2. No Relation with Sales – It is not possible to predict reliably the marginal impact of advertising on sales. The effect of advertising is rarely so clear cut that a non-purchaser immediately becomes a purchase of the brand as a result of advertising exposure alone, except in the case of a new or improved product, or when a promotional offer is made.

3. Effect of Personal Experience – It is difficult to divorce the advertising effect from the effect of product usage or the consumer's attitude to the product, formed either by physical performance or the emotional satisfaction derived from it. In other words, the effect of advertising on the decision/to re-purchase a brand cannot be separated by research from the effect of previous experience of the brand on the purchase decision; nor can it be accurately predicted.

4. Low Consumer Involvement – The consumer's involvement with advertising communication is relatively low in most cases. He generally has stable attitudes, which are amenable to change over time, but not generally to over night change. This poses obvious problems for meaningful quantification, for one study may show little result, and many studies may be too expensive.

5. Competitive Factors – These are the unpredictable competitive factors that change the market environment in which the ad has to work, and thus make it impossible for one to predict the specific effect of the advertising.

6. Complex Blend – Advertising is a complex blend of sensuous, rational and emotional elements. With the relationship between them as important as the elements themselves, testing the elements in isolation cannot give a true picture of the totality of advertising. The quantitative factors are likely to elude mathematical precision.

GUIDELINES

The realties of advertising measurement have to be recognized and accepted before any plans for evaluation can be formulated. Measurement and evaluation are certainly possible within limits. The following guidelines are essential to do so:

1. The definition of advertising as "mass, paid communication, the ultimate purpose of which is to impart information, develop attitude and induce action." has to be accepted. It must be recognized that advertising performs a communication task, not a direct sales role.
2. It is necessary to separate an advertising objective from the total marketing objectives.
3. A clear-cut distinction should be made between advertising objectives and advertising goals. An objective is a broad general aim, while a goal is a specific pinpointed task. It is necessary to accept the following definition of an advertising goal: "a specific goal to a give degree in a given period of time."
4. The basis of setting a goal should be a close and correct knowledge of the market and the potential of the brand/product, not unrealistic expectation.
5. Advertising goals and task should be agreed upon by everyone, directly concerned with the advertiser and the advertising agency, and put down in writing.
6. Benchmarks and methods of measurement should be a part of the plan and not left for a later date.
7. Experience and common sense should never be sacrificed at the alter of techniques and jargon. One should never be "blinded by science" nor "killed by techniques" while dealing with advertising research. Skills and techniques should be harnessed to serve the needs of advertising men, and not the other way around.
8. The basic goal of advertising is to do something— to modify consumer attitudes or behaviour. Therefore, when we deal with the evaluation of advertising effectiveness, we should be more concerned with measuring its ability to influence these attitudes and behaviour rather than with measuring the extent to which consumers recall a given advertisement.

Though many of these measurement devices have enjoyed some degree of success, however, there is still a long way to go before really effective evaluation tools and techniques are developed for adverting. The hope of the future lies in the more effective use of psychological and sociological testing methods and in the use of mathematical models and operations research.

LEGAL FRAME WORK OF ADVERTISING

There are there institutions to protect consumers from frauds in advertising.

1. Government agencies acting to enforce laws, against offenders.
2. Industry associations imposing self regulation upon their members.
3. Advertisers working through enlightened self-interest and a sense of social responsibility.

SELF REGULATION

Advertising has an organisation to promote self regulation and to establish professional standards for industry. As advertising is not used for marketing but as a communication process, the third form is useful as a supreme protection. Most advertisers prosper on repeated business for their survival. Truthful advertising has a good place in strategies. Robert J.

Keith made five recommendations to chief executives to ensure that advertising and promotion practices of their corporation show the belief and principle of the corporation as given below:

(i) The chief executive of the corporation should be involved in the development of statements of advertising policy and procedure.

(ii) The statements should be reduced to writing.

(iii) The statements should be disseminated to all individuals involved in the organisation's advertising and promotion functions.

(iv) The statements should be made available to interested individual outside the organisation.

(v) The statements should be subject to counting review and revision.

LEGAL RESTRICTIONS ON ADVERTISING

By the end of nineteenth century public attitude was different towards business. Several business activities had come under the governmental regulations. More laws were enacted and judicial interpretations extended the areas of control. Every fact of business operation were under contract of the regulations. This included laws and judicial rulings which control the buying and selling processes, pricing, selling below cost, quantity discounting, terms of sale, trade marking, labelling and advertising.

Advertising, a well established mode of modern business technique, is often used to deceive the customers.

Advertisers and business face several legal restrictions. Consumers movement leads to passages of such laws. The central government passes laws uniform throughout the country.

REGULATION OF FALSE AND DECEPTIVE ADVERTISING

Regulations under advertising false and misleading facts are controlled by union governments.

Union Act says:

"Be it enacted.........that unfair methods of competition in commerce are hereby declared unlawful." The commission is hereby empowered and directed to present persons partnerships or corporation to regulate commerce from using unfair methods of competition in commerce and unfair or deceptive acts or practices in commerce were declared to be unlawful."

The Act further added:

(a) It shall be unlawful for any person, partnership or corporation to disseminate or cause to be disseminated any false advertisement—

(i) by mails or in commerce by any means for the purpose of inducing or which is likely to induce directly or indirectly the purchase of food, drugs, devices or cosmetics or

(ii) By any means from the purpose of inducing or which is likely to induce directly or indirectly the purchase of food, drugs devices or cosmetics.

(b) The dissemination or the causing to be disseminated of any false advertisement with in the provisions of sub-section (a) of this action shall be an unfair or deceptive act or practice in commerce.

DEFINITION OF FALSE ADVERTISEMENT

The term false advertisements means an advertisement other than labelling which is misleading in a material respect and in determining whether any advertisement is misleading. There shall be taken into account (among other things) not only representations made or suggested by statement, word, design, device, sound or any combination there of but also the extent to which the advertisement fails to reveal facts material in the light of such representations or material with respect to consequences which may result from the use of the commodity to which the advertisement relates under the conditions prescribed in the said advertisement or under such condition as are customary or usual.

The Commission Act may prescribe—(A) interpretative rules and general statements of policy with respect to unfair or deceptive acts or practices in or affecting commerce and (B) rules which define with specificity acts or practices which are unfair or deceptive acts or practices or affecting commerce...........Rules under this sub-paragraph may include requirements prescribed for the purpose of presenting such acts or practices.

The Acts continue with detailed provisions dealing with having procedures rules of evidence, judicial review and so forth.

These Acts left a great deal of advertising irregulated, hence revisions were made.

"Any person, firm, corporation or association or agent or employee there of, who with intent to sell, service, employment or anything offered by such person, firm, corporation or association or agent or employee there of directly or indirectly, to the public for sale, purchase, distribution or the hire of personal services, or with intent to increase the competition of or to contract with reference to induce the public in any manner to enter in to any obligation relating there to or to acquire title thereto, or an interest therein, or to make any loan makes, publishes, disseminates, circulates or places before public or causes directly or indirectly, to be made published, disseminated, circulated or placed before the public, in this state in a book, notice, circulated or other publication or in the form of a book, notice, circular, pamphlet, letter, hand hill, poster, bill, sign, placard, card label or over any radio or television station or other medium of wireless communication or in any other way similar of dissimilar to the foregoing an advertisement, announcement or statement of any sort regarding merchandise, securities, service, employment or anything so offered for use purchase or sale or the indirect terms or conditions upon which such loan will be made to the public, which advertisement contains any assertion, representation or statement of fact which is untrue, deceptive or misleading, shall be guilty of misdemeanor".

Laws patterned after these specifications provide the basic mechanism for the control of misleading advertising at state municipal levels.

Advertisements become misleading when things are intentionally omitted or false claims are made. For example, it is untrue to claim that "Our T.V. sets would provide life long trouble free service" or "Our washing soap or powder washes 50 or 60 per cent more clothes whitest, brightest and safest". If a consumer is thus falsely induced to buy goods that do not possess the quality advertised, it can only be treated as a false representation. Therefore, efforts should be made to eradicate this kind of frauds against the consumers. The Federal Trade Commission Act, 1914 (USA) bans this kind of selling methods "to prevent the public from being made victims of falce class of products blatantly advertised even though it may not have an adverse effect on the competition."

In India, a growing concern is being felt against this kind of deceptive advertisements. Appointed to revise The Companies Act and MRTP Act Sachar Committee opined, "The objection taken is not to the advertisement of the product which it may be necessary to do in order to acquaint the public with the articles. What is however insisted on is that, there is an objection on the seller, namely, that if he advertises, he must speak the truth."

In its report, the Commission treated the various devices used for sales promotion methods also as deceptive. For example price may be advertised as greatly reduced and cut when in reality the goods are being sold at seller's regular prices.

Recommendations of the Sachar Committee- Following acts of the sellers should be declared as Unfair Trade Practices:

1. Misleading advertisement and false representation. A seller should not falsely represent;

   (a) That the goods are of a particular standard, quality, grade, composition , style or model;

   (b) That the rebuilt, second hand goods are new goods.

2. Offering of gifts or prizes with the intention of not providing them and conducting productional contests.

The Committee is of opinion that all the aforesaid unfair trade practices should be punishable as an offence and any person or under-taking indulging in any of them should be liable to be prosecuted before the Commission.

LEGAL PROTECTION TO TRADE MARKS

Trade marks are closely connected with advertising. Advertisement reproduces the trade mark for the featured product they want and they are stimulated in desire. Hence, legislation is designed to protect trade marks.

REGISTRABLE ON PRINCIPAL REGISTER

Two registers are kept for trade marks. Trade marks referable on the Principal Register are listed here under:

"No trade mark by which the goods of the applicant may be distinguished from the goods of other, shall be refused registration on the principal register on account of its nature unless it-

(a) Consists or comprises immoral, deceptive or scandalous matter, or matter which may disparage or falsely suggest a connection with persons, living or dead, institutions, beliefs or national symbols or bring them into contempt or disrepute.

(b) Consists of or comprises the flag or coat of arms or other insignia of the nation or of any state or municipality or of any foreign nation.

(c) Consists or comprises a name, portrait or signature identifying a particular living person except by his written consent or the name, signature or portrait of a deceased person during the life of his widow, if any, except by the written consent of the widow.

(d) Consists or comprises a mark which so resembles a mark registered in the patent office or a mark, a trade name previously used by another and not abandoned as to be likely when applied to the goods of the applicant, to cause confusion or mistake or to deceive purchasers.

TRADE MARKS REGISTRABLE ON THE SUPPLEMENTAL REGISTER

There, include "All marks capable of distinguishing applicant's goods or services and not negotiable on the principle register provided in this chapter, except those declared to be unregistrable. Under sub-sections (a), (b), (c) and which have been in lawful use in commerce by the proprietor thereof, upon or in connection with any goods or services for the year proceeding the filling of the application, may be registered on the supplemental register upon the payment of the prescribed fee and compliance with the provisions of the title, so far as they are applicable.

CONNECTED CONCEPTS

1. Trade Mark – It includes any word, name, symbol or device or any combination there of adopted and used by a manufacturer or merchant to identify his goods and distinguish them from those manufactured or sold by others.

2. Service Mark – It means a mark used in the sales or advertising of services to identify the services of one person and distinguish them from the services of others and includes without limitation of marks, names, symbols, tittles, designations, slogans, character names and distinctive features of radio or other advertising used in commerce.

3. Certification Mark – It means a mark used or incantation with the products or services of one or more persons other than the owner of the mark to certify regional or other origin material, mode of manufacture, quality, accuracy or other characteristics of such goods or services or that the work or labour on the goods or services was performed by members of a union or other organization.

4. Collective Mark – It signifies a trademark or service mark used by the members of a cooperative, an association or other collective group or organization and includes marks used to indicate membership in a union, an association or other origination.

REGULATION OF ADVERTISING ALLOWNACES

It was to control the practice of price discrimination among buyers. The manufacturer should treat all intermediaries equally while giving advertising allowances. Suppliers would make available on proportionally equal terms, promotional allowances to retailers who buy from wholesalers and who compete with a favoured direct buying retailer. Hence, some of the buying advantage of large buyers has been taken away by the Act. There is a possibility that some sellers avoided the use of advertising allowances due to legal uncertainties involved in their use.

"It shall be unlawful........to discriminate in price between different purchasers..........where the effect of such discrimination may be to substantially lesson competition or to tend to create a monopoly. There were provisions for price variation when the sale involved products of different quantity and a differential in price was permitted when the costs of selling or transportation varied among competing buyers.

Some intermediaries were given an allowance for promotion of the manufacturer's products while many buyers may have actually expended these funds for this purpose; some took the allowance as a form of price discrimination. People thought of chain stores, which were driving small independent merchants out of business. Hence Act added:

"It shall be unlawful for any person engaged in commerce to pay or contract for payment of any thing of value to or for the benefit of customer or such person in the course of such comers as compensation or inconsideration for any services or facilities furnished by or through such customer in connection with the processing, handling, sale or offering for sale of any products or commodities manufactured, sold or offered for sale by such person, unless such payment or consideration is available on proportionally equal terms to all other customers competing in the distribution of such products or commodities."

"It shall be unlawful for any person to discriminate in favour of one purchaser against another purchaser or purchasers of a commodity brought for resale with or without reprocessing by contracting to the furnishings of any services of facilities connected with the processing, handling, sale, or offering for sale of such commodity so purchased upon terms not accorded to all purchasers on proportionally equal terms".

ADVANTAGES OF REGISTRATION ON PRINCIPAL REGISTER

1. Ownership – The registrant can claim ownership. After registration date, no other party can use the mark even if done in good faith or without knowledge.

2. Exclusive Use – A mark may become incontestable after five years and give exclusive right to its use even though another party may have used the mark prior to its registration by the registrant.

LEGISLATION ABOUT THE CONTENT OF ADVERTISING MESSAGE

The law of defamation governs the advertising copy. No untrue statements may be made about other persons nor, may they be held up to contempt. The use of an individuals name, picture or statement without his or her consent is an invasion of the right of privacy and grounds for action for damages. Hence, one must get legal releases from persons pictured or mentioned in an advertisement. But if the advertisement exposes the person to ridicule or contempt or is otherwise defamatory the publisher, the advertiser and the agency are all liable even though standard releases have been obtained.

Fraudulent advertisement and absence materials are denied the use of mails. They have also controlled the lotteries. A lottery is present if a prize, some form of consideration and chance are present. Advertisement promoting lotteries may be ruled illegal. At present, lotteries have been taken under the state governments. They have controlled misrepresentation in the offering of securities to the public. It has also control over the false or misleading advertising, which reaches the public through radio or television. The law also restricts the advertising of cigarettes without quoting the statutory warning and hence we find every packet has the words: "Cigarette smoking is injurious to health." These are health warnings which are exhibited on package also.

SELF REGULATION OF ADVERTISING

Laws are not to solve problems unless they are enforced through the channels of courts and by rulings of administrative authorities. Court decisions have helped in the development of advertising. People used advertising agencies for publicizing their products. Hence, the rule was made that the advertising agency should make certain, that claims in the advertising created for client should be true.

Sometimes, actors performed the functions as doctors to show the use of the medicine, which inspired people to use the product. Hence, such cases were scrutinized. A case of milk powder had come to the legal proceedings wherein it was found as has been depicted by Marries L. Mayer Joseph B. Mason and Einar A. Or beck: "The case is in the nature of a land mark decision as it recognizes the fact that value has been created for a product by promotion. Though there is no change in the grade or quality, there may be an economic value attached to a brand name product over its private brand counterpart" In another case, the following factors were deemed to be present in advertising: "Those persons affected do not constitute a particularly vulnerable group. There are no health and or safety considerations that might legitimately demand further expenditure of public funds; there was no significant economic pattern to a consumer who purchased and found it 'less dry' than anticipated: the advertising in question was terminated over four years earlier; there was no indication on the record that competition was adversely affected by whatever deception might be proved; here was the case dealing with intentional wrong doer."

ADVERTISING SUBSTANTIATION

Advertiser must supply the documents is support of claims made in its advertising about product safety performance, efficacy, quality or comparative price. They must also show that. They relied on the documentation while preparing the advertising in question. Substantiation is determined on such issues as the potential effect of the advertising and the product on consumer health, safety or economic well-being, the state of the art regarding test of the particular product and the extent to which consumers will rely on the advertising claim.

Uniqueness of product can not be implied unless it can be supported. According to Robber E. Wilkies and James B. Wilcox uniqueness "...........differs, sharply from the unique selling point approach to developing advertising copy first advocated. This concept challenges an advertiser to make a proposition to consumers that competition cannot or does not make; one that is unique to the brand or is not already being made. Under the substantiation programme, however, non-supported claims as well as preemptive claims that imply uniqueness when none exist are likely to be challenged by the Commission."

AFFIRMATIVE AND FULL DISCLOSURE OF INFORMATION

Consumers should have sufficient, information to make valid comparison between purchasing alternatives. Laws have been passed and regulatory body rulings promulgated to require that specific kind of informations be provided to them. The label on packages of processed food should first list the nutritional value of the contents. Nutritional information should appear in all food advertising.

Affirmative disclosure will lead advertisers to tell not only the positive story about their products but salient negative side also. This will lead to full disclosure of their weaknesses.

FRAUDULANT ADS

1. Bait and Switch Advertising – The retailer advertises an object at low price for a consumer item but when the consumer goes to the store he learns that:

(i) The item is not in stock.

(ii) It is inferior in quality.

The salesman then proceeds and makes an attempt to switch over the prospect's interest to another model of high price. This gives high rates of compensation to salesmen.

2. Comparison Advertising – It is defined by William L. Wilkie and Parl W. Farris as it:

(i) Compares two or more specifically named or recognizably presented brands of the same generic product or service class, and

(ii) Make such a comparison in terms of one or more specific product or service attributes.

The competitive product was just as effective, yet was being sold at much lower prices. This practice was encouraged by consumers under the theory that such messages give consumers additional information upon which to make purchasing decisions. But Thomas E. Barry and Roger L. Tremblay, remark, "What the comparative spot does tell the user of the compared to brand that he or she is in fact using the product that a wrong brand being advertised, the comparison spot focusing on cognitive dissonance might be alienating the consumer."

COUNTER MEASURES

1. Corrective Advertising – The rationale of corrective advertisements is given by Stanley E. Cohen as follows:

(i) Dispel the 'residual effects of such deceptive advertising.

(ii) Restore competition to the stage that prevailed before the unfair practice.

(iii) Deprive firms from falsely attained gains to which advertising may have contributed.

2. Better Business Bureaus – These are concerned to fight illegal advertising and to raise the standards of advertising practice at local and national levels. The effectiveness varies from city to city. Each bureau depends only on the voluntary contributions of advertisers, media and agencies. The focus of interest is upon people operating with in the local are, retailers and service establishments. National Advertising Boards influence the national advertising, while local bureaus deal with local and retail advertising.

3. Self-regulation by Advertising Media – All advertising media reserve the right to reject any advertising submitted if it is considered objectionable. The advertising agencies owe great responsibility to the people in general that the message they seek to convey is not misleading and false. It is in their own interest that they should reject advertisements, the authenticity of which is doubtful. Advertising media adopt the following self-regulation, code:

(i) Trust

(ii) Responsibility

(iii) Taste, decency

(iv) Disparagement

(v) Bait advertising

(vi) Guarantees and Warranties

(vii) Price claims

(viii) Unprovable claims

(ix) Testimonials under self-regulation.

CHAPTER

19 PERSUASIVE COMMUNICATIONS

I explain quietly,
You hear me shouting
You try a new track,
I feel new wounds reopen.
You see both sides,
I see your blinkers.
I am placatory,
You sense a new selfishness.
I am a dove,
You recognise a hawk.
You offer an olive branch,
I feel the thorns.
You bleed,
I see crocodile tears.
I withdraw,
You feel from the impact.

— **Roger McGough**

Energy Drinks: The Real Thing or Just Bull?

Forget about the cola wars between Pepsi and Coke. The new threat to the stagnant cola market is an international cult drink—and that's no bull—it's Red Bull, actually. And the large soft-drink manufacturers have taken notice.

Red Bull is just one of the many "energy" drinks now on the market. Others include Extreme Energy Shot, Venom, Dark Dog, Energy, AMP, and KMX, just to mention a few. In fact, it seems that every company wants to introduce its own energy drink in an attempt to take advantage of a new market that is growing at an amazing rate. Consider that when Red Bull first introduced its product in 1997, there was no such thing as an energy-drink category. By 2001, estimates are that the market was somewhere between $140 million to $200 million, with forecasts that it will be $500 million in just a few years. Also consider that Red Bull has about 70 percent of the market share. While these figures may pale in comparison to the overall carbonated-beverage market (approximately $45 billion), there is enough concern for competitors to take notice.

Red Bull has been variously described as "an international cult drink," "a kinky concoction," and "the new sex drink," all of which suit the company just fine. It is exactly the mystique attributed to the drink that helps create the "buzz" that makes it sell. Many marketers feel that it is Red Bull's alternative image that accounts for much of its success. Even the company's marketing department likes to maintain the illusions while claiming the product is a "non-marketed brand."

But while the mystique part of Red Bull may be true, the "non-marketed" claims may not necessarily be so. As noted by the Economist, it takes a lot of marketing money to sustain this image. The magazine notes that Red Bull's founder, Dietrich Mateschitz (an Austrian) "spent three years developing the drink's image, its packaging and its low-key, grassroots marketing strategy." Further, Red Bull puts about 35 percent of its revenues back into advertising—about $19 million according to Advertising Age. And advertising is not the only IMC component the company successfully employs. At launch in Europe, students were persuaded to drive around in Volkswagen, Beetles or Minis with a Red Bull can strapped on the top and to conduct Red Bull parties using wild and unusual themes. A marketing director from Procter & Gamble was hired to oversee strategic planning for the brand in North America (he later was named one of Brandweek's Marketers of the Year).

At present, Red Bull's marketing efforts still employ grassroots efforts but have expanded to include more traditional media as well. What seems to make Red Bull successful, however, is that the efforts assume a very non-traditional approach to its messages—essentially attempting to do the opposite of what everyone else does. The first order of business in any market is to determine four or five accounts in a particular market area that sustain the image—underage discos, surf shops, and so on—rather than attempting to gain widespread distribution. Spokespeople (deejays, alternative sports stars, etc.) are recruited to spread the word and to be seen using the product. Sponsorship of alternative sports like the Red Bull Streets of San Francisco (a street luge event) and Red Bull Rampage (a free-ride mountain bike competition) has also been shown to be effective, as has the use of "education teams"—hip locals who drive around in a Red Bull auto handing out samples and promoting the brand.

The more mainstream media are also used— though on a market-by-market basis rather than through mass media and even these traditional efforts may take on a less traditional form. For example, the advertising campaign ("Red Bull gives you wings") uses animated television and radio spots featuring the devil trying the product and sprouting wings. The company also sponsors a number of more traditional events ranging from soapbox derbies to Formula 1 racing cars, as well as extensive public relations programs to reach youth.

Now that Mateschitz and Red Bull have created a new beverage category, can they hold on to it? Success attracts competitors—many who have the potential to provide more marketing clout than Red Bull. Coca-Cola, Pepsi, and Anheuser Busch have all recently introduced their own energy drinks. Hansen Beverage's "Energy" and Sobe have both been gaining sales, and Snapple's "Venom" is getting more marketing support from Cadbury. Mateschitz is not oblivious to the competition. He and his marketing team are continually developing more wacky ideas to maintain Red Bull's alternative and mystical image. Others feel that expanding the category can only benefit Red Bull. It may depend on how large the cult grows!

Sources: "Selling Energy," Economist, May 11, 2002, p. 62; Kenneth Hein, "Red Bull Charging Ahead," Brandweek, Oct. 15, 2001, pp. 38-42; Hillary Chufa, "Grabbing Bull by Tail," Advertising Age, June 11, 2001, pp. 4-6; David Noonan, "Red Bull's Good Buzz," Newsweek, May 14, 2001, p. 39.

Communication is something we indulge in every day, but the most impending question is: What exactly is this most widely and commonly talked routine? If we look on the lighter side of this issue, Anne Morrow Lindbergh (Argonauta, Gift From the Sea, 1955) has very aptly annunciated the core value by stating that 'Good communication is stimulating as black coffee and just as hard to sleep after.'

On the other side of the coin, communication is the unique tool that market communicators use to persuade consumers, both existing and potential, to act in a desired fashion. Communication is such a lethal weapon that puts the consumer in a morereceptive frame of mind, thereby arresting his logic. It is a multi facet bridge between consumers and marketers on the one hand and between socio cultural environment and the consumer on other hand. Being so important communication is a difficult function for the simple reason every one assumes that he or she can communicate well — while others have difficulties.

The Magic Potion

We have quite often seen a number of times that some people are more effective in communicating than others. A man on one hand may motivate the people by the strength of his speech to do unlawful feats, while another man may not succeed in even creating a ripple on the surface of human action. The persisting question that arises is: Why does this happen? After all both are talking and sending some kind of message and has a large audience yet one moves mountains while the other doesn't even succeed in moving an inch.

Communication is like water to a fish that surrounds us. We constantly communicate with others and except for biological functions that sustain us; there is no activity more pervasive and critical than communication. As the Chinese proverb says, 'Talk does not cook rice', we all assume that talking is a kind of communication, but it will be erroneous to declare it true. This is so, because of a very simple reason, talk does not persuade others to get through them. It should be equipped with the ability of persuasive communication. If one goes about digging a bit, the answer is evident enough. Persuasive communication is the magic potion that brings about the enormous difference.

Communication, as we have already, discussed in detail, next on the agenda is the mind-boggling words, 'persuasion persuasive communication and persuasibility.'

Fig. 19.1

Persuasion in its simplest term means to convince, to make some one agree with your point of view. In Hindi, the synonym for persuasion is *'Manana.'* If we break this word into two parts, humorously, we get a very effective meaning of the word persuasion, in the following manner:

'Manana' = *'Mana'* + *'Na'*
= **Do not say No.**

By the above, we get to learn that persuasion is an art of presenting your point of view in such an effective and efficient manner that the other person is not able to say 'no' to it, i.e., he or she gets thoroughly convinced by your ideas.

Thus, combining communication and persuasion, we can say persuasive communication, simply means, to communicate in such a fashion so that others can be influenced to such an extent that they willingly perform the required task. Thus, any communication process in which a source attempts either to secure a change in one's belief or attitude or induce an overt behaviour in one or more receivers, is a persuasive communication.

It would be difficult to overestimate the role that persuasive communication has in our lives. The central function of most communication is to influence. The issue of influence is directly related to the definition that communication is purposive, that it is directed towards the achievement of goals. For example, students attempt to influence teachers to give high grades on their papers and exams. Teachers try to persuade students that their classes have praxis, relational partners spend an exorbitant amount of time attempting to influence each other. Employees spend a great deal of their work related conversations, attempting to convince their superiors that they have what it takes to make it. Most communication events are attempt to manipulate the environment around us. Our ability to get what we want in life is to a large extent, is based upon our ability to manage the impressions others have of us honesty, trustworthiness, capability, and so on.[1]

Persuasion is an important part of our daily communication. To persuade is to change a receiver's attitudes, beliefs, or behaviour (Bettinghaus 1980, p.1). Advertisement is a type of persuasive message which tries to draw consumers to certain products or services by affecting their attitudes.

Publicis, a TVC Ad company created the commercial for HP using headline: Have Fun & All That Jazz and baseline: The Computer is Personal Again . Just push the quick play button...music, movies, mails, is what HP is promising you this time. In short, 'fun & all that jazz' is a guarantee from HP on this latest remote-controlled HP Pavilion•DV 2046TU Notebook. The power idea is to play on the current wave amidst consumers for using the computer for wholesome entertainment. The eye catching visual display showcases a beam balance, with diverse features hanging from its different strings. The body copy further elucidates on the laptop's features. The reward to the prospect is clear: 'the computer is personal again'. Of course, HP wants to cash in its remote control empowered laptop. So, all set to become a couch potato?

Tea Board of India, uses headline: For That Hourglass Figure, Drink More Tea and baseline: Chai Piyo Mast Jiyo in the TVC created by JWT. Someone rightly said, 'Tea is liquid wisdom' and according to this ad, it is the cup of life too. The power idea is to unshackle the myth of tea being a staid and boring drink, instead making young consumers aware that tea actually is a hip drink, which even helps you burn calories. In fact, the copy has perfect clarity on the tea's positioning and relates its clinching benefit: 4-5 cups of tea everyday, helps you spend energy faster and that it is a 'zero calorie drink'. The photograph displaying a cup of the hot brew, increases the visual appeal of the ad. The body copy further urges you to drink tea, and 'flaunt that bod'. Now that's what we call appealing to the target audience, in their lingo!

Bates Enterprise created a TVC ICICI Credit Card using headline: The Sea Paces in Anticipation... The World Can Wait and baseline : Own the World for An aspirational headline, combined with a striking B&W visual, equals a winning communication for potential ICICI Platinum Card holders. The power idea is to convince the target audience (in this case high net worth individuals) that ICICI's Platinum Card offers you the exclusivity reserved for the privileged. The ad provides clinching benefit to the brand by positioning it such that it enables its esteemed holders to reserve tables at the finest restaurants in the city; and for making every moment cherishable. Oh! what a feeling to be spoilt rotten... yet another winsome ad from the ICICI stable!

GM was no way behind. They used the headline: When you buy a Chevrolet, you become a part of GM, the world's No. 1 car with baseline: For a special journey called life created by Rediffusion DY&R. GM is out with a huge ad this time, flaunting all its brands, awards and products. If that wasn't enough, they have painstakingly listed all their performance and achievements too. The power idea is crystal clear: if Toyota Corolla can claim to be the global leader for 40 years, why should GM deprive itself from claiming its rightful glory? GM's brand personality is eminently visible: it wants to flex its muscles as the world's largest car manufacturer. The positioning is clearly to establish Chevrolet as GM's flagship brand in India. No wonder the headline extolls: when you buy a Chevrolet, you become a part of the GM family! Wonder if that's reason enough to buy a Chevrolet?Brand : TVS

Break free with GLX 125 and Sachin with a baseline: New GLX 125 with electric start. Saatchi & Saatchi created this for TVS mobikes. Sachin signifies 'speed' and the power idea in this ad, flouting Sachin as TVS' brand ambassador, is to create a common brand association of 'speed' between Tendulkar and the mobike. The reward to the prospect comes in the form of a dinner with the master blaster (of course on a lucky draw basis) for prospective TVS buyers. Apart from the promise of Tendulkar, this one successfully captures the USP (undoubtedly speed and style) of the Victor GLX 125 model too. There is complete product positioning clarity, and thank God for the missing 'woman' in this bike ad!

In a TVC of Surf Excel washing powder, created by LOWE, children have been used as persuasive agents using the baseline 'Daag Achche Hain'. Two boys are fighting over a piece of paper that has 10/10 written on it (it's a form for the 10 on 10 contest that gives out a Rs. 5 lakh scholarship to the lucky winner).While wrestling in the muddy lawn, one of them catches sight of a poor boy observing them from across the fence. They ask if he wants to go to school. The boy nods affirmatively; they hand him the contest form. The TVC ends with all three going to school together, and one kid asking the 'lucky' boy whether he has completed his homework.

Surf Excel now-a-days seems to only bank on kids when it comes to advertising, and this time too, it delivers a power-packed performance! Cute kids are the flavour of the day. However, this ad not only depends on the cuteness quotient but combines it with a heart wringing storyline too. While the power idea is the 10/10 contest scholarship, the ad doesn't miss on its product benefit, which is its stain removing ability. While the brand personality of Surf Excel is visible through and through, the strong emotional factor, the clarity of communication and its high visual appeal work wonders for the concept. An extension of the winning campaign Daag achche hain commercials, this one may not be the best in the series but touches hearts for sure.

Persuasive communication may be defined as the process through which people attempt to influence the beliefs or actions of others. In many cases, persuasive communication involves people who are important to each other—parents influence children, children influence parents, and friends influence each other. Persuasive communication such as advertising frequently involves strangers. Those involved in designing ads or producing commercials will attempt to "know" the target audience, but this is generally limited to a few important details about potential customers, such as where they live or how much money they are expected to spend on certain items in a given year.

People begin to influence others early in life. Preschool children learn that they can influence other children and adults by crying, smiling, whining, pointing, tugging, and, eventually, talking. By the time children enter school, they use a variety of strategies to influence others.

During elementary school years children grow in their ability to adapt persuasive messages to the people they wish to influence. Research has shown that kindergartners and children in the first grade tend to use the same strategies when trying to influence different people. Children in grades two and three adapt their persuasive messages by adding words like "may I" and "please." Children who are in the fourth and fifth grades begin to adapt their messages to specific people. For example, they begin to use strategies when trying to gain favours from teachers that differ from those they use in trying to gain favours from friends.

By the time most students are in the sixth grade, they can adapt their persuasive messages to specific listener characteristics. In one study, most 12-year-olds used different strategies when trying to get a ball back from the yard of an angry-appearing man than they did when addressing a pleasant-appearing man.

In high school, students continue to grow in the number and sophistication of persuasive strategies used. The average high school senior, for example, anticipates and responds to arguments that disagree with his or her own. High school seniors, however, still have much to learn about influencing others and responding critically to attempts to influence them. Since persuasive communication is complex, learning about it is a lifelong process. Much of that learning can begin by participating on school debate teams and studying rhetoric.

According to Bettinghaus' definition of persuasion, a receiver is the target audience of a persuasive message. Therefore, how each individual perceives and reacts to the persuasive message is important to advertisers. Personality differences affect the levels of influence that each persuasive message has on each individual.

Communication scholars have found that personality structures are organizations of beliefs and attitudes that become pervasive for the individual and affect the way in which the individual behaves in many kinds of situations (Bettinghaus 1980, p.53). The definition of personality is the relatively long-lasting distinctive personal qualities that allow us to cope with, and respond to the world around us (Burnett, Moriarty & Wells 1995, p.188). Personality is conceived of as a predisposition to particular modes of behaviour and its measurement potentially allows us to predict behaviour (Byrne & Cherry 1977, p.109). As mentioned above, personality differences will affect the level of influence that persuasive messages have on each person. Therefore, in additional to situation factors, scholars have identified several personality factors that are correlated with persuasion.

Two of the goals of human communication are: to be understood and to be believed. In persuasive communication, both of these acts are fulfilled. Pragmatists have investigated the first goal and how it is carried out, while social psychologists have focused on the second goal. This paper attempts tossed new light on persuasion by reviewing work from both fields and sketching the outline of a model integrating such work. Relevance theory bridges communication and cognition and, as such, provides a solid foundation for further research on persuasion. Marketing communication offers a rich domain of investigation for this endeavour: we show that pragmatics can only benefit from an analysis of persuasive communication in an "optimized" context such as marketing.

One of our goals, when we communicate, is to be understood. Another goal is to be believed: we try to affect our audiences' beliefs, desires and actions. Persuasion is the communicative act that carries out both these goals – an audience that has been persuaded has understood an utterance, and believed its message. Accounting for the understanding aspect has typically been the work of pragmatic theorists, while explaining how attitudes change has been the focus of social psychologists.

Persuading someone is performing an act (roughly, that of affecting someone's beliefs or desires) using some form of communication, usually language. As such, persuasion constitutes a "speech act," an act performed in, or by speaking. The notion of speech act and the theory that was developed around it were first introduced by J. L. Austin in his 'William James Lectures' at Harvard in 1955, and published in 1962 in his 'How To Do Things With Words'.

Austin (1962). The verb "to persuade" is typically given as one of the first examples of perlocution by speech act theorists. Indeed, Austin (1962), when he develops speech act theory and introduces the term "perlocutionary act", uses the utterance "He persuaded me to shoot her" as his first example (Austin 1962: 102).

Perlocutionary acts are the third in Austin's tri-partite nomenclature of speech acts. After locutionary acts, which are simply "saying something," and illocutionary acts, which are performed "in saying something," perlocutionary acts are performed "by saying something." Here is an example from the world of advertising:

(i) Locutionary act: A young woman holds up a bottle of Coca Cola and shouts "Coke is the real thing" in front of a television camera.
(ii) Illocutionary act: In shouting "Coke is the real thing," the young woman asserted that a product called "Coke" is the real thing.
(iii) Perlocutionary act: By shouting "Coke is the real thing," the young woman persuaded millions of television viewers around the world that drinking Coke is a worthwhile experience.

Austin specifies the effects of perlocutionary acts as "certain consequential effects upon the feeling, thoughts or acts of the audience, or of the speaker, or of other persons". In other words, the production of cognitive, affective or behavioral effects on an audience by a speaker's utterance constitutes a perlocutionary act. Austin goes on to state that "it may be done with the design, intention or purpose of producing them (the effects)", suggesting that the speaker's intention to produce these effects is not necessary, in his view. To better understand Austin's notion of perlocutionary act, we need to look more closely at how he distinguishes illocutionary and perlocutionary acts. Such a distinction cannot be made purely on the basis of effects resulting from the utterance, according to Austin, because illocutionary acts produce their own effects which are not perlocutionary in nature. The expected effects from illocutionary acts are the utterance's "uptake" (i.e., "bringing about the understanding of the meaning and of the force of the locution"), "taking effect" ("bringing about states of affairs in the normal way"), and "inviting a response". Clearly then, in Austin's framework, all that is required for successful communication is the performance and identification of an illocutionary act – whereby the hearer will understand a speaker's utterance, the normal state of affairs will be brought about, and appropriate responses will be 'invited.' Perlocutionary acts are peripheral to the study of communication proper.

However, it is generally agreed that Austin fails to draw a consistent line between illocutionary and perlocutionary acts, so the status of persuasion remains problematic in his framework.

Persuasive communication plays a central role in a number of professions. Lawyers, salespersons, advertising specialists, public relations experts, and politicians use persuasive communication very oftently. While persuasive communication may not be the central ingredient in many careers, most people need to be able to influence others in work-related settings.

The most prominent form of persuasive communication in contemporary life is advertising. Consumers are confronted by advertisements from a variety of directions. While newspapers are thought of as informative sources, local, national, and classified advertising take up about 65 percent of their average total space. In many magazines 45 to 50 percent of the space is given to advertising. As people drive to and from work, radio advertising rides with them. The roadsides are filled with billboards, neon signs, or banners in store windows that compete with traffic for attention. After arriving home and sorting through the advertisements in the day's mail, people view numerous commercials on prime-time television and attempt to filter e-mail advertisements (known as "spam") from the e-mails they wish to read.

When we focus our attention at history, we find several examples of persuasive communication. The great example can be found from the events of public communications. Greatest of all the examples of persuasive communication, can be found in the famous play, Julius Caesar by William Shakespeare. In the play an instantaneous change was observed in the overt behaviour of the mob through persuasive communication, in the following two situations:

(*a*) Ceasar, the King, was murdered by the conspirators. His assassination by Brutus, Cassius and others created confusion, Citizens were demanding reasons for the King's assassination. Brutus, who was one of the noble man and a great orator, who enjoyed great respect among the crowd, came forward to explain the reason for King's death. He explained that the future of the country was at stake because of the ambitious nature of the king. Brutus, with his persuading skills was able to satisfy the crowd.

(*b*) Then came the turn of Antony, a friend of Ceasar. He came in the crowd to give the funeral speech, though his intention was to change the belief of the crowd about Ceasar. Antony, too, was a good orator and possessed high persuasion skills. He with the clever and timely use of words and with the sarcastic statement was able to highlight the qualities of Ceasar as a good King. He aroused the feeling of crowd to such an extent that they started searching the conspirators to revenge the King's death.

Persuasive communication sometimes fails to be effective even when logically and directly planned and heavily substantiated by reasons for change. Basketball great Earvin, 'Magic' Johnson, after being diagnosed HIV positive, returned to play for the Los Angels lakers. Health care professional argued that the risk of other players contacting the HIV virus from Magic Johnson while on the court were remote and rare. Professional basketball players from around the league were given the latest medical information available concerning the risk of contacting HIV. Not all of the players were convinced by these persuasive messages. Questions, anxiety and previously learned stereotyped images of HIV infected persons were too strong for any rational argument to persuade some players that playing with Magic Johnson was safe. Amid much controversy, Magic Johnson decided to retire from professional basketball. This example is matched by numerous other curiosities in the area of persuasive communication. Why, how and in what ways people are persuaded to change.

Next comes the persuasibility factor. Persuasibility factor means any variable attribute within a population that is correlated with consistent individual differences in responsiveness to one or more classes of influential communications.[2] The meaning of the key words become clear if we consider an analysis of the communication process involved in successful persuasion.

Whenever an individual is influenced to change his belief, decisions or attitudes, certain evident external events occur which constitute communication stimuli and certain behavioural changes occur constituting communication effects. The communication stimuli include not only what is said but even the unintentional and intentional cues which influence the audience. Information — as to what is said, why he said it and how do people react to it forms a part of it.

On the other hand communication effect inculcates all perceptible changes in the receivers verbal and non-verbal behaviour. This even includes all changes in private judgment and opinion, learning effects for example, increased knowledge, a superficial conformist behaviour for example, public expression of agreement even though there is a private rejection of it.

However, our main focus is on the behavioural change which is considered as component of genuine change in opinion or verbalised attitude. Here we need to observe whether the recipient is giving an internalised response or just a superficial change in opinion and attitude.

Thus, a clear cut attitude change is indicated when the recipient has internally absorbed a valuational message and there is a change in the person's perception, affect and overt action. In addition, his verbalised judgment too show a distinct change. When we get indications of a genuine change in verbalised belief or value judgment we term it as opinion change, which usually consists of one component of attitude change.

Neither opinion change nor attitude change include surface conformity in which a person pretends to adopt a point of view though does not agree privately.[3]

There are two major factors which account for the interrelationship between the communication stimuli and observable effect, they are: Predispositional factors and internal mediating process. 'Pre dispositional factors are used to account for individual differences in observable effect when all communication stimuli are held constant. Constructs referring to internal or mediating processes are used in order to account for the differential effect of different stimuli on a given person or group of persons.'

In other words, internal processes have been coined primarily to account for different effects attributable to different types of communication focusing on the same people while predispositions are needed to account for the different effects seen in different people who have been radiated with the same communication. There are two major kinds of predisposition 'topic bound including all those factors which effect a person's readiness to accept or reject a given point of view on a particular topic. The other main type called 'topic free' is relatively independent of the subject matter of the communication.[4]

The difference between topic-bound and topic-free is not necessarily the same as the dimension of specificity-generality. Some topic-bound predispositions-positions may be very narrowly confined to those communications expressing a favourable for unfavourable judgment toward a specific trait of a particular person (for example, the members of an organisation, after having been embarrassed by the gauche manners of their highly respected leader, would be disposed to reject only those favourable statements about him which pertain to a limited aspect of his social behaviour). Other topic-bound predispositions may be extremely general (for example, certain types of persons may be inclined to accept any comments which express optimism about the future). A topic-bound predisposition, however, is always limited to one class of communications (a narrow or a broad class) which is defined by one or another characteristic of the content of the conclusion.

Similar restrictions hold for some of the topic-free factors. For example, Hovland, Janis, and Kelley point out that many topic-free factors may prove to be bound to specific characteristics of the communication.

Some to the hypotheses concerning topic-free predispositions deal with factors which predict a person's responsiveness only to those persuasive communications that employ certain types of argumentation. Investigations of topic-free predispositions ultimately may reveal some that are associated primarily with the nature of the communicator, others that are associated with the social setting in which the communications takes place, and perhaps still others that are so broad in scope that they are relatively independent of any specific variables in the communication situation.

Thus, for any communication, it can be assumed that there are likely to be several different types of personality predispositions, topic-bound and topic-free, whose joint effects determine individual differences in responsiveness. The essential point is that, by also taking an account of topic-free factors, it should be possible to improve predictions concerning the degree to which members of the audience will be influenced by persuasive communications. Such factors have generally been neglected in analyses of audience predispositions.

We shall briefly consider those topic-free factors which are bound to other features of the communication situation before turning to an examination of the unbound, or communication-free, factors.

Content-Bound Factors

The content of a communication includes appeals, arguments, and various stylistic features, as well as the main theme or conclusion which defines its topic. The effectiveness of each of these content characteristics is partly dependent upon certain pre dispositional factors which have been designated as 'content-bound.'

Appeal-Bound Factors

In the content of many communications one finds appeals which explicitly promise social approval or threaten social disapproval from a given reference group.[5] Responsiveness to these social incentives partly depends upon the degree to which the person is motivated to be affiliated with the reference group. Personality differences may also give rise to differences in responsiveness to special appeals concerning group consensus and related social incentives. Different types of personalities may be expected to have different thresholds for the arousal of guilt, shame, fear, and other emotions which can be aroused by special appeals. For example, Janis and Feshbach[6] have found that certain personality factors are related to individual differences in responsiveness to fear-arousing appeals, Experimental studies by Katz, McClintock, and Sarnoff[7] indicate that the relative effectiveness of rational appeals, and of self-insight procedures designed to counteract social prejudices, depend partly upon whether the recipient rates low, medium, or high or various measures or ego defensiveness.

Argument-Bound Factors

Many variables have been investigated which involve stimulus differences in the arrangement of arguments and in the logical relationship between arguments and conclusions. There are evidences indicating that pre dispositional factors play a role in determining the extent to which an individual will be affected by the order in which information is presented. Individuals with low cognitive-need scores were differentially influenced by variations in order of presentation while those with high scores were not. One would also expect that individual differences would affect the degree to which a person will be influenced by such variations as the following: (1) The use of the strictly rational or logical types of argument *vs*. propagandistic devices of over generalisation, *innuendo, non-sequitur,* and irrelevant *ad hominem* comments. (2) Explicitly stating the conclusion that follows from a set of arguments *vs*. leaving the conclusion implicit.

Style-Bound Factors

Differences in social class and educational background probably account for some of the individual differences in the responsiveness to variations in style, for example, a literary style as against a 'folksy' approach. Other variations in treatment that may be differentially effective are technical jargon *vs.* simple language; slang *vs*. 'pure' prose; long, complex sentences *vs*. short, declarative sentences.

Communicator-Bound Factors

The effectiveness of a communication depends on the recipient's evaluation of the speaker. The phase of the problem which has been most extensively studied is that concerned with the authoritativeness of the communicator. That personality differences in the recipients are associated with the extent to which particular communicators are effective. The subjects who are more influenced by authority figures tended to have both higher self-confidence and stronger authoritarian tendencies than those who are more influenced by peers.

The affiliation of the communicator is also an important factor in interaction, of course, with the group membership of the recipient. Thus the communicator who is perceived as belonging to a group with which the recipient is also affiliated will be more effective on the average than a communicator who is perceived either as an outsider or as a member of a rival group. When, for example, a speaker's affiliation with a political, religious, or trade organisation becomes salient to the audience, persons who are members of the same organisation will be most likely to be influenced by the speaker's communication.

Finally, the intent of the communicator is perceived differently by different members of the audience, with a consequent influence on the speaker's effectiveness. A number of studies have shown that the fairness and impartiality of the communicator is viewed quite differently by individuals with varying stands on an ideological issue, and this in turn is related to the amount of opinion change effected.

Media-Bound Factors

It seems probable that some persons will be more responsive to communications in situations of direct social interaction, whereas others may be more readily influenced by newspapers, magazines, radio programs, television, movies, and mass media in general, concerning the psychological differences between propaganda emanating from mass media and from informal social contacts. Other media characteristics that may evoke differential sensitivities involve variations in the sense modalities employed, e.g., some people may be more responsive to visual than to auditory media. There is some evidence that individuals with less education may be more influenced by aural presentations (e.g., by radio and lectures) than by printed media.

Situation-Bound Factors

There are indications that some persons tend to be more influenced when socially facilitative cues accompany the presentation of a persuasive communication (for example, presence of others, applause). The experiments by Asch[8] and other investigators contain some indirect implications bearing on individual differences in responsiveness to an expression of consensus on the part of others in the audience. Some studies indicate that some people are affected by the pleasantness or unpleasantness of the situation in which a communication is received. For example, the effectiveness of persuasive message was found to be enhanced if they were expressed at a time when the subjects were eating a snack. We might expect to find some personality factors associated with low *vs.* high sensitivity to extraneous stimulation of this type.

Just as in the case of topic-bound factors, each of the above content-bound, communicator-bound, media-bound, and situation-bound factors may include some predispositions that are very narrow in scope (e.g., applicable only to communications which emanate from one particular communicator) and other predispositions that are broadly applicable to a large class of communications (e.g., to all communications emanating from purported authorities or experts). It is the predispositions at the latter end of the specificity-generality continuum that are of major scientific interest, since they are the ones that increase our theoretical understanding of communication processes and help to improve predictions of the degree to which different persons will be responsive to social influence.

Aproaches to Persuasion[9]

There are various different approaches to understanding how one goes about changing people's opinions, beliefs, values and/or behaviours. The different models of persuasion assumes different assumptions about the underlying psychological mechanism that explain why certain persuasive strategies are effective and why others fail. These models make different assumptions about the nature of people, how information is processed, and how various communication strategies ought to operate.

There are a number of theoretical perspectives that provide an explanatory framework from which we might understand some of the dynamics of persuasive communication. However, there is a likelihood that some of the following models might be appropriate in some persuasive situations and not in others.

LEARNING THEORIES

Infants are born without any opinions, beliefs, or values. Through the socialisation process, they learn to respond to the environment, to behave acceptably, and yet, in their own self interest, to accept certain ideas as true or false, good or bad. In fact, learning can be defined as the process of acquiring or changing behaviour in response to individual encounters with people, events, and things.

Yet much that is said about persuasion, and about communication in general, implies that the person being persuaded already holds an opinion, belief, or value and that the communicator is simply trying to induce a change. A stimulus, in this context, is anything that occurs in the communication transaction and is perceived by the receiver; a response is what the receiver does as a result of the stimulus.

The stimulus-response relationship can be manipulated in order to enhance learning.[10] For instance, most learning theories assume that reinforcement is necessary to induce learning. There are two general kinds of reinforcement; positive and negative. Suppose as any one came to your door and asked you to allow your name to be listed in an advertisement supporting a political candidate. If you were told that you would be listed as a 'prominent' citizen along with the mayor, several movie stars, and other celebrities, that your participation would make you a patriotic person; and that you would be paid Rs.10,000 for allowing your name to be used, you would be offered positive reinforcement or rewards. If you were told that anyone not allowing their name to be used will be considered unpatriotic and, further more might find themselves under investigation by the Central Bureau of Investigation, you would be offered negative reinforcement, that is, you would be offered an opportunity to escape from an undesirable situation. Negative reinforcement is not the same as punishment. Negative reinforcement leaves open the door to the desired behaviour; punishment takes place only after the receiver has behaved in an undesired way. If you rejected the offer to be listed in the ad and the next day found that you had been fired from you job because CBI agents had made some unsavoury suggestions to your boss, that would be punishment.

Most learning theories also assume that the time between response and reinforcement affects the speed of learning. If you know that by signing the political advertisement you will be paid Rs. 10,000 in cash on the spot, you might be more willing to sign than if you learned you would get a Rs. 10,000 tax rebate the following year. Negative reinforcement is also more effective if escape from the undesired state will be immediate. For instance, telling young people that they will live to be 75 years old instead of 60 years old if they stop smoking is not likely to be as effective as telling them that smokers are automatically disqualified from a social/cultural group they wish to join.

Learning theory also emphasises the importance of feedback. Positive feedback can work as a form of reinforcement. Rewarding the receivers and helping to ensure that they will continue to respond in the desired way. For example, a press agent whose job is to persuade writers and reporters to do stories about his or her client may reward the authors of favourable stories with praise for their fine abilities or with complimentary gifts, like a ticket to a rock show being organised in the city.

Learning theory does not offer the only explanation for human change. In fact, much about learning theory has been criticised for its stimulus-response model, which critics believe is a simplistic view of the nature of human beings. In addition to raising questions about who would control the conditioning process, this theory also raises questions about the nature of the human species. Other theories about human change assume that people make decisions and engage in behaviour that does not depend on the stimulus response relationship. These theories deny that people merely respond to stimuli in their environment; in fact, some theories suggest that people do not always respond in the way that would bring them the best reward.

Advertisers often use positive reinforcement to link products (Stimuli) to increased sexuality, likability, and other supposedly desirable states in order to increase the sales (desired response). They also use negative reinforcement, for example, by linking a mouthwash to escape from the supposedly undesirable state of having 'morning breath.' Both positive and negative reinforcers are likely to have impact on the receiver's behaviour. If the communication can demonstrate to a person the way he or she will be rewarded or will escape an undesirable state by complying with the communicator's request, behaviour will probably change. Punishment, however, does not usually work so well. People who do not escape the undesirable state and who are punished tend to withdraw from the situation. In other words, the use of punishment might be very effective in insuring that an unwanted behaviour ceases however, using punishment alone does not necessarily produce other behaviours that might be desirable.

CONSISTENCY THEORIES

Although some learning theorists prefer to ignore variables within the receiver's mind that might interfere with the stimulus-response relationship, other persuasion theorists have focused on the mind as a 'middleman' between the stimulus and the response. For example, cognitive theory sees the mind as a complex mechanism that organises past learning and present stimuli into meaningful units. Thus, the mind is not simply being bombarded with unrelated stimuli; it is always organising information into patterns.

A mind operating in this fashion evaluates persuasive communication in terms of the way it fits into an organisational pattern.[11] If a new communication fits into the pattern, the receiver's internal state remains balanced. For instance, if a man recently lost several thousand rupees because of shady and irresponsible dealings by his stockbroker and if he then hears a speech proposing stricter regulation of brokerage firms, he can fit the speaker's proposals into the pattern of his experience and feel comfortable with the conclusions. He does not need to be persuaded. His attitudes are probably already consistent with the positions being advocated by the message, that is, there is internal consistency. If the message does not conform to prior attitudes and/or presents a position opposing, or unfamiliar to, the receiver, internal inconsistency is likely to occur. For instance, if stockbrokers or investors who had been successful in the market heard the same speech advocating stricter control, they might have great difficulty in resolving the speaker's proposals with prior beliefs and experiences regardless of how logical the communicator was. Strategies must be employed to persuade the receiver; one such strategy would be to maximise internal inconsistency.

Another consistency theory of persuasion that deserves special attention because of the unique perspective it takes on communication and persuasion is cognitive dissonance. The theory of cognitive dissonance assumes that people feel uncomfortable when they hold opinions or ideas that are psychologically inconsistent. It is further assumed that when people experience this discomfort called cognitive dissonance, they will be motivated to change attitudes or behaviours to reduce that inconsistency, for example, a person who is faced with some conflict in making a choice about a car to purchase. Once the decision is made and a car purchased, however, dissonance is aroused. The person probably is somewhat unsure of whether or not the right decision was made and is aware that there are positive and negative aspects about both the purchased car and the car he or she decided not to buy.

Another example might help make the point about how people operate to reduce dissonance and support what they have been persuaded to do. Let us stress again that we are only discussing how people seek to support what they have already been persuaded to do. Suppose that someone persuaded you not to engage in an activity that you enjoyed. Let us further suppose that this persuasion was accompanied with a mild threat outlining the harms that would befall you if you went ahead and did the enjoyable task. Would you be likely to change your attitude toward the task itself more if the threat were mild than if the threat was severe and you were advised of the extremely harmful results of the behaviour? The attitude toward the enjoyable task itself would be more likely to change if you refrained from doing it if you had been given a mild threat.

SOCIAL JUDGMENT THEORY

Social judgment theory differs from learning theory and consistency theories in several ways.[12] First, it views attitude change as a two-stage process. In the first stage, the receiver judges the relationship of a communication to his or her own currently held or most preferred attitude about an issue. For instance, if X believes that the death penalty for convicted murderers is a good idea and if he hears someone argue that the death penalty is itself tantamount to condoning murder, he will judge the communication to be widely discrepant from his view. In the second stage of attitude change, X makes changes in his opinions, beliefs, or values, how much change he makes will depend on how much discrepancy he perceives between his view and the source's view.

Social judgment theory treats attitudes as more compiles than favourable-unfavourable or positive-negative reactions. It claims that attitudes are best represented by a continuum as represented in Table 19.1

TABLE 19.1

Social Judgment Theory/Acceptance-Rejection Continuum

Attidude of Acceptance	*Attidude of Non-commitment*	*Attidude of Rejection*
1. The death penalty should be invoked for convicted murderers. 2. The death penalty should be invoked only for pre-mediated murders. 3. The death penalty should be invoked only if committed during the perpetration of a felony.	4. The death penalty should only be invoked if the victim is a juvenile.	5. Convicted murderers should pay restitution to families of their victims. 6. Convicted murders should face prison sentences. 7. All convicted murderers should receive psychiatric counselling in order to reassimilate them into society.

Social judgment theory also predicts the ways in which the receiver's ego-involvement affects his or her attitude change. High ego-involvement corresponds to a wide latitude of non-commitment. For example, a person awaiting trail on a murder charge would be highly ego-involved on the subject of the death penalty. Because an ego-involved person has a wide latitude of rejection, persuasive messages are more likely to fall into that range and be contrasted with the prime attitude. Thus, attitude change is difficult. A receiver who lacks ego-involvement, however, has a wide latitude of non-commitment into which persuasive messages, are likely to fall. Such messages can then be assimilated into the acceptable range, and persuasion is more successful. Common sense certainly supports the conclusion that people are more reluctant to change their attitudes on issues that are directly important to them.

Elaboration Likelihood Model

The Elaboration Likelihood Model (ELM) of persuasion is another approach that focuses on the ways in which people process information contained in persuasive communication.[13] According to this model, the impact of persuasive communication depends upon the amount of issue-relevant thinking, or elaboration, in which individuals will engage. Essentially, ELM posits that under different conditions, individuals will employ one of two types of elaboration, either central or peripheral routes to persuasion. Sometimes, individuals engage in extensive elaboration or issue-relevant thinking about an issue.

The Elaboration Likelihood Model (ELM) of persuasion argues that the effects of persuasive communication depend upon the amount of issue-relevant thinking, or 'elaboration', in which individuals engage. Under different conditions, individuals will engage in either central or peripheral-route processing, receivers focus on the validity and evidence contained in the persuasive message and other issue relevant concerns. Central-route processing occurs when individuals are highly involved with the topic of interest. Attitude change that occurs through central-route processing is robot and more resistant to persuasive counter arguments. In peripheral-route processing, receivers tend to use simple decision rules that require little information processing as the basis for acceptance or rejection of the persuasive argument. These decision rules focus on extrinsic features of the communication situation, such as the characteristics of the source (i.e., attractiveness and credibility) while paying limited attention to message attributers. Attitude change under these conditions is less enduring and often easily changed by counter arguments.

Language Expectancy Theory

One of the few language-based theories of persuasion is Language Expectancy Theory (LET).[14] (The logic that underlies LET argues that because language is a rule-governed symbolic system, people develop sociological and cultural norms and expectations about language use is given persuasive situations. In most communication transactions, language use confirms these norms and expectations, which enhances the normative status of those individuals engaged in those behaviours. For example, you probably have developed expectations about the language your close friends, parents, teachers, and so on, will use when they attempt to persuade you. Over time, because these expectations for language use by these individuals are usually confirmed, fairly rigid forms of the appropriate use of language develop and the normative status of these individuals becomes reinforced. LET asserts that communicators may intentionally or accidentally violate the norms governing language use, which in turn violates receivers' expectations. These violations of receivers' expectations will affect their receptivity to persuasive messages. Depending upon a variety of variables, violations of language expectations can either enhance or inhibit the effectiveness is whether the language choice of the source positively or negatively violates the target of persuasion's expectations.

Language Expectancy Theory (LET) argues that because language is a rule-governed symbolic system, people develop expectations about appropriate language usage in given persuasive situations. These expectations are based on cultural and societal norms of language behaviour and form a bandwidth of appropriate communication behaviours for individuals. Persuasive effectiveness is influenced by the violations of expectations. Violations can either inhibit or enhance persuasive effectiveness. Negative violations occur when a source uses culturally or socially inappropriate language, which decreases his or her persuasive effectiveness. Positive violations occur when a source, who is expected to use either socially inappropriate language or to conform to normative language expectations, employs language that is evaluated in a positive manner. This type of violations will increase the persuasibility of the message.

Persuasions: Applications and Message Strategies

We do not think that all communication is persuasive by nature; that view is too simplistic. We also are not interested in simply training people to be manipulators. Many people find our strong emphasis on the persuasive function of communication to be somewhat irritating, if not offensive, and we are willing to speak to that issue. Persuasion is a persuasive part of our daily lives, and much of our communication is suasory in nature. The suggestions we make in this context are likely to be useful to the would-be huckster who wishes to use the tool of communication for ends that we might personally find reprehensible.

Knowledge of how to construct persuasive messages and how those messages are likely to affect people.

Finally, given the alternatives to persuasion — that is, the sue or threat of force and violence we believe that persuasion is an acceptable and desirable tool by which we can influence our environment.

The Components of a Persuasive Message

If we can understand how people evaluate logical arguments, we are more likely to construct messages that will be seen as logical and increase the probability of those message being persuasive. Toulmin (1959) has created a model of critical thinking that has great utility in persuasive discourse. It is appropriate to argue that a persuasive message that facilitates this kind of critical thinking is most likely to be effective.[15] Every persuasive message presents an idea or course of action that the communicator advocates; it then suggests reasons that listeners should agree with it. Thus, it can be argued that most persuasive message, in their simplest form, are made up of the three components in the Toulmin model: claim, warrant, and data. These elements work to reinforce each other in persuasive attempts.

Claim

A claim is any statement, implied or explicit, that a communicator wants his or her audience to accept or agree to. A particular claim can serve as the major point of several related arguments, or it may be used by the communicator in one part of an argument to support an assertion (claim) made in another part.

There are several kinds of claims that can be used in a message a policy claim, a fact claim, or a value claim.

Warrant

To persuade, the communicator must support each claim with two other message parts: a warrant and date. A warrant is a general belief or attitude stated in support of a claim. To be effective, a warrant must be implicitly accepted by the audience; otherwise, it remains jut another claim. For example, a communicator who says, 'Schools should not be racially integrated', is making a claim. The claim can then be supported with the general statement, 'Blacks are genetically inferior to whites in mental ability.' Such a statement would be a warrant. Members of the KU Klux Klan might accept this warrant and so accept the claim. But it is highly likely that a convention of anthropologists or a group of African Americans might not belie the warrant and so would reject the claim as unwarranted. In this case, the warrant itself (that African Americans are mentally inferior) becomes a claim and needs a new warrant to justify it.

Data

Data are specific beliefs stated in support of a claim. Similar to the warrant, the data must be accepted by the audience to be persuasive. McCroskey (1968) has suggested that there are three types of data: first order, second order, and third order.[16]

First order data are specific beliefs or knowledge shared by the communicator and the audience. It may be claimed, for example, that all cigarette advertising should be hanged. Such a claim might be warranted by the generally accepted belief that cigarette smoking causes lung cancer. The communicator might then offer as data the information that cigarette advertising encourages smoking.

Second order data are beliefs held by the communicator but not necessarily known or shared by the audience. This type of data is often called 'source assertion', because it asks the audience to accept something just because the speaker, or source, says it is so. The important message component in this case is the warrant that the speaker is a credible source. For example, a speaker might asserts that consistently poor nutrition retards the mental development of children. If his or her credibility is high enough that the audience knows the speaker to be an established and respected member of the medical profession.

When the communicator has low credibility and the audience does not share his or her views, third order data must be used to persuade. This type of data is called 'evidence.' It comes from a third party, a source outside the communicator and the audience. Third order data ask the audience to accept warrants for two separate claims.

Appeals Based on Evidence

Is it important to present evidence (third order data) to support a claim? the answer depends on the situation. Research has shown that sometimes evidence is very persuasive, whereas at other times different kinds of supporting material are more effective. It is possible to extract from the research some generalisations about the usefulness of evidence.[17]

There are two final points that should be made about the use of evidence. The first is that little research is available that distinguishes between 'good' and 'bad' evidence. However, it is probably common sense to suggest that evidence is more likely to be perceived as good evidence when it is relevant to the claim being advanced properly linked to that claim by an appropriate warrant. The second point is that the sources of evidence also help people make judgments about the quality of the evidence. Evidence obtained from a source low in credibility can have an adverse effect on the persuasiveness of your message, and it can also reduce your credibility. Many times a person can increase communicative effectiveness, however, by relying on evidence and examples from other high-credible sources.[18]

Appeals Based on Fear

Many communicators try to pervade by stimulating fear in their audiences. Public health pamphlets, for example, predict a frightening future of blindness, sterility, paralysis, or the possibility of contracting the virus that leads to Acquired Immune Deficiency Syndrome (AIDS) as the reward for sexual promiscuity (or even occasional indiscretions) unless one takes the recommended precautions. Gun-control advocates talk of unleashed violence, and their opponents talk of first steps down the road to totalitarianism. Students in a driver's education course watch a state highway department film that graphically portrays the results of reckless or negligent driving, complete with blood and bodies and intimations of one's own mortality. Because people do react strongly to fear in everyday life, much research has been done to see if fear can be used to change attitudes.

A fear appeal says that harm will befall the listener or someone important to him or her unless the claim of the communicator is adopted. A strong fear appeal shows this harm dramatically. A film intended to make people stop smoking that shows a close up of a cancerous lung being removed from a corpse is an example of high fear appeal. A moderate fear appeal states the same message less dramatically, as in the case of a film that shows people smoking and then coughing. A low fear appeal states the message in a fairly calm way; for example a printed advertisement claiming that scientists have established a link between smoking and lung cancer. It is important to note here that we are talking about the construction of messages that vary on the degree to which they contain vivid or frightening consequences associated with failure to accept the claim of the persuader, which is not necessarily isomorphic with the amount of fear that the receiver experiences after exposure to the message.[19] Fear Appeal increases viewer interest in the ad and the persuasiveness of the ad. Advertisers frequently use such appeal factor with health and beauty products, idea marketing, and insurance. Most experts believe that a moderate level of fear is most effective.

Appeals Varying in Language Intensity

Some of our closest friends and most respected colleagues believe we have obtained whatever modicum of success we have because people have confused the intensity of our claims with the validity of our positions. People have choices to make about kinds of language that will be used in any given persuasive message, and there is evidence to suggest that those language choices will have a great effect on whether the persuasion attempt succeeds. One important language variable that influences persuasion is language intensity. Language intensity can be rated by measuring the distance between a claim and a neutral position. For example the claim, 'Unions are destroying the newspaper industry,' is certainly less neutral than saying, 'Unions create problems in the newspaper industry.' There are different ways to vary the intensity of language in a message.[20]

One method to vary intensity of language is to insert qualifiers. One kind of such qualifiers expresses probability. For example, consider the opening line of a press news, 'Recent decisions of the apex court of the country on the fundamental rights of accused will certainly lead to more crime in the country.' Such statement can be made less intense by replacing the word 'certainly' to 'perhaps' and dropping 'fundamental.' Another kind of qualifier expresses extremity. If the spokesperson of a particular party says, 'The party vigorously condemns bias in the news media,' the attitude implied is certainly greater, more intense and perhaps threatening than if it would have been said, 'The party frowns upon bias in the news media.'

A second way to increase intensity of language is to use metaphors, especially those with sexual or violent connotations. Claims such as, 'The president is raping the Constitution,' 'The recent incursion by Iraq is a molestation of the country's territorial waters,' 'Public school teachers suffocate student creativity,' or 'Prejudice in the system has brutalised the minds of young children,' go beyond a representation of the facts as they stand and attempt to persuade through the intensity of images.

Whether such high-intensity language does, in fact, achieve the speaker's goal is difficult to say. One study showed that very intense communicators seem more credible and that their messages seem clearer and more intelligent; however, the study did not indicate that such communicators were actually more effective in persuading people to accept the positions being advocated.[21] Other research has found that messages employing low levels of language intensity are actually more persuasive than those using highly intense language.

Making Strategic Decisions about what to Include in a Persuasive Message

To communicator must make a strategic decision as to whether or not it is best to cite opposing arguments. In a one sided message, a claim is made and the communicator attempts to support it. In a two sided message, the same claim can be made but there is at least the acknowledgment the opposing arguments exist, with some attempt to demonstrate why the claim being advocated is superior to those in opposition.

Let us also stress the communicator must make decisions about how discrepant the message is to be from the help beliefs of the receivers. To the extent that at least recognising opposing arguments makes the receiver seem more informed and logical, it may also work to make the communication and the communicator seem less radical and polarised. When this happens, there is less likelihood of simply rejecting the message because it appears to be too discrepant from privately held beliefs.

Revealing your Desire to Persuade

The question of whether it is wise to tell someone we want to change an opinion is complex. If the members of the audience are strongly opposed to our claim, warning them in advance that we intend to persuade them is not effective.[22] A person speaking to a group of radical feminists would be ill advised to state that he or she intended to change their minds about job discrimination against women.

However, if a speaker and an audience are known to be in strong mutual sympathy (e.g., if they are friends), the speaker may be more persuasive by openly admitting the intent. If the audience dislikes the speaker, the speaker will probably do better to keep quiet about this intent. Sometimes, an apparent lack of intent to persuade can become a powerful persuasive tool. When someone is made to believe that the message what he accidentally overheard, such a person tends to be persuaded by it.[23] Political gossip columns often work this way. A government official 'leaks' information to the columnist, who then pretends it is a secret that has been accidentally uncovered. In such a case, our belief that the official had no intent to persuade us can lead us to accept the claim.

Presenting Problems and Solutions

Suppose that a speaker wants to convince people that the problems of mothers on welfare can be solved by government funded Day Care centres. He or she could structure the message in two ways. The speaker might discuss the problems of welfare mothers and then propose day care centres as the solution, or could first discuss the merits day care centres and then explain the problems of welfare mothers.

Research indicates that the first pattern is much more effective in changing attitudes, both immediately following the message and over a period to time.[24] The problem to solution message is more interesting and the solution is more understandable when presented as the answer to a specific problem or need. When the solution is presented first, people may not understand its relevance until they hear about the problem. By that time, they may have lost interest.

Stating Conclusions

A speaker who makes an explicit conclusion creates more attitude change than one who lets the audience deduce which beliefs or actions are favoured.[25] There are some experts who say that listeners will have more lasting change of attitude if they 'participate' in the communication by drawing their own conclusions. But this method is risky for there is no assurance that the listener will arrive at the conclusion the communicator desires. Thus in persuasive communication situations, it is usually wise for the speaker to state all conclusions clearly and specifically.

The Win-Win Strategy

It is often said that advertising is the art of making people buy that you want to sell. In other words it is the art of persuasive communication which is incorporated in the field of marketing. The best way to design the persuasive communication process is that, 'the sponsor, who may be an individual, a for-profit company or a not-for-profit organisation, must first establish the objectives of the communication; then select the appropriate audience for the message and appropriate media through which to reach them and then design (i.e., encode) the message in a manner that is appropriate to the medium and to the audience. The communication strategy should also include on a prior control plan which provides for prompt feedback, to enable the sponsor to make modifications and adjustments to the media and the message if and as needed.'[26]

1. Setting of Objectives

Thus, we see that the primary function of the sponsor is to set primary communication objectives. This encompasses creating awareness of a service, attracting retail patronage, goodwill creation, a favourable image, increasing post purchase satisfaction etc. There might be an amalgamation of two or more objectives into one. This applies equally to commercial, non-profit and other organisations, both for formal and informal communication.

Audience Selection

It must be noted that audience is a set of unique individuals who have their own set of interests, needs, experience, knowledge etc. Thus, an effort to reach the general mass by a common message in simple language is not effective. Instead the sponsor must segment the market into homogeneous groups in terms of some relevant characteristics. Thus these market segments which are homogeneous in nature give the advertisers the opportunity to form advertisements only for the target segment, thereby getting a far better response in return. This also helps them decide the media to which that target segment is maximum exposed, e.g., hostile advertising. Here the advertisement is focused towards the hostile segment which is not ready to accept the sponsor's viewpoint as it is opposed to his own. As a result of such advertising firstly, the people for the product are not affected, secondly people refrained from further hostility to the product, thirdly the new consumers do not join the bandwagon of hostile audience. A study of a 1986 Chevron campaign, directed at hostile audiences indicated that the company's promotional efforts resulted in more positive attitudes as well as increased sales of the firm's gasoline. The campaign's greatest impact in terms of attitude change and increased purchase behaviour was observed among a market segment described as inner directed — those consumers who 'think for themselves'.[27]

Some companies which have a variety of audience require an umbrella communication which consists of an overall communication message directed to diverse audience, for example, SAIL is a company manufacturing steel which is used in different walks of life in different ways. So its advertisement consists of a rough crayon sketch of diverse uses, e.g., anchors in ship, and safety pin in diapers etc., thereby encircling people from all walks of life into its purview.

Some giant organisations go to the extent of maintaining public relation departments etc., to ensure positive communication between the company and the audience. Thus, publicity campaigns focused towards companies' popularity enhancement are becoming increasingly popular.

Fig. 19.2(A). Ad for Youth Target Segment

Fig. 19.2(B). Audience Selection

Media Strategy

Media strategy is the process of selecting the right media to which the target audience are most exposed. While making such a decision the marketer must consider issues like overlapping audiences, characteristics of the audience and effectiveness of their advertisement. The selection of media obviously depends on the type of product. Thus, the marketer must first select a general media before determining the specific media. A multi media usage has become a common trend today, where one prime category carries the main campaign which some supplementary categories support it. Therefore this rule is for certain that for a successful advertising campaign the

Fig. 19.2(C). Audience Selection

marketers should choose that specific media which has the highest probability to reach the target segment, e.g., people dealing in curtain and drapes must advertise in magazine like Inside-Outside, marketers dealing in precious designer jewellery must advertise in magazines like, Filmfare, Femina, Stardust, etc., people selling fitness machines must advertise on television like Abisolators, an abdominal exercise machine is being demonstrated on Asian Television Network.

Each time a new communications technology is developed merchants are quick to devise ways of exploiting the medium for advertising purposes. Advertisers move rapidly to exploit the commercial possibilities of radio, television and cable. Facsimile machines are now used to transmit ads. Sports arenas' and stadiums' electronic scoreboards carry product names in yards-high lettering. The developing technologies of teletext, electronic mail, and interactive cable television are now being used to sell products as well. Research suggests that as a result of these developments, advertising is now less likely to contain meaningful product information, and more likely to be intermingled with other kinds of messages (Sepstrup 1986). Consumers, as the targets of these increasingly complex promotional strategies, must become much more aware of the persuasive nature of advertising.

There are two major factors which must be considered while selecting media strategy:

(i) Overlapping Audiences

There are a number of media vehicles which have overlapping audience due to similar features and format. So the marketers putting their ads in such media, simultaneously or sequentially, which tend to achieve reach (i.e., a heterogeneous group is exposed to it) and frequency (i.e., the number of times a person is exposed to it). Thus, effective reach is a minimum of three confirmed vehicle exposures to an individual member of a target group over an agreed upon time period. The effective reach threshold suggests that 45% of the target group should be reacted over the agreed upon time period.[28]

(ii) Characteristics of the Audience

A wise marketer makes a balanced assessment of the audience characteristic and product characteristic and only then decides the best media category to be used. There are a number of ways of making a data base of various audience characteristics which in turn assists in precision targeting wherein the marketers cater to highly refined target segment. Some methods are:

(*a*) *Direct Marketing:* Herein different media like mail, television, telephone etc. are used for the purpose of soliciting a direct response from the consumer, **e.g.**, on the release of Vipin Honda's directoral debut film *'Uff Yeh Mohabbat'*, they offered free ticket to anyone who got the advertisement clipping from Lucknow Times Selection of Times of India, Lucknow Edition with a small coupon to be filled which provided the data base and response which Times of India required.

(*b*) *Mail Order Catalogues:* Here catalogues are send to the prospective consumers. Its a prime example of direct marketing, e.g., Burlington Home Shopping catalogue is sent to certain niched customers. In order to building up 'relationship marketing' these catalogues at times contain certain articles like fabric manufacturing process, recipes etc., too.

(*c*) *Electronic Shopping:* This too is a facet of direct marketing. Here the audience data base is received from responses of the ads on the home shopping TV channels, e.g., TSN Tele Shopping Network is a fine example from the Indian scenario. This method is a piece of cake, as busy people prefer this kind of relaxed and laid back avenue of shopping.

Message Strategies

Message is defined as the idea that the sender wishes to convey to the receiver. It is of prime importance for the sender to know his mind and the audience characteristic. Only then will he be able to achieve the precise understanding with the receiver.

In order to formulate a persuasive message one should initiate with an appeal to the needs and interests of the audience and with an appeal relevant to the marketer's own needs, *e.g.*, 'contact your favourite dealer as soon as possible, offer open only till stock lasts' or 'Dial immediately on the number next to the flag of your country.'

Thus, an ad which is bracketed by action on the part of the audience is highly persuasive and achieves high response. Photographs, illustrations etc. add on to the meaning and persuasibility of the message. One study showed that when verbal information was low in imagery, the inclusion of pictures that provided examples increased recall of the verbal information on both an immediate post test and a delayed post test. However, when the verbal information was high in imagery, the addition of pictures did not increase subjects' ability to recall the verbal information contained in the ad.[29]

Fig. 19.3. High Imagery Presentation

A number of studies have tried to manipulate the proportions of illustration and body copy used in print ads to determine the impact on recall and persuasion, but the findings have been fragmented and inconclusive. For example, one study showed that in some instances, body copy alone induced more favourable consumer evaluations than body copy used in conjunction with a picture; in other instances the reverse was true.[30] Another study found that all copy print ads were rated as more utilitarian/rational, and all visual print ads were rated as more familiar.[31] Other researchers found that the attractiveness of the picture in the print ad influenced brand attitudes.[32] Although the evidence is somewhat inconclusive as to what makes a print ad memorable or persuasive, therefore, creativity and successful positioning are essential components in persuasive communications. Marketers are beginning to use high imagery copy with creative typography to evoke favourable moods. Fig. 19.3 is an example of high imagery copy underscored by creative typography makes a thrilling sensation to consumers for a uninteresting product which lack in beauty-shoes.

Method of Presentation

The method in which an ad is presented has a lot to do with the persuasiveness of the ad. The semantics (i.e., meaning of words used and its inferences) alone does not constitute a persuasive message, its syntax (sentence structure) holds importance at part. It has been seen that simple syntax sentences have higher recall value than complex ones, for example, Ruffles Chips with simple message like 'Get your own bag' is recalled faster than the long ad of Hello Chips. Different methods of presentation have different effect. For example, people are much more influenced by word-of-mouth communications than they are by a printed format. However, research indicates that this effect is reduced or eliminated when a prior impression of the target brand is available from memory.[33]

Researchers study not only the semantics of ad messages (i.e., the meanings of the words used and resulting inferences) but also the syntax (the sentence

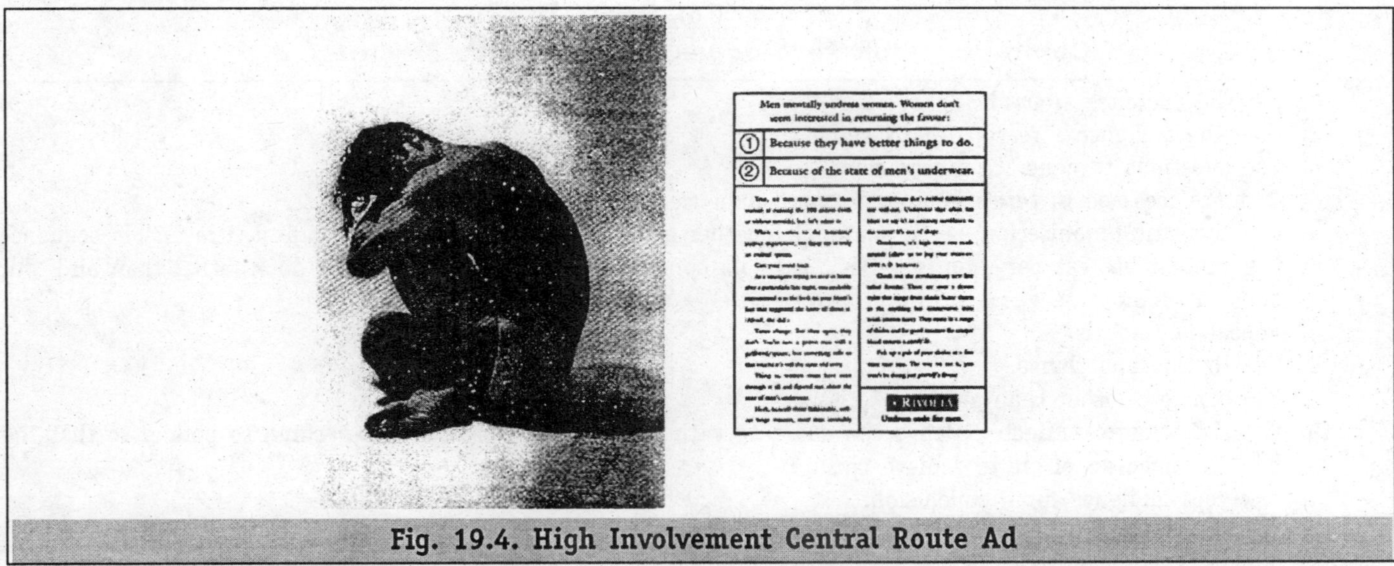

Fig. 19.4. High Involvement Central Route Ad

structure). One study found that ads using simple syntax produced greater levels of recall, regardless of the strength of the argument, than ads of greater complexity.[34] A study designed to explore the differences between persuasive and non-persuasive TV commercials found that highly persuasive commercials tended to have stronger linkages between the visuals in the advertising.[35] The findings concluded that this 'wholeness' provided a more complete or unified experience for the consumer.

Message and Involvement Theory

The vital theory we need to discuss here is the involvement theory. According to this theory statements individuals devote active cognitive process in evaluating high involvement products thus marketers should use central route persuasion, i.e., use strong arguments and informative ads while products involving low involvement make the audience focus on the peripheral message cues thus marketers must use peripheral route and emphasise on background scenery, music etc. Fig. 19.4 is an example of central route ad and Fig. 19.5 is a peripheral route ad.

Fig. 19.5. Low Involvement Peripheral Route Ad

Despite the fact that many marketers have found that action closings tend to be more effective in encouraging consumer response, researchers have also found that, for high-involvement audiences, open-ended advertisements (that is, ads that do not draw explicit conclusions) are more effective in terms of creating positive brand attitudes and purchase intentions.[36] The results from another study found that peripheral advertising cues can affect brand choice, but the extent of this influence depends on the particular brand-relevant information available at the time of choice.[37] Table 19.2 lists 12 techniques summarised from the literature on communications to make a message more memorable and persuasive.[38]

TABLE 19.2

Communication Techniques for Persuasive Advertising

1. Get the audience aroused.
2. Give the audience a reason for listening.
3. Use questions to generate involvement.
4. Cast the message in terms familiar to your audience and build on points of interest.
5. Use thematic organisation — tie material together by a theme and present in a logical, irreversible sequence.
6. Use subordinate category words — that is, more concrete, specific terms (Example: duck rather than bird, duck being a subordinate word to bird.)
7. Repeat key points.
8. Use rhythm and rhyme.
9. Use concrete rather than abstract terms.
10. Use the Zeigarnik effect — leave the audience with an incomplete message, something to ponder so that they have to make an effort to achieve closure.
11. Ask your audience for a conclusion.
12. Tell the audience the implications of their conclusion.

Source : James MacLachian, 'Making a Message Memorable and Persuasive,' *Journal of Advertising Research,* 23 December 1983-January 1984). pp. 51-59.

Message framing is an important factor. Positively framed messages reface more persuasive in low involvement situation and *vice versa.* It has been found that inclusion of quantitative information in the message stimulates people to rely on the spokesperson etc., while non-quantitative information stimulates individual to process the context of the message centrally, e.g., in the ad of Tata Cafe, here is a lot of quantitative information delivery by Renuka Shahane thereby leading the audience to relay on the spokesperson.

Studies which examined message framing effects on persuasion have had mixed results. Some studies show that positively-framed messages (those which specify benefits to be gained by using a product) are more persuasive than negatively-framed messages (which specify benefits last by not using a product); other studies have found the reverse to be true. One study found a tentative explanation for these mixed results by factoring in the level of involvement (i.e., cognitive processing). It found that positively-framed messages are more persuasive when there is little emphasis on detailed processing (low-involvement situations), and negatively-framed messages more persuasive when detailed processing is required (high involvement situations).[39]

Researchers also have found that the presentation of messages that are consistent with the consumers' self image triggers the cognitive processing of information.[40] Other studies have found that the inclusion of quantitative information in the message stimulates people to rely on a peripheral cue, such as the spokesperson, while non-quantitative information stimulates individuals to process the content of the message cognitively (centrally).[41]

Some researchers tend to oversimplify the two-route approach by recommending the exclusive use of either emotional (i.e., right-brain, peripheral route) or rational (left brain, central route) message appeals. The distinction between these two approaches is readily seen in advertisements that make heavy use of emotional, symbolic cues in their formats, as opposed to straightforward, factual presentations. For example, De Beer's Diamond company's ad has an ad where a man gives an exquisite ring to his wife and at that very moment his son calls up to confirm, thereby arousing a family emotion among audience. Fig. 19.6 is also an ad to the same effect arousing emotions and feelings of closeness.

However, some researchers argue that it is not possible to deliver either a completely rational or a completely emotional message, and suggest that makers incorporate both routes to persuasion in their advertisements. These researchers believe that ads incorporating both factual, objective product messages (the central route) and highly visual symbolic cues that support the product claim (the peripheral route) are likely to be more persuasive than ads that use either the central or peripheral route exclusively.[42]

But today, the marketers use both the emotional and factual facets in the ad thereby forming a more persuasive ad, e.g., the latest Cielo ad has a lady describing the refreshing change in her life since she bought the car, side by side facts are displayed in small prints through the time span of the ad.

Comparative advertising is another strategy that the marketers use. Here the ad proclaims the superiority of the product over explicit and implied complicity and implied competitors' either on overall basis or selective attributes, e.g., Fig. 19.7. The advertisement of Dove is a fine example of this strategy.

It has been found that comparative advertising has a positive effect on challenger brands, e.g., The 'Captain Cook' 'Namak' has challenged in a implied manner, 'Tata Namak' is its comparative ad by showing its free flow quality as compared to moisture laden salt of 'Tata' in order to compete with the 'Tata Namak' ad stating it to be 'Desh Ka Namak'. At times, two companies bring out ads for their product comparing the mutual characteristic, e.g., Pepsi states 'Nothing official about it' and Coca Cola on the other hand says 'The Official Drink.'

Order effect is a prerequisite for persuasive communication. Researches have shown that the order of the appearance of the ad is vital. Some says that ads shown first have a stronger effect due to primacy effect while the others say that ads shown last are more lasting due to recency. On T.V. the commercial shown first and last retain for a longer time that the ones in middle slot. Hence, the order is highly critical in nature.

ADVERTISING APPEALS

There are two major types of appeals. They are: Emotional and Rational appeals.

Emotional Appeal relates to the customers' social and/or psychological needs for purchasing a product or service. This appeal is so effective because many consumers' motives for purchase decisions are emotional. Many advertisers believe an emotional appeal to work better at selling brands that do not differ markedly from competing brands. Within the emotional appeal, there are two subsets - the personal and the social.

Rational Appeals focus on the consumer's practical, functional, or utilitarian need for the product or service and emphasize features of a product or service and/ or benefits or reasons for owning or using a particular brand. Print media is well-suited for rational appeals. Such appeals are normally used by business-to-business

Fig. 19.6. Use of Emotion in Ad

Or, use Dove.

Whether you wash your face or take a bath, Dove gives your skin all the comprehensive routine it may need. You see, Dove is not a soap. It is a gentle blend of 1/4 moisturising cream and mild cleansing ingredients. It cleanses thoroughly, yet helps the skin retain its moisture. With soap your skin feels dry after every bath, but with Dove, it feels soft and smooth all over, all through the year. So you don't have to use a moisturiser. The silky feeling you are left with is proof that Dove is at work. Try Dove, and discover the difference yourself.

Dove does not dry your skin like soap can.

Fig. 19.7. Comparative Ad

" One second we were having the time of our lives. The next, everything collapsed around us. "

Saffola

Fig. 19.8. Use of Fear Appeal

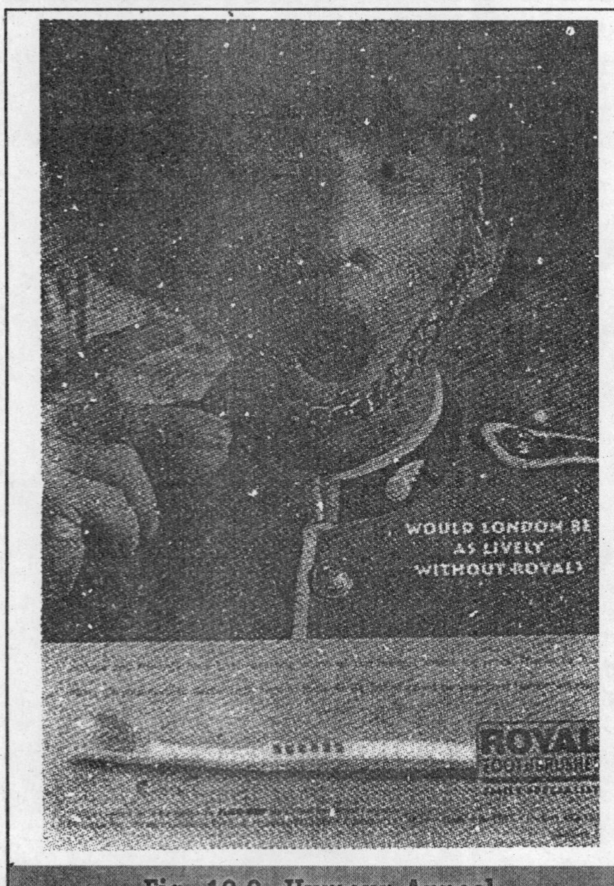

Fig. 19.9. Humour Appeal

Fig. 19.10. Humour Appeal

Fig. 19.11. Abrasive Appeal

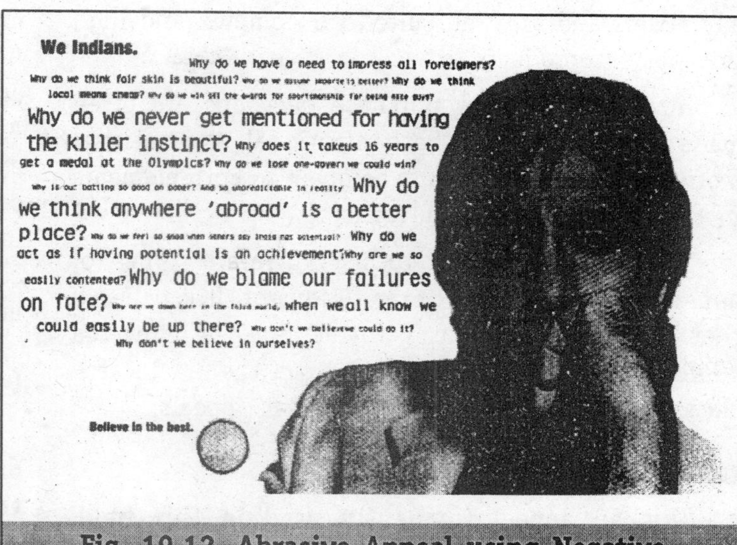

Fig. 19.12. Abrasive Appeal using Negative Conotations

19.Fig. 13. Sex Appeal

Fig. 19.14. Sex Appeal

advertisers and are well-suited for complex and high involvement products.

However, consumer purchase decisions are often made on the basis of both emotional and rational motives, and attention must be given to both elements in developing effective advertising.

The marketers have to use different types of appeals to reach different target segment. It is believed that logical appeal is used to en rope the educated while emotional bait is used to attract the uneducated class. Let us discuss a few emotional appeals.

(a) Fear Appeal

This an appeal frequently used in this field. Researchers have found an inverse relationship between intensity of fear appeal and their ability to persuade. So strong fear appeal leads to less effectiveness and *vice versa*. For example, 'Cigarette Smoking is injurious to health' does not make the audience to give up smoking instead leads to point blank denial of aftermath. Some other researchers have discovered that fear appeal and persuasion are directly related if the idea is of controlling the danger and not fear e.g., The Saffola Ad (Fig. 19.8) has the same appeal. If the ad is focussed towards prevention against social embarrassment as compared to prevention against the crippling disease, then it is a sure short success, for example the Revlon Deodorant ad is focussed towards the preventing social embarresment by eradicating bad body odour. Thus, it is far more appealing.

(b) Humour Appeal

This is a very delicate instrument which should be used cautiously to avoid any backfire. Some believe that humour increases the persuasiveness while the other end believes that humour in the ad might make their product an object of ridicule. Evidences have shown that humour appeal in ad is more acceptable by the younger, upscale, educated, professionals, e.g., Kwality Wall's Feast ad has a humour appeal where the guy asks the girl on the busstand when her parents got married and the girl replies that she was not taken there and takes a huge bite from the guys chocobar feast. Thus, this appeal should be administered to a target market only. Some researches on the behaviour effect or humorous propaganda shows that relevant humour in an ad increases consumer loyalty but irrelevent humour has a negative impact. A good example to this effect is of Royal Toothbrush and Bigen hair colour. It is estimated that 'Humour Appeal' is used in 30% of all advertisements and are excellent at capturing attention. Such appeals comparatively score high in recall tests, however, it is important that they should be related directly to customer benefit or else, the joke can overpower the message.

(c) Agony Appeal

Quite often we one time or another have been driven off by so-called agony advertisements on our television sets. These commercials depict in diagrammatic details the internal and intestinal effects of indigestion, heat burn, clogged nose, hammer induced headache, sprain, stiff joints and many more ailments. Recall the commercials of Hajmola, Aciguard, Pudin Hara, Iodex, Amritanjan etc. to name a few. The complaints are legitimised by advertisements with which they spontaneously identify and persuade the consumers to purchase the product. Such advertisements posses tremendous persuassive power as they are directed towards the specific segment of the consumers that suffers from ailments that are not visible and therefore elicit no sympathy from other members of the society. This appeal is widely used by the pharmaceutical companies in which detailed information regarding the ailment and the effect of the drug on it are shown, e.g., Vicks Sinex shows the diagramatic effect of Vicks Vapours on sinus congestion. This type of ad helps the people sympathize towards the sufferer, whose disease is not overt and the sufferer identifies with the ad.

(d) Abrasive Appeal

This is a negative ad where the sentences fade out of memory over time and only the brand name remains, e.g., BPL Ad (Fig. 19.12). The sleeper effect gives a cue that the efficacy of an ad message increases over a period of time, despite the presence of a negative cue. However, this goes with the old dictum of public relations, 'it matters not whether they think well of you or ill of you so long as they remember your name.' Accordingly, the memory of an unpleasant advertisement that antagonises the viewers or listeners will disappear at last, leaving only the brand name along with the persuasive message in the minds of customers.

(e) Sex Appeal

Since time unknown sex advertising has been practised world wide. The sexual themes at first catch the reader's attention, but do not arouse curiosity. The sex factor pulls away the reader's attention from the product or the message and in turn hampers the cognitive process. If the sexual implications in the ad are not relevant to the product they lead to decline in the reader's attention and impression. Ads in which sex is used to draw the attention have a low recall value, while ads in which sex has been used for fantasy fulfilment or product function (e.g., for bra, panties etc.) then the recall value of the product goes up.

The men and the fairer sex respond differently to sexual appeal. For women it has been found that romantic ads are sexy, e.g., Monti Carlo ad featuring a couple drifting on boat, candle light dinner with seducing looks is considered sexy. Women can recall the product of erotic ads so the ad of cosmopolitan shows a bed, an office and states the best everywhere while the male are found to forget brand name of erotic ad, thus playboy magazine has no erotic ads. Thus, the companies should use sex with utmost care and finesse.

Research Results have shown that sex and nudity do increase attention. They are rated as being more interesting and often lead to strong feelings about the advertisement but brand recall is lower. Sex appeals often interfere with message comprehension.

While using sex appeals effectively, be aware of differences in the international arena. Sex Appeals should be an integral part of the product and utilize a variety of models in terms of age, size, ethnicity and gender. It is advisable that one should consider using "regular person" models. Be careful sex does not overpower advertisement and consider shifting to more sensuality.

Audience Participation

Audience participation is the last block in persuasive communication strategy. The provision for feedback transforms the communication from one way to two way communication. Feedback is of vital nature to the receiver because it enables him to participate in the process, and even to the sender who is able to judge whether the information has been received in the right perspective.

Thus, it is a challenge for marketers to involve the audience in the process. Incomplete ads are an important example to this effect, for example, BPL ad where Mr. Amitabh Bacchan is at the Piccadilly Station of London forgets the name of the company and just states that the name of the company starts with B. Thus, audience participation is incorporated.

In the TVC of Coca Cola produced by McCann Erickson displays with a Coca-Cola factory in the backdrop, Aamir Khan talks about his reasons for still endorsing the brand in this ad. He takes a round of the Coca-Cola factory, and explains how this 'Thanda' drink goes through many quality checks and also about the precautions that are taken in the process of making this carbonated drink. The TVC ends with Aamir inviting customers to come and visit any of the Coca-Cola factories if they are still in doubt. Unable to resist any more, Aamir picks up a bottle, opens it and takes a sip as he says, 'Jab bhi man kare, befikar ho kar peejiye'.

In the wake of the pesticide controversy, if Pepsi brought its CEO Rajeev Bakshi out of the boardroom to talk to consumers, Coke is not far behind either. But, for Coke, Aamir Khan does the trick and that's where it scores a point over Pepsi. When it comes to screen presence and convincing power, Aamir being Aamir takes the lead over Bakshi. That's celeb power for you.

The power idea is clearly to damage control measure and establishes how safe Coke is. The single-minded focus of the ad ensures that Khan does his job effectively. Simple yet powerful, this one might not be remembered for its storyline, but for its convincing power! In all the above TVC's the persuasive technique is employed very intelligently and effectively.

Celebrity endorsements: An Effective Tool for Persuassion?

Celebrity endorsements pull in hundreds of crores every year, and are widely preferred by marketers to promote their products. Using celebrities for endorsing brands has become a trend for building the brands as well as the company's image. Who are these celebrities? And what does celebrity endorsement mean? A celebrity is a person who is well recognized by the public, and has a reputation for his/her expertise in his/her chosen silos. Sports persons and film stars fit the bill perfectly. Promotion of a company's products through these celebrities is termed as celebrity endorsement. The company makes use of the celebrity's characteristics and qualities to establish an analogy with the products specialties with an aim to position them in the minds of the target consumers. Celebrity endorsement, thus, is one of the powerful tools adopted by companies/ marketers to consolidate their brand(s) in the crowded marketplace.

Consumers prefer to own a brand that has a good reputation, and when someone like a famous film star or a sport star is associated with that particular brand, it is obvious that the consumers will get attracted to it, because the consumer wants to maintain some status, and feels that using a brand promoted by a star can satisfy that longing.

Why Celebrities

There is a myth that celebrity endorsement is used to give a brand advantage over its competitors. However, choosing a celebrity for this purpose requires considerable amount of calculations. There should be something common between the brand and the celebrity promoting it. Let us come to the main question as to why marketers use celebrities to promote their brands. Is there a real need to associate a celebrity with the product? Yes seems to be the resounding answer. This is because a company needs to create awareness and interest in the consumers mind when it unveils a new brand or product. To be successful, brands need to convince consumers that they carry a different image and value from other competing products. In other words, brands have to show their true personality to the potential consumer(s).

An effective way to do this is through celebrity endorsements. As MG Parmeswaran, executive director of FCB Ulka says, "As advertising professionals, we recommend celebrity endorsements when the case is justified. There are many cases where you need to use the celebrity to break out of a category clutter. At times, celebrity endorsement is used to build credibility to the brand offer." People always wish to see their favorite stars and marketers, and advertisers are quick to capitalize on such ideas. Endorsement of a product/ service by a celebrity gives out the message that it is as authentic and credible as the celebrity is. The urge that people have of enjoying the same recognition and status like their favourite stars is often the main reason for the increasing use of celebrities for products/ services endorsement.

JWT India saw the ad for Kurkure Xtreme as the perfect opportunity for the brand to take a leap. The FritoLay Division of PepsiCo India Holdings Pvt. Ltd's television ad for the Xtreme variant of its snack brand Kurkure has been created by advertising agency JWT India Ltd. The ad features brand ambassador Juhi Chawla jumping off rooftops and performing other stunts to reach the Kurkure delivery van. In the ad, the actor's sudden ability to perform these stunts has been powered by one bite of the snack's flavours, which has her craving for more-lending itself to the tag line: "Seriously thoda zyada". Creative director Sonia Bhatnagar takes us behind the frames of the advertisement.

She explains "Since this product was meant to be an in-and-out flavour launch (would be in the market for two to three months), the client obviously wanted us to make sure the extreme flavours flew off the shelf. They wanted us to create a strong impact during the short stay of Xtreme, so that it stays in the mind of consumers. They gave us a lot of freedom to do what we thought was best, while staying true to the full-on taste the "electric nimbu" and "risky chilli" flavours promised.We saw this as the perfect opportunity for the brand to take a leap, literally. So, the concept we went with was of a family on holiday in Jodhpur, where the housewife, Juhi, takes a leap off the fort in true extreme-sport style. I think the rest of it just flew as we took off on the name Xtreme, which is exactly what our clients wanted us to convey. Everything was unique about the shoot. Jodhpur had never seen anything like it. All of Jodhpur was on holiday that day and we had the toughest time taking the simplest of shots. The film was directed by Abhijit Chaudhary of Black Magic Productions". Isn't the concept of jumping off buildings to reach the product delivery van similar to rival CocaCola India Inc.'s brand Thums Up ad featuring actor Akshay Kumar?

See, the whole idea is to do a take on all things extreme. That includes James Bond, Jackie Chan,

Bollywood action movies, the works. If Akshay Kumar is a part of that world, it will seem like we're taking off on him, too. But that's hardly the intention. The differentiating factor is obviously Juhi! Nobody's ever seen her jump off a chair, let alone a fort wall, over a cannon. Good old, smiley, bubbly, housewifey Juhi goes extreme... just for these flavour.

For Nestle Munch, JWT created an interesting TVC. Actor Rani Mukherjee sings of the country of crunch. A building collapse, a cricket shot, a military salute-all end in a crunch, and a jingle: "Yeh desh hai crunchy, crunchy sa".

A montage of visuals of the LIC man-shielding children from sudden rain, securing belts on a merry-go-round, giving helmets to the elderly. All showcasing the promise of protection designed by RK Swamy of BBDO.

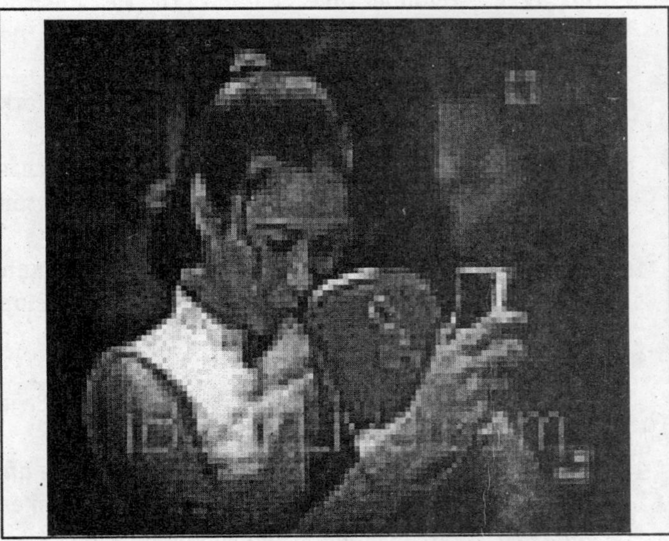

For Surf Excel Quick Wash. Agency: Lowe. A boy who has got his clothes dirty disarms his mother, sympathising with her plight, playing doctor and offering his prescription: Use the Surf Excel sixer pack for six days.

For Pond's Age Miracle, Agency Ogilvy & Mather created a TVC depicted below. Red tick marks float around women in a restaurant, a couple in a corridor, a pregnant woman exercising. Voice-over: About 99.9% of the women who took on the challenge are satisfied.

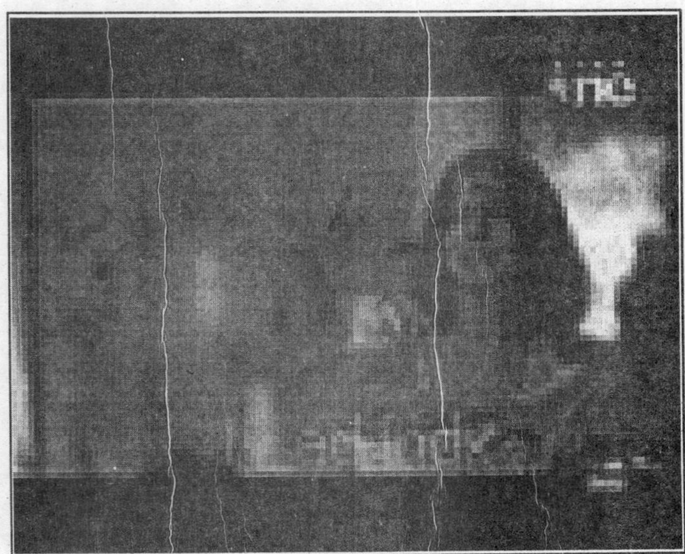

Bates India uses actor Shah Rukh Khan declares Nokia a friend of 10 years' standing because it has helped him share some of the special moments of his life with loved ones.

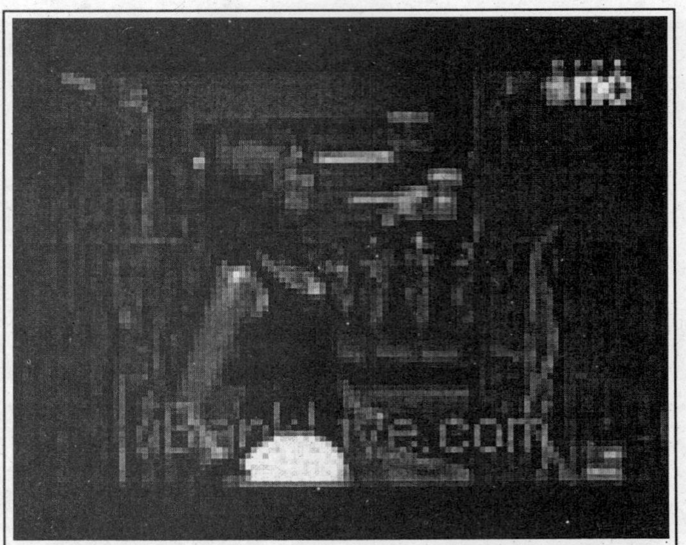

For Nokia 1208 Bates India once again uses an elderly lady successfully plays saviour when battery failure leaves a bus stranded at night. Her "torch" cellphone helps her call for a new battery and provides light.

Actor Bipasha Basu, riding a red scooter, pulls the plug on an assembly line of pink "girlie" scooters-today's girls, she declares, are neither girlie nor delicate for Kinetic SYM Flyte created by Ambience Publicis.

Thus, a complete understanding of the strategy is a win-win situation for both the advertisers and the audience. Hence, persuasive communication is the Magic Potion.

REFERENCES

1. Michael Burgoon, Frank G. Hunsaker, Edwin J. Dawson, *Human Communication,* Sage Publications, New Delhi, 1994, p. 175.
2. Irvin L. Janis, Carl I. Hovland and Others, *Personality and Persuasiveness,* Yale University Press, New Haven, Feb. 1962, p. 1.
3. *Ibid.,* p. 4.
4. C.I. Hovland, I.L. Janis and H.H. Kelly, *Communication and Persuasion,* Yale University Press, New Haven, 1953, pp. 189-195.
5. T. M. Newcomb, *Personality and Social Change,* Dryden Press, New York, 1943, pp. 9-27.
6. I.L. Janis and S. Feshbach, 'Personality Differences Associated with Responsiveness for Fear Arousing Communication', *Journal of Personality,* 1954, Vol. 23, pp. 154-166.
7. D. Katz, C. McClintock and I. Sarnoff, 'The Measurement of Ego Defense as Related to Attitude Change,' *Journal of Personality*, 1978, Vol. 25, pp. 265-474.
8. S. E. Asch, *Social Psychology,* Prentice Hall, New York, 1952, pp. 12, 143, 245.
9. This part has been adopted and condensed from Michael Burgoon, Frank G. Hunsaker and Edwin J. Dawson, *op.cit.,* pp. 175-247.
10. J.K. Burgoon, M. Burgoon, G. R. Miller and M.Sunna Frank, 'Learning Theory Approaches to Persuasion,' *Human Communication Research,* 1981, Vol. 7., pp. 161-175.
11. D. J. O' Keefe, *Persuasion, Theory and Research,* Sage, 1990.
12. C.W. Sherif, M. Sherif and R.E. Nebergall, *Attitude and Attitude Change: The Social Judgment — Involvement Approach,* W. B. Saunders, Philadelphia, 1965.

13. R.E. Petty and J.R. Cacioppo, *Communication and Persuasion: Central and Peripheral Routes to Attitude Change,* Springer, New York, 1986.
14. M. Burgoon, Social Influence in H. Gales and P. Robinson [Eds.], Handbook of Languages and Social Psychology, John Wiley, London, 1989, pp. 51-72 and M. Burgoon and G. R. Miller, *An Expectancy Interpretation of Language and Persuasion,* in H. Giles and R. St. Clair [Eds.], *Recent Advances in Language, Communication, and Social Psychology,* Lawrence Erlbaum, London, 1985, pp. 199-229.
15. S. Toulmin, *The Uses of Argument,* Cambridge University Press, 1959.
16. J.C. McCroskey, *An Introduction to Rhetorical Communication,* Prentice Hall, Englewood Cliffs, N.J., 1968.
17. J.C. McCroskey, 'A Summary of Experimental Research on the Effects of Evidence in Persuasive Communication,' *Quarterly Journal of Speech,* Vol. 55, 1969, pp. 169-176 and The Effects of Evidence as an Inhibitor or Counter Persuasion, *Speech Monographs,* 1970, Vol. 37, pp. 188-194.
18. J.C. Rineard, 'The Empirical Study of Persuasive Effects of Evidence: The Status After Fifty Years of Research,' *Human Communications Research,* Vol. 15, 1988, pp. 3-59.
19. D. J. O' Keefe, *op. cit.,* G. R. Miller, 'Studies in the Use of Fear Appeals, A Summary and Analysis,' *Central States Speech, Journal,* Vol. 14, 1963, pp. 117-125 and K. Witte, 'Putting The Fear Back Into Fear Appeals: The Extended Parallel Model,' *Communication Monographs,* Vol. 59, 1992, pp. 329-349.
20. J.W. Bowers, Some Correlates of Language Intensity, Quarterly Journal of Speech, Vol. 50, 1964, pp. 415-420.
21. W.J. McEwen and B.S. Greenberg, 'The Effects of Message Intensity on Receiver Evaluation of Source, Message and Topic,' *Journal of Communications,* Vol. 20, 1970, pp. 340-350.
22. J. Allyn and L. Festinger, 'The Effectiveness of Unanticipated Persuasive Communication,' *Journal of Abnormal and Social Psychology,* Vol. 62, 1961, pp. 35-40.
23. E. Walster and L. Festinger, 'The Effectiveness of Overheard Persuasive Communications,' *Journal of Abnormal and Social Psychology,* Vol. 65, 1967, pp. 395-402.
24. A.R. Cohen, 'Need for Cognition and Order of Communications as Determinants of Opinion Change,' in C.I. Hovland (Ed.), *The Order of Presentation in Persuasion,* Yale University Press, New Haven, 1957, pp. 102-120.
25. G. Cronkhite, *Persuasion: Speech and Behavioural Change,* Bobbs-Merrill, Indianapolis, 1969.
26. Leon G. Shiffman and Leslie Lazar Kanuk, *Consumer Behaviour,* Prentice Hall of India Pvt. Ltd., New Delhi, 1995, p. 293.
27. Lewis C. Winters, 'Does it Pay to Advertise to Hostile Audiences with Corporate Advertising?' *Journal of Advertising Research,* May-June, 1992, pp. 11-18.
28. George B. Murray and John R.G. Jenkins, 'The Concept of 'Effective Reach' in Advertising,' *Journal of Advertising Research,* May-June 1992, pp. 34-42.
29. H. Rao Unnava and Robert E. Burnkrant, 'An Imagery-Processing View of the Role of Pictures in Print Advertisements,' *Journal of Marketing Research,* Vol. 28, May 1991, pp. 226-31.
30. Jolita Kisielius and Brain Sternthal, 'Detecting and Explaining Vividness Effects in Attitudinal Judgments,' *Journal of Marketing Research,* 21 February 1984, pp. 54-64.
31. Elizabeth C. Hirschman and Michael R. Solomon, 'Utilitarian, Aesthetic, and Familiarity Responses to Verbal Versus Visual Advertisements,' in Thomas C. Kinear, ed., *Advances in Consumer Research,* 11 (Provo, UT: Association for Consumer Research, 1983), pp. 426-31.
32. Yehoshua Tsal, 'Effects of Verbal and Visual Information on Brand Attitudes,' in Elizabeth C. Hirschman and Morris B. Holbrook, Ed., *Advances in Consumer Research* 12 (Provo. UT: Association for Consumer Research, 1984), pp. 265-267.
33. Paul M. Herr, Frank R. Kardes, and John Kim, 'Effects of Word-of-Mouth and Product Attribute Information on Persuasion: An Accessibility Diagnosticity Perspective,' *Journal of Consumer Research* 17, March 1991, pp. 454-62.
34. Tina M. Lowrey, 'The Relation Between Syntactic Complexity and Advertising Persuasiveness,' *Advances in Consumer Research* 19, 1992, pp. 270-74.
35. Charles E. Young and Michael Robinson, 'Visual Connectedness and Persuasion,' *Journal of Advertising Research,* March/April 1992, 51-59.
36. Alan G. Sawyer and Daniel J. Howard, 'Effects of Omitting Conclusions in Advertisements to Involved and Uninvolved Audiences,' *Journal of Marketing Research* 28, November, 1991, pp. 467-74.
37. Paul W. Miniard, Deepak Sirdeshmukh, and Daniel E. Innis, 'Peripheral Persuasion and Brand Choice', *Journal*

of Consumer Research 19, September 1992, pp. 226-39.

38. James MacLachlan, 'Making a Message Memorable and Persuasive,' *Journal of Advertising Research* 23, December 1983, January 1984, 51-59.
39. Durairaj Maheswaran and Joan Meyers-Levy, 'The Influence of Message Framing and Issue Involvement,' *Journal of Marketing Research* 27, August 1990, pp. 361-67.
40. John T. Cacioppo, Richard E. Petty, and Joseph A. Sidera, 'The Effects of a Salient Self-Schema on the Evaluation of Pro Attitudinal Editorials: Top-Down Versus Bottom-Up Message Processing, ' *Journal of Experimental Social Psychology* 18, 1982, pp. 324-38.
41. Richard F. Yalch and Rebecca Elmore-Yalch 'The Effect of Numbers on the Route to Persuasion,' *Journal of Consumer Research* 11, June 1984, pp. 522-27.
42. Shiffman and Kanuk, *op. cit.*, pp. 302-303.

CHAPTER 20

EXHIBITIONS AND TRADE EVENTS

A trade show is an excellent opportunity to meet your target market, build relationships, study competitors and their products, study responses to your products, make sales, generate leads, and, in general, increase product awareness.

The term "exhibition" covers a very wide range of events in the commercial and non-commercial field but they all present rather similar challenges and opportunities to those involved.

Conferences are for discussing and "selling" ideas instead of products and services. However, it has become usual for a conference to incorporate an exhibition, and *vice versa*. This is both from financial considerations and the conviction that these events are mutually supportive.

It is believed that exhibitions or trade fairs began almost 600 years before the birth of Christ. While no precise record is available, 'The book of Ezekiel' (in the Bible) written in 588 BC, contains many references to merchants trading in a "multitude of the kinds of riches with silver, iron, tin and lead". Ezekiel also talks about the city of Tyre which was an important centre of trade and commerce.

There is also a close connection between fairs and religious celebrations and holy days. The word "feria" comes from the Latin meaning "holy day" and the term is still commonly used to describe what we might otherwise refer to as an exhibition or trade fair.

Today, trade shows & exhibitions provide a forum for companies to display and demonstrate their products to potential buyers who have a special interest in buying these products. The compacted time frame and concentrated location of trade shows are cost-effective for exhibiting companies and convenient for buyers.

Since the 1960s, Trade shows and exhibitions are extensively used as prominent part of marketing strategy. Their relative importance is reflected in their promotional expenditures. Larger amounts are spent each year on trade exhibitions than on magazine, radio, and out-door advertising.

The primary role of trade shows in the marketing strategy is that of a selling medium. Depending on the type of product being exhibited, selling activities can involve booking orders or developing leads for future sales. If show regulations permit, they can even involve selling products directly at the exhibit.

Exhibitions provide a natural and nearly perfect platform for the delivery of solutions to the buyers. More and more exhibition organizers are providing learning content, demonstration theaters, and consultative opportunities as important features of their events. More and more exhibiting companies are taking full advantage of these opportunities.

Trade shows also serve as vehicles for advertising and publicity. Exhibits can be very effective three-dimensional ads as well as collection points for names for direct-mail lists. They can also command the attention of the news media, which regularly cover shows in search of stories on new products and new approaches. Participating companies can also accomplish non-promotional marketing objectives at trade shows. Market research data can be collected from show visitors. Competitors' offerings can be evaluated. And contacts can be made with potential suppliers and sales representatives.

In the twenty-first century, exhibitions, trade events and trade fairs have attracted the interest of almost all companies, consumer goods manufacturers and industrial goods manufacturers. Even concept marketers are not left behind. These fairs/shows are now regularly organized on every conceivable aspect, topic, product or idea. They attract a good number of exhibitors and visitors, offering a platform for trade, business enquiries, awareness, consumer education and sales promotion. These trade fairs have the advantage of attracting an active audience that is basically willing to come across the latest products etc., being available in the market. See their live demonstration and comparing it with various other products being offered by other companies. The another advantage to prospective consumers that these trade fair offers is to get a product not only at a cheaper price than the open market but also get it at a discounted price that most of the companies offers in these trade fairs/ shows. Trade fairs also offer a great advantage to manufacturers and producers of their goods. In these trade fairs the companies introduce themselves to new prospects, give live as well as still demonstration of their products, generate excitement about the company on one hand, they are able to motivate their sales force on the other hand.

Some emerging trends for trade fairs indicate that visitors are more interested in benefits of the product offer, solutions and are more focused on business. They are inclined to concentrate on fewer exhibits and increasingly driven by needs and not by freebies and other attractions. In recent years, in some cities these trade shows and events have taken the shape of 'Night Bazars'.

Specialised trade shows and Business-to-business trade shows - exhibitions in the areas of health care, computer products, electronics, advertising specialties, heavy equipment, agriculture, fashions, furniture, and toys -focus on goods and services within an industry or a specialized part of an industry. They are targeted to wholesalers and retailers with the intent of pushing products through the channel of distribution. Most attendees at these shows are actively looking for products and have the authority to buy. Consumer trade shows, like business-to-business expositions, also have an industry focus. They are different that they target the general public and, accordingly, are designed to stimulate end-user demand. The kinds of products exhibited at these open shows include autos, housewares, boats, antiques, and crafts.

Several trade show organizations provide information and assistance to exhibitors and those considering exhibiting. The Center for Exhibition Industry Research is an umbrella organization that represents the entire exhibition and convention field. It sponsors research on the effectiveness and cost-efficiency of trade shows and has a resource center and serves as a referral point for more specialized groups. The International Association of Exhibit Managers is the association of individuals within companies who are responsible for exhibit arrangements. Others, like the Healthcare Convention and Exhibitors Association, concentrate on the organization and promotion of shows for specific industries.

The exhibitors consider is whether his product or service should be presented at horizontal - or vertical-based shows, or both. Horizontal shows are shows with vendors who are selling a broader variety of products or services, and the attendees usually come from a single market segment and are looking for either very specific products or services or a broader variety. Vertical shows are more narrowly focused to just one type of product and market. The advantage of vertical shows is that the attendees are all from a very specific market, and your objectives for the show can be more focused. The disadvantage is that your product or service must fall exactly within the focus for the show, or you won't get the results you want.

Here is an example of these two types of markets: Shows for physical therapists or boating would be vertical, while shows for occupational safety and health services would most likely be horizontal because the attendees would be from all types of markets. There are also variations, with shows that bring in vertical sellers and horizontal buyers and *vice versa*. This is usually apparent when you look at the list of vendors and the list of attendees. Just remember to keep it in mind when making your choices.

Different companies exhibit at various events for differing reasons, but there are seven main objectives:

(i) to meet existing and potential customers;
(ii) to secure the largest possible number of inquiries which can be followed up after the event;
(iii) to publicise the company's name and products(This is a long-term benefit which will assist future business);
(iv) to avoid being conspicuous by absence, thus preventing competitors insinuating that you are no longer in business in the field and your own customers believing it;
(v) to aid market research and long-range planning(Discussions with visitors to the stand and analytical inspection of other exhibitors' stands help in this.);
(vi) to take orders;
(vii) to back up the company's agents or local distributors, or to secure new and better agents or distributors.

Some companies exhibit products or machines on their stand, which they hope to sell during the event, thus covering their costs of participation and avoiding return freight costs. This can be very satisfying in the short term, but the main objective should be to secure inquiries and orders for trial consignments which are likely to lead to continuing business and an increasing degree of market penetration.

TYPES OF EVENTS

Exhibitions have many different names. They may be called a Trade Fair, Salon, Fair, Show, Exhibition, Samples Fair, etc, but the title is not necessarily an indication of the nature of the event. One of the most important differences between these shows is whether or not they are open to the public. Consumer goods events obviously benefit from attracting as many members of the public as possible but specified trade fairs, particularly in the capital goods field, are likely to be much more successful without public admission. In some cases, the organisers compromise with certain days or parts of the day restricted to trade buyers.

The trend in trade fairs throughout the world is towards specialised events of short duration, and the general trade fair has lost its support except for consumer goods and other events primarily of public appeal. Where there is a choice in a particular territory, participation in a specialised event is likely to yield better results than a general exhibition.

Some "international" trade fairs are international in name only. Unless international participation from exhibitors and visitors is substantial, the event is only a national show, and to name it an international trade fair can be misleading. On the other hand, many of the leading international trade fairs in the world started with only a handful of foreign exhibitors and slowly built up to a truly international content.

Most specialised trade fairs now last three to five days only, the idea being that the customers who really want to attend will do so anyway and will benefit from the presence of the top executives from the exhibiting companies, who can afford to be on duty throughout a fair of such short duration. This in turn is better for visiting buyers. A rather similar idea is current at some of the Indian trade fairs where a number of related but different product groups are the subject of trade fairs each lasting only a few days but following in quick succession. This is very convenient for both exhibitors and trade buyers since, in so many instances, interest is not confined to narrow industry categories.

Exhibitions and trade shows provide a temporary forum for sellers of a product category to exhibit and demonstrate their products to prospective buyers. Agricultural shows fulfil a similar function, but are usually biased more towards competitions among livestock breeders and other types of farmer rather than being purely about promoting products.

Some exhibitions exist as marketplaces where buyers and sellers meet; these are called selling exhibitions. Others (Expo Auto or Expo Engineering etc., held oftenly at Pragati Maidan, New Delhi) exist purely as promotional vehicles, with no actual buying and selling taking place at the exhibition (non-selling exhibitions). Some exhibitions are open to the public, while others are business-to-business vehicles.

Considerable controversy exists as to whether exhibitions are cost-effective and which promotional objectives they best address; the area is considerably under-researched by academics, and much of the existing research has been conducted by parties with vested interests who may or may not be entirely unbiased in their findings. Nonetheless, exhibitions are used by most firms at one time or another and therefore merit at least as much consideration and preparation as any other communication tool.

Why Do Trade Shows?

Exhibiting at a trade show offers you one of the best ways to get in front of a lot of customers and prospects in a relatively short amount of time. Trade shows give you the opportunity to not only show your product or describe your service, but also create that all important first impression. According to a Simmons Market Research Bureau study, 91% of respondents ranked trade shows as "extremely useful" as a source for product purchasing information. This was higher than any other source, including on-site visits from reps. Also, nearly half of the respondents had purchased products or services at the trade show.

At a typical national trade show, with 10,000 attendees and 1,000 exhibitors, you can realistically have 200 visitors per day. If you were making sales calls, you could not even approach that number. Granted, you don't always have the opportunity to go into as much detail in your presentation as you would like, but it opens the door for future communications — a door that sometimes is very difficult to get your foot into.

So for most companies, trade shows are worth the effort. In fact, before you decide to nix a show your company has attended for years, think about what that might say to your current customers who expect to see you there. This is especially damaging if your company has been through recent staffing/ management changes, mergers, acquisitions, or other changes your clients may have caught wind of. Your competition will use your absence to their advantage. This doesn't mean you can't ever stop attending a show, but just be sure you think about whom you see there and what your company's absence may lead them to believe.

Exhibitions in the communications mix

Exhibitions and trade fairs are widely regarded as a powerful way for firms to reach a large number of potential customers face-to-face at a cost far below that of calls by salespeople. Exhibitions do, indeed, bring together buyers and sellers under one roof in a way that is unique; it is probably the closest thing most modern businesses have to the mediaeval marketplace, which is so often held up as an example of ideal marketing practice.

Substantial sums of money are devoted to exhibitions. During 1995, £750 million was spent at trade, consumer and agricultural shows in the UK, which was double the amount spent on outdoor and transport advertising (£378 million) and more than the advertising spend in consumer magazines (£533 million) or business directories (£639 million). If private events are included (£266 million), the spend approaches that of the advertising spend on national newspaper advertising (Advertising Association, 1997). On an average, approximately 8 per cent of UK firms' marketing budget is spent on exhibiting on average (Campaign Report, 1992).

Despite the widespread use of exhibitions as promotional tools (for exhibitors) and as sources of up-to-date information about the latest developments (for visitors), relatively little research has been conducted into them. This may be due to the difficulties of obtaining a definitive answer as to whether exhibitions are really an effective way to promote; it may be due to the difficulty of reconciling the aims of exhibitors with the aims of visitors; or it may be due to entrenched attitudes *on* the part of exhibitors, non-exhibitors and exhibition managers. One of the areas in which conflict occurs is in the split between activities that directly relate to personal selling (lead generation, appointment making and closing of sales) and activities that relate to other marketing functions such as public relations, promotion, new product launches and marketing research.

Certainly, attitudes among exhibitors and non-exhibitors can be extremely polarised. There are firms that have no other promotional activity than exhibitions, so strong is their belief in the efficacy of the medium; equally, there are marketers who do not believe that exhibitions serve any useful purpose as a promotional tool.

Exhibitions and trade fairs are concerned with two main areas of marketing communications: activities directly related to making sales, and areas that relate to more general promotional activities. Some exhibitions are intended primarily as selling events, where visitors would expect to be able to buy goods directly from the exhibitors, while other exhibitions (called non-selling exhibitions) exist primarily to show the latest developments in the industry.

Exhibitions occupy a key role in business-to-business marketing, since they allow contact with buyers who otherwise would be seen infrequently due to geographical or time constraints. This is particularly the case with international exhibitions such as those held in Germany, where exhibitions occupy a more important role than in most other countries. In many cases, these exhibitions bring together people who otherwise would not have met at all, and who might not have known of each other's existence.

Since contact at exhibitions is on neutral territory, both parties may feel more relaxed, so that the exhibition allows the relationship between buying company and selling company to develop more fully and often in unexpected directions. Meetings at exhibitions can therefore be important factors in relationship marketing, and certainly exhibitions present opportunities for strengthening personal bonds between buyers and salespeople. Networking opportunities between exhibitors are also commonly available; firms with complementary products may be able to make contact with each other.

Sometimes, exhibitions also allow contact with clients who only order occasionally, but who have strategic importance (for example major construction projects or defence projects).

Exhibitions and PR

As a public relations exercise, exhibitions have a great deal to offer. Although, not everyone who visits an exhibition is planning on making a purchase (in fact, some research shows that buyers are in a minority at most exhibitions), it can be said that almost everyone who visits is interested in the industry exhibiting. For example, not everyone who visits the Boat Show in London each January is about to buy a yacht, but those who are not in the market are probably dreaming about buying a yacht. Many of them will crew for friends at weekends, perhaps will sail dinghies, and may one day be in a position to buy. At the very least, they will be talking to their friends about what they have seen.

There is considerable evidence that exhibitions are most useful to visitors at the information-gathering stage of the decision process rather than at the buying stage. This means that exhibitions should be regarded as a sought communication. The emphasis therefore needs to be on supplying factual information, answering queries and ensuring that the firm's products become part of the consideration set.

Research into exhibitions

As in many other areas of marketing, the bulk of the published research originates in the USA. Although there might be cause for caution when dealing with US research, on the grounds that exhibitions acquire a somewhat different nature in a large country, where comparisons exist with UK research the findings are broadly similar.

Most research into managers' perceptions of trade shows and exhibitions confirms the view that managers see exhibitions in terms of making sales. This is true of both US and UK research: even when managers do not expect to take orders at the shows, they still tend to expect to obtain leads, qualify prospects and open sales. This is particularly apparent in the staffing of stands: managers predominantly staff them with salespeople, even though there is evidence to suggest that visitors do not like this (Tanner and Chonko, 1995).

Shipley, Egan and Wong (1993) identified 13 reasons for exhibiting, of which seven were directly related to selling, with six representing non-selling activities. Table 21.1 shows their ranking of reasons for exhibiting; the mean scores refer to the scores out of 7 given by the respondents.

This research showed that taking sales orders ranked low on the list (although, of course, this depends on the nature of the exhibition itself). This is despite the fact that much of the strategy-orientated research into exhibitions focuses on the level of resources committed to participation (Herbig, O'Hara and Palumbo, 1994; Bonoma, 1983), with the decision being made according to the number of sales leads the show is likely to generate (Kijewski, Yoon and Young, 1992; Cavanaugh, 1976).

Trade fairs and exhibitions tend to be regarded as selling opportunities in much of the literature, particularly in the practitioner textbooks (Waterhouse, 1987; Cotterell, 1992), with an emphasis on the low cost per contact made, as compared to cold calling in the field. The problem with this view of exhibitions is that it does not take account of the strength of the contacts; contacts obtained in the field are likely to be stronger, if only because competitors are not present when the contact is made.

Sharland and Balogh (1996), for example, define effectiveness as the number of sales leads generated, followed up and successfully closed, and efficiency as the comparison between the cost of trade show participation versus other sales and promotion activity. Some rather elderly US research by the Trade Show Bureau estimates the cost of a qualified prospect at a trade show to be $132, compared with $251 per call in the field (Trade Show Bureau, 1988). UK research by the Centre for Leisure and Tourism Studies (1994) showed the UK figures to be £30 per useful contact, compared to £150 for a field call. These figures may not be exactly comparable, since a 'useful contact' is not necessarily a qualified lead, but the general conclusion drawn by the researchers is that exhibition contacts are cheaper than field contacts.

This view of exhibitions as selling tools is certainly borne out by other UK research, managers typically talk about selling and meeting new customers, rarely about the PR value of exhibitions, in fact, in one research study some managers expressed surprise that there could be any other reason for exhibiting (Blythe and Rayner, 1996).

Having said that, Kerin and Cron (1987) found that non-selling activities are considered by some exhibitors to be more important than selling activities. Many firms view exhibitions as an opportunity to enhance the company image, for example, or to carry out some general marketing research - to find out what the competition are offering, for instance. Although it can be argued that the purpose of all marketing activity is, ultimately, to make sales, not all activities relate directly to the personal selling function. Therefore, although the received wisdom (and the prevailing view) is that exhibitions are tools for personal selling, not all exhibitors agree. Table 20.1 shows the importance accorded to various trade show aims by Kerin and Cron's respondents.

TABLE 20.1

UK(n = 124)	*Overseas (n=61)*		*Objective*	
	Mean	***Rank***	***Mean***	***Rank***
Meet new customers	6.02	1	6.11	1
Enhance company image	5.62	2	5.56	2
Interact with customers	5.55	3	5.43	4
Promote existing products	5.49	4	5.51	3
Launch new products	5.11	5	4.79	5
Get competitor intelligence	3.71	6	3.90	6
Get edge on non-exhibitors	3.65	7	3.38	9
Keep up with competitors	3.61	8	3.46	8
Enhance personnel morale	3.30	9	2.82	13
Interact with distributors	3.02	10	3.89	7
General market research	2.92	11	3.10	11
Take sales orders	2.74	12	2.90	12
Meet new distributors	2.15	13	3.20	10

Source: Shipley, D., Egan, C. and Wong, K. S. (1993), 'Dimensions of Trade Show Exhibiting Management', Journal of Marketing Management, Vol. 9, No. 1.

The dissidents may well be right. For example, there is a conflict between the exhibitors' view of exhibitions and the visitors' view. Many visitors do not have any role in purchasing (Gramman, 1993) and in fact the majority has no direct role. Some are students on visits from their universities and colleges, some are competitors who are not themselves exhibiting, some are consultants or others who are trying to make contact with exhibitors in order to sell their own services. They are therefore unlikely to become qualified leads although they might well be 'useful contacts'.

In the US, Bello and Lohtia (1993) report similar findings. Other researchers report visitors complaining of 'too much sales pitch (Chonko, Tanner and McKee, 1994); many visitors are on information-gathering expeditions rather than intending specifically to purchase anything. Moriarty and Spekman (1984) identify trade shows as being most useful to purchasers in the information-gathering and vendor selection stages of the decision-making process. Given this conflict between visitor expectations and exhibitor expectations, it is presumably up to the market-orientated exhibitor to adapt the approach on the stand (Tanner, 1994). Exhibitors really need to ask themselves why the visitors come (Godar, 1992) and in most cases will find that they did not come to be sold to.

It is therefore entirely possible that non-selling aims are more important (or at least more realistic) in exhibiting. The main non-selling activity that firms do report as an aim is enhancing the corporate image; for some this is the most important aim (see Table 21.2). Shipley, Egan and Wong (1993) found that it ranked second for both domestic and overseas exhibitors, and 25 per cent of respondents in a US survey reported 'establishing a presence as their primary goal in exhibiting (Tanner and Chonko, 1995).

This background of dissent about the true value of exhibitions naturally leads some exhibitors to question whether there is a value at all, and of course some exhibitors have moved away from exhibitions and towards road shows or other means of promotion or lead generation (Couretas, 1984; Industrial Marketing, 1979). Equally, there is dissent among academics as to the value of exhibitions. Sashi and Perretty (1992) express doubts about the overall usefulness of trade shows, Bonoma (1983) is critical of them, yet Gopalakrishna et al. (1995) are of the opinion that trade shows are effective. Not unnaturally, the exhibition industry itself reports that exhibitions are very effective in generating sales leads and other benefits (Trade Show Bureau, 1988; Exhibition Industry Federation, 1989).

TABLE 20.2
Importance of trade show aims.

Aim	*Mean score (out of 10)*	*Standard deviation*
Identify new prospects	5.08	1.521
Servicing current customers	4.69	1.956
Introduce new products	5.14	1.695
Selling at the show	2.79	2.294
Enhancing corporate image	5.32	1.384
New product testing	2.17	1.955
Enhancing corporate morale	3.75	1.816
Getting competitive information	4.94	1.392

(*Source:* Kerin and Cron, 1987).

Planning an exhibition

Although exhibitions are expensive activities, many firms do not put sufficient time and effort into planning them. In some cases this is because the management believes that the exhibition is merely a flag-waving exercise and does not expect to get anything tangible from it; in other cases the exhibition is a one-off or infrequent activity and thus imposes an extra burden on the marketing team which disrupts their usual routine.

In fact, a properly planned and executed exhibition is likely to take up six months or more in total, both in the preparation beforehand and in the follow-up activities afterwards. The first stage is to decide what the objectives of the exhibition are; this goes beyond merely deciding what the reasons are for exhibiting. The objectives need to be realistic (bearing in mind the visitor profile of the exhibition), they need to be achievable (within the context of the firm's resources) and they need to be quantifiable (and mechanisms must be in place to monitor their achievement).

Formal objective setting appears to be influenced by a combination of the importance of the activity and the ease or difficulty of assessment. Most exhibitors state that personal selling is the main aim of exhibiting, or indeed the only aim; most are able to set formal objectives for taking sales orders, but the majority (more than two-thirds) are unable or unwilling to set objectives for interacting with existing customers. If most firms do not set objectives for this activity, clearly even fewer would set objectives for non-selling activities such as enhancing the company image (Blythe, 1997).

The second stage of the planning process is to decide which exhibition to attend. This decision will rest on the following factors:

- The number of available exhibitions to choose from. In some industries, there are only one or two suitable exhibitions each year.
- The visitor profile of the exhibition. Most exhibition organisers will provide this information based on the previous year's attendance. Obviously, information from this source will need to be treated with some circumspection; exhibition organisers are unlikely to give a negative picture.
- The cost of exhibiting.
- The availability of suitable space in a good location.
- The timing of the exhibition relative to the firm's business cycle and other communication projects.
- The profile of exhibitors (i.e., which competitors will be exhibiting and which will not).
- The prestige level of the exhibition. It would be hard to imagine a British car manufacturer not exhibiting at the London Motor Show, for example.

The third stage is to plan the staffing of the exhibition stand. Most managers tend to use the sales force to staff the stands, but this has the disadvantage of taking salespeople off the road. Also, the research evidence shows that most visitors are not actually in a position to buy, but are probably engaged in the information search stage of the buying process. Unless the show is primarily a selling show, therefore it is more productive to staff the stand with technical people, with perhaps one salesperson to handle buyers and collect leads.

The fourth stage is to plan the support promotions around the exhibition. These may include direct mail shots to potential visitors, advertising campaigns in advance of the exhibition, press releases in the trade or consumer press as appropriate, and extra activity by the salesforce both before the exhibition (inviting existing customers to visit the stand) and afterwards (following up new enquiries).

The fifth stage is to decide on the layout of the stand and its contents. Since visitors are usually information gathering, the stand needs to be eye-catching and attractive, but should also convey solid information. Exhibitions are often good places to launch new products, so the firm's latest offerings need to be on the stand. It is often useful to have an area that is away from the public view so that potential customers can discuss their needs with the salesperson in private. Some refreshments can be available and the quiet area can also serve as a rest area for stand staff. Some exhibitors employ temporary staff for the exhibition period; this has the advantage of freeing up the firm's permanent staff and avoiding the disruption of routine that exhibitions often cause, but can mean that the stand is staffed with people who have no long-term commitment to the firm and its success. A way around this is to use the temporary staff for leaflet distribution around the exhibition, to encourage visitors to visit the firm's stand.

The sixth stage of planning is to arrange for follow-up activities after the exhibition. A surprising number of exhibitors fail to do this, with the result that the sales force is unable to follow up on leads generated (Blythe and Rayner, 1996). The main problem with delaying follow-ups is that the prospects will undoubtedly have contacted the firm's competitors as well (since they will almost certainly be at the same exhibition). This may mean that a delay allows the competition to get the business, so sales people should clear their appointment books for about a month after the exhibition in order to have time to do follow-up visits.

The final stage of planning is to arrange the logistics of the exercise. This means ensuring that the equipment, furnishings, promotional material and staff are all transported to the exhibition at the right time and arrive in good condition to make the exhibition a success.

Once the exhibition is over, two activities need to be carried out: first, the follow-up sales activities (where appropriate) or follow-up promotional activities in the case of non-selling show; second, evaluating the success of the show. This can be carried out by formal market research, or by counting the number of leads generated, or the number of visitors to the stand, or whatever other means is appropriate to the objectives. Many exhibitors do not have systems in place for evaluating their activities (Blythe and Rayner, 1996).

It transpired that few companies had any formal evaluation systems in place, even for selling activities; still fewer had systems for tracking non-selling activities. The reasons given for this varied from a belief that the variables are too vague, through to a view that the lead times involved in converting exhibition leads to sales made tracking impossible.

Undoubtedly these difficulties are perfectly valid, and of course for an individual firm in the field it may well be more expensive to find out the answers than it is to live with the problem.

More research is indicated into the reasons for firms not evaluating but some possible reasons have been identified, as follows:

1 The firm lacks the resources to carry out the evaluation.
2 The activity is not important enough to warrant evaluation.
3 The evaluation would be too difficult or expensive.
4 The firm is owner managed and therefore the owner feels able to estimate the effectiveness of the exhibition without formal evaluation (Blythe, 1997).

Non-evaluation of such an expensive, time-consuming and (often) disruptive activity would seem to be perverse, to say the least. It would be hard to imagine a firm conducting; for example, a nationwide billboard campaign without evaluating the results, yet exhibiting represents mere than double the national exp billboard and outdoor advertising.

Managing the exhibition stand

Stand management is straightforward provided that the planning has been carefully carried out and the necessary equipment and staff have arrived. Stands are usually regarded as stressful environments; the noise and crowds at most exhibitions put a strain on those staffing the stand and they will therefore need frequent rest periods.

Designing the layout of the stand is an important part of the process; most exhibitors tend to make the company name the most prominent feature, with brand names and product specifications lower on the list of priorities. This is a reasonable policy if the purpose of the stand is to raise the corporate profile, but in most cases (as research shows) the company is actually aiming to make sales or generate leads. In those circumstances, the visitors' need for solid information will dictate the design and layout of the stand.

In many cases, firms assume that visitors will recognise the company's name and will know what products are available. This is something of a leap of faith; overseas visitors to exhibitions may not be familiar with the firm and its products, and even domestic visitors may be more familiar with brand names than with company names, since that is what is usually given the heaviest promotion.

Exhibitions are tiring for the visitors as well as for the exhibitors, so visitors usually only spend significant time at a few stands. This may be as few as 10 or 12 stands, and this figure does not rise if the exhibition is larger since most visitors only spend one day at an exhibition. This means that large exhibitions with many stands do not lead to an increase in the number of visitors who will see the stand; statistically, large exhibitions actually reduce the chances of particular visitors seeing a particular stand since there are more stands to choose from. The problem of clutter is probably greater at exhibitions than in any other environment, as exhibitors all compete for the visitors' limited attention. For this reason the stand must be designed with the visitors' needs in mind as well as the exhibition's objectives.

For example, if the exhibition objective is to raise corporate awareness, the company name needs to be prominent and a plentiful supply of brochures and leaflets needs to be available. Temporary promotion staff could be employed to hand out leaflets in other parts of the exhibition so that exhibitors who do not visit the stand might be encouraged to do so, or at least go away with some information about the firm. The stand might have some kind of stunt or gimmick to raise awareness; a product demonstration or some spectacular event will attract attention.

On the other hand, if the aim is to make sales or generate leads, the stand should show the brand names prominently, with plenty of information on product benefits. The stand should be staffed with some technical people and some salespeople, and brochures should only be given to visitors who are prepared to leave their names and addresses (some exhibitors will only mail out brochures rather than give them out on the stand). This ensures that follow-up calls can be carried out. Promotions and stunts should be used to collect names and addresses; for example, a free draw for a prize. Special 'exhibition-only' discounts or promotions can be used, and pre-publicity can reflect this in order to get buyers on to the stand. In these circumstances, casual non-buying visitors are less important and might even be actively discouraged - although this may be a short-sighted policy, since most exhibitions are probably not good selling venues and the casual visitors may be the exhibitor's best future customers.

The following is a checklist for organising the stand itself:

- Ensure that displays are easily accessible and are informative.
- Check that stand members have a clear brief.
- Have clear objectives in place and, where possible, set targets for stand members.
- Have an area where prospects can be taken for a private conversation if necessary.
- Ensure an adequate supply of drinking water and other refreshments.
- Establish a rota for stand staff to ensure regular breaks.
- Have a record-keeping system for leads and useful contacts.
- Have a feedback system for visitors' comments.
- Set up some 'fun' activities for stand staff.

It is useful for stand staff to have the opportunity to tour the rest of the exhibition (this also gives them a break) and it is worthwhile to give them objectives for doing this, for example making it the time for gathering information about competitors. Staff will need a break at least every hour; long periods of standing, smiling and relating to large numbers of people are both physically and psychologically exhausting. This requires careful planning to ensure that there are enough suitably qualified people left to staff the stand during breaks.

The main problem concerning stand staff is maintaining their motivation over the period of the show. After a few hours on the stand, the visitors seem to meld into a single mass, most of the enquiries seem like a waste of time and the smile begins to wear a little thin. For this reason it is a good idea to have some activities running that keep stand personnel interested. For example, a competition for collecting business cards, with an appropriate small prize, can motivate staff. Demonstrations throughout the day can help to break the monotony for staff as well as visitors, particularly if the demonstrations are given by stand members in rotation. Again, a small prize could be offered for the best demonstration.

Exhibitions are often held away from the firm's home base and therefore away from staff's homes and families. Sometimes it might be appropriate to allow staff to bring their partners with them, but in most cases this is problematic, so every opportunity should be given for staff to telephone home and it almost goes without saying that their accommodation and meals should be of a high standard- this compensates to a small extent for being away from home, but in any case it reflects better on the firm.

Overall, exhibitions need to be planned in fine detail, with everything leading towards the planned objectives. Choice of exhibition, pre-publicity, follow-up, stand design, staffing and choice of what to exhibit should all be decided with clear objectives in mind.

Alternatives to exhibitions

Because of the cost and commitment attached to exhibiting, not least the disruption to the exhibitors' normal routine, firms are beginning to look for alternative routes for meeting buyers and promoting their products. Since one of the main advantages of exhibitions is the 'neutral territory' aspect, allowing buyers and sellers to discuss matters in a more relaxed way, many exhibitors are moving towards private exhibitions or road shows to exhibit their products.

Private exhibitions

Private exhibitions are sometimes run at venues near to the public exhibition, and coincide with the main event. Typically, such events are held in hotels or small halls where the buyers are invited. The main advantages are as follows:

- The atmosphere is usually more relaxed and less frenetic than that in the main exhibition.
- No competitors are present to distract the visitors.
- The exhibitor has much more control over the environment than would be the case at the public exhibition, where the organisers may impose irksome regulations.
- Superior refreshment and reception facilities are available.
- If the event is held in a hotel, the staff will have access to their rooms and can easily take breaks.
- Sometimes the overall cost is less.

The main drawback of the private event is that visitors will only come to it if they are given advance warning, and even then may decide only to visit the main exhibition. The invitations need to be sent out early enough so that visitors can set time aside for the event, but not so early that they forget about it, and some incentive to make the necessary detour may also need to be in place. It is extremely unlikely that the list of desirable visitors will be complete- one of the main advantages of a public exhibition is that some of the visitors will be unknown to the exhibiting company and a first contact can be made.

Private exhibitions work best in situations where the company has a limited market, where the costs of the main exhibition are high and where a suitable venue is available close to the main site.

Road shows

A road show is a travelling exhibition that takes the product to the buyer rather that the other way round. In some cases these are run in hotels, in other cases trailers or caravans are used. Road shows are useful in cases where large numbers of buyers are concentrated in particular geographical areas, and where many of them would not make the journey to visit a national exhibition. For example, many householders would not take the trouble to visit a national Ideal Homes exhibition, but might be interested in visiting an hotel in their home town to see the latest imported furniture.

Like private exhibitions, road shows allow the exhibitor to control the environment to a large extent. Road shows can be run in conjunction with other firms, which reduces the cost and increases the interest level for the visitors; this can be particularly effective if the firms concerned are complementary rather than competing.

Also like private exhibitions,-the exhibitor is entirely responsible for all the publicity. In the case of a major public exhibition, the organisers and even the firm's competitors will ensure that a certain minimum level of visitors will attend; in the case of a road show, the exhibitor will need to produce considerable advance publicity and even send out specific invitations to individual buyers and prospects. This adds to the risk as well as the cost.

Companha da Electrofera

Each year, around August, the Brazilian city of Porto Alegre hosts Expo Inter, the biggest agricultural show in South America. Ranchers and breeders from Brazil, Argentina, Chile, Uruguay and Paraguay come to show their prize animals and to see the latest offerings from equipment manufacturers.

The world's major manufacturers of tractors and machinery are there: John Deere, Massey-Ferguson, David Brown, Caterpillar. The world's leading producers of fertilisers and pesticides also exhibit there: ICI, Belgo-Mineira, DuPont For the manufacturers, it is an opportunity to show their products to potential customers from a wide range of countries who are all in one place for this one occasion, it reduces traveling time for salespeople in a part of the world where roads *art* not always good and where distances are vast (Brazil alone is as large as Australia or the USA). In some cases, the ranchers themselves are coming from remote parts of the Andes or the Amazon forest, where the main access to the outside world is either by light aircraft or by boat.

For the gauchos who accompany the ranchers, Expo Inter provides an opportunity to travel and see the big city; for these traditional cowboys, the open plains of the pampas are their usual home and many of them rarely sleep inside a building, let alone see a city the size of Porto Alegre. The show gives them the opportunity to meet old friends from other parts of the country, to swap stories and to take part in the competitions and games that form part of the event.

For the ranchers, the show offers a chance to meet the manufacturers, to discuss the merits of the latest equipment and chemical products, and to meet other ranchers from other countries and exchange ideas and techniques. Above all, the show enables people who otherwise rarely see each other to interact and refresh their thinking about agricultural issues.

Walter Pereira is the sales manager for Companha da Electrofera, a firm which manufactures welding equipment, specifically electrodes for welders. Every year he visits Expo Inter, but not to exhibit, nor to buy. His purpose is to visit the major companies who exhibit and to make contacts which he can later follow up in the hope of selling electrodes. Last year he met an old friend, a salesman for an agricultural implement firm, who now works in Argentina, The friend pointed out that virtually all of the ranchers and farmers at the show have their own welding equipment, since they often need to repair machinery themselves - many of them are a long way from repair shops. Up until now Walter's firm had concentrated on selling to industrial users, and through wholesalers, but Walter decided that there might be scope for selling direct, or at least raising the profile of the firm so that the ranchers will specify Electrofera electrodes when ordering from their suppliers.

His boss authorised him to book a stand at this year's Expo Inter. Walter sent out a mailing to the ranchers who visited the show last year and arranged for his salespeople to keep their diaries free for the month following the show. The stand design was subcontracted to a specialist firm from Rio de Janeiro, and the brief specified that the purpose of the exhibition is to raise the corporate profile.

After the exhibition was over, Walter was pleased to find that, apart from general interest displayed in the stand, more than 200 actual sales enquiries resulted. Most of these were from ranchers wanting to order equipment directly, but 11 were from light 'engineering firms based in Uruguay and Chile. Business resuming from these 11 contacts alone is expected to come close to covering the cost of the show, and Walter's boss is happy about authorising attendance next year. The future of Electrofera's attendance at Expo Inter seems assured.

While most writers agree that exhibitions are a powerful communications tool, since no other medium brings so many buyers and sellers together under one roof, there are many voices of dissent.

Much of this dissent arises from the problem of deciding what should be the criteria for deciding whether an exhibition has been successful or not. A firm that sets unrealistic objectives (for example setting sales objectives for a non-selling exhibition) or that fails to plan properly for following up the enquiries generated is likely to blame the exhibition for lack of success. Equally, many managers place blind faith in exhibitions while not actually having any mechanisms in place for evaluating the activity.

Exhibitions require a considerable degree of commitment, not just for the week or so of the exhibition but for the months preceding and following the event. As an activity it is too expensive and too high profile to be left to chance.

Here is a list of the key points:

- Visitor expectations and exhibitor objectives may not complement each other.
- Exhibitions are often seen as information sources by visitors; it is therefore too early in the decision-making process for selling activities to be effective.
- Visitors spend time on relatively few stands.
- Exhibition-related activities will probably span a period of six months.

- Setting objectives is as important in exhibiting as anywhere else; the difficulty lies in measuring the success of the objectives.
- Stunts, gimmicks and demonstrations can help keep staff involved as well as attracting visitors.

In recent years exhibitions and events have grown into a core position of the strategic business plan in the modern organisation. They attract customers and potential business to your company. It is an enabler for pre-qualified prospects and allows you to meet the market face to face. Visitors can touch and feel your products; you can demonstrate them in real-time and answer questions and offer solutions during dialogue. There is no "shotgun" approach in terms of target audience definition, as the vast majority of people who attend exhibitions and events – including suppliers, buyers and procurement influencers, consultants and the media – want to be there in the first place. The fact that visitors are there by choice underscores the power of exhibitions and events, contrary to other means of communications where messages and solutions have to be pushed into the business environment, where decision makers are preoccupied with other business matters.

Exhibitions are effective and deliver measurable value. This extends from personal selling to potential buyers, networking, building prospect databases, confirming relations with existing customers and education. Many visitors, including students, use the exhibition forum as a source for information. Other motivations are demonstrating products and services, building brand awareness and generating media exposure, product launches, corporate image – to mention a few. Exhibitions have the potential to deliver a significant measurable return on investment, including cost per lead and cost per sale. The recall factor due to personal experience also lasts much longer – up to three years – compared to other forms of communication. In many instances exhibitions form the platform for companies to create other marketing opportunities.

PLANNING A TRADE SHOW PARTICIPATION

You've just been put in charge of planning the company's trade show activities for the year and you have no idea where to begin. May be you've attended a trade show before so you have an idea of what they are, but planning and managing the process is a whole other animal. Trade shows are one of the best ways to get in front of your customers and prospects, but how do you decide which shows are best? How do you budget for them, how do you decide what kind of display you need, and how do you make sure you get back more than you put into it?

In this article, we'll take a look at why trade shows are so effective, how to select the best shows, and how to manage the process from start to finish. We'll also provide tips, checklists and web links that will make the job a heck of a lot easier for you. Let's start with why it makes sense to attend trade shows.

Why Do Trade Shows?

So for most companies, trade shows are worth the effort. In fact, before you decide to nix a show your company has attended for years, think about what that might say to your current customers who expect to see you there. This is especially damaging if your company has been through recent staffing/management changes, mergers, acquisitions, or other changes your clients may have caught wind of. Your competition will use your absence to their advantage. This doesn't mean you can't ever stop attending a show, but just be sure you think about whom you see there and what your company's absence may lead them to believe. If necessary, send a post card to your primary clients that you know attend that particular show, and explain your decision to attend show B rather than show A.

Before you even start looking for shows, you need to set your goals. To help you do this, there are four questions you need to ask yourself:

- Why are you exhibiting?
- Are you trying to extend your relationship with existing customers? Introducing a new product? Positioning your company within the market? Generating qualified leads for new sales? Countering a competitor's claim?
- Who is your target audience?
- What is the message you want to convey?
- What do you want to get out of the show?
- Do you want to bring home leads, sell your product/service, or create/improve/build upon your company image?

Selecting the Right Shows

When thinking about travelling to trade shows, your first thought is probably, "Okay, which shows are being held in Pragati Maidan at New Delhi?" However, with a large number trade shows being held every year in every nook and corner of India, nationally or internationally or regionally, you have to make your choices wisely to stretch your marketing dollar, because even though trade shows give you a great bang for the buck, they also cost quite a bit to attend. You and your booth staffers (those are the people who stand in the booth and tell visitors about your business — and hopefully sell your products or services) may not want to go to Lucknow or New Delhi in June or July; may be because of the extensive heat wave; but if that's where the best show is, then that's where you have to send them. But which shows are the best shows?

The first place to start is with your industry's associations. These shows will typically be targeted right to your market, and often are reasonable in cost. You can also check with the trade publications you advertise in (or perhaps should be advertising in). Another resource is, of course, the Web. Go for directories of shows around the world in all types of industries. No list is entirely complete; however, so make sure you go to more than one directory.

Narrowing the List

Unless you have unlimited budgets and resources, once you have a list of potential shows to attend, you need to find out which of those shows are the best. The key to finding the best shows lies in finding the shows that pull in the most decision makers for your industry. For example, you may find that one of the very large shows in your industry brings in a lot of non-decision makers because their union specifies that members get to attend one national conference each year, and that's the show most of them choose.

To find out who attends, ask the show management for a demographic profile of their attendees. Typically, show literature will list only the numbers and general titles of their attendees. Check the titles and purchasing responsibility if that information is available.

Another route to finding the best shows is to contact past attendees if you have the data and basic information of the trade shows held earlier. Have a list of questions ready that will tell you if they are indeed the decision makers, and what value they placed on their time spent in the exhibit hall. You can also check out the exhibitor list from the previous year, and ask those non-competing exhibitors what their impressions of the show were and whether they will be attending again. Or, if possible, go to the show as an attendee and walk the exhibit floor so you'll know if you want to attend it next year. You can get an exhibit-only pass for many shows, so you're not paying the entire fee.

You also need to check with the show managers and ask how they are promoting the show and about their strategy for getting people to the exhibit hall. If it's a new show, there has to be very good promotion to get the traffic you need to make it worthwhile. Often, the conference schedules are set up so that luncheons and socials are held in the exhibit hall to ensure that attendees spend time with vendors. While it is nice to get them into the exhibits (and to your booth), food-related functions aren't always the best arenas for talking with prospects, mainly because it's hard to handle a plate of food, a drink, and your company's literature at the same time. Make sure the schedule allows for plenty of time around those events so attendees can eat and visit your booth. If it doesn't, let the show management know so they can plan better the following year. (Or better yet, if it's a show that you do well at, volunteer for the planning committee, if there is one.)

Once you've nailed down the best shows to attend, you need to figure out what you're going to be standing in front of.

Designing and Caring for Your Booth

There are lots of things to take into consideration when purchasing and designing your booth. These include the size and type of booth; that is, do you need a floor model or tabletop model? And, if you need a floor model, does it need to be a large custom booth to communicate the right corporate image, or will a smaller, more versatile floor model work? There is a huge variety of configurations for booths. You can have a large custom booth built that will require multiple booth spaces and a crew of workers to assemble, or you can opt for a smaller, 10-foot (3-meter) size that can be easily shipped and assembled and disassembled by your booth staffers. Often, these smaller, modular versions can be broken down and used as two tabletop booths as well.

Here are the main things to think about when deciding what type of booth you need:

- What are your functional needs for the booth?
- Do you need seating so you can sit and discuss at length with prospects the great benefits of your services or products? If your product or service is more complicated or technical, this functionality might work well for you.
- Do you need shelving for books or product displays, video capability, or storage?
- Do you need the booth to be easily assembled, disassembled and packed?
- Do you need to be able to reconfigure it for different shows or other uses?
- What kind of traffic flow do you need through your booth?
- What are your aesthetic needs?
- Do you need a display with movement to illustrate your product?
- Does it need to be backlit to illustrate the detail of your product?
- Does your corporate image necessitate a certain "look" that would require curves, sharp/crisp lines, or colors?
- What are your marketing needs?
- What is the message you need to communicate?
- Do you have strong name/logo recognition already?
- Are you a start-up trying to make a name for yourself?

What is your booth budget?

Booth prices vary greatly depending on the size and format. Graphics make a big difference in pricing. Once you've answered these questions, you should have a better idea of the type of booth you need, but the trickiest part of all is determining how the booth will look.

Graphics - Less is More

How do you get your exhibit booth to communicate who you are, what you do, and what your product or service is — all in three seconds? Sounds impossible, but it isn't. Think about the billboards that you pass on the highway. They have the exact same job. They have to tell you who the company is and what it's selling as you zoom past at 75+ kilometers per hour. Some work and some don't. The key is usually in the graphics.

Graphics can communicate a whole host of impressions at a single glance. Think about the billboard with the cows painting the "Eat More Chicken" sign. It's quick, and to the point. Think of your booth in the same way. Trade show attendees are strolling down the aisle looking at hundreds of booths, and unless you've pulled them to your booth with a pre-show promotion, you have to very quickly make them notice you and want to walk over to your booth.

- To make your booth graphics have impact and work for you rather than against you, remember:
- Focus on your product's or service's "benefits" rather than "services."
- Use text very sparingly. You want your booth to look more like a billboard than a brochure.
- Make sure there is a single focal point. Find the essence of your business and make sure everything revolves around that central idea.
- Make sure your name and your positioning statement are very prominent in the design. Remember, if you're a new company, you have to create an impression, and if you're an existing company you have to maintain and build on that impression.

The trends these days in booth graphics are large visual backdrops with only the most concise, key text statements to communicate a message or theme. For example, a company that manufactures scissors or chain saws could use a single, larger-than-life photograph of its product as the background for the booth. The message is immediately obvious, as opposed to the booth that posts several small photos of its products with descriptive text along side them that can only be read at a distance of 2 feet (0.6 m).

Now, if your company is a service-oriented company, you may have more difficulty posting a single image, but think hard about it. You can usually come up with an image or simple montage that can communicate the essence of your business.

Making It Happen

So now you have an idea about the type of booth you want and how you want it to look. How do you make it happen?

First, check with booth vendors in your area. It is important to have local access to your vendor so you can easily go to the showroom to see the products, get ideas, and also be able to easily get support, extra parts, and supplies. Most sales reps will also bring a booth to your office and set it up so you can see it firsthand in your own environment. Many times, booth sales reps are also great resources for ideas for designing your booth. They know what works and how to make your booth effective. Use their experience and advice — it's typically free! Check references of the vendors you speak with. Talk to their customers and see if they are happy with both their booth and the service from the vendor. Or, go to a local trade show and ask some of the show vendors about their booths and whom they work with. You are about to make a potentially large investment, and a little product research is very valuable.

Also, many vendors will store your booth in their warehouse or showroom while it's not in use, for no additional charge. Some will also make sure it's clean and in good shape, and ship it for you when you need it. Make sure you know what they charge for this service (if anything — some vendors provide it free) because those fees can add up.

Usually, the booth vendor can either create your graphics from images you supply, or they may offer services to create the images for you. Here, cost is usually the key difference. If you have an internal graphics staff, you'll save money, but make sure they are in good communication with the vendor graphics staff to ensure that the appropriate sizes and formats are supplied.

Other Things to Keep in Mind

It seems there are always little things you didn't think about that greatly affect how much you love or hate a product you've purchased. Exhibit booths are no exception. First, if you plan on shipping the booth yourself, know the size and weight limitations of your shippers, as well as the conference locations for the trade shows you are attending. One company purchased a large custom 20-foot (6-meter) booth that could be broken down into two 10-foot booths for smaller shows, but didn't take into consideration the weight and size of each of the 10-foot sections. The company shipped a 10-foot section to a small regional show that did not have the equipment in their facility to move a 300-kg) carton into their exhibit hall. The company's sales reps had to quickly and creatively come up with a good reason for why they were standing in an empty booth space!

Second, know the tools you need to put the booth together, as well as the muscle required to do it. This comes into play both from your booth staffing standpoint, and the convention center requirements. Always check to see if the conference facility requires that union labor assemble the booths. Typically, if a facility has an agreement with the labour union, then anything that requires tools to put together or can't be carried without the help of a hand truck or dolly must be put together by union labour.

Third, if you get a portable booth, make sure the cases that your booth ships in are very durable, as well as replaceable. Shippers never give your shipments the tender loving care you would like, and it won't take long for cases to start showing wear. Once this happens, you stand the chance of having your booth damaged, which can be a disaster if it's en route to an important show.

Now you have your booth, and it's time to start getting out there in front of customers. How do you manage this process? Let's go over the nuts and bolts of paperwork, scheduling, and all of the other dirty work of trade shows.

Managing the Show Schedule & Materials

The most tedious part of any job is usually the paperwork, so if you're involved in managing the company's trade shows — be prepared! There are forms to be filled out for everything imaginable.

So, where do you start? First, you'll contact the show management for the shows you've planned to attend, and ask for an exhibitor application. You should do this as soon as you know you are attending the show because many show managers require paperwork to be turned in and deposits to be paid months in advance. Plus, some shows base your booth location on a first-come, first-served basis. Others use a point system based on the number of years you've attended the show. You put down your choices, but if someone with more seniority wants the same spot, then you're out of luck and get the next closest thing.

The Exhibitors Application Form

Fill out the forms completely and carefully. It is usually with the application forms that you have the opportunity to choose the all-important booth location (if not, it will be in the exhibitor package, which we'll talk about next). Usually, you'll list at least three locations in order of preference, and list any competitors you don't want to be near. When choosing the location, think about the traffic flow into the exhibit hall. Select areas toward the front, near food stands, near restrooms, break areas, etc. — any area that will naturally have more traffic. Also, try to get a corner location. A corner gives you twice the visibility and usually costs more, but is worth it. You also have a better opportunity for traffic flow through your booth.

At this point, you also need to know how big of a space you need. If it's a large show and you expect a lot of traffic, then you probably want the most space you can afford. Fortunately, there is a formula the help determine the necessary space, as well as the number of booth staffers to send. It goes like this:

Studies by CEIR have shown that, on average, 16% to 20% of the show attendees will have a special interest in your products/services. Therefore, multiply the number of show attendees by .16 to get your "high interest attendees." Take this number and multiply it by .53 for vertical shows or .37 for horizontal shows, and you get your "potential audience." Divide the potential audience by the total number of show hours and you'll get the number "visitors per hour." Divide the visitors per hour by the number of presentations your booth staffers can do in an hour, and you'll get the number of staff you need. Multiply the number of staff you need by 50 (square feet) and you get the amount of open space you need. Add the space your display and the space your products will take up to this number and you'll get the total space required. Presto!

[***Source:*** Skyline Displays]

Or, you can assume that since you only have a 10-foot booth, then your booth space only needs to be 10 to 20 feet, and you only need two to four people. But the formula is there if you need it.

The Big Book

Shortly after the application has been sent in and processed, you'll receive your exhibitor packet/binder/folder of information. Unless you're a paperwork junkie, you may be a little overwhelmed by the volume of information you're going to have to wade through. The show information will include forms for everything from booth cleaning and rented floral arrangements, to advertising and promotion opportunities. Just take them one at a time and flag all of the deadlines. Some shows will actually provide you with a checklist and schedule of deadlines. If they don't, take this advice: Create your own! Also, be sure you really need all of the services offered. You probably only need your booth cleaned after the initial setup day, and you may want to just purchase and ship some of the other things you can rent.

What If You Miss a Deadline?

It's amazing how things like deadlines will creep up on you. Missed deadlines aren't always a catastrophe, however; you'll just have to pay more for the service if you sign up for it later, and even more if you decide you need it once you get to the show. Many times, there are early-bird discounts or prepayment discounts for a lot of the show items, so flag all of those so you won't miss out on some savings. Also, be aware of the convention centers that require you to use union labour. Usually, for those locations, if your booth requires any tools to be put together, union labor must do it. If you have a portable, pop-up or modular panel system booth, you're probably fine. Just check the requirements before you go so you are prepared.

Booth Staffing

Part of the paperwork you'll be filling out in "the big book" will be the total number and the names of the booth staff you will be sending to the show. Assuming you worked through the formula provided above, you now know how many to send. The problem now is to decide whom. This is always one of the trickiest parts of managing your trade show activities.

Depending on the locations of the shows you have planned to attend, you may have people begging to go, or begging not to go.

So how do you decide which of your sales reps to send? The first thing to think about is who among your sales reps are the most "people-oriented," and who are the most knowledgeable about your company. If those two overlap, problem solved! If they don't, and if you have your sales staff divided up as product specialists, it may make sense to send someone else who has more of an overall knowledge of the company (unless it happens to be a very specialized show). Putting your technical people in the booth isn't always the answer either, because technical people often don't have those very necessary people skills. If yours do, you're very lucky!

Packing and Shipping

You've sent in all of the forms, everything is ready and paid for, so now you just have to pack it up and ship it. Your show paperwork will have explicit instructions for precisely how and when your booth must arrive. Make sure you review them. If your booth arrives early, you may have to pay to have it transferred and stored; if it arrives late, well... you don't want that to happen. Make sure you know all of the requirements for your shipper, as well as the convention centre. Also, make sure you send everything together in the same shipment. Your drayage charge (what the convention centre charges you to take your booth shipment from the loading dock to your booth space) works on a minimum charge basis. Every time something comes in that has to be taken to your booth, there is a minimum charge of usually about $200 or more. If you can keep everything together, you'll just get charged once, based on the shipment's weight. So remember to send last minute incidentals to the hotel where your staff is staying instead of the convention hall.

The Trade Show Tool Kit

Another thing that will help your booth staffers is a Trade Show Tool Kit. This kit includes all of the incidental things you never remember and always need. It should include: packing tape, scissors, Band-Aids, aspirin, extra extension cords, extra illuminations devices like bulbs, pot lights, display signs etc., business cards of various staff members, pens, paper, a highlighter, a stapler and staple remover, shipping labels filled out for the return shipment, extra lead forms, a disposable camera... There could be a long list of things your staff may need, but not always the space to include everything. Decide on the most important items, and make sure the supply is always replenished and packed with the booth. Your booth staff will thank you for it.

Company Literature, Giveaway Items, etc.

How many brochures, giveaway items and other handouts you need to bring depend on how many people you expect to see. Once again, you can refer to the handy formula listed above. If you expect to see 300 visitors per hour, then estimate how much literature you'll need based on that number. Keep in mind that about 90% of all literature never makes it back to the attendees' offices anyway. Depending on the quality and expense of your company literature, perhaps it's best to train your staff to always offer to send the literature by mail to the attendee's office. Many times, attendees don't want to lug your precious marketing materials all over the exhibit hall and will jump at the chance (and sometimes request it themselves) that you send the information to them the following week.

Back-to-Back Shows

Normally many trade shows are scheduled in the winter or just start of winter season, that you're bound to have problems with scheduling. Usually, the best thing to do is take advantage of the storage services and have your booth and supplies shipped directly from one show to the next and stored until show time. Make sure the staff from the first show makes a list of everything that needs to be replenished, like literature, candy, giveaways, etc., so you can pack it up and send it to the second show. If it's not too bulky, your booth staffers may be able to take it with them when they travel to save the additional drayage charges, or it could be shipped to the hotel where they are staying.

Basic Training

So you've selected the most promising candidates, detailed what the show goals are, and explained in detail how the company should be presented. Now you need to put your candidates through some simple training exercises to show them how to engage show attendees so that they actually get to use the information you've armed them with. There are four phases in trade show selling:

- Engagement
- Qualification
- Presentation
- Closing
- Engagement.

First, as we mentioned above, engaging the show attendee is not as simple as you might think. Assuming you don't have a magic show, a live animal promo, or other crowd magnet, the burden of getting people to stop at your booth is on your booth staff. The first rule of engagement is: Don't ask a question that will allow the attendee to simply give you a one word answer and keep on walking. Ask them what product they are looking for at the show, whether this show has been as helpful for them as another show, if they are familiar with your company, etc. Be creative — this is a critical step, and the goal is to get them to stop and talk to you.

Qualification

Phase two is the qualifying phase. You certainly don't want to waste your time on someone who isn't really interested in your product, so it pays to ask some qualifying questions right off the bat. There's nothing worse than seeing six good prospects walk by while you're politely listening to someone who you suspect doesn't even need your product. (Yes, this can happen, especially if you have cool giveaways at your booth.)

So to qualify your prospect, take one to two minutes to ask some specific questions like, "Tell me about what you're looking for at the show." "Tell me about how your company does ______." Essentially, just ask them whatever you need to ask to identify whether or not they need your product or service.

Presentation

Phase three is show time! Time to do your top dance and dazzle the prospect with the many benefits of using your product as opposed to the other guys. Remember to limit your presentation to about five minutes or less and make your message as memorable as possible. If you've done a good job identifying your show goals, product message and competitive advantages, then this phase should be a cake walk. It's typically the easiest phase for your staff because, if they're sales reps, it's basically a condensed version of what they do every day.

Closing

The final phase is probably the most important of all, and the key to a successful closing is making sure you and your prospects are in common agreement about the next step. Ask them how they would like for you to follow up. That puts the ball in their court and forces them to say, "Yes, send me a package of information" or "Yes, call me on Tuesday about a quote." And yes, you do want to get specific with call back times. The more specific you can get, the more likely they will remember who you are when you call.

So those are the basic steps involved in trade show presentations. Go through the process with your booth staff and rehearse with each other. Pull in office mates to play the role of the trade show attendees and assign them personality types to make it more fun and challenging for your booth staffers. Having prepared booth staffers can make the difference between a very successful show and a not-so-successful show.

Organizing Your Staff

Now that everyone is trained and ready, you need to get them organized. First you need to assign a Show Captain to be in charge and manage the other staff members. Even if you are attending a small show and are only sending two staffers, it still makes sense to do this so they know who is responsible for what.

Part of the Captain's job will include organizing booth rotations and breaks. There are always other activities during the show such as vendor meetings, client luncheons, training sessions, etc., that warrant sending a booth staffer to attend. The Captain should review the show schedule and set up an appropriate schedule for the booth staff based on the exhibit hours and competing events. Once everyone arrives, the captain will also lead a pre-show meeting to go over the show objectives, strategies, special booth presentations, etc., and to answer any last minute staff questions. It's also a good idea to meet each morning prior to the show to talk about experiences and problems from the previous day.

You'll also need to assign someone the job of managing the show leads. This person will ensure that follow-up letters are written, information packets are prepared for mailing, and lead forms are filled out correctly and completely (including assigning a priority code based on your own pre-determined system). You'll find that a lead management system will work much better and you'll have a much higher percentage of closures if you assign one person the responsibility of managing it.

Additional Tips

- Here are few additional tips that your booth staff should keep in mind while at the show.
- Don't eat in the booth.
- Don't talk on the phone in the booth.
- Watch your body language. (Don't stand with your arms folded across your chest — it's not an "inviting" stance.)
- Remember breath mints!
- Take breaks — about five minutes per hour.
- Wear comfortable shoes.
- Dress depending upon your industry and market.
- Don't carry on conversations with other booth staff while prospects are walking by.
- Don't sit down while attendees are in the exhibit hall.
- Do venture out into the aisle to greet attendees.
- Make sure you have a pen and a lead form handy at all times.
- Okay, your staff is armed and ready. Now go make some money! Next, we'll help you set up a system to get the most out of your show leads.

Lead Tracking

Did you know that 80% of all leads are never followed up? If you've ever attended a trade show and asked for information from a lot of vendors, then most likely you've personally experienced that response rate (or lack of response). Did you make the effort to track that company down and ask for the information again? No, probably not.

So, now you're in charge of the lead management process for your company. You know you don't want that feeble level of responsiveness to be the case for your company. But, how do you set up a system that ensures adequate follow-up, and ultimately closure of sales, without overtaxing your resources and sending materials to people who really don't want them? You know that lots of people dropped their business cards into the fish bowl at your booth so they would be entered into your drawing for a free Palm Pilot, but they have no interest whatsoever in your product. While fish bowl givea-ways are a good way to get people's business cards, they don't qualify prospects and they don't guarantee loyal customers. The dilemma you're faced with is how to determine who is interested and who isn't when all you have is a pile of business cards.

There are some steps you can take to make the lead management process a lot easier and your trade show (and other lead-generation efforts) much more profitable.

First, assign one person the responsibility of managing your company lead system so you won't have so many leads falling between the cracks. If you've followed the previous session on training your booth staff, you may have already assigned one of your booth staffers the responsibility for managing the leads for a specific show. That person should work closely with your Lead Manager.

The Lead Manager should be responsible for:

- Writing/editing lead response letters.
- Determining the fulfillment package contents.
- Making sure the fulfillment packages are sent out in a timely manner — not a month after the show, but a week after the show.
- Distributing leads among sales reps (or, if your budget allows for lead-qualification staff, managing the qualification process and then distributing the qualified leads to sales reps).
- Developing a lead form to collect exactly the information your company needs (or, reviewing the individual show's electronic lead collection systems that are usually available for rent).
- Setting up a timetable/flowchart for following the leads once they hit the field so you can come up with a return on investment for the show.

Writing Response Letters

Writing a lead response letter is usually a much less painful process than writing letters for direct response mailings or other media. In the case of response letters, you know the people have shown interest in your product or service, and now you just have to make sure you answer all of their questions and give them the desire to act on your offer. A few quick tips include making the letter short, your voice and verbs active, and making the closing compelling.

Filling the Fulfillment Package

How do you decide what to put in your fulfillment packages? It's never as easy as it sounds. For one thing, you don't want to simply send the same things your visitors picked up at the show (reason number one for not displaying every piece of literature your company offers at your trade shows). You also don't want to overload them with expensive literature that they will just throw in the trash. About 90% of all literature picked up by people at trade shows never makes it back to their office.

For these reasons, a well done but economical overview piece for your company is essential. It can be used for either pre- or post-show mailings, as well as for a simple informational piece for your "general" response packages and other mass mailings.

There should be some variation in the contents of your fulfillment packages. If you did a pre-show mailing, you should first take that mailing list and pull out the names of those who actually came to the booth (excluding the fish bowl people). To the remainder of that list, send a very basic package outlining your company's product or service line. Speak specifically about the success of the show and make sure you include an offer in the letter to encourage the reader to act. Sometimes, the electronic lead systems that trade shows rent to exhibitors don't collect phone numbers because the attendees do not want to provide them. Make sure you know exactly what information the system automatically collects, and pay the additional charges to customize as much as possible the information.

To the contacts you made at the booth, send letters and contents specifically addressing their requests. These packages need to be personalized and should also include a specific offer that will encourage the contact to take action. Also, remember to state that a representative will be contacting the person by phone, and provide a range of dates for the contact time.

Following Up After Follow-Up

You need to make sure your sales reps are actually calling the contacts you've turned over to them. The top reasons sales reps give for not following up on leads are that the leads haven't been qualified, the information is not complete, or they just don't have the time because they're following up on leads they feel have more potential.

If you've provided your reps with phone numbers, then you have a better chance of getting somewhere. If you have a telemarketer in place to qualify the leads first, even better. Having a person dedicated (or at least responsible) for lead qualification is a luxury for many companies, and often is not an option. However, selling the idea for the position can be made easier if it is identified that it is also instrumental in the building of a client/prospect database. (In some companies, lead qualification is part of the client database manager's job.)

One solution is to have your booth staffers ultimately responsible for following up on their own leads, which makes sense from a consistency standpoint. Many show attendees will expect to get follow-up information from the same person they spoke with at the show. But, what if your sales organization is divided up into regional territories, and the show attendee fell into another rep's territory. These are all questions you have to wrestle with when coming up with your own system. The main thing is to get these contacts called. A personal phone call is typically the best way to get the response you want.

The Lead Sheet

To address one of the complaints of sales reps about the contact information not being complete, you can develop a lead sheet that includes spaces for all of the specific information your reps need in order to make a sales call. These sheets should be small enough to fit in a coat pocket, and typically work best in a notepad form. One critical piece of information to add to the sheet is the priority code or lead assessment. Come up with a simple 3-to-5 level rating system to assess how "hot" this lead really is. Make sure your booth staffers understand and use this rating system when they talk with show attendees.

If you are planning on renting one of the electronic lead-collection systems that gather information from the attendee's swiped nametag, pay the additional costs for customizing the data that it can collect. All of these systems tend to be slightly different, so study the literature well, and make sure you can record as much specific information as possible. If you can't customize the information, it might make sense not to rent one at all and simply use your own lead sheet.

Follow-Up Flow Charts

Before you know it, hot prospects will be cold, and lukewarm prospects will have absolutely no recollection of who you are. Therefore, it behooves you to move quickly with your lead follow-up process. Make sure you have a schedule in place for lead follow-up. This means:

- Getting fulfillment packages out within five days after the end of the show.
- Allowing two to five days for lead qualification (if you have that option) .
- Allowing no more than two weeks to pass before phone contact is made by your sales reps
- Getting an initial sales report on the likeliness of a sale.
- Closing the sale.
- Getting the final report of closed sales for the show report.

How a company can derive maximum benefits out of exhibitions and trade events can be well elaborated by the Pix Printers experiences. Pix Printers is one of the largest automation products company that offers a variety of printers and scanners both for office and commercial use. Pix Printers have produced videos of their various products display and demonstration stalls at regular intervals for all equipments using high end laser, graphic and special effects. They generate a high level of attendance and are shown at their stalls at various trade shows at regular intervals.

Pix Printers tried another novel concept in their upcoming exhibitions and trade events. Pix Printers hired seminar hall and gave numerous presentations as many as twenty five presentations of these videos supplemented by massive promotional techniques. This effort enabled them to attract more than three thousand visitors in three days that may be their prospective clients.

The sales manager of Pix Printers remarked to this strategy as "The visitors sitting in the seminar hall are representatives of their company and may be the prospective customers of ours." He further added, "We were able to have their exclusive attention for just 10 minutes. The three day presentation was able to attract a couple of thousand prospecting customers, They are now aware of our product along with their benefits and applications. However, if our sales force are able to contact them. The potential customers, we would have spent 100 times more effort and time."

Pix Printers were able to generate about 2,500 potential customers leads. Pix Printers were also able to project itself as a growing as well as a professionally managed company. However, the trade shows or trade events do not always give the benefits of more business awareness. These are certain issues that come up and often affect the whole concept of exhibiting. Hence. Some companies have started evaluating their participation and effectiveness of trade fairs/shows and trade events as well as cost implications of such participation.

Some major issues thus arise are;

(a) The number of trade shows are increasing day by day. Therefore, it is important for any company to evaluate which trade show or event participation will give them an advantage of costs, audience and type of visitors attracted by these exhibitions or trade events.

(b) The costs of participation in these events/ shows have risen rapidly; therefore, the cost of reaching potential customers must be evaluated.

(c) A lot of companies now believe that ignoring routine sales activities and current customers increases costs, as the entire sales force is diverted attending such shows.

(d) Companies are of the opinion that superficial enthusiasm is built up in trade shows lasts longer and normal sales get affected for a longer period. They also feel that the sales force do not follow-up on inquiries and therefore many leads are lost.

(e) Industrial manufacturers opine that for them sales mature after long and hectic negotiations. Therefore, they are not in a position to measure the impact of trade shows in clear terms.

(f) It is generally felt that for the majority of companies there exist no reliable way to measure the performance of exhibitions.

REFERENCES

1. Advertising Association, (1997) Marketing Pocket Book Henley-on-Thames: NTC Publictions.
2. Bello, D. C. and Lohtia, R., (1993) 'Improving trade show effectiveness by analyzing attendees', Industrial Marketing Management, 22, pp311-18.
3. Blythe, J., (1997) 'Does size matter? Objectives and measures at UK trade exhibitions', Journal of Marketing Communications, 3 (1, March).
4. Blythe, J. and Rayner, T., (1996) 'The evaluation of non-selling activities at British trade exhibitions - an exploratory study', Marketing Intelligence and Planning, 14 (5).
5. Bonoma, T. V., (1983) 'Get more out of your trade shows', Harvard Business Review, 61,Jan./Feb. 75-83.
6. 'Campaign' Report (1992).
7. Cavanaugh, S., (1976) 'Setting of objectives and evaluating the effectiveness of trade show exhibits', Journal of Marketing, 40 (October) pp. 100-103.
8. Centre for Leisure and Tourism Studies (1994) The Exhibition Industry Research Report: The Facts 1994. London: Centre for Leisure and Tourism Studies.
9. Chonko, L. B., Tanner Jr., J. F. and McKee, J., (1994) 'Matching trade show staff to prospects', Marketing Management, 3, 40-43.
10. Cotterell, P., (1992) Exhibitions: an Exhibitor's Guide. London: Hodder and Stoughton.
11. Couretas, J., (1984) 'Trade shows and the strategic mainstream', Business Marketing, 69. pp. 64-70.
12. Exhibition Industry Federation (1989) EIF Exhibition Effectiveness Survey. London: Centre for Leisure and Tourism Studies.
13. Godar, S. H., (1992) 'Same time next year? Why industrial buyers go to trade shows', in Marketing: Perspectives for the 1990s, Annual Proceedings of the Southern Marketing Association.
14. Gopalakrishna, S., Lilien, G. L., Williams, J. D. and Sequeira, I. K., (1995) 'Do trade shows pay off ?' Journal of Marketing 59 (July), pp. 75-83.
15. Gramann, J., (1993) 'Independent market research', Birmingham: Centre Exhibitions with National Exhibition Centre.
16. Herbig, P., O'Hara, B. and Palumbo, E, (1994) 'Measuring trade show effectiveness: an effective exercise?' Industrial Marketing Management, 23, pp. 165-70.
17. Industrial Marketing, (1979) 'Trade shows are usually a form of n Industrial Marketing 64, p. 4.
18. Kerin, R. A. and Cron, W. L., (1987) 'Assessing trade show functions and performance: exploratory study', Journal of Marketing, 51, July, pp. 87-94.
19. Kijewski, V., Yoon, E. and Young, G., (1992) Trade Shows: How Managers pick their winne Institute for the Study of Business Markets.
20. Moriarty, R. T. and Spekman, R. E., (1984) 'An empirical investigated of the informatics sources used during the industrial buying process', Journal of Market pp. 37-47.
21. Sashi, C. M. and Perretty, J., (1992) 'Do trade shows provide value?' Industrial Market Management, 21, 3, pp. 249-55.
22. Sharland, A. and Balogh, P., (1996) The value of non-selling activities at international tars shows'. Industrial Marketing Management, 25, 1, pp. 59-66.
23. Shipley, D., Egan, C. and Wong, K. S., (1993) 'Dimensions of trade show exhibitn management', journal of Marketing Management, 9 (1, Jan.) pp. 55-63.
24. Tanner, J. F., (1994) 'Adaptive selling at trade shows', Journal of Personal S Management, XIII, pp. 15-24.
25. Tanner, J. F. and Chonko, L. B., (1995) 'Trade show objectives, management and staffer practices', Industrial Marketing Management, 24, pp. 257-64.
26. Trade Show Bureau (1988) Attitudes and Opinions of Computer Executives Regarded Attendance at Information Technology Events. Study no. 1080, East Orleans, Massachusett Trade Show Bureau.
27. Waterhouse, D., (1987) Making the Most of Exhibitions,, Aldershot: Gower.
28. Deep, Sam and Lyle Sussman, Close the Deal: Smart Moves for Selling. Cambridge, MA: Perseus Publishing, 1999.
29. Vanderleest, Henry W., "Planning for International Trade Show Participation: A Practitioner's Perspective." SAM Advanced Management Journal 59, No. 4 (1994).

CHAPTER 21

EMERGING TRENDS IN MARKETING COMMUNICATIONS: A NEW FACE

"An Army of One" Campaign Accomplishes Its Mission

During the early to mid 1990s, the U.S. 'Army had little trouble attracting enough young men to enlist military service. The collapse of the Soviet Union had all but ended, and the cold war and military warfare was becoming more high-tech, which meant that fewer soldiers were needed. Thus, the Army was downsized by 40 percent, making it easy to reach modest recruitment goals. Recruitment advertising used the "Be All That You Can Be" tagline and relied primarily on expensive television commercials to deliver the self-actualization message. The ads also emphasized how joining the Army provided opportunities for career training, college scholar-ships, and other financial incentives.

While its recruitment marketing strategy worked well in the early to mid '90s, by the later part of the decade the Army found itself losing the battle to recruit America's youth. The military recruiting environment had changed as the booming economy of the '90s created many other opportunities for high school graduates. The Army's financial package was not enough to attract qualified recruits, and many high school graduates were not willing to endure the demands of basic training. However, the core challenge facing the Army was deeply rooted negative perceptions of the military. Research showed that 63 percent of young adults 17-24 said there was no way they would enlist in the military, and only 12 percent indicated an interest in military service. Comments such as, "not for people like me," "for losers," and, "only for those with no other options" were typical of the feelings young people held toward military service. Moreover, even for many of those who would consider enlisting in the service, the Army was their fourth choice among the branches of the military as it had major image problems on key attributes considered important in a post-high school opportunity.

All of these factors resulted in the Army missing its recruiting goals three out of the five years during the late '90s, despite spending more money on recruitment advertising than any branch of the military. In early 2000, Secretary of the Army Louis Caldera announced that: "We are totally changing the way we do Army advertising. We have to adopt the kinds of practices that the best marketing companies use to attract today's youth." His new marketing strategy called for a new advertising campaign and a new media strategy that included less reliance on television ads and greater use of the Internet, and "e-recruiting" to complement the Army's transformation into a more mobile, high-tech force. In June of 2000, Caldera announced the hiring of Leo Burnett USA, Chicago, as its new agency, replacing Young & Rubicam which had created Army ads since 1987.

One of the first decisions facing Leo Burnett was whether the long running "Be All That You Can Be" tagline. Although highly recognizable, the agency felt that the tagline had lost its relevance with young adults and could not be used to reposition the Army and forge a connection with this target audience. The agency came up with a new advertising and positioning theme that would be the basis for the inte-grated marketing campaign- "An Army of One." The creative strategy behind the theme is that it would bring to the forefront the idea that soldiers are the Army's most important resource and high-light that each individual can and does make a difference; that his/her contributions are important to the success of the whole team. The "An Army of One" campaign would send a message that a soldier is not nameless or faceless, but part of a unified group of individuals who together create the strength of the U.S. Army.

A major goal of the "An Army of One" campaign is to provide young adults with an accurate look into what it means to be a soldier in today's Army. A key phase of the campaign was called "Basic Training" which uses a reality based television format made popular by the hit show Survivor. The unscripted TV spots feature brief profiles of six actual army recruits as they progress through basic training, giving viewers a glimpse of their personal experiences and opinions as they transform from civilians into soldiers. The ads also encourage prospective recruits to visit the Army website (GoArmy.com) to experience a complete, in-depth multimedia "website" presentation including commentary from the recruits. The Web site was re-designed in early 2001 by Chemistri, an interactive agency which is a subsidiary of Leo Burnett, with the goal of making it a more effective recruitment tool. The site serves as a resource for potential recruits interested in learning about the Army and helps them overcome fears about basic training, increases their understanding of career opportunities available, and introduces them to soldiers similar to themselves.

The "An Army of One" campaign has been a great success. Although its media budget was 20 percent lower than the previous year, the Army fulfilled its 2001 recruiting goal of 115,000 new recruits one month early. Television, print, radio and online ads were effective in driving traffic to GoArmy.com as visits to the Web site doubled and online leads were up by 75 percent. The Web site has won several awards including a prestigious Cannes Cyber Lion and has become a focal point for the Army's recruitment efforts. The overall "An Army of One" integrated campaign also won an Effie Award as one of the most effective marketing programs of the year. Mission accomplished.

(***Sources:*** 2002 Effie Awards Brief of Effectiveness, Leo Burnett USA; Kate MacArthur, "The 'Army of One' meets 'Survivor,'" Advertising Age, www.AdAge.com February 02, 2001; Michael McCarthy, "Army enlists Net to be all it can be," USA Today, April 19, 2000, p. 10B).

The opening vignette illustrates how the roles of advertising and other forms of promotion are changing in the modern world of marketing. In the past, marketers such as the U.S. Army relied primarily on advertising through traditional mass media to promote their products. Today, many companies are taking a different approach to marketing and promotion: They integrate their advertising efforts with a variety of other communication techniques such as websites on the Internet, direct marketing, sales promotion, publicity and public relations (PR), and event sponsorships. They are also recognizing that these communication tools are most effective when they are coordinated with other elements of the marketing program.

The various marketing communications tool used by the U.S. Army as part of its recruitment efforts exemplify how marketers are using an integrated marketing communications approach to reach their customers. The U.S. Army runs recruitment advertising in a variety of media including television, radio, magazines, newspapers, and billboards. Banner ads on the Internet as well as in other media encourage consumers to visit the GoArmy.com website which provides valuable information about the U.S. Army such as career paths, the enlistment process, and benefits. Direct marketing efforts include mailings to high school seniors and direct response television ads which encourage young people to request more information and help generate leads for Army recruiters. Publicity for the U.S. Army is generated through press releases and public relation activities as well as in movies and television shows. At the local level the Army sponsors athletic events and participates in activities such as career fairs to reach its target audience as well as other groups or individuals who can influence its brand image. Recruiters work in local recruitment offices and are available to meet individually with potential recruits to answer questions and provide information about the Army. Recruitment efforts for the U.S. Army also include promotional incentives such as cash enlistment bonuses and educational benefits.

The U.S. Army and thousands of other companies and organizations recognize that the way they must communicate with consumers and promote their products and services is changing rapidly. The fragmentation of mass markets, the explosion of new technologies that are giving consumers greater control over the communications process, the rapid growth of the Internet and electronic commerce, the emergence of global markets, and economic uncertainties are all changing the way companies approach marketing as well as advertising and promotion. Developing marketing communications programs that are responsive to these changes is critical to the success of every organization. However, advertising and other forms of promotion will continue to play an important role in the integrated marketing programs of most companies.

Alvin Toffler in his best seller "Future Shock" suggested that how we have already landed in the world of information. If we have information we are considered smart, if we are smart, we earn good money, which can buy power. Every morning average humans bombarded with information in form of Newspaper, Radio, Television etc. This continues till the time he goes to bed. Shiv Khera in his book "You can Win," suggested numerous ways to gather this information.

In the competitive environment of today, it is now an established fact that winners are the one's who can disburse this information in the most powerful way. Modern world saw numerous ways in which this information can be imparted. One of the most powerful forms of spreading information is advertising.

Post Independent India has seen a lot of change in almost all walks of life. With the competition gradually rising day by day, Indian producers and manufactures also identified the difficulty in selling their products or services. It was gradually being understood by the late 80s that more innovative ways have to be identified to not only understand the need of the consumer but also satisfy them. The growing awareness among masses was making the job of sellers even more tough. Sending the message precisely and crisply became a challenge and early 90s saw a revolution in Indian Advertising. As by now it was established that advertising was a vital marketing tool as well as powerful communication force. The head for developing various channels of information and persuasion was also understood to help sell goods, services, images and ideas.

It was also realized that power of advertising communications can also be used for public utility services in the form of social advertising that can make people aware of the various social evils and problems. Also messages like promoting national integration, creating awareness of traffic rules, fighting diseases were effectively promoted and are still being used extensively.

Indian today, in the world community is the only country catering to diverse habits, tests, needs, valued and beliefs. The journey that started with an absolute non-professional attitude has since then changed, and changed for the better. As one of the top advertising companies said sometime back.

"We work not for ourselves, not for the company, not even for a client; we work for Brands. We work with the client, as Brand teams. These teams represent the collective skills of our clients and ourselves. On their performance our client with judge the whole agency. We encourage, individuals, entrepreneurs and inventive mavericks. With such members, teams thrive. We have no time for prima donnas and politicians. We value candor, curiosity, originality, intellect, rigor, perseverance, brains and civility.

We see no conflict between commitment to the highest professional standards in our work and to human kindness in our dealings with each other. We respect the intelligence of our audiences, "The consumer is not a moron."

The words as they may read, definitely project maturity and enthusiasm. The message comes sharp, hitting to the point and precise.

Today marketing calls for more than developing a good product, price it attractively, and marking it available to target customer. Companies must also communicate with their present and potential customer, retailers, suppliers and other shareholders and the general public.

Thanks to technological breakthrough, people can now communicate through traditional media (radio, newspaper, telephones, televisions) as well as through newer media forms (computers, fax, e-mail, mobile phones, pager). By decreasing communication costs, the new technologies have encouraged more targeted communication and one-to-one dialogue. As Marshall McLuchon remarked, "The medium is the message" that is the media will affect the message's content. This Chapter in "The Emerging Trends in Marketing Communication- A New Face," resulted from shift to marketing strategies and advances in computer and information technologies.

Using Contests to Build Brand Equity

Building and/or maintaining brand equity has become an important goal for marketers as they develop their sales promotion strategies. Companies are asking their promotion agencies to think strategically and develop promotional programs that can do more than just generate short-term sales. They want promotions that require consumers to become more involved with their brands and offer a means of presenting the brand essence in an engaging way. Many marketers are recognizing that a well-designed and executed contest can be a very effective way to engage consumers and differentiate their brands. Contests are experiencing resurgence as marketers focus less on awareness and more on ways to engender consumer interaction and get their branding messages across.

One of the reasons for the growing popularity of contests is that they can be used to get consumers to think about a brand and how they can relate to it. Some companies are using contests rather than sweepstakes as the latter are seen as less involving and less motivating. Because of the additional work involved in participating, contests attract brand loyalists who are not just entering to win a big prize. The right type of contest can also transcend its role as a promotional tool and help build the brand franchise. For example, the Pillsbury Bake-Off, which has been around since 1949, requires participants to whip up their favorite dishes featuring Pillsbury ingredients. The contest has been adapted to fit the times, and now includes an "Easy Cook Night" for contemporary on-the-go eating habits and a $1 million grand prize. The final round brings 100 chefs together for a televised bake-off, and thousands of recipe books are distributed annually. Eighty percent of the female entrants now have careers, and 10 percent of the entries in recent years have come from men. The director of corporate promotion and marketing for Pillsbury notes, "Prizes are certainly part of the incentive, but the real motivation is the fundamental desire for recognition."

Contests can also be helpful in rejuvenating struggling brands by creating interest and excitement that can get consumers to become involved with them. When the Georgia-Pacific Corp. acquired the Brawny paper-towel business a few years ago, it inherited a declining brand. As part of its effort to rebuild the brand, the company wanted to leverage the Brawny Man icon as well as gain insight into the modern-day woman's opinions as to what makes a man brawny. In the summer of 2002, Georgia-Pacific conducted the "Do You Know a Brawny Man™?" promotion, which included a contest asking women to send in photos and 150-word descriptions explaining why their guys are as rugged as the product. More than 40,000 entry forms were downloaded from the Brawny-man.com website, and over 4,000 people wrote to the company to nominate someone to be the Brawny Man. Five finalists were selected, and consumers were able to vote online and through the mail to choose a winner, whose picture appeared on the package for a few weeks. Information gathered from the entrants was used by the Brawny marketing team to develop a permanent Brawny Man image to replace the smiling lumberjack, who was long overdue for a makeover.

Marketers feel that contests can often provide them with insight into consumers who use their brands. Campbell Soup Co. has run a "What Do You Do With Your Pace?" recipe contest for several years as a way of understanding how its customers actually use the salsa brand. The contest averages about 12,000 entries and has produced some interesting tidbits into how consumers use the product. A recent grand-prize winner submitted a recipe for banana bread that included salsa as an ingredient. Thales Navigation, manufacturer of the Magellan GPS navigation system, ran a contest requiring entrants to write an essay about their off-road adventures. The winner was sponsored in the Jaos Adventure Road Rally, an annual high-tech scavenger hunt that sends participants into the Nevada desert looking for cues with GPS devices.

More marketers are realizing that contests can get consumers to think more about a product than about the prize they might win. As the brand manager for Brawny paper towels notes: "For the winner, the contest provides 15 minutes of fame. For the consumer, it provides a better opportunity to relate to the brand than just seeing it as they walk down the aisle."

Sources: Evan Perez and Chad Terhune, "Today, 'Brawny' Men Help with the Kids and the Housework," The Wall Street Journal, Oct. 4, 2002, p. B2; Matthew Kinsman, "May the Best Brand Win," Promo, August 2002, pp. 45-47.

WHAT IS COMMUNICATION VIS-A-VIS MARKETING COMMUNICATIONS

Communication is the base of all human activity. Talking, singing, teaching, public speaking and virtually all types of human activity has communication content. Communication, in general is the act of conveying a message. The process involves not first conveying the message, but involves a complete cycle from the sender of the message to the receiver and feedback from the receiver to the sender.

Communication is a unique tool in the hand of marketers, which they can use very effectively and intelligently to persuade their present and prospective consumers to act in a desired way to make a purchase to a certain product or to partonise a certain store. Marketing communications plays a pivotal role in bridging the gap between marketers and consumers. It also bridges the gap between consumers and their social cultural environments.

Today, companies practicing modern management concepts realise the role which marketing communication play to corporate success. For example, Du Pont, the giant US Company describes collecting information from the market and distributing communication department suggests that marketing communication is treated as a strategic resource of being planned and integrated with other critical corporate decisions and not just as something that is done to accomplish current needs.

From the managerial angle, we may define the process of marketing communications as :

(a) It is a complex process of presenting an integrated set of stimuli to the target market buyers with the intentions of evoking positive set of responses within the target market and

(b) Setting up appropriate channels to receive, interpret and merely act upon the message sent by the company and also identifying new communication opportunities.

A company has many tools at its disposal to chalk out a comprehensive communication programme for its product. All these go in to make a company's promotional effort. A brief description will amply clarify the indistinctions among these promotional elements.

"Advertising": Any paid form of non-personal presentation and promotion of ideas' goods or services by an identified sponsor.

"Personal Selling": Personal presentation by the firm's salesforce for the purpose of making sales and building customer relationship.

"Sales Promotion": Short-term incentives to encourage the purchase or sale of a product/service.

"Public Relations": Building good relations with the company's various publics by obtaining favourable publicity, building up a good 'corporate image" and handling or heading off unfavourable rumours, stories and events.

Each of these elements has its specific tools. A blend of the above referred activities is known as a promotional mix which is actually a part of the marketing communications mix. Advertising includes print, broadcast, outdoor, and other forms. Personal selling includes sales presentation, trade shows, and incentive programs; sales promotion includes point-of-purchase displays, premiums, discount, coupons, specialty advertising and demonstrations.

At the same time, communication goes beyond these specific promotion tools. The product's design, its price, the shape and colour of its package, and the stores that sell it—all communicate something to buyers.

The Changing Face of Marketing Communication

During the past several decades, companies around the world have perfected the art of mass marketing-selling highly standardised products to masses of customers. In the process, they have developed effective mass media advertising techniques to support their mass marketing strategies. These companies routinely invest millions of dollars in the mass media, reaching tens of millions of customers with a single ad. However, as we move toward the twenty-first century, marketing managers are facing some new marketing communications realities. In India also millions of Rupess are being invested in the mass media to create awareness.

The Changing Communication Environment

Two major factors are changing the face to today's marketing communications. First, as mass markets have fragmented, marketers are shifting away from mass marketing. More and more, they are developing focused marketing programmes designed to build closer relationship with customers in more narrowly defined micro markets. Second, vast improvements in computer and information technology are speeding the movements towards segmented marketing. Today's information technology helps marketers to keep closer track of customer needs— more information about consumers at the individual and household levels is available than ever before. New technologies also provide new communication avenue for reaching smaller customer segments with more tailored messages.

The shift from mass marketing to segmented marketing has had a dramatic impact on marketing communications. Just as mass marketing gave rise to a new generation of mass media communications, the shift toward one-on-one marketing is spawning a new generation of more specialised and highly targeted communication efforts.

Given this new communication environment, marketers must rethink the roles of various media and promotion mix tools. Mass Media advertising has long dominated the promotion mixes of consumer product companies. However, although television, magazines, and other mass media remain very important, their dominance is now declining. Market fragmentation has resulted in media fragmentation— in an explosion of more focused media that better match today's targeting strategies. For example, in 1960, by purchasing commercial time on the three major television networks, an advertiser could reach 90 percent of the U.S. population during an average week. Today, that number has fallen to less than 60 percent, as cable television systems now offer advertisers dozens or even hundreds of alternative channels that reach smaller, specialized audience. Similarly, the relatively few mass magazines of the 1940's and 1950s - Look, Life, Saturday Evening Post - have been replaced by more than 11,000 special interest magazines reaching smaller, more focused audience. And, beyond these channels, advertisers are making increased use of new, highly targeted media, ranging from video screens on supermarket shopping carts to on-line computer services and CD-ROM catalogues. In India also, numerous channels have resulted in the reach drop at a particular time. This has created a greater challenge for the advertiser to reach his target audience.

More generally, advertising appears to be giving way to other elements of the promotion mix. In the glory days of mass marketing, consumer product companies spent lion's share of their promotion budgets on mass media advertising. Today, media advertising captures only about 25 percent of total promotion spending. The rest goes to various sales promotion activities, which can be focused more effectively on individual consumer and trade segments. In all, companies are doing less broadcasting and more narrow casting. They are using a richer variety of focused communication tools in an effort to reach them in many and diverse target markets. Some observers envision a future in which today's advertising supported mass media will be replaced almost entirely by one-line computer services and two-way television.

Growth of Direct Marketing

The new face of marketing communications is most apparent in the rapidly growing field of direct marketing. Now the fastest growing form of marketing, direct marketing reflects the trend towards targeted or one-on-one marketing communications. As discussed in the previous section, direct marketing consists of direct communications with carefully targeted consumers to obtain an immediate response. Through direct marketing, sellers can closely match their marketing offers and communications to the needs of narrowly defined segments. All kings of consumers and business-to-business marketers use direct marketing - producers, wholesalers, retailers, non-profit organisations, and government agencies. Direct marketers employ a variety of communications tools. In addition to old favourites, such as television, direct mail, and telephone marketing, direct marketers employ powerful new forms of telecommunications and computer-based media. These tools are often used in combinations that move the customer from initial awareness of an offer to purchase and after sale service.

One of the fastest-growing sectors of the economy is direct marketing, in which organizations communicate directly with target customers to generate a response and/or a transaction. Traditionally, direct marketing has not been considered an element of the promotional mix. However, because it has become such an integral part of the IMC program of many organizations and often involves separate objectives, budgets, and strategies, we view direct marketing as a component of the promotional mix.

Direct marketing is much more than direct mail and mail-order catalogs. It involves a variety of activities, including database management, direct selling, telemarketing, and direct-response ads through direct mail, the Internet, and various broadcast and print media. Some companies, such as Tupperware, Discovery Toys, and Amway, do not use any other distribution channels, relying on independent contractors to sell their products directly to consumers. Companies such as L.L. Bean, Lands' End, and J. Crew have been very successful in using direct marketing to sell their clothing products. Dell Computer and Gateway have experienced tremendous growth in the computer industry by selling a full line of personal computers through direct marketing.

One of the major tools of direct marketing is direct-response advertising, whereby a product is promoted through an ad that encourages the consumer to purchase directly from the manufacturer. Traditionally, direct mail has been the primary medium for direct-response advertising, although television and magazines have become increasingly important media. Direct-response advertising and other forms of direct marketing have become very popular over the past two decades, owing primarily to changing lifestyles, particularly the increase in two income households. This has meant more discretionary income but less time for in-store shopping. The availability of credit cards and toll-free phone numbers has also facilitated the purchase of products from direct-response ads. More recently, the rapid growth of the Internet is fuelling the growth of direct marketing. The convenience of shopping through catalogs or on a company's website and placing orders by mail, by phone, or online has led the tremendous growth of direct marketing.

Direct-marketing tools and techniques are also being used by companies that distribute their products through traditional distribution channels or have their own sales force. Direct marketing plays a big role in the integrated marketing communications programs of consumer-product companies and business-to-business marketers. The companies spend large amounts of money each year developing and maintaining ad-bases containing the addresses and/ or phone numbers of present and prospective customers. They use telemarketing to call customers directly and attempt to sell them products and services or qualify them as sales leads. Marketers also send out a mail pieces ranging from simple letters and flyers to detailed brochures, catalogs, and videotapes to give potential customers information about the Direct-marketing techniques are also used to distribute product of a competing brand.

Forms of Direct Marketing Communication

The four major forms of direct marketing are direct mail and catalogue marketing, telemarketing, television marketing and on-line shopping.

DIRECT-MAIL AND CATALOGUE MARKETING

Direct mail marketing involves mailings of letters, ad samples, foldouts, and other "Salespeople on wings" sent to prospects on mailing lists. The mailing lists are developed from customer lists or obtained from mailing lists houses that provide names of people fitting almost any description—the super wealthy, mobile-home owners, veterinarians, pet owners, or about anything else.

Direct mail is well suited to direct, one-on-one communication. Direct mail permits high target-market selectivity, can be personalised, is flexible, and allows easy measurement of results. Whereas the cost per thousand people reached a higher, than with mass media such as television, or magazines, the people who are reached are much better prospects. Directly mail has proved very successful in promoting books, magazine subscriptions, and insurance. Increasingly, it is being used to sell novelty and gift items, clothing, gourmet foods, and industrial products. Direct mail also is used heavily by charities, which raise billions of dollars each year and account for about 25 percent of all direct-mail revenues.

Catalogue Marketing

This involves selling through catalogues mailed to a select list of customers or made available to stores. Some huge general-merchandise retailers - such as BPL and Lakme - sell a full line of merchandise through catalogues. But recently, the giants have been challenged by thousand of special catalogues that serve highly specilised market niches. As a result, Business Directory discontinued its 40-year old annual "Big Book" Catalogue in 1993 after years of unprofitable operation.

Over 14 billion copies of more than 8,500 different consumer catalogues are mailed out annually, and the average household receives some 50 catalouges a year. Consumers can buy just about anything from a catalogue. However, House sends out 22 different catalogues selling everything from shoes to decorative love birds. In America, Sharper Image sells $2,400 jet-propelled surf boards. The Banana Republic Travel and Safari Clothing Company features everything you would need to go hiking in the Sahara or the rain forest.

Recently, special department stores such as venue, Neiman Macus, Bloomingdales, and Ask Fifth Venue, have begun sending catalogues to cultivate upper middle-class markets for high prices, often exotic, merchandise. Several major corporations also have developed or acquired mail-order divisions. For example, Avon now issues ten women's fashion catalogues along with catalogues for children's and men's clothes and Walt Disney Company mails out over 6 million catalogues each year featuring videos, stuffed animals, and other Disney items. It is now being observed that in India too, such a kind of an activity of posting catalogs to potential buyers is now being actively pursued. Even in India now companies like Lakme, Oriflame, BPL, Philips, HCL- HP, Amway, Hindustan Lever and many more are joining the bandwagon of this upcoming group of marketers.

Many consumers enjoy receiving catalogues and will sometimes even selling their catalogues at book stores and magazine stands. Some companies, such as Royal Silk, Neiman Marcus, Sears, and Speigel, are also experimenting with videotape, computer diskette, and C-R catalogues. Royal Silk sells a 35 minute video catalogue to its customers for $ 5.95. The tape contains a polished presentation of Royal Silk Products, tells customers how to care for silk, and provides ordering information. Solo flex uses a video brochure to help sell its $ 1,000 in-home exercise equipment. The 22-minute video shows an attractive couple demonstrating the exercise possible with the system. Solo flex claims that almost half of those who view the video brochure later place an order via telephone, compared with only a 10 per cent response from those receiving regular direct mail.

Many business-to-business markets also rely heavily on catalogues. Whether in the form of a simple brochure, three-ring binder, or book, or encoded on a videotape or computer disk, catalogues remain one to today's hardest-working sales tools. For some companies in fact, catalogues have even taken the place of sales people. In all, companies mail out more than 1.1 billion business-to-business catalogues each year, reaping more than $50 billion worth of catalogue sales.

Telemarketing

Telemarketing-using the telephone to sell directly to consumer has become the major direct marketing communication tool. Telemarketing sometimes called telephone selling refers to a sales person initiating contact with a shopper and closing a sale over the telephone. That is telemarketing involves the use of the telephone and cell centers to attract prospects, sells to existing customers and provide service by taking orders and answering question. Many products that can be bought without being seen are sold over the telephone. Telemarketing helps companies increase revenue, reduce selling cost and improve customers satisfaction.

Today, some companies have a sales force that goes to the customers, but not in persons. These sales representatives, "going to the customers" by means to telephone, computer, etc. Thus, outside selling is becoming has become a major marketing tool. Telemarketers should have pleasant voices and project enthusiasm. Effective telemarketing depends on choosing the right telemarketers, training them well and providing performance incentives. Telemarketing is growing because; (a) many buyers prefer it over personal sales calls, and (b) many markets find that it increases selling efficiency. Sellers face increasingly routine selling by telemarketing allows the field sales force to devote more time to creative selling major account selling and other more profitable selling activities.

Marketers used outbound telephone marketing to sell directly to consumer and businesses. Outbound toll-free 800 numbers are used to receive orders from television and radio ads, direct mail, or catalouges. The average household receives 19 telephone sales calls each year and makes 16 calls to place orders. During 1990, AT & T logged more than 7 billion 800 number calls.

Other marketers use 900 numbers to sell consumers information, entertainment, or the opportunity to voice an opinion. For example, for a charge, consumers can obtain weather forecasts from American Express (1-900 Whether-75 cents a minute); pet care information from Quaker Oats (1-900-900S-PETS-95 cents a minute); advice on snoring and other sleep disorders from Somnus (1,900-USE-SLEEP $2-for the first minute, the $1 a minute); or Golf lessons from Gold Digest (1,900-454-3288-95 cents a minute). Altogether, the 900-number industry now generates $860 million in annual revenues.

Business-to-Business marketers use telemarketing extensively. In fact, more than $115 billion worth of industrial products were marketed by phone last year. For example, General Electric users telemarketing to generate and quality sales leads to manage small accounts. Releigh Bicycles uses telemarketing to reduce the amount of personal selling needed for contacting its dealers; in the first year, sales force travel costs were reduced to 50 percent, and sales in a single quarter increased by 34 per cent.

Most consumers appreciate many of the offers they receive by telephone. Properly designed and targeted telemarketing provides many benefits, including purchasing convenience and increased product and service information. However, the recent explosion in unsolicited telephone marketing has annoyed many consumers who object to the almost daily "junk phone calls" that pull them away from the dinner table or clog up their answering machines. Lawmakers around the country are responding with legislation ranging from banning unsolicited telemarketing calls during certain hours to letting households sign up for national "Don't Call Me" list. Most telemarketers support some action against random and poorly targeted telemarketing. As a Direct Marketing Association executive notes, "We went to target people who want to be targeted." The position is same in India too where TRAI has made obligatory to mobile service providers to give "Do Not Call' registry in order to avoid general subscribers to be not disturbed by unsoliciting telemarketing calls.

Television Marketing

Television Marketing takes one of two major forms. The first is direct response advertising. Direct marketers air television spots, often 60 or 120 seconds long that persuasively describe a product and give customers a toll-free number for ordering. Television viewers often encounter 30-minute advertising programs, or information commercials for a single product. Such direct-response advertising works well for magazines, books, small appliances, tapes and CDs, collectibles, and many other products. For example, the "Telebrand," "Asian Sky Shop" has become very favourite site for television viewers in India.

Some successful direct-response ads run for years and become classics. For example, Dial Media's ads run for years, and become classics. Let us consider another example, Dial Media's ads for Ginsu knives ran for seven years and sold among 3 million sets of knives worth more than $40 million in sales; its Armourcote cookware ads generated more than twice that much. And the now familiar 30 minute Psychic-friends information commercials have aired more than 12,00 times during the past two years, offering callers access to its national network of psychics and generating more than $100 million worth of business. For years, information commercials have been associated with somewhat questionable pitches for juicers, get-rich-quick schemes, and nifty ways to stay in shape without working very hard at it. Recently, however a number of top marketing companies – GTF, Johnson & Johnson, MCA Universal, Sears, Revlon, Philips Electronics, and others – have begun using information commercials to sell their wares over the phone, refer customers to retailers, or send out coupons and product information. In all, information commercials produced almost $ 1 billion sales in 1994, which increased to $ 26 billion in 2007.

Home shopping channels, another form to television direct marketing, are television programs or entire channels dedicated to selling goods and services. Some home shopping channels, such as the Quality Value Channel and the Home shopping Network, Broadcast 24 hours a day. On HSN, the programs' hosts offer bargain power tools and consumer electronics—usually obtained by the Home shopping channel at closeout price. The show is upbeat, with the hosts honking horns, blowing whistles, and praising viewers for their good taste. Viewers call an 800 number to 1,200 incoming lines, entering order directly into computer terminals. Order are shipped within 48 hours. Sales through home shopping, channels grew from $ 450 in 1989 to an estimated $ 2 million in 1994. More than half of all U.S. homes have access to QVC, HSN, or other home shopping. Mail, or Teleshopping, Sears,

Kmart, J.C. Penney, Spiegel, and other major retailers are not looking into the home shopping industry. Many experts think that advances in two-way, interactive television will make video shopping one of the major forms of direct marketing in this century.

On-Line Shopping

On line computer shopping is conducted through interactive on-line computer services, two-ways systems that link consumers with sellers electronically. These services create computerized catalogues of products and services offered by producers, retailers, bank, travel organisation, and others. Consumers use a home computer to hook into the system through cable or telephone lines. For example, a consumer wanting to buy a new compact-disc player could request a list of all brands in the computerised catalogue, compare the brands, then order one using a change card—all without leaving home. Such on-line services are till in their infancy. In recent years, several large systems have failed because of a lack of subscribers or too little use.

Relationship marketing

Selling is an old profession but of late, marketing concepts have pushed sales into a very small part of the total function of doing business with customers. While selling primarily means disposing of whatever one has of produces to customers by convincing them, marketing involves identifying customer's needs and tailoring products and services to their satisfaction. The new approach to marketing is that people do not buy things but buy solutions to problems and that to succeed corporations need unique insights into customers and their problems. When things are viewed in this way, relationships with customers become the key to attracting and holding them. Building relationships with key customers is not a new idea; the neighbourhood grocery store owner has known this approach to marketing. It is just those big corporations which have mass marketing methods have forgotten these basic lessons. The critical difference between the grocery store owners and the big corporations is that the latter has to set up systems in place which will allow it to do relationship marketing with a very large number of customers in a cost effective manner. Almost all corporations can make a start with relationship marketing by identifying their key customers. Here the thumb rule is that the revenue pattern of most organizations flow the 80/20 rule. 20% of the customers bring in 80% of the revenue. At Modi Xerox, one of the few Indian companies which puts a lot of stress on relationship marketing 900 of its accounts form 30% of its turnover.

Creating customer care and building relationships is a never ending odyssey. Most organisations are better at talking to their customers than listening to them. The marketer's preferred means of communication was the monologue. Now they protected economy where monopolists reigned supreme. Monopoly is almost invariably associated with high cots, high prices, over-manning and indifference to customers. Even if you do enjoy a monopoly position today, it makes strategic sense to act as if you don't as privatization exposes both organisations and their internal working to the competitive forces, customers will go elsewhere. The customer needs and expects customers' friendly systems, and the secret of turning customer service into a competitive advantage is to do something that makes you memorable and different. If customer relationship is put across during induction as a veneer will be lifted and forgotten.

Lastly, a note of caution regarding relationship marketing—the customer wants a single interface with his supplier—he doesn't want to deal with several different departments.

Direct Marketing Databases

Successful direct marketing begins with a good customer database. A marketing database is an organised set of data about individual customers or prospects, including geography, demographic, psychographic, and buying behaviour data. The data base can be used to locate good potential customers, tailor products and services to the special needs to targeted consumers, and maintaining long-term customer relationships. Many companies are now building and using customer database for databases for targeting marketing communication and selling efforts. A recent survey found that more than one-half of all large consumer products companies are currently building such database. For example, in India Eureka Forbes can be referred as one of the companies based on Direct Marketing practice.

Integrated Direct Marketing

Many direct marketers use only a "one-shot" effort to reach and sell a prospect, or a single vehicle in multiple stages to trigger purchases. A more powerful approach in integrated direct marketing, which involves using multiple-vehicle and multiple-stage campaign. Such campaigns can greatly improve response.

More elaborate integrated direct marketing campaigns can be used. Consider the following multimedia, multistage campaign:

Paid ad with a Direct outbound face-to-face response channel mail, telemarketing, sales call

Automatic Vending

The sale of products through a machine with no personal contact between buyer and seller is called automatic vending. The appeal of automatic vending is convenient purchase. Products sold by automatic vending are usually well-known, per sold brands with a high rate of turnover. Automatic vending is used for a variety of merchandise, etc. Vending machines can expand a firm's market by reaching customers where and when they cannot come to a store. Thus, vending equipment is found almost everywhere, particularly in schools, factories, officers, large retail stores, gasoline stations, hotels, restaurants and many others places. They officer 24 hour selling, self-service and merchandise that is always fresh. Automatic vending has high operating costs because of the need to replenish inventories frequently. The machine also requires maintenance and repairs.

E-Business

As computers had become common business tools in the late 1950s, firms were able to collect, store and manipulating larger amount of data to aid marketing decision makers. Out of this capability developed the marketing information system- an outgoing, organized procedure to generate, analyze, disseminate, store and retrieve information for use in making marketing needs of a business are organized into what is called "Management Information System" (MIS). A management information system consists of inter-connected sub-systems. They provide the information necessary to be competitive. The computer is an electronics tool that is used to collect, organize, analyze, interpret and communicate mounts of information with great speed.

E-Business describes the use of electronic means and platforms to conduct company business. The advent of the internet has greatly increased the ability of companies to conduct their business faster, more accurately, over a wider range of time and space, at reduced cost and with the ability to customize and personalize customers offerings. Many companies have set up Web site to inform and promote their business value by combining the system and process that run core business operations with the simplicity and reach made possible by internet technology."

E-Business can be (a) within the organization , that is intranets facilitate employers company computers. (b) Business to business dealings, that is extranet consists to two intranets connected via the internet, whereby two organizations are allowed to see confidential data of the other (c) Business to customer transition, that is selling the goods and services through internet to the innumerable customers spread all over the world.

Electronics business is a super-set of business case. E-Commerce is one of the aspects of E-business. Some other important aspects of E-business, which are successfully carried through the internet, are e–auctioning, e–banking, e-mailing, e-marketing, e-trading, etc.

Interactive/Internet Marketing

As the new millennium begins, we are experiencing perhaps the moost dynamic and revolutionary changes of any era in the history of marketing as well as advertising and promotion. These changes are being driven by advances in technology and development have led to dramatic growth of communication through interactive media, particularly the Internet. Interactive media allow for a back-and-forth flow of information whereby users can participate in and modify the form and content of the information they receive in real time. Unlike traditional forms of marketing communications such as advertising, which are one-way in nature, the new media uses to perform a variety of functions such as receive and alter information and BCS, make inquiries, respond to questions, and of course, make purchases. Other forms of interactive media include CD-ROMs, kiosks, and interactive television. However, the interactive medium that is having the greatest impact on marketing is the Internet, especially through the component known as the World Wide Web.

While the Internet is changing the ways companies design and implement their entire business and marketing strategies, it is also affecting their marketing communications programs. Thousands of companies, ranging from large multinational corporations to small local firms, have developed websites to promote their products and services, by providing current and potential customers with information, as well as to entertain and interact with consumers. Perhaps, the most prevalent perspective on the Internet is that it is an advertising medium, as many marketers advertise their products and services on the websites of other companies and/or organizations. Actually, the Internet is a medium that can be used to execute all the elements of the promotional mix. In addition to advertising on the Web, marketers offer sales promotion incentives such as coupons, contests, and sweepstakes online, and they use the Internet to conduct direct marketing, personal selling, and public relations activities more effectively and efficiently.

While the Internet is a promotional medium, it can also be viewed as a marketing communications tool in its own right. Because of its interactive nature, it is a very effective way of communicating with customers. Many companies recognize the advantages of communicating via the Internet and are developing Web strategies and hiring interactive agencies specifically to develop their websites; of their integrated marketing communications program. However, companies that are using the Internet effectively are integrating their Web strategies with other aspects of their IMC programs.

An excellent example of this is the award-winning whatever" campaign developed by Nike and its advertising agency. Weiden & Kennedy to introduce the Air Cross Trainer II shoes. The ads featured star athletes such a sprinter Marion Jones in dramatic situations, and as each spot ended the words "Continue at whatever nike.com" appeared on the screen. When viewers visited the site, they could select from six or seven possible endings to the commercial, read information on the sports and athletes featured in the ads, or purchase the shoes. The integrated campaign was very effective in driving traffic to both Nike's main website and the whatever.nike.com site created specifically for the campaign. The "whatever" campaign was also very effective in terms of sales as it helped make the Air Cross Trainer II Nike's best-selling shoe soon after the ads debated.

Publicity/Public Relations

Another important component of an organization's promotional mix is publicity /public relations.

Publicity Publicity refers to non-personal communication regarding an organization, product, service, or idea not directly paid for or run under identified sponsorship. It usually comes in the form of a news story, editorial, or announcement about an organization and/or its products and services. Like advertising, publicity- involves non-personal communication to a mass audience, but unlike advertising, publicity is not directly paid for by the company. The company or organization attempts to get the media to cover or run a favourable story on a product, service, cause, or event to affect awareness, knowledge, opinions, and/or behaviour. Techniques used to gain publicity include news releases, press conferences, feature articles, photographs, films, and videotapes.

An advantage of publicity over other forms of promotion is its credibility. Consumers generally tend to be less skeptical toward favourable information about a product or service when it comes from a source they perceive as unbiased. For example, the success (or failure) of a new movie is often determined by the reviews it receives from film critics, who are viewed by many movie-goers as objective evaluators.

Another advantage of publicity is its low cost, since the company is not paying time or space in a mass medium such as TV, radio, or newspapers. While an organization may incur some costs in developing publicity items or maintaining a staff to do so, these expenses will be far less than those for the other promotional programs.

Publicity is not always under the control of an organization and is sometimes unfavorable. Negative stories about a company and/or its products can be very damaging. For example, a few years ago negative stories about abdominal exercise machines appeared on ABC's "20/20" and NBC's "Dateline" newsmagazine TV shows. Before these stories aired, more than $3 million worth of the machines were being sold each week, primarily through infomercials. After the negative stories aired, sales of the machines dropped immediately; within a few months the product category was all but dead.

Public Relations: It is important to recognize the distinction between publicity and public relations. When an organization systematically plans and distributes information in an attempt to control and manage its image and the nature of the publicity it receives, it is really engaging in a function known as public relations. Public relations is defined as "the management function which evaluates public attitudes, identifies the policies and procedures of an individual or organization with the public interest, and executes a program of action to earn public understanding and acceptance." Public relations generally has a broader objective than publicity, as its purpose is to establish and maintain a positive image of the company among its various publics.

Public relations uses publicity and a variety of other tools—including special publications, participation in community activities, fund-raising, sponsorship of special events, and various public affairs activities to enhance an organization's image. Orga-nizations also use advertising as a public relations tool.

Traditionally, publicity and public relations have been considered more supportive than primary to the marketing and promotional process. However, many firms have begun making PR an integral part of their predetermined marketing and promotional strategies. PR firms are increasingly touting public relations as a communications tool that can take over many of the functions of conventional advertising and marketing.

Relationship Marketing

Today, most marketers are seeking more than just a one-time exchange or transaction with customers. The focus of market-driven companies is on developing and sustaining relationships with their customers. This has led to a new emphasis on relationship marketing, which involves creating, maintaining, and enhancing long-term relationship with individual customers as well as other stakeholders for mutual benefit.

The movement toward relationship marketing is due to several factors. First, companies recognize that customers have become much more demanding. Consumers desire superior customer value, which includes quality products and services that competitively priced, convenient to purchase, delivered on time, and supported by excellent customer service. They also want personalized products and services that are tailored to their specific needs and wants. Advances in information technology, along with flexible manufacturing systems and new marketing processes, have led to mass customization, whereby a company can make a product or deliver a service in response to a particular customer's needs in a cost-effective way. New technology is making it possible to configure and personalize a wide array of products and services including computers, automobiles, clothing, golf clubs, cosmetics, mortgages, and vitamins. Consumers can log on to websites such as Mattel Inc.'s barbie.com and design their own Barbie pal doll or Fingerhut's myjewelry.com to design their own rings. Technological developments are also likely to make the mass customization of advertising more practical as well.

Another major reason why marketers are emphasizing relationships is that it is often more cost-effective to retain customers than to acquire new ones. Marketers are giving more attention to the lifetime value of a customer because studies have shown that reducing customer defections by just 5 percent can increase future profit by as much as 30 to 90 percent.

Promotional Management

In developing an integrated marketing communications strategy, a company combines the promotional-mix elements, balancing the strengths and weaknesses of each, to produce an effective promotional campaign promotional management involves co-ordinating the promotional-mix elements to develop a controlled integrated program of effective marketing communications. The marketer must consider which promotional tools to use and how to combine them to achieve its marketing and promotional objectives. Companies also face the task of distributing the total promotional budget across the promotional-mix elements. What percentage of the budget should they allocate to advertising, sales promotion, the Internet, direct marketing, and personal selling?

Companies consider many factors in developing their IMC programs, including the type of product. The target market, the buyer's decision process, the stage of the product life cycle, and the channels of distribution. Companies selling consumer products and services generally rely on advertising through mass media to communicate consumers. Business-to-business marketers, who generally sell expensive, risky, and often complex products and services, more often use personal to-business marketers such as Honeywell do use advertising to perform important functions such as building awareness of the company and its prod-mg leads for the sales force, and reassuring customers about the purchase they have made. Conversely, personal selling also plays an important role in consumer-product marketing. A consumer goods company retains a sales force to call on marketing intermediaries (wholesalers and retailers) that distribute the product or service to the final consumer. While the company sales reps do not communicate with the ultimate consumer, they make an important contribution to the marketing effort by gaining new distribution outlets for the company's product, securing shelf position and space for the brand, informing retailers about advertising and promotion efforts to users, and encouraging dealers to merchandise and promote the brand at the local market level.

Advertising and personal-selling efforts vary depending on the type of market being sought, and even firms in the same industry may differ in the allocation of their promotional efforts. For example, in the cosmetics industry, Avon and Mary Kay Cosmetics concentrate on direct selling, whereas Revlon and Max Factor rely heavily on consumer advertising. Firms also differ in the relative emphasis they place on advertising and sales promotion. Companies selling high-quality brands use advertising to convince consumers of their superiority, justify their higher prices, and maintain their image. Brands of lower quality, or those that are hard to differentiate, often compete more on a price or "value for the money" basis and may rely more on sales promotion to the trade and/or to consumers.

The marketing communication program of an organization in generally developed with a specific purpose in mind and is the end product of a detailed marketing and promotional planning process.

Integrating Marketing Communications

For many years, the promotional function in most companies was dominated by mass media advertising. Companies relied primarily on their advertising agencies for guidance in nearly all areas of marketing communication. Most marketers did use additional promotional and marketing communication tools, but sales promotion and direct-marketing agencies as well as package design firms where generally viewed as auxiliary services and often used on a per-project basis. Public relations agencies were used to manage the organization's publicity, image, and affairs with relevant publics on an ongoing basis but were not viewed as integral participants in the marketing communications process.

Many marketers built strong barriers around the various marketing and promotional functions and planned and managed them as separate practices, with different budgets, different views of the market, and different goals and objectives. These companies failed to recognize that the wide range of marketing and promotional tools must be co-ordinated to communicate effectively and present a consistent image to target markets.

There have been dramatic changes in formation technology over the past ten or fifteen years consumer and business — people no longer need to be near a computer to send and receive information. All they need is a cellular phone. While they are on the move, they can be in touch with their field personal no matter where they are. Advances in information technology are revolutionizing the modus operandi of marketing and the business system. The business horizon is humming with buzzwords like internet, World wide web (www), Cyberspace, information superhighways, etc., which are changing the way of contacting customer; order receiving and processing; and networking and interchanging business system. The revolutionary changes being ushered in by the internet are indeed exciting. The revolutionary changes in the information technology is sweeping across the global business. New information technology modes include electronic mail, corporate and public database, application system, fax, video and computer conferencing. These modes are considered to be some of the driving forces of internationalization. These new information technology modes have a major impact on the co-ordination of head- quarter- subsidiary relations. In fact, most of the MNCs have developed these new modes of information technology. The internet is a world wide, self - governed network connecting thousands of smaller networks and millions of computers and people to mega sources of information. Quite simply, it is a technology no nation or enterprise can ignore. Technology experts are anticipant that the internet and the www would become the centre of commercial universe. Electronic markets will eliminate the need for the intermediaries and that cost of final product. The internet has the potential to evolve into an inter-connected electronic market place (cyberspace) bringing buyers and sellers together to facilitate commercial exchanges.

It is needless to say that the internet is a world-wide network of computer networks. Imagine a network of five computers in your office which are linked up together in a manner that you can exchange data, correspondence (mail) and even soft-ware, between these computers. Now imagine that you have business associates or friends who also have several computers spread over different locations linked up in manner so that they (meaning you) can communicate between each other. This is what internet is all about. Except as mentioned earlier, this is a global network linking millions of computers and people cutting across all barriers and boundaries of countries, race, class or sex. The networking of computers that allow the managers, Employers, customers, vendors,, dealers, bankers, suppliers to deal with each other even across the globe. The networking of ATMs allow the customer to deposit money in Delhi, to withdraw money in Lucknow, to deposit cheques for clearance in Kolkatta and to get his statement of accounts in Mumbai.

Today, however, more companies are adopting the concept of integrated marketing communication. Under this concept, the company carefully integrates and co-ordinates its many communications channels-mass media, advertising, personal selling, sales promotion, public relations, direct marketing, packaging and others to deliver a clear, consistent, and compelling message about the organisation and its products. The company works out the roles that the various promotional tools will play and the extent to which each will be used. It carefully coordinates the promotional activities and the timing of when major campaigns take place. It keeps track of its promotional expenditures by product, promotional tool, product life-cycle stage and observed effect in order to improve marketing strategy, the company appoints a marketing communications director who has overall responsibility for the company's communication efforts.

Integrated marketing communications produces better communications consistency and greater sales impact. It places the responsibility in someone's hands-where none existed before—to unify the company image as it is shaped by thousands of company activities. It leads to total marketing communications strategy aimed at showing how the company and its products can help customers solve their problems.

The Evolution of IMC

During the 1980s, many companies came to see the need for more of a strategic integration of their promotional tools. These firms began moving toward the process of integrated marketing communications (IMC), which involves co-ordinating the various promotional elements and other marketing activities that communicate with a firm's customers. As marketers embraced the concept of integrated marketing communications, they began asking their ad agencies to co-ordinate the use of a variety of promotional tools rather than relying primarily on media advertising. A number of companies also began to look beyond traditional advertising agencies and use other types of promotional specialists to develop and implement various components of their promotional plans.

Many agencies responded to the call for synergy among the promotional tools by acquiring PR, sales promotion, and direct-marketing companies and touting themselves as IMC agencies that offer one-stop shopping for all their clients' promotional needs. Some agencies became involved in these no advertising areas to gain control over their clients' promotional programs and budgets and struggled to offer any real value beyond creating advertising. However, the advertising industry soon recognized that IMC was more than just a fad. Terms such as new advertising, orchestration, and seamless communication were used to describe the concept of integration. A task force from the American Association of Advertising Agencies (the "4As") developed one of the first definitions of integrated marketing communications:

A concept of marketing communications planning that recognizes the added value of a comprehensive plan that evaluates the strategic roles of a variety of communication disciplines —for example, general advertising, direct response, sales promotion, and public relations and combines these disciplines to provide clarity, consistency, and maximum communications impact.

The 4As' definition focuses on the process of using all forms of promotion to achieve maximum communication impact. However, advocates of the IMC concept such as Don Schultz of Northwestern University, argue for an even broader perspective that considers all sources of brand or company contact that a customer or prospect has with a product or service. Schultz and others note that the process of integrated marketing communications calls for a "big-picture" approach to planning marketing and promotion programs and co-ordinating the various communication functions. It requires that firms develop a total marketing communications that recognizes how all of a firm's marketing activities, not just promotion, communicate with its customers.

Consumers' perceptions of a company and/or its various brands are a synthesis of the bundle of messages they receive or contacts they have, such as media advertisements, price, package design, direct-marketing efforts, publicity, sales promotions, websites, point-of-purchase displays, and even the type of store where a product or service is sold. The integrated marketing communications approach seeks to have a company's entire marketing and promotional activities project a consistent, unified image to the marketplace. It calls for a centralized messaging function so that everything a company says and does communicates a common theme and positioning.

Many companies have adopted this broader perspective of IMC. They see it as a way to co-ordinate and manage their marketing communications programs to ensure that they give customers a consistent message about the company and/or its brands. For these companies, the IMC approach represents an improvement over the traditional method of treating the various marketing and communications elements as virtually separate activities. However, as marketers become more sophisticated in their understanding of IMC they recognize that it offers more than just ideas for co-ordinating all elements of the marketing and communications programs. The IMC approach helps companies identify the most appropriate and effective methods for communicating and building relationships with their customers as well as other stakeholders such as employees, suppliers, investors, interest groups, and the general public.

Tom Duncan and Sandra Moriarty note that IMC is one of the "new-generation" marketing approaches being used by companies to better focus their efforts in acquiring, retaining, and developing relationships with customers and other stakeholders. They have developed a communication-based marketing model that emphasizes the importance of managing all corporate or brand communications, as they collectively create, maintain, or weaken the customer and stakeholder relationships that drive brand value. Messages can originate at three levels corporate, marketing, and mar — keting communications — since all of a company's corporate activities, marketing-mix activities, and marketing communications efforts have communication dimensions and play a role in attracting and keeping customers.

At the corporate level, various aspects of a firm's business practices and philosophies, such as its mission, hiring practices, philanthropies, corporate culture, and ways of responding to inquiries, all have dimensions that communicate with customers and other stakeholders and affect relationships. For example, Ben & Jerry's is a company that is rated very high in social responsibility and is perceived as a very good corporate citizen in its dealings with communities, employees, and the environment. Ben & Jerry's capitalizes on its image as a socially responsible company by supporting various causes as well as community events.

At the marketing level, as was mentioned earlier, companies send messages to customers and other stakeholders through all aspects of their marketing mixes, not just promotion. Consumers make inferences about a product on the basis of elements such as its design, appearance, performance, pricing, service support, and where and how it is distributed. For example, a high price may symbolize quality to customers, as may the shape or design of a product, its packaging, its brand name, or the image of the stores in which it is sold. Montblanc uses classic design and a distinctive brand name as well as a high price to position its watches and pens as high-quality, high-status products. This upscale image is enhanced by the company's strategy of distributing its products only through boutiques, jewellery stores, and other exclusive retail shops.

At the marketing communications level, Duncan and Moriarty note that all messages should be delivered and received on a platform of executional and strategic consistency in order to create coherent perceptions among customers and other stakeholders. This requires the integration of the various marketing communication's messages and the functions of various promotional facilitators such as ad agencies, public relations firms, sales promotion specialists, package design firms, direct-response specialists, and interactive agencies. The goal is to communicate with one voice, look, and image across all the marketing communications functions and to identify and position the company and/or the brand in a consistent manner.

Many companies are realizing that communicating effectively with customers and other stakeholders involves more than traditional marketing communications tools. Many marketers, as well as advertising agencies, are embracing the IMC approach and adopting total communication solutions to create and sustain relationships between companies or brands and their customers. Some academics and practitioners have questioned whether the IMC movement is just another management fad. However, the IMC approach is proving to be a permanent change that offers significant value to marketers in the rapidly changing communications environment they are facing in the new millennium.

Reasons for the Growing Importance of IMC

The move toward integrated marketing communications is one of the most significant marketing developments that occurred during the 1990s, and the shift toward this approach is continuing as we begin the new century. The IMC approach to marketing communications planning and strategy is being adopted by both large and small companies and has become popular among firms marketing consumer products and services as well as business-to-business marketers. There are a number of reasons why marketers are adopting the IMC approach. A fundamental reason is that they under-stand the value of strategically integrating the various communications functions rather than having them operate autonomously. By co-ordinating their marketing communications efforts, companies can avoid duplication, take advantage of synergy among promotional tools, and develop more efficient and effective marketing communications' programs. Advocates of IMC argue that it is one of the easiest ways for a company to maximize the return on its investment in marketing and promotion.

The move to integrated marketing communications also reflects an adaptation by marketers to a changing environment, particularly with respect to consumers, technology, and media. Major changes have occurred among consumers with respect to demographics, lifestyles, media use, and buying and shopping patterns. For example, cable TV and more recently digital satellite systems have vastly expanded the number of channels available to households. Some of these channels offer 24-hour shopping networks; others contain 30- or 60-minute direct-response appeals known as infomercials, which look more like TV shows than ads. Every day more consumers are surfing the Internet's World Wide Web. Online services such as America Online and Microsoft Network provide information and entertainment as well as the opportunity to shop for and order a vast array of products and services. Marketers are responding by developing home pages on which they can advertise their products and services interactively as well as transact sales. For example, travellers can use American Airlines' AA.com website to plan flights, check for special fares, purchase tickets, and reserve seats, as well as make hotel and car-rental reservations.

Even as new technologies and formats create new ways for marketers to reach consumers, they are affecting the more traditional media. Television, radio, Magazines, and newspapers are becoming more fragmented and reaching smaller and more selective audiences. A recent survey of leading U.S. advertising executives on trends that will shape the industry identified the segmentation of media audiences by new media technologies as the must important development.

In addition to facing the decline in audience size for many media, marketers are facing the problem of consumers' being less responsive to traditional advertising. They recognize that many consumers are turned off by advertising and tired of being bombarded with sales messages. These factors are prompting many marketers to look for alternative ways to communicate with their target audiences, such as making their selling messages part of popular culture. For example, marketers often hire product placement firms to get their brands into TV shows and movies. MGM/United Artists created special scenes in the recent James Bond movie Die Another Day to feature the Aston Martin V12 Vanquish sports car. It is estimated that the British automaker, which is owned by Ford Motor Company, paid $70 million to have the car featured in the movie. In an arrangement with Columbia Pictures, Daimler-Benz agreed to spend several million dollars on commercials, private screenings, and other promotions to have the redesigned Mercedes-Benz E500 automobile featured in the movie Men in Black II.

The integrated marketing communications movement is also being driven by changes in the ways companies market their products and services. A major reason for the growing importance of the IMC approach is the ongoing revolution that is changing the rules of marketing and the role of the traditional advertising agency. Major characteristics of this marketing revolution include:

- A shifting of marketing dollars from media advertising to other forms of promotion, particularly consumer and trade-oriented sales promotions. Many marketers feel that traditional media advertising has become too expensive and is not cost-effective. Also, escalating price competition in many markets has resulted in marketers' pouring more of their promotional budgets into price promotions rather than media advertising.
- A movement away from relying on advertising-focused approaches, which emphasize mass media such as network television and national magazines, to solve communication problems. Many companies are turning to lower-cost, more targeted communication tools such as event marketing and sponsorships, direct mail, sales promotion, and the Internet as they develop their marketing communications' strategies.
- A shift in marketplace power from manufacturers to retailers. Due to consolidation in the retail industry, small local retailers are being replaced by regional, national and international chains. These large retailers are using their clout to demand larger promotional fees and allowances from manufacturers, a practice that often siphons many away from advertising. Moreover, new technologies such as checkout scanners give retailers information on the effectiveness of manufacturers' promotional programs. This is leading many marketers to shift their focus to promotional took feat can produce short-terra results, such as sales promotion.
- The rapid growth and development of database marketing. Many companies are building databases containing customer names; geographic, demographic, and psycho graphic profiles; purchase patterns; media preferences; credit ratings; and other characteristics. Marketers are using this information to target consumers through a variety of direct-marketing methods such as telemarketing, direct mail, and direct-response advertising, rather than relying on mass media. Advocates of the approach argue that database marketing is critical to the development and practice of effective IMC.
- Demands for greater accountability from advertising agencies and changes in the way agencies are compensated. Many companies are moving toward incentive-based systems whereby compensation of their ad agencies is based, at least in part, on objective measures such as sales, market share, and profitability. Demands for accountability are motivating many agencies to consider a variety of communication tools and less expensive alternatives to mass-media advertising.
- The rapid growth of the Internet, which is changing the very nature of how companies do business and the ways they communicate and interact with consumers. The Internet revolution is well under way, and the Internet audience is growing rapidly. The Internet is an interactive medium that is becoming an integral part of communication strategy, and even business strategy, for many companies.

This marketing revolution is affecting everyone involved in the marketing and promotional process. Companies are recognizing that they must change the ways they market and promote their products and services. They can no longer be tied to a specific communication tool (such as media advertising); rather, they should use whatever contact methods offer the best way of delivering the message to their target audiences. Ad agencies continue to reposition themselves as offering more than just advertising expertise; they strive to convince their clients that they can manage all or any part of clients' integrated communications needs. Most agencies recognize that their future success depends on their ability to understand all areas of promotion and help their clients develop and implement integrated marketing communications programs.

The IMC Planning Process

As with any business function, planning plays a fundamental role in the development and implementation of an effective promotional program. The individuals involved in promotion design a promotional plan that provides the framework for developing, implementing, and controlling the organization's integrated marketing communications programs and activities. Promotional planners must decide on the role and function of the specific elements of the promotional mix, develop strategies for each element, and implement the plan. Promotion is but one part of, and must be integrated into, the overall marketing plan and program.

A model of the IMC planning process is shown in Figure 21.1.

Review of Marketing Plan

Examine overall marketing plan and objectives
Role of advertising and promotion
Competitive analysis
Assess environment's influences

Analysis of Promotional Program Situation

Internal analysis	*External analysis*
Promotional department	Analysis of communications process
Consumer behaviour analysis organization	Analyze receiver's response processes
Market segmentation and target marketing	Analyze source, message channel factors
Firm's ability to implement promotional program	Establish communications goals and objectives
Market positioning	
Agency evaluation and selection	
Review of previous program results	

Budget Determination

Set tentative marketing communications budget
Allocate tentative budget

Develop Integrated Marketing Communications Program

Advertising	*Sales promotion*
Set advertising objectives	Set sales promotion objectives
Determine advertising budget	Determine sales promotion budget
Develop advertising message	Determine sales promotion tools
Develop advertising media strategy	and develop messages
Direct marketing	Develop sales promotion media strategy
Set direct-marketing objectives	Public relations/publicity
Determine direct-marketing budget	Set PR/publicity objectives
Develop direct-marketing message	Determine PR/publicity budget

Develop direct-marketing media strategy	Develop PR/publicity messages
interactive/internet marketing	Develop PR/publicity media strategy
Set interactive/Internet marketing objectives	Personal selling
Determine interactive/Internet marketing budget	Set personal-selling and sales objectives
Develop interactive/Internet message	Determine personal-selling/sales budget
Develop interactive/Internet media strategy	Develop sales message
	Develop selling roles and responsibilities

Integrate and Implement Marketing Communications Strategies

Integrate promotional-mix strategies
Create and produce ads
Purchase media time, space, etc.
Design and implement direct-marketing programs
Design and distribute sales promotion materials
Design implement public relations/publicity programs
Design and implement interactive/internet marketing programs

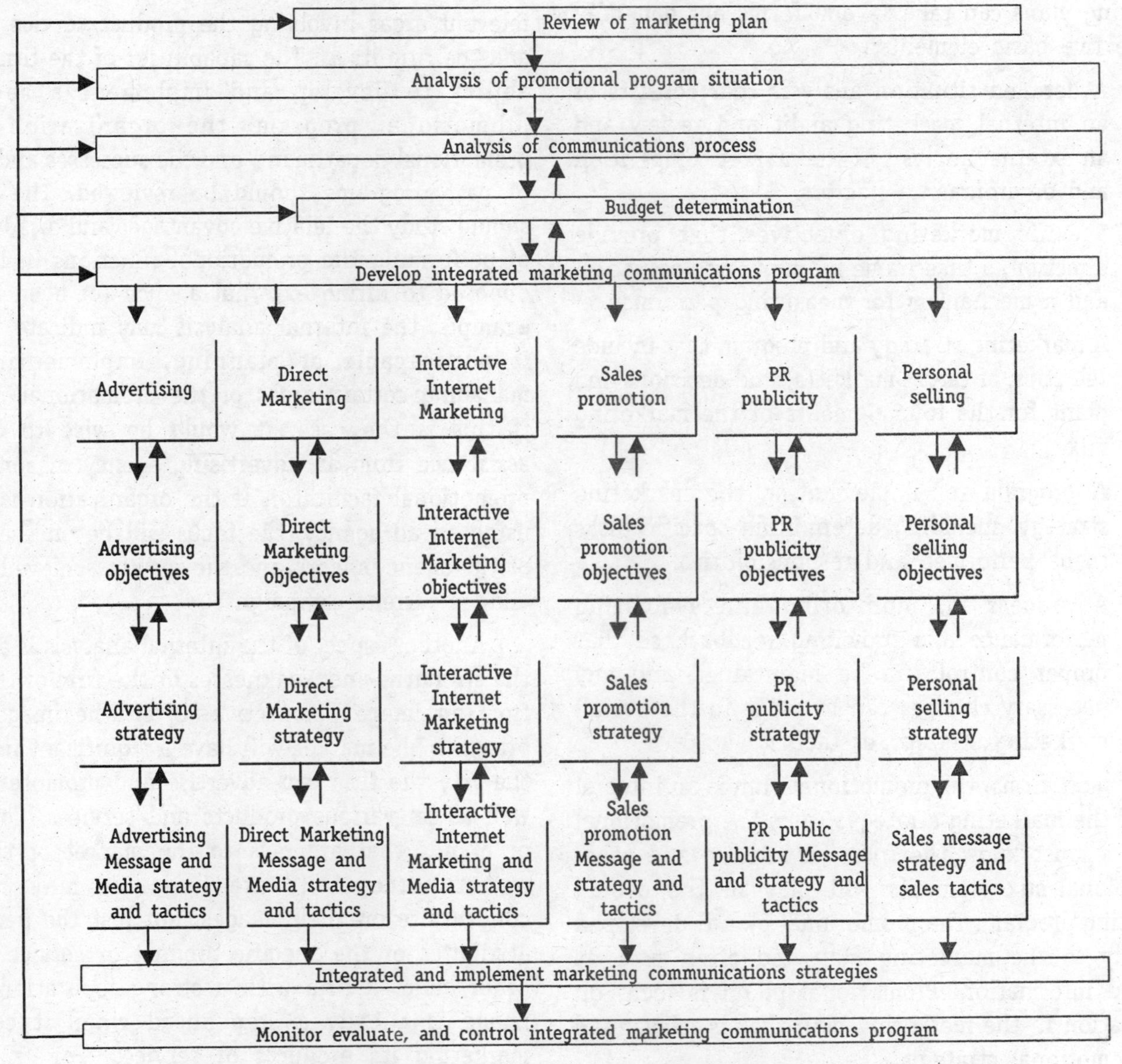

FIG. 21.1. An integrated marketing communications planning model

Monitor, Evaluate, and Control Integrated Marketing Communications Program

Evaluate promotional program results/effectiveness
Take measures to control and adjust promotional strategies

Review of the Marketing Plan

The first step in the IMC planning process is to review the marketing plan and objectives. Before developing a promotional plan, marketers must understand where the company (or the brand) has been, its current position in the market, where it intends to go, and how it plans to get there. Most of this information should be contained in the marketing plan, a written document that describes the overall marketing strategy and programs developed for an organization; a particular product line, or a brand. Marketing plans can take several forms but generally include five basic elements:

1. A detailed situation analysis that consists of an internal marketing audit and review and an external analysis of the market competition and environmental factors.
2. Specific marketing objectives that provide direction, a time frame for marketing activities, and a mechanism for measuring performance.
3. A marketing strategy and program that include selection of target market(s) and decisions and plans for the four elements of the marketing mix.
4. A program for implementing the marketing strategy, including determining specific tasks to be performed and responsibilities.
5. A process for monitoring and evaluating performance and providing feedback so that proper control can be maintained and any necessary changes can be made in the overall marketing strategy or tactics.

For most firms, the promotional plan is an integral part of the marketing strategy. Thus, the promotional planners must know the roles advertising and other promotional-mix elements will play in the overall marketing program. The promotional plan is developed similarly to the marketing plan and often uses its detailed information. Promotional planners focus on information in the marketing plan that is relevant to the promotional strategy.

Promotional Program Situation Analysis

After the overall marketing plan is reviewed, the next step in developing a promotional plan is to conduct the situation analysis. In the IMC program, the situation analysis focuses on the factors that influence or are relevant to the development of a promotional strategy. Like the overall marketing situation analysis, the promotional program situation analysis includes both an internal and an external analysis.

Internal Analysis- The internal analysis assesses relevant areas involving the product/service offering and the firm itself. The capabilities of the firm and its ability to develop and implement a successful promotional program, the organization of the promotional department, and the successes and failures of past programs should be reviewed. The analysis should study the relative advantages and disadvantages of performing the promotional functions in house as opposed to hiring external agency (or agencies). For example, the internal analysis may indicate the firm is not capable of planning, implementing, and managing certain areas of the promotional program. If this is the case, it would be wise to look for assistance from an advertising agency or some other promotional facilitator. If the organization is already using an ad agency, the focus will be on the quality of the agency's work and the results achieved by past and/or current campaigns.

Another aspect of the internal analysis is assessing the strengths and weaknesses of the firm or the brand from an image perspective. Often the image a firm brings to the market will have a significant impact on the way the firm can advertise and promote itself as well as its various products and services. Companies or brands that are new to the market or those for whom perceptions are negative may have to concentrate on their images, not just the benefits or attributes of the specific product or service. On the other hand, a firm with a strong reputation and/or image is already a step ahead when it comes to marketing its products or services. For example, a nationwide survey found that the companies with the best overall reputations among American consumers include Johnson & Johnson, Coca-Cola, Hewlett-Packard, Intel, Ben & Jerry's, and WalMart. WalMart was rated very high in the area of social responsibility, which involves perceptions of the company as a good citizen in its dealings with communities, employees, and the environment. WalMart enhances its image as a socially responsible company by supporting various causes at both local and national levels.

The internal analysis also assesses the relative strengths and weaknesses of the product or service; its advantages and disadvantages; any unique selling points or benefits it may have; its packaging, price, and design; and so on. This information is particularly important to the creative personnel who must develop the advertising message for the brand.

Figure 21.2 is a checklist of some of the areas one might consider when performing analyses for promotional planning purposes. Addressing internal areas may require information the company does not have available internally and must gather as part of the external analysis.

External Analysis

The external analysis focuses on factors such as characteristics of the firm's customers, market segments, positioning strategies, and competitors, as shown in Figure 21.2 An important part of the external analysis is a detailed consideration of customers' characteristics and buying patterns, their decision processes, and factors influencing their purchase decisions. Attention must also be given to con-sumers" perceptions and attitudes, lifestyles, and criteria for making purchase decisions. Often, marketing research studies are needed to answer some of these questions.

A key element of the external analysis is an assessment of the market- The attrac-tiveness of various market segments must be evaluated and the segments to target must be identified. Once the target markets are chosen, the emphasis will be on determining how the product should be positioned. What image or place should it have in consumers' minds?

This part of the promotional program situation analysis also includes an in-depth examination of both direct and indirect competitors. While competitors were analyzed in the overall marketing situation analysis, even more attention is devoted to promotional aspects at this phase. Focus is on the firm's primary competitors: their specific strengths and weaknesses; their segmentation, targeting, and positioning strategies; and the promotional strategies they employ. The size and allocation of their promotional budgets, their media strategies, and the messages they are sending to the marketplace should all be considered.

The external phase also includes an analysis of the marketing environment and current trends or developments that might affect the promotional program.

ADVERTISING TO CONSUMER MARKETS

National Advertising

Advertising done by large companies on a nationwide basis or in most regions of the country. Most of the ads for well-known companies and brands that are seen on prime-time TV or in other major national or regional media are examples of national advertising. The goals of national advertisers are to inform or remind consumers of the company or brand and its features, benefits, advantages, or uses and to create or reinforce its image so that consumers will be predisposed to purchase it.

Retail/Local Advertising

Advertising done by retailers or local merchants to encourage consumers to shop at a specific store, use a local service, or patronize a particular establishment Retail or local advertising tends to emphasize specific patronage motives such as price, hours of operation, service, atmosphere, image, or merchandise assortment. Retailers are concerned with building store traffic, so their promotions often take the form of direct-action advertising designed to produce immediate store traffic and sales.

Primary- versus Selective-Demand Advertising

Primary-demand advertising is designed to stimulate demand for the general product class or entire industry. Selective-demand advertising focuses on creating demand for specific company's brands. Most advertising for products and services is concerned with stimulating selective demand and emphasizes reasons for purchasing a particular brand.

Internal Factors	*External Factors*
Assessment of Firm's Promotional	Customer Analysis
Organization and Capabilities	Who buys our product or service?
Organization of promotional department	Who makes the decision to buy the product?
Capability of firm to develop and execute promotional programs	Who influences the decision to buy the product?
Determination of role and function of ad agency and other promotional facilitators	How is the purchase decision made? Who assumes what role?
What does the customer buy? What needs must be satisfied?	
Review of Firm's Previous Promotional?	
Programs and Results	Why do customers buy a particular brand?
Where do they go or look to buy the product or service?	
Review previous promotional objectives	When do they buy? Any seasonality factors?
Review previous promotional budgets and allocations	What social factors might influence the purchase decision?
Review previous promotional-mix strategies and programs	Do the customers' lifestyles influence their decisions?
Review results of previous promotional programs	How is our product or service perceived by customers?
Assessment of Firm or Brand Image and?	How do demographic factors influence the purchase decision?
Implications for Promotion	
Assessment of Relative Strengths and Competitive Analysis	
Weaknesses of Product or Service	
Who are our direct and indirect competitors?	
What are the strengths and weaknesses of product or service?	What key benefits and positioning are used by our competitors?
What is our position relative to the competition?	
What are its key benefits?	How big are competitors' ad budgets?
Does it have any unique selling points?	What message and media strategies are competitors using?
Assessment of packaging, labelling, and brand image	**Environmental Analysis**
How does our product or service compare development that might effect the promotional programme?	Are there any current trends or with competition?

Fig. 23.2. Areas Covered in the Situation Analysis

An advertiser might concentrate on stimulating primary demand when, for example, its brand dominates a market and will benefit the most from overall market growth. Primary-demand advertising is often used as part of a promotional strategy to help a new product gain market acceptance, since the challenge is to sell customers on the product concept as much as to sell a particular brand. Industry trade associations also try to stimulate primary demand for their members' products, among them cotton, milk, orange juice, pork, and beef.

ADVERTISING TO BUSINESS AND PROFESSIONAL MARKETS

Business-to-Business Advertising

Advertising targeted at individuals who buy or influence the purchase of industrial goods or services for their companies, industrial goods are products that either become a physical part of another product (raw material or component parts), are used in manufacturing other goods (machinery), or are used to help a company conduct Its business (e.g., office supplies, computers). Business services such as insurance, travel services, and health care are also included in this category.

Professional Advertising

Advertising targeted to professionals such as doctors, lawyers, dentists, engineers, or professors to encourage them to use a company's product in their business operations. It might also be used to encourage professionals to recommend or specify the use of a company's product by end-users.

Trade Advertising

Advertising targeted to marketing channel members such as wholesalers, distributors, and retailers. The goal is to encourage channel members to stock, promote, and resell the manufacturer's branded products to their customers.

Keeping up with The New Advertising Media

Today, as new forms of media and communication emerge, the mass market has fragmented into millions of mini markets. To target these micro markets effectively, advertisers going beyond network TV, radio, print, and billboard advertising to shout their messages from buses and subways, sports stadiums, movie screens, clothing and supermarket shelves. They are also sending their messages to our mailboxes, telephones, computer screens and fax machines. Some of the new electronic media that advertisers have begun to explore are as:

- Digizines (or e-zines)
- Interactive TV
- Fax-on demand.

Advertising seek Alternative Media

As network television costs soar and audience shrinks, many advertisers are looking for new ways to reach consumers. And the move toward micro marketing strategies, focuses more strategies, focused more narrowly on specific consumer groups also has fuelled the search for alternative media to replace or supplement network television. Advertisers are shifting larger portions of their budgets to media that cost less and target more effectively.

Two media benefiting most from the shift are outdoor advertising and Cable television. Billboard have undergone a resurgence in recent years. Although outdoor advertising spending recently has leveled off, advertisers now spend more than $1.1 billion annually an outdoor media, a 25 percent increase over ten years ago. Gone are the ugly eye-sores of the past, in their place we now see cleverly designed, colourful attention-grabbers. Outdoor advertising provides an excellent way to reach important consumer segments.

E-commerce

Electronic commerce (E-commerce) is "the exchange of business information using electronic formats, including Electronic formats, including Electronic Mail. Electronic Bulletin Boards and Electronic Funds Transfer.

E-commerce technologies are designed to replace traditional paper based work flow with flow with faster, more efficient and reliable communication between computers." He further stated that "e-commerce" is the process of two or more parties making business transaction via computer and some type of network, e.g., a direct connection or the internet.

E-Commerce (electronic commerce) is the buying and selling of goods and services via the communications capabilities of private and public computer networks including the internet. Global business indexes is increasingly become e-business. This helps both the parties to efficiently co-ordinate their actives. Extract also links dealers, retailers and distributors so that the company can have better control on the delivery, on finished goods. All consulates, ad agencies and market research agencies are linked with the company though the extract making it possible for them to provide service of value to the company.

E-commerce is more specific than e-business; it means that in addition to providing information to visitors about the company, its history, policies products and job opportunities, The company or site officers to transact or facilities the selling of product, and service online. E-marketing describes the company efforts to inform, communicate promote, and sell its products and services over the internet. The 'e' term is also used in terms such as e-finance, e-learning and e-service. But as someone observed, the 'e' will eventually be dropped when most buys practice is online.

Electronic Data Interchange

The term electronics data interchanging has many definitions. American National Standards Institute has defined it as. "Electronic Data Interchange (EDI) is the transmission, in a standard syntax, of unambiguous information of business or strategic significant between computers of independent organisation".

The period of EDI is simple, it is a set of standard that define the easy the paper forms should be rendered electronically. For example, EDI can be used to send an invoice or an order from one company to another. The "sending computer" located at a customer's premises, used telecommunication technology to transfer order data instantly to the receiving computer:, located at the suppliers distribution centre. Software on each company's computer translates the item into standard codes, so it would not matter if one company calls a product a cog and the order calls the same things a sprocket, EDI will make sure that the right part is ordered. After the order is received data are manipulated and formatted to match the order entry files, in the "order data base" of the supplier. The information is then transferred into the data entry files, in the order data base of the supplier. The information is then transferred into the data base and appropriate error messages, and/or expection reports are generated. The "sending computer" stores the order and follows up on it. The "receiving computer" automatically transfers the data to the warehouse of the factory, the accounting and billing department and the shipping department. Electronic Data Interchange is the transfer of business documents, such as purchase orders and involves, between computers as per a set of standards. EDI facilitates the transfer of business documents stored in structured format through mutually agreed messaging protocols—from one computer application to another.

E-Mail

E-Mail is the exchange of text message and computer files over a communication network such as local area network or the internet, usually between computers or terminals." It is also defined as "an electronic text message". Communication is the basic of all business. The internet breaks into the traditional communication. Postal services and telecommunication are losing market share to the electronic communication, especially e-mail. E-mail combines he strength of phone calls and letter. The internet enables combines the strength of phone calls and letters. The internet enables instant communication in written form, either by e-mail or online chat.

Internet

Internet is "the world wide collection of networks and gateways that use the TCP/IP suite of protocols to communication with one another". At the heart of the internet is a backbone of high - speed data communication lines between major modes or host computers, consisting of thousand of commercial, government, educational and other computer system, that route data and messages. One or more internet nodes can go off line without endangering the internet as whole or causing communication.

E-Auctioning

Auctioning on the internet has become popular now-a-days. In traditional methods of auctioning, all those who would like to participate in the auction gather at one place or bid over the phone. Some who are busy may find it difficult to spare time to participate in the auction by sitting at home itself. The internet enables everyone, irrespective of the country to which he belongs and where he is located, can visit the auction web site with a click and participate in the auction and auctioning the people who want to participate in the auction visit the web site with a click and participate in the auction. In e - auctioning the people who want to participate in the auction visit the web site with a click, go through the details of the goods offered on the concerned web pages and place the price or price they would like to offer on the web page.

E-Marketing

In traditional marketing, the marketing team could not get immediate results on the customer reaction. They conducted market surveys, processed the data prepared the reports. On the basis of those reports the management took decisions, Formulated the polices, prepared the plans and implemented them. For all these they took lot of time. The internet allows companies to react to individual customer demands immediately without any loss of time. It does not matter where the customer is located. This is called e-marketing.

E-Banking

Electronic banking is one of the most successful online business. E-banking allows customers to access their accounts and execute orders through a simple to use web site. Electronic banking saves individuals and companies time and money from an Automated Teller Machine (ATM) instead of walking upto the cash counter in the bank, can view their accounts, transfer funds and can pay bills.

E-Trading

E-Trading, where the basic requirements are a PC, a modem and the internet connection, the investor can log on to an online trading portal, go through a comprehensive database of information use the online analytical tools and pass on instruction to a friendly and reliable online broker. Online trading is the perfect combination of net catering to a real life concept. Online trading is the perfect solution to investor needs. It brings together under one site all the relevant factors to enable an informed investment, rather cheaply to the user.

Behavioural Targeting

Behavioural targeting is a technique used by online publishers and advertisers to increase the effectiveness of their campaigns.Behavioural targeting uses information collected on an individual's web-browsing behavior, such as the pages they have visited or the searches they have made, to select which advertisements to display to that individual. Practitioners believe this helps them deliver their online advertisements to the users who are most likely to be influenced by them.

Behavioural marketing is used on its own or in conjunction with other forms of targeting based on factors like geography, demographics or the surrounding content. Examples of behavioural targeting in advertising targeting systems include: nugg.ad, AdLINK 360, Boomerang, DoubleClick, and WunderLoop. These targeting systems allow two main ways of using the technology.

Firstly, they allow advertisers\site owners to display different creative to different people. Secondly, they allow publishers to sell inventory against specific segments of their audiences to advertisers of other e-commerce. Behavioural targeting techniques is also applied to content within a retail or website as a technique for increasing the relevance of product offers and promotions on a visitor by visitor basis. Again, behavioural data can be combined with demographic and past purchase history in order to produce a greater degree of granularity in the targeting.

Self-learning onsite behavioral targeting systems monitor visitor response to site content and learn what is most likely to generate a desired conversion event. Some good content for each behavioural trait or pattern is often established using numerous simultaneous multivariate tests. Onsite behavioural targeting requires relatively high level of traffic before statistical confidence levels can be reached regarding the probability of a particular offer generating a conversion from a user with a set behavioural profile. Some providers have been able to do so by leveraging its large user base, such as Yahoo!. Some providers use a rules based approach, allowing administrators to set the content and offers shown to those with particular traits.

Examples of onsite behavioural targeting systems include: Maxymiser, Netmining and Touch Clarity. Unique for Netmining is that they add an interaction layer on top of their solution so you can get in touch with your webvistor at the right time and with the right interaction. Yahoo! Inc. has been offering onsite behavioural targeting for many years as well.

Network Behavioural Targeting

Advertising Networks use behavioural targeting in a different way to individual sites. Since they serve many adverts across many different sites, they are able to build up a picture of the likely demographic makeup of internet users. An example would be a user seen on football sites, business sites and male fashion sites. A reasonable guess would be to assume the user is male. Demographic analyses of individual sites provided either internally (user surveys) or externally (Comscore\netratings) allow the networks to sell audiences rather than sites. Although advertising networks used to sell this product, this was based on picking the sites where the audiences were. Behavioural targeting allows them to be slightly more specific about this.

Contextual Advertising

Contextual advertising is the term applied to advertisements appearing on websites or other media, such as content displayed in mobile phones, where the advertisements are selected and served by automated systems based on the content displayed by the user.

Google AdSense was the first major contextual advertising program. It worked by providing webmasters with JavaScript code that, when inserted into web pages, called up relevant advertisements from the Google inventory of advertisers. The relevance was calculated by a separate Google bot that indexed the content of the page. Since the advent of AdSense, the Yahoo! Publisher Network, Microsoft adCenter and others have been gearing up to make similar offerings.

Contextual advertising has made a major impact on earnings of many websites. As the ads are more targeted they are more likely to get clicked, thus generating revenue for the owner of the website (and the server of the advertisement). A large part of Google's earnings are from their share of the contextual ads served on the millions of webpages running the AdSense program.

A contextual ad system scans the text of a Web site for keywords and returns ads to the Web page based on what the user is viewing, either through ads placed on the page or pop-up ads. For example, if the user is viewing a site about sports, and the site uses contextual advertising, the user might see ads for sports-related companies, such as memorabilia dealers or ticket sellers. Contextual advertising also is used by search engines to display ads on their search results pages based on what word(s) the users has searched for.

Contextual advertising has attracted some controversy through the use of techniques such as third-party hyperlinking, where a third-party installs software onto a user's computer that interacts with the browser by turning keywords on a Web page into links that lead to advertisers that are not paying the Web site to advertise on its pages. A contextual ad is the advertisement that dynamically appears on a Web site.

DISPLAY ADVERTISING

Display advertising is a type of advertising that may, and most frequently does, contain graphic information beyond text such as logos, photographs or other pictures, location maps, and similar items. In periodicals it can appear on the same page with, or a page adjacent to, general editorial content; as opposed to classified advertising, which generally appears in a distinct section and was traditionally text—only in a limited selection of typefaces (although the latter distinction is no longer sharp).

Display advertising uses static and animated images in standard or non-standard sizes called web banners as well as interactive media that might include audio and video elements. Flash by Adobe (originally Macromedia, which was bought by Adobe) is the preferred format for interactive ads on the internet.

Display ads do not have to be rich in images, audio or video. Text ads are also used where text is more appropriate or more effective. An example of text ads are commercial SMS messages to mobile devices users.

E-mail marketing

E-mail marketing is a form of direct marketing which uses electronic mail as a means of communicating commercial or fundraising messages to an audience. In its broadest sense, every e-mail sent to a potential or current customer could be considered e-mail marketing. However, the term is usually used to refer to:

- Sending e-mails with the purpose of enhancing the relationship of a merchant with its current or old customers and to encourage customer loyalty and repeat business.
- Sending e-mails with the purpose of acquiring new customers or convincing old customers to buy something immediately.
- Adding advertisements in emails sent by other companies to their customers.
- E-mails that are being sent on the Internet (E-mail did and does exist outside the Internet, Network E-mail, FIDO etc.)
- Researchers estimate that US firms alone spent $400 million on e-mail marketing in 2006.

Advantages

E-mail marketing (on the Internet) is popular with companies because:

- The advantage of a mailing list is clearly the ability to distribute information to a wide range of specific, potential customers at a relatively low cost.
- Compared to other media investments such as direct mail or printed newsletters, it is less expensive.
- An exact return on investment can be tracked ("track to basket") and has proven to be high when done properly. E-mail marketing is often reported as second only to search marketing as the most effective online marketing tactic.
- It is instant, as opposed to a mailed advertisement, an e-mail arrives in a few seconds or minutes.
- It lets the advertiser "push" the message to its audience, as opposed to a website that waits for customers to come in.
- It is easy to track. An advertiser can track users via web bugs, bounce messages, un-subscribes, read-receipts, click-throughs, etc. These can be used to measure open rates, positive or negative responses, correlate sales with marketing.
- Advertisers generate repeat business affordably and automatically.
- Advertisers can reach substantial numbers of email subscribers who have opted in (consented) to receive e-mail communications on subjects of interest to them.
- Over half of Internet users check or send e-mail on a typical day.
- Specific types of interaction with messages can trigger other messages to be automatically delivered.
- Specific types of interaction with messages can trigger other events such as updating the profile of the recipient to indicate a specific interest category.
- Green-e-mail marketing is paper-free.

Disadvantages

Many companies use e-mail marketing to communicate with existing customers, but many other companies send unsolicited bulk e-mail, also known as spam.

Illicit e-mail marketing antedates legitimate e-mail marketing, since on the early Internet it was not permitted to use the medium for commercial purposes. As a result, marketers attempting to establish themselves as legitimate businesses in e-mail marketing have had an uphill battle, hampered also by criminal spam operations billing themselves as legitimate.

It is frequently difficult for observers to distinguish between legitimate and spam email marketing. First off, spammers attempt to represent themselves as legitimate operators, obfuscating the issue. Second, direct-marketing political groups such as the U.S. Direct Marketing Association (DMA) have pressured legislatures to legalize activities which many Internet operators consider to be spamming, such as the sending of "opt-out" unsolicited commercial e-mail. Third, the sheer volume of spam e-mail has led some users to mistake legitimate commercial e-mail (for instance, a mailing list to which the user subscribed) for spam — especially when the two have a similar appearance, as when messages include HTML and flashy graphics.

Due to the volume of spam e-mail on the Internet, spam filters are essential to most users. Some marketers report that legitimate commercial e-mails frequently get caught by filters, and hidden; however, it is somewhat less common for e-mail users to complain that spam filters block legitimate mail.

Opt-in email Advertising

Opt-in email advertising or permission marketing is a method of advertising via electronic mail whereby the recipient of the advertisement has consented to receive it. It is one of several ways developed by marketers to eliminate the disadvantages of e-mail marketing.

Email has become a very popular mode of communication across the world. It has also become extremely popular to advertise through. Some of the many advantages of advertising through e-mail are the direct contact with the consumer and is "inexpensive, flexible, and simple to implement" (Fairhead, 2003). There are also disadvantages attached to email advertising such as, alienating the consumer because of overload to messages or the advertisement getting deleted without getting read.

Permission email marketing may evolve into a technology that uses a handshake protocol between sender and receiver (Fairhaed, 2003). This system is intended to eventually result in a high degree of satisfaction between consumers and marketers. If opt-in email advertising is used, the material that is emailed to consumers will be "anticipated." It is assumed that the consumer wants to receive it, which makes it unlike unsolicited advertisements sent to the consumer (often referred to as spam). Ideally, opt-in email advertisements will be more personal and relevant to the consumer than untargetted advertisements.

A common example of permission marketing is a newsletter sent to a firm's customers. Newsletters like this are a way to let customers know about upcoming events or promotions, or new products. In this type of advertising, a company that wants to send a newsletter to their customers may ask them at the point of purchase if they would like to receive this newsletter.

With a foundation of opted-in contact information stored in a database, marketers can automatically send out promotional materials. The marketers can also segment their promotions to specific market segments.

Interactive Advertising

Interactive Advertising is the use of interactive media to promote and/or influence the buying decisions of the consumer in an online and offline environment. Interactive advertising can utilise media such as the Internet, interactive television, mobile devices (WAP and SMS), as well as kiosk-based terminals.

Interactive advertising affords the marketer the ability to engage the consumer in a direct and personal way, enabling a sophisticated and dimensional dialogue, which can affect a potential customer's buying decisions particularly in an e-commerce environment.

Perhaps one of the most effective implementations of interactive advertising is so-called Viral marketing. This technique uses images, texts, web links, Flash animations, audio/video clips etc., passed from user to user chain letter-style, via email. A notable example of this is the Subservient Chicken, a campaign by Burger King to promote their new line of chicken sandwiches and the "Have It Your Way" campaign.

Interactive advertising is also assuming other avatars, such as online directories for brands. These directories presently perform a complementary role to conventional advertising, helping viewers recall and compare brands primarily seen on television. Response is mediated usually through forms and click-to-call technologies.

In early 2008, Pay per play advertising launched online. This type of advertising uses audio ads to get a website visitor's attention. Now, advertisers have one more way to interact with the senses of their target demographic.

Affiliate Marketing

Affiliate marketing is a web-based marketing practice in which a business rewards one or more affiliates for each visitor or customer brought about by the affiliate's marketing efforts. Affiliate marketing is also the name of the industry where a number of different types of companies and individuals are performing this form of internet marketing, including affiliate networks, affiliate management companies and in-house affiliate managers, specialized 3rd party vendors, and various types of affiliates/publishers who promote the products and services of their partners.

Affiliate marketing overlaps with other internet marketing methods to some degree, because affiliates often use regular advertising methods. Those methods include organic search engine optimization, paid search engine marketing, email marketing and in some sense display advertising. On the other hand, affiliates sometimes use less orthodox techniques like publishing reviews of products or services offered by a partner.

Affiliate marketing — using one site to drive traffic to another — is a form of online marketing, which is frequently overlooked by advertisers. While search engines, e-mail and RSS capture much of the attention of online retailers, affiliate marketing carries a much lower profile. Still, affiliates continue to play a significant role in e-retailers' marketing strategies.

The Beginning of Affiliate Marketing

The concept of revenue sharing, paying commission for referred business, predates that of affiliate marketing and the Internet. The translation of the revenue share principles to mainstream ecommerce happened almost four years after the World Wide Web was born in November 1994, when CDNow launched its BuyWeb program. With its BuyWeb program, CDNow was the first non-adult site to introduce the concept of an affiliate or associate program with its idea of click-through purchasing.

CDNow.com had the idea that music-oriented web sites could review or list albums on their pages that their visitors might be interested in purchasing and offer a link that would take the visitor directly to CDNow to purchase them. The idea for this remote purchasing originally arose because of conversations with music publisher Geffen Records in the fall of 1994. The management at Geffen wanted to sell its artists' CDs directly from its site but did not want to do it itself. Geffen Records asked CDNow if it could design a program where CDNow would do the fulfillment. Geffen Records realized that CDNow could link directly from the artist on its Web site to Geffen's web site, bypassing the CDNow home page and going directly to an artist's music page.

Affiliate marketing was used on the internet by the adult industry before CDNow launched their BuyWeb program. The consensus of marketers and adult industry insiders is that Cybererotica was either the first or among the early innovators in affiliate marketing with a cost-per-click program.

Amazon.com launched its associate program in July 1996. Amazon associates would place banner or text links on their site for individual books or link directly to the Amazon's home page.

When visitors clicked from the associate's site through to Amazon.com and purchased a book, the associate received a commission. Amazon.com was not the first merchant to offer an affiliate program, but its program was the first to become widely known and served as a model for subsequent programs.

In February 2000, Amazon.com announced that it had been granted a patent (6,029,141) on all the essential components of an affiliate program. The patent application was submitted in June 1997, which was before most affiliate programs but not before PC Flowers & Gifts.com (October 1994), AutoWeb.com (October 1995), Kbkids.com/BrainPlay.com (January 1996), EPage(April 1996), and a handful of others.

Historic Development

Affiliate marketing has grown quickly since its inception. The e-commerce website, viewed as a marketing toy in the early days of the web, became an integrated part of the overall business plan and in some cases grew to a bigger business than the existing offline business. According to one report, total sales generated through affiliate networks in 2006 was £2.16 billion in the UK alone. The estimates were £1.35 billion in sales in 2005. Marketing Sherpa's research team estimated that, in 2006, affiliates worldwide earned $6.5 billion in bounty and commissions from a variety of sources in retail, personal finance, gaming and gambling, travel, telecom, education, publishing and forms of lead generation other than contextual ad networks such as Google AdSense.

Currently the most active sectors for affiliate marketing are the adult, gambling and retail sectors. The three sectors expected to experience the greatest growth are the mobile phone, finance and travel sectors. Hot on the heels of these are the entertainment (particularly gaming) and internet-related services (particularly broadband) sectors. Also several of the affiliate solution providers expect to see increased interest from B2B marketers and advertisers in using affiliate marketing as part of their mix. Of course, this is constantly subject to change.

Web 2.0

The rise of blogging, interactive online communities and other new technologies, web sites and services based on the concepts that are now called Web 2.0 have impacted the affiliate marketing world as well. The new media allowed merchants to get closer to their affiliates and improved communication between each other. New developments have made it harder for unscrupulous affiliates to make money. Emerging black sheep are detected and made known to the affiliate marketing community with much greater speed and efficiency.

Predominant Compensation Methods

80% of affiliate programs today use revenue sharing or cost per sale (CPS) as compensation method, 19% use cost per action (CPA) and the remaining 1% are other methods, such as cost per click (CPC) or cost per mille (CPM).

Diminished Compensation Methods

The use of pay per click (PPC/CPC) and pay per impression (CPM/CPT) in traditional affiliate marketing is far less than 1% today and negligible. CPM and CPC are today still heavily used in display advertising and paid search.

Cost per mille (thousand) (CPM/CPT) requires the publisher only to load the advertising on his website and show it to his visitors in order to get paid a commission, while PPC requires one additional step in the conversion process to generate revenue for the publisher. Visitors must not only be made aware of the ad, but also pursue them to click on it and visit the advertiser's website.

Cost per click (CPC/PPC) used to be more common in the early days of affiliate marketing, but diminished over time due to click fraud issues that are very similar to the click fraud issues modern search engines are facing today. Contextual advertising, such as Google AdSense are not considered in this statistic. It is not specified yet, if contextual advertising can be considered affiliate marketing or not.

CPM/CPC versus CPA/CPS (performance marketing)

In the case of CPM or CPC, the publisher does not care if the visitor is the type of audience that the advertiser tries to attract and is able to convert, because the publisher already earned his commission at this point. This leaves the greater, and, in case of CPM, the full risk and loss (if the visitor cannot be converted) to the advertiser.

CPA and CPS require that referred visitors do more than visiting the advertiser's website in order for the affiliate to get paid commission. The advertiser must convert that visitor first. It is in the best interest for the affiliate to send the best targeted traffic to the advertiser as possible to increase the chance of a conversion. The risk and loss is shared between the affiliate and the advertiser.

For this reason affiliate marketing is also called "performance marketing", in reference to how employees that work in sales are typically being compensated. Employees in sales are usually getting paid sales commission for every sale they close and sometimes a performance incentives for exceeding targeted baselines. Affiliates are not employed by the advertiser whose products or services they promote, but the compensation models applied to affiliate marketing are very similar to the ones used for people in the advertisers' internal sales department.

The phrase, "Affiliates are an extended sales force for your business", which is often used to explain affiliate marketing, is not 100% accurate. The main difference between the two is that affiliate marketers cannot, or not much influence a possible prospect in the conversion process, once the prospect was sent away to the advertiser's website. The sales team of the advertiser on the other hand does have the control and influence, up to the point where the prospect signs the contract or completes the purchase.

Multi-tier Programs

Some advertisers offer multi-tier programs that distribute commission into a hierarchical referral network of sign-ups and sub-partners. In practical terms: publisher "A" signs up to the program with an advertiser and gets rewarded for the agreed activity conducted by a referred visitor. If publisher "A" attracts other publishers ("B", "C", etc.) to sign up for the same program using her sign-up code all future activities by the joining publishers "B" and "C" will result in additional, lower commission for publisher "A".

Snowballing, this system rewards a chain of hierarchical publishers who may or may not know of each others' existence, yet generate income for the higher level signup. This sort of structure has been successfully implemented by a company called Quixtar.com, a division of Alticor, the parent company of Amway. Quixtar has implemented a network marketing structure to implement its marketing program for major corporations such as Barnes & Noble, Office Depot, Sony Music and hundreds more.

Two-tier programs exist in the minority of affiliate programs; most are simply one-tier. Referral programs beyond 2-tier are multi-level marketing (MLM) or network marketing.

Even though Quixtar compensation plan is network marketing & wouldn't be considered 'affiliate marketing', the big company partners are considered and call themselves affiliates. Therefore, you may argue that the Quixtar company is the affiliate marketer for its partner corporation.

From the Advertiser's Perspective Pros and cons

Merchants like affiliate marketing because in most cases, it uses a "pay for performance" model, meaning that the merchant does not incur a marketing expense unless results are accrued (excluding any initial setup cost). Some businesses owe much of their success to this marketing technique, a notable example being Amazon.com. Unlike display advertising, however, affiliate marketing is not easily scalable.

Implementation options

Some merchants run their own affiliate programs (In House) while others use third party services provided by intermediaries to track traffic or sales that are referred from affiliates. Merchants can choose from two different types of affiliate management solutions, standalone software or hosted services typically called affiliate networks.

Affiliate management and program management outsourcing

Successful affiliate programs require a lot of maintenance and work. The number of affiliate programs just a few years back was much smaller than it is today. Having an affiliate program that is successful is not as easy anymore. The days when programs could generate considerable revenue for the merchant even if they were poorly or not at all managed ("auto-drive") are over (with the exception of some verticals).

Those uncontrolled programs did aid (and continue to do so today) rogue affiliates, who use spamming, trademark infringement, false advertising, "cookie cutting", typosquatting and other unethical methods that caused affiliate marketing to get a bad reputation.

The increase of number of internet businesses in combination with the increased number of people that trust the current technology enough to do shopping and business online caused and still causes a further maturing of affiliate marketing. The opportunities to generate considerable amount of profit in combination with a much more crowded marketplace filled with about equal quality and sized competitors made it harder for merchants to get noticed, but at the same time the rewards if you get noticed much larger.

Recently, the internet advertising industry has become more advanced. Online media has in some areas been rising to the sophistication of offline media, in which advertising has been largely professional and competitive for many years already. The requirements to be successful are much higher than they were in the past. Those requirements are becoming often too much of a burden for the merchant to do it successfully in-house. More and more merchants are looking for alternative options which they find in relatively new outsourced (affiliate) program management or OPM companies that were often founded by veteran affiliate managers and network program managers.

The OPM are doing this highly specialized job of affiliate program management for the merchant as a service agency very much like Ad agencies are doing the job to promote a brand or product in the offline world today.

FIG. 23.3. Companies and websites in affiliate marketing

Types of affiliate websites

Affiliate sites are often categorized by merchants (advertisers) and affiliate networks. There are no industry-wide accepted standards for the categorization. The following list is very generic but commonly understood and used by affiliate marketers.

- Search affiliates that utilize pay per click search engines to promote the advertisers offers (search arbitrage).
- Comparison shopping sites and directories
- Loyalty sites, typically characterized by

providing a reward system for purchases via points back, cash back or charitable donations.
- Coupon and rebate sites that focus on sales promotions.
- Content and niche sites, including product review sites.
- Personal websites (these type of sites were the reason for the birth of affiliate marketing, but are today almost reduced to complete irrelevance compared to the other types of affiliate sites).
- Blogs and RSS feeds.
- Email list affiliates (owners of large opt-in email list(s)).
- Registration path or Co-Registration affiliates who include offers from other companies during a registration process on their own website.
- Shopping directories that list merchants by categories without providing coupons, price comparison and other features based on information that frequently change and require ongoing updates.
- CPA networks are top tier affiliates that expose offers from advertiser they are affiliated with to their own network of affiliates (not to confuse with 2nd tier).

Past and current issues

In the early days of affiliate marketing, there was very little control over what affiliates were doing, which was abused by a large number of affiliates. Affiliates used false advertisements, forced clicks to get tracking cookies set on users' computers, and adware, which displays ads on computers. Many affiliate programs were poorly managed.

Email spam

In its early days many internet users held negative opinions of affiliate marketing due to the tendency of affiliates to use spam to promote the programs in which they were enrolled. As affiliate marketing has matured many affiliate merchants have refined their terms and conditions to prohibit affiliates from spamming.

Search engine spam/spamdexing

There used to be much debate around the affiliate practice of spamdexing and many affiliates have converted from sending email spam to creating large volumes of autogenerated web pages, many-a-times, using product data-feeds provided by merchants. Each devoted to different niche keywords as a way of "SEOing" (search engine optimization) their sites with the search engines. This is sometimes referred to as spamming the search engine results. Spam is the biggest threat to organic search engines whose goal is to provide quality search results for keywords or phrases entered by their users. Google's algorithm update dubbed "BigDaddy" in February 2006 which was the final stage of Google's major update dubbed "Jagger" which started mid-summer 2005, specifically targeted this kind of spam with great success and enabled Google to remove a large amount of mostly computer generated duplicate content from its index.

Sites made up mostly of affiliate links are usually badly regarded as they do not offer quality content. In 2005, there were active changes made by Google whereby certain websites were labelled as "thin affiliates" and were either removed from the index, or taken from the first 2 pages of the results and moved deeper within the index. In order to avoid this categorization, webmasters who are affiliate marketers must create real value within their websites that distinguishes their work from the work of spammers or banner farms with nothing but links leading to the merchant sites.

Affiliate links work best in the context of the information contained within the website. For instance, if a website is about "How to publish a website", within the content an affiliate link leading to a merchant's ISP site would be appropriate. If a website is about sports, then an affiliate link leading to a sporting goods site might work well within the content of the articles and information about sports. The idea is to publish quality information within the site, and to link "in context" to related merchant's sites.

Adware

Adware is still an issue today, but affiliate marketers have taken steps to fight it. Adware is not the same as spyware although both often use the same methods and technologies. Merchants usually had no clue what adware was, what it did and how it was damaging their brand. Affiliate marketers became aware of the issue much more quickly, especially because they noticed that adware often overwrites their tracking cookie and results in a decline of commissions. Affiliates who do not use adware became enraged by adware, which they felt was stealing hard earned commission from them. Adware usually has no valuable purpose nor provides any useful content to the often unaware user that has the adware running on his computer. Affiliates discussed the issues in various affiliate forums and started to get organized. It became obvious that the best way to cut off adware was by discouraging merchants from advertising via adware. Merchants that did not care or even supported adware were made public by affiliates, which damaged the merchants' reputations and also hurt the merchants' general affiliate marketing efforts. Many affiliates simply "canned" the merchant or switched to a competitor's affiliate program. Eventually, affiliate networks were also forced by merchants and affiliates to take a stand and ban certain adware publishers from their network.

Resulting from this were the Code of Conduct by Commission Junction/BeFree and Performics, LinkShare's Anti-Predatory Advertising Addendum and ShareASale's complete ban of software applications as medium for affiliates to promote advertiser offers. Regardless of the progress made, adware is still an issue. This is demonstrated by the class action lawsuit against ValueClick and its daughter company Commission Junction filed on April 20, 2007.

Trademark bidding / PPC

Affiliates were among the earliest adopters of pay-per-click advertising when the first PPC search engines like Goto.com (which became later Overture.com, acquired by Yahoo! in 2003) emerged during the end of the nineteen-nineties. Later in 2000, Google launched their PPC service AdWords which is responsible for the wide spread use and acceptance of PPC as an advertising channel. More and more merchants engaged in PPC advertising, either directly or via a search marketing agency and realized that this space was already well occupied by their affiliates. Although this fact alone did create channel conflicts and hot debate between advertisers and affiliates, the biggest issue was the bidding on advertisers' names, brands and trademarks by some affiliates. A larger number of advertisers started to adjust their affiliate program terms to prohibit their affiliates from bidding on those type of keywords. Some advertisers however did and still do embrace this behaviour of their affiliates and allow them, even encourage them, to bid any term they like, including the advertisers trademarks.

Lack of self-regulation

Affiliate marketing is driven by entrepreneurs who are working at the forefront of internet marketing. Affiliates are the first to take advantage of new emerging trends and technologies where established advertisers do not dare to be active. Affiliates take risks and "trial and error" is probably the best way to describe how affiliate marketers are operating. This is also one of the reasons why most affiliates fail and give up before they "make it" and become "super affiliates" who generate $10,000 and more in commission (not sales) per month. This "frontier" life and the attitude that can be found in such type of communities is probably the main reason, why the affiliate marketing industry is not able to this day to self-regulate itself beyond individual contracts between advertiser and affiliate. The 10+ years history since the beginning of affiliate marketing is full of failed attempts to create an industry organization or association of some kind that could be the initiator of regulations, standards and guidelines for the industry. Some of the failed examples are the Affiliate Union and iAfma.

The only places where the different people from the industry, affiliates/publishers, merchants/advertisers, networks and 3rd party vendors and service providers like outsources program managers come together at one location are either online forums and industry trade shows. The forums are free and even small affiliates can have a big voice at places like that, which is supported by the anonymity that is provided by those platforms. Trade shows are not anonymous, but a large number, in fact the greater number (quantitative) of affiliates are not able to attend those events for financial reasons. Only performing affiliates can afford the often hefty price tags for the event passes or get it sponsored by an advertiser they promote.

Because of the anonymity of forums, the only place where you are to get the majority (quantitative) of people in the industry together, it is almost impossible to create any form of legally binding rule or regulation that must be followed by everybody in the industry. Forums had only very few successes in their role as representant of the majority in the affiliate marketing industry. The last example of such a success was the halt of the "CJ LMI" ("Commission Junction Link Management Initiative") in June/July 2006, when a single network tried to impose on their publishers/ affiliates the use of Javascript tracking code as a replacement for common HTML links.

"Threat" to traditional affiliate networks

Increasingly, voices in the industry are recommending that "affiliate marketing" be substituted with an alternative name. The problem with the term affiliate marketing is that it is often confused with network-marketing or multi-level marketing. "Performance marketing" is a common alternative, but other recommendations have been made as well. A similar attempt was made to rename search engine optimization, but with little success.

Affiliate marketers usually avoid this topic as much as possible, but when it is being discussed, then are the debates explosive and heated to say the least. The discussion is about CPA networks (CPA = Cost per action) and their impact on "classic" affiliate marketing (traditional affiliate networks). Traditional affiliate marketing is resources intensive and requires a lot of maintenance. Most of this includes the management, monitoring and support of affiliates. Affiliate marketing is supposed to be about long-term and mutual beneficial partnerships between advertisers and affiliates. CPA networks on the other hand eliminate the need for the advertiser to build and maintain relationships to affiliates, because that task is performed by the CPA network for the advertiser. The advertiser simply puts an offer out, which is in almost every case a CPA based offer, and the CPA networks take care of the rest by mobilizing their affiliates to promote that offer. CPS or revenue share offers are rarely to be found at CPA networks, which is the main compensation model of classic affiliate marketing.

Some of these alternative media has seen a farfetched, and they sometimes irritate consumers. But for many marketers, these media can save money and provide a way to hit selected consumers where they live, shop, work and play. Of course, this may leave wondering if there are any commercial-free havens remaining for adweary consumers. The back seat of a tax, perhaps, or public elevators, or stalls in a public restroom? Forget it! Each has already been invaded by innovative marketing communicators.

Marketers Respond to 9/11

Marketers often have to deal with events that have a significant impact on the economy as well as the psyche of the consumer. However, the tragedy created by the horrific events of September 11, 2001, caused an environment unlike anything most businesspeople have ever experienced. The aftershocks of the terrorist attacks ripped through nearly every sector of the U.S. economy, with certain industries, such as travel, tourism, media, and entertainment, being particularly hard hit.

After the attacks, the major television networks, including CBS, NBC, ABC, and Fox, went commercial-free for several days, an approach costing them a combined $35 to $40 million a day in lost revenue. Adding in cable news networks and local stations, the television industry's cost for covering the attacks and their immediate aftermath was more than $700 million in canceled advertising. The major broadcast and cable news operations face growing expenses to cover the war on terrorism, including the costs of creating new bureaus abroad, improving technology, and widening coverage.

The terrorist attacks also have had a significant impact on the advertising industry and created major problems for ad agencies as well as media companies, both of which were already reeling from the soft economy and dot-com bust that resulted in lower advertising spending. Advertising agencies and their clients have had to determine how to appeal to consumers facing economic uncertainty, rethinking their priorities, and feeling anxious about their safety. Marketing after a tragedy is always a tricky business and was even more so because of the scale of the September 11 events. Marketers who alluded to the tragedy risked alienating consumers who might think they were trying to capitalize on it, while those who ignored it ran the risk of seeming insensitive and out of touch.

Consumers emitted mixed signals regarding their feelings about the terrorist attacks. Researchers found a resurgence of patriotism, a renewed desire to connect with family and friends, and a strengthened belief in old-fashioned values such as community service and charity. In a survey conducted six months after the attacks, 80 percent of the consumer respondents indicated that 9/11 was still affecting their professional and personal lives. Though their lives were returning to normal and few people radically modified their day-to-day activities, changes included keeping cell phones handy, installing more locks, watching more 24-hour news channels, and looking more for products that were made in the United States.

Some marketers decided that the best way to respond to the new times was with messages offering appeals to patriotism, the promise of escape, or tribute to those who died or were involved with the tragedy. One of the most popular commercials during the 2002 Super Bowl was an Anheuser Busch spot featuring stately Clydesdales trotting across serene snowy landscapes and over the Brooklyn Bridge to pause before the Manhattan skyline and bow in tribute to New York City. Not surprisingly, New York City firefighters and police officers became popular advertising spokespersons.

The U.S. government used the public's outrage over the terrorist attacks as part of its efforts to fight drug abuse. The White House Office of National Drug Control Policy developed an advertising campaign suggesting that illegal drug sales have become a major means of raising money for terrorism. The idea behind the campaign is that people will be less likely to use drugs if they understand that by using them they may be supporting terrorism.

Marketers have now had time to reflect on how they responded to the nation's worst terrorist tragedy and how their marketing communications during the chaotic months after the attacks were received by consumers. Appeals to patriotism were unwelcome if they were seen as attempts to cash in on the tragedy. However, companies whose advertising programs were already identified with patriotism, the flag, and other U.S. symbols and those whose marketing efforts were tied to charitable donations destined to I the recovery effort were perceived favourably.

Sources: Steve Jarvis, "Red, White and the Blues," Marketing News, May 27, 2002, pp. 1,9; Hillary Chura, "The New Normal," Advertising Age, Mar. 11,2002, pp. 1,4; Gwendolyn Bounds, "Marketers Tread Precarious Terrain," The Wall Street Journal, Feb.5, 2002,pp_Bl,4; Jon E. Hilsenrath, "Terror's Toil on the Economy," The Wall Street Journal, Oct. 9, 2002, pp_ Bl, 4.

Sponsorship

This is a new trend in marketing communications. Sponsorship is the fastest growing form of marketing communications in India. However, it is still very much in its infancy, especially in the trade show arena. With this in mind, you can find unlimited opportunities to broaden your competitive advantage by increasing your credibility, image and prestige in sponsoring events attracting your target market.

Some trade show promotional opportunities include sponsorship of the press room, an international lounge, a speaker or VIP room, an awards reception, educational programs, banners, badge holders, audio visual equipment, display computers, tote bags, shuttle buses, napkins and drink cups.

So, why should your company be interested in sponsorship? When done well, it offers significant opportunities for distinct marketing and competitive advantages, as well as showing support of the event.

What is sponsorship?

Sponsorship is the financial or in-kind support of an activity, used primarily to reach specified business goals. According to IEG's Complete Guide to Sponsorship, "Sponsorship should not be confused with advertising. Advertising is considered a quantitative medium, whereas sponsorship is considered a qualitative medium. It promotes a company in association with the sponsee."

A large number of events these days use sponsorship support to offer more exciting programmes and to help defray rising costs. Sponsorship allows you to reach specifically targeted niche markets without any waste. In addition, it is a powerful complement to other marketing programs, in addition to having a dramatic influence on customer relations.

Why sponsor?

Sponsorship offers the possibility of achieving several goals at once. According to Schmader and Jackson in their book, 'Special Events: Inside and Out', a company can benefit from sponsorship in many ways, such as:

- **Enhancing Image/Shaping Consumer Attitudes**

Often companies are looking to improve how they are perceived by their target audience. Sponsoring events that appeal to their market are likely to shape buying attitudes and help generate a positive reaction. Coca Cola, for example is always looking to generate a positive influence of their products in the minds of their consumers and as such, regularly support events they feel can influence consumer opinions.

- **Driving Sales**

Sponsorship geared to driving sales can be an extremely potent promotional tool. This objective allows sponsors to showcase their product attributes. Food and beverage companies often use sponsorship to encourage samplings and sales.

IEG's Complete Guide to Sponsorship cites Visa's fund-raising effort around its sponsorship of the Olympic Games and the U.S. Olympic Team. They promoted their association by offering to make a donation to the team each time consumers charge a purchase to their card. American Express used a similar strategy by donating to needy causes with their "Charge Against Hunger" campaign. As a result, both companies experienced a significant rise in sales volume.

- **Creating positive publicity/heightening visibility**

Every sponsor is seeking wide exposure in both electronic and print media. Positive publicity helps create heightened visibility of products/services. Various media covering the event may include sponsors names and/or photos. In addition, the kind of media coverage a sponsor may get is often unaffordable if the company were to think of purchasing it, and if it were available. To maximize this objective, it is important for the sponsoring company to have a comprehensive media campaign to augment the regular media coverage promoted by the organizers. Sponsorship can often generate media coverage that might otherwise not have been available.

- **Differentiating from competitors**

The mere act of sponsoring an event, especially an exclusive sponsorship, is a significant way to create competitor differentiation. Your company name has the opportunity to stand out head and shoulders above the competition. This is particularly helpful if your company wants to combat a competitor with a larger ad budget. Sponsorship allows smaller companies to compete with their industry giants.

Target audiences often perceive sponsorship in a positive way. They see you as making a greater effort to support the event, often allowing more or better activities to take place as a result of your sponsorship.

- **Helping with good "Corporate Citizen" role**

Another powerful sponsorship objective allows companies to be viewed as a "good neighbour." To be seen supporting the community and contributing to its economic development is extremely powerful and creates enormous goodwill.

- **Enhancing business, consumer and VIP relations**

Sponsorship that offers hospitality opportunities is always very attractive to companies. Perks may include special exclusive networking settings such as VIP receptions or golf tournaments – opportunities to meet key customers and solidify business relationships. It is important to evaluate each opportunity and look for ways it could tie into your marketing objectives. (Susan Friedman, http://www.Buzzle.com/).

Sponsorship: the Key to Powerful Marketing

Sponsorship provides a great means of broadening your competitive edge by improving your company's image, prestige and credibility by supporting events that your target market finds attractive. In recent years, corporate sponsorship has become the fastest growing type of marketing in India.

Part of this growth can be attributed to the increasing numbers of small and medium-sized businesses involved. Previously, only large businesses could afford to sponsor cause marketing, for instance, as a way of boosting profits as well as establishing goodwill. However, now smaller companies are sponsoring everything from local volleyball and softball teams to fairs, festivals and clean-ups of parks as an effective method of boosting their visibility in their community. Most of these sponsorships help these companies to enhance their public profile relatively cheaply.

Irrespective of the size of the company, however, experts in the field tout a broad spectrum of benefits that can be gained by sponsorship aside from enhancing visibility and image, such as differentiating the company from competitors, helping to develop closer and better relationships with customers, both existing and potential ones, showcasing services and products, and even getting rid of outdated inventory. These experts go on to say that when sponsorships are strategic and well-conceived, they can boost both short-term and long-term sales.

Event Sponsorship Benefits

Sponsorship of events in particular can be especially effective as a marketing tool because it can be a means of accessing a wide range of audiences such as decision makers in business, government entities, and of course customers. It can be particularly beneficial for companies that take part in international trade, because sponsorship transcends cultural and language barriers.

A growing number of marketers think that corporate sponsorship is better than other methods as it provides opportunities to gauge customer response to products immediately. Events allow business owners or executives relate directly with their customers, while they give customers the opportunity to try out the products of a company firsthand. In comparison, marketing research methods such as focus groups are usually costly and may not focus on the right kind of people, while market surveys or questionnaires usually do not allow prospective customers the opportunity to try out products.

Heightened visibility due to positive publicity through the media is another reason corporate sponsorship of events — especially those that attract large numbers of people like popular sports events - can be the most effective marketing tool. Every corporate sponsor seeks the widest exposure possible in both print and electronic media. This publicity increases the visibility of the company's products and services. The various kinds of media that cover the event usually include the names, and even pictures, of the sponsors. This kind of mass coverage by the media that the sponsor gets is usually unaffordable, if the company were to purchase it. Therefore, in order to maximize the impact, the company sponsoring the event should augment the media coverage the organizers arrange. In fact, sponsorship often can generate media coverage which may not have been otherwise available.

Sponsorship and Consumers

Given the propensity of consumers to associate sponsors with the event they promote, it is important for companies to select events that are appropriate with their product or corporate image. Therefore, before signing up, check out how the show is perceived. Does it have an up-scale, classy image? Does it have a clean image, or is its reputation less than what it should be? Companies should not be associated with any event or cause without first determining if the sponsorship has the potential of having any negative effects on them.

In addition, the organizers should also provide you with details like the target audience that are expected, media coverage plans, and what obligations you have as a sponsor. It is also important to find out the kind of support the organizers will provide, and exactly what your sponsorship money is buying.

Sponsorship that involves hospitality always appeals to companies. The advantages may involve exclusive networking opportunities like golf competitions or receptions of VIP's, which can be used to meet significant customers and consolidate business associations. It is essential to appraise every opportunity and seek ways to marry them with your business and marketing goals.

Sponsorships are a time-honoured method of winning favour with the public by associating the name of your business with an event. When strategically selected and intelligently executed, event sponsorships help persuade your target market to do business with you. Like every marketing technique, however, sponsorships have numerous pitfalls that can mean you're wasting your money. Most businesses don't have a specific goal when they sponsor an event, just a vague idea that it will bring them tons of new business.

Sponsorships are a great way to go for two reasons: First, the person will be buying a smaller number of commercials per day than he or she would with a regular non-sponsoring schedule, and these reports are run in excellent time slots to provide audiences with critical information, so the person is not going to get any crummy placements. And second, audiences tend to hear a sponsoring message because they're in a listening mode - that is, they're focused on the special report and will most likely hear the message more clearly than if it had just popped up between songs.

Corporate sponsorship can be increased through aligning the property with business objectives, measuring and quantifying performance, select and renew properties, designing a solid activation strategy. Hence, Sponsorship marketing is a medium that corporations can use to build brand awareness and customer loyalty. Companies that develop an integrated marketing plan, using sponsorship marketing and a related activation strategy as important components of their overall plan, are the most successful over the long term.

Companies game for sports sponsor+ships: Indian Perspective

Marketers are always experimenting with new ways to reach and satisfy customers. Imagine putting your logo on billboards, banners and T-shirts, and handing out free product samples to countless potential customers—all for next to nothing. With event sponsorship, you can do all that and more since through such an activity the brand mileage is high.

The demand that marketing programs be fully accountable and prove their value has never been greater. When traditional marketing and PR methods miss your mark, it's time to converge those efforts with sponsorship.

Sponsorship is a more effective messaging tool than ever. Still, it falls below the radar in terms of use within marketing and PR strategies. For all the gains sponsorship has made in becoming an integral part of the mix, many companies hold a limited view of the discipline and its potential impact.

While India might not be known as a 'sporty' nation, the near religion status of cricket with an occasional detour towards hockey, football, tennis and F1, are reasons enough for companies to put in mega bucks into sports events. Following the success of movies like 'Chak De! India', and with the upcoming Commonwealth Games, etc., companies are putting in place their strategies to gain maximum brand mileage out of sports events.

But how big is the sports sponsorship market in India? The figures vary. Arun Sharma, General Manager-Marketing and Head-Media, Bharti Airtel Ltd., said, "The sports sponsorship market in India is approximately worth Rs. 700 crore."

And what is the brand mileage from sponsoring sports events? Corporates firmly agree that sponsoring sports events added value to the brand and one also found a committed and sustained viewership.

Vijay Narayan, Vice President-Marketing Communication, Havells India Ltd, said., "Sponsoring sports events is more secured than having a sportsperson as brand ambassador. The popularity of a brand ambassador might fluctuate according to his/her performance, which could put the identity of the company at stake."

After acquiring Sylvania in March 2007, it was essential for Havells India, which manufactures and supplies lighting products and electrical equipment in India and abroad, to create brand awareness beyond the Indian shores. And the company did that through an "advertising blitzkrieg on television", according Anil Gupta, Joint Managing Director, Havells India Ltd.

Gupta further said, "Cricket sponsorship is the magic formula for grabbing the largest number of eyeballs as advertisers get good mileage for their sponsorship deals." Havells was the co-presenting sponsor of the Natwest Series as well as the Twenty20 Championship. The company is also sponsoring the telecast of the ongoing India's tour of Australia.

Some companies have gone beyond cricket for brand associations. PepsiCo's Mountain Dew is one such example. The aerated beverage brand from the company has been successful in associating itself with alternative adventure and extreme sports like river rafting, paintball and biking events like 'Crusty Demons'. However, PepsiCo has not overlooked cricket altogether. Through several innovative campaigns like 'Toss ka Boss', 'Khufiya' and 'Blue Billion', Pepsi has been able to unite the passion of cricket fans across the country and kept its brand association with the game alive.

Punita Lal, Executive Director-Marketing, PepsiCo India, said, "Similarly, with Gatorade Pacers, we have been able to facilitate the growth of budding sports talent while driving the linkage of Gatorade as a sports drink."

Bharti Airtel has also been sponsoring cricket events for quite some time now. The company recently also got into sponsoring football events with an investment of about Rs. 100 crore. Bharti Airtel's Sharma said, "The spending on sports sponsorship is high as the ROI on one media dwindles after a point and one needs to add more media vehicles for more impact media multiplier effect."

Maj Vinod Krishna, Head of Sports at ONGC, opined, "Sponsors spend a lot of money on such events as they find the returns worth the expenditure. In the case of ONGC, we spend roughly Rs. 10 crore on sports sponsorship annually."

Sports equipment and apparel manufacturing companies like Adidas, Nike and Reebok have been sponsoring some of the biggest sporting events for several decades. Adidas was one of the main sponsors of the FIFA World Cup and the French Open 2007. In 2008, they will be the sponsors of the Beijing Olympics as well as the European League football championships.

Hartwin Feddersen, Director-Marketing, Adidas, said, "It is fair to say that sports are a unique platform where people with different backgrounds engage with sports events and sports brand at an emotional level."

Commenting on the association of Reebok, the official partner for ICC events, with cricket, Puneet Sewra, Brand Manager, Reebok India, said, "In India, cricket grabs the maximum attention, which is evident from the TRPs during major matches. However, to harness sports events just to get brand awareness is not the right strategy. We at Reebok make sure that we only take part in events or campaigns related to sports."

REFERENCES

1. Robert J. Coen, Insider's Report: Robert Coen Presentation on Advertising Expenditures (New York: Universal McCann. McCann Erickson Worldwide. December 2002).
2. "AMA Board Approves New Market-ing Definition," Marketing News, March 1, 1985, p. 1.
3. Richard P. Bagozzi, "Marketing as Exchange," Journal of Marketing 39 (October 1975), pp. 32-39.
4. L Leonard L. Berry, "Relationship Mar-keting of Services—Growing Interest, Emerging Perspectives," Journal of the Academy of Marketing Science 23, no. 4,1995, pp. 236-45; Jonathan R. Capulsky and Michael J, Wolfe, "Relationship Marketing: Positioning for the Future," Journal of Business Strategy, July-August 1991. pp. 16-26.
5. James H. Gilmore and B. Joseph Pine II, "The Four Faces of Customization." Harvard Business Review, 75(1) (January-February 1997), pp. 91-101.
6. Robert J. Lavidge. "Mass Customization' Is Not an Oxy-Moron." Journal of Advertising Research, (July-August 1999), pp. 70-72.
7. B. Joseph Pine II, Don Peppers, and Martha Rogers, "Do You Want to Keep Your Customers Forever?" Harvard Business Review, 73 (2) (March-April 1995), pp. 103-14.
8. Adrienne Ward Fawcett, "Integrated Marketing—Marketers Convinced: Its Time Has Arrived," Advertising Age, November 6,1993, pp. S1-2.
9. "Do Your Ads Need a Super Agency?" Fortune, April 27,1991, pp. 81-85; Faye Rice, "A Cure for What Ails Advertising?"' Fortune, December 16, 1991,pp.119-22.
10. Scott Hume, "Campus Adopts 'New' Advertising," Advertising Age, September 23,1991, p. 17.
11. Don E. Schultz, "Integrated Marketing Communications: Maybe Definition Is in the Point of View," Marketing News, January 18,1993, p. 17.
12. Tom Duncan and Sandra E. Moriarty, "A Communication-Based Model for Managing Relationships," Journal of Marketing 62, (2), (April 1998). pp. 1-13.
13. Ronald Alsop, "The Best Corporate Reputations in America," The Wall Street Journal, September 29, 1999, pp. B 1,6.
14. Harlan E. Spotts, David R. Lambert, and Mary L. Joyce, "Marketing Deja Vu: The Discovery of Integrated Marketing Communications," Journal of Marketing Education, Vol. 20, (3) (December 1998), pp. 210-18.
15. Kate Fitzgerald. "Beyond Advertising," Advertising Age, August 3, 1998, pp. 1, 14; Jane Smith, "Integrated Marketing," Marketing Tools, November/December 1995, pp. 63-70; Thomas R. Duncan and Stephen E. Everett, "Client Perception of Integrated Marketing

Communications," Journal of Advertising Research, May/June 1993, pp. 30-39.

16. Anthony J. Tortorici, "'Maximizing Marketing Communications through Horizontal and Vertical Orchestration," Public Relations Quarterly, Vol. 36, (1) (1991), pp. 20-22.
17. Robert H. Ducoffe, Dennis Sandier, and Eugene Secunda, "A Survey of Senior Agency, Advertiser, and Media Executives on the Future of Advertising," Journal of Current Issues and Research in Advertising 18, No. 3 (Spring 1996) pp. 1-19.
18. Earle Eldridge, "These cars want to be in pictures," USA TODAY, May 24, 2002, p. 3B,
19. Sergio Zyman, The End of Marketing As We Know It (New York: Harper Business, 1999); Joe Cappo, "Agencies: Change or Die," Adverting Age, December 7,1992, p.26.
20. Don E. Schultz, "Be Careful Picking Database for IMC Efforts," Marketing News March 11, 1996, p. 14.
21. Kevin Lane Keller, "The Brand Report Card," Harvard Business Review, 78 (1) (January/February 2000) pp. 3-10.
22. Kevin Lane Keller, "Conceptualizing, Measuring, and Managing Customer-Based Brand Equity/' Journal of Marketing, Vol. 57 (January 1993), pp. 1-22.
23. Michael L. Ray, Advertising and Communication Management (Engle-wood Cliffs. NJ: Prentice Hall, 1982).
24. Ralph S. Alexander, ed. Marketing Definitions (Chicago: American Marketing Association, 1965), p. 9.
25. "Network Television Cost and CPM Trends," Trends in Media, Television Bureau of Advertising, New York. http://www.tvb.org
26. Richard Lewis. "Absolut Vodka Case History," A Celebration of Effective Advertising: 30 Years of Winning EFFIE Campaigns (New York: American Marketing Association, 1999). pp. 20-23.
27. Janis Maya, '-Nike: Best Integrated," Brandweek, June-5;
28. "Slow + Steady: Promo's Exclusive Annual Report of the U.S. Promotion Industry," Promo, April 2002.
29. Jefferson Graham, "Abs Machine Sales Go Flabby," USA Today, October 22,1996, p. D1.
30. H. Frazier Moore and Bertrand R. Canfield, Public Relations: Principles, Cases, and Problems, 7th ed. (Burr Ridge, IL: Irwin, 1977), p. 5.
31. Jack Ncff, "Ries' thesis: Ads don't build brands, PR does,'" Advertising ' Age, July 15, 2002, pp. 14-15; Art Kleiner, "The Public Relations Coup," Adweek's Marketing Week, January 16, 1989, pp. 20-23.
32. Ronald Alsop, "The Best Corporate Reputations in America." The Wall Street Journal. September 29, 1999. pp. B1-6.
33. DMA: "The Power of Direct Marketing: ROI, Sales, Expenditures and Employment in the U.S., 2006-2007 Edition", Direct Marketing Association, October 2006.
34. Brownlow, M: "Why do email marketing?", Email Marketing Reports, January 2008.
35. Pew Internet & American Life Project, "Tracking surveys", March 2000 – March 2007.
36. Fairhead, N., (2003) "All hail the brave new world of permission marketing via email" (Media 16, August 2003)
37. Dilworth, Dianna. (2007) Ruth's Chris Steak House sends sizzling e-mails for special occasions, DMNews retrieved on February 19, 2008
38. O'Brian J. & Montazemia, A. (2004) Management Information Systems (Canada: McGraw-Hill Ryerson Ltd.)
39. Guide to E-Commerce Technology, 2007-08, Edition by Internet Retailer.
40. Jason Olim, Matthew Olim and Peter Kent, "The Cdnow Story: Rags to Riches on the Internet", Top Floor Publishing, January 1999 ISBN 0-9661-0326-2
41. Shawn Collins (November 10, 2000), History of Affiliate Marketing, ClickZ Network, retrieved October 15, 2007.
42. Frank Fiore and Shawn Collins, "Successful Affiliate Marketing for Merchants" , from pages 12,13 and 14. QUE Publishing, April 2001 ISBN 0-7897-2525-8.
43. Daniel Gray, "The Complete Guide to Associate and Affiliate Programs on the Net", McGraw-Hill Trade, November 30, 1999 ISBN 0-0713-5310-0.
44. October 2006, Affiliate Marketing Networks Buyer's Guide (2006), Page 6, e-Consultancy.com, retrieved June 25, 2007.
45. Anne Holland, publisher (January 11 2006), Affiliate Summit 2006 Wrap-Up Report — Commissions to Reach $6.5 Billion in 2006, Marketing Sherpa, retrieved on May 17 2007 February 2007, Internet Statistics Compendium 2007, pp 149-150, e-Consultancy, retrieved June 25, 2007.
46. Dion Hinchcliff (15.July, 2006),Web 2.0's Real Secret Sauce: Network Effects,SOA Web Services Journal, retrieved on 14.May, 2007.
47. Dion Hinchcliff (29.January, 2007), Social Media Goes Mainstream, SOA Web Services Journal, retrieved on 14.May, 2007.
48. AffStat Report 2007. Based on survey responses from almost 200 affiliate managers from a cross-section of the industry.
49. CellarStone Inc. (2006), Sales Commission, QCommission.com, retrieved June 25, 2007.

50. Tom Taulli (9 November 2005), Creating A Virtual Sales Force, Forbes.com Business. Retrieved 14 May 2007.
51. Jeff Molander (June 22, 2006), Google's Content Referral Network: A Grab for Advertisers, Thought Shapers, retrieved on December 16th, 2007.
52. Danny Sullivan (June 27 2006), The Daily SearchCast News from June 27 2006, WebmasterRadio.fm, retrieved May 17 2007.
53. Wayne Porter (September 6 2006), NEW FIRST: LinkShare- Lands' End Versus The Affiliate on Typosquatting, ReveNews.com, retrieved on May 17 2007.
54. Jennifer D. Meacham (July/August 2006), Going Out Is In, Revenue Magazine, published by Montgomery Research Inc, Issue 12., p., 36.
55. Marios Alexandrou (February 4th, 2007), CPM vs. CPC vs. CPA, All Things SEM, retrieved November 11, 2007.
56. Ryan Singel (October 2 2005), Shady Web of Affiliate Marketing, Wired.com, retrieved May 17 2007
57. Jim Hedger (September 6, 2006), Being a Bigdaddy Jagger Meister, WebProNews.com, retrieved on December 16, 2007.
58. December 10, 2002, Online Marketing Service Providers Announce Web Publisher Code of Conduct (contains original CoC text), CJ.com, retrieved June 26, 2007
59. December 12, 2002, LinkShare's Anti-Predatory Advertising Addendum, LinkShare.com, retrieved June 26, 2007.
60. ShareASale Affiliate Service Agreement, ShareASale.com, retrieved June 26, 2007
61. April 20, 2007, AdWare Class Action Lawsuit against - ValueClick, Commission Junction and BeFree, Law Firms of Nassiri & Jung LLP and Hagens Berman, retrieved from CJClassAction.com on June 26, 2007.
62. Carsten Cumbrowski (November 4 2006),Affiliate Marketing Organization Initiative Vol.2 - We are back to Step 0, Reve News, retrieved May 17 2007.
63. Alexandra Wharton (March/April 2007), Learning Outside the Box, Revenue Magazine, Issue: March/April 2007, p. 58, link to online version retrieved June 26, 2007.
64. Shawn Collins (June 9, 2007), Affiliate Millions - Book Report, AffiliateTip Blog, retrieved June 26, 2007.
65. March/April 2007, How Do Companies Train Affiliate Managers? (Web Extra), RevenueToday.com, retrieved June 26, 2007.
66. April 10, 2006, UM Announces $50K Business Plan Competition Winners, University of Maryland
67. Jeff Molander (November 15, 2006), Are CJ and Linkshare Worth Their Salt?, CostPerNews.com, retrieved May 17 2007.
68. November 17 2006, Affiliate Networks vs CPA Networks-Official statements to CostPerNews.com post from 11/15/2006 and comments, CostPerNews.com, retrieved May 17 2007.
69. January 2006, There Must Be a Better Way - Thread at ABestWeb affiliate marketing forums, A Best Web, retrieved May 17 2007.
70. Vinny Lingham (11.October, 2005), Profit Sharing - The Performance Marketing Model of the Future,Vinny Lingham's Blog, retrieved on 14.May, 2007.
71. Jim Kukral (18.November, 2006), Affiliate Marketing Lacks A Brand - Needs A New Name, Reve News, retrieved on 14.May, 2007.
72. Danny Sullivan (5.November, 2001), Congratulations! You're A Search Engine Marketer!, Search Engine Watch, retrieved on 14.May, 2007.
73. Danny Sullivan (3.December, 2001), Search Engine Marketing: You Like It, You Really Like It, Search Engine Watch, retrieved on 14.May, 2007.

CHAPTER 22 THE FUTURE MEDIUM OF COMMUNICATION: WEBS & INTERNET

Intel Inside: The Co-op Program That Changed the Computer Industry

If you were to ask most owners of personal computers what is inside their PCs, chances are they would respond by saying, "an Intel," And there's a good reason why. Over the past decade, consumers have been exposed to hundreds of millions of dollars' worth of ads for personal computers each year that carry the "Intel inside" logo. The logo has become ubiquitous in PC ads as a result of a landmark co-operative advertising program that is lauded as the most powerful ever and the definitive model for successful "ingredient" branding.

In 1989, Intel was the first computer chip manufacturer to advertise directly to consumers. Its goal was to persuade PC users to upgrade to Intel's 386SX chip from the 286. Known as the "Red X" campaign, the ads depicted the number 286 with a bold, spray painted X over it. In 1990, Intel selected a new agency, Dahlin Smith White, Salt Lake City, which created the now famous tagline "Intel. The Computer Inside." The goal of the campaign was to build awareness and position Intel as the real brains of the computer. In early 1991, Intel began pitching the program to PC makers, and IBM, creator of the first Intel-powered personal computer, became the first computer maker to use the logo. Intel then began talking to PC makers about the creation of a co-op fund in which Intel would take 5 percent of the purchase price of processors and put it in a pool to create funds for advertising. The "Intel Inside" co-op program was officially launched in July 1991 and works as follows: In return for showing the logo in print ads and on the PCs, a computer maker can get back 5 percent of what it pays Intel for chips, with the money to be applied to ads paid for jointly by the PC vendor and Intel. More than 150 computer makers signed on to the program and began using the "Intel Inside" logo in their ads.

As the program began, Intel started playing up the logo in its own print ads as well. In November 1991, it moved the campaign to television with the classic "Power Source" spot, which magically took viewers on a whirlwind tour of the inside of a computer to show how the Intel chip streamlined upgrading of a PC. In 1993, Intel introduced the Pentium processor brand with a national TV campaign. However, the company was putting the bulk of its advertising budget into the "Intel Inside" co-op program, in 1995 Intel expanded the co-op program to include TV, radio, and in-flight ads. The move led to a boom in PC ads on television featuring the Intel auditory signature at the end of each commercial. In 1997, Intel expanded the co-op program to include Internet ads and provided incentives to PC makers to place ads on media-rich websites. Intel has also extended the co-op program into retail promotions as well.

Since the co-op program began, Intel has pumped into it an estimated $4 billion, and this has been an awfully smart investment. Intel's share of the micro-processor market has grown from 56 percent in 1989 to nearly 80 percent in 2002, and the company's revenue has gone from $3 billion to nearly $30 billion. Nearly 90 percent of more than 17,000

PC print ads run in the United States carry the "Intel Inside" logo. The program has influenced a generation of PC users and propelled growth of the entire computer industry.

According to positioning expert Al Ries, "Intel Inside" will go down in history as one of the most magnificent campaigns of the century. He notes, "It's brilliant, and, in a sense, it pre-empted the branding of personal computers." Branding guru Jack Trout notes, "They took an old idea-ingredient branding-which Du Pont pioneered, and took it into technology." Trout was an early believer in the program; he told Advertising Age in a 1991 interview that conceptually it was a good idea, although Intel would need consistent advertising overtime for the logo to have much meaning.

Intel's advertising has been consistent over the past decade as its various ad campaigns have strengthened its brand image and demonstrated the power of various generations of Intel Pentium processors. These campaigns have featured the "Bunny People," who were a takeoff on the workers who wear so-called bunny suits to keep chip labs sterile, as well as the Blue Man Group performance artists, in fate 2002, Intel launched a new global brand campaign called "Yes" that is designed to connect with young adults and showcase the benefits of a digital lifestyle.

The commercials capture today's digital lifestyle by showing people using their computers for digital photography, CD-Burning, instant messaging and movie making. The ads play off the famous tagline by showing people burning CD's and then cutting to the copy line "Intel inside your music" or by showing how a digital photo can be used followed by the line "Intel inside your photos." The commercial ends with the line "Can a better computer really change your life? YES."

In its early stages, the Intel Inside programme encountered criticism, as many advertising and computer marketing executives were skeptical about Intel's ability to differentiate its chips. The head of one agency note: "Most people who buy computers don't even know that chip is there. They care about the performance of their computer. It really doesn't matter what the chip is." Well, some may still not know exactly what a microprocessor chip does, but apparently it does matter if there is an "Intel Inside."

Sources: Tobi Elkin, "Intel Goes for a New Overall Branding Look," Advertising Age, Sept. 1, 2002, pp.3,43. Tobi Elkin, "Co-op Crossroads" Advertising Age, Nov. 15, 199, pp. 1,24,26.

Borderless, Barrierless, Boundaryless. An accident mega market it may be born of technology rather than of economic needs. But the Internet today offers India Inc., its best-ever opportunity to expand into global markets. This planet-encircling Network of computers represents a perpetually open market place where neither geographical frontiers nor tariff barriers can prevent CEOs with a global vision from reaching out to customers all over the world. For, there are no hurdles in this virtual market, where trade and transactions, cash commodities, all flow in the form of electronic impulses.

What must India Inc., do to break into this market of opportunities? Well, as the scientific aid, which the Internet began life as, is transformed into a global market. It is spawning a unique set of products and services which Indian companies with global mind sets can manufacture and sell. Besides, the unusual economics of doing business on the Net to advertise, market, sell, and distribute products, reaching out to customers once completely beyond their reach. Following these role models, after mastering the technical aspects of establishing a presence on the Net, will offer ways to size the unique opportunities for globalising through the Net, on the pages that follows.

THE NET AS A GLOBAL MARKET

The Mega-Network is now a Mega Market. Once a little-known lattice of computers on academic and defence campuses in the U.S., the Internet — the Net in today's fast forward vocabulary — has morphed into the world's newest, and strangest, global bazar. No longer confined to the 11,000 locations that it spanned until as recently as 1991, the once-shimmering frontiers of the Net are now dotted by shopping windows wherever in the world there is a computer, a modem, and a telephone line. Cyberspace has been fused with the market, and the result is — what else? — the market space. This market space is truly global. Its principle commodity, data, understands no international borders, no customs duties, and no import barriers.

Stripped to its basics, of course, the Net is just what it was — albeit much larger than ever before:

a fault-tolerant system of 10 million computers, interconnected through a pish-pash of commercial phone lines, satellite links, undersea cables, *et al.*, accommodating about 33 million uses (growing at the rate of 10 per cent per month) worldwide. Beginning life as a decentralised Network of computers, most of them located at the Universities of Berkeley and Standford and at the Massachusetts Institute of Technology, the Net has spread its tentacles at a blindingly high speed. Today, its reach is no longer static: its borders wink in and out of existence wherever a computer is attached, via a phone line and a modem, to the basic backbone of the Net.

And while the old Net viewed surffers as mere cyberpros, business is beginning to look at them as customers who can visit this market space simply by switching on their computers and using their modems to connect to the Net. They come and go in this cybermart at the click of a mouse. Seated at their computer terminals all over the globe, ordinary people — who use soap, drive cars, and eat breakfast in everyday life — are being converted into cyber-consumers as soon as they enter the market space.

Two developments have enabled this transition. First, the links between the computers on the Net are being made faster and wider than even before. With the original creaky, copper phone-line connections being systematically supplanted by a global fiber-optic and satellite link, the data carrying capacity of the Net is exploding. The second factor is the emergence of the World Wide Web — a.k.a. the Web — a portion of the Net where the data that pass back and forth comprise not just sterile words, but a combination of text, pictures, and video and audio clips. This is the real home of the business transactions in the market space.

A feature named hypertext worked the miracle behind the Web, which, at one stroke, cut through the arcane complexity of Unix, the AT & T-owned operating system on which computers connected to the Net ran. For, in the per-Web days, only a minority of computer experts around the world could bend Unix to their needs, thus limiting the use of the Net among themselves. In 1990, however, Time Beners-Lee, a researcher at CERN, The Particle Research Laboratory in Geneva, invented Hyper Text Markup Language (HTML), which freed the Net from the tyranny of plain data, and allowed pictures, sound-bytes, video clips — anything, in short, that can be encoded digitally as strings of 0s and Is — to be transmitted. Says Craig R. Barrett, 55, CEO, Intel: "For 30 years, the Internet didn't show up because the user interface was too complex, you had to be in a need to use it." The shift also enabled users to jump from one digital document or page to another by simply clicking on a word, a phrase, a visual-the hyper-link-respective of which computer in the world the second document was physically stored in. As the Web Burst into colour and sound, following the invention of a graphical interface named Mosaic — the brainchild of researchers at the National Center for Super Computer Applications in Illionis, US — it offered a way to stimulate real life retail shops. Just as a buyer can browse through a brick-and-mortar store, so too can a Web surfer explore a digital shop set up by a company?

The Consumer on the Net

Even in 1993, over 70 per cent of Net traffic were between educational institutions: highspeed exchanges of information without a commercial concern. In three short years, the ratios have been reversed, with over 65 per cent of traffic now headed for — or origination from — a business related site. Naturally, today's Web surfer is a much more powerful consumer than his predecessor. As a recent University of Georgia survey points out, over 40 per cent of the 22 million wired customers in the US have annual incomes of over $ 80,000 members of the richest 48 per cent in that country. Adds Arvind Agarwala, 36, CEO, Vedika Software: "The profile is diversifying very quickly. A few years ago, most Internet users were the same kind of people. Not anymore."

But numbers don't really define the virtual consumer, who actually belongs to a borderless world, joining up with others to form cross-country clusters of virtual communities linked by common interests. While geographical classifications are possible — for instance, 73 per cent of Net-users belong to the US, Europe contributes 11 per cent, and Asia, 2.4 per cent — they're irrelevant in the frontier-free world of the Web, says Subhash Palsule, 37, Director, Panalink, which publishes a Web magazine named India-conned: "You just don't think of Web surfers as belonging to a particular place anymore. They're on the Internet period." Ranging across frontiers, age-groups, gender, and cultures, many of them are in search of companionship, trying to build virtual friendship, or simply, to advertise their presence. And almost the only distinguishing factor about Web surfers is an interest in specific issues, ranging from the fashion to food receipts, from music to the Indian elections, from cars to Hillary Clinton's hairstyles, from the Calvin and Hobbes comic strip to management consultancy. And companies are utilising these very triggers to attract consumers.

In its decade long presence in India, Internet usage has evolved more in 'depth' than in 'spread'. That is, its impact and growth is being driven through 'increased usage' by existing users rather than assimilation of newer ones. Eighty per cent of urban net users have been wired for more than three years now, while only 8 per cent joined the bandwagon less than a year ago.

These and other key insights have emerged out of one of the largest online surveys conducted by JuxtConsult in April 2005 among Internet users in India.

The survey sampled more than 30,000 users with the aim to unravel the identity of the net user along with his lifestyle choices. To estimate the penetration of Internet among urban Indians, a telephonic survey spread across 10 cities with over 3,000 participants was also conducted.

The study finds that around 17.5 million urban Indians are using the Internet with certain consistency. With another 5.2 million using it sparingly, its upper limit is around 23 million urban users at present. This puts the penetration of Internet among urban Indians at around 9 per cent. Assuming marginal usage in rural areas, the national penetration level stands at a potential 2 per cent.

In terms of 'depth' of usage, almost a third of urban Internet users are heavy users with log time of more than three hours every day. Interestingly, one out of every three heavy Internet users is connected 'throughout the day' and a third of those log in at least five times a day. Clearly, urban India is witnessing the emergence of the 'netoholic'. 7.5 million almost always connected with Net.

The profile of a characteristic net user is exceedingly inconsistent with the projected notion that he/she is a 'white collared professional'. The professional most likely does not represent more than the 'tip' of the iceberg of the urban Indian net users.

The typical net user is more the average person. However, he does represent a 'reasonably' decent purchasing power. Every three out of four net users own an automobile of some kind and every second net user has a credit card.

There are 37million mobile users (Source COAI) and 25 million Indians online (Source IOAI). Taking an estimate on the lower side there are 15 million Indians online and another 22 million mobile users that are in the 20-40 age group, a keen movie penchant audience with a sizeable disposable income, and with numbers expected to swell to 165 million (55 million online users + 110 million mobile users) by 2007 will make them an interactive demographic impossible to ignore.

Whilst many a traditional marketer has catered to the influence of this growing demographic it was pertinent to show case the importance of integrating Internet and Mobile as medium in the traditional media mix to highlight the new age patterns that influence decision making process.

The Internet has become part of every day lexicon in India too. It is this new nervous system of mother earth linking up any amounts of facets of humanity with a highlight of Information Technology and Business becoming intrinsically interwoven.

The Internet and Online Association of India estimated, that there will be a 100 million Internet users by the year 2007. 73 per cent Indian net users are online buyers: first Indian net users survey reported.

eMarketer, a research house specializing in e-business and the Internet, reported that China's Internet population reached 176.5 million in 2007, compared to 188.1 million in the United States. The tally for China included Hong Kong. Ben Macklin, senior analyst at eMarketer, said China would "overtake the United States as the most populous Internet nation in the world" this year. The Internet market in the Asian country, he added, is still relatively immature and together with countries such as Brazil and India, will drive growth in the number of Internet users globally. Macklin noted that the number of Internet users in the Asia-Pacific region is also expected to grow by about 14.1 percent to 543.8 million, from 476.6 million last year. The region's Internet population is forecast to grow at a compound annual growth rate of 11.4 percent—the second highest in the world after Latin America—between 2007 and 2012. By 2012, nearly one in four persons worldwide will access the Internet at least once a month. About half of the total Internet population will come from the Asia-Pacific region.

The Internet & Online Association, a not-for-profit organization of India, has released its latest research on internet user's proclivity for the entertainment industry. This research, conducted in collaboration with Cross-Tab Marketing Services, pioneers of Online Research in India is a first of a series addressing various industries. The research was undertaken to understand the 25-million strong internet user's and above 37-million mobile users media habits and will serve as a resource for marketers for film channels and production houses.

The research assumes significance since marketers have endeavoured to cater to this growing segment of consumers. The study would help showcase the importance of integrating the internet and mobile as a vital medium in the traditional media mix to highlight new age patterns that influence the decision making process.

Commenting on the release of the research Preeti Desai, president, Internet and Online Association, said, "The Indian entertainment industry stands at over 20,000 crore and is expected to reach 45,000 crore by 2009. Film marketers already have a substantial presence online but do not promote their films online with almost negligible focus on advertising-related. film related ecommerce (online ticketing, film merchandise inclusive of audio and video VCD's and DVD's, posters and star clothes).

The research was undertaken with a view to empower this sector with actual statistics and to create a realisation amongst movie house and film channels that their prime demographic is online and thus "e" and the "m" of marketing should be an integral part of their media mix.

Desai further added, "IOAI estimates that there will be 165 million interactive users in the 20-40 years age group by 2007, an affluent demographic who cannot be ignored anymore."

Some Research Highlights

• **Age:** 94 per cent of the audience lies within the 18-45 age group. A generation accustomed near to instantaneous keeping in touch i.e., via email, SMS and instant messaging. A prime demographic of moviegoers.

• **Education and profession:** 78 per cent of the audience is either a graduate / postgraduate with 56 per cent of them are executives in their professional capacity representing an assured spending power.

- metro divide

• **Technology and television:** 68 per cent of the audiences have a personal computer, with 50 per cent part of a two television set household.

• **Internet familiarity:** 92 per cent of the populations have been using the internet

Regional representation: An aberration from the perceived norm of a metro bias. Responses were evenly divided between a 51 per cent: 49 per cent metro and non metro.

- for one to five years, highlighting an online pedigree. 52 per cent access internet from home.
- 80 per cent are online for more than 5 hours a week with 30 per cent use the internet for more than 20 hours a week. An indication of online activity as becoming part of daily activity.

• **Internet activity:** 55 per cent use the internet for chatting, a very vocal community which can be used to promote viral marketing - as they can handle "multiple conversations". Internet & mobile plays a very important role into this generation's wish for flexible communication at home, work and during down time. 58 per cent use the internet "to answer surveys" - A market researcher's dream - which has hardly been used.

• **Media consumption:** Numbers are a confirmation that internet and mobile marketing should be integrated into "Integrated Media Budgets".

- 30 per cent are online for more than 20 hours a week,
- 34 per cent spend 5-10 hours a week watching television,
- 32 per cent reading newspapers for 3-5 hours a week.

Clearly showcasing that Internet is a permanent part of media consumption habits along with TV & Print.

The Net as a Shopping Mall

In 1995, US consumers are believed to have spent between $ 135 million (Rs. 480 crore) and $ 250 million (Rs. 888 crore) — the two extremities of several estimates — on the market space, barely a drop in the $ 57-billion (Rs. 1,99,500 crore) home-shopping market, which is itself a tiny niche in the country's $ 1.8 trillion (Rs. 6,30,000 crore) retail sales. However, projections suggest that the takings from on-line retailing could rise to $ 4 billion a year by the year 2000. Information providers Gartner Group of US expect Internet commerce to become as acceptable by 1999 as ordering products over a toll-free number now is in the US. And by the turn of the century, predicts the Gartner Group, virtually every business in the world will be using electronic transactions.

Of course, the benefit will not be counted in revenues for a long time yet.

More important, therefore is the opportunity for business to build relationship with potential consumers, which can be translated into transactions either in the physical market place or in the virtual market space. After all each of the over 2.5 million consumers who have already done business in the market space provided by the Web are major buyers in the physical world too, heightening the opportunity to interact with them. Business thinks so too. On June 1, 1996 there were 100,000 Corporate sites on the Web, covering over 10 million separate sub-sites between them. According to an estimate made by the Gartner Group, 15 per cent of the world's large enterprises will be present on the Web by the end of 1996. And the proportion will rise to 50 per cent over the next two years. Most of these mega corps are using a home page as their signpost a multimedia package of text, graphics and increasingly, audio and video, embedded within which are features ranging from advertising to product descriptions, from company profiles to financial, from interactive games to pure trivia.

The primary purpose of most companies, so far, is to attract consumers to their sides rather than directly boost sales. For the consumer of the virtual world is using the Web's digital depths to search out the information on what to buy and whom to buy it from. And once she — whether she's an executive in search of a car, a tourist hunting for a hotel room, or an importer trawling the global seas for low cost suppliers has used the Web as her Yellow Pages, she will never again turn to another source of data. Says Sumeet Kapoor, 31, Director of Chipsoft Technology, a Web-hosting consultancy: 'once one of your competitors is on line, you don't really have a choice. You must join in.' Particularly since the future of the Net promises to be even more business friendly than it is today. Predicts Nandan M. Nilekani, 40, Joint Managing Director of the Rs. 88.56 crore Infosys: 'As bandwidth increases and the cost of bandwidth drops, the Net will see another transformation of the kind that the Web has brought' and the only losers will be companies, which don't set up shop in the Web mart.

"Shopping on The Net - Will it work in India?

A lot of people nowadays who are absolutely fascinated by the kind of business Net can offer. Many have pressing questions to ask about "how this whole thing works", a lot of them influenced by so much that they hear, see and read about e-commerce all around them. Behind such curiosity and fascination, one can notice is something uppermost on everyone's mind - how relevant is it and will it work in India?

Lets look at Shopping on the Net, perhaps the most well known type of e-commerce, and see how this can work in a place like India. Notwithstanding all the hype surrounding e-commerce and The New Economy, the fact remains that just like in existing Brick-and-Mortar physical retail, it is still the customer who has the power to decide if a business will work or not.

All of us, including you and me, are used to shopping in physical stores. It's a habit and part of our lifestyles. And we all know how tough it is for us to change habits built over years. It is therefore important for e-tailers to think hard and see if there are any compelling value propositions they can offer to consumers on a sustained basis, so that customers can consider shifting parts of their shopping online.

The good news is that web stores come with many advantages over physical stores. Many of these are relevant anywhere including India, but some are more relevant here than elsewhere. Let's look at a few of them.

When was the last time you walked into a bookstore, which had on display, say, a few hundred thousand books? Chances are never - and unlikely you will be able to do so in future as well. But you can easily enter online bookstores like amazon.com, which has over four million books and counting! Physical stores, including large retail outlets will always have limited shelf space and in time will run out of it, whereas for web stores, you just need to keep adding SKUs (Stock Keeping Units) to a database without limits. Such incredible range and selection makes online shopping a real pleasure.

Information is another big plus for online shoppers. The Internet is best suited to deliver all the information that collateral that can be made available along with trained sales persons, it is impossible for a physical store to provide all the information in a convenient manner, such that prospective shoppers can make a better and informed choice.

A lady had an interesting experience to narrate. On her way back from work in the evening, she dropped by her favourite music store to pick up the latest Hindi film album. As she reached the store, she found the store closing up for the day. Despite her pleas, the store politely yet firmly refused to allow her to come in and pick up the title she wanted to buy. That night, in a peeved mood, this lady ordered the same CD at fabmall.com - today she's an enthusiastic online shopper and a big evangelist amongst her circle of friends for online stores, which remain open 24×7. And as moving around in congested roads through bumper-to-bumper traffic in polluted environments and a paucity of parking lots becomes the rule rather than the exception in most Indian cities and towns, the convenience of choosing your own time and place to shop and in complete privacy will start becoming more and more attractive.

All of us like a good deal. And the best place to get good deals and bargains is the Net. Most web stores have some promotion or other running almost always and if you check out a few stores for the product of your interest, you should be able to find something attractive. Price is a good reason to start shopping online, although you will probably continue to shop on the web for reasons other than just attractive deals.

Sending gifts is a very satisfying experience but all of us at some time or other must have decided against sending a gift to someone residing in some other place, just because it is quite cumbersome. The Internet is a great option to send gifts simply because it removes most of the hassles in the process of gifting. It has been observed that many customers have tried Net shopping first for gifting music, books and jewellery to their friends in other cities - over time, Net shopping has become their destination store for buying items for their own use.

While some of these reasons are relevant everywhere, some are more relevant in India. Unlike in countries like USA where huge shopping malls are available everywhere, such large format retail outlets which offer a good shopping experience are just beginning to sprout up. For them to be able to reach large segments of the Indian population across many towns and cities will take a few years, as it is not easy to expand physically in a rapid manner. For many consumers in smaller towns and cities, where retailers will take a longer time to reach out, online stores are their first taste of a good shopping experience. In other words, unlike in the USA, where an Amazon.com had to attract customers already used to excellent Barnes & Noble bookstores, it is possible that in India, stores like fabmall.com may become the benchmark against which consumers will evaluate new and big retail outlets for a good shopping experience - more so in smaller towns.

Sceptics of course submit a few reasons, which they believe will prevent online shopping to take off in India. Low PC and credit card penetration, high Internet access rates when you take telephone costs into account, poor infrastructure, lack of secure payment gateways are some of the more popular excuses. The good news is that just like in the past few years, PC penetration will grow at a rapid pace and the security of paying online over payment gateways using secure links like SSL (Secure Socket Layer) will keep increasing the online transacting population. Initiatives like Internet banking, online stock trading, booking of Railway tickets on the Internet will all help remove the initial discomfort that consumers may have with this new medium.

What about the issue of touch-and-feel? Customers certainly prefer to see a product physically and maybe touch- and feel the item before buying. There is of course, no way that the web can offer touch and feel (not yet anyway!) and because of this, sceptics use this as the more compelling part of their arguments as to why they believe that online shopping will just not work in India. I do believe it is a myth that physical touch and feel always means a better shopping experience.

A housewife shopping for shampoo in a large departmental store was faced with several shampoo brands and almost all of them offered various types of shampoos. Some were for natural hair, some for sticky or moist hair, some for dry hair and so on. This consumer was at a loss to pick the right shampoo since she was not too clear about her type of hair in the first place.

Now imagine the same housewife buying shampoo on the Net. The amount of information that can be presented on the types of hair, how to determine ones own hair type, which shampoo to select and why different hair types need different shampoo types for best results will help her make an informed choice. A clear case where physical touch-and-feel is not able to help a consumer make a superior and informed choice as compared to on-line shopping. Many such examples are available if we think about it.

This is not to reduce the importance of touch and feel. It will be tough to make the same housewife buy (say) salwar-kameez over the web. She will most likely want to touch and feel the texture and also the actual color on the garments before she buys the item.

The point is that some product categories require touch and feel and some don't. It is important for e-tailers to replicate physical shopping as much as possible and in some areas go beyond what is available in brick-and-mortar stores, to compensate for the lack of touch-and-feel aspect. If e-tailers can create such overwhelming value, it will help consumers shop regularly on the Net.

Our experience with jewellery has been exactly that. When we started the jewellery store after the music store and book store, many people told us that Indian customers will just not buy jewellery without touching it physically and trying it on. Instead, customers have not only bought jewellery online, but have bought more traditional gold items than branded jewellery! Like mangalsutras and thalis also, something you would expect customers to try it on before buying, isn't it?

The point is that online stores are only an alternative to physical stores and certainly not a replacement. In future, customers will certainly use the Net for shopping regularly for many items, which are suited to Net buying. Of course, physical stores and retail outlets will continue to exist and flourish. Just like TV never replaced print and radio, despite concerns to this effect, similarly, online stores and physical stores will co-exist together. And between them Indian consumers, who are increasingly being offered more and more choices across every product category will now have a choice of medium as well. So, what's your choice?

ONLINE sales during the festival season jumped a whopping 117 per cent to Rs. 115 crore from Rs. 53 crore in 2004-05, as more Indians shopped on the Internet, according to the Internet and Mobile Association of India (IAMAI).

"Online sales clocked across over 8,10,000 transactions in three weeks and delivered a 135 per cent increase in transactions. These figures clearly show that online shopping has truly come of age and consumers are keen to shop on the Net. Festival shopping is the prime time for multi-channel retailers to attract new shoppers," an IAMAI release said here.

Effective customer communication on products, reduced shipping costs and timely delivery helped online marketers to seize a slice of the Rs. 115-crore sales. These purchases accounted for over 10 per cent of total Indian online sales estimated at Rs. 1,180 crore for this year sans travel categories over a three-week festival period.

"With e-commerce revenues set to cross Rs. 1,180 crore for 2005-06 and a growing Internet user base currently at about 32 million, it has been a sparkling Diwali and Eid in 2005-06, as e-commerce sales crossed to a whopping Rs. 115 crore in the three-week period. "Online retailers have consistently seen growing consumer interest in buying Diwali and Eid gifts online. Each festival season, Indians seem to be leaving their shopping for the last minute and this year was no exception, as we sold 61 per cent of the gifts in the two weeks prior to Diwali day, compared to 54 per cent last year," the IAMAI President, Ms. Preeti Desai, said.

E-commerce figures are going through the roof, especially Delhi and Mumbai and its volumes are expected to exceed by 150 per cent to touch Rs 5,500 crore in 2007-08 from Rs. 2,200 crore in 2006-07, with share of Delhi e-shoppers going beyond 30 per cent, which was 20 per cent in last fiscal, according to the Associated Chambers of Commerce & Industry of India (ASSOCHAM).

As traffic for e-commerce sites is mostly coming from the two metros of Delhi and Mumbai, convenience must be the major reason to explain this rush. Other reasons for e-shoppers numbers multiplying are because of factors such as home delivery, which saves time, and '24x7' hours shopping with ease and availability of product comparisons.

In 2006-07, Delhi's e-shoppers population was 20 per cent, in Mumbai it was 24 per cent with maximum e-shopping taking place in electronic gizmos, apparel & design purchases, railways, airlines & movie tickets. The number in percentage increase for e-shoppers in 2007-08 would touch at least 40 per cent in case of Mumbai while in Delhi it is expected beyond 30 per cent. Products that will gain popularity in e-sale could include gems & jewellery, accessories, gift items, online books sale, music and movies, hotel room and tickets for various transportation mediums.

ASSOCHAM findings show that in Chennai 7 per cent of its population chose to buy daily routine products through e-commerce in 2006-07, which will go to 11-12 per cent in current fiscal for railway tickets, airline tickets, magazines, home tools, toys, jewellery, beauty products & sporting goods categories. Similarly, Kolkata share was 7 per cent, which can go up another 3-4 per cent in 2007-08. Online music sales and movies are the highest e-sale in the Kolkata. Bangalore's share is 6 per cent for books, electronic gadgets, accessories, apparel, gifts, computer peripherals, movies, hotel booking, home appliances, movie tickets, health & fitness products and apparel gift certificates in 2005-06 and they are expected to touch 9 per cent in 2007-08.

Actually, a major reason why metros are contributing to e-shopping growth is literacy rates. Most cities in India have a higher literacy rate as compared to the national average of 64.8 per cent. In fact, Mumbai has a highest literacy even amongst the cities (86 per cent). Delhi too has a high literate population (81.2 per cent). Oddly, although Bangalore has a higher literacy rate than Delhi, at 83 per cent, the city's share of e-commerce is not very high. Kolkata, too, has a high literacy rate (80.8 per cent) and so does Chennai (80.1 per cent).

The rapid development of e-commerce is compelling companies to adopt business strategies revolving around the internet. Today, the internet population is more than 120 million and is likely to grow to 200-plus million by 2008. Experts believe that this business module is cost effective, easily accessible and profitable in many functional areas. Consumers and retailers both desire safe, simple and comprehensive online shopping that will truly realise the range of power of the internet.

DIGITAL ECONOMY

Mastering the market space could be India Incorporation's passport to globalisation. Classically, as the textbooks will remind you, a market exists wherever there is a demand for, and a supply of, a product or a service. In the material world, the market place represents a physical convergence of buyers and sellers where products built with tangible resources are bought and sold, the market space, by contrast, does not exist in the physical world at all. Its home, instead, is cyber space the virtual real, where products and services exist in digitised form and not as corporeal objects or, as bits, and not as atoms. And consumers gather here, using their computer to enter it, in order to exchange, access and, increasingly mere strings of 0s and Is: it adds up thousands of items of commerce. Such as —

Stock market quotations from the Bombay Stock Exchange. Masterpieces from the London Museum of Arts. Computer Software. The facility to order from

Paris, a gift to be delivered to a relative in Calcutta. The New York philharmonic orchestra's recording of Beethoven' Fifth Symphony, News from Reuters, Bank loans, Order forms for importing jewellery from India while living in the U.S. Catalogues of property that can be bought in Kerala or Connecticut, Bangalore or Boston. Details about the latest cars. The opportunity to test a new computer. Buying tickets for the Olympic Games in Atlanta. Booking a plane ticket from Bussets to Bonn. Concludes Bill Gates, 40, CEO, Microsoft: 'the Internet is likely to become the electronic highway of business. Every kind of electronic commerce will go on the Internet from picking real estate to finding a professional that you want to work with allowing people with expertise, even if they want to stay at home most of the time to offer that expertise and work through the screen. It's really very, very, very, different from anything that's happened before.'

Emergence of Digital Economy

Economy refers to a systematic way of describing how goods and services are exchanged among members of a given community. Digital means anything that can be fully expressed using digits, or numbers. Effectively this means anything that can be translated into numerical form, and can be retranslated back to its original state without losing its essential aspects. For instance, a book or a photograph can be expressed digitally but cars or fresh flowers cannot be expressed digitally because they possess physical aspects that cannot yet be turned into digital form without radically altering their inherent qualities.

Any macroeconomic theory consists of explaining the inter-workings of four principal components - land, labour, capital and technology - as they facilitate the exchange of goods and services within a specific community. Though all of these components are necessarily involved in all economic systems, the extent to which each one impacts a specific economy varies dramatically. For example, the agricultural economy was centred on producing, exchanging, and consuming products derived from working with the natural world. In these economies, land and labour were the most precious components for determining economic success. Capital - or money - did play a part, as did technological innovations such as the plough, the train or the thresher. However, an agricultural community could subsist with a minimum of money and technology, but could not survive at all without land or labour. Later, with the Industrial Revolution, technology assumed a more important role, as proved with the inventions of electricity and the telephone. However, because the economy was primarily driven by the ability to produce goods for the mass market, capital (possessing enough money) and labour (commanding an adequately trained workforce) were by far the most important ingredients for success.

Industrial economy gradually evolved from the agricultural economy, and now the industrial economy is making way for the digital economy. With the advent of the digital economy, information has become the driver of value and wealth creation and therefore information technology (IT) is considered the key to success in a growing number of industries. Manufacturers may compete less on their manufacturing skill and more on the ability to streamline their procurement and distribution processes by electronically connecting to suppliers and customers and exploit IT for process improvement. Four types of economic activities would drive the growth of digital economy in future:

Building out the Internet

In 1994, three million people, most of them in the U.S.A., used the Internet. In 1998, hundred million people around the world used the Internet. Some experts believe that about one billion people may be connected to the Internet by 2005. This expansion is driving dramatic increases in computer software, services and telecommunication investments.

Electronic Commerce Among Businesses

Business organisations have begun the use of Internet for commercial transactions with their business partners since 1994. Early users already reported significant productivity improvements from using Internet to create, buy, distribute, sell, and service products and services.

Computer software programs, newspapers, and music CDs no longer need to be packaged and delivered to stores or homes, but can be delivered electronically over the Internet. Other industries such as, consulting services, entertainment, education and health-care, face some hurdles at present, but are also beginning to use the Internet to change the way they do business. Over time, the sale and transmission of goods and services electronically is likely to be the largest and most visible driver of the new digital economy.

Retail Sale of Tangible Goods

The Internet can also be used to order tangible goods and services that are produced, stored and physically delivered. Though Internet sales at present is less than 1% of total retail sales, sales of certain products such as books, etc., are growing rapidly.

Traditional Commerce

Traditional commerce perhaps started before recorded history when our ancestors first decided to specialise their everyday activities. Instead of each family unit having to grow crops, search for food, and make tools, families developed skills in one of these areas and traded some of their production for other needs. It started with bartering, which eventually gave way to the use of currency, making transactions easier to settle. However, the basic mechanisms of trade were the same. Some body created a product or provided a service, which somebody else found valuable, and therefore was willing to 'pay' for it in exchange. Thus, commerce, or doing business, is a negotiated exchange of valuable products or services between at least two parties and includes all activities that each of the parties undertakes to complete the commercial transaction.

Any commercial transaction can be examined from either the buyer's or the seller's viewpoint. These two sides of a commercial transaction are shown in the figure 22.1 and 22.2 given below.

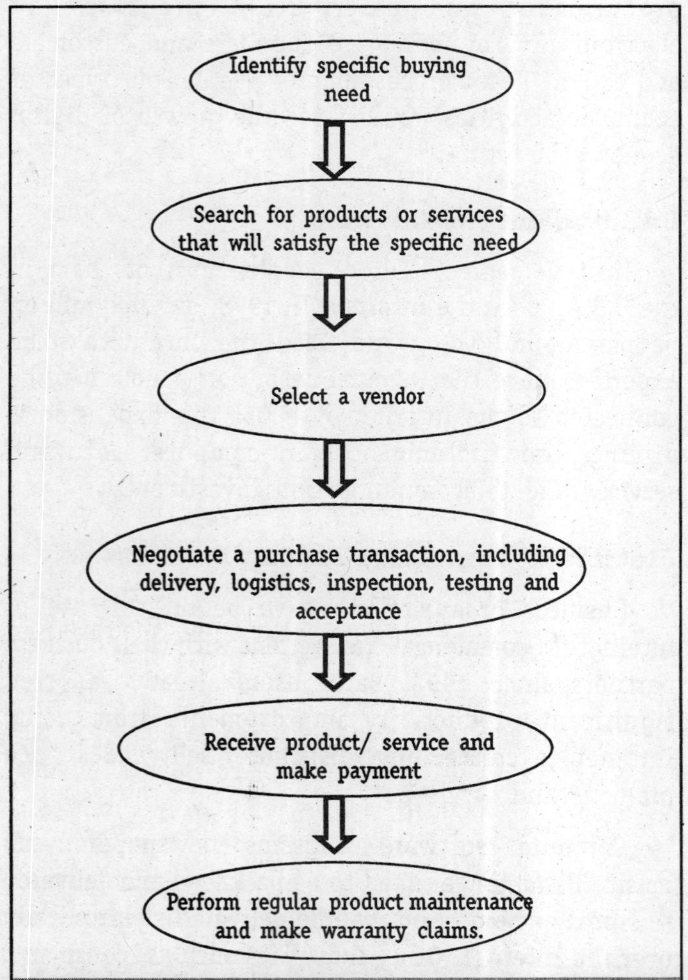

Identify specific buying need

↓

Search for products or services that will satisfy the specific need

↓

Select a vendor

↓

Negotiate a purchase transaction, including delivery, logistics, inspection, testing and acceptance

↓

Receive product/ service and make payment

↓

Perform regular product maintenance and make warranty claims.

Fig. 22.1. Buyer's Side of Traditional Commerce

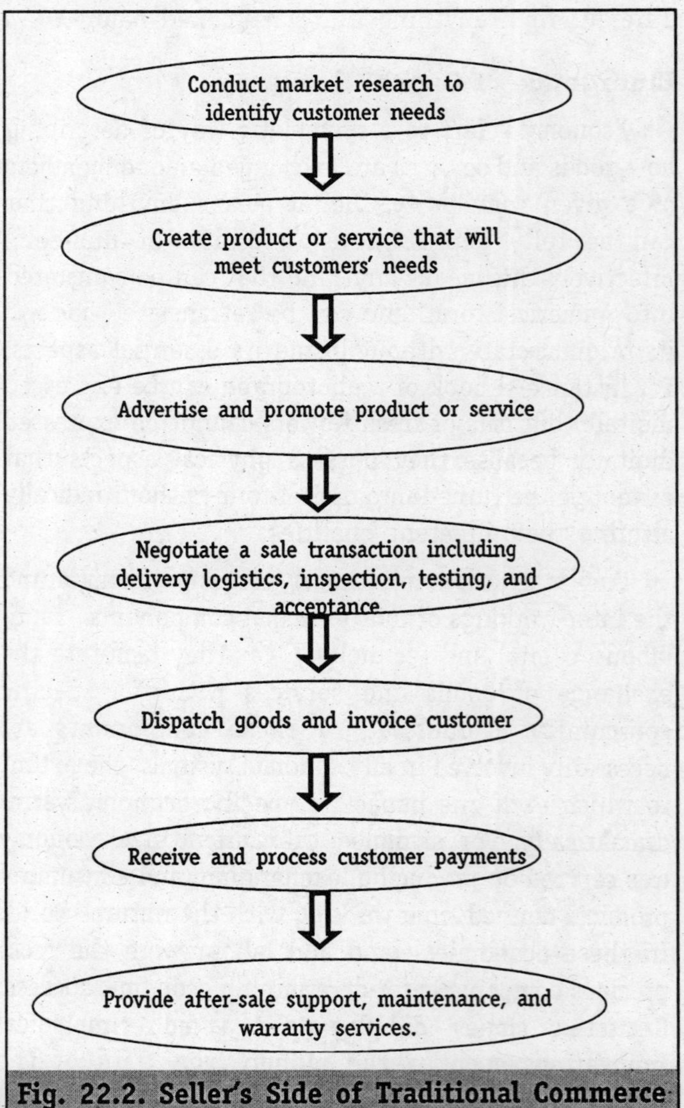

Fig. 22.2. Seller's Side of Traditional Commerce

Electronic Commerce (e-commerce)

It can be loosely defined as 'doing business electronically'. More rigorously, e-commerce is buying and selling over digital media. It includes electronic trading of physical goods and of intangibles such as information. This encompasses all the trading steps such as online marketing, ordering, payment, and support for delivery. It includes the electronic provision of services, such as after-sales support, as well as electronic support for collaboration between companies, such as collaborative design (Fig. 22.3).

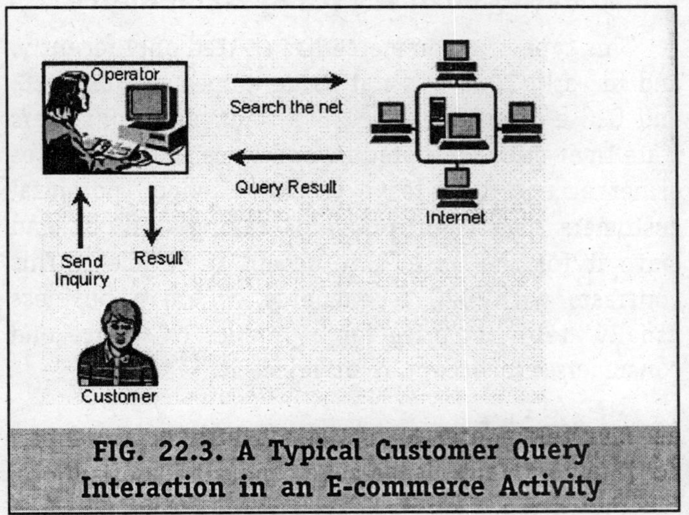

FIG. 22.3. A Typical Customer Query Interaction in an E-commerce Activity

A further definition of e-commerce is provided by the European Union website; which defines 'Electronic commerce as a general concept covering any form of business transactions of information exchange executed using information and communication technology, between companies, between companies and their customers, or between companies and public administrations. Electronic commerce includes electronic trading of goods, services and electronic material.

Some people use the term Internet commerce to mean electronic commerce that specifically uses the Internet as its data transmission medium. E-commerce did not just happen in the last five years. Automobile companies and supermarkets in the Western countries have been doing e-commerce for many years; their e-commerce technology is called electronic data interchange (EDI). Airline seats have also been sold using e-commerce systems; and the French have also been using e-commerce since 1983, but they do it in French with a system called Télétel.

How do you know which products can be sold more effectively using traditional commerce, and which using electronic commerce? Products that buyers prefer to touch, smell, or examine closely are difficult to sell using e-commerce. For example, customers might be reluctant to buy high fashion garments and perishable food products, if they cannot examine the products closely before agreeing to purchase them. Retail merchants may have long traditional commerce experience in creating store environments that help convince customers to buy. This combination of store design, layout, and product display knowledge is called merchandising. Many salespersons have developed skills that allow them to identify customer needs and find products or services that meet those needs. The art of merchandising and personal selling can be difficult to practice over an electronic link.

However, branded merchandise and products, such as books or music CDs, can be easily sold using e-commerce. Customers are willing to order a book title without examining the specific copy they will receive, because one copy of a new book is identical to other copies of the same book, and because the customer is not concerned about its other qualities such as freshness, or smell. Furthermore, e-commerce also offers the advantage of providing the ability to offer a wider selection of book titles than even the largest physical bookstore; which outweighs the advantage of a traditional bookstore, such as the customer's ability to browse the book.

Typologies of E-commerce

A common classification of e-commerce is by the nature of business transaction. E-commerce can be business-to-business, business-to-consumer, consumer-to-consumer, or consumer-to-business.

Business-to-Business (B2B) E-commerce

In business-to-business e-commerce, business organisations buy and sell goods and services to and from each other. In this type of e-commerce, buyers can place their requests for new bids for suppliers on their e-commerce sites, and the sellers from all over the world have a chance to bid. The more buyers there are, the better off sellers will be and *vice versa.* More buyers means sellers will have more customers for their products and services. More sellers means there will be more choices for buyers. The more sellers, the better it is for all sellers, especially when they can learn from each other or produce complementary products or services.

However, if there are too many small buyers and sellers (i.e. buyers and sellers are highly fragmented) a seller may not even know who all the buyers are. Similarly a buyer may not know who all the sellers are either. Each seller has to search through all the e-commerce sites (could be Web pages) of all the buyers to find out what they want, give them the product descriptions that they need, find out about their credit worthiness, complete the buyers' requests for quotation (RFQs), and so on. Thus, the more sellers and buyers and the more fragmented both are, the higher the transaction costs. In order to reduce this transaction cost, we use what is called the 'B2B hubs' — also known as B2B intermediaries or B2B exchanges. They provide a central point in the value chain where sellers and buyers can go to find each other (Fig. 22.4).

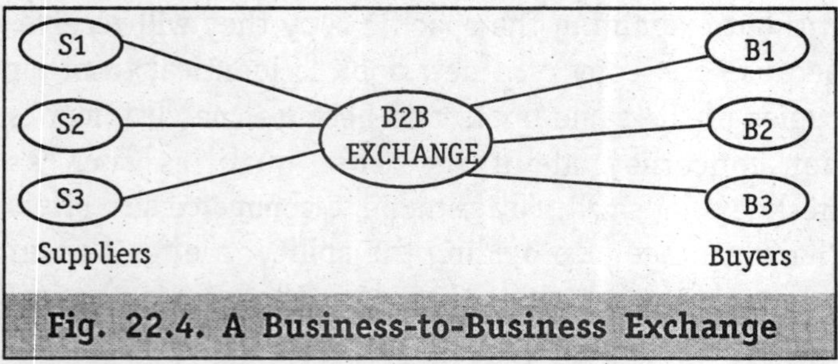

Fig. 22.4. A Business-to-Business Exchange

Business-to-Consumer (B2C) E-commerce

In business-to-consumer e-commerce, business organisations sell to consumers. These are retailing transactions with individual shoppers. The advantage of this type of e-commerce is that consumers have access to the 'electronic shops' 24 hours everyday. The consumers also do not face any queues anytime they go shopping! Also there is almost no limit to the number of goods that an on-line retailer can display on its 'electronic storefront or mall'. Furthermore, the sellers also get an opportunity to collect rich data about their customers while they are interacting, and use it to 'personalise' service for these customers and, in case of some goods bought electronically, such as music and computer software, they can be received instantaneously. Since the consumers can interact from their home computers, they can shop electronically in the privacy of their homes.

Consumer-to-Consumer (C2C) E-commerce

In consumer-to-consumer e-commerce, consumers sell to other consumers. Since there could be a large number of consumers who want to sell different goods, as well as a large number of consumers who want to buy these goods; the cost to sellers and buyers of finding each other could be exorbitant. The solution is to have an intermediary. Rather than having an exchange in this case, 'electronic auction houses', such as eBay, act as an intermediary among the buyer and seller consumers.

Consumer-to-Business (C2B) E-commerce

This type of e-commerce has started only recently, and in early 2000 was not as developed as B2B, B2C, and C2C e-commerce. In C2B e-commerce, consumers state their price for a product or service, and businesses either accept it or leave it. For example, potential customers give their price for taking a flight and leave it for the airlines to accept it or reject. This contrasts with B2C e-commerce, where a business usually states its price for a product or service and consumers can accept it or reject it.

Managing E-Business

Organizations today face major challenges of constantly reducing their costs, introducing new and innovative products on a regular basis and satisfying increasing customer demands. Customers are demanding lower prices, more product options and customization, improved level of services and personalized treatment. To meet all these challenges, the top management at most organizations is examining their enterprises operations in the context of e-business opportunities.

Till recently, e-business had been narrowly viewed by most organizations as establishing a website to offer more information about the company and its products. The maximum efforts made by organizations were to develop the website into just another marketing and sales channel. However, e-business has a much broader scope. It involves digitization of an organization's internal business processes as well as its external interfaces with customers, suppliers and partners. E-Business is about transforming an organization for the information age where value is created by effectively managing intangible assets rather than just physical assets. It offers significant potential to transform companies by creating new value chains and business processes or redesigning existing ones.

The top management at most corporates are now recognizing that e-business is one of the biggest transitions for businesses. They are worried that if they do not handle this transition in the right manner, it could mean losing significant business in the short term or even going out of business in the longer term. To manage this e-business transition successfully, requires developing effective e-business strategies by the top management including the three 'Os' (CEOs, CIOs and CFOs) of all organizations.

DIGITAL ECONOMY INITIATIVES IN INDIA

In the Inaugural Address delivered at the ASSOCHAM Seminar on 11.07.2001 Mr. N. Vittal, Central Vigilance Commissioner so remarked:

"Digital economy is the economy in which digital technology is prominent. Information technology is based on digital technology and thanks to its pervasive impact over the wide spectrum of the economy, we can talk about the economy having become digital. India, like any other country has to face the challenge of the digital economy.

The initiatives needed for preparing India to enter the digital economy can be studied from two sets of angles. One set will relate to the hardware and the software aspects of preparing the country for the digital economy. The second set will relate to specific sectors like e-business or e-commerce and e-governance.

The most important initiative to be taken from the software angle was to bring a change in the mindset and the organisational culture for India to flourish in the digital economy. The permit licence raj which was introduced immediately after Independence had created a culture of corruption involving delay and lack of transparency in decision-making so far as the government is concerned. Business and industry in India has got accustomed to operating in a closed economy, which provided a ready to exploit seller's market. Digital economy means that we must be able to use information technology in every aspect of manufacturing and services. The Internet is the new medium for business. The culture of the digital economy requires transparency and speed. This is what was lacking in the earlier era of the permit licence raj.

From 1991 onwards we are witnessing the process of economic liberalisation, which is proceeding at the pace of two steps forward and one step backward. The progress made so far is uncertain but the trend and the direction of the reform are clear. There will be less protection and greater competition so far as business is concerned. The pressure for the e-governance also calls for the government to rethink its strategy and culture.

The Government of India declared 2001, as the year of e-governance. The Government of India as well as many state governments are taking initiatives to introduce egovernance in their respective areas. E-governance basically amounts to applying information technology (IT) in government functions. In short, e-governance is IT enabled governance.

E-governance, brings a major change in the way the government functions. So far government has been accustomed to conduct its operations on paper. Cynics have observed that the 'paperless office' in government organisations normally results only under two circumstances. Firstly, when there is no budget to buy paper and secondly, when the paper is misplaced. But any serious attempt at application of IT in government functions will have to take into account the hidden resistance to the whole process. Change is always resisted and this resistance, among other things can come from the culture of the government organizations.

There are at least four sources, which gives rise to cultural resistance to e-governance. The first is the government culture of secrecy. The culture of secrecy is further strengthened by the Official Secrets Act. One of the issues, which social activists and NGOs have been highlighting, is the need for bringing greater transparency in government functioning and also empower the citizen by way of enacting the Right to Information Act – 2005. If there is greater application of IT in government operations, then access to information to the public also will become easier. But the question is can the extensive use of IT take place against a culture of secrecy? There could be resistance both overt and covert on this issue. In fact, the application of e-governance itself should be looked upon as a means of bringing greater transparency in the system. This could be even one of the stated objectives of e-governance like the entire purpose being to achieve SMART – small, moral, accountable, responsive and transparent – Government.

The second source of cultural resistance is from corruption. Red tape and delays have bred corruption and in fact the lack of transparency also has been a source of corruption. Egovernance tries to remove these basic factors that promote corruption in the governmental system. But vested interests who are deriving benefits under the present system may resist the extensive application of e-governance because of this factor. If government were to announce that one of the objectives of e-governance is also going to be a more transparent and to that extent a faster moving and less corrupt government, there will be widespread public acceptance and welcome to this measure. Public opinion therefore can thus be generated to overcome this aspect of resistance to e-governance.

The third source of resistance is the culture of seniority, which is very rigidly observed in government. When it comes to IT, it may be the junior officers and staff who may be more familiar and comfortable with computers and IT systems but it is the seniors who take all policy decisions. For example, in one of the states an initiative was taken to have a computer based centre at the heart of the city whereby citizens dealing with seven organizations of the state government could go and make their payment instead of going to the individual offices. The process also was faster. Even though the centre was functional for more than two months, none of the secretaries to the government concerned with those seven departments ever took the care to go and see the working of the center. This is a classic example of the neglect and indifference if not the total lack of interest in the whole effort at introducing e-governance. On the other hand, a suggestion was made that the introduction of the computerised centre amounted to front end computerization where the department interacts with the citizens and back end computerization should take precedence for effective e-governance. This was a classic example of trying to kill a good idea by coming up with a better idea, so that ultimately even the good idea is not implemented.

The fourth source of cultural resistance for e-governance would be sheer lack of imagination. The emphasis in government most of the time is on red tape, procedures and systems. Doing a thing rightly is more important in government than doing the right thing. Innovation is the key for success and generally the bureaucratic culture discourages innovation. On the other hand, if e-governance has to succeed, we need a lot of innovation. How are we to overcome this problem?

Perhaps the best solution would be to first identify the four sources of cultural resistance and initiate specific action so that the appropriate environment for success in e-governance is created. The problem of secrecy can be overcome by either a more liberal freedom of information act or a simple device by which there could be small negative list of items that could be secret and the rest could be accessible to the public. This could be done by a regular administrative order. The issue of corruption can be overcome by mobilizing committed public servants within the system and also cultivating public opinion. The issue of seniority can be overcome by adopting models similar to that adopted by Sam Pitroda when CDOT was set up by which even within the government system, an organization on a mission mode can be created. However, the problem in e-governance would be that while introduction of the systems can be done through a mission mode organization, the operations have to be also seamlessly integrated with the general routine of the government system. In this context, encouraging knowledgeable youngsters and identifying champions for IT in governance at fairly senior levels in government may be the way out. As regards innovation, the change made for overcoming the problem of seniority itself would have created the requisite environment.

So far as Indian business is concerned, the initiatives for the digital economy will be centred on six 'Cs'. These are:

(i) computer density
(ii) connectivity
(iii) contents
(iv) cyber laws
(v) costs, and
(vi) common sense.

E-Government - The Emerging Paradigm

E-government is more than just offering public services over the Internet. It is about making transition from the industrial society to the emerging information society. The use of IT can significantly enhance a government's dealings with its citizens, businesses as well as its employees. The article explains in detail what e-government is and discusses about the strategies for achieving government enterprise transformation. It also discusses the technological aspects e-governments must address and the key issues faced by them.

The Internet has brought in a fundamental change in our personal and professional lives. We are in the midst of an information and communications technologies revolution. Now, Internet is radically changing the way governments operate across the globe. The new millennium had brought forward unprecedented opportunities for innovative, result-oriented government sector.

E-government refers to the use of IT to deliver public services and information in a more convenient, citizen-centric, cost-effective, and manner. The past decade witnessed many government departments all over the world embrace the digital revolution. E-government is a way for governments to use the new technologies to provide citizens and businesses with more convenient access to government information and services, to improve the quality of their services and provide greater opportunities to participate in the democratic processes. However, e-government is more than just offering government services over the Internet. It involves a significant organizational change, a change that can bring about Government Enterprise Transformation (GET).

It is good that the Government of India has taken the initiative to declare the year 2001 as the 'Year of E-governance'. This brought in the greater degree of IT in government administration which is very vital for developing a vigorous economy which can compete in this digital age.

In fact, the pace of development of the infrastructure needed for the digital economy would depend upon the pace with which telecom infrastructure is developed. This will call for an enlightened approach to licensing. There is need for a new approach focussed on convergence in licensing, in this context.

Convergence in technology is one of the most important features of modern telecommunications.

The Government has recognized this and is also ready with a Convergence of communication Bill which has been thrown open for debate. While Government has taken a significant and imaginative step forward in the area of legislating for convergence of communication when it comes to the policy of licensing in telecommunication, it is trapped in the legacy of the past. The recent controversy over the limited mobility for the wireless in local loop permitted for the fixed telephone line operators, resulted finally in the GOTIT giving a report which proved its objectivity by dissatisfying the lobbies of both the cellular operators as well as the basic telecom operators. The matter will continue to remain unresolved for the foreseeable feature because regulatory agencies like the TRAI and TDSAT have been or will be approached by the parties concerned.

In this situation, the best way to resolve the issue and move ahead is to go back to the basics of the current telecom scene and re-think the strategy. Four engines are driving the telecom process all through the world. These are; technology, political will, regulatory activism and market dynamics. We have seen their inter play in India right from 1994 when the National Telecom Policy was announced. The recent controversy about the limited WILL mobility is also part of the same process.

The licensing policy adopted should be in tune with the technological development and the ground realities in telecommunication. The convergence in technology underlines the need for convergence in licensing. There are four 'Cs', which should be the basis for regulating the emerging telecom scene in the era of convergence. The First 'C' is the consumer who is the most important person. It should be ensured that all policies which are adopted, benefit the consumer of telecom services. The second 'C' is convergence, which is a technical reality.

Licensing should take care of this aspect and ensure what technology unites by convergence is not divided by licenses based on the earlier approach to technology. The third 'C' is competition which means that there should be plurality of players in the market place, plurality of services and even plurality when it comes to the quality and price of the telecom services. One cannot adopt a procrustean approach in this area. Competition is also the best guarantee to ensure that the first 'C' consumer interests, are not sacrificed.

The fourth 'C' is commitment which includes both legal commitments entered into by the Government as well as the licensing agency or the Regulatory Authorities and financial commitments entered into by the licensees.

The need for course correction in the approach to licensing and regulation arises because of the emerging realities in the telecom scene. Technology is changing constantly and mistakes made either by the Government or by the investors have to be also corrected. Looking to the large financial stakes involved, it may not be possible for the Government to adopt a hands off attitude and say that the market forces will prevail. This was the spirit behind the Government's 1999 New Telecom Policy whereby the cellular operators who had bid enormous amounts for license fees were bailed out by the Government by giving them an opportunity to come over a revenue sharing system.

The emerging convergence of technology has also given rise to a new telecom service. This is the Internet Telephony where the computer is linked with the Public System Telephone Network (PSTN) or voice over Internet Protocol (VOIP) which does not link with PSTN. This service is not permitted by the Government because it affects adversely the finances of Government organizations like VSNL, BSNL and MTNL. Adopting the King Canute attitude and banning technology is not in the long term interest of the country. It is said that the Internet Telephony can bring down the cost by 1/500th of the wire line cost and will thus make the telephone tariff very affordable to the poor especially in rural areas. In Thailand the rural Internet telephony has brought rural telecom costs down to one fifth of the normal rates. As the poor and the rural areas are sacred cows in any democracy, why should there be any hesitation at all in permitting.

Internet telephony and VOIP?

Another policy restriction which is preventing the economics of the telecom operations becoming more viable, is the restriction on the inter connecting of the networks of the private sector operators and PSTN. There should be total freedom given for the telecom operators in the private sector whether they are cellular services or in basic telephony to interconnect freely so that the national network which is today dependent on the traditional infrastructure put up by the Government and operated by BSNL and MTNL will get a further boost. What is more, such networking will ensure that without going in for a separate national long distance operator, long distances services would automatically flow from the existing investments already made by both the Government and private sector operators.

The next step needed to resolve all the present and future controversies about the different type of licenses is to introduce a single license concept with a cafeteria approach for different services which could be provided by the license holders. All the existing operators should be permitted to migrate to the single licence system just as the cellular operators were permitted to migrate from the license fee regime to the revenue sharing. Before the parameters and the conditions for each type of service and the conditions for transmission to a single licensing regime are introduced, full opportunity must be given to all the stake holders in the Indian telecom scene to come up with their suggestions about the terms and conditions for such a shift. Once all these options are placed on the table, the TRAI go into them and make suggestions which will be acceptable to all.

The final solution should be based on the principle of entitled self interest and the four 'Cs'. The age of convergence in telecom technology also calls for a convergence in the concept of licensing and harmonising the interests of all stake holders.

So far as cyber laws are concerned, the Government of India have already enacted the Information Technology Act 2000 on the anvil is the Communication of Convergence. With these two laws in place, at least we have created the legal infrastructure needed for ushering in the digital economy".

THE GLOBE IS A SQUARE

Bad geometry is good economics when networks make a plaza out of the planet. Marshal McLuhan's dream of a global village has come true and with it has emerged the concept of a 'global economy'.

This 'global economy' has happened mostly because of phenomenal advances in computing and telecommunications. Of course, there have been other circumstances responsible for the death of distance like the end of the Cold War and the setting up of the World Trade Organisation. But information technology, by far, has been the most significant in the creation of what we have come to call the 'global economy'.

What exactly do we mean by 'globalisation' in a 'global economy'? Globalisation essentially involves free movement across international borders of four specific elements of an economy. These are (i) physical capital in terms of plant and machinery; (ii) financial capital in terms of finances invested in the capital markets; (iii) technology and (iv) labour.

International computer and telecommunication networks have not only opened access but also speeded up the free movement of these elements. Take the case of financial capital. Thanks to optic fibre cables, it literally moves at the speed of light. Unfortunately, the recent currency crisis in Southeast Asia can also be traced to this particular 'boon'. But before we discuss the implication of this any further, let us sharpen our focus a bit. The global economy has already morphed into the 'digital' global economy. Here we must recognise the most significant development in the technology of this century, the technology of information.

Information technology is nothing but the coming together of computers and communications. If railroads were the decisive technology of the 19th century and automobiles of the 20th, information technology will fashion the century to come. The Internet is already making the prophecy come true. According to one estimate, the Web has about a 100 million users. When so many people are over a particular kind of network, will they not take their economies over it? This should in fact change the meaning of commerce. Already, the first mutation of commerce as we know it has appeared. Large businesses have begun to worry about the implications of e-commerce or electronic commerce!

Massachusetts Institute of Technology Media Labs chief Nicholas Negroponte was among the first to dramatically outline e-commerce in his best-selling book 'Being Digital'. He speaks of commerce where more and more businesses trade 'bits' of information instead of 'atoms' of products.

Here's a pointer. In the US, about 45 per cent of the investments in office equipment go into purchase of computers and information technology systems. This rising presence of information technology in businesses translates directly into the creation of what we may call the 'digital global economy'. But not all countries are equally developed. When it comes to technology, the differences become more severe. This raises the issue of the widening divide between the information rich and the information poor. There is also talk about information apartheid.

The increasing pace of technology could become an opportunity for a country like India. Dr Vikram Sarabhai had pointed out that developing nations like India stand to gain by reaching the technological scene late then they can leapfrog through the intermediate stages that the developed nations had to go through.

For instance, India is not very much wired. We can therefore increasingly use modern wireless technology for our communications needs. Again, we probably missed out on the mainframe revolution. But now for the same reason, we can take advantage of the network revolution in the absence of legacy systems. Information technology is highly versatile. After all, any economy comprises manufacturing and services. One can say there is no activity, no area of manufacturing or services, where one can apply information technology and not immediately gain advantage in terms of improvement in productivity and savings in costs and energy.

According to a recent publication of the US government, 'The Emerging Digital Economy', one of the most notable economic developments in recent years has been the rapid increase in investment in the IT sectors, computing and communications and their contribution to the gross domestic product. It grew from 4.9 per cent of the economy in 1985 to 6.1 per cent in 1990 as the PC began to penetrate homes and offices. The next spurt started in 1993 with a burst of commercial activity driven by the Internet. From 1993 to 1998, IT's share of the economy would have risen from 6.4 per cent to an estimated 8.2 per cent. With such rapid expansion, IT's share of total nominal GDP growth has been running at about double its share of the economy at close to 15 per cent. This growth has been possible because IT is tailor-made to enhance the key elements of competitiveness in the global economy. Today, competitiveness depends on speed and IT is speed. Competitiveness depends on reducing costs, and a primary objective of IT is to do exactly that.

Email has eliminated the need for bothering about time zones in communication. In fact, multinational companies have become entrepreneurial Webs spread over the world only because of the nervous system that IT can provide.

As economies develop, the share of the service industry becomes more than that of manufacturing. In fact, developed economies like the United States have a very large percentage of the GDP in services, sometimes over 70 per cent. Because of this, some people fear about the hollowing of the US economy. Nevertheless, it is a fact that the higher the percentage of the service economy, the greater is the state of economic development.

It is in the service industry, that IT provides the most opportunities because of its capacity for instant communication, random access and ability to handle large amounts of data. In fact, computer aided design, computer aided manufacturing or management practices like the just-in-time technique would not be possible without IT. Tough IT is increasingly becoming an integral part of the manufacturing process or the service industry, people have their fears. Jeremy Rifkin writes in 'The End of Work' that computers may lead to jobless growth. This is being experienced especially, in Europe.

It is IT, which has also made possible the fantastic growth of software in India. The US companies find it easier to outsource work without any loss of their competitiveness in the global context.

The significance of the IT in global trade can also be deducted from the fact that one of the earliest agreements entered into after the WTO was formed was the Information Technology Agreement. India is a part of ITA.

In a recent testimony to the US Congress, Federal Reserve Board Chairman Alan Greenspan noted "Our nation has been experiencing a higher growth rate of productivity output per hour worked in recent years. The dramatic improvements in computing power and communication and information technology appear to have been a major force behind this beneficial trend." It has been suggested that these advances will create a "long boom" which will take the economy to new heights over the next quarter of the century.

Other economists remains sceptical of the contribution of the IT industry to overall productivity and yet there is limited direct evidence in government data of the United States that the investments made in IT have substantially raised productivity in many non-IT industries. The increasing use of IT, particularly the Internet, demonstrates the need for designing and amending existing legal structure so as to have a set of appropriate cyber laws.

E-commerce also provides opportunities for frauds. One has to guard against cyber frauds. After all, as Oscar Wilde said "The thief is the artist. The policeman is only a critic." The issues of cyber laws are going to become increasingly important in the context of the global digital economy.

An interesting observation brought out in the US publication 'The Emerging Digital Economy' is that IT has also helped to control inflation. In fact, inflation in the United States would have been 3 per cent but this has been reduced by at least 1 per cent because of the increasing application of IT.

The Internet has really been the harbinger of e-commerce. Some facts about the Internet and e-commerce are really breathtaking:

- Fewer than 40 million people around the world were connected to the Internet during 1996. By the end of 1997, over 100 million people were using the Internet.
- As of December 1996, about 627,000 Internet domain names had been registered. By the end of 1997, the number of domain names more than doubled to reach 1.5 million.
- Traffic on the Internet has been doubling every 100 days.
- Cisco Systems closed 1996 having booked just over $100 million in sales on the Internet. By the end of 1997, its Internet sales were running at a $3.2 billion annual rate.
- In 1996, Amazon, the first Internet bookstore, recorded sales of less than $16 million. In 1997, it sold $148 million worth of books to Internet customers. One of the nation's largest book retailers, Barnes and Noble, launched its own online bookstore in 1997 to compete with Amazon for this rapidly growing online market.
- In January 1997, Dell Computers was selling

less than $1 million worth of computers per day over the Internet. The company reported reaching daily sales of $6 million several times during the December 1997 holiday period.

- Auto-by-Tel, a Web-based automotive marketplace processed a total of 345,000 purchase requests for autos through its Web site in 1996, for $1.8 billion in auto sales. As of the end of November 1997, the Web site was generating $500 million a month in auto sales ($6 billion annualised) and processed over 100,000 purchase requests each month.

Where does India stand in this emerging global digital economy?

The importance of Digital Society as an integral part of development and prosperity of the whole society is increasing day-by-day. E-Economy has seamlessly integrated with the Economy which we know of and gaining in its share of the market.

Conceptually, Digital Economy in India became visible around 1997 with the Internet becoming available to common public. Legally, Digital Economy became a reality in India in 2000 with the passage of ITA-2000 digital contracts possible. The Recasting of the Global I-Governance system with the ICANN giving way to a new system under WSIS is now on the horizon.

It has been repeatedly pointed out for several years that when it comes to basic hardware we have miles to go. India have only 1.8 computers per 1,000 of the population while the world average is 25. The world telephone density is 10 per cent and India's is 1.6 per cent. Policy measures to increase the availability of information infrastructure are the only way out for the country. It is a healthy sign that the National Agenda for Governance has taken note of the significance of IT. What is important is the need to initiate policy changes quickly, so that we don't miss out on the global digital economy.

India cannot participate effectively in the global digital economy unless the Indian government, both at New Delhi and the state capital, become technology minded. It is healthy that apart from the India's recognition as a software source, visionary leaders like Chandrababu Naidu of Andhra Pradesh are trying to push IT in state administration. One simple solution that is needed is that at least 2 to 3 per cent of the budget of every department must be earmarked for the application of IT. In this way, the culture of IT will spread right across the entire spectrum of government and public administration.

Equally important for India to participate effectively in the digital economy is the need for a very large size computer literate manpower. Today, the attrition rate in the software industry is 20 per cent and some claim it is as high as 50 per cent. To overcome this situation we will have to massively increase a number of computer literate students.

It would therefore suggest that full credits be given to computer studies in both the 10th and 12th classes. Further, practically in every degree course, there should be a module of information technology. In this way, we will ensure that a whole generation of students which will come in the next three years, will be computer literate. This will provide the substantial manpower needed for bringing a transformation in the nation's own economy and make it a part of the global digital economy. Otherwise, today when we talk about global digital economy in the Indian context, we are mostly talking about software or those aspects of the Indian economy that are related to exports.

But ultimately, India cannot afford to play a very effective role unless the Indian economy also falls in line with the global digital economy. That means increasing application of IT in all aspects of manufacturing and services, right across the entire spectrum of our economy. The global digital economy is a reality. The question is whether India will be able to make it in the brave new world.

If India has to remain in the map of the Digital World, a focused approach to the needs of Digital Society is therefore considered essential. Today E-Commerce or E-Governance is no longer an option. It is a critical necessity.

THE ECONOMICS OF THE MARKET SPACE

While transactions involving each of these items can and do take place in the physical market place, a growing proportion is now being conducted in the market space too. As in any new bazaar, there are few established relationships yet. Buyers search for the products or services they need, all of which reside in the data banks of computers. Leaping from Delhi to Detroit, or from Tokyo to Turin in search of the best bargain is just as simple as walking to the next shop if the first one doesn't offer a good price. Thousands no, millions of transactions take place within the shimmering contours of the market space every hour as every new forces of demand and supply spring into existence, meet for a moment to conclude a deal, and disappear into the unknown into existence, from whence they came. Importantly, the classical laws of economics just don't hold in this market space. As Harvard Business School Professors Jeffrey F. Rayport and John J. Skioval write in the Harvard Business Review: 'The conventional understanding of the economies of scale and scope does not apply to the virtual value chain, managing information allows companies to create new value for customers and serve a broader set of needs.'

In the physical world, production is always associated with the consumption of resources. There, so long as your company is climbing up the ladder of economies of scale, the incremental cost of each additional unit will fall until the law of diminishing returns sets in. After that, your brick and mortar factories will produce less with every additional rupee, man hour, or kilograms of raw material you put in. Naturally, profit making in the physical market place is bound by these restrictions. The contrast with the market space couldn't be starker. Companies that manufacture digital products don't even have to produce additional units. All that they need is a master copy of the product, stored digitally, which can be copied again and again by consumers through their computer connections. Music companies, for instance, only need to create one copy of the package. Software companies only need to create, one copy of a package. An information vendor only needs to maintain one database without even spending money on making copies of it on CD-ROMS.

Since no additional resources will be spent on each unit of a product that your company sell in the market space, the conventional equations of costs and revenues will crumble too. And once your company has recovered its development cost for a product, every unit of additional sales will mean pure profit a mirage in the market place, but reality in the market space. Moreover, in this virtual market, physical distance which usually adds to cost of transportation, is immaterial. So long as your product is information, it can be transferred at the same cost anywhere in the world. One outcome of this digital level playing field is that being physically close to your market offers no benefits, just as thousands of miles create any handicaps either. Pronounces Nichloas Negroponte, 51 Director, MIT Media Lab: 'the distribution and movement of bits is much easier than atoms. But delivery is only part of the issue. The physical distributor performs the tasks of selections and promotion, which the Network itself supercedes.'

THE VALUE CHAIN ON THE NET

Equally important are the opportunities that the Net provides companies to exploit the market space for managing their value chain from raw materials to after sales services more efficiently. For, the market space offers the possibility of creating a virtual value chain in addition to the real value chain that starts with raw materials and tarverses inbound logistics, production processes, outbound logistics, marketing and sales, ending with after sales services. While each stage of value addition in the real value chain takes place in the physical world, in the virtual value chain, all value is added in the form of information in the market space. How can companies make the shift? The first of the two stages of the migration involves adding value simultaneously in the real and virtual worlds during some of the stages. For instance, if your company manufactures and markets high fashion clothing you can accept orders from the customer connecting to your home page on the Web, just as you do when customers walk into your retail stores. Here, the value addition from selling the product can be accomplished in both the physical and electronic worlds.

In the second stage, companies can use the market space to add value in ways, which are impossible in the physical world. For instance, a publisher who's planning to print a novel by a new author can post a chapter from the novel on his company's home page on the Web, using the response from readers to plan the print run and the form of promotion that will optimise his revenues from the publication. Or, an automobile company can use the information from its computer stimulated test drives to design games for consumers in virtual space, thus building relationships with them which will improve the quality of their marketing. Of course, companies cannot expect to abandon the market place altogether: they will have to maintain a presence in both the physical and the digital market to ensure that they do not miss out on the opportunities of either.

How can Corporates respond to the emergence of the market space? By moving in very quickly. Warm Mckinsey & Co.'s Lorraine Harrington and Grey Greed in the Mackinsey Quarterly: "As E-commerce spreads those who understand and use the economics of the electronic market place will gain a competitive advantage. The rise of intermediaries exploiting electronic channels to circumvent and, in some cases, replace physical channels represents a wake up call for incumbent businesses or, as Lousi Gerstener, 54, CEO, IBM, declared recently: 'The interent has to be near the centre of most businesses' future plans. The power of the Network to change structures will be the strongest force in the environment." For India Inc., the paradigm shifting economics of the brave new market space offers a clear chance to compete with manufacturers — big and small — from any part of the world, on an equal footing. Here, using the powerful search systems of the market space, potential customers will seek out Indian companies that have the right products. Here, reputations will be built not from past transactions, but from the speed of response to digital deals. Here, big brands will hold no edge over unknown labels. Here, the tools of satisfying the customer will be available to a Rs. 10 crore exporter as easily as to the $ 168.90 billion General Motors. To the world's mega corps the market space is still too small to divert major resources from the physical market place. But India Inc., which has few markets to protect globally, can homestead the electronics frontier before its larger competitors. For, the market space is the ultimate democracy for business. Everyone is equal but India Inc., can be more equal than others can.

THE MARKET SPACE — BUSINESS ON THE NET

The hottest emerging — Albeit confusing — market space for the world's mega corps, the Net is becoming a global gateway for India Inc. Dip, for a moment, into the wish list of the would be global Indian entrepreneur. The power to reach out to new consumers. A method for overcoming the handicap of being small. A low cost strategy for establishing a brand. As already recognised by a handful of visionary CEOs in the country, the Net now offers these very opportunities to Corporate India. While the physical market place — comprising distribution and retail channels in countries around the world — is difficult to access and even harder to stake a presence in the market space will prove far more receptive to Corporate India's globalisation. Just what is the business that Indian companies can conduct profitably in the market space?

Selling information of various hues — from huge databases to addresses and phone numbers of potential business partners, from music and images to electronic versions of magazines and newspapers. For instance, Ravi Database's 'Indiaworld' and advertising agency Rediffusion Dentsu Young and Rubicam's 'Rediff on the Net' are both digital compendia of news, trivia, and other data which subscribers can buy over the Net.

Retailing financial products like equity offerings, bond issues, fixed deposit schemes for Non-Resident Indians (NRI) *et al.* The classic examples: in February 1998, Kotak-Mahindra Finance, part marketed the Rs. 5,071.04 crore Industrial Development Bank of India's Rs. 1,000 crore bonds issue through the Net. A large proportion of the applications came from investors from the US and Europe who scouting the market space for investment opportunities in India, have spotted Kotak Securities' Web-site and applied electronically.

Vending real estate to NRIs, the K. Raheja Group and the Rs. 2,500 crore Videocon Group of Mumbai, as well as the Rs. 159.67 crore Ansal Group of Delhi, are using the Net to offer detailed information about their products. Once initial contact is established with prospective buyers, the companies deal by following up through conventional means such as fax and phone.

Distributing products that, typically, involve Networking with people — such as educational services. A pioneer: the Rs. 145 crore software and computer training company NIIT, which has set up virtual classrooms with a global reach, using the Web as the medium, starting with free courses at the lowest level to build customer interest, NIIT has designed a complete menu of courses to provide just-in-time education into the form of skill-tests.

Micro-niche services cashing in on the unique global and distance-demolishing information conduits what the Net has created. For instance, the Mumbai based Pacific Gift Service which invites people outside India to visit its home page, pick a gift from the menu, enter the name and address of a recipient in India, and make the payment. The company's job is delivering the gift.

Scouting of collaborations with global partners. The Rs. 600 crore Eicher Group's Website, besides offering company-related information, has launched into a statement inviting responses from prospective partners — technical or financial — for two new units: a ferrous foundry for automotive units, and a cam-shaft machining unit. Searching globally for knowledge workers: companies like Rs. 7,908.73 crore TELCO and market researchers mode research have been using the Net to post recruitment ads in a bid to reach people who are beyond the reach of conventional devices like appointment ads and head-hunting.

Clearly, cyberwise Corporates are not only ringing up sales on their cash registers through innovative products and distribution channels, they're also expanding their business horizons by using the Web as a medium for establishing contact with potential customers, collaborators, employees and shareholders. Says Sugata Mitra, 44, head of research NIIT: Given the low costs and the reach of the Internet, an Indian Company is at no disadvantage in his business. In fact we can fully leverage all our cost advantages in this model. The typical platform for the pitches: the Web magazine a compendium of news and features — either on specific subjects, or originating from specific countries such as India. Currently, there are at least 10 India-related Webzones on the Net, all of them watering holes for Indian and foreign Websurfers. Like their cousins in print or television, these digital magazines will accept ads from your company. And these ads can act as gateways to your Website with a simple click on the ad immediately transporting the visitor to your home page, wherever it may be located.

The classic forms of cold-call marketing, using the Net beats conventional distance-selling in one fundamental way. In physical markets, no Indian exporters can effort to simply post an ad in suitable media and wait for responses to pour in. He must also proactively seek out potential customers and establish relations with them. But in the market space, customers roaming the world for sellers of the products and services will track you down and set up business links with you. For instance, over 3,500 merchants log into Industry Net-a Web-based service designed to put business in touch with one another — every day, and search its databases for companies manufacturing or marketing products that they are interested in. Establishing your company's presence on these digital yellow pages will immediately bring in customers and queries.

Your Customer

Remember: with just 8,000 Internet subscribers in the country, conventional marketing techniques have a far wider reach among Indian consumers. It is home in on customers in other countries in general — and the US and Europe, where 84 per cent of the 33 million Web surfers form, in particulars — that India Inc. must do business on the Net. And while many among them are retail purchasers of products and services, the real opportunity for Indian business buyers and closing deals with them. The economics of contacting such customers in the market space are vastly different. For, the cost of establishing an outpost on the Web in the form of a home page, is a fixed one. But since its reach is global, there is no multiplication of media spends for different countries. Imagine, for instance, the bill and the logistic that Kotak Securities would have to manage in order to advertise in countries as far apart as New Zealand, Malaysia, and Canada — each with its own media targeting a handful of NRIs in each country. But because the market space is not geographically fragmented, it requires only one medium, the Net and only one digital signpost, the home page and reaching even a single potential customer in, say Japan, involves no additional costs. Says Anmol Teneja, 38, Director of the Delhi-based web service provider DSF Internet: The kind of reach that the Net provides is impossible to duplicate through conventional media.

He is right for instance, having started out by advertising itself and its activities on India world Kotak Securities added electronic forms, complete with serial numbers for the IDBI issue. And while IDBI spent Rs. 6 lakh on 55,000 mailers, receiving a near-zero response, the Website cost under Rs. 50,000 generating between 10,000 and 15,000 hits every week. Says C. Jayaram, 39, CEO Kotak Securities: we tried out the Internet as an experiment. The results surprised us pleasantly. Likewise the Rs. 200.04 crore Lloyd Finance received more than 1,000 applications through the Net to its Rs. 190 crore rights issue in February 1996. All that the respondents had done was click on the company's ad on Indiaworld, which allowed them to download a digital form, fill it up and zap it across the Net to the company. And the Rs. 32.23 crore ICICI Bank receives 20 e-mail responses every day from NRIs who have logged onto its home page from Hong Kong, Malaysia, and New Zealand, seeking information on saving products back home. Says S. Solomon Raj, 42, Managing Director, Indusland Bank: The Net holds great potential as a marketing tool given its wide reach. Adds Rajesh Jain 30, Managing Director of Ravi Database, the company that hosts Indiaworld: This is not just a better medium for reaching the NRI market. It is the only reasonably priced medium to reach that audience.

While these companies have developed Web-selling with Web-marketing, even the power to communication with the customer — whether the deal is closed or not is a Net granted benefit that can be leveraged effectively. Agrees K. Vijay Rahavan, 26, Group Manager (merchant banking), Llyods Finance: A part from the response we got from the NRI market via the Net, even the ability to draw a lot of people to our Website is an advantage. With 20 e-mail queries coming in every day the company has dedicated four persons to manage its Website and process on-line response.

Market Methodologies — 4 Ps Web Marketing

No wonder, then, that the Net is brimming over with Corporate Websites. While current estimates peg the number of business-related home pages — belonging to big corporations, small exportes and importers, retail-chains, electronic shopping malls, Web order services, information providers *et. al.,* — at over 1,00,000 over half the Fortune 500 companies have also established a direct presence on the Web. Just what are these Corporates doing on the Net — besides directly selling their products and services — that provide a role model for India Inc., for marketing to the wired customer?

Offering Information

Many companies that haven't yet managed to work out the best way to cash in on the opportunities on the Net, but nevertheless realise that they cannot afford to stay out of this market space, are building Websites with detailed information about themselves. Corporates manufacturing low-involvement products such as soaps and detergents, for instance, cannot really expect info-hungry Web surfers to explore the details about their products. So the $ 49.47 billion Unilever, for one, is disseminating information about its brands, its financial performance and its organisational structure.

Potraying Products

As a company's wares climb up the involvement scale, the Web is the perfect medium for enabling interactivity with customers. The DM 25.10 billion automaker Opel for example, has created a multimedia museum of its own as well as competitors' cars, with lavish picture and detailed spacesheets of the vehicles, all designed to appeal to the quite essential motor-maniac's lover for such information. Sure, the company doesn't sell its motor this way, but it is using the Web to build relationships, some of which could be translated into purchases. Equally important, its presentation is creating for it a top of the mind presence among global customers who will react positively to the brand name.

Alluring Customers

A Company's products and services needn't be its only hook for sharing customers. The $290-million industrial tool maker N.C. Dawson, for instance, not only has a full colour detailed catalogue of its tools, but employees. The result: home pages that are devoted to, *inter alia,* the cult computer game Doom and the rock group Pink Floyed. These unexpected contents help attach Websurfers outside Dawson's core target audience.

Providing Entertainment

Companies can delve into their inventories for startlingly Web-compatible products with which to compete with the vast multitudes of multimedia entertainment that Net serves up. The Rs. 911.68 crore Gujarat Cooperative Milk Marketing Federation, the manufacturer of Amul butter, for instance, has erected a gallery of its legendary of outdoor advertisement with fun driven punch lines on topical issues. The gallery receives more than 5,000 visitors a day. Among other companies with the same Web-marketing strategy are the $ 18.02 billion Coca-Cola the $ 19.52 billion Boeing, and the $ 32.20-billion BMW, all of whom seek to entertain and edify rather than hard sell their products through the Net.

But while these are strategic ways to grab the attention of Websurfers and divert them, companies cannot expect real benefits unless they use the market space for business transactions, and not just as multimedia billboards. Just how, then can Indian companies market their products and services on the Net?

The Four Ps of Web-Marketing are as follows:

The Product

Exporters and manufacturers of physical products from commodities to handicrafts, from leather to tea, from sea food to tobacco can use the market space only to contact customers and not to deliver their wares. So the Net need not define their product strategy. However, vendors of products, which can be digitised and distributed directly over the Net, can cash in on the market space by designing appropriate offerings. Pure information, relating to Indian markets, the economy, and their stock markets are not among users of such data, who routinely use the Net as their primary shopping spot. Says Arvind Agarwala, 36, CEO Vedika Software: "The Interent can be the delivery vehicle for providing business information." Information products like newspapers and magazines from the country are already on the Web, although most of them are free at the moment, the trend is being set by on-line publications from US and UK which charge users a fee to access their news articles and data banks. Such paid services clearly point to the development of an info mart that Indian companies can exploit. Already, information sellers like Mumbai-based Centre for Monitoring India Economy (CMIE) are running Websites which surfess can access for data on the Indian economy. Says Ajay Shah, 34, former President, CMIE : "The Web is a natural first-choice for the specialised information vendor." And Indiaworld and Rediff on the Net which open up their detailed information bases and full range of services only to paid subscribers offering a glimpse to free loaders for sampling purposes are pointing the way to the future.

Among the other ideal products for the market space is, of course, software, as countless software companies form all purpose giants like the $ 5.94 billion Microsoft to specialised game designers ID Software are demonstrating. Since software, like information, can be downloaded directly over the Net, the acts of marketing, sampling and selling are fused together seamlessly in the market space. Indian software companies thirsting for global buyers, can use the Web effectively to advertise and vend their products, as companies like the Rs. 93.41 crore Infosys and NIIT are doing already. So too can publishers of books and music. And to cash in on the multi-media capabilities of the Web CD-ROM publishers are designing special products. For instance, Microsoft's Cinemania and Music central CD-ROM, are sold shinkwrapped as complete multimedia packages, which them update themselves with details on new films and new music releases, respectively by connecting to the company's Website. Educational courses are Web-compatible too. Says Ganesh Natarajan, 38, CEO, Aptech: "we plan to use the Net for conducting on line examinations for students, and for delivering on line courses through multimedia." And even as the Net brims over with information, providing an easy way to access it searches engines, for instance — is among the hottest Net businesses today. That's why Vedika Software, in association with the Videsh Sanchar Nigam, is setting up on line clearing house of all India-related information on the Net: a one stop shop of data buyers.

The Price

Since the economics of manufacturing products for the market space are unique, primarily because a product has to be created only once and stored digitally thereafter, so is the pricing. As in any competitive new market, demand and supply — rather than the cost plan formula — will determine the premium. The real innovation, however, will be in the fact the sales will, typically, be in small units rather than complete packages: One item of information instead of the entire database. A small application instead of the entire program. Individual songs instead of an entire course. Be prepared, therefore, to draw up a pricing formula that factors in this characteristic: NIIT's Netvarsity, for instance, will vend its just-in-time training modules at prices as low as $2 each.

The Promotion

The simplest form of advertising on the Web is the strip-ad: a small panel of visual and text on popular Websites, which attract your company's target audience. The difference, however, is that the technology of the Web allows this ad to act as a gateway to your home page. Since ads that lead nowhere efforts on the Net, it is essential to follow up your ad with your own Website. And this Website must act as your company's profile for anyone in the world. Says Ajay Batra, 31, Director of the Delhi-based Web-hosting service provider Boolean Solutions: "the homepage is your permanent face to the world. There's no limit on the amount of information you can give. Corporate analysts are getting used to the idea that whenever you want any information on a company, you just hit its homepage." Echoes P.V. Maiya, 49, Chairman, ICICI Bank: "We want to develop our homepage as a site for analysts and foreign institutional investors who need information on banking and finance in India." Just how do you get your Website right?

Function, and not appearance, must be the guiding factor when planning it. Start by bench marking your needs against those being served by Corporate sits already on the Web. Do you need a Website to disseminate information about your company? Sample the $ 111.05 billion Toyota's homepage (http// www.Toyota.Com) for information about the company and its products, including a car care advisory, a travel section, and a glossary of auto speak. Does your business strategy involve posting digital product catalogues? Learn from the $ 47.58 billion Sony Music (http://www. music. Sony.com), where visitors can get information on and sample, every one of the 11,300 albums and more than 200 artists in the company's repertoire. Planning to sell your products directly to customers on receipt of on-line orders? Explore The Virtual Vineyard (http://www.wombat.com.au/wombat/ showcasel) — an Australian trading company which has transformed its site into a comprehensive database on Australian business resources. Only after a thorough reconnaissance should you start planning the contents and appearance of your Website. Then, by packing in as much information and innovation as possible, you can ensure that the traffic doesn't die out. For instance, Kotak Securities and Indiaworld have launched a stock market game named Cybex on their site, "The idea," explains Suraj Mishra, 32, Vice-President, Kotak Securities, "is to build up focused audience that visits the site daily."

The Place

The most powerful boost to cross-border marketing comes from the fact that the Net makes the physical distance between the buyer and the seller immaterial. No longer do Indian companies targeting global customers need to set up expensive distribution channels — usually the highest entry-barriers in open markets — in different countries. One Website, located in any computer in the world, can service consumers all over the world. However, so long as distribution and payment weren't integrated on the Net, the power of the market space was curbed: payments had to made in the real world, either through cash or credit cards. Now, however, secure on-line payments systems, in the form of both credit cards and electronic cash, are emerging with companies like Digicash, Cybercash, and e-cash, as well as credit card giants like Visa and Mastercard evolving electronic payment systems. Says Hatim Tyabji, 49, CEO of the $ 3.09-billion-transaction automation company Verifone, which is developing on-line payment systems for both Nescafe and the $ 5.93-billion Microsoft: "Internet based transactions will be as secure as conventional credit card transactions very soon." After that your distribution dilemmas will only be technical: What kind of hardware should you use for your Web sever? How close to the backbone of the Net can you find room for it? And how large a bandwidth — which will determine how long the queues will be — can you accommodate? Adds Ravi Database's Jain, "It is important to structure a Web-based business in such a way that the transaction can be completed on the Web itself."

Value-Added Services

Crucially, opportunities for differentiating your

products or services also lie beyond the four Ps. For, exploiting their unique powers of the market space, users and products can be brought together, bridging time and space effortlessly and by moving three custom-related parts of their value chain advertising, marketing, direct selling, sampling, and after sales for instance into the market space, companies can deliver greater value to consumers and gain an edge over competitors. For any information-based product from news and stock market quotes to music, pictures, computer software, and education digital sampling is not only simple, but also economical unlike physical products, house-to-house distribution is not necessary.

It is by seizing these opportunities that India Inc., can force the Net to deliver its full basket of benefits many companies around the world still view the market space as a frustrating, confusing and unprofitable arena, where the type is yet to match the hard figures. They're right. But early entrants have the advantage of setting the rules, which will then have to be followed by late commerce. For, make no mistake, as the computer population around the world explodes, even as Web TVs' invade living rooms, exponentially rising access to the Net will expand the frontiers of the market space to envelope the majority of consumers around the world. This is not an opportunity that India Inc., can afford to miss.

Construction of Web Site

The buck stops here. Having devised your game plan for riding the Net into global markets, just how do you actually plant your stake in Web-land? However immaculately you might have planned your Internet strategy, however imaginatively you might have transferred your value chain to the market space, just how efficiently and economically you manage to place each page of your testament homepage in Webspeak-in cyber space will make all the difference between success and failure. So, you'll need a dedicated team, continuous attention, constant surveillance, and regular validation of the effectiveness and implementation of your Internet strategy, Consels Dorab Sopariwala, 54, Market Research Consultant: "Getting on the Net isn't exactly the job of your EDP department. Hiring a consultant, or even putting one on your payroll, is essential." Just where, then, do you begin?

Attracting Traffic

While pretty sites are easy to design, your focus must be on creating an interesting site that earns a reputation among Web surfers and invites repeat visits. Observe Ajay Batra, 31, Director, Bollean Solutions: "The real challenge lies in designing a site that, while essentially being an ad, makes people return to it." So, the solution is to provide the staple that all Webcrucisers are hungry for information. Repeat visits to your site are ruled out unless your site can hold its own against the thousands of data banks that dot the Web. But just how will your consumer be aware of the wealth of information on your Website? That's where the hyperlink the quintessential feature of the Web which allows a user to click on a highlighted phrase, world, or visual in one document to leap to another one comes in. For, the richer and more diverse the information on your company's homepage is the more other sites devoted to any of those subjects create links to yours.

Putting provocative strip-ads each hyperlinked to your site on popular Website in general, and those related to the information presented in your site in particular, is a powerful and mandatory way to publicize your presence on the Net. Try, too, — to include contents that will put your site in the indices of the most-used search engines like Alta Vista, Yahoo and Lycos. Adds Anmol Taneja, 36, Director, DSF Internet: "Many sites will put links to your site if you return the favour."

The potent strategy for ensuring repeat visits of course is to change both the contents and the appearance of your Website at regular intervals. After all, your site is competing with the 5,000 new sites that join the Web every day, which makes frequent changes imperative to hold people's interest. Advises Rajesh Jain, 31, CEO, Ravi Database: "There must be something new a on a Website every day." Virtually as powerful a hook is interactivity, which enables your customers not just to passively view the pages, but also to answer questions, play games and involve themselves with your Website.

Designing the Site

The real touchstones of user-friendly design lie not in colours, text or spatial arrangement, but in the speed at which each of your pages can be downloaded. Remember, in our low bandwidth world, your website must be created so as to be zapped as quickly as possible from the server on which it is hosted to the user's computer. For, the majority of Web surfers are connected to the Net at bandwidths between 14 and 29 kilobytes per second (KBPS). Translation : if the patience threshold for downloading a page the average length of time that a user will happily wait before clicking on the stop button is assumed to be 30 seconds. Or, whatever can be down-loaded in that period, even if it is only part of the page must be interesting enough to warrant a longer wait. Keeping a light page involves using as few bandwidth-hogging graphics and photographs as possible. Prefer the second strategy? Put the most exciting part of your content right on top of the page, or, alternatively, use a device called a frame, which effectively splits the user's screen into several portions and units different sets of contents on each. Smart Web page designers use one frame to list the entire menu of options available on that site. While the Web surfers explores the menu, the rest of the frames fill up with text and images. A thumb rule: If your homepage takes one minute to download, its contents must keep your visitor hooked for at least five minutes.

Ensure too that your site is designed to accept feedback usually in the form of electronic questionnaires which visitors can fill in on screen so that you can tailor your content according to your customers' needs. As Jain says: "The feedback that a Website generates must help tune the changes." Besides, digital records of visitors will build a database of potential customers quickly, cheaply, and automatically. With the personal preference of every Web surfer who's made a hit on your site available, customising your products, Services, or communication for her/his will also become easier. Explains Pradeep Singh, 37, CEO of Netquest, a Bangalore-based company that provides technical support for software: "In a short period you can build a very valuable database of exactly who your potential customers are."

Finding the Host

Whether you want a one page bare-bones homepage or an elaborate 50 page Website, picking a host — the computer, or Web server, where the pages will be stored — is not difficult. Even two years ago, you would have been compelled to set up your own Web server and connect it to the Net. No longer, today, Web-hosting is a fast growing business, and hundreds of service-providers-over — 20 of them having operations in India with their Web serves already connected to the Net, are marketing disk-space on their computers to companies. How do you choose between them? Use two crucial parameters: location and speed of access. The location of the Web server is important because the closer the PC is to the backbone of the Net — a core of links offering bindingly high speed to data zipping across them, most of it lying in the US, with a few tendrils floating out to Western Europe and Japan the smarter is your choice, since your homepage will be downloadable faster. That, effectively, rules out Web servers located in India, which are a long way from the backbone. As for speed of access, it depends on how quick both the computer and connecting links leading to it are. While technical specifications can obfuscate, the best strategy is to benchmark sites on your short-listed servers against the waiting time for downloading data from two of the fastest Corporate Websites Microsoft (www. Microsoft.COM.) and Netscape (home. Netscape Com). The more the difference, the less wise it is to pick that server. Companies offering Web-hosting services fall into three genres.

Full service-providers will provide turnkey management, suggesting a Web-strategy, translating your ideas into text and graphics, and preparing them for the Web by converting them into Hypertext mark up Language — the lingua franca of picking sites to placing your strip ads, also thrown in, this service will cost between Rs. 1,00,000 and 5,00,000 per month for a site of about five to fifteen pages. The cost will also depend on the frequency with which you change your content and design.

Content designing and hosting, which most India service-providers are focusing on, exclude strategic issues from their ambit. Their focus is on converting your content for the Web and arranging the hosting. For a site of between 5 and 15 pages, expect to pay between Rs. 10,000 and Rs. 30,000 a month.

Pure hosting services will only arrange server space,

leaving conceptualisation, designing, and conversion of your contents to you. Meant for companies which can perform these services in-house, bottom of the scale prices offering one megabyte, or about 50 normal pages can be as low as Rs. 2,000 a month. This option has become more viable with the emergence of easy to use Web authoring software packages like Hot Dog and Hot Metal, and Web-authoring modules in popular work processors like Microsoft Word and Lotus Word Pro.

With the first wave of Corporates having washed up on the sands of the Web, establishing a beachhead on it is becoming increasingly difficult. Explains Ravish Bajaj, 33, CEO of Wide World Commissions, a Delhi-based Web hosting service: "Good Web design is a moving target. There is so much innovation that only those who actively monitor the Net can keep up. "Be warned: one off Website-building projects results in static efforts that hold no one's interest. Your decision to join the market space must be a strategic choice, not an experiment. And your Website will be your retail store, operations room, design lab, digital assemble line, and creative communications centre rolled into one. Unless this, virtual infrastructure is set up, monitored, and fine-tuned with attention to quality, how can you win over the world with the Web.

THE FUTURE IS NOW: ON LINE MARKETING FOR THE TWENTY-FIRST CENTURY

With the promise of a brighter fiscal tomorrow, like corporate American, the corporate India too stands ready to pounce on internet users and inundate them with product information on demand. The future holds a new digital marketplace in store for Americans. An existence in which everyday errands are underaken not in the family Caravan but through the modem and mouse. Shopping, paying bills, entertainment, and banking are all ready to enter the American home through a more efficient channel, offering their services to the world for nominal cost in advertising. Interesting, many have noted, but how soon are we to see these changes appear on the net? The harbaringers of change are already in place and they promise to redefine the lifestyles of every man, woman, and child on the planet.

The internet network is becoming increasingly popular among businesses as an avenue for marketing their products and services. The system is growing rapidly, with twenty-five million users in ninteen-niney four, a number which increased over the years. An Internet expert stated that the number of commercial users on the Internet reached fifty million by ninteen nintety-eight; a fifty percent rise in only four years. What implications and effects are in store for the future of marketing with such a rapid advance in technology?

Experts express both concerns and breathless anticipation. This computerized information boom has enormous potential to boost economies world-wide, but it also has the possibility of being expolited. Advertising and marketing on the Internet makes obtaining huge profits possible. Id Software Inc., for example, sold several thousand copies of its Doom cliff-hanging software game the first weekend that it made the game available on the Internet. The company now has sold about ten million dollars worth of software via the net, while avoiding the costs of overhead that generally consume profits. Sellers, though, are not the only ones to reap benefits from the internet. Purchasing products over the net is also beneficial. It is faster than the traditional process of mail ordering, and the on-line support forums provide advice that is not found in manuals, catalogs, or brochures.

To have marketing success on the internet does not require the abandonment of traditional marketing methods; innovation and placement are the prime components in the formula for acquiring internet revenues. Those businesses who devise a successful marketing plan are guaranteed a large profit for their efforts: commercial trade on the net is currently estimated at $200,000 per day, and is expected to substantially increase over the years.

To make the network work to thier advantage, direct marketers have more to consider than just developing a sound financial plan of action. Internet experts lay out several suggestions to generate profit and be a net success. Marketers should avoid being intrusive or sending unwanted messages, for practically noting else annoys internet users more. Instead, an affective approach is to use the internet for building higher levels of relationships with consumers through dialogue. Furthermore, Oglivy & Mather Direct has developed six rules for advertising on the Internet: consumers should only be given information which they have requested, data derived from a consumer interaction should never be resold, advertising should be limited to pre-specified newsgroups and list servers, promotion and direct selling must be preceded by full disclosure, consumers must be informed of end uses of market research, and communications software must not contain hidden functions.

What does all of this mean for the future of marketing? The internet, as of now, is a free enterprise network. Neither government nor big business owns or regulates its content or procedures, thus allowing for a liberal dissemination of information. The costs for marketers or purchasers to use the net is very low, thus enabling both groups to make or save money. There are, however, problems to consider in this cyberspace wonderland. Commercial interests are flocking to the internet, and are directing their aims to the distribution of services and information to mainstream commercial audiences. Marketers should, experts of the net worn, be more cautious before starting internet sites and pages. Rather than automatically assuming the benefits of the medium, they should realize that many Internet sites offer poor data. They are much less accessible than interactive TV services, and they often include outdated information. Marketers should experiment with the medium but not blindly embrace it for the sake of their image.

Rushing to set up shop on the web could be disasterous without the proper research and attitude, because the technology lacks such mission critical features as management, backup, security, and performance management. Some businesses, such as Pizza Hut, simply may not have internet-using customers; however, the low cost of setting up on the internet still remains a good argument in favor of doing so anyway. A good guage of what advertisers should focus upon comes from what type of audience they are playing to on the internet. Net users want advertising to be informative. A reason for this advertising approach focuses upon an internet user profile with notes that internet users are predominantly educated, discerning individuals.

A survey of internet users by a commercial marketing firm found that eighty-seven percent possess a college degree and sixty-seven percent earn more that 50,000 per year. According to Miniwatts Marketig Group survey of the total Net users 27.6% were in USA alone.

Internet Usage Statistics for the Americas Internet User Statistics and Population Stats for 51 countries and regions- North America, Central America, South America and the Caribbean -

TABLE 22.1

INTERNET USERS AND POPULATION STATS FOR THE AMERICAS

THE AMERICAS	*Population (2007 Est.)*	*% Pop.of World*	*Internet Users, 2007 Data%*	*Population (Penetration)*	*% Usage of World*	*Use Growth (2000-2007)*
All the Americas	903,793,105	13.7%	364,219,243	40.3%	27.6%	188.7 %
Rest of the World5,	703,178,554	86.3%	955,652,866	16.8 %	72.4%	307.0%
WORLD TOTAL	6,606,971,659	100.0%	1,319,872,109	20.0%	100.0%	265.6%

Notes: (1) Internet Usage and Population Statistics for the Americas were updated for December 31, 2007. (2) Population numbers are based on data contained in the US Census Bureau. (3) The most recent usage comes mainly from data published by Nielsen//NetRatings , by ITU , and other local sources. (4) Data on this site may be cited, giving due credit and establishing an active link back to Internet World Stats © Copyright 2008, Miniwatts Marketing Group.

INTERNET USAGE STATISTICS

The Internet Big Picture

World Internet Users and Population Stats

TABLE 22.2

WORLD INTERNET USAGE AND POPULATION STATISTICS

World Regions	*Population (2007 Est.)*	*Population % of World*	*Internet Usage, 2007 Data*	*% Population (Penetration)*	*Usage% of World*	*Usage Growth 2000-2007*
Africa	941,249,130	14.2 %	44,361,940	4.7%	3.4%	882.7%
Asia	373,378,347,45	6.5 %	510,478,74	313.7%	38.7%	346.6%
Europe	801,821,187	12.1%	348,125,847	43.4%	26.4%	231.2%
Middle East	192,755,04	52.9%	33,510,500	17.4%	2.5%	920.2 %
North America	334,659,63	15.1%	238,015,529	71.1%	18.0%	120.2 %
Latin America/ Caribbean	569,133,474	8.6%	126,203,714	22.2%	9.6%	598.5 %
Oceania/Australia	33,569,718	0.5%	19,175,836	57.1%	1.5%	151.6%
WORLD TOTAL	6,606,971,659	100.0 %	1,319,872,109	20.0%	100.0%	265.6 %

NOTES: (1) Internet Usage and World Population Statistics are for December 31, 2007. (2) CLICK on each world region name for detailed regional usage information. (3) Demographic (Population) numbers are based on data from the US Census Bureau . (4) Internet usage information comes from data published by Nielsen//NetRatings, by the International Telecommunications Union, by local NIC, and other reliable sources. (5) For definitions, disclaimer, and navigation help, please refer to the Site Surfing Guide, now in ten languages. (6) Information in this site may be cited, giving the due credit to www.internetworldstats.com. Copyright © 2000 - 2008, Miniwatts Marketing Group.

TOP 43 COUNTRIES WITH THE HIGHEST INTERNET PENETRATION RATE (OVER 50 PERCENT OF THE POPULATION USING THE INTERNET)

TABLE 22.3

TOP 43 COUNTRIES WITH THE HIGHEST INTERNET PENETRATION RATE

	Country or Region	*Penetration (% Population) 2007 Data*	*Internet Users*	*Population (2007 Est.)*	*Source and Dateof Latest Data*
1	Norway	88.0%	4,074,100	4,627,926	ITU - Sept/07
2	Netherlands	87.8 %	14,544,400	16,570,613	ITU - Sept/07
3	Iceland	85.4%	258,000	301,931	ITU - Sept/06
4	New Zealand	77.7%	3,200,000	4,115,771	ITU - Sept/05
5	Sweden	77.3%	6,981,200	9,031,088	ITU - Sept/07
6	Antigua & Barbuda	76.3%	53,000	69,481	ITU - Dec/07
7	Australia	75.9 %	15,504,532	20,434,176	Nielsen//NR - Dec/07
8	Portugal	73.1%	7,782,760	10,642,836	IWS - Mar/06
9	United States	71.7%	215,935,529	301,139,947	Nielsen//NR - Dec/07
10	Faroe Islands	71.6%	34,000	47,511	ITU - Sept/07
11	Korea, South	71.2%	34,910,000	49,044,790	ITU - Dec/07
12	Luxembourg	70.6%	339,000	480,222	ITU - Aug/07
13	Hong Kong	69.9 %	5,230,351	7,554,661	Nielsen//NR - Sept/07
14	Falkland Islands6	9.4%	1,900	2,736	CIA - Dec/02
15	Switzerland	69.2%	5,230,35	17,554,661	Nielsen//NR - Sept/07
16	Denmark	68.8 %	3,762,500	5,468,120	ITU - Sept/05
17	Japan	68.7%	87,540,000	127,433,494	ITU - Sept/07
18	Taiwan	67.4%	15,400,000	22,858,872	TWNIC - June/07
19	Greenland	67.4%	38,000	56,344	ITU - Dec/05
20	United Kingdom	66.4%	40,362,842	60,776,238	Nielsen//NR - Nov/07
21	Canada	65.9%	22,000,000	33,390,141	ITU - Mar/07

22 Germany	64.6%	53,240,128	82,400,996	Nielsen//NR - Dec/07
23 Liechtenstein	64.2%	22,000	34,247	ITU - Mar/07
24 Bermuda	63.5%	42,000	66,163	ITU - March/07
25 Finland	62.7%	3,286,000	5,238,460	ITU - Sept/05
26 Slovenia	62.2%	1,250,600	2,009,245	ITU - Sept/07
27 Monaco	61.2%	20,000	32,671	ITU - Sept/07
28 Malaysia	60.0%	14,904,000	24,821,286	MCMC - June/07
29 Estonia	57.8%	760,000	1,315,912	ITU - Sept/07
30 Israel	57.6%	3,700,000	6,426,679	TIM - July/06
31 Italy	57.0%	33,143,152	58,147,733	Nielsen//NR - Nov/07
32 Barbados	57.0%	160,000	280,946	ITU - Sept/06
33 Austria	56.7%	4,650,000	8,199,783	C.I. Almanac - Mar/05
34 Spain	56.5%	22,843,915	40,448,191	Nielsen//NR - Nov/07
35 Belarus	56.3%	5,477,500	9,724,723	ITU - Sept/07
36 Guernsey & Alderney	54.9%	36,000	65,573	ITU - Oct/05
37 France	54.7%	34,851,835	63,718,187	Nielsen//NR - Nov/07
38 Singapore	53.2%	2,421,800	4,553,009	ITU - Sept/05
39 Belgium	52.8%	5,490,000	10,392,226	ITU - Dec/07
40 Niue	52.3%	900	1,722	RockET - Sept/05
41 San Marino	52.0%	15,4002	9,615	ITU - Sept/07
42 Ireland	50.1%	2,060,000	4,109,086	C.I.Almanac - Mar/05
43 Czeck Republic	50.0%	5,100,000	10,228,744	ITU - Dec/05
TOP 43 in Penetration	66.7%	676,306,057	1,013,272,507	IWS - Feb/08
Rest of the World	11.5%	643,566,052	5,593,699,152	IWS - Feb/08
World Total Users	20.0%	1,319,872,109	6,606,971,659	IWS - Feb/08

Notes: (1) Only countries with a Penetration Rate (p.r.) higher than 50% qualify for this list. At present only 43 countries meet this condition, and 226 countries do not. (2) The Internet Penetration Statistics were updated as of December 31, 2007. (3) Population numbers are based on the data contained at the U.S. Census Bureau. (4) The most recent usage information comes from data published by Nielsen//NetRatings, ITU, Computer Industry Almanac and other trustworthy sources. For definitions please refer to the surfing guide. (5) Data in this table is copyrighted. It may be cited, giving due credit and establishing an active link back to Internet World Stats. © Copyright 2008, Miniwatts Marketing Group.

What are the best ways for business to market goods and services on a computer network occupied by such individuals? Experts on the use of the internet, some of whom have played major roles in linking its twenty-five million users, are uncertain. Some experts stress the unique cultural norms which are evolving among internet users as the best way for business to develop an internet customer base. Among the major barriers to successful marketing are security concerns and the absence of a definitive look and feel that will appeal to consumers.

While the net is viewed as more user friendly than interactive TV, transactions are, as yet, few because of technology hurdles. For one, the net is not a closed system, which raises concerns of security. In addition, the differing computers and networks that comprise the net makes developing transactions difficult. The internet also requires increased competitive effort from enterpeneurs because government bureaucrats and their associated tax payer-supported groups will not provide the best information superhighway. This leads to widespread concerns that the internet will become a breeding ground for monopolies as groups struggle to gain the most control and profit from the net.

The concerns about achieving success via the internet are realistic, but the positive aspects of using the Internet as a marketing tool outweigh the negative ones. The Internet problems discussed above are simply issues which entrepeneurs need to consider before venturing into cyberspace.

The net still offers low cost benefits, high profit margins, quick exchange of information, and user friendliness. It is for these reasons that the internet is the wave of the future. If businesses wish to remain competitive and successful, they must eventually make the move to riding the ever-evolving computer highway, for that is where their consumer market is heading.

The Indian Scenerio

eMarketer, a research house specializing in e-business and the Internet, reported that China's Internet population reached 176.5 million in 2007, compared to 188.1 million in the United States. The tally for China included Hong Kong. Ben Macklin, senior analyst at eMarketer, said China would "overtake the United States as the most populous Internet nation in the world" this year. The Internet market in the Asian country, he added, is still relatively immature and together with countries such as Brazil and India, will drive growth in the number of Internet users globally.

There is a lot of buzz around us about the Internet just as there was about the mobile phones some years ago. It was followed by a boom in the mobile industry. Internet is growing at a fast pace and increasingly becoming part of an ordinary Indian's life. Infrastructure level constraints are being removed, and every morning we see some new developments in this domain. The mobile boom arrived in India after low cost mobile sets and cheap tariffs were in place. Today broadband connections are made available at rock bottom rates. New innovations are on to develop low cost PCs. There are a lot of efforts on the content front, too. So, is the Internet in India is following the same path mobile followed? Are these efforts going on to mark a new epoch in development of Internet in India?

In a recent remark Google CEO Eric Schmidt has said that India will be the largest Internet market in the coming 5-10 years, and Hindi will be on the three most important languages on the web. A recent study by IOAI (Internet and Online Association of India) estimates there will be 100 million net users in India by 2007. Today it is at 25 million and a four-fold growth is estimated in less than 2 years. All these remarks float hope, but don't provide any clear-cut answer about the future of Internet.

Regarding usage of Internet, there are many other questions, too. What are the Indians doing on the web? Who are they and what is their profile? What is the online behaviour of Indians? How is the Internet shaping the lives of millions of Indians? Has it entered their lives or not? Which are the areas mostly touched by the web wave and which are the abandoned areas?

Till recent, we had no clear answers to all these questions. But now two pieces of research are available, which offer some valuable insights. Among these, the first is India Online 2005, prepared by an online research company JUXT CONSULT. Another is India E-commerce Report 2005 prepared by the Internet and Online Association of India (IOAI). Though the domains of these studies are different, but both offer insights into what is happening on the Web in India. Both the reports are based on online surveys. These surveys were done in the middle of 2005.

The E-commerce Report has given two important estimates: first, the number on Net users in India will reach 100 million by 2007 and second, the value of e-commerce in India will reach Rs. 2300 crore by the same period. It is surprising to know that e-commerce was just Rs. 130 crore in 2002-03. In 2005-06 it stood at Rs. 1180 cr. In a span of five years, e-commerce is expected to grow 18 times. Similarly, online transactions have increased from 20,7000 in 2003-04 to 79,5000 in 2005-06. These estimates are encouraging.

The India Online Report 2005, prepared on the basis of more than 30,000 responses from 10 cities, reveals some new facts about Internet usage in India. Here are some excerpts:

1. Internet is touching the lives of Indians, but not entering them. For most net users logging on to the net has become a daily routine. But they use it mostly for personal communication and 'work' related activities.
2. About a third of net users spend more than 3 hours on the net, use it throughout the day and log on at least five times a day. This is the class of net users, which can be called netoholics.
3. Unlocking the speed barrier is must for growth of Internet here. To keep people hooked up, technical problems such as 'slow speed' and 'frequent disconnections' should be resolved.
4. The image of the Internet has to change. Most people treat it as a 'work' tool, searching for professional information than as a tool for personal information.
5. E-commerce is increasing, but security is the most common fear in the mind of net users. This fear is the greatest impediment for the growth of on-line transaction.

The report concludes that to achieve the expected growth, particularly in urban India, Internet would have to break two barriers. First, resolve the technical constraints, second, make it relevant for users' lives.

This report breaks many myths related to Internet usage. The first is about what people do on the Net. It concludes that porn is not the most popular activity. Most popular activities are e-mail, news/events, career development, downloading application forms, sports/ cinema, job search etc.

Some other results of this report are also very interesting to understand the situation of Internet usage in India. The 19-40 years age group is the major section (85%) of the total net users. Similarly, office is the most preferred place to go online. About 62% users access the Internet from there workplace. 90% of the net users are highly educated. Graduates comprise 46% of the total net users, while Post-Graduates 26% and people with Professional qualification 19%. It has made in-roads among all sections of life. 83% users have no car and only 25% use credit cards. Similarly, 70% of the total users have a monthly income near Rs. 10,000, only 13% have a monthly income of more than Rs. 50,000.

However, the Internet is largely a male bastion. Only 15% users are women. About half among them are working. Housewives comprise only 2%.

Seventy per cent users come from the biggest 8 cities - Mumbai, Delhi, Chennai, Kolkata, Banglore, Hyderabad, Pune and Ahmedabad. Mumbai, Delhi and Bangalore alone account for 51% users. The eastern zone of India is most backward regarding to Internet usage. Only 7% users come from this area. Western zone accounts for 36%, Southern zone for 31% and Northern zone for 26%. Executives and students are the largest categories using Internet.

Logging-on has become a daily routine for most users. Eighty five per cent users use the Net at least once in a day. Three in 10 users use net for more than 3 hours a day. There is no prime time on the net. Users use it all the time except between midnight to morning. The survey notes some barriers that users feel while using the net: difficulty in getting connected, slow speed, unsolicited ads and cumbersome navigation are main ones. Users feel irritated due to these problems and this psychological problem creates a big barrier to Internet usage.

Internet, though has not entered deep into the Indian's lives, but it has become a working tool for most users. Users utilise the Net for their professional requirements and communication, but the least for entertainment, learning and personal information search. E-mailing is what, people use most. However, the report says that the scenario is not disappointing. Forty six per cent users are experienced in buying something online. Eighteen per cent are buying regularly. Another positive sign is that a lot more people are using the Net to search for their personal needs. 35%-45% net users regularly search information related to purchase of products or services. Similarly, the number of users using net for their personal needs is also increasing. In India, 60% activities on Net are related to job and career activities, 48% each for net banking and product information, and 46% each for computer skill enhancement, market info and downloading/listening music. Nearly 40% activities are done for health/lifestyle info and booking of train/air tickets, while 30% activities are done for downloading or playing games and paying bills.

As per the annual I Cube report from the Internet and Mobile Association of India (IAMAI) and IMRB International, the number of active Internet users in India had reached 32 million in September 2007, up only 10.9 million from 21.1 million in September 2006.

With number of Internet users increasing in India at a fast pace, it is accurate to say that India will become the largest market for Internet. Like mobile, the Web fever is grappling Indians. Constraints are being resolved and no doubt, India will soon see a web wave.

Technology is the word that dominates life in the 21st century. Internet is one such product of this technology. Internet today is no longer a medium of the elite. It has found its place in every business, household or office and is being used for almost every purpose from business to entertainment, education to shopping. Internet today has its dedicated surfers everywhere across the globe.

Internet is the best medium to capture maximum audience. And when it is used for brand promotion and advertising it becomes advertising media internet. People now-a-days prefer to go for advertising on internet has it helps in easy brand building and also maximum exposure. In this cut throat competitive world only the fittest can survive and for surviving you have to be on your toes and also equipped with the latest advertising tools.

For all those who have till now declined to believe in the power of the internet as mass medium, the recent report of ZenithOptimedia must have had a sobering impact. As per the latest estimates, Internet Advertising will more than double to Rs. 450 crore by the end of the year and will be pegged at around Rs. 2,250 crore by the end of 2010. This means that atr its current growth rate Internet will actually the media spends of radio, cinema and outdoor and advertising in less than two years. The report has indeed resulted in a wave of optimism and more and more companies in India have started using the internet to advertise their products.

Internet is the best medium to capture maximum audience and when it is used for brand promotion and advertising, it becomes advertising media internet. People now-a-days prefer to go for advertising on internet has it helps in easy brand building and also maximum exposure. In this cut throat competitive world only the fittest can survive and for surviving you have to be on your toes and also equipped with the latest advertising tools.

In addition to buying and selling products, Business Internet Services also helps in handling other traditional business aspects. The use of electronic chat as a form of technical and customer support is an excellent example of this. An ebusiness which uses chat to supplement its traditional phone support finds a system which saves a lot of time while providing opportunities unavailable through the traditional support. By using virtual computer systems, technical support operators can remotely access a customer's computer and assist them in correcting a problem. And with the downloading of a small program, all pertinent information about the hardware and software specifications for a user's computer may be relayed to the support operator directly, without having to walk a customer through personally collecting the data.

Using email and private websites as a method for dispensing internal memos and white sheets is another important aspect of advertising on the Internet. Rather than producing time-intensive and costly physical copies for each employee, a central server or email list can serve as an efficient method for distributing necessary information.

In the past few years, virtually all businesses are making use of eServices. The penetration of Internet technology, readily available solutions, and the repeatedly demonstrated benefits of electronic technology has made Business Internet Services the obvious path. This trend continues with new technologies, such as Internet-enabled cell phones and PDAs. The popularity of ebusiness is likely to continue.

The latest and perhaps a fast emerging segment in Indian advertisement sector is online media advertising. With Internet being accessible in all the nooks and corners of the country online media advertising is on an upward swing. Considering the growing number of Internet users, one may safely assume that the country will experience a boom in online media advertising very soon.

Therefore, naturally, the future medium of communication for any business is Web and Internet.

REFERENCES

1. Cross, Richard. "Internet: The Missing Marketing Medium Found." *Direct Marketing*, Oct. 1994, Vol. 57 p. 20.
2. Donaton, Scott, "Mucking up Marketing on the Net" *Advertising Age*, Jan. 23, 1995, p.18.
3. Ellsworth, Jill H., "Business on a Virtual Rush to the Virtual Mall" *PC Magazine* Feb. 7, 1995 p. 190.
4. Fryer, Bronwyn., "Net Sales" *Computerworld*. Sept 5, 1994 p. 118.
5. La Monica, Martin. "Business needs new models before profitting from Internet" *Advertising Age*. Dec. 19, 1994 p. 57.
6. Lang, Curtis. "Cashing in: The rush is on to Buy and Sell on the Internet" *Infoworld*. Oct. 24, 1994 p. 53.
7. Metcalf, Robert M., "Commercialization of the Internet opens gataeways to Interpreneurs" *Infoworld*, Aug. 8, 1994, p. 44.
8. Nisenholtz, Martin. "How to Market on the Net" *Advertising Age*, July 11, 1994. p. 28.
9. Semich, J. William, "The WWW: Internet Boomtown?" *Datamation* Jan. 15, 1995. p. 37.
10. Steinart-Threikeld, Tom, "The internet should not be a breeding ground for onopolies" *Interactive Week*, Nov. 7, 1994.
11. Vijayan, Jaikumar, "Internet Support Soars" *Computerworld*. Oct. 10, 1994, p. 45.
12. Vis, David. "On line Advertisers Should Provide Information, not Hype" *Travel Weekly*, Jan. 9, 1995 p. 40.